A
History of the
Ecumenical
Movement Volume 3

1968-2000

A
History of the
Ecumenical
Movement *Volume 3*
1968-2000

Edited by

John Briggs, Mercy Amba Oduyoye and Georges Tsetsis

World Council of Churches, Geneva

Cover design: Rob Lucas

Cover illustration: "La tempête apaisée", by Claude Gastine, published
in *Dessine-moi la Bible*, Paris, Desclée de Brouwer, 2000, p.107

ISBN 2-8254-1355-0

Printed in Switzerland

This volume is dedicated to
Jan H. Kok
publications manager of the World Council of Churches 1973-2002
and director of its department of Communication 1987-1999

Table of Contents

The Editors

John Briggs, a Baptist layman, is currently emeritus professor of the University of Birmingham, UK, and senior research fellow and director of the Baptist History and Heritage Centre at Regent's Park College in the University of Oxford. He was principal of Westhill College of Higher Education from 1997 to 1999, and pro vice-chancellor of the University of Birmingham, Westhill, from 1999 to 2001. He has served on both the central and executive committees of the WCC, and acted as drafter of the report of its Special Commission on Orthodox Participation in the WCC.

Mercy Amba Oduyoye, a Methodist from Ghana, is director of the Institute of African Women in Religion and Culture of Trinity Theological Seminary, Legon, Ghana. She was on the faculty of the Department of Religious Studies, University of Ibadan, Nigeria, for twelve years, and has served as visiting faculty in theological institutions in Africa, Europe and North America. The Circle of Concerned African Women Theologians was founded on her initiative. Previous professional responsibilities include presidency of the Ecumenical Association of Third World Theologians, membership of the WCC's Faith and Order Commission, and seven years as deputy general secretary of the WCC.

Georges Tsetsis is Grand Protopresbyter of the Ecumenical Patriarchate. From 1965 to 1984 he served the WCC, first as secretary for the Middle East and later as deputy director of the Commission on Inter-Church Aid, Refugee and World Service. From 1985 to 1999 he was permanent representative of his church to the WCC. After his retirement he directed the Orthodox Centre of Chambésy, Geneva, and its Institute of Post-Graduate Orthodox Theological Studies for a short time. From 1991 to 2001 he was a member of the WCC's central and executive committees of the WCC.

***

Hugh McCullum, an Anglican from Canada, is an author and journalist. After serving as editor of the two largest circulation church publications in Canada, he spent more than 14 years in Africa, first in southern Africa as a foreign correspondent, then in Kenya with the All Africa Conference of Churches, and finally in Zimbabwe as a correspondent for several overseas publications and in journalism training. He is the author and editor of 14 books and has had a long association with the WCC's department of Communication.

Preface

We are often reminded that, as the pioneers of the ecumenical movement of the 20th century pass from the scene, we are in danger of losing "ecumenical memory". Even those committed to the ecumenical cause often work with only limited knowledge of past ecumenical efforts.

With the publication now of this third volume of *A History of the Ecumenical Movement 1968-2000* we have a reflective and analytical body of history dating back to the Reformation. The first two volumes, covering the periods 1517-1948 and 1948-1968, presented a detailed and systematic survey of the ecumenical initiatives by the churches down through history.

This latest volume brings us to the end of the second millennium and it reminds us of the increasingly controversial and complex period of time we have just passed through. Presented as they are, these three volumes together will not only remind us of our "ecumenical memory" but will broaden our view and widen our perspective.

There is a danger that, in the times in which we live and in our attempts to respond to ever more demanding and varied issues, we can lose the essential memory, the essence and basics of our movement. For, if the past is forgotten, the present loses perspective and the future then lacks direction.

Through this third volume and the republishing of the first two volumes, the ecumenical movement and the World Council of Churches can experience again the vision and the challenges of earlier times and enthusiasm may be renewed.

Geneva, 2004   Samuel Kobia
                                                         General Secretary
                                                         World Council of Churches

Introduction

This third volume of *A History of the Ecumenical Movement* comes thirty-five years after its immediate predecessor which covered the first twenty years following the inaugural assembly of the WCC at Amsterdam in 1948. This volume will be available in preparation for the ninth assembly of the WCC, to be held at Porto Alegre, Brazil, in February 2006.

Originally, this third volume should have been published in time for the celebration of the 50th anniversary of the WCC at the Harare assembly in 1998. Unforeseen circumstances delayed the completion of the project. During the long years of preparation it has become clear that the writing of contemporary history is a risky enterprise, even more so if the authors have been actors who were directly involved in shaping the events and developments under review. Perceptions, evaluations and emphases are bound to change with greater distance. Yet, the account of contemporaries becomes an important source for later historical research. Furthermore, after thirty-five years there is an urgent need to take stock and to preserve the ecumenical memory for the benefit of a new generation.

In looking back at the fourth assembly of the WCC at Uppsala in 1968, the general secretary at the time, Eugene Carson Blake, wrote at the end of the second volume of this history: "Uppsala marked the end of an era of the ecumenical movement. It also marked a new beginning." Thirty-five years later, we see clearly that another phase of the ecumenical movement has ended and a new chapter has been opened. An attempt in the early 1980s to continue the account of the history of the ecumenical movement beyond 1968 was abandoned; the time was not yet ripe, and the main contours of the period under review were still a matter of controversy. Since then, the dust has begun to settle and it appears possible to offer a comprehensive perspective on this exciting phase in the development of the ecumenical movement.

Such an account has been urgently awaited by many. We live again in a time of accelerated change – some would even speak of an epochal change. A new generation has moved into positions of leadership in church and society. There is the danger of a loss of "ecumenical memory", of the common tradition which has evolved through the ecumenical movement. The formation of new ecumenical leadership must include the effort to repossess the past, even though the result may be a critical assessment.

This volume is intended to preserve the markers on the way and thus to assist a new generation in coming to terms with the legacy of those who have gone before. To characterize these last thirty-five years as a period of change amounts almost to a truism. Since its beginnings, a hundred years ago, the ecumenical movement has been caught up in the turmoil, hopes and despair of the 20th century. There has been the most explicit effort on the part of the Christian churches to discern the "signs of the time". Thus the movement has been profoundly affected by the crises and advances of the human community.

The second volume of this history, composed around the time of the Uppsala assembly of the WCC, was marked by the optimism and revolutionary excitement of that period. Shortly afterwards, however, the climate began to change. The development conflict, the struggles for liberation, the nuclear and political confrontation between the superpowers, and the emerging consciousness of threats to ecological survival, became the dominant features of an increasingly conflictual and antagonistic view of the world situation which left its marks on the ecumenical movement. The unexpected collapse and dissolution of the communist system in 1989-90, especially in Eastern Europe and the former Soviet Union, brought about another radically new constellation.

Perceptive historians consider that the 20th century, which started late in 1914, ended prematurely in 1989. Not only has the human community at the world level entered a period of transition; the same is also true for the ecumenical movement. The first chapters of this volume provide a survey of these changes in the global context and how they are reflected in the life of the churches and in the ecumenical movement.

The very structure of this volume is an expression of the changes in the profile of the ecumenical movement over the last thirty-five years. While all the fifteen authors of the preceding volume were men from Europe or North America, the more than thirty contributors in the present volume include eight from the South and five women. The Orthodox churches and the Roman Catholic Church today are considered an integral part of the ecumenical movement and are, therefore, no longer treated in separate chapters. On the other hand, the expansion and diversification of ecumenical activity on the regional (and national) level made it necessary and advisable to include nine chapters on "regional ecumenism" covering all the major ecumenical regions. While the "oneness" of the ecumenical movement is being affirmed by all involved, it is equally clear that this oneness and integrity eludes any centralizing structure. It is realized in and through networks of sharing and bonds of mutual accountability between very diverse partners, among whom the WCC has assumed the role of a "trustee" of the integrity and sense of purpose of the ecumenical movement.

The last thirty-five years has also been characterized by a significant widening of the scope and agenda of the ecumenical movement. It is significant to note the list of topics and areas of ecumenical concern which are being recognized in their own right for the first time in this volume. These include: inter-religious dialogue; racism and ethnicity; science, technology and ecology; the Bible (surprisingly); spirituality; ecumenical formation; and women (under the heading of "inclusive community").

Since this volume, like the preceding ones, is being published by the World Council of Churches, it is clear that the topical chapters reflect primarily the activities and priorities of the WCC during this period. The selection, however, does not simply follow the programmatic structure of the WCC, which has changed several times during this period, but is intended to offer a representative cross-section of the ecumenical agenda since 1968. The fact that many of these activities have sprung originally from initiatives of the Uppsala assembly verifies in retrospect the assessment that Uppsala was the end of an era and a new beginning at the same time.

"Has the ecumenical movement a future?" This question, which the first general secretary of the WCC, Willem A. Visser 't Hooft, chose as the title of a series of lectures given in the Netherlands in 1972 (published in English in 1974), is being asked again to-day as we have entered the 21st century. Talk about the "crisis" of the ecumenical move-ment has been with us throughout this period, and a whole chapter has been devoted to the sharply critical voices which have been heard inside and outside the movement. The critical questions about institutional paralysis, religious plurality and the politicization of the ecumenical movement which Visser 't Hooft addressed in his lectures are still with us. But conscious as he was of previous crises and transition periods in the history of the ecumenical movement, he was able to articulate clearly the sense of vision and purpose which has kept it alive.

The epilogue, therefore, appropriately addresses the present-day question of a vision of ecumenism. It draws on an extensive process of reflection and dialogue which the central committee of the WCC initiated in 1989 with and among its member churches and ecumenical partner organizations. The process has resulted in a policy statement, "Towards a Common Understanding and Vision of the WCC", which was adopted by the central committee in 1997 and reconfirmed by the eighth assembly at Harare in 1998. This statement does not pretend to remove all the ambiguities and uncertainties which have characterized the ecumenical way in the last decades. But it has begun to serve the churches and the wider networks of ecumenical partner organizations as a frame of ref-erence and orientation to acknowledge again their common calling and to renew their commitment to the ecumenical vision. In an increasingly global context, the ecumenical imperative has become more urgent than ever before.

It is fitting to conclude this introduction with an expression of thanks. First, of course, to the authors of the twenty-seven chapters who have generously contributed their time and knowledge. Each chapter has been read and commented upon by at least one other unnamed person, and as a consequence has undergone some revision. Par-ticular thanks are due to the editors, John Briggs, Mercy Oduyoye and Georges Tsetsis, who beyond their own signed contributions have helped to develop the plan for this vol-ume and have watched over its realization.

This volume is dedicated to the memory of the late Jan Kok who, as director of the WCC communication department and publications manager, together with his friend and colleague, the late Marlin VanElderen as chief editor of the WCC, had the courage to embark on this project and accompanied it until the last days of his life. Both dedi-cated all their extraordinary skills and ecumenical commitment to this enterprise, but their premature deaths did not allow them to see it through to completion. Among the many friends who stepped into the breach and helped the project to continue, mention should be made of Norman Hjelm, former director of Faith and Order with the National Council of Churches of Christ in the USA, who served as an interim editor during a crit-ical period. Final responsibility for the entire volume was carried by Hugh McCullum, a Canadian editor, author and journalist with extensive experience in the WCC.

The publication bears the mark of the difficulties encountered in the process of pro-duction. But the ecumenical movement itself is an unfinished project; how much more does this apply to the writing of ecumenical history! We now present this volume in the hope that it may inspire a new generation to carry forward the ecumenical vision and thus to honour the memory of those who have gone before them.

Geneva, 2004

Konrad Raiser
General Secretary (1993-2003)
World Council of Churches

From the Editors

WCC Publications, the publishing house of the World Council of Churches, first proposed this third volume of the *History of the Ecumenical Movement* to mark the fiftieth anniversary of the founding of the Council in 1948. For various unexpected and very human reasons which are detailed in Konrad Raiser's introduction, the publication has been delayed for some years but is now complete and covers the period 1968 to 2000.

Volume I (1517-1948), edited by Ruth Rouse and Stephen C. Neill, appeared in 1954; Volume II (1948-68), edited by Harold E. Fey, appeared in 1970. They have been reprinted several times (with an updated bibliography in 1986, and in a one-volume edition in 1993). This third volume presents a comprehensive review and analysis of the immense variety of ecumenical events and activities of the last third of the second millennium.

Our focus has been, from the beginning, on the ecumenical movement as it has manifested itself in all traditions, continents and regions. The present volume endeavours to provide an authoritative account and consolidated interpretation of ecumenical developments during the three decades covered. Since space does not permit extensive detail, writers were asked to "discover" and convey the "texture" of the events and activities they describe and interpret.

Rather than being aimed solely at an academic and scholarly audience, this volume aims to present the history of the ecumenical movement in a manner that makes it accessible to the general reader, whether or not they have been participants in ecumenical events and organizations. Nevertheless, the analysis arises out of a meticulous study of both the documentary evidence and already published research, and the topics treated attempt to meet generally agreed criteria for historical scholarship. While WCC Publications is the originating publisher, the book deals with the entire ecumenical movement; it makes no claim to be an "official history" either of the WCC or of the movement.

The editorial board appointed in 1995 agreed that this portrait of the ecumenical movement should be critical, and avoid as far as possible a structure of the chapters reflecting or justifying the programmatic structure of the WCC. It was important to acknowledge a range of critical voices: thus each chapter endeavours to tell the story of pro-ecumenical developments but also takes into account contrary influences.

This is a work of church history, albeit church history of a distinctive kind. The ecumenical focus is not intended in any way to eclipse the story of the churches themselves. What we believe gives this volume its vitality is precisely the fact that the ecumenical movement has been in "crisis" since 1968. For that reason, and also because very few people have been doing reflection on this period of ecumenical history, the volume concentrates on the 32 years from the key date of 1968 until the beginning of the new millennium.

We have attempted to focus on specific events and episodes, and to integrate selected case studies into the narrative. We have had many discussions of the role of "people" in the history. It is clearly impossible and undesirable to omit all references to individuals. At the same time there are obvious pitfalls: how to evaluate, to decide in terms of balance and significance, which people are mentioned or not mentioned, how to avoid self-justification and deal fairly with the contributions made. This history attempts to give the ecumenical movement a human face, by not falling into the temptation of the "technical historian" of dealing only with concepts and movements; yet the central thrust is not biographical.

The volume is divided into three interconnected sections. The first section attempts to provide context and overview, and is followed by a series of thematic chapters which seek to address the major streams within the ecumenical movement. A "strengthened awareness" of regional ecumenism comprises the third part. A final essay or epilogue, "The Changing Shape of the Ecumenical Movement", looks to the future.

The methodological and hermeneutical questions have been complex. The editorial board worked through the major sections and subject matter. We were cognizant throughout that this was to be a history of the ecumenical movement rather than a programmatic history of the WCC, and we tried to ensure that the role of the churches is clearly recognizable so that they, and not the ecumenical organizations, are the "main players". The hermeneutical questions included: where to begin, who have been the main players, what has been the interaction between different themes, what have been the respective roles of institutions and individuals, how to give voice to the poor and the powerless alongside more powerful players, indeed is it possible for there to be a common hermeneutic?

Potential authors were contacted and lengthy discussion held about criteria, length, deadlines and the like, and through it all the massive changes and crises of the last part of the 20th century loomed darkly over our work.

In seeking primary and secondary sources, the documentation available in the library and archives of the Ecumenical Centre and the Bossey Institute have been widely used, but material from beyond also finds its place. Solidly annotated bibliographies for each chapter have been developed by retired Centre librarian Pierre Beffa, as well as an overall bibliography for the entire volume. Some of this may appear repetitious but it provides the reader of one chapter with as complete a bibliography as possible.

We have received many suggestions for making this history better and more complete, all of which have been considered carefully, keeping in mind the constraints of space and time available. The language and tone of the third volume attempt in every way possible – within the bounds of accuracy of quotations – to be inclusive. Some authors have maintained the traditional use of the pronouns "he, him, his, himself" when referring to God; others have avoided it.

We three editors have had invaluable assistance and support from many people without whom we could not have completed this important work. As Konrad Raiser has mentioned in his introduction, much of the preliminary and conceptual work was done by the late Jan Kok, WCC Publications manager, and his close colleague, Marlin VanElderen, senior editor of the WCC. Their untimely deaths within 18 months of each other were a serious setback, yet their vision and focus can be seen throughout the book. We are deeply indebted to a number of professional people within WCC Publications – Joan Cambitsis, Evelyne Corelli, Theodore Gill, Yannick Provost, Regina Rueger Surur – as well as colleagues with long association with the ecumenical movement whose names appear in the list of editorial board members or as additional contributors to chapters.

Following the deaths of Jan Kok and Marlin VanElderen, we required the services of a coordinating editor to work on the manuscripts as they came in. Norman Hjelm of the United States was able to fulfill this role only partly, and the major responsibility in this area has been carried by Hugh McCullum from Canada.

Each chapter bears the name of its principal author and in some cases reference is made to a number of people who have contributed material. All the chapters have been subject to editorial revision, often with advice from professional readers in a given area. We are grateful both to authors for allowing us to employ such a method and to those who have helped us with comments and advice.

Finally, a very sincere word of thanks goes to the Council for World Mission in London, which made a substantial grant to the production costs of this volume in order to make it available in the third world at an affordable price.

We three editors express our deep gratitude to everyone who contributed to this long-awaited third volume of *The History of the Ecumenical Movement*.

John Briggs   Mercy Oduyoye   Georges Tsetsis

Part I

1
The Global Context of Ecumenism 1968-2000

Martin E. Marty

FRAMING THE PERIOD AS A TIME OF "CENTRIPETALITY" AND "CONVERGENCE"

An observer of those world historical trends that frame the ecumenical movement could well use two arrows to indicate the main directions of historical forces. The first, depicting the motion of circumstances surrounding the generation that prevailed between the end of the second world war in 1945 and the approximate period covered by this book, beginning in 1968, would be well-described with an arrow spiralling towards a centre or a set of arrows converging on each other. The direction was centripetal. The second arrow, for the thirty-year period after 1968, is best described with an arrow spiralling outward towards undetermined ends or a set of arrows diverging from each other. The direction this time has been centrifugal.

Of course, it is impossible to reduce all the major forces and trends to something as simple as two sets of arrows. The world is full of diversity, pluralism, ambiguity and contradiction. Whoever wishes to look can always find phenomena that complicate generalizations. The choice of those generalizations also depends somewhat upon the theses that the various generalizers propose after studying the movements, events, personalities and inventions of a time. Between 1945 and 1968, many elements fit the "centrifugal" theme and between 1968 and 2000 there have continued to be "centripetal" agents and agencies – the ecumenical movement itself being one of these. Yet some reference to events of the two sets of years helps reinforce the point about the arrows of history.

Thus, to the theme of centripetality. During and after 1945, the United Nations was formally organized in San Francisco, California, to replace an old and ineffective League of Nations. The intention of the general assembly of the UN was to provide a forum for positive argument on the model of a parliament. Three years later, a United Nations Declaration of Human Rights was agreed upon to help ensure an extension of rights in all the nations. Peace-keeping forces of the United Nations were designed to counter militancies that threatened world peace. A number of sponsored or spin-off organizations extended the spiritual and material scope of the UN, among them the United Nations Educational, Scientific and Cultural Organization (UNESCO) and the United Nations Relief and Rehabilitation Administration (UNRRA). The UN and its corollaries embodied dreams of human unity in a war-weary world.

One could point to any number of forces parallel to what the United Nations was to represent: decolonialization and movements for liberation that would bring new nations to the parliamentary forum would be among them. Racial integration was a dream in many nations. Numbers of metaphors were advanced during this period or soon after, as it was ending, to encapsulate the trends: "global village", "the human family", "spaceship earth". Philosophers and historians like Arnold Toynbee, Sarvepalli Radhakrishnan, Julian Huxley and Pierre Teilhard de Chardin acquired international readerships for their visions of human convergence and unity.

The modern ecumenical movement came to fruition in this period as well. While its stirrings are often traced to some 19th-century efforts and certainly to the international missionary conference at Edinburgh in 1910, it was the post-second world war era that saw it mature. Early in the period the most vivid example was the formation of the World Council of Churches at Amsterdam in 1948. Meanwhile, the various confessional bodies around the world regrouped and became freshly articulate in the post-war world. While there had been national "united" and "uniting" churches before the war, in the generation after the war they gained new momentum and found fresh favour. The invention and support of a large number of national, regional and local councils of churches further matched the "centripetal" motif and promoted convergences across old boundaries. The Second Vatican Council (1962-65), while officially involving only the Roman Catholic Church, exemplified so many gestures towards non-Catholics that it has to be seen as thoroughly ecumenical. Its close coincided with the end of the period of convergences.

So much for the period before 1968. Before the ink on the "uniting" documents had dried and before the post-war pioneers of secular and religious – especially Christian – ecumenism alike got to sit back and enjoy their achievements, any number of counter-forces and trends became manifest and disturbed their peace and their dreams. If it is possible to state credibly that the ecumenical movement both prospered from and promoted the secular dreams of unity, henceforth it became clear that ecumenical agencies would suffer from and often be set back by what was occurring in the secular context that surrounded religious institutions. Ecumenical endeavours had never been easy, but now they were complicated both by a world of secular divergences around the churches and particularist tendencies within them. An advocate of Christian ecumenism, whether on theological or humanistic grounds, could now credibly argue that precisely because the times and the odds were against it, at least against it in its earlier forms, it was more necessary than ever before – and that it demanded fresh devotion and energies.

THE PERIOD 1968-2000 AS A TIME OF "CENTRIFUGALITY" AND "DIVERGENCE"

To anticipate the larger story: In the secular context, the United Nations, symbol of convergence dreams, continued to serve as peace-keeper and relief agency. But progressively, or regressively, it often turned into a platform for forensic polemics, of mutually contradictory monologues or representations of established positions as opposed to theses for parliamentary debate by the ever-increasing number of nations. The secular metaphors about the global village and spaceship earth came to be challenged by descriptions of the world scene as characterized by tribalisms and atavisms. Post-colonialism was less an expression of outcome that allowed for liberated nations to reduce their claims of sovereignty and work towards common purposes, and more a development of conflict between nation and tribe, tribe and tribe. Movements designed to advance racial integration came to be opposed by movements promoting separate racial and ethnic identities and often self-chosen re-segregations.

Before chronicling some of these developments, it is necessary to ask why the sudden turn occurred from the centripetal to the centrifugal both as an ideal and a strategy around much of the globe. Why did what we have called "tribalism" in national and ethnic affairs or what we might call "new particularism", not always on confessional lines, emerge in ecumenical Christianity? It would be impossible to give a complete and satisfying answer to any set of questions as complex as those. But several widely supported suggestions might advance reflection on them. Among these:

First, the patterns of convergence were, or were perceived to have been by many minorities in formerly colonial powers, or by overlooked and repressed individuals, the efforts of those long in power. Thus the "first" and "second" worlds of blocs dominated by the United States and the Soviet Union had set the terms on the basis of which the "third"-world nations were to find their destinies determined. In the eyes of many in the poor world, these determinations originated too frequently in Europe and North America, where technology, wealth and habits based on colonialism were too reflexively (or calculatedly) imposed on others. It was time for them to react, and they could do this only by extravagant compensatory gestures. For example, "racial reconciliation" in the United States came to be countered or complicated by cries of "black power", "Chicano power", and the like.

Alongside this explanation based on perceptions of negative liberty, meaning opposition to oppressions past, present and potential, many adduced a positive one. The code word for it was "identity politics". This meant that people and peoples who had long been all but invisible to others, races and ethnic groups that had been disdained by others, or individuals who had experienced "identity diffusion" when they had been alone and at the mercy of technological and other homogenizing forces, were now free to react. As if by a signal apprehended worldwide, many groups that came to be organized around race, religion, ethnicity, gender, class, taste or ideology began to take command of their stories and histories in efforts to reinforce identities and gain power.

While many such particular expressions were designed for mutual enrichment – "you tell your story so that I know who you are and I'll tell you my story so that you know who I am" – others were mutually exclusive: "Unless you are born of *xxx* group and grew up on *xxx* soil, you have no right to tell our story and you have little possibility of understanding it." The exclusive version was especially complicating for Christian ecumenism. The old sectarian lines of division may have been reduced between 1910 and 1968, but others were renewed or were paralleled by distinctions based on categories of race or gender.

Alongside the explanations having to do with liberation and identity, a third one is often adduced: much of the move towards convergence was conducted along the lines of bureaucratic models that, in the name of dominance or efficiency, suppressed the particularity, individuality and self-expression of those who did not want to be pushed into conformities or manipulated. Thus, in a fashion that many would call paradoxical at this moment in history, the potential for "cosmopolitanism" that came with the United Nations era and the interaction made possible by modern media of communication and modes of rapid transportation appeared on the scene just as a compensatory "localism" developed. One book title expressed this paradox well. Referring to the Arabic word for holy mission, action or war, *Jihad* on the one hand, and then, on the other, a symbol of international corporate life, Benjamin Barber envisioned the future as one of a contest: *Jihad Versus McWorld.*[1]

---

[1] B. Barber, *Jihad Versus McWorld: How Globalism and Tribalism Are Reshaping Our World*, Andrea Schulz ed., New York, Ballantine, 1996.

Implications of these developments for ecumenical endeavours are obvious. Radio, television, audio and video recordings and transmission, and, most of all, the Internet, make possible the cosmopolitan experience once denied all but global travellers. Events among Christians in Rwanda and Burundi or Northern Ireland are as vivid to television viewers everywhere as are the activities of a Christian church of another denomination a couple of blocks away. At the same time, communication among people on local levels also serves to build community. Many a pastor can convoke a congregation at the press of a laptop key, apprise members of events or call on them for participation.

On the ecumenical scene, the contesting between cosmopolitan and local forces often produced resistance to the world or national councils of churches or the curial enforcements of Vatican decrees, on the grounds that they were being administered by impersonal, remote and unresponsive agents who could not possibly understand local differentiations or comprehend why the locals chose their own modes of adaptation to circumstances. People who were or wanted to be religious, whether in areas of the world where individualism ran strong or in those where local communities wanted to be the determiners, often noted that it was only in the religious field that they could express themselves and have a measure of power. They did not want to be dictated to by "headquarters", by "Rome" or "Geneva" or "Nairobi" or "New York"; by experts who, it was charged, homogenized and exploited them. Whether these resistances to bureaucratic and rationalized models in the secular or Christian world were always soundly based is not the issue; that they took form on the basis of perceptions of forced conformity became obvious.

THE SPECIAL CASES OF FUNDAMENTALISMS AND TRIBALISMS

A fourth set of explanations has to do with ideology. The most familiar illustration is militant fundamentalism, usually within religious orbits but having counterparts in the secular world. (Thus, it is to be noted that it is credible to define the term in such a way that it might include scientific, communist or capitalist, environmental and feminist fundamentalisms – and their oppositions.)

What is fundamentalism thus perceived and defined? It is not to be equated with conservatism, traditionalism or orthodoxy, though some of its evidences may look like these. Rather, it develops in the hands of those who diagnose the modern world as an assault on all that they are and hold dear. For example, religious pluralism often brings the stranger too near; it threatens individual and group identity. A consequence of pluralist awareness is often relativism; relativism is destructive of the faith of the group; modernizers within the group begin to make too many accommodating gestures. So fundamentalisms arise, always as reactive (though not necessarily reactionary) movements.

They are called fundamentalisms or fundamentalist-like movements because at a certain stage they reach back and retrieve, on a selective basis, some previously approved authoritative teachings, usually from a scripture or a script used scripturally. This may mean the Quran, Torah, the New Testament, papal documents from the 19th century, or the writings of Marx or Mao. Such writings are perceived as empowering those responsive to them; in religious terms, the empowered become "chosen", the instruments of the deity, agents of God or the good, and are then given a mission, often over against the other. This impulse leads them to draw boundaries and erect thick walls against outside influences and to help keep the people together. A Manichaean world-view develops, a preference for dualities that tolerates no moderation or moderates, no compromise and no compromisers.

That such fundamentalist impulses have an appeal ought to be obvious to anyone who looks at the world scene. In open competition, movements that bear "family resemblances" to fundamentalisms gain converts at the expense of ecumenical, tolerant and mutually responsive religious groups. The terrors of identity diffusion, absence of power and the threats of pluralism and relativism are so ominous to so many that they take refuge in absolutisms, and from such bases often turn aggressive. The result is, to say the least, a direction towards "divergence" on "centrifugal" lines. And ecumenical movements find everything more difficult, even as their leaders adapt and yield power to those who offer new models for interchurch or inter-religious interaction.

A fifth reason often brought forward to explain the divergent trends in the age that ought to have been cosmopolitan and ecumenical is coded under a word we have already used several times: "tribalism". Tribalism has to be voiced with caution, since it can be misused or misheard. The problem is the "ism". The tribe can be a beautiful, necessary, empowering reality, and it has been honoured from the days of ancient Israel to modern nationhood. The tribe more than the family passes on traditions and values without which the family in its generation could hardly know what to pass on. The tribe, when it works effectively, enhances trust: in it, one gains the security to find and enjoy one's identity, to celebrate the rites proper to the stages of life and the times of year and to help ward off the power of Leviathan and all agencies that would force homogenization.

Tribalism, however, is a doctrinaire, ideological and aggressive defence of the tribe. Those who advocate it magnify the difference from "the other". They promote exclusivism and enmity. In religious and ethno-nationalist spheres, the advocates tend to arrogate to their tribe the attributes or the sanctions of the divine: "God or the gods are on the side of my tribe – and you are ruled out." Tribalism often became the expression of clusters of peoples who resented artificial national boundaries that had been imposed on them by people of power in the colonial age, people who had been heedless of tribes and territories. Afterwards, post-colonially, the tribes would redraw boundaries on the map, sometimes "ethnically cleansing" those who did not match their interests or who would resist their claims. So tribalism became one more agency complicating the work of those who promoted convergences, cooperation, mutuality – and ecumenism.

A LOOK AT THE MAP AND THE CHRONICLES

To give some body to these generalizations, at least on a highly selective basis, we can look at some events that produced new chronicles, new maps, in an era of centrifugal movements and divergent trends.

Between 1968 and 2000, the event with most implications in secular and religious worlds alike was the break-up of the Soviet Union, the gaining of independence on the part of nations that had long been in the Soviet sphere of power and the rise of newly independent states. So long as Soviet communism prospered, one could say that two sets of convergences coexisted. The one, self-designated as "the free world", saw itself as united in opposition to the slave states under Marxist-Leninist influence and communist control. Having a common enemy serves to force people together into unities that they might not have chosen to experience were it not for the threat. Similarly, the Soviet Union, under harsh patterns of enforcement, imposed conformity on all nations that came under its control – along the way harassing dissenters or suppressing "tribal", ethnic or religious distinctions that would have disrupted the artificial unity that came from the powers.

During the 1980s, under the governance of Mikhail Gorbachev, movements of Soviet reform quickly went out of control and, in common parlance, the iron curtain was torn and the Berlin wall was breeched. In retrospect, any number of leaders received credit for having contributed to the implosion of the Soviet system and state: Pope John Paul II through his being a Pole and supporting Polish solidarity at the Russian borders; Gorbachev for effecting *glasnost,* a spirit and policy of reform; Ronald Reagan for cold-war policies that led to arms build-ups on both sides to the point that the Soviet Union could no longer afford it. Still others saw that the resistance had a religious base, as in the former East Germany.

Whatever credence one gave to such explanations, it also appears, or fundamentally appears to be, that the "implosion" came about because the ideology that was to produce a productive economy failed to do so. So the ideology was less believed in; the ideologues came under criticism as being elites or failures; the vision of economic freedom in the West whetted the appetite for other freedoms; all these, and more, contributed to the fall of communism on Soviet models.

What replaced the enforced homogenization was not a new homogenization, now more freely chosen than before. Instead, there re-emerged all the national and ethnic groups gathered into the Soviet sphere between 1917 and the 1990s: Ukrainian, Armenian, Arzerbaijani, Chechnyan, Turkistani, Orthodox and Jewish and Catholic and Baptist and Jehovah's Witnesses and more – all of them still articulate and many of them freshly militant.

The devastation of Soviet power and communist claims outside of China, North Korea, Cuba and a few lesser outposts left what might be called a spiritual vacuum or a desert landscape, not to be filled by any single replacement ideology, creed or force. The only sufficiently potent alternative, code-named "capitalism" or "free-market economics", had its ideological defenders and practical implementers across the globe. From a great distance one could make some generalizations about the "essence" or "nature" of capitalism. But since some of its self-advertised features are competition, individualism and freedom, it was not capable of being reduced to a credal form that might unify the world.

Capitalism, therefore, meant something quite different in China, where it became a name for relative economic freedoms unaccompanied by political freedom, through "democratic capitalism" in some of the Western nations and welfare-state capitalism in others of them, to unmonitored and utterly free-formed individualist support for laissez-faire and libertarian capitalism – hardly a creed for those who favoured convergence, or at least not a realistic embodiment of such a creed. Late-capitalism, then, could no more offer a picture of an international community or an ideal of convergence than could post-communism. The spiritual, moral and intellectual vacuum or desert remained, not to be left simply empty and bare but to begin to be filled with all kinds of conflicting competitors for attention and loyalty.

Unfortunately, much of the tribal and neo-national tension issued in open conflict. Future historians may look back at the last third of the 20th century as a period in which not only the cold war and its ending dominated the world scene, but as a time of ethno-nationalist conflict. All efforts made by the ecumenical movement across national boundaries and often within them were coloured by the fact that somewhere in the world people were shooting at each other, more often than not in the name of God or the gods. Sometimes the shooting was done by people in the name of one Christian faction versus another – as in Protestant and Catholic northern Ireland, or in white and coloured and black Protestant Reformed South Africa. Not all the shooting was inspired by religious tribalism, but religious justifications often intensified conflicts that were already present, as in the former Yugoslavia where Serb and Croat were at war, but also where Muslim, Orthodox Christian and Roman Catholic were names of contending parties. Similarly, Christian fought Christian in the mid-1990s in Rwanda and Burundi, where Hutu and Tutsi alike were more often than not Christian. It is hard to speak or think of ecumenical movements advancing under the guns.

A chronicle of warfare in these years suggests something of the following outbreaks:[2]

Between 1965 and 1969: in India-Pakistan, Mozambique, Namibia, Chad, Indonesia, Uganda, Nigeria, Middle-East (six-day war), Israel and Egypt, El Salvador and Honduras, USSR-China border, Northern Ireland, Philippines; between 1970 and 1974: Jordan, Cambodia, Pakistan, India-Pakistan, Sri Lanka, Uganda, Rhodesia, Burundi, Chile, Middle East (Yom Kippur war), Pakistan, Cyprus, Ethiopia, Iraq, Philippines; between 1975 and 1979: Lebanon, Cambodia, Indonesia, Western Sahara, Angola, Argentina, Turkey, Somalia and Ethiopia, Nicaragua, Iran (revolution), Afghanistan, Cambodia, Tanzania and Uganda, El Salvador, Iran and Iraq, China and Vietnam; between 1981 and 1988: Nicaragua, Mozambique, Syria, Falklands, Lebanon, Peru, Sri Lanka, Sudan, India, South Yemen, Somalia, Burundi – and from there into what are "current events", a dreary catalogue of traumas in a horrifying saga.

If religion intensified these conflicts, it should also be noted that there were instances where religious people worked for reconciliation. Thus, lay groups of Protestant and Catholic women in Northern Ireland won a Nobel Peace Prize for their efforts; leaders named Carter and Begin and Sadat used religious motivations discernible in each other as warrants towards peace in the Camp David Agreements; Popes Paul VI and John Paul II on occasion intervened in peace efforts, and so on. But future ecumenical strivings for decades to come may have to deal with this generally under-estimated set of conflicts and setbacks for reconcilers.

It would be difficult to present a fair and believable picture of the whole landscape surrounding ecumenical Christianity without noting that on many occasions the inter-tribal and inter-religious conflicts proceeded not through armies but through the terrorist acts of the few. Frustrated in their efforts to gain large followings, indiscriminate trouble-makers have intentionally taken history into their hands and killed. This introduced irrational and unpredictable elements onto a scene where the word of reconciliation and concord was already hard to spread or to have its works effected. To speak of this all happening in a secular world hardly does justice to the fact that very often religious names were associated with terrorism.

So another catalogue of terrifying acts would evoke images designed to disturb anyone who had held to serene and sunny views of human nature. Thus the decade of the 1980s opened with Iranian embassy seizures by Iraqis in London, fascist and neo-Nazi bombing at Munich, Armenian terrorists injuring themselves in Geneva, Armenians assassinating a Turkish consul-general, a Zionist-owned hotel in Nairobi bombed; in 1981, there was an assassination attempt on Pope John Paul II, President Anwar Sadat was assassinated in Egypt by fundamentalist terrorists, a Muslim Brotherhood car bomb killed

[2] Patrick Brogan, *World Conflicts: A Comprehensive Guide to World Strife Since 1945*, 3rd ed., London, Bloomsbury, 1998, pp.569-70.

68 in Damascus, Abu Nidal gang members hijacked a jet over India, others massacred 21 in an Istanbul synagogue, and more.

Just beyond the historical period we are reviewing, nothing did more to disturb the security of the United States and allied nations than the attack on the World Trade Center in New York and the Pentagon in Washington by terrorists who crashed jet airplanes into the buildings on 11 September 2001. The Al-Qaeda movement, an excrescence of Islamic fundamentalism influenced by Wahhabism in Saudi Arabia and the Muslim Brotherhood's Sayyid Qutb from Egypt, was held responsible. Some observers saw the attack as an expression of a "clash of civilizations", one that might unite Christians into defensive and even aggressive alliances against Islamic movements and nations. At the same time, many used the resources of Christian ecumenism to work against anti-Islamic counter-movements of high-risk character.

The purpose in this citing of events in September 2001 is to suggest how the odds work against peace-makers in a time when a few fanatics can through random activities disrupt constructive efforts by those who would work for justice and peace.

COUNTERVAILING FORCES: LEVELLING MULTICULTURALISM AND POST-MODERN RELATIVISM

Militancies, military actions and terror in the name of God did not have the landscape or news scene all to themselves throughout this period. Sometimes, the anti-ecumenical and anti-homogenizing forces worked to effect the opposite of what they claimed to be about. This is particularly the case in capitalist societies like the American. There a new word challenged the earlier-favoured and somewhat more domesticable term "pluralism": it was "multiculturalism". Few people were killed in its name, but many claimed to find their identity, acquire their interpretations of life and gain their power through multicultural advocacies.

After mentioning IRA bombings and Middle East terrorism, it may seem frivolous to draw attention to movements that often combined genuine attempts to recover lost histories and identities with extravagant claims for the virtue of one's own group defined by rather precise boundaries. A case study: In the United States, which continued to show its digestive capacity to find ways for new immigrants to make their way, where intermarriage across group boundaries was higher than ever and where mass media imagery worked erosive effects on those defined by ethnic and religious or gendered boundaries, multiculturalism came to be promoted in colleges and universities as well as in media.

The cynical could say that, for some, multiculturalism was an expression of weak egos that found their strength only when they were bonded to stronger ones. Or that it was an instrument of power, so that there could be caucuses and provisions for a pentagon of peoples who bore signs of hyphenation: Native-, Euro-, African-, Hispanic- and Asian-American. They could have their seats in congress, their visages in advertisements, their share of scholarship and curricular slots, their houses of study, if they banded together. They could make sense of literary texts if these were interpreted in community. And they could make a display of decorations from a sphere whence came the decor of life, the suggestion of slightly "other" menus, recipes, dances and the like, "other" meaning that different groups did not possess them, or possessed different versions of them.

It is often pointed out that this form of multiculturalism is to be taken only semi-seriously. It is an expression in cultures which were once *really* multicultural, as when, in Australia or Argentina or Canada and the United States, Jews talked Yiddish, ethnic groups did not know each others' cuisine and religious groups were utterly alienated from each other. Today, a consumer and capitalist culture reduces the various expressions and makes them equally accessible. The cultural icons within multiculturalism may happen to be Muslim athletes, Jewish comics, Hispanic musicians, Indigenous spiritual leaders and so on, yet they all are marketed to all in pursuit of a profit.

As valued and valuable as are the separate cultural traditions, when their particularity is insisted upon in civic or religious order, they serve again to complicate efforts at bringing people together or having them represented on grounds independent of their natural, putative or acquired and chosen "tribe". Ecumenical leaders have again learned that multicultural representation both enriches denominational and other bodies, or it can paralyze them or mute their distinctively Christian orientation and expression. However regarded, and the regarding is often done on polemical grounds, multiculturalism is part of the cultural landscape that will provide the setting for future ecumenical work in Australia, the Americas, Europe and elsewhere.

THE MOVE FROM "MODERN" TO "POST-MODERN"

In any effort to be ecumenical, one must take special pains not to let the inevitable perspective of the individual viewer unwittingly colour all attempts to do justice to a larger world. So to speak of some intellectual and spiritual trends that spread from the west of Poland across northern and western Europe through Canada and the northern United States to Japan – what I call "the spiritual ice-belt" – as being normative or characteristic of the whole world is hazardous. Many of the trends that Europeans and Americans experience in mild ways or not at all, including tribal conflict with live ammunition, are part of the daily experience of millions of people, which means also many Christians, every day. Similarly, many of the intellectual fashions that shape the moral landscape in this "ice-belt" are luxuries beyond the scope or even the imagination of those in the poor world or in other worlds with different cultural backgrounds.

Still, it is from this northern sphere that so many elements in world affairs issue. It has been the heartland of secularization, industrialization, modernization, technological production, mass communication revolutions, the development of the Internet and the like. From northern climes are exported some of the selective yields and liabilities that become part of daily life at least in some locales and on some levels – e.g., among the intellectuals, the jet-setters, the managerial elites, the middle classes – from Nairobi through Singapore to Tokyo or Santiago. Only when this is kept in mind do we feel ready to venture to name a trend most discussed and noticed in what is often called the West: the rise of the post-modern.

When such a word is introduced in a world where "the modern" has not arrived or been appropriated on any even scale, one must do some explaining. In the present context, we may speak of the years between 1945 and 1968 as "high-modern" towards "late-modern" times and from 1968 to 2000 as an ambiguously defined "late-modern" into "post-modern" time. Whoever uses these terms must be aware that a kind of arbitrary and subjective game is being played. But to refuse to play it is to miss some important signals in many parts of global culture.

In the present context, then, one speaks of the modern as a time of an international style, as seen especially in architecture. Buildings designed by Mies van der Rohe, Walter Gropius, Le Corbusier and their contemporaries, could have been anywhere and tend to be anywhere. This style is marked by rationality, coherence, coordination, an aspiration towards practicality, a mininum of decorative accretions. Such design has produced skyscrapers that make it hard for one to know whether she is in Asian, African, Latin American or European cities. Such design also erases the recall of what had been distinctive in the local cultures. "Modern art", especially in its abstract form, had a similar character. The expressions displayed a kind of integrity based on an inner logic.

The intellectual, moral and spiritual worlds have subsequently taken on more of the style architects allow to be called or choose to call "post-modern". Decoration is back, and "style" has returned. So have elements of tradition. But the inner logic and rationality have been replaced by an eclectic jumble of elements. An architect can in the same building evoke but not really represent Gothic, Romanesque, colonial, Greek and modern aspects in juxtaposition. The result can be pleasing to the eye and useful for intended purposes, yet it is anything but coherent. In visual arts, collage, montage, assemblage and similar expressions are characteristically post-modern.

In literature and philosophy, the post-modern sensibility creates doubt and promotes suspicion as to the connection between the sign and the signified: "c-a-t" and "G-o-d" are arbitrarily chosen sounds; they could have been anything else; they do not point in any intrinsic and integral way to a reality. No meanings are stable. Such a concept, over-promoted for a time in the 1980s in Western academies, is being called into question. But where it dominates, it is hard for the ecumenical intention to be worked out. Ecumenists certainly are capable of selective appropriations and introducing measures of eclecticism themselves. But they have taken seriously the meanings of the texts of the various traditions, something that is hard to do when the interpreter of the text dominates the legacy of the original creator of each.

Another feature of the post-modern posture, one that shares with all the others both some assets and some liabilities for those who would work ecumenically, is the hermeneutical realization. In pre-modern (and pre-ecumenical) and modern (ecumenical) times – both the parenthesized terms being used in a special time-ly sense here – more attention was paid to the uni-vocal character of texts. Pioneer ecumenists expressed the belief that if people of rational outlook, good will and intentions, and with the Holy Spirit's blessing, would sit down to confront a text or a textual tradition, sooner or later they would see each other's viewpoint and maybe move towards agreement about its meanings. Of course, there was room for local colour: one expected the word "freedom" to mean something different where modern liberation movements were in effect than where earlier revolutions had long before produced situations that assured individuals their freedom. One expected Eastern Orthodox after nine centuries or more to have different cultural norms for measuring validities in worship than Westerners employed. But it was assumed that East and West could come to a kind of objective agreement on the essentials.

In the hermeneutical revolution that colours everything on the global landscape that ecumenists face, all this is different. The hermeneutical or interpretive arts begin with the assumption that texts are multivocal and that readers have multiple perspectives. What is more, they interpret the texts in no small measure in the light of their own experience and, perhaps more, the experience of the "interpretive community" to which they belong. This is the case with readers and leaders who have dominated others and also with their victims or underlings. So a prosperously patriarchal senior male in power will read a biblical text or a civil constitution differently than will, say, an abused woman, a victim of slavery or wage slavery, and so forth. What one gets from a text depends in part on what one brings to it, or what, more particularly, one's identity group brings to it.

Post-modern instability of interpretations and hermeneutical perspectives can be designations that illumine why it is so difficult to get Spirit-filled, rational, well-intended people to unite, put energies into councils or seek a uniting church around the world. There is no question but that feminist, Africanist and other interpretations have greatly enriched the understanding of texts, including biblical writings. It is quite likely that many of the sub-groups within Christianity or a specific civil order have more access to a hearing and to rites than do those that exclude all readings but one and are forcefully anti-hermeneutical. But grant the hermeneutical revolution and reading, and you find that ecumenical endeavours are more complex at the same time. It is not likely that this hermeneutical insight will disappear completely as a new rationalism or objectivism finds its way in the Western and, through it, global communities.

THE SECULAR ECUMENISM OF THE MARKET AND THE IMBALANCE OF TRADE

In the mid-century decades, Sino-Soviet communism was very much alive. With its satellites, this complex governed – many would have judged then and judge now, en-thralled – more than a third of the human race. At its root was the notion of a controlled collective economy; at its top, adherence to its ideology and practices was coerced. Alongside communism, there were any number of more moderate and less violently supported socialisms, wherein some measure of collective economic pattern was pres-ent. Still more moderate were the welfare states of the sort most recognized in Scandi-navian polities and economies.

Enemies of the regimes on the left were often critical of any who made religious de-fences of any aspect of them. In the brutal and totalitarian cases, the critique had to do not only with economic coercion but religious restriction: Soviet and Chinese regimes persecuted, harassed, controlled or limited most religious expression, including that of Christians. Those who kept Christian witness alive in the more repressive circum-stances either had to go into dissent, be seen as compromisers or, as it turns out they were in some cases, be suspected as agents of the government. In the moderate and elected governments where socialisms and welfare states were present, there was much more Christian support for planned and distributive economies. And, of course, from the right there was a criticism of any such support on various economic and theologi-cal grounds.

In Latin America, the Christian support for socialisms was most frequent, character-istic and intense. After mid-century, there developed schools of thought and action that came to be known as liberation theology. This is not the place to detail such thought, pat-terned as it was after biblical prophetic assertions that God has a "preferential option for the poor" along with some Marxian analysis and criticism. It is the place to notice it, however, as a mode of adaptation to and promotion of something in the secular context that coloured ecumenical work. Most of the support was vigorously nonviolent in ethos and intention. There were exceptions, however, and in some cases Christian leaders gave support to the idea and even the realization of violent revolution. Such support evoked vehement criticism from the religious and political right across the globe and led to cau-tion and nervousness among many who supported the economic moves with some hope and some reserve.

Between 1968 and 2000, but closer to the end than to the beginning of the period, the Christianity of the left began to wane along with the economies and polities to which it was attached or which it had advocated. Some of those who had been on the left in many nations read the signs of the times and switched to the economic and political right. More continued their critique of unfettered and unmonitored capitalism and refused to give it their word of blessing as being the uniquely favoured if not the only way of God in human economic affairs. They sought ways to transcend the communist/capitalist duality as an exclusive set of options.

Meanwhile, towards the end of the period, as the left was in retreat and its most articulated and coerced forms came to defeat, many religious people including Christians did begin to favour laissez-faire capitalism as God's chosen instrument for human good. Just as the left had used prophetic language to provide theological justification for its stand, the right, as its predecessors through the century had done, selected a different set of texts to legitimate the unqualified right to private property; the removal of government from economic participation; the ethics of work and private stewardship; and the claim that capitalism allowed for the most creativity and human development or freedom.

In both cases of the left and the right, the economies and polities would no doubt have existed and prospered without the blessings of the people of God. So these belong fundamentally to what is our topic: the secular context or environment for Christian ecumenism. Let us assume here that some form of economy to be called capitalist will prevail for an indefinite future, perhaps to be replaced eventually by something not now clearly envisioned. This means that Christians in most parts of the world will make decisions against the background of market economies and business-oriented ethics.

If the left's controlled or welfare economies represented the patterns of convergence or centripetality, their replacements are, by definition and in their unfolding, part of the centrifugality of direction. By definition? Because capitalisms stress competition more than cooperation; they pit companies and people and classes against each other. Yet it must also be noted that, paradoxically, the business economy also has an ecumenical character.

First, one notes that this economy has reduced the size of the world and enlarged the need for signals to pass around it. This is the McWorld of which Benjamin Barber spoke as he posed it over against *Jihad*. The invention of satellite communication and then the electronic Internet makes possible instant transacting around the globe. People far from Japan wake up in the morning seeing how the dollar does against the yen. People far from Arab Middle East pipelines watch how the price and flow of oil varies. When the Arabs "stepped on the pipelines" in 1973-74 and threatened an oil shortage, users of oil around the world were suddenly alerted to the fact that they shared a small and interactive oikoumene.

The market is also ecumenical in that it knows no religious boundaries. Shi'ite Muslim fundamentalists in oil-rich countries know that their law, Sharia, forbids the taking of interest. Yet to be in a world economy they deal with interest. So they invent elaborate, often computerized, terminologically nuanced descriptions to make it seem as if they are conforming to religious law while, in effect, taking interest. Israeli Orthodox Jews, for reasons of adaptation to a market world, invent elaborate ways to compromise without overtly violating the law. Christians, who once opposed life insurance because it signalled doubt in God's providence, during this century often established highly successful fraternal life insurance companies of their own.

As evident as these negotiations with modernity were in this period, even more evident has been the development of what social scientists and the pope alike call "a consumerist mentality". When economies depend upon the market, what people buy and sell is more important than what they save or give. The development of advertising and public relations encourages frequent – indeed, constant – consumption. In the prosperous world, this leads to an almost obsessive use of the shopping mall, an agency that often acquires a kind of religious cast.

Pope John Paul II could regularly criticize the tendency to reduce humans to market objects through advertising and social pressure. This meant that the human might become "nothing but..." a consumer. The papal warnings had little effect; early in this period, many movements among Christians to seek the simple life were displaced by those that gloried in consumption as a market stimulant.

If many of the market goods issue from the rich world, they are offered for sale in the poor, and status of persons often depends upon the goods they come to possess. Gone, then, are the phenomena once known as "Protestant this-worldly asceticism", "the work ethic", much of the idea of stewardship, and much charitable activity and giving. Whatever ecumenical-minded Christians decide is the biblical or Christian thing to do in the economy, a safe predicter would say that the leadership is likely to come up with rationales for whatever economists and the market determine will be the direction.

While papal, episcopal, preacherly and leftist critiques of consumerism issue forth and consumers keep consuming and keeping the world economy going, the prophet and other critical voices will also find much to depict concerning imbalances in the world economy. There is a "rich world" in which many are poor and there is a "poor world" in which some are rich. Ecumenical Christianity is one of the agencies that can make people in both aware of each other. While much of the Christian literary production and setting of terms was formerly of European and North American varieties, a feature that often made the Christian movements seem more convergent and similar to each other than they were, the centrifugal thrust in recent decades has spun observers to scenes long unfamiliar to them, or misnamed and misperceived. So long as ecumenical Christians of Europe and America after 1910 still spoke of "foreign missions" and then "younger churches", they did not need to see the missionized on their own terms, the younger churches through their own eyes. And the missionary and younger churches were often reduced to dependency upon the Northern Christian world for goods and gifts, personnel, terminology and theology.

In recent years, this has changed. The Christian momentum is now in the southern hemisphere. While it is not strictly our business to account for Christian growth in this chapter, some mention of the relative size of Christian communities in various continental locales will frame our act of framing. Thus in the best reckoning, in 2002 the Christian census that cited the number of adherents read like this:[3]

Africa	352,886,000
Asia	320,439,000
Europe	537,656,000
Latin America	490,701,000
North America	215,633,000
Oceania	21,898,000

[3] *International Bulletin of Missionary Research*, 26, 1, 2002, p.23.

It is shocking to many North Americans to see that, except for lightly populated Australia, their continent has the fewest Christians, and it does little for the accuracy of their perceptions to see the large number in Europe, until they are made aware of the nominal and vestigial character of many Christian populations there compared to the dynamism of sub-Saharan and Latin American Christian movements and churches. Any glance at such statistics will suggest to the informed that Christianity is either the religion of elites in the poor world – which a second glance will show is not the case – or that most Christians are among and of the poor. And if so, there will be a special poignancy to appeals to do justice and love mercy in respect to the poor neighbour elsewhere. Given the rapid population growth elsewhere, it is likely that alert Christians will have to find new focus in the light of changes in the power bases of Christians. Thus one set of computer-using prognosticators foresees that in 2025 the continental configuration will be as follows:

Africa	669,526,000
Asia	459,029,000
Europe	532,861,000
Latin America	635,271,000
North America	235,112,000
Oceania	28,152,000

If there is anything at all to these projections based on population growth and churchly vitality, it is envisioned that Europe would see a net loss of Christian numbers and a move from first to fourth place among the continents. And North America, with small population growth and a settled secular orientation in many of its parts, would experience but slight growth and would remain the second least Christianly populated continent.

Back to the secular motif that is our assignment: Christians in the European and American worlds, if they care about their church ecumenical, will be alert to and identified with what goes on in Latin America or the southern Asian sub-continent as much as they have been concerned with each others' homelands. And African, Latin American and southern Asian church people, while less dependent than before on goods and outreach from the North, will find new reasons to appraise their posture and sometimes extend empathy for their travail and relative decline.

Along with concerns for the environment, population, planning and development, this kind of petite-global view, enhanced in McWorld by satellite and Internet communication, is also going to provide reasons for paying more attention than before to world health problems. To take but one illustration: half way through the period under discussion, a new tendency and a new disease developed, HIV and AIDS. It may have broken out first in Africa and was soon exported to Europe and North America and then throughout the world. While agitation for addressing the AIDS problem and summoning resources for treatment and cure have come from the United States and Europe, the huge mortality rates are in Africa where, transmitted by homosexual and heterosexual contact and the needles of drug users, it has spread to millions upon millions in some nations. Similarly, new strands of tuberculosis and viral infections that developed in the poor world became threats everywhere. Christians who claim to be devoted to healing cannot continue in mindlessly divergent directions but will be looking for ways to return to some concept of a holistic-minded "one world" if there is to be a reduction of these threats and a human address to the diseased. To all this one might add the ever more urgent questions of pollution, deforestation, desertification and defoliation in some parts of the world as they will have a bearing on others.

HOW SECULAR IS THIS "SECULAR ENVIRONMENT"?

Throughout this survey and analysis, we have used the assigned word "secular" to describe the intellectual, moral, "spiritual" and practical envelopes that surround the world of Christian ecumenism. It is not any more likely that we can satisfyingly define the term "secular" than that we can let it go and do away with it or find a satisfactory replacement. But enough change has occurred in the usages of the concept to warrant some examination of its present and possible future utility.

The term has roots in the word *saeculum*, which simply means the present age, the world of this time and the time of this world. In the Middle Ages in European Christendom, the term acquired specific uses as a kind of cognate for "profane", which meant *pro+fanum* = that which was outside the sanctuary. So there was a "secularization" of land when ecclesiastical properties were removed from church ownership and control. There were secular priests, who moved around the landscape as compared to the religious who stayed cloistered or close to the altar. In due course, the term acquired a slight post-Enlightenment tinge and came to mean, as some theologians put it, that the world "rounds itself off" the same whether or not God exists, and God does not have to be reckoned with. In modern times, when an "ism" got attached to it, "secularism" came to mean a systematic, often belligerent acting as if God did not exist or played no role in human affairs. That is a rarer use, however; ordinarily, "secular" is a more neutral, matter-of-factly employed term for practical god-lessness in societies and cultures.

At the end of the period 1945-68, in the writings of some theologians in the Western Christian sphere at least, "secular" came to be appropriated positively in the Christian vocabulary and was seen as a designation for a world in which magic and miracle, metaphysics and mysticism and mystery, played waning roles. The human of the future was going to become a kind of "computer with legs" and the societies of the future would characteristically act unmindfully about God or the gods. Yet on such a scene, it was reasoned, biblical proclamation could have fresh effect. This remained a minority view, however.

Not all scholars and trend-spotters were content with the employment of the word "secular" to describe the ethos and mentality of everyone in sight, nor then to project that as an inevitably pervasive style in the world's future. Vying with it through the late modern and into the most recent period have been various concepts associated with "modernization". These are not the same as the notions connected with "modern" in architecture, efficient engineering of lives or bureaucratization in organization, since these sought conformity and organicism. Instead, "modernization" came to be associated with the directions we have called "divergent" or "centrifugal" for they worked against coherence and the integral.

Modernization of this sort related to "differentiation", the chopping up of life into sectors, the separation, for example, of "religious" from "secular", "this world" from "after-life", clergy from laity, fact from value, economics from politics, work place from home place, and the like. Denominations were part of this kind of differentiated Christianity, and ecumenism was to minimize this differentiation and promote more common styles. The period from 1968 to 2000, however, saw an increase, not a decrease, in denominations; five a week were added, say some statisticians, and the number of separate Christian denominations in the world was growing, right through the "ecumenical century", towards the 25,000 mark. Some have predicted the demise of denominations in the world of the centrifugal, because denominational organizations are still too coherent, routinized, static, unitive or coordinated to survive in the competition of a market economy of religion. Competition and supply-side religious economies lead to para-churches and post-denominational entities. (We envision that these will become quasi-denominations in due course. "Denomination" is the slot that most societies have for religion after disestablishment occurs, when the non-established can no longer be conceived of and called "dissenters".)

Denominational proliferation has not helped Christians cover all the spiritual bases, however. So, as the century came towards its end and more and more people found the secular model wanting, they turned to a variety of options. The code word for their turning, in North America and Europe, is "spiritual" or "spirituality", but it has cognates in all the cultures, also in those where secularization had not spread so far or gone so deeply. Spirituality is of a heightened centrifugal character; those who favour it outside the traditions – as they had previously dominated within the traditioned instances of Christian, Jewish or Muslim spirituality – invented or reclaimed very individualized and even idiosyncratic forms of expression. Spirituality has come to be used as a term for alternatives to "organized religion", "the institutional church" and often even for religion itself. Religion is too coherent and communal; it stifles the individual's spiritual journey, say the advocates of the journey-in-isolation.

While such spirituality may not be the mark of sub-Saharan African Christians or of believers in New Delhi, it is likely to be an indicator of still another complication for ecumenical Christianity. If the spiritual searchers disdain all institutions, they will have little patience for interaction between Orthodoxy and evangelicalism, Catholicism and Presbyterianism, or even Christian-Buddhist dialogue. Whoever supports Christian ecumenism may well first have to work for the conversion of many people from isolation to community, from independence and individualism to association and commitment.

Of course, the secular designation will continue to describe aptly many dimensions of many elements in world cultures. That most science proceeds secularly is evident when one notices how much is made of the rarer scientist who finds it important to speak of God. That most literature, arts, entertainment and athletics phenomena join the market in being independent of God-talk is equally obvious when one notes the celebrity that is extended to the exceptional Christian or other religious person among elites in these worlds.

"Secular rationality" is an apt descriptive term for efforts in the higher academy to utilize and promote the sceptical mode in the search for learning. Mass communicators and those who govern in a pluralist society find it convenient to restrict themselves to using such modes of reasoning. Even in the world of health care, where faith has, it is said, a certified bearing on how people cope with death, deal with illness or face suffering, much of the medical enterprise, including the fashioning of ethical discourse, proceeds under the secular canopy. It might be noted with irony that precisely the people who get paid to give an accounting for and an address to the culture are the last to hear of the main spiritual trends and tendencies of publics. Church leadership was also caught off guard, much of it having promoted secular styles precisely at the moment when they were being called into question elsewhere.

COMMUNITIES OF WORLD RELIGIONS AND CONVERSATION IN A SECULAR WORLD

While questioning the purity of the secular designation, we do well to note not only the differentiating, fissiparating and diverging forms of spirituality apart from religion, but also to see the renewed growth of many of the communities of world religion. A quick canvass of these and of projections for their future will reinforce the point. Again, we will compare 1970 with 2002 and 2025. While Christians have gone on holding their (roughly) 33.1 percent or 34 percent of humanity – moving towards 2025's possible 36.9 percent, other religions, some of which were observed being sleepy and caught off guard in the 19th-century missionary era, slumber no more.

The most dramatic growth in the religious world that we call secular has been Muslim: from 553,528,000 in 1970, earlier in our period, to 1,239,029,000 in 2002 to 2025's envisioned 1,784,876,000. Jews, who in 2002 numbered only 14,670,000 worldwide and potentially will count only 16,053,000 in 2025, along with Hindus and Buddhists in greater numbers, at best keep pace with population growth and are more likely to experience percentage decline than are Christians and Muslims, to whom so much of the world's future and, alas and probably, conflict's future, belong. That is one of the biggest features of the world envisioned a decade and more from now.

To speak only of growth and conflict does not do justice to one other element that has entered the inter-religious scene in this period: dialogue, conversation and mutual influence. One may attribute the increase in such dialogue to a number of elements. First, many leaders and adherents have become aware of how dangerous militant religion is. Second, many individuals are truly tolerant and respectful of others. They look for better ways to relate to each other. To these two we may add curiosity. For many people to whom the tradition of their culture and family does not speak satisfyingly, there is a quest; thus, Westerners may explore Hinduism or Buddhism through travel, literary pursuits, retreats or even by joining companies of people who represent faiths far from their own. Post-modern relativism may be a fourth contributing factor: if nothing can be assured or assuredly true within a faith tradition, then everything can be conceived of as true. One may as well dabble in other traditions and appropriate from them what is pleasing and satisfying.

Ecumenical leaders are aware of great changes on the inter-religious front, changes that affect the way they go about their own work. For example, at the Second Vatican Council the bishops approved a decree, *Nostra Aetate* ("The Relation of the Church to Non-Christian Religions"), which spoke in friendly terms of witness and light beyond Christianity, Judaism and Islam, the Abrahamic and Jerusalemaic faith of "the peoples of the book". That declaration emboldened many Catholic scholars to explore the faiths in which some light also shines and to show an openness to re-examining their own postures. (Such questioning has also accompanied some decline in the impulse to send missionaries beyond historic Christian homelands. "Proselytization" has been much criticized, and there is an increasing diffidence about interrupting other cultures and religions and "imposing" one's own faith. Implications of such alterations for Christian ecumenism are vast.)

An intellectual agenda has been set forth in recent decades: systematic theologians within the Christian tradition, looking at the "secular" (but also really religious) environment have begun to conceive theologies that take "the faiths of other people" seriously. Few of them look forward to a synthesis of religions and few suggest that "truth" in religion is to be found half-way between the faith communities. They do not picture it easy to affirm the faith of "the other" to its final end. Thus the final word in Christianity is *theos*, the God who is a Thou; in Buddhism it is something like "holy emptiness". So there is no foundational meeting point. But the years 1968-2000 have left on the table the charter for further inquiry about how the faiths relate to each other in the "religio-secular" world.

RELIGIO-SECULAR ISSUES CLOSEST TO THE PERSON

To speak in global terms about the faiths of peoples and of dramatic secular forces risks the possibility of missing how most people conceive of what is most important to them. To write about interfaith conflict, tribal warfare and dialogue between leaders is to overlook the priorities of ordinary people. For a study of fundamentalisms around the world, R. Scott Appleby and I conceived a way to look at these priorities.[4] We imagined an individual and asked what was closest to her (or him). Then we moved towards outer edges of this personal experience to the social, following a set of concentrics. Assessments of the secular environment of Christianity might adapt this scheme.

Thus closest to one is one's "world-view," one's *Ur-* or foundational view of reality. This may come with one's genetic package, early upbringing or conversion experiences. Finding enlightenment, becoming "born again", turning to see hope – all these go into a world-view. Threats to a world-view in a world of pluralism, media assaults and relativism or proselytization, inspired reaction between 1968 and 2000.

Next to this is the experience of relating to one's personal and social identity: To whom do I belong and who belongs to me? Whom do I trust and on whom can I count? Much of the tribal conflict issued from this immediate sphere in the three decades being reviewed.

Third is the question of one's gender, a fundamental issue of differentiation. "Male and female he created them." During these decades, in many cultures there has been a more frank accounting than before of other differentiations: gay, lesbian and bi-sexual. Whatever touches on anything this close to individuals will occasion religious response and reaction.

A fourth circle extends this set of perceptions and occasion for reaction to the most intimate bonding, as in the family. "Family values" may be a code word in North America, but it represents an issue everywhere, as people and peoples improvize new ways of being intimately together or call old ones, e.g., the polygynous, into question. All over the world, these family issues are threatened or full of the promise that accompanies change.

How to propagate the tradition, whatever we hold dear. How to have it confirmed in the next generation? Education represents the next concentric circle of awareness and action. Everywhere debates over schooling affect the religious scene. Muslim fundamentalists, West Bank Jews, Roman Catholics in Peru, Canadians of all faiths, Europeans where Muslim populations crowd Christian ones are only a few of the populations that illustrate the volatility of educational issues.

If education represents the extension of such issues through time, mass media of communication extend faith issues in space, as radio, television, cinema and the Internet bring the distant near, the remote close to hand. Since mass media invade traditional cultures, homes and consciousnesses, they often are the main agents of cultural revolutions and the main sources for new agendas on the table of Christian ecumenists. One might well add the clinic, the hospital, the world of medical research and care as a sixth zone. Around the world, the secular environment has become religio-secular as people in technological societies re-inquire about the religious roots of traditional medicine and traditionalists try to acquire the benefits of technology and modern health-care delivery.

It is only at this point that the "macro" themes form the outer zones of one's consciousness: economics, politics, warfare and terrorism. Appleby and I noticed that

---

[4] M.E. Marty and R.S. Appleby eds, *Fundamentalisms Observed*, Chicago, Univ. of Chicago Press, 1991.

religion made news in the secular world when terrorists acted in God's name, or when godly fought godly in tribal religious conflict, or when political orders and constitutions were assaulted by the religious and religions or when the economy changed. But politics was increasingly an expression of what had been part of the private sphere: people cared most and fought most over the closest-to-the-centre zones. There world-view, identity, gender, family, education, media and health care preoccupied every sentient and responsible person. Politics? Yes. But a book title of these years, *Everything Is Politics but Politics Isn't Everything*,[5] put well the way most people conceive of the reality around them.

Of course, people in poor worlds determine the priorities differently than do those in prosperous and politically more secure ones. In order to stay alive, some will seek to effect revolution or drastic political change, often in the name of God, if they are hungry enough. The "filled" may seek no more than minor adjustments in their political order and work to assure security for themselves and their values through other than military means. Both cases and all those between them have implications for Christians as they relate to their environment.

One can look at the United Nations conferences on population and development at Cairo in 1994 and the conference on women at Beijing in 1995 to see how the secular agenda impinges upon religion and how much the religious feel they have a stake in the secular order. The Vatican and Islamic fundamentalists challenged most of the "progressive" items on the agendas at these conferences. They reacted against "family planning" and "population planning" and "reproductive rights" issues as United Nations conferees proposed and debated them. Meanwhile, other religious forces supported the proposals.

Just as these issues of gender and family are prime on the secular table, they serve to inspire controversy within the various communities of faith. Most Christian communions are in bitter conflict over them. How to define and relate to homosexuality, abortion, non-marital sex, divorce, female circumcision and scores of other tense matters are questions that sunder religious bodies. They accompany their fighting over these questions with the whole issue of ecclesiastical authority. At mid-century, it would not have been foreseen by many that sex-plus-authority would be a prime element on the social agenda of the religious, thanks to change in the secular cultural environment. But it is now likely that for decades to come Christians, but not only Christians, will relate to that combination of themes in ways that inspire conflict between reactionaries and progressives, holders to what they conceive of as the tradition and those who would improvise.

CONCLUSION ABOUT THE RELIGIO-SECULAR ENVIRONMENT

We have conceived the secular environment as "religio-secular". Of course, one apologises for using such an inelegant construct, and there is no need to wish it into the dictionaries. But for present purposes, it signals something of importance. The late modern (or post-modern) world that responsible Christian ecumenists inherit, after the experiences of 1968-2000, is indeed an unstable one. Instability brings with it threats, for it is bewildering and can be devastating. The historian who looks at twenty centuries of Christianity and almost a century of modern ecumenical invention, however,

---

5 H.M. Kuitert, *Everything Is Politics but Politics Isn't Everything*, London, SCM Press, 1986.

also sees possibilities in the experiment that such times of ferment and instability evoke. The ancient dreams of a world that would be wholly and utterly religious, by any definition, came to be denied in the secular unfolding after the second world war, when "the West" exported its secular styles. But the modern dreams of a world that would be satisfyingly secular have also been denied. They are replaced by visions of a world in which in some modes people and cultures will be content with the ordinarily rational and practical approaches to life – and, at the same time, alert to the signals we associate with words like "spiritual", "soul", "transcendence" and, yes, God.

BIBLIOGRAPHY

Berger, Peter L. ed, *The Desecularization of the World: Resurgent Religion and World Politics*, Grand Rapids MI, Eerdmans, 1999, 135p.

Bevans, Stephen B., *Models of Contextual Theology*, Maryknoll NY, Orbis, 1992, 146p.

Burce, Jerome E., *Proclaiming the Scandal: Reflections on Postmodern Ministry*, Harrisburg PA, Trinity, 2000, 123p.

Edwards, David L., *The Futures of Christianity: An Analysis of Historical, Contemporary and Future Trends within the Worldwide Church*, London, Hodder & Stoughton, 1987, 479p.

Featherstone, Mike, *Undoing Culture, Globalization, Postmodernism and Identity*, London, SAGE, 1995, 178p.

Geffré, Claude and Jossua, Jean-Pierre eds, *The Debate on Modernity*, London, SCM Press, 1992, 130p.

Gill, Robin, *Christian Ethics in Secular Worlds*, Edinburgh, T&T Clark, 1991, 159p.

Hardy, Daniel W. and Sedgwick, P. H. eds, *The Weight of Glory: A Vision and Practice for Christian Faith: The Future of Liberal Theology*, Edinburgh, T&T Clark, 1991, 316p.

Histoire du christianisme des origines à nos jours, sous la direction de Jean-Marie Mayeur, Charles et Luce Pietri, André Vauchez, Marc Venard. Tome 13, Crises et renouveau, de 1958 à nos jours, Paris, Desclée, 2000, 794p.

Jaspert, Bernd ed. *Ökumenische Kirchengeschichte: Probleme, Visionen, Methoden*, Paderborn, Bonifatius, 1998, 218p.

Lawrence, Bruce B., *Defenders of God: The Fundamentalist Revolt against the Modern Age*, Columbia SC, Univ. South Carolina Press, 1989, 306p.

Marty, Martin Emile and Appleby, R. Scott eds, *Fundamentalisms Observed*, Chicago, Univ. Chicago Press, 1991, 872p.

Newbigin, James Edward Lesslie, Sanneh, Lamin and Taylor, Jenny, *Faith and Power: Christianity and Islam in "Secular" Britain*, London, SPCK, 1998, 177p.

Osborn, Lawrence, *Restoring the Vision: The Gospel and Modern Culture*, London, Mowbray, 1995, 210p.

Raiser, Konrad, *To Be the Church: Challenges and Hopes for a New Millennium*, WCC, 1997, 104p.

Regan, Hilary D. and Torrance, Alan J. eds, *Christ and Context: The Confrontation between Gospel and Culture*, Edinburgh, T&T Clark, 1993, 269p.

Sacks, Jonathan, *The Persistence of Faith: Religion, Morality and Society in a Secular Age*, London, Weidenfeld & Nicolson, 1991, 118p.

Snyder, Howard A. ed, *Global Good News: Mission in a New Context*, Nashville TN, Abingdon, 2001, 269p.

Stark, Rodney and Finke, Roger, *Acts of Faith: Explaining the Human Side of Religion*, Berkeley CA, Univ. California Press, 2000, 343p.

Tilley, Terrence W. ed., *Postmodern Theologies: The Challenge of Religious Diversity*, Maryknoll NY, Orbis, 1995, 182p.

Weinrich, Michael, *Ökumene am Ende? Plädoyer für einen neuen Realismus*, Neukirchen-Vluyn, Neukirchener, 1997, 182p.

Wengert, Timothy J. and Brockwell, Charles W. eds, *Telling the Churches' Stories: Ecumenical Perspectives on Writing Christian History*, Grand Rapids MI, Eerdmans, 1995, 134p.

2
Major Trends in the Life of the Churches

Lukas Vischer

To understand the history of the ecumenical movement, we must first look at the history of the churches themselves. The ecumenical movement is inseparable from that history, which it depends on, reflects on, stands out from or even contradicts. Accordingly, we have to ask what has happened in the churches even though it is impossible to offer anything like a full account of those events. This chapter can provide only an outline of major trends. The following pages are, therefore, no more than an initial survey of the manifold strands in the history of the churches from 1968 through 2000.

A TIME OF GROWTH

The decades under review saw an expansion of Christianity, however astonishing this may sound to many people, especially in the "Christian nations" of the West. The number of Christians increased throughout the world. In the countries of East Asia, in particular, the Christian faith took root in ways never anticipated. In Korea, Christians increased from around 3 million in 1970 to more than 12 million in 1997: Christians represented by 2000 about 25 percent of the country's total population. Moreover, several thousand Korean missionaries were active in many countries. In China, the churches not only survived the period through the Cultural Revolution but emerged strengthened from persecution and repression. Thousands of churches were reopened or newly opened after 1979, when a policy of toleration of religion was restored. Estimates are always uncertain, but it is safe to say that the increase in the number of Christians in China was proportionally considerably greater than the growth in population. Similar developments may be observed in other parts of the world, too. The number of Christians rose significantly in Indonesia and India as well as in African countries such as Nigeria and the Democratic Republic of the Congo.

The Roman Catholic Church undoubtedly saw the largest overall increase. The Second Vatican Council strengthened the church's position in the southern hemisphere. Reforms, especially in liturgy, laid the foundations for a new self-confidence on the part of local Catholic churches. In many countries, those churches came to play an important role in national integration; where disintegration and insecurity prevailed, the stability proper to the Roman Catholic Church as a worldwide community exerted immense

• This text was translated from the original German by John Cumming.

drawing power. Its consistent witness for justice was, in many places, a source of appeal among the disadvantaged and oppressed.

This growth is certainly not restricted to the Roman Catholic Church. In both Korea and China, for example, Protestant churches in particular had grown and continued to grow. Protestant missionary work, mainly "evangelical", bore fruit in many parts of the world. But the most powerful growth in the non-Roman Catholic sphere was experienced by Pentecostalism – in the widest sense of the word. In many countries this was not only the largest but the most rapidly developing non-Roman Catholic religious community. This growth occurred in many different forms since Pentecostal spirituality was not confined to communities organized as Pentecostal churches. It was also the decisive characteristic of several spontaneous and independent movements, especially in Africa and Latin America. In the shape of the charismatic movement, it found a place in the mainline churches, especially Anglican and Roman Catholic. Informed observers believe that the number of persons identified as Pentecostalists by 2000 may be estimated at more than 300 million.

A quite different course was to be observed in the Western churches. Almost without exception, the membership of the historic churches diminished in the last three decades of the second millenium. Identification with Christian tradition had clearly receded. The idea of "Christian nations", always somewhat dubious, had become close to meaningless. Secularization, with its general acceptance of modern values and attitudes, made the churches de facto minorities and the proclamation of the gospel became a defensive activity. The venerable "drapery" inherited from the past no longer fit the situation of the historic churches. Their influence on public life was contracting, and the need in more than one Western country to redefine and restructure church-state relationships was certainly not accidental. Trends towards the privatization of religious life intensified. Informal modes of religious life and practice were increasingly evident, and society as a whole seemed ever more prone to a proliferation of religious movements and communities extending all the way to sects and secret societies.

The tendency to identify less and less with ecclesiastical tradition did not exclude the possibility of new breakthroughs. Precisely because their witness no longer evoked an automatic response, wide circles within the churches were increasingly aware of their missionary vocation. The rising number of committed groups – whether monastic communities or movements committed to specific causes – showed the gospel's extraordinary capacity to inspire alternative ways of life even, indeed precisely, in secularized societies. The longing for another kind of life found expression in large assemblies of young people such as the German *Kirchentag* or popular pilgrimages to Taizé or Santiago de Compostela.

Yet the part now played by conservative movements in almost all Western churches may have come to be more characteristic of the late 20th-century situation. Conservative options had become more attractive, many people feeling that tradition, whatever its actual form, was a source of certainty and credibility. Conservative movements, to be sure, did not see themselves merely as defending traditional values but, like the evangelical movement, sought faithfully to witness to the gospel both in their own countries and throughout the world.

Things were different in Eastern Europe in these decades. The churches were repressed, and their witness was severely impeded under communist regimes. Yet they represented one of the few institutions able to survive as relatively independent bodies. For many people, therefore, they were symbols of resistance to the state's totalitarian grip on society. The collapse of the communist system created an entirely new situation. Whereas many in both East and West had assumed that the secularization of society in the East was the result of coercion and governmental constraint, it was now clear that the effect of secularization on society went much deeper than that. Henceforth, the challenges posed by modern society to the churches had to be confronted on a new level.

All this implies a considerable shift of emphasis in the Christian world. Churches in Africa, Asia and Latin America were by the year 2000 numerically in the majority; they were also sources of new and creative initiatives. Western theology and church life no longer showed the way. Increasingly, Christianity has become polycentric and theology has taken on a wide variety of forms. Having to face up to their own particular context led churches to adopt new approaches to both theological reflection and ecclesiastical practice.

WHAT CAN WE HOPE FOR?

The general expectation in the 1960s was the eventual arrival of a new and better society. Though social change inevitably required victims, the ongoing struggle was expected to lead in the end to horizons filled with promise. New technologies and a steady increase in the production of goods appeared to guarantee an ever-greater degree of universal well-being. This confidence in technological and industrial development was common to both rival ideological systems, adverse critics of the systems generally making the same assumptions. The civil-rights movement in the US seemed to prove that society could indeed be changed. Similarly, the vision offered by the 1968 revolts and demonstrations in France and other European countries relied on an assumption that a new division of power was within the realm of possibility. The dark forces blocking the way to a favourable outcome of historical progress could be vanquished, if only imagination was granted access to power.

Step by step, this confidence eroded in the following decades. It became clear that injustice has much deeper roots than many had suspected. Above all, it was found necessary to scrutinize and suspect technological and industrial development. At the end of the 20th-century, as Western Christians looked back, many asked whether the entire course society had taken since the 1950s had to be completely reconsidered.

The favourite theme of the 1950s and 1960s was development. The technological, industrial and, therefore, economic development of the Northern nations was to be universalized. Justice was to be realized by giving the "underdeveloped" countries a share of the good things that comprised the new well-being. The churches, including the World Council of Churches and the Roman Catholic Church, also dedicated themselves to this project. But the obstacles in its way soon became all too harshly evident. The North-South divide between rich and poor nations showed no signs of narrowing; indeed, it grew wider. Initiatives for structural change proved illusory. Revolutionary movements that tried to force changes were suppressed by military dictatorships. Even when individual countries, particularly in Eastern Asia, leaped to the level of industrial nations, the structure of economic dependence was not broken. It was made worse by the growing indebtedness of the poor countries in the 1970s and 1980s. Moreover, in those decades people once again – as in the 1950s – became conscious of the danger of a third world war waged with nuclear weapons. The armaments race between the superpowers, legitimized by the theory of mutual deterrence, exacerbated the worst possible fears. In these circumstances, not only commitment to justice but witness for peace became increasing concerns of the churches. Détente between the superpowers became a necessity if the human race was to be prevented from destroying itself. The churches – mainly in Western countries – played an active part in peace initiatives of all kinds. Awareness of the ecological crisis took longer to penetrate the churches. Only in the 1980s did it become clear that the survival of humanity was fundamentally exposed to a threefold danger: injustice by exploitation, extermination by war, and self-destruction by irresponsible use of natural resources. If the churches were to perceive and act on their responsibilities, they had to bear witness on all three fronts. This insight was behind the movement for "Justice, Peace and the Integrity of Creation" proposed at the WCC's Vancouver assembly (1983).

From the 1970s onwards, comprehensive prospects for the future proved less and less plausible. Christian witness was increasingly faced with a complex range of contradictory forces. Injustice was deeply inscribed in "structures of sin". To a great extent, therefore, Christian commitment became participation in specific movements: the struggle against apartheid, solidarity with liberation movements, the defence of the rights of Indigenous Peoples and identification with the poor and oppressed who were trying to break out of their bondage. The great Christian figures of these decades were people who inspired such movements of protest and solidarity: Dom Helder Camara, Mother Teresa, Dom Evaristo Arns, Desmond Tutu and C.H. Kao.

Many Christians lost their lives in this struggle without seeing their commitment bear fruit. As was true of the 20th century in general, the last decades of the century were a time redolent with the blood of martyrs. In many places and in very diverse contexts Christians, and not only Christians, paid with their lives for their witness and commitment to justice. To mention only three names: under Idi Amin's dictatorship in Uganda the Anglican Archbishop Janani Luwum was killed; under Mengistu's Marxist regime in Ethiopia Gudima Tumsa, the general secretary of the Mekane Yesu Church, "disappeared"; and in 1980 in El Salvador, Archbishop Oscar Romero was assassinated by a "death squad" while celebrating mass.

Human rights became an increasingly significant issue in the 1970s. If a comprehensive transformation of the social order was unattainable, protection of at least the most fundamental rights had to be secured. In the early 1960s Amnesty International was founded and gained wide acceptance, especially in the Western world.

These changes in people's expectations also may be detected in the development of theology. In the 1960s the theology of revolution made its appearance. It was concerned with the part played by the Christian tradition in the overall transformation of social conditions. At the beginning of the 1970s this was followed by theologies which tried to articulate the hopes and protests of specific oppressed groups in the light of the gospel – for example, black theology in the US and minjung theology in Korea. The Latin American theology of liberation, first formulated by Gustavo Gutiérrez in 1971, tried to demonstrate the potential of the gospel in situations of repression. In doing so, it opened the way for an identification of the church with those who are bereft of freedom. Because of this perspective, liberation theology awakened a response far beyond the confines of Latin America. In the 1980s, increasingly, critics asked to what extent liberation could be seen as an historical project for the forseeable future. Were we really living in a time of revolutionary renewal? More and more frequently, theologians suggested that attention should not focus exclusively on the prospect of an exodus from oppression, but that it was necessary also to recognize the enduring ambivalence of history – change may be delayed. There was need for developing "a culture of waiting for justice" (Juan Luis Segundo).

DEVELOPMENTS IN THE ROMAN CATHOLIC CHURCH

The history of the Roman Catholic Church in the last three decades was largely deter-mined by the Second Vatican Council and its decrees. The most important change prob-ably came in reforms of the liturgy. These reforms were given priority both in the con-ciliar procedures and in their reception throughout the church: introduction of the vernacular, refocusing of the mass as a communal eucharistic celebration and, above all, growing participation of the faithful in worship. The Bible, now almost every-where translated into the vernacular – often on an ecumenical basis – was given a new weight in the life of the church. The role of the laity was expressed in new forms of parish life such as the base communities developed in Latin America.

Bishops conferences began to exercise a much more independent role. In several countries national synods met to put the decisions into effect. Latin American bishops arranged continental meetings at which attempts were made to elicit the implications of the Council for the continent (Medellín 1968; Puebla 1979). In several countries, during the 1970s and 1980s, the bishops conferences became full members of national coun-cils of churches.

The style of Roman Catholic theological reflection was profoundly affected by these developments. Whereas, before the Council, theology sought to reproduce the official doctrine of the church in as faithful a manner as possible, the task of theology was now increasingly seen as reflecting in the light of the gospel on the realities of each context. Acculturation became a privileged topic of Roman Catholic theology. Liberation theology broke new methodological ground by its emphasis on the perception and analysis of the Latin American social and political context.

For many, the image of the church changed within a short time. Instead of a system in which doctrine and practice were defined down to the last detail, a church emerged that saw itself as a community in the making. A Catholicism closed in on itself was seen as dissolving into a number of "Catholicisms". All at once, wide debate and experimen-tation became present. Many looked on Vatican II as merely a beginning, and it was hoped that large unresolved issues would be brought closer to decisions taken in the spirit of the Council. Free discussion on problems such as married priests, the ordina-tion of women, divorce and birth control opened up. Indeed, it became possible even to raise such prohibited doctrinal topics as the infallibility of the pope. A rich variety of the-ological publications appeared. The journal *Concilium* deserves special mention. In 1967, *A New Catechism*, authorized by the Roman Catholic Church in the Netherlands, provoked wide debate. Reformulation of doctrine in the light of today's world appeared on the agenda of many.

However, as reform began to affect dimensions of the church's life, opposition grew. An increasing number of voices declared illegitimate the idea of "a church on the way". The Council, according to this viewpoint, had been concluded, and its results had now to be applied in accordance with the norms of previously approved and interpreted tra-ditions. Both among laity and hierarchy, there was a reaction against the "unrestrained will to change". It would be a mistake to dismiss this counter-tendency simply as ob-scurantism, intellectual narrow-mindedness or political conservatism. Movements such as Opus Dei and the schismatic ultra-traditionalism of Archbishop Marcel Lefebvre were shaped by intellectual and political notions of earlier centuries. In general, however, these counter-tendencies were a matter of loyalty to the church in its traditional form. These critics asked if, in the reforms, values had been lost which hitherto had been re-garded as essential. Did an arbitrary treatment of tradition not inevitably result in the loss of uniformity? And was that not precisely what had been the strength of the Roman Catholic Church in the past? Increasing emphasis was placed on these questions, especially when renewal began to lead to signs of disintegration. The number of priests and religious diminished. Declining church attendance in Western countries led many people to think that the process of reform was leading to a profound crisis.

Roman pontificates since the Council have been marked by tensions between the renewal of church life and the reinforcement of tradition. After Vatican II, popes had the difficult task of keeping the mutually opposed forces together in the same church. They tried to achieve this by ensuring a credible continuation of the Council, on the one hand, and doing justice to the need for continuity in the life of the church, on the other. The papal office was marked by new characteristics. In contradistinction to previous popes, the successors of John XXIII were eager to interpret their task as one of trying to present themselves to church and world as dynamic symbols of unity. "Pastoral visits" to all parts of the world have become a permanent feature especially of the peripatetic John Paul II. However strong the tendency of the Council to see the pope primarily as the bishop of Rome, in late 20th-century dialogue he had, at least at a symbolic level, become a "universal bishop" to a degree never before witnessed, while the prestige of the papal symbol had grown considerably in public opinion.

Paul VI sought to promote the Council's pastoral instructions, and norms of implementation were published for most of the decrees. His encyclical *Populorum Progressio* ("Development of Peoples", 1967) spoke emphatically of the need for worldwide solidarity with the countries of the South. Through a series of international synods, he attempted to pursue debates of Vatican II. A synod on evangelization (1975) led to the publication of an important document which in many respects went beyond the Council's decree on the missionary activity of the church. The new "Ostpolitik", the attempt to normalize relations with communist regimes in Eastern Europe, was also his initiative.

Yet Paul VI also constantly drew attention to traditional teachings and practices of the church. In 1968 he caused a stormy debate in church and society with his encyclical *Humanae Vitae* ("Regulation of Birth"). With the aim of preventing any impression of discontinuity in the exercise of the papal *magisterium*, he spoke out against all forms of artificial birth control. To counteract decay in devotion to the Virgin Mary, in 1974 he reaffirmed traditional Marian dogmas in a special apostolic injunction. The last years of his pontificate saw a proliferation of reprimands to theologians who, in the eyes of the Vatican's Sacred Congregation for the Doctrine of the Faith, had overstepped the bounds of permissible teaching.

Despite such measures, many felt that Paul VI was too weak and indecisive. At the end of 1978 John Paul II was elected pope. After a long period, the church now had a non-Italian pope who was an extremely dynamic and robust personality. He continued the dual approach of his predecessor, though with new emphases. He was primarily concerned to affirm in new ways the presence and witness of the Roman Catholic Church throughout the world.

On the one hand, he sought to give the church a new thrust through the way in which he actually exercised his office. In a series of encyclicals he tried to give a new orientation to the social witness of the church. As the former archbishop of a church under communist domination in Poland, he wanted to strengthen the determination to survive, and even more the active witness of the churches under communist oppression. Particularly impressive in this respect were his several visits to Poland and in 1998 to Cuba. Alongside his unequivocal rejection of all forms of Marxism, he was equally unsparing in his criticism of Western materialism and lack of solidarity. This double papal witness evoked an enormous response, especially at the level of politics and in the media.

On the other hand, from the outset the pope had been concerned to preserve traditional Roman Catholic teaching and order. He quickly put an end to further discussion of papal infallibility by the condemnation in December 1979 of Hans Küng, the Tübingen theologian. Other such condemnations followed. In September 1984 the Latin American theology of liberation was subjected to official criticism. Classical Roman Catholic teaching on sexual issues was reaffirmed on every possible occasion. The *Catechism of the Catholic Church* was published in English in 1992, a summary account of teaching and ethics in which new approaches developed since the Vatican Council received only scant consideration. Scarcely less important was the papal policy in filling vacancies so that as many dioceses as possible were given to bishops committed to conservative leadership. The first of these two won as much approval as the second evoked criticism. In Western countries in particular, papal policy led occasionally to open protest and even rebellion.

The unity of the Christian churches remained an explicit objective under both Paul VI and John Paul II. A long list of papal declarations testified to the Holy See's desire to move closer to the goal made explicit by Vatican II of reconciliation between divided Christian traditions. Official dialogues, reciprocal visits and symbolic gestures were intended to remove obstacles. Yet a certain asymmetry predominated with other churches. The clarification of their relations was an issue of prime importance for their own self-understanding, but ecumenical dialogue had far less existential significance for the Catholic church. Its primary concern was quite clearly its own witness. Basically, it assumed that the ecumenical movement must finally lead to an integration of all churches into the one Catholic church.

The role of the pope was of particular significance in this context. The Roman Catholic Church considered both the doctrine and the institution of the papacy as not merely essential; it was convinced that the unity of the church could be realized *only* under the authority of the successor of Peter. Conscious of the fact that this doctrine was unacceptable to other churches, the theme was avoided in official contacts in the first years after Vatican II. Theological conversations on a ministry of unity within Christianity began only in the 1970s. A new stage was reached with the publication in 1995 of the encyclical *Ut Unum Sint* ("On Commitment to Ecumenism"). This pronouncement offered an open ecumenical dialogue regarding the papal office. In reality, however, it soon became clear that the potential for such a discussion was limited. The debate was not to call into question the institution as such; instead, it should suggest alternative forms of its exercise. In this respect, the numerous colloquies which have been called in response to the encyclical had little actual impact. In consequence, the non-Roman churches faced the question of the extent to which they were prepared, for the sake of Christian unity, to make use of the papal ministry in its historical form.

As open as the Catholic church was to dialogue and exchange, it was equally reticent with regard to all forms of collaboration which might call into question its claim to uniqueness. At the end of the 1960s, the Holy See briefly considered membership in the WCC but soon concluded that it was out of the question. Projects of common witness which were bound to engage the Roman Catholic Church at the international level had little chance of being accepted. In the late 1960s the joint programme on Society, Development and Peace (SODEPAX) raised high hopes but they were not fulfilled and it was discontinued in 1980. After the Vancouver assembly in 1983, the WCC proposed a "conciliar process for justice, peace and the integrity of creation" but the Catholic church refused to co-sponsor the initiative.

The unresolved tensions which characterized Roman Catholic ecumenism were particularly manifest in the way in which the holy year 2000 was conceived and celebrated. Since the holy year 1975, hope had been expressed that the transition into the third millennium would provide a common witness of all Christian churches. Despite all efforts and appeals, this hope did not materialize. The year was used by the Catholic church for its own witness and the traditional framework, including the practice of indulgences, was maintained. A few impressive manifestations gave the year a certain splendour, but these were overshadowed by traditional positions. These included the beatification of Pope Pius IX, but above all Cardinal Joseph Ratzinger's letter, explicitly approved by John Paul II, *Dominus Iesus:* On the Unicity and Salvific Universality of Jesus Christ and the Church", underlining limits to ecumenism. Although criticism of this document was sharp and sometimes harsh, even within the Catholic Church, the fact remained that the common witness of divided Christendom was still far from being solved.

CHURCHES OF THE REFORMATION, THE EVANGELICAL MOVEMENT AND PENTECOSTAL CHURCHES

In the last few decades, the image of the Protestant world changed no less profoundly than that of the Roman Catholic. Indeed, this period may be described as one of self-discovery as Protestant churches posed key questions of themselves. What does it mean to be the church of Jesus Christ? What is the task of the Protestant churches in the context of present-day challenges? How, in terms of changed relations between the churches, are we to interpret the meaning of the Reformation and the manifold traditions that derive from it? Such questions provoked intense controversies and answers proved anything but uniform, both theologically and ecclesially. The image of the Protestant world at the beginning of the new millennium was more diversified than ever before. A reinvigorated evangelical movement consolidated old battle-lines, and the rise of Pentecostalism added new promontories to the contours of the Protestant world.

A major feature was the tension between commitment to the ecumenical movement and loyalty to particular church traditions. Several Protestant churches experienced something of the greater community in the ecumenical movement. In the early days, many Christians hoped that the foundation of the World Council of Churches might in the foreseeable future put an end to the division of the churches. Answers to the major challenges of the time were sought in the context of a more inclusive community.

This expectation was, however, increasingly called into question in the course of the 1960s. It became ever more obvious that unity would not be reached as soon as anticipated, and that the churches would have to work out their own answers. Several Protestant churches set about this task and tried theologically to translate the inherited faith into contemporary confessions. Attempts at such statements were made, for example, in North America by the United Presbyterian Church (1967), the Reformed Church in America (1974) and the Presbyterian Church in Canada (1984).

Vatican II created a new situation for the Protestant churches. Dialogue, exchanges and cooperation were soon taken for granted in many places. The ecumenical community began to be extended beyond the membership of the WCC. But the ecumenical opening of Vatican II was more than an invitation to cooperation. It represented a challenge to the self-understanding of the Protestant churches. How far was it necessary to re-examine and revise earlier Protestant positions in view of the new formulations of the Council? To answer such questions appropriately, it became essential to revisit one's own tradition.

Consequently, the commitment of Protestant churches to the ecumenical movement became much more complex. On the one hand, they continued to acknowledge their indebtedness to the vision that had taken visible form in the WCC and they still looked on its assemblies as major events. Suggestions emerging from discussions within the framework of the WCC were taken up by various churches and could result in pointed controversies. At the same time, churches found themselves increasingly forced to have recourse to their own traditions, and to develop them in dialogue with other churches, especially the Roman Catholic Church.

The participation of the Roman Catholic Church in ecumenical encounters also had structural consequences for Protestant churches. It led to an increased significance and role of the international confessional associations, the so-called Christian World Communions (CWCs). In the 1940s and 1950s, these associations did not play a major role. The WCC was not conceived as a fellowship of world confessional families but intentionally as a council of national or regional churches. But now these communions became active partners in relation to the Catholic church and thus took on increased weight also within their own constituencies. General assemblies of confessional groups became occasions to articulate specific identities in an ecumenically responsible way. The first world communions to enter into dialogue with the Roman Catholic Church were the Lutheran World Federation (LWF) and the worldwide Anglican communion. Others soon followed. A wide network of bilateral conversations came into existence. Most dialogues resulted in partial agreements. The most spectacular breakthrough with the Catholic church was achieved by the Lutheran World Federation with the adoption in 1999 of a Joint Declaration on the Doctrine of Justification. Justification had been the central theme of the 16th-century Lutheran Reformation. Though the text created atmospherically a new situation between the two traditions, it did not lead to immediate steps towards full communion. Unreconciled divergences in the understanding of the nature of the church continued to block further progress.

Efforts to consolidate unity among the Protestant churches continued and bore fruit. In 1970 the World Alliance of Reformed Churches (WARC) and the International Congregationalist Council united. In 1973 the Lutheran, Reformed and United churches of continental Europe, with the adoption of the Leuenberg agreement, declared full communion. Though this step did not immediately have spectacular consequences, it placed the long-term relations of the churches of the Reformation in Europe on a new footing. At the beginning of the 1990s the Evangelical-Methodist churches also joined the agreement and in 1997 a comparable Lutheran-Reformed agreement, called "A Formula of Agreement", was adopted in the US. Moreover, the formation of united churches continued in these last three decades: the Church of North India (1970), the Church of Pakistan (1970), the Church of Bangladesh (1971), the Church of Christ in Zaire (1971), the Uniting Church in Australia (1977), the United Church of Belgium (1979), the United Reformed Church UK (1972) and the United Church in Jamaica and the Cayman Islands (1992). In spite of all obstacles, efforts within the framework of the Consultation on Church Union (COCU) in the US never faltered and by 2000 led to tangible results at least in some areas of the life of the nine church bodies involved. With the implosion of communism in Europe in 1989, an almost natural consequence was a European evangelical assembly held in Budapest in 1992 to assess the common witness that was now required of Protestant churches.

On the whole, the Protestant churches of the southern continents faced other questions. Their concern was not primarily to open up denominational identity for the ecumenical movement. The question of the relationship between the legacy received from Western missions and local traditions was more to the fore. For many Protestant churches of the South, the last three decades of the century proved to be the "second phase of independence". After achieving structural independence, they now had to determine their places in their own cultural and political environments in order to develop credible forms of witness. The theological work carried out in this connection was substantial, its effects being felt far beyond confessional boundaries. Several churches experienced new vitality. In many places appropriate witness in political crises led to discrimination and persecution. New confessions of faith were produced in individual churches. The Belhar confession of the (Coloured) Uniting Church of South Africa (1986-90) was an especially impressive example of a new form of confession of faith. Yet the process of attaining authentic self-awareness had by no means been achieved everywhere. Some churches remained embedded in received traditions without the inner freedom and creativity required for credible witness. In general, the continuing divisions of the Protestant churches had a paralyzing effect.

Protestantism's image was decisively co-determined by conservative movements which had always been opposed to the ecumenical movement. The influence of fundamentalism in the narrower sense of the word had on the whole tended to recede. Even in conservative circles, movements such as Carl McIntyre's International Council of Christian Churches (ICCC) met with rejection by century's end. The constantly repeated summons to leave the godless world, the premillennialist expectation of the end, the overall avoidance of contacts with "unbelievers" and therefore with the ecumenical movement, as well as militant anti-communism, lost their attraction and found acceptance only in ever smaller groups. The evangelical movement, however, experienced a remarkable upturn in the three decades from 1970 to 2000. Given the upheavals of the period, it proved increasingly attractive, not least of all because it explicitly demarcated itself from the fundamentalist tendency. Conservative forces in Protestantism were disturbed by a perception of dissolution of the Christian message by liberal theology and catholicizing tendencies. Evangelicalism had stood for an uncompromising recognition of the authority of the Bible, emphatically rejecting any "watering down" of the truth by ecumenical considerations. However, it concentrated particularly on fulfilling its missionary commitment.

The evangelical movement took on decisive vigour in the 1960s, initially in the US when that country was unsettled both internally and externally. In 1976, Jimmy Carter, who referred to himself as an evangelical, was elected president and the evangelical influence became an important factor in forming political opinion. Whereas some historical churches adopted critical attitudes to some government policies, the evangelical movement left little or no room for doubt concerning the vocation of the country. It was able to confirm its position in public life under subsequent presidents, especially Ronald Reagan and George W. Bush.

Even though it had strong roots in the US, the evangelical movement was not a solely American phenomenon. The International Congress on World Evangelization inspired by Billy Graham (Lausanne 1974) made this clear. Evangelicals from all over the world assembled to re-commit themselves to the evangelization of the nations. They agreed on the Lausanne covenant, a short text summarizing the main evangelical tenets and outlining the great common task of reaching the 2.7 billion people to whom the gospel had not yet been proclaimed. Although the congress distanced itself from the ecumenical movement, it avoided explicit polemics. It sought to establish as wide a basis as possible that would prove amenable to Evangelicals of every provenance and, above all, conservative forces from the churches of the South. In subsequent years the movement also became increasingly open to social and political considerations. In 1989 a second and even more representative world conference was held at Manila under the theme "Proclaim Christ Until He Comes".

In many respects the evangelical movement adhered to the revivalist tradition of the 19th century. It considered revival convictions indispensable and sought to renew them in present-day contexts. It accepted that its goals could not be attained without polarization. The unity of the church was a secondary consideration for evangelical Christians.

In these same decades the Pentecostal movement spread just as effectively as did the evangelical. It experienced rapid growth in many forms in almost all countries and developed into a global phenomenon within a short period of time. Its vitality was demonstrated at major international gatherings – Dallas 1970; Seoul 1973; London 1976; Vancouver 1979; Nairobi 1982; Zurich 1985; Singapore 1989. Pentecostalism's real effectiveness, however, was most evident at the local level. The movement shared the basic convictions of the evangelical movement, yet was distinct from it in that its hallmark was the direct experience of the Spirit. For this reason, traditional Protestantism –the historic churches and the evangelical movement – often treated Pentecostal spirituality with scepticism and mistrust. In its manifestations they saw an uncontrolled and therefore dangerous exaggeration of the emotional side of religion. But they, too, overlooked the reason for the movement's actual strength: the holistic nature of devotion. Piety may draw not only on mental capacities but on the dimension of emotion, and on all human impulses that would otherwise remain untapped. The stress on personal faith, congregational life and personal mission was capable of evoking a new awareness of worth precisely in the disadvantaged and oppressed.

It is hard to say whether Pentecostalism can really be classified as a form of Protestantism, or whether it represents a new way of being Christian. Even though it has its roots in the Protestant world, it has in the form of the charismatic movement also found acceptance in Roman Catholic circles. It definitely has affinities with the Protestant tradition, yet there has been constant disagreement there about the movement's message. Several churches divided over the question of the significance of experiencing the Spirit. On the other hand, in many countries Pentecostal churches are beginning to approximate more traditional Protestants, in both teaching and practice. Some Pentecostal bodies have become members of councils of churches, including the WCC. Reformed or Presbyterian theology especially has been accepted and is being developed in some Pentecostal churches.

The African Independent Churches (AICs) constitute a comparable case. In more than one respect they can be assimilated into the Pentecostal movement. But at the same time they have very different – social, political and cultural – roots and therefore represent a phenomenon that is *sui generis*. During the closing decades of the 20th century they acquired new weight in many African countries. While in the past they were considered to be on the fringe of Christianity, they were increasingly recognized as partners in the ecumenical movement and played a key role in the debate concerning the future of Christian thinking and witness on the African continent. The changing attitudes found expression in new designations. In order to underline the African character of these groups, they had come to be called African Instituted (Independent) Churches (AIC).

DEVELOPMENTS IN THE ORTHODOX CHURCH

Orthodoxy bore Christian witness under difficult external conditions over the last three decades of the 20th century. Most Orthodox churches had only limited space in which to operate freely, and this put a strain on mutual relations and made joint initiatives difficult.

The Ecumenical Patriarchate of Constantinople, commanding a dwindling minority in Turkey itself, had only limited freedom of action. The Cyprus conflict of 1974 increased tension between the Orthodox church and the Turkish regime. However, through the support of the diaspora which belongs to its jurisdiction, the Patriarchate was able to fulfil its role for the whole of Orthodoxy. The Orthodox churches in the Soviet Union, Romania, Bulgaria, Yugoslavia, Poland and Czechoslovakia lived under communist governments, and their witness was systematically obstructed by the state. The Orthodox church of Albania was entirely dissolved in the regime's radical policy on religion. The ancient church of the Middle East, no less than Muslims and Jews of the region, sought to maintain faith and community in a particularly violent era. The Church of Greece had to cope with a military dictatorship and conflicts with a secularized government about its historic rights in Greek society.

It is all the more surprising, therefore, that the efforts of the Ecumenical Patriarchate to bring about pan-Orthodox union made slow but continual progress in these decades. Four pan-Orthodox conferences were held in the 1960s. Far-reaching resolutions were passed at the fourth of these conferences, which took place in 1968 in the newly-opened Orthodox centre of the Ecumenical Patriarchate at Chambésy, near Geneva. The churches agreed then that a serious start should be made on preparations for a great and holy council of the Orthodox church and set up at Chambésy a permanent secretariat to implement the project. The fourth pan-Orthodox conference also established a basis for common witness by the Orthodox churches in the ecumenical movement.

Vigorous inter-Orthodox work now began. An agenda for the future council was confirmed at Chambésy in 1976. At a second pan-Orthodox pre-conciliar conference, six years later, it became evident that very little progress was being made, the only real outcome being approval of a text on impediments to marriage. In 1986, however, the third conference reached agreement on four texts: fasting, bilateral conversations with other church traditions, the role of Orthodoxy in the ecumenical movement, and the Orthodox churches' contribution to peace. The complex questions of the date of Easter, the Orthodox diaspora, the proclamation of autocephaly and autonomy, and diptychs (the ranking of Orthodox churches in reciprocal intercession) had to be left open.

The ecclesial status of the Orthodox diaspora, a matter of great urgency, remained controversial. Since the 19th century, and especially since the beginning of the 20th, Orthodoxy spread far beyond the bounds of the "East". Orthodox mission churches were founded in some African countries (Kenya, Uganda and Zaire). Above all, Orthodox minorities came into existence as a result of migration to Western countries. What was their status? Under whose authority could national Orthodox churches be formed in such countries? However strong the desire to reach agreement about these questions, it was obvious that a solution could be reached only in stages. In 1993 an inter-Orthodox conciliar preparatory commission proposed that the bishops of the different minorities should form national or regional conferences and work within this framework towards a more comprehensive solution.

The part played by the Orthodox churches in the ecumenical movement took on new features. The fourth pan-Orthodox conference of 1968 did a great deal to promote bilateral dialogue with other Christian traditions. Inter-Orthodox commissions were founded for official dialogues with Anglicans, Old Catholics, Oriental Orthodox, Lutherans and, later, Reformed churches. Official discussions with the Roman Catholic Church were especially significant. After some delays, these talks began in 1980 and continued, despite obstacles that have arisen over the years. For the relationship between the Orthodox and the Roman Catholic Church mutual visits were of great significance, perhaps more so than the formal dialogue. Following his first meeting with Patriarch Athenagoras, the ecumenical patriarch, in Jerusalem in 1964, Pope Paul VI visited Constantinople in 1966, as did John Paul II in 1979. In the course of these years almost all Orthodox patriarchs paid visits to the Roman see. Papal and patriarchal visits were exchanged in 1967. In the last years of the millennium the pope began to extend his visiting programme to countries which are traditionally considered to be Orthodox – Romania 1999, Georgia 1999, Greece 2001, Ukraine 2001.

Through all this, the preconciliar process and, especially, the ecumenical activities of the Orthodox churches had to cope with the resistance of conservative circles in their churches. Loyalty to tradition was certainly characteristic of the spirituality of the Orthodox church, to an even greater extent than in the churches of the West. Therefore it was scarcely surprising that the monks of Mount Athos, for instance, constantly objected to innovations of all kinds. But the conservative tendency in individual churches also had other roots. During the years of persecution, the preservation of tradition was a condition for survival in some churches. This indicates the specific value of national considerations in the Orthodox churches. Whereas conservative opposition remained more in the background in the 1970s and 1980s, it became increasingly evident after the demise of communism in Europe in 1989.

Against this background, it was not surprising that after 1989 Orthodox participation in the life and witness of the WCC was increasingly called into question. Since the foundation of the WCC, the role of the Orthodox churches in the ecumenical movement had been a recurrent theme. What were the implications for the Orthodox church, which considers itself to be the true church, to have communion with other Christian traditions? Both in the context of the third preconciliar conference of 1986 and at other assemblies, the special status of the Orthodox church was emphasized. At the same time more scope for its witness in the community of the WCC was requested. However severe their criticisms, the Orthodox churches remained faithful to the ecumenical vision underlying the WCC. The situation, however, deteriorated in the 1990s. In 1997 the patriarch of the Georgian Orthodox Church was forced by conservatives, especially from monastic circles, to withdraw the church from both the WCC and the Conference of European Churches. The Bulgarian Church took the same decision. By the time of the WCC's eighth assembly (Harare 1998) and the fiftieth anniversary of the founding of the WCC, there was widespread fear that the ecumenical fellowship could break apart. However, the commitment of the Orthodox churches to the ecumenical movement prevailed. After Harare, a mixed commission of persons from the Orthodox churches and other WCC member churches went to work, seeking to lay the ground for a viable relationship within the ecumenical fellowship.

Planning for the great and holy synod was also affected by tensions between individual Orthodox churches, especially between the Patriarchates of Moscow and Constantinople. After joining the ecumenical movement at the start of the 1960s, the Russian Orthodox Church began to play an increasingly active role in international relations. With the agreement of Soviet authorities, it developed its own ecumenical programme and its significance in the life of the ecumenical organizations grew. It increasingly established relationships with particular churches. For instance, regular bilateral talks ensued between the Russian Orthodox Church and the Evangelical Church in Germany, and later several meetings were held with representatives of the National Council of the Churches of Christ in the US. But Russian Orthodoxy also tried to make its influence felt within the communion of the Orthodox churches themselves. At the beginning of the 1970s, the decision of the Moscow Patriarchate to grant autonomy to the Orthodox churches of America and Japan led to conflict, since in the eyes of the Ecumenical Patriarchate of Constantinople this decision ran counter to traditional canonical regulations. For some years, strained relations made communication extremely difficult.

With the end of the Soviet Union the Russian Orthodox Church had to face new conflicts. Certain Orthodox communities that had been under the jurisdiction of Moscow were now part of independent states. Old disputes were revived as these new situations arose, particularly in the Ukraine and Estonia. In the Ukraine several churches were established – one recognizing the jurisdiction of the Moscow Patriarchate, another claiming the status of autocephaly and a third recognizing the authority of the Roman Catholic see. The wish of the Orthodox church in Estonia to be received into the jurisdiction of the Ecumenical Patriarchate also led to a sharp conflict between Moscow and Constantinople.

The Oriental Orthodox churches found themselves in a perhaps even more complicated situation in the last three decades. The Coptic Orthodox Church in Egypt was subjected to increasing pressure from the Islamic majority, at the same time experiencing deep spiritual renewal. In order to avoid open religious conflicts, President Anwar Sadat put Coptic Pope Shenouda III under house arrest in 1980. The Ethiopian Orthodox church lost its privileges after the fall of Emperor Haile Selassie to a Marxist regime at the beginning of the 1970s. It had to find an entirely new role in Ethiopian society. The Armenian Orthodox church continued to be divided into the catholicosate of Etchmiadzin in the former Soviet republic of Armenia and the catholicosate of Antelias in Lebanon. The two jurisdictions separated largely for political reasons, which also resulted in severe tensions in the Armenian diaspora. In 1970, a split occurred in the Syrian Orthodox church in India: in order to relate more credibly to its own Indian context, part of the church in India withdrew from the jurisdiction of the patriarch in Syria, which led to a conflict lasting several years.

Plans for closer cooperation among the Oriental Orthodox churches that had been proposed in the 1960s could scarcely develop under these circumstances. The fact that the dialogue between the Eastern and Oriental Orthodox churches was not only maintained but gradually drew closer to the stated goal of union was all the more promising. A mixed theological commission met four times between 1985 and 1993. After it had proved possible to formulate a common theological declaration at the second assembly in 1989, an explicit agreement was reached on the central disputed question of Christology in the following year. On the whole, that agreement met with a favourable response in churches on both sides. Reactions, comments and criticisms were treated at the fourth meeting in 1993 and by the century's end it had become a matter of implementing the agreement. But a certain rapprochement of the two families of churches had already occurred, and there was some reason to hope that further steps would be taken in the foreseeable future.

THE CHURCHES IN THE EAST-WEST CONFLICT

During the period under review, the confrontation of the superpowers impinged decisively on the life of the churches. In many respects, the churches' witness was determined by the way they viewed the conflict. Differing assessments of communism within the churches often resulted in tensions and led to bitter disputes.

With a few exceptions, the common assumption was that the ideological and political situation which had emerged from the second world war would for an indefinite time be an unchangeable fact of life; the confrontation between the two systems was bound to last. Of course, the relationship might change and the face of communism might take on new features, but neither side thought that the Eastern system would come to an end. The major concern was the danger of a military confrontation – a third world war in which there would no victors but only losers. Accordingly, everything had to be done to prevent such an escalation of the conflict. From the 1960s on, the view dominated that a modus vivendi had to be found that would both avoid war and not harm the integrity of these systems – at least for the time being. It was necessary to promote and extend the peaceful coexistence of mutually opposed systems. This vision found political and institutional expression and scope in the Conference for Security and Cooperation in Europe established at Helsinki in 1973. This conference reduced the risk of warlike conflicts and above all provided a framework for an international debate on the protection of human rights in both East and West. The reliability of the Helsinki agreement, however, was ultimately thought to owe less to the partners' readiness for peace than to "mutual deterrence", military preparedness on both sides that rendered any armed action counter-productive. The question now was how to bring about a step-by-step extension of the Helsinki framework.

The churches that were forced to live under communist regimes were those primarily affected by the East-West conflict. They were faced with the task of deciding how to survive as the church of Christ under a traditionally hostile system. The cold war that characterized the first two decades after the second world war was long past, and both governments and churches were now interested in rapprochement, though for different reasons. As far as the governments were concerned, it became less a matter of persecuting than of controlling the churches and using them for their own political objectives. The churches were faced with the problem of deciding how far to go in recognizing the communist regimes without being disloyal to their own mandate. Answers differed from country to country. Some churches – the Roman Catholic Church in Poland and the Protestant churches in the German Democratic Republic – succeeded in maintaining a relatively high degree of self-determination. Other churches were forced to work much more closely with state authorities. The Russian Orthodox Church already had decades of persecution behind it and now had to defend the limited recognition it had regained as a result of the second world war against renewed waves of ideological restriction. On the whole, the life and witness of most churches in the East remained confined to the sphere of worship.

Many of these churches began to play a more active part in the international ecumenical movement. The office for external relations of the Russian Orthodox Church became a veritable centre of international ecumenical activities during the 1970s and 1980s. The Christian Peace Conference in Prague provided a platform for Christian witness in the context of the communist world. Though officially supported by some churches, in particular the Russian Orthodox and the Czech Republic churches, its statements were received by church constituencies with reservation.

In all churches, local parishes bore the main burden of confrontation. State measures against religious life often failed at the point of decisive resistance by those members of parishes who were prepared to suffer disadvantages for the sake of the gospel. An increasing number of "dissidents" spoke out in the 1970s and 1980s. Priests, ministers, writers and scientists, encouraged by the Helsinki agreement, protested against the violation of basic human rights in their countries.

But how was the conflict between the systems viewed in the West? On the one hand, there were those for whom a constantly and clearly stated *No* to communism was the obvious duty of any Christian. On the other hand, a more nuanced understanding of things became increasingly apparent. However necessary it was to reject Marxist materialism, it was essential not to ignore the darker aspects of the Western system itself. The churches had to resist the temptation to play down inadequacies on their own side by referring to the much greater evil of communism. Above all, it was their responsibility to ward off the danger of nuclear war. Instead of mere rejection, they needed to engage in dialogue and "confidence-building". Throughout the 1970s and 1980s the WCC and the majority of its member churches represented this viewpoint. In the 1980s, it became the basis of the movement that sought to call into question the East-West conflict in the name of peace – with special success in the German Democratic Republic.

The attitude of the Roman Catholic Church had begun to change with Vatican II. Although the critique of Marxist ideology was confirmed, the Council avoided straightforward rejection and opened up the way for new relations with communist regimes. At the end of the 1970s, a new *Ostpolitik* towards the Soviet bloc became apparent at the Vatican. It was inspired by a concern for the best way to guarantee the future of the churches. The Roman Catholic Church fully supported the Helsinki agreement. Through a number of concordats, the appointment of new bishops in Eastern Europe was made possible. Rome increasingly stressed the fundamentally Christian character of Europe. John Paul II decided to engage in more dynamic witness in relation to the communist states. In 1979, shortly after his election, he visited Poland and spoke before 3.5 million people; his vigorous presence strengthened the self-confidence of all those in Eastern Europe who hoped for a better future.

The East-West conflict was perceived and experienced quite differently by the churches in the third world. The struggle for dominance between the great powers had clear ramifications for the South where a bitter contest for spheres of influence took place. The West showed its most odious side in this confrontation in terms of economic exploitation. Whoever stood for justice had to oppose the economic machinery of the dominant Western system. Marxism, on the other hand, seemed to be a source of hope. Third-world theologians resorted to Marxist philosophy in order to understand more deeply their own situation of oppression and to provide a structure for resistance by the poor and marginalized. This affinity enabled them also to see the communist regimes of Eastern Europe in another light. In their eyes, those regimes came to represent the political power that consistently supported liberation and revolution in the third world.

A further complication in this conflict occurred with the Chinese revolution. On the one hand, it created a new constellation since the conflict of the superpowers was no longer limited to the confrontation of the US and the Soviet Union. Communism now had a new and independent centre and began to exert a considerable attraction in developing countries. On the other hand, the Chinese Cultural Revolution, with its radical suppression of all forms of religious life, awakened great concern in the churches. At the end of the 1960s and early 1970s, the fate of the churches in China appeared to be sealed. Communication was so restricted that the capacity for survival of the small Christian minority was scarcely perceptible.

The common witness of the churches was made difficult and occasionally even paralyzed by differing assessments and attitudes towards this ideological struggle. There could be sharp clashes of opinion over political developments and actual events, such as the apartheid regime in South Africa or the entry of Soviet troops into Afghanistan. In some countries, especially in the third world, actual divisions occurred within certain churches over the issue of communism and anti-communism. This debate created areas of tension between the churches which had a disastrous effect on authentic Christian witness.

JUSTICE, RACISM AND APARTHEID

A certain radicalization of the commitment to justice was a characteristic mark of church life in the last three decades of the 20th century. It had long been clear that a just order could not be established through well-meaning declarations and proposals, but the late 1960s and the 1970s made it evident that obstacles to a more just order had deeper roots than hitherto suspected. The power of economic interests was so great it could withstand all intellectual and religious pressure. The struggle for justice had to assume new features to arouse the forces needed for change.

In the 1970s violence imposed itself on the Christian conscience with increasing urgency. Can the use of force be justified when oppression and exploitation become unbearable? Is the violence in the struggle of the oppressed, or among oppressors equipped with all the resources of power? And how was the church to react to this dilemma? Inevitably, there were different answers and the 1970s were marked by bitter confrontations, especially in the West, over precisely these issues.

At the heart of the struggle for justice was racism, especially the apartheid system in South Africa. Though the churches officially rejected racism, at the end of the 1960s new dimensions of this evil became apparent. It became increasingly clear that it was impossible to count on the power of persuasive argument alone to combat racism – above all, the association between racism and economic interests was becoming evident. In 1969 the WCC launched its Programme to Combat Racism (PCR). This was an attempt by the churches to put themselves unequivocally on the side of the underprivileged and oppressed. Something of the basic tenor of those years was expressed in the following declaration:

> Our struggle is not against flesh and blood. It is against the principalities, against the powers of evil, against the deeply entrenched forces of racial prejudice and hatred... the demons operating through our social, economic and political structures. But the root of the problem is as deep as human sin and only God's love and man's dedicated response can eradicate it.

The focus of church commitment throughout these years was southern Africa, not least because there the credibility of Christian witness was at stake to a particularly high degree. However, the fight against racism also engaged other situations of oppression: the movement of the Palestinians for their own independent state; the rights of Australian

Aborigines; the Indigenous Peoples of South and Central America threatened with extinction; the marginalization of racial minorities and aboriginal peoples in the North, and so on. This overall commitment was guided by the concept of an "inclusive society", i.e. a society guaranteeing equal rights for all without exception. Accordingly, the struggle was extended to other forms of discrimination. At the beginning of the 1970s the position of the disabled in society received increasing attention. With the growing flood of refugees from the South to the industrial nations of the North, the churches' struggle began for the right of asylum in situations where people's existence was endangered by war and poverty. In the 1980s in some churches, especially in the US and Western Europe, another dimension of the inclusive society became increasingly important – the recognition of the rights of sexual minorities, gays, lesbians and others. The debate on this latter issue is far from concluded; in several churches it has been a cause of tension, even involving the risk of new divisions. Seen as a whole, the witness against injustice, against all forms of oppression, was readily accepted in the countries of the third world. For many Christians in situations of such oppression, the WCC and its various programmes became a symbol of hope – their significance and weight were perhaps sometimes even over-estimated.

Things were, however, quite different in the Western countries. The fight for worldwide justice led to polarizations in the churches during the 1970s and 1980s. The intensification of this struggle brought traditional ideas into question and created uncertainty. Many conservative circles in the churches reverted to "safe" biblical or theological positions. Above all, the perceived closeness of this new concern for justice to "communist" viewpoints awakened the fear that the churches could be exploited by communist regimes as a usefully undiscerning tool.

For many Christians in the West the commitment to justice for the underprivileged and oppressed in the third world became the point at which a critical confrontation with their social and economic system could develop. The churches in Eastern Europe, however, found themselves in a quite different situation. At the level of the international ecumenical movement, it was not difficult for them to engage in anti-racist discussions since in so doing they were in harmony with their governments' official positions. At the parish level, however, only a limited engagement with questions concerning the struggle for a society of equal rights was possible. Therefore traditional prejudices could persist without being fundamentally challenged. The collapse of the communist regimes revealed a past – even within the churches – with which no one as yet had come to terms.

The period from 1968 to 2000 certainly refined the churches' conscience in respect to justice. The struggle for the rights of the disadvantaged to some degree has borne fruit, and there is a new awareness that society must be inclusive if it is to survive. The peaceful eradication of the apartheid system showed that the struggle for a new social order is not always a hopeless undertaking. Yet it remained obvious that racism is anything but banished. It was still present in new forms which in certain respects were more difficult to assess and to deal with. Precisely because racism is "as deep as human sin", it was as difficult as sin to abolish.

THE POSITION AND WITNESS OF WOMEN

The feminist movement certainly became one of the most significant developments in the life of the churches in the last decades of the century. Its propositions and demands had a far-reaching influence. Its contribution to Christian theology was among the most creative to appear in recent years.

The beginnings of feminist theology coincided chronologically with those of liberation theology. Nevertheless, though it shared some basic assumptions and viewpoints with liberation theology, it had its own roots, topics and questions, resulting as it did from a generally new consciousness on the part of women in modern society. A new role for women, new relations between men and women and a new form of society seemed to have become possible as antiquated patriarchal structures eroded. What does this mean for the church? Will it remain a bulwark of patriarchal structures? Or will new forms of community come about within it too? Perhaps the Christian faith may even prove to be the leaven as a new reality arises?

The question of women's contributions to Christian witness within the ecumenical movement had been under discussion since the early 20th century. Christian women's organizations sought to promote women's rights in church and society. Individual women such as Sara Chakko (1905-54), Madeleine Barot (1909-95) and Kathleen Bliss (1908-89) played significant roles in the history of the WCC. After the second world war, a special secretariat on the role of the woman in church and society was established in the Council. The feminist movement as such, however, went far beyond these early initiatives. It became a matter of questioning Christian tradition and asking how far it was moulded by patriarchal ideas and continued to contribute to their maintenance. To what extent was the free development of women in the church possible? Answers varied. "Reformist" women theologians merely drew attention to hitherto hidden aspects of Christian tradition in order to make a new image of women possible. Others went farther in their criticisms, assuming that patriarchal ideas were so deeply rooted in Christian tradition that a totally new interpretation was needed. Women's hidden experience of God, and its history throughout the centuries, had to be uncovered.

This debate over the burden of tradition was soon expressed in a controversy about inclusive language. The demand was for an eradication of sexist prejudices that had taken hold of language itself. Colloquial language had to be reformed. Terms signifying "male" must no longer be used for "men and women". Moreover, the argument was extended to the ways in which people talk of God. How was it possible to redress the misunderstanding that had led to God being conceived in male terms? How was "he" to be spoken of so that women could recognize themselves, in terms of their own experience, in discourse about God?

Following the lead of pioneering thinkers like Simone de Beauvoir and their writings, most of the first feminist publications appeared in the US. For a time, it seemed possible that the movement of Christian feminism would remain restricted to North America. But it soon became evident that the movement was spreading. Variations on its propositions and demands were put forward in other countries. In many places two projects of the WCC, the study on the Community of Women and Men in the Church (1978-81) and, later, the Ecumenical Decade of the Churches in Solidarity with Women (1988-98) offered frameworks for the movement.

In some churches the situation began to change. Within a relatively short time, the number of women in church decision-making bodies increased. A major contribution to this process was made by the quota rule introduced and recommended to the churches by the WCC. New forms of non-inclusive language began to win acceptance. In some churches, hymnals and even translations of the Bible were revised on feminist lines.

The ordination of women remained a controversial issue. Even though the practice had already been adopted in many Protestant churches, more conservative churches, especially those of an evangelical persuasion, still rejected it. The question was undecided in the Anglican church for some time. The idea of women priests remains unacceptable for the Roman Catholic Church, as well as for the Orthodox churches. Those two churches continue to feel that they must hold to the centuries-old practice of the church. They have declared that the decision of the Church of England to ordain women to the ministry (1994) was an "obstacle" to ecumenical dialogue. (The Anglican Church of Canada and the Episcopal Church in the US were officially ordaining women priests as early as 1976 and both now have fully recognized female bishops.) The highest leaders of both Roman Catholic and Orthodox churches have recorded their negative attitude in public declarations.

New developments became discernible by 2000 even in those churches that cling to traditional positions. The part played by women was growing stronger. In more and more places, for example, they shouldered the main responsibility for parishes; one need think only of the role of pastoral assistants in the Roman Catholic Church. Members of religious orders and congregations, in the past the very image of subordination, were often seen in the front ranks of the women's movement. Even though aspects of the feminist movement may be debatable, there was every reason to think by the year 2000 that changes in the life of the church which feminism has brought about had become irreversible.

FROM CONFRONTATION TO DIALOGUE AND COOPERATION

The churches' awareness of non-Christian religions had been radically transformed in the 20th century. There was an ever-growing readiness in the churches not only for inter-religious dialogue but for practical cooperation between religions. Inter-religious encounters increasingly formed part of the obvious pattern of things. A new relationship was developing. Of course, how far this was possible in the way of common endeavour with representatives of other religions remained a vexed question. Many people thought that dialogue and cooperation inevitably tended to lead to syncretism and necessarily reduced the uniqueness of the Christian message. Yet, whatever their assessment of the task and possibilities of dialogue, all parties agreed that encounters between religions must start from a more secure basis of respect and openness than in the past.

Relations with other religions had long been a central task for many churches, especially the Christian minorities in Asia. A new feature of life by 2000 was that a growing number of people in all countries were being exposed to a variety of religious expressions. Religious pluralism was now a fact of life; a whole range of religious beliefs was available in almost every nation. These also included new movements attached to one religious tradition or another, or to several traditions at the same time.

Religious convictions had historically been one cause of conflicts. Even in the late 20th century, there was no lack of violent confrontations that were religious, or at least partly religious, in origin. Integrist movements almost inevitably involved the potential of violence, and ethnic conflicts were often heightened by antagonism between religions. Modern pluralist societies were especially vulnerable in this respect since they depend on tolerance for survival. The greater the insecurity, the more frequent the outbreaks of religious enmity. The desecration of Jewish cemeteries and other institutions, like threats and the use of force against Muslims in some industrialized nations, came to be ominous examples of this tendency.

In many countries the relationship between Islam and Christianity was strained. The reasons for this varied from country to country. Certain conflicts had their origin in the period of Christian colonial domination but they could also be due to the religious claims of Islamic states or to the quest of political power. In many places minorities – both Christian and Muslim – found themselves in precarious situations. Again and again tension exploded and led to violent confrontation. The Balkan wars were one illustration of this; Nigeria, Egypt and Indonesia have been the scene of acts of violence. Against this background many Christians tended to see in Islam a threat to the future of the church.

Nevertheless, the number of people perceiving a certain unifying power in the religious dimension of life was growing. They hoped that religions, once purged of exclusivity, would become a factor of peaceful coexistence. More and more people were experiencing a desire for an exchange of ideas and a deeper understanding of the religious aspect of existence. In Western society especially, religious eclecticism – expressed in movements such as New Age spirituality – proved increasingly attractive. A striving for agreement between religions was also one of the central concerns of Sun Myung Moon's Unification Church.

Dialogue between the churches and representatives of the Jewish people began immediately after the second world war. The failure of European churches to speak out during the period of Nazi persecution of the Jews played a major role in these initiatives. How was it possible that the churches did not immediately recognize the evil gathering over the Jewish people? The conviction that the relation of the church to Judaism had to be entirely rethought spread through broad areas of opinion, particularly in the Netherlands, Germany and later in the US. Direct dialogue with Jewish counterparts developed gradually, initially taking place at an individual church level and later in the WCC. A study document published by the WCC in 1982 reflected the growing readiness of the churches to acknowledge present-day Judaism as a God-given partner without ignoring the divergences which continue to exist. The relationship between the church and Judaism remained fragile in the late 20th century and demanded constant vigilance from both sides. Israel and Israeli policy proved especially controversial in many churches. Christian commitment to the rights of the Palestinians could easily be misunderstood as a renunciation of solidarity with Judaism.

For the Roman Catholic Church, Vatican II was the beginning of a new relationship with Judaism. The decree *Nostra Aetate* ("Relation of the Church to Non-Christian Religions") was promulgated in 1965 and a dialogue began in which the main questions raised were theological and spiritual. In 1986 John Paul II visited the synagogue in Rome, a symbolic step of far-reaching significance sometimes referred to as the "pope's longest journey". For a long time, relations between the Vatican and the state of Israel remained unresolved. Out of consideration for the Arab states, the Holy See greatly delayed its official recognition of the Jewish state, but this finally took place at the end of 1993.

In the 1970s and 1980s, dialogue extended far beyond Judaism. Both the Vatican, in 1964, and the WCC, in 1971, provided structures to foster relations with other religions. A long series of dialogues subsequently took place – both bilaterally with individual religions, and multilaterally with representatives of various religions at the same time. Whereas the bilateral talks were mainly concerned with promoting deeper reciprocal understanding, common commitment to peace was in the forefront in multilateral meetings. Dialogue between the Eastern Orthodox and Jews and Muslims at Chambésy was especially helpful. The Russian Orthodox Church took the initiative in arranging meetings between different religions in the area of the Soviet Union. An inter-religious service of common prayer for peace, for which the pope issued invitations to Assisi in 1986, aroused special interest. In evident contrast, the letter of Cardinal Joseph Ratzinger *Dominus Iesus*, on the "unicity of the church" crafted by Opus Dei and issued in 2000, recalled the conviction of the Roman Catholic Church that in the world of multiple religions Christ was to be considered the only and unique source of salvation.

There has been a marked reinvigoration of inter-religious movements and organizations in the last few decades. The World Conference on Religion and Peace was founded at the end of the 1960s, primarily on the basis of American initiatives, with the intention of bringing representatives of different religions together in common witness for peace. It was inspired by the hope that the outgoing century would be remembered for inter-religious dialogue instead of "inter-religious disaster". A series of international assemblies was held (Kyoto 1970, Louvain 1974, Princeton 1979, Nairobi 1985, Melbourne 1989). In recent years, however, this movement seems to have lost much of its initial thrust. Clearly, a still fragile common witness for peace could not entirely cope with the complicated circumstances that arose after the fall of communism in 1989. More recent inter-religious initiatives have put common responsibility for the integrity of creation to the fore, as, for example, contacts between the World Wide Fund for Nature and representatives of various religions, or the Pax Christi conferences at Klingenthal near Strasbourg in 1995 and 1997.

However dialogue and movements may develop in particular instances, the fundamental questions remained: What does it mean to be a Christian in this fragile world which we share with other religions and convictions? How is the gospel to be proclaimed without devaluing other religious approaches and thus possibly encouraging enmity? How can the exclusivity that seems to go with Christian belief be overcome? And, conversely, how is it possible to have relations in common with the representatives of other religions without harming the identity and integrity of the Christian message? As in the past, these questions were still being answered in different ways. New interpretations of Christian faith were put forward, whereas more conservative circles maintained traditional theological and biblical views. An "either-or" approach to mission and dialogue had become one of the points of controversy between the evangelical movement and the traditional churches. Both the Congress on World Evangelization in Lausanne in 1974 and that in Manila in 1989 spoke emphatically and exclusively of Jesus Christ as the one source of salvation.

There was increasing agreement that dialogue between religions had to be pursued for the sake of the future of humanity. All constructive forces must act in concert if humanity were to overcome the dangers that threaten to overwhelm the world. Dialogue and cooperation between religions were essential parts of this process. But the task demanded more than that. When the WCC founded a secretariat for dialogue with other religions, it was correctly pointed out that not only religions but also ideologies had to come within the purview of the churches. Exchange between religions could bear fruit for the construction of a "responsible society" only if dialogue were undertaken at the same time with the secular forces which were deciding the present pace of development. Dialogue with other religions could help to clarify one's own tradition and such dialogue could also open up realities that had hitherto been obscured. Nevertheless, the nature of the contribution to dialogue to be made by the churches was not a matter of looking for salvation in the religious dimension alone, thus playing off the religious against the secular, but rather it was meant to testify to God's love in all areas of human life.

FALL OF COMMUNISM: NEW DEPARTURE FOR THE CHURCHES

The collapse of the communist regimes in Eastern Europe in 1989 was a critical turning-point for the churches too, the consequences of which are still unresolved. True, the peace movement of the 1980s was sustained by the hope that antagonisms between the two global systems would grow less intense and diminish. Yet not even the most daring of forecasts could have imagined that the *perestroika* experiment in the Soviet Union could lead to the system actually imploding. As it turned out, the breakdown of communism resulted in a shift in the distribution of power that had determined political issues since the second world war. The well-established division of the globe into first, second and third worlds became meaningless. All at once, the Western powers were confronted with a polycentric world.

The churches, too, had to face a new situation. The collapse of communism showed how profoundly their witness had been marked by four decades of ideological and political conflict. A process of reorientation was necessary. Seen as a whole, the churches in Eastern Europe had concentrated their efforts on surviving as Christian communities. In almost all countries, radical resistance to the regime was restricted to small circles of dissidents. In Poland the church, not least of all after the election of Pope John Paul II, was a real factor of resistance. In individual countries, particularly in East Germany, the churches provided opposition groups with space for alternative demonstrations.

After the fall of the communist regimes, the churches were inevitably faced with the task of confronting their past. To what extent could church leaders having served under the communist rule remain in office? What was to be done about bishops and ministers who had cooperated with the regime? Since secret archives were being opened up in some countries, facts were revealed that had remained hidden until then. In the former German Democratic Republic, in particular, it was a matter of a veritable settling of accounts with "collaborators".

Confrontation with the past was not restricted to individuals. Claims arising from injustice unresolved in the past now came into the open. Oppressed nations which had fought – often with active Western support – for minimal recognition under communist regimes, now demanded independence. In many cases, especially among the Orthodox, the churches joined in this movement. The conflicts in Armenia, Georgia, Ukraine, Estonia, Moldavia and, above all, the former Yugoslavia put the churches in an almost intolerable state of tension between commitment to peace and solidarity with one's own nation.

On Pentecost 1989, a few months before the Berlin wall came down, an all-European ecumenical assembly was held in Basel, Switzerland. It was imbued with great hopes for a common Christian witness in Europe. However, the confusion that ensued in the years that followed represented so vast a challenge for the churches that they were now forced to decide for themselves the exact nature of the tasks that were confronting them. Assemblies were held in 1992 by Catholics, Protestants and Orthodox in an attempt to assess the new situation – a Roman Catholic bishops' synod in Prague, a European Protestant assembly in Budapest, and a meeting of Orthodox primates in Istanbul. It took five more years until the agenda for a second European ecumenical assembly, held in Graz, Austria, in 1997, had matured. This event provided new opportunities for collaboration but also made manifest the continuing complexity of relations among churches in Europe.

The Orthodox churches, in particular, faced enormous challenges. After the fall of communism they were given new access to all areas of society: schools, hospitals, prisons and, not least of all, the media. After so many years on the periphery, the churches had to make considerable adjustment in their lives and administrative structures. A process of renewal had to take place. At the same time tensions that for many years had been suppressed became visible. Conservative voices made themselves heard, questioning the involvement of the Orthodox churches in the ecumenical movement. Western churches and church movements contributed to these internal tensions by their sometimes inconsiderate – even arrogant – attempts to promote spiritual renewal in Eastern Europe, giving rise to charges of proselytizing. John Paul II called for the re-evangelization of Europe – with a special emphasis on Eastern Europe. Numerous Roman Catholic and Protestant groups started missionary activities in Eastern Europe and sects of all sorts began to promote their particular messages. A survey showed that in 1995 in Albania, the one state where atheism had been given the status of a "state religion", around 150 different Western groups were at work. The restoration in Ukraine and Romania of the uniate churches which had been suppressed under the communist regime could not be realized without causing considerable tensions, adding new difficulties to the dialogue between Orthodoxy and the Roman Catholic Church. The political changes and conflicts which followed the implosion of the communist system had far-reaching consequences for the churches. They primarily affected the Patriarchate of Moscow. With the dissolution of the Soviet Union an autonomous Orthodox church came into being in Ukraine, and in 1996 the previously mentioned tensions occurred between the Patriarchates of Moscow and Constantinople over the issue of the jurisdictional status of the Orthodox church in Estonia.

The Western churches, too, had to face the challenge of this new situation. The Western social and economic model appeared to have emerged victorious from the confrontation between the two rival systems. An unrestricted development of the free market seemed to many in the West the only appropriate answer to contemporary needs. Yet growing contradictions were emerging at the same time. Not only was the North-South divide unresolved, but social problems were increasing: new poverty, vast numbers of unemployed people, drug addiction, etc. The development of the market was accompanied by constraints which made society look increasingly inhuman. The more evident this course of events became, the less permissible seemed any attempt to justify it by citing the much greater evil of the centrally controlled communist system which had dominated some nations in the past.

The countries of the third world now faced a single Western system and had to come to terms with it. Not so long ago, the great project of "liberation" had offered a common perspective to broad constituencies in the churches of the third world. This perspective, however, was now fast beginning to seem less attractive and increasingly gave way to either either inward-looking piety or to pragmatic realism. While a number of Asian countries achieved accelerated economic growth, the churches in several African countries were experiencing a rapidly progressive collapse of state and economic structures. In consequence of the fact that the advance towards modernization required an appropriate theological analysis, a "theology of reconstruction" was proposed increasingly as a substitute for the theology of liberation.

One great sign of hope was the overwhelming change that took place in South Africa. The apartheid system came to an end without leading to the blood-bath that had been feared for so many years. Despite its immense economic and political power the system had, in fact, lost its moral legitimacy. In light of the new global situation caused by the demise of communism as a world power, it was also in the interest of the West to seek and support new solutions in South Africa. Decisive initiatives, however, came from in-side. In a relatively short time, through free elections, a government of the black major-ity came into power. A variety of factors fostered this relatively peaceful transition to a democratic society. The outstanding figure of Nelson Mandela played a major role in this process. The consistent witness of broad church groups was a decisive contribution to the change-over. It is highly significant that Archbishop Desmond Tutu was asked to preside over the Truth and Reconciliation Commission set up to investigate the crimes of the former system. Though the wounds of the past, the legacies of the time of op-pression, were not yet healed, a new situation arose through the work of this unique commission. New forces for the construction of a new order have been set free. Yet the magnitude of the tasks still to be faced by the country exceeded all expectations. Social tensions, poverty, ecological destruction, criminality and AIDS weighed heavily on the agenda of the new South Africa. ·

THE MORE PROFOUND ASPECTS OF THE CRISIS

In the years following the collapse of communism in Europe, people in the churches in-creasingly began to realize the threats caused by the technological and industrial society to nature both in the immediate and the more distant future. It became clear that the maintenance of the bases of life on this planet had to be one of the central tasks of Chris-tian witness.

That there are limits to human activity in God's creation was not a new insight. At the least it had become an inescapable theme with the epoch-making book by the Club of Rome in 1971, *Limits to Growth*. At the time, however, the debate evoked only a lim-ited response in the churches. In the 1970s, to be sure, detailed studies had been carried out within the WCC – the now commonplace term "sustainability" originated from those studies. The WCC assembly in Nairobi in 1975 went so far as to make the issue central to its programmes. For a long time, however, the notion of the limits to human activity in creation had little effect on the public testimony of the churches.

At the Vancouver assembly in 1983 it was proposed that the churches should join to-gether in a "conciliar process of mutual commitment" for "justice, peace and the in-tegrity of creation". This summons was based on the acknowledgment that the witness of the churches for justice and peace must be accompanied by a new attitude towards the Creator's gifts. But connecting the three aims of the proposal proved extremely dif-ficult. In view of economic exploitation which required redress and justice, and the dan-ger of a nuclear war, attention was focused primarily on the two goals of justice and peace. The churches of the third world suspected that the reference to the ecological re-sponsibility of humanity represented a toning down of the struggle for justice and liber-ation. The churches of the Western world saw their primary duty in witness for peace. Even at the two major conferences devoted to the conciliar process, at Basel in 1989 and Seoul in 1990, the ecological crisis was not more than a subordinate theme.

For a long time, the conflict between ideological systems had obscured the crisis of technological and industrial society. Both sides shared the same goal of economic growth. Only the collapse of communist rule brought a new situation into existence – the Western concept of the free-market economy was now unopposed and the Eastern states adopted it. The fact that far greater environmental destruction had occurred under the administrative system of the communist governments seemed to support the notion that the Western system could master the ecological crisis.

At the same time, however, a growing number of critical voices were heard. In 1992, only a few years after the fall of communism, the UN Earth Summit on Environment and Development took place in Rio de Janeiro. There an attempt was made to define the concept of sustainability more adequately and also to apply it politically. In a sense, Rio de Janeiro can be seen as a secular version of the ecumenical "conciliar process" for justice, peace and the integrity of creation. Compared with the 1970s and 1980s, the witness of the churches to integrity of creation was now more active and well-defined.

The crisis of technological and industrial society was deepened after the 1980s by an unprecedented leap in technology which opened undreamed of possibilities. The technological advantage of the West undoubtedly contributed to the fall of the communist system but an answer was needed to the question of how to deal with new scientific achievements. The image of society was profoundly altered within a few years; other changes were sure to come, with the further development of computers, the growth of mobility, the new telecommunications facilities, the prospects of bio-technology and so on. New circumstances were arising with effects that were still hidden.

THE CHRISTIAN THIRD MILLENNIUM: A NEW BEGINNING?

The transition into a new millennium did not open up new horizons. The factors which determined history in previous years and decades continued to be operative in the new millennium, challenging the churches with radically new and unresolved questions. How were the churches to arrive at a common witness in this situation of uncertainty and confusion?

On the one hand, inherited divisions still needed to be overcome. In the last three decades of the century, efforts to consolidate a consensus on doctrine steadily continued in multilateral and bilateral discussions. The publication in the early 1980s of the "convergence text", *Baptism, Eucharist and Ministry*, evoked an unexpectedly impressive response from the churches. A wide range of doctrinal agreements were reached in bilateral conversations. Some churches have found it possible explicitly to declare that anathemas, mutually proclaimed in the past, no longer apply to today's partners.

But these results alone will not lead to communion. The events of 1968 to 2000 did not mark steady movement towards ever greater unity. All the ecumenical achievements could not conceal the simultaneous existence of new tendencies to break apart. Christian communion continued to be exposed to many threats.

The major question remained how the churches would deal with the problems confronting them. In order to enter the new millennium credibly and responsibly, developments of the last few decades would have to be faced and dealt with together. What did true community between women and men mean? What would be the attitude of the church of Jesus Christ to the great world religions? What was the position of human beings in God's creation? And, finally, what hope did the gospel allow and enable humanity to hold for the future – or, more concretely, for the first century of the third millennium? The credibility of Christian proclamation would depend largely on the answers to these questions.

The picture emerging in the year 2000 was contradictory. On the one hand, the urgency of a new commitment was recognized on all sides. On the other hand, uncertainty and confusion grew so strong that the churches were inclined to concentrate on themselves alone. Traditional and even traditionalist positions were in the ascendant. The energies required for the building-up of true unity seemed to be diminishing.

In consequence, a new beginning for ecumenical Christianity was far from assured. As the churches enter a new millennium they are confronted with the unresolved issues of the past. The contradictions in the life of the churches are manifest. The reluctance of an increasing number of Christians to face these contradictions was perhaps the greatest danger to which the churches of 2000 were left exposed.

BIBLIOGRAPHY

Battle, Michael, *Reconciliation: The Ubuntu Theology of Desmond Tutu*, Cleveland, Pilgrim, 1997, 255p.
Beeson, Trevor, *Discretion and Valour: Religious Conditions in Russia and Eastern Europe*, Philadelphia, Fortress, 1982, 416p.
Braaten, Carl E. and Jenson, Robert W. eds, *Church Unity and the Papal Office: An Ecumenical Dialogue on John Paul II's Encyclical "Ut Unum Sint"*, Grand Rapids MI, Eerdmans, 2001, 166p.
Braaten, Carl E., *No Other Gospel: Christianity among the World's Religions*, Minneapolis, Fortress, 1992, 146p.
Brash, Alan Anderson, *Facing Our Differences: The Churches and Their Gay and Lesbian Members*, WCC, 1995, 75p.
Brockman, James R., *Romero: A Life*, Maryknoll NY, Orbis, 1990, 284p.
Burgess, Stanley M. and MacGee, Gary B. eds, *Dictionary of Pentecostal and Charismatic Movements*, Grand Rapids MI, Zondervan, 1996, 914p.
Camara, Helder, *Hoping against All Hope*, Maryknoll NY, Orbis, 1987, 82p.
Cooey, Paula M. ed., *After Patriarchy: Feminist Transformations of the World Religions*, Maryknoll NY, Orbis, 1991, 169p.
Cox, Harvey, *The Silencing of Leonardo Boff: The Vatican and the Future of World Christianity*, Oak Park IL, Meyer Stone, 1988, 208p.
Fitzgerald, Timothy and Connell, Martin eds, *The Changing Face of the Church*, Chicago, Liturgy Training Publications, 1998, 244p.
Grootaers, Jan, "An Unfinished Agenda: The Question of Roman Catholic Membership of the World Council of Churches, 1968-1975", in *The Ecumenical Review*, 49, 3, July 1997, pp.305-47.
Häring, Hermann, *Hans Küng, Breaking Through*, London, SCM Press, 1998, 377p.
Hennelly, Alfred T. ed., *Liberation Theology: A Documentary History*, Maryknoll NY, Orbis, 1990, 547p.
Hick, John and Hebblethwaite, Brian eds, *Christianity and Other Religions: Selected Readings*, London, Collins, 1980, 253p.
Hunter, Alan and Chan, Kim-Kwong, *Protestantism in Contemporary China*, Cambridge, Cambridge Univ. Press, 1993, 291p.
Irvin, Kevin W., *Context and Text: Method in Liturgical Theology*, Collegeville MN, Liturgical Press, 1994, 388p.
Joint Declaration on the Doctrine of Justification: Official Common Statement and Annex to the Official Common Statement of the Lutheran World Federation and the Roman Catholic Church, Grand Rapids MI, Eerdmans, 2000, 47p.
Joppien, Heinz-Jürgen ed., *Der Ökumenische Rat der Kirchen in den Konflikten des Kalten Krieges: Kontexte, Kompromisse, Konkretionen*, Frankfurt am Main, Otto Lembeck, 2000, 325p.
Krapohl, Robert H. and Lippy, Charles H., *The Evangelicals: A Historical, Thematic, and Biographical Guide*, Westport CT, Greenwood, 1999, 366p.
Küng, Hans ed., *Christianity and World Religions: Paths of Dialogue with Islam, Hinduism, and Buddhism*, Maryknoll NY, Orbis, 1993, 460p.
Legrand, Hervé ed., *Les conférences épiscopales: théologie, statut canonique, avenir: actes du colloque international de Salamanque, 3-8 janvier 1988*, Paris, Cerf, 1988, 530p.
Moon, Cyris Hee-Suk, *A Korean Minjung Theology: An Old Testament Perspective*, Maryknoll NY, Orbis, 1985, 83p.
Mottu, Henri ed., *Confessions de foi réformées contemporaines et quelques autres textes de sensibilité protestante*, Genève, Labor et Fides, 2000, 361p.

Nicholls, Bruce J. ed., *The Unique Christ in Our Pluralist World*, Grand Rapids MI, Baker Book House, 1994, 288p.

O'Brien, David J. and Shannon, Thomas A. eds, *Catholic Social Thought: The Documentary Heritage*, Maryknoll NY, Orbis, 1992, 688p.

Park, Seong-Won, *Worship in the Presbyterian Church in Korea: Its History and Implications*, Frankfurt am Main, Peter Lang, 2001, 205p.

Pobee, John Samuel and Ositelu II, Gabriel, *African Initiatives in Christianity. The Growth, Gifts and Diversities of Indigenous African Churches: A Challenge to the Ecumenical Movement*, WCC, 1998, 73p.

Provost, James H. and Walf, Knut eds, *Catholic Identity*, London, SCM Press, 1994, 147p.

Ramshaw, Gail, *God beyond Gender: Feminist Christian God-Language*, Minneapolis, Fortress, 1995, 144p.

Runge, Rüdiger and Kässmann, Margot eds, *Kirche in Bewegung: 50 Jahre Deutscher Evangelischer Kirchentag*, Gütersloh, Gütersloher, 1999, 222p.

Russell, Letty Mandeville and Clarkson, J. Shannon eds, *Dictionary of Feminist Theologies*, Louisville KY, Westminster/John Knox, 1996, 351p.

Schwarz, Klaus ed., *Bilaterale theologische Dialoge mit der Russischen Orthodoxen Kirche*, Hermannsburg, Missionshandlung Hermannsburg, 1996, 396p.

Spink, Kathryn, *A Universal Heart: The Life and Vision of Brother Roger of Taizé*, London, SPCK, 1986, 196p.

Tang, Edmond and Wiest, Jean-Paul eds, *The Catholic Church in Modern China: Perspectives*, Maryknoll NY, Orbis, 1993, 260p.

Thual, François, *Géopolitique de l'Orthodoxie*, Paris, Institut de relations internationales et stratégiques, 1993, 123p.

Tomos Agapis: Vatican-Phanar, 1958-1970, Rome, Imprimerie Polyglotte Vaticane, 1971, 734p.

Tschuy, Theo, *Ethnic Conflict and Religion: Challenge to the Churches*, WCC, 1997, 160p.

Tschuy, Theo, *World Development in the 1980s: Disaster or New Life?*, WCC, 1980, 201p.

Walker, Andrew and Carras, Costa eds, *Living Orthodoxy in the Modern World*, London, SPCK, 1996, 246p.

Weigel, George, *Witness to Hope: The Biography of Pope John Paul II*, New York NY, Cliff Street Books, 2001, 1016p.

Witte, John and Bourdeaux, Michael, *Proselytism and Orthodoxy in Russia: The New War for Souls*, Maryknoll NY, Orbis, 1999, 353p.

3
Assessing the Ecumenical Movement

Michael Kinnamon

It is difficult to know what overall assessment to make of the ecumenical movement from 1968 to 2000. On the one hand, this was a period of astonishing achievements and advances:

- The Roman Catholic Church – once a distant, even hostile, observer of the movement – became a central participant following the Second Vatican Council (1962-65). Catholic, Protestant and Orthodox Christians now make "common witness" in various parts of the world.
- The movement has left the era when "third-world concerns" were merely incorporated into a basically Western agenda, in favour of a more genuine partnership between North and South, East and West.
- The document *Baptism, Eucharist and Ministry*, produced by the WCC's Commission on Faith and Order, represents a new level of theological convergence on issues crucial to church unity; and bilateral conversations (e.g., between Roman Catholics and Lutherans or between Eastern Orthodox and Oriental Orthodox) resulted in once-unthinkable consensus on such matters as justification by faith and the two natures of Christ. For those churches that have taken the ecumenical movement seriously, a common tradition of shared theological convictions has begun to emerge.
- Ecumenical dialogue helps to forge a broad commitment to reject racism and sexism and to stand in solidarity with the poor; and concerted ecumenical action contributed to the collapse of apartheid in South Africa. Issues that once would have been regarded as "theirs" now became "ours" thanks to relationships developed through the movement.
- Local ecumenical initiatives – including councils of churches, social justice networks and joint worship on special occasions – so proliferated that it was impossible to keep track of them. In many places and many churches, a spirit of dialogue and cooperation had, in a remarkably short time, replaced centuries of estrangement and condemnation.

On the other hand, any historical assessment of these years must also acknowledge that "the disappearance of a general interest in ecumenical themes, events and publications is appreciable and almost universal".[1] The very achievements noted above made it easier for a new generation of Christian leaders to minimize "the scandal of division"

[1] *Crisis and Challenge of the Ecumenical Movement: Integrity and Indivisibility: A Statement of the Institute for Ecumenical Research, Strasbourg*, WCC, 1994, p.2.

that so troubled the movement's pioneers and to demote ecumenical organizations and initiatives on their list of priorities. The exhilaration of the movement's early years had, in large measure, given way to the hard task of acting on the results of dialogue and of confronting what are often called "fundamental differences". "For my generation," wrote the WCC's first general secretary, Willem A. Visser 't Hooft, in 1974, "the ecumenical movement had all the attraction of something unexpected and extraordinary. For the present generation it is simply part of the church's design."[2] Participation in ecumenical structures had become part of the job description for many church bureaucrats, whether or not they have ecumenical understanding or commitment.

In some quarters, churches sought to emphasize confessional identity in the face of declining numbers and cultural influence. Issues such as human sexuality opened new divisions within, as well as between, the churches. In other places, the pressure of economic or political oppression made ecumenical conversation, at least as traditionally practised, seem like a luxury the churches could not afford. In still others, "being ecumenical" was equated with tolerant cooperation in a way that failed to challenge the churches to deeper commitment and renewal. To some degree, faltering commitment and the multiplication of ecumenical agencies were responsible for a falling-off of financial support to traditional conciliar organizations like the WCC.

Equally troubling, the movement over the last third of the 20th century often seemed to lack an orienting vision capable of integrating the disparate priorities – church unity, social justice, peace-making, cooperative evangelism – brought by its wider array of participants. It was not surprising that the WCC repeatedly sought during these years to articulate "a vital and coherent ecumenical theology" or to identify "a common understanding and vision" for its work.

It is impossible to understand the story of the ecumenical movement in the late 20th century without reviewing the incredible transitions that took place between the WCC's third assembly in 1961 (New Delhi) and its fourth assembly seven years later in Uppsala.

- As nations in Africa, Asia, Latin America and the Pacific gained their independence following the collapse of colonialism, churches in these regions also claimed a new selfhood and began to assert their priorities for the ecumenical movement. Eighteen "younger churches" joined the WCC at its New Delhi assembly in 1961; but the first major ecumenical meeting with full representation from outside Europe and North America was the 1966 world conference on Church and Society. This conference, which spoke in its theme of the churches' participation in "the social revolutions of our time", signalled a new level of disillusionment with Western culture. It was not long before the same critique was coming from within the Western churches themselves, especially from women and racial minorities.

- These were also the years, as we have noted, when the Roman Catholic Church committed itself to seek the "restoration of unity among all Christians" (*Unitatis Redintegratio* – "Decree on Ecumenism") and entered into various working relationships with the WCC. Meanwhile, those Orthodox churches that were not original members of the WCC joined the Council in the early 1960s; and the fourth pan-Orthodox conference (1968) underlined Orthodoxy's unequivocal commitment to ecumenism. Many members of these churches were active participants in struggles for social justice. It was, after all, the Roman Catholic bishops from Latin America who first spoke

---

[2] W.A. Visser 't Hooft, *Has the Ecumenical Movement a Future?*, Belfast, Christian Journals, 1974, pp.40-41.

about the church's "preferential option for the poor". In general, however, the Roman Catholic and Orthodox churches tend to place highest ecumenical priority on realizing unity in faith through a recovery of the church's apostolic tradition. This stands in considerable tension with those who emphasize solidarity and dialogue among contemporary cultures and who often view tradition as at least potentially oppressive.

* The New Delhi assembly also witnessed the integration of the International Missionary Council with the WCC, a confluence that seemed to promise a closer relationship between unity and mission on the ecumenical agenda. This indeed happened, at least to some extent; but another less-anticipated outcome was a more visible split between ecumenical and evangelical approaches to mission and evangelization. Major gatherings of evangelical Christians in Berlin (1966), Lausanne (1974) and Manila (1989) set themselves over against the work of the WCC's Commission on World Mission and Evangelism. This tension was exacerbated by a growing emphasis within the ecumenical movement on the importance of interfaith dialogue and of interfaith cooperation in response to human need.

By the turn of the 21st century, the ecumenical movement was still working out the implications of these transitions. Three themes, reflective of these efforts, ran throughout the decades following the Uppsala assembly (and, thus, throughout the pages of this history).

Expanded definition

According to the classic definition of "ecumenical", written by the WCC's central committee in 1951, the term refers to "the whole task of the whole church to bring the gospel to the whole world". Focus in this formulation is on the church as the universal body of Christ and on the church's proclamation of Christ throughout the oikoumene (a Greek word, meaning "the whole inhabited earth", that is the root of "ecumenical"). By the late 1960s, however, new emphasis was being placed on (a) the trinitarian nature of God, including the Holy Spirit's sustaining and renewing presence in all of creation (the theme of the WCC's assembly in 1991), and (b) the new humanity, revealed in Christ, which God intends for the entire human community. The World Council's third general secretary, Philip Potter, put it this way in a 1977 address to the central committee:

> The whole burden of the ecumenical movement is to cooperate with God in making the oikoumene an oikos, a home, a family of men and women, of young and old, of varied gifts, cultures, possibilities, where openness, trust, love and justice reign.[3]

In retrospect, this expanded definition seems inevitable given the shifting centre of world Christianity. The goal of uniting churches separated by patristic, medieval and Reformation-era disputes often appears restrictive to those whose histories are shaped less by Europe than by struggles for political and economic freedom in other parts of the world. Gustavo Gutiérrez makes this point forcefully in his seminal book of 1970, *A Theology of Liberation*:

> Meetings of Christians of different confessions but of the same political opinion were becoming more frequent. This gave rise to ecumenical groups, often marginal to their ecclesiastical authorities, in which Christians shared their faith and struggled to create a more just society. The common struggle made the traditional ecumenical programmes seem

---

[3] "One Obedience to the Whole Gospel", in *The Ecumenical Review*, 24, 4, Oct. 1977, p.303.

obsolete ("a marriage between senior citizens" as someone has said) and impelled them to look for new paths towards unity.[4]

Expanded participation

We have already noted that the movement's cultural and confessional diversity increased dramatically in the last third of the century. One symbol of this was the succession of general secretaries of the WCC. Visser 't Hooft from the Netherlands, and Eugene Carson Blake from the US, were followed by Potter, a native of Dominica in the Caribbean, Emilio Castro from Uruguay, and Konrad Raiser from Germany. Ecumenical participation also expanded in another way, however. Persons who were not in official church leadership, including many women, came to play a much larger role in the life of councils and other ecumenical instruments.

These developments produced a plurality of voices and visions that both enriched and complicated the movement's agenda. To the list of "Northern" concerns – the challenge of a scientific technological culture, the challenge of secularism, the challenge of nuclear confrontation, the challenge of declining churches – was added a new set of priorities: endemic poverty, interfaith relations, the lingering effects of colonialism... And along with an expanding agenda came new methodologies. An action-reflection method that took seriously the experiences of those historically excluded from power was a hallmark of the WCC from the late 1960s onward. "Victims" were no longer just talked about, but listened to, in many ecumenical settings.

Chastened expectations

The third shift is harder to name and somewhat more subjective. At Uppsala 1968, there was talk of the Roman Catholic Church joining the WCC; bilateral dialogues were springing up in unexpected places (e.g., between Roman Catholics and Pentecostals); and new ecumenical efforts to combat such social evils as racism were being born. Despite enormous international problems, including the war in Indochina, positive change seemed in the air (as indicated by the assembly's theme, "Behold, I make all things new"). Yet as early as 1974 Visser 't Hooft would publish a book under the ominous title, *Has the Ecumenical Movement a Future?*;[5] and a generation after Uppsala much of its report has come to sound naive or triumphalistic. Uppsala's final report looked confidently towards the day (in our life-time?) "when a genuinely universal council may once more speak for all Christians". By contrast, preparatory documents for the WCC's eighth assembly (Harare 1998) urged the churches to declare, in the year 2000, their intention to move towards such a council – and to repeat this declaration "in every generation until the goal is attained".

In the early 1980s, many church leaders thought that the crises of that time – hunger, nuclear threat, environmental destruction – would compel the churches to respond together. Some church leaders called for the convening of an ecumenical peace council, while others had high hopes that the Justice, Peace and Integrity of Creation initiative, launched by the WCC, would lead to substantive covenants between the churches. While much work was done, by 2000 these expectations also had been greatly diminished.

4 *A Theology of Liberation: History, Politics and Salvation*, transl. by Caridad Inda and Joohn Eagleson, New York, Orbis, 1973, p.104.
5 Belfast, Christian Journals, 1974.

The reasons for this were complex. One had to do with a new awareness of "the limits of growth" and the persistence of human suffering despite achievements in science and technology. The claim made in the Uppsala report that "new advances in agriculture hold the promise of freedom from hunger" has been tempered by subsequent history.

Within the movement itself, each gain seemed to produce new problems. The end of the cold war was accompanied by charges of proselytism in Eastern Europe and by burgeoning ethnic conflicts that pitted Christian against Christian. The growing number of Christians in the South included a significant growth of churches not involved in ecumenical organizations. Concerns over ecumenical commitments have helped precipitate splits within churches, many of which may prove to be more intractable than divisions inherited from the Reformation.

The remainder of this chapter is organized thematically in order to anticipate the more detailed essays that follow. This division of material is, of course, artificial and is not meant to suggest that worship can be divorced from mission or ecclesiology from ethics in any adequate vision of ecumenism. The limitations of space require a focus on global developments, but at least some reference will be made to the rich texture of local ecumenical life.

CHURCH UNITY

When it comes to the unity of the church, the period from 1968 to 2000 witnessed a remarkable amount of activity, considerable theological convergence, and several significant examples of increased communion. Generally speaking, this work was carried out in four types of conversations.

Faith and Order

The Faith and Order movement has been a major expression of ecumenism since its first world conference in 1927. At its second world conference, ten years later, the decision was made to join with Life and Work in the formation of a world council of churches; and, since 1948, Faith and Order has continued as a department of the WCC, specifically committed to calling the churches to "the goal of visible unity in one faith and one eucharistic fellowship" (bylaws). Though part of the WCC, Faith and Order has its own Commission, whose membership includes representatives from churches that do not belong to the World Council (the Vatican has appointed members since 1968), and it has the right to convene periodic world conferences.

The third and fourth in this series of international gatherings were held in 1952 (Lund, Sweden) and 1963 (Montreal); but thirty years were to elapse before the fifth world conference on Faith and Order took place in Santiago de Compostela, Spain, under the theme "Towards Koinonia in Faith, Life and Witness". The work of Faith and Order over those three decades, which the Santiago meeting sought to assess and extend, centred in large measure around "three marks of a witnessing unity" (Vancouver assembly, 1983):

- a common understanding of the apostolic faith and an ability to confess it together;
- a full mutual recognition of baptism, the eucharist and ministry sufficient to allow common celebration; and
- common ways of decision-making and of teaching the faith authoritatively.

The apostolic faith, understood not as a fixed formula but as the dynamic reality of Christian faith through the ages, was an explicit focus of study in Faith and Order from the late 1970s. Most attention was dedicated to an explication of the Nicene-Constanti-nopolitan Creed in hopes that it could serve as a means for discerning unity of faith among the diversity of contemporary expressions. This study was preceded by a re-markable "Common Account of Hope", written at the Commission's meeting in 1978, which drew heavily on the input of local study groups.

Faith and Order's major achievement of the last third of the century, however, was the document *Baptism, Eucharist and Ministry* (BEM),[6] which addressed the second of the three marks noted above. Indeed, BEM is widely regarded as the most influential the-ological text of modern ecumenism. It has been translated into nearly forty languages, used as an unofficial teaching document in many churches, and has contributed to litur-gical renewal among Protestants and served as a resource for numerous dialogues.

The Commission invited all churches to prepare an official response "at the highest appropriate level of authority" to four statements including "the extent to which your church can recognize in this text the faith of the church through the ages" (BEM pref-ace). More than 190 churches did so, their responses published in six volumes by the WCC. In a survey of these responses, the Faith and Order Commission identified three over-arching issues on which further study is needed: the relationship of scripture and Tradition, the meaning of sacrament and sacramentality and ecumenical perspectives on ecclesiology. Work was undertaken, throughout the 1990s, in each of these areas.

Church union conversations

This heading is usually reserved for the "organic union" of separated denominations into a single new structure and identity. There have been a number of these involving churches of the same confessional family (e.g., the union of three US Lutheran churches to form the Evangelical Lutheran Church in America in 1988). Perhaps more ecumeni-cally significant, however, are unions involving churches of different confessional her-itages (e.g., the United Church of Canada [1925] and the Church of South India [1947]). The heyday of interconfessional church unions was the late 1960s when united churches were born in such places as Zambia and Jamaica, Papua New Guinea and North India. Since that time, there are few to report – probably the most influential be-ing the United Reformed Church in the United Kingdom (1972) and the Uniting Church in Australia (1977).

One reason for this reduction in church union activity was the entry of the Roman Catholic Church into the ecumenical movement. Since the Roman Catholic Church is a global communion, the idea of union in national or regional settings is at odds with its ecclesiology. Far preferable from Rome's perspective are theological conversations be-tween globally organized church families, often called Christian World Communions (CWCs). Thus, the ecumenical role of CWCs (e.g., the World Alliance of Reformed Churches) grew while church union conversations received less ecumenical attention.

Another reason for this trend was the growing appreciation within the ecumenical movement as a whole for diversity, including diversity of denominational heritage. In the US, for example, the nine-party Consultation on Church Union (COCU) shifted its focus from a plan of organic union to a covenantal relationship which involved eu-charistic sharing, common mission and a commitment to continuing dialogue on min-istry, while leaving intact the churches' decision-making structures and denominational

---

[6] Faith and Order paper no. 111, 1981.

labels. Proponents refer to this as "church union in a new form", but it represents a decided change from the vision of a previous generation.

Bilateral theological dialogues

These official church-to-church conversations aimed at overcoming divisive doctrinal differences mushroomed in the last thirty years. A collection, published in 2000, contained reports from 27 international "bilaterals", eleven involving the Roman Catholic Church as an official partner. Other church families engaged in international dialogues included the Adventist, Anglican, Baptist, Disciples, Eastern Orthodox, Lutheran, Methodist, Old Catholic, Oriental Orthodox, Pentecostal and Reformed. These dialogues have a specificity not possible in the multilateral work of Faith and Order; but, generally speaking, they share the same goal of full communion in faith, sacramental life and witness.

Brief mention of three bilaterals may indicate the kind of convergence that was being achieved in this period.

- The Anglican-Roman Catholic International Commission (ARCIC), which began its first round of dialogue in 1970, had by 1981 reached "substantial agreement" (i.e., unanimity on essential matters) with regard to eucharist, ministry and ordination and had identified a great deal of common ground on the sticky question of authority (later expanded in the influential publication, *The Gift of Authority*.[7] Subsequent conversations tackled such issues as salvation, moral decision-making, and the church as communion – although the dialogue was overshadowed by the decision of various Anglican provinces to ordain women to the priesthood.

- Four unofficial conversations between Oriental and Eastern Orthodox theologians (1964-71) set the stage for an official joint commission to declare agreement on the Christological dogma which had divided them doctrinally since the council of Chalcedon (451). Though the anathemas pronounced on each other were not yet formally lifted, it is fair to say that 1500 years of estrangement have come to an end.

- Thirty years of Lutheran-Roman Catholic dialogue led to an agreed statement on justification, the doctrine that was at the heart of Reformation controversies. In 1999, at a ceremony in Augsburg, Germany, representatives of these two communions publicly declared that the condemnations pronounced on each other in the 16th century were no longer church-dividing.

The big challenge – as the moderator of Faith and Order, Mary Tanner, put it at Santiago de Compostela in 1993 – is "to turn the ever-growing pile of ecumenical texts into shared life".[8] Thus, there has been a great deal of discussion about the "reception" (the process of legal and spiritual appropriation) of ecumenical documents.

Multilateral dialogues at a regional level

Best known of these is the Leuenberg agreement (1973) which declared "pulpit and altar fellowship" among Lutheran, Reformed and United churches in Europe. The Church of England reached significant agreement with the Evangelical Church of Germany (the Meissen common statement 1988) and inaugurated a relationship of full communion

---

[7] *The Gift of Authority, Report by the Anglican-Roman Catholic International Commission (ARCIC III)*, 1999.
[8] "The Tasks of the World Conference in the Perspective of the Future", in Thomas F. Best and Günther Gassmann eds, *On the Way to Fuller Koinonia*, WCC, 1994, p.22.

with all but two of the Lutheran churches of the Nordic and Baltic countries (the Porvoo common statement 1992). Similar agreements, which go beyond mutual recognition without attempting structural integration, have been reached in the US between the Evangelical Lutheran Church in America (ELCA) and the Episcopal Church, the ELCA and three Reformed churches, and the ELCA and the Moravian Church.

BROAD QUESTIONS ON UNITY

Along with these dialogues, two general questions have dominated the church unity agenda over the past generation.

1. What is the nature of the unity we seek? This was by no means a new ecumenical discussion! The most influential definition was that of the WCC's New Delhi assembly (1961) which spoke of the church being one when it lives as a "fully committed fellowship" of "all in each place", a fellowship marked by common baptism, confession, prayer, service and eucharistic celebration.

Two WCC assemblies of the years under review explicitly attempted to build on this definition. At Nairobi (1975), the one church was envisioned as "a conciliar fellowship of local churches which are themselves truly united". In other words, locally united churches, separated from one another by such things as geography and language, should from time to time come together in councils in order to speak with authority on issues of common concern. Then at Canberra (1991), assembly delegates approved a statement describing the unity of the church as *koinonia* (communion), a biblical term widely used in bilateral conversations, that focuses less on institutional structures than on a quality of relationships, relationships modelled on the love which binds Father, Son and Holy Spirit.

The Canberra statement also summarized a generation of ecumenical dialogue and biblical scholarship when it affirmed that diversity was not just acceptable in, but constitutive of, authentic unity. That, however, gave rise to a number of questions frequently heard in the following years: What are the limits to legitimate diversity? How, and by whom, are such limits determined? How much agreement is needed on what issues before one may speak of diversity rather than division? What needs to happen before diversity is sufficiently "reconciled" that one may speak of unity in the midst of churches' continuing differences?

2. What is the relationship between the unity of the church and the unity or renewal of the wider human community? There is now general agreement that the issues which divide the world (e.g., racism, sexism, economic disparity, violence) also divide the church. Racism, to take one example, is recognized as an issue of ecclesiology, not simply a question of social justice. Far from being "non-theological", racism signals a radical distortion of the Christian faith and of the church that proclaims it.

Many participants in ecumenical discussion would also agree with the Uppsala assembly report (as well as Vatican II) that the church is called to be "the sign of the coming unity of [human]kind" – which, of course, it cannot be in its divided state. For others, however, this formulation claims too much, or at least is too one-directional. The ecumenical movement, they contend, is not only a matter of the church getting itself together in order to carry the gospel of wholeness to the world; it is also a matter of the church participating in God's mission of wholeness and, thereby, discovering its own unity. From this perspective, unity is to be accomplished less through the recovery of tradition and the patient building of consensus than through shared social struggle.

Subsequent WCC studies on "ecclesiology and ethics" attempted to bridge these different approaches. Perhaps their key affirmation was that "the church not only has, but is, a social ethic" ("Costly Unity"[9]). The church is not constituted by the moral activities of its members, but Christian faith should be embodied in a corporate discipleship that resists threats to life. The studies' ecumenical challenge was posed this way:

> Is it enough to say that if the church is not engaging responsibly with the ethical issues of its day it is not being fully church? Must we not also say: If the churches are not engaging these ethical issues together, then none of them individually is being fully church?[10]

MISSION AND EVANGELISM

A major shift in the theology and practice of mission was already well underway by the late 1960s. Key elements of this new perspective included the following.

1. Mission is not so much an activity of the church as it is an activity of God in which the church participates. The aim of mission, to put it another way, is the realization of God's purposes for the world (e.g., justice, peace and wholeness) not simply the growth of the church. Evangelism, while important, is by no means the sole mission priority. The church also participates in God's mission when it serves the poor, helps build human community, or challenges the structures that perpetuate suffering and domination. This understanding gained prominence in ecumenical discussion from the time of the Willingen (Germany) conference of the International Missionary Council (IMC) in 1952.

2. Participation in this mission of God is the responsibility not just of specialized agencies and societies, but of the whole church, including each of its congregations. The real question, said the report from Uppsala, is not "Does the church have the right structures for mission?" but "Is the church totally structured for mission activity?" This understanding helps explain why the IMC became part of the WCC in 1961 (mission should not be separated from the search for the unity and renewal of the church); and it was further developed through a widely influential study, "The Missionary Structure of the Congregation", sponsored by the newly created WCC Division on World Mission and Evangelism.

3. The preceding point means that mission should take place on every continent; it is not simply a matter of churches in traditionally Christian countries sending missionaries and resources to other parts of the world. Past understandings created patterns of dependency that now must give way to reciprocal, partner relationships. In fact, it may be that Europe – home to the idolatries of the Western, scientific world-view – is the great new mission field of this era! "Witness in Six Continents" was the theme of a 1963 world conference on mission and evangelism held in Mexico City.

The more than thirty years of ecumenical discussion following Uppsala did not alter, but expanded on, these themes. One way to trace this development is to examine the series of international missionary conferences sponsored by the WCC's Division (subsequently, Commission) on World Mission and Evangelism (CWME). While Faith and Order held only one world conference since the 1960s, the CWME organized four such gatherings.

---

[9] In Thomas F. Best and Martin Robra eds, *Ecclesiology and Ethics: Ecumenical Ethical Engagement, Moral Formation and the Nature of the Church*, WCC, 1997, p.5.
[10] *Ecclesiology and Ethics*, p.29.

1. *Bangkok (1973):* Meeting in the shadow of the Vietnam war, the delegates in Bangkok affirmed what is now a familiar theme in ecumenical discussions: Salvation must be understood in a "holistic" way.

> The salvation which Christ brought, and in which we participate, offers a comprehensive wholeness in this divided life. We understand salvation as newness of life – the unfolding of true humanity in the fullness of God (Col. 2:9-10). It is salvation of the soul and the body, of the individual and society, humanity and the "groaning creation" (Rom. 8:19).[11]

The gospel manifests itself, they argued, in justification of the sinner and in social-political justice, and thus demands from us both evangelism and active struggle on behalf of the oppressed. Either alone will not do justice to the reign of God which Jesus announced and inaugurated.

2. *Melbourne (1980):* It is hard to think of a more dominant ecumenical theme over the last three decades of the century than "the poor". The general conference of Latin American bishops – meeting in Medellín, Columbia, in 1968 – set the tone by speaking of "God's preferential option for the poor", a key concept for theologies of liberation. During the 1970s, a series of WCC studies, programmes and publications (e.g., *Towards a Church of the Poor*[12]) echoed this concern. But it was at Melbourne that "the poor" received full attention as a crucial criterion for mission.

The church's relation to the poor, said Melbourne, is not only a question of social ethics; it is a question of gospel faithfulness. Jesus established a clear link between the coming of the kingdom and the proclamation of good news to the poor. Christ is the centre of the world's life, but paradoxically he demonstrates that centrality by moving towards those who are on the margins – to the point of dying "outside the gate" (Heb. 13:12). The church, therefore, cannot speak of God's kingdom, or of its own missional task, without a deep concern for those who live in material poverty. Such concern is not only a matter of speaking to them or for them, but of listening to their distinctive voices and of standing with them against political and economic systems of oppressive inequity.

3. *San Antonio (1989):* The themes of previous meetings were by no means absent in San Antonio, but the dominant tone was "concern for the fullness of the gospel, namely: to hold in creative tension spiritual and material needs, prayer and action, evangelism and social responsibility, dialogue and witness, power and vulnerability, local and universal".[13] Particular attention was paid to the tension between witnessing that "salvation is offered to the whole of creation through Jesus Christ" and entering into a genuinely open, searching dialogue with neighbours of other faiths (see next section). "We appreciate this tension", said the delegates in the conference report, "and do not attempt to resolve it."[14]

4. *Salvador (1996):* The relationship between gospel and culture has become a theme of great importance in recent ecumenical conversation. The ecumenical movement as a

---

[11] *Bangkok Assembly 1973: Minutes and Report of the Assembly of the Commission on World Mission and Evangelism of the World Council of Churches, December 31, 1972 and January 9-12, 1973*, WCC, 1973, p.20.
[12] Julio de Santa Ana ed., WCC, 1979.
[13] Frederick R. Wilson ed., *The San Antonio Report: Your Will Be Done: Mission in Christ's Way*, WCC, 1990, p.20.
[14] *Ibid.*, p.33.

"dialogue of cultures" was the focus of discussions at the time of Philip Potter's retirement as WCC general secretary in 1984, has been the topic of two sessions of the graduate school at the Bossey Ecumenical Institute, was addressed in several publications of the WCC's Bible studies desk (e.g., *Immanuel* and *On a Friday Noon*[15]) and sparked considerable controversy at the Canberra assembly 1991. At that assembly, a keynote address by Korean theologian Chung Hyun Kyung made use of images from Shamanism and Buddhism in order to reflect on the activity of the Holy Spirit. Intense debate ensued. Delegates asked whether such a "contextual" presentation runs the risk of syncretism, of compromising the gospel? On the other hand, is not the liberating message of the gospel always shaped by one's cultural setting? If so, can Christians effectively communicate across the vast cultural differences that now mark the global church? Examples of Aboriginal spirituality incorporated into the worship at Canberra also raised issues of appropriate inculturation.

The question of cultural identity, dramatically posed by Vatican II's affirmation of the mass in the vernacular, was on the agenda of the Bangkok conference in 1973. ("Culture", said the delegates at Bangkok, "shapes the human voice that answers the voice of Christ.") But the meeting in Salvador (Brazil) made "the gospel in diverse cultures" its central theme. It is not simply that the gospel must be taken to every culture; it must be understood within a culture so that its power may be unleashed.

A second key concern in Salvador was proselytism, understood as the perversion of witness through improper persuasion or coercion. An emphatic rejection of proselytism was published in 1970 by the Joint Working Group between the Roman Catholic Church and WCC; but aggressive evangelistic tactics by foreign missionaries since the collapse of communism in Eastern Europe and the former Soviet Union brought the issue to the fore with fresh urgency. In a series of "commitments", the conference denounced proselytism and coercion "which neither recognize the integrity of local churches nor are sensitive to local cultures".

As noted in the introduction to this chapter, the period from 1968 to 2000 also witnessed a series of evangelical "congresses", international gatherings of Christians from different churches aimed at promoting evangelization of the "unreached". The challenge to the ecumenical movement posed by these meetings (especially Lausanne 1974 and Manila 1989) was reflected in "open letters" written by evangelical participants at the Vancouver and Canberra assemblies – including the need for greater emphasis on the invitational dimension of evangelism, and the need for more attention to the spiritual alienation of individuals from God and, thus, to the redemptive dimension of Christ's suffering on the cross.

These differences will be familiar to readers since they eventually permeated most churches. At the same time, however, there were a number of signs of significant convergence. At the Nairobi assembly, M.M. Thomas, then moderator of the Council's central committee, identified three points of agreement between the report of the Bangkok conference, the Lausanne Covenant (produced by the evangelical congress) and the apostolic exhortation *Evangelii Nuntiandi* ("Evangelization in the Modern World"): (1) their affirmation that the gospel addresses both the spiritual and material dimensions of life (though the Lausanne Covenant emphasizes that social action is not evangelism and political liberation is not salvation); (2) their effort to relate evan-

---

[15] Hans-Ruedi Weber, WCC, 1984 and 1979.

gelism to the unity and renewal of the church; and (3) their recognition of the realities of the contemporary world, including the renaissance of cultures and religions.[16]

The most notable attempt to bridge differences and reflect common affirmations was the text *Mission and Evangelism: An Ecumenical Affirmation*,[17] produced by CWME and sent to the churches for consideration and implementation by the WCC's central committee in 1982. It was widely regarded as the most important ecumenical mission statement of the generation and was generally reviewed with appreciation by evangelical Christians. An updated convergence statement, "Mission and Evangelism in Unity Today", was adopted by CWME and sent to the churches in 2000.

INTERFAITH DIALOGUE

The relationship between Christians and people of other faiths has been a concern of the modern ecumenical movement – especially, in the movement's early years, through the International Missionary Council. While there was by no means unanimity, the dominant perspective (particularly following the IMC's world conference in 1938) was to regard such relations as an element of, or preparation for, evangelism.

Once again, the 1960s mark a time of transition. Religious diversity, always the experience of Christians in Asia and Africa, became increasingly characteristic of Europe and North America as well. Church leaders in the West were now aware that the spread of Western civilization, contrary to the expectations of previous generations, was not leading to the extinction of non-Christian religions. In fact, with the end of colonialism, these faith communities were beginning to assert their own validity with growing zeal.

Meanwhile, Christians outside the North Atlantic region were also finding their voice, and many of them were using it to encourage a more cooperative approach to other religions. Their primary agenda was often nation-building and/or the struggle against oppression, activities that were, in many cases, directed in opposition to other Christians and undertaken alongside persons of other faiths.

The first WCC assembly to speak about "dialogue" as a way of relating to these neighbours was New Delhi in 1961 (the first assembly held outside Europe or North America); but the seminal ecumenical document was the Declaration on the Relation of the Church to Non-Christian Religions from Vatican II. The key theological motif, one echoed in many subsequent ecumenical statements, was set forth in the Declaration's opening paragraph:

> All people form but one community. This is so because all stem from the one stock which God created to people the entire earth, and also because all share a common destiny, namely God... Since all are created in God's image, it is incumbent upon Christians to treat all people in a brotherly [and sisterly] fashion.[18]

A Vatican Secretariat for Non-Christians was established by Pope Paul VI following the Council, and by 1971 the WCC's central committee was ready to create a new Sub-unit

---

[16] M.M. Thomas, "Jesus Christ Frees and Unites", in *Towards a Theology of Contemporary Ecumenism*, London, CLS, 1978, p.296.

[17] *Mission and Evangelism: An Ecumenical Affirmation: A Study Guide*, WCC, 1983.

[18] In Michael Kinnamon and Brian Cope eds, *The Ecumenical Movement: An Anthology of Key Texts and Voices*, WCC, 1997, p.399.

on Dialogue with People of Living Faiths and Ideologies, thus removing interfaith relations from the framework of mission and evangelism.

Behind the idea of dialogue stands a crucial methodological conviction: Other faiths should not be judged in the abstract, on the basis of doctrinal principle, but should be experienced through living encounter. Partners in dialogue must be allowed to define themselves. This conviction was spelled out in a set of guidelines on dialogue developed by the sub-unit at a conference in Chang Mai, Thailand (1977), and subsequently commended to the churches for study and action by the WCC's central committee. The World Council organized numerous bilateral and multilateral dialogue meetings with Jews, Muslims, Hindus and Buddhists, and issued specific guidelines on Jewish-Christian and Muslim-Christian relations.

The churches involved in the ecumenical movement are not of one mind, however, on the question of interfaith relations. Nairobi (1975), the first WCC assembly with guests from other religions, was also the site of considerable controversy over this topic. How does dialogue avoid the danger of syncretism (the inappropriate blending of religions)? Does dialogue undermine Christian mission? What about the uniqueness of God's revelation in Jesus Christ? Differing responses to such questions helped define the theological divide (often spoken of as liberal versus conservative) that opened in many churches. Other questions concerning dialogue were raised (e.g., at the WCC's Canberra assembly in 1991) by Christians who suffer at the hands of fundamentalist Muslims in parts of Africa and the Middle East or militant Hindus in India.

Even when Christians agreed that dialogue was appropriate, there often was disagreement about its purpose. Within the WCC, for example, there was broad support for challenging prejudices, eschewing triumphalist forms of evangelization and working with others to build a better human community; but there was less willingness to affirm that dialogue can be a "common pilgrimage towards truth" (W. Ariarajah). The dialogue office attempted in the 1990s to speak with greater clarity about the theological significance of other faiths, especially through a four-year study programme entitled "My Neighbour's Faith – and Mine", but no one suggested that such work was complete.

The final three decades of the 20th century, in sum, witnessed an astonishing transformation in the way Christians relate to people of other faiths. Interfaith dialogues and activities could be found in communities around the world. Interfaith events such as the Parliament of Religions in 1993 and 1999, with its attempt to produce a "global ethic", generated considerable excitement. Many churches have expanded their ecumenical departments to include an interfaith desk and numerous churches in Europe and North America developed statements on interfaith (especially Jewish-Christian) relations. In some places, former councils of churches expanded their membership to include representatives from other faith traditions. All of this activity also pointed, however, to another unresolved tension: Does the concern for such "wider ecumenism" undermine or detract from the movement's historic focus on intra-Christian unity?

ECUMENICAL SOCIAL THOUGHT AND ACTION

As noted in the introduction to this chapter, one of the truly pivotal ecumenical events of the 1960s was the Geneva conference on Church and Society (1966). The participants, half of whom did not come from the North Atlantic regions, argued that political and economic justice require not just revision but dramatic, systemic change. This marked a decisive shift away from the notion of "the responsible society" that had dominated ecumenical social thought for the preceding generation.

To put this transition in thinking another way, a theology of "Christian realism", in which the churches seek to contribute to relative justice in a sinful world, gave way at the global level to "eschatological realism", in which the churches seek to live in anticipation of God's intended shalom. The reign (kingdom) of God is to be found in our midst, challenging the pseudo-reality of the world's systems. The task of the church is therefore to bring the values of God's reign to bear on economic, social and political life, to embody and confess the eschatological demands of Christian faith as an alternative to the powers and principalities. In practice, this meant a shift within the ecumenical movement, from attempting to influence those with power, to participating in the struggles of those without it. Critics within the movement insisted that such a stance was often ineffectual – a case of idealism undermining the possibility of actual change. But after Geneva, they were clearly swimming upstream.

By the 1970s, ecumenical conferences began to speak of the search for "a just, participatory and sustainable society" as the new framework for ecumenical social thinking. Given the increasing awareness of the environment's vulnerability, and new understanding of the limits to growth, it was hardly surprising that "sustainability" would emerge as a key element of the churches' social vision. This image was more fully developed at a WCC-sponsored conference on "Faith, Science and the Future" (Boston-MIT 1979). Nearly half the participants at that meeting were from the fields of science and technology, which enabled the conference to speak with credibility about the threat, as well as the promise, of scientific developments.

The Vancouver assembly (1983) pressed this vision further by calling on the WCC "to engage member churches in a conciliar process of mutual commitment (covenant) to justice, peace and the integrity of creation" (JPIC). The JPIC process, a central priority of the Council in subsequent years, was intended to keep the churches' social witness from fragmenting into competing emphases (peace versus justice, justice versus ecology). The idea of a "council" through which the churches would make mutual commitments proved too lofty, but the participants at a global convocation (Seoul 1990) did enter into "an act of covenanting" on four issues: (1) a just economic order, including "liberation from foreign debt bondage", (2) a culture of nonviolence, (3) "a culture that can live in harmony with creation's integrity" (ecological responsibility), and (4) the eradication of racism. JPIC also proved to be an umbrella for various initiatives outside the auspices of the WCC; and it spawned a number of national and regional conferences, including a highly celebrated gathering of European churches in Basel in 1989. The Council itself attempted to build on the Seoul convocation, and to integrate its array of affirmations, through a programme entitled "Theology of Life".

There is not room to discuss the actual acts of common social witness that marked the years in question: Catholics and Protestants working together for political justice in Latin America; Christians of different colours and confessions acting together to oppose racism in Africa, North America and Australia; churches with histories of animosity joining in protest of nuclear weapons in Europe and the Pacific; churches witnessing together in Eastern Europe against the destructive effects of Marxism; Christians working with neighbours of other faiths on behalf of the poor in Asia... The picture may be rather more complete, however, if we note that broad ecumenical consensus emerged in these decades on three particular issues.

Recognizing a preferential option for the poor

This phrase (referred to above) signalled the beginning of a new era in the church's struggle with poverty. Indeed, the terminological shift from "poverty" to "the poor" is itself indicative of new directions. Poverty focuses attention on the reform of impersonal economic systems. By the late 1960s, however, there was "a growing conviction that the remedy for poverty was not top-down reforms but changes of structure [including political structure] emanating from among the poor, acting as agents of their own emancipation".[19]

The ecumenical consensus that has developed around the need for solidarity with the poor has already been touched on in our discussion of mission and evangelism. This "preferential option" has been repeatedly affirmed as

> a guideline for the priorities and behaviour of all Christians everywhere, pointing to the values around which we should organize our lives and the struggle in which we should put our energy.[20]

Perhaps the dominant concern of the WCC's Harare assembly (1998) was "globalization", especially the emerging global economy that provided wealth for some while widening the gap between rich and poor. The assembly contrasted this "oikoumene of domination" with the "oikoumene of faith and solidarity" that marks the ecumenical movement at its best; and it echoed the Jubilee 2000 movement (itself an example of grassroots ecumenism) in calling for a cancellation of the debt owed by poor countries to Western governments and international lending institutions.

Combating racism

The ecumenical movement has overtly opposed racism and shown support for its victims since the 1920s. Ecumenical thinking about racism, however, underwent two major shifts in the last third of the 20th century.

First, until the late 1960s, ecumenical leaders assumed, in line with Enlightenment culture, that racism could be eradicated through education. A significant change was first articulated at a WCC-sponsored consultation in Notting Hill, England, in 1969. Visser 't Hooft summarized the prevailing attitude:

> We have believed too much in persuasion by declarations and have not been sufficiently aware of the irrational factors of the situation... We have insisted too little on the very considerable sacrifices which have to be made if racial justice is to prevail.

The WCC's response was the Programme to Combat Racism (PCR) which through its special fund supported groups around the world, though especially in southern Africa, that were fighting against racism. (Grants for humanitarian assistance to groups engaged in armed struggle in such places as Rhodesia [now Zimbabwe] and South Africa made the PCR the most controversial WCC programme of these decades.) Just as it is not enough to aid the victims of economic oppression, so it is not enough to educate racial oppressors. Just as there must be a preferential option for the poor, so there must be a privileged listening to the racially oppressed. When it comes to racism, said the WCC's central committee, "neutrality is not an option".

---

[19] Richard D.N. Dickinson, "Poverty", in N. Lossky et al. eds, *Dictionary of the Ecumenical Movement*, 2nd ed.WCC, 2002, p.917.
[20] *Mission and Evangelism: An Ecumenical Affirmation*, WCC, 1982, §35.

The second shift was expressed a decade later at a world consultation on racism held in Amsterdam. Racism had generally been seen within the ecumenical movement as a problem of mission (i.e., it undermines the church's witness). Ecumenists, as noted above, now began to see that it is also an issue of ecclesiology (i.e., racial inclusiveness is a fundamental mark of the church and its unity). It is not surprising, given this shift, that the 1977 assembly of the Lutheran World Federation spoke of apartheid as status confessionis, an issue on which it is not possible to differ without jeopardizing the church's shared confession. Then, in 1982, the World Alliance of Reformed Churches suspended the membership of its apartheid-supporting churches in South Africa, contending that their theological apology for apartheid was a heresy that placed them outside the fellowship of churches and made eucharistic communion impossible.

Promoting peace with justice

In one of the most insightful books written about ecumenism in the period we are discussing, *And Yet It Moves*,[21] Ernst Lange declared, "The ecumenical movement is a movement for peace. Far wider than the Geneva association, it is in fact the way in which the Christian churches really serve the cause of peace." But how is peace-making related to other ecumenical priorities? And what particular steps should the churches take together to promote it? Two areas of consensus emerged in response to such questions.

First, there was broad agreement that peace and justice are fundamentally inseparable. This did not mean, of course, that churches involved in ecumenical dialogue affirmed the same priorities in particular situations (both the Vancouver and Canberra assemblies were marked by severe tension over how to relate peace and justice); but there was a shared recognition that peace was not simply the absence of overt combat since the status quo has often been violently unjust in the suppression of dissent. This issue was perhaps most fully explored by the WCC in a two-year study on "Violence, Nonviolence and the Struggle for Social Justice", completed in 1973. A new initiative, the Decade to Overcome Violence, called for by the Harare assembly, was to be launched at the beginning of 2001.

Second, there had been, at least since the Vancouver assembly, a widespread condemnation in ecumenical documents of the production and deployment, not to mention potential use, of nuclear weapons. This, too, was understood as a justice issue since spending on armaments syphons off money that could have been used for building up the human family.

INTERCHURCH AID AND DIAKONIA

The idea of interchurch aid as more than help given to the mission churches of one's own communion developed in response to the needs created by the second world war. The demand for refugee resettlement following the war helped further expand the churches' understanding of service (diakonia) to include assistance for people of whatever faith who were in need.

---

[21] Ernst Lange, *And Yet It Moves: Dream and Reality of the Ecumenical Movement*, transl. by Edwin Robertson, Grand Rapids MI, Eerdmans, 1979, p.147.

A 1966 conference in Swanwick, England, sponsored by the WCC, is generally seen as a watershed in discussions of interchurch aid and ecumenical diakonia because of its forceful challenge to lingering forms of colonial paternalism. Swanwick also called on the churches to move beyond the giving and receiving of aid to a shared concern for changing structures that perpetuate poverty. This theme was urgently underscored twenty years later at a WCC conference in Cyprus which issued what is known as the Larnaca declaration:

> We have all experienced, in one way or another, the transforming power of Christian service... we dedicate ourselves, from this day forward, to work for justice and peace through our diakonia.[22]

Two closely related debates dominated ecumenical thinking on this topic over the 35 years after Larnaca.

The debate over development

The term "development" suggests that poor nations can achieve economic and social prosperity if technical skills and economic support are made available to them by affluent (developed) countries. Development was strongly endorsed by the Uppsala assembly, leading to the establishment within the WCC of the Commission on the Churches' Participation in Development (CCPD).

Since that time, however, "there has probably been more criticism than praise within ecumenical circles for economic and technical development and for reproducing the Western economic system with its economic successes in the South"[23] – even as faith in the development model has grown in other quarters. While some may benefit, traditional understandings of development also reinforce patterns of dependence and actually widen the gap between rich and poor. By the early 1970s, the CCPD had identified three inter-related objectives: justice, self reliance and economic growth. The churches' task, the Commission argued, should be to participate with the poor in the struggle for that kind of development.

A significant initiative that should not be forgotten in any history of the period is the joint committee on Society, Development and Peace (SODEPAX), formed in the years after Vatican II as an instrument for collaboration between the Roman Catholic Church and the World Council. The potential of SODEPAX was never realized, in part because of differing understandings of development and what the churches should do to promote it, and the programme was eventually terminated in 1980.

The debate over the sharing of resources

In the early 1970s, church leaders in both Africa and Asia, concerned about relationships of dependency and inequality, called for a "moratorium" on the receiving of money and personnel from churches in the North Atlantic regions. The debate this provoked at the WCC's Nairobi assembly led to a study programme known as the Ecumenical Sharing of Resources (ESR). A world consultation on ESR (El Escorial, Spain, 1987) produced a set of "guidelines for sharing" which affirmed (1) that all

---

[22] Klaus Poser ed., *Diakonia 2000: Called to be Neighbours*, WCC, 1987, p.124; *The Ecumenical Movement: An Anthology of Key Texts and Voices*, p.317.
[23] Michael Taylor, *Not Angels but Agencies*, WCC, 1995, p.69.

churches are both givers and receivers, (2) that the resources to be shared include not only material wealth but such things as theological insights, forms of spirituality, testimonies of faith and suffering, and cultural gifts, and (3) that decisions about sharing must be marked by broad participation and mutual accountability. The guidelines were widely discussed and a number of churches committed themselves to such a framework of relationships.

These debates over the meaning of diakonia, development and sharing should not obscure the fact that churches, over the decades, came to one another's assistance repeatedly. Two most notable examples of these years are support for the victims of drought in northern Africa during the early 1980s and for the people of the war-torn Balkans in the 1990s.

EDUCATION

Education, though sometimes neglected in discussions of ecumenical history, is one of the four "streams" that flowed together to make up the modern ecumenical movement. Beginning in the late 19th century, the World Sunday School Association and its successor body, the World Council on Christian Education (WCCE), held numerous international conventions/assemblies that brought together educators from different cultures and confessions. The 1960s, that decade of transitions, saw increased collaboration between the WCC and the WCCE, culminating in the integration of the latter into the World Council of Churches in 1971. It was clear to the leaders of both organizations that concern for education, both in society and the church, could not be separated from other ecumenical activities and conversations.

Looking back over this period, three themes marked education in ecumenical perspective:

1. Education, wherever it takes place, is never neutral. It can be, and often is, used to socialize people into oppressive systems; however, by the same token, it can be an important tool in the process of human liberation. With this in mind, the ecumenical approach to education stressed what former WCC staff member Paulo Freire called "conscientization", i.e., the process of helping people to recognize that they are subjects, not objects, and therefore able to take an active role in changing their social-political situations. "Education", as the Uppsala assembly put it, "must play a constructive and at times radical part in the process of changing the world."

2. Education must involve "learning in community". This phrase from the Vancouver assembly implies a collaborative approach that takes account of the diversity of human gifts. Education, to put it another way, is a two-way process and cannot be reduced to the transmission of knowledge from experts to pupils.

3. Increasing attention was also given to the importance of "ecumenical formation" (i.e., the nurturing of an ecumenical spirit, the knowledge of ecumenical agreements, a sense of the faith and culture of other churches), though this remained an underdeveloped part of the movement's agenda. Various studies, including one by the Joint Working Group between the Roman Catholic Church and the WCC, emphasized the need to learn to think globally, while relating global issues to local experiences, and to learn to receive the riches of other traditions and cultures.

These three points constituted the animating perspective of the many "lay academies" or ecumenical centres found throughout Europe and in parts of Asia, Africa and North America.

PARTICIPATION

In one of the most celebrated ecumenical speeches of the period, Philip Potter contended in his general secretary's address to the Vancouver assembly (1983) that the ecumenical journey is a "fellowship of participation" beyond diversities of culture and confession.

> We have reminded each other that the church is, as Peter affirmed, the people, *laos*, of God, and not principally the ordained ministry which, though indispensable, constitutes less than one percent of the house of living stones. We have endeavoured to encourage the churches to recognize that young people are not the church of tomorrow but of today. More insistently in recent years, we have painfully tried to come to terms with the fact that the house of living stones is a community of women and men fulfilling a common ministry of witness and service to the world.[24]

These assertions accurately identify a key concern of the years from 1968 to 2000: genuine church unity ought to require the full participation of people historically excluded from positions of power. The actual record of achievement, however, was somewhat more ambiguous.

1. While women played a significant role in the early development of modern ecumenism through such organizations as the YWCA and such movements as the Women's World Day of Prayer, they remained largely absent from official leadership positions until the 1970s. By way of example, only 9 percent of the delegates at Uppsala in 1968 were women; and, until that assembly, only one woman had been a president of the Council.

The times, however, were clearly changing. The first major indication of new sensitivities came in 1974 with a WCC-sponsored an all women's consultation on "Sexism in the 1970s". The following year at the Nairobi assembly a plenary session was, for the first time, devoted to the concerns of women and a recommendation was made for an international study on "The Community of Women and Men in the Church".

The Community study (1978-81), as it was known, centred around local study groups ("the most extensive grassroots participation of any such project in WCC history"[25]) and, thus, helped to foster dialogue about women's participation in various parts of the world. A culminating consultation in Sheffield, England (1981), denounced the "web of oppression" (sexism, racism and classism) which traps many women, highlighted the gifts which women bring to the community of the church, and set a goal (subsequently affirmed by the WCC central committee) of equal participation between women and men in decision-making bodies of the WCC. At Vancouver in 1983, 30 percent of the delegates were women; fifteen years later in Harare, the figure was nearly 40 percent.

The 1974 conference had been prompted, in part, by a UN-sponsored Decade for Women, beginning in 1975. By the mid-1980s, however, it seemed clear that this initiative had been ignored by many of the churches; and, thus, in 1988 the WCC launched its own Ecumenical Decade of the Churches in Solidarity with Women. The Decade included team visits by people who were called "living letters" to nearly every WCC

---

[24] Philip Potter, "Report of the General Secretary", in David Gill ed., *Gathered for Life: Official Report, 6th Assembly, World Council of Churches, Vancouver, Canada, 1983*, p.202; *The Ecumenical Movement: An Anthology of Key Texts and Voices*, p.57.

[25] Dorothy Harvey, "Participation", in *Dictionary of the Ecumenical Movement*, 2nd ed., p.883.

member church; and it prompted several major events on various continents, including a highly controversial "Re-Imagining" conference in North America in 1993.

2. Student movements and organizations, like those of women, were instrumental in the formation of the ecumenical movement, nurturing generations of leaders with an ecumenical outlook. Again, however, the 1960s were a time of decisive transition. Many Christian youth, reflecting the revolutionary spirit of the age, expressed a deep alienation from the church and church-related ecumenism. Those who remained involved were less interested in separate youth structures and conferences than in greater participation in the movement as a whole. The WCC's youth department, for example, was greatly reduced in the early 1970s with the assumption that youth concerns would be taken up throughout the Council. The percentage of delegates under thirty years of age did increase from 4 percent at Uppsala to 11 percent at Vancouver, but it is hard not to conclude that the overall influence of youth in the WCC and the ecumenical movement has actually lessened as a result in this shift of philosophy. The percentage of youth delegates to the Canberra assembly in 1991 was lower than in Vancouver, prompting a protest (reminiscent of Uppsala twenty-three years earlier) on the part of youth delegates and stewards.

The late 1960s were a particularly painful and divisive time for the World Student Christian Federation, one of the pioneering bodies of modern ecumenism. Leaders called for a shift in emphasis, away from educational institutions and towards solidarity in social-political struggles, with the result that the student movement's organizational base weakened around the world, disappearing altogether in such countries as the US. Groups with far fewer ties to the ecumenical movement, including Campus Crusade for Christ and Inter-Varsity Christian Fellowship, moved into the void.

The story is not complete without mention of positive developments. The *Kirchentag*, for example, continued to draw large numbers of youth to ecumenical gatherings in Germany. A Council of Youth, started in 1974 by the Taizé community in France, brought tens of thousands of youth to that ecumenical monastic centre for common prayer, study and fellowship.

3. The first WCC assembly to take seriously the participation of persons with disabilities was Nairobi (1975) which issued a powerful statement on "The Handicapped and the Wholeness of the Family of God". Following the Vancouver assembly in 1983, the WCC appointed a full-time consultant to promote awareness of this issue within the Council and its member churches. Local ecumenical efforts also acknowledged that "the refusal to receive [disabled] sisters and brothers as full human beings and contributing members of Christ's body is a form of apostasy"[26] (US Consultation on Church Union). But such recognition is by no means universal in the churches and ecumenical bodies.

4. Many of the early ecumenical leaders were lay people, and the "rediscovery of the laity" was a key dimension of the renewal sought by the movement in the 1940s and 1950s. By the time of the Uppsala assembly, however, the focus was less on laity per se than on the mission of the whole people of God in the social struggles of the era. Two other factors contributed to the diminishing emphasis on laity: (1) As the ecumenical movement became ever more institutionalized in the churches, ecumenism was

---

[26] Gerald F. Moede ed., *The COCU Consensus: In Quest of a Church of Christ Uniting, approved and commended to the churches by the 16th Plenary of the Consultation on Church Union, November 30, 1984, Baltimore MD*, Princeton, Consultation on Church Union, 1985, p.10.

increasingly seen as something that is done by "specialists", usually ordained. (2) A focus on particular constituency groups (e.g., women) began to replace concern for the laity as a whole. When the WCC was reorganized in 1971, the former Department on the Laity was absorbed into the new Sub-unit on Renewal and Congregational Life. Only in the 1990s did the issue re-surface as an explicit item of ecumenical study.

Perhaps the most accurate summary of "participation" as an ecumenical theme of the era is to say that it has enriched the movement while also causing inevitable tensions. Demands for participatory diversity within ecumenical organizations were often out of sync with continuing patterns of leadership in the churches. This meant, for example, that delegates to a WCC assembly frequently did not speak with authority to or for their churches – which was a factor in the marginalization of the ecumenical agenda back home.

The movement also lived with the irony that its commitment to inclusive community meant including those who did not agree about the meaning of inclusivity. The wider the range of participants, for example, the more divided the ecumenical movement seemed over the participation of homosexuals.

ORTHODOX PARTICIPATION

Various Orthodox churches have been involved in the modern ecumenical movement from its beginning, but the 1960s saw a dramatic increase in Orthodox participation. Several official statements over the past years insisted that such participation, far from being revolutionary, was consistent with Orthodoxy's historical attempts to apply the apostolic faith to new situations.

One form of involvement was through bilateral theological dialogues. The Eastern Orthodox church, for example, had official dialogues with Oriental Orthodox, Roman Catholic, Anglican, Old Catholic, Lutheran, Reformed and Methodist churches. The Roman Catholic dialogue focused during the 1990s on the problem of "uniate" churches (i.e., Eastern rite churches that have – at times, under pressure – broken communion with Orthodox communities in order to establish full communion with Rome). In 1993, the Eastern Orthodox-Roman Catholic dialogue commission recognized that the Orthodox and Roman Catholic are "sister churches", argued that there should be "no question of conversion of people from one church to the other in order to ensure their salvation", and proclaimed uniatism an unacceptable model of unity – while also affirming the right of Eastern Catholic churches to exist with full religious liberty.[27]

A second form of Orthodox involvement in ecumenism was through councils of churches – locally, nationally, regionally and internationally. With the exception of the churches in Georgia and Bulgaria, every autocephalous Orthodox church, Eastern and Oriental, was a member of the WCC in 2000, and individuals from these churches have played major leadership roles in the Council. Orthodox scholars have been particularly active in Faith and Order and CWME.

There is no doubt that these contacts had a significant impact on ecumenical statements (e.g., in the way the WCC now highlights the trinitarian nature of God) and, at the same time, helped prevent Orthodox isolation, especially during the period of communist control in Eastern Europe, and in the Muslim-dominated Middle East. On the

---

[27] *Growth in Agreement II: Reports and Agreed Statements of Ecumenical Conversations on a World Level, 1982-1998*, Jeffrey Gros, Harding Meyer and William G. Rusch eds, WCC, 2000, pp.680-85.

occasion of the WCC's twenty-fifth anniversary (1973), the Ecumenical Patriarchate acknowledged that the Orthodox had been enriched by the encounter with Western church life and theology as well as by the "generous material expressions of Christian solidarity, help and love. These have all helped to build up Christ in the hearts of millions of distressed Christians and their fellow sufferers."[28]

Despite such positive developments, Orthodox leaders repeatedly expressed concerns about their relations with other churches through the ecumenical movement. The following four concerns seemed to be most troubling.

1. Within the life of a council, issues "alien to the Orthodox tradition and ethos", including the ordination of women, inclusive language and the place of homosexuals in the church, may be given programmatic attention. Concern over such matters led Eastern Orthodox churches in the US temporarily to suspend membership in their national council in 1992 and two churches to withdraw from membership in the WCC and the Conference of European Churches in the late 1990s.

2. The structures and procedures of conciliar life often seem at odds with Orthodox ecclesiological self-understanding. According to the third preconciliar pan-Orthodox conference (one in a series of meetings intended to prepare for a great and holy synod), the Orthodox church "does not accept the idea of the 'equality of confessions' and cannot consider church unity as an interconfessional adjustment... God calls every Christian to the unity of faith which is lived in the sacraments and the Tradition, as experienced in the Orthodox church."[29] A council's activity must allow the Orthodox to live in fidelity to this self-understanding. For some, this raised issues concerning the extent of Orthodox participation in "ecumenical worship" at world conferences and assemblies.

3. The modern movement tends to emphasize "ecumenism in space" (i.e., the dialogue among contemporary churches, each shaped by a particular culture and history), while the Orthodox clearly favour "ecumenism in time" (i.e., the common recovery and affirmation of the apostolic Tradition). This hermeneutical divide was particularly evident in the negative Orthodox response to the keynote address delivered by Chung Hyun Kyung at Canberra, referred to above in the section on mission and evangelism.

4. The Orthodox strongly objected to what they perceive as proselytism in historic Orthodox lands. Our experience in the 20th century, they argued, was one of martyrdom. Now that such persecution has ended, it is time to exhibit ecumenical solidarity and encouragement, not evangelistic competition. Instead, Western churches, including some involved in the ecumenical movement, sent missionaries and material aid to the former Eastern bloc without apparent regard for the indigenous Christian communities. Such activity "has led to an almost complete rupture of the ecumenical relations developed during the previous decades".[30]

With these concerns in mind, a gathering of Orthodox leaders six months before the 1998 Harare assembly called for the creation of a theological commission, made up of Orthodox and non-Orthodox, to discuss Orthodox involvement in both the Council and the movement. The assembly endorsed the idea, and a Special Commission on Orthodox Participation in the WCC thereafter identified five areas of work: (1) issues related to membership in the WCC, (2) the WCC's decision-making process, (3) worship and

---

[28] Gennadios Limouris ed., *Orthodox Visions of Ecumenism*, WCC, 1994, p.51.

[29] In *Orthodox Visions of Ecumenism*, p. 113

[30] Metropolitan Kirill of Smolensk and Kaliningrad, "Gospel and Culture", in Christopher Duraisingh ed., *The Gospel in Diverse Cultures*, WCC, 1998, p.91.

common prayer in the WCC, (4) ecumenical methodologies for approaching social and ethical issues, and (5) issues of ecclesiology. The final report of the Special Commission to the WCC's central committee was completed in 2002.

ROMAN CATHOLIC PARTICIPATION

It would be difficult to overstate the ecumenical transformation wrought by the Second Vatican Council. Pope Paul VI confirmed, during a historic 1969 visit to the WCC headquarters, that centuries of estrangement have now given way to growing contact and understanding. This visit, said the pontiff, is "a clear sign of the Christian fellowship which already exists between all the baptized, and thus between member churches of the World Council and the Catholic church". This fellowship is, at present, "imperfect", but the Spirit is "guiding all Christians in the search for the fullness of that unity which Christ wills for his one and only church..."[31]

Catholic involvement in the ecumenical movement at the end of the 20th century took a variety of forms, including the following.

1. The Roman Catholic Church was by 2000 a full member of more than fifty national councils of churches, as well as regional councils in the Pacific, Caribbean and Middle East. A 1975 text from the Vatican Secretariat (now Pontifical Council) for Promoting Christian Unity and the 1993 Ecumenical Directory provided guidelines and encouragement for such participation.

2. By 2000 the Roman Catholic Church also participated in numerous national-level theological dialogues and had undertaken global dialogues from the late 1960s with the Anglican, Assyrian, Baptist, Disciples, Lutheran, Methodist, Orthodox, Pentecostal and Reformed communions. As noted elsewhere in this chapter, several of these conversations produced substantial agreements, though "official reception" proved more difficult than many ecumenists had hoped.

3. The Roman Catholic Church worked closely with the WCC, especially through the Council's Faith and Order Commission (where Catholic theologians sat as full members), the Commission on World Mission and Evangelism (which had a series of Catholic consultants), and the Joint Working Group, which in addition to coordinating other activities between Rome and Geneva produced notable studies on such topics as common witness, proselytism, ethics, ecumenical formation and the "hierarchy of truths". In 1972, the Roman Catholic Church declined to ask for WCC membership "in the immediate future", citing its self-understanding as a globally organized communion (WCC members are, for the most part, nationally structured churches). Similarly, the Roman Catholic Church participated in such events as the world convocation on "Justice, Peace and the Integrity of Creation", but backed away from co-sponsorship.

4. Common witness is a good general description of local relations between Catholics and other Christians, despite several highly publicized trouble spots (e.g., Northern Ireland and the former Yugoslavia). It is now commonplace, especially in Europe and North America, for Catholics and Protestants to study one another's theologians as part of their ministerial education and to cooperate in local mission projects.

5. Much of this period under review was dominated by the pontificate of John Paul II, a pope who, in the eyes of some of his critics, carried forward the letter more than the spirit of Vatican II's commitment to ecumenism. Episcopal appointments over the last

---

[31] *The Ecumenical Movement: An Anthology of Key Texts and Voices*, p.35.

two decades of the century, they charged, often reflected a cautious, conservative tone that discourages creative ecumenical initiative. At the same time, however, this pope met frequently with leaders of other communions during his many trips abroad, including high-profile visits to the Ecumenical Patriarchate (1979), Canterbury cathedral (1982) and the WCC headquarters (1984). During a visit to Rome by Patriarch Dimitrios I (1987), the pope recited the Nicene Creed without the historically divisive filioque clause ("... the Spirit proceeds from the Father *and the Son*") – a sign of growing rapprochement with Eastern Orthodoxy.

In his 1995 encyclical, "On Commitment to Ecumenism" *(Ut Unum Sint)*, John Paul II exhorted the church's bishops to be vigilant in "promoting the unity of all Christians by supporting all activities or initiatives undertaken for this purpose, in the awareness that the church has this obligation from the will of Christ himself". (A 1998 Vatican document, "The Ecumenical Dimension in the Formation of Pastoral Workers", mandated a thorough education in ecumenism for all Catholic leadership.) The encyclical also welcomes the call, made by the fifth world conference on Faith and Order (1993), for "a new study of the question of a universal ministry of Christian unity" – a topic that the movement had generally avoided up to that time. While reaffirming the Roman Catholic conviction that the bishop of Rome, as successor to Peter, is a "perpetual and visible principle and foundation of unity", the encyclical acknowledged that the papacy had been a stumbling block and suggested that primacy would need to be exercised in the future in a way that is "open to a new situation".[32]

SPIRITUALITY AND WORSHIP

Leaders of the modern ecumenical movement long affirmed, in the words of the WCC's Evanston assembly (1954), that "the measure of our concern for unity is the degree to which we pray for it. We cannot expect God to give us unity unless we prepare ourselves to receive God's gift by costly and purifying prayer." Emphasis on spirituality as the foundation of all ecumenical endeavour grew, however, over the closing decades of the century. The WCC, for example, made "spirituality" one of its guidelines for future activity following the 1983 Vancouver assembly. The 1991 assembly in Canberra marked the first time that an assembly theme had either taken the form of an invocation or been focused on the third person of the Trinity ("Come, Holy Spirit – Renew the Whole Creation"). Communities that stressed prayer for unity (e.g., the Taizé community in France) grew in popularity. And the idea that *koinonia* involves not just an accumulation of consensus but a spiritual "conversion of the churches" (Groupe des Dombes) also received wide support.

The reasons for these developments are complex, but they would seem to include a growing hunger for spiritual depth in the secularized West and the increased ecumenical participation of Orthodox churches whose ecclesial life centres on liturgy. The presence of the Roman Catholic Church had an undeniable impact. The Second Vatican Council's Decree on Ecumenism spoke of prayer as "the soul of the ecumenical movement" and declared that "there can be no ecumenism worthy of the name without a change of heart". This was echoed in John Paul II's 1995 encyclical on ecumenism:

---

[32] Joannes Paulus II, *Ut Unum Sint: Encyclical Letter by the Supreme Pontiff John Paul II on Ecumenism*, Vatican City, Libreria Editrice Vaticana, 1995, §§ 89 and 95.

Along the ecumenical path to unity, pride of place certainly belongs to common prayer...
If Christians, despite their divisions, can grow ever more united in common prayer around
Christ, they will grow in the awareness of how little divides them in comparison to what
unites them. (§22).

The following observations give further detail to this picture of the last decades of the
20th century.

1. Special occasions of ecumenical prayer grew to be commonplace in local communities around the world. The Week of Prayer for Christian Unity, which from 1966 had
been jointly produced and promoted by the WCC and the Vatican, was by 2000 observed
in at least 75 countries. The WCC also produced an ecumenical prayer cycle, *With All
God's People*, designed to enhance the "growing fellowship of mutual intercession" (L.
Vischer) and to encourage the sharing of spiritual resources.

2. The nature of worship was not an explicit focus of much international ecumenical
study after the Uppsala assembly. A great deal of work was done, however, on the theology of sacraments. The Lima liturgy, which expressed the theological convergence found
in *Baptism, Eucharist and Ministry*, was used at many ecumenical gatherings, including
a widely praised service at the WCC's Vancouver assembly (1983).

3. Vancouver, known as "the praying assembly", deserves additional mention as an
example of effective worship in an ecumenical setting. Reports on the event stressed that
worship was every bit as important as the sessions of business. Vancouver's respectful,
authentic incorporation of non-Western materials, including hymns and chants, influenced worship in a number of Western churches.

4. A key motif of these decades was the integration of worship and service, spirituality and social justice. Worship was understood as an offering of praise, but this offering
could not be divorced from active concern for the world God loves.

- A central theme of the Nairobi assembly was "spirituality for combat", a "holiness in
  action combining struggle with contemplation" (M.M. Thomas).
- Vancouver stressed the need for a "eucharistic way of life" that integrates *leiturgia*
  and diakonia.
- "The liturgy after the Liturgy", a phrase first used by Orthodox theologians, frequently was quoted as a description of the church's life of mission.
- *Baptism, Eucharist and Ministry* was typical of this period's ecumenical texts when it
  acknowledged that "the eucharist is precious food for missionaries" and that "all
  kinds of injustice, racism, separation and lack of freedom are radically challenged
  when we share the body and blood of Christ".
- Those who favoured the term *koinonia* as a description of "the unity we seek" pointed
  out that the word was used by the apostle Paul to denote both sharing in Christ at the
  table (1 Cor. 10) and sharing with sisters and brothers in need (Rom. 15).

COUNCILS OF CHURCHES

Councils of churches, generally regarded as one of the most significant expressions of
modern ecumenism, were certainly prevalent in most parts of the world, nationally and
locally, in the late 1960s. The following 35 years, however, saw several developments (in
addition to the increasing participation of the Roman Catholic Church, noted above) that
warrant attention.

1. Regional councils played an important role during this period in fostering indigenous forms of theology and mission and in providing a point of contact for churches

separated by regional conflicts. By the time of the Uppsala assembly, there were regional councils in Asia, Europe, Africa and the Pacific. After Uppsala, three more were formed: in the Caribbean (1973), Middle East (1974) and Latin America (1982).

2. New models of conciliar life developed in these years in several parts of the world. In the "classical" model, representatives of the member churches meet periodically in order to decide how to carry out tasks on behalf of the churches. The danger is that the council, guided and staffed by ecumenical enthusiasts, might assert its own agenda alongside, or even over against, the churches. With this in mind, councils in the United Kingdom, Australia, New Zealand and Canada adopted a new type of structure, one designed not to do things for the churches but to be the place where churches do things together. This "churches together" model generally means that the council does not act unless there is a consensus among the member churches to do so and that church leaders play a more prominent role in decision-making. The question is whether councils organized in this fashion can still be "the thorn in the flesh of the churches" (L. Vischer), prodding them, through mutual commitment, to expand their vision and self-understandings.

Other councils (e.g., the Middle East Council of Churches and the Christian Council of Sweden) structured themselves according to "families" of churches – Roman Catholic, Orthodox, Protestant. This model allows for representation that is not based solely on the size and resources of individual churches.

3. A good deal of attention was paid over this third of a century to "the ecclesiological significance" (the theological self-understanding) of councils of churches, especially through three international consultations sponsored by the WCC and through the World Council's own attempt to speak of a "common understanding and vision" (CUV) in preparation for the Harare assembly. Affirmations made by the WCC as a result of the CUV process may serve as a summary of these discussions:

- The essence of a council of churches is not the organization per se but the relationship of the churches to one another.
- The churches' fellowship, expressed through the council, is a dynamic, relational reality that ought to change and deepen as a result of life together.
- The churches, through their mutual engagement in the council, should challenge one another to more costly ecumenical commitment.
- While membership in a council need not imply that a church recognizes the other members as true churches, it does imply a recognition (1) that the other members belong to Christ, (2) that membership in the church of Christ is more inclusive than the membership of one's own church, and (3) that the others possess, at the very least, elements of the true church.

4. There was widespread recognition in these years that the ecumenical tent is too narrow, especially given the rapid increase of churches not traditionally Involved in conciliar ecumenism – including Pentecostal, Evangelical and African Indigenous churches. With this in mind, the WCC initiated discussion of a "forum" of churches designed to create space for conversation without the obligations of membership in an ecumenical organization. A similar idea was explored in the US.

It should be noted that many Pentecostals and evangelicals do take part in ecumenical dialogues and common witness, and that some churches from these traditions do participate in conciliar life. One-quarter of the members of the Latin American Council of Churches are Pentecostal.

LOCAL ECUMENISM

Perhaps the most profound ecumenical change of these three decades was the extent to which Christians of different confessional backgrounds could work and pray together in local settings. What once was novelty became commonplace in many parts of the world. Various initiatives identified in other sections of this chapter (e.g., the Week of Prayer for Christian Unity) could easily fit under the heading "local ecumenism", but there are three additional developments that deserve special mention.

1. The term Local Ecumenical Project (LEP) refers to a form of local ecumenical life prevalent in England, though a similar initiative is also found in New Zealand where such projects are called "cooperative ventures".

> A local ecumenical project may be said to exist where there is, at the level of the local church, a formal, written agreement affecting the ministry, congregational life and/or buildings of more than one Christian denomination, and where that agreement has been recognized by the appropriate denominational authorities.[33]

By the year 2000, there were approximately 700 LEPS, generally involving congregations from the Methodist, Church of England, United Reformed, Roman Catholic and/or Baptist traditions. LEPs trace their roots to a British Council of Churches conference in 1964, but the numbers grew dramatically following the failure of national-level dialogues in 1972 and 1982. A national "consultative committee" for LEPs was established in 1973.

In the US, Ecumenical Shared Ministries (ESMs) mushroomed over these three decades, often without much denominational support. The term ESM includes yoked parishes, in which congregations of different denominations share a pastor and (sometimes) programmes; federated churches, in which persons holding membership in two or more denominations form a single congregation; and union churches, which are similar to federated churches but with only one membership role. A 1995 survey discovered that there are close to 800 ESMs affiliated with the United Methodist Church alone. In the survey, members spoke of enhanced ministry and worship, wise stewardship of resources, credibility of witness and expanded mission as benefits of ESMs.

2. One of the most innovative and influential developments in the church was the growth of church base communities (CBCs, also known as basic Christian communities). CBCs are groups of lay Christians, generally poor, who meet regularly to reflect on scripture, build community, and plan for political/social action in their communities. CBCs are not understood by their members as an alternative to congregational participation, but as a new pattern of church life among those who are often marginal to the institutional church.

CBCs are ecumenically significant in that they downplay denominational differences (in some places, Catholics and Protestants participate in the same base communities) and stress the importance of shared practice. Estimates have run as high as 150,000 for such communities in Brazil and Central America alone. Following their appearance in the mid-1960s, CBCs spread throughout Latin America and even to parts of Africa and Asia.

3. Christians of various confessional and cultural backgrounds found it natural to work together through grassroots movements or associations for social renewal (e.g.,

---

[33] Hugh Cross, "Eucharist Experiences Today: Local Ecumenical Projects in England", in *The Ecumenical Review*, 44, 1, 1992, p.48; *The Ecumenical Movement: An Anthology of Key Texts and Voices*, p.253.

Habitat for Humanity). Mention of these highlights a tension that runs throughout the modern ecumenical movement: Is ecumenism primarily a matter of committed individuals who cross traditional boundaries for the sake of mission, or of churches growing together through the efforts of official representatives? This tension is often acute since renewal movements (e.g., of women in the church) frequently stand in opposition to official church policies and practices.

In the 1990s, the ecumenical importance of these movements and associations was stressed by (among others) the general secretary of the WCC, Konrad Raiser. At the fifth world conference on Faith and Order, Raiser observed,

> Experiences shared under persecution and in the common struggle for justice and respect for human rights as well as in movements for peace and the healing of God's creation – all these things have helped to create an awareness of solidarity and belonging together to which the old forms no longer correspond.[34]

TENSIONS AND TRANSITIONS

The year 1968 will go down as a seminal year in the history of the 20th century: the Tet Offensive in Vietnam, the Soviet invasion of Czechoslovakia, the assassinations of Martin Luther King, Jr, and Robert Kennedy in the US, student revolt in the streets of Paris and on university campuses worldwide, the first circling of the moon... This year was also, as we have seen, a seminal year in the history of ecumenism. For many observers, the WCC's Uppsala assembly signalled a move in the right direction, the first sign that the movement was breaking free from Western domination. For others, Uppsala was the point at which the WCC in particular went astray, the moment when it subordinated its historic focus on church unity to a revolutionary political agenda. Just when the movement "has entered into a period of reaping an astonishingly rich harvest", said Visser 't Hooft in his address at Uppsala, the movement "is more seriously called into question than ever before. And once again the basic issue is that of the relation between the church and the world."[35]

This issue has run throughout our discussion of various dimensions of the ecumenical movement after 1968. When these parts are looked at together, several tensions become readily apparent, tensions that marked past discussions and hinted at future directions.

- Is the ecumenical movement to be best understood as a forum where conflicting perspectives meet in dialogue or as a renewal effort that boldly declares the gospel's partisanship on behalf of the excluded and oppressed? Actually, the ecumenical tent of 2000 did not take in a significant portion of the Christian family, e.g., many Pentecostals and Protestant evangelicals (not to mention fundamentalists). How would ecumenical conversations be changed if these communities were included? How widely, and with what conditions, should the invitation to ecumenical participation be extended?
- Is catholicity (a key ecumenical value) best understood in terms of the church's adaptability to diverse local contexts or in terms of transcontextual consensus (often understood as fidelity to the apostolic Tradition)? The danger with the former is fragmentation, an inability of churches to talk meaningfully with one another. The

---

[34] "The Future of the WCC and the Role of Faith and Order within the Ecumenical Movement", *On the Way to Fuller Koinonia*, p.170.
[35] *The Uppsala Report 1968*, N. Goodall ed., WCC, 1968, p.316.

danger with the latter is domination of the agenda by those holding the power. The ecumenical movement must surely be both local and global, must affirm both the church's diversity and its commonality, but this tension is often difficult to sustain.

- Should the ecumenical movement focus primarily on the unity and renewal of the church as a sign and instrument of God's intention for the world or on God's mission of wholeness for the world in which the church is privileged to participate? To put it another way, is unity in faith and order the basis for effective service and witness, or is shared witness and service the soil out of which Christian community grows? At its best, the movement has refused to see this as an either/or choice but, once again, the tension can be difficult as well as creative.

- Is ecumenism at its best when it seeks to do what is possible given the inevitable brokenness of human history or when it seeks to be guided by an eschatological vision of a new world and a transformed church? We have seen how this tension surfaced in discussions of ecumenical social thought; but it also characterized the debate over church unity. Should the emphasis be on commitment to the fullness of Christian communion (which requires the patience of saints) or on manifestation of the *koinonia* that is currently possible (which requires the impatience of prophets)?

- Is the unity of the church, so central to the ecumenical vision, a fellowship based on agreement or a fellowship of those who are unlike and not necessarily agreed? Even those who favour the former understanding might well disagree on whether the agreement required is a matter of doctrine or of socio-political commitment – or both. This tension is by no means new, but it is also by no means resolved.

- Is the pursuit of justice the foundation of authentic Christian witness, or is explicit witness to Christ the context for authentic ministries of justice and service? This question, which contributes to the liberal-conservative divide running through most churches, calls out for more discussion within the ecumenical movement itself.

- Should the ecumenical emphasis remain on intra-Christian communion and cooperation or should it shift more in the direction of solidarity and struggle with people of other faiths?

Stephen Neill ended his epilogue to the first volume of *The History of the Ecumenical Movement: 1517-1948*, with these words:

> We may venture to hope that if, in fifty years time, a further volume of this history comes to be written, those who undertake it, looking back over the second half of the 20th century, will find no less cause than we to rejoice, and to glorify God for what he has wrought.[36]

Surely this brief survey of ecumenical developments gives plenty of cause for rejoicing at what God has accomplished through our efforts and in spite of our shortcomings.

BIBLIOGRAPHY

Baptism, Eucharist and Ministry 1982-1990: Report on the Process and Responses, WCC, 1990, 160p.
Bekes, Gérard and Vajta, Vilmos eds, *Unitatis Redintegratio, 1964-1974: The Impact of the Decree on Ecumenism*, Rome, Anselmiana, 1977, 176p.

---

[36] London, SPCK, 1953.

Burgess, Joseph A. and Gros, Jeffrey eds, *Growing Consensus: Church Dialogues in the United States, 1962-1991*, New York, Paulist, 1995, 688p.

Carden, John ed., *With All God's People: The New Ecumenical Prayer Cycle*, WCC, 1989, 2 vols.

Cashmore, Gwen and Puls, Joan, *Clearing the Way: En Route to an Ecumenical Spirituality*, WCC, 1990, 64p.

The Challenge of Dialogue: Papers and Resolutions of the Dialogue Working Group Meeting: Casablanca, Morocco, June 1989, WCC, 1989, 170p.

Craig, Maxwell ed., *For God's Sake, Unity: An Ecumenical Voyage with the Iona Community*, Glasgow, Wild Goose 1998, 185p.

Crisis and Challenge of the Ecumenical Movement: Integrity and Indivisibility: A Statement of the Institute for Ecumenical Research Strasbourg, WCC, 1994, 41p.

Döring, Heinrich ed., *Ist die Ökumene am Ende?* Regensburg, Friedrich Pustet, 1994, 129p.

Duchrow, Ulrich, *Conflict over the Ecumenical Movement: Confessing Christ Today in the Universal Church*, WCC, 1981, 443p.

Edwards, David L., *The Futures of Christianity*, London, Hodder and Stoughton, 1987, 479p.

Fatio, Olivier ed., *Pour sortir l'oecuménisme du purgatoire*, Genève, Labor et Fides, 1993, 93p.

Francis, Leslie J. and Williams, Kevin, *Churches in Fellowship: Local Councils of Churches in England Today*, London, British Council of Churches, 1990, 104p.

Fraser, Ian M., *Many Cells, One Body: Stories from Small Christian Communities*, WCC, 2003, 118p.

Fraser, Ian M., *Strange Fire: Life Stories and Prayers*, Glasgow, Wild Goose, 1994, 189p.

Halter, Hans ed., *Neue ökumenische Eiszeit?* Zürich, Benziger, 1989, 153p.

In Spirit and in Truth: A Worship Book: World Council of Churches Seventh Assembly 1991, WCC, 1991, 198p.

Jesus Christ, the Life of the World: A Worship Book for the Sixth Assembly of the World Council of Churches, WCC, 1983, 166p.

Joppien, Heinz-Jürgen ed., *Der Ökumenische Rat der Kirchen in den Konflikten des Kalten Krieges: Kontexte, Kompromisse, Konkretionen*, Frankfurt am Main, Otto Lembeck, 2000, 325p.

Kilcourse, George, *Double Belonging: Interchurch Families and Christian Unity*, New York, Paulist, 1992, 179p.

Lemopoulos, Georges ed., *The Ecumenical Movement, the Churches and the World Council of Churches : An Orthodox Contribution to the Reflection Process on "The Common Understanding and Vision of the WCC"*, WCC, 1996, 63p.

Meyer, Harding ed., *Fundamental Differences, Fundamental Consensus: The Impact of Bilateral Dialogues on the Ecumenical Movement*, Indianapolis, Council on Christian Unity, 1986, 96p.

Míguez Bonino, José, "The Concern for a Vital and Coherent Theology", in *The Ecumenical Review*, 41, 2, 1989, pp.160-76.

Newbigin, James Edward Lesslie, *The Other Side of 1984: Questions for the Churches*, WCC, 1983, 75p.

Niederstein, Peter, *Christen am runden Tisch: Ermutigungen zur ökumenischen Bewegung*, Zürich, Benziger, 1990, 211p.

Raiser, Konrad, *Ecumenism in Transition: A Paradigm Shift in the Ecumenical Movement?* WCC, 1991, 132p.

Raiser, Konrad, *For a Culture of Life: Transforming Globalization and Violence*, WCC, 2002, 173p.

Raiser, Konrad, *To Be the Church: Challenges and Hopes for a New Millennium*, WCC, 1997, 104p.

Robra, Martin, *Ökumenische Sozialethik*, Gütersloh, Mohn, 1994, 255p.

Ryan, Thomas, *A Survival Guide for Ecumenically Minded Christians*, Ottawa, Novalis, 1989, 163p.

Survey of Church Union Negotiations 1954-2002.

Stormon, E. J. ed., *Towards the Healing of Schism: The Sees of Rome and Constantinople: Public Statements and Correspondence between the Holy See and the Ecumenical Patriarchate 1958-1984*, New York, Paulist, 1987, 559p.

Tsompanidis, Stylianos, *Orthodoxie und Ökumene: Gemeinsam auf dem Weg zu Gerechtigkeit, Frieden und Bewahrung der Schöpfung*, Münster, LIT, 1999, 266p.

Vassiliadis, Petros, *Eucharist and Witness: Orthodox Perspectives on the Unity and Mission of the Church*, WCC, 1998, 115p.

Visser 't Hooft, Willem Adolf, *Has the Ecumenical Movement a Future?* Belfast, Christian Journals Ltd., 1974, 97p.

Wainwright, Geoffrey, *The Ecumenical Moment: Crisis and Opportunity for the Church*, Grand Rapids MI, Eerdmans, 1983, 263p.

Weinrich, Michael, *Ökumene am Ende?: Plädoyer für einen neuen Realismus*, Neukirchen-Vluyn, Neukirchener, 1997, 182p.

Welch, Elizabeth and Winfield, Flora, *A Handbook on Local Ecumenical Partnerships*, London, Churches Together in England, 1995, 128p.

Willaime, Jean-Paul ed., *Vers de nouveaux oecuménismes: les paradoxes contemporains de l'oecuménisme, recherches d'unité et quêtes d'identité*, Paris, Cerf, 1989, 250p.

Yearbook of the World Council of Churches, WCC, 1995-2003.

4

The Unity We Share, the Unity We Seek

Melanie A. May

The search for the visible unity of the church was the heartbeat of the 20th century ecumenical movement. Since its early stages, questions continued to be asked: What *is* the unity we seek? What does it look like? How much agreement is necessary? How much diversity is possible? In what form is unity to be made manifest?

Until the 1960s ecumenical conversation tended to focus on nurturing the growing recognition that the churches' divisions both contradict the gift of unity given in Christ and threaten the credibility of the churches' witness to the world. But during the 1960s, several significant shifts in the ecumenical conversation occurred. First, at the third assembly of the World Council of Churches (New Delhi 1961), talk about visible unity began to describe "the nature of the unity we seek" – "all in each place". This was consistent with previous attempts to make concrete what is meant by the visible unity of the church and to specify steps to be taken towards the fullness of unity. The innovation in terminology had a catalytic effect on discussions of the church's unity.

A second shift was also signalled at New Delhi. A number of so-called "younger churches" from Africa, Asia and Latin America and the Orthodox churches of Eastern Europe were welcomed as members of the Council. This significant growth in ecclesial diversity and ecumenical partnership continued the year after the assembly when Pope John XXIII convened the Second Vatican Council (1962-65), emphasizing the church's duty to work for "full visible unity in truth" among all Christians in a "fullness of charity". By virtue of *Unitatis Redintegratio* ("Decree on Ecumenism", 1964), the Roman Catholic Church officially became a faithful ecumenical partner, bringing to the table the vision and commitment of the documents of Vatican II, and later of the remarkable 1995 encyclical by John Paul II, *Ut Unum Sint* ("On Commitment to Ecumenism", 1995).[1]

Further, during more recent decades the ecumenical conversation has been enriched by many Pentecostal and some evangelical voices, and also by a new attentiveness to the free-church tradition. In short, beginning in New Delhi in 1961, the ecumenical

---

[1] An even more recent statement, *Dominus Iesus: On the Unicity and Salvific Universality of Jesus Christ and the Church*, issued by the Office of the Doctrine of the Faith in September 2000, has been more controversial. Some, including Pope John Paul II, are convinced the statement expresses the ecumenical passion of *Ut Unum Sint*. Some, to the contrary, are convinced that it fails to take into account the past forty years of ecumenical dialogue. For three diverse Roman Catholic perspectives on *Dominus Iesus*, see *Ecumenical Trends*, 29, 11, Dec. 2000. For reflections on the significance of Vatican II for Roman Catholics and the ecumenical movement, see Thaddeus D. Horgan ed., *Walking Together: Roman Catholics and Ecumenism Twenty-five Years after Vatican II*, Grand Rapids MI, Eerdmans, 1990.

movement became, ecclesially, increasingly diverse at world, regional, national and local levels.

Along with this newly emerging ecclesial diversity came a more visible and vocal cultural diversity. This diversity led in time to a third shift. From the 1960s, ecumenical conversations took place in a variety of arenas – bilateral dialogues, multilateral initiatives, local partnerships, etc. As a result, the WCC and other councils of churches were no longer primary or privileged instruments but were, instead, one among the many instrumentalities of the ecumenical movement. These included new structures that had arisen around unresolved tensions regarding mission, unity in mission and mission in unity.

Having briefly identified some of the most significant shifts that began in the 1960s, this discussion will focus on subsequent ecumenical conversations about unity, beginning with a review of descriptions and models that found prominence in both multilateral and bilateral discussions, along with WCC Faith and Order studies that have significantly shaped, and been shaped by, these discussions.

Finally, the chapter explores a persistent point of tension in ecumenical conversations about unity. This point of tension developed between those who understood the search for visible church unity primarily in terms of divisions defined by doctrine and polity, and those who were convinced that cultural, gender, historical, political and socio-economic factors were the most divisive of churches. In the past, this tension was frequently referred to as between two streams within the one ecumenical movement: Faith and Order, and Life and Work. The first WCC assembly (Amsterdam 1948), declared in its message, "We are divided from one another not only in matters of faith, order and tradition, but also by pride of nation, class and race." This tension persisted in a tendency to view Faith and Order and Life and Work as having separate agendas, even though most discussion of the unity of the church continued to assume that church division was primarily a matter of disagreements about doctrine, sacraments or ministry.

VISIBLE UNITY IN CONCEPT AND CONVERSATION

The Faith and Order report on "Unity" at the New Delhi assembly stated:

> We believe that the unity which is both God's will and his gift to his church is being made visible *as all in each place* who are baptized into Jesus Christ and confess him as Lord and Saviour are brought by the Holy Spirit into one fully committed fellowship, holding one apostolic faith, preaching the one gospel, breaking the one bread, joining in common prayer, and having a corporate life reaching out in witness and service to all and who at the same time are united with the whole Christian fellowship in all places and all ages in such wise that ministry and members are accepted by all, and that all can act and speak together as occasion requires for the tasks to which God calls his people. (italics added)

"The achievement of unity", the report declared, "will involve nothing less than a death and rebirth of many forms of church life as we have known them."

The key and most often cited phrase in this report is "all in each place". This depiction of unity was appropriate for the occasion on which the Orthodox churches of Russia, Bulgaria, Romania and Poland became members of the WCC, since from the perspective of Orthodox ecclesiology the local community that gathers to celebrate the eucharist *is* the church. This picture of unity also highlighted the particular places where Christians live and work. The New Delhi statement on "all in each place" originated within the International Missionary Council which merged with the WCC at New Delhi.

The "local situation" – "each school..., each factory or office..., each congregation" – is identified as the place where "the common life in Christ is most clearly tested". In this picture, the unity given in Christ is to be made manifest not only in the church but also in the world: that "every wall of race, colour, caste, tribe, sex, class and nation" be broken down. This picture was also fitting for New Delhi when churches from Africa, Asia and Latin America became WCC members, helping shape a Council which was in every respect beginning to be more diverse.

The New Delhi report also clearly set before the churches the obligation to make this unity manifest by identifying "marks" of, or "requirements" for, the *visible* unity of the church: the confession of the apostolic faith, eucharistic fellowship, recognition of one another's baptism and ministry, as well as common preaching, prayer, witness and service. The report, rather remarkably, set forth what has since the 1960s become a common agenda for ecumenical conversations on unity.

Despite the call for the unity in each place of a fully committed fellowship to be linked as one everywhere, by the time of the fourth WCC assembly (Uppsala 1968), it was clear that the New Delhi picture was incomplete. The focus at Uppsala shifted from "all in each place" to unity "in all places" and "in all ages". The Uppsala report stated:

> We must continue to seek the unity of all Christians in a common profession of the faith, in the observance of baptism and the eucharist, and in recognition of a ministry for the whole church... This calls the churches in all places to realize that they belong together and are called to act together. In a time when human interdependence is so evident, it is the more imperative to make visible the bonds which unite Christians in universal fellowship.

The 1968 assembly invoked the idea of conciliarity as a model for the wider unity of the church in all places, and called on member churches to "work for the time when a genuinely universal council may once more speak for all Christians and lead the way into the future".

In speaking of the goal of visible unity in terms of a "genuinely universal council", the fourth assembly was prompted by Vatican II and its promulgated documents. Uppsala included Roman Catholic theologians as participants who were full members of the Comission on Faith and Order. The Second Vatican Council raised the issue of conciliarity afresh, not only in order to clarify the goal of church unity, but also to clarify an understanding of the church and its witness to a divided human community. The concept and theory of conciliarity first appeared only in the 14th and 15th centuries, at the time of the schism within the Western church. The Russian notion of *sobornost*, meaning "conciliarity" or "ecumenicity", is defined as spiritual unity and religious community based on free commitment to a tradition of catholicity interpreted through ecumenical councils of the Eastern Orthodox Church.[2] Thus Vatican II and later Uppsala linked the issue of conciliarity to the notion of the church as "sign". As Uppsala put it, "The church is bold to speak of itself as the sign of the coming unity of mankind."

The notion of a universal council, together with the notion of church as sign, was welcomed in many arenas of ecumenical conversation, including the Lutheran World Federation, the World Alliance of Reformed Churches, the Old Catholic Congress and the

---

[2] See "Conciliarity and the Future of the Ecumenical Movement, Commission on Faith and Order, Louvain 1971", in *The Ecumenical Review*, 24, 1, 1972. See also Anthony Ugolnick, "Unity and the Orthodox Sensibility", in *Mid-Stream*, 25, 3 July 1986, pp.260-75.

Lambeth conference of Anglican bishops. Consequently, in 1971 the central committee of the WCC requested further clarification in response to which Faith and Order offered this statement:

> By conciliarity we mean the coming together of Christians – locally, regionally or globally – for common prayer, counsel and decision, in the belief that the Holy Spirit can use such meetings for his own purpose of reconciling, renewing and reforming the church by guiding it towards the fullness of truth and love.[3]

This statement also noted that conciliarity takes different forms in different places and at different times. Stressing the need for a form appropriate to the present, the report emphasized conciliarity as a model of unity in which there is "ample space for diversity and for open mutual confrontation of differing interests and convictions".

The visible unity described by the fifth WCC assembly (Nairobi 1975) brought together the emphases of New Delhi and Uppsala:

> The one church is to be envisioned as a conciliar fellowship of local churches which are themselves truly united. In this conciliar fellowship each local church possesses, in communion with the others, the fullness of catholicity, witnesses to the apostolic faith, and therefore recognizes the others as belonging to the same church of Christ and guided by the same Spirit. As the New Delhi assembly pointed out, they are bound together because they have received the same baptism and share in the same eucharist; they recognize each other's members and ministries. They are one in their common commitment to confess the gospel of Christ by proclamation and service to the world. To this end, each church aims at maintaining sustained and sustaining relationships with her sister churches, expressed in conciliar gatherings whenever required for the fulfilment of their common calling.

Prior to Nairobi, the term "conciliarity" had been used to describe an instrument, model or expression of the unity of the church. Nairobi, however, used the term "conciliar fellowship" to describe that unity: the churches "united by a common understanding of the apostolic faith, by a common ministry, and a common eucharist". Not since the "Appeal to All Christian People" by the 1920 Lambeth bishops had the goal of visible unity been so precisely defined.[4]

Deliberate steps towards fuller fellowship

The Nairobi assembly, in an unprecedented action, also decided to send the Faith and Order statement on "Baptism, Eucharist and a Mutually Recognized Ministry" to the churches for response. This was an attempt to enact at least one of the requirements for convening a council: encouraging the churches to take "deliberate steps towards a fuller fellowship with other churches". Many responses were received, anticipating the

---

[3] "Conciliarity and the Future of the Ecumenical Movement", in Günther Gassman ed., *Documentary History of Faith and Order, 1963-1993*, WCC, 1993, p.236. See also *The Ecumenical Review*, 22, 4, 1970.

[4] "Appeal to All Christian People" in Michael Kinnamon and Brian E. Cope eds, *The Ecumenical Movement: An Anthology of Key Texts and Voices*, WCC, 1997, pp.81-83. The appeal restated, without attribution, the portion of the Chicago-Lambeth Quadrilateral that lists the four "essentials" for Christian unity: "1. The holy scriptures of the Old and New Testament as the revealed word of God. 2. The Nicene Creed as the sufficient statement of the Christian faith. 3. The two sacraments – baptism and the supper of the Lord – ministered with unfailing use of Christ's words of institution and the elements ordained by him. 4. The historic episcopate, locally adapted in the methods of its administration to the varying needs of the nations and peoples called of God into unity of his church."

churches' response to the later convergence text, *Baptism, Eucharist and Ministry* (BEM).

Three years after Nairobi, Faith and Order's plenary meeting in Bangalore, India (1978), recognized the need for yet further clarification, but agreed that "the actual requirements for the unity of the church" should receive primary attention. These requirements were seen as: (a) consensus in the apostolic faith; (b) mutual recognition of baptism, eucharist and ministry; (c) structures making possible common teaching and decision-making.

True, the New Delhi and Nairobi assemblies had anticipated these requirements, but not precisely in the form of the Bangalore report. Subsequently, and in the Bangalore form, these three requirements were affirmed at the sixth WCC assembly (Vancouver 1983). They significantly shaped the studies of the Faith and Order commission as well as many of the themes of bilateral dialogues for the next twenty years. Work towards the "mutual recognition of baptism, eucharist and ministry" had already taken on a degree of intentionality in Accra, Ghana (1974), in three statements agreed by Faith and Order on the topic "One Baptism, One Eucharist and a Mutually Recognized Ministry". It now became a focal Faith and Order study, along with common confession of the apostolic faith and the relationship of the unity of the church to the renewal of human community.

Baptism, Eucharist and Ministry, approved by the Faith and Order Commission at its meeting in Lima, Peru, in 1982, and sent to the churches for "an official response... at the highest appropriate level of authority",[5] is arguably the major milestone of the 20th century search for unity. The significance of the document is at least fourfold:

- First, it was unprecedented for theologians from Orthodox, Protestant and Roman Catholic traditions to speak together substantively about matters so deeply at the heart of Christian faith and life.
- Second, this was the first time that churches of different traditions and polities had been asked to respond to an ecumenical document at "the highest appropriate level of authority". Nearly two hundred official responses to the document were made by churches, including churches not members of the WCC.[6] These responses reflect the many local, regional and global settings in which ecumenical conversation has been taking place. Moreover, it is clear that discussions of BEM were instrumental in initiating new ecumenical contacts and relationships at all levels.
- Third, BEM made use of insights from several bilateral dialogues between Christian World Communions, and subsequently the document was used in a number of bilateral talks as a point of reference and framework. In a more general sense, BEM became a focal point for many ecumenical meetings, statements and texts.
- Finally, *Baptism, Eucharist and Ministry* inspired an unofficial "Lima liturgy" which has been used widely and has informed liturgical life in numerous member churches of the WCC. The Lima liturgy revived the centrality of ecumenical worship at WCC

[5] Michael Kinnamon ed., *Towards Visible Unity: Commission on Faith and Order, Lima, 1982*, vol. I: *Minutes and Addresses*, Faith and Order Paper no. 112, WCC, 1982, p.83.
[6] See Max Thurian ed., *Churches Respond to BEM*, vols I-VI, WCC, 1986-88; cf. *Baptism, Eucharist and Ministry, 1982-1990: Report on the Process and Responses*, Faith and Order Paper no. 149, WCC, 1990; cf. also "Report of an Inter-Orthodox Symposium: 'Baptism, Eucharist and Ministry,' Boston, USA, 11-18 June 1985", in Gennadios Limouris ed., *Orthodox Visions of Ecumenism: Statements, Messages and Reports on the Ecumenical Movement, 1902-1992*, WCC, 1994, pp.105-109.

assemblies, gave rise to renewed studies of ecumenical worship and spirituality, and stimulated consideration of the social-ethical implications of sacraments, worship and spirituality.

The BEM document and responses also clarified continuing points of controversy. Among these points, some of which are particular to confessional families or regional contexts, three major issues appeared. First, while all churches affirm the authority of scripture, the responses made it clear that there are different ways of describing both that authority and the issue of how "scripture" is to be interpreted in relation to "tradition". A second issue was the need to clarify the meanings of sacrament and sacramentality. Third, various and divergent ecclesiologies were assumed or implied in the churches' responses. The "BEM process", consequently, provided new and active momentum to the conviction that ecclesiology was integral to the goal of visible church unity.

There is a fourth and often unaddressed issue that continued to be controversial in the ecumenical era opened by BEM: the question of the ordination of women to the sacramental ministry of the church. The New Delhi assembly asked Faith and Order, in conjunction with the WCC's Department on Cooperation of Men and Women in Church and Society, to study "the theological, biblical and ecclesiological issues involved in the ordination of women". There was one consultation, in 1963, at which study papers were prepared for the fourth world conference on Faith and Order, held at Montreal the same year. Thereafter the issue was discussed by Faith and Order together with the WCC women's sub-unit and in consultations dealing with the ministry section of BEM. In 1979, at a consultation held at Klingenthal, near Strasbourg, France, and sponsored by the WCC's Community of Women and Men in the Church study, a thorough discussion of "Ordination of Women in Ecumenical Perspective" took place.[7]

More recently, the fifth world conference on Faith and Order, in Santiago de Compostela, Spain, in 1993 recommended that "continuing work on the *issue of the ordination of women*" be conducted. The next year the standing commission of Faith and Order, also echoing the plenary commission meeting in Budapest in 1989, recommended that a consultation "on the specific theological question of the representation of Christ in the ordained ministry" be held in relation to the Commission's ecclesiology study. Not until the 1999 standing commission, meeting in Toronto, was it again recommended that a consultation on ministry and the ordination of women be held, in 2002, to bring together "theological reflection and hearing the experiences of the churches as they reflect on this topic". This recommendation was widely debated, indicating that the issue continued to be controversial. For example, one Orthodox speaker said, "any ecumenical debate on the topic of the ordination of women could become not a contribution but rather an obstacle..." It came to the fore of the ecclesiastical and ecumenical debate mainly due to sociological causes: to recognize and apply an equal status for women and men, in all walks of life, including the church. The speaker continued with the suggestion that any Faith and Order discussions on this theme should concentrate on a theological approach in the wider context of priesthood, including "the difference between the universal priesthood and the ordained ministry".

---

[7] Constance F. Parvey ed., *Ordination of Women in Ecumenical Perspective: Workbook for the Church's Future*, WCC, 1980.

Common expression of apostolic faith

A second Faith and Order study following BEM addressed the requirements for visible unity – "The Common Expression of the Apostolic Faith". Work on common confession was underway as early as the mid-1960s. After Uppsala and through the 1970s, this work examined both the diversity of confessions of faith and "accounts of hope" around the world.[8] The study, "Giving Account of the Hope that Is in Us", was intended to start from actual contexts and move towards a common account of hope. Accordingly, at its meeting in Bangalore, in response to a request from the Nairobi assembly to enable the churches to "receive, reappropriate and confess together... the Christian truth and faith, delivered through the apostles", the Faith and Order Commission proposed a study on "The Common Expression of the Apostolic Faith".

One of the earliest consultations in this study was a joint meeting in 1978 between Faith and Order and the Joint Working Group between the Roman Catholic Church and the World Council of Churches (JWG). It drafted a document "Towards a Confession of the Common Faith", which addressed the difficult issue of plural, even contradictory, confessional traditions among the churches. The result centred attention on the *regula fidei* (rule of faith) transmitted through the centuries, in relation to which time- and place-bound expressions of faith must be measured.

By the time of the Faith and Order Commission meeting in Lima, the Nicene-Constantinopolitan Creed of 381 had emerged as the foundation for a new study project, "Towards the Common Confession of the Apostolic Faith Today". This study had three inter-related goals: (1) recognition of the 381 creed as *the* ecumenical creed of the church; (2) explanation of this creed for the sake of contemporary understanding and relevance to the search for unity; and (3) finding ways to express the common faith today. After a series of consultations and drafts, a document and study guide were sent to the churches for reaction.[9]

The third study at the forefront of Faith and Order's response to the Bangalore statement of requirements for visible church unity came to maturity as "The Unity of the Church and the Renewal of Human Community". As noted at the outset, the commitment to relate the church's call to visible unity to the church's call to witness and service within the human community has been at the heart of 20th-century ecumenism, although the 1910 world missionary conference in Edinburgh intentionally did not place the matter of church unity on its agenda. Only in the early 1960s did this commitment become an explicit theme in ecumenical conversation. It was in New Delhi that the unity of the church was clearly spoken of in connection with the unity of humankind:

> The love of the Father and the Son in the unity of the Holy Spirit is the source and goal of the unity which the triune God wills for all men and creation. We believe that we share in this unity in the church of Jesus Christ.

This connection was explored in the study project on "God in Nature and History", a study that set forth an interpretation of history that opened a way for new understandings of the church's relationship to the world.

---

[8] See *Confessing Our Faith around the World*, vols 1-4, WCC, 1984-86; *Giving Account of the Hope Today*, Faith and Order Paper no. 81, WCC, 1977; *Giving Account of the Hope Together*, Faith and Order Paper no. 86, WCC, 1978.

[9] See *Confessing the One Faith: An Ecumenical Explication of the Apostolic Faith as It Is Confessed in the Nicene-Constantinopolitan Creed (381)*, Faith and Order Paper no. 153, WCC, 1991; and *Towards Sharing the One Faith: A Study Guide for Discussion Groups*, Faith and Order Paper no. 173, WCC, 1996.

The growing awareness of being involved in one universal history appeals to the church, particularly because this fact also has an ethical thrust. It inspires people to react against all kinds of social, racial and economic discrimination and to strive with all their strength for world peace and world cooperation. In all this can be seen realizations of God's purposes for this world, signs of the coming kingdom.

The church as sign or sacrament

This catalytic turn in the 20th-century ecumenical conversation is indebted to the Second Vatican Council's view of the church as "sign" or "sacrament", continued with Uppsala's declaration: "The church is bold in speaking of itself as the sign of the coming unity of mankind." Thus Faith and Order decided to "pursue its study programme on the unity of the church in the wider context of the study of the unity of mankind and of creation".

In 1971, the Commission, meeting in Louvain, Belgium, placed the traditional themes of church unity in the context of human as well as confessional divisions, the human divisions having hitherto been frequently referred to as "non-theological factors". At Louvain, the discussion continued in five sections on the inter-relatedness of the unity of the church and (1) the struggle for justice in society; (2) the encounter with living faiths; (3) the struggle against racism; (4) the handicapped in society; and (5) differences in culture. An important insight emerged from this meeting: the method should not simply be contextualization but *intercontextualization*, since multiple contexts mutually craft interpretive frames for one another.

This process faltered because deep disagreements about the study itself had surfaced by the time a report reached the 1974 Commission meeting in Accra which affirmed that church unity is not for the sake of the churches themselves. Accra insisted that unity be understood within God's design for justice, reconciliation and the renewal of human community. To this extent, the Commission confirmed the concept of church as sign. But its statement, "Towards Unity-in-Tension", also looked long and hard at possible tensions between the commitments to church unity and to justice and reconciliation. The statement concludes, "We must resolutely refuse any too easy forms of unity or any misuse of the 'sign', that conceal a deeper disunity."

Deep disagreement runs through the lines of this statement. The substance of the disagreement becomes clearer when it is remembered that it was at Accra that "three agreed statements" on baptism, eucharist and ministry were affirmed as requirements for visible unity, with the recommendation that the Nairobi assembly forward them to the churches for study and response. This coincidence suggests the disagreement is related not only to differing understandings of factors affecting church division or unity, but ultimately to differing ecclesiological perspectives. During the 1960s and into the early 1970s, talk of the church as "sign" helped hold commitment to unity together with commitment to the healing of human community. However, at Accra the emerging focus on baptism, eucharist and ministry moved a more sacramental understanding of the church to the forefront.

"The Unity of the Church and the Renewal of Human Community" was revived as a major study at Lima in 1982. This would not have happened without the impulse and insights created by the study on "The Community of Women and Men in the Church". Accra had agreed to "undertake a study of the theological and practical aspects of the community of women and men in the church", most immediately in response to a 1974 consultation in Berlin on "Sexism in the 1970s". Here too there was disagreement.

Some members considered the issues raised in Berlin to be "non-theological matters", arguing that "the woman problem" had nothing to do with the church and its unity. But led by women delegates, Accra in 1974 held firm; after considerable debate, the Commission agreed to sponsor a study. Not until Nairobi in 1975, however, under the assembly theme "Jesus Christ Frees and Unites", did Faith and Order clearly affirm that the unity of the church "requires that women be free to live out the gifts which God has given them and respond to their calling to share fully in the life and witness of the church".

Community of women and men

In addition to its crucial role in reviving the "Unity of the Church and the Renewal of Human Community" study, the Community of Women and Men study was remarkable for at least two reasons. First, the method of the study was experience-based, an unusual but not unprecedented method for a Faith and Order study. In the 1970s, the Commission undertook the study "Giving Account of the Hope that Is in Us" which drew on the experiences and discussions of local study groups. The method of the two studies was similar, although the experiences on which the Community study drew were strikingly different: women's experiences of exclusion, silence and violation in the churches. Dialogically engaging, these experiences were the "meeting point and end point of the study". Accordingly, at the heart of the Community study were several hundred local group reports. But in contrast to the method of the later BEM, which was focused on response to a text, the Community study made it impossible to imagine models of unity in abstraction from conversation around the concrete experiences of women and men as conditioned by various ecclesial and cultural circumstances. The method of the study was interdisciplinary, not least in that it was sponsored by Faith and Order in cooperation with the WCC Sub-unit on Women in Church and Society. In this study it became clear that the search for the visible unity of the church cannot be undertaken without attention to the realities of the world in which the church lives and to which it witnesses. There are, in this sense, no "non-theological factors".

A second point of significance was the study's inclusion of new and previously unheard-of constituencies. Many women of different ages and cultures, races and confessions – trained theologians, laity and clergy – participated in what had hitherto most often been closed ranks of older, mostly Western male theologians. Methodologically, this inclusion witnessed to growing recognition that "doing theology" is a task for the whole people of God.

In this way, then, the consultations and conferences that constituted this study process were themselves "ecclesial events" or eschatological embodiments of the church life and unity for which we seek. The significance of this study's method and its welcome of a wide diversity of voices must not be under-estimated in relation to subsequent discussions of visible church unity.

Eucharistic vision unites heaven and earth

This became evident at the sixth WCC assembly in Vancouver (1983). Here as never before the integral relationship of the unity of the church and the healing and reconciliation of the world's divisions was stressed:

> Peace and justice, on the one hand, baptism, eucharist and ministry, on the other, have claimed our attention. They belong together. Indeed the aspect of Christian unity which

has been most striking to us here in Vancouver is that of a *eucharistic vision*. Christ – the life of the world – unites heaven and earth, God and world, spiritual and sacred.

Reiterating the by-now familiar three requirements or marks of unity, the Vancouver report also recognized, "Such a unity – overcoming church division, binding us together in the face of racism, sexism, injustice – would be a witnessing unity, a credible sign of the new creation." Indeed, the concept of the church as sign was specified as "prophetic 'sign'", thereby challenging the churches to "actions which advance towards the goal" and confirming the church

> ...as a prophetic community through which and by which the transformation of the world can take place. It is only as a church which goes out from its eucharistic centre, strengthened by word and sacrament and thus strengthened in its own identity, resolved to become what it is, that it can take the world on to its agenda. There never will be a time when the world, with all its political, social and economic issues, ceases to be the agenda of the church.

Vancouver's affirmation of the church as eucharistic community is an indication of the growing significance of Orthodox participation in the search for unity. Indeed, the Orthodox contribution to the theme of the sixth assembly – "Jesus Christ – the Life of the World" – anticipated and contributed to that assembly's articulation of the integral relation between the life of the world and the life of the church.

At Vancouver a "conciliar process of mutual commitment (covenant)" to Justice, Peace and the Integrity of Creation" (JPIC) was initiated. The two ecumenical streams, Faith and Order and Life and Work, were brought together in a specific proposal of the assembly's programme guidelines committee. JPIC called member churches (and later also non-member churches) to commitment and coordinated action in response to injustices and threats to survival throughout the world. This commitment is at the heart of what it means to be the church. Indeed, for the churches to take such actions together is to nurture *koinonia* and thus build up that unity for which the churches seek.

In 1987 the central committee asked Faith and Order to undertake "a fresh consideration of the concepts and forms of the unity we seek" and to prepare a draft statement for the seventh assembly in Canberra (1991) where, after debate and redrafting, a new statement on unity emerged: "The Unity of the Church as *Koinonia*: Gift and Calling". The statement at once echoed earlier expressions and opened a new era of ecumenical conversation, an era characterized by a new emphasis on *koinonia*, communion:

> The unity of the church to which we are called is a *koinonia* given and expressed in the common confession of the apostolic faith; a common sacramental life entered by the one baptism and celebrated together in one eucharistic fellowship; a common life in which members and ministries are mutually recognized and reconciled; and a common mission witnessing to the gospel of God's grace to all people and serving the whole of creation. The goal of the search for full communion is realized when all the churches are able to recognize in one another the one, holy, catholic and apostolic church in its fullness. This full communion will be expressed on the local and the universal levels through conciliar forms of life and action. In such communion churches are bound in all aspects of their life together at all levels in confessing the one faith and engaging in worship and witness, deliberation and action.

Striking a distinctive note, the Canberra statement affirms the significance of diversity to this communion: "Diversities which are rooted in theological traditions, various cultural, ethnic or historical contexts, are integral to the nature of communion." At the same time, the issue of the limits to diversity is addressed:

Diversity is illegitimate when, for instance, it makes impossible the common confession of Jesus Christ as God and Saviour the same yesterday, today and forever (Heb. 13:8); and salvation and the final destiny of humanity as proclaimed in holy scripture and preached by the apostolic community.

"In communion," this section of the statement concludes, "diversities are brought together in harmony as gifts of the Holy Spirit, contributing to the richness and fullness of the church of God."

KOINONIA IN FAITH, LIFE AND WITNESS

The nature of the church as *koinonia* had already entered ecumenical conversations in the 1920s. However, it was first made explicit in the 1961 New Delhi report on unity:

> The word "fellowship" *(koinonia)* has been chosen because it describes what the church truly is. "Fellowship" clearly implies that the church is not merely an institution or organization. It is a fellowship of those who are called together by the Holy Spirit and in baptism confess Christ as Lord and Saviour. They are thus "fully committed" to him and to one another.

As we have seen, this description was further developed at Nairobi as "conciliar fellowship" based on the activity of the triune God who draws Christians, in all their diversity, into a communion in the Spirit around the eucharistic presence of the Lord.

Viewed against the backdrop of these earlier statements, the Canberra statement is distinctive in several ways. First, it puts "the unity we seek" in a broader framework, both with regard to the world the church is called to serve and with regard to the church itself as the foretaste of communion with God and the whole creation. Second, the mission of the church is lifted up with renewed urgency, in light of the damage done to this mission because "the churches are painfully divided within themselves and among each other".

Third, and again distinctively, the Canberra statement acknowledges that there is "a certain degree of communion already existing" among the churches, and goes on to challenge the churches to take "specific steps together" towards full visible unity. Among these challenges are recognition of one another's baptism as affirmed by BEM, the recognition of the apostolic faith as expressed in the Nicene-Constantinopolitan Creed, mutual recognition of ministries, recommitment to work for justice, peace and the integrity of creation, and re-dedication to the search for sacramental communion.

The revival of an emphasis on *koinonia* in ecumenical conversation had been firmly established by Vatican II. In *Lumen Gentium* ("Dogmatic Constitution on the Church") and more explicitly in *Unitatis Redintegratio* ("Decree on Ecumenism") relationships among Christians were characterized as *koinonia*. The idea of *koinonia* also came to the forefront in several subsequent bilateral dialogues in which the Roman Catholic Church participated, most especially in conversations with the Orthodox church and with the Anglican communion, but also with Methodist, Lutheran and Reformed churches. The prevalence of the theme of *koinonia* also characterized dialogues not involving the Roman Catholic Church. Indeed, the report of the fifth forum on bilateral conversations asserted that "*koinonia* is the fundamental understanding of the church emerging from the bilateral dialogues".

In fact, the Nairobi assembly's use of *koinonia* appropriated a positive outcome of the bilateral dialogues. This in turn confirmed that the bilaterals were shaping a new reality in the movement towards *koinonia* in faith, life and witness even before 1975. Bilateral dialogues, between Christian World Communions on the international level and between churches on regional and national levels, began to emerge in the 1960s as one of the consequences of the post-Vatican II entrance of the Roman Catholic Church into the ecumenical movement.

Among the bilateral dialogues is that between the Roman Catholic Church and the autocephalous Orthodox churches. Nine weeks before New Delhi, in 1961, Ecumenical Patriarch Athenagoras I of Constantinople (1949-72) convened a pan-Orthodox conference on the Greek island of Rhodes which decided that the Orthodox churches would adopt a common stance in future relations with other Christian churches. This decision – and the Jerusalem meeting between the patriarch and Pope Paul VI in January 1964 where they exchanged blessings and the kiss of peace after reading Jesus' prayer in John 17 – opened the door for the Orthodox delegating observers to the Second Vatican Council. The meeting also led to the December 1965 common declaration by the patriarch and pope to "erase from the memory" of the church the mutual excommunications of 1054 and to express "a practical desire to reach a common understanding of the apostolic faith and its demands". The continuing " loving dialogue of charity" resulted in the official bilateral dialogues in 1980 whose goal was "the re-establishment of full communion". The first two documents from these dialogues described a common approach to the relation between the eucharist and the Trinity, the church and the eucharist, and the local church to the universal church.

Bilateral dialogues: indispensable instrument of visible unity

Bilaterals have now emerged as an indispensable instrument of the movement towards visible unity. Their agreements and convergences have contributed to improved understanding, to growing communion, and in a number of cases to full communion between churches.[10] A recent instance of churches entering into full communion, including a ground-breaking mutual recognition of ordained ministries, is an agreement between the Evangelical Lutheran Church in America and the Episcopal (Anglican) Church in the United States, "Called to Common Mission", formally approved in 1999 and 2000 by the respective churches, and celebrated in a joint liturgy in January 2001.

Bilateral dialogues have undertaken diverse tasks for various purposes. The Leuenberg agreement of 1973, for example, addressed past histories of "family" conflict and division among Lutheran, United and Reformed churches of continental Europe and Argentina, renounced mutual condemnations from the Reformation era, and affirmed a relationship of full church fellowship. Another "family" conflict, between Oriental and Eastern Orthodox churches, addressed in bilateral dialogues, led to the resolution of ancient Christological controversies and to recognition in one another of the one Orthodox faith of the church.

Other bilateral dialogues have responded to local or regional circumstances and have led to the rediscovery of commonalities and on occasion to mutual recognition. For example, Anglican-Lutheran dialogue in Europe, begun in 1909, has led Anglican churches in the British Isles and, with two exceptions, Lutheran churches in

---

[10] Harding Meyer and Lukas Vischer eds, *Growth in Agreement: Report and Agreed Statements of Ecumenical Conversations on a World Level*, Faith and Order Paper no. 108, WCC, 1984; and Jeffrey Gros, Harding Meyer and William G. Rusch eds, *Growth in Agreement II: Reports and Agreed Statements of Ecumenical Conversations on a World Level, 1982-1998*, Faith and Order Paper no. 187, WCC, 2000.

Nordic and Baltic countries to agree, in what is called the Porvoo declaration of 1992, on interchangeable ministries and full eucharist. As of 2000 the signatory churches were the Anglican churches of England, Ireland, Scotland and Wales; and the Lutheran churches in Estonia, Finland, Iceland, Lithuania, Norway and Sweden. Along the same lines, although it is not an agreement of full communion, the Meissen agreement, concluded in 1988 between the Church of England and what were then the Evangelical churches in the German Democratic Republic and the Evangelical Church in Germany in the Federal Republic of Germany, enabled these churches to work out a basis for closer relations.

Bilateral dialogues have also healed deep differences as, for example, regarding justification, the doctrine that most divided the Western church during the Reformation. Lutheran-Roman Catholic dialogues, beginning with the first international bilateral dialogue in 1972, reached a milestone on Reformation Day, 31 October 1999, when representatives of the churches of the Lutheran World Federation and of the Roman Catholic Church signed the historic Joint Declaration on the Doctrine of Justification at Augsburg, Germany. This was the site of the presentation in 1530 of the *Confessio Augustana* by the Lutheran Reformers to the Roman Catholic Emperor Charles V. The 20th-century statement declared that the 16th-century condemnations concerning justification, promulgated by Lutherans and Roman Catholics against each other, are no longer to be seen as church-dividing.

Other bilateral dialogues initiated new relationships. A foremost example is the dialogue between Pentecostals and Roman Catholics. The 1976 report of this dialogue clearly reflected this:

> The dialogue has a special character. The bilateral conversations which the Roman Catholic Church undertakes with many world communions (e.g. the Anglican communion, the Lutheran World Federation, etc.) are prepared to consider problems concerning church structures and ecclesiology and have organic unity as a goal or at least envisage some kind of eventual structural unity. This dialogue has not.... Its purpose has been that "prayer, spirituality and theological reflection be a shared concern..."[11]

This dialogue has continued through three five-year periods, and has addressed topics such as baptism in the Holy Spirit, giving of the Spirit and Christian initiation, scripture and Tradition, public worship, discernment of spirits, prayer and praise, evangelism and proselytism.

The remarkable contribution of bilateral dialogues to the search for unity has not been without difficulties. Although it was not envisaged that Faith and Order would need to convene a forum for the review and coordination of bilaterals, in 1994 the sixth forum on bilateral dialogues identified a number of difficulties with the ecumenical methodology of the bilaterals:

- the consistency of churches' affirmations in dialogues with various partners;
- the relevance of dialogues to churches in Asia, Africa, Latin America and the Pacific;
- the relevance of international agreements to the life of local churches;
- the asymmetry of relationships where links of communion are partial and not reciprocated with all churches;
- the increasing strain brought to bear on ecumenical relations by political and economic realities, most especially post-cold war realities in Eastern Europe and increasing poverty in many places; and

---

[11] *Growth in Agreement*, p.422.

– the question of the churches' readiness to assume mutual accountability for all issues raised in a dialogue and the challenge of creating consensus in the process of reception rather than the simple exercise of power by majority vote.

Bilateral dialogues have also added complexity to discussions of the nature and form of the full visible unity of the church. Before Nairobi, discussions had centred around the model of "organic union" and "conciliar fellowship" as a vision of how organic unity could be realized among local united churches. However, the bilateral discussions of Christian World Communions developed models such as "reconciled diversity" and "a communion of communions". In contrast to the model of organic union, based on the New Delhi declaration that such unity would "involve nothing less than a death or re-birth of many forms of church life as we have known them", the bilateral models tended to affirm that unity was expressed when confessions were reconciled to one another, even though maintaining their discrete identities.[12]

Nonetheless, for much of the 20th century the favoured model of visible church unity was "organic union" and from the mid-1960s through the mid-1970s United and Uniting churches were born in Ecuador, Papua New Guinea, Great Britain, Jamaica, Belgium, North India, Pakistan, Bangladesh, Zaire, Zambia, Madagascar, the Solomon Islands and Grand Cayman. However, during this same period of time there was also considerable criticism of organic church union. Some church leaders, especially in Africa, Asia, Latin America, the Caribbean and the Pacific, argued that overcoming confessional differences through corporate union was not and should not be a primary agenda. Energy spent on church union would be better spent in the struggle against social and political injustice. Some church leaders, moreover, reasserted the value of separate confessional identities, an assertion that enhances power in separated churches. Such realities, in combination with the growing influence of bilateral dialogues which have themselves at times tended to reinforce confessional identity, have since the mid-1970s slowed down or even reversed movements for organic church union.

Additionally, since the mid-1970s it has also become apparent that visible unity may be achieved in stages. United and Uniting churches include both those churches for which the process has a definite organic goal and those which do not have a definite vision of structure but which persevere nonetheless towards authentic expressions of unity. Several church union efforts have established "covenants" as a way of making a commitment to stay together in movement towards fuller communion. In one instance – the Consultation on Church Union (COCU) in the US, later to be known as Churches Uniting in Christ – the covenant was itself an expression of unity and not simply a stage on the way to union.

Whatever the difficulties, the very existence of United and Uniting churches posed a challenge to other churches committed to the ecumenical search for unity. Moreover, United and Uniting churches were by their very nature inclusive churches. They welcomed people from a variety of Christian traditions and understood how to receive confessional diversity as a source of richness rather than of division. In the closing decades of the 20th century, this inclusiveness widened to enable fuller participation of women, to incorporate into common worship expressions of faith that reflect many societies and

---

[12] For a fuller discussion of models of unity, see Paul A. Crow, Jr, "Reflections on Models of Christian Unity", in Thomas F. Best ed., *Living Today towards Visible Unity*, WCC, 1988. Cf. also Harding Meyer, *That All May Be One: Perceptions and Models of Ecumenicity*, Grand Rapids MI, Eerdmans, 1999.

cultures, and to affirm persons regardless of sexual orientation, although this latter issue remains deeply controversial.[13]

Other controversial issues will confront United and Uniting churches in the future. These include resurgent confessionalism or denominationalism, and *episcope* and the non-recognition of ministries.

THE UNITY OF THE CHURCH AND THE HUMAN COMMUNITY

The United and Uniting churches are not alone in facing the persistent tension between the search for church unity and the need to address struggles within the whole human community. Indeed, as noted at the outset, this tension has been present in the ecumenical movement through much of the 20th century. Some have held, and still hold, the strong conviction that the ecumenical movement is a movement whose primary purpose is to enable the churches to realize the visible unity of the church. Others have held, and still hold, the strong conviction that the search for church unity is inseparable from witness and service and from struggles for justice and peace, not least because of the concern for both unity and mission evident in Jesus' prayer (John 17:21).

Several attempts have been made in Faith and Order, as well as in other ecumenical arenas, to articulate understandings of the church that would be able to heal this division in the search for unity. The concept of the church as sign, for example, was intended to hold in creative tension *intra ecclesia* and *extra ecclesia*. *Baptism, Eucharist and Ministry*, in contrast, sets the division within the context of eucharistic celebration which is said to embrace all aspects of life.

The report of the Faith and Order study on the "Unity of the Church and the Renewal of Human Community", *Church and World*, is one late-20th-century attempt to build a bridge across the divide.[14] The key question was this: "How can the church be understood in such a way that the nature of the church and the mission of the church are seen as integral and inter-related elements of the being (the *esse*) of the church itself?" In response, the report set forth an understanding of the church as both mystery and prophetic sign.

The church is at once a divine reality transcending time and space and thus prefiguring God's reign, and a human reality of institutions and communities existing in time and space. As human reality, the church struggles together with the world amid brokenness, injustice, oppression and discrimination. And so the church knows that the search for unity can never be for the sake of the church alone: "It is in and for the world that God calls the church that it may be a sign and bearer of the triune God's work towards the salvation and renewal of all humankind." Thus, continued the report, "the church participates in the mystery and mission of God, and thereby can be understood as mystery and prophetic sign".

But the tension within the ecumenical movement persists, particularly as many of the deepest divisions within, as well as between, the churches and Christians can be

---

[13] For fuller discussion of United and Uniting churches, see Michael Kinnamon and Thomas F. Best eds, *Called to Be One in Christ: United Churches and the Ecumenical Movement*, Faith and Order Paper no. 127, WCC, 1985; *Growing towards Consensus and Commitment: Report of the Fourth International Consultation of United and Uniting Churches*, Colombo, Sri Lanka, Faith and Order Paper no. 110, WCC, 1981; and Thomas F. Best ed., *Living Today towards Visible Unity: The Fifth International Consultation of United and Uniting Churches*, Faith and Order Paper no. 142, WCC, 1988.
[14] Faith and Order Paper no. 151, WCC, 1990.

identified as moral and ethical, political and ideological, differences. One arena in which an honest reckoning of these differences between Christians and churches has taken place is within the conversations of the Joint Working Group (JWG), the official consultative forum of the Roman Catholic Church and the WCC. Established in 1965, the JWG has submitted official reports to its two authorities and has sponsored its own studies. In the late 1990s, the JWG engaged in an ecumenical conversation on "personal and social ethical issues", viewing such issues as causes of new divisions and thus as potential areas of common witness. A report of the JWG conversation, submitted in 1991 to the Canberra assembly and to the Roman Catholic Church, offered guidelines for ecumenical dialogue on difficult and potentially divisive moral issues. The report ended, "The deep desire to find an honest and faithful resolution of our disagreement is itself evidence that God continues to grace the *koinonia* among disciples of Christ."

The reference to *koinonia* is noteworthy, for reflection concerning the unity of the church as *koinonia* marked attempts to hold together what was by the 1990s, most often discussed in terms of "ecclesiology and ethics". Accordingly, at Canberra the unity of the church as *koinonia* was integrally connected to the church's mission. *Koinonia* was, according to "The Unity of the Church as *Koinonia*: Gift and Calling",

> ...given and expressed in the common confession of the apostolic faith, a common sacramental life... and a common mission witnessing to the gospel of God's grace to all people and serving the whole of creation.

Two years later at the fifth world conference on Faith and Order, held in Santiago de Compostela, Spain, the unity of the church as *koinonia* was more fully elaborated as "*koinonia* in faith, life and witness".

Earlier in 1993, at a consultation in Rønde, Denmark, yet another attempt was made to close the chasm between ecumenical commitments focused on visible church unity and those focused on witness, service and moral struggle. The resulting report argued for an integral connection of ecclesiology and ethics on the basis of understanding the church as *koinonia*. Significantly, the report of the consultation speaks of the church as *koinonia* with regard to its moral existence as well as with regard to faith, life and witness:

> Faith and discipleship are embodied in and as a community way of life. The memory of Jesus Christ *(anamnesis)*, formative of the church itself, is a force shaping of moral existence. The Trinity is experienced as an image for human community and the basis for social doctrine and ecclesial reality. Such explication could continue, but need not, since it all comes to the same point: the church not only has, but is, a social ethic, a *koinonia* ethic.

The report goes on to clarify:

> *Koinonia* in relation to ethics does not mean in the first instance that the Christian community designs codes and rules; rather that it is a place where, along with the confession of faith and the celebration of the sacraments, and as an inseparable part of it, the gospel tradition is probed permanently for moral inspiration and insight...[15]

A year and a half later, at another consultation on ecclesiology and ethics, at Tantur near Jerusalem, the voices of those who wished to frame an understanding of *koinonia* in terms of trinitarian communion were stronger. Moreover, despite the disavowal of

---

[15] Thomas F. Best and Martin Robra eds, *Ecclesiology and Ethics: Ecumenical Ethical Engagement, Moral Formation and the Nature of the Church*, WCC, 1997, pp.4-5,9.

"codes and rules" at Rønde, many expressed fear that discourse concerning the church as moral community could lead to the prescription of particular ethical positions. Consequently, a new phrase was put forward: in the church as *koinonia*, a constant process of "moral formation" becomes a "way of life".

The concept of *koinonia* has been helpful to this discussion of ecclesiology and ethics for at least two reasons. First, it conveys unity as dynamic and thus shifts the focus of the search for the unity of the church from structures to relationships. *Koinonia* features a deepening of life together, rather than a set of requirements for visible unity.

Secondly, *koinonia* is not merely a recent attempt to hold together what has too often been held apart in the ecumenical movement. The word "*koinonia*" was introduced by the Ecumenical Patriarchate in its 1920 encyclical "Unto the Churches of Christ Everywhere" to hold together what was then referred to as the invisible church and the visible church, or the being of the church and the function of the church.[16] This early, indeed foundational, Orthodox contribution to the ecumenical movement has helped those committed to the search for unity to embrace the communion of the church with the tri-une God along the consequence of that communion: *koinonia* must be evident among the members of the church and, in anticipation, among all God's people who await the fullness of communion in God.

Church unity in tension: justice, reconciliation and renewal

However fundamental the notion of *koinonia* is to the ecumenical movement, those committed to the continuing search for the unity of the church still confronted deep tensions as humankind embarked upon a new century and a new millennium. The term *koinonia*, like the term *sign*, was not able fully to catalyze the bold creativity called for in the midst of what continued to be, at root, an ecclesiological crisis.

As early as 1974 the Accra statement "Towards Unity-in-Tension" was clear that church unity must be viewed from the perspective of God's design for justice, reconciliation and the renewal of human community. But the statement was sober about the church's witness in the world:

> We may believe in and give witness to our unity in Christ, even with those from whom we may, for his sake, have to part. This means to be prepared to be... a "unity-in-tension" – dependent on the Spirit for the strength to reconcile within the one body of the church all whom the forces of disunity would otherwise continue to drive apart.

This is to say, the search for unity in the 21st century may need to enact what has subsequently been referred to as the "Accra principle": the commitment to stay in dialogue with persons who represent differing perspectives and traditions, cultural and ecclesial, even in the face of serious disagreements about belief and practice.

If this be so, perhaps the most urgent question of the search for unity at the end of the 20th century was not the customary one: What can we say together?, but rather: What will keep us together as we move into the depths of our differences?

In conclusion, several themes found in the ecumenical thinking of this period may function as signposts to indicate a way ahead in the search for unity. First, the search for unity will be sustained as it is suffused by prayer. This was powerfully expressed by John Paul II in *Ut Unum Sint*. Indeed, prayer is explicated as a "change of heart and holiness

---

[16] *The Ecumenical Movement: An Anthology of Key Texts and Voices*, pp.11-14.

of life, along with public and private prayer for the unity of Christians". Prayer, this is to say, is intimately connected to conversion.

And so a second response for the future presented itself: conversion. The connection of prayer and conversion that was elaborated in *Ut Unum Sint* was anticipated by the Roman Catholic Ecumenical Directory, published in 1993 by the Pontifical Council for Promoting Christian Unity. But a call to conversion was put perhaps most powerfully by independent French ecumenists, Catholics and Protestants, the Groupe des Dombes (the Dombes group), which had been meeting at Les Dombes, northeast of Lyons, France, for many years. In *Pour la conversion des Eglises (For the Conversion of the Churches)* published first in French in 1991 and in English in 1993, the Groupe des Dombes challenged churches Protestant and Roman Catholic alike to listen, to remember and to move towards mutual recognition in ways that require relinquishment of unilateral understandings of faith, life and witness.

The direction indicated by these signposts ran counter to another course some saw for the new century. Orthodox churches were only the most articulate among many that were increasingly asking about the "theological and ecclesiological criteria for membership" in the World Council of Churches. In the face of growing ecclesiological diversity – new churches, independent churches, small house churches, Christian communities – not conversion, but clarity, became the paramount concern in the search for the visible unity of the church.

Against this backdrop, amid contending calls for conversion and for clear criteria, a whole range of thorny theological and, especially, ecclesiological issues integral to the search for visible unity stood out in sharp relief: uniatism, proselytism, nationalism and ethnicity, poverty, human sexuality and religious pluralism. (Ecumenical consideration of national identity and "race" can be traced to the first world conference on Faith and Order in Lausanne in 1927.) These issues, taken individually or together, indicate the extent to which the question of the church, its nature and its mission in the world, was the central problem of ecumenism in 2000. They thus confirmed the imperative for ecumenical reflection on ecclesiology. This reflection was already underway in various arenas. But one crucial question had yet to be addressed adequately: What ecclesiology would sustain the search for unity, especially since the ecclesial diversity that burst onto the ecumenical scene in New Delhi had continued to grow and the deepest differences within and between churches had become more and more apparent?

Another question followed from the first: What ecclesiology would enable growth towards the fullness of that communion for which the churches prayed as did their Lord? Here another set of issues appeared: structures for mutual accountability and common decision-making; primacy and the Petrine ministry; *episcope* and episcopacy; apostolicity and succession; interpretation of scripture and Tradition; the community of women and men in the church, including women's call to ministries; authoritative teaching. Despite much study of these issues, more work was needed and this need was made even clearer as the Orthodox churches asked whether the instrumentality of the World Council of Churches remained appropriate for the task. The need for more work was also articulated as the voices of churches from the Pacific, Latin America, the Caribbean, Asia and Africa – the new Christian majority – brought forward their new experiences, new methods and new perspectives on the search for unity.

To attend to the tension running throughout the 20th century search for visible church unity was to confront the hardest issues that still lay ahead: Had attempts to describe and embody the unity of the church taken sufficient account of ever-changing and conditioned contexts in the churches and in the world? Had descriptions and models of unity to date been so burdened with Western – mainly Protestant – cultural forms as to make the search for unity impositional and unity itself "an instrument of domination"? As these and other issues were addressed, questions that had become the heartbeat of the ecumenical movement would be posed anew: What *was* the unity we seek? What would it look like?

BIBLIOGRAPHY

Aram I, *Conciliar Fellowship: A Common Goal*, WCC, 1992, 125p.
Baptism, Eucharist and Ministry, WCC, 1982, 33p.
Best, Thomas F. ed., *Beyond "Unity in Tension": Unity, Renewal and the Community of Women and Men*, WCC, 1988, 171p.
Best, Thomas F. ed., *Living Today towards Visible Unity*, WCC, 1988, 135p.
Best, Thomas F. and Gassmann, Günther eds, *On the Way to Fuller Koinonia: Official Report of the Fifth World Conference on Faith and Order*, WCC, 1994, 318p.
Best, Thomas F. and Granberg-Michaelson, Wesley eds, *Koinonia and Justice, Peace and Creation: Costly Unity. Presentations and Reports from the World Council of Churches' Consultation in Rønde, Denmark, February 1993*, WCC, 1993, 104p.
Best, Thomas F. and Robra, Martin eds, *Ecclesiology and Ethics: Ecumenical Ethical Engagement, Moral Formation and the Nature of the Church*, WCC, 1997, 121p.
Bouteneff, Peter C. and Falconer, Alan D. eds, *Episkopé and Episcopacy and the Quest for Visible Unity*, WCC, 1999, 129p.
Church and World: The Unity of the Church and the Renewal of Human Community: A Faith and Order Study Document, WCC, 1990, 90p.
Confessing the One Faith: An Ecumenical Explication of the Apostolic Faith as It Is Confessed in the Nicene-Constantinopolitan Creed (381), Faith and Order Paper no. 153, WCC, 1991, 1999, 139p.
Confessing Our Faith around the World, WCC, 1984-1986, 4 vols.
Congar, Yves Marie Joseph, *Diversity and Communion*, London, SCM Press, 1984, 232p.
Cullmann, Oscar, *Unity through Diversity: Its Foundation, and a Contribution to the Discussion Concerning the Possibilities of Its Actualization*, Philadelphia, Fortress, 1988, 109p.
Duquoc, Christian, *Provisional Churches: An Essay in Ecumenical Ecclesiology*, London, SCM Press, 1986, 116p.
Falconer, Alan D. ed., *Faith and Order in Moshi: The 1996 Commission Meeting*, WCC, 1998, 339p.
Fries, Heinrich and Rahner, Karl, *Unity of the Churches: An Actual Possibility*, Philadelphia, Fortress, 1985, 146p.
Gassmann, Günther ed., *Documentary History of Faith and Order, 1963-1993*, WCC, 1993, 325p.
Gassmann, Günther, *Konzeptionen der Einheit in der Bewegung für Glauben und Kirchenverfassung 1910-1937*, Göttingen, Vandenhoeck & Ruprecht, 1979, 311p.
Gassmann, Günther and Radano, John eds, *The Unity of the Church as Koinonia: Ecumenical Perspectives on the 1991 Canberra Statement on Unity*, WCC, 1993, 33p.
Gros, Jeffrey, Meyer, Harding and Rusch, William G. eds, *Growth in Agreement II: Reports and Agreed Statements of Ecumenical Conversations on a World Level, 1982-1998*, Faith and Order Paper no. 187, WCC, 2000, 941p.
Groupe des Dombes, *For the Conversion of the Churches*, WCC, 1993, 97p.
Horgan, Thaddeus D. ed., *Walking Together: Roman Catholics and Ecumenism Twenty-Five Years after Vatican II*, Grand Rapids MI, Eerdmans, 1990, 148p.
Hüffmeier, Wilhelm and Podmore, Colin eds, *Leuenberg, Meissen and Porvoo: Consultation between the Churches of the Leuenberg Church Fellowship and the Churches Involved in the Meissen Agreement and the Porvoo Agreement – Leuenberg, Meissen und Porvoo: Konsultation zwischen den Kirchen der Leuenberger Kirchengemeinschaft und den an der Meissener Erklärung und der Porvoo-Erklärung beteiligten Kirchen, Liebfrauenberg, Elsass, 6.-10. September 1995*, Frankfurt am Main, Otto Lembeck, 1996, 192p.

Hurley, Michael, *Christian Unity: An Ecumenical Second Spring?*, Dublin, Veritas, 1998, 420p.

John Paul II, *Ut Unum Sint: Encyclical Letter by the Supreme Pontiff John Paul II on Commitment to Ecumenism*, Vatican City, Libreria Editrice Vaticana, 1995, 117p.

Kinnamon, Michael and Best, Thomas F. eds, *Called to Be One in Christ: United Churches and the Ecumenical Movement*, Faith and Order Paper no. 127, WCC, 1985, 77p.

Limouris, Gennadios ed., *Church, Kingdom, World: The Church as Mystery and Prophetic Sign*, WCC, 1986, 209p.

Meyer, Harding and Vischer, Lukas eds, *Growth in Agreement: Reports and Agreed Statements of Ecumenical Conversations on a World Level*, Faith and Order Paper no. 108, WCC, 1984, 514p.

Meyer, Harding, *That All May Be One: Perceptions and Models of Ecumenicity*, Grand Rapids MI, Eerdmans, 1999, 156p.

Minutes of the Meeting of the Faith and Order Standing Commission, 9-16 January 2002, Gazzada, Italy, WCC, 2002, 128p.

Müller-Fahrenholz, Geiko, *Unity in Today's World: The Faith and Order Studies on "Unity of the Church – Unity of Humankind"*, WCC, 1978, 240p.

One Baptism, One Eucharist and a Mutually Recognized Ministry, Three Agreed Statements, WCC, 1975, 65p.

Parvey, Constance F. ed., *Ordination of Women in Ecumenical Perspective: Workbook for the Church's Future*, WCC, 1980, 96p.

Podmore, Colin ed, *Community, Unity, Communion: Essays in Honour of Mary Tanner*, London, Church House Publishing, 1998, 294p.

Pope, Stephen J. and Hefling, Charles eds, *Sic et Non, Encountering Dominus Iesus*, Maryknoll NY, Orbis, 2002, 204p.

Puglisi, James F. ed., *Petrine Ministry and the Unity of the Church: Toward a Patient and Fraternal Dialogue*, Collegeville MN, Liturgical Press, 1999, 211p.

Rusch, William G. and Gros, Jeffrey eds, *Deepening Communion: International Ecumenical Documents with Roman Catholic Participation*, Washington DC, US Catholic Conference, 1998, 653p.

Rusch, William G. and Martensen, Daniel F. eds, *The Leuenberg Agreement and the Lutheran-Reformed Relationships: Evaluations by North American and European Theologians*, Minneapolis, Augsburg, 1989, 154p.

Thurian, Max ed., *Churches Respond to BEM*, WCC, 1986-1988, 6 vols.

Tillard, Jean-Marie Roger, *Church of Churches: The Ecclesiology of Communion*, Collegeville MN, Liturgical Press, 1992, 330p.

Tjørhom, Ola ed., *Apostolicity and Unity: Essays on the Porvoo Common Statement*, WCC, 2002, 284p.

Together in Mission and Ministry: The Porvoo Common Statement with Essays on Church and Ministry in Northern Europe. Conversations between the British and Irish Anglican Churches and the Nordic and Baltic Lutheran Churches, London, Church Information Office, 1993, 218p.

Uniting in Hope: Reports and Documents from the Meeting of the Faith and Order Commission, 23 July-5 August 1974, University of Ghana, Legon, WCC, 1975, 144p.

What Kind of Unity?, WCC, 1974, 131p.

Yannaras, Christos, *Vérité et Unité de l'Eglise*, Grez-Doiceau, Belgium, Axios, 1989, 175p.

5

Christian World Communions

Harding Meyer

Any description of the ecumenical movement and its developments in the last 35 years would be incomplete without taking full account of the involvement of Christian World Communions (CWCs). Their strength and involvement in the movement had a formative influence on church and world throughout the period from 1968 to 2000.

The previous volume of this history contains an excellent essay by Harold E. Fey, "Confessional Families and the Ecumenical Movement", giving a certain chronological order of the development of Christian world alliances up until 1968. Fey gives the essential details about "confessional world families", which since 1979 have commonly been called Christian World Communions.

FORMATION

The formation of the individual CWC, each different from others both in character and structure, began towards the end of the 19th century and reached fruition towards the middle of the 20th century. This took place concurrently with the formation of the global ecumenical movement and the World Council of Churches.

From the very beginning, there was tension between "confessionalism and ecumenism", which nevertheless did not mean that there were conflicts of principle. The ecumenical movement had at one and the same time two "faces", *interconfessional* and *intraconfessional*. Insofar as the CWCs brought together churches of the same confession over national, ethnic and cultural borders in worldwide "universal" fellowships, they had an ecumenical function and could even be seen as "the principal existing form of the ecumenical movement".

This tension between confessionalism and ecumenism continued. It determined the current structure of the WCC, which was organized quite consciously not according to the principle of confessional representation, but according to that of the geographical or territorial representation of the churches. For the most part, this brought about mutual respect and coexistence between the WCC and the CWCs and the desire to coordinate their programmes and work together on their activities.

In 1957, with support from the WCC, the world fellowships began the annual conference of confessional representatives. It was an unofficial body which had no

---

• This chapter was translated from the German by the WCC Language Service.

authority, but its existence aided consultation and exchange of information. The conferences created space for meetings between confessions, and in this respect had quite a clear ecumenical character from the outset.[1] This was also true of the themes of these annual conferences. The role of the CWCs in the ecumenical movement, and the relationship of the CWCs to the WCC were, to some extent, continually recurring themes, as was the issue of religious freedom, the question of church unions and later bilateral dialogue. By 1968, 14 world communions regularly participated in the conferences.

The tension between confessionalism and ecumenism was felt particularly strongly in the younger churches. The churches' efforts to promote a more effective and credible Christian mission led them to encourage individual denominations in a particular country or region to unite into a single church. The powerful and influential world confessional organizations seemed to be a hindrance to this form of organic unity. The East Asia Christian Conference (Bangalore 1961, Bangkok 1964) criticized CWCs for hindering church union in various declarations that attracted considerable attention. In particular, the EACC directed a call to three of the confessional world families to support the churches of that region in their ecumenical endeavours.

Both the EACC's criticism and its appeal were taken up by the confessional families. In 1967, a conference of CWC representatives wrote a short statement on "The place of world confessional families in the ecumenical family".[2] It became apparent at last that the CWCs were ready to encourage and help their member churches to form unions, making it clear that the old form of "confessionalism", with pretensions to exclusivity, was "a thing of the past".

WORLD CHRISTIAN COMMUNIONS IN 2000

By the end of the 20th century, 17 CWCs were represented at the annual conference of CWC representatives. Compared with 1968, the number had risen only slightly, but the overall composition had changed markedly. In 2000, representatives came from:
- General Conference of the Seventh-day Adventist Church
- International Old Catholic Bishops Conference
- Anglican Consultative Council
- Baptist World Alliance (BWA)
- Church of the Brethren
- World Convention of Churches of Christ
- Salvation Army
- Lutheran World Federation (LWF)
- Mennonite World Conference
- World Methodist Council (WMC)
- Ecumenical Patriarchate (Constantinople)
- Moscow Patriarchate
- Pentecostal World Fellowship
- Friends World Committee for Consultation (Quakers)

---

[1] For the history of this "conference" see also the exhaustive study by Edmond Perret covering the period to 1978, "The History and Theological Concerns of Confessional Family Organizations", in *LWF Reports*, Geneva, LWF, 1978, pp.43-72.
[2] *Study Encounter*, 4, 1, 1968, pp.46-47.

– World Alliance of Reformed Churches (WARC), into which the International Congregational Council had been integrated in 1970
– Reformed Ecumenical Council
– Pontifical Council for Promoting Christian Unity of the Roman Catholic Church

The differences between individual CWCs were substantial in some cases. This refers not only to classic Faith and Order matters but to other differences as well.

- Individual CWCs varied a great deal in size. For the largest of them, such as the Anglican communion, the WARC, the LWF, the BWA and also the WMC – leaving to one side the Orthodox churches and the Roman Catholic Church – the total number of members claimed in the 1990s lay at between 70 million for the Anglican communion and around 50 million for the Methodists. For the smaller CWCs it was significantly less: for instance, the Adventists claimed 12 million members and the Old Catholics half a million.

- Considerable structural divergences also existed between the different CWCs. The majority, the unions of Reformation and post-Reformation churches, had for the most part clear federal structures. However, the Anglican communion was much different and this was even more pronounced among the Orthodox, with their conciliar structures, and for the Roman Catholic Church with its conciliar and primatial structure.

- These structural differences reflected the self-understanding of each one. Some understood themselves to be "churches", including the Adventists and of course the Orthodox and the Roman Catholics. Others, such as the Anglican communion and the LWF, may be seen as increasingly developing an "ecclesial depth", without having a self-understanding of themselves as "churches". On the other hand, the WMC, the WARC and the BWA put more emphasis on, or quite clearly stated, their nature as free associations of churches.

- Individual CWCs had differing views regarding the bonds that held them together. Elements identified by the different communions as binding ran from a general sense of spiritual belonging, having the same worship traditions, characteristic forms of piety or a shared ethos, all the way to shared church structures or a shared doctrine through binding dogmas or confessions of faith.

- Within individual CWCs there have been disagreements over interpretation and application of the common confessional tradition which have threatened its unity. During the late 20th century, issues that provoked new explorations of ecclesial depth and confessional unity included, but were not limited to, the ordination of women, presuppositions behind interfaith dialogue and the role of homosexual persons in the churches. In 1977 the LWF identified apartheid as a status confessionis (fundamental issue of faith), and in 1982 the WARC declared it a heresy, causing alienation between the CWC and some members in South Africa.

These differences were overstated on more than one occasion, even to the extent of claiming that there was "extreme heterogeneity"[3] within the CWCs. In reality, these differences did not mean that a common term or definition could not be used to describe them all. Moreover, the differences were counteracted by common foundational concerns, through which a common self-understanding of the CWCs could be stated. This

---

[3] See the Salamanca report of the Faith and Order Commission in "Unity of the Church – Next Steps", in *What Kind of Unity*, WCC, 1974, pp.119-31.

self-understanding was clarified in a process which continued through the 1960s and 1970s and which was triggered by two determining factors: on the one hand, the criticism that the CWCs experienced and, on the other, the ecumenical opportunity offered by the opening up of the Roman Catholic Church and the beginning of bilateral dialogue.

CRITICISM OF THE CHRISTIAN WORLD COMMUNIONS

As Harold Fey has made clear, criticism of the CWCs was expressed, particularly in the years 1961-64, and had considerable repercussions at the 1961 New Delhi assembly of the WCC.[4] Complaints focused on two particular areas: criticism of the CWCs as world organizations, and the much more fundamental criticism of what one could call "confessionalism".

Criticism of the CWCs as worldwide organizations

This was the main focus of the declaration of an enlarged continuation committee of the East Asia Christian Conference in 1961. The worldwide confessional movements were not criticized as such. Quite the contrary. The declaration said, "It has been a natural development that, with the growth of the ecumenical movement, there should also be an increased consciousness and a desire to come together as confessional families."[5] It was hoped that there would be a fruitful interaction between "ecumenical" and "confessional" ways of thinking. The positive role of the world alliances was recognized in breaking down "local isolation", overcoming "national barriers" and "protecting against dangerous introversion and narrow-minded nationalism".

Over and against this, "fear and anxiety" were aroused by the confessional world organizations which offered structures to these confessional movements. Three danger points were listed:

1. The expression of world confessionalism in "increasingly institutional structures" might prevent the younger churches from finding their independence and identity.
2. Churches' membership of different and clearly structured confessional world organizations risked undermining work towards regional church unions and thus threatened effective communication of the gospel.
3. In the area of Christian service for the sake of humanity it seemed more important for churches in individual countries or regions to come together in transconfessional church unions than to insist upon their loyalty to confessional world organizations.

By the end of the 1960s the sharp criticism of the CWCs as world organizations had considerably lessened, though it had by no means ceased. One of the reasons for this was that the key question of church unions had been taken up again by the CWCs and responded to in ways that were new and fundamentally positive.

---

[4] In the unity section report to the assembly mention is made of leading men and women "who see the world confessional bodies as a threat to wider unity in particular areas, a view which some Asian and African Christians have expressed with vigour". W.A. Visser 't Hooft, *The New Delhi Report: The Third Assembly of the World Council of Churches, 1961*, WCC, 1962, p.132.

[5] Minutes of the enlarged continuation committee of the East Asia Christian Conference, Bangalore, 7-12 Nov. 1961, p.38.

Criticism of "confessionalism"

Behind the criticism of the confessional world organizations lay fundamental critical reservations which had always existed in the ecumenical movement. These concerned denominations, the formation of confessions and the existence of confessional churches. There were serious reservations about confessionalism generally.

These criticisms took the form of a gradual and growing challenge to the CWCs. They began with the demand for "new interpretation" of traditional church confessions, continued with the demand for "new, common confessions" and led from there to the demand for "contemporary confession". Thus, they led to a calling into question, implicitly at least, of the historical relevance of confessions and the formation of denominations generally, as well as a questioning of the current raison d'être and justification for the existence of denominational churches and confessional church unions.

This criticism amounted to a new interpretation of traditional confessions of faith. Looking back at the Bangalore declaration of 1961 or at the statements from the WCC youth committee in 1962-63, one is easily astonished at the positive evaluation of historical confessions. They were regarded as being "of highest importance" for the present day as they "confront the churches with the question of truth itself". The youth statements asked for *translation* of historic confessions of faith into their respective historical and cultural situation, because confessions could not sufficiently respond to the challenge of contemporary society in the form in which they had been handed down.

At about the same time, calls could be heard for new common confessions of faith. The inadequacy of the historic confessions of faith at bearing witness in the current situation was strongly underlined. There was a demand no longer simply to make a new interpretation of the historical confessions but to reformulate a common confession of faith for the Asian churches which would then leave confessional divisions behind.

But doubts soon arose as to whether the formulation of a common confession could really be the goal of a regional ecumenical organization. Several consultations in the 1960s called for ongoing, open "contemporary confessions of faith". Being tied to confessional formulations or to confessional loyalties or world communions could only stand in the way of contemporary confessing.

At two large consultations in 1963 and 1965, the CWCs made it clear that they no longer supported the "confessionalism" of earlier times, with its claim to exclusive confessional loyalty and its "fundamentalist" position on the historic confessions. They encouraged member churches to engage in church union discussions.

THE CHALLENGE OF VATICAN II

It was during the same period of the CWCs trying to respond to critical questions that the Second Vatican Council was convened. It was the wish of Pope John XXIII that the Council should have a clear ecumenical direction and that representatives of churches who had split with Rome should be invited to attend as observers. Discussions between Cardinal Johannes Willebrands, secretary of the Secretariat for Promoting Christian Unity, and W.A. Visser 't Hooft, general secretary of the WCC, led to invitations being extended to the CWCs.

For the CWCs this was a new ecumenical challenge and opportunity, one to which almost all responded. During the years of Vatican II the observers continually reported back to their respective communions on progress, often in published form, with lively participation from churches and their members as well as the wider public.

During Vatican II some thought was given to how contacts made between the Roman Catholic Church and the CWCs could be continued and what form these should take. The 1965 "Decree on Ecumenism" (*Unitatis Redintegratio*) offered the term "dialogue". By doing so it used language not yet common in the ecumenical movement. In September 1964 the LWF decided to propose general bilateral Roman Catholic-Lutheran dialogue. Other bilateral dialogues followed, not only with the Roman Catholic Church but also between other CWCs or confessional churches at both international and national levels. By the end of the 1970s, an ever greater network of bilateral dialogues existed, including almost all confessions. This has been a large and important undertaking within the ecumenical movement.

What were the implications of all this? Lukas Vischer noted in *The Ecumenical Review* of January-April 2002,

> In this way, a completely new situation emerged. Increasingly, the world confessional bodies became the partners of the Roman Catholic Church. Having once been regarded as an obstacle to ecumenical fellowship, they now became agents of the ecumenical movement. This development has altered the nature of world communions more than any other, so much so that the world communions of the 1980s and 1990s were no longer the same kind of bodies as they were after the second world war.

BASIC CONCERNS AND SELF-UNDERSTANDING OF CWCS

Both the criticism and the ecumenical opportunity of the 1960s were cause for the CWCs to reflect on their self-understanding and basic concerns in the light of their acknowledged responsibility. This reflection took place as a series of events in the 1970s began to help form a broader picture. Particularly noteworthy is the October 1978 conference of CWC representatives where a broad picture was approved as an accurate portrayal of the role of CWCs.

CWC representatives began by accepting two "working definitions" which had been used in the 1960s to try both to describe the common (distinctive) features and basic concerns of the CWCs and also to answer the question concerning the CWC's raison d'être.

This was the definition of confessional families proposed by Visser 't Hooft in 1962:

> These bodies have this in common:
> a) that their member churches share together not only the general tradition which is common to all Christian churches, but also specific traditions which have grown out of the spiritual crises in the history of the church;
> b) that they desire to render witness to specific convictions of a doctrinal or ecclesiological character which they consider to be essential for the life of the whole church of Christ.

And this was the definition adopted in 1967:

> Each World Confessional Family consists of churches belonging to the same tradition and held together by this common heritage; they are conscious of living in the same universal fellowship and give to this consciousness at least some structured visible expression.[6]

---

[6] "The Place of World Confessional Families in the Ecumenical Movement", in *Study Encounter*, IV, 1968, p.46.

Even if these "working definitions" were not completely satisfactory, they could nevertheless, if taken together, be used as a starting point to show up the common concerns of the CWCs which underpinned their self-understanding. There were three basic concerns which came particularly to the fore: CWCs could be described by the terms "universality", "continuity" and "diversity". The following summaries sketch the ecclesiological significance of each term as they contribute to CWCs' self-understanding.

The universality of Christian fellowship

As the people that God has brought together from among all the peoples, the church is a fellowship which crosses and goes beyond the dividing lines between nations, races, cultures and countries. This universal dimension, which is part of the nature of Christian fellowship, is visible within the CWCs. Given the diversity of the confessions, each of the CWCs can demonstrate only a partial realization of this universality. It is nevertheless true that each communion shows proof of a common faith that has the power to overcome barriers.

Whatever one may wish to call a union of churches from the same confessional background – a world alliance, a world family or a worldwide communion – all of these terms include reference to universal breadth; and this for the most part is how the individual CWCs understand themselves. The second "working definition" of confessional families (1967) says that the churches of one confessional family "are conscious of living in the same universal fellowship and give to this consciousness at least some structured visible expression". This was the strongest driving force behind the formation of the CWCs. Across national, ethnic and cultural barriers churches recognized the close ties of their faith and applied pressure to live out this fellowship: through interchurch aid in times of emergency, mission and service in the world and for human beings, and overcoming dangers which arose from political, cultural and ethnic isolation. The common ground of each one's particular tradition, and the consciousness of belonging together as churches sharing responsibilities towards one another, proved to be strong enough to achieve a liberation from the narrowness of their national borders and ethnic realities.

Even the East Asia Christian Conference recognized that the world families helped to "lift Christians out of local isolation and aid them in surmounting national barriers of separation". In the WCC also, in the years between the assemblies of New Delhi (1961) and Uppsala (1968), the confessional families and their ecumenical role began to be seen in a new and positive light. After a period when there was much concentration on "unity in every place", more emphasis began to be given to "unity in all places" in order to underline the "catholicity" of the church. The WCC's Uppsala assembly (1968) recognized in the world confessional families a "real experience of universality", even if this experience remains "unavoidably incomplete" because of the remaining divisions between the confessions.

The constitutions of the CWCs were also shaped by this consciousness of universality. In their "aims" or "tasks" there was constant reference to how the worldwide fellowship between member churches had been maintained and deepened in various ways. The WMC formulated this quite clearly. The first of its aims was "to deepen fellowship between Methodists across the divisions of race, nationality, skin colour and language".

This intensive and vigorous push for a structured, visible consciousness of the universality of Christian fellowship was something new. For most of the Protestant churches, up to this point, the *ecclesia universalis* had seemed to be something invisible, a sort of communion of hearts. By 2000, this was no longer the case.

The significance of the universality of Christian fellowship (communion) has been deepened for those involved in the life and work of the CWCs because of the way this fellowship has been lived out and nurtured. This is reflected in the new name given to these confessional associations, "world communions". It was recognized that "association" was in many ways too weak a term to describe adequately the depth of belonging experienced by the Christians and churches of these associations. This belonging was characterized by the following marks of communion:

- The individual confessional families were so closely linked through their common faith that common witness, mission and service became direct consequences creating occasional problems but no fundamental ones.
- There was full sacramental communion within each CWC and membership in one member church meant that one had, *ipso facto*, the right to membership in any other member church.
- Within individual confessional families there was a common ministry, meaning that the exchange of ministers was accepted in principle while respecting the usual church regulations.
- Each of the confessional families – not only the Orthodox and Roman Catholic churches – had a leadership structure (assemblies or synods, executive committees, president, moderator, general secretary, etc.) which upheld and took care of the fellowship.
- Each – not just the Roman Catholic Church – could, and in some cases had the constitutional right to, undertake tasks when asked to do so on behalf of its member churches. These tasks were mainly of an ecclesiological nature (interconfessional dialogue, mission, Christian education, etc.).

From this perspective, most of the CWCs clearly had features characteristic of "ecclesiality" without being fully "churches". Their "ecclesial density" was often mentioned, closely followed by questions concerning their "ecclesial nature". The LWF was a particularly good example of this. The question of its "ecclesial nature" accompanied the Federation almost from its beginnings and was again widely discussed in the years following 1979. This led to the LWF no longer understanding itself to be – in the words of its constitution – "a free association of Lutheran churches" but "a communion of churches which confess the triune God, agree in the proclamation of the word of God and are united in pulpit and altar fellowship".

Authority remained an open question for nearly all CWCs except the Roman Catholic Church. Almost none of them possessed church decision-making or leadership powers as such. This rightly rested with the independent, autonomous or autocephalus member churches (national churches, provinces or patriarchates). Thus, for CWCs, in order to be binding, decisions had to be accepted officially by member churches. However, such decisions were doubtless "implicitly" binding – "morally" was frequently the term used – which follows from agreeing to enter universal fellowship.

The historical continuity of faith and the church

The universality of Christian fellowship as expressed through the CWCs involved more than physical unifying dimensions ("synchronism"). It was understood as more than the sum of its "geographical" universality and extended beyond national, ethnic, cultural, political and societal lines. Christian communion also unified "across time". It had a "diachronic" dimension which transcended the dividing lines between times and generations.

Just as the church was seen by CWCs as God's people gathered together from all the peoples, so it was also to be seen as the people guided and preserved by God throughout time and across generations. Even when members of one generation confessed faith and lived out Christian fellowship in new ways, this always took place in a way closely linked to Christians of previous generations and with a sense of responsibility to past witnesses who handed down the gospel of Christ.

Emphasizing this dimension of historical continuity and the roots of Christian faith and Christian fellowship brought out a second basic concern that was decisive for the life and work of the CWCs and what they stood for.

This was spelled out in the "working definitions". They spoke of "tradition", of "tradition which is common to all Christian churches", and also of "specific traditions" which individual CWCs have as a result of their history and to which they know themselves to be committed. In the latter of the two working definitions (1967) the words "tradition" and "heritage" became the key terms in determining the nature of the confessional families: "Each world confessional family consists of churches belonging to the same tradition and held together by this heritage."

The constitutions of the individual CWCs demonstrated this consciousness of historical continuity. Whether in sections on membership criteria or criteria for setting their aims, they clearly stated that their current life and work was a fulfilment of their responsibility in the face of history and in terms of their confessional heritage. Maintaining this heritage is an important foundation of their universal fellowship as it significantly contributes to their witness and work in the given moment. Even in those instances where the "backward-looking nature" of the CWCs was criticized and when links to their historical heritage were regarded as harmful for present-day witness, this specific concern of the CWCs was nevertheless recognized. For example, at the WCC fifth assembly in Nairobi (1975) it was stated in a very positive way that the confessional organizations stressed "the necessity for faithfulness to the truth as it has been confessed to us in the past and as it is embodied in the received traditions".

The legitimacy of different manifestations of faith and church

Besides the rather secondary differences between the individual CWCs – size, structure, "ecclesial" self-understanding and the binding nature of their fellowship – each CWC naturally valued its own confessional differences which were mainly doctrinal or ecclesiological. The question is how to understand the fact that these primary differences between the CWCs exist. An attempt at an answer was proposed by the 1962 working definition which gave an impression of the "specific convictions of doctrinal or ecclesiological character... as essential for the life of the whole church of Christ", and interpreted them as specific contributions to the life of the whole church.

This is the correct interpretation and any other interpretation could be seen as too "static" or "pre-ecumenical". However, in order to understand the confessional families properly – especially their diversity – one should use their particularities as a starting point. "A satisfactory definition can only be given by using the creed as a basis, 'I believe in the Holy Spirit, in one holy catholic and apostolic church.'"[7]

This is a much more appropriate starting point and one which has stood the test of time throughout the development of the self-understanding of the CWCs. Without

---

7 Lukas Vischer, "The Place and Task of Confessional Families in the Ecumenical Movement", in *Duke Divinity School Review*, winter 1968, p.37.

denying that the particular convictions of the individual CWC are to be understood as a "specific contribution" to the life of the whole church, it is first and foremost stated that each individual CWC, or all of their member churches, are a *particular* manifestation of the *one* catholic and apostolic church.

The 1930 Lambeth conference of Anglican bishops already understood the Anglican communion in this way, as "a communion within the one, holy, catholic and apostolic church", made up of dioceses and regional churches which have the same particular "common characteristic". Similarly, the Lutheran World Federation states,

> Lutheran churches consider themselves to be part of the one holy, catholic church. The apostolic witness is the basis of their life and proclamation and they use the creeds of the ancient church to confess their own faith. At the same time, however, they constitute a distinctive fellowship of churches, united by common confessions and a common history. The LWF is an organized instrument and an expression of this fellowship.[8]

Vatican II also helped this interpretation to break through in the Roman Catholic Church. However one may wish to interpret the well-known statement that the one holy, catholic and apostolic church "is realized in" *(subsistit in)* the Roman Catholic Church, it at least implies that the one church can and does exist beyond the walls of the Roman Catholic Church.

From the Orthodox perspective there are also representative statements which point in the same direction. At a conference in Crete in 1975, Orthodox church leaders stated,

> So the Orthodox church does not expect that other Christians be converted to Orthodoxy in its historical and cultural reality of the past and the present and to become members of the Orthodox church. Its desire is that all should strive in their own churches and traditions to deepen the fullness of the apostolic faith embodied in a fully ecclesial life. No church is therefore required to uproot itself, to cut itself off from its cultural heritage or to lose its distinctive character. Each would contribute to the enrichment of all.[9]

Thus one may say that all CWCs basically share the conviction that they are each a particular manifestation of the church of Christ. They see themselves, or the totality of their member churches, not as primarily separate entities defined by their difference, but rather as specific manifestations of one and the same given reality: the one, holy, catholic church and the one apostolic faith.

This basic conviction, which characterizes the self-understanding of the CWCs, is also expressed in their new description of themselves. This no longer emphasizes the differences, as did the earlier title "World *Confessional* Families". The first, foundational and common characteristic of these fellowships is much more in their relationship to the one, holy, apostolic and catholic church of Jesus Christ; they are *Christian* World Communions.

It is true that not all CWCs are able to recognize each other mutually as legitimate and authentic manifestations of the one, holy, catholic and apostolic church. However, none of them upholds the exclusive claim, sometimes maintained in the past, of being

---

[8] "Ecumenical Relations of the Lutheran World Federation", preparatory booklet for the LWF assembly 1977, p.31. To quote a representative of the World Alliance of Reformed Churches, "According to our understanding a confessional church is a catholic church with a particular theological discipline, a church which confesses its faith to the world in particular structural and doctrinal ways" (Lewis S. Mudge, lecture at the consultation on world confessionalism and the ecumenical movement, *Lutheran World*, 10, 1, 1963, p.54).

[9] *Orthodox Contributions to Nairobi*, WCC, 1975, p.32.

the only manifestation of the Christian church, nor denies the existence or possibility of other legitimate and authentic manifestations of the church.

Two important, even decisive, ecumenical developments were expressed through this self-understanding of the CWCs.

First, this self-understanding made it clear that the earlier intransigent confessionalism, characterized by its claims to exclusivity, had been surmounted. Although this was of course connected with wider ecumenical thought, it was the separate development of the CWCs which contributed decisively to this. For the *inner* diversity and the *inner* variability of the individual CWC, which arose from the universal fellowship of churches of different cultural, ethnic and historical influences, had to call into question any narrow confessionalism. The "refuges" of confessionalism, as the East Asia Christian Conference still referred to them at the beginning of the 1960s, could in no way persist in the many-sided and in no way homogeneous or monolithic CWCs. For this reason some CWCs decided to change their constitutions to describe the confessional criteria for membership in a more open and less formal way. Other CWCs could allow churches to join who did not strictly correspond to their criteria[10] or who had distanced themselves from these criteria as a result of their development. The occasional possibility for a church of "double membership" in two different CWCs is also part of this picture, as is the possibility of membership for united churches. One eloquent indication for overcoming this narrow and intransigent confessionalism is that some CWCs – such as the WARC and the LWF – experienced a real "confessional opposition" from churches which voted to reject membership applications and accused "their" world federation of watering down the confessional inheritance. What the WCC's Norman Goodall had already said at the 1963 consultation on world confessionalism and the ecumenical movement proved to be apposite:

> It could be contended that most of these family-colloquies [by which he meant the discussions within confessional families] have provided their own impetus to self-criticism and to something more than conversation, not least through the discovery at close quarters of the many differences represented within the one group.[11]

It is certainly the case that the self-understanding of the CWCs as being differing manifestations of the one church of Jesus Christ no longer corresponded with claims to confessional exclusivity.

Secondly, this self-understanding of the CWCs signified not only the fundamental overcoming of "confessionalism"; at least equally important was the fact that at the same time the principle of equating confessional diversity with church division was both rejected and definitively breached.

This principle of equating confessional diversity and church division was rarely explicitly stated in the official documents of the ecumenical movement. But such a view had at least implicitly characterized the ecumenical movement in the first part of the 20th century, right up to the 1960s. "Confession" and "ecumenism" were seen as polar opposites. Both the debates and decisions that led to the formation and structure of what became the WCC and the prevalence of the explicitly "transconfessional" models of "organic" or "corporate union"[12] are two of the particularly obvious indications of this tendency.

---

[10] For example, the Lutheran World Federation allowed churches to join who did not have the *Confessio Augustana* as their confession.
[11] *Lutheran World*, 1965, p.55.
[12] H. Meyer ed., *That All May Be One: Perceptions and Models of Ecumenicity*, Grand Rapids MI, Eerdmans, 1999, pp.94-100.

The self-understanding of the CWC, however, expressed itself through the conviction, even the assertion, that confessional differences not only do not contradict the unity of the church but are instead legitimate differences that have their place in the unity that is sought. Already the "working definition" of the World Confessional Families (WCFs) from 1962 expressed the conviction that the confessional world bodies desired "to render witness to specific convictions of a doctrinal or ecclesiological character which they consider to be essential for the life of the whole church of Christ".

There was awareness nevertheless that both in the past and today these confessional differences were – and remained – the main foundation for the existing church divisions. There was the conviction that this need not be the case, but that these differences could lose their church-dividing severity and that the condemnations or anathemas with which such differences were linked could be overcome. If this could be achieved then the confessional differences could become part of the sought-for-unity, which in the ecumenical movement was never seen as "uniformity" but always as a unity that could encompass such legitimate differences.

This conviction that confessional differences could be reconciled with the unity of the church would become a central element of the CWCs' ecumenical endeavour.

THE ROLE OF CWCs IN THE ECUMENICAL MOVEMENT

Three basic considerations, and the self-understanding of CWCs which is expressed in them, clearly have implications for the communions' relationship to the ecumenical movement and the form of their own ecumenical participation.

Positions on church union

Even before the CWCs developed their own form of ecumenical involvement, about the beginning of the 1970s, they had to clarify their position on church union negotiations and the formation of united churches in which their member churches were involved or in which they wished to become involved. This took place, in part, as a direct response to criticism from these churches which accused the then World Confessional Families of obstructing local or regional church unions by the positions they were taking. At the consultation in November 1965 on confessional movements, mission and unity, in which the WCC and some mission societies took part, the WCFs were asked whether they were prepared "to fully encourage and assist their member churches when they sought union with other churches". The issue was about the continuation of financial support and the continuing membership in the respective World Confessional Family. This question was answered in the affirmative by practically all those confessional families affected.

The position from the beginning of the 1970s was that most CWCs had also officially declared their readiness, in the framework of their constitutional requirements for membership, to accept or to maintain united churches in their fellowship. The constitutions, for example, of the World Alliance of Reformed Churches, the World Methodist Council and the Anglican Consultative Council make provision for membership by united churches. Corresponding decisions were taken at the 1968 Lambeth conference and at the LWF assembly of 1970.

Through such means, the important question of the continuation of both financial and personnel support of united churches by the respective CWCs received a positive response.

The old and the new ecumenical role of CWCs

It has often been pointed out that the formation of the CWCs and the WCC took place at the same time, the first through the coming together of confessional movements and the second as a result of the ecumenical movement for unity. When one takes into account that it was the same churches and often the same people who were involved in both movements, it becomes clear that it was not a question of movements in opposition to each other; in the final analysis, both movements, despite their differences, grew from the same roots. They were said to be "two expressions" of the one ecumenical movement, "an interconfessional and an intraconfessional" form.

This suggests that the ecumenical task of CWCs was seen as being to prepare, promote and support the "interconfessional" gathering and the actual "ecumenical" coming together of *all* churches, through the "intraconfessional" gathering of their own churches. In this sense, Visser 't Hooft said in his greeting to the founding assembly of the Lutheran World Federation in 1947,

> The World Council [in formation] is deeply aware of the fact that the ecumenical task can only be performed if the main confessional federations and alliances perform their task of bringing the churches of their confessional family together in close fellowship and so prepare the way for the even greater and more difficult task of establishing the wider ecumenical Christian brotherhood.

For their part, the CWCs appeared to be content with this role. Most of them had constitutions that contained and still contain a passage stating in these or similar words that their "tasks" included those of "promoting the participation of member churches in the ecumenical movement" (World Methodist Council), "encouraging their ecumenical involvement" (World Conference of Churches of Christ), "to enable them to make a contribution to the ecumenical movement" (World Alliance of Reformed Churches) or "to promote... their interest and participation in the ecumenical movement and strengthen their responsibility for this" (Lutheran World Federation).

Each of these statements demonstrates what the "ecumenical role" of CWCs was at that time. They engaged in more or less *indirect participation in the ecumenical movement* through their member churches, for example, in the way they encouraged their member churches to join the WCC or to participate in regional church union negotiations. But there was no thought, or hardly any, given to the idea that the CWCs should participate actively and directly in the ecumenical movement *in their own right*.

Towards the end of the 1960s, however, there was a fundamental change. The CWCs were offered the historic "challenge and opportunity" to play a new ecumenical role, which they seized with eagerness and determination. Having been indirect promoters and supporters of the ecumenical movement they became its active and direct protagonists. This happened as all CWCs were gradually drawn into official interchurch discussions, so that a comprehensive network of worldwide and national bilateral dialogues was quickly established, without which it would be impossible to imagine the ecumenical movement.

Bilateral dialogues

The form of bilateral discussions

Official church bilateral dialogue, that is, dialogue between two partner churches, may be seen to be an ecumenical innovation which had considerable repercussions. The conscious decision to embark on this form of dialogue was intended not to replace, but rather to complement, the form of "multilateral" dialogue that had been dominant until then – with equally conscious intent. It was based on the conviction that a discussion between only two partner churches was a more appropriate way of dealing with confessionally specific controversial issues that had divided, and still divided, two churches, as opposed to a discussion between many partner churches. It would also be possible in a bilateral discussion to deal with such issues in more detail, to treat them in a more differentiated way and better resolve them. At the same time it was thought that the specific commonalities that existed and remained between two churches could be more adequately affirmed.

These convictions have been confirmed on the whole by the way in which the dialogues proceeded. There had certainly been an awareness of the possible disadvantages of such bilateral discussions. For example, there was a danger of becoming isolated and losing sight of the wider ecumenical horizon, so the results of multilateral dialogues – such as the Lima text (1982) on *Baptism, Eucharist and Ministry* – were taken into consideration. Above all a forum for bilateral dialogues was formed in 1978 and over the next two and a half decades met eight times with the task of bringing together the individual bilateral dialogues through an exchange of information. This forum also dealt with common theological and methodological questions and discussed the implications of the results of bilateral dialogues for the whole ecumenical movement.

The levels and the abundance of dialogues

The bilateral dialogues conducted by the CWCs themselves naturally took place at the international level. The results of these dialogues have been fully documented.[13] The documentation refers to about thirty such dialogues or series of dialogues since 1967 that have taken place or were taking place at the dawn of the 21st century. From this it can be seen that some confessions have been intensively involved in such dialogues, while others have been less so. The reasons for this seem to be linked above all to the size and the level of organization as well as to the capacity in finance and personnel of the participating confessions. The Roman Catholic Church was intensively involved by 2000 (with ten international dialogues), followed by the Lutheran World Federation, the (Oriental) Orthodox church, the World Alliance of Reformed Churches and the Anglican communion (each with six or seven international dialogues).

Alongside these international dialogues, there were also a large number of national bilateral dialogues whose results have often been published. However, there is no full and comprehensive documentation of such dialogues. Moreover, many were only short-term, had consequences limited to a small geographical area, and often their results remain unpublished. Recent estimates have counted up to fifty national dialogues.

The character and themes of the dialogues

In formal terms, the overwhelming majority of bilateral dialogues have an official ecclesial character. They have been mandated by the churches which nominate the participants, and their results are immediately conveyed to church leaders. This official eccle-

---

[13] Harding Meyer and Lukas Vischer eds, *Growth in Agreement: Reports and Agreed Statements of Ecumenical Conversations on a World Level*, WCC, 1984; Harding Meyer, Lukas Vischer and Jeffrey Gros eds, *Growth in Agreement II: Reports and Agreed Statements of Ecumenical Conversations on a World Level, 1982-1998*, WCC, 2000.

sial character of such dialogues does not mean that their results immediately become binding for churches. It *does* mean that the churches have committed themselves to take note and to examine these results and to be open to formally accepting them.

In the beginning at least, a number of dialogues focused on getting to know each other better and overcoming existing prejudices. But most dialogues are – given their subject matter – from the outset doctrinal discussions in which the aim is to overcome theological and ecclesiological differences. The starting point is that confessional, church-dividing differences need to be dealt with in order to arrive at a sustainable and long-lasting fellowship between churches.

The five main areas discussed in the last three decades of the 20th century were: (1) the sacraments, in particular the eucharist; (2) the ordained ministry, mostly including the issue of the *episcope* and occasionally also touching on the issue of papal primacy; (3) the nature of the church, which included a series of other questions such as authority in the church, church structures or the norms for the proclamation and teaching of the church; (4) the understanding of salvation, in dialogues that included Lutheran-Catholic dialogue on the question of justification; (5) how marriage was to be understood and the issue of confessionally mixed marriages. Issues of Christian ethics and responsibility for the world were discussed more at the national rather than the international level.

Reaching consensus as the task of dialogue

In the end, the majority of bilateral dialogues took the form of trying to reach consensus on each of the existing divergences. Thus bilateral dialogue assumed that attempts at church unity might take different forms but that they could not bypass efforts at consensus. Of course, arriving at such consensus did not imply the removal or levelling-out of all differences. The sought-for consensus could actually allow more space for remaining differences, provided that these differences lost their capacity to be church-dividing and were recognized as genuine differences. This is why in earlier times this kind of consensus was referred to as "differentiated consensus". It indicated a consensus which left room for remaining differences because of basic and fundamental agreement, so long as these differences were "carried" by, and did not undermine, the basic and fundamental agreement. This form of consensus corresponded with the visible unity of the church that gave direction to the ecumenical movement. That unity which the ecumenical movement seeks can certainly find room for legitimate differences and is not to be seen as "uniformity" but as "fellowship".

The ecclesial reception of the results of dialogue

On many individual issues the dialogues managed to arrive at understandings that for the most part could be described as achieving sufficient consensus to be acceptable to church fellowships. In these cases attempts to reach consensus did not then need to be taken further. It was up to the churches whether or not to accept or to "receive" the results of dialogue. In a number of cases that took place. Since 1973 the Leuenberg agreement in Europe made it possible – thanks to bilateral dialogue – to establish full church fellowship for more than 100 churches in many countries. This fellowship between Reformed, Lutheran and even Methodist churches, is also to be found between Anglicans in Britain and Ireland and Lutherans in the Nordic and Baltic countries, and between the Evangelical Lutheran Church and the Episcopal (Anglican) church in both the US and Canada.

Nevertheless, the ecclesial reception of the results of dialogue continued to encounter all manner of difficulties and resistance, not least in attempting to reach consensus through dialogue with the Roman Catholic Church. But even here there was a crucial breakthrough when, in 1999, the consensus that had been achieved in the Catholic-Lutheran dialogue was approved and received in a solemn Joint Declaration on the Doctrine of Justification officially signed by the Roman Catholic Church and the member churches of the Lutheran World Federation.

Visions of church unity

Soon after they started their bilateral dialogues, the CWCs were faced with the question of what their vision of unity was in regard to their ecumenical endeavours. This question was officially posed to the CWCs in 1973 by the Commission on Faith and Order of the WCC. In the report of its meeting in Salamanca, Spain, the Commission had the "vision of a united church as a conciliar fellowship".[14] This concept of "conciliar fellowship" was entirely based on what was said in the well-known and influential "statement on unity" concerning the unity of the church and its constitutive elements, made at the WCC's 1961 New Delhi assembly. The unity being sought was described in the Salamanca report as being a "conciliar fellowship of local churches themselves truly united". This description both expanded the New Delhi statement on unity and made it more precise in two areas: the idea of the "conciliar fellowship of local churches" was stressed more strongly; and the reference to "truly united local churches" meant that the concept of "church union" – i.e. an overtly transconfessional concept – was now explicitly being made part of the conception of the unity of the church in a way that had not been the case in New Delhi. The Salamanca report made clear in other places as well that "conciliar fellowship" both presupposed and required "organic union".

Even though the CWCs had already acknowledged as a legitimate concept the idea of church union as "organic union" and had pledged their support for church unions, they did not see this transconfessional approach as the *only* way to achieve church unity "in any one place". Still less did they see it as being an approach that reflected their own self-understanding. They could not answer the request they had received from Faith and Order "to clarify their understanding of the quest for unity", by simply giving blanket support to the idea of a "conciliar fellowship" that was linked to the concept of church union. Certainly they supported the idea that the universal unity of the church needed to take the form of a "conciliar fellowship" of churches. But they could not agree to the idea that the members of this fellowship should be exclusively united churches or local churches. Rather they placed alongside this concept of transconfessional church union the concept of a confessionally based church union that could give space to confessional differences and identities rather than giving them up and leaving them behind.

This position was clarified at two consultations in 1974. The critical section of the "discussion paper" about "the ecumenical role of the World Confessional Families in the one ecumenical movement" reads as follows:

> We consider the variety of denominational heritages legitimate insofar as the truth of the one faith explicates itself in history in a variety of expressions. We do not overlook the fact that such explications of the faith have been marked by error which has threatened the unity of the church. On the other hand, it needs to be seen that a heritage remains legiti-

---

[14] *What Kind of Unity?*, Faith and Order paper no. 69, WCC, 1974, p.121.

mate and can be preserved if it is properly translated into new historical situations. If it is, it remains a valuable contribution to the richness of life in the church universal. In the open encounter with other heritages the contribution of a particular denomination can lose its character of denominational exclusiveness. Therefore, unity and fellowship among the churches do not require uniformity of faith and order, but can and must encompass a plurality or diversity of convictions and traditions. This idea is as old as the ecumenical movement itself, but only in the last decade has it been taken seriously. On the basis of the old idea has emerged a new conception of the relationship between "confession" and "ecumenism". Confessional loyalty and ecumenical commitment are no contradiction, but are one – paradoxical as it may seem. When existing differences between churches lose their divisive character, there emerges a vision of unity that has the character of a "reconciled diversity".[15]

This confessionally based vision of church unity, summarized by the slogan "unity in reconciled diversity", completely corresponded with the way the CWCs understood their new ecumenical role and sought to reach unity and consensus in their bilateral dialogues. The discussion paper pointed to the Lutheran-Reformed Leuenberg agreement as one way of achieving such unity. Through this instrument, church fellowship had been established the previous year (1973) between European Lutheran and Reformed churches with continuing confessional differences. Even if not all CWCs accepted the slogan of "unity in reconciled diversity" in the way in which the LWF assembly did in 1977, the slogan still corresponded to their basic concerns.

The CWCs now had not only an ecumenical role but also an ecumenical goal that corresponded to their own self-understanding. Certainly both the ecumenical role and the ecumenical goal had specific characteristics, but finally they were able to fit into the ecumenical movement as a whole, both expanding and enriching it.

This goal of "unity in reconciled diversity" was something that became recognized in various ways in the course of 1978, initially at the first forum on bilateral conversations, then at the Bangalore, India, meeting of Faith and Order and finally at a consultation between representatives of the WCC and the World Confessional Families. Drawing on the discussion paper, it was stated,

> Those placing emphasis on organic union want to stress that unity must be close enough to make possible the common witness at the local level. Those defending the concept "unity in reconciled diversity" want to promote the view that the confessional traditions, though they obviously need to be transformed, can have a continuing identifiable life within the one church.[16]

Both concepts "may be two different ways of reacting to ecumenical necessities and possibilities of different situations and of different traditions".

This specific concern of the CWCs, namely that the unity of the church that was being sought should also allow space for confessional differences, received support at the WCC Canberra assembly in 1991. In its statement on "The Unity of the Church as Koinonia: Gift and Calling" it was explicitly stated that those "diversities which are rooted in theological traditions" are differences that "are integral to the nature of communion".[17]

[15] G. Gassmann and H. Meyer, "The Unity of the Church: Requirements and Structure", in *LWF Report*, June 1983, p.31, §30.
[16] Ibid., p.52, §8; and p.46.
[17] "The Unity of the Church as Koinonia: Gift and Calling", in Michael Kinnamon ed., *Signs of the Spirit: Official Report, Seventh Assembly*, WCC, 1991, pp.172-74.

The relationship between CWCs and the WCC

The issue of the relationship between CWCs and the WCC is something that was discussed repeatedly both at the conferences of CWCs secretaries and at WCC assemblies. But in all important respects this relationship appears to have remained the same as in the first two decades following the formation of the WCC as described by Fey: a relationship based on respect and, as Visser 't Hooft described it at the foundation of the LWF, a necessary coexistence which, particularly in the area of the projects and activities undertaken by the two parties, became a relationship of cooperation.

Certainly in the 1960s, following the criticism directed by Asian and African churches at the then World Confessional Families, there had been both tensions and polarizing tendencies. But by the time of the WCC assembly at Uppsala in 1968 a more positive view of WCFs appeared to have become accepted. The assembly more or less adopted the statement of the conference of WCF secretaries from the previous year:

> The World Council of Churches reminds the world families of their limits and their role in the ecumenical movement. It provides the churches with a place to meet and cooperate and thus to realize a fuller universality than any single world family will ever be able to realize. The world families remind the World Council of Churches that there is true universality only if it is rooted in truth. This interdependence needs to be mutually recognized.

This more positive view of the World Confessional Families continued at the WCC assembly in Nairobi in 1975 and at the assemblies that followed. An important factor in this was the standpoint of the CWCs on church union, something that by 1970 had been clearly stated. Even the brusque debate between 1974 and 1978 about the common vision of church unity eventually led to an understanding.[18]

Some may find it surprising that the new and more intensive role played by the CWCs in the ecumenical movement did not fundamentally change their relationship to the WCC, although it would have perhaps been a good thing to rethink this relationship completely. Still it remained at a general level of a relationship based on "partnership" – a "consultative" or a "mutually supportive" relationship that could become more concrete on a one-off basis in particular projects, but which had no structural expression. This situation is one that was thought by many to be unsatisfactory. That appears to have been the case at the WCC assembly in Harare (1998) which produced the "recommendation" that

> a process be initiated to facilitate and strengthen the relationships between the WCC and CWCs as called for in the document "Towards a Common Understanding and Vision of the World Council of Churches". The assembly recognizes the unique historical and ecclesiological contribution of CWCs to the one ecumenical movement. The proposed process aims to foster cooperation, effectiveness and efficiency in the quest for visible unity. The assembly noted with appreciation the important work already done by the conference of secretaries of CWCs, and encouraged that this conference be called upon to contribute to this work in the future.[19]

---

[18] See also Tom Stransky, "Christian World Communions", in N. Lossky et al. eds, *Dictionary of the Ecumenical Movement* 2nd ed., WCC, 2002, pp.174-75: the CWCs' secretaries' group "now organizes periodic forums to analyze bilateral conversations and compare their results with the F&O studies [of the WCC Commission on Faith and Order]. The fourth forum (1985) compared the WCC's baptism, eucharist and ministry statement (BEM) with the same three subjects in bilaterals; the fifth (1990) focused on the understanding (coherence or divergence) of the church; the sixth (1994) on the dialogues and their reception in the churches; the seventh (1997) on the emerging visions of unity; the eighth (2001) on the implications of regional agreements for international bilaterals."

[19] Diane Kessler ed., *Together on the Way: Official Report of the Eighth Assembly of the World Council of Churches*, WCC, 1999, p.165.

This process, approved by the conference of secretaries of the CWCs, was underway by late 2000, though it had still not become clear where it would lead.

BIBLIOGRAPHY

Acts of the 12th Reformed Ecumenical Synod at Yogyakarta, 2000, Grand Rapids MI, Reformed Ecumenical Synod, 2000, 480p.

Bachmann, E. Theodore and Bachmann, Mercia Brenne, *Lutheran Churches in the World: A Handbook*, Minneapolis MN, Augsburg, 1989, 631p.

Bauswein, Jean-Jacques and Vischer, Lukas eds, *The Reformed Family Worldwide: A Survey of Reformed Churches, Theological Schools, and International Organizations*, Grand Rapids MI, Eerdmans, 1999, 740p.

Bremer, Thomas, Oeldemann, Johannes and Stoltmann, Dagmar eds, *Orthodoxie im Dialog: Bilaterale Dialoge der orthodoxen und der orientalisch-orthodoxen Kirchen, 1945-1997: Eine Dokumentensammlung*, Trier, Paulinus, 1999, 578p.

Coleman, Roger ed., *Resolutions of the Twelve Lambeth Conferences: 1867-1988*, Toronto, Anglican Book Centre, 1992, 247p.

Ehrenström, Nils and Gassmann, Günther, *Confessions in Dialogue: A Survey of Bilateral Conversations among World Confessional Families 1959-1974*, WCC, 1975, 266p.

Falconer, Alan D. ed., *Eighth Forum on Bilateral Dialogues : The Implications of Regional Bilateral Agreements for the International Dialogues of Christian World Communions : John XXIII Centre, Annecy-le-Vieux, France, 14-19 May 2001*, WCC, 2002, 116p.

Frei, Hans A. ed., *Bericht über den XXV. Internationalen Altkatholiken-Kongress in Genf, 27.-31. August 1990*, Bern, Internationale Kirchliche Zeitschrift, 1990, pp.249-336.

Gassmann, Günther ed., *International Bilateral Dialogues 1965-1991: List of Commissions, Meetings, Themes and Reports*, WCC, 1991, 53p.

Gros, Jeffrey, Meyer, Harding and Rush, William G. eds, *Growth in Agreement II: Reports and Agreed Statements of Ecumenical Conversations on a World Level, 1982-1998*, WCC, 2000, 941p.

Hale, Joe ed., *Proceedings of the Seventeenth World Methodist Conference, Rio de Janeiro, Brazil, August 7-15, 1996*, London, World Methodist Council, 1996, 394p.

Ishida, Yoshiro, Meyer, Harding and Perret, Edmond, *The History and Theological Concerns of World Confessional Families*, Geneva, LWF, 1979, 80p.

Lienemann-Perrin, Christine, Vroom, Hendrik M. and Weinrich, Michael eds, *Reformed and Ecumenical: On Being Reformed in Ecumenical Encounters*, Amsterdam, Rodopi, 2000, 189p.

Meeking, Basil and Stott, John eds, *The Evangelical-Roman Catholic Dialogue on Mission, 1977-1984: A Report*, Exeter, Paternoster, 1986, 96p.

Meyer, Harding, *That All May Be One: Perceptions and Models of Ecumenicity*, Grand Rapids MI, Eerdmans, 1999, 156p.

Meyer, Harding and Vischer, Lukas eds, *Growth in Agreement: Reports and Agreed Statements of Ecumenical Conversations on a World Level*, WCC, 1984, 514p.

Nelson, E. Clifford, *The Rise of World Lutheranism: An American Perspective*, Philadelphia, Fortress, 1982, 421p.

The Official Report of the Lambeth Conference 1998: Transformation and Renewal, July 18 to August 9, 1998, Lambeth Palace, Canterbury, England, Harrisburg PA, Morehouse, 1998, 534p.

Official Report of the Ninth Assembly of the Lutheran World Federation, Hong Kong, 8-16 July 1997: In Christ – Called to Witness, Geneva, LWF, 1998, 262p.

Opocensky, Milan, *Faith Challenged by History: Reports, Lectures, Sermons and Bible Studies Given by Rev. Dr. Milan Opocensky, while General Secretary of the World Alliance of Reformed Churches*, Geneva, WARC, 2001, 296p.

Opocensky, Milan ed., *Proceedings of the 23rd General Council of the World Alliance of Reformed Churches (Presbyterian and Congregational) Held in Debrecen, Hungary, 8-20 August 1997*, Geneva, WARC, 1997, 268p.

Pradervand, Marcel, *A Century of Service: A History of the World Alliance of Reformed Churches, 1875-1975*, Edinburgh, Saint Andrew, 1975, 309p.

Puglisi, James F. ed., *A Bibliography of Interchurch and Interconfessional Theological Dialogues*, Rome, Centro Pro Unione, 1985.

Rusch, William G. and Gros, Jeffrey eds, *Deepening Communion: International Ecumenical Documents with Roman Catholic Participation*, Washington, United States Catholic Conference, 1998, 627p.

Samuel, Vinay and Sugden, Christopher eds, *Anglican Life and Witness: A Reader for the Lambeth Conference of Anglican Bishops 1998*, London, SPCK, 1997, 260p.

Schjörring, Jens Holger, Kumari, Prasanna, Hjelm, Norman A. and Mortensen, Viggo eds, *From Federation to Communion: The History of the Lutheran World Federation*, Minneapolis MN, Augsburg Fortress, 1997, 552p.

Stephenson, Alan M. G., *Anglicanism and the Lambeth Conference*, London, SPCK, 1978, 343p.

Tesfai, Yacob, *Liberation and Orthodoxy: The Promise and Failures of Interconfessional Dialogue*, Maryknoll NY, Orbis, 1996, 196p.

Vischer, Lukas, "World Communions, the WCC and the Ecumenical Movement", in *The Ecumenical Review*, 54, 1-2, Jan.-April 2002, pp.142-61.

What Kind of Unity? WCC, 1974, 131p.

World Methodist Council, *Handbook of Information*, London, World Methodist Council, 2001, 256p.

Wyrwoll, Nikolaus ed., *Orthodoxia*, Regensburg, Ostkirchliches Institut, 1998, 256p.

Part II

6

From Missions to Mission

Birgitta Larsson and Emilio Castro

The change of the title of the *International Review of Missions* to the *International Review of Mission* in 1969 might appear a minor matter. The dropping of an "s", however, represented an important development which characterizes this whole period. It reflected the change in attitude from "missions", meaning organized missionary work from Western Christendom to what were regarded as non-Christian countries, to "mission" as the task of the one, holy, catholic and apostolic church through its members wherever they are located. No longer was the world to be divided in simple fashion into "senders" and "receivers".[1]

The dropping of an "s", however, was itself not enough to change the practice of mission. It was a movement and that is one of this chapter's themes. The other, partly interwoven with the first, deals with the controversy about mission being the work of the whole church, with the whole gospel addressed to the whole person in the whole world.

MEXICO CITY 1963

The first mission and evangelism conference, after the integration of the International Missionary Council (IMC) into the World Council of Churches in 1961 and the creation of the Division, later the Commission, on World Mission and Evangelism (CWME), took place in Mexico City in 1963. Its theme was "Mission in Six Continents". This signalled a change in the focus of mission, leading to a new perception that "the missionary frontier runs around the world. It is the line that separates belief from unbelief, the unseen frontier which cuts across all other frontiers and presents the universal church with its primary missionary challenge." The conference also gave strong focus to the missionary role of the local congregation, initiating a study on "The Church for Others".[2]

The shift from missions to mission raises the question of missionary priorities. "What is to be the instrumentality of the church's obedience to the command to preach the gospel to those who have not even had a chance to hear it for the first time? If the

---

[1] Philip Potter, "From Missions to Mission: Reflections on Seventy-Five Years of the IRM", in *International Review of Mission*, April 1987, 302, p.155.

[2] *The Church for Others and the Church for the World: A Quest for Structures for Missionary Congregations*, WCC, 1967. On the missionary structure of the congregation, see also Harold E. Fey ed., *A History of the Ecumenical Movement*, vol. 2, 1948-1968, 2nd ed., WCC, 1986, pp.11, 193-95, 406-409, 424.

business of mission is every Christian's business, there is the danger that no one will make it his [or her] business to go to the two billions who still have not heard the gospel."[3]

BANGKOK 1973

Meeting under the shadow of the Vietnam war, the next CWME conference was in Bangkok in 1973 under the theme "Salvation Today". The main concerns had been debated at the WCC's Uppsala assembly in 1968, but what had ended in stalemate at Uppsala moved forward in Bangkok into a new openness of discussion.

> Uppsala failed to resolve the argument between those who hold that the gospel, primarily concerned with that in man which is eternal, is an offer of personal forgiveness and atonement with God, and those who hold that mission is not so much telling as doing – joining the God of history in what he is doing to create the kingdom of righteousness and freedom in the life of this world. By choosing the title "Salvation Today" for its 1973 conference, the Commission on World Mission and Evangelism went boldly to the heart of this theological problem.[4]

To a remarkable extent the Bangkok conference released its participants from the old polarization between personal and social salvation. A great number of third-world participants contributed to this by objecting to being involved in a theological division that had never been their reality. Bangkok said more revolutionary things than any previous conference but said them in more conservative language than had been used for a long time in WCC statements. Consider, for example, the way in which the conference spoke of salvation:

> The salvation which Christ brought, and in which we participate, offers a comprehensive wholeness in this divided life. We understand salvation as newness of life – the unfolding of true humanity in the fullness of God (Col. 2:9-10). It is salvation of the soul and the body, of the individual and society, humanity and the "groaning creation" (Rom. 8:19).

The gospel manifests itself, the Bangkok conference argued, both in the justification of the sinner *and* in socio-political justice, and thus demands both evangelism *and* active struggle on behalf of the oppressed. Alone, neither does justice to the reign of God which Jesus announced and inaugurated.

Bangkok set up a number of signposts for the future, indicating new types of relationships and organization:

1. No longer could a clear-cut distinction be made between the foreign and home mission enterprises.
2. Mission across national borders, however, was not seen as having come to an end. New possibilities of international cooperation underlined the need to see the whole world as mission territory.
3. Western countries needed the help of formerly designated missionary nations in the fulfilment of their missionary duty in the now secularized societies.
4. The "moratorium" debate began and became the focus of major concern.

---

[3] William H. Crane, Editorial, in *International Review of Mission*, April 1969, 230, p.142.
[4] John V. Taylor, "Bangkok 1972-1973", in *International Review of Mission*, 267, July 1978, p.366.

THE MORATORIUM DEBATE

The 1973 Bangkok conference was followed by lengthy discussions concerning the potential impact of a temporary moratorium on the sending, in certain situations, of mission personnel and funds. It was held that this would be a means of breaking unequal power relationships between mission agencies and local churches. Such a moratorium might provide space for local churches to reflect on their self-identity, their calling to mission, and their need to develop their own authentic response to the gospel in their individual contexts. Properly implemented, it would have the power to break patterns of dependency. At the same time a moratorium on the sending of funds and people would give the sending agencies extra resources to devote to education in mission for the members of their own churches and also to invest in new ecumenical mission initiatives.[5]

> A moratorium as the withdrawal of personnel and funds from a particular country is not advocated as a general principle nor as a solution to be implemented in many places. It is only one suggestion among many from the arsenal of the possible ways of going forward in the fulfilment of our mission. A moratorium is justified only... [if] it is the best way to fulfil our Christian mission... It must be a moratorium *for* mission, never a moratorium *of* mission.[6]

A moratorium, either total or partial, was applied in a few situations. For instance, in 1974 the United Church of Christ in the Philippines, as it moved towards self-reliance, declared a moratorium on foreign missionaries and foreign grants. However, relationships with churches and institutions abroad continued, though these gradually assumed new shapes such as exposure programmes, solidarity conferences, internships, fact-finding missions and information exchange. That same year moratorium was also the focus of major discussions at meetings of the All Africa Conference of Churches (AACC), discussions that evoked fear even as they became a catalyst for some change in bilateral relationships. But, more importantly, issues raised by the moratorium discussions were taken up in many mission bodies and local churches and proved helpful in provoking change.

Even as mission agencies affiliated with CWME cut back on numbers of missionaries, evangelical and independent missionary societies unrelated to CWME were increasing. The establishment of consortia of mission agencies relating to particular churches increased the power of the foreign bodies and limited the freedom of the local churches. New structures in fact often perpetuated patterns of domination and dependency.

MELBOURNE 1980

"The era of world missions is over; the era of world mission is beginning." With these words Emilio Castro summarized the import of the Bangkok conference in his opening address at the next CWME conference, held at Melbourne in 1980 under the theme "Your Kingdom Come".

Delegates came to Melbourne with evident frustration over the discrepancy between rhetoric and action. Persons committed for decades to the ecumenical movement had made valiant efforts to develop relationships in mission consonant with the calling to

---

[5] John Brown, "International Relationships in Mission: A Study Project", in *International Review of Mission*, 86, 342, July 1997, pp.207-48.
[6] Emilio Castro, "Bangkok, the New Opportunity", in *International Review of Mission*, 246, April 1973, pp.142-43.

share a common life in the body of Christ, but in fact little progress had been made towards an ecumenical sharing of resources. Thus it was an earnest hope that the Melbourne conference would carry forward in a meaningful way "the quest for true cooperation and unity".

One strong focus of this conference was derived from the conviction that Jesus had established a clear link between the coming of the reign of God and the proclamation of good news to the poor. It is, in fact, hard to think of a more dominant ecumenical theme over the past thirty years than "the poor". The second general conference of Latin American bishops – meeting in Medellín, Columbia, in 1968 – had coined the phrase "God's preferential option for the poor", a key concept for theologies of liberation. During the 1970s, a series of WCC studies, programmes and publications echoed this concern.

It was at Melbourne that "the poor" were singled out as the crucial criterion for testing the effectiveness of mission. It was affirmed that the church's relation to the poor was not simply a question of social ethics; it was also a matter of faithfulness to the gospel itself. Christ is the centre of the world's life, but he paradoxically demonstrates that centrality by moving towards those who are on the margins – to the point of dying "outside the gate" (Heb. 13:12). The church, therefore, can speak neither of God's reign nor of its own mission without a deep concern for those who live in physical and material poverty. Such concern is not only a matter of speaking to the poor or for them, but of listening to their distinctive voices and standing with them against political and economic systems of oppressive inequity.

At Melbourne it was affirmed that

> [t]he church of Jesus Christ is called to preach good news to the poor, even as its Lord has done in his ministry announcing the kingdom of God. The churches cannot neglect this evangelistic task. Most of the world's people are poor, and they are waiting for a witness to the gospel that will really be good news. (section 1)

The mission which is conscious of the kingdom will be concerned for liberation, not oppression; justice, not exploitation; fullness, not deprivation; freedom, not slavery.

> Who but the church of the poor can preach with integrity to the poor of the world? In these ways we see the poor churches of the world as the bearers of mission: world mission and evangelism may now be primarily in their hands. (section 4)

THE CHURCH'S HEALING MISSION

One of the vital dimensions of the church's mission which was reaffirmed strongly and creatively was the healing ministry of the church, especially through the work of the Christian Medical Commission (CMC) of the WCC. From apostolic times, healing has been an essential component of the ministry of the church, tracing its origin to Jesus' own ministry of healing. That ministry set in motion a long history of services, both through prayers for the sick in the liturgical life of the church and through the caring solicitude of diaconic ministers and the hospitality provided by monastic orders. In the revival of the cross-cultural mission of the Western churches, especially in the 19th and early 20th centuries, mission also meant the propagation of Western forms of medicine. Clinics and hospitals were a normal sign of missionary outposts in Asia, Africa and Latin America.

In the 1960s, two developments called for the renewed attention of church leaders to these ministries of the church. First, the overall processes of decolonization that brought new independent nations into being made those countries eager to affirm their national identity by linking responsibility for health concerns to the state. In many countries, especially in Africa, health facilities were nationalized and those provided by the churches integrated into national planning. Second, technological progress in Western medicine produced an enormous growth in the cost of hospital services. In what seemed an inevitable pattern, health services that were intended for the poor became more and more a privilege of the social and economic elite. It was necessary to think afresh, both to reaffirm that health care belongs to the core of Christian mission, and also to redefine the prophetic servant ministry of the churches in new circumstances. This process of reflection and consultation was initiated in 1964, taking ecumenical thinking and missionary practice into new areas.

The CMC became a pioneer movement in helping not only churches but even the World Health Organization to rethink healing priorities for today. An initial consultation on the healing ministry of the church, called by the Lutheran World Federation and the Division of World Mission and Evangelism of the WCC, took place in Tübingen, Germany, in 1964 and another was held in 1968. The concern of the first consultation was to provide an agenda for an extended programme of consultations, training and organization in all continents. The findings of consultations were made available through *Contact*, a magazine distributed widely in several languages, which became a successful WCC publication, both in its wide circulation and the impact of its contents. The CMC was created following the second Tübingen consultation in 1968 to assist the member churches to deal with questions being raised about medical missions in the third world and to encourage church-related health programmes to develop ecumenical cooperation.

According to the report of the CMC to the WCC central committee in Dresden in 1981, recurring themes in these broadly ecumenical meetings included:

1. Health and wholeness: "Health is a dynamic state of well-being of the individual – physical, mental, social and spiritual – of being in harmony with each other, with the natural environment and with God".
2. Traditional healing systems are being explored to maximize useful and effective practices and discourage harmful ones, and help these find their place in today's concern for healing.
3. The relationship of health to justice has emerged as a concern in many parts of the world.
4. Responsibility for health must be shared by all those who live together, enabling all to realize fully their human potential.
5. The church has its role to play; renewal of the church's mission and ministry can be helped with a new concern for healing, moving all towards "life in all its fullness".[7]

This synthetic agenda, formulated at Dresden, was discussed at local and regional levels all over the world, and several findings emerged from the process, including the following:

1. An inclusive definition of health which does justice to the human person, both in recognizing him/her not only as a person with an illness, but also as a person in relationship with neighbours, with nature and with God, so that health is not only a private matter but a matter of solidarity, both in the individual's responsibility to take care of himself or herself as a contribution to the health of society, and also in the responsibility of the whole society to care for each of its members.

---

[7] WCC Central Committee, *Minutes of the Thirty-Third Meeting, Dresden, GDR*, 1981, p.31.

Above all, the affirmation of the whole person is the commanding value to be preserved, and it is the health of society at large which is the target of the whole endeavour.

2. This definition of health, involving all relationships, immediately raises the issue of justice in relation to health policies. Most nations are marked by impressive technologically developed institutions of health care alongside millions of deprived people who do not have access to those facilities. Since most of the pharmaceutical industry operates under the profit motive, the poor often do not have access to advanced products of medical research, and that research itself concentrates on the search for medicines or stimulants which will produce immediate financial gain at the expense of efforts to combat diseases, like malaria, which basically afflict poor people and poor countries. The CMC addressed these issues at different levels. It challenged the ministries of the church to exercise imagination in order to put resources at the service of the poorest of the poor. In many countries, national coordinating committees were established in order to maximize efficiency and to provide a place where Christian concern for poor people could be brought to the attention of all health-care professionals at work in the area.

At the world level, the CMC challenged governments and international institutions to accept *health for all* as a motivation and goal to be reached by humanity as a whole over a short period of time.

At the national level, there was insistence on the need for national health planning agencies to prioritize existing resources, both state and private, in service to the less privileged. The Vancouver assembly of the WCC in 1983 dealt with healing and sharing life in community. The report states:

> Many nations, with only limited resources, must order their national priorities accordingly; others, with adequate resources, have not justly managed their priorities. In all cases the question of justice in the distribution of these resources is of paramount importance. In so many countries only a privileged few have access to such health care. Where the doctrine of national security based on the force of arms prevails, the possibilities of meeting basic health care needs decrease. In such cases, the urban and rural poor always lose out. While the emphasis on distributive justice is vital for developing countries, many industrialized and affluent states also have the problem of unjust distribution of resources. The urban poor living alongside health care institutions of high excellence still suffer from malnutrition and appalling health conditions. The church expresses its concern over the growing hunger and malnutrition in *all* regions and recognizes the need to tackle the complex questions surrounding the local and global supply of food.[8]

At community levels, the CMC emphasized the need to direct the existing resources of the community to provide basic primary health care. In 1977 the Chiang Mai, Thailand, consultation on dialogue with people of living faiths and ideologies stated,

> In traditional culture, disease and sickness are not only physical, but affect the whole person. Healing is therefore not only a response to the physical manifestation of sickness and disease but is related to the whole mental and spiritual outlook of the person. When a person falls ill, it is moreover not only the problem of the individual and his or her family, but is a concern of the community. It is the community which provides the active, dynamic context for healing to take place. The response to sickness in such communities points towards the hidden dimension upon which all interpersonal relations are founded, and both

---

[8] David Gill ed., *Gathered for Life: Official Report, Sixth Assembly World Council of Churches, Vancouver, Canada, 24 July 10 August, 1983*, WCC, 1983, p.65.

the above aspects help to sensitize the Christian community to the importance and relevance of the biblical understanding of sickness and healing for our own times.[9]

The CMC has encouraged the establishment of community health-based programmes which incorporate not only professionals but, more than that, involve the training of gifted people both to provide elementary fundamental services and to create an atmosphere of reciprocal support at every local level. Symbolic but effective actions, such as ongoing surveys of pharmaceutical products so as to produce a select list of appropriate commodities for use in basic primary health care, have been offered by the Christian Medical Commission. Also, experiments in popular medicine, as in China, have been the object of careful analysis and publicity so that people already doing the work could learn from such alternative health care services. The stimulus to train national, provincial or local workers in health needs has been a constant element of the work of the CMC.

At local levels, parishes were challenged to become caring communities where reciprocal support is given and received, where resources are made available for the health of the whole community, and where in a participatory process all assume responsibility for the wellbeing of the whole of society. Churches are encouraged to rediscover afresh their ministry of concern for the poor and the sick through prayer and symbolic actions, releasing spiritual strength to support those who are suffering. Intercessory prayer for the sick and anointing with oil are practices which should be considered afresh and even though these Christian acts have been misused in many quarters, their potential for conveying profound meaning and new spiritual depth needs to be fully explored and encouraged. The healing ministry of the church remains a normal, essential component of the total mission of the church. In new situations, this must be done in interaction with all other sectors of society concerned with the promotion of humanity as a whole and with justice for all.

URBAN RURAL MISSION

During this period, one of the best illustrations of the missionary concern for the poor, as enunciated at Melbourne, was the movement called Urban Rural Mission (URM). The 1961 assembly of the WCC in New Delhi placed on the agenda of the Council for the first time the issue of urbanization and industrialization.

From its beginning URM was not merely a programme creation of the WCC, but was a discovery of the living reality of Christian communities all over the world dedicated to the common struggle for a new day under the inspiration of the reign of God. What the WCC provided was recognition, cross-fertilization, aid for training, and above all emphasis on the need to organize ordinary people to overcome their oppression. Organization was always a key word in the life of URM groups.

Initially, this movement was named Urban Evangelism because a first discovery was the alienation of the church and its message from the reality of the oppressed poor in newly urbanized and heavily industrialized situations. A second stage was to widen the scope of the groups which then called themselves Urban Mission, embracing in this way the conviction that mission is the sending of Christians into the world in the steps of

---

[9] *Dialogue in Community: Statement and Reports of a Theological Consultation, Chiang Mai, Thailand, 18-27 April 1977*, WCC, 1977, pp.37-38.

Jesus and with his same aim of announcing the reign of God. Later it was discovered and recognized that the urban poor had common roots and close relations with the rural poor. It would have been a failure not to recognize this dynamic relationship between the rural and urban populations. From this recognition came the present name of the movement, Urban Rural Mission:

> Urban Rural Mission is a movement of human communities organized for and with the poor to manifest God's liberating purpose in specific situations where people are struggling to overcome oppression and alienation of all kinds. It is a worldwide movement in the sense that it has a certain common vision, but it is not like a political party or a central office with central authority to organize the activities carried out by all those connected with it. The Urban Rural Mission office of the World Council of Churches repeats and repeats: "We do not have a network; we do not have anything. We are in relation to people who gather together in concrete struggles, and we are there to be servants, to provide some service, some liaison. In that sense, a worldwide movement – yes; but one which only exists in and through the many and various local groups which are consciously participating in God's missionary movement, in the proclamation of the gospel in the midst of struggles for justice and human community."
>
> It is a spiritual movement of solidarity expressed in specific communities which have organized themselves for the struggle to overcome specific forms of alienation. They may be neighbourhood groups, students, professional people or trade unions, but common to all of them in one way or another are: the knowledge of sharing in God's mission, a real community of mutual support, and organization for action and involvement in clearly defined activities and struggles.[10]

It is clear that the main aim of every group belonging to URM is to be concerned with local struggles, particular battles to overcome injustice, and particular ways to plant signposts of the kingdom which is to come. But precisely because of this frontier character of their mission, it is unavoidable that their relations to the institutional churches are marked by creative tension. These groups have come out of the churches and have been nurtured and inspired by the churches, but in their concrete engagements they assume a freedom of operation that the official church is sometimes not able to follow or recognize. In a sense, then, these groups are exploratory forerunners of the Christian mission in the world, running the risk of being so immersed in the world that they might forget from where they come, but bringing to the human situation something of the light of the gospel of Jesus Christ.

This tension has raised important theological questions that have enriched the missiological discussion of the last decades. URM raised

> penetrating and sharp questions about the appropriateness and relevance of current mission thinking and strategy; about the relationship of the human struggle to the kingdom of God; about the ecclesiological implications of community organizing; about theological, political and social attitudes to the ownership and use of church land and property, etc. There can be no doubt, however, that the central question which was raised time and time again was that of justice and the church's understanding of and preparedness to support, identify and put itself on the line with the struggles for justice of the poor, Indigenous Peoples, women, peasants and workers. These are not entirely new questions, but they have again been raised, with renewed passion and anger, from the perspective of the oppressed and those who daily live, work and struggle with them.[11]

---

[10] *Celebration and Challenge: URM '87 Manila, April 1-6, 1987*, WCC, 1987, pp.44-45.
[11] *Ibid.*, p.3.

A similar kind of tension has arisen in several parts of the world with city or state political authorities where URM groups are at work. From the self-understanding of people organized to struggle against poverty and oppression inevitably comes confrontation with the existing situation of oppression or deprivation. URM, at least in its own self-understanding, is not a partisan political group, but it is a component of society's struggles and tensions that points towards a solution to prevailing problems. In a certain sense, then, conflict seems to be unavoidable.

But in a second area of tension it is the other way around. There is always a temptation to act politically, especially in those countries where URM groups have been successful in influencing the struggles of workers or peasants – the considerable temptation to recruit the leadership of URM, or even the URM organization itself, for a particular political purpose.

> This being so, there is bound to be a necessary – and hopefully constructive – tension with the secular political movements which are likewise engaged in promoting the participation of marginal sectors in the social and political struggles of the community. URM does not set itself up in competition with these movements – much to the contrary! – but neither is it ready to let itself disappear, absorbed by popular organizations of particular political signs... The debate between losing ourselves in the new political instrument or the preservation of our [URM] identity as a... contribution to the kingdom of God that embraces that movement but is not limited to it [is an ongoing one].[12]

URM makes

> no claim to hold the solution to all human problems, nor to be God's only instruments in the transformation of society... Because our horizon is the kingdom of God, which consequently involves and invites all human beings, we are open and eager for the gifts and abilities which God has certainly given to the popular organizations which are trying to transform human history. In supporting or collaborating with others in this way we do not lose our identity, but enrich it through this vision and awareness which give the strength to resist, to endure, to persevere... The word "resistance" is used here as a synonym for mission in URM's historic experience...[13]

In another document from the WCC, the notion of "resistance" is elaborated:

> The double – reactive and proactive – character of resistance is seen as a prophetic task. The *denouncement* of a situation of injustice and inhumanity is simultaneously accompanied by the *announcement* of possibilities of overcoming that situation – even when there seems to be no objective basis or corroboration for such an announcement... Jesus' proclamation, in word and deed, of the kingdom of God was the announcement of the dream (or vision) of God and of people that life, not death, reigns. Worship (ascribing to God worth, honour and obedience) is therefore a form of resistance to all that is false, to all that negates life. It says no to injustice and yes to life, through the proclamation of the cross and resurrection of Jesus.[14]

URM is an excellent illustration of the prevailing emphasis of the World Council of Churches on God's preferential option for the poor and on the privileged position they hold in God's own missionary plan. In the search for a church for the poor, with the poor, of the poor, URM plays a vital role.

---

[12] *Ibid.*, pp.48-49.
[13] *Ibid.*, p.49.
[14] Report of a consultation on resistance as a form of Christian witness, Recife, Brazil, 1985, in Hugh Lewin ed., *A Community of Clowns: Testimonies of People in Urban Rural Mission*, WCC, 1987, p.302.

THE MISSIONARY VOCATION OF ORTHODOXY

Another point of emphasis at the 1980 CWME conference in Melbourne was an affirmation of the church as a sacrament of the kingdom, the sacramental reality of the church manifested in the celebration of the eucharist. The invitation at the eucharist is to share in the pilgrim loaf, missionary bread, food for people on the march.[15]

This eucharistic language points to the important contribution of Orthodox theology and missionary practice to the ecumenical debate. While there is a long tradition of Orthodox missionary witness, it must be acknowledged that in neither Protestant nor Roman Catholic circles has there been strong awareness of that witness. For generations, if not centuries, there has been a tradition of reciprocal caricature. In the West, a view of Orthodoxy as quietistic has prevailed, while in Orthodox churches Protestant and Roman Catholic missionary activity has been rejected as proselytism rather than evangelism. The ethnic lines which define most Orthodox churches, their frequent location in Muslim territories which inhibits visible evangelistic initiatives, the limitations and persecutions inflicted by communist regimes in Eastern Europe, and practical limitations to work in the diaspora for the preservation of the Orthodox faith of migrants – all of these factors have contributed to the distorted view of Orthodoxy frequently held by Western churches.

To be sure, the Orthodox also have a distorted vision of Protestantism and Roman Catholicism because in a number of regions they have experienced the presence of Protestant and Catholic missions as a de facto attempt to convert Orthodox from one church to another. This helps to explain the rich debate on common witness and proselytism which has taken place during the last thirty years, not only among churches related to the WCC but also with Evangelicals and, of course, with Roman Catholics. This perception of Western missions may well have been the reason for Patriarch Athenagoras's negative vote in relation to the integration of the International Missionary Council and the World Council of Churches in 1961.

From the very beginning of the modern ecumenical movement, there has been important Orthodox participation. The Orthodox theological view of the being and identity of the church – ecclesiology – has contributed greatly to the work of Faith and Order. Nevertheless, a vital, polemic and fruitful encounter concerning missiological issues began to take place immediately after the 1973 CWME conference in Bangkok where "Salvation Today" was the theme. This fundamental theological issue, salvation, is obviously of central importance for the life and teaching of all churches, but especially for the Orthodox churches. They participated fully in the conference, but immediately on its conclusion an official letter from the Russian Orthodox Church indicated deep concern over what they held to be serious shortcomings of the event. In a letter to the moderator of the central committee of the WCC, M.M. Thomas, they affirmed:

> Perplexity and great regret are aroused by the fact that in the "Letter to the Churches" [from the Bangkok conference] there is no significant reference – and primarily from the pastoral point of view – to that dimension of the process of salvation without which the very concept of salvation loses its implication. Nothing is said about the ultimate goal of salvation, in other words, about eternal life in God; nor does anything point to the moral

---

[15] Editorial, in *International Review of Mission*, Oct. 1980-Jan. 1981, pp.276-77.

improvement and perfection as an indispensable condition for the achievement of this goal.[16]

While the Bangkok findings could be defended as being more holistic and spiritual than this and other interpretations recognized at the time, the issues raised both in the conference and in the letter of Patriarch Pimen and the holy synod of the Russian Orthodox Church were important enough to bring about a serious encounter of differing missiological perspectives. It was necessary to overcome the barriers of different theological languages in order to address together the common missionary reality in the world. On the one hand, the liturgical and mystical language of the Orthodox churches had to be seen as able to address concrete historical realities and, on the other hand, the so-called "secular" theological language of the West, using so much of the terminology of the social sciences, had to be seen as able also to give testimony to the eternal kingdom of God.[17] After the long consultative process concerning missiology which succeeded this exchange, it is possible to summarize conclusions – not always agreements – in three points.

First, the churches all came to appreciate Tradition, not simply as a reference to past ages or as limited to the canonical authority which assesses doctrinal truths, but more fundamentally as the actual missionary transmission of the faith of the church from past generations to present and future generations. Tradition is to be understood precisely as the word indicates: to transmit, to pass on, to handle. It is a missionary concern. In countries where evangelization was prohibited, Orthodox churches have nevertheless been able to keep the loyalty and faithfulness of the Christian community, passing on the witness of faith through generations. One could speak of a chronological dimension of mission. In the former Soviet Union where all organized Christian education for children was forbidden, it was left to the *babushkas*, the grandmothers, to explain the liturgy and to transmit the story of the gospel and the life of the saints to the children at home. This chronological, generation-wide perspective on mission is not to be confused with quietism; it is resistance, endurance, faithfulness, and has much to teach to the whole of Christianity.

Second, together with the missionary understanding of Tradition, the churches came to appreciate the centripetal dimension of mission. Protestants and Catholics have emphasized the centrifugal, activist side of the missionary calling, its sending aspect. The Orthodox, remembering the situation of the early church where "the Lord added daily those that were being saved", have underlined the beauty and depth of liturgical life conceived as an evangelistic invitation. The Romanian Orthodox theologian Ion Bria has emphasized that it is this sense of praise and beauty in the divine liturgy of the Orthodox church that is central to the centripetal mission:

> One of the most impressive elements in Orthodox spirituality is the impulse of the faithful of all categories and ages to be totally involved in the action of the liturgy as a feast, the desire to see, to enter into the holy place, to concelebrate and to take holy communion. Liturgy is not a matter of time, but of moving towards the glorious high throne to praise the presence of God. In this physical movement towards the altar it is impossible to be uninvolved or to remain motionless. Here is a unique spirit of conviviality and collective pil-

[16] "Message of Patriarch Pimen of Moscow and All Russia and the Holy Synod of the Russian Orthodox Church to the Central Committee of the WCC", in Constantin G. Patelos ed., *The Orthodox Church in the Ecumenical Movement*, WCC, 1978, p.49.

[17] Ans J. van der Bent, *Vital Ecumenical Concerns*, WCC, 1986, pp.36-37.

grimage in a space which symbolizes the beauty of God. People need to rediscover the beautiful sacred nature of their life and milieu. This is not simply a matter of popular religiosity perpetuating humble piety. It is the biblical understanding of the church as a priestly people standing before God, an inexhaustible people who are receiving divine resources. Often people place food and drink in the middle of the church to be blessed by the priest – food for pilgrims.[18]

Finally, the churches have come to appreciate the emergence of the expression used by Bria as the title of his book, "the liturgy after the Liturgy". Here is an attempt to express a sacramental understanding of life and of Christian participation in history. The phrase does not simply connote a traditional affirmation that good works follow from liturgical practice. It leads, rather, to a consideration of the world as an extension of the altar and of service rendered to one's neighbour as a sacramental service rendered to God. Boris Bobrinskoy has written,

> The sending forth of the faithful at the end of the liturgy has a profound symbolic and sacramental significance. The *ite misa est* of the Roman mass or the "let us go in peace" of the Byzantine liturgies, this "sending out" of the faithful, is only the announcement of the end of the first stage of the eucharist... What follows is not so much an "exit" from the church as an "entrance" by the church into the world, continuing the sending forth of the disciples by the risen Lord (Matt. 28:18-20; Mark 16:15-20) in the power of the Spirit of Pentecost. When we leave the church, we enter another mode of the liturgy which is the "liturgy after the Liturgy". This is the passage from Sunday, the day of the Lord, to the week.[19]

Ion Bria's own summary of the Orthodox understanding of mission is eloquent:

> There is a liturgy after the Liturgy because Christians pursue their witness and vocation outside the temple, in the street, in social halls, in the wider society. Nourished by the eucharist, the pilgrim bread, the food for missionaries and evangelists, Christians are sent out – "Go forth in peace, in the name of the Lord" – to witness in faithful discipleship in the common round of daily life. Their authority flows from their liturgical sending, which becomes fruitful through personal authenticity. The typology of mission as liturgy after the liturgy can help us to understand the connections among the various forms and definitions of mission: as proclamation and invitation emphasizing personal salvation, as response to God's merciful will for the whole of humanity, as actions of service aimed at the transformation of society, as witness to God's justice and righteousness against inhuman conditions and unjust social structures, as a means for personal discipleship and holiness, as pastoral care responding to God's compassion for lost humanity.[20]

The full participation of Orthodox believers and theologians in the missiological debate has enriched ecumenical thought and Christian practice. The Bangkok conference of 1973 attempted to formulate a concept of mission and salvation that avoided a schizophrenic division between faith as eternal salvation and justice for the poor. It attempted to set forth a holistic understanding of salvation. Today, after years of debate and common search, Orthodox, Roman Catholics and Protestants are able deeply to communicate a shared responsibility and hope for God's entire creation.

---

[18] Ion Bria, *The Liturgy after the Liturgy: Mission and Witness from an Orthodox Perspective*, WCC, 1996, p.76.
[19] Boris Bobrinskoy, "Prière du coeur et eucharistie", in Ioan I. Ica ed., *Person and Communion: Homage to Fr D. Staniloae,* Sibiu, Romania, 1993, p.631. Quoted in Bria, *The Liturgy*, p.85.
[20] *The Liturgy*, p.87.

ECUMENICAL AFFIRMATION

Years of ecumenical reflection on evangelism culminated in the document "Mission and Evangelism: An Ecumenical Affirmation" adopted by the WCC's central committee in 1982. This statement made clear that "the spiritual gospel" and "the material gospel" are identical in the gospel of Jesus. "Liberation, development, humanization and explicit evangelism are all integral parts of mission."[21] The document demonstrates that churches of diverse traditions can not only share certain basic convictions but also engage in common practice of mission and evangelism. Both the document's trinitarian basis and its Christological concentration attracted the support of many WCC member churches. The mission of the church was not to be found in an activist busyness devoted to assigned institutional tasks; rather mission is participation in the inner life of the Trinity.

Mission and Evangelism: An Ecumenical Affirmation, which emphasized the importance of planting local congregations as the fundamental Christian missionary strategy, was an attempt to break false dichotomies.

> A proclamation that does not hold forth the promises of the justice of the kingdom to the poor on earth is a caricature of the gospel; but Christian participation in the struggles for justice which does not point towards the promises of the kingdom also makes a caricature of a Christian understanding of justice.[22]

SAN ANTONIO 1989

The CWME conference in San Antonio, US, in 1989 was held under the theme "Your Will Be Done: Mission in Christ's Way". This conference confirmed the perspective of the ecumenical affirmation,

> We are called to exercise our mission in this context of human struggle, and challenged to keep the earth alive and to promote human dignity, since the living God is both Creator of heaven and earth and Protector of the cause of the widow, the orphan, the poor and the stranger.[23]

To respond to all this was part of mission, even as inviting people to put their trust in God was part of mission. The material gospel and the spiritual gospel were to be one even as they were equal parts of the ministry of Jesus.

Some say that for the first time since the 1963 Mexico City conference, evangelical voices were heard at San Antonio. Groups of concerned Evangelicals at San Antonio wrote a letter to the conference of the Lausanne movement meeting at the same time in Manila, the Philippines, urging that it become more holistic. These Evangelicals expressed appreciation for the rich diversity of those present at San Antonio – youth, people from the third world, a balance of lay and ordained, and women whose gifts were equal to those of men. All this was commended to the Lausanne movement. Through worship and Bible studies Evangelicals had, at San Antonio, the chance to hear and learn from other Christian traditions equally committed to following Christ. They felt that the expression of concern for the rights of the poor must not be understood as showing that

---

[21] Emilio Castro, "Evangelism", in Nicholas Lossky et al. eds, *Dictionary of the Ecumenical Movement*, 2nd ed. WCC, 2002, p.448.

[22] WCC, 1982, §34.

[23] Frederick R. Wilson ed., *The San Antonio Report: Your Will Be Done: Mission in Christ's Way*, WCC, 1990, p.26.

the WCC had relinquished the central concern of devotion and faithful witness to Jesus. For too long, they said, the WCC has

> been perceived as being involved with justice without relation to the justification of sin-
> ners; and the Lausanne movement has been perceived as being concerned for personal jus-
> tification without reference to the personal and corporate sin at the root of injustice. With-
> out an affirmation of the invitation of Jesus to repentance, faith and discipleship, mission
> among the poor for justice can become indistinguishable from the economic development
> notion of eradicating poverty without respect to the many cultural and human values of
> poor communities.[24]

Delegates were also invited to appreciate the tension between evangelism and dialogue, affirming both that "salvation is offered to the whole of creation through Jesus Christ" and the need to enter into a genuinely open, searching dialogue with neighbours of other faiths. "We appreciate this tension", said the delegates in the San Antonio report, "and do not attempt to resolve it."

THE LAUSANNE MOVEMENT AND THE EVANGELICAL CRITIQUE OF CWME CONFERENCES

The understanding of mission as the work of the whole church proclaiming the whole gospel to the whole person in the whole world has been challenged in different ways. The Uppsala assembly had reinforced Evangelicals' negative evaluation of the WCC and CWME in particular. They therefore organized their own International Congress on World Evangelization, meeting at Lausanne in 1974 under the theme "The Unfinished Task of World Evangelization". Although the formation of a new version of the Interna-tional Missionary Council was not envisaged, the Lausanne Committee for World Evan-gelization (LCWE) was formed at this meeting with an expressed concern for both transnational and national evangelism, in particular the evangelization of the "un-reached". The desire to "frame a biblical declaration on evangelism" led to the writing of the Lausanne Covenant, which was extensively discussed and subsequently accepted by those present. While no single document can represent all Evangelicals, this covenant is widely acknowledged as a milestone that reflects the spirit and stance of the evangelical community in the late 20th century.[25]

The LCWE sponsored a consultation of more than eight hundred participants in Pat-taya, Thailand, in 1980 at a time close to that of the Melbourne missionary conference. A third international congress was held in Manila in 1989 shortly after the San Antonio conference. There was increased attention both in the programme at Manila and in what came to be known as "the Manila Manifesto" to the social implications of the gospel as integral to but not superseding its proclamation.

The critique of CWME that provoked the establishment of the Lausanne Movement was, to be sure, also heard elsewhere. There was at Bangkok in 1973 a wholeness of the truly human and truly holy, the personal and social, that seemed to be lacking at Mel-bourne in 1980 and San Antonio in 1989. Melbourne seemed to offer a clear sign that the constituency had forgotten or was ignoring that essential part of CWME's mandate which dealt with the explicit proclamation of the gospel to the "unreached". Melbourne

[24] "Letter from Those with Evangelical Concerns at San Antonio to the Lausanne II Conference", in *In-ternational Review of Mission*, 78, 311-12 July-Oct. 1989, pp.431ff.
[25] Robert T. Coote, "Lausanne Covenant", in *Dictionary of the Ecumenical Movement*, pp.673-74.

was criticized for having a deep passion for the poor but not for the lost, and for having more concern with the renewal of the church than with the evangelistic mobilization of congregations for mission. At Melbourne and San Antonio the classical terms "mission" and "evangelism" became overloaded, so that mission and evangelism, being burdened with too much meaning, ended up meaning and signifying too little. CWME conferences became mini versions of WCC assemblies, with little that was distinctive in their agendas.

The challenge to the ecumenical movement posed by the LCWE meetings, especially Lausanne and Manilla, was reflected in "open letters" written by evangelical participants at the Vancouver (1983) and Canberra (1991) assemblies of the WCC. These letters asked the WCC to put greater emphasis, in its work on mission, on the invitational dimension of evangelism, and to give more attention to the spiritual alienation of individuals from God and, thus, to the redemptive dimension of Christ's suffering on the cross.

Such differences have become familiar since they divide most churches. At the same time, however, there have been significant signs of convergence. At the WCC's Nairobi assembly, M.M. Thomas, then moderator of the central committee, identified three points of agreement between the report of the Bangkok conference, the Lausanne Covenant and the 1975 encyclical of Paul VI, *Evangelii Nuntiandi* ("Evangelization in the Modern World"). Thomas drew attention to: (a) their affirmation that the gospel addresses both the spiritual and material dimensions of life, although the Lausanne Covenant emphasizes that social action is not evangelism and political liberation is not salvation; (b) their effort to relate evangelism to the unity and renewal of the church; and (c) their recognition of the realities of the contemporary world, including the renaissance of cultures and religions.

The Roman Catholic missiologist Tom Stransky, however, has significantly observed that the paradigm of "Christian power" is shifting from a simple competitive Roman Catholic versus Protestant/Orthodox, to mainstream Protestant/Roman Catholic/Orthodox versus Evangelical. Both sides are serious about the whole gospel of the whole church to the whole world. However, at a distance – not through dialogue – each side has made too many over-facile generalizations concerning the other.[26]

GOSPEL AND CULTURE

The relationship between gospel and culture became a theme of great importance in later ecumenical conversations. The ecumenical movement as a "dialogue of cultures" was the focus of discussions at the time of Philip Potter's retirement as WCC general secretary in 1984. It was also the topic of two sessions of the graduate school of the Bossey Ecumenical Institute, and was addressed in two publications of the WCC's Bible study secretariat, *On A Friday Noon* and *Immanuel*, both by Hans-Ruedi Weber.[27] The issue sparked considerable controversy at the WCC Canberra assembly in 1991.

The question of cultural identity, dramatically posed by Vatican II's instruction that the mass should normally be said in the vernacular , was on the agenda of the Bangkok conference in 1973: "Culture", said the delegates, "shapes the human voice that answers

---

[26] Thomas Stransky, "From Mexico City to San Antonio", in *International Review of Mission*, 313, Jan. 1990, pp.40-53.

[27] *On a Friday Noon: Meditations under the Cross*, WCC, 1979; *Immanuel: The Coming of Jesus in Art and the Bible*, WCC, 1984.

the voice of Christ." From the beginning of the modern ecumenical movement, the missionary imperative has usually provided the framework for considering issues of gospel and culture. The ignorance of, insensitivity to and outright rejection of other cultures as "primitive and pagan" in early mission history has been well documented. Yet this is only one side of the story of missionary engagement in other lands. Some missionaries laboured tirelessly to preserve local culture by committing ancient stories to writing and making them known to the world. Some tried, together with converts, to work out the meaning of the gospel in the context of a specific culture. In almost all early missionary debates strong voices challenged insensitivity to other peoples and traditions, appealing for a new look at the assumptions that undergird the missionary enterprise. It is surprising, however, that little or no specific discussion of gospel and culture is to be found in the reports of the early mission conferences.[28]

The Bangkok conference had a section on "Culture and Identity", stating in its report,

> "[c]ulture shapes the human voice that answers the voice of Christ". Many Christians who have received the gospel through Western agents continue to ask the question "Is it really I who answer Christ?"... How can we responsibly answer the voice of Christ instead of copying foreign models of conversion – imposed, not truly accepted?[29]

The Nairobi assembly emphasized cultural plurality as a blessing that should be preserved, arguing that "[n]o culture is closer to Jesus Christ than any other culture. Jesus Christ restores what is truly human in any culture and frees us to be open to other cultures". Vancouver provided a great step forward through its section on "Witnessing in a Divided World". The report offered a useful summary of the steps to be taken in the study of gospel and culture, incorporating many elements of the debate up to that time – recognition of the cultural imperialism of the past, issues of theological plurality as the gospel took root in several cultures, and the problems of cross-cultural mission.[30]

Even though it was decided that the question of gospel and culture should permeate the work of every section at the San Antonio conference, the WCC did not show itself to be successful in dealing with the issue until the Canberra assembly in 1991. The presence and direct challenge of the Aboriginal peoples in Australia made gospel and culture a living reality that had to be encountered, not just another intellectual issue to be discussed. In addition to that was the controversial presentation by the young Korean theologian Chung Hyun Kyung. She challenged the assembly by relating the gospel to contemporary attempts to understand the faith in context. Her exploration of dance in Korean and Australian Aboriginal spirituality, and her Asian pneumatology drawing on popular understandings of the *han* spirits of righteous anger and *ki* (or *ch'i*) as life-affirming energy, excited the imagination of some listeners while prompting suspicion of religious syncretism in others.[31] The subsequent debate at Canberra brought a renewed urgency into the ecumenical exploration of gospel and culture. The worldwide study project that followed resulted in about sixty study groups around the world and

---

[28] S. Wesley Ariarajah, *Gospel and Culture: An Ongoing Discussion within the Ecumenical Movement*, WCC, 1994, pp.2-3.

[29] *Bangkok Assembly 1973 : Minutes and Report of the Assembly of the Commission on World Mission and Evangelism of the World Council of Churches, December 31, 1972 and January 9-12, 1973*, WCC, 1973, p.73.

[30] *Gospel and Culture*, p.39.

[31] Chung Hyun Kyung, "Come, Holy Spirit, Renew the Whole Creation", in Michael Kinnamon ed., *Signs of the Spirit: Official Report, Seventh Assembly*, WCC, 1991, pp.37-47.

produced, among other things, a series of 18 small booklets or pamphlets, *Gospel and Cultures*. All this formed the background for the final 20th-century world conference on mission and evangelism.

SALVADOR 1996

At the end of the century it was appropriate that a global mission conference also deal with the issue of gospel and cultures. The world was being torn apart by two opposing forces: a search for cultural roots and ethnic identities that was becoming increasingly separatistic and destructive, and globalization, the force of which stifles struggles for the autonomy of the local and the particular.[32] Accordingly, the conference on world mission and evangelism at the end of 1996 had the theme "Called to One Hope: The Gospel in Diverse Cultures". The venue for the conference, Salvador de Bahia, Brazil, a microcosm of the world's diversity of cultures and spiritualities, was well suited for the work of a conference in which participants tried better to understand the way in which the gospel challenges all human cultures and how culture itself can give a clearer understanding of the gospel. "The gospel in diverse cultures" was a central theme – not simply that the gospel must be taken *to* every culture; it must be understood *within* a culture for its power to be unleashed. This eleventh and last mission conference of the century stood in stark contrast to the first held in Edinburgh in 1910, where the vast majority of participants were European and North American. At Salvador, more than six hundred Christians participated from a wide spectrum of cultures spanning sixty nations.

The conference concluded

> that it is still the church's primary calling to pursue the mission of God in God's world through the grace and goodness of Jesus Christ. Yet this mission, history-long, worldwide, cannot be seen today in narrow ways – it must be an every-member mission, from everywhere to everywhere, involving every aspect of life in a rapidly changing world of many cultures now interacting and overlapping.[33]

The conference showed clearly that for the gospel to be most fruitful it needs to be both true to itself and incarnated, rooted in the culture of those to whom it is addressed.

Thus Salvador explored the creative tension between contextuality and catholicity. Identity and context, on the one hand, and communion and catholicity, on the other, do not necessarily stand in opposition to one another – they could be complementary. The gospel is not the property of any particular culture. The unique spiritualities of different people have to be respected as integral expressions of their life and faith.

To be sure, the dynamic interactions between gospel and cultures in the process of cross-cultural witness inevitably raise questions of syncretism and power. For Indigenous People, determined to make connections between their own spirituality and their Christian faith, the question of who establishes the criteria for testing the appropriateness of contextual expressions is crucial. The following criteria were suggested in one of the sections at Salvador:

> faithfulness to God's self-disclosure in the totality of scriptures; commitment to life-style and action in harmony with the reign of God; openness to the wisdom of the communion of saints across space and time; relevance to the context.[34]

---

[32] Christopher Duraisingh, in *Gospel and Culture*, p.ix.
[33] Christopher Duraisingh ed., *Called to One Hope: The Gospel in Diverse Cultures*, WCC, 1998, p.20.
[34] *Ibid.*, p.67.

The Salvador conference emphasized the need for local churches to be transformed so that the primary responsibility for mission and for discovering contextual expressions of the gospel comes to the top of their agenda. At the same time it was emphasized that the catholicity of a church was enhanced by the quality of the relationships it established with churches of other traditions and cultures. This has implications for mission and evangelism and also requires respect and sensitivity for Christian churches already located in the region.

The matter of relationships in mission that has been dealt with in one way or the other at almost all the mission conferences through the century was also discussed at Salvador. This in turn led to an analysis of proselytism, a subject of increasing concern in the post-cold-war period, especially as it bears on the relationship between the Orthodox and other Christian traditions. Proselytism in this context can be defined as the perversion of witness through improper persuasion or coercion. In a series of "commitments", the Salvador conference denounced proselytism and coercive evangelism, because they "neither recognize the integrity of local churches nor are sensitive to local cultures".

TOWARDS RESPONSIBLE RELATIONSHIPS IN MISSION

What did the change from missions to mission mean in practical terms? Why have mission structures across the world proved so difficult to modify? This question was asked in a 1987 editorial in the *International Review of Mission* devoted to the theme, "Sharing in One Mission: Partnership in Practice". The theme was illustrated by two examples of the restructuring of mission societies in an attempt to create more mutual and inclusive relationships.

From the 1910 Edinburgh conference onwards, calls for changes in relationships of dominance and dependency had been formulated. Early meetings criticized the foreign character of churches established by foreign mission agencies. Concern was expressed that genuinely indigenous church expressions be developed. This would, it was said, involve changes in decision-making, more consultation, encouragement of self-support and training of indigenous leaders. A parallel issue throughout was the question of the cooperation of mission agencies among themselves. The theme of "partnership" had emerged at the Jerusalem conference of 1928, and the notion of joint action for mission, in which the various churches and missions at work in any area would assume mutual responsibility, was put forward in Tambaram 1938. The meeting in Whitby, Ontario, in 1947 was entirely devoted to the theme "Partners in Mission". Increasingly, mutual relationships were seen to originate in obedience to the living Word of God in Jesus Christ.

Some of the assemblies and conferences of the 1960s – the WCC at New Delhi in 1961 and the DWME at Mexico City in 1963 – underscored the conviction that mission had to be one united task throughout the world. While every church was called to mission in its own locality, it was also compelled to share its gifts for mission in the larger world. When the Bangkok conference of 1973 identified moratorium as a valuable tool for mission in certain places, it in effect called for radical reforms and new ways of conceiving mission. These were to find expression in the restructuring of several missionary agencies whose purpose was to send out missionaries, e.g., the Evangelical Community for Apostolic Action (Cevaa) and the Council for World Mission (CWM).

After the Mexico City conference the churches related to the Paris Missionary Society began to work through the implications for their common life of "mission from six continents to six continents", "mutuality in mission", and "every church a missionary church". These churches acted on the conviction that mission could no longer be one-directional. Cevaa was formed in 1971 as a community of churches committed to mission in every place, bringing together a group of about 25 largely francophone churches in Europe, Africa and the Pacific that covenanted to share resources and engage in "joint apostolic action". Decision-making was to be shared – one church, one vote. The executive staff team was to be international in character. Each member church committed itself to theological reflection on mission in its own context. There was to be an overall commitment to joint reflection and study, to the pooling of financial resources and available personnel, and to the evaluation of past and current activities. Together the members of Cevaa were to promote the education of the whole church in and for mission, missionary action focused on those outside of the faith, and a unity of witness and action designed to reflect both unity in Christ and respect for human dignity.

Another of the bodies which took seriously the demand of Bangkok for a radical restructuring of missionary-sending agencies was the Council for World Mission (formerly the London Missionary Society and Congregational Council for World Mission). In 1977 a new, fully representative CWM was formed, each participating church being represented according to its size and degree of involvement. Each church would contribute funds, personnel and other resources. This restructuring was an attempt to move away from donor-recipient relationships to a community within which each partner contributed its gifts and in which power was shared. "Mutuality, not moratorium" was the slogan with which CWM was launched, for there was to be genuine sharing and participation by all, with decision-making the responsibility of all.

These organizations were pioneers and for some time no more restructuring of mission societies occurred. In five regional consultations held between 1988 and 1992, the CWME made a renewed effort to define rules for relationships. Issues of relationships were looked at critically. In any partnership, all partners need to be seen as having both needs and gifts to be shared reciprocally (El Escorial, Spain, 1986). All are enriched in such sharing as they are discovered to be equal partners in the exchange of ideas and resources (Chiang Mai, Thailand, 1989). Resources of personnel and finances are to be shared between partner churches in mutually acceptable ways respectful of the dignity of all sides. All must have equal access to decision-making. Relations within such partnerships should be as transparent as possible from both sides concerning finance, theology, personnel, struggles, dilemmas, fears, hopes, ideas and stories.

These principles have been most openly practised in a second wave of restructuring which involved two European agencies, the Basel Mission and the United Evangelical Mission (VEM). In 1988 a "united in mission" committee of 13 members was formed, including five members from Africa and Asia and three from Germany. Its purpose was to study ways in which the structure of the United Evangelical Mission could be reformed to allow for shared decision-making. In 1996, the board of the former VEM was dissolved and all rights and responsibilities, including all funds, reserves and real estate, were transferred to the international decision-making bodies and mission agencies of this communion of churches on three continents. The official name of the new organization was to be United Evangelical Mission – Communion of Churches in Three Continents

(UEM).[35] While recognizing that these fellowships have developed more transparent and mutual relationships, the criticism remains valid that to a great extent ongoing patterns of work continue to reflect old colonial connections and denominational lines.

There have also been many churches which have not restructured radically but have nevertheless responded with more or less integrity to the call to change their relationships with partners so as to enable shared decision-making and to achieve more mutual, reciprocal and transparent relationships. That has taken the form of a one-mission-board model, and the combining of mission overseas and mission within the country. To give just one example: in Canada and the United States, the United Church of Christ (UCC) and the Christian Church (Disciples of Christ) have committed themselves to structures that express mutuality and are globally responsible, ecumenically accountable, and inclusive of God's concern for all persons.

Recognizing that they have primary responsibility for mission in their own setting, some churches in the South have restructured or taken measures to enhance their own self-identity. Examples are the Presbyterian Church of Kenya which has negotiated a moratorium on receiving personnel and financial resources from overseas, and the United Church of Papua New Guinea and the Solomon Islands which has claimed total autonomy in making decisions on the receipt and use of resources from outside.[36]

In spite of attempts to find renewed structures for mission with new emphases on mutuality, shared decision-making and more genuine partnership, the 1990s were characterized by a number of initiatives completely outside the established pattern. There was widespread interest and active expression of mission in many parts of the world manifested both through broad voluntary movements or para-church groups, and by churches themselves as they exploited new possibilities. While the importance of this new wave of spiritual awakening was recognized and respected, there was also a concern about others who deployed a methodology of "hit and run". Their activities demonstrated both ignorance of the receiving culture and of the churches that were, and had long been, present in a given geographical area. Such agencies showed little concern about creating new patterns of dependency and were furthering divisions in both churches and communities.

COMMON WITNESS AND PROSELYTISM

On a number of occasions over the last forty years the churches have had to address the issue of common witness and proselytism. Unfortunately, these efforts have not yet persuaded all Christian churches to enter into more cooperative ways of being in mission together, nor to refrain from proselytizing others' members. In 1961 the WCC's New Delhi assembly condemned proselytism as "a corruption of witness". The assembly received and commended a document on "Christian Witness, Proselytism and Religious Liberty". Thereafter the Joint Working Group between the Roman Catholic Church and the WCC (JWG) issued a number of study documents, the first one, from 1970, being *Common Witness and Proselytism*. After several years of collecting reports from churches about new initiatives in common witness, the JWG in 1981 issued another important study document, *Common Witness:*

---

[35] "International Relationships in Mission", p.234.
[36] *Ibid.*, pp.246-47.

Common witness is deeply rooted in our faith and is a demand of the very gospel we proclaim. Its urgency is underlined when we realize the seriousness of the human predicament and the tremendous task waiting for the churches at present. Common witness is not an abstract theological concept. It is very much more than friendly ecumenical relations. It is a responsible way of relating the human problems of today... We discover that those challenges touch each and all of the churches when we look beyond our own and see the millions of people who do not know the gospel of Jesus Christ.[37]

Many voices were raised in the mid-1990s concerning various forms of proselytism. Another study document was published in 1995 by the Joint Working Group, "The Challenge of Proselytism and the Calling to Common Witness". The issue is raised largely by the effort – usually by conservative and even politically reactionary groups – to "evangelize" the formerly communist countries of Eastern and Central Europe following floods of missionaries from the United States, Western Europe and South Korea who entered these countries, often acting as if the whole population were atheist and there were no local churches. Yet in Russia, for example, 70 percent of the population are baptized members of the Russian Orthodox Church, which itself has established about 10,000 new parishes in recent years and is determined to deepen the faith of its own baptized members.

A common complaint has been that the inducement to change religious affiliation has frequently been made with the offer of material resources. For example, a researcher with the Moscow Patriarchate has claimed that at some non-Russian churches in Moscow everyone who attends worship receives a gift. Leaders of local churches in Moscow spoke of this process as "Americanization" or "Koreanization" rather than evangelization. Similarily a church leader in Nepal has reported that an American pastor resident in the US had offered scholarships to seventy children in a Nepalese congregation and provided the salary of the pastor, and so was able to persuade a majority of the congregation to join his church.[38] Yet again, a report on relationships in mission in the Philippines has focused almost entirely on relationships with the Korean missionaries there who in 1995 numbered 455. Relationships between these missionaries and the United Church of Christ in the Philippines have been particularly difficult; when Korean missionaries have not found a local church with theological views similar to their own, they have on occasion founded their own churches, seminaries and schools.

There are many reasons why people may be vulnerable to such persuasion to change their church affiliation, including a need for material assistance, a lack of knowledge and conviction concerning the content of their own faith, and an inability to enter into dialogue with those coming to evangelize. Local churches may well need to ask whether some of the problem may lie with them: whether, for example, they are offering the spiritual and pastoral care their people need, and whether they are adequately preparing their people for service in church and society. For many churches proselytism is to be looked upon as a source of suffering which should be condemned. However, some churches acknowledge that proselytism may well be a call to them to renew and enrich the spiritual lives of their people in their own tradition and cultural context. It is also a call for renewed dialogue between churches and missionary organizations, especially on the local level, on

[37] *Common Witness: A Study Document of the Joint Working Group of the Roman Catholic Church and the World Council of Churches*, WCC, 1982, p.28.
[38] *Preparatory Papers for Section Work, Conference on World Mission and Evangelism*, Salvador, 1996, p.79.

the subject of policies and styles of mission, in order to overcome misunderstandings, mutual ignorance and prejudice in order to "speak the truth in love" to one another.[39]

Dialogical encounter may provide a context for the exploration of new patterns of mission. Proclamation and witness are improved through dialogue, within and among the churches as well as beyond the boundaries of Christian community. Sharing diverse experiences of Jesus Christ, believers come to broader, richer understandings of the significance of God's love for individuals, churches and society. Among missionary organizations of varying approaches and traditions, it is reasonable to expect the same common values that are increasingly recognized in inter-religious dialogue:

> We expect reciprocal knowledge that will help us to understand and accept each other. We expect the development of a climate of relationship in which everyone has the right to convince and to be convinced. We work towards the development of a... relationship that will eliminate the reciprocal caricatures and the real danger of using our emotional religious loyalties as divisive elements... In such a permanent dialogue we bring from our respective traditions the best contributions to enable humankind to overcome tensions and to affirm a new day of justice.[40]

As the ecumenical movement has learned to read the Bible and see the world "with new eyes" – in a fellowship welcoming poor and rich, marginalized and powerful, women and men, South and North – so too is the one, holy, catholic and apostolic church being enriched, empowered and transformed in mission through encounter among Christians and in dialogue with people of other faiths.

BIBLIOGRAPHY

Anderson, Gerald Harry ed., *Witnessing to the Kingdom: Melbourne and Beyond*, Maryknoll NY, Orbis, 1982, 170p.

Ariarajah, S. Wesley, *Gospel and Culture : An Ongoing Discussion within the Ecumenical Movement*, WCC, 1994, 50p.

Bangkok Assembly 1973: Minutes and Report of the Assembly of the Commission on World Mission and Evangelism of the World Council of Churches, December 31, 1972, and January 9-12, 1973, WCC, 1973, 118p.

Barrow, Simon and Smith, Graeme eds, *Christian Mission in Western Society : Precedents, Perspectives, Prospects*, London, CTBI Inter-Church House, 2001, 270p.

Bauerochse, Lothar, *Learning to Live Together: Interchurch Partnerships as Ecumenical Communities of Learning*, WCC, 2001, 196p.

Beek, Huibert van and Lemopoulos, Georges eds, *Turn to God, Rejoice in Hope: Orthodox-Evangelical Consultation, Hamburg, 30 March - 4 April, 1998*, WCC, 1998, 109p.

Bosch, David, *Transforming Mission: Paradigm Shifts in Theology of Mission*, Maryknoll NY, Orbis, 1996, 587 p.

Bria, Ion ed., *Go Forth in Peace: Orthodox Perspectives on Mission*, WCC, 1986, 102p.

Bria, Ion, *The Liturgy after the Liturgy: Mission and Witness from an Orthodox Perspective*, WCC, 1996, 88p.

Bria, Ion ed., *Martyria – Mission: The Witness of the Orthodox Churches Today*, WCC, 1980, 255p.

Brown, John, "International Relationships in Mission: A Study Project", in *International Review of Mission*, 86, 342, July 1997, pp.207-48.

Bühlmann, Walbert, *With Eyes to See: Church and World in the Third Millennium*, Maryknoll NY, Orbis, 1990, 162p.

---

[39] *Ibid.*, p.79.
[40] Emilio Castro, *A Passion for Unity*, WCC, 1992, p.44.

Camps, Arnulf ed., *Missiology: An Ecumenical Introduction: Texts and Contexts of Global Christianity*, Grand Rapids MI, Eerdmans, 1995, 498p.
Castro, Emilio, *A Passion for Unity: Essays on Ecumenical Hopes and Challenges*, WCC, 1992, 94p.
Castro, Emilio, *Sent Free: Mission and Unity in the Perspective of the Kingdom*, WCC, 1985, 102p.
Celebration and Challenge: URM '87, Manila, April 1-6, 1987, WCC, 1987, 242p.
"The Challenge of Proselytism and the Calling to Common Witness: A Study Document of the Joint Working Group", in *The Ecumenical Review*, 48, 2, April 1996, pp.212-21.
Christian Understanding of Health, Healing and Wholeness: Report on the North-East Asia Regional Consultation held in Kyoto, Japan, 21-26 April 1987, WCC, 1987, 57p.
The Church for Others and the Church for the World: A Quest for Structures for Missionary Congregations, WCC, 1967, 135p.
Common Witness: A Study Document of the Joint Working Group of the Roman Catholic Church and the World Council of Churches, WCC, 1982, 54p.
David, Kenith A., *Sacrament and Struggle: Signs and Instruments of Grace from the Down-Trodden*, WCC, 1994, 126p.
Dorr, Donal, *Mission in Today's World*, Maryknoll NY, Orbis, 2000, 308p.
Douglas, J.D., *Proclaim Christ until He Comes: Calling the Church to Take the Whole Gospel to the Whole World: International Congress on World Evangelization*, Minneapolis MN, World Wide Publications, 1990, 463p.
Duraisingh, Christopher ed., *Called to One Hope: The Gospel in Diverse Cultures*, WCC, 1998, 234p.
Fackre, Gabriel, *Ecumenical Faith in Evangelical Perspective*, Grand Rapids MI, Eerdmans, 1993, 230p.
Fung, Raymond, *Evangelistically Yours: Ecumenical Letters on Contemporary Evangelism*, WCC, 1992, 260p.
Fung, Raymond, and Lemopoulos, Georges eds, *Not a Solitary Way: Evangelism Stories from Around the World*, WCC, 1992, 80p.
Hunsberger, George Raymond, *Bearing the Witness of the Spirit: Lesslie Newbigin's Theology of Cultural Plurality*, Grand Rapids MI, Eerdmans, 1998, 341p.
Lewin, Hugh ed., *A Community of Clowns: Testimonies of People in Urban Rural Mission*, WCC, 1987, 303p.
Linn, Gerhard ed., *Hear What the Spirit Says to the Churches: Towards Missionary Congregations in Europe*, WCC, 1994, 139p.
"Mission and Evangelism: An Ecumenical Affirmation", in *International Review of Mission*, 71, 284, 1982, pp.427-51.
Nalunnakkal, George Mathew and Athyal, Abraham P. eds, *Quest for Justice: Perspectives on Mission and Unity*, Delhi, ISPCK, 2000, 134p.
Newbigin, James Edward Lesslie, *The Gospel in a Pluralist Society*, WCC, 1989, 244p.
Nicholls, Bruce J. and Ro, Bong Rin eds, *Beyond Canberra: Evangelical Responses to Contemporary Ecumenical Issues*, Oxford, Regnum, 1993, 144p.
Paterson, Gillian, *Whose Ministry? A Ministry of Health Care for the Year 2000*, WCC, 1993, 120p.
Potter, Philip, "From Missions to Mission: Reflections on Seventy-Five Years of the IRM", in *International Review of Mission*, 302, April 1987, pp.155-172.
Sauca, Ioan ed., *Orthodoxy and Cultures: Inter-Orthodox Consultation on Gospel and Cultures*, Addis Ababa, Ethiopia, 19-27 January 1996, WCC, 1996, 186p.
Scherer, James Arnold and Bevans, Stephen B. eds, *New Directions in Mission and Evangelization*, vol. 1: Basic Statements 1974-1991, Maryknoll NY, Orbis, 1992, 324p.
Stackhouse, Max L., Dearborn, Tim and Paeth, Scott eds, *The Local Church in a Global Era: Reflections for a New Century*, Grand Rapids MI, Eerdmans, 2000, 218p.
Stromberg, Jean ed., *Sharing One Bread, Sharing One Mission: The Eucharist as Missionary Event*, WCC, 1983, 79p.
Thomas, Norman E. ed., *Classic Texts in Mission and World Christianity*, Cambridge MA, Boston Theological Institute, 1995, 346p.
Thorogood, Bernard ed., *Gales of Change: Responding to a Shifting Missionary Context: The Story of the London Missionary Society 1945-1977*, WCC, 1994, 345p.
Todd, Kathleen, ed., *Crossing Boundaries: Stories from the Frontier Internship in Mission Programme*, WCC, 1985, 108p.

Werner, Dietrich, *Mission für das Leben, Mission im Kontext: Ökumenische Perspektiven missionarischer Präsenz in der Diskussion des ÖRK 1961-1991*, Rothenburg, Ernst Lange Institut für Ökumenische Studien, 1993, 540p.

Wieser, Thomas ed., *Whither Ecumenism? A Dialogue in the Transit Lounge of the Ecumenical Movement*, WCC, 1986, 103p.

Wilson, Frederick R. ed., *The San Antonio Report: Your Will be Done: Mission in Christ's Way*, WCC, 1990, 214p.

Yates, Timothy, *Christian Mission in the Twentieth Century*, Cambridge, Cambridge Univ. Press, 1994, 275p.

Your Kingdom Come: Mission Perspectives: Report on the World Conference on Mission and Evangelism, Melbourne, Australia, 12-25 May 1980, WCC, 283p.

7

Interfaith Dialogue

Israel Selvanayagam

The establishment of interfaith dialogue on the agenda of the WCC and the ecumenical movement corresponded closely with the beginning of the period covered by this volume. Neither the term itself nor any equivalent expression is found in the indexes to the first two volumes of *A History of the Ecumenical Movement*, and references there to other world religions and their significance for the ecumenical endeavour are few. Thus a brief overview of the historical and theological antecedents may help to set the stage for discussing developments during the final third of the 20th century.

Interfaith dialogue has a short history, but it may be said to have a long past, going back to the earliest period of the Judaeo-Christian tradition. The biblical accounts suggest that when the Hebrew nomads encountered people of other religions they rejected beliefs and practices counter to their own but were nevertheless ready to incorporate elements of the cultic systems of their neighbouring peoples – a pattern that continued when the Israelites settled in Canaan. In the New Testament, the gospels record Jesus' commendation of the "faith" he found in some Samaritans, Romans and Canaanites of his day; and the epistles echo the affirmation of the early Christians that God was the Creator of the whole universe, and that among all peoples and in every nation God has not been without witnesses. The Bible however also includes sharp condemnations of the beliefs and practices of people of other religious traditions such as idolatry and polytheism. Often-cited verses in the New Testament point to Jesus as the only way to God and God's name as the only source of salvation.

Protagonists of these two extreme views are found throughout the history of the Christian church – the one side following the dictum of Cyprian of Carthage (d. 258) that there is "no salvation outside the church", the other guided by the insights of those early Christian thinkers who detected in other religions and philosophies scattered seeds of the "cosmic word" or rays of the supreme light or traces of the presence and activity of the one God.[1] The controversy has continued in the ecumenical movement.

When the disciples were mandated by Jesus "to go to the ends of the earth" as witnesses to him and his gospel, they were unaware of the contemporary living religions of Asia – Jainism, Buddhism, Zoroastrianism and Hinduism. Nor of course could they

---

[1] For a brief survey of early thinkers and their views see Carl F. Hallencreutz, *Dialogue and Community: Ecumenical Issues in Inter-religious Relationships*, Uppsala, Swedish Institute of Missionary Research, 1977, pp.12-16, and Eric J. Sharpe, *Faith Meets Faith: Some Christian Attitudes to Hinduism in the Nineteenth and Twentieth Centuries*, London, SCM Press, 1977, pp.1-7.

have projected the emergence six hundred years later of Islam, much less of Sikhism nine hundred years after that – a unique synthesis of Islamic belief in one God and Hindu belief in reincarnation.

Responding in the 19th century to the biblical "great commission" (Matt. 28:16-20), the Protestants who initiated the missionary endeavours that would later give birth to the ecumenical movement were motivated by an evangelical piety which thought in terms of winning all people for Christ and his church. The simultaneous colonial expansion of the West gave them a status in which few seemed to develop a sensitivity to the theological and intellectual challenges posed by the existence of the ancient religions they encountered.

Missionaries were often the first to engage in serious studies of religion, language and other aspects of culture. Some of these studies clearly aimed to prove the inferiority of these religions and their need to be replaced (or perhaps "fulfilled") by Christianity. But even these unsympathetic attempts often elicited systematic apologetic studies from the indigenous followers of these religions. And some missionary studies and translations of sacred texts displayed a fairness and empathy which are still recognized both by scholars of religion and the adherents of the religions concerned. Soon the study of religion found a place in the academic world. The historical, psychological, sociological, anthropological, philosophical and phenomenological approaches to religion produced by this new science aided the development of new approaches to people of other faiths and of a Christian theology of religions. But they also became increasingly controversial in many quarters.

Friedrich Max Müller (1823-1900), a pioneer of the scientific study of religion who edited and translated numerous sacred texts, described the World's Parliament of Religions, convened in Chicago in 1893, as "one of the most memorable events in the history of the world".[2] While the host committee was predominantly Christian, they were committed to the conviction that all the great historic faiths could cooperate in manifesting the unity of humankind. Audiences in Chicago were impressed by the presentations from representatives of religions other than Christianity. The most colourful figure, Swami Vivekananda, captured the attention not only of those present but also of observers around the world with his brief discourse on universal tolerance and spirituality as the essence of human existence as expounded in the Hindu philosophy of Vedanta.

WORLD MISSIONARY CONFERENCES

The world missionary conference in Edinburgh in 1910 is often called the birthplace of the modern ecumenical movement. Less well known is that it provided the setting for the first ecumenical discussion of other religions. Commission 4 in Edinburgh was entitled "The Missionary Message in Relation to Non-Christian Religions", and those preparing it had sent out a questionnaire to both missionaries and converts to Christianity. The response was overwhelming. With a few exceptions, the overall position emerging from the responses was that sympathy and respect should characterize the

---

[2] For a reflective report of the Parliament, see Marcus Braybrooke, *Pilgrimage of Hope: One Hundred Years of Global Interfaith Dialogue*, London, SCM Press, 1992, pp.7-42; on Müller's views and achievements, see Eric J. Sharpe, *Comparative Religion: A History*, London, Duckworth, 1975, pp.27-46.

Christian approach to persons of other faiths.[3] The general conclusion of this commission emphasized that (1) the proper Christian approach to other religions is one of appreciation and love; (2) training is necessary for such an approach; (3) the theology of the churches should be reformulated in the light of the theologies found in other religions; (4) the study of religion is urgent for theological education.

The next world mission conference (Jerusalem 1928) focused on the growing challenge of secular ideologies – whose spread was as much a concern of Asian church leaders as of the Western missionaries. Ten years later, at the third world mission conference in Tambaram, India, the attitude towards other religions was shaped by the position set out by the Dutch missiologist Hendrik Kraemer in his preparatory book *The Christian Message in a Non-Christian World*.[4]

Kraemer drew on the theologies of Karl Barth and Emil Brunner, both of whom saw a radical discontinuity between God's revelation in Christ and world religions. Kraemer's burden was the crisis of Christian mission in the wake of a discredited West and the resurgence of Asian religions. For him, every religion is a living and indivisible unity, with distinctive myths, rituals and ethics. It is thus inappropriate to try to establish "points of contact" with them.

While there were missionaries and others who disagreed with Kraemer, his influence could be seen in the succeeding missionary conferences – in Whitby, Ontario, Canada, in 1947, with its hopeful post-war emphases on "expectant evangelism" and "partnership in obedience" in the missionary task to the non-Christian world; and in Willingen, Germany, in 1952, which called for an end to "church-centric" mission, but gave no serious consideration to the religions of those whom this mission was to reach.

When the IMC merged with the WCC in 1961 at the New Delhi assembly, the special concern of the new WCC Division of World Mission and Evangelism was "to further the proclamation to the whole world of the gospel of Jesus Christ, to the end that all men may believe in him and be saved".[5]

The section on "The Church's Witness to God's Design" at the WCC's first assembly in Amsterdam discussed "The Approach to Other Faiths"; and the section report received by the assembly asserted that while much of God's purpose "is still hidden from us", three things are clear:
– all we need to know about God's purpose is already revealed in Christ;
– it is God's will that the gospel be proclaimed to all people everywhere;
– God is pleased to use human obedience to fulfill his purpose.[6]
In describing the present situation in the world, the assembly spoke of "the millions of Asia and Africa, filled with new hope..., determined to seize now the opportunity of shaping their own destiny... The religions of Asia and Africa are being challenged and profoundly modified. In the period of transition, the minds of millions are more than usual open to the gospel."[7]

---

[3] *WMC 1910: Report of Commission, The Missionary Message in Relation to Non-Christian Religions*, Edinburgh and London, Oliphant, Anderson & Ferrier, p.2; an analysis of the responses is offered by Kenneth Cracknell, *Justice, Courtesy and Love: Theologians and Missionaries Encountering World Religions, 1846-1914*, London, Epworth, 1995, pp.196-286.

[4] London, Edinburgh House Press, 1938.

[5] Quoted by Lesslie Newbigin, "Mission to Six Continents", in H.E. Fey ed., *A History of the Ecumenical Movement*, vol. 2, 1948-1968, 2nd ed., WCC, 1986, p.190.

[6] W.A. Visser 't Hooft ed., *The First Assembly of the World Council of Churches*, London, SCM Press, 1949, p.64.

[7] *Ibid.*, p.65.

One of the books by the first general secretary of the WCC, W.A. Visser 't Hooft, was entitled *No Other Name*, in which he warned against the growing threat posed by syncretism and liberalism to the uniqueness and universal significance of the Christian gospel. The "no other name" theme appears in the section on non-Christian faiths in the report of the WCC's second assembly in Evanston in 1954 ("in Jesus Christ God has given to man the full and only sufficient revelation of himself"). But there is also evidence of a struggle by the assembly to confront the tension between a missionary commitment and openness to people of other faiths. A spokesperson for younger churches at the WCC's third assembly in New Delhi 1961, Paul Devanandan, stressed the importance of inter-religious encounters at the local level, in which a reconception of the fundamental message of the gospel would take place.

The New Delhi report on "witness", one of the three assembly sections, states:

> The church is sent, knowing that God has not left himself without witness even among men who do not yet know Christ, and knowing also that the reconciliation wrought through Christ embraces all creation and the whole of mankind. We are aware that this great truth has deep implications when we go out to meet men of other faiths. But there are differences of opinion amongst us when we attempt to define the relation and response of such men to the activity of God amongst them. We are glad to note that the study of this question will be a main concern in the continuing study on "The Word of God and the Living Faiths of Men"... In the churches we have but little understanding of the wisdom, love and power which God has given to men of other faiths by their long encounter with Christianity. We must take up the conversations about Christ with them, knowing that Christ addresses them through us and us through them.[8]

THE SECOND VATICAN COUNCIL

The Second Vatican Council (1962-65) is well known as a watershed in terms of the attitude of the Roman Catholic Church to other churches and to the ecumenical movement. But it also marked an important new stage in the relationship of the Catholic church with other religious traditions. One of its sixteen official documents was *Nostra Aetate*, a declaration on the Catholic church's attitude towards other faiths. The declaration affirms the "common humanity" which Catholics share with all people of any religious tradition. The theological basis of this affirmation is God's creation of all human beings in God's own image, and the quest of people everywhere for the ultimate meaning and goal of human life in the face of the problems of evil, suffering and death. The declaration points to the hidden power or transcendental awareness in every human being, and says that the truth that enlightens every human being is the same for all religions.

In its comments on particular religions, *Nostra Aetate* recognizes Hinduism's elaborate philosophy and vision for life, Buddhism's endeavour to overcome human suffering, Islam's emphasis on absolute surrender to the Almighty, its acceptance of Jesus as a prophet and the similarities of its eschatological vision to that of the Judaeo-Christian tradition. The common roots of Jews and Christians are recognized and all forms of antisemitism are denounced. Christians should recognize the elements of truth and spiritual values in all these religions and cooperate with them in efforts to establish justice, peace and freedom for all, while proclaiming Jesus Christ as the Way, the Truth and the Life.

---

[8] W.A. Visser 't Hooft ed., *The New Delhi Report*, London, SCM Press, 1962, pp.81-82.

WCC: PROGRAMMES AND CONTINUING DISCUSSIONS

The change of attitude towards people of other faiths signalled by the Vatican helped to widen the scope of ecumenical concerns on dialogue; and a consultation on the Living Faiths study in Kandy, Sri Lanka, in 1967 brought together for the first time Catholic, Orthodox and Protestant theologians to discuss the relationship between Christians and people of other faiths, including such experienced scholars as Kenneth Cragg, Lyn de Silva and Johannes Blauw. The consultation statement on "Christians in Dialogue with Men of Other Faiths"[9] affirms one common humanity and acknowledges the possibility of Christ speaking through Christians to neighbours of other faiths and vice versa. It describes dialogue as an authentic life-style in a multifaith context. Transcending simple coexistence, it calls for a "positive effort to attain a deeper understanding of the truth through mutual awareness of one another's conviction and witness" and also envisages dialogue within the framework of nation-building with people adhering to secular ideologies – so long as the transcendental dimension of life remains in view. In indicating its approval of the statement from Kandy, the WCC central committee added a warning against the temptation of trying to establish a "common religious front".

Shortly after the 1968 Uppsala assembly, Stanley J. Samartha of India became the WCC staff person responsible for the study on "The Word of God and the Living Faiths of Men". It would not be long before the approach to people of other faiths became a central question in ecumenical mission discussions and interfaith dialogue gained its distinctive identity in the work of the WCC.

The 1969 meeting of the central committee welcomed "the increased emphasis on dialogue" and approved a plan for a ground-breaking encounter – held in Ajaltoun, Lebanon, in March 1970 – which was the first WCC consultation to bring together Hindus, Buddhists and Muslims with Christians. The objective, as summarized in the "Ajaltoun Memorandum on Dialogue between Men of Living Faiths",[10] was "to gather together the experience of bilateral conversations between Christians and people of the major faiths of Asia, with the full participation of members of these faiths, to experiment with a multilateral meeting and to see what could be learned for future relations between people of living faiths". The value of the experiment is attested by the summary of the participants' comments in the memorandum.

Two months later, a consultation in Zurich brought together a group of theologians from different Christian traditions and cultural backgrounds to examine specific issues arising for Christians in interfaith dialogue. Their report[11] speaks of the "truly universal context of common living and common urgency" and the clear human demand for common action, which is authenticated by Jesus Christ, who "has assumed humanity on behalf of all men of all ages and all cultures". It goes on to state:

> Christ releases us to be free to enter into loving, respectful relation with all human beings. Dialogue is but part of that encounter with other men, and sets the tone for all other forms of relationships, including proclamation of the gospel, service to mankind, and the struggle for justice. It is the grace of God that draws us out of our isolation into genuine dialogue with other men.

---

[9] See *Study Encounter*, 3, 2, 1967, pp.52-72.
[10] The full text is in Stanley J. Samartha ed., *Living Faiths and the Ecumenical Movement*, WCC, 1971, pp.15-32.
[11] For the full text, "Christians in Dialogue with Men of Other Faiths", see *ibid.*, pp.33-45.

The document recommends witness in the place of one-way patterns of mission, urges genuine love and a search for truth under the guidance of the Holy Spirit, and calls for urgent theological consideration of the relation between God's economy of salvation in Jesus Christ and the economy of his presence and activity in the whole world, particularly in the lives and traditions of people of other faiths. While seeing dialogue as part of mission, the document declares that all mission requires an approach of "openness to and respect for the other", which includes "our being open to the realities and possibilities of [the other's] mission to us".

On the basis of these encounters, the WCC central committee took up dialogue as one of the major themes for its meeting in Addis Ababa in January 1971, adopting "An Interim Policy Statement and Guidelines".[12] Reflecting the growing ecumenical concern with interfaith dialogue, the new WCC programme structure, in its Unit on Faith and Witness, included a Sub-unit on Dialogue with Men (later changed to People) of Living Faiths and Ideologies, alongside three sub-units continuing aspects of the ecumenical agenda that were part of the WCC mandate from the beginning: Faith and Order, Church and Society, and World Mission and Evangelism.

A controversial theme

Samartha, the sub-unit's first director, made a significant contribution over the next decade in both programmes and publications – though, despite the central committee's affirmation of it, dialogue remained a controversial theme. The Sub-unit on Dialogue had to maintain its independence within the WCC structure to dispel suspicions among partners of other faiths that dialogue was designed as a camouflage for new strategies of evangelism. At the same time, the sub-unit had to explore how the perspectives and insights of people of other faiths might be brought into ecumenical discussions of a wide variety of priority issues which were on the agenda of other WCC units and sub-units.[13]

A second multilateral dialogue (this time including Jews) took place in Colombo in 1974 on the theme "Towards World Community: Resources and Responsibilities for Living Together". "World community" in this dialogue was not regarded as a "super-organization". Rather the emphasis was on the "interdependence of communities", and of their need to "work together for immediate goals".[14] The participants presented resources found in their own religious traditions which could promote life-in-community and could be mobilized for establishing a society based on justice and peace.[15]

Such a quest for "world community" would prove ecumenically controversial, appearing as it did to many as shattering the claims for Christian uniqueness and missionary validity. The tensions came into the open at the fifth assembly of the WCC at Nairobi in 1975. Nairobi marked the first time the WCC gave attention to interfaith dialogue at the assembly level and was the first assembly to which representatives of other world religions – a Jew, a Muslim, a Hindu, a Buddhist and a Sikh – were invited as observers. One of the six sections in which the assembly worked focused on "Seeking Community – the Common Search of People of Various Faiths, Cultures and Ideologies".

---

[12] *Ibid.*, pp.47-54.
[13] Cf. A.J. van der Bent, *Vital Ecumenical Concerns*, WCC, 1986, pp.50f.; and, on the place of dialogue in theory and practice during the WCC's world mission conference at Bangkok in 1972-73, *Dialogue and Community*, pp.83f.
[14] Van der Bent, *Vital Ecumenical Concerns*, pp.52f.
[15] See Stanley J. Samartha ed., *Towards World Community: The Colombo Papers*, WCC, 1975, esp. pp.117ff.

A preparatory document spoke about the potentiality of a "world community" as a "community of communities".[16] The section discussed this preparatory document as well as a number of related issues regarding inter-religious relations, the encounter between different cultures and the relationship between Christianity and systems of secular ideology, and drafted a report for discussion by the whole assembly which touched off a heated debate in the plenary. The report had to be revised with an addition of a preamble recognizing the missionary obligation of the church. The negative reactions, mainly from northern European theologians, elicited Asian rejoinders. The tension between adherents of Christian uniqueness and religious plurality was clearly evident. On the one side was an apologetic tendency, apprehensive that excessive openness to interfaith dialogue would move in the direction of a "wider inter-religious ecumenism". On the other side were theologians, mainly from Asia, who emphasized the significance of dialogue for the authentic existence and spiritual maturity of the church. Russell Chandran of India lamented that in Nairobi the pendulum had swung back to the position of Tambaram in 1938.[17]

In the face of the apparent breakdown of ecumenical communication on interfaith dialogue, the sub-unit recognized the need for further clarification on issues such as "the nature of the unity of humankind", and "world community as a community of communities". The need to clarify the relationship between dialogue and Christian witness led to a consultation in Chiang Mai, Thailand, in 1977, on the theme "Dialogue in Community". It brought together 85 Christian thinkers from 36 countries to share their perceptions and experiences of dialogue with people of particular religious traditions and ideologies. The reality that Christianity is a "faith in the midst of faiths" was reflected in the choice of these words for the title of the report and statement of the consultation.[18]

The Chiang Mai consultation reaffirmed the basic concerns expressed in Colombo and Nairobi. World community is a community of communities, including the Christian community. Dialogue is an attitude in relationship, and it need not lead to syncretism, although Christians should be positive about all the good values found in other religious communities, since God is the Creator of all and is actively present everywhere. The consultation also developed guidelines for interfaith dialogue which were subsequently received by the WCC central committee and commended to the churches.[19] These guidelines explain dialogue as a basic life-style involving commitment and openness, which encourages Christians to see the diverse ways in which God has been dealing in human history through the experience and traditions of different communities. The terms "mission" and "evangelism" are avoided because of wrong notions attached to them in the past, but the emphasis is on Christian witness, which might include sharing of the gospel in a dialogical encounter. Comprehensive and persuasive, these guidelines have been translated into a number of languages and studied by Christian groups around the world, and have served as a basis for further reflection both locally and internationally.

---

[16] *Dialogue and Community*, p.92; cf. A.J. van der Bent, *The Utopia of World Community*, WCC, 1974.
[17] On the Nairobi debate see *Dialogue and Community*, pp.96ff. and *The Utopia of World Community*, pp.55ff.
[18] Stanley J. Samartha ed., *Faith in the Midst of Faiths: Reflections on Dialogue in Community*, Chiang Mai, Thailand, 18-27 April 1977, WCC, 1977.
[19] *Guidelines on Dialogue with People of Living Faiths and Ideologies*, WCC, 1979; revised as *Ecumenical Considerations for Dialogue and Relations with People of Other Religions*, WCC, 2003.

Contemporary statements from other consultations and conferences recognized dialogue as an important component of affirming faith in Christ, common humanity and rich mutuality in community.[20] The seventh assembly of the Christian Conference of Asia (Bangalore 1981), however, expressed some unease with the term "dialogue":

> It gives the impression of mutual interchange of ideas and beliefs more on the intellectual level. We need a more suitable word which can convey the sense of mutual cooperation between people of living faiths and ideologies in coping with social evils in concrete measures for building truly human communities.[21]

While it is true that "dialogue" can be understood in the narrow sense of two parties conversing (a similar connotation can attach to other terms such as "encounter"), the ecumenical use of the term has followed the lines of Samartha's description of dialogue as "a mood, spirit and attitude in relationship". Thus, although several related terms have been used in discussions of interfaith relationships, "dialogue" continues to be an umbrella term covering different perspectives and issues. *Current Dialogue*, the sub-unit's publication, continuing an earlier newsletter of the Committee on the Church and the Jewish People (CCJP), came into being in 1980, and includes news and reflection concerning dialogue.

Vancouver 1983

For the sixth WCC assembly (Vancouver 1983), the number of official guests from other faiths was increased to fifteen. To prepare them for participating in an assembly whose theme was "Jesus Christ – the Life of the World", the Dialogue sub-unit organized a special meeting in Mauritius, which brought them together with an equal number of Christians who would be in Vancouver. The consultation drafted a special message, affirming life in unity with diverse visions of and resources for it.[22] Despite the gains in understanding the concept of dialogue over the preceding seven years, vigorous debate about dialogue emerged over the draft report of the assembly's issue group on "Witnessing in a Divided World". Several speakers criticized it for not taking sufficient account of recent WCC work on mission and evangelism. Some wanted a clearer statement on the role of Christ; others expressed unease that certain paragraphs might be construed as advocating "universalism". The report was said to be "too negative in speaking of the work of the missionaries". It was also criticized for not being "more scriptural" in its approach and for not being more critical of the "un-Christian aspect of local cultures".[23]

The report was sent back for reworking, and a revised version reached the plenary on the last day of the assembly. The most striking changes in the revision were the addition of an opening sentence, "The starting point for our thinking is Jesus Christ"; the reaffirmation that "Christians are called to witness to Christ in all ages"; and the modification of a sentence which recognized God's creative work in the "religious experience" of people of other faiths to refer instead to their "seeking of religious truth". Because of the pressure of time, this revised report was referred to the new central committee which

---

[20] Cf. *The Utopia of World Community*, pp.58ff.
[21] Quoted by van der Bent, *ibid.*, p.59.
[22] Cf. Allan R. Brockway, *The Meaning of Life: A Multi-Faith Consultation in Preparation for the Sixth WCC Assembly*, WCC, 1983.
[23] David Gill ed., *Gathered for Life: Official Report of the Sixth Assembly of the WCC*, WCC, 1983, p.31.

subsequently approved its substance and commended it to the churches for study and action.

In addressing the concern of "witnessing among people of living faiths", the Vancouver report notes that the presence of friends from others faiths in the assembly "has raised for us questions about the special nature of the witness Christians bring to the world community". It acknowledges the urgency of common action and cooperation between Christians and persons of other faiths especially in areas of human dignity, justice and peace, economic reconstruction, and the eradication of hunger and disease. Areas identified for further attention included dialogue with people from traditional religions, highlighted by the presence of a large number of Canadian Aboriginal peoples at the assembly, interfaith prayer and worship, the phenomenon of New Religious Movements, and issues of gospel and culture. The report described dialogue as

> that encounter where people holding different claims about ultimate reality can meet and explore these claims in a context of mutual respect. From dialogue we expect to discern more about how God is active in our world, and to appreciate for their own sake the insights and experiences people of other faiths have of ultimate reality.[24]

The document *Mission and Evangelism: An Ecumenical Affirmation,* adopted by the central committee in 1982, was prepared by the WCC's Commission on World Mission and Evangelism in extensive consultation with Roman Catholic and evangelical missiologists. Within the framework of the missionary obligation of the church, it affirms that God is the Creator of the whole universe and has been left by no means without witness "at any time or in any place", and that the Spirit of God is constantly at work "in ways that pass human understanding and in places that to us are least expected". In entering into dialogue with others, therefore, "Christians seek to discern the unsearchable riches of God and the way [God] deals with humanity". The statement also speaks of the encounter of commitments, mutual witness and the need for a spirit of openness and trust.[25]

In implementing the recommendations from the controversial Vancouver report, the Dialogue sub-unit gave particular attention to the debate on the theological significance of other faiths. In 1986 it launched a four-year study programme in the churches with a study guide entitled *My Neighbour's Faith – and Mine: Theological Discoveries through Interfaith Dialogue*, whose nine sections presented themes ranging from creation to hope and vision as expounded by different religious traditions. This was translated into 18 languages and made widely available. Reports were received from a number of study groups around the world on their use of and response to the material.

Findings of this study were part of the input for a consultation on the theology of religions held in Baar, Switzerland, in early 1990, which addressed three major theological issues: "the theological significance of religious plurality, the meaning of Christ in a religiously plural world, and the implications of the belief that the Holy Spirit works out-

---

[24] *Ibid.*, p.40.
[25] For further reflections on interfaith dialogue from this sector of the ecumenical constituency, see the report of the 1989 world mission and evangelism conference, F.R. Wilson ed., *The San Antonio Report*, WCC, 1990, esp. the report of the section "Towards Renewed Communities in Mission" (pp.68-79) and the plenary presentations on "Gospel and Culture" (pp.122-24) and "Christian Relationship to People of Other Great Religious Faiths of Humankind" (pp.124-26).

side the boundaries of the institutional church".[26] While the theological perspectives articulated at this consultation were clear enough to form the basis for continued exploration, the tensions between commitment to Christ as God's decisive revelation and openness to God's cosmic presence and work remained. Also unresolved was the tension between the church's missionary obligation and willingness to learn from people of other faiths. Nevertheless, bilateral and multilateral interfaith discussions continued.[27] In his short book *The Bible and People of Other Faiths*[28] WCC Dialogue sub-unit director Wesley Ariarajah sought to suggest a scriptural basis for a dialogical relationship with others. While the book, published in 1985 and regularly reprinted, and translated into 12 languages, confirmed and encouraged the convictions of many people regarding the need for a ministry of dialogue at various levels, its approach and emphasis made it unacceptable for many conservative Christians.

Canberra 1991

Fifteen official guests of other faiths who attended a preparatory meeting to the seventh WCC assembly (Canberra 1991), similar to the one before Vancouver, and were welcomed in a plenary session at the assembly itself. A number of them spoke in section plenaries and special events. The framework set by the assembly agenda, however, led to some questioning of the effectiveness and value of bringing a small number of guests to such large Christian assemblies.[29]

Although one sub-section was devoted to "Dialogue with People of Other Faiths", interfaith issues had a high profile elsewhere as well. Some of the issues from the earlier debate on the theological significance of other faiths reappeared in vigorous exchanges on the inter-relationship of gospel and culture:

> The presence of the Aboriginal people of Australia and the incorporation of their perspectives and practices into the life of the assembly produced considerable reaction among many Christians. Some saw this as the introduction of "pagan" practices, even though it was understood that such practices are used by Aboriginal Christians as part of the heritage which they have brought into the life of the church. Controversy also arose over the presentation by Chung Hyun Kyung of Korea, who brought in Korean Buddhist cultural reflections on the main theme. The lively debate it produced at the assembly and in the follow-up period showed that Christian relations to other faiths and cultures continue to be an important and divisive issue.[30]

The identification of the Holy Spirit with the ancestral spirits of the Aboriginals and some of the symbols used in speeches and ceremonies at the assembly elicited sharp criticism, even if few assembly participants would have gone so far as a handful of protesters who carried placards that read, "Dialogue is satanic".

Another issue which preoccupied the participants was Christian-Muslim relations. The first Gulf war had broken out two weeks before the assembly. Statements on the Gulf war, the Middle East and other situations threatening world peace emphasized the

---

[26] T.F. Best ed., *Vancouver to Canberra, 1983-1990: Report of the Central Committee of the WCC to the Seventh Assembly*, WCC, 1990, p.132.

[27] For details, see *ibid.*, pp.132-40.

[28] WCC, 1985. Risk Book Series no. 26.

[29] See S. Wesley Ariarajah, "Dialogue Concerns at the Seventh Assembly of the World Council of Churches, Canberra", in *Current Dialogue*, 20, July 1991, pp.34-37.

[30] *Ibid.*, p.36.

contribution of religious resources for world peace,[31] but for a number of participants from several parts of the world the experience of interfaith relations, especially between Christians and Muslims, was one of tension and even conflict.

Within the overall Canberra theme, "Come, Holy Spirit – Renew the Whole Creation", the section "Spirit of Unity – Reconcile Your People" dealt more specifically with interfaith encounter. Echoing earlier affirmations of the freedom of the Spirit at work "in ways that pass human understanding", the report says that "dialogue challenges us to discern the fruit of the Spirit in the way God deals with all humanity". It also seeks to give a scriptural basis for dialogue:

> The Bible testifies to God as sovereign of all nations and peoples as the one whose love and compassion include all humankind. We see in the covenant with Noah a covenant with all creation. We recognize God's covenant with Abraham and Israel. In the history of this covenant we are granted to come to know God through Jesus Christ. We also recognize that other people testify to knowing God through other ways. We witness to the truth that salvation is in Christ and we also remain open to other people's witness to truth as they have experienced it.

Recognizing how religious language and symbols are being used to exacerbate conflicts in many parts of the world, the report emphasizes "dialogue as a means of reconciliation", calling for a "culture of dialogue" that goes beyond meetings, exchanges and formal encounters. Such a culture begins with knowing the other and then trusting one another – "telling their stories of faith and sharing their concerns and service to the world". This is put in the context of discerning God's will: "Part of dialogue is standing together under God and leaving space for us to be touched by the Holy Spirit. We enter into dialogue with the other asking God to be present among us."

One part of the report addresses "dialogue with ideologies" – a mandate which was on the agenda of the sub-unit in 1971 but which had never received the level of focused attention that was given to inter-religious dialogue. The attention in Canberra to dialogue with ideologies was obviously related to the new situation created by "the obvious failure of communism as a state ideology". The report sees this as a fresh challenge to the churches "to discriminate between constructive and destructive elements in any ideology and to clearly express the criteria of truth and justice as a basis for critical dialogue" with ideologies. The collapse of Marxism as a likely partner in dialogue with Christianity should lead neither to triumphalism about the free-market system, whose negative effects are all too obvious, nor to the supposition that there are no other ideologies. The report points to "ideological trends" found in fundamentalism and nationalism and lists five "hidden ideologies" – patriarchy, economic materialism, achievement-oriented individualism, uncritical pluralism and aggressive modernization:

> The tasks of the community of faith are: (1) to name the hidden ideologies and to expose the contradiction between the ideological claims and the realities of people's lives; (2) to enter into critical dialogue with the exponents of such ideologies on the basis of the biblical criteria of God's preferential option for the marginalized and for the well-being of creation. It is the power of truth as encounter with reality which brings these hidden ideologies to accountability.

---

[31] See M. Kinnamon ed., *Signs of the Spirit: Official Report of the Seventh Assembly*, WCC, 1991, pp.202-34. A recommendation that the WCC "immediately seek to bring together leaders of the Christian, Muslim and Jewish communities to explore ways of working together for peace and justice in the present context of the Middle East crisis" was made in the report of the assembly section which discussed interfaith dialogue (p.107). The following references to Canberra from pp. 104,105,106.

During the years following the Canberra assembly, the WCC went through two major programmatic restructurings. The first, instituted in January 1992, organized programmes and activities according to four thrusts: unity, mission, justice and sharing. The former Sub-Unit on Dialogue was replaced by an Office on Inter-Religious Relations (OIRR), attached to the General Secretariat. Its mandate was to enable and encourage the churches in their relationships to people of other faiths...; [to] monitor developments in inter-religious relations at different levels, including other religious traditions and international interfaith organizations; and respond to specific issues, such as the use of religion in conflict situations and the problems of religious minority communities, and concrete situations of conflict where religions play a role.[32]

Some advocates of interfaith dialogue criticized the changed mandate as blurring the visible identity of the programme of interfaith dialogue (and a few suggested that this was a consequence of the controversies surrounding it over the previous twenty years). A more positive assessment saw the possibility for the concerns of interfaith dialogue to permeate all the programmes of the WCC, recognizing that an ecumenical approach to issues as varied as worship and spirituality, gospel and culture, mission and witness, Indigenous Peoples, racism, solidarity with women, peace, human rights and social transformation require a new ethos characterized by comprehensive and interdependent thinking and action, including input from other religious traditions.

Though its size was reduced because of financial constraints, OIRR initiated a number of new programmes and continued others. Its task of enabling and encouraging the churches in their dialogue work, clarification of perspectives and issues in dialogue was a continuing one. A group of Christians involved in interfaith dialogue in different parts of the world were brought together in Colombo, Sri Lanka, in 1992 for sharing and discussion in this connection.[33] In collaboration with the WCC programme on churches in mission, a consultation on the theological significance of other religions was held in Baar, Switzerland, in 1993, building on the consultation there on the same theme in 1990.[34] This fitted into the WCC study process on "Gospel and Culture", in preparation for the world conference on mission and evangelism in Salvador de Bahia, Brazil, in November-December 1996. Two of the conference sections in particular – "Local Congregations in Pluralistic Societies" and "One Gospel – Diverse Expressions" – addressed the vexing but unavoidable question of Christian commitment and approaches in a multi-faith context.

Following the Canberra assembly, the OIRR further strengthened its collaboration with the Pontifical Council for Inter-Religious Dialogue (PCID), holding annual joint staff meetings and exploring two specific issues: inter-religious marriage and inter-religious prayer. The result of these studies was two documents issued in 1997-98 which have elicited favourable reactions from churches. The OIRR and the PCID worked with several other bodies to organize consultations on the significance of Jerusalem for the three Abrahamic faiths and on the significance of the Jubilee theme for Christians and Jews.

Harare 1998

Fifteen official guests of other faith traditions were invited to the WCC's eighth assembly (Harare 1998). Some eight presentations related to interfaith dialogue were made at

---

[32] *WCC Resource Sharing Book 1993: Programmes/Projects and Services*, WCC, 1992, p.9.
[33] For a report and some articles, see *Current Dialogue*, 23, Dec. 1992.
[34] See report and papers in *Current Dialogue*, 26, June 1994.

the *padare* – the open forum at the assembly where a broad cross-section of churches and ecumenical groups made presentations on a wide range of concerns.

The importance of continuing the work of interfaith dialogue was repeatedly affirmed. The assembly amended the WCC constitution which for the first time explicitly identified relations with communities of people of other faiths as one of the functions of the fellowship of churches within the Council.

In specifying guidelines for the WCC's future work, the Harare assembly said the primary focus in inter-religious relations should be to help "member churches who find themselves increasingly confronted with the theological, missiological and political challenges of living in situations of religious pluralism". Echoing a theme that had emerged around the 1993 centenary of the World Parliament of Religions, it called for ecumenical participation in "the development of a global ethic that further applies human-rights commitments to an increasingly interconnected world community".[35]

On globalization – signalled as a major priority for the WCC as a whole in the post-Harare period – the assembly called on the Council to "build relations with partners of other faiths to explore how commitments to human rights and dignity can be built into a global framework of values". The importance of interfaith perspectives in conflict resolution and in education also was underscored. At the same time, Harare reaffirmed a traditional ecumenical emphasis that "mission and evangelism should be at the centre of the life of the churches and thus also of the work of the WCC" – suggesting that the tension between dialogue and mission will continue to face the Council. The hope, of course, is that the tension would be creative.

The post-Harare period began in January 1999 with a further restructuring of the WCC. The former OIRR was changed into the team on Interreligious Relations and Dialogue to restore specific mention of the word "dialogue".

THE ORTHODOX CONTRIBUTION

As a segment of the churches that constitute the WCC, the Orthodox churches have been part of the overall programmes of the Sub-unit on Dialogue. Metropolitan Georges Khodr of Lebanon was one of two key speakers (the other being Stanley Samartha) who advocated a programme on dialogue at the WCC central committee meeting at Addis Ababa (1971) which brought the sub-unit into being. Representatives of the Orthodox churches have played significant roles in the advisory groups of the sub-unit since its formation.

At the first pre-conciliar pan-Orthodox conference in Chambésy, Geneva, in 1976, the Orthodox churches unanimously declared their desire "to contribute to inter-religious understanding and cooperation, and in this way to eliminate fanaticism in all aspects, and in every way to contribute to the reconciliation of peoples." Dialogue was seen in this meeting as a way to achieve the "ideals of freedom, peace on earth, and service to humanity irrespective of race and religion". These proposals were renewed and developed more systematically at the third pre-conciliar pan-Orthodox conference in 1986.

Many of these initiatives, as well as others proposing meetings with Muslims and Jews, were based at the Orthodox centre of the Ecumenical Patriarchate in Chambésy

---

[35] The world parliament produced a "Declaration of the Religions for a Global Ethic", drafted by German theologian Hans Küng and signed by most of the parliamentary delegates. See *Towards a Global Ethic: An Initial Declaration*, Chicago, Council for a Parliament of the World's Religions, 1993.

under the leadership of Metropolitan Damaskinos (Papandreou) of Switzerland, show-ing the commitment of the Ecumenical Patriarchate to promoting relationships with neighbours of other faith traditions.

These were also part of more sustained Orthodox-Jewish dialogue meetings organ-ized by the Orthodox centre of the ecumenical patriarchate and the World Jewish Con-gress, both based in Geneva. There have also been several Orthodox-Muslim meetings in the regions where they live in close proximity, and national dialogue initiatives in countries where the Orthodox church forms the Christian majority.

Orthodox involvement and interest in dialogue centre primarily on such issues as mutual understanding, cooperation, religious liberty, concerns of minorities, anti-semitism, peace, etc. The Dialogue sub-unit's attempts to rethink theology in the context of plurality has at times met with resistance from some within the Orthodox con-stituency. This has been identified as one of the issues that need clarification in the WCC's internal Orthodox-Protestant conversations on the meaning of oikoumene and the nature and purposes of the WCC.

BILATERAL ENCOUNTERS

While certain issues arising in interfaith dialogue are common to all religious traditions, some are specific to the Christian relationship with a particular religion.

Jewish-Christian relations

The fact that Christianity was an offshoot of the Jewish religious tradition makes the re-lationship an extremely complicated one. Christian theological affirmations – for exam-ple, that the scripture of the Jewish people has no validity unless it is understood in terms of its fulfilment in Jesus Christ – have combined with a host of social, economic and political factors to create a legacy of Christian tolerance of, and complicity in, anti-semitism, climaxing in the Shoah or Holocaust, the genocide of six million European Jews during the second world war.

The 1910 world missionary conference did not mention Judaism in its list of "non-Christian religions". It was thought that a different approach was needed to win converts from Judaism. The Committee on the Christian Approach to the Jews, formed in 1930 as a sponsored agency of the International Missionary Council, developed a full pro-gramme of training and consultation, which took a missionary approach, while de-nouncing antisemitism in any form. At New Delhi in 1961 this committee was recon-stituted as the WCC's Committee on the Church and the Jewish People.

Some Christians and churches spoke out against antisemitism in the period between two world wars, and a Council of Christians and Jews (CCJ), set up in 1942, did foster some mutual understanding, goodwill and collaboration between Christians and Jews.[36] The WCC's first assembly (Amsterdam 1948) deplored "the failure of the churches to oppose antisemitism" and affirmed Israel's unique position in God's design:

> It was Israel with whom God made his covenant by the call of Abraham..., to whom God revealed his name and gave his law. It was to Israel that he sent his prophets with their message of judgment and of grace..., to whom he promised the coming of his Messiah. By the history of Israel, God prepared the manger in which in the fullness of time he put

---

[36] Cf. *Pilgrimage of Hope*, pp.178ff.

the Redeemer of all mankind, Jesus Christ. The church has received the spiritual heritage from Israel and is therefore in honour bound to render it back in the light of the cross.[37]

This tension between the recognition of the Jews as the first to receive divine revelation and the desire to persuade them about the newer revelation in Jesus Christ is a recurring theme in ecumenical statements. Moreover, the establishment of the state of Israel in 1948 complicated the Christian approach to the Jews with political fears and enmities. Amsterdam stated that,

> On the political aspects of the Palestine problem and the complex conflict of "rights" involved we do not undertake to express a judgment. Nevertheless, we appeal to the nations to deal with the problem not as one of expediency – political, strategic or economic – but as a moral and spiritual question that touches a nerve centre of the world's religious life.[38]

Persistent calls for peace in the Middle East and a series of consultations and statements on topics ranging from the status of Jerusalem to the significance of biblical Jubilee illustrate that the Jewish-Christian dialogue comprises difficult political as well as complex theological concerns and problems.

A number of ecumenical and Christian-Jewish organizations were formed in order to give focused attention to building mutual understanding and fostering cooperation, most notably the International Council of Christians and Jews (ICCJ), which involved Protestants and Roman Catholics and Jews. Roman Catholic attitudes were revolutionized after the Second Vatican Council by the follow-up to *Nostra Aetate*, with its affirmation of the common "spiritual patrimony of Jews and Christians" and its repudiation of the idea that the Jewish people bore a unique responsibility for the passion and death of Jesus Christ. Several European and North American church bodies made official statements on these issues, including the synod of the Protestant churches in the Rhineland, Germany, which called for an end to the efforts to convert Jews to Christianity. Within the WCC, the shift away from a primarily missionary approach was signalled in 1973 by lodging the CCJP in the Dialogue sub-unit, rather than the Commission on World Mission and Evangelism.

A document on "Ecumenical Considerations on Jewish-Christian Dialogue" was received by the WCC central committee and commended to the churches in 1982. This widely circulated text, growing out of conversations between the CCJP and the International Jewish Committee for Inter-religious Consultations (IJCIC – an umbrella organization of mainly American Jewish organizations established for dialogue with major Christian bodies), affirms the general principles of dialogue set forth in the WCC's "Guidelines on Dialogue". It acknowledges the fateful historical consequences of the perception of Israel in classical Christian theology and teaching, recognizes the "wide spectrum of opinions, options, theologies and styles of life and service" within both Judaism and Christianity, and calls Christians and Jews to mutual witness and corporate mission. It notes that,

> Christians in parts of the world with a history of little or no persecution of Jews do not wish to be conditioned by the specific experiences of justified guilt among other Christians.

---

[37] Quoted in Allan Brockway, Paul van Buren, Rolf Rendtorff, Simon Schoon eds, *The Theology of the Churches and the Jewish People: Statements by the World Council of Churches and Its Member Churches*, WCC, 1988, p.6.

[38] *Ibid.*, p.8.

Rather, they explore in their own ways the significance of Jewish-Christian relations, from the earliest times to the present, for their life and witness.[39]

Several subsequent consultations on Jewish-Christian dialogue from a third-world perspective, drawing on the lived experiences of Asian Christians and Jews, shed new light on this and pointed to creative areas of further dialogue.[40] From a socio-political perspective, the question of how far the Jewish community is able to identify with the powerless nations in today's world is extremely significant. From a cultural perspective, the common heritage, including art and wisdom shared by Jews and others in Asia, has attracted serious attention. From a theological perspective, Jews and Christians have been challenged to work together to develop a more convincing theology of religions as they share faith in one God. So also from a missionary perspective, they have a common mission in the whole world notwithstanding the covenant of God made with Noah.[41]

Within the Vatican, Christian-Jewish relations are the responsibility of the Pontifical Council for Promoting Christian Unity. Similarly, there were suggestions at the time of the 1992 restructuring of the WCC that exploration of the theological dimensions of Jewish-Christian relationships should become part of the task of Faith and Order. Already in 1964, following the world conference on Faith and Order in Montreal, a study on "The Church and the Jewish People" had been approved within the framework of the overall Faith and Order study of the nature of the church. But the implementation of the suggestion in the 1990s went largely unrealized due to practical considerations of limited resources.

Christian-Hindu/Buddhist dialogue

Hinduism and its associated religions that grew out of it like Buddhism, Jainism and Sikhism are dialogical in nature. As Vivekananda said in Chicago, Hinduism represents a plurality within, and tolerance of, other traditions. Nevertheless, although not often openly admitted in dialogue, there have been periods of tension and intolerance in its development, some forms of which re-surfaced during the 1990s. The internal reason for taking a tolerant and open attitude towards other faiths is twofold: first, the presence of diverse visions, traditions and cults within Hinduism; second, its claim from the Vedic times that Reality is one and that people call it by different names – in other words, that the essence of all religions is the same and that different religions are different ways to the same goal. The consequent Hindu attitude of neither acceptance nor rejection of the Christian message perplexed and upset many missionaries who worked in India.

To speak of Hindu-Christian dialogue in the singular can lead to confusion since more than any other world religion the umbrella of Hinduism embraces several major traditions – the Vedic religion of ritual, Vaishnavism, Saivism, popular cults – each one of which is distinctive although there has been interaction and integration between them. In this respect there is some justification for the claim of some Hindus that Buddhism, Jainism and Sikhism were originally part of their pan-mythic tradition. Within

---

[39] For the text, see *ibid.*, pp.36ff. Here p.41.
[40] See I. Selvanayagam, "Jewish-Christian Relationship from a Third World Perspective", in *Current Dialogue*, 25, Dec. 1993, pp.20-31; Hans Ucko ed., *People of God, Peoples of God*, WCC, 1996.
[41] On these issues see also Hans Ucko, *Common Roots – New Horizons: Learning about Christian Faith from Dialogue with Jews*, WCC, 1994.

the ecumenical movement, dialogue with particular traditions of Hinduism has not been widely developed.[42]

Already at the time of Edinburgh in 1910, Hinduism was the main point of reference for discussions of a missionary approach to religions and the theology of religious pluralism. The resurgent Hinduism which acknowledged the great value of the teachings of Jesus and the profound meaning of his cross attracted the attention of Christian thinkers to the extent that some attributed this change to the work of the Holy Spirit. Later observations regarding an "opportune moment" (P.D. Devanandan), the "acknowledged Christ" (M.M. Thomas), and "response to the unbound Christ" (Stanley Samartha) emerged from studies of the Christian Institute for the Study of Religion and Society in Bangalore. Theological models like "the crown of Hinduism" (J.N. Farquhar) and "the unknown Christ of Hinduism" (R. Panikkar) remain popular. The world mission conference in Tambaram in 1938, the WCC assembly in New Delhi in 1961 and a major consultation in Tambaram in 1988 to commemorate the 50th anniversary of the 1938 event recognized the importance of Hindu-Christian dialogue.

While Ariarajah argues that Hindu-Christian dialogue has yet to find the place it deserves in ecumenical discussions on dialogue, Hinduism has been well represented in all the WCC's multilateral dialogues and inter-religious encounters. A consultation in Rajpur, North India, in 1981 brought together Christians and Hindus from areas of the world where people of these two religious traditions live together in significant numbers – theologians and philosophers, spiritual leaders and pastors, social workers and others – to discuss "Religious Resources for a Just Society". The Hindu idea of *dharma* was expounded in a comprehensive way as covering all aspects of a liberated life and life in its fullness, paralleling the biblical vision of *shalom*.[43] The WCC's OIRR cooperated with dialogue groups in India and elsewhere in consultations and programmes of peacemaking and organized together with the National Council of Churches in India two Hindu-Christian consultations in Madurai (1995) and in Varanasi (1997). These initiatives took on added urgency during the late 1990s in the wake of the emergence of Hindu revivalist groups which resorted to violence and persecution of Christians and members of other religious communities.

The "Missionary Message" of Edinburgh 1910 mentioned Buddhism in its treatment of religions in Japan and China, pointing out that its sectarian forms and pantheistic beliefs are unable to meet spiritual needs, but acknowledging that "there are several points in Chinese Buddhism which have prepared men's minds for the fuller and clearer teachings of Christianity". Such points of contact include "the new Buddhist teaching regarding paradise", "the incarnations of the Divine in human form" and the teaching of "pity for all living things". Buddhists have subsequently become regular partners in the WCC's interfaith dialogue initiatives; indeed, of ten representatives of other faiths at the historic Ajaltoun meeting in 1970, four were Buddhists.

---

[42] The first major attempt to bring together the principal themes of Hindu-Christian discussion both in India and ecumenically was Eric Sharpe, *Faith Meets Faith*; these issues are further developed in S. Wesley Ariarajah, *Hindus and Christians: A Century of Protestant Ecumenical Thought*, Grand Rapids MI, Eerdmans, 1991. Cf. also the survey in Harold Howard ed., *Hindu-Christian Dialogue: Perspectives and Encounters*, Maryknoll NY, Orbis, 1989. A critical view from the Hindu perspective of Christian approaches to Hinduism is Sita Ram Goel, *History of Hindu-Christian Encounters*, New Delhi, Voice of India, 1989.

[43] For the report see *Religious Resources for a Just Society: A Hindu-Christian Dialogue*, WCC, 1981.

The Buddhist contribution to world peace, emphasis on compassion and interpretation of *nirvana* as a "positionless position" signifying an authentic existence have fascinated their Christian interlocutors in dialogue. The consultations in Kandy, Colombo and Chiang Mai provided opportunities to encounter Buddhist monks and believers in their living context. Other consultations have addressed specific issues. For example, Christians, Buddhists and Cao Daists discussed the theme "Christian and Buddhist Contributions for the Renewal of Society in Vietnam" at a meeting at Geneva in 1972. A group of Buddhists and Christians discussed the religious dimensions of humanity's relation to nature in Colombo in 1978, at a time of growing awareness of the dominance of science and technology in human life.[44] This resulted for the WCC in the 1979 world conference on "Faith, Science and the Future". Nevertheless, intensive ecumenical encounter with Buddhists and representatives of other Asian religious communities diminished during the 1990s – again, partly due to resource constraints on the side of the WCC. Ongoing contacts and cooperation has been established with Rissho Kosei-Kai and Myochikai, two Japanese lay movements.

Christian-Muslim dialogue

The Edinburgh "Missionary Message" acknowledged that while Islam "borrowed not a little both from Judaism and Christianity, it cannot be regarded as a merely corrupt form of the one or the other". The universal appeal of its belief in one Almighty God and of its religious duties – confession of faith, regular prayer, fasting, alms-giving and pilgrimage to Mecca – were noted. The Edinburgh message also noted that, like Christianity, Islam is a missionary religion. It saw some tendency among Muslims who are dissatisfied with their faith to wish to embrace Christianity. But it also recognized that the presence of Christianity challenged the Muslims to purify their faith in order to be more successful in Islam's own missionary effort.

Besides the "contest" there was also "conversation", as Muslims participated in multilateral and bilateral meetings.[45] A Christian-Muslim dialogue in Broumana, Lebanon, in 1972, for example, prepared a memorandum calling for the protection of religious liberty for individuals and religious minorities:

> While we accept that both religious traditions have a missionary vocation, proselytism should be avoided, whether by a majority intent upon pressing a minority to conform, or whether by a minority using economic or cultural inducements to swell its ranks. It is especially unworthy to exploit the vulnerability of the uneducated, the sick and the young. Open to the inexhaustible nature of the grace of God..., we work together for self-critical re-evaluation of our roles and of our mutual relationships.[46]

Subsequently, interest in Islam increased among many churches in the light of the growing influence of political Islam and what came to be called "Islamic fundamentalism" in their own contexts. After the WCC's Vancouver assembly in 1983, the Sub-unit

---

[44] For the papers and aide-mémoire, see Stanley J. Samartha and L. de Silva eds, *Man in Nature: Guest or Engineer?*, Colombo, Ecumenical Institute for Study and Dialogue, 1979.

[45] For details of consultations held from 1974 to 1982 see *Vital Ecumenical Concerns*, pp.54ff; for a documentary record of Christian-Muslim dialogue, see *Christians Meeting Muslims*, WCC, 1977; and Stuart E. Brown ed., *Meeting in Faith: Twenty Years of Christian-Muslim Conversations Sponsored by the WCC*, WCC, 1989.

[46] Stanley J. Samartha and J.B. Taylor, eds, *Christian-Muslim Dialogue: Papers from Broumana*, WCC, 1973, p.159.

on Dialogue began a long-term project to develop guidelines for Muslim-Christian relations. It organized five regional meetings between Christians and Muslims on the themes of religion and family, religion and education, and religion and the state. Findings from these consultations were incorporated into an exploration of theological and political considerations. At the same time the sub-unit worked with the Pontifical Council for Inter-Religious Dialogue in an effort to create a liaison group between the WCC and the Vatican and world Islamic bodies. The churches' increasing interest in Islam was reflected in initiatives taken outside the WCC as well, including a series of Christian-Muslim encounters involving the Orthodox centre in Chambésy beginning in the mid-1980s and a Lutheran-Reformed consultation on Islam in Asia in the early 1990s.

Like its counterpart for Jewish-Christian relations, the document "Ecumenical Considerations on Christian-Muslim Relations" (1992) is shaped by the general WCC "Guidelines on Dialogue". Among common convictions affirmed by both Christians and Muslims, the document identifies belief in God as "the source of all life and of everything that exists", in God's oneness and in God's revelation to humanity through several prophets. At the same time it details the "real and substantial differences between Christian and Islamic teaching", particularly on the Trinity, which Muslims consider as tritheism, on the divine sonship of Jesus, which has no quranic sanction, on God's definitive revelation – for Christians, in Christ and his continuing work; for Muslims in the immutable Quran – and proselytism.

A central area of concern in the document, reflected in the work of the OIRR in the 1990s, was the situation of Christians in countries where Islamic law (sharia) is in force and how this relates to the call for Christians and Muslims to live and work together to establish love and justice in the world. A number of colloquia were organized on religion and law and on broader questions of human rights.[47] At the same time, several situations of political conflict in areas where the Muslim presence is prominent attracted the special attention of the OIRR.

Dialogue with primal religious traditions

The missionary attitude towards what are now generally called primal or traditional religions is reflected in some of the other names used for them: "tribal", "primitive", "animistic", "pagan". Indeed, some Christians have seen these religious expressions as superstition, not even deserving of the name religion. Moral, intellectual and social hindrances are seen as standing in the way of their conversion to Christianity. But signs of a more sympathetic attitude and approach can be seen in the "Missionary Message" of Edinburgh, based on the conviction that there is a modicum of truth in all religious systems, since God has not been left without a witness anywhere. Among the points of contact for the preaching of the gospel, it was suggested, were the belief in a higher power or supreme being, belief in an after-life, the practice of sacrifice, a "rudimentary moral sense and a dim consciousness of sin" in some cases, and the use of prayer to the chief or Great Spirit. Subsequent decades would bring into sharper relief the realization that no religion is exempt from elements of "superstition" and that

---

47 Cf. Tarek Mitri ed., *Religion, Law and Society: A Christian-Muslim Discussion*, WCC, 1995; Tarek Mitri, "A Christian-Muslim Consultation on 'Religion and Human Rights'", in *Current Dialogue*, 27, Dec. 1994, p.15; "Patient Dialogue, Urgent Dialogue", in *Current Dialogue*, 28, June 1995, pp.21-26; "Reports on Christian-Muslim Meetings in Tashkent, Abidjan and Geneva", in *Current Dialogue*, 29, pp.33-36.

the primal traditions had a holistic vision of life, community bonds, natural methods of healing and spontaneous expressions of religious life which are often absent in most other religious traditions, including Christianity.

In 1973 the Sub-unit on Dialogue joined with the All Africa Conference of Churches and the Theological Education Fund to organize a consultation in Ibadan, Nigeria, on "The Wholeness of Life: Christian Involvement in Mankind's Inner Dialogue with Primal World Views". The group reports concentrated on:

- humans in relation to tradition, nature, myths and symbols, divine presence and freedom;
- community in relation to Christ and Christianity; and
- sickness and healing.[48]

It was hoped that this consultation would be followed up locally and regionally, not only in Africa, but also in those parts of Asia and Oceania where Christians are influenced by primal world-views.

In its approach to the encounter with African religions, the Sub-unit on Dialogue worked in close consultation with the Vatican. The dialogue with primal religious traditions was seen primarily as an "internal dialogue", in which "the Christian interlocutor is confronted with authentic native tradition in his own life, in his social circle and in the Christian congregation".[49] "Some Reflections on African Experience of Salvation Today" was the title of one of the essays included in the materials for the world mission conference in Bangkok in 1972 on the theme "Salvation Today".[50]

While the WCC's fifth assembly (Nairobi 1975) deliberated on the issue of dialogue within the broad spectrum of world community, the venue afforded opportunities for encountering certain aspects of African religions and for taking dialogue with primal traditions more seriously. Similarly, a Native Canadian spiritual leader was one of the participants in the multifaith meeting held in Mauritius in 1983, in preparation for the Vancouver assembly later that year; and the Indigenous religion of Canada had a significant profile at the assembly itself – though not without raising objections in some quarters. Symbolic of this was a tall, intricate cedar totem pole, carved for the assembly by Aboriginal Canadian prisoners and given to the WCC. It was not placed within the confines of the Ecumenical Centre in Geneva as is customary with assembly gifts, but was erected at the Ecumenical Institute in Bossey, after considerable delay and controversy over the issue of possible syncretism.

After Vancouver, a consultation in Kitwe, Zambia, in 1986 brought together twenty African Christians from fourteen countries to consider the church's approach to traditional religion. It was acknowledged that "all African Christians have an ongoing dialogue with their traditional beliefs... a true encounter between Christianity and traditional beliefs may help incorporate the values, wisdom and understandings of community which have been essential to African culture in the life of the church".[51] The next year the sub-unit brought together in Sorrento, British Columbia, Canada, traditional elders from North America for a sharing on issues relevant to their life. To

---

[48] J.B. Taylor ed., *Primal World-Views: Christian Involvement in Dialogue with Traditional Thought-Forms*, Ibadan, Daystar, 1976.
[49] *Dialogue and Community*, p.88.
[50] John Mbiti, repr. in S.J. Samartha ed., *Living Faiths and Ultimate Goals*, WCC, 1974, pp.108-19.
[51] *Vancouver to Canberra*, p.136; see also the report *Towards a Dialogue between Christians and Traditionalists in Africa*, WCC, 1986.

suit their style there was no fixed agenda or presentation of papers. Yet the conversation was found to be very enriching.

The encounter with Australia's Aborigines and their beliefs and practices at the WCC's Canberra assembly in 1991 produced considerable reaction. But there was no detailed discussion of the specific issues of a dialogue between Christians and the Aboriginal communities. The assembly statement on Indigenous Peoples dealt primarily with their land rights, with only a passing mention of cultural, missiological and theological issues in connection with their historical mistreatment at the hands of missionaries and the need to protect their sacred sites from desecration. Indigenous Peoples felt their concerns were treated in a somewhat trivializing manner.

Some of these issues did receive a certain amount of ecumenical attention in the study process on gospel and culture in preparation for the world mission conference in Salvador, Brazil, in 1996, though the scope was broader than the area of primal religions.[52] There has been increasing realization ecumenically that the gospel, both in its original form and in its later presentations through the missionary movement, has always been culture-bound in one way or other. Thus, the primal religions should be given their rightful place in the main discussions on interfaith dialogue. Moreover, interfaith dialogue with only the classical traditions of the world's religions has serious limitations; for example, proper awareness of the dynamics of the Hindu religious traditions requires encounter with the distinctive characteristics of diverse cults and folk traditions; and, to a lesser extent, "folk Islam" in its different forms exposes a process of integration between the traditional tenets of Islam and local beliefs and practices. The increased involvement of the WCC with the concerns of Indigenous Peoples around the world in the period after the Canberra assembly, reaffirmed by the Harare assembly in 1998, has included issues of religious expressions and spirituality as one of the key areas for ecumenical focus and has initiated a process of cooperation with the desk for Indigenous Peoples.

DIALOGUE WITH PEOPLE OF SECULAR IDEOLOGIES

The secular ideologies of the 20th century have often been regarded as a form of religion or quasi-religion. Stephen Neill, Anglican missionary to India and ecumenical pioneer, is a case in point. Neill included Marxist communism as one of the "other faiths" which Christians encounter. In doing so, he gave the word "religion" a wider meaning than many traditional definitions, understanding it "in terms of man's ultimate concern for his life and that of others" – a concern which he found in Marxist communism.

> Still more, if we understand religion in terms of faith and particularly faith in a purpose, we must recognize that Marxist communism can awaken a burning and devouring faith, devotion and self-sacrifice, such as are best understood in religious categories.[53]

---

[52] For an overview see S. Wesley Ariarajah, *Gospel and Culture: An Ongoing Discussion within the Ecumenical Movement*, WCC, 1994, the first of a series of 18 Gospel and Cultures pamphlets emerging from the WCC study process; others included Stan McKay and Janet Silman, *The First Nations: A Canadian Experience of the Gospel-Culture Encounter* (no. 2, 1995); Juan Sepúlveda, *The Andean Highlands: An Encounter with Two Forms of Christianity* (no. 17, 1997); and Anne Pattel-Gray and John P. Brown eds, *Indigenous Australia: A Dialogue about the Word Becoming Flesh in Aboriginal Churches* (no. 18, 1997).
[53] Stephen Neill, *Christian Faith and Other Faiths: The Christian Dialogue with Other Religions*, Lucknow, Lucknow Publ. House, 1966, p.153.

Already at the world mission conference in Jerusalem in 1928, the idea of a common religious front against the growing trends of materialism and secularism had gained currency. Moreover, a large number of studies on Christianity and Marxism by churches and academic groups had been carried out, with regional variations, in different parts of the world.[54] However, it was difficult to find partners for discussions on the issues raised by the "secular faiths" in terms of social changes and the assumptions of science and technology. Seeing the need to approach this issue from various perspectives, steps were taken after the Uppsala assembly to make this a joint enterprise of several sectors within the WCC.

When the central committee approved the plan to create a Sub-unit on Dialogue with People of Living Faiths in 1971, concern was expressed that the bilateral and multilateral dialogues already being undertaken should be balanced by a dialogue with ideologies; as a result, the words "and ideologies" were added to the sub-unit's name – and its brief. But from the outset there were problems with working out a solid programme of dialogue with secular ideologies. Such issues as the definition of ideologies, the identification of partners for dialogue, the lack of finance and a suitable person to translate the mandate into a programme were serious difficulties but the concern never died out. In 1984 the central committee approved a recommendation to delete the words "and ideologies" from the title of the Sub-unit on Dialogue in favour of forming a staff team to coordinate the work on ideologies, with administrative responsibility vested in the Commission on the Churches' on Participation in Development. Several efforts were made through small consultations,[55] but the issue remained largely dormant on the WCC agenda. By 1992, when a new structure for the WCC came into being, communism as a state ideology had collapsed and the states which had been founded on the basis of Marxism in Eastern Europe had disintegrated.

> In effect, there was no longer a *partner* for Christian-Marxist dialogue – this possibility on which so much thought and energy had been expended by the WCC over a period of nearly two decades. It was a termination rather than a conclusion, an end without a beginning.[56]

Ecumenically, there has been a recognition that the failure of Marxism in Europe is not an occasion for rejoicing in the triumph of the "religious" over the "ideological", but rather an opportunity for in-depth discussion of the nature and destiny of human life and history.

Neill's question of the transcendental dimension or sense of the sacred, mentioned earlier, comes up repeatedly in the context of Christian dialogue with secular ideologies. On this point Ucko reminds Marxists that Marx once said, "as long as humankind reflects, it reflects religiously". Then he continues:

> And even if we set all prisoners free, fed all the hungry, clothed all the naked, healed all the wounds and banned all the wars, we would still always hear the voice within us: "Who am I? From where do I come and where do I go?" This voice is a voice of spirituality which keeps on asking us if we are not more than ashes. Someone has rightly called it... an ocean-like feeling.[57]

---

[54] Cf. Stanley J. Samartha, *Between Two Cultures: Ecumenical Ministry in a Pluralist World*, WCC, 1996, p.64, 84ff. An essay on "A Marxist View of Liberation" was included in *Living Faiths and Ultimate Goals,* 1974, pp.56ff.
[55] See *Vital Ecumenical Concerns*, pp.162-74; and *Churches among Ideologies: Report of a Consultation and Recommendations to Fellow Christians*, WCC, 1982.
[56] *Vital Ecumenical Concerns*, pp.88f.
[57] Ucko, "Christian-Marxist Dialogue: Crisis or Kairos?", in *Current Dialogue*, 18, June 1990, p.25.

This is an example of the possibility of Christianity correcting Marxist materialism. From the other side, however, Marxists – or anyone professing a "secular" ideology – can offer a corrective to forms of religion, including Christianity, which tend to be introverted and oppressive, to hinder social progress and scientific advance, to follow only narrow political interests.

Mention should be made of dialogue with certain north Asian traditions, in Japan and China, where radical changes have taken place due to wars and cultural revolution. Christians in these countries have sometimes been hesitant to initiate dialogue with certain traditions in their context. The WCC has, however, sought to maintain contact and develop cooperative work with the Christian centres for the Study of Chinese and Japanese religions and cultures in Hong Kong and China, and a few conferences have taken place.[58]

DIALOGUE IN PARTNERSHIP

While this chapter has concentrated on the role of the Sub-unit on Dialogue (in its successive organizational manifestations within the structure of the WCC), this work has never been undertaken in isolation – not only for the practical reason that this has always been one of the smaller WCC staff teams, but more importantly because the very idea of interfaith dialogue implies a style and ethos of working in partnership. Three aspects of this cooperation and contact are mentioned briefly.

Collaboration within the WCC

Especially in the period following the Vancouver assembly in 1983, priority was given to collaborative programmes integrating the interfaith dimension into other aspects of the work of the WCC.[59] Participants from other faith communities contributed to the WCC's priority discussion on Justice, Peace and the Integrity of Creation (JPIC), including the world convocation on the subject in Seoul in 1990.[60] To the discussions on contextualization within the Programme on Theological Education, dialogue provided a reminder of the multifaith context.[61] In collaboration with the WCC Sub-unit on Women, a consultation in Toronto, Canada, in 1988 brought together fifty women from eight different faiths to discuss issues such as scripture and Tradition, authority and leadership, and identity and sexuality, that affect women across religious lines. In another consultation, at Kyoto, Japan, the Dialogue sub-unit explored the issues of "Spirituality in Dialogue" along with the Sub-unit on Renewal and Congregational Life.[62] In several cases advice and consultation from an interfaith perspective have been critical for the WCC's dealing with international affairs when tensions or conflict arise around sensitive issues per-

---

[58] For a report on an international Confucian-Christian conference held in California in 1991, see Peter K.H. Lee, "Breaking New Grounds in Confucian-Christian Dialogue", in *Current Dialogue*, 21, Dec. 1991, pp.12-15.
[59] For examples see *Vancouver to Canberra*, pp.137ff.
[60] See *Current Dialogue*, 15, Dec. 1988, pp.4-15; 20, July 1991, pp.41-47.
[61] See the report of a consultation sponsored by PTE and the Sub-unit on Dialogue on the implications for interfaith dialogue for theological education, in Kuala Lumpur, in 1985, S. Amirtham and S. Wesley Ariarajah eds, *Ministerial Formation in a Multi-Faith Milieu: Implications of Interfaith Dialogue for Theological Education*, WCC, 1986.
[62] For the report and papers, see T. Arai and S. Wesley Ariarajah eds, *Spirituality in Inter-Faith Dialogue*, WCC, 1989.

taining to other faith communities. And, as noted earlier, ecumenical discussion of mission and evangelism issues has been an arena in which the issue of the approach to people of other faiths is always present.

Such collaboration has also sometimes taken the form of working together with the WCC's related organizations in Geneva. A key example was the consultation jointly facilitated by the Dialogue sub-unit and the Lutheran World Federation in Amsterdam in 1986 on New Religious Movements.[63] The LWF subsequently launched a major study project on the church and people of other faiths.

Collaboration with the Vatican

When the Second Vatican Council (1962-65) led to greater openness on the part of the Roman Catholic Church to collaboration with the WCC, one of the areas in which this was realized was interfaith dialogue. The Pontifical Council for Inter-religious Dialogue (previously known as the Secretariat for Non-Christians) has regularly been invited to meetings of the advisory bodies for the WCC Dialogue sub-unit and its successors, and vice-versa; and there are annual joint meetings of the staff of the two bodies. The OIRR has encouraged Protestant participation in the ministry of dialogue organized by Roman Catholics at national, regional and local levels. As noted earlier, the two staff groups launched common studies on interfaith prayer and interfaith marriages.

Collaboration with other interfaith networks

Many organizations and networks on interfaith dialogue have grown up around the world, attesting to the breadth of interest in this encounter, especially since religious plurality has become evident in many more places in the past thirty years (though the oldest of these initiatives antedates the organized ecumenical movement of the 20th century). The Interfaith Network for the United Kingdom, established in 1987, links some seventy organizations. The *Guide to Inter-Religious Activities in Israel,* published in 1994, mentions more than fifty organizations.

The International Association for Religious Freedom (from 1900), the World Congress of Faiths (from 1936), the Temple of Understanding (from 1960) and the World Conference on Religion and Peace (from 1965) have been working at the international level to promote inter-religious understanding and peace.[64] The WCC's Dialogue programme kept in touch with these organizations and participated in their major events. Some of these organizations jointly convened a cluster of events in 1993 in different parts of the world to mark the centenary of the Chicago Parliament of the World's Religions. An attempt was made in this context to formulate a "global ethic" acceptable to all religious communities in dialogue, and, while there have been differences of opinion on the nature of this ethic and its applicability, the discussion continues.

In recent years, the OIRR has been organizing meetings in collaboration with national and regional interfaith dialogue centres and groups.[65] There are indications to suggest that this collaborative style will become increasingly prominent in the years to come, and that groups of people adhering to other faiths will take more and more ini-

---

[63] For the report and papers see Allan Brockway and J. Paul Rajashekar eds, *New Religious Movements and the Churches,* WCC, 1987.
[64] For their origin and activities see *Pilgrimage of Hope,* pp.44ff.
[65] E.g., for meetings held in India in 1995 see Hans Ucko "Travel Report from India", in *Current Dialogue,* 29, Jan. 1996, pp.2-6; cf. p.35.

tiatives in interfaith dialogue, for which the impulse still comes overwhelmingly from the Christian side.

LOOKING TO THE FUTURE

While the controversy within the ecumenical movement over interfaith dialogue is not over, no one can deny its significance and influence on the thinking and doing of the ecumenical movement. Despite the opposition from many quarters, the WCC's sub-unit, from its beginning in the 1970s, has enabled a sustained "dialogue on dialogue" within the churches and has opened up new avenues of conversation and cooperation with communities of other religious traditions. Much of the widespread interest in interfaith dialogue today and many initiatives that come from a great variety of sources can no doubt be traced to the impact that the sub-unit has had on the churches and other faith communities.

BIBLIOGRAPHY

Arai, Tosh and Ariarajah, S. Wesley eds, *Spirituality in Interfaith Dialogue*, WCC, 1989, 103p.
Ariarajah, S. Wesley, *The Bible and People of Other Faiths*, WCC, 1985, 71p.
Ariarajah, S. Wesley, *Hindus and Christians: A Century of Protestant Ecumenical Thought*, Amsterdam, Rodopi, 1991, 244p.
Ariarajah, S. Wesley, *Not Without My Neighbour: Issues in Interfaith Relations*, WCC, 1999, 130p.
Bent, A. J. van der, *The Utopia of World Community*, London, SCM Press, 1973, 150p.
Braaten, Carl E., *No Other Gospel! Christianity among the World's Religions*, Minneapolis MN, Fortress, 1992, 146p.
Braybrooke, Marcus, *Pilgrimage of Hope: One Hundred Years of Global Interfaith Dialogue*, London, SCM Press, 1992, 367p.
Brockway, Allan R., *The Meaning of Life: A Multi-Faith Consultation in Preparation for the Sixth WCC Assembly*, WCC, 1983, 20p.
Brockway, Allan, van Buren, Paul, Rendtorff, Rolf and Schoon, Simon eds, *The Theology of the Churches and the Jewish People: Statements by the World Council of Churches and Its Member Churches*, WCC, 1988, 186p.
Brown, Stuart E., *Meeting in Faith: Twenty Years of Christian-Muslim Conversations Sponsored by the World Council of Churches*, WCC, 1989, 181p.
Brown, Stuart E., *The Nearest in Affection: Towards a Christian Understanding of Islam*, WCC, 1994, 124p.
Brueggemann, Walter and Stroup, George W. eds, *Many Voices, One God: Being Faithful in a Pluralistic World*, Louisville KY, Westminster John Knox, 1998, 202p.
The Challenge of Dialogue: Papers and Resolutions of the Dialogue Working Group Meeting: Casablanca, Morocco, June 1989, WCC, 1989, 170p.
Dhavamony, Mariasusai, *Interfaith Dialogue: Christianity and Other Religions – Dialogue interreligieux: Christianisme et autres religions*, Rome, Pontifical Gregorian University, 1994, 362p.
Dialogue in Community: Statement and Reports of a Theological Consultation, Chiang Mai, Thailand, 18-27 April 1977, WCC, 1991, 16p.
Dupuis, Jacques, *Toward a Christian Theology of Religious Pluralism*, Maryknoll NY, Orbis, 1997, 433p.
Eck, Diana L., *Encountering God: A Spiritual Journey from Bozeman to Banaras*, Boston, Beacon Press, 1993, 259p.
Ecumenical Considerations for Dialogue and Relations with People of Other Religions, WCC, 2003, 15p.
Guidelines on Dialogue with People of Living Faiths and Ideologies, WCC, 1979, 30p.
Gort, Jerald Dale ed., *Dialogue and Syncretism: An Interdisciplinary Approach*, Grand Rapids MI, Eerdmans, 1989, 228p.

Gort, Jerald Dale et al. eds, *On Sharing Religious Experience: Possibilities of Interfaith Mutuality*, Grand Rapids MI, Eerdmans, 1992, 304p.

Hallencreutz, Carl F., *Dialogue and Community: Ecumenical Issues in Inter-Religious Relationships*, WCC, 1977, 109p.

Heim, S. Mark, ed., *Grounds for Understanding: Ecumenical Resources for Responses to Religious Pluralism*, Grand Rapids MI, Eerdmans, 1998, 227p.

Küng, Hans, *Christianity and World Religions: Paths of Dialogue with Islam, Hinduism, and Buddhism*, Maryknoll NY, Orbis, 1993, 460p.

Kuschel, Karl-Joseph, *Abraham: A Symbol of Hope for Jews, Christians and Muslims*, London, SCM Press, 1995, 286p.

May, John D'Arcy, *Pluralism and the Religions: The Theological and Political Dimensions*, London, Cassell, 1998, 99p.

Mitri, Tarek, ed., *Religion, Law and Society: A Christian-Muslim Discussion*, WCC, 1995, 137p.

My Neighbour's Faith – and Mine: Theological Discoveries through Interfaith Dialogue: A Study Guide, WCC, 1986, 53p.

Ruokanen, Miikka, *The Catholic Doctrine of Non-Christian Religion according to the Second Vatican Council*, Leiden, Brill, 1992, 169p.

Samartha, S.J. and Taylor, J.B. eds, *Christian-Muslim Dialogue: Papers Presented at the Broumana Consultation, 12-18 July 1972*, WCC, 1973, 167p.

Samartha, S.J., *Courage for Dialogue: Ecumenical Issues in Inter-Religious Relationships*, WCC, 1981, 157p.

Samartha, S.J. ed., *Faith in the Midst of Faiths: Reflections on Dialogue in Community: Consultation, Chiang Mai, 1977*, WCC, 1977, 198p.

Samartha, S.J. ed., *Living Faiths and the Ecumenical Movement*, WCC, 1971, 183p.

Samartha, S.J. ed., *Living Faiths and Ultimate Goals: A Continuing Dialogue*, WCC, 1974, 120p.

Samartha, S.J., *One Christ, Many Religions: Toward a Revised Christology*, Maryknoll NY, Orbis, 1991.

Samartha, S.J. ed, *Towards World Community: The Colombo Papers*, WCC, 1975, 165p.

Selvanayagam, Israel, *A Dialogue on Dialogue*, Madras, CLS, 1995.

Selvanayagam, Israel, *A Second Call: Ministry and Mission in a Multifaith Milieu*, Madras, CLS, 2000.

Sharpe, Eric J., *Faith Meets Faith: Some Christian Attitudes to Hinduism in the Nineteenth and Twentieth Centuries*, London, SCM Press, 1977, 178p.

Sherwin, Byron L. and Kasimow, Harold eds, *John Paul II and Interreligious Dialogue*, Maryknoll NY, Orbis, 1999, 236p.

Singh, David Emmanuel and Singh, Robert Edwin eds, *Approaches, Foundations, Issues and Models of Interfaith Relations*, Delhi, ISPCK, 2001, 499p.

Sperber, Jutta, *Christians and Muslims: The Dialogue Activities of the World Council of Churches and Their Theological Foundation*, Berlin, Walter de Gruyter, 2000, 484p.

Taylor, John Bernard, *Primal World Views: Christian Involvement in Dialogue with Traditional Thought Forms: Consultation, Ibadan, September 1973*, Ibadan, Daystar, 1976, 131p.

Thomas, M.M., *Risking Christ for Christ's Sake: Towards an Ecumenical Theology of Pluralism*, WCC, 1987, 122p.

Tillich, Paul, *Christianity and the Encounter of World Religions*, Minneapolis MN, Fortress, 1994, 79p.

Ucko, Hans ed., *People of God, Peoples of God: A Jewish-Christian Conversation in Asia*, WCC, 1996, 112p.

Willebrands, Johannes Gerardus Maria, *Church and Jewish People: New Considerations*, New York, Paulist, 1992, 280p.

8
Ecumenical Formation

Ulrich Becker

Ecumenical formation is "an ongoing process of learning within the various local churches and world communions". This process is aimed at informing and guiding people in the ecumenical movement which, inspired by the Holy Spirit, seeks the visible unity of Christians. This is how the study document of the Joint Working Group between the Roman Catholic Church and the World Council of Churches, published in 1993, described ecumenical formation. It went on to explain,

> As a process of learning, ecumenical formation is concerned with engaging the experience, knowledge, skills, talents and the religious memory of the Christian community for mutual enrichment and reconciliation... The language of formation and learning refers to some degree to a body of knowledge to be absorbed. That is important; but formation and learning require a certain bold openness to living ecumenically as well... ecumenical formation takes place not only in formal educational programmes but also in the daily life of the church and people.[1]

It is in this broad understanding that the term "ecumenical formation" is used here, covering all programmes, publications and other activities of the ecumenical movement, whether or not terms like "ecumenical education", "education for ecumenism", "ecumenical learning", "ecumenical theological education", "ecumenical training" and so on, are used.

> Since the term was first used ecumenically in the 1965 Gazzada statement on "lay formation", it has been understood that "formation" is not to be limited to programmes of instruction; it is more than training or even education. It refers to the whole process of equipping, enabling, raising awareness, shaping or transforming attitudes and values.[2]

ECUMENICAL FORMATION: RECALLING A MEMORY

As one dimension of the movement, ecumenical formation has always formed part of, and been related to, all activities carried out in the ecumenical context. Involvement in interconfessional questions – e.g., interchurch aid, activities to combat racism, an ecumenical work camp or a team visit – has been for many even more educational than spe-

---

* Some material for this chapter has been provided by Simon Oxley.
[1] "Ecumenical Formation: Ecumenical Reflections and Suggestions", in *The Ecumenical Review*, 45, 4, 1993, p.490, §§9,11,12,13.
[2] K. Raiser, "Fifty Years of Ecumenical Formation: Where Are We? Where Are We Going?" in *The Ecumenical Review*, 48, 4, Oct. 1996, p.440.

cial programmes and conferences. Discerning, admitting and overcoming past and present theological, socio-political and cultural differences and barriers is possible only where comprehensive learning takes place. The ecumenical movement has, therefore, to be understood as a learning movement.

In the years after the second world war, the main "breeding-grounds" (H.R. Weber) for ecumenical learning were the Student Christian Movements, but other centres were found in lay movements such as the YWCA, the YMCA, initiatives like the German *Kirchentag*, missionary service overseas of ecumenically committed persons from "older" to "younger" churches and vice-versa, ecumenical service through fraternal workers in CIMADE (Comité inter-mouvement auprès des évacués – Inter-movement Committee for Evacuees), Friend's Service, Refugee Service, the Fellowship of the Least Coin, the Week of Prayer for Christian Unity and other spontaneous actions within the ecumenical movement. Since the WCC is a major instrument of this movement, the knowledge, values, awareness and perspectives that were generated through its many and varied activities had far-reaching implications for the development of ecumenical formation. The Ecumenical Institute, established in 1946 at Bossey, Switzerland, as "a centre of ecumenical education", has been particularly influential as "a sort of laboratory where ecumenism is being lived".[3]

It was noted at the Belfast assembly of the World Council of Christian Education (WCCE) in 1962 that the ecumenical movement and especially the WCC were already involved in a wide variety of special educational activities. In 1961 the Commission on World Mission and Evangelism (CWME) created a desk on education. In 1958 the IMC created the Theological Education Fund (TEF), which after 1961 became a service of the CWME. In 1977 it became the Programme on Theological Education (PTE) and then Ecumenical Theological Education (ETE). The WCC started its scholarships programme in 1945, and undertook joint youth work with the WCCE in 1957. From 1961 there was cooperation between the Ecumenical Institute, the Laity and the Youth departments with the WCCE and sponsorship jointly with the WCCE of the Education Renewal Fund in 1969 which would "seek to encourage renewal and reform of education in the churches and in society".[4]

The fourth world conference on Faith and Order (Montreal 1963), after receiving a document on "The Revision of Catechism in the Light of the Ecumenical Movement", recommended cooperation between Faith and Order and the WCCE, a consequence of which was a report on "Ecumenical Commitment and Christian Education" (1967). One of its conclusions was that

---

[3] Visser 't Hooft called the Ecumenical Institute "a centre of ecumenical education" in his speech at the opening of Bossey in 1946 and he explained further: "...the centre must have a truly ecumenical character. It should be the place where men and women of all the member churches of the ecumenical movement learn together, receiving and giving, learn to struggle one for the other, and where they thus accept the tension between truth and unity which is at the basis of any true ecumenical community. The programme of the institute, therefore, has three main subjects: the Bible, the world and the universal church..." Cf. K. Raiser, op. cit., p.440. It was Suzanne de Diétrich who called this institute a sort of laboratory... cf. H. R. Weber, "A Laboratory of Ecumenical Life", in *The Ecumenical Review*, 48, 4, 1996, p.435.

[4] Proposal for the establishment of an Education Renewal Fund, jointly sponsored by the World Council of Churches and the World Council of Christian Education, appendix VII to the Minutes of the Central Committee meeting in Canterbury 1969, p.177.

"ecumenical commitment" and "Christian education" are inextricably linked. Christian education which is not ecumenical is not truly Christian, for it lacks engagement with the world in which men live and with their "separated brethren".[5]

In spite of all these various educational activities, Christian education is only mentioned once in a more detailed form in the second volume of *A History of the Ecumenical Movement*. In connection with the Uppsala assembly (1968) and in the context of the final report of the joint study commission on education (1969), it is stated,

This will for the first time put the World Council squarely into the technical problems of education. Until Uppsala the World Council had stayed out of the field partly because of the existence of the World Council of Christian Education.[6]

The challenge of involving in an ecumenical learning process those who did not actively share in the life of the ecumenical movement was addressed in "The Revision of Catechisms". It raised the question which still remains pertinent: How far do the teaching materials which are used in our churches reflect their ecumenical commitments and intentions?[7]

The search for a concept of ecumenical formation within the WCC occurred as early as the 1950s. In a statement to the central committee in 1957, the Division of Ecumenical Action tried to describe "(1) what 'ecumenical education' really means, and (2) who should have the responsibility for it".[8] The answers offered there were:

The term "ecumenical" envisages the one missionary church in process of renewal. Therefore, "ecumenical education" can no longer be limited to the history of attempts to reunite churches or the growth of ecumenical organizations. Ecumenical education essentially means fostering understanding of, commitment to and informed participation in this whole ecumenical process.

Responsibility for implementing ecumenical education does not rest only with a division of the WCC, nor with the WCC as a whole, nor with the member churches, but with Christian parents, teachers, pastors, theological colleges, lay training centres and so on, and also with national councils of churches and with the whole WCC. Thus ecumenical education is aiming at a far wider participation, and such participation includes not only educational activities, but also ecumenical worship, service and creative experiments.

This statement denoted a shift from "teaching about" to "fostering understanding of, commitment to and informed participation in" the ecumenical process. The background in formulating this goal was that the vision of the one missionary church in process of renewal, when it is apprehended, leads all members of the church to an ecumenical commitment.

In the following years a comprehensive understanding of ecumenical formation was only slowly accepted; in discussions the need for a special programme activity in this field surfaced more and more. So the New Delhi report of 1962 described as one of the functions of the WCC's Division of Ecumenical Action "to help the churches to relate

[5] *Ecumenical Commitment and Christian Education, A Report to the WCC Commission on Faith and Order*, WCC, 1967, p.31.
[6] E. Carson Blake, "Uppsala and Afterwards", in Harold E. Fey ed., *A History of the Ecumenical Movement*, vol. II 1948-1968, WCC, 1970, p.438.
[7] Patrick C. Roger and Lukas Vischer eds, *The Fourth World Conference on Faith and Order, Montreal, 1963*, Faith and Order Paper no.42, London, SCM Press, 1964, p.61.
[8] WCC Central Committee, *Minutes of the Tenth Meeting*, New Haven, 1957, p.105.

ecumenical thinking to Christian concern for education in all its aspects, and to encourage experiments in new methods of ecumenical education".[9] Furthermore, this report distinguished explicitly between ecumenical education, Christian education and education in general, and tried to define ecumenical education as "information about the history and present expressions of the ecumenical movement and education for personal participation in ecumenical responsibilities for witness, service and unity". Therefore, churches were asked "to work out in terms of Sunday school curricula, catechetical instruction and other forms of Christian education, substantial material which enables young people and adults to understand and appreciate the ecumenical movement and prepares them to share it". The following discussions mentioned in this report noted, however, that producing substantial materials could only be part of the unsolved task. More attention should be given to the "real heart of the task", namely, "to open the eyes of the teacher to a new dimension". And further, "consultations and cooperation can bring a true ecumenical perspective even better than written materials".

ECUMENICAL FORMATION AFTER 1968

A new beginning: education on the agenda of the ecumenical movement

Ecumenical formation was given a new focus when education was placed explicitly on the agenda of the ecumenical movement. Following the WCC's fourth assembly at Uppsala in 1968, the Office of Education was established within the Division of Ecumenical Action in 1969.

> Step by step the insight had grown that not only is the traditional way of the WCC in itself a learning process, but that also the concrete questions of general, Christian and theological education demand considerate special attention within the ecumenical framework.[10]

Three additional factors encouraged this new beginning. Firstly, the role of education became increasingly important in societies. In the 1960s, discussion centred on the "explosion in education... as part... of the explosions in knowledge, technology, population and expectations"[11] and a "world crisis in education" threatened the responsible persons in governments, universities and the churches. A joint study commission on education of the WCC and the WCCE worked between 1964 and 1968. Its secretary, Theodore A. Gill, addressed the Uppsala assembly in 1968, saying,

> It is in education, among those being educated, that the protest comes against a spiritually, morally, humanly underdeveloped world, just in those countries we are most used to thinking of as developed. It is in education where this ultimate underdevelopment is being attacked. Much more is wrong than the curricula and communications, just as much more will finally have to give besides schools and the mass media. But once again it is in and around education where all the main problems surface...[12]

[9] W.A. Visser 't Hooft ed., *The New Delhi Report: The Third Assembly of the World Council of Churches 1961*, London, SCM Press, 1962, p.198. Following quotes from pp.198, 199, 201.
[10] K. E. Nipkow, "Christian Education and Ecumenical Faith", in *Education Newsletter*, 2, 1983, p.1.
[11] *Work Book for the Assembly Committees*, prepared for the Fourth Assembly of the World Council of Churches, Uppsala, Sweden, 4-19 July 1968, WCC, 1968, p.166.
[12] A. H. van den Heuvel ed., *Unity of Mankind*, WCC, 1969, p.69. Cf. Norman Goodall ed., *The Uppsala Report: Official Report of the Fourth Assembly of the World Council of Churches, Uppsala July 4-20, 1968*, WCC, 1968, pp.134ff.

The assembly's final report maintained that the church has urgent responsibilities in three inter-related sectors – the explosive situation in general education; pressing issues in church educational institutions at all levels; the enormous challenges in the churches' nurture and training of their members of all ages in congregational life and in other ways.

Secondly, it was recognized that the churches, although they had a long history and involvement in education, were not prepared to deal with the crisis in education. The churches had to "come to new terms with a cultural institution long familiar but suddenly novel in its size and its dynamism, and not waiting a minute for the churches' attention, suggestions or adjustment".[13] The prevailing impression in the ecumenical movement was of a vast variety of educational programmes, but no concentration.

> All our major conferences..., our principal reports to the assembly, most of the papers prepared... invoke education in their prescriptions for action, but there is no address on their invocations. We must do better. For our own sake, if no one else.

Thirdly, after ten years of conversations and negotiations, the WCCE decided in Lima 1971 to merge itself into the educational work of the WCC.

The Office of Education in the WCC

In the light of the theme of the Uppsala assembly, "Behold, I make all things new", the distinctive task of the Office of Education was "to stir up and equip all of God's people for ecumenical understanding, active engagement in renewing the life of the churches, and participation in God's work in a changing world".[14] This dual focus on the renewal of the churches and the transformation of the societies determined the educational policy. The report of the first consultation organized by the new office in Bergen, Norway, in 1970, "Seeing Education Whole", laid out the principles of a new approach:
- a critical analysis of schools as systems and a new priority for non-formal education combined with the development of alternatives to school education;
- the recognition that there is no neutral education and, therefore, a need to understand the role of church education in liberating or domesticating people; churches should ally themselves with other forces in society that are working for education towards freedom and transformation;
- the urgent necessity for the churches to renounce the use of religious education as a means of self-preservation;
- a broader participation of all in making educational decisions and of problem-solving with people rather than for them;
- a fundamental reappraisal and reshaping of educational processes with conscientization rather than indoctrination and a reflection-action process;
- the rediscovery of the global dimension and responsibility of the Christian faith with a consequence that education develops intercultural awareness and counters purely nationalist or confessionalist attitudes; and
- a basic reconsideration and reformulation of the concept of leadership-training in the church and in society in the light of the changing perception of "the whole people of

---

[13] *Work Book*, p.168.
[14] *Ibid.*, p.246.

God"; the development of a mature and effective body of Christians in the world demands a reappraisal of the separated systems of training for clergy and laity.[15]

These principles must be seen in the general context of the 1960s with its widespread hope for change and transformation, especially for the poor, dispossessed, marginalized and powerless. The writing of Ivan Illich on "de-schooling" and Paulo Freire's *Pedagogy of the Oppressed*[16] gave a conceptual and methodological challenge to the educational status quo.

Later some of the one-sidednesses of these principles had to be corrected or at least interpreted to avoid false alternatives. This began at the WCC's Nairobi assembly (1975) which was held against the background of several world crises – the widening gap between rich and poor, growing environmental pollution, and the food, urban and energy crises of 1973. The fifth assembly was the first where educational questions were raised before the ecumenical forum as a whole, confirming the increasing importance of education in the ecumenical movement and in the churches all over the world. At the same time, it became obvious that a critical analysis of the world situation and the will to change structures is not enough. "At the centre of the learning experience in the church stands worship and liturgy. This is the joyous expression of the Christians' dependence on God and Christ's presence in the life of his community."[17] The education section report in Nairobi was entitled "Education for Liberation and Community". Its image is of an ellipse "comprising two poles, world and worship, liberation and community, action-reflection processes (including 'doing theology') and prayer, finally coming back to the beginning, holding together both fundamental aspects as one joint perspective."[18] One of the results of an urgent request for a better theological basis of all educational activities was linking the portfolio of biblical studies with the new Sub-unit on Education to enable better biblical reflection on education and renewal.

In spite of such clarifications and corrections, there is no question that the holistic approach influenced the educational policy of the WCC and the ecumenical movement as a whole and strengthened the attempts to put ecumenical formation in the centre of the educational policy. This was supported by the pedagogical insights provided by Paulo Freire between 1969 and 1980 as a consultant to the Office of Education. Programmes were built on the aspirations of those who were not engaged through existing patterns of ecumenical engagement. Freire's methodologies enabled the awakening of "the consciousness of people to situations in which their own silence and submissiveness contributed to their continued bondage".[19]

---

[15] *Seeing Education Whole:* An Invitation from the First Consultation of the Office of Education of the World Council of Churches, to Share in an Attempt to Understand the Distinctive Tasks and Challenges Facing Education throughout the World Today and to Envisage the Particular Contribution of Christians, WCC, 1970.

[16] Paulo Freire, *Pedagogy of the Oppressed*, London, Continuum, 1972. I. Illich, *Deschooling Society*, Harmondsworth, Penguin, 1973.

[17] D.M. Paton ed., *Breaking Barriers: Nairobi 1975: The Official Report of the Fifth Assembly of the World Council of Churches, Nairobi, 23 November-10 December, 1975*, London, SPCK, 1976, p.91.

[18] "Alienation, Liberation, Community: The Educational Policy of the WCC before and after Nairobi", in *The Ecumenical Review*, 30, 2, 1978, p.139.

[19] D.E. Johnson ed., *Uppsala to Nairobi 1968-1975: Report of the Central Committee to the Fifth Assembly of the World Council of Churches*, New York, Friendship Press, 1975, p.184.

Development education: actions of solidarity

It is not possible to speak about the ecumenical formation activities which were strongly influenced by Paulo Freire without mentioning the fast growing work of development education within the Commission on the Churches' Participation in Development (CCPD), established in 1970. It defined development as a process aimed at social justice, self-reliance and economic growth and "was quick to point to the need for a supportive educational programme".[20]

Although similar to related educational activities (e.g., global education, education for international understanding, education for justice, peace education) this programme was rooted in the practical work of various churches with projects and programmes in developing countries. It was clear that "people had to learn how to participate and what to struggle for... It was necessary to inform and educate people about the issues at stake and to encourage and stimulate them to bring pressure to bear on political decision-making processes."[21]

The desk for development education started its work in 1971 linked to fund-raising activities "for educational programmes, the mobilization of public opinion and the financing of political action, especially in the affluent countries, to foster world cooperation for development".[22] In the beginning the attempt was made to work at every level, e.g., the revision of church educational programmes in the light of the criteria of justice, self-reliance and participation; appropriate training for local personnel by missionary and interchurch aid agencies; encouraging governments to revise curricula; support for political action groups (working on specific issues relating to trade and aid); encouraging literacy campaigns based on Paulo Freire's methodology. Reinhild Traitler comments in an assessment of development education in this period, "Needless to say, this state of enthusiastic innocence could not, and did not, last long."[23]

Two reasons for this observation should be mentioned. This approach, which strongly advocated social justice, brought development education into conflict with those who believed in neutrality. There was also an enormous underestimation of the scale of the task of education in processes of social change. "Changes of attitudes are not to be achieved in a matter of years, not even of decades, especially if the total social environment militates against such a change."[24] Nevertheless, the desk for development education pioneered a kind of alternative education based on liberating experiences, involvement in actions that express solidarity with the poor and the search for alternatives in social organization and life-styles. This new type of alternative education grew rapidly in churches and in networks of the ecumenical movement. With its strong emphasis on non-formal education, it influenced the educational policy of donor-and-interchurch aid agencies and challenged traditional religious and theological education programmes.

---

[20] R. Traitler ed., *Leaping over the Wall: An Assessment of Ten Years' Development Education*, WCC, 1982, p.1.
[21] *Ibid.*, pp.22-23.
[22] P. Gruber ed., *Fetters of Injustice: Report of an Ecumenical Consultation on Ecumenical Assistance to Development Projects, 26-31 January 1970, Montreux, Switzerland*, WCC, 1970, p.126.
[23] *Leaping Over the Wall*, p.3.
[24] *Ibid.*, p.24.

A MORE COHERENT CONCEPT OF ECUMENICAL FORMATION

Some old and new tensions

A tension between a teaching-oriented approach to ecumenical formation and a more holistic model continues to surface in discussions and programmes: one understands and practises ecumenical formation as formal instruction and cognitive learning where a teacher with subject matter, curriculum resources and structured classes is the norm. It might relate to training for a particular task in church or society or to the formation of those with a certain responsibility for ministry and leadership in the church.

The other model puts an emphasis on fostering understanding of, commitment to and informed participation in the ecumenical process by informal processes involving learning by sharing and by participating. It is interested in lifelong learning and enabling people to lead a responsible and mature life.

One has to have these different educational concepts in mind to understand the terminology which is used in the discussions on ecumenical formation. In the period after Nairobi, "learning", understood in a broad sense, was often preferred to the term "education" and appeared frequently in ecumenical documents.

> ... Learning means an approach, both to knowledge and to life... It encompasses the acquisition and practice of new methodologies, new skills, new attitudes and new values necessary to live in a world of change. Learning is the process of preparing to deal with new situations. It may occur consciously or often unconsciously usually from experiencing real life situations, although simulated or imagined situations can also induce learning. Practically every individual in the world, whether schooled or not, experiences the process of learning...[25]

Ecumenical formation as liberating and spiritual renewal, as it was developed after the Nairobi discussions, expanded the concern for the renewal of the church to the renewal of the human community. For some it was a natural development. For others, the rediscovered spirituality was a significant revision of Uppsala. The threats to human survival produced a new awareness of the coming world, of the common responsibility of all Christians and of the global dimensions of the Christian faith. The urgency of the task seemed to be clear to the delegates to the Nairobi assembly: "All member churches must be helped to participate in the process of ecumenical education that is so fundamental to our pilgrimage."[26] In response, "education and renewal in search for true community" became one of the four major programme thrusts of the WCC for the period after Nairobi. Ecumenical education was the special task of the Unit on Education and Renewal.

This task was unambiguous only in so far as there was an acceptance of a common ecumenical vision. In the 1950s there had been a discussion as to whether ecumenical education is concerned both with the life of the churches and the relations of Christians to the world. Now there was a significant diversity in the way in which "ecumenical" was understood. Hans-Ruedi Weber, reflecting on the work of the Ecumenical Institute at Bossey,[27]

---

[25] J.W. Botkin, M. Elmandjra, M. Malitza, *No Limits to Learning, Bridging the Human Gap: A Report to the Club of Rome*, Oxford, Pergamon, 1979, p.8.

[26] *Breaking Barriers*, p.7, cf. also the reports from the hearing on Unit III and the Unit III core groups report.

[27] H. R. Weber, "A Laboratory for Ecumenical Life", in *The Ecumenical Review*, 48, 4, 1996, p.435; similarly K. Raiser, "Fifty Years of Ecumenical Formation," p.447, where he resumes: "What is important also for the present and future orientation... is to acknowledge that we can no longer take a common understanding of the ecumenical vocation for granted. Ecumenical formation will increasingly have to focus on finding ways of responding creatively to these tensions and diversities."

identifies four different understandings of the term. It may refer exclusively to Christian unity. It may be expanded to include the unity of all humankind. From a different starting-point, it may be seen in the context of a movement which like a river maintains its name but changes its character as it flows through different landscapes. It can also encompass all the world's cultures and faiths. To these one must add understandings of "ecumenical" which place an emphasis on building links of support and solidarity between rich and poor churches and preparing people for commitment to the struggle for justice and peace at a local level.

In order to understand what happened in the field of ecumenical formation after Nairobi, one must have these different interpretations of "ecumenical" in mind. This would help to discern the objectives of different ecumenical formation activities and to understand why the discussions on ecumenical education/learning/formation have sometimes been so difficult, not to say frustrating.

There were still more obstacles to enlarging the ecumenical experiences of people in the member churches, especially at the local level. Nairobi delegates noticed the great disparity between WCC studies and actions and those of the member churches. It became obvious that many of the ecumenically committed delegates, commission members and staff had not received their ecumenical vision in the local churches but in other training grounds such as the World Student Christian Federation or in ecumenical work camps. The implication of this was that ecumenical awareness would be available only to a very few people as such opportunities declined or became less attractive. The development of an ecumenical consciousness would remain the privilege of a few ecumenical insiders. Ernst Lange, for some years director of the Division of Ecumenical Action, articulated the dilemma: "To educate and train ecumenical 'multipliers' in sufficient quality and in sufficient numbers to produce the needed 'forward leap' in public opinion in the member churches, would itself presuppose that 'forward leap'!"[28] He argued that, as the parochialism of a person's world-view begins in early childhood, there needed to be radical changes in religious education from the earliest years.

Although the lessons Lange taught were never fully learned, the questions he raised remained relevant:

• How can the whole people of God and local communities participate in the ecumenical experience?
• How can people, while remaining rooted in a specific denominational, cultural, historical and socio-political context, become ecumenically committed and share the experiences of others?
• How can they become both local and universal, so that they think globally and act locally?
• What are the obstacles to this learning process and how could they be overcome?

Therefore,

> The question to which it [the WCC Office of Education] needs to find an answer is how Christians can grow so as to continue to be adequate for the world in which they are called to believe, to love and to hope.[29]

Some new answers

The various reports from the Nairobi assembly underlined the special responsibility of the programme on Education and Renewal for ecumenical formation. "Education for

---

[28] E. Lange, ... *And Yet It Moves, Dream and Reality of the Ecumenical Movement*, WCC, 1979, p.110.
[29] *Ibid.*, p.135.

ecumenism is, in the first instance, the enabling of the whole people of God to partici-pate in the church's life and mission, to discover Christian unity where they live and work and to share in the creation of a community justice and liberation.[30] There was to be a special focus on laity with particular attention to the fuller participation of women, youth and children. The unit had as its concerns education, women in church and soci-ety, and youth, to which was added renewal and congregational life. In 1977 the Pro-gramme on Theological Education (PTE) relocated from England to Geneva. It joined the unit on Education and Renewal in 1981 and widened its scope to theological educa-tion for the whole people of God and to ministerial formation. Although these structural changes did not resolve the issues around ecumenical formation, they did make possi-ble a new type of collaboration. This provided a greater coherence, a more intensive dis-cussion and a more dynamic interaction between the different but related constituen-cies. A wider collaboration and interaction was made possible by a staff working group on education which brought together representatives of Education and Renewal with col-leagues from the Ecumenical Institute, Bossey, the Commission on World Mission and Evangelism (CWME), the CCPD, the Christian Medical Commission and the education desk of the Lutheran World Federation.

A number of cooperative programmes, consultations and other activities developed which also involved other ecumenical organizations such as the YWCA and the WSCF. The guiding principles which emerged were the participation of all church members (women and men, clergy and laity, all ages and persons with disabilities), the under-standing of ecumenical renewal as a process of lifelong learning, concrete involvement on a regional or local level, and learning understood as a two-way process in which every-body is taken seriously in their specific context.

Such a common approach became all the more urgent as the ecumenical movement entered a phase of new sensitivity to the basic conditions of human life. The message of the WCC sixth assembly in Vancouver (1983) stated "how critical this moment is in the life of the world, like the turning of a page of history". The message continues,

> We hear the cries of millions who face a daily struggle for survival, who are crushed by mil-itary power or the propaganda of the powerful. We see the camps of refugees and the tears of all who suffer inhuman loss. We sense the fear of rich groups and nations and the hope-lessness of many in the world rich in things who live in great emptiness of spirit. There is a great division between North and South, between East and West. Our world – God's world – has to choose between "life and death, blessing and curse".[31]

As collective life was threatened, a collective response was required. The assembly therefore had to pay special attention to children as those who carry the gift of life. Struggling together for life is possible only where children and adults learn together and from one another. Common learning in the church is demanded. Learning between and among different churches, Christian groups and movements could become a symbol for the learning capacity of humankind.

The issue group in Vancouver in which all educational programmes found their focus, "Learning in community", formulated future goals for ecumenical formation, grounded in the faith in "Jesus Christ as the source of life":

---

[30] Cf. *Breaking Barriers*, p.31.
[31] D. Gill ed., *Gathered for Life: Official Report to the Sixth Assembly of the World Council of Churches*, WCC, 1983, pp.1-2.

- to discover together that God has given us *one world*;
- to participate in the struggle for global justice and peace;
- to participate in communities of prophetic witness;
- to relate our local struggles to global perspectives.

"This is the overarching vision we see for the future of the ecumenical movement as a fellowship of learning."[32]

At Nairobi, education had been one theme besides others. However, in Vancouver, learning became a constitutive dimension for the church as church. In his report to the assembly, the then general secretary Philip Potter described the churches in the ecumenical movement as a fellowship of learning.

> Learning in the Bible is a process by which people relate to God and God's way of truth, righteousness and peace, that they may in obedience practise that way in relation to each other and extending to the nations... learning does not simply mean acquiring knowledge or skills, or being intellectually equipped, or just memorizing some catechism of faith. Rather it means so entering with our whole being and with all the people into a relationship with God through God's self-revelation, that our horizons are widened and our wills are strengthened to be right with God and with one another in word and deed... Such learning is a precondition for any effective action in the cause of truth, peace and justice, and the building of true community.

This deep and broad vision of learning was accompanied by an admission that it

> has not been sufficiently built into the programmes of the World Council and that the churches themselves have not sufficiently appropriated the insights and perspectives received through this process of ecumenical learning.[33]

EXPRESSIONS OF ECUMENICAL FORMATION, 1976-90

Education and renewal

As early as 1976 the WCC central committee had asked staff "to explore further with member churches a revision of their curricula and educational programmes so that they promote education for ecumenism, particularly on the local level". Several activities were undertaken to follow this up, including a worldwide survey of common catechetical programmes. In some parts of the world, for example in Australia and England, substantial projects of ecumenical curricula and learning material for use with local congregations had been developed. Workshops and seminars on ecumenical learning were held in collaboration with Bossey, the CCPD and PTE to test didactic models and to offer help at local level on the goal definition, content and methods of ecumenical learning. Guidelines were produced on Christian participation in education in a multifaith environment with the intention of enabling Christian people to respond creatively to the situation of growing diversity. These and other activities reinforced the conviction

> that ecumenical learning cannot be limited to mere communication of facts, history, background, structures and functions of the ecumenical movement. Rather, it is the comprehensive task of equipping Christians to live as a liberating and reconciling community in a divided world.[34]

---

[32] *Gathered for Life*, p.94.

[33] *Ibid.*, pp.200-201, Cf. also K.E. Nipkow, "Verantwortung für Kinder und ökumenisches Lernen, Pädagogische Schwerpunkte in Vancouver", in *Ökumenische Rundschau*, 33, 1984, pp.87ff.

[34] *Nairobi to Vancouver 1975-1983: Report of the Central Committee to the Sixth Assembly of the World Council of Churches*, WCC, 1983, p.183.

The need to recognize that ecumenical formation is an indispensable part of processes of Christian formation and nurture for all, whether they be laity, clergy, women, youth, children or local congregations, became more apparent. The attempt was made by the programme on Education and Renewal to collaborate across its areas of education, women, youth, renewal and congregational life, and PTE in a programme on formation for participation in ecumenism. In this context they would deal with a variety of issues such as learning for justice, peace and the integrity of creation, developing a new vision for the ecumenical youth movement, following up the insights gained from the study on the community of women and men in the church, developing liturgical activities and spiritual formation as ecumenical concerns, and preparing lay people and the clergy for ecumenical activities. Such cooperation was affirmed and strengthened by the programme guidelines committee of the Vancouver assembly which identified ecumenical learning as crucial for the coming years and as a priority to all WCC programmes.[35]

This new attempt at cooperation in furthering ecumenical formation suffered from the tensions mentioned earlier. It was difficult for everyone involved to understand and accept the new ways of cooperating and of learning demanded by ecumenical formation that challenged traditional patterns of formal Christian education.

Development education

Perhaps the obstacles to ecumenical formation were most clearly seen and analyzed in the field of development education. As has been mentioned, new educational approaches had been introduced in congregations, communities and groups which were based on liberating experiences, involvement in actions that express solidarity with the poor and marginalized, the struggle for justice and participation in the renewal of ethical perspectives in relation to the world. Community-oriented action-reflection processes could not easily be accommodated within existing educational systems. Consequently the assessment of ten years of development education in the WCC came to the conclusion that the structured and fragmented approach of school learning could not easily adapt to this other educational process.

> This has given development education the freedom to experiment in adult education programmes, organized by Christian lay training institutes, action groups and specialized church-related agencies. It has largely taken on a pioneering function, both in the pedagogical debate and in the practical work. But this implies also that there is still a considerable gap between a new pedagogy, focusing on "learning" as an active, participatory, action-oriented, contextual activity, and "education" as a more or less passive transfer of knowledge, which has no contextual relevance and thus does not receive in the process of "reflection" the necessary stimulus for "action to transform the reality".[36]

Since that was written in 1982, school education has changed considerably in some places but not in others. Similarly, some programmes of Sunday school teaching and religious instruction have been influenced by this development and have tried to help young people to understand their own life experiences in the context of the whole inhabited earth.

---

[35] *Gathered for Life*, p.256.
[36] *Leaping over the Wall*, p.32.

Justice, peace and the integrity of creation

The attempt made at the end of the 1980s to incorporate the ecumenical focus on Justice, Peace and the Integrity of Creation (JPIC) in the Christian and theological education activities in churches and congregations revived tensions between those working in development education and teachers in Sunday schools or religious education. The intention to learn to do justice and build peace, rather than simply learn about it, revealed a continued reluctance on the side of many churches, congregations and schools to open themselves to this broader understanding of learning.

The multiplicity and political character of issues raised in development education was often seen as another problem. Issues such as human rights, militarism, racism, transnational corporations, sustainability and the ecological crisis are inter-related and can only be analyzed and taken up in a holistic approach to education. This presented development education with a dilemma.

> On the one hand, staggering injustices, contradictions and threats to survival confronting persons and communities have been revealed at an ever faster rate; on the other hand, it is clear that true education requires long-term processes, where people can learn to cope with complex issues as they unfold.[37]

Much of what has been said about development education in the ecumenical movement could have been used to describe the programmes of UNESCO or other organizations working towards creating global awareness. The difference was not only that adult education was located in part of the WCC structure associated with "renewal". Development education as ecumenical formation brought:

– a deeper exploration of "Christian modes of resistance" to the power of oppression...;
– an ongoing theological reflection which emerges in the struggles for justice and wholeness...;
– a sharing of experiences of faith made in the struggle: Bible study, liturgical materials, prayers, meditations and hymns;
– learning to live with a set of different values, which traditionally have often been considered negative... to see that limitations can be a source of competence and creativity;
– encouraging the formation of small communities, where people can worship, act, live and learn together...[38]

Ecumenical theological education

From the very beginning it was clear that innovative approaches to learning had to be brought also into programmes of theological education. The Theological Education Fund and then the Programme on Theological Education (PTE)[39] stimulated and supported attempts to include ecumenical perspectives, commitment for justice and peace, education for the whole people of God, participation of women in leadership, contextual theologies and the spiritual dimension in ministerial formation as new emphases in traditional theological education programmes. In consultations, conferences and publications it became obvious that each of these emphases had far-reaching consequences for the role of theological learning institutions for church and society and for the teaching

---

[37] *Ibid.*, p.55.
[38] *Ibid.*, pp.81-82.
[39] Cf. John S. Pobee, "Some Forty Years of Ecumenical Theological Education", in *Ministerial Formation*, 38, July 1997, pp.25ff.

of classical theological disciplines. New forms of theological education for all were developed where the learning process was related to the context in which it occurred, relationships were established between students and teachers with community groups, and education became a true action-reflection process involving the participation of the wider community. Study and lay training centres and academies, supported by the World Collaboration Committee of Christian Lay Centres, Academies and Movements for Social Concern (Wcolc), were seen as models for this kind of ecumenical ministerial formation.

Lay training

Lay training centres and academies had developed in the 1950s and 1960s in Western Europe to meet the spiritual and intellectual development needs of the laity. Many ran courses to help people relate their faith to their work and to daily life. They also trained lay workers for parishes and schools. In this period, the idea spread to the rest of the world, taking on forms appropriate to the context, e.g. training community development workers or agricultural specialists; the contextual popular reading of the Bible; providing open spaces for reflection on the economic and societal issues affecting their community. They provided an alternative ecumenical formation track to that of the established ecumenical movement.

The Wcolc had been formed in 1972 to build up relationships between them. A network of regional associations emerged for Asia, Africa, Europe, North America, Middle East, Caribbean and South America and the Southern Cone of South America. The committee identified issues of common concern and identified models of education for transformation.

One example of a new model was the Course for Leaders of Lay Training (CLLT) organized by regional associations of laity centres. In 1976, for example, a global CLLT brought together 36 participants from lay training centres, seminaries and urban rural mission programmes. The objective of this form of ecumenical formation was to equip participants to become agents of change. The course was demanding, requiring participants to spend nine days in an exposure visit followed by seven weeks in Bangalore, India, for an ecumenical learning programme. The process included the exploration of expectations, sharing experience, exposure, encounter, reflection and synthesis. A second global CLLT was held in Tanzania in 1986. From these global programmes would come the animateurs of regional and local CLLTs.

The experiments in new forms of theological education and leadership formation failed to compensate for the disappearance or decline of activities, such as ecumenical youth work, the Student Christian Movements and the WSCF, which had given people an ecumenical vision. Konrad Raiser, writing in 1996 while WCC general secretary, commented,

> Almost a whole generation has grown up without being offered opportunities for ecumenical learning and encounter... we are presently in a situation in which a fair number of those who have moved into positions of leadership in the churches are little acquainted with the ecumenical movement and have not been exposed to any kind of ecumenical formation. This is particularly true for the male leadership of the churches, whereas the expanding ecumenical women's movement has in fact become one of the main promoters of ecumenical formation in the present generation.[40]

---

[40] K. Raiser, "Fifty Years of Ecumenical Formation", p.448.

Throughout the period under review, the WCC Scholarships programme served as an agent of ecumenical formation. Hundreds of people were not only equipped with new knowledge and skills relating to their own area of service but were also given an exposure to other cultures and expressions of church life. Churches in receiving countries were enriched by the presence of these students and given new perspectives on global Christianity. Scholarship holders returned home with broader visions and ecumenical sympathies.

Missionary congregations

The ecumenical study on "The Missionary Structure of the Congregation", developed after the New Delhi assembly, was the starting point for various activities in the Commission on World Mission and Evangelism (CWME) and in the ecumenical movement to enable local congregations to define their own agenda for evangelism and mission in a secularized or a multifaith society or in a context where people struggle for justice and liberation. Congregations and local groups associated with Urban Rural Mission (URM) committed themselves to live following God's mission in partnership with the world for justice, peace and the integrity of creation. They raised questions about the structure of their community or congregation and about their proclamation, worship and service, and searched for the meaning and shape of their witness and service in the context of a culturally and religiously plural world. This could be properly described as an ecumenical formation process.

The study document of the Joint Working Group between the Roman Catholic Church and the World Council of Churches on ecumenical formation, quoted at the start of this chapter, emphasized that "ecumenical formation must also address the matter of religious plurality and secularism, and inform about inter-religious dialogue which aims at deeper mutual understanding in the search for world community".[41] The urgency to build creative relationships was seen as a new challenge in many parts of the ecumenical movement. Those involved in mission, education and dialogue within the WCC worked together to respond to educational questions raised by the increasing plurality of the world. It became obvious that it was not enough to help Christians to understand people of other faiths and ideologies by strengthening traditional teaching. Rather, it was necessary to take seriously the comprehensive understanding of ecumenical formation and to enter into dialogue.

> People engaged in dialogue have felt their own faith challenged and deepened by the new dimensions of religious life which they have observed, and may find in inter-religious encounter a new impetus for doing theology and reviving spirituality. Communities in dialogue function as the leaven in the larger community, facilitating the creation of a society transcending religious barriers.[42]

ECUMENICAL FORMATION AT THE END OF THE CENTURY

The structural reorganization of the WCC in the period immediately after the Canberra assembly of 1991 was undertaken with an understanding that the whole work of the Council is in some way educational. Consequently the specific strands of work on education were separated across the newly formed units. In spite of efforts by the mechanisms set in place to link educational work across the Council, the WCC's work on

[41] "Ecumenical Formation", p.494, §23.
[42] Wesley Ariarajah, *My Neighbour's Faith – and Mine: Theological Discoveries through Interfaith Dialogue*, WCC, 1986, p.viii.

ecumenical formation lost its sense of cohesion and the symbiotic energy of collaboration. An opportunity to re-energize and integrate work on ecumenical formation was created in a further reorganization following the Harare assembly in 1998.

At the start of the 1990s the churches of Central and Eastern Europe and the former Soviet Union were facing an educational challenge. After many years of restrictions on teaching the faith, they now had the possibility of resuming this but without trained personnel and contemporary learning resources. An ecumenical consultation in Moscow in 1992, hosted by the Russian Orthodox Church, identified four areas where help from the WCC was required – curriculum development; leadership and teacher training; the teaching process; ecumenical teacher training. Various activities were held over the next few years to meet these needs. Inadequate relationships between churches meant that the full ecumenical potential could not be realized. However, the activities relating to Orthodox curriculum development, teacher training and the teaching process were enriched by the participation of representatives and experts from the wider constituency of the WCC.[43]

This account illustrates a dilemma faced by the WCC in regard to ecumenical formation. Is it the role of the WCC to support an approach to education, nurture or formation within its member churches that is limited to their own tradition? It is a question that surfaced constantly during this period. A resurgence of denominationalism in various parts of the world resulted in churches establishing their own theological education institutions, sometimes in competition with ecumenical institutions in which they already had a stake. Ecumenically developed courses and learning resources for adults and children were being supplanted by denominationally oriented equivalents. In parts of Africa and Asia, churches whose schools were taken over by newly independent states received them back again as their government sought to reduce expenditures. This was seen by some as an opportunity to reassert a denominational identity. In all of these areas requests came to the WCC to give assistance. If the WCC simply existed to serve its membership, the answer would have been simple. However, the imperative of ecumenical formation in education and the limited human and financial resources of the WCC meant that many were disappointed.

In the 1990s, developments in the profile of the work of Ecumenical Theological Education (ETE) became apparent. From an orientation to the South, the programme took on a global concern. Issues such as contextualization had become equally important for theological institutions in the North. The tradition inherited by ETE "represents the reminder that there can be no renewal of theology without honouring the standards and demands of the academy and the church, without concern for mission, unity and viable education and formation in the global context".[44]

For ecumenical formation, as with theological education in general, such discussions raised the question of the control exercised by higher education institutions, sometimes secular in establishment, over the content and methodologies of learning and accreditation. The liberalization of the "educational market" resulted in the academic validation of many contextual courses which build on and integrate participants' experience with a received body of knowledge. In these developments relating to the academy, one can see the influence of less institutionalized forms of education.

---

[43] Teny Pirri-Simonian, *Canberra to Harare: On the Trail of Education Work in the World Council of Churches*, WCC, 1998.
[44] Pobee, "Some Forty Years of Ecumenical Theological Education", p.27.

The World Collaboration Committee, which exercised oversight for the CLLTs, organized a world convention of laity centres and movements in 1993 at Montreat, North Carolina, US. Addressing the convention, Konrad Raiser recognized that the ecumenical movement had been institutionalized and professionalized. A new profile of the committed laity in the ecumenical movement was required.

The goal of lay commitment is the rebuilding of viable non-exclusive social forms that will produce a community with a human face in which human dignity is recognized, basic human needs are satisfied and the diversity of cultural identities and human talents are duly recognized.[45] The World Collaboration Committee celebrated the twenty-fifth anniversary of its founding in 1997 in Argentina and changed its name to Oikosnet.

The 1990s ended with a search for new paradigms and methodologies for ecumenical formation. Work being done in different parts of the world in holistic education and a renewed interest in indigenous ways of learning offer challenges to some formal practices of ecumenical formation.

There were important differences in style between the Festival to mark the end of the Decade of the Churches in Solidarity with Women and the WCC Harare assembly which immediately followed it in 1998. These differences were an indication that it was not only the location of ecumenical formation in women's groups which was significant but the manner in which women learn.

The century ended with ecumenical formation as found in denominational and ecumenical educational structures in need of new vision, concepts and methodologies. However, outside those official structures there were signs of educational creativity which might provide the seeds of renewal for ecumenical formation.

CONCLUSIONS

This chapter has made an attempt to describe the major developments in ecumenical formation during the last three or four decades. It is also attempting to identify some of the lessons learned. In spite of the problems and tensions inherent in many of the ecumenical formation programmes or activities, what has been achieved cannot be disregarded. On the contrary, it must be acknowledged that much has happened in equipping and enabling Christian people, congregations, movements and groups to participate in the ecumenical experience and to become ecumenically committed. Without these varied activities of ecumenical formation, the ecumenical movement would have totally lost its liveliness and its creativity.

Those who are working in the field of ecumenical formation have learned a lot. Some conceptual questions have been answered and there is a more sophisticated perception of the interacting elements and of the difficulties, tensions and obstacles to the ecumenical formation process. However, a coherent concept is hardly visible and several important theological and pedagogical questions are still left unanswered.

Ecumenical formation activities were built around major programme issues and their respective constituencies. Sometimes these were treated by sustained, long-range efforts but sometimes they were picked up like changing fashions.[46] All too frequently

---

[45] Konrad Raiser, "Towards a New Definition of the Profle of the Laity in the Ecumenical Movement", in *Report of the World Convention of Christian Lay Centres and Movements*, WCC, 1993, p.27.
[46] Cf. *Leaping over the Wall*, p.78.

programmes of the WCC, Bossey and other ecumenical institutions or organizations approached the same issues in their own way, with their preferred method and with regard to their own constituency. There was no admission that a common approach or at least a common strategy would be much more effective. Nor was it possible to learn from one another and to assist one another. The more visible the convergence of these various ecumenical issues becomes, the less possible it is to justify an isolated and fragmented approach.

Learning from the experience of these years, a coherent concept of ecumenical formation is necessary and requires:
- intensified theological reflections on eccelesiological questions such as an understanding of the church as a fellowship of learning and on the relationship between education and renewal, action and spirituality (ecumenical formation as an experience of faith);
- an interdisciplinary approach to analyze the various issues related to ecumenical formation and to explore their educational implications;
- a thorough reflection about the ecumenical formation process – how people learn by being taught, by sharing, by participating and by experiencing; how learning can be motivated; the role of the learning community; the limits of education; and
- a clearer answer to the question of what "ecumenical" really means.

This latter may be the key issue. Until we are clear what it is that is being formed with and in people, ecumenical formation will remain problematic. Hans-Ruedi Weber sums this up in his account of the story of Bossey:

> Neither the ecumenical movement at large nor the governing bodies of the World Council of Churches, neither the headquarters staff nor the Bossey board and teaching team can give a common answer to that question. The Institute must, therefore, work with an open mind and different understandings of what "ecumenical" means. All talk about ecumenical education and ecumenical learning becomes frustrating unless this dilemma is recognized and faced.[47]

BIBLIOGRAPHY

Amirtham, Samuel and Ariarajah, S. Wesley eds, *Ministerial Formation in a Multifaith Milieu: Implications of Interfaith Dialogue for Theological Education*, WCC, 1986, 122p.

Amirtham, Samuel and Pobee, John S. eds, *Theology by the People: Reflections on Doing Theology in Community*, WCC, 1986, 143p.

Assad, Maurice ed., *Tradition and Renewal in Orthodox Education: Report of the Consultation on "Tradition and Renewal in Orthodox Education" Held in the Neamt Monastery, Roumania, 6-12 September, 1976*, Syndesmos, 1977, 130p.

Becker, Ulrich, "The WCC and the Concept of Ecumenical Learning", in *Education Newsletter*, 14, 1, 1985, pp.1-5.

Becker, Ulrich ed., *Projekt Ökumene: auf dem Weg zur Einen Welt: Arbeitsbuch Religion, Sekundarstufe I*, Düsseldorf, Patmos, 1997, 192p.

Bröking-Bortfeldt, Martin, *Mündig Ökumene lernen: Ökumenisches Lernen als religionspädagogisches Paradigma*, Oldenburg, Isensee, 1994, 279p.

Dauber, Heinrich and Simpfendörfer, Werner eds, *Eigener Haushalt und bewohnter Erdkreis: ökologisches und ökumenisches Lernen in der "Einen Welt"*, Wuppertal, Hammer, 1981, 399p.

---

[47] H.-R. Weber, *A Laboratory for Ecumenical Life: The Story of Bossey 1946-1996*, WCC, 1996, p.125.

Engel, Lothar and Werner, Dietrich eds, *Ökumenische Perspektiven theologischer Ausbildung*, Frankfurt am Main, Otto Lembeck, 1990, 231p.

Freire, Paolo, *Learning to Question: A Pedagogy of Liberation*, WCC, 1989, 142p.

Gossmann, Klaus ed., *Ökumenisches Lernen in der Gemeinde*, Gütersloh, Gütersloher Mohn, 1988, 128p.

Joint Working Group between the Roman Catholic Church and the World Council of Churches, "Ecumenical Formation: Ecumenial Reflections and Suggestions", in *The Ecumenical Review*, 45, 4, October 1993, pp.490-494.

Kinsler, F. Ross ed., *Ministry by the People: Theological Education by Extension*, WCC, 1983, 332p.

Koerrenz, Ralf, *Ökumenisches Lernen*, Gütersloh, Gütersloher, 1994, 228p.

Lange, Ernst, *Leben im Wandel: Überlegungen zu einer zeitgemässen Moral*, Gelnhausen, Burckhardthaus, 1971, 111p.

Learning in Context, The Search for Innovative Patterns in Theological Education, Bromley, UK, New Life, 1973, 195p.

Lienemann-Perrin, Christine, *Training for a Relevant Ministry: A Study of the Contribution of the Theological Education Fund*, WCC, 1981, 252p.

Oxley, Simon, *Creative Ecumenical Education: Learning from One Another*, WCC, 2002, 156p.

Pirri-Simonian, Teny, *Canberra to Harare: On the Trail of Education Work in the World Council of Churches*, WCC, 1998, 95p.

Pobee, John S., "Some Forty Years of Ecumenical Theological Education", in *Ministerial Formation*, 38, July 1997, pp.25ff.

Raiser, Konrad, "Fifty Years of Ecumenical Formation: Where Are We? Where Are We Going?", in *The Ecumenical Review*, 48, 4, Oct. 1996, pp. 440-56.

Richey, Russell E., *Ecumenical and Interreligious Perspectives: Globalization in Theological Education*, Nashville TN, QR Books, 1992, 152p.

Schipani, Daniel S, *Religious Education Encounters Liberation Theology*, Birmingham AL, Religious Education, 1988, 276p.

Schlüter, Richard, *Ökumenisches Lernen in den Kirchen: Schritte in die gemeinsame Zukunft: Eine praktisch-theologische Grundlegung*, Essen, Blaue Eule, 1992, 143p.

Seeing Education Whole: An Invitation from the First Consultation of the Office of Education of the World Council of Churches, to Share in an Attempt to Understand the Distinctive Tasks and Challenges Facing Education throughout the World Today and to Envisage the Particular Contribution of Christians, WCC, 1970.

Stotter, Pamela D., *Called beyond Ourselves: The Importance of Ecumenical Learning*, Dublin, Irish School of Ecumenics, 1991, 122p.

Sutcliffe, John M., *Learning Community*, Nutfield, Denholm, 1974, 124p.

Traitler, R. ed., *Leaping over the Wall: An Assessment of Ten Years' Development Education*, WCC, 1982, 83p.

Wingate, Andrew, *Does Theological Education Make a Difference?: Global Lessons in Mission and Ministry from India and Britain*, WCC, 1999, 116p.

World Council of Churches, *Alive Together: A Practical Guide to Ecumenical Learning*, WCC, 1989, 95p.

World Council of Churches, *Doing Theology in Different Contexts: Latin American and Eastern/Central European Theologians in Dialogue: A Report of a Programme on Theological Education Consultation in Prague, June 1988*, WCC, 1988, 126.

9

The Bible in the Ecumenical Movement

Hans-Ruedi Weber

> The ecumenical movement of the 20th century has found in the Bible a dynamic force, making for that unity which God wills. The common language of Christian prayer and liturgy is a scriptural language, and in our time many have come to a fresh appreciation of the biblical content of the churches' liturgy.[1]

The United Bible Societies (UBS) and the World Council of Churches (WCC) affirmed this in 1968. Indeed, the Bible played a crucial role in the early ecumenical movement, especially in its pioneering youth movements, but was this still the case by the late 1960s?

THE BIBLE IN 1968

In 1968, that symbolic year of change and unrest, the Bible did not make headlines.[2] True, the UBS could publish impressive statistical surveys, but circulation does not necessarily mean reading, appropriation or real influence. Many young people in China and persons involved in the revolutionary movements of the West read the little Red Book of Chairman Mao's thoughts with more hope and excitement than the Bible. They were scarcely aware of the fact that Jesus and the Old Testament prophets challenge both the existing world order and personal directions of life more fundamentally than Mao's Cultural Revolution. Shortly after 1968, a widely read analysis was published, bearing the provocative title *The Strange Silence of the Bible in the Church*.[3]

Nevertheless, certain little-publicized events of that year became stimuli for the use of the Bible in the ecumenical movement. The most important was undoubtedly the publication of *Guiding Principles for Interconfessional Cooperation in Translating the Bible*,[4] jointly issued in 1968 by the UBS and the Vatican Secretariat for Promoting Christian Unity. Five years of intensive discussions had led to this document, made possible by

---

[1] Joint Committee of the UBS and the WCC, "The Bible in the Ecumenical Movement", in *Workbook: WCC Uppsala Assembly*, WCC, 1968, pp.124-26.
[2] Olivier Béguin, "Uppsala 68 and the Bible", in *UBS Bulletin*, 76, 1968, pp.177-83. "The Bible Distributed and Translated: 1968", in *UBS Bulletin*, 79, 1969, pp.88-93.
[3] James D. Smart, *The Strange Silence of the Bible in the Church*, London, SCM Press, 1970.
[4] *Guiding Principles for Interconfessional Cooperation in Translating the Bible*, London/Rome, UBS/Secretariat for Promoting Christian Unity, 1968. Walter M. Abbott, *Roman Catholics and the Bible Societies*, Vatican City, Office for Common Bible Work, 1970.

three main developments. First, the Second Vatican Council had decreed in its "Dogmatic Constitution on Divine Revelation" (*Dei Verbum* VI.22) that "easy access to sacred scripture should be provided for all the Christian faithful" and recommended that, wherever possible, Roman Catholics should cooperate with other Christians in the work of translation so that a common Bible to be used by all could emerge. Second, in order to serve all churches, many Bible societies had agreed to make available editions of the Bible that met divergent requirements with regard to the canon of holy scriptures. Third, many Bible societies were abandoning the policy of publishing "no notes or comment", providing helps for readers and non-doctrinal annotations which also satisfied Roman Catholic needs.

The *Guiding Principles* indicate which editions of the Hebrew and Greek biblical texts are to be translated, and they specify with regard to the canon that common editions of the Bible should include the deuterocanonical books as a separate section before the New Testament. For exegesis, annotations, helps for readers and supplementary features, mutually acceptable commentaries and critical studies are to be used. Suggestions on how to overcome confessional divergences with regard to orthography, proper biblical names and styles of language are added. The statement also lays out procedures for joint translations and revisions. There is a common concern that versions of scripture should, as far as possible, be in the living, current languages of the people and be based on the best scholarship available to all Christian traditions.

The ecumenical importance of the implementation of these *Guiding Principles* can hardly be over-emphasized. During the 19th century, the work of Protestant Bible societies had been strongly condemned in papal encyclicals. Although cooperation between Roman Catholic and Protestant biblical scholars had begun before the Second Vatican Council, prior to 1968 no great progress had been made towards a common Bible. Two years later, however, a progress report could list many initiatives taken for joint translation and distribution on all continents. The Vatican helped the UBS financially to continue research on biblical manuscripts in their original languages. To have a common biblical text in Hebrew and Greek and to work for common translation and distribution were ecumenical breakthroughs. Many believe that to have a common Bible for study and worship is as important for the unity of the church as a – still unattained – common eucharist.

In the UBS, the mainly Protestant Bible societies had since 1946 possessed a world organization. Roman Catholic Bible associations also gradually came to be linked in a global network. In 1967, the Vatican Secretariat for Promoting Christian Unity initiated the practical implementations of the "Dogmatic Constitution on Divine Revelation", especially of its sixth chapter, "Sacred Scripture in the Life of the Church". As a result of this, the World Catholic Federation for the Biblical Apostolate was founded in 1969; since 1990 it has been known as the Catholic Biblical Federation (CBF).

There were other little-publicized events around 1968 that positively affected the role of the Bible in the ecumenical movement. The findings of a worldwide study process under the auspices of the UBS and the WCC, on the Bible in mission and evangelism, were notable.[5] They show concretely – especially in Latin America, Africa and Asia, but also in Western industrial missions – that the Bible had become not only a best-seller but a source of new life. The report summarizes, for instance, what had been accomplished

---

[5] G.H. Wolfensberger, *Multiplying the Loaves: The Bible in Mission and Evangelism*, London/Glasgow, Fontana, 1968.

through the Penzotti institutes that had been founded in 1956 for biblical teaching and evangelization in local churches. It also reports on work done through Bible correspondence courses and through such Bible reading movements as the Scripture Union, the International Bible Reading Association and the Bible Reading Fellowship.

Despite the strong emphasis on the centrality of Bible study in the early days of the WCC, it was only in 1961 in section meetings at the New Delhi assembly that corporate Bible study became a feature of WCC assemblies. New Delhi also extended the basis of the WCC to include the statement that the Council is a fellowship of churches which confess Jesus Christ "according to the scriptures". At Uppsala in 1968 the whole assembly engaged, both in plenary sessions and section meetings, in participatory study of biblical passages on the main theme. The UBS was given space to present its work, and the statement on "The Bible in the Ecumenical Movement", quoted at the beginning of this chapter, was received. The assembly resolved that means be developed "by which the World Council could more effectively help the member churches to encourage the distribution, reading and study of the Bible by their members".[6] This led in following years to the circulation of much Bible study material by the WCC publication office and to the establishment of a WCC secretariat on biblical studies.

The power of the prophetic biblical message also became evident at Uppsala in quite an unexpected way. The critical issues of racism and racial conflict had made it imperative at the last minute to add an extra session on "White Racism or World Community?" This was scheduled just prior to the presentation of *On That Day*, a drama concerning the prophet Amos.[7] The combination of the testimonies given during that session with the dramatic message of the prophet put before the assembly an inescapable challenge. More than words and statements were now needed. The decision by the WCC to establish its Programme to Combat Racism (PCR) came at least partly out of that biblical summons.

MAJOR DEVELOPMENTS SINCE 1968

What has influenced most strongly the role of the Bible in the ecumenical movement since 1968? People from different continents, confessions and organizations for Bible work have contributed to the following review of some miscellaneous trends which have emerged.

Growing biblical illiteracy

In world history, no book has received such a concerted and continuing effort for translation, dissemination and interpretation as the Bible. During these last decades, this effort has even been intensified. Nevertheless, in the West one often speaks now about the Bible as the "least read best-seller". The Bible continues to be respected as a classic which has made a deep impact on literature, art and society. New translations and revisions are still being made and bought by many. However, the disciplines of private and corporate Bible study and meditation have regressed. There are of course exceptions to this trend, but the fact of growing biblical illiteracy, especially in the North, must be faced.

[6] Norman Goodall ed., *The Uppsala Report: Official Report of the Fourth Assembly of the World Council of Churches, Uppsala, July 4-20, 1967*, WCC, 1968, p. 187; cf. pp.100 and 135.
[7] *Ibid.*, pp. 101, 129f. and Olov Hartman, *On That Day*, Philadelphia, Fortress, 1968.

Seen from a world perspective, the present pattern of population growth has caused Christians to become, in terms of percentages, an ever smaller minority. Even with increased translation and distribution, the percentage of available Bibles per each million inhabitants has decreased. In many parts of the world, the churches have lost their former influence in society. A European ecumenical conference in 1970 coined the slogan, "We are the only Bible which the general public still reads!", yet the message communicated by the life of Christian communities and their members often belies the gospel. In East Europe and China, moreover, programmes of translation and distribution as well as public biblical teaching were difficult or impossible until the political changes of the 1990s. With the emergence of fundamentalist tendencies in other world religions, similar difficulties for Bible distribution and biblical teaching have arisen in some regions where formerly such hindrances did not exist.

However, the foremost reason for growing biblical illiteracy in formerly "Christian" regions is undoubtedly the worldwide process of secularization. While this process helps to liberate people from sacralized structures of domination and fundamentalism, it also may lead to purely secularist ideologies in which all is conceived to be enclosed in a merely this-worldly space and time. The dimension of mystery and transcendence wastes away. Biblical concerns for the origin and the purpose of creation and history and biblical testimonies about God's direction for present life become unintelligible for many. The effect of secular ideologies is intensified by the fact that in the urban and industrial world the pace of life has been greatly accelerated. New scientific discoveries and their technological applications bring growing unrest, a faster life-style and disorientation into daily life. New products, possibilities and messages compete for attention through communication media. This leads to constant fragmentation and diversion and loss of the ability to concentrate. Time and quietness for reflection and for biblical nurture and meditation becomes rare. Many among the masses marked by this secularism have gradually become aware of a spiritual void, a fear of life under what appears to be an empty heaven. Alongside biblical illiteracy one notices, therefore, a search for new certainties and new directions. The present rise of fundamentalism and sectarianism ironically manifests fear and disorientation.

The growth of conservative evangelicalism

What is often called "evangelical Christianity" has gained momentum, first in North America but gradually throughout the world. There are different emphases in this type of Christianity, but in all of them the Bible and the discipline of some kind of Bible reading play important roles.

A number of faith missions, movements around TV evangelists and groups relating to the International Council of Christian Churches adhere to a fundamentalist view of scripture that teaches the verbal inspiration, inherence and infallibility of the Bible. This is often combined with both militant evangelistic activities and conservative political positions. Such a fundamentalist tendency holds strongly anti-ecumenical and anti-Roman Catholic presuppositions, excluding itself from the ecumenical movement. The role of the Bible among fundamentalists, therefore, falls outside the scope of this chapter.

Many evangelical Christians distance themselves from such fundamentalism. Suspicious of what they see as excessive biblical criticism and loss of substance among liberal Protestants, they work for individual conversion, a personal testimony to Christian faith and a life of obedience. Their understanding of the Bible is based on conservative biblical scholarship. Within the Orthodox and Protestant churches that have covenanted in the WCC, as well as within the Roman Catholic Church, many live by such an evangelical faith. These persons seldom participate actively in the ecumenical movement, but they do serious biblical work with which too few ecumenical leaders have sufficient contact. A new trend in this evangelical Christianity is demonstrated in groups – especially in North and Latin America – in which a strong evangelical faith is combined with increasingly courageous and progresssive stances in social and political affairs. Such groups may provide new initiatives with regard to the Bible in the ecumenical movement.

A shift from North to South

At the beginning of the 20th century, approximately four-fifths of all Christians lived in the Northern hemisphere. Immediately after 2000, more than half live in the South. With regard to keen interest in the biblical message, such a shift from the North to the South may also be observed, for instance in the field of biblical translation. While translations have been published in almost all northern languages as well as in the main languages of the South, large areas have remained in Africa, Asia and Latin America where the Bible was not accessible to people in their own languages. This situation is rapidly changing. By 1980, 80 percent of existing Bible translations were being made into languages of the Southern hemisphere. Formerly, the main translators had been missionaries from the North working in languages which they first had to learn. Now it is UBS policy to have such translations made by indigenous people working in their own languages, outsiders serving only as consultants on specific linguistic and theological questions.

This shift has deep implications for the churches and their interpretation of scripture. Each Bible translation is not only a linguistic but a fundamentally theological event, a transculturation of the gospel. New questions are raised and new insights won. With every new transculturation, the Bible brings ecumenicity. The shift from the North to the South causes related shifts. Formerly, traditional confessional divisions and interconfessional debates had deeply marked the work of translation and interpretation. Now the question of inculturation has come much more to the fore, leading to a dialogue of understandings of the Bible which develop in different socio-economic and cultural environments. Formerly, ways of doing biblical interpretation were mainly set by Northern academic theologians and by Northern church authorities. Now, biblical interpreters in the South have begun to challenge and complement such established ways of reading and interpreting the Bible. Thus, scripture is increasingly becoming the treasure of the whole, worldwide church.

Developments in biblical scholarship

In the mid-1940s, two ancient libraries from biblical and immediately post-biblical times were discovered: the Coptic tractates of Nag Hammadi in upper Egypt (end of the 2nd to the 4th century CE) with several gospels not included in the biblical canon; and the library of the Jewish community of Qumran in the Judean desert (about 150 BCE to CE 68) with prescriptions, biblical commentaries, hymns and apocalyptic texts. They also include a copy of the whole book of Isaiah from the end of the 2nd century BCE, the oldest large biblical manuscript found so far. In the course of the ensuing fifty years, the insights gained from these two libraries led to much reflection and debate concerning the period from 300 BCE to CE 300, a period crucial for both Old and New Testament studies. The Qumran interpretation of the Hebrew scriptures sheds new light on early Christian interpretation. Both the rootedness of Jesus and the early Christians in their time and the specificity and newness of the gospel appear in clearer relief. It also has become evident that during the early Christian centuries the frontiers between "orthodoxy" and "heresy" were much more fluid than formerly assumed.

With regard to exegesis, there has been a certain shift from studies concerning the sources of the biblical writings to studies examining the theology of the redactors, for instance, of the Deuteronomistic historians in the Hebrew scriptures and of the evangelists in the New Testament. Critical historical-exegetical studies have, to be sure, continued, examining what the authors/redactors wanted to say to the first hearers/readers in their particular historical contexts. Yet besides such a "diachronic" understanding of the Bible more "synchronic" analyses have been made. The text as it has been transmitted to us has been examined: What do its structure and rhetoric communicate? These analyses have made strong use of insights from literary criticism, psychology, sociology, gender studies and various "post-modern" and "post-colonialist" theories. Further, in respect to New Testament exegetical and historical work, it should also be indicated that in various forms and various ways "the quest for the historical Jesus" continued, with controversial and unclear results.

New interpreters

Throughout history, the Bible has been interpreted not only by scholars but by whole churches in communal undertakings. Nevertheless, the expositors and authors of historical and exegetical commentaries have been predominantly academics, ordained and male. This reality has been changing in the course of the last decades. Christian "base communities" have developed in rapid succession in Latin America, Asia and Africa as well as in parts of Europe and North America. In these very diverse communities, much Bible study is being done in connection with worship and socio-political action. Those now turning towards the Bible are ordinary women, men and children from different social classes; some are seekers of no confessional background, others are members of different churches.

The context in which such communities do their biblical interpretation is often one of oppression marked by a struggle for liberation. Concrete social and personal life experience becomes the commentary for the stories in scripture. What is received from the biblical messages finds expression in acts of worship, in community life and in involvement in the affairs of this world. The biblical messages are correlated with the realities of daily life. This kind of biblical interpretation has uncovered hidden ideological presuppositions and biases in the traditional teaching of the churches and in academic scholarship. Some of these groups follow what is inadequately called a "materialist reading of the Bible", using a Marxist analysis of society that is applied both to biblical times and current situations. Analogies to power struggles are thus discovered and new perspectives on the person and ministry of Jesus revealed.

Reading and interpreting the Bible on the basis of women's experience has in recent years raised new and exciting challenges, not only in many base communities but more generally for the life of whole churches. What is at stake far exceeds the struggle against "sexist language". Feminist students of the Bible are examining whether traditional teachings about women, authority, church and society are consistent with the biblical text or whether such traditions are actually based on age-old patriarchal prejudices. This approach opens up new perspectives on how God has acted in history, and it provides surprising new glimpses of the real identity of Jesus. Reading the Bible with women's eyes also leads to a deeper appreciation of typical biblical ways of communication – images, gestures, stories and poetry.

From print to electronic media

Most biblical messages were originally transmitted not by writing but, rather, orally – as sermon, song and recitation, sign, gesture or liturgical enactment. Even when messages had been fixed in written manuscripts, scripture was still read aloud and illuminated for visual communication. Nevertheless, with the invention and development of printing, the Bible became more and more merely a book, "incarnate" in paper, most often read privately and silently.

What impact can a book have now in a world where communication happens mostly through audiovisual and electronic media? No one is yet able clearly to foresee how present revolutions in communication will affect future ways of learning and understanding. Nevertheless, all observers are convinced that a fundamental change is taking place that may well have a deeper impact than that of the invention of movable type. What does this mean for the translation, dissemination and teaching of the Bible? How will this affect biblical understanding and interpretation? Bible societies and those who enable biblical study are struggling with this issue.

A difficult new task of translation [or "transmediatization"] lies ahead. Over the centuries, artists and dramatists have undertaken the task. More recently, those working with radio, films and cassettes have joined them, and now computer specialists and telecommunication experts are making new contributions. Additionally, innovative performance artists are rediscovering old biblical ways of communicating with the whole body, with ears and eyes, gestures and walking, with dramatization, and memorization leading to meditation. Gradually, the Bible is again becoming much more than a book. In these new circumstances, a perennially critical question again arises: What happens to a message when it is transposed from one medium to another? The affirmations of biblical faith in painting and sculpture led at times to idolatry. Medieval passion plays degenerated into cheap banter. Nor was the print medium itself completely innocent, often leading to bibliolatry, worship of the book. What will happen to the message of scripture as it is translated into the media – electronic and otherwise – of the 21st century? Are there deeply effective means of communication that must not be used because their coercive influence contradicts the message? These are questions not to be evaded by those who are committed to the truth and vitality of biblical messages.

SOME AGENTS OF GLOBAL BIBLE WORK

Bible study and Bible meditation remain essentially personal and communal exercises best done in the contexts of worshipping, witnessing and serving local communities. Education departments of churches and national and regional ecumenical councils together with Bible reading fellowships and similar movements can facilitate but never replace personal and corporate study of the Bible. The following three worldwide agencies, which serve the use of the Bible in the ecumenical movement, can do no more than a similar work of enabling and stimulating.

The United Bible Societies

In 1996, the UBS celebrated its jubilee, looking back on fifty years of remarkable service.[8] Alongside its primary task of translating and distributing scripture, the UBS, working with all Christian confessions and groups, has a special ministry of unity, although among Protestants the gap between Christians of conservative-evangelical persuasion and those who are ecumenically involved is not yet completely bridged. Collaboration with Roman Catholic Bible agencies has continued; in 1987, a revision of the earlier mentioned *Guiding Principles* was made. Protestants and Roman Catholics now work together on Bible translations in many languages. In recent years, collaboration with Orthodox churches has also been strengthened, especially in Bible translation and distribution in the former Soviet Union and in Central and Eastern Europe.

Working relationships with such a wide range of theologically different churches and groups have at times created tensions within the UBS. In the mid-1970s, when the WCC Programme to Combat Racism caused conservative Evangelicals sharply to criticize that ecumenical initiative, the fellowship of Bible societies had to pass through a "test of elasticity". Nevertheless, the UBS was invited to present its work and cause both at the 1974 Congress on World Evangelization in Lausanne and at the fifth assembly of the WCC in Nairobi in 1975. In some countries with heavy Roman Catholic influence, it has thus far proven impossible to start common Protestant-Catholic translation projects although Catholics increasingly also use Bible Society editions.

The UBS continues to review and re-edit the original Hebrew and Greek texts of the Bible on the basis of new manuscript discoveries and new insights in textual studies. A series of translators' handbooks is being published, and training seminars for translators are being organized. Traditional translations emphasized formal equivalence with both the biblical messages and the special features of the source language, but the special characteristics of the receptor languages were then often disregarded, and the translated text on occasion became incomprehensible to common readers. Accordingly, within the UBS the theory and practice of "dynamic-equivalent translation" (now often called "functional equivalence") was developed. In 1966, *The New Testament in Today's English Version* and in 1976 the whole *Good News Bible*, translated according to this theory, were published and immediately found an unexpectedly large readership. In these versions, the meaning of the original biblical text is rendered in words and forms accepted as standard by people everywhere who employ English as a means of communication, not least those who use English as an acquired language. Similar common language translations have been made for many other language areas. This translation theory is constantly being refined. While formerly analysis of the sentence structure and the informative function of language were specially emphasized, more attention is now given to rhetorical structures and to the expressive function of language; e.g., most of the key vocabulary of the Bible is figurative, and thus poetry is to be translated as poetry.

By 1996, the UBS had become a world fellowship of 135 societies operating in more than 200 countries and territories. It works with a structure of regional service centres, regional conferences, a global service centre, and world assemblies. These assemblies

---

[8] The UBS publishes two quarterlies, the *UBS Bulletin* and *The Bible Translator*. On history: Edwin H. Robertson, *Taking the Word to the World: 50 Years of United Bible Societies*, Nashville TN, Nelson, 1996. On Bible translation: Eugene A. Nida and Charles R. Taber, *The Theory and Practice of Translation*, Leiden, Brill, 1969. Articles in *The Bible Translator* and *Bulletin* 1970/71, 1994, 182/83, 1997. Reports from UBS world assembly at Mississauga 1996 in *UBS Bulletin* no. 178/79, 1997.

took place in Addis Ababa in 1972, in Chiang Mai, Thailand, in 1980, in Budapest in 1988, and the jubilee assembly met at Mississauga, Canada, in 1996 under the theme "God's Word: Life for All". There the original vocation of the UBS for Bible translation and distribution was reaffirmed and new emphases for future work specified. Among these the following have special relevance for the role of the Bible in the ecumenical movement:

- More human need-centred scriptures are to be provided for the ministry of the churches for worship, nurture, service and evangelism. This includes scripture programmes for suffering people such as refugees, victims of violence, the terminally ill; programmes of scriptures with study notes for people of other religions and those seeking to know God; programmes which affirm and celebrate life as God-given and which foster responsibility to care for all of God's creation.
- With regard to communication, the objective is to make use of the achievements in the field of information technology and electronic media so that new channels be developed for spreading the word of Life.
- The UBS is to work with churches in developing programmes that will counter a growing lack of biblical knowledge with active reading, listening and study of the Bible.

The Catholic Biblical Federation

After the Second Vatican Council, there was a vigorous rediscovery of the Bible among many Roman Catholics.[9] A number of ordained and lay theologians along with religious who felt imprisoned in traditional Catholic structures and institutions discovered a new ministry, that of biblical performance as *animateurs*. This led to creative Bible movements and programmes in many dioceses, to regional bishops' conferences centred around scripture, and to Catholic biblical associations all over the world, most of which are now joined together in the Catholic Biblical Federation (CBF). Twenty-five years after its foundation in 1969, the Federation had become a fellowship of 253 member movements and institutions in 95 countries. According to canon law, it is "an international Catholic organization of a public character to further the pastoral implementation of *Dei Verbum*". Like the UBS, the CBF works through coordinating offices in regions and sub-regions, through a world office, and through plenary assemblies, the last three of which took place at Bangalore in 1984, Bogota in 1990, and Hong Kong in 1996. The Vatican II "Constitution on Divine Revelation", *Dei Verbum*, remains the foundation document for the CBF, further explicated in a statement issued in 1993 by the Pontifical Biblical Commission on "The Interpretation of the Bible in the Church".[10] There, a continuing, pastorally oriented use of historical-critical exegesis is advocated and a fundamentalist approach to scripture strongly rejected.

During the first phase of CBF work, much emphasis lay on collaboration with the Bible societies for joint translation and distribution. This continues, but the accent of CBF is now put more on the reading of the Bible, its relation to worship and its role in

---

[9] "Dogmatic Constitution on Divine Revelation" (1965) in Walter M. Abbott ed., *The Documents of Vatican II*, New York, Guild, 1966, pp.111-28. Articles on the implementation of this Vatican Decree in the CBF quarterly *Dei Verbum*. And the survey *Audiens et Proclamans: Serving the Biblical-Pastoral Ministry*, Stuttgart, 1994. Current orientations of CBF work: Pontifical Biblical Commission, *The Interpretation of the Bible* (English in *Catholic International* 5, 3, 1994, pp.109-47) and final document of the CBF plenary assembly, *Word of God – Source of Life*, Hong Kong, 1996.

[10] *Origins: CNS Documentary Service*, Washington DC, 23, 29, 6 Jan. 1994.

biblical-pastoral ministry. At the Hong Kong assembly, there was great sensitivity for what it means to read the Bible in different cultural, religious and socio-political environments. Proposals were made for bridging the gulf between academic biblical scholarship and biblical-pastoral ministry; e.g., on the training of priests and laity and the revision of the lectionary. The hope was expressed that a future synod of bishops would concentrate on the theme of biblical-pastoral ministry and work towards such an event has commenced.

The World Council of Churches

The WCC has never confined itself to being a Bible movement. Bible study has not been done as an end in itself but has been conducted with a view to the churches' worship, witness and service in the world.[11] Implementing the 1968 statement from the Uppsala assembly, "The Bible in the Ecumenical Movement", the WCC has developed special work in four areas.

First, since 1946, the Ecumenical Institute in Bossey, Switzerland, has been deeply involved in biblical training and interpretation. What had been learned in pioneering ecumenical youth movements was continued at Bossey: a type of participatory Bible study based on the best insights gained in biblical scholarship and at the same time addressing current issues facing the church in the world. After 1968, such a discipline of Bible study became more difficult to maintain. Nevertheless, whether it was popular or not, most course programmes at Bossey continued to include some biblical studies. The themes of the 1970-71 and 1980-81 Bossey graduate school for ecumenical studies concentrated on the Bible in our time and some training courses for ecumenical Bible study *animateurs* were organized. The following themes of Bossey consultations are symptomatic of the last decades: "Prophecy in the New Testament and Today", "God's Justice and the Justice of Man", "Biblical and Theological Perspectives on Power" and "Reading the Bible with Women's Eyes".

Second, WCC Publications have provided considerable Bible study material for use in local congregations and ecumenical groups. An example is the series "Word for the World", published in 1970 in cooperation with the Bible Reading Fellowship. In this series, written by a group of ecumenical leaders from all confessions and continents, biblical and ecumenical education are combined: for each day of the year, a biblical text is introduced for study and an ecumenical event or insight singled out for continuing remembrance. Such material has since been followed up by a variety of other resources. Preparatory Bible study outlines for large ecumenical gatherings have been widely circulated and used. The studies "Images of Life", prepared for the 1983 WCC assembly in Vancouver, have been translated into over thirty languages. Often it is only through such material that individual Christians, local churches and ecumenical groups can participate through thought, prayer and action in what is happening on the larger ecumenical scene.

Third, a secretariat for biblical studies was established by the WCC in 1971, functioning until 1990. Initially, its main emphasis lay in consultative work, helping to

---

[11] Richard C. Rowe, *Bible Study in the World Council of Churches*, WCC, 1969. On Bossey and the Biblical Studies Secretariat: H.-R. Weber, *Experiments with Bible Studies*, WCC, 1981. Idem, "Bossey, the Bible and Culture", in *The Ecumenical Review*, 39, 2, 1987, pp.197-205. For Faith and Order studies on the Bible: Ellen Flesseman-van Leer ed., *The Bible: Its Authority and Interpretation in the Ecumenical Movement*, WCC, 1980. Günther Gassmann ed., *Documentary History of Faith and Order*, WCC, 1993, and bibliography at the end of this chapter.

strengthen the biblical orientation of various programmes. The secretariat also conducted a worldwide study on how cultural factors influence biblical interpretation, concentrating on the meaning of the crucifixion. Multiple ways of learning and teaching biblical testimonies, e.g. through oral tradition and art, were explored.[12] In response to requests from churches, the main emphasis of the secretariat later shifted from biblical consultancy work to the training of leaders for participatory Bible study. In the 1970s and 1980s, about a hundred ecumenical residential training courses were organized in all continents.

Fourth, even before the WCC was officially founded, its future study department had initiated an enquiry on the theme "From the Bible to the Modern World". This led to the ongoing study of this theme mainly under the auspices of the Faith and Order Commission. At the end of this chapter more will be said about that study process.

BIBLE STUDY AROUND THE WORLD

Biblical texts and stories do not address Christians in the same way all over the world. There is no universally valid objective interpretation of scripture. Throughout history believers of every century have approached the Bible with their own particular questions, expectations and prejudices. The same is currently true for readers living in different socio-political and cultural situations. This "circle of interpretation" – back and forth from present context to biblical text – gives rise to the danger of misusing the Bible as a quarry of proof-texts for preconceived ideas and dogmas. Yet wherever attentive listening and study is done, the Bible begins to challenge hearers and readers with its own questions and truth. The different situations and preconceptions of the world's regions together with the specific biblical challenge to each region account for the great diversity of understandings of the biblical messages today.[13]

Middle East

Several unique circumstances influence Bible reading in the Middle East. First, the Semitic languages spoken, especially Arabic and Hebrew, give readers a more direct and congenial relationship to the original biblical texts than is possible for speakers of Indo-Germanic, Finno-Ugaritic or other languages. This is true not only for the Hebrew scriptures but also for understanding Jesus, who almost certainly spoke Aramaic, and for appreciating the strongly Semitic background of the Greek New Testament. In addition, the Middle East is the land of the Bible with its archeological richness and its holy places which give Middle Eastern readers a sense of historic continuity with biblical origins. This continuity is accentuated by the fact that some of the oldest Christian churches, the Eastern and Oriental Orthodox, are comparatively strong in this region. The first Bible

---

[12] H.-R. Weber, *Immanuel: The Coming of Jesus in Art and the Bible*, WCC Publications, 1984.

[13] No full survey on this theme exists. The following generalizations are made on the basis of the author's experience of Bible study on all continents and in interviews with Bible study enablers. Compare many detailed reports from all continents in UBS and CBC publications and, among many others, the following: *Traduction oecuménique de la Bible*, Cerf/Société Biblique, Paris, 1972/75. Manfred Lundgren, *Proclaiming Christ to His World: The Experience of Radio Voice of the Gospel, 1957-1977*, Geneva, LWF, 1983. John Mbiti, *Bible and Theology in African Christianity*, Nairobi, Oxford Univ. Press, 1986. *Bibliografia Biblica Latino-Americana*, Sao Benardo do Campo, since 1988. R.S. Sugirtharajah ed., *Voices from the Margin: Interpreting the Bible in the Third World*, Maryknoll NY, Orbis, 1991. O. Ch. Lee ed., *Women of Courage: Asian Women Reading the Bible*, Seoul, Asian Women's Resource Centre, 1992. Howard C. Kee ed., *The Bible in the Twenty-First Century*, Philadelphia, Trinity, 1993.

translations were made in this region and, moreover, ancient Jewish worship strongly influenced the Orthodox liturgies, as demonstrated by the central place given to the Bible in Orthodox worship.

Two other circumstances play a role in the understanding of the Bible in the Middle East. First, both Jews and Christians live as minorities in a Muslim environment. The relation of Jewish and Christian scripture to the Quran is, therefore, important. Secondly, the explosive political situation existing since the establishment of the state of Israel and the consequent plight of Arab refugees pose urgent questions for biblical interpretation. According to the Hebrew scriptures, an intimate link exists between God's chosen people and the chosen land of Canaan; this theology can be one-sidedly accentuated as a "theology of the land". Yet an equally strong emphasis lies on a "theology of the poor" which in the New Testament becomes even more prominent. In today's Middle East, these two biblical traditions come into conflict. Reflection is needed on what promise, election and justice mean with regard to land, poverty and peace. Such reflection should be done corporately by Jews, Christians and Muslims. Although the present situation makes this exceedingly difficult, attempts at such corporate inter-religious studies are made in, among a few other places, the Ecumenical Institute at Tantur near Jerusalem.

Africa

Two factors characterize rapidly growing African Christianity, especially the mushrooming African Instituted (Independent) Churches (AICs): the central role of the Bible, and the interpenetration of biblical and African world-views. The greatest increase of Bible circulation and the largest output of new translations have occurred in Africa. Case studies reveal that the Bible often precedes the church: as soon as parts or the whole of the scripture are available in the African language of a given area, independent churches grow almost spontaneously. These are no longer dependent on outside authorities – expatriate missionaries or Westernized African church leaders – for leadership, support or governance. Translated scripture speaks to such African churches with its own authority and with emphases often strange to Christians of the West. New converts discover striking affinities between their own heritage and biblical beliefs, culture and customs. The Bible functions as an oral message, not as a written text, and African theology thus appears most genuinely in prayers, hymns and sermons. Salvation is seen as the power of Christ the Exorcist who defeats life-destroying forces and liberates believers from the bondage of evil. Faith is not primarily defined in creeds but is experienced, often in dreams, as the presence of God, as a shield against suffering and a power for healing. Faith is celebrated in joyful worship where rituals and holy places play an important part.

This affinity between biblical and African customs and the consequent popularity of the Bible can lead to special dangers. There are instances of a magical use of the Bible in healing ceremonies. The proliferation of AICs becomes a threat to Christian unity. As elsewhere, in African political rhetoric biblical quotations are at times used for quite unbiblical purposes. The gravest misuse of the Bible on that continent was made by Christians of European descent when some theologians and politicians of the Afrikaner churches attempted to justify apartheid by biblical arguments. Remarkably, the strongest positive message comes now from the same country, South Africa: in its biblically inspired way of dealing with the violence of racial discrimination by a process of establishing truth through judgment, confession of sin, forgiveness and reconciliation.

The numerical growth of African churches and their thirst for biblical nurture requires considerable biblical training. Traditional theological seminaries with their one-sided intellectual approach have responded only insufficiently to this demand. Radio and cassettes play a crucial role, and the Lutheran World Federation's Radio Voice of the Gospel (RVOG) in Addis Ababa fulfilled an important ministry until it was nationalized in 1977. Since then many local radio stations, some of which are former studios of RVOG, continue the work of biblical nurture. The South African Council of Churches organizes special training for leaders of independent churches. The Lumko Institute of the Catholic bishops conference of South Africa has developed simple ways of pastorally studying the Bible which are now being used on other continents as well. Another Roman Catholic initiative, the Centre for the Biblical Apostolate in the Democratic Republic of the Congo, fosters encounter between biblical and African thought and indigenous ways of studying and celebrating the biblical messages.

Asia

Except in the Philippines, Christians in Asia form only a tiny minority among large populations that have their own holy scriptures. Both Christian faith and modern secularism are being challenged by the revival of Hinduism, Buddhism and militant Islam. Asian Christians face questions such as: What is the relationship of the Bible to ancient Asian holy scriptures? To what extent could these scriptures function as the "Old Testament" for churches in Asia? What is the role of the Bible for the probably large number of "anonymous Christians" who do not have or want to have any contact with organized Christianity? (In this connection, the Japanese Mukyokai, the "non-church movement", is symptomatic.)

The Bible speaks strongly to Asian women and people involved in urban-rural mission. The experiences of the enslaved people of Israel in Egypt, as well as that of women and marginalized poor in Jesus' time, are seen to be revealing analogies for the present situation of suffering and groaning among the masses in Asian cities and villages. In the minjung theology of Korea, this analogy functions as a key for biblical interpretation. Other ways of understanding the Bible come to the fore in the encounter with believing Hindus or Buddhists who have a cyclical view of history and a long tradition of meditation. Western theology, especially in mid-20th century, emphasized a linear view of salvation history *(Heilsgeschichte)* that often leads to an activist, prophetic involvement in history. This, however, is not the whole of biblical faith. Especially in the wisdom and priestly traditions of the Old Testament, there is a less linear view of history combined with a great concern for all created things and beings, for wise decision-making, and for a daily life nurtured by worship and meditation. Such often neglected aspects of the Bible are rediscovered when it is read in an Asian context.

Undoubtedly the most noteworthy development with regard to the Bible in Asia is what has happened since the 1980s in China. During the so-called Cultural Revolution, Bibles had been declared "poisonous literature"; they were confiscated and at times burned. As a kind of remnant, Christians could meet only secretly and their sole nurture was memorized passages of scripture. With recent changes, Christians and seekers began in many parts of the country to meet in house churches for Bible study and prayer. When former church buildings were restored for worship, these soon proved to be much too small for almost miraculously growing congregations. Now the majority of Christians in China are first generation Christians who never knew denominational Christianity – their common link is the Bible, and their first priority is to secure Bibles and biblical teaching. When in 1981 the Nanjing Union Theological Seminary could start work again, it organized, in addition to its resident courses, a nationwide biblical-theological correspondence course that within three years had thousands of students. The UBS became instrumental for launching Amity Press in China which by 1993 had printed its five millionth copy of the Chinese Bible. Yet many more millions are needed in response to the thirst for scripture.

Oceania

For most of the small societies and oral cultures in the Pacific islands, the largest geographic area of the world, the Bible became the first book and for a long time the only book known. In the popular mind, it was vested with *mana*, a holy power. On the basis of biblical prescriptions, law codes and customs were shaped, and on several islands a kind of "Christendom" developed in which it was difficult to separate either church and state or Christian spirituality and customary law. For a long time now, translations of the Bible have existed for all major island groups, prepared mainly by missionaries. Archaic language and many transliterations of Hebrew, Greek and English words enhanced the mystery of the book, yet they hardly developed a true understanding of biblical messages. Scripture continued to have a central place, yet functioned mainly as law and not as gospel.

The second world war, nuclear testing, negative experiences of migration, invasion by tourists, electronic media, the threat of rising water levels due to climate change – all this is now shaking the foundations of formerly closed, traditional cultures. It does not suffice any longer simply to have the Bible as a holy book. What is needed is biblical understanding, thinking and discernment to safeguard the wisdom and values of the island cultures and to meet the challenges of the invading "modern world". New translations of the Bible are urgently required and training of Bible study enablers has also become a high priority. The Pacific Theological College in Suva, Fiji, which trains church leaders and teachers for local theological schools in the whole region, has developed a master's programme especially geared to Bible translation and biblical thinking in the field of gospel and culture.

Latin America

By the 1960s, the biblical renewal movement which had developed in Europe, largely in association with neo-orthodox theology, began to make its impact in Latin America, among Roman Catholics mainly via France, and among Protestants mainly through the World Student Christian Federation. For most Latin American Christians, the traditional situation had been longstanding: among the Catholic majority there was very little knowledge of the Bible, and among the growing number of Protestants there was a strongly conservative evangelical love for the Bible, often combined with legalistic and fundamentalist attitudes. The "liberation theologies" which were just developing were, at first, seldom based on serious biblical studies. For two reasons this situation changed.

First, many Christian base communities began to grow all over Latin America and the Caribbean. The poor and oppressed masses listened to biblical stories, now available in vernacular translations. These were discussed and interpreted in the light of common oppression. This led to communal prayer and worship, to mutual support and common action. Through such Bible study, a new way of being the church began to grow, relatively unhindered by confessional barriers. The Bible ceased to be the exclusive property of clergy and academic theologians and was less often used for providing proof texts for dogmatic convictions or legalistic moral conduct. It became a source for new insight, for discerning the signs of the times and an encouraging inspiration for socio-political involvement.

The second reason for the present advance in biblical renewal was through the initiative of those Latin American and Caribbean liberation theologians who had a special concern for biblical nurture. They met for the first time in 1984 to take stock of the very diverse work in Bible circles throughout the continent, to foster interchange and to stimulate further growth. From the beginning, Catholics and Protestants worked together and women exegetes began to play an important role. A Latin American network was created, supported by the WCC and other agencies. The ecumenical Centro de Estudos Bíblicos, established in Brazil in 1978, had already done pioneering work for a community-based popular reading of the Bible and became a rallying point for biblical renewal. In the late 1980s, it organized for biblical *animateurs* three intensive continent-wide training courses, each for six months. Since 1991, similar but shorter intensive courses became itinerant, in Mexico, Colombia, Chile, Brazil, Bolivia and subsequently planned for other sub-regions. Alongside training, there is a flourishing development of published literature on biblical interpretation and study.

North America

Much of North America, especially the US, is strongly influenced by the conservative evangelical mood. In the US, moreover, the fundamentalist movement has many links with civic religion, biblical arguments, often based on questionable exegesis, playing a large role in political debates and public discussions on abortion, sexuality, capital punishment, etc. The "battle for the Bible" fostered by entities such as the Christian Coalition with its support of conservative political action has made headlines. In sharp contrast, Christians more involved in the ecumenical movement have been active in the struggle for racial justice, in women's liberation causes and in actions of solidarity with Native Americans and Inuit – all movements against social exclusion. In such involvement, the Bible is seen as a prophetic challenge for justice, equality and inclusion.

What characterizes North American biblical scholarship is a shift from history to story. The original oral, narrative form of biblical testimonies and their "theopoetic" quality are being rediscovered. This is accompanied by much interest in the psychology of learning and in theories of communication. Insights gained have immediately been applied to Bible study programmes. Christians are, for instance, taught again to become biblical story-tellers and to link their personal and their society's stories with the stories in the Bible. A popular programme, launched in 1977 by Roman Catholics in Canada, is called "The Journey": in forty lessons it introduces members of self-taught groups to the whole of the biblical story.

Nowhere else in the world is the impact of electronic media so deep as in North America. No wonder that the most creative thinking and experimenting with regard to the "transmediatization" of the Bible was initiated in 1990 by the American Bible Society. In its "multi-media translation project", critical questions have been asked about the complex relationship between message and medium. Translations of biblical stories into other than print media are being made with an attempt to remain faithful to the original Hebrew or Greek both with regard to message and to the original media, oral tradition and manuscripts.

Europe

With the fall of the Berlin wall and the disintegration of the former Soviet Union and communist Eastern Europe, not only the political map of Europe changed but also Bible work. A UBS survey of 1993 shows how deeply this has affected the life of churches in Central and Eastern Europe where the demand for Bibles overwhelms available stocks and budgets despite intensive new efforts at local printing and distribution. Ultimately, perhaps the most important long-term impact of these developments will be an increasing participation of Orthodox churches in general Bible work. The essential link between Bible and liturgy, between Bible study and the worshipping community, will be more clearly appreciated.

In Western Europe, traditional Bible study groups in local parishes have in the last decades diminished and often even disappeared. At the same time, promising new initiatives are being taken. The publication of *Traduction oecuménique de la Bible*, in 1972 for the New Testament and 1975 for the whole Bible, was an ecumenical event. For many years, Protestant and Catholic biblical scholars had together translated, introduced and theologically annotated the scripture, and for the French-speaking world this teamwork made not only a lasting impact on biblical scholarship but also laid the basis for ecumenical Bible study in local groups. The two following examples are typical.

Among Protestants in France, the 1960s saw the start of *équipes de recherche biblique*, local groups of lay people engaged in biblical study utilizing the best available resources and various ways of interpretation. Some biblical scholars became full-time itinerant advisers for these groups. A number of lay people learned Greek and Hebrew simply to have more direct access to and a better basis for studying scripture. Soon, members of other denominations and agnostics joined this type of intellectually demanding exploration.

A second and quite different, more meditative way of biblical nurture started in 1980 among Italian Roman Catholics in Milan. It was an adapted form of the ancient *lectio divina* (originally a Benedictine process of communal prayer and meditation) which throughout the centuries has been practised in monasteries. Its emphasis lay in listening to a biblical passage in an atmosphere of silence so that what was heard was imprinted on mind and heart and its message led both to prayer and commitment for action. Such "schools of the word" are now spreading to other countries and involve participants from various confessions, especially drawing together young people for series of large evening gatherings in city cathedrals.

BIBLICAL INTERPRETATION AND THEOLOGY

Ecumenical Bible study primarily means to listen together to biblical messages and to be corporately judged, corrected, encouraged and guided by them. Letting the biblical witnesses speak to us, even if we do not yet agree on what we think *about* the Bible and how we should approach it, is the primary task. Such study becomes converting and uniting. To speak first about the Bible is usually divisive. Nevertheless, sooner or later Christians from different confessions and cultures must also face persisting disagreements about the nature of scripture, critically examining the variety of hermeneutics in use. This requires an honest investigation of the way in which methods of interpretation are conditioned dogmatically and philosophically as well as socio-economically and culturally.[14]

---

[14] "Guiding Principles for the Interpretation of the Bible", in *The Bible: Its Authority and Interpretation*, pp.13-17. Daniel C. Arichea, "Theology and Translation", in *UBS Bulletin*, 140/41, 1985, pp.7-24. Pontifical Biblical Commission, *The Interpretation of the Bible*. R.S. Sugirtharajah, *Asian Biblical Hermeneutics and Postcolonialism: Contesting the Interpetations*, Maryknoll NY, Orbis, 1998.

Which Bible?

Biblical testimonies are not merely literary texts. They point to living communities, historical events of judgment and salvation, feasts to be celebrated, acts of obedience demanded by faith, the life and hope of a pilgrim people in particular cultural and socio-political contexts. Ultimately, they point to the person in whom God became incarnate. Moreover, behind these texts is usually a whole pre-history of oral tradition, written sources, compilation and redaction. Additionally, the texts have their own history – for instance, as an Old Testament passage is interpreted in the New Testament, or as they have impact on the subsequent history of the church, of persons and of nations.

In biblical interpretation, the history and development of these different dimensions and layers of textual material must be considered. However, what is to be *translated* are the original Hebrew (part Aramaic) and Greek texts as they have been accepted into the canon of scripture. Renditions into languages of today will obviously differ in a variety of ways: the translation theories used, the possibilities and structures of the receptor language, the differing audiences and purposes envisaged. Thus Bibles for children, for liturgical use, for a wide readership outside the churches or for study groups must have their individual styles. They may or may not require limited or full sets of introductions and annotations. Yet all these different Bibles must be based on the original texts. Immediately, two controversial questions arise.

First, how much weight should be given to the Septuagint, the ancient Greek translation of the Hebrew scriptures made in Alexandria during the 3rd and 2nd centuries BCE? Some scholars always give priority to the Hebrew text, while others believe that the Alexandrian translators had access to manuscripts older than those on which the present Hebrew text is based. Though definitely a translation, the Septuagint is often helpful for discovering a clearer sense of what the original authors and redactors wanted to convey. Additionally, for early Christians the Septuagint was the Bible, and Old Testament quotations in the New Testament are more often based on the Septuagint than the Hebrew text. Moreover, this is not only a matter of language, since the Septuagint has its own theological emphases; there is a unique "Septuagint spirituality" which developed in the Hellenistic-Jewish world.

A second difficulty with regard to the translation and ecumenical use of the Bible lies in the fact that there is no complete agreement concerning what constitutes the canon, the particular books which have authority for the life and teaching of the churches. In respect to the New Testament there is almost total agreement, although the canon of the Ethiopian Orthodox Church includes several writings thought to originate later than the universally acknowledged 27 books. Differences arise mainly with regard to the canonical status of a group of writings from the intertestamental period. These "apocryphal" or "deuterocanonical" books do not form part of the Hebrew canon although almost all are included in the Septuagint. Roman Catholics consider them to be canonical; most Orthodox also follow the Septuagint; Protestants generally do not give much authority to these books.

Studying the Bible ecumenically requires a readiness to work with different understandings of the canon. This readiness is part of ecumenical spirituality: as communities join a common pilgrimage they must, as it were, suspend traditional definitions and canons. This suspension is a witness that the truth possessed by different groups within the pilgrim people is partial in light of the fuller truth to which the people hope to be led. Such mutual openness is all the more needed when questions about the right interpretation of the Bible are faced.

Towards common interpretation

The quick survey, above, of how Bible study is done around the world shows that interpretation is influenced by geographical and cultural factors. Confessional traditions also provide different prisms for understanding scripture. For Orthodox Christians, the fathers of the early church and the seven ecumenical councils go far to determine the perception of biblical texts. Roman Catholics understand the Bible within the framework of what bishops, councils and the pope – the *magisterium* – teach as the apostolic deposit of faith. Protestants consciously or unconsciously read and interpret biblical testimonies with the eyes of the Reformers or, often, of current influential exegetes. Through ecumenical experience such divergent confessional approaches and their particular, and limited, angles of vision become less operative. Bible translators and biblical scholars of different confessions and cultures have in fact developed a degree of cooperation and common interpretation which goes far beyond the present state of the official ecumenical movement. The work of the UBS and the CBF point to this, and the comprehensive document on "The Interpretation of the Bible in the Church", issued in 1993 by the Pontifical Biblical Commission, expresses much with which Orthodox and Protestant scholars can agree.

The 1963 report from the fourth world conference on Faith and Order, "Scripture, Tradition and Traditions",[15] describes the Bible as the testimony to and the written form of the normative, living Tradition of the gospel by which Christians live and which is transmitted by the church through the power of the Holy Spirit. This Tradition (with capital T) has to be transmitted and interpreted in and for every new situation. A plurality of traditions (with small t) is expressed in widely varying forms of worship, missionary proclamation, creeds, spiritualities, etc. It also is expressed in the variety of particular church confessions.[16] This general insight from Faith and Order has proven to be helpful for bilateral and multilateral discussions between representatives of different confessional families. However, the last part of the 1963 report, "The Christian Tradition and Cultural Diversity", has not yet been fully appropriated in ongoing ecumenical debate about "gospel and culture". Further work is needed on how to discern what is or is not a manifestation of the living Tradition of the gospel when, in conflicting cultural situations, differing interpretations of biblical faith confront one another. In the ecumenical situation at the end of the 20th century, this question is as important as the clash of conflicting confessional traditions themselves. In other words, what does the phrase "according to the scriptures" in the WCC basis mean and how does it become operative as a criterion?

---

[15] *The Bible: Its Authority and Interpretation*, pp.18-29.

[16] "(6)There is an historic Christian Tradition to which every Christian body inevitably appeals in matters of faith and practice. In this Tradition three aspects can be distinguished, although they are inseparable. [a] By *"Tradition"* (with a capital "T") is meant the whole life of the church insofar as, grounded in the life of Christ and nourished by the Holy Spirit, it manifests, confesses and testifies to the truth of the gospel (John 1:1-4). This uniting Tradition comes to expression in teaching, worship, witness, sacraments, way of life, and order. [b] Tradition is also the *process of transmitting* by which this living reality of Christ is handed on from one generation to another. [c] And, since Tradition is this continually flexible and growing reality as it is reflected, known, and handed on in the teaching and practice of the church, Tradition is also embodied and expressed more or less adequately in a variety of concrete historical *traditions* (lower case "t")... Scripture is the focal and definitive expression of the Tradition of the apostles. As such, it is the supreme norm and corrector of all traditions. The church has acknowledged this by binding itself to the scripture as its canon." From Consultation on Church Union, *The COCU Consensus*, Princeton NJ, 1985, chap. V, §§ 6,7.

The 1971 Faith and Order report on "The Authority of the Bible" viewed authority and inspiration in a dynamic and relational way. The biblical testimonies prove themselves authoritative in the midst of human experience. Through them, God's authority, promise and will are experienced as normative. The inspiration of scripture, usually affirmed as a dogmatic assumption, is here seen as the action of the Spirit in the whole process that led to the biblical testimonies. This Spirit is also at work in interpretive processes within the community of Christ's church throughout the ages. This similarly raises the question: what in present conflicting interpretations of the Bible is or is not "of the Spirit"?

A much debated issue for ecumenical biblical interpretation concerns "The Significance of the Old Testament in Its Relation to the New", as the issue was stated in a little known Faith and Order statement of 1977.[17] Is there simply a historic continuity between the two, or does the relationship between the Testaments have specific theological significance? Should this relation be seen, for instance, as one of promise and fulfilment? If so, what is to be fulfilled? The statement describes various understandings of the matter that are operative in biblical interpretation. It insists that the Old Testament is an integral and indispensable part of the one authoritative scripture but emphasizes the specificity of each Testament. There are central affirmations of biblical faith in the Old Testament that must not be neglected although in the New Testament they may receive little emphasis, and, to be sure, central affirmations of Christian faith – primarily concerning Jesus Christ – go far beyond the Old Testament. Such a view is important for any attempt to see the Bible as a whole. Indeed, it is also important in Jewish and Christian dialogue on the relation of the Hebrew scriptures and the New Testament.

The search for a biblical theology

Through the 1950s, a broad agreement existed within the ecumenical movement about how to see the Bible as a whole. "Salvation history" (Heilsgeschichte) was for many the thread running through the Old and the New Testaments, linking the two and becoming, with Christ at the centre, the frame for constructing a biblical theology from the biblical messages.

Since then, no such broadly accepted common framework regarding "biblical theology" has been in place. Biblical exegesis has become ever more fragmented and specialized. In the Bible there are various, theologically divergent versions of salvation histories. The study of redaction history has shown how each evangelist gave different accents to the gospel. Analyses of Old Testament wisdom literature have indicated that, for the people of Israel, wisdom could become an alternative theological option, standing apart from and in tension with salvation histories and prophetic traditions. The "Tradition" about which the 1963 Montreal report had spoken appeared in the Bible itself as a bundle of constantly transmitted and reinterpreted biblical traditions of faith. This diversity and the theological tensions within the Bible were honestly described in the 1967 Faith and Order report on "The Significance of the Hermeneutical Problem for the Ecumenical Movement".[18]

On the basis of such exegetical insights, it is difficult to conceive of a theology of either the Old or the New Testament. Even more impossible is any attempt to expose the "biblical theology" – there are several possible ones, and none can claim entirely to capture the rich diversity of the Bible. Are we then condemned to live only with diversity? In recent Faith and Order studies, there has been a concentration on "the apostolic

---

[17] *The Bible: Its Authority and Interpretation*, pp.58-76.
[18] *Ibid.*, pp.30-41.

faith".[19] Can a common confession of apostolic faith as expressed in the Nicene Creed become the criterion for theological work and for discerning what is of the Spirit? Can it help to find the common vision that the ecumenical movement desperately needs? For theologians in different confessional families, this is indeed a way forward. Yet for the large membership of the churches, especially those in cultures which have been little influenced by Greek philosophy, the language of the Nicene Creed and of the ancient ecumenical councils is much more foreign than the language of the Bible.

Alongside reflection on the apostolic faith looms another great task: the ecumenical movement again needs ways to see the Bible as a whole so that its diverse witnesses may together address Christians and churches today. The Bible as a whole has been received by the universal church and is given to its members for nurture and encouragement. Exegetes and theologians must therefore not be allowed to work only on small pieces without seeing that whole. In the field of biblical scholarship, the pendulum is again swinging back from an almost exclusive concentration on texts, individual biblical books and themes to a new search for a biblical theology.

Despite the earlier mentioned disagreements about the delimitation of the canon, a new emphasis on the importance of the canon as a framework for biblical theology may be noticed. Biblical thinking should be guided not by a dogmatically or contextually conditioned "canon within the canon", but by the whole of canonical scripture. This implies that one cannot start with just one centre to the Bible. Nor can all the biblical messages be summed up by just one central theme. The 1971 Faith and Order statement *The Authority of the Bible* pointed to the fact that biblical statements have internal connections around a few "relational centres" which together witness to a key biblical affirmation; for instance, to a saving act or to the coming kingdom. There are several such internal connections around a rallying point and message. Biblical theology has to discern this network of such "relational centres", describing how with their diversities and inner tensions they form a whole. In the statement of 1977, "The Significance of the Old Testament in Relation to the New", the major themes of covenant, hope and wisdom are mentioned as testimonies which together link the two Testaments and point to the Bible as a whole.

Another way of seeing the whole is to discover different trajectories of faith running through the Bible.[20] For the Old Testament, the two trajectories centring around Sinai and Zion have often been described: on the one side the Mosaic, and on the other the Davidic tradition, each standing at a centre. There are other such trajectories as, for instance, those marked strongly by priestly and cultic traditions, those of the wisdom tradition, those emphasizing the spirituality of the poor and those of the often neglected apocalyptic tradition. Biblical theology must discern how such various trajectories of faith developed and were transmitted, how each one was challenged by prophetic protest and how in the New Testament all are critically taken up and radically reinterpreted in the light of the teaching, death and resurrection of Jesus. Besides such a descriptive survey, a further step is then needed in response to the question, what is canonical in the canon? Usually, one thinks only about the content of the biblical affirmations of faith. Yet is not also the biblical process of constant transmission and reinterpretation canonical? Biblical affirmations are not timeless truths. In the Bible itself, these affirmations

---

[19] Hans-Georg Link ed., *The Roots of Our Common Faith: Faith in the Scriptures and in the Early Church*, WCC, 1984. *Confessing the One Faith: An Ecumenical Explication of the Apostolic Faith as it is Confessed in the Nicene-Constantinopolitan Creed (381)*, Faith and Order paper 153, rev. ed., WCC, 1999.
[20] Weber, *Power: Focus for a Biblical Theology*, WCC, 1989.

have been transmitted not only from one generation to the other, they have also been reinterpreted and re-emphasized for new times and circumstances.

Biblical theology would therefore be less than biblical if it limited itself to a kind of descriptive inventory. Again and again it will have to be *ad hoc*, focused on immediate situations of and for confession. The discussion on hermeneutics continues.[21] How, for example, does the Bible – in diversity and unity – guide and enlighten churches when they struggle for liberation? When they are involved in safeguarding God's creation? Or when they seek a responsible use of power? As such attempts at doing biblical theology focus on today's urgent questions, certain parts of the Bible and certain traditions of biblical faith will be emphasized more strongly than others. They are not wrongly employed today if the churches maintain disciplines of Bible study and if the whole canon is used as a constant corrective.

BIBLIOGRAPHY

Amirtham, Samuel and Moon, Cyris H.S. eds, *The Teaching of Ecumenics*, WCC, 1987, 142p.

Berger, Teresa and Geldbach, Erich eds, *Bis an die Enden der Erde: Ökumenische Erfahrungen mit der Bibel*, Zürich, Benziger, 1992, 160p.

Braaten, Carl E. and Jenson, Robert W. eds, *Reclaiming the Bible for the Church*, Edinburgh, T&T Clark, 1996, 137p.

By Our Lives: Stories of Women, Today and in the Bible, WCC, 1985, 57p.

Confessing the One Faith: An Ecumenical Explication of the Apostolic Faith as It Is Confessed in the Nicene-Constantinopolitan Creed (381), Faith and Order paper 153, rev. ed., WCC, 1999, 139p.

"Dogmatic Constitution on Divine Revelation", (1965) in Walter M. Abbott ed., *The Documents of Vatican II*, New York, Guild, 1966, pp.111-28, 794p.

Flesseman-van Leer, Ellen, *The Bible: Its Authority and Interpretation in the Ecumenical Movement*, WCC, 1980, 79p.

Gassmann, Günther ed., *Documentary History of Faith and Order 1963-1993*, WCC Publications, 1993, 338p.

Guiding Principles for Interconfessional Cooperation in Translating the Bible, London/Rome, UBS/Secretariat for Promoting Christian Unity, 1968, 20p.

Haudel, Matthias, *Die Bibel und die Einheit der Kirchen: Eine Untersuchung der Studien von Glauben und Kirchenverfassung*, Göttingen, Vandenhoeck & Ruprecht, 1993, 470p.

Houlden, James Leslie, *The Interpretation of the Bible in the Church*, London, SCM Press, 1995, 163p.

Neuhaus, Richard John ed., *Biblical Interpretation in Crisis*, Grand Rapids MI, Eerdmans, 1989, 190p.

Robins, Wendy S. ed., *Through the Eyes of a Woman: Bible Studies on the Experience of Women*, WCC, 1995, 145p.

Rowe, Richard C., *Bible Study in the World Council of Churches*, WCC, 1969, 81p.

Schneider, Theodor and Panneberg, Wolfhart eds, *Verbindliches Zeugnis: Schriftverständnis und Schriftgebrauch*, Göttingen, Vandenhoeck & Ruprecht, 1992-98, 3 vols.

Sugirtharajah, R.S. ed., *Asian Biblical Hermeneutics and Postcolonialism: Contesting the Interpretations*, Maryknoll NY, Orbis 1998, 148p.

Sugirtharajah, R.S. ed., *Voices from the Margin: Interpreting the Bible in the Third World*, Maryknoll NY, Orbis, 1991, 454p.

A Treasure in Earthen Vessels: An Instrument for an Ecumenical Reflection on Hermeneutics, Faith and Order Paper no. 182, WCC, 1998, 40p.

Weber, Hans-Ruedi, *Experiments with Bible Studies*, WCC, 1981, 319p.

Weber, Hans-Ruedi, *Power: Focus for a Biblical Theology*, WCC, 1989, 204p.

---

[21] *A Treasure in Earthen Vessels: An Instrument for an Ecumenical Reflection on Hermeneutics*, Faith and Order Paper no. 182, WCC, 1998.

10
The Contemporary Search for Spirituality

K.M. George

"Spirituality" is one of the most widely used terms in contemporary religious speech and literature. The decades following the mid-20th century witnessed the increasingly popular, if unspecific, use of the word, cutting across confessional, religious and ideological boundaries. Still largely free floating and fluid, the word "spirituality", however, evokes some common ground of meaning and reflects a certain religious-cultural consensus. On that basis this chapter seeks to trace the outlines of the major changes occurring in the character and orientation of "Christian spirituality" in the latter part of the 20th century. Inevitably some areas and themes related to spirituality are highlighted while others are simply mentioned and still others completely passed over.

TOWARDS A DEFINITION

Attempts to define the term defy consensus. In the 25-volume *World Spirituality*, no attempt was made by the editors and writers to arrive at a common definition of spirituality acceptable to all in the same way.[1] Yet the inner dimension of the being called by certain traditions "the spirit" is recognized as the common core of various spiritualities. Some key words like transcendence, experience, ultimate reality, prayer, meditation, spiritual journey and spiritual ascent provide the meeting point for different religious traditions and movements. The attempt to provide a working description of the term which takes into account all religious perspectives, and not merely Christian views, shows the pluralistic orientation of contemporary spirituality.[2] In some cases religion and the spiritual quest are placed at opposite poles.[3] The institutional and collective character of religion sometimes puts off those who seek the deeply personal and the transcendent. Only those who can transcend denominational loyalties can subscribe to "meta-religious" spirituality. The shift of emphasis from theological and doctrinal particularity to the commonality of different spiritual traditions marks a new horizon in the

---

- Gwen Cashmore and Joan Puls have also contributed material for this chapter.
[1] Ewert Cousins, Preface to the Series in L. Dupre and D. Saliers eds, *World Spirituality: An Encyclopedic History of the Religious Quest*, 25 vols, New York, Crossroads, 1985.
[2] Ewert Cousins, "What Is Christian Spirituality?" in Bradley C. Hanson ed., *Modern Christian Spirituality: Methodological and Historical Essays*, Atlanta GA, Scholars, 1990, pp.39-44.
[3] Cf. Robert M. Torrance, *The Spiritual Quest: Transcendence, Myth, Religion and Science*, Berkeley CA, Univ. of California Press, 1994.

ecumenical vision. The search for contemporary Christian spirituality must be surveyed against this backdrop.

Before the 1960s the Christian use of the English word "spirituality" and its equivalents in other European languages was restricted largely to Roman Catholic circles, especially to its religious congregations. Expressions like "Franciscan spirituality" and "Ignatian spirituality" were regularly used with a rather clear meaning. After the Second Vatican Council, the term began gradually to be adopted by other Christian traditions and religions and also by secular movements like Amnesty International and ideologies like feminism and Marxism. Sandra M. Schneiders points to the "the unavoidable ambiguity of the term spirituality" as it refers to

a) a fundamental dimension of the human being;
b) the lived experience that actualizes that dimension; and
c) the academic discipline that studies that experience.[4]

Rejecting suggestions from some scholars that the term should be reserved for the lived experience while the discipline should be referred to as "spiritual theology", Schneiders opts for retaining the term spirituality for both the experience and the academic discipline. Specifications could be made whenever the context does not provide adequate clarity. On the academic side the last three decades have seen a phenomenal rise in publications, courses, seminars and worship related to the theme of spirituality. Research tools like dictionaries and bibliographies have proliferated.

The editor of the *New Dictionary of Catholic Spirituality* concedes that spirituality is a rather unwieldy term and emphasizes the following as constituting his understanding the central elements:[5]

a) Since spirituality is concerned with the *human person* in relation to God, the relational and the personal (inclusive of the social and political) dimensions of the human-divine relationship are decisive.
b) The new spirituality, expressing the dynamic and concrete character of the relationship of the human person to God in actual life situations, is distinguished from conceptual theology. As a religious experience it is capable of growth. This spirituality abolishes the old distinction between the *credenda* (what is to be believed, treated in dogmatic or systematic theology) and the *agenda* (what is to be done as a result of belief, area of moral theology or ethics). The new spirituality considers the agenda of a Christian life in relation to God as its focus and integrates into it the traditional domain of theology.
c) The fundamentally interdisciplinary character of the new spirituality is reinforced by ecumenical and inter-religious dialogues.

There are also simpler definitions of spirituality, such as "the endeavour to live in obedience to the gospel – in a word, in discipleship",[6] a term of longer and more common usage among Protestant and evangelical Christians. According to this definition of Gwen Cashmore and Joan Puls, the spirituality of discipleship is the lived response to the question of Jesus, "Who do you say that I am?" Obedience requires listening to the

---

[4] Sandra M. Schneiders, "Spirituality in the Academy" in *Modern Christian Spirituality*, p.17.
[5] Michael Downey, ed., "Editor's Preface" in *The New Dictionary of Catholic Spirituality*, 25 vols, New York, Crossroad, 1985, p.viii. And Cousins, "What Is Christian Spirituality?"
[6] Gwen Cashmore and Joan Puls, "Spirituality in the Ecumenical Movement", in N. Lossky *et al* eds., *Dictionary of the Ecumenical Movement*, 2nd ed., WCC, 2002, pp.1070-73.

Holy Spirit and living the gospel in one's own cultural and socio-political context. The living of the gospel implies Christian participation in the struggle of the people with the goal of transformation. A broader description is then provided:

> Spirituality, then, is the way people take to be Christian, fulfill their Christian vocation. It embraces ministry and service, relationships, life-style, prayer and response to the political and social environment.

Roman Catholic writers dealing with the evolution of contemporary spirituality almost invariably find the Second Vatican Council as the decisive historical landmark. So they qualify the old stream of spirituality as preconciliar and the new as post-conciliar. As to the mainline Protestant churches and the Orthodox tradition, there are no such precise landmarks. The Reformation tradition was more susceptible than others to the secularizing tendencies unleashed by the rise of an urban technological civilization. Post-second world war changes in the religious sensitivity of the people, the events of the 1960s, the growth of the ecumenical movement, the evangelical-charismatic revival are all inter-related and contributory factors in provoking a search for new forms of spirituality.

The Orthodox churches, except certain segments of their Western diaspora, do not generally acknowledge any radical change in their spiritual ethos. They firmly hold that their present spirituality is nothing but the faithful continuation of an age-old spiritual tradition. However, Orthodox churches would gladly acknowledge a renewal of spiritual life in the 20th century through the rediscovery of the ascetic-monastic life-style, meditation on the *Philokalia*, liturgical-theological interpretations of the icons, etc. History, change and growth are understood differently in the Orthodox liturgical and theological tradition. In consequence, Western criteria for judging the evolution in spirituality can hardly be applied to the Orthodox world.

The English word "spirituality" has no equivalent in the New Testament or the early patristic period. The origin of the word, however, is generally traced to Paul's use of "spiritual" *(pneumatikos)* as an adjective of spirit *(pneuma)* where spirit refers to the Spirit of God, clearly seen in his distinction between the "spiritual person" *(pneumatikos)* and the "carnal one" *(psychikos)* in 1 Corinthians 2:14-15. It is significant that the Pauline use does not contrast the "spiritual" with the "material". The contrast is between the person whose life is governed by the Holy Spirit and the one who lives merely under the sway of natural impulses.

In the West, the evolution of the word spirituality at various stages placed it in opposition to temporality and materialism. Thus a heavy sense of otherworldliness was attached to it. In its modern phase the word denoted the interior life of individual Christians who sought perfection by the practice of certain conventional spiritual principles and techniques. This was perhaps the most prevalent notion, especially in Roman Catholic circles some thirty years ago when the floodgates of contemporary spirituality were opened in every conceivable direction.

In the Orthodox tradition of the East, there is no equivalent word for spirituality. Spiritual as an adjective is traditionally and meaningfully used in Orthodoxy as in other traditions. Expressions like "spiritual person", "spiritual experience" and "spiritual reality" are commonly used with the context illuminating the meaning. Spirituality may be used in a given context to convey a sense of the total spiritual ethos. The Orthodox tradition, largely unaffected by secularization as far as its doctrinal discourse and liturgical practices are concerned, would easily translate spirituality in familiar words as "life lived in the power of the Holy Spirit". Spiritual masters like St Seraphim of Sarov (Russia, 19th century) would define the very aim of the Christian life as the acquisition of the Holy Spirit. Appropriating the gifts and fruits of the Spirit of God in one's personal life and submitting one's life to the direction of the Spirit are important for spiritual growth. The intensely personal experience is fully integrated into the life of the community that is pre-eminently the church. The worship of the church is in spirit and truth. Church, the body of Christ, constantly calls (epiclesis) upon the Holy Spirit for power from above, for guidance into all truth and for the total transformation of human beings, society and the whole creation.

FROM THEOLOGY TO SPIRITUALITY

Theological literature today reflects the change from theology to spirituality over the last decade or so. It seems in many cases that where the word "theology" was once used, one can now substitute "spirituality". During the rise of "genitive and adjectival theologies" from the theology of liberation to chaos theology, theology broke off from the classical singular and became theologies in the plural. Now apparently, in these contexts, spirituality with its diversified connotations takes the place of theology.

The present resurgence of interest in spirituality has been attributed to a number of reasons like the crisis of meaning provoked by the events of the 1960s (B. Hanson) among Catholics, the spiritual maturation of Catholics since Vatican II (Joann Conn), the increased desire to integrate faith and life, especially the justice agenda (John Heagle) and the impact of both biblical and liturgical renewals (Eugene Megyer). The fact that this renewed spiritual quest is not confined to some countries or some religious traditions but is a global phenomenon is significant. The fascination of young people especially from the West for ancient Asian religious traditions like Hinduism and Buddhism and for the spiritual experience and wisdom communicated by gurus, yogis and Zen masters came as a rude shock to the older generation used to classical Christian spiritual practices. However, it signalled the need for a thorough re-examination of human spiritual needs and sensitivities in the latter half of the 20th century.

It is generally recognized that the high tide of secularization associated with industrialization, urbanization and scientific-technological revolutions, especially in economically advanced countries, deprived people of their traditional religious certainties, and altered the social and familiar landscapes that once provided support for the life of the spirit. "The eclipse of God" (Martin Buber) became so real in the wake of massive secularization that many people began listening to the "rumour of angels" (Peter Berger) to reawaken their dormant spiritual sensitivity. If God has been banished from public discourse in respectable society, spirituality has returned to the academy and the agora in greatly diversified and subtle ways of God-talk.

The emergence of the contemporary interest in spirituality within the Christian world was provoked to a great extent by the dogmatism and provincialism of theology that marked church traditions. The theology of a particular church often took as its task to distinguish, if not always to contrast, the church's particular identity and character from that of other churches. The apologetic and defensive attitude of theology in fulfilling this task did not always serve the ecumenical vision. In spirituality, on the other hand, many people found a suitable vantage point from which they could perceive other traditions and appreciate their riches in a spirit of fellowship. This happened largely in worship and Bible study, especially in the gatherings of the World Council of Churches.

This new entry-point in ecumenical settings gave fresh insights for traditional theological positions. Theology was reminded of its source and norm in the corporate worship of the church, meditation on the word of God, and the sharing of spiritual and material gifts.

Theology as taught in the dominant traditions of the West had been shaped in the context of either scholastic or Enlightenment rationality. In the 19th and 20th centuries, theology in university settings sought academic respectability by adopting the methods followed by scientific disciplines. Whether this yielded results or not is disputed. Theology as taught in the academy moved away from liturgical and pastoral contexts and discovered in doing so that the old, rational, scientifically objective and critical theological discourse did not respond to the deep spiritual yearning of ordinary people. People faced with urban anonymity and fragmentation were looking for integration in their lives at both personal and corporate levels. The intuitive and the inarticulate spiritual quest craved expression. Intensely personal and radically transcendent dimensions of human life were sought after. Young people made a broad range of experiments from psychedelic drugs to transcendental meditation. Academic and cerebral theology was thought by many to be incapable of responding to the changed situation. Again, spirituality became the crux of the issue. While academic and dogmatic theology had created its own spirituality with elitist, other-worldly, anti-secular and individualistic tendencies, the newly emerging spirituality of the age is qualified as

> intensely personal, without being private. It is visionary without being theoretical. It is prophetic without being partisan and it is incarnational without being worldly. It emphasizes personal response and interior commitment, but it readily changes the context within which this response takes place.[7]

LITURGICAL SPIRITUALITY

One of the most significant aspects of ecumenical spirituality is its increasing appreciation of liturgical worship as central to Christian faith and practice. The liturgical movement in the Roman Catholic Church, spearheaded chiefly by Dom Lambert Beauduin (d. 1960) in Belgium, the work of the Second Vatican Council, the rise of the ecumenical movement, and the formation of the WCC, gave the impetus to Western Christians, both Catholic and Protestant, to rediscover elements of liturgical spirituality.

Western Christianity encountered the East anew in ecumenical gatherings after a millennium of mutual alienation and suspicion. In spite of the fact that the Orthodox did not deliberately start a "liturgical mission" among Western Christians, more and more people were attracted to the rich spirituality of the Christian East through the beauty and transcendent quality of its liturgy, even though often offered in a special ecclesiastical language rather than in a vernacular. By and large many Protestants overcame traditional suspicions of rituals and symbols in liturgical worship and joyfully participated in the Orthodox worship in ecumenical settings. "Participate" is probably too strong a word to use, since eucharistic communion, the central experience of Orthodox liturgy, is not yet shared between the Orthodox and the others, for doctrinal reasons arising mainly on the Orthodox side. However, there are a number of other non-eucharistic Orthodox liturgical occasions – the blessing of the water, blessing of the bread, canonical offices and specially planned prayers and devotions – in which all Christians usually participate dur-

---

[7] John Heagle, "A New Public Piety: Reflections on Spirituality", in *Church*, 1, 1985, pp.52-55.

ing ecumenical gatherings. It should be recognized that there are Orthodox Christians who express strong reservations about "ecumenical prayers" and joining other Christians even for non-eucharistic worship. Yet in the experience of the WCC and the ecumenical movement in general, common non-eucharistic prayer with the Orthodox has become a regular feature.

The rediscovery of Orthodox spiritual classics like the *Philokalia*, the devotional practice of the Jesus prayer, meditation on icons, the ascetic practices of fasting and vigil, and the involvement of all the senses – seeing, hearing, smelling, touching and tasting – in worship, have contributed to the present shape of ecumenical spirituality.

An attempt to appropriate positively the sacramentality of the material universe is made in ecumenical spirituality. This is part of a holistic approach in which the traditionally perceived dichotomy between matter and spirit is overcome. In the Orthodox view, sacramentality is directly derived from the mystery of the incarnation. That God chose to assume human flesh in Christ and perfectly united divinity and humanity without division or fusion is central to the spiritual-theological vision. So in Christ all matter is given the possibility for transfiguration and for participation in the glory of God. The liturgical celebration of Christ's transfiguration and the paschal mystery of his death and resurrection underscore the Eastern Christian spirituality of *theosis* or divinization. No part of creation is excluded from this total and ultimate experience. This eschatologically oriented spirituality places emphasis on the hope that the subjection of creation to futility (cf. Rom. 8:20) will be broken and the created world will fully share in the freedom of the children of God.

The Orthodox tradition, true to its character, did not invent any new theology in the 20th century but simply brought out the spiritual wisdom and insight of its own patristic and ascetic-monastic traditions. However, the interactions in ecumenical settings with Christians of Reformation and Roman Catholic traditions have brought a new self-awareness among many Orthodox with implications for spirituality. They have been challenged by Western Christians to shed the light of celebrated Orthodox ideas of transfiguration and *theosis* on contemporary social and economic issues such as poverty, apartheid, social injustice, economic-political oppression and human rights. This has provided a genuinely ecumenical give-and-take in the shaping of present-day ecumenical spirituality.

The old saying *lex orandi, lex credendi*, what the church believes (doctrine) is derived from what the church prays (worship), is particularly true in respect to ecumenical spirituality. Any arbitrary or academic distinction between worship, doctrine and practice is false. Theological articulation has its source in the worshipping community. A theology that arises from the praise of God cannot be distinguished from spirituality. Worship of the triune God, the spiritual experience and practice of the community, and theological reflection are but one single reality. Favourite Orthodox expressions like "theology is doxology" and "liturgy after the Liturgy" epitomize this understanding. One reason why the word spirituality in our times defies definition is precisely that there is a creative fusion of liturgical experience, faith practice, and rationally articulated theology in the emerging spirituality that challenges neat academic compartmentalization.

What one author describes as the shape of the post-conciliar Roman Catholic liturgy may be applied to the ecumenical understanding of liturgical spirituality in general:

> In contrast to the highly rubrical approach to liturgy that preceded Vatican II, the shape of the reformed liturgy fosters a spirit of devotion that avoids cultic self-consciousness, rubrical scrupulosity, or a functional approach to rites. The present rites lend themselves to em-

phasis on the proclamation of the word, involvement of a variety of ministers, and qualitative participation of the whole assembly...[8]

Ecumenical prayers and acts of worship have necessitated the introduction of new hymns, canticles and liturgies. An ecumenical tradition of hymn-singing, formed largely at assemblies of the WCC, has integrated elements from a variety of sources, ranging from the ancient chanting of monastic circles to popular hymns from almost all parts of the world. Two compilations of hymns deserve special mention: *Cantate Domino* and *Thuma Mina*. The first edition of *Cantate Domino* was published in 1924 by the World Student Christian Federation with hymns mainly from the European and North American Protestant tradition. In successive editions efforts were made to make the book more adequately representative of the world Christian community. Difficulties arose as to the adaptation of Asian music, for example, to an "international style", showing the cultural rootedness of hymns and melodies used by various churches. What was considered universal was often found to be deeply culture-specific. The last edition of the book in 1974 was entrusted to the Faith and Order Commission of the WCC and it still did not include many hymns from the southern hemisphere. Since 1990 the WCC has been using *Thuma Mina*, an ecumenical hymn book published by the Evangelisches Missionswerk, Germany, in cooperation with the Basel Mission. It contains a wide variety of songs from all continents and traditions, giving their texts not only in the original languages, but also in translations into English, German, French, Spanish and sometimes other languages. Both hymn books have helped make ecumenical prayer a rich experience of the diversity of ways of praising God.

ECUMENICAL SPIRITUALITY

The roots of ecumenical spirituality precede the 20th century. The intense desire of many Christians in different parts of the world not only to pray for unity but also to pray together with people from different Christian churches and denominations resulted in the formation of various fellowships.[9] These groups and prayer movements, which took the high priestly prayer of Jesus for unity (John 17:21) as the missionary task of Christians living with the reality of divided churches, became a major spiritual resource for the ecumenical movement and ecumenical institutions such as the World Council of Churches.

The transition that took place in the last quarter of the 20th century in ecumenical spirituality can be linked to the "paradigm shift" marking the ecumenical movement in general. Konrad Raiser identifies several features of this change of paradigm. Some of them relate to the evolution of ecumenical spirituality.

1. *Christocentrism and religious pluralism.* The ecumenical movement's concern for the unity of all Christians has gradually taken on a universal perspective of openness to all humanity. By the time of the Uppsala assembly of the WCC (1968), the question of the place of many religions within the one humanity became pivotal in the search for genuine community. In 1971 the WCC launched its programme for dialogue with people of

---

[8] Kewin W. Irwin, "Liturgy", in Michael Downey ed., *The New Dictionary of Catholic Spirituality*, Collegeville MN, Liturgical Press, 1993, p.605.

[9] For the connection between ecumenical spirituality and spiritual ecumenism, see G. Wainwright, "Ecumenical Spirituality" in C. Jones et al eds, *The Study of Spirituality*, London, SPCK, 1986, pp.540ff.

other faiths. An increasing awareness of pluralism has brought to the ecumenical movement a greater appreciation of the spirituality and life-style of people who belong to religions other than Christianity. An ill-conceived "Christomonism", heir to an old ideology of Christendom and the colonial-missionary era, has slowly given way to a trinitarian vision of God and a deeper perception of the work of the Holy Spirit in interpreting the Christ event. The Spirit as the "pledge" or "foretaste" for the universal rule of God leads us out of all institutional parochialism. Raiser observes that the Spirit's work is particularly important in preventing an imbalanced Christ-centred belief from becoming a church-centred belief. He notes that the Orthodox tradition constantly appealed to the theology of the Holy Spirit for relations with other faiths.[10]

Inter-religious dialogue has shaped a spirituality of its own over the last three decades of the 20th century. The core of this spirituality is undoubtedly the mutual respect and sharing of different spiritual experiences from different religions. A renewed understanding of the trinitarian God, "the giver of all good gifts", and of the creative and inspiring work of the Holy Spirit in the entire creation has helped many Christians to develop a healthy attitude to the emerging spirituality of inter-religious dialogue.

2. *Christian universalism and the global system.* Christian claims of universalism have undergone critical soul-searching as false global structures have emerged in the name of unity and interdependence. The Faith and Order Commission meeting in Accra 1974 thought it would be "more accurate to speak of human brokenness than of mankind's unity".[11]

Debates in the WCC in the 1970s involving world models of development, modernization and economic growth, as well as critical political situations in places like Vietnam and South Africa, "marked the transition from the classic perspective of 'the kingship of Christ' over the church and the world to God's kingdom seen in messianic perspective".[12] The logic of global systems erected in the name of one market, one economy or one world could be disappointing as they are often geared to power, control and domination. The emerging paradigm is more inclined to a logic of life, relationships, sharing, stewardship and solidarity. It points to "the oikoumene of the house of life, of the habitable earth" (Raiser). Life is understood as a web of reciprocal relationships. The messianic vision of God dwelling with humankind (cf. Rev. 21:3) indicates this transition and also sets an orientation for ecumenical spirituality.

3. *Universality and diversity in the church.* In the classical ecumenical paradigm, the search for unity in the church was always based on the universal significance of the Christ event. Thus the visible unity of the church was perceived as a crucial witness to the incarnate Christ in whom a perfect union of divinity and humanity was accomplished. Moreover, the global unity of the church was correlated to the unity of all humankind under God's rule. According to Raiser, this ecclesiological centrality coupled with elements such as Christomonism and emphasis on history as the central category of interpretation gave rise to a "triumphalist" understanding of the church which was hard to verify by appeal to actual experience.[13]

---

[10] Konrad Raiser, *Ecumenism in Transition: A Paradigm Shift in the Ecumenical Movement*, WCC, 1991, p.59.
[11] Geiko Müller-Fahrenholz ed., *Unity in Today's World: The Faith and Order Studies on "Unity of the Church – Unity of Humankind"*, WCC, 1978, p.91.
[12] *Ecumenism in Transition*, p.62.
[13] *Ibid.*, p.72.

In the ecumenical debates, expressions such as "one fully committed fellowship" and "church as sign of the kingdom of God" became openings to a new understanding of the church. The transition was from a vertical model of the unity of the church to a horizontal one, taking into account a variety of different traditions and positions. The concept of fellowship or communion *(koinonia)* in recent ecclesiological discussion incorporates both the actual element of the vertical dimension, i.e., participation in the divine reality through Jesus Christ in the Holy Spirit, and the horizontal dimension of sharing with one another in solidarity. Contemporary ecumenical spirituality has a close affinity with this dynamic and open model of fellowship or communion oriented to relationship with the Other. A doctrine of the Trinity that evokes infinite possibilities for interpersonal relationship while maintaining the distinct identity of each person in a dynamic movement of *perichoresis* has a fresh appeal for Christian spirituality as well as for the ecumenical search for unity in diversity. The decisive role of the Holy Spirit in nurturing unity while fully recognizing the diversity of gifts, persons and positions in God's household is being restored in ecumenical spirituality.

As in other aspects of Christian experience and reflection, the 1960s were a major landmark in the evolution of ecumenical spirituality. The WCC, which began as a fellowship of predominantly white North Atlantic Protestant churches, became in the 1960s a world forum with the entry into its membership of almost all of the Orthodox churches and the "younger churches" of the third world. Different streams of Christian worship and spirituality were thus introduced into the life of the WCC. Classical Western theological and social assumptions were challenged. The cries of the poor and the oppressed were powerfully expressed in forms of worship that significantly altered the style and ethos of traditional Western worship.

THE VERTICAL AND THE HORIZONTAL

The powerful waves of secularization of the 1960s and 1970s hastened the search for a new spirituality as the relevance and value of classical discourse on doctrine and piety was called into question. Many Christian groups developed a new awareness of the secular world, and turned to social, economic and political issues with activist zeal. This created a widening gulf between socially active, usually ecumenical "mainstream" churches and the newly powerful evangelical-Pentecostal-charismatic movement. The former, stressing "costly discipleship" and radical obedience to the gospel, turned to total involvement in the struggle of the people in various situations. "Spirituality and theology for combat" (WCC Nairobi assembly 1975) dominated the thought processes and action strategy of these groups and movements. The evangelical wing, however, sensing the alienation of the individual in secularized, urban-technological society, emphasized themes of personal conversion and certainty of salvation. Evangelicalism, with a clear priority for God's agenda as revealed in scripture, centred on the message of eternal salvation to the fallen human beings and adding converts to the church. Church unity, social action, and involvement in the social-political struggle of the people received at most a low priority in many evangelical communities although, to be sure, some evangelical groups had a long tradition of social engagement. The ecumenical movement was looked down on as a deviation from the gospel mission. This divergence became more and more pronounced in the so-called "ecumenical-evangelical divide". Evangelical groups were seen by those involved in socio-political action as fundamentalists evading the call of the gospel to transform the world.

The ecumenical movement clearly opted for the agenda of the world and this became evident in the WCC's New Delhi assembly in 1961. As David J. Bosch put it,

> The 1960s was the period in which the ecumenical movement and many churches related to it celebrated the idea of secularization, of involvement in the world, of the world providing the church with its agenda, and also of the presence of God in other religions.[14]

Bosch would describe the years following (1966-74) as "the period of confrontation" and the years from 1974 to the end of the 20th century as "the era of convergence". In respect to spirituality, the convergence continued. The ecumenical movement and the evangelical movement have grown to the point of recognizing the spiritual values in both movements and thus their reciprocal influence. Perspectives apparently opposed to each other are reconciled in a converging ecumenical spirituality. Fine distinctions had to be made: the cry of the poor and the cry of the spiritually lost; human disorder and God's design; corporate sin and individual sin; humanizing liberation and redeeming justification; the mixing of church and world and the separation of church from the world; and the world as the arena of God's activity and the church as the only field of divine operation. Because the human race appeared everywhere divided into rich and poor, resort had to be made to the language of oppressor and oppressed on the one hand, and "peoples' groups" on the other, witnessing where the church *is* and witnessing where the church is *not yet*, preferring the "Jesus language" of the gospels yet still deploying the "theological language" of Paul. Concern for the macro-ethical and that for the micro-ethical – these are some of the characteristically conflicting positions of "the ecumenicals" and "the evangelicals" now being brought together on the basis of a holistic ecumenical spirituality.[15]

Recent ecumenical dialogues between the Orthodox and Evangelicals have found a *modus operandi* based on a shared spirituality drawn from the authority of scripture, the witness of holy men and women to the power of the Holy Spirit, uncompromising faith in Jesus Christ as the only begotten Son of God and unique Saviour of humanity, and an emphasis on the church and its key role in the salvation of the world.

REVIVAL OF ASCETIC–MONASTIC ASPECTS OF SPIRITUALITY

Spirituality in the Roman Catholic tradition owes its strength in large measure to its numerous religious congregations. The long monastic tradition starting with St Benedict in the 6th century cultivated a diversity of spiritual practices and insights which continue to enrich the Western Christian tradition. In the ecumenical movement many Reformation churches also appreciate some of the positive elements in that tradition. Reciprocally, the Roman Catholic Church has assimilated several elements of Reformation spirituality including the rediscovery of the role of scripture in the daily life of Christians. Another element contributing to current ferment concerning spirituality comes from the Orthodox tradition. The spirituality of the Orthodox has its sources in the biblical-patristic interpretation of the triune God, the mystery of the incarnation of the word of God, the work of the Holy Spirit, ascetic-monastic practice, and the liturgical-sacramental experience. The great emphasis placed on the continuing presence and activity of the

---

[14] David J. Bosch, "Ecumenicals and Evangelicals: A Growing Relationship?", in *The Ecumenical Review*, 40, 3-4, 1988, pp.458-472.
[15] *Ibid.*, p.72.

Holy Spirit throughout the whole of creation provides Orthodox spirituality with a sense of freedom and wholeness that is opposed to all legalism and individualism. The corporate as well as personal character of this spirituality has been particularly appealing to various emerging communitarian and creation theologies searching for holistic models.

Two prominent sources of the ascetic-monastic revival in the recent past are Mount Athos, the 1000-year-old Orthodox monastic republic on the Aegean sea, and the Coptic Orthodox monasteries in the Egyptian deserts, the cradle of Christian monasticism. Non-discursive and non-iconic ascetic spiritual techniques like hesychasm, and its search for deep inner silence and direct experience of the uncreated light of God, as well as the school of prayer, spiritual exercises, and spiritual direction recommended by the famous texts of the *Philokalia* are part of the Athonite monastic heritage which is being rediscovered in contemporary spirituality. The Egyptian deserts have come alive with new Coptic monasteries peopled with young and educated monks who have left "the world" to devote themselves to the life of the spirit. These revivals attract a large number of people, young and old, who are desperately looking for new spiritual resources. Monastic spirituality is centred on deep prayer, community living and eucharistic-liturgical experience. The social implication of this spirituality for the daily life and struggle of people is quite important, but generally speaking no conscious attempt is made to make that connection directly evident. The impact of ascetic-monastic spirituality on people's lives – in contrast to direct social-economic activism – is held to be the long-term fruit of the life of disciplined prayer and sharing in community.

Icons, specially painted religious pictures with strict norms for both the choice of motifs as well as technique for preparation, have been introduced to the wider oikoumene in the second half of the 20th century. Regularly used in Orthodox liturgical worship, they have revived interest in a largely ignored area of authentic Christian spirituality, namely, the aesthetic dimension, miserably absent in many traditional spiritualities. Icons help to perceive the beauty and splendour of the Transcendent in which created reality is invited to participate. They are "windows on eternity" and remind us that human beings are co-creators with God in freedom and love.

The world is seen not as hostile to the spirit but as its bearer and as capable of becoming the icon of the glory of God. The Eastern Orthodox tradition integrates icons in worship with a profound sacramental view of creation and the incarnation of the Son of God. Even Christian traditions which historically do not share the theology of icons have now begun to appreciate the iconic dimension of worship and the material-aesthetic aspect of a holistic spirituality. Orthodox spirituality has generally refrained from moving out of its traditional moorings and many people would consider this as a source of strength rather than weakness in a world threatened by constant change and upheavals.

SPIRITUALITY AND NEO-MONASTIC COMMUNITIES

The experiments being made in communities of recent origin like Taizé in France, Iona in Scotland, and Grandchamp in Switzerland are of great importance for ecumenical spirituality. Arising out of basically Protestant spiritual roots, these communities have integrated into their life elements from classical monasticism, both Western and Eastern, and from Roman Catholic and Orthodox spiritual traditions, and transformed them in ways appealing to the spiritual sensitivities of the present age.

Brother Roger Schutz, who founded the Taizé Community in 1940, wanted it to be a "parable of communion" in the midst of Christian divisions. With a core group of "brothers", drawn from Catholic, Anglican and various Protestant churches, who take monastic vows, the community is engaged in creating trust and reconciliation within and between societies around the world. The Taizé life of worship and meditative reflection on scripture with links to human solidarity in our times attracts a large number of young people to the weekly meetings and other events.

The Iona Community, not strictly monastic, is committed to a spirituality of engagement reflecting the Celtic church's insight that God is in the midst of everything. The Community, in seeking "new ways to touch the hearts of all", as one of its frequently used prayers puts it, sees work and worship, prayer and politics, the religious and the secular as inextricably bound. Members of the Community, living throughout Britain and beyond, are bound by a fivefold rule which includes a daily devotional discipline, mutual accounting for the use of time and money, meeting together periodically, and action for justice and peace.

The Grandchamp Community of sisters in its monastic setting and engagement in the world reflects the same spirit as Taizé and Iona. Nourished by worship and committed to service in areas of conflict and poverty, the sisters are sent by the Community to live in places of special need. Their quiet presence and their openness to the great spiritual traditions of both Western and Eastern Christianity renew the emphasis on a refreshing communitarian and ecumenical spirituality.

SPIRITUALITY AND CONTEXT

Whatever definition we give to "spirituality", some form of worship and devotional practice is considered constitutive. The WCC from its very beginning in 1948 wished to reconcile the vertical or the "Godward vocation of the church in worship and its horizontal or humanward vocation in witness and service". The intention to overcome divergences in the relationship between these two dimensions has always been at the heart of ecumenical worship, causing a new style of spirituality to grow. Conventional and deep-seated notions like the incompatibility of spirit and matter, of the sacred and the secular, of worship and work, had to be dislodged to make place for healthy, holy living. The assembly of the East Asia Christian Conference held in Bangkok in 1964 stated,

> The continuing call to holy living comes from worship where takes place the true meeting between the sacred and the secular. Here the call is heard, maintained and renewed. In worship, the whole community, which is the church, receives the promise and the demand, "I will be your God and you shall be my people", and finds itself entrusted with the Holy Name to which by word and deed it must witness... The result is a life of work and worship in which work is done as an offering of worship and worship becomes part of the work to be performed...The call to holy living then, is both a promise and a demand; it is a consequence of God's apartness in holiness as well as his involvement in love.[16]

This statement is representative of the orientation of the worship-based and integrative spirituality that emerged in the 1960s and flourished from the 1970s on. In Africa

---

[16] Christian Conference of Asia, *The Christian Community within the Human Community, Containing Statements from the Bangkok Assembly of the EACC, March, 1964*, Bangalore, CLS, 1964, p.47. Cf. also the analytical and bibliographical survey of the discussions on spirituality within the constituency of the WCC in Ans J. van der Bent, "The Concern for Spirituality", in *The Ecumenical Review*, 38, 1, 1986, pp.101-14.

and Asia there was a simultaneous search for more indigenous and authentic forms of worship that took a critical distance from the liturgies, hymnody and rituals imported by Western missionaries. African Christians felt that what the missionaries offered in respect to worship was inadequate to express the deep yearnings of the African religious spirit, since those liturgies did not grow out of a living church in Africa and also because they were unable to reach the emotional depths of Africans.[17]

The global assemblies and other meetings of the WCC continued to explore the theme of worship, work and spirituality. Especially noteworthy were the fourth world conference on Faith and Order, Montreal (1963), the Bossey consultation on "Eastern and Western Spirituality" (1962), and three consultations (Jaizi, Syria, 1966, Delemont, Switzerland, 1967, Geneva, 1968) on the "Worship of God in a Secular Age" which culminated in the Uppsala assembly of 1968. These consultations struggled with issues like secularization, intelligibility of liturgical texts in contemporary intellectual settings, living out a daily spirituality in the industrialized, urban context, participation of lay people, appeal of worship and spiritual life to particular groups of people like students, industrial workers, scientists, journalists, etc. At the Uppsala assembly, representatives from the non-Western world were uncomfortable with the heavy stress laid on the secular context for the consideration of worship and spirituality. They had expressed a pressing concern for bringing Christian worship to their own multi-religious cultural contexts. By the early 1970s, worship and spirituality were no longer considered as privileged topics for Faith and Order alone. The central committee in Berlin 1974

> welcomed the decision of the Commission on Faith and Order to give more attention to problems of worship and spirituality than before. Problems of the Christian's spiritual life go far beyond matters of worship. Worship and spirituality cannot and should not be seen as matters exclusively related to Faith and Order and will require the cooperation of several departments of the WCC.[18]

THE VANCOUVER ASSEMBLY AND AFTER

The world assemblies of the WCC have exhibited increasing awareness of common worship and liturgy. The Vancouver assembly (1983) is generally considered the high point of ecumenical worship. The tent, erected as space for daily worship, became the symbol of the dynamism, freshness and vitality of common worship. Drawing on resources from various cultures, confessions, liturgical traditions, contexts of suffering and struggle, hope and courage, the tent worship celebrated a new sense of human community and the glimpses of a new spirituality. A description of it is as symbolic as it is literal:

> Although most of the highlights of worship were in the tent, yet worship penetrated the whole assembly. As we moved from the tent to the plenary we were already a community of faith... through personal testimonies, through the beautiful and simple Orthodox rite of breaking bread, through a prayerful act of repentance or a joyful hymn. We found our roots and we found our context. We are the church, a world assembly of those who confess Jesus as Lord and Life of the World, gathered and marvelling in our unity and diversity.

---

[17] *Drumbeats from Kampala: Report of the First Assembly of the All Africa Council of Churches, Kampala, April 20-30, 1963*, London, Lutterworth, 1963, pp.35-36.
[18] WCC Central Committee, *Minutes of the 27th Meeting, West Berlin, August 11-18, 1974*, WCC, 1974, p.28. Cf. also "The Concern for Spirituality", p.107.

> We learned a new way of participating, less clerically dominated, with women and children and disabled in visible roles, and we saw with respect the humility of many renowned church leaders ready to be simply part of the whole.[19]

The story of worship, prayer and spirituality in the ecumenical movement has not for the most part been as ecstatic and exhilarating as the one suggested here. It has, rather, been down to earth, involving painful struggle and combat, cries of despair and division, of shared joy and ever rising solidarity.

> It is the full immersion in the chaos of humanity, a holy "worldliness" which enables them [churches and their faithful] to speak to humankind at large in a prophetic role. Our desperate struggles against classism, racism and sexism became a part of our spirituality and liturgy.[20]

A significant follow-up of the Vancouver emphasis on spirituality was the Annecy consultation on "Spirituality for Our Times" organized in 1994 by the WCC Sub-unit on Renewal and Congregational Life.[21] That consultation, which brought together some 12 church representatives who strove to live out the gospel in diverse ways and circumstances, reflected the contours of key issues in ecumenical spirituality in the post-Vancouver period. The consultation encouraged a common search for the direction in which the church was being led, and attempted "to discern the call of our times to enflesh the gospel and to cooperate with the Spirit in the building up of the body of Christ".

The consultation made the following assumptions as marks of a genuine, holistic spirituality for today: first, the source and guiding force of a true spirituality is action by the Holy Spirit; secondly, spirituality is lived and sought in community; and thirdly, this spirituality involves an ongoing process of formation and discipleship.

As to the specific marks of such a spirituality, it was affirmed that it is to be incarnational with a proper emphasis on the here-and-now of our existence. Informed by a sensitivity to culture and language and by the history and symbols of a people, it should not be excessively cerebral, but celebratory. This spirituality is life-giving and is sustained by the life of the Trinity. The true spirituality we seek is rooted in scripture and nourished by prayer. This spirituality calls us to suffering for others' sake, to take risks in the cause of justice. Open to the wider oikoumene, it is joyful and hopeful.

In faithfully following such ecumenical concerns for spirituality, the Harare assembly in 1998 reaffirmed a pervasive spiritual hunger. The integral connection between worship and spirituality was to be a priority matter demanding further exploration. The formation of theology as the intertwining of ecumenical hermeneutics, worship, spirituality, ecclesiology and ethics was affirmed. Concern for an authentic spirituality included a number of ethical questions requiring urgent attention such as genetic engineering, the information revolution and various aspects of human sexuality.[22]

---

[19] Gwen Cashmore, "The Worship of the Sixth Assembly", in *Midstream*, 23, 1, 1984, pp.74-89, quoted in "The Concern for Spirituality", p.111.

[20] "The Concern for Spirituality", p.113.

[21] *A Spirituality for Our Times: Report of a Consultation, Annecy, France, December 3-8, 1984*, WCC, 1985.

[22] Diane Kessler ed., *Together on the Way: Official Report of the Eighth Assembly of the World Council of Churches*, WCC, 1999, pp.131-36.

SOME PROMINENT EXAMPLES

Some of the major currents of spirituality that became prominent in the closing decades of the 20th century can be highlighted. The following selection is somewhat arbitrary except that these currents of spirituality cut across confessional and cultural divides and marked the ecumenical scenario in a significant way.

Spirituality for liberation

The rise of various liberation theologies since the 1960s was accompanied by a keen interest in spirituality. Both "theology" and "spirituality" were until then heavily loaded words carrying the baggage of rationalism and pietism respectively. In the process envisaged by various liberation theologies, these words also underwent a "detheologization" and "despiritualization" to become the proper tools of a theology and spirituality of liberation. Thus the spirituality of liberation has been a liberation of spirituality as well.

Liberation theology originated in Latin America in the 1960s in the context of rampant poverty, grave social injustice, marginalization and oppression of the poor, and an alliance between the ruling class and the church. As an active and liberating awareness of the poor people of their condition of bondage, liberation theology drew its spiritual strength from people's actual experience. The base communities *(communidades eclesiales de base)* were essentially communities of poor peasants and workers, mostly unlettered, supported by the active participation of some priests and theologians. Reading scripture in the light of their daily experience of misery, these communities evolved a new way of understanding the message of the Bible as liberative. Their reflection and common worship were no longer theoretical and cut off from the daily struggle of the people. Instead, every new reading of scripture, together with prayer and reflection, motivated them to live a spirituality of action, combat, resistance and solidarity on behalf of the suffering and oppressed people. In an action-reflection process (praxis) they received new empowerment. The source of this empowerment is God's gracious love and God's preferential option for the poor. Throughout history, as witnessed in the Bible, God's identification with the poor was translated into liberating action by prophets like Moses. The exodus experience of the people of Israel in the land of bondage became a central theme in liberation thinking. The praxis or the action-reflection process of communities engaged in liberation theology, produced a spirituality with a distinctly prophetic-communal flavour.

If classical theology often portrayed God as a neutral judge of both the rich and the poor, liberation theology does not find any positive meaning in a God who is objectively neutral. It is God's preferential option for the poor and solidarity with the victims of history that constitute the cornerstone of liberation spirituality. Neutrality is suspect because it means, more often than not, identification with the oppressor and with the interests of exploitative systems. Traditional spirituality is generally characterized by passive acceptance of social inequality and oppressive systems in the name of obedience to divine authority, by respect for the prevailing order of society, and by subservience to certain religious-spiritual hierarchies. Liberation spirituality, on the contrary, believes in active resistance to such forces in the name of both God's compassion for the weak and the costly demands of the justice of the kingdom of God.

Rereading the gospels from the perspective of the poor and the marginalized, liberation theologians have discovered a Jesus who has identified himself with the poor and the powerless. His life and ministry consisted in a series of confrontations with the corrupt power of political and religious leaders. Jesus put himself in the place of the hungry, the thirsty, the alien, the naked and the imprisoned. He made it clear that the norm of the last judgment will be our response and attentiveness to these categories of people who exist in our real life (Matt. 25:31-46). Freedom, justice and compassion to "the least" become the driving force of liberation spirituality. Solidarity is the key in this mode of spirituality as it brings to active focus the power of the community. While traditional and institutional spirituality sought to nourish the "soul" of the individual Christian who could then conveniently ignore the demands of the gospel, liberation spirituality begins with a commitment to authentic life in community in terms of practising solidarity with the least and the lost. In Christ's identification with the poor it is God's own nature that is manifested, a God who is actively involved in the daily struggle of ordinary people. Thus in liberation spirituality God and human beings are brought to a new dynamic inter-relationship for the visible transformation of society.

One of the offshoots of liberation theology and spirituality has been the rise of third-world theologies which highlighted a spirituality drawn from local third-world situations. While the validity of the concept of the third world as a political-economic-cultural category is challenged by some thinkers in the economically poor countries, a group of theologians drawn mainly from Asia, Africa and Latin America have deliberately begun to adopt the term as a focal point for their theological articulations. The Ecumenical Association of Third World Theologians (EATWOT), formed in 1976, holds that third-world theologies are born out of a *spiritual experience*. All the churches of the third world are demonstrating an awakening and a new appreciation of the importance of spirituality.[23]

The common situation of oppression suffered by the people of Latin America, minorities in North America, the peoples of Asia and Africa forms the backdrop of deeply spiritual experience. In faithfulness to this experience, any theology that speaks to these people must start "from a meeting with God that takes place in a situation of challenge, a situation that awakens Christians to a *contemplative commitment*".[24] This spirituality participates in the mystery of the suffering, death and resurrection of Christ through the people's experience of humiliation, deprivation and death and through their sense of dignity and hope for liberation.

The Oaxtepec, Mexico, assembly of EATWOT in 1986 was a landmark in understanding third-world spirituality. A key document from the assembly spoke of "spirituality which is at the source of third-world theology" as consisting "in a passionate commitment to God's reign on earth, and therefore to the earth and to its liberation and transformation. It is a spirituality which challenges the oppressed to throw off their yoke and be free."[25]

The document points to the spiritual and mystical understanding of reality by the "little ones", the unsophisticated masses of the people, prior to reflection and analysis. This holistic, uniting and intuitive approach that goes beyond the merely rational-logical

[23] Maria Clara Luccheti Bingemer, "Preface: Third World Theologies: Conversion to Others", in K.C. Abraham ed., *Third World Theologies: Commonalities and Divergences. Papers and Reflections from the 2nd General Assembly of the Ecumenical Association of Third World Theologians, Oaxtepec, Mexico, December 1986*, Maryknoll NY, Orbis, 1990, p.viii.
[24] *Ibid.*
[25] "Commonalities, Divergences and Cross Fertilization among Third World Theologies: A Document Based on the 7th International Conference of EATWOT, Oaxtepec, Mexico, December 7-14, 1986", in *Third World Theologies: Commonalities and Divergences*, pp.209-210.

is at the source of symbol, dance, poetry, liturgy and institutions. The document affirms a "lived heroic holiness" that unfolds in the struggle for life. In the very combativeness of liberation movements spirituality comes alive. A major thrust of this spirituality is to overcome the dichotomies – legitimized by academic theology – between nature and history, word and silence, action and contemplation, the mystical and the logical, between doctrine and devotion, heaven and earth, a teaching church and a taught church. Repudiating all historical idealisms, all alienating and soporific spiritualities, all theologies without a passionate love for land and people, third-world spirituality names its martyrs and draws its strength from the thousands of children, women and men who have been humiliated and killed because of their committed concern for the poor, the people, and the justice of God here and now.[26]

Summarizing all that third-world spirituality implies, the EATWOT Asia experience of 1989 verges on the rhapsodic:

> Spirituality for us is bound up with life
> and all that life involves.
> It is freedom and food,
> dignity and equality,
> community and sharing of resources.
> It is creativity and celebration of the God of life and liberation.

> Spirituality originates from the Spirit of God who fills the earth, who gives, guides and accompanies, who blesses, accepts and works with the created order. Spirituality is contemplation and praxis. It is all that can contribute to the balance and blossoming, the healing and wholeness of life, of the human race, the earth, the cosmos....[27]

Feminist spirituality

Spirituality that is specific to the feminist movement may be considered within the broad frame of liberation spiritualities. The powerful wave of feminist thinking that emerged in the 1970s in the US penetrated Europe within a decade and is now vigorously present in the rest of the world. Striking a common ground with other liberation theologies, feminist theology and spirituality have arisen out of women's experience of oppression as women. Methodologically, feminism undertakes a radical critique of the patriarchal structures of society and proposes an alternative vision of humanity. This vision includes concern for the environment and the whole created order. The intertwining of feminist spirituality with ecological and holistic motifs has made it, in many parts of the world, one of the most significant spiritual currents of the closing decades of the 20th century.

The age-old dichotomy between spirit and body is recognized by feminist spirituality as the source of the dominant ideology of patriarchy. This oppressive system, according to this way of thinking, has identified the female body with the sexual-reproductive physicality of women and excluded them from the sphere of the spirit. The intellectual-rational-spiritual has became a "male mystery". The male concept of God became the cornerstone for all the patriarchal and exclusivist notions of male domination both in religion and society.

It is precisely at the level of female bodiliness that the feminist spiritual reconstruction of reality begins. The woman's body is reclaimed by advocates of this spirituality as the habitation of the spirit and her physicality as the medium of the transcendent. In some streams of Christian feminist spirituality the figure of the Virgin Mary takes on a

---

[26] *Ibid.*
[27] "The Search for Liberation Spirituality: The EATWOT Asia Experience", in *Voices from the Third World*, 13, 1, June 1990, pp.1-9.

new dimension of meaning as the connection between the bodiliness of women and human salvation. Because each woman bears a body which shares bodily features with the body of Mary who gave birth to Jesus, the Saviour, every woman's body, it is argued, becomes an inseparable part of salvation history.[28]

By overcoming the dichotomy between body and spirit, woman's identity is rehabilitated; all that had been broken, exploited and marginalized by patriarchy is reintegrated. Old hierarchical symbols such as ladder, climbing, mountain, ascent, combat and conquest are repudiated. Instead, feminist spirituality speaks in terms of connectedness employing such images as web, network, weaving, dancing, circles and spirals.[29]

It is unfair to speak about feminist spirituality as if it were a monolithic block. In fact, it continues to branch out into a number of different streams depending on the context and its demands. Christian feminist spirituality is linked with the global feminism that arose without any particular religious or institutional affiliations.

Many of the early Christian feminists were professional theologians or scholars in the field of religion. They realized that the patriarchal order reigned so exclusively in such traditional centres of power as the church and the academy that women's experience was either negated or underestimated. The language these centres had hitherto used, the leadership they trained, and the general ethos they cultivated were all judged oppressive, suppressing or at best indifferent to women's perceptions and their sense of wholeness. However, because of the central emphasis of the "spirit" in feminist understanding, spirituality became the interlinking force for different streams of feminism irrespective of religion and academy. Some feminists in the church had the hope of transforming these institutions with a fresh breath of spirituality, while others totally rejected them as anti-women and so not conducive to the emerging feminist spirituality.

In the search for alternatives some Western streams of feminist spirituality place a heavy emphasis on "goddess" research. This involves the recovery of the primordial divine spirit and power imaged in terms of women's fundamental experience and self-understanding. Travelling beyond Christian revelation, the goddess emerges as the Great Mother worshipped in pre-patriarchal cultures as the source of life and death. The sexist language used by the Judaeo-Christian tradition in relation to the ungendered word "God" is radically altered by the recovery of the goddess image and language. Goddess recovery, to be sure, developed in different directions. Sandra M. Schneiders has identified at least three.

In one of its forms, theology (discourse on *theos*, a masculine noun) has been changed to *thea*logy where discourse about goddess recaptures the divine power in terms of feminist perceptions and over against all male manipulation of the transcendent.

A second direction in which this recovery has developed is seen in the introduction by some, in an attempt to reappropriate God experience for women, of a new way of verbally representing the deity as god/dess. Their intention is to highlight those feminine aspects of the divine which are deliberately obscured in male theological language. Thus feminine metaphors and symbols used in the Bible – e.g., Wisdom as a personification of God, the Holy Spirit as feminine, and so on – are used to create new theological conceptualizations as instruments of an alternate vision of the feminine as the image of

---

[28] Cf. Judith Gray, "Seeking a Real Mary of Nazareth Today", in *The Way*, 37, 2, April 1997, pp.158-65.
[29] Sandra M. Schneiders, "Feminist Spirituality", in *The New Dictionary of Catholic Spirituality*, pp.394-406. Cf. also S. Purvis, "Christian Feminist Spirituality" in L. Dupre and D. Saliers eds, *World Spirituality: An Encyclopedic History of the Religious Quest*, vol. 18, New York, Crossroads, 1989, pp.500-19.

god/dess. Feminists who adhere to this position continue to relate to the Judaeo-Christ-ian tradition while repudiating its patriarchal and masculine thrust.

A third expression of goddess reflection is psychological, finding its base in the archetypal theory proposed by Karl Jung concerning the *anima-animus* relationship or the reciprocal presence of male and female principles in the psychic field of men and women. The feminist critique of this theory is that it is culturally too stereotypical of masculine and feminine qualities and so leads to the confirmation of the cultural hier-archy of the masculine over the feminine and thus perpetuates the dichotomy between matter and spirit. Goddess language works against the stereotyping of women's psyche and locates spirit and reason, initiative and leadership and such other stereotypical mas-culine traits within women themselves.[30]

Schneiders has provided a summary of the general characteristics of feminist spiri-tuality. This summary underlines both how far such spirituality has travelled from more traditional spiritualities, and at the same time its commonalities with other emerging spiritualities. The following general characteristics of feminist spirituality, as identified by Schneiders, recognize the distance it has taken from the traditional Christian spiritu-ality and its commonalties with other emerging spiritualities:

1. Feminist spirituality is rooted in women's experience of disempowerment and re-empowerment. Story-telling becomes a means of consciousness-raising, and in turn the personal and the private assume political dimensions.

2. Feminist spirituality fosters a reintegration of body and spirit, overcoming the male reductionism of woman's body which confines its functions to sexuality, with asso-ciated ideas of shame and impurity.

3. Since female bodiliness is related to the status of non-human nature, the reintegra-tion of the former with the spirit and its qualities transforms the material creation into the spiritual realm. The raping of the earth and the raping of women by the aggressive male are not simply coincidental. Male possessiveness has relegated both women and the material creation to passivity as objects of pleasure and exploitation. Feminist spirituality, by rediscovering the dignity and value of the feminine, restores the active identity of nature and all created reality, liberating them from the aggres-sion and domination of male power.

4. Participatory, circular, incarnate, communicative, life-enhancing and joyful ritual is the key to feminist spirituality. This implies a radical revision of all liturgical practice that is hierarchical, excessively verbal, unemotional and male-dominated; it extends to all aspects of church life from the simple gesture in worship to the governance of global church communities.

5. Feminist spirituality recognizes the intimate relationship between personal spiritual growth and the politics of social justice. It starts with a commitment that grows simultaneously inward and outward unlike the traditional spiritualities that develop personal spiritual growth and commitment to social justice in parallel tracks, hoping to a find a meeting point on the way.

The ecumenical movement has been influenced by feminist theology and spirituality to such a point that, in present attempts to find a new shape and thrust for the movement, feminist spiritual visions are playing a crucial role. In the WCC, the study on the "Community of Women and Men in the Church" fostered a concern to integrate the holistic and communi-

---

[30] "Feminist Spirituality".

tarian aspects of feminist spirituality into both the quest for the unity of the human community and the promotion of an inclusive and participatory ministry of the church.

Creation spirituality

In the last quarter of the 20th century, the ecumenical movement added to its concern for Christian unity a concern for "justice, peace and the integrity of creation". Passionate concerns for justice and peace, disarmament and international solidarity, and the eradication of racism and poverty, were always at the heart of the WCC alongside its original goal of Christian and human unity. But the worldwide awareness of a profound crisis in the global environment and the attendant search for alternative paths to human survival are now deeply shared by the ecumenical movement as constitutive of its agenda. Moreover, the stream of creation spirituality that has arisen from an ecological perception of created reality as the gift of God in which all human beings gratefully participate has contributed to the search for new dimensions of ecumenical Christian spirituality. It draws from both Judaeo-Christian resources of scripture and liturgy, and from ascetic devotional practices.

The Vancouver assembly had already made the call "to engage member churches in a conciliar process of mutual commitment (covenant) to justice, peace and the integrity of all creation". In projecting ecological concerns together with the issues of justice and peace, the WCC provided a solid basis for a spirituality centring around God's creation. The world convocation on "Justice, Peace and the Integrity of Creation" held in Seoul in 1990 sought to bind the churches in a covenantal relationship with each other.

Creation-centred spirituality, like feminist spirituality, seeks to overcome all dualistic approaches to reality. It takes body and, indeed, all material reality as capable of manifesting the Spirit in a sacramental way. Human creativity is participation in the work of the Creator Spirit. Human and non-human realms, art and architecture, science and technology, politics and sexuality are all integral to the holistic vision of God's creation.

A keen perception of intrinsic inter-relatedness within the cosmos is characteristic of creation spirituality. A view of organic wholeness, it attempts to move human consciousness away from the anthropocentric view of nature that believes in the domination of nature by human beings, especially males, who understand themselves as the only image of God and as the crown of creation. Creation spirituality moves beyond this parochial attitude to join hands with the original Judaeo-Christian vision that conceived the created reality as good and pervaded by the power of the Holy Spirit of God. Human beings, as part of this creation, can gratefully and joyfully celebrate it and care for it with a profound sense of justice and humility.

Ecumenical spirituality in recent years has been enriched by this view, particularly its recognition of the limitations of such models as master and steward for the relationship between humanity and creation. The change is obviously from a merely ethical and objective attitude regarding the environment, nature and non-human creation to one of participation and spiritual communion.

Within the ecumenical movement, the Orthodox spiritual and liturgical tradition has provided access to some forms of a creation-centred spirituality that is aligned with a holistic ecological vision. Unlike classical Western theology, Orthodox theology has never seen dichotomies between nature and grace, reason and revelation, faith and works, etc. The Eastern Orthodox tradition has espoused a view of creation as flowing out of God's infinite goodness and will, and thus has not conceived of a natural realm as opposed to the supernatural. Nature is understood as grace-filled. Human freedom is not necessarily opposed to God's authority; rather, freedom is one of the chief characteristics of the image of God in humanity so that women and men can work together with the Spirit of God in a synergy on behalf of all creation. According to this view human reason is not necessarily estranged from the mystery of God and God's operations *(energeia)* in creation. Creation, because of its fundamental goodness as God's work, is called to share in the divine glory. The transfiguration of matter and its *theosis* (divinization) are major themes running through Orthodox spirituality. The dynamic nature of all that is created and its capacity for holiness and for participation in the triune splendour, underline the sacramental spirituality of the Orthodox tradition. Historically, the Orthodox tradition, unlike its Western counterparts, was not fundamentally altered by currents set in motion by movements such as Renaissance humanism, the Reformation, or the rationalism and scientific-secular world-view shaped by the Enlightenment. Hence, it is somewhat difficult for the Orthodox churches to resonate to some contemporary questions that arise in basically Western terms. Recent efforts of the Patriarchate of Constantinople in cooperation with the World Wide Fund for Nature (WWF) towards creating ecological awareness among people and initiating such projects as organic farming have been understood as arising from this Orthodox spiritual vision of the wholeness and harmony of creation.[31]

Monastic communities – marked by a simple life-style, prayer, a eucharistic attitude to creation and communal styles of work – are called to be living models for a humanity struggling with the issues of sustainability, over-consumption, pollution and violence to the environment. A new human asceticism with regard to nature arises in many instances from the experience of monastic spirituality. While it is important to use available resources to meet the needs of the present generation, it is equally important not to deprive future generations of their right to share the earth's resources. An eco-ascetic spirituality can inculcate such a caring and future-oriented attitude, rejecting cultures of consumption, violent exploitation of material resources, and selfish and parochial views of development. This spirituality, rather, promotes the common good, the disciplining of one's needs in new life-styles, a sharing and solidarity with the poor, and a deep sensitivity to the health and wholeness of creation. The ecumenical movement has not yet fully articulated its perceptions in this regard, but it has definitely begun to integrate eco-spiritual insights into its own vision of the future.

Pentecostal and charismatic spirituality

A major force that continues to influence Christian spirituality throughout the world comes from Pentecostal and charismatic circles. It is not the organizational aspects of these movements which are of interest in this present context, but those main features that have made an impact on the way Christians experience community, worship, prayer and spiritual fellowship.

Contemporary Pentecostalism is an early 20th-century phenomenon, born in the US. It traces its origin to the ministry of Charles Fox Parham (1873-1929) in Kansas and Texas and to the famous Azusa Street revival in Los Angeles in 1906 although its theological roots go back to various developments in the 18th and 19th centuries. The search for a "Spirit-filled, Spirit-led first-century church" has crystallized over the years into var-

---

[31] *Orthodoxy and the Ecological Crisis*, Gland, WWF International, 1990.

ious Pentecostal churches and movements. Some of these churches, chiefly from Latin America, are now members of the WCC.

In popular usage, "Pentecostal" and "charismatic" are interchangeable terms. While many Pentecostals traditionally consider Spirit baptism and glossolalia (speaking in tongues) as the chief expressions of faith, charismatics generally insist on speaking in tongues as the confirmation of Spirit baptism. While most Pentecostals would understand themselves as belonging to institutionalized church communities, charismatics cut across denominational lines. Since charismatics do not usually move out of their original church affiliation, there is today a charismatic movement that embraces Roman Catholic, Anglican and Protestant churches in more or less the same way. The Orthodox churches are also affected but to a much lesser degree. Pentecostal and charismatic movements are bound together by an emphasis on the work and gifts of the Holy Spirit as extended to both individuals and communities.

The contemporary charismatic movement originated in the United States, towards the end of the 1950s in Protestant churches and in 1967 in the Roman Catholic Church; it has subsequently spread to different countries and churches. Its growth, especially among Roman Catholics, has been phenomenal. Spiritual and liturgical renewal in the post-Vatican II church prepared fertile soil for the flourishing of charismatic groups. Charismatics or "neo-Pentecostals" have expressed a strong desire, based on devoted study of the Bible, to return to the model of apostolic community described in the Acts of the Apostles.

When some members of the hierarchy, like Joseph Cardinal Suenens of Belgium, came to its leadership, the new movement became increasingly integrated into the Roman Catholic Church. More and more people, including many from the clergy, joined the charismatic fellowship. Pope Paul VI himself greeted a large charismatic assembly in Rome in 1975. One Roman Catholic theologian has observed with sympathy:

> [T]he charismatic movement is a grace of God touching every aspect of the Christian life and is found across all the Christian churches... The reappearance of the spiritual gifts thus represents something dramatically new in church history. Once you admit they are authentic and are the work of the Holy Spirit, you have to recognize that something of possibly unparalleled importance is happening.[32]

It is claimed by many charismatics and Pentecostals that direct experience of the Holy Spirit is manifested in, for example, baptism in the Spirit, speaking in tongues and healings of all sorts, although Roman Catholic groups generally place less emphasis on such phenomena as glossolalia, shouting and dancing. Sacramental participation in the Catholic stream has moderated typical Pentecostal features. Deep interest in the Bible, mutual participation of clergy and laity, the abolition of strict hierarchy in worship, intensity of personal relationships, and transdenominational fellowship have helped the movement to continue to exercise a decisive influence on the shaping of a global spirituality for the new millennium.

While ecumenical spirituality as understood in WCC circles attached crucial importance to such concerns for social justice, Pentecostals and charismatics have rarely been enthusiastic about "spirituality for combat". However, recent dialogues and encounters between these different spiritual trends may prove mutually complementary and produce a more balanced and truly ecumenical spirituality. The fact of the "totally unanticipated penetration or diffusion of the Pentecostal experience into the estab-

---

[32] Peter D. Hocken, quoted in S.M. Burgess and G.R. McGee eds, *Dictionary of Pentecostal and Charismatic Movements*, Grand Rapids MI, Zondervan, 1989, pp.3-4.

lished denominations", as described by David du Plessis of South Africa at the Evanston 1954 assembly of the WCC, stands true in the case of the charismatic movement as well.[33]

CONCLUSION

The interactions between various spiritual currents are extremely subtle and often intractable. The continuous osmosis between different life-styles, ideas and practices related to human spiritual aspirations seems to defy the familiar signposts of dogmatic definitions, confessional statements and ecclesiastical borders. This is clear from the very indefinability of the word "spirituality." The experiential dimension, however, provides a common and pivotal point. All major trends in the domain of spirituality seem to point to the old wisdom that religious belief is essentially a matter of profound human *experience,* both personal and corporate: an experience that is never adequately expressed in human language and logic. The familiar distinction between theology and spirituality is no longer tenable since it seeks to perpetuate the wrong polarity between rationality and life of the spirit. Late 20th-century spirituality claims to have overcome this polarity by appealing to the wholeness of human experience that links the transcendent to the historical, the struggle for justice to the bliss of meditation, the pain of the planet earth to the health of the soul.

The ecumenical movement is tremendously enriched by this new spiritual quest as it makes possible a free and joyful sharing of prayers, hymns, devotional practices and spiritual wisdom not only between many churches and ecclesial communities but on occasion between various religious traditions as well. Critical questions, however, have recently been raised in some Christian circles about the assumptions and practices of an "ecumenical spirituality". Common worship involving different Christian groups, for example, is considered by some to be a violation of ecclesiological principles. Dialogue and spiritual exchange with other faith traditions are suspected by some of being syncretistic corruptions of Christian faith. New geo-political configurations, the emergence of a uni-polar world, and phenomena like globalization and pluralism have induced, in many places, feelings of anxiety and fear. In many cultures, religious traditions are seeking a reinforcement of identity. Emerging spiritualities will certainly bear the marks of such a global scenario.

While doctrinal disagreements and institutional identities continue to defeat ecumenical aspirations and obstruct true human community, the new search for authentic spirituality has begun to build a common household. The God-question has regained a tremendous importance in the "post-Christian" world. Art and poetry, music and celebration, living together and listening to one another's stories, speaking out for the oppressed alongside the search for justice for the most wretched of the earth will be of equal importance in determining the emerging spirituality of the oikoumene, the whole inhabited earth.

---

[33] R. Quebedeaux, *The New Charismatics II*, San Francisco, Harper & Row, 1983, p.8.

BIBLIOGRAPHY

Abraham, K.C. ed., *Third World Theologies: Commonalities and Divergences. Papers and Reflections from the 2nd General Assembly of the Ecumenical Association of Third World Theologians, Oaxtepec, Mexico, December 1986*, Maryknoll NY, Orbis, 1990, 216p.

Amirtham, Samuel and Pryor, Robins eds, *Resources for Spiritual Formation in Theological Education*, WCC, 1989, 249p.

Appleton, George, *The Oxford Book of Prayer*, Oxford, Oxford Univ. Press, 1985, 397p.

Bent, Ans J. van der, "The Concern for Spirituality", in *The Ecumenical Review*, 38, 1, 1986.

Berger, Peter L., *A Rumour of Angels: Modern Society and the Rediscovery of the Supernatural*, New York NY, Doubleday, 1969, 132p.

Bria, Ion, *People Hunger to Be Near to God: Common Convictions about Renewal, Spirituality, Community*, WCC, 1990, 93p.

Cantate Domino, an Ecumenical Hymn Book, Basel, Bärenreiter, 1974, 379p.

Carden, John, *With All God's People: The New Ecumenical Prayer Cycle*, WCC, 1989, 2 vols.

Cashmore, Gwen and Puls, Joan, *Clearing the Way: En Route to an Ecumenical Spirituality*, WCC, 1990, 64p.

Castro, Emilio, *When We Pray Together*, WCC, 1989, 86p.

Celebrating Community: Prayers and Songs of Unity – Gemeinschaft feiern: Gebete und Lieder der Einheit – Célébrer la communauté, WCC, 1993, 86p.

Collins, Owen, *2000 Years of Classic Christian Prayers: A Collection for Public and Personal Use*, New York, Orbis, 2000, 342p.

Evans, Gillian Rosemary, Fuchs, Lorelei F. and Kessler, Diane C. eds, *Encounters for Unity*, Norwich, Canterbury Press, 1995, 234p.

Falardeau, Ernest, *That All May Be One: Catholic Reflections on Christian Unity*, New York, Paulist, 2000, 192p.

Fraser, Ian M., *Salted with Fire: Life-Stories, Meditations, Prayers*, Edinburgh, Saint Andrew, 1999, 152p.

Harling, Per, *Worshipping Ecumenically: Orders of Service from Global Meetings with Suggestions for Local Use*, WCC, 1995, 183p.

Hinson, E. Glenn ed., *Spirituality in Ecumenical Perspective*, Louisville KY, Westminster John Knox, 1993, 200p.

In Spirit and in Truth: A Worship Book – En esprit et en vérité: louanges et prières – Im Geist und in der Wahrheit: Ein Gottesdienstbuch – En Espíritu y en Verdad: Libro de Culto, WCC Seventh Assembly, 1991, WCC, 1991, 198p.

Jesus Christ, the Life of the World: A Worship Book for the Sixth Assembly of the World Council of Churches, WCC, 1983, 166p.

Jones C. et al. eds, *The Study of Spirituality*, London, SPCK, 1986, 634p.

Kaan, Fred, *The Only Earth We Know: Hymn Texts*, Carol Stream IL, Hope, 1999, 145p.

Limouris, Gennadios, *Icons: Windows on Eternity. Theology and Spirituality in Colour*, WCC, 1990, 228p.

Maas, Robin and O'Donnell, Gabriel eds, *Spiritual Traditions for the Contemporary Church*, Nashville, Abingdon, 1990, 464p.

Newton, John A., *Heart Speaks to Heart: Studies in Ecumenical Spirituality*, London, Darton, Longman and Todd, 1994, 132p.

Potter, Jean and Braybrooke, Marcus eds, *All in Good Faith: A Resource Book for Multi-faith Prayer*, Oxford, World Congress of Faiths, 1997, 165p.

Prayers Encircling the World: An International Anthology, Louisville, Westminster John Knox, 1999, 278p.

Puls, Joan, *Seek Treasures in Small Fields: Everyday Holiness*, Mystic CT, Twenty-Third, 1993, 149p.

Report on the Consultation on Christian Spirituality for Our Times, Iasi, Romania, 27 April-4 May 1994, WCC, 1994, 28p.

Rowthorn, Jeffery W. ed, *The Wideness of God's Mercy. Litanies to Enlarge Our Prayer: An Ecumenical Collection*, Harrisburg PA, Morehouse, 1995, 384p.

Ryan, Thomas, *Disciplines for Christian Living: Interfaith Perspectives*, New York, Paulist, 1993, 274p.

The SPCK Book of Christian Prayer, London, SPCK, 1995, 490p.

A Spirituality for Our Times: Report of a Consultation, Annecy, France, December 3-8, 1984, WCC, 1985, 23p.

Taylor, John V., *Weep Not For Me: Meditations on the Cross and the Resurrection*, WCC, 1986, 46p.

Thomas, M.M., "Spirituality for Combat", in *The Ecumenical Review*, 42, 3-4, July-Oct. 1990, pp.216-224.

Thuma Mina: Singing with Our Partner Churches, Basel, Basileia, 1995, 432p.

Torrance, Robert M., *The Spiritual Quest: Transcendence, Myth, Religion and Science*, Berkeley CA, Univ. of California Press, 1994, 367p.

Vischer, Lukas, *Intercession*, WCC, 1980, 66p.

Weber, Hans-Ruedi, *The Way of the Lamb. Christ in the Apocalypse: Lenten Meditations*, WCC, 1988, 58p.

11
Inclusive Community

By Elisabeth Raiser

The second general secretary of the WCC, Eugene Carson Blake, once said that "the ecumenical movement is a result of concerns of ordinary church people who find their ecumenical aspirations limited by church structures".[1] The point is that the ecumenical movement gets nowhere unless and until ordinary church people are involved in it, embrace it and carry the torch of ecumenism. But there are no "ordinary Christians": all are equal and created in the image of God, making up an inclusive community from which the impenetrable walls of exclusion are removed. We have seen the appalling violence and pain caused by barriers of race, ethnicity and religion. But among ordinary church people there are no second-class baptisms, no conditional memberships in the body of Christ. Exclusion, however, has prevented the community from coming together because of differences – gender, disability, sexual orientation, origin, age and gifts. Ministry which belongs to the whole people of God has been denied to laity and leadership and too often given over to clerical leaders, ecclesiastical bureaucrats and executives, academics and pastors. Exclusion is not an ecumenical stance.

The process of transforming the ecumenical community of churches into a truly "inclusive" community gained momentum during the 1960s. Often ecumenical endeavours in this respect ran parallel to political struggles for liberation and participation, and were inspired by the anti-apartheid and civil-rights movements, and not least by the emerging women's movement. The churches' search for an "inclusive community" can only be understood against this background of a widespread desire for a participatory and healed community without barriers. "Liberation" and "inclusive community" are reverse sides of the same coin.

In the period covered by this chapter the determined, and at times militant, engagement for the participation of women, youth and elderly, gays and lesbians, lay people, the differently abled and the sick gave rise to a number of conflicts within the ecumenical movement. The way in which the individual churches, and with them the ecumenical community, dealt with the reality of a broken community, characterized by structures of domination and inequality, and the various effects of emancipation, became in itself a touchstone of inclusivity – of the churches' understanding of authority and ministry, of representation and witness.

• This chapter contains material which has been supplied by the editorial team.
[1] See "Eugene Carson Blake Dies, Was WCC Leader 1967-72", *Ecumenical Press Service*, 85.08.12, 11-20 July 1985, year 52, issue 27.

The most clearly articulated discussions, full of tensions, emerged in connection with the search for the "community of women and men" in the church. These discussions will take centre stage in the first part of this chapter. The second part will deal with ecumenical conversations and actions about the role of lay people and youth, an inclusive community with differently abled people, and with men and women identifying themselves as gays and lesbians.

WOMEN AND MEN

The WCC Uppsala assembly (1968) took place at a time when support and solidarity for liberation movements against colonialism and oppression were at their peak. The women's movement, similarly struggling against patronizing attitudes and economic and social injustices, gained a powerful voice within these movements. Finding focus in the concept of "sexism" (coined as a parallel to racism and classism), it linked women's rights and human rights. Christian women began rediscovering their sisters in the Bible. They raised questions about women's ministry and ordination and gave new impetus to demands for a wider and more just participation of women in the decision-making of the churches.

Within ecumenical institutions, the WCC's women's department (Cooperation of Men and Women in Church and Society) under the leadership of Madeleine Barot played a pioneering role. The department and its commission shared with most women in the churches of the oikoumene the hope that the advancement of women's competencies would of itself lead to a strengthening of their participation. New approaches to anthropology and sexual ethics and new interpretations of the biblical basis of partnership were to change firmly held role models in church and society. But by the end of the 1960s partnership had become an ambiguous concept.

It could be asked whether "partnership" was not in reality a matter of complementarity between the dominating and the dominated. Even after twenty years of efforts by the Department on Cooperation of Men and Women in Church and Society, the structures of power were still the same, i.e. the churches had not responded to the challenges which had been brought to them through the oikoumene and no real changes had taken place.[2] Women's circles became convinced that a new and inclusive community would be attained only if women were to separate themselves from men for a time and develop both capabilities and strategies in their own protected and unsupervised space.

At Uppsala, the WCC became much more inclusive in relation to the Orthodox churches and to the churches of the third world. The large majority of their membership – lay people, women and youth – were, however, represented only by a small minority (women made up 9 percent of the assembly, up somewhat from the 3 percent at New Delhi). At the same time, youth protested visibly and loudly with demonstrations and

---

[2] Cf. the report of the Division of Ecumenical Action to the WCC central committee 1969: "... there is a conflict between women and men in a man-made world. Premature harmonization in concepts like 'complementarity' have not solved the problem; they have dimmed it." World Council of Churches Central Committee, *Minutes of the Twenty-Third Meeting, Canterbury, 1969*, p.167. Cf. Marga Bührig, "Discrimination against Women", in Ronald H. Preston ed., *Technology and Social Justice: An International Symposium on the Social and Economic Teaching of the World Council of Churches from Geneva 1966 to Uppsala 1968*, London, SPCK, 1971, p.295.

banners during the formal closing worship in the Uppsala cathedral.[3] Those responsible for the Department on Cooperation of Men and Women lobbied to get women nominated for leadership.

The assembly expressed its "great dissatisfaction" that so few women, lay people and youth had participated as official delegates, and demanded a more equitable representation at the next assembly.[4] Subsequently, a first decision concerning the idea of quotas was made in relation to the structural changes approved in 1971 and 1973: that 60 percent of the number of assembly delegates nominated by the WCC itself should be women.[5] The question of women's participation was now irrevocably placed on the agenda of the churches.

The Uppsala assembly resulted in six seats for women out of the total of 120 members of the central committee, and Pauline Webb of the UK was elected to the executive committee and appointed vice-moderator. From the beginning, Webb understood her role as being an advocate for women's concerns and as an "opener of doors" for more women.[6] The intentional strategy of calling women to work separately from men in order to assert their identity and plan their strategy was put into action for the first time at the central committee meeting in 1972.[7] The most important gain at the gatherings without the presence of men was mutual encouragement and solidarity. "Worldwide sisterhood" had become a key term in ecumenical women's work.[8]

This new community of women was, however, not always in harmony. In spite of many similarities, strong differences became obvious and with them tensions between women from different cultures, traditions and socio-political situations. The women in the North were struggling for more self-determination and greater material and spiritual independence from the men. Abortion and the search for self-realization and recognition became hotly debated issues. Questions of survival and liberation for all from oppression were predominant in the South: hunger and persecution, colonial and racist domination, and the deadly effects of increasing militarism. The women felt solidarity with the men in the liberation struggle and often had little empathy with their Northern sisters' efforts to achieve what appeared to be liberal emancipation. Women had to develop an inclusive community among themselves.

Brigalia Bam of South Africa, who had worked in the Women's Department since 1967 and been its director since 1970, was convinced that only face-to-face meetings be-

[3] D.E. Johnson ed., *Uppsala to Nairobi 1968-1975: Report of the Central Committee to the Fifth Assembly of the World Council of Churches*, WCC, 1975, pp.197f.

[4] Cf. Norman Goodall ed., *The Uppsala Report 1968: Official Report of the Fourth Assembly of the World Council of Churches, Uppsala, July 4-20, 1968*, WCC, 1968, p.191.

[5] Cf. Robert McAfee Brown, "Lessons from the Assembly", in *Christianity and Crisis*, 28, Sept. 1968, p.206. For the resolutions of central committee in 1971, 1972 and 1973, see Janet Crawford, *Rocking the Boat: Women's Participation in the World Council of Churches, 1948-1991*, PhD Thesis, Wellington, New Zealand, 1995, unpubl., pp.236-37.

[6] Cf. Pauline Webb's self-evaluation in her book *She Flies Beyond: Memories and Hopes of Women in the Ecumenical Movement*, WCC, 1993, p.20: "I realized that I had been chosen as a token woman rather than through any particular ability of my own, but I had to accept that in all humility. Often it was through tokenism at first that any of us women would be given the experience of working in committees, and through that experience might be enabled to push open doors of opportunity for other women..."

[7] Pauline Webb, "Committed to Fellowship – But of What Sort?", in *The Ecumenical Review*, 25, 1973, p.263.

[8] See Brigalia Bam's evaluation of these meetings in Susannah Herzel, *A Voice for Women: The Women's Department of the World Council of Churches*, WCC, 1981, p.63.

tween women from the first, second and third worlds could set this learning process in motion. Liberation from racial discrimination and poverty were just as important to her as women's liberation itself. She helped to build bridges between white and black women, between women of the North and of the South, and between secular women and women in the church. An inclusive community of women without political and social solidarity was unthinkable for her, and she was always urging women of the North to translate their own experiences of oppression into an active engagement in their sisters' struggle against hunger and racism.[9]

It is significant that the 1971 restructuring of the WCC renamed the department Women in Church and Society. In the following years it concentrated on the situation of women, and this shifted the perspective away from partnership between women and men to more justice for women.

A pioneering WCC conference "Sexism in the Seventies" took place in 1974 in Berlin to locate the struggle of Christian women in the context of women's liberation movements. Not only women from member churches but also Roman Catholics and women from secular movements were invited. Men were not allowed to attend – a decision which met with some misunderstanding, but was supported by the WCC's general secretary Philip Potter. The expression "sexism", which first entered the ecumenical discussion in 1971,[10] was intended to signal every discrimination or devaluing of a person for reason of gender. Using an analysis drawn from liberation theology, the liberation of women was understood as also implying the liberation of men, in the belief that only after such a double liberation from the sin or heresy of sexism would the unity of the church become visible.[11]

The theme of the WCC's 1975 assembly, "Jesus Christ Frees and Unites", was thus already operative at the Berlin conference, and the impulse for the later study on the Community of Women and Men in the Church came out of a working group on women and theology.[12] Unravelling the links between sexism, racism and economic exploitation – the "web of oppression" – seemed, however, to be the most urgent task, and the critical attitude towards patriarchal structures both in society and in the church was easier to articulate than the visions of a new community. Only a radical renewal could offer visibility and an audible voice to women, make space for their spirituality, make them equal partners in decision-making and thus able to deal responsibly with sensitive socio-ethical issues such as sex education, family planning, abortion, and women in the work-

---

[9] *Ibid.*, p.64, quotes Bam: "Women have achieved a solidarity they should now use. From their experience of oppression, women can enter into the experience of blacks more immediately and work for their liberation. I am saying that, if we have the platforms, we must also speak on behalf of others who have no platform. I do not know how we can enjoy our liberation while we live amidst their oppression. Our solidarity must express itself in the fields and on the frontiers."

[10] Anna Marie Aagaard seems to have brought this concept into the ecumenical discussion for the first time in her "Unscientific Postscript" to the Cartigny consultation, 1971. In any case, this is what Melanie May implies in *Bonds of Unity: Women, Theology and the Worldwide Church*, UMI Dissertation Information Service, 1986, p.56. Cf. also Aagaard in *Gladly We Rebel*, WCC, 1971, pp.59-63.

[11] See the opening address by Pauline Webb in *Sexism in the Seventies: Discrimination against Women: A Report of a World Council of Churches Consultation, West Berlin 1974*, WCC, 1975. Also pp.10 and 33.

[12] *Ibid.*, pp.59f. Cf. Constance F. Parvey, "Journey of a Dream: Beginning Again", in *Report of the All African Regional Consultation on the Community of Women and Men in the Church Study*, Ibadan, Nigeria, Sept. 1980, Nairobi, AACC, 1980, p.6. I refer here to an indication by Parvey who, against the leadership of the conference, must have carried through/enforced the creation of a theological working group on the spot. In *Gladly We Rebel*, p.6.

place.[13] In retrospect, many of the participants experienced the growing sense of community among women in Berlin itself before the blossoming of a more widespread renewal.[14]

The Berlin experience of community and women's ecumenical creativity was in itself not a first. National and confessional women's organizations, including women's mission societies, had offered women the opportunity to acquire experience in taking responsibility and developing democratic decision-making processes, as well as providing a strong sense of belonging together.

In many of the earlier networks, particularly the World Day of Prayer and the Fellowship of the Least Coin, the old expression "pray and act" became a basic principle, i.e. linking information sharing, common prayer, and practical engagement for specific solidarity projects. The ever-increasing number of church collections for such projects provided a visible expression of a worldwide concrete solidarity of women. In addition, Orthodox, Roman Catholic, Old Catholic and Protestants participating in the World Day of Prayer provided the most inclusive international ecumenical network which had ever existed.

The Women's Ecumenical Liaison Group (WELG) founded in 1968 worked for closer relationships between non-Roman Catholic and Catholic women. Contacts were developed during and after Vatican II between the WCC Women's department and the Council's women observers. Cardinals Augustin Bea and Johannes Willebrands, at that time the outgoing and incoming presidents of the Vatican Secretariat for Promoting Christian Unity, encouraged and supported these contacts.[15]

A first conference, on the theme "The Christian Woman, Co-Artisan in a Changing Society", took place in 1967 at Taizé, France. It resulted in the formation of a steering committee, with 14 members appointed each by the WCC and the Vatican Secretariat. Two further conferences took place, both with a great deal of commitment on both sides. Vienna (1971) on "The Image of Woman in the Mass Media" expressed the growing concerns about the influence of Western television on the role models of women and men in all cultures. The second conference in Cyprus (1972) on "Women's Role in Peace Education" took up women's commitment to the peace movements and development initiatives.[16] It consciously risked conflicts between women of different political outlooks. In style and content this was indicative of the working method of the Women's desk in Geneva, which the Vatican perceived as being a dangerous strategy for Catholic women. The Cyprus conference, consequently, turned out to be the last for the WELG. The Secretariat for Promoting Christian Unity demanded that the liaison group be dissolved. The controversy strengthened the resolve of ecumenically committed women to create self-reliant forms of organizations that would be completely independent of the churches.

Regional ecumenical women's conferences had been formed in Asia, Africa, the Pacific, Latin America and the Caribbean in the 1960s and early 1970s. The Ecumenical Forum of European Christian Women (EFECW), founded in 1982, was created partly to

---

[13] Nelle Morton, in *Sexism in the Seventies*, pp.61,64. Webb, *ibid.*, p.10. Cf. also recommendation on full partnership in the church, *ibid.*, p.108. Webb raised these questions sharply in her essay "Committed to Fellowship – But of What Sort?"
[14] *She Flies Beyond*, pp.20f.
[15] *A Voice for Women*, p.55.
[16] *Ibid.*, p.58.

offer a platform transcending the boundaries of political systems, confessions and nationalities, and partly as a means of speaking publicly to the churches.

The choice of independence from the ecumenical and church-related institutions generated controversial discussions. Did the Forum and other ecumenical women's organizations want a women's oikoumene, along the lines of the "Women's Church" in the US, or did they want to apply women's perspectives to the men's oikoumene? On several occasions constructive models of cooperation with the ecumenical bodies were found. For example, the European Ecumenical Assembly in Basel in 1989 had women participate at all levels, developing their own spirituality and their own reading of the issues, due to the active participation of the EFECW in the planning of the conference.

If the World Day of Prayer, the YWCA, the European Women's Forum and similar movements in other parts of the world offered ecumenical learning and an action field for Christian women at the grassroots level, the World Student Christian Federation provided students and educated young women with a wide range of possibilities of gaining international and ecumenical experience. The WSCF attempted real partnership between men and women, including sharing of leadership tasks with women, and it is not by chance that some of the strongest women personalities of the oikoumene came from this movement.[17]

The study on the "Community of Women and Men in the Church"

During the Sexism conference in Berlin, participants in the working group on women and the churches started from their own lived experiences as they considered liberation theology for and by women. Women's lives spoke more loudly about the brokenness of the community than all theological statements could do.

It became, as Madeleine Barot was to say later, the moment of birth of the study on the "Community of Women and Men in the Church", which was to determine the search for an inclusive community far beyond the framework of the WCC for the next eight years.

The Faith and Order Commission adopted the idea of such a study (1974). The International Year of Women helped to give women's concerns visibility during the 1975 WCC assembly in Nairobi. For the first time in the WCC's history women were able to conduct a whole plenary session, bringing home the real situation of women to the delegates through a number of very impressive testimonies and analyses.[18] Most of the delegates began to realize that the Indian proverb, quoted by Prakai Nontawasee from Thailand, was valid in the churches: "Men are the front legs of the elephant and women are the back legs", meaning that women carry the whole burden but have no say in choosing which direction to follow. One of the sections reported, "As long as women are largely excluded from decision-making processes, they will be unable to realize a full partnership with men, and therefore the church will be unable to realize its full unity."

The assembly accepted the idea of the so-called Community study. The fact that, one year later, the study was placed within Faith and Order and not within the scope of the

---

[17] Cf. the evaluation by Milan Opocensky, WSCF Europe secretary 1968-73, quoted in Gudrun Kaper et al., *Eva, wo bist du? Frauen in internationalen Organisationen der Ökumene* (Kennzeichen 8), Laetare, Gelnhausen, 1981, p.130.

[18] David M. Paton ed., *Breaking Barriers: Nairobi 1975: The Official Report of the Fifth Assembly of the World Council of Churches, Nairobi, 23 November-10 December, 1975*, London, SPCK, and Grand Rapids MI, Eerdmans, 1976, pp.19-21.

Women's desk[19] provided clarity about its ecclesiological character. The initiators considered it a "victory". Constance F. Parvey, later to be director of the study, took the placement to be one of the conditions for its success. Contrary to the interpretation that women's concerns had nothing at all to do with the theological questions of the unity of the church, the study was to become a programme "to rescue the church from its masculine barriers". In a new approach to unity it would be pioneering a common venture of women and men struggling to "image God" in a more true way.[20]

The Community study was launched in January 1978, when Parvey joined the secretariat of Faith and Order. The study process was to run on these levels:

- For local church groups and women's organizations, those most widely invited to participate, a study booklet was produced with questions about the church and community life.
- Regional gatherings were planned, as well as four thematic consultations.
- After four years, an international conference was to mark the culminating point of the process.

The depth of the process was overwhelming. The study booklet (in English, French and German) was translated by volunteers into 13 additional languages and printed in 65,000 copies. No other study reached the grassroots to this extent. Grateful that the WCC had finally put women's concerns on the agenda of the churches, women everywhere received the booklet enthusiastically. It included a series of personal and cultural questions about identity, sexuality, family, marriage, community, while other questions dealt with biblical exegesis and the tradition of the church in relation to the community of women and men. The last section dealt with women's participation in church structures: religious education, worship, decision-making, the understanding of ministry and renewal movements within the church.

The study groups were invited to formulate their visions and hopes for a renewed community of women and men. The replies to these questions expressed less anger and frustration than those that surfaced at the Berlin meeting in 1974, but focused much more on the suffering caused by the brokenness of community. Philip Potter read in these responses the "incredible pain and agony of it all – and with it the extraordinary love and patient endurance and perseverance which lie behind it".[21] The variety and richness of the women's reports showed what unity looks like as seen from the margins or from below. Similar ecclesial structures were experienced differently in different contexts – sometimes helping to create community, sometimes destroying it. Traditional ways of exercising authority in the church were, for example, seen by some as linked to oppression and patriarchal power and, consequently, definitely rejected. In another context, authority was experienced as a protection against the deterioration of values, or against persecution, and as the only certain guarantee for the continuation and maintaining of community.[22] No one model could be derived either from tradition or experi-

---

[19] See WCC Central Committee, *Minutes of the Twenty-Ninth Meeting, Geneva 1976*, p.28. The Women's desk would have preferred to begin a programme to combat sexism. The question of community seemed premature to them. Personal communication from Constance Parvey, director of the CWMC study.

[20] See *Bonds of Unity*, pp.75f.

[21] Constance F. Parvey ed., *The Community of Women and Men in the Church: The Sheffield Report*, WCC, 1983, p.25.

[22] See Janet Crawford and Michael Kinnamon eds, *In God's Image: Reflections on Identity, Human Wholeness and the Authority of Scripture*, WCC, 1983, pp.96,105.

ence which could command universal respect as a model for global community between women and men.

The African regional consultation recalled the strength of the women in tribal communities and regretted both Christianity's weakening of their position in society and the Westernization of the image of women. The Middle East placed the emphasis on the Orthodox interpretation of women in scripture and Tradition, while the Latin American consultation turned to the political and economic analyses of the women's situation, and the European consultation gave the East-West conflict a major role.[23]

Specialized consultations debated ministry, Mariology and biblical hermeneutics, the ordination of women from an ecumenical perspective, "towards a theology of human wholeness" and "the authority of scripture in the light of the new experiences of women". They drew on the experiences of the participants, as did the 1981 international conference "A Chance for Change" in Sheffield. This brought some underlying conflicts to the surface. Women from the South revolted in Sheffield against the Northern and too church-related view taken by the conference, believing that their questions about survival were not taken seriously enough.

The struggle for a new vision of community was not easy. This became evident shortly after Sheffield at the WCC's central committee in Dresden in 1981. The presentation of the Sheffield conference's report began with the words,

> At Berlin, the "Community of Women and Men in the Church" study was born. It was not a programme *against* sexism, but *for* more participation of women; that was Berlin 1974. Sheffield 1981 is about women and men becoming a new community and the means to bring that about. Since the beginning of the study process in 1978, its framework has not been illness, but health and healing, not brokenness, but new community.[24]

New community and healing were the key words, but demands for the ordination of women and a 50 percent quota of women's representation at the next WCC assembly set the central committee into an uproar for several days. Half of the delegates to be women at an official ecumenical assembly and three women presidents? Some central committee members considered it as absurd, extravagant or too radical.[25]

The Orthodox representatives especially expressed themselves vehemently, and even a conciliatory amendment proposing the principle of "equal representation" was debated for days before it was adopted – without the votes of the Orthodox whose participants feared, rightly, that growing influence of women in the decision-making processes of the WCC would bring issues onto the agenda that they perceived as endangering unity – such as the ordination of women.[26]

A consultation in Prague in 1985 focused upon the fact that "our words 'strain, crack and sometimes break'; that they may 'decay' and may be 'assailed'".[27] A new language needed to be found which would help the churches to move beyond the "unity-in-tension" which characterized the discussions around the community between

---

[23] A resumé of the regional consultations in *Bonds of Unity*, p.80.
[24] Parvey in an unpublished paper, quoted in *Bonds of Unity*, p.93.
[25] See *She Flies Beyond*, p.24, and Mary Tanner, "The Community Study and the Unity of the Church and Renewal of Human Community", in Michael Kinnamon ed., *Towards Visible Unity: Commission on Faith and Order, Lima 1982, vol. 2: Study Papers and Reports*, WCC, 1982, p.163.
[26] Reinhild Traitler, "An Oikoumene of Women?", in *The Ecumenical Review*, 40, 1988, p.180.
[27] Cf. Thomas F. Best ed., *Beyond Unity-in-Tension: Unity, Renewal and the Community of Women and Men*, WCC, 1988, p.27.

women and men, and especially around the issues of the ordination and participation of women.

The ordination of women

The ordination of women became a bone of contention – some Orthodox saw the Dresden discussion as an expression of the unwillingness of women to enter into dialogue with them, and it led to a temporary halt in the Community study. Elisabeth Behr-Sigel, one of the most outspoken among Western Orthodox women theologians, observed, "The Orthodox felt they could not make themselves heard... They underestimated the importance of the problem of women's ordination for their Protestant partners who, in their turn, thought they could treat Orthodox reticence with disdain"[28] – a tough judgment upon the inability of both sides to listen to one another.

Some Protestant churches had ordained women since the end of the 1940s or even earlier. They put the issue of women's ordination on the ecumenical agenda. The Roman Catholic Church as well as the Orthodox churches felt they were being forced into a discussion which inevitably addressed the self-understanding of the church: embracing questions about the nature of God, the order of creation, the understanding of ministry, the doctrine of men and women as created in God's image, and the relationship of the church with the surrounding society. These churches consider the ordination of women as endangering the search for the unity of the church.

In the bilateral conversations between the Church of England and the Swedish Lutheran Church, between Anglicans and Old Catholics, and more recently between Anglicans and the Roman Catholic Church, the ordination of women presented a stumbling block as it did in the multilateral ecumenical conversations conducted by the Commission on Faith and Order.[29]

The last decades have, however, provided some clarification in relation to these conflict-ridden issues.

As a follow-up to a recommendation at Uppsala, Brigalia Bam organized an ecumenical consultation on the ordination of women in 1970 in Cartigny, Switzerland. It was to draw up positive reasons for women's ordination and gather experiences from the churches which were already ordaining women. "A church which seeks to be the people of God, a sacrament or sign of his presence in the world, must be a body where there is full cooperation between men and women. Today this is possible only if ordination of women is permitted." The theological arguments for the ordination of women highlighted the notion of man and woman made in God's image (Gen. 1:27) and the baptismal confession of men and women as one in Christ Jesus (Gal. 3:28). The leading role of women in the early church was lifted up and the classical anthropological arguments for linking Jesus' maleness with the sacramental priestly office were questioned. The influence of changing patterns of behaviour in many societies played a major role at the consultation – making impossible the use of earlier anthropologies. The "burden of proof" was beginning to pass from the advocates of women's ordination to those who re-

---

[28] Elisabeth Behr-Sigel, *Le ministère de la femme dans l'Eglise*, Paris, Cerf, 1987, p.18. English translation Jane E. Crawford, *Rocking the Boat: Women's Participation in the World Council of Churches 1948-1991*, p.364, and *The Ordination of Women in the Orthodox Church*, WCC, 2000.

[29] Cf. Mary Tanner, "Ordination of Women", in Nicholas Lossky et al. eds, *Dictionary of the Ecumenical Movement*, 2nd ed., WCC, 2002, pp.854-57.

jected it, and the assertion that women's ordination was a threat to the unity of the church was questioned.[30]

The consultation suffered, however, from the same weakness as the one that later was to weigh down the Community study: the Orthodox voice, with only one Orthodox participant, was not sufficiently audible. A reaction was inevitable. It came, predominantly, from Faith and Order. The Commission's meeting in 1971 reported that "strong emotions are aroused when this subject is discussed" – nineteen hundred years of Tradition against the ordination of women could not simply be cast aside without any consideration. It was, however, acknowledged that traditions could be changed, and that the time had come to face the question.[31]

The Orthodox took up the challenge a few years later and in 1976 organized a consultation in Agape, Romania, on the role of women in the church. Prominent Orthodox clergy as well as lay men and women participated. As in all later Orthodox consultations and statements, the representatives of the churches asserted the particular dignity and strength of women in the early church in which women deaconesses had important liturgical functions, and they suggested reactivating the non-sacramental ministries of women. The participants recommended that (1) theological education be made available to women; (2) the "office of deaconess be studied and considered for 'reactivation' in churches where the needs of society could be met more effectively by such a service", and (3) women be placed on the decision-making bodies in which lay people are included, e.g. parish councils.[32]

A "change of paradigms", as Letty Russell called it in retrospect,[33] was indeed achieved at the consultation in Klingenthal near Strasbourg in 1979. For the first time ordination and ministry were discussed from the perspective of women, rather than beginning with the viewpoints of the male ordained church representatives. The equality of men and women in baptism was emphasized and most Orthodox participants were agreed that the diaconate could offer new possibilities for an ordained ministry for women in the church.[34]

At the beginning of the 1980s the question of women's ordination did not seem to get any easier, but on the contrary became more complicated – and the impatience of Protestant (and Anglican) women was pitted against an increasingly defensive stand of the Orthodox churches that neither felt understood nor sufficiently integrated into the WCC framework.[35]

The convergence text on *Baptism, Eucharist and Ministry* (1982) dealt with the ordination of women in the main text and in a commentary (M18), listing the diverse interpretations (including the Roman Catholic) without coming to a convergence on this

---

[30] Brigalia Bam ed., *What Is Ordination Coming To? Report of a Consultation on the Ordination of Women, Cartigny, Switzerland, 21-26 Sept. 1970*, WCC, 1971, pp.1,72,64,60,59.

[31] "The Ordained Ministry", in *Faith and Order Louvain 1971: Study Reports and Documents*, Faith and Order paper no. 59, WCC, 1971, p.93.

[32] *Orthodox Women, Their Role and Participation in the Orthodox Church: Report on the Consultation of Orthodox Women, September 1976, Agapia, Romania*, WCC, 1977.

[33] Letty M. Russell: "Women and Unity: Problem or Possibility", in *Mid-Stream: An Ecumenical Journal*, 21, 1982, p.303.

[34] Constance F. Parvey ed., *Ordination of Women in Ecumenical Perspective: Workbook for the Church's Future*, WCC, 1980, pp.13-15.

[35] "Orthodox Churches Express Desire for More Participation in WCC", in *The Ecumenical Review*, 33, 1981, p.398.

point. The commentary mentions specifically that none of the churches which ordain women to the priestly function have had reason to reconsider their decision.[36]

The 1988 Orthodox conference in Rhodes (called by the Ecumenical Patriarchate of Constantinople) on the "Place of Women in the Orthodox Church and the Question of the Ordination of Women" deepened the theological argumentation in favour of a better understanding and a renewal of the role of women in the Orthodox church. The ministry of deaconesses was again put up as an example of a possible step in this renewal. In the story of salvation Mary is the all-important female figure, not Eve, and it follows that discrimination against women has no biblical justification. Rather, dignity, respect and space are due to women for their full development. The reflection on the lower orders has continued since Rhodes. On the other hand, the conference again drew upon the classic arguments against women's ordination to the priesthood.[37]

Neither at Agape 1976 nor at the Rhodes conference 12 years later did Orthodox women question their exclusion from the priesthood. The situation was different in the Roman Catholic Church. In 1976 the Vatican's Congregation for the Doctrine of the Faith had pronounced itself against the ordination of women. The reactions from Catholic lay people, both women and men, to these declarations led in some countries to campaigns for an altogether new shape of the Roman Catholic Church. Millions of signatures asked for more democracy in the church and especially for the ordination of women.

The ordination of women continues to be a controversial subject in the ecumenical movement, even if a certain silent agreement on avoiding the issue in official meetings has been reached. Nevertheless, in 1992 there were strong Roman Catholic and Orthodox reactions to the Church of England's decision in favour of the ordination of women to the priesthood – which had been preceded in 1976 by the national Anglican churches of Canada, the US and New Zealand, and in the 1990s by decisions to admit women to the episcopate: according to these reactions the unity of the church and the respective bilateral conversations were put in jeopardy.[38] Many women are currently asking how they should react. Keep silent, or rather build on maturing ecumenical relationships in an open and honest search for truth in love? The dialogue on the ordination of women has not come to an end.

The participation debate: theological assumptions, advocacy and enablement

The ordination debate generated passions, not least because the exclusion of women from ordained ministries implied exclusion from power. More serious and far-reaching, however, were the discriminatory practices in many member churches of the WCC.

In 1985, in her retrospective on five years as director of the WCC's Women's desk, Bärbel von Wartenberg wrote,

> There are some churches where young girls are not brought to the altar during baptism; this honour is reserved for the boys, thus initiating a pattern of subjugation that will plague

---

[36] *Baptism, Eucharist and Ministry*, WCC, 1982, pp.23f,25.

[37] *The Place of the Woman in the Orthodox Church and the Question of the Ordination of Women: Inter-Orthodox Symposium, Rhodos, Greece, 30 October-7 November 1988*, Istanbul, Ecumenical Patriarchate, 1988, p.5. See also Gennadios Limouris in *One World*, 150, Nov. 1989.

[38] Cf. the message of the primates of the holy Orthodox churches which identifies two major stumbling blocks to the unity of the church: the ordination of women and the use of inclusive language in speaking about God. The Vatican threatened to break off Anglican-Roman Catholic conversations. See also "Ordination of Women" by Mary Tanner in *Dictionary of the Ecumenical Movement*.

women throughout their lives in the church. In such a structure, no community of partners is possible.[39]

In 1975 the Nairobi assembly had foreseen needs consistent with this later insight in drafting the following guidelines for the future work of the Women's department:

1) to work on the theological assumptions held by the churches and by individuals which limit the participation of women;

2) to advocate the fuller and better participation of women within the WCC and the member churches and to draw attention to women's concerns;

3) to enable women, who are often emotionally, educationally and politically inadequately prepared for full participation; and

4) to communicate with churches, women's groups and within the WCC structures and so to strengthen the advocacy for women's concerns.[40]

The WCC's Women's desk organized a consultation of women in church leadership in 1977 in Glion, Switzerland. It was thus no longer a matter of talking about such women but rather of talking with them, in order to develop new perspectives.[41]

Conscious of the theological stances implied in the subordination of women in many churches, the Women's department increasingly emphasized the theological dimension of the justice question. Women could no longer accept the assignment of the oppression of women to a purely cultural level, as had been attempted by some church leaders over and over again in the past.

An ecumenical theology of women was to be developed: "The world is not seen as a whole if only seen and named by the male half of humanity."[42] This could happen only internationally, and the Women's department of the WCC energetically supported every attempt by women theologians to network beyond the barriers of confession and culture. The women's commission of the Ecumenical Association of Third World Theologians (EATWOT), the European Society of Women doing Research in Theology (ESWTR) and other networks were established, and a consultation on women in church and society in Egypt in 1978 debated women's role from the perspective of the Bible, as well as church history and canon law, and the relationship between mission and development. Development of grassroots theology emerging from the life experience of ordinary people and new forms of theological language and Bible study was high on women's ecumenical agenda.[43]

This work was broadened by attention to other religions. A study in connection with the UN Decade for Women (1975) confirmed that religious values were not the least significant factor in hindering women's equal participation in public life, and that these values were tied to moralizing judgments on women's physical body. Cultural taboos were often reinforced through religious teachings. In order to examine some of these connections, the WCC, under the leadership of Marie Assaad, sponsored a study on the theme "Female Sexuality and Bodily Functions in Different Religions". A small

[39] In *Women in a Changing World*, 20, Nov. 1985, p.3.
[40] Cf. *Breaking Barriers: Nairobi 1975*, section I, §26, section II, §9, section V, §§39-56.
[41] *Half the World's People: A Report of the Consultation of Church Women Executives, Glion, Switzerland, Jan. 1977*, WCC, 1978, p.15.
[42] Bärbel von Wartenberg, in *Women in a Changing World*, 20, Nov. 1985, p.3.
[43] *We Listened Long Before We Spoke, Report of the Consultation of Women Theological Students, Cartigny, Switzerland, July 1978*, WCC, 1979. *By Our Lives... Stories of Women – Today and in the Bible*, WCC, 1985. John S. Pobee and Bärbel von Wartenberg-Potter eds, *New Eyes for Reading: Biblical and Theological Reflections by Women from the Third World*, WCC, 1986.

group of women theologians and anthropologists from various Christian churches, and from the great religions of Judaism, Islam, Buddhism and Hinduism, looked at the official teachings of their respective religions regarding the nature of woman and her relationship to man; the female life-cycle; women's rites on reaching puberty, adulthood or menopause; a woman's place in the family, religious community and society; and women's expectations for themselves. The study, published in 1990, gathered a wealth of findings about cultural differences and the ever-returning pattern of a patriarchal value system which has everywhere a dominant impact on religious teachings. The study makes evident how urgently women in all religions need to be more involved in the interpretation of their religious scriptures and tradition, especially when these deal with women's role and sexuality. The study argues that women need to discriminate between the central and unchanging essence in religious teaching and what has been incorporated in each religion through the powerful impact of culture, particularly regarding values which relegate women to an inferior position.[44]

Inclusive language

Language is the most effective mirror of cultural reality. It creates as well as interprets relations between human beings in a particular cultural context; every current language expresses superiority and subordination, reveals or keeps quiet about particular realities of life. In connection with the women's movement of the 1960s, the feminist language-critique emerged first in the US with the demand for a non-discriminatory "inclusive" language, which was taken up in Western Europe during the 1970s.[45] With regard to semantics and morphology, it has been shown to what degree women have either been limited, made invisible or devalued in the use of vocabulary and idioms. Women in the churches quickly took up such reflections ("Don't call us brothers!") and began to look for new inclusive forms of liturgical expression. In the US, at the behest of the National Council of the Churches of Christ, an *Inclusive Language Lectionary* was developed, which contained the readings for a three-year cycle in a non-sexist version.[46]

Particularly explosive in terms of the ecumenical discussion was the attempt to develop new images and names for the Persons of the Trinity, and to widen the traditional male image of God. Some women liturgists and theologians suggested adding the name of mother to the name of God the Father, while others focused on images of God which derive from the living reality experienced by women – as for example in the parable of the kingdom of God, where God is compared with a woman who was looking for her lost coin and who rejoices with her friends when she had found her treasure (Luke 15:1-10).

Although liturgical texts have been produced in editions acceptable to women, they have rarely found an entry into the general liturgy and they have been unable to permeate official ecumenical texts. Orthodox church representatives see "inclusive lan-

---

44 See Jeanne Becher ed., *Women, Religion and Sexuality: Studies on the Impact of Religious Teachings on Women*, WCC, 1990, p.x.

45 Cf. Hildburg Wegener: "Language/Language Change", in Elisabeth Gössmann et al. eds, *Wörterbuch der Feministischen Theologie*, Gütersloh, Gütersloher/Mohn, 1991, p.387ff.

46 *An Inclusive Language Lectionary*, Division of Education and Ministry, NCCCUSA, Atlanta, 1983 Year A, 1984 Year B, 1985 Year C.

guage" as damaging the holy Tradition brought down to them and some women's groups from the East and the South have also opposed Western demands for inclusive language.[47]

However, ecumenical texts and speaking use inclusive language forms to a great extent – provided that they do not refer directly to God.[48]

The discussion about participation and quotas

In order to achieve full participation of women, the Women's department of the WCC, as well as countless women in the churches around the world, have invested a great deal of energy, time and fantasy on securing quotas of representation. At the WCC assembly in Canberra (1991) women had 38 percent of the delegates' seats. "Participation means representation, numbers of positions occupied by women."[49] It follows that men must give up these seats, and in so doing must renounce some power and influence and become accustomed to relate to women in leadership positions.[50]

Following Pauline Webb's appointment as vice-moderator of the central committee at Uppsala (1968), Kiyoko Takedo Cho was elected a president in 1970, the second woman after Sarah Chakko to serve in this office. In Nairobi (1975) two women were elected presidents, while Vancouver (1983) and Canberra (1991) each elected three women presidents.[51] However, Harare (1998) slipped back to two women.

At the end of the 1970s, the WCC's Geneva staff was strengthened with an increased number of women in executive positions, and in 1980 Marie Assaad of the Coptic Orthodox Church in Egypt was appointed deputy general secretary. Significantly more women became involved in the work of the commissions as moderators and members.

The quota system represents a successful method for reaching equal representation. Women and youth argued that quotas would help identify women and young people in the churches and involve them in ecumenical work.[52] Intensified after Nairobi, the demands for quotas achieved their real breakthrough in 1981 at the Dresden central committee where the 30 percent clause for women's participation at all WCC levels was accepted. It became visible for the first time in 1983 at the WCC's Vancouver assembly.

---

[47] *The Sheffield Report*, p.163. Constance Parvey tried to mediate between the different positions in saying that steps towards inclusive language must certainly be taken, but that they need not be seen merely as an adoption of Western language patterns. They can provide an opening to learn more from non-Western languages about how God is expressed, experienced and understood.

[48] One example is the blessing that Lois Wilson formulated at the beginning of the 1980s and which has since found acceptance in ecumenical worship as well as in the worship of many churches, parishes and groups: "The blessing of the God of Sarah and of Abraham, the blessing of the Son, born of the woman Mary, the blessing of the Holy Spirit who broods over us as a mother with her children, be with you all. Amen." In Iben Gjerding and Katherine Kinnamon eds, *No Longer Strangers: A Resource for Women and Worship*, WCC, 1983, p.45.

[49] Bärbel von Wartenberg-Potter, in *Women in a Changing World*, 20, Nov. 1985, p.3.

[50] Cf. the report by Marie Assaad (WCC deputy general secretary from 1980) about her first experiences in this position. "I don't know whether it is... because I am a woman, but on numerous occasions I found myself automatically excluded..." Worship on "Leadership: A Question of Power", in *Women in a Changing World*, 22, Oct. 1986, p.8.

[51] Nairobi 1975: Justice Annie Jiagge (Ghana) and Cynthia Wedel (US); Vancouver 1983: Nita Barrow (Barbados), Marga Bührig (Switzerland), and Lois Wilson (Canada); Canberra 1991: Anna Marie Aagaard (Denmark), Priyanka Mendis (Sri Lanka), Eunice Santana (Puerto Rico).

[52] Cf. Reinhild Traitler, "An Oikoumene of Women?", in *The Ecumenical Review*, 40, 2, April 1985, p.184.

Women made themselves heard and seen at all levels and made an impression on the style and climate of the assembly as never before.[53]

The Vancouver programme guidelines committee recommended that, in the future work of the WCC, "The concerns and perspectives of women should become integral to the work of all WCC units and sub-units." The principle of "mainstreaming" was thus introduced into WCC bodies much before it gained momentum in the secular world, as for example in the European Union. The Women's department had successfully struggled to get this principle accepted – even if it was the first step towards the goal of making its own existence superfluous, as Bärbel von Wartenberg, then director of the Women's desk, admitted later.[54] Women's concerns were subsequently given attention in every WCC programme planning and assessment.

The world conference on resource sharing in El Escorial, Spain, in 1987 accepted a guideline which provided for a 50 percent quota of women in all decision-making or consultative bodies that would be set up as a result of the conference. The decision was to a great extent realized, with the support of the Decade of the Churches in Solidarity with Women (1988-98). The Canberra assembly visibly illustrated the success achieved by the quota system: it significantly changed the face of the oikoumene. But it was controversial from the beginning. A major problem was the representativeness of the women or youth sent to ecumenical conferences on behalf of their churches. How could they create links between the churches and the oikoumene if they had no access to decision-making bodies in their churches and possessed no forum of their own? Implicit in the heated discussions was the concern that the WCC would lose its authority in relation to the member churches, if the churches were represented by women who had no influence back home.[55]

In 1988 the WCC's executive committee urged the member churches to name only such delegates to Canberra who were recognized by their own churches, who were aware of their church's opinion about the issues (and would be able to present them) and who were in a position to bring back to their churches the decisions of the assembly.[56] At the same time, the criticism was reiterated that the strong representation of women and youth made the WCC no longer a council of churches. The quotas were seen as driving the WCC into meaninglessness;[57] the numbers game was considered prejudicial to the search for truly competent personalities into leadership roles. Women participants at Canberra raised self-critical questions about quotas at WCC assemblies because churches used these rules as an alibi for not increasing women's participation in their own structures. They advocated that the task of bringing women and youth into decision-making positions was therefore to be given back to the member churches.

---

[53] Women delegates to WCC assemblies (total number of delegates in brackets): Amsterdam 1948: (350) 22, 6% – Evanston 1954: (502) 44, 8.7% – New Delhi 1961: (581) 42, 8.5% – Uppsala 1968: (688) 50, 7.2% – Nairobi 1975: (677) 148, 22% – Vancouver 1983: (835) 247, 29.9% – Canberra 1991: (852) 298, 35%. At the 1998 Harare assembly, which celebrated the Council's fiftieth anniversary, participation by women plummeted to 28%, while men surged back to their accustomed control at 62%.

[54] See von Wartenberg-Potter, "Be Wise as Serpents...", in *Women in a Changing World*, 20, Nov. 1985, p.3.

[55] Constance Parvey, "Participation: A Pilgrimage of Agony and Hope", in *The Ecumenical Review*, 40, 4, 1988, pp.500-501.

[56] Quoted by David Gill, "Participation: Beyond the Numbers Game", in *The Ecumenical Review*, 1988, 40, 4, p.492.

[57] Elisabeth Raiser, "Spiritualität und Partizipation, Eindrücke von der Vollversammlung in Canberra aus Frauensicht", in *Ökumenische Rundschau*, Heft 3, Juli 1991, p.386.

"Serious concern" about the quota system was again expressed in the document "Costly Unity" (1993), issued as a reflection on the interdependence between ecclesiology and ethics. While acknowledging the quota system as a means of achieving participation, the document judges that the system had become self-defeating and actually narrowed, rather than ensured constructive exchange.[58] But where would the participation of women be today without the quota system?

Women in the conciliar process

The conciliar process for justice, peace and the integrity of creation (JPIC) began at Vancouver (1983), but justice, peace and creation issues had occupied the oikoumene of women for many years beforehand.

The period of military dictatorships in Latin America, Asia and Africa witnessed a rapid growth of militarization with disastrous consequences for women and children. Simultaneously, the feminization of poverty, increasing prostitution and trade in women were all becoming major concerns.

During the 1970s a number of women's solidarity groups were established in democratically ruled countries, and the ecumenical movement served as a clearing-house for networking and planning. The women's departments of the various ecumenical organizations began to work closely together and to coordinate their contacts with women's groups in the NGOs.

Such contacts were used to plan the very effective anti-apartheid campaigns which lasted for 15 years. These campaigns linked conscientization about the apartheic system in South Africa with concrete actions of solidarity. Countless numbers of women in the North were able to mobilize themselves. "Don't buy the fruits of apartheid! Politics with a shopping basket" became part of their programme. Political consciousness-raising and concrete actions also characterized women's campaigns in the South, e.g. the Chipko movement to save the trees in India, or the Green Belt movement to replant trees in Kenya.

In the solidarity campaigns for women victims of sex tourism, forced prostitution and trade in women and children, the ecumenical institutions worked closely with local groups especially in the Philippines, Thailand, Japan and Indonesia.[59] In 1979, at a human-rights conference organized by the Women's department, Sister Mary John Mananzan, OSB, described the desperate situation of prostitutes in Asia, especially those in the tourist centres and near military bases.[60] In accordance with a 1981 recommendation from the central committee, the Women's department, together with the human rights office and the Commission on the Churches' Participation in Development undertook a study, later presented to the UN Human Rights Commission,[61] of sexual exploitation and the desperate situation of women in specific countries.

The ecumenical efforts called attention to many concrete examples of human-rights violations against women visible and brought them to the attention of member churches and the international community: rape and torture of imprisoned women, sexual mis-

---

[58] "Costly Unity", in Thomas F. Best and Martin Robra eds, *Ecclesiology and Ethics: Ecumenical Ethical Engagement, Moral Formation and the Nature of the Church*, WCC, 1997, p.22.
[59] Cf. "Prostitution and Tourism – Women Act in Solidarity", in *Women in a Changing World*, Dec. 1981.
[60] "Sexual Exploitation in a Third World Setting", in *Human Rights: World Council of Churches Documentation*, WCC, 1979, and the report of the conference on women, human rights and mission, Venice, Italy, June 1979.
[61] "Sexual Exploitation in a Third World Setting", in *ibid.*, p.7.

use, killing of "witches", female circumcision, domestic violence, exploitation of household employees, the burning of widows, forced labour and judicial dependency, lack of health care especially for young girls.

As a partial fulfilment of its focus on "enablement", in 1978 the WCC Women's Department initiated a programme on "Women in Rural Development" which, in the period up to 1983, accompanied 91 small self-help projects aiming at women's analysis of their economic and social situation and autonomous self-reliance.[62]

The international peace movement of the 1970s and early 1980s encouraged the growth of women's peace groups. In Israel women founded the "Women in Black", in Argentina the "Mothers of the Plaza de Mayo". Networking done by these groups represented important attempts at breaking through the sometimes paralyzing isolation. The central focus of the work of the Women's desk, which had become an important partner in this network, was a determined opposition against the arms race and war. At the WCC Women's consultation in 1981 in Nassau, Bahamas, on the theme "Choose Life – Work for Peace", women drew attention to the close link between the – both nuclear and conventional – arms race of the past decade and the growing injustice, the "weaponless war" against the poor in every region of the world. With the words "the threats to peace grow out of a deep lack of social justice on a global level", they recognized a link which later became a principal part of the agenda of the conciliar process.[63]

The abundance of studies, declarations and Bible studies by women on the themes of justice, peace, reconciliation and creation led the Sub-unit on Women in Church and Society in 1984 to focus on the conciliar process from women's point of view and, consequently, it organized between 1986 and 1990 women's conferences in all regions which worked on specific questions related to the JPIC process.[64]

In the course of the process, women from the South kept drawing attention to the disastrous effects of unbridled capitalism which were just as obvious as were the fatal consequences of the cold war, with its continuing process of atomic tests in the Pacific. Asian women concentrated on the effects of militarism on women and children. The Africa meeting was concerned with apartheid, deforestation, the refugee problem, the exploitation of women workers, and the dumping of atomic waste. A group of Swiss women developed some feminist theses on JPIC, which were to influence the discussion in numerous European church women's groups. The theses stated that women have a different fault to confess than men, namely their passive complicity with capitalism and environmental destruction, and the lack of readiness to take responsibility; hence, women must seek a different kind of liberation.

Although some felt that women's contribution to the JPIC process was not taken seriously enough at the official WCC level,[65] the world convocation on JPIC in Seoul in

---

[62] *Towards Self-Reliance: A Handbook on Rural Development I*, and *Mobilising Rural Women for Awareness, Analysis, Action: A Handbook on Rural Development II*, WCC, 1980.

[63] "A Letter from the Participants", in *Choose Life – Work for Peace*, Nassau, Bahamas, Dec. 1981, WCC, 1982, p.6.

[64] Cf. Thomas F. Best, *From Vancouver to Canberra: 1983-1990*, WCC, 1990, p.227; see pp.229-30 for the list of these meetings relating to the JPIC process.

[65] Cf. for example the critique of the preparatory process for Seoul by Jane Carey Peck and Jeanne Gallo, in "JPIC: A Critique from a Feminist Perspective", in *The Ecumenical Review*, 46, 1989, pp.573-81; Margot Kässmann: "The Process Leading to Seoul and Canberra: Points of Strength and Weakness", in Preman Niles ed., *Between the Flood and the Rainbow*, pp.8-16; and Marga Bührig: "The World Convocation: Problems, Achievements", in *ibid.*, pp.17-25.

1990 did respond to a certain degree to the challenge: the fourth of the ten affirmations in which the churches committed themselves to covenant for life referred explicitly to the community of women and men and highlighted the strength and power of women in their struggles for life and dignity.[66]

The Ecumenical Decade: Churches in Solidarity with Women

In 1985 the UN Women's Decade came to an end with a conference in Nairobi, at which the WCC played an active role. Reports arguing that the women had made no progress, especially in religious communities including the churches, made the WCC propose a church-related women's decade.[67] In 1987 the WCC's central committee called upon the churches, for a period of ten years, to take active steps in favour of women, to pay more focused attention to their concerns and cooperate closely with women's organizations and groups. The Decade was officially launched at Easter 1988 with the following objectives:

- empowering women to challenge oppressive structures in the global community, their churches and communities;
- affirming – through shared leadership and decision-making, theology and spirituality – the decisive contributions of women in churches and communities;
- giving visibility to women's perspectives and actions in the work and struggle for justice, peace and the integrity of creation;
- enabling the churches to free themselves of racism, sexism and classism, and from teachings and practices that discriminate against women; and
- encouraging the churches to take actions in solidarity with women.

In its aim and conception, the Decade had close links with the Community of Women and Men in the Church study initiated at the Nairobi assembly. The Decade call assumed that there is an "unsegregated" church and asked the churches to care for the totality of its membership. It was a call for inclusiveness in all aspects of church life which included the challenge to show economic solidarity with women. In addition, a further emphasis emerged, that of violence against women.[68]

From the beginning the Decade had difficulties becoming a decade *of* the *churches*. Because it dealt with the situation of women, it was almost everywhere passed on to women's organizations and was scarcely taken up at all in the decision-making bodies of the churches.[69] In spite of several women-related programmes of the WCC, the concept of inclusive community had hardly realized a foothold in most of the churches. Women's concerns remained in the "women's corner".

At the Canberra assembly (1991) the Decade received a good deal of visibility, but the pressures on some female delegates to withdraw their candidature for the new central committee in favour of male candidates brought disillusion and disappointment. It became clear that the Decade needed a new stimulus. Aruna Gnanadason from India, di-

---

[66] "Final Document", world convocation on "Justice, Peace and the Integrity of Creation", Seoul 1990, WCC, 1990, Affirmation no. 4.

[67] Mercy Oduyoye, *Who Will Roll the Stone Away? The Ecumenical Decade: Churches in Solidarity with Women*, WCC, 1990, p.1. Cf. World Council of Churches Central Committee, *Minutes of the Thirty-Seventh Meeting, Buenos Aires, Argentina, 1985*, p.57.

[68] For the whole issue cf. Aruna Gnanadason, *No Longer a Secret: The Church and Violence against Women*, WCC, 1993.

[69] Cf. the "Report of Regional Women's Desk Meeting, Geneva, February 1992". See also the letter of 27 April 1994 by the mid-Decade consultant, Nicole Fischer, to the regional women's desks.

rector of the Women's department since 1990, convened an evaluation consultation in January 1992, where the ambitious idea of team visits to every member church was born. A first Decade visit to four countries of West Africa in 1989 had proved quite effective both in making the Decade known and in supporting the local women. It offered women one of the very first opportunities to make church leaders aware of the culturally conditioned traditional practices against women in everyday village life and to ask them to intervene in matters that had hitherto been taboo, as for example the exclusion of widows from active participation in village communities.

The systematic team visits began in 1993 and were more or less completed by the end of 1996. Each of the seventy teams was set up separately, mostly with four to five members, wherever possible including two men and two women, a staff member and a woman from the receiving country. The teams travelled as so-called "living letters", using the apostle Paul's image, to some 330 churches, 68 national councils of churches and 650 women's groups in all regions of the world to discuss the concerns of the Decade (including violence against women) and the concerns of local women's groups.[70] In many churches the Decade was successful in mobilizing women, and in some the Decade has led to developing women's desks and training programmes for women. A change of consciousness may have taken place and solidarity with women may have grown. However, much remains to be done. Violence against women seems to be a very difficult issue almost everywhere, and many churches are reluctant to uncover it in their own circles and to become advocates for the victims in society.[71]

The Decade concluded as planned in December 1998 with a festival held at Harare, just before the WCC's eighth assembly. More than a thousand women joined by about thirty men assessed what the Decade had achieved, outlined the remaining tasks, and urged the churches to move into the new millennium proceeding "from solidarity to accountability". The festival challenged the ecumenical movement to continue to raise the many issues women wrestle with. There was also a strong call to deal more consistently with the ecclesiological and theological challenges that are at the heart of the true community of women and men.

A new impetus for solidarity is to be the concept "Towards Building a Just Community", and the invitation to men to take up more strongly than heretofore the consequences of patriarchal thinking and doing, which put limitations on their own lives. There is a rethinking of the concept of women's work. "If men are part of the problem, they should become part of the solution also" became a growing conviction of many women and led to a new gender approach. If women do not succeed in convincing men of the promises of a new community in partnership, then little will change in the long term. Only together can men and women build this new community.

The Decade had come to an end in 1998. But there was now an opportunity to listen to and learn from its insights and from women as they continued to explore fundamental questions about what sort of church God calls us to be. A reflection and action process, entitled "Women's Voices and Visions: On Being Church", has been initiated to bring before the churches some insights from women's perspectives on ways of being church that were revealed in the Decade, in such a way that the churches themselves

---

70 Cf. *Living Letters: A Report of Visits to the Churches during the Ecumenical Decade – Churches in Solidarity with Women*, WCC, 1997.
71 Cf. "Implications of the Decade Team Visits on the World Council of Churches: Paper of the Working Group on Women", La Longeraie, Nov.-Dec. 1995.

take account of these perspectives and respond to women's deepest aspirations for community *(koinonia)*, justice and solidarity.

With women (and men) around the world, this new study explores: what it means to be called by God to live in and for the world; what forms of spirituality would nurture the life of the church as community; how the ministry of the whole church might be renewed to include the gifts that God gives to both men and women for service; and what structures would better equip the church for faithfulness in its task of witness and service in the world. The hope is that out of this listening to, and engagement with, women's voices and visions may come renewal and greater unity.

LAITY

The concern for lay participation has been present in the ecumenical movement from the beginning. The second assembly of the WCC (Evanston 1954) gave prominence to this concern and the affirmation, "The laity stand at the very outposts of the kingdom of God: they are the missionaries of Christ in every secular sphere"[72] was repeated and strengthened at the third assembly (New Delhi 1961). After Evanston, the WCC accepted the challenge to stimulate the involvement of lay people in the whole life and mission of the church by establishing a department of the Laity as a part of the new Division of Ecumenical Action. While the terminology and interest focused mainly on lay *men*, the programmatic emphases – centred on the laity's missionary responsibility in the secular sphere – presupposed the cooperation of women and men. There was also a clear recognition that rediscovery of the laity had implications for the understanding of the ministry. The department's major study, "Christ's Ministry and the Ministry of the Church", thus served as a starting point for the section on ministry at the third world conference on Faith and Order at Montreal (1963) which stated,

> A recovery of the doctrine of the laity has brought with it a recognition that ministry is the responsibility of the whole body, not only of those who are ordained. This recovery is one of the most important facts of the recent church history...[73]

The spirit of the whole period up to the WCC Uppsala assembly in 1968 is well captured by the following paragraph:

> There is increasing evidence within and among churches throughout the world that an enlightened and committed laity hold the key to the renewal of the church. It is through the engagement of the laity as the church in the world that the mission of Christ in today's world is most effectively carried out. Therefore, to be concerned about laity is to be concerned about the renewal and mission of the church.[74]

The concern for lay participation has found many expressions beyond the WCC and its Department on the Laity, e.g. the older Christian lay movements among youth, like the YMCA, the YWCA, the WSCF and, since 1953, Syndesmos, the World Fellowship of Orthodox Youth. Two of the pan-Orthodox conferences (1961 and 1968) considered the

[72] W.A. Visser 't Hooft ed., *The Evanston Report: Second Assembly of the WCC*, London, SCM Press, 1955, p.103.

[73] P.C. Rodger and L. Vischer eds, *The Third World Conference on Faith and Order: The Report from Montreal 1963*, New York, Association Press, 1964, p.62.

[74] *New Delhi to Uppsala: 1961-1968. Report of the Central Committee to the Fourth Assembly of the World Council of Churches*, WCC, 1968, p.91.

topic of "more complete participation of the laity in the devotional and other life of the church", but it was not included in the agenda of the envisaged pan-Orthodox synod.

Within the Roman Catholic Church, Vatican II underlined the mission of the laity, especially in its Decree on the Apostolate of the Laity (1965), by placing it in the context of an understanding of the church as the "people of God".

Even before the promulgation of the Council's decree, in 1965 the Permanent Committee for International Congresses of the Lay Apostolate and the WCC's Laity department had begun cooperation and sponsored a consultation on laity formation. Common efforts regarding lay training became the central focus of an increasingly close cooperation, also with the Pontifical Council for the Laity (established in 1967), leading up to a major joint consultation on "New Trends in Laity Formation" (1974). The more recent apostolic exhortation *Christifideles Laici* of Pope John Paul II (1988) returned to the traditional Roman Catholic position according to which the vocation of the laity and of ordained ministry is different "not only simply in degree, but in essence".

For the WCC, Uppsala was a turning point. The assembly initiated a discussion on "new styles of living" which reflected many concerns of Christian lay people. Further consideration of the laity and their self-understanding became less important than the content of their mission and service in the world in the struggle against racial, political and economic injustices. The plan to continue the discussion with a study project of the Division on Ecumenical Action about contemporary morality ("Participation in Change") moved the focus of interest from "the laity" to grassroots initiatives, people's movements and base communities with commitment to social change and church renewal.[75]

While Uppsala expressed concern about the participation of lay people in the life of the WCC,[76] the re-examination of the Council's structures after the assembly led to the gradual disappearance of the Laity department which was absorbed into the Sub-unit on Renewal and Congregational Life. Thus began a period when the word "laity" virtually disappeared from ecumenical discussions.[77] The main issue of the sub-unit was spiritual and liturgical renewal; it conducted workshops and related to church base communities and networks. In 1968 the Association of Directors of Evangelical Academies and Lay Institutes in Europe together with the Department on the Laity organized a Course for Leaders of Lay Training (CLLT) from Africa, Asia and Latin America. This and a subsequent course encouraged the formation of associations of Christian lay training centres and institutes for social concern in Asia (ACISCA 1970) and in Africa (ACLA 1970). The sub-unit had a desk for lay and study centres, which functioned as a secretariat for the World Collaboration Committee of Christian Lay Centres, Academies and Movements for Social Concern, founded in Crete in 1972. The academy movement spread into many parts of the world, and continental associations were formed. Other issues, initially linked with a focus on the laity, developed into ecumenical programmes, e.g. education, development, dialogue.

Since the beginning of the WCC, its Ecumenical Institute at Bossey played an important role in exploring work with and among lay people, especially through its courses for lay leaders. In Germany the "Kirchentag" (begun in 1949-50) turned into an impressive forum of discussion about the vocation of lay people in the life of church and society.

---

75 Cf. Ian M. Fraser, *The Fire Runs: God's People Participating in Change*, London, SCM Press, 1975.
76 *The Uppsala Report*, pp.189f.
77 Cf. Hearing on Unit III: Education and Renewal, in *Breaking Barriers*, pp.310f.

The academies and laity centres and their worldwide network became decisive laboratories for "ecumenical learning" by their struggle to make "this whole inhabited earth – the oikoumene – inhabitable for all people". The most important in these efforts were the courses for leaders in lay training (CLLT) in Bangalore, India (1976), and Dodoma, Tanzania (1985), the world consultations on lay training at Naramata, Canada, in 1977 and Ibadan, Nigeria, in 1982, and ecumenical team visits in the form of "visiting communities".

By the end of the 20th century, the "new lay movement" linked almost six hundred centres of lay training in all parts of the world.[78] An evaluation (1990) led to the affirmation of the three "Ls", i.e. lay training, leadership and ecumenical learning as priorities for empowering the laity. The evaluation also called for the re-establishment of the Laity department in the WCC which would imply a renewed recognition of the "lay question" and its importance for the ecumenical movement. "The new form of lay activities – base communities, justice and peace movements, solidarity and ecological groups, women's movements, all often outside traditional church structures – are as decisive as the position of the official church."[79]

The programmatic reorganization of the WCC following the Canberra assembly (1991) led to the formation of a "stream" on "lay participation towards inclusive community" as part of the new programme unit on Unity and Renewal. The WCC thus acknowledged as a priority the task to contribute to the "formation and participation of lay people in the life and mission of the church, in close cooperation with Christian lay centres and movements".[80] The message from the world convention of Christian lay centres and movements in 1993 unfolds a "vision of the visiting God" as the source of hope for the network of communities. It states,

> It has often been said that in Christ's church there are clergy and laity who each have to fulfill their special tasks. Frequently this distinction between clergy and laity has led to a separation, linked with an uneven distribution of power and influence. We experienced and remembered, however, that the biblical stories at their core do not contain such division, separation or abyss between clergy and laity. Clergy and lay people together are all members of the one people of God, members of the one body of Christ and endowed with the one Spirit of God.[81]

A new profile of the laity in the ecumenical movement is emerging which sees lay people as "agents of the ecumenical learning process".[82]

A special session on the *laos* at the WCC's central committee in Johannesburg (1994) highlighted the ecumenical concept of the laity and its new profile. It underlined the need for further clarification of the terms, especially in view of the strong ecclesiological

---

[78] Cf. the comprehensive presentation in Werner Simpfendörfer ed., *The New Fisherfolk*, WCC, 1988.

[79] Ans J. van der Bent, "Where Do We Come from? Our Background: Contribution to the Consultation on "New Ecumenical Perspectives on Laity", Orthodox Academy of Crete, February 1990, in Gert Rüppell ed., *Mooring for New Provisions – Sailing to New Venues*, WCC, 1991, p.9. Cf. also Ans J. van der Bent, *Laity in the Ecumenical Movement: An Analytical and Documentary Survey* (mimeographed paper).

[80] WCC Central Committee, *Minutes of the Forty-Fourth Meeting, Geneva, 1992*, p.82.

[81] *The World Convention of Christian Lay Centres and Movements: "Weaving Communities of Hope", Montreat, 30 August-10 September 1993: Final report*, compiled and edited by Nico Peterse and Evelyn Appiah, WCC, 1995, pp.134f.

[82] Konrad Raiser, "Laity in the Ecumenical Movement: Redefining the Profile", in *The Ecumenical Review*, 45, 4, Oct. 1993, p.382. This issue of *The Ecumenical Review* attempts to reopen the ecumenical discussion of the laity.

implications attached to the term "laity", and further discussion on the general issue of lay movements and their relationship with the church.[83]

"PARTNERS IN LIFE": THE DIFFERENTLY ABLED

While definitions vary, the term "disability" is generally used in church and ecumenical networks to refer to any emotional, mental or physical impairment that can prevent a person from participating fully in life and society. The usage "differently abled persons" is preferred in the WCC to the term "disabled persons" (or, earlier, "handicapped persons") as a way of affirming the wholeness and recognizing the potential of the person.

In the 1960s Christians began discussing how the differently abled could be liberated from their passive role as receivers of diaconal care, and rather become self-reliant persons and independent partners in church life. Movements such as "L'Arche" fostered the idea of home-communities and groups that would include both the differently abled and those in good health. These movements aimed at integrating the differently abled in normal social life and at creating possibilities for having differently abled persons live together with abled persons regardless of religious persuasion.[84]

Within the ecumenical movement, the Faith and Order study "Unity of the Church, Unity of Mankind" launched a fundamental enquiry into the self-understanding of the churches. At the Commission meeting in Louvain (1971) a whole section dealt with the ecclesiological significance of community with the differently abled. Their marginalization reveal the incompleteness of the unity of the church.[85] The report of section II of the Nairobi assembly (1975) stated,

> The disabled are treated as the weak to be served, rather than as fully committed, integral members of the body of Christ and the human family; the specific contribution which they have to give is ignored. This is the more serious because disability – a worldwide problem – is increasing...[86]

The WCC took several initiatives in the period between the Nairobi and Vancouver (1983) assemblies in order to sensitize the churches and to encourage them to take their own steps. A consultation on "The Life and Witness of the Handicapped in the Christian Community" in 1978 in Bad Saarow in the former East Germany, whose churches had a long tradition of work with the differently abled, focused on their spiritual contribution, and a second consultation in 1981 dealt with the "wholeness of the person" of the differently abled. In 1979 Faith and Order published *Partners in Life* with theological reflections, reports and testimonies from local situations which served as an exchange of experiences and insights among the churches.

The Year of the Handicapped (1981), the subsequent UN Decade and the movements of the differently abled led both society and the churches to a new appreciation of them as partners and citizens with equal rights. In several countries, such as Great Britain,

[83] Cf. Elisabeth Adler and Jonah Katoneene, "Laity", in *Dictionary of the Ecumenical Movement*, p.662.
[84] See Jean Vanier in *The Challenge of L'Arche*, London, Darton, Longman & Todd, 1982, pp.1-10.
[85] Cf. Ernst Lange, *Die ökumenische Utopie oder Was bewegt die ökumenische Bewegung?*, Stuttgart, Kreuz, 1972, pp.155ff.; and L. Newbigin, "Not Whole without the Handicapped", in G. Müller-Fahrenholz ed., *Partners in Life: The Handicapped and the Church*, WCC, 1979, p.25. Cf. further "The Unity of the Church and the Handicapped in Society", report of Section IV at the Faith and Order Commission meeting in Louvain, in *Study Encounter*, 7, 4, 1971, p.3.
[86] *Breaking Barriers*, p.62.

Ireland, Canada and Scandinavia, this development led to the closing of most of the large institutions for the differently abled,[87] as well as to an entirely new orientation for church-related work with them. More and more differently abled persons were becoming active in participating in worship life, the ordination of the differently abled was introduced in some churches or increased, as for example in the Church of England or in the Lutheran and Reformed churches in most countries in Europe.

Meanwhile, the economic, political and societal causes of handicaps increased in the so-called third world. More and more adults and children have to live with life-long disabilities, but in 1985 only 2 percent of all the differently abled in the developing countries were able to take advantage of direct state or church assistance.[88]

Twenty-one differently abled persons took part in the WCC's Vancouver assembly (1983) as delegates, observers, advisers or visitors – a small but visible number.[89] The role of the differently abled as full members of a "healing community" – a concept which stood at the centre of the general secretary's report – received a new emphasis. The advocacy role of the churches and the necessity to include the differently abled in decision-making bodies in order to give them the possibility to speak for themselves was articulated. As in the women's and children's work of the WCC, advocacy and participation also became leading concepts of the WCC's work with the differently abled.

The work (lodged after the Vancouver assembly in the Education sub-unit) concentrated on developing partnership relations and networks. A full-time staff consultant was appointed from 1984 to the end of 1991 to coordinate further work in the Council and its member churches. Two regional consultations (Montevideo 1987 and Bangkok 1989) served this end. Lobbying in favour of a stronger participation of the differently abled did not meet with much success.[90] The hard-won quota of ten delegates to the Canberra assembly (1991) was far from being achieved, and the disillusion, which also affected women's and youth work at the end of the 1980s, led to the recognition that the psychological and social resistance to a stronger involvement of marginalized groups – in this case, the differently abled – must be better understood and brought closer to the churches' purview if any progress was to be made in the search for greater inclusivity.[91]

Canberra brought hardly any new impetus. In the assembly report the concerns of the differently abled appear at various places – sometimes they are mentioned alongside the youth, then with people of all age groups, then again with women, youth, indigenous peoples. The impression is given that the question did not play any central role but was dealt with in a purely formal way, and always only under the aspect of participation. The statement by the differently abled asks the WCC to take their concerns anew into consideration in all areas of its programmatic work.

In the process of the restructuring of the WCC's work, the unit on Unity and Renewal took up the challenge in the framework of its stream on Lay Participation towards Inclusive Community. According to the guidelines of the assembly the programme

---

[87] Nancy Robertson, "Report from Europe", in *Differently Abled Consultation, Cartigny, Geneva, Switzerland, 21-24 November 1994*, WCC, 1994.
[88] Lynda Katsuno, "The Church and People with Disabilities", in *Education Newsletter*, 2-3, 1985, p.1.
[89] On the issue of the differently abled in Vancouver, cf. *Gathered for Life*, pp.8,10,57,60,66-67,70,93.
[90] *From Vancouver to Canberra*, p.211.
[91] Cf. *Education Newsletter*, 1, 1988, and report by Evelyn Appiah in *Differently Abled Consultation, Cartigny 1994*.

turned the emphasis away from specified quotas to a vision of a full and healed community including the differently abled.[92]

A new consultant continued the work from 1994 to 1996, building networks and organizing regional consultations so that there was a visible presence of ten advisers with disabilities at the eighth assembly at Harare (1998). Their presence influenced a number of documents, including the programme guidelines report. These advisers formed the Ecumenical Disability Advocates Network (EDAN), that later linked up with the WCC; the network's coordinator is based at the national council of churches of Kenya in Nairobi, and is also a staff member of the WCC's Justice, Peace and Creation team where the concerns for differently abled people was based after Harare. EDAN, whose major concern is to stimulate and engage in theological reflection on issues concerning people with disabilities, has organized several consultations and cooperated with a number of partners within the WCC, the wider ecumenical movement and disability organizations around the world. The network has also sent advisers to central committee meetings.

The formation of the network and its cooperation with the WCC has led to a new working style for the concerns of people with disabilities in the WCC. It remains to be seen what effect that will have for the Council, the member churches and the larger ecumenical movement. Within the WCC concerns of the differently abled have been considered both from the perspective of inclusive community and as an issue of justice. It became apparent that member churches working in this area have different starting points and approaches, based largely on culture. Theological understandings of what causes a person to have or encounter a disabling condition vary greatly from society to society, which in turn affects how that society views and treats persons with disability and how differently abled people participate in the life and work of local congregations. Ecumenically, the Consultation on Church Union in the US has been notable for its intensive work done concerning disabilities.

Amidst this diversity, the WCC has sought to serve as a focal point to coordinate materials and work, conscientize and mobilize churches and thus emphasize a new and deeper spirituality, transforming and renewing people. Regrettably, lack of funds and limited human resources in member churches and the WCC itself have often made ecumenical progress on regional and international levels slow; at the local level, more informal ecumenical work and sharing has in fact occurred, usually out of necessity. The challenge is for national councils of churches to incorporate the concern for differently abled people into their agendas. The problem is often financial and, because the issue is so diverse, it tends to become lost in the list of programme priorities.

THE CHURCHES AND THEIR GAY AND LESBIAN MEMBERS

The WCC has no official policy statement on homosexuality and the public inclusion of gays and lesbians in the community of faith. There is no consensus among the member churches on the reading of scientific data on sexual orientation, let alone on the resources from Bible and Tradition which guide the churches in forming ethical judgments.

---

[92] Statement from the Differently Abled Consultation, Cartigny, Geneva, Switzerland, 21-24 November 1994.

The lack of consensus between – and within – the churches does not equal an absence of theological inquiries on human sexuality, including homosexuality.[93] Indeed, as far back as the New Delhi assembly (1961), at the request of member churches the WCC began to address issues of human sexuality. At Uppsala (1968) the debate on birth control was the entry-point and the delegates asked for materials "elaborating the problems of polygamy, marriage and celibacy, birth control, divorce, abortion and also of homosexuality to be made available for responsible study and action".

Research has documented that controversies on "churches in solidarity with their homosexual members" began when changes in social attitudes, especially after the second world war, led a number of predominantly Western countries to accept laws and regulations guaranteeing non-discrimination against homosexual people and the decriminalization of homosexuality.

The WCC's Nairobi assembly in 1975 called for a "theological study of sexuality, taking into account the culture of the member churches". And it urged the churches "to affirm the personhood and mutual interdependence of individuals in families and the personhood and worth of people living in different life situations". Vancouver (1983) and Canberra (1991) came up with similar recommendations. Vancouver called for a thorough re-examination of values in sexuality and initiated a study on female sexuality. A second study was commissioned by the 1989 central committee meeting in Moscow, "Sexuality and Human Relations", to be circulated for comment in the regions. The result was a carefully edited publication which came out in 1990 on *Living in Covenant with God and One Another: A Guide to the Study of Sexuality and Human Relations.*[94]

Linking human rights with the prohibition of discrimination against gays and lesbians, the United Church of Canada, for example, situated sexual orientation as a "given" aspect of human identity within an overall theological affirmation of "all human beings as persons made in the image of God".[95] During the 1990s some churches, not least in Scandinavia, allowed for a "blessing" of registered same-sex partnerships or unions and, accordingly, produced prayers and rites to be used by pastors. The heated internal discussions in the Norwegian Lutheran Church, Anglican churches in Canada, the US, England and a significant number of Protestant churches especially in the West on homosexual partnership and acceptance of gay and lesbian pastors testify to a general, and unquestionably controversial, theological component in almost all discussion of homosexuality within the churches, namely the understanding and exercise of authority in the churches. Who decides by which criteria and through what means of decision-making? These questions about authority link the search for forming Christian teaching on homosexuality with the previous discussions on churches as inclusive communities of women and men.

Against society's changing sexual mores some churches have affirmed heterosexual, indissoluble marriage as the only life-situation for sexual relationships. The Roman Catholic Church has included a unitive (and not merely procreative) meaning of marital sex in its understanding of marriage, but sex belongs to marriage. Nevertheless, the

---

[93] Cf. Birgitta Larsson, "A Quest for Clarity: The World Council of Churches and Human Sexuality", in *The Ecumenical Review*, 1, 1998, pp.30-40.
[94] Robin Smith, *Living in Covenant with God and One Another: A Guide to the Study of Sexuality and Human Relations Using Statements from Member Churches of the World Council of Churches*, WCC, 1990.
[95] *Gift, Dilemma and Promise. A Report and Affirmations on Human Sexuality*, United Church of Canada, 1984.

churches acknowledged that sexual orientation is not a matter of free choice or preference and, consequently, neither in itself a matter of moral evaluation nor of exercising rights.[96]

The Orthodox churches have, generally, either ignored research on sexual orientation or, when "homosexual inclinations" have been recognized, confirmed – on biblical and theological grounds – a tradition judging homosexuality as a sinful distortion of human nature.[97] The attitude to the human-rights component of the discussion varies within Orthodoxy. The official position of the Russian Orthodox Church states that the church does not deny "anybody the fundamental rights to life, respect for personal dignity and participation in public affairs", but believes it inadmissible for homosexual persons to work with children and youth or hold superior jobs in prisons or in the army. On the other hand, the United Church of Canada, the United Church of Christ in the US and some other denominations have moved to full recognition of "self-declared, practising gay and lesbian persons" being eligible for both ordination and marriage. Four Canadian jurisdictions (provinces) allow legal same-sex civil marriages. Elsewhere in the West similar legal options exist, putting heavy pressures on churches to move with society. On the other hand, the numerically burgeoning churches of the South generally are adamantly opposed to any such consideration and in many cases have split or threatened to split world communal and confessional bodies.

While some churches expected the WCC to contribute more clarity and perhaps a common position, it proved extremely difficult for the Council to respond. The member churches were more successful in identifying a range of key issues that needed to be addressed in different contexts and in creating opportunities for careful consideration of the various aspects and perspectives involved. However, the WCC functioned well as a space for facilitating and enabling the dialogue on issues related to human sexuality.

In the period from Canberra (1991) to Harare (1998) homosexuality moved higher on the agenda. There was a gay and lesbian caucus at Canberra which drafted a letter to the central committee asking that work on sexual orientation be transferred from family-life education to justice. At the Johannesburg central committee (1994) a heated debate in plenary took place in response to references to violence against women, particularly lesbians. The announcement that Harare was to be the venue for the eighth assembly gave rise to remarks in the media that Zimbabwe's human-rights record regarding gays and lesbians was abysmal. Increasingly, as preparations for the assembly were under way, the WCC was confronted within the host country by strong reactions from gay groups and anti-gay members as well as their supporters internationally.

Following a chaotic discussion at the central committee in 1995, the WCC's general secretary, Konrad Raiser, took responsibility for devising some means of at least an orderly debate on homosexuality. A series of staff workshops, conducted by Alan Brash, provided material for the book *Facing Our Differences: The Churches and Their Gay and Lesbian Members*, which appeared in 1995. Like a later (1998) survey, done by the Swiss ethicist Wolfgang Lienemann,[98] the book documents a number of church statements on

---

[96] James P. Hanigan, "The Centrality of Marriage: Homosexuality and the Roman Catholic Argument", in *The Ecumenical Review*, 50, 1, Jan. 1988, pp.54-68.

[97] Cf. *Bases of the Social Concepts of the Russian Orthodox Church*, Jubilee Bishops' Council of the Russian Orthodox Church, www.mospat.ru/text/e_conception/id/4047.html, XII.9.

[98] "Churches and Homosexuality: An Overview of Recent Official Church Statements on Sexual Orientation", in *The Ecumenical Review*, 50, 1, Jan. 1998, pp.7-21.

homosexuality. Summarizing the various arguments from Bible and Tradition and the discussions of the human-rights angle, the book encourages a constructive dialogue on homosexuality. The survey article makes it undeniable, however, that the diverse theologies and attitudes pose a problem in the common search for Christian unity, and the ecumenical situation is not made any easier by the fact that many churches also have problems with the inner consistency of their teachings, not least with biblical hermeneutics and the interpretation of the relation between public law and Christian morals.

Fears of having discussions about homosexuality rock the ecumenical boat into sinking made the WCC leadership take comprehensive and considered steps towards defusing a possible conflict on homosexuality at the Harare assembly. The conflict did not materialize, because while a number of workshops run by gay and lesbian activists and support groups were held at the *padare* or market-place of ideas, the issue did not reach the plenary floor. The churches were, in general, determined to stay together, and although no consensus is in sight on this potentially divisive issue both the material published in connection with the Harare assembly and the more recent church statements testify – in general – to "the efforts to allow each side to express itself and to listen to one another... On issues of sexual morality there is no alternative to the readiness to search together, in struggle, conversation and study for possible agreements and a modus vivendi within and between the churches."[99]

Harare made it clear that the churches did not feel it was appropriate to establish a specific programme on human sexuality. The mandate of the assembly was not to start a programme but to "provide space" through which the member churches were enabled to discuss the difficult issues related to human sexuality. For this reason, after Harare the general secretary with the support of the officers of the WCC approached the issue as follows.

Representatives from a number of member churches were invited to form a reference group on human sexuality. Its terms were:
– to advise the general secretary on the development and content of the WCC work related to human sexuality, taking into account the link with all other areas of WCC work that have bearing on the implementation of the governing bodies recommendations;
– to advise and accompany the WCC's human sexuality staff group in carrying out the recommendations of the WCC governing bodies, helping to evaluate its work and offering advice on further development of the work; and
– to ensure the participation of representatives from WCC member churches in their confessional, cultural and religious diversity.

The group met on several occasions during and following the year 2000 and developed a considerable body of work and analysis in theological, pastoral and ethical reflections, and established a timeline of work for the ninth WCC assembly in 2006. The staff group on human sexuality was required to "develop a process that responds to the mandate from the [Harare] assembly in ways which will enable the member churches to engage in dialogue with one another as well as with congregations".

Three seminars at Bossey were organized as laboratories for testing and developing the approach chosen by the programme guidelines committee and the reference group as a comprehensive contribution to the process between the eighth and ninth assem-

---

[99] *Ibid.*, p.15.

blies. All three seminars were introduced by a meditation on the theme of "pilgrimage" developed from the guidelines for the *padares* at Harare. The seminars were facilitated by a professional from outside the WCC who tested the consensus of the group.

An *aide memoire* prepared as an update covering the background to the central committee covering the post-Harare period also makes reference to two other related concerns.

The first is the worldwide HIV/AIDS pandemic which challenges the churches to a deeper level than the many excellent care, education and counselling programmes existing at the end of the century.

> As the pandemic has unfolded, it has exposed fault-lines that reach to the heart of our theology, our ethics, our liturgy and our practice of ministry. Today churches are being obliged to acknowledge that they have – however unwittingly – contributed both actively and passively to the spread of the virus. The difficulty of addressing issues of sex and sexuality has often made it painful to engage, in any honest and realistic way, with issues of sex education and HIV prevention. The tendency to exclude others and certain interpretations of the scriptures have all combined to promote stigmatization, exclusion and suffering of people with HIV or AIDS. This has undermined the effectiveness of care, education and prevention efforts and inflicted additional suffering on those already affected by the HIV. Given the extreme urgency of the situation and the conviction that the churches do have a distinctive role to play in response to the pandemic, what is needed is a rethinking of the mission, and the transformation structures and ways of working.
>
> The work on curricula for theological education that has begun includes the need for more positive affirmation of the human body and of sexual relationships. HIV/AIDS forces the churches to engage more openly and in a pastoral way with issues of human sexuality.[100]

The second concern is violence against women which had been on the agenda of the WCC for more than a decade. In their analysis of the violence, women increasingly make a link with issues related to human sexuality and violence. Whenever there is war or conflict, there is reference to rape and sexual violence against woman.

> What makes it even more difficult to bear is the evidence of sexual violence against women and children even in refugee centres in the hands of humanitarian aid workers. But sexual violence against women is a reality in times of peace too.
>
> Regrettably sexual violence takes place even in the so-called safe environment of the church. Women in the WCC constituency also point to violence that lesbian woman experience in most societies. All this has made women identify more clearly the link between the violence they experience and their sexuality. The WCC is committed to working with women in challenging the churches to speak out more clearly on these issues and to offer solidarity and pastoral support to women who experience violence.[101]

YOUTH

The presence of young people in the ecumenical movement has been apparent from earliest days in such institutions as the Young Men's and Young Women's Christian Associations (YMCA and YWCA), the World Student Christian Federation, the World Alliance for Promoting International Friendship through the Churches, the Life and Work movement and youth activities of various churches worldwide. Less visible has been the participation of youth in the initiation and development of the ecumenical movement at

---

[100] Aide memoire: World Council of Churches and Human Sexuality, 2003 (internal document).
[101] *Ibid.*

various levels of church life. Cross-denominational relationships and common witness started in many communities, towns and nations through encounters of young people in the churches for Bible study, discussion, entertainment, social service and sports.

"Youth" has a different meaning in various cultures. For example, in the West, especially North America, youth is often equated with teenage years and adolescence, while in many African countries some assert that as long as one is young in heart one can still be a youth. But while setting age limits can be arbitrary, there is no way to avoid it. Over the years the ecumenical movement has come to see youth as persons between the ages of 15 and 30 (or in some cases, even 35).

The development of youth participation in the ecumenical movement at the global level can be traced through four principal means:

- land-mark events;
- life and activities of a number of ecumenical organizations;
- participation of young people in a number of major ecumenical institutions (e.g. the WCC and regional ecumenical bodies); and
- through the engagement of youth in issues that affect the communities in which they live.

Youth participation in WCC assemblies dates back to the Amsterdam founding assembly in 1948 and gradually increased until Uppsala in 1968. There, sparked by an all-European seminar held for youth in East Berlin in preparation for the fourth assembly, young people concentrated on section 4, "Towards New Styles of Living". They submitted six proposals concerning greater personal sacrifices in time, thought and money, new life-styles, more universal education, greater involvement in changing oppressive political structures, an open-mindedness continually questioning the information flow and ended with the ringing words: "Church structure is dead; long live movement! Let us all take part in the Lord's supper in Uppsala."[102] As the assembly began, 127 young people from all over the world held another preparatory conference to deal with themes and sub-themes in their role as official youth delegates with the right to speak but not to vote. Ten Roman Catholics and 12 Orthodox were part of the delegation, and half their numbers come from the third world. By this time the WCC Youth department, which had been first established at Amsterdam as part of the general secretariat, was included within the department of ecumenical action and at Uppsala had 345 stewards, mostly from Sweden. From the beginning all these young people, with their 1960s basic distrust of institutions and bureaucracy, made life hard going for the more sedate delegates. They insisted on voting for their own programmes. In the whole history of the ecumenical movement youth had never been so visibly present and clearly critical of adult deliberations as at Uppsala. Some were taken into custody by police for public protests and their constant message loudly expressed was clear: "Put up or shut up." They demanded that at least 25 percent of delegates to the next assembly be under 35, noting that Visser't Hooft was only 38 when he became the WCC's first general secretary. They demanded full unity in worship and full participation by all delegates at the daily eucharist. They sanctioned common service to the poor and exploited, demanded an emphasis on justice and peace, and predicted the demise of the WCC if it did not implement their motions.

---

[102] Ans J. van der Bent, *From Generation to Generation: The Story of Youth in the World Council of Churches*, WCC, 1986, p.81.

The final resolutions of the youth participants were heard by the assembly in plenary session the last day: they were received with thanks but not discussed. On the whole the bureaucracy and the leadership were somewhat less than enchanted with the protestors' confrontation of the established delegations. The Youth desk noted hat "a real integration, which would require or at least allow critical participation, is more than most adults can take and more than most young people can muster".

The fact that the Council was financially unstable at the time and that there was no constitutional provision for the participation of youth made the future bleak. Indeed, from 1969 to 1974 the staff of the Youth department was severely curtailed, losing financial allocations and programme resources given over to other assignments. "Youth as a constituency was obscured and seemed to become the object of benign neglect."

Ecumenical youth work became an increasingly hazardous enterprise although *Uppsala to Nairobi* analyzed the world situation as follows:

> Massive protests, students and young workers challenging the values (or lack of them) of an industrial order, just demands for a more human society and anti-war movements all characterized an unprecedented epoch in the 20th century that has given way to what the churches and society are now witnessing among the young.[103]

Since 1962 when the first international youth meeting was held at Taizé, France, with 200,000 people in attendance, to the council of youth in 1974 when 40,000 people from 100 countries gathered again at Taizé for an "inner adventure", youth were on the churches', if not the WCC's, agenda. A declaration of the young people contained the words "...Reconciled in one universal community, Christians will be able to be a living word at the heart of the tragedies of war, injustice, segregation and hunger."[104] Before the Nairobi assembly (1975) youth gathered at Arusha, Tanzania, for a pre-assembly conference. Although still not voting members, they got membership on the assembly business committee, and the programme guidelines committee received reports from the youth workshops. Finally, the assembly approved a change in structure allowing youth work some autonomy. High priority from youth was given to: (1) youth participation in ecumenism at local and international levels, (2) youth for social justice; (3) youth and personhood; (4) violence and nonviolence; and (5) youth and spirituality. Another high priority was given to encounters and contacts with youth and youth leaders around the world and building a network of communication among them. Special emphasis was given to YM-YWCAs, WSCF, Intervarsity Fellowship, Roman Catholic organizations and especially to Syndesmos, the World Fellowship of Orthodox Youth founded in 1953.

Four significant events took place between 1977 and 1979: an international conference at Bossey on the theme "Christian Witness for Social Justice" (1977); a regional ecumenical seminar on "Christian Youth in a Troubled Society" at Ayia Napa, Cyprus (1978), with the Middle East Council of Churches; a gathering on the theme "Christian Vigilance and Solidarity on Six Continents" at Bossey, also in 1978; and a meeting of seventy students of natural and social sciences prior to the world conference on "Faith, Science and the Future" at Cambridge, Massachusetts, in 1979. This last conference declared,

> What is needed is a new vision of a global community, a new society in which the horizons of moral concern and accountability extend not only to every human, but also to every other

---

[103] *Uppsala to Nairobi*, pp.200 and 202.
[104] *Ecumenical Youth News*, 7, September 1975, p.2.

aspect of the natural order... The greatest part of scientific research and the development and use of technology should be directed towards meeting basic human needs.[105]

Youth participation in WCC assemblies gradually increased, especially after Uppsala and Nairobi, up to Harare (1998) but in a much more integrated way as member churches increased the number of youth on their delegations. Through the 1980s young people were showing a marked preference against holding large events unless they were made part of the process and encouraged to respond to the issues of the day. They sought more and more "critical participation" rather than mere integration into church structures. Indeed, at Harare youth were critical of the failure to establish participation of youth in the ecumenical movement: "The level of youth participation in many aspects of the Council's life stands in glaring contrast to the firm commitment made by the central committee in 1988 for 20 percent involvement of young people."[106] Pointing out that in many countries young people are leaving the historic churches because they feel excluded and ignored, the youth recommended:

- equitable participation of young people in all aspects of ecumenical life by maintaining the requirement of 20 percent youth membership at assemblies, committees and meetings;
- assigning one staff person on each staff team to monitor youth participation within its programmes, and forming a new staff coordinating group on youth;
- assuring resources only for those activities which reflect goals for inclusiveness and maintaining affirmative action policy in employment of young people in all areas of work;
- maintaining the position of a youth president within the presidium of the Council;
- retaining programme staff for youth work;
- providing opportunities for ecumenical formation at all levels and further developing the stewards and internship programmes to serve as models for future work in the WCC; and
- maintaining programmes which respond to particular concerns of youth as well as affirming their participation in addressing wider issues; this is best done through pre-meetings for youth participants prior to all WCC consultations and events.

Young people have been active ecumenically for many years in their own regions and contexts and have been at the forefront of raising environmental and economic issues. At the All Africa Conference of Churches in the 1980s and 1990s the youth desk established a programme to promote a culture of peace on the continent against the backdrop of many ethnic and political conflicts, holding youth gatherings at Douala (1984) and Kinshasa (1989) which were collaborative efforts ecumenically. The 1984 Asian youth assembly was sponsored by the Christian Conference of Asia, along with Catholic students, and elected the first ever position of CCA youth president. Latin Americans formed the Union of Latin American Ecumenical Youth with Roman Catholic participation in 1970, with priorities set for rural and urban youth and participation in the process of people's liberation. In the Middle East ecumenical work camps brought together Orthodox and Protestants and emphasized concern for regional political issues coordinated by the Middle East Council of

---

[105] Paul Abrecht ed., "Report of the Science Students Conference", in *Faith and Science in an Unjust World, vol. 2: Reports and Recommendations*, WCC, 1980, p.173.
[106] In Diane Kessler ed., *Together on the Way: Official Report of the Eighth Assembly of the World Council of Churches*, WCC, 1999, pp.261-64.

Churches youth department. In North America ecumenical youth work depended on denominations and national councils of churches since there was no regional structure. In the 1980s Young Christians for Global Justice was formed as a means of filling this void. A 1987 North American consultation of ecumenical groups and denominational youth bodies expressed new commitment to ecumenical cooperation but little formal structure existed to try and make impact in the highly secular cultures. The Ecumenical Youth Council in Europe (EYCE) was formed in 1968 and worked closely with the WCC, the WSCF, and the Conference of European Churches as a forum for encounter and dialogue.

In 1993, the Ecumenical Global Gathering of Youth and Students (EGGYS) in Brazil brought together young people from the networks of the WCC, the regions, the WSCF, the YW-YMCAs, Syndesmos, Young Catholic Students and the youth programmes of the World Alliance of Reformed Churches and the Lutheran World Federation for the first time in such a large gathering – more than 500 young men and women from 101 countries. In a sense it was in continuity, if not style, with the first youth conferences held in 1936 in Amsterdam and again in Oslo in 1947, but this one was fully ecumenical for the first time. They called themselves the "traumatized generation" which is "morally confused". They were seeking dialogue, humility and a simpler life-style. It was a less than formal gathering and its results were difficult to quantify.

EGGYS did not come up with concrete plans of action, nor even a commitment to continue to meet in such a way. However, the youth did see themselves as a microcosm of the day's world racial, gender, cultural and ideological diversity and richness, so it became a forum for diversity and differences. Afterwards, delegates returned home to continue maintaining global solidarity in various locations, and to network and continue structural support through their own organizations for cooperative programmes which "will allow the ecumenical vision to spread among young people seeking a future made whole in the Spirit of God, without whom we will perish".[107]

In late summer 1995, ecumenical youth and many of the young at heart gathered in Ivory Coast for the centennial assembly of the World Student Christian Federation, under the theme "A Community of Memory and Hope: Celebrating God's Faithfulness".[108]

Youth engagement in the ecumenical movement has mostly been through concrete activities, not just words and papers. Older generations found this kind of involvement threatening, and tended to condemn youth without trying to discern the importance of their activism for the whole community.

At the end of the 20th century, it was clear that ecumenically engaged youth had been an asset to their communities and a strong force for transformation. Where they were listened to and given space to contribute, both church and society have experienced signs of new life.

BIBLIOGRAPHY

Amirtham, Samuel, *Stories Make People: Examples of Theological Work in Community*, WCC, 1989, 99p.

---

[107] *Seeds of Hope and Transformation, Official Report of the Ecumenical Global Gathering of Youth and Students*, Geneva, EGGYS, 1993, p.60.
[108] See Philip Potter and Thomas Wieser, *Seeking and Serving the Truth*, WCC, 1997, pp.286-87.

Apostola, Nicholas ed., *A Letter from Christ to the World: An Exploration of the Role of the Laity in the Church Today*, WCC, 1998, 147p.

Becher, Jeanne ed., *Women, Religion and Sexuality: Studies on the Impact of Religious Teachings on Women*, Philadelphia, Trinity, 1991, 265p.

Behr-Sigel, Elisabeth and Ware, Kallistos, *The Ordination of Women in the Orthodox Church*, WCC, 2000, 96p.

Bent, Ans J. van der, *From Generation to Generation: The Story of Youth in the World Council of Churches*, WCC, 1986, 136p.

Best, Thomas F. ed., *The Search for New Community: Consultation on Models of Renewed Community, Ecumenical Institute, Bossey, Switzerland, 1987: A Bossey Seminar*, WCC, 1987, 127p.

Brash, Alan Anderson, *Facing Our Differences: The Churches and Their Gay and Lesbian Members*, WCC, 1995, 75p.

Crawford, Janet, and Kinnamon Michael eds, In God's Image: Reflections on Identity, Human Wholeness and the Authority of Scripture, WCC, 1983, 108p.

Devadas, David, *Ecumenism and Youth*, WCC, 1995, 98p.

Directory of Ecumenical Conference Centres, WCC, 1994, 200p.

Ecumenical Decade 1988-1998: Churches in Solidarity with Women. Prayers and Poems, Songs and Stories, WCC, 1988, 99p.

Fraser, Ian M., *The Fire Runs: God's People Participating in Change*, London, SCM Press, 1975, 152p.

Gift, Dilemma and Promise: A Report and Affirmations on Human Sexuality, United Church of Canada, 1984, 6 vols.

Gjerding, Iben and Kinnamon, Katherine eds, *No Longer Strangers: A Resource of Women and Worship*, WCC, 1983, 80p.

Gnanadason, Aruna, *No Longer a Secret: The Church and Violence against Women*, WCC, 1993, 79p.

Grohs, Gerhard and Czell, Gernot eds, *Kirche in der Welt – Kirche der Laien?*, Frankfurt am Main, Otto Lembeck, 1990, 214p.

Herzel, Susannah, *A Voice for Women: The Women's Department of the World Council of Churches*, WCC, 1981, 197p.

Kanyoro, Musimbi R.A. ed, *In Search of a Round Table: Gender, Theology and Church Leadership*, WCC, 1997, 187p.

Kanyoro, Musimbi R.A. and Robins, Wendy eds, *The Power We Celebrate: Women's Stories of Faith and Power*, WCC, 1992, 102p.

Kaper, Gudrun et al., *Eva, wo bist Du? Frauen in internationalen Organisationen der Ökumene* (Kennzeichen 8), Gelnhausen, Laetare, 1981, 188p.

Katsumo-Ishii, Lynda, Keay, Kathy and Ortega, Ofelia eds, *God Has Called Us: A Report from the Ecumenical Workshop for Women Theological Educators, Bossey, Switzerland, May 7-17, 1991*, Singapore, ATESEA, 1994, 192p.

Katsuno-Ishii, Lynda and Orteza, Edna J. eds, *Of Rolling Waters and Roaring Wind: A Celebration of the Woman Song*, WCC, 2000, 142p.

Living Letters: A Report of Visits to the Churches during the Ecumenical Decade Churches in Solidarity with Women, WCC, 1997, produced by the Mid-Decade office, 50p.

May, Melanie Ann, *Bonds of Unity: Women, Theology, and the Worldwide Church*, Atlanta GA, Scholars, 1989, 196p.

May, Melanie Ann ed., *Women and Church: The Challenge of Ecumenical Solidarity in an Age of Alienation*, Grand Rapids MI, Eerdmans, 1991, 197p.

Müller-Fahrenholz, Geiko ed., *And Do Not Hinder Them: An Ecumenical Plea for the Admission of Children to the Eucharist*, WCC, 1982, 81p.

Müller-Fahrenholz, Geiko ed., *Partners in Life: The Handicapped and the Church*, WCC, 1979, 184p.

Oduyoye, Mercy Amba, *Who Will Roll the Stone Away? The Ecumenical Decade of the Churches in Solidarity with Women*, WCC, 1990, 69p.

Ortega, Ofelia Miriam ed., *Women's Visions: Theological Reflection, Celebration, Action*, WCC, 1995, 182p.

Parvey, Constance F. ed, *The Community of Women and Men in the Church: The Sheffield Report*, WCC, 1983, 201p.

Parvey, Constance F. ed, *Ordination of Women in Ecumenical Perspective: Workbook for the Church's Future*, WCC, 1980, 96p.

Peterse, Nico and Appiah, Evelyn eds, *The World Convention of Christian Lay Centres and Movements: "Weaving Communities of Hope", Montreat, 30 August-10 September 1993: Final Report*, WCC, 1993, 151p.

Pobee, John Samuel ed., *Theology, Ministry and Renewal of God's People: Sixteen Bible Studies*, WCC, 1995, 127p.

Potter, Philip and Wieser, Thomas, *Seeking and Serving the Truth: The First Hundred Years of the World Student Christian Federation*, WCC, 1997, 307p.

Raiser, Elisabeth and Robra, Barbara eds, *With Love and with Passion: Women's Life and Work in the Worldwide Church*, WCC, 2001, 183p.

Raiser, Konrad, "Laity in the Ecumenical Movement: Redefining the Profile", in *The Ecumenical Review*, 45, 4, Oct. 1993, pp.375-83.

Robins, Wendy S. ed., *Through the Eyes of a Woman: Bible Studies on the Experience of Women*, rev. ed., WCC, 1995, 145p.

Schulze-Wegener, Gernot, *Kirche als Basisbewegung: Die Bedeutung der Laien für die Kirche innerhalb der Diskussion im Ökumenischen Rat der Kirchen von 1948-1968*, Frankfurt am Main, Peter Lang, 2000, 282p.

Seeds of Hope and Transformation. Official Report of the Ecumenical Gathering of Youth and Students, Geneva, EGGYS, 1993, 72p.

Sexism in the Seventies: Discrimination against Women, WCC, 1975, 150p.

Simpfendörfer, Werner ed., *The New Fisherfolk: How to Run a Church-Related Conference Centre*, WCC, 1988, 130p.

Smith, Robin, *Living in Covenant with God and One Another: A Guide to the Study of Sexuality and Human Relations Using Statements from Member Churches of the World Council of Churches*, WCC, 1990 182p.

Thompson, Betty, *A Chance to Change: Women and Men in the Church*, WCC, 1982, 121p.

Wartenberg-Potter, Bärbel von, *We Will Not Hang Our Harps on the Willows: Engagement and Spirituality*, WCC, 1987, 124p.

Webb, Pauline Mary, "Committed to Fellowship – But of What Sort?", in *The Ecumenical Review*, 25, 1973, pp.256-65.

Webb, Pauline Mary, *She Flies Beyond: Memories and Hopes of Women in the Ecumenical Movement*, WCC, 1993, 72p.

Weber, Hans-Ruedi, *Living in the Image of Christ: The Laity in Ministry*, WCC, 1986, 79p.

World Council of Churches, Sub-Unit on Women in Church and Society, *By Our Lives: Stories of Women – Today and in the Bible*, WCC, 1985, 57p.

World Council of Churches, Sub-Unit on Women in Church and Society, *Half the World's People: A Report of the Consultation of Church Women Executives, Glion, Switzerland, January 1977*, WCC, 1978, 64p.

World Council of Churches, Sub-Unit on Women in Church and Society, *Orthodox Women, Their Role and Participation in the Orthodox Church: Report on the Consultation of Orthodox Women, September 11-17, 1976, Agapia, Romania*, WCC, 1977, 55p.

12
Ecumenical Social Thought

Lewis S. Mudge

Ecumenical social thought[1] needs to be considered in both its institutional and theological aspects. Institutionally speaking, it is thinking about the social implications of Christian faith carried on by the various administrative units and official gatherings of ecumenical bodies such as the World Council of Churches. Theologically speaking, it is thinking that wrestles with the challenges of realizing the oikoumene (inhabited earth, the whole world) as a global household of life for all human beings living under the reign of God. Ideally, the theological vision, with its methods and ends, shapes the institutional means. But the institutional setting, by defining a social location, also helps shape the theological vision.

From these considerations alone the reader will readily understand how intricate and ramified this subject has been from its 19th-century beginnings until now. And the last thirty years of the 20th century have seen it become even more complex. Ans J. van der Bent, in his helpful book *Commitment to God's World*, writes:

> It goes without saying that the complexity of the evolution of ecumenical social thought is extremely difficult to unravel and explain in all its agreements and disagreements, certainties and uncertainties, ups and downs, commitments and abstentions.[2]

The total literature is "extremely vast". The relevant material comes not only from the successor programmes to the Life and Work movement, but also at times from Faith and Order studies as well. The present account must therefore be selective in several ways, singling out the main trends, tracing the important relationships and teasing out the chief dilemmas. The important subject of Roman Catholic social thought – a vast canvas in its own right – is examined where it intersects, or runs parallel to, thought within the WCC or closely related programmes. Likewise, the Orthodox churches conceive of

---

[1] The writer is grateful to Paul Abrecht, Thomas F. Best, Alan Falconer, John Huber, Larry Rasmussen, Martin Robra, Julio de Santa Ana, Charles West and Philip Wickeri for providing information, documentation and insight, as well as for reading the penultimate manuscript of this chapter, helping to eliminate errors and making numerous salutary suggestions. They are absolved, nonetheless, of any responsibility for the final result. He is also grateful to Daniel McFee, a doctoral student at Marquette University, USA, for sharing source materials from his dissertation research on this subject.
[2] Ans J. van der Bent, *Commitment to God's World: A Concise Critical Survey of Ecumenical Social Thought*, WCC, 1995, an "in house" account, topically organized with a nearly exhaustive listing of WCC meetings and other international gatherings, an extensive bibliography, and additional useful information, to all of which this chapter is indebted.

what the West calls "social action" mainly as a continuation of the liturgy.[3] This contributes an important alternative perspective, but makes their participation in Western-dominated social-thought dialogues difficult, a point which is mentioned repeatedly in documents of this period. It became especially salient in the late 1990s as Orthodox member churches pressed for changes in the language, thinking and institutional shape of the WCC.

Michael Kinnamon and Brian Cope describe the last three decades of the 20th century as marked by a new experience of pluralism, a dialogue of cultures and ideologies within the global church at a time of growing disparities within the human family. Human and ecclesial dialogues alike have become less East-West in orientation and more North-South.

> If there is a central motif, it is the rediscovery of the church's relationship to God's creative and redemptive work throughout creation, a rediscovery occasioned by deeper encounter with secular liberation struggles and with people of other faiths.[4]

This contrasts with the strongly Christocentric character of ecumenical theological work in preceding periods, with its stress on the church as "the universal body of Christ and the proclamation of Christ throughout the oikoumene". Now, instead, we see stress on the trinitarian nature of God, on the humanity of Jesus Christ, including his suffering and solidarity with those who live on the margins of history. The focus is on "the new humanity of Christ, and on new forms of human community marked by such things as sharing, healing and participation".

Accompanying these moves is a shift from analytical reflection by theologians and human scientists, usually meeting far from the situations they think about, to a commitment to direct ecumenical involvement and action in specific localities. Thought is now expected to emerge in the midst of action rather than apart from it. From reflection *about* the conditions and causes of poverty, ecumenical social thought begins to call for active identification *with* the poor, solidarity with their cause and acceptance of their perspectives as normative.

In the end, it has probably been no easier to derive specific social positions from the new, more involved theological perspective than from the older, more remote one. The sheer variety of circumstances, perspectives and ideologies both inside the churches and beyond has posed new, formidable and, in many ways, unexpected challenges for ecu-

---

[3] See Ion Bria, *The Liturgy after the Liturgy: Mission and Witness from an Orthodox Perspective*, WCC, 1996. The publisher's back-cover comment summarizes: "Chrysostom spoke of two altars, one within the sanctuary and one outside in the public square. The 'liturgy after the Liturgy' is thus a way of expressing how Christian worship is inseparable from committed engagement in society and culture." Bria comments that, forgetting this, and "under the guise of avoiding the temptation of 'horizontalizing' the Christian message or subjecting it to 'social' and 'political' concerns, the Orthodox have often proposed a way of life which cannot be translated into action in society. They place the social order and secular issues in the hands of the state and the political parties. Hence they are unable to translate their theological vision into the terms of the prevailing intellectual and political culture. They have ignored the social and political consequences of *theosis* (deification) and disregarded the historical concretization of eucharistic spirituality. In so doing, they interrupt the flow of the liturgical act, breaking off diakonia at the end of worship, at the door of the church" (p.23). See also Alexander Schmemann, *For the Life of the World*, Crestwood NY, St Vladimir's, 1973, and *The Historical Road of Eastern Orthodoxy*, Crestwood NY, St Vladimir's, 1977. Also John Meyendorff, *The Orthodox Church: Its Past and Its Role in the World Today*, 3rd ed., Crestwood NY, St Vladimir's, 1981.

[4] Michael Kinnamon and Brian E. Cope, *The Ecumenical Movement: An Anthology of Key Texts and Voices*, WCC, 1997, p.4.

menical social thinking. And a "loyal opposition" representing a more Western academic style of social thought has continued to press the claims of something like the former "responsible society"[5] vision.

THE LEGACY

It is not possible to understand the situation of ecumenical social thought from 1968 without brief reference to the seminal contributions of the 1966 Geneva Church and Society conference described by Paul Abrecht in the second volume of this History.[6] This gathering marked an effort "to understand the revolutionary realities which shape the modern world": economic, political, technological and scientific realities. Grappling with issues such as these raised unprecedented theological and social-ethical questions which dominated the years since 1968. To paraphrase Abrecht: Geneva 1966 questioned the nature of Christian responsibility for world economic and social development. How do we understand revolutionary social transformations? How do churches with different moral traditions and contemporary attitudes cooperate in facing such questions? What modes of cooperation are possible with the Roman Catholic Church?

Among other things the Geneva conference criticized the concept of "responsible society" – a social-ethical watchword of the ecumenical movement since Amsterdam 1948 – because it failed to grasp the character of revolutionary social change and tended to support the status quo. An address by Richard Shaull[7] (in what may have been the earliest witness to what came to be called "liberation theology" in a formal ecumenical meeting) argued that the churches' participation in radical historical existence through social revolution had made it clear that neo-orthodoxy, as expressed in "responsible society" language, supports the maintenance of traditional social structures and categories in the name of stability.

In the decolonization process, for example, "responsibility" is taken to connote the maintenance of political and economic relations between European powers and their former colonies. What had formerly meant something like "good governance" now was being taken to mean stability at all costs. It seemed to fail to appreciate the need for structural changes to foster economic justice. This critique set in motion a long-term movement from concern for policy formation at the top to solidarity with the poor and oppressed which has marked the last three decades.

---

[5] The term "responsible society" is thoroughly treated in volume 2 of *A History of the Ecumenical Movement 1948-1968*, 2nd ed., WCC, 1986. It refers to the original, classic frame of reference for ecumenical social thought, reaching back as far as J.H. Oldham's contributions to the 1937 Oxford conference on Life and Work (at which it superseded the "social gospel" optimism of the 1920s) and continuing virtually unchallenged through the formation of the WCC at Amsterdam in 1948 until the late 1960s, when it began to be confronted by the first appearances of liberation theory. Amsterdam stated that the responsible society is one "where freedom is the freedom of men who acknowledge responsibility to justice and public order and where those who hold political authority or economic power are responsible for its exercise to God and to the people whose welfare is affected by it". The assembly went on to say that "responsible society" is "not an alternative social or political system, but a criterion by which we judge all existing social orders and at the same time a standard to guide us in the specific choices we have to make". *The Ecumenical Movement: An Anthology*, pp.282-87.

[6] "The Development of Ecumenical Social Thought and Action", in *A History of the Ecumenical Movement*, vol. 2, 1948-1968, pp.250-58.

[7] Richard Shaull, "The Revolutionary Challenge to Church and Theology", world conference on Church and Society, Geneva, 1966, excerpted in *The Ecumenical Movement: An Anthology*, pp.299ff.

Words from the report of the working group on theological issues and social ethics capture the 1966 vision:

> ...the church is called, in the world, to be that part of the world which responds to God's love for all men, and to become therefore the community in which God's relation to man is known and realized. The church is in one sense the centre and fulfilment of the world. In another it is the servant of the world and the witness to it of the hope of its future. It is called to be the community in which the world can discover itself as it may become in the future. When it does not fulfil this mission and reflects the prejudices of the world, as is often the case, it is not faithful to its calling.[8]

While Geneva 1966 marked a clear advance in ecumenical social thought, fundamental theological issues remained unresolved. Again to paraphrase Paul Abrecht: How is agreement among the churches on practical questions of social witness possible when there is little concord in the arenas of Faith and Order? Can the theological assumptions underlying social witness be made explicit? Is it not hazardous to proceed without doing this? Or may it be that practical social-ethical agreements are evidence of accord at a deeper level: a level which Faith and Order dialogues do not often reach? In any case, the debate between deductive and inductive forms of moral reasoning, or between an ethic of principles and an ethic of contextual experience, continued to be problematic.[9]

Abrecht, surely the most significant instigator and architect of ecumenical social witness within and by the WCC, ended his account in 1968 with a realistic appraisal. Ecumenical social thinking remained "a precarious enterprise". Many in the churches were opposed to the directions it had taken. Events were likely further to polarize attitudes in the churches on basic social questions. All this weakened the possibility of substantial Christian social witness on a global scale. Things would become more, rather than less, difficult. But the "search for an ecumenical community of ideas and witness will proceed...even in situations where opposing points of view [seem] to make real encounter impossible".

UPPSALA AND ITS AFTERMATHS

Heir to this legacy of insight and warning, the WCC's Uppsala assembly (1968) met at a time of tumultuous world events. It was said that "the world set the agenda for Uppsala". Preparations for this fourth assembly took place at the height of social optimism symbolized by the American civil-rights movement and the "Prague springtime". Yet, before the assembly could meet Martin Luther King Jr, scheduled as a keynote speaker, had been assassinated. And, as the assembly closed, Soviet tanks were rumbling into the Czech capital. Despite all the ambiguities of the moment, it still seemed that anything was possible: even an application for WCC membership by the Roman Catholic Church.

Social issues surfaced in several of the section reports. Section 1 on "The Holy Spirit and the Catholicity of the Church" asserted,

> We cannot be isolated from the shocks and turmoils of our time, as conflicts between races and nations tear apart the fabric of our common life, as developed and developing countries become more and more alienated from each other, and ideologies and crusades clash in deadly struggle for survival. The miseries of men multiply.

---

[8] *Christians in the Technical and Social Revolutions of Our Time: World Conference on Church and Society, Official Report*, WCC, 1967, p.202.

[9] Abrecht, in *A History of the Ecumenical Movement*, vol. 2, pp.257f.

And from section 3 on "World Economic and Social Development":

> For the first time in history we can see the oneness of mankind as a reality. For the first time, we know that all men could share in the proper use of the world's resources. The new technological possibilities turn what were dreams into realities.[10]

Significant parallels with Roman Catholic social thought also marked the assembly which adopted, in revised form, an important formula from *Lumen Gentium* ("Dogmatic Constitution on the Church") of Vatican II: "The church is bold in speaking of itself as the sign of the coming unity of mankind."[11] This action was in line with the underlying question of the whole period: How is profound social concern of the *essence* of being church? How is the search for justice *integral* to the preaching of the gospel? This issue reappeared in myriad forms during the next thirty years.

The assembly met the same year as the Medellín, Colombia, conference of Latin American Catholic bishops (Celam) recognized the "preferential option for the poor". The phrase was to become a watchword: the single most perduring and influential formula in ecumenical social ethics over the next thirty years, as much alive at the opening of the 21st century as the day it was first announced.

Uppsala thus marked the surfacing of a new perspective. Alongside continuing research into social questions drawing upon Western theological and technical expertise, the WCC began to make commitments to various actions intended to be in solidarity with the victims of oppression. Both Niebuhrian caution about revolutionary social change and "responsible society" rhetoric began to give way in favour of biblical themes available to anyone. The biblical story as a whole began to be seen as one of exodus from oppression, repeated in ever-new situations. As Geiko Müller-Fahrenholz has since put it,

> God is confessed as the Lord of change and renewal hence the church is called to be an agent of change and renewal. Since God is at work, [God's] disciples must work also. Salvation history is not something to think about but something to work out in concrete solidarity with the poor and oppressed.

Salvation history is "less... a hermeneutical clue to *understand* history than... a prophetic tool to *change* it."[12]

Not all post-Uppsala programmes adopted this revolutionary-justice perspective. Following the assembly a remarkable number of creative initiatives occurred in continuity with "responsible society" reasoning, even though the term was seldom used. Uppsala touched on issues of world economic development, the study of nonviolent strategies in effecting social change, the elimination of racism and an inquiry into "science and the problems of worldwide change".

Meeting at Canterbury in August 1969, the central committee confirmed several Uppsala emphases by turning them into organized and funded programmes. An inquiry was begun into "The Future of Man and Society in a World of Science-Based Technol-

---

[10] N. Goodall ed., *The Uppsala Report: Official Report of the Fourth Assembly of the World Council of Churches*, WCC, 1968, p.12, §12; p.45, §1.

[11] *Ibid.*, p.17, §20. The original passage in *Lumen Gentium* runs as follows: "By her relationship with Christ, the church is a kind of sacrament or sign of intimate union with God and of the unity of all humankind. She is also an instrument for the achievement of such union and unity" (Walter M. Abbott ed., *The Documents of Vatican II*, New York, Guild Press, 1966, p.16.

[12] Geiko Müller-Fahrenholz, "Salvation History" in Nicholas Lossky et al. eds, *Dictionary of the Ecumenical Movement*, WCC, 1991, 2nd ed., 2002, p.1014.

ogy", as well as a programme on "Violence, Nonviolence and the Struggle for Social Justice". The committee also commissioned a Programme to Combat Racism, which was soon to embody the new spirit by combining reflection with decisive and often controversial action.

A parallel, post-Uppsala reappraisal of the methodology employed in Christian social theory is found in the "Humanum Studies" published between 1969 and 1975 in the journals *Study Encounter* and *Anticipation*. These studies argued that the incarnation of Jesus Christ affirms "that the nearer we come to reality the nearer we come to God, and that the more accurately we achieve an analysis of reality the more closely we come to suffering and sharing with God in his redemptive and creative work".[13] The Humanum Studies called for a theological anthropology based in a new appreciation of the sciences of sociology and psychology, as well as in a profound engagement with particular peoples, their cultural contexts and Indigenous theologies.

By any standards, before or after, this was an unprecedented array of programmes and objectives.

The unity of the church, the unity of human community

Why mention a Faith and Order study prominently in a history of ecumenical social thought? First, because the underlying issue of this whole period is the manner in which social witness is intrinsic to ecclesiology; and, second, because the Faith and Order Commission produced a study paper titled "Unity of the Church – Unity of Mankind" immediately after Uppsala whose conclusions powerfully informed the Commission meeting at Louvain, Belgium, in 1971. This gathering took up a number of social issues in an ecclesiological context.

The Louvain meeting is brilliantly analyzed by Ernst Lange in one of the classic studies of the workings of the ecumenical mind, *And Yet It Moves...: Dream and Reality of the Ecumenical Movement*. Lange displays the capacity of Faith and Order conversation for engaging underlying issues of social thought, striving to clarify the ecclesiological significance of engagement with the social world. Yet, at the same time, he notes the obstacles to any genuine sharing of social thought between the WCC and its member churches imposed by the character of the Council's institutional base:

> ...the WCC pays for its freedom of action by its impotence vis-a-vis the member churches, and the churches pay for their freedom from obligation by foregoing any close control over the Geneva headquarters and its actions.[14]

At Louvain, an effort was made to frame traditional Faith and Order questions in the light of the world situation – to view the historic theme of church unity in a new context, specifically in the context of human, not simply denominational, divisions. Section themes deliberately moved discussion into territories unfamiliar to many regular Faith and Order participants: justice, encounters with living faiths, the struggle against racism, inclusion of the handicapped, differences in culture. Preoccupation with the nature of the church gave way to discussion of its social function. Was concentration across the board on moral issues in the WCC a sign of retreat by theologians from their proper task? Was it tantamount to dissolving gospel into law, theology into anthropol-

---

[13] Quoted by Dietrich Werner, "Humanum Studies", in *Dictionary of the Ecumenical Movement*, p.552.
[14] Ernst Lange, *And Yet It Moves... : Dream and Reality of the Ecumenical Movement*, Grand Rapids MI, Eerdmans, 1979, p.71. Abridged by Konrad Raiser and Lukas Vischer, and translated by Edwin Robertson from *Die ökumenische Utopie oder was bewegt die ökumenische Bewegung?*, Stuttgart, Kreuz.

ogy? Louvain was the scene of a famed debate on just these issues between John Meyendorff, representing the traditional Faith and Order position, and José Míguez Bonino, favouring an ecclesiology of social engagement. Meyendorff maintained that the important thing is eucharistic presence in the world rather than active intervention. Míguez Bonino argued that there could be no going back to earlier, purely ecclesiocentric, understandings of the unity agenda.[15]

Louvain proclaimed that the church *is* the unity of humankind in the form in which this is realizable in this penultimate age. Studying the role of the church for survival of humankind *is* seeking church unity, only by a new method. The old question of what no longer divides became the new question of what we are to do together. And that included working out the preconditions for a true ecumenical council and trying to lay the groundwork for an ecumenical confession of faith, perhaps as soon as the WCC's Nairobi assembly in 1975.

What certainties about the church and its role in the world were now emerging?[16] It is striking how much these ruminations at Louvain anticipated the call for a *conciliar* affirmation of justice, peace and the integrity of creation preceding the Seoul convocation of 1990. The meeting was also the first to use the term "ecumenical space" which became prominent only in the late 1990s. But the theologians at Louvain were amateurs on the practical social-ethical questions. A year before, a conference on technology and futurology[17] had convened in Geneva at which, according to Lange, the theologians were almost completely silent. It was left to other initiatives flowing from Uppsala to tackle the practical questions, and in these efforts persuasive links to theological foundations were only sporadically made.

The revolution and violence debate

The rise of consciousness in the WCC concerning liberation struggles brought with it the question of theological justifications for revolutionary violence. Bearing in mind the long history of debate between Christian pacifism and proponents of "just-war" theory, the 1960s saw the churches drawn into a new phase of discussion regarding violence as a reality in the struggle for social justice.[18] The 1966 world conference on Church and Society had asked "whether the violence which sheds blood in planned revolutions may not be a lesser evil than the violence which, though bloodless, condemns whole populations to perennial despair".[19] Roman Catholic documents, e.g. *Gaudium et Spes* and *Populorum Progressio*, at the same time were praising those who renounced the use of violence in the justice struggle. King's assassination four months before the Uppsala assembly dramatized the issue.

The 1971 central committee asked the Department on Church and Society to pursue a study of these moral dilemmas, a study which produced the 1973 report "Violence, Nonviolence and the Struggle for Social Justice". Stressing that the goal of revolutionary action is not the destruction of the enemy but a more just social order, this document

---

[15] *Ibid.*, p.88.
[16] *Ibid.*, p.118f. The call, by Lukas Vischer, for work on a common confession of faith met resistance and became, finally, an experimental process of challenging groups in different localities across the globe "to account for the hope that is in [us]" (1 Pet. 3:15).
[17] See the report of this conference by David M. Gill, *From Here to Where: Technology, Faith and the Future of Man*, WCC, 1970.
[18] See David Gill, "Violence and Nonviolence" in *Dictionary of the Ecumenical Movement*, pp.1189-92.
[19] *Ibid.*, p.1189.

analyzed, without reconciling, three distinct points of view about the use of force in resistance to oppression: (1) absolute, exclusive nonviolence, (2) violence only in extreme circumstances, (3) violence as unavoidable in certain situations. In any case, it taught, one must not foreclose the possibility of reconciliation with one's opponents, or fail to see that nonviolence can be a highly political and controversial stance. Christians far away from tense situations should also hesitate to offer gratuitous advice.

More recent consideration of these issues has tended to uphold the 1973 conclusions. Yet ecumenists have begun to see the achievement of justice in many parts of the world as even more difficult than it seemed in the mid-1970s. "Both pacifism and just war theory", wrote David Gill in 1990, "are feeling their inadequacies in the developing ecumenical debates about militarism, weapons of mass destruction and revolutionary conflict."[20]

The Programme to Combat Racism

The WCC's 1969 central committee at Canterbury, UK, also took steps to establish a Programme to Combat Racism (PCR), destined to become ecumenism's most controversial foray into material solidarity with the oppressed. At once, the emphasis fell on "white racism", and the racist character of white wealth and power. This move signalled an attempt to analyze and expose the institutionalized racism at work in government and corporate power structures, as well as to acknowledge the churches' complicity in perpetuating racist attitudes and structures. The churches were called to support organizations representing the racially oppressed and those supporting the victims of racism.[21]

Controversy began as the WCC called for economic and other sanctions on South Africa, held consultations between church and liberation movement leaders, investigated the plight of Indigenous People and land-rights issues in Australia, formed a programme for the support of women under racist oppression, pointed to the resurgence of racism in Europe together with global racism in education, and took other actions in numerous similar situations. Controversy boiled over as the WCC set up a "special fund" which made grants to anti-racist organizations and movements. From 1970 to 1990, approximately 9.2 million US dollars were expended for these purposes, focusing mainly on southern Africa. "Charity", it was said, had been "replaced by solidarity".

It appeared to many that the nuanced conclusions flowing from the violence-nonviolence debate were not being consistently honoured by the PCR. Its assumption seemed to be that the WCC's commitment to solidarity with various struggles for justice and liberation meant approval of the means chosen, even if violent in nature.[22]

Such assumptions and actions severely tested the ecumenical fellowship. Member churches and groups within them, as well as outside media, protested. But, strained as it was, the fellowship did not break.[23] It is worth noting to what great extent the PCR remained for many a paradigm, positive or negative, of the WCC's social engagement.

---

[20] Quoted on p.1192 of the 2nd ed. of the *Dictionary of the Ecumenical Movement*.
[21] See Baldwin Sjollema, "Programme to Combat Racism," in *Dictionary of the Ecumenical Movement*, pp.935-37.
[22] *Commitment to God's World*, p.182.
[23] Sjollema, in *Dictionary of the Ecumenical Movement*, pp.935-37. The "fellowship did not break", but the Presbyterian Church in Ireland withdrew from the WCC on account of PCR, and the Salvation Army reduced its level of participation.

Development, poverty and the poor

From 1948 to 1974 the WCC had placed emphasis on the problem of "poverty", a general structural-analysis term used, largely irrespective of specific context, in debates about why people are marginalized and destitute. Section III at Uppsala on "World Economic and Social Development" urged that development must be at the heart of the churches' social witness, observing that this is a political challenge to sovereign nations. Concern for distributive justice, Uppsala said, needed to be paramount, and this would call for changes in social structures. The churches could help by demonstrating politically potent, but nonviolent, means for bringing about such change. "White racism" was recognized as a serious obstacle to the needed transformations.[24]

The Indian economist Samuel Parmar had urged the assembly to "move from a welfare state to a welfare world". Quoting the encylical *Populorum Progressio* ("Development of Peoples"), he declared that "development is the new name for peace". Yet "development is disorder because it changes existing social and economic relationships.... Order so often provides a camouflage for injustice that the very quest for justice generates disorder."[25]

These initiatives led to the establishment, in 1970, of the Commission on the Churches' Participation in Development (CCPD). Under its auspices the development debate gained focus, at first following secular economic prescriptions such as those of Walter Rostow's *Stages of Economic Growth*, but later, under Parmar's influence, beginning to question the sufficiency of that secular academic analysis. More power was to be given to "recipient" groups for setting their own agendas, emphasis began to be placed on socially comprehensive, rather than purely economic, perspectives, and social transformation was judged more measurable by what happened to actual people than by official statistics. A "people-centred" approach became characteristic of ecumenical development discourse.

This move continued the basic shift in perspective noted for this period, placing the "preferential option for the poor" alongside more traditional sorts of ecumenical social thinking.[26] Analyses of poverty's causes continued, but there occurred a shift of emphasis from top-down solutions to solidarity with the poor themselves, stressing the need for peoples' movements to define and fight for their own destinies. This theme reached classic expression and wide circulation in Paulo Freire's *Pedagogy of the Oppressed*, published in English in 1970[27] and destined to impose enormous influence on ecumenical social thought.

Central to Freire's argument was the conviction that the poor have the right to name their own world, to become subjects of their own history. One must foster this renaming of the world, or "conscientization", not with formulas from European and North American universities but through a cooperative pedagogy that names and enacts a new world. The poor are all who are victimized by the way the world is politically, militarily and economically organized. Latent, but unavoidable, was the question whether, or how,

---

[24] *Uppsala Report*, pp.49-50.
[25] Quotations in *Commitment to God's World*, p.37f.
[26] This account draws upon the article "Poverty" by Richard D.N. Dickinson in *Dictionary of the Ecumenical Movement*, pp.916-18. See also Julio de Santa Ana ed., *Towards a Church of the Poor*, WCC, 1978; and Gustavo Gutiérrez, *The Power of the Poor in History*, London, SCM Press, 1983.
[27] Paulo Freire, *Pedagogy of the Oppressed*, New York, Seabury, 1970.

such commitment to the poor lay at the very core of ecclesiology, and hence formed an essential part of what it means to be the people of God.

One began with the conviction that a passion for social justice is fundamental to the covenant histories of both Israel and the church. One could point to the calling of an enslaved people, to prophetic denunciations of wealth, to the calling of many (but not all) disciples from disadvantaged classes. The assumption was that disadvantaged people, being free from the anxiety to maintain wealth and social position, might well be able to understand the gospel, and hence the very being of the church, better than others. Hence an "epistemological privilege of the poor", the capacity of the poor to achieve their own emancipation, reflecting Freire's notion.

Yet it was recognized that this awareness often comes initially from outside the communities of poverty as such. In the then-emerging liberation theology one saw a type of analysis, socialist or at least suspicious of the West in its tendencies, used to raise the consciousness of the poor to be their own liberators. "Participation" and "solidarity" became watchwords, although not without the sort of criticism that asks whether the poor have genuine wisdom about social policies and the best methods for carrying them out. Should Christians endorse *every* strategy adopted by poor people and their leaders?[28] These questions continued to be asked, through subsequent developments in the understanding of the "preferential option", at the Nairobi assembly (1975) and beyond.

Cooperation with the Holy See: Society, Development and Peace

As already indicated, social thought in the WCC proceeded in many ways in parallel with the different modes of social thought in Roman Catholicism. The "preferential option" and the church as "sign and sacrament" were fundamental orientations derived from Roman Catholic sources. Another product of the energy and creativity of the period around 1968 was the Joint Committee on Society, Development and Peace (SODEPAX). In operation until 1980, this body was for a time the only agency responsible both to the WCC and the Holy See, and hence well positioned to bring WCC social thought further into encounter with Catholic reflection and practice. Drawing on the findings of the 1966 Church and Society conference and the work of the Uppsala assembly along with the social encyclicals of John XXIII and Paul VI[29] and the Vatican II document on the church in the modern world, *Gaudium et Spes* (1965), SODEPAX made significant contributions in the fields of economic development research, education, communications and peace. Its theological work also dramatized the differences in social thought between the Protestant and Roman Catholic traditions. Above all, the experiment made clear the structural and institutional difficulties of WCC-Roman Catholic cooperation, not least in the enterprise's independent style of operation which sometimes duplicated other work and disturbed those on both sides who desired more programmatic control.

The tensions contributed to the eventual demise of SODEPAX. Diminishing financial support made matters still more difficult. After the initial three years of funding from international financial institutions, SODEPAX had to depend mainly on what the WCC and the Vatican could make available. In time, both sponsoring bodies began to see the needed support as an unnecessary burden.

---

[28] See Richard D.N. Dickinson, "Development" in *Dictionary of the Ecumenical Movement*, pp.298-303.
[29] See *Mater et Magistra* (1961) on Christianity and social progress, *Pacem in Terris* (1962) on peace, and *Populorum Progressio* (1967) on development of peoples.

Thomas Sieger Derr's book *Barriers to Ecumenism: The Holy See and the WCC on Social Questions*,[30] published three years after the end of the SODEPAX, uncovers some of the underlying tensions. There were remarkable areas of agreement on human rights, religious liberty, economic development, racism and the like, yet rarely joint actions or statements arising from such regions of accord. Derr attributes mutual hesitation to differences both of doctrine and of style. The Vatican, after long and careful study, speaks cautiously and in generalities. The WCC convenes short-term meetings that speak specifically and prophetically. Behind these differences of style are more profound theological and ecclesiological tensions.

Lutheran theologian Mark Ellingsen has noted that since Vatican II, Catholic social thinkers have begun to subordinate creation to Christology, while the WCC, since the onset of the limits-to-growth debate, has shown more openness to "natural law" perspectives.[31] The question of relationships between reflection within the WCC and Roman Catholic social thought will emerge again with reference to the 1990 Seoul gathering on "Justice, Peace, and the Integrity of Creation".

"The Future of Man and Society in a World of Science-Based Technology"

The WCC's 1969 central committee also approved a prospectus from Church and Society responding to the Uppsala initiative to focus attention on "The Future of Man and Society in a World of Science-Based Technology". Funds from a Swedish source enabled the department to convene an exploratory conference on the theme "From Here to Where? Technology, Faith and the Future of Man". The 120 participants included scientists, social thinkers, philosophers, theologians and political leaders. Introducing the published report of this meeting, conference chairperson Samuel Parmar wrote:

> ...Our concerns lead us into new and uncharted areas. Man must not be made subservient to "progress" which is taken as a blessing of modern science. More important than the autonomy of science and technology is the autonomy and freedom of man, of the human spirit. We have to transcend the narrow materialistic concepts that have governed decisions about the use of technological power. The scientist who can see beyond the present level of knowledge, the social scientist who dreams of a new order, the humanist who is concerned about dehumanization of our structures and values, the theologian who struggles to incarnate the transcendental into the existing situation, all of them are engaged in acts of faith. Therein lies our unity as we begin to understand the complexities of society and the exercise of all modes of power: technological, economic, political, in today's world.[32]

The recommendations of this meeting advanced plans for a WCC programme of study and action in this field, leading to a series of working conferences on theoretical and practical issues relating to developments in fields such as genetics, nuclear energy and the environment. Inquiries were also launched concerning the impact of science and technology in various regions, including East Asia (Malaysia, 1973) and America-Europe (France, 1973).[33]

---

[30] Thomas Sieger Derr, *Barriers to Ecumenism: The Holy See and the World Council on Social Questions*, Maryknoll NY, Orbis, 1983.

[31] For more, see Mark Ellingsen, *The Cutting Edge: How Churches Speak on Social Issues*, WCC, 1993, p.143f. Also *Commitment to God's World*, pp.155ff.

[32] S.L. Parmar, "Foreword" to David M. Gill ed., *From Here to Where? Technology, Faith, and the Future of Man*, WCC, 1970, p.8.

[33] The findings of these preparatory meetings were duly reported in the Church and Society publication *Anticipation: Christian Social Thought in Future Perspective*.

A world conference to review and sum up the results of these meetings met in 1974 in Bucharest on the theme "Science and Technology for Human Development: The Ambiguous Future and the Christian Hope". It was this meeting – the first ecumenical conference held in Romania – that introduced the concept of a "just and sustainable society" as a goal for the churches, later transformed into a programme to promote the "Just, Participatory and Sustainable Society" (JPSS).

In 1975, Church and Society organized a hearing in Sweden on "The Risks and Potentialities of the Further Expansion of Nuclear Energy". Nuclear scientists and engineers on both sides of the question took part. Reports of all these meetings were made available to the WCC's fifth assembly at Nairobi in late 1975.

NAIROBI (1975): RECAPITULATION AND NEW EMPHASES

Many of the programme thrusts begun at or soon after Uppsala continued beyond Nairobi. Fewer fresh initiatives appeared than had been the case after Uppsala. But new emphases were now placed on the issues of faith, science and technology, militarism and disarmament, ecology and human survival, and the role of women in church and society. Nairobi also marked the growing impact of liberation perspectives on many aspects of WCC thought and action. Philip Potter, who had become general secretary of the WCC in 1972, was beginning to emerge as a key voice in the transition from the older to the newer paradigms of ecumenical social thought.

In the interim between Uppsala and Nairobi the works of Gustavo Gutiérrez, Paulo Freire and others had also begun to make their mark. The PCR and the special fund had become public tokens of WCC commitment to the cause of the poor. Development thinking was moving away from Western paradigms towards participatory postures. Nairobi saw a sharpening focus and consolidation of certain programme thrusts, directing ecumenical social thought and action towards a "church of the poor", towards a "Just, Participatory and Sustainable Society" (JPSS), and towards a coming conference on "Faith, Science and the Future".

Towards a church of the poor

An action-reflection programme on "The Church and the Poor" was undertaken that quickly produced three important published studies. Santa Ana's *Good News to the Poor*[34] explored the relationships between the poor and the organized church in the ancient and medieval periods. This was followed by *Separation without Hope?*,[35] a set of essays under Santa Ana's editorship dealing with the industrial age and Western colonial expansion. Finally *Towards a Church of the Poor*, reporting the conclusions of a 1978 consultation in Cyprus, recorded the crucial turn towards the idea of a church *of* the poor: that is, a church identified with the poor, in solidarity with the poor, composed of the poor. Among other things, this report said,

> The poor now know that traditional Christian institutions have resulted in an overly Westernized, overly materialized and overly institutionalized Christianity. Along with the poor's demand for a critical approach to the gospel message, there is an equal call for a "decolo-

---

[34] Julio de Santa Ana, *Good News to the Poor: The Challenge of the Poor in the History of the Church*, WCC, 1977.

[35] Julio de Santa Ana ed., *Separation Without Hope? Essays on the Relation Between the Church and the Poor during the Industrial Revolution and the Western Colonial Expansion*, WCC, 1978.

nialization of Christianity." ... The challenge is not only to identify with the poor, but to become poor and above all else to become the church as it ought to be.[36]

Some questioned the literal possibility of this prescription, while also raising the
question whether thinking from the perspective of the poor always produces the most
effective strategies for dealing with their poverty. A continuing concern for economic
development of a sort able to deliver distributive justice on a world scale was also a preoccupation. At the close of the "church of the poor" study, the CCPD staff, in collaboration with Church and Society, launched the Advisory Group on Economic Matters
(AGEM), an international group of noted economists and social scientists which produced a series of significant studies. The notion of a "preferential option for the poor"
was honoured here in terms of "identification" and "solidarity" but not, at least until the
late 1980s, as the literal "epistemological privilege" some saw in the theology of life programme.

Participation and sustainability

Since the period immediately after Uppsala the WCC had taken part in the international
development debate about a new international economic order through its Commission
on the Churches' Participation in Development. But developmentalism as such was
soon seen to have come to an impasse between demands from the West that the third
world limit population, and demands from the third world that the first world reduce
consumption. Nairobi authorized its new programme, "Towards a Just, Participatory
and Sustainable Society (JPSS)", which was intended to move beyond this conundrum.
At the same time it was to capture the several ingredients of the international debate in
one brief phrase, with the hope that member churches would commit to working for a
sustainable future without polarization. The search for *participatory* justice and *participatory* sustainability was meant to continue the theme of solidarity.[37]

The "participation" theme became prominent just as the experience of estrangement
and powerlessness was coming to a head in a variety of ways in different parts of the
world: demonstrations against nuclear energy projects, pressures towards governmental
decentralization in France, "states rights" or "new federalism" interests in the US, assertions of regional, national and local distinctiveness across the third world, new
emphasis on local ecumenism within the churches.[38] This sheer variety of concrete
experience complicated the task of thinking globally about the meaning of the word
"participatory", raising questions about the appropriate institutions for participation by
the people, and hence questions of democratic theory and practice.

The "sustainability" theme pointed to the acknowledged fact that levels of consumption in first-world societies have been achieved by exploiting the resources of the rest of

---

[36] *Towards a Church of the Poor*, p.102.
[37] The phrase "sustainable society" seems initially to have come upon the world stage at the WCC's initiative, while the WCC always avoided the phrase "sustainable development", because it seemed a contradiction in terms. The distinction was between the sustainability of just, livable and environmentally
friendly *communities* – the WCC vision which saw matters from "below" – and the notion of a sustainable *development* process focused on rising gross domestic product numbers as seen from the
standpoint of the World Bank or the International Monetary Fund. The latter perspective has since
been condemned by Larry Rasmussen as not only "too economistic" but "bad economics" as well. See
Rasmussen, *Earth Community, Earth Ethics*, WCC, 1996, p.146, as well as the whole chapter, "Message from Geneva".
[38] See Richard D.N. Dickinson, *Poor, Yet Making Many Rich*, WCC, 1983, p.170.

the earth.[39] Furthermore, what worldwide level of consumption, and what principles of just distribution, would be compatible with environmental limits? Could acceptable global life-styles be achieved without risking adverse long-term consequences? And what about the issue of justice towards future generations? The need for structural change, perhaps "revolutionary" structural change, was more clearly inherent in the JPSS perspective than in that of CCPD.

In the hands of Preman Niles, director of the WCC's Justice, Peace and the Integrity of Creation Programme in the late 1980s, JPSS marked one more shift away from "responsible society" rhetoric, which Niles saw as engendering political pessimism about the possibilities of change in the world. "Responsible society" talk was ostensibly focused on maintaining democracy rather than achieving justice. JPSS reversed these priorities. Yet, Niles wrote,

> To give prominence to the JPSS model is not to reject the concerns of responsible society, but rather to modify and subordinate them to the concerns of the former. Christian realism cannot be discarded. We live in an imperfect world and have to envision proximate goals which will be achieved through less than perfect means. However, it is necessary to move beyond the political pessimism engendered by the concept of the responsible society by using the kingdom perspective inherent in the JPSS model.[40]

It proved difficult for the JPSS theme to coalesce into new programmatic thrusts for social action. The report of this programme to the 1979 Jamaica central committee meeting led to a spirited debate concerning the relation between the kingdom of God and the processes of history. On the one hand, the JPSS report was praised for having seen history and eschatology from the perspective of the poor, for whom the struggles for justice, participation and sustainability were matters of life and death. On the other hand, it was argued that distinctions between history and eschatology were not made clearly enough, that the report tended at times to an unexamined "messianism", and that generally insufficient attention had been given to the problems connected with moving from theological to political categories.[41] The central committee proceeded to call for a study of political ethics, that is "an examination of the structures of power, participation and political organization on local, national and international levels". A consultation on this subject took place in Cyprus. Philip Potter, by now frequently the best articulator of underlying issues, asked three questions in the report's foreword: Can Christians and churches go beyond generalities to make specific political judgments and, if so, on what basis? How do we deal with the qualitatively new situation brought about by science and technology? And how do we evaluate peoples' movements across the world; is the revolutionary option the only one?[42]

"Faith, Science and the Future" at MIT

Meanwhile, the 1979 conference on "Faith, Science and the Future" convened at the Massachusetts Institute of Technology (MIT) in Cambridge, Massachusetts. This meeting was the fruit of the intensive work in this field done by Church and Society since 1968. Nearly

---

[39] See *Commitment to God's World*, p.65.
[40] Preman Niles, "Rerum Novarum: One Hundred Years", in *The Ecumenical Review*, 43, 4, Oct. 1991, p.454, quoted in van der Bent, *Commitment*, p.66.
[41] *WCC Central Committee Minutes*, 1979, pp. 17ff., quoted in *Commitment to God's World*, p.66f.
[42] *Ibid.*, p.48f.

half the delegates came from the fields of science and technology – so much so that the theologians present seemed, to some observers, to be intimidated into relative silence.

The Jamaica central committee meeting of the WCC in 1979 had called for "a peaceful community of all humankind in which every human being finds true fulfilment of life". The MIT conference affirmed that while science itself implies values, it needs a larger setting of values and purposes. Despite the ambiguities and differences noted at Jamaica, the MIT meeting took up the themes of JPSS in a less "messianic" tone. To paraphrase the meeting's official report,

> We do not expect the full achievement of such a society within human history. We must pay attention to the specific circumstances of our own historical situation, and to the specific situations of those who engage in ethical reflection. We sometimes find that, in particular social locations, insights emerge that "official" interpretation has missed. We have an obligation to give attention to moral insights from outside the Christian community, including those of Marxists. Yet keeping the identity of Christians as a distinct community is essential. We cannot learn from others, or others from us, without such distinctness. We struggle to find an ethic more secure and authoritative than our feelings and our social location.[43]

Christian ethical decisions, the report continues, combine faith in Jesus Christ, by which one is committed to live or die, with the uncertainty of knowing what actions will work to human benefit in a given situation. Sometimes we know what is right: the problem then is to do it. Uncertainty can undercut the basis for action, i.e. provide us a pretext for escape from what we do know we should do. Self-deception is easy. Claims to a sort of universality through the diffusion of science and technology may take attention away from peoples' cultural roots, to the detriment of adequate moral reflection.

What, then, is the ethical relation between justice and sustainability? We seek justice both for our contemporaries and for those who come after us. But, in the short term, there may be conflicts between the two. DDT may prevent deaths from malaria now, but insert poison into the ecosystem to cause even more deaths in the future.

Human authority is exercised within creation, not over it. "We should perhaps think of ourselves as the self-conscious intelligence of the whole created order, with authority to act with and for it, not over it. We are therefore to care for nature, as if it were the body of humanity. This is good theologically, and it is good biologically." This implies that we see nature as "the context for moral judgment, not a world from which human beings can take their values".[44]

How, then, does the vision of the kingdom of God relate to human decisions and political actions?

> We try to recognize in events the activity of God, [which means acknowledging the continuous radical judgment of Christ upon our efforts.] ...the task of the Christian mission and of Christian moral judgment is constantly to point the world to the God who is active within it to bring righteousness and peace. The Christian community does this only when it is itself a community of love, which is prepared to suffer for the sake of its Lord.[45]

---

43 Paul Abrecht ed., *Faith and Science in an Unjust World: Report of the World Council of Churches' Conference on Faith, Science and the Future*, vol. 2, WCC, 1980, pp.147-65.
44 *Faith and Science in an Unjust World: Report of the WCC's Conference on "Faith, Science and the Future": 2. Reports and Recommendations*, Paul Abrecht ed., WCC, 1980, p.162. It is striking how anthropocentric this language (humanity "as the self-conscious intelligence of the whole created order") sounds less than a quarter-century later, in the light of present convictions that creation has its own intrinsic value and increasing doubts as to humanity's ability to "manage" nature. Humanity seems smaller in the universe today than in 1979.
45 *Ibid.*, p.162.

One may recognize here questions of the sort that earlier surfaced in "responsible society" debates under the influence of J.H. Oldham, Reinhold Niebuhr and others, now woven into the discussion of justice, participation and sustainability. How does one translate love into structures, or structure love into justice? At most, we are experiencing the birth-pangs of new order in the world, in which insecurity, pride and ambiguity remain very much with us.

Militarism, disarmament and peace

Nairobi also recognized, as did all previous WCC assemblies, the continued concern about global militarism, noting the close connections between real or perceived economic injustice and the resort to warfare. This discussion, of course, like all other ecumenical attempts to deal with this subject, took place against a background of divided opinion in the churches. On one side lay the ancient tradition of just-war theory, according to which the use of force in certain situations can be ethically justified as a lesser evil. On the other side lay the different varieties of pacifism, including that of the historic peace churches for which any preparation for or participation in war is morally wrong. The advent of nuclear weapons and the pursuit of cold-war politics only made matters more complex, difficult and contentious.

A concentrated effort to deal with this matter followed Nairobi, with consultations in successive years (1977-78) at Glion, Switzerland, and a presentation by the Programme on Militarism and the Arms Race to the central committee in 1979. In 1980, the central committee requested the Sub-unit on Church and Society and the Commission of the Churches on International Affairs to "arrange jointly an international public hearing on the current threat to world peace with special focus on the increased danger of nuclear war, where authoritative witnesses can be cross-examined in an effort to assess the present situation".

The hearing took place at the Free University of Amsterdam in November 1981, with a representative hearing group of some 18 church leaders and concerned lay persons, under the moderatorship of John Habgood, then bishop of Durham in the Church of England. Forty expert witnesses were invited to give their views: a roster of eminent politicians, scholars, activists and others including such figures as McGeorge Bundy, Olof Palme, Brent Scowcroft, Edward Schillebeeckx and Roger Shinn. The voluminous and detailed report of this meeting appeared under the title *Before It's Too Late: The Challenge of Nuclear Disarmament*.[46] The central committee had received the unpublished document the preceding year and commended it to the churches for study, a routine action. But the committee on this occasion went beyond routine in singling out a list of points on which the churches "should take clear positions":
- the unjustifiability of nuclear war under any circumstances;
- "limited" nuclear war is unlikely to remain limited;
- policies of "first use" should be renounced by all present or future nuclear powers;
- the concept of deterrence is morally unacceptable;
- production of nuclear weapons should be halted;
- all nations should ratify a comprehensive test ban treaty; and

---

[46] Paul Abrecht and Ninan Koshy eds, *Before It's Too Late: The Challenge of Nuclear Disarmament*, WCC, 1983. This volume contains the full text of each of the presentations made at the Amsterdam meeting as well as records of the discussions that took place.

– all means leading to both nuclear and conventional disarmament should be welcomed as complementary and mutually reinforcing.

Finally, the central committee declared that a conviction expressed by the public hearing should become "an official position for churches and for Christians" in the following words:

> We believe that the time has come when the churches must unequivocally declare that the production and deployment as well as the use of nuclear weapons are a crime against humanity and that such activities must be condemned on ethical and theological grounds... [S]uch a position supports the struggle to make one's own nation commit itself never to own or use nuclear weapons, despite the perils of nuclear vulnerability, and to persuade Christians and others to refuse to cooperate with or accept employment in any projects related to nuclear weapons and nuclear warfare.[47]

Subsequent events showed that even this ringing pronouncement did little to resolve the fundamental differences between just-war thinkers and those inclined to one or another version of pacifism. The debate was to re-surface, in particular, at the Canberra assembly (1991).

The Community of Women and Men in the Church

The position of women in church and society had been an ecumenical social concern since the WCC's first assembly at Amsterdam in 1948, which heard a report based on an extensive survey of viewpoints and circumstances among the member churches. A Department on the Cooperation of Women and Men in Church, Family and Society was established in 1954, and in 1974 the WCC Women's desk sponsored a world consultation titled "Sexism in the 1970s: Discrimination against Women". This meeting lifted up the fact that women are over-represented among the world's disadvantaged and oppressed. Potter likened the oppression of women to the effects of racism, calling on women to take their liberation into their own hands, thereby assisting in the liberation of their oppressors.

Between 1978 and 1981 a study was launched under the joint auspices of Faith and Order and the Sub-unit on Women in Church and Society[48] on "The Community of Women and Men in the Church". This study culminated at an international consultation in 1981 at Sheffield, England, "to consolidate the initial findings and to formulate recommendations for critical follow-up activities".[49] The preliminary study material attracted global attention, involving more local groups than any other WCC study up to that time. Here, for the first time in major ecumenical settings, the powerful critique of patriarchal social structures by feminist theologians took centre stage. Delegates saw the need for liberation from sexist oppression as parallel in every way to the need for liberation from economic oppression, and often as one and the same struggle. Frustration and anger were expressed at the exclusion of women from ordained ministry in many churches. In response to the Sheffield event, and under the pressure of the frustration and anger expressed there and elsewhere, the 1981 central committee

---

[47] Action of the central committee, 27 July 1982, as recorded in *Before It's Too Late*, p.384.

[48] The choice of these joint auspices was designed to help overcome the perennial reflection/action split in ecumenical discourse and to show that issues of women in the church are fundamentally ecclesiological in nature.

[49] See Constance F. Parvey ed., *The Community of Women and Men in the Church: A Report of the World Council of Churches Conference, Sheffield, England, 1981*, WCC, 1983.

meeting at Dresden established a quota for the representation of women at all WCC events, a pioneering decision at the time.[50]

Feminist witness took diverse forms in different parts of the world. The "revolt" by third-world women that took place half-way through the Sheffield meeting showed, not that feminist consciousness was undeveloped outside the West, but that it expressed itself differently in relation to different cultural situations. Leaders at Sheffield found it difficult to establish linkages between this concern and other sectors of ecumenical social thought. Male theologians in many parts of the world with strong economic liberation concerns – Latin America being perhaps the most striking example – continued in their patriarchal ways.

The initiative was surely among the most widely-responded-to of WCC programmes, and led to concern for fuller representation of women in all deliberations of the churches and in the ecumenical movement.[51] At the sixth assembly (Vancouver 1983), 12 of the plenary speakers were women, and the proportion of women elected to WCC policy-making bodies rose to 29 percent. At Easter 1988, the WCC launched an Ecumenical Decade of Churches in Solidarity with Women which focused particularly on local programmes and emphases. The Decade concluded with a presentation at the eighth assembly in Harare in 1998.

THE SIXTH ASSEMBLY, VANCOUVER 1983

Vancouver 1983 – unlike previous assemblies with their multiple programmatic thrusts towards science and technology, environment and energy – is remembered for one basic insight: that the confession of Jesus Christ as the life of the world and Christian resistance to the powers of death are one and the same thing. Among many other actions, this conviction led to two quite different, but ultimately inter-related, decisions in the area of social thought. It authorized a Faith and Order study on the "Unity of the Church and the Renewal of Human Community". And it called for an engagement by member churches in "a conciliar process of mutual commitment to justice, peace and the integrity of creation" (JPIC), which led eventually to the Seoul convocation of 1990.

Social thought in the context of Faith and Order

The new Faith and Order study on the "Unity of the Church and the Renewal of Human Community" built upon previous experience, but also reflected frustration with the former theme "Unity of the Church – Unity of Humankind". The notion of a "unity of humankind" had begun to appear distressingly abstract. What could be meant by it? No single, shared conception of the human essence was emerging in any of the natural-science or human-science disciplines. Theological conceptions were similarly diverse.[52] The Humanum Studies authorized at Uppsala had produced little consensus. The notion of a "renewal of human community" seemed more graspable, and it also brought social issues and social thought once again into the Faith and Order agenda.

---

[50] See the chapter on inclusive community in this volume for a more detailed discussion of the reaction.

[51] Janet Crawford's thesis *Rocking the Boat: Women's Participation in the World Council of Churches, 1948-1991*, Wellington, NZ, 1995, is a substantial and detailed history. See also an article by the same author on women's issues in relation to Faith and Order: "Women and Ecclesiology: Two Ecumenical Streams?" in *The Ecumenical Review*, 53, 1, Jan. 2001, pp.14-24.

[52] See the report of the earlier Faith and Order studies edited by Geiko Müller-Fahrenholz, *Unity in Today's World*, Faith and Order paper no. 88, WCC, 1978.

Faith and Order had recently begun to avail itself of an "intercontextual method"[53] that sought, in solidarity, to share the testimonies to suffering and hope coming from around the world, bringing them as far as possible into conversation with the developing ecumenical tradition. Intercontextual method did not mean that contextual theology was the only theology, nor that "situation" became theology's primary source. Rather, two moves were involved. Testimonies to specific local or issue-oriented efforts to overcome human brokenness in the light of the gospel were brought into the effort to recover and extend the common Christian tradition. And, in turn, insights gained in that tradition-making process were brought to bear upon the efforts of these communities to address their particular concerns.

The clear implication was that the churches of the Western world, with their university-related theological faculties and deep relationships to dominating cultures, came to represent but one context among others. While the long Faith and Order tradition had been related to that Western context, intercontextual method in effect decentred the conversation. Now insight could come from any source.

Some, of course, continued to insist that justice issues belonged somewhere else in the institutional structure. Critics from outside asked what Faith and Order could do with issues like racism, poverty and sexism beyond blunting their cutting edge by assimilating them into esoteric ecclesiological dialogue, burying them under mountains of prelatical prose. Purists inside the movement feared a dilution of traditional church unity concerns. Yet the Vancouver decision to place "renewal of human community" on Faith and Order's agenda once again, as at Louvain, posed the question of how involvement with justice issues could be seen as intrinsic to the church's being rather than as a concern only for those interested in such questions.

An elaborate working paper, "The Church as Mystery and as Prophetic Sign", appeared in 1985. Simultaneously the Commission sought to bring testimonies from several arenas of liberation struggle into the unity-fostering dialogue process. This effort included a series of regional consultations intended to hear the testimony of Christians working at the forefront of struggles to renew the human community in justice and inclusivity. Such issues were studied at Singapore (1986), Porto Alegre, Brazil (1987), and Harlem, US (1988). Questions concerning the community of women and men brought groups together in Prague (1985) and Porto Novo, Benin (1988).

The 1990 "Unity of the Church and the Renewal of Human Community" incorporated, edited and enlarged versions of previous inquiries, with many quotations and references from the issue-oriented local studies. Chapters with the titles "Unity and Renewal and the Search for Justice" and "Unity and Renewal and the Community of Women and Men" were added. Something new was happening. In the past, the tradition of Faith and Order had not often sought to embrace local and issue-focused forms of witness. It had tended instead to dissolve them conceptually into ecclesiological and even ontological generalizations. Faith and Order was now testing its fresh articulations

---

[53] Faith and Order had begun to develop "intercontextual method" after the Accra plenary commission meeting (1974) in the process of eliciting confessions of faith from churches across the globe, later published in four volumes as *Confessing Our Faith around the World*, WCC, 1976. This process was linked to the section report "Confessing Christ Today" at the Nairobi assembly (1975), which, in a Christological perspective, holds together as inseparable the concerns of theology, worship, justice and peace (see esp. §43).

of tradition for their capacity to sponsor at least a "convergence", if not "fusion", of horizons, this time not only between past and present and between the different historic communions, but also with all the new expressions of faith in movements of human inclusion and liberation. New horizons of faith were having their impact upon the growing ecumenical tradition: pressing it, extending it, enriching it.

A fundamental question arising from these efforts was whether the sacramental and the socio-ethical dimensions implied in the study could be held together. Could one speak of the consequences of the church's signifying presence in the world and at the same time do justice to the church's inherent being as sacramental reality in its own right? These questions were to surface again at Seoul in 1990 and in the studies of a "theology of life" and "ecclesiology and ethics" after the Canberra assembly in 1991.

Did these Faith and Order studies produce a theological basis for ecumenical social thought and action? This precise result had not been intended. And, furthermore, the studies in question had not yielded unambiguous results. Faith and Order had not spoken with one voice. Moreover, Church and Society and its successor units in the WCC would not often draw upon these materials for their rationale. Rather, the tendency was to take for granted the simple yet powerful biblical prophetic passages on justice and peace instead of detouring through the controverted notion of an ecclesiology for which social witness is of the essence. Ecumenical social thinkers implicitly believed the latter understanding to be valid, but did not often take on Faith and Order's ways of wrestling with this issue. Yet, as we shall see, the notion of a "conciliar process" for achieving a covenant around "Justice, Peace and the Integrity of Creation" once again would bring the social thinkers close to ecclesiological concerns.

Justice, Peace and the Integrity of Creation (JPIC)

JPIC as a programmatic emphasis marked a conceptual shift from the earlier CCPD and JPSS programmes. What was going on as the Council moved from one acronym to another? Konrad Raiser, at the Jamaica central committee in 1979, had likened these combinations of concerns to the scientific "paradigms" of Thomas Kuhn: comprehensive perspectives or ways of putting concerns together that characterize different ages and give rise to new ways of asking old questions, as well as to questions never before asked. Perhaps the WCC's thematic clusters were not quite that. They did not quite represent comprehensive world views or *epistemes*. Rather, they signalled ensembles of concerns that belong together, yet all too often are considered separately by groups with passionate concerns for justice, or peace, or the environment as such. In particular, these ecumenical acronyms served to make the institutional point that various programmes were supposed to interact, that reconfigurings of departments and staff were supposed to yield new insights about the interconnections of factors constituting the human situation at any given moment.

It is apparent that in the new formula the concerns for "justice" and "peace" remained, and in that order. But "participation" was now missing and the focus on "sustainability" had shifted towards a concern for the "integrity of creation". It is probably correct to argue that the notions of "participation" and "sustainability" had proved both controversial and difficult to define in the preceding decade, giving rise to interminable debates among experts in political theory and resource management. "Development" as a theme involved both and, as we have seen, gave rise again and again to an impasse between consumption limiters and population limiters, both parties arguing for behavioural changes in parts of the world other than their own.

If, as the delegates to Vancouver wished, issues of justice, peace and sustainability were now to become the subject of a "conciliar process", it seemed best not to include matters on which there had been so much argument, definitional, procedural and otherwise. The notion of "conciliar process" linked the JPIC studies to the theme of "conciliar unity", developed by Faith and Order and endorsed at Nairobi in 1975. In short, a step was taken that made these social concerns incipiently ecclesiological as well. The churches were invited into a process that might eventually define these commitments as being of the *essence* of the faith itself and therefore of the church universal.

The same point can be put in a different way. Vancouver had said that the confession of Jesus Christ as the life of the world and Christian resistance to the powers of death are one and the same activity. This expressed conviction countered the view that Christian involvement in world affairs is largely a matter for those interested in "Christian ethics" as a distinct discipline of its own. Rather, confessing the faith together became integral to a missionary *and* moral task of resisting the powers of evil in the world, including all the newly recognized powers at work in a global society.

Already moves to link social righteousness to the integrity of the faith as such had been made by two affiliated world communions with reference to apartheid in South Africa. The Lutheran World Federation (LWF) in 1977 and the World Alliance of Reformed Churches (WARC) in 1982 had both declared that support by the South African churches for, or complicity in, the social policy of apartheid raised a status confessionis: meaning that such attitudes and practices constituted a fundamental denial of the Christian faith which, if persisted in, would place the ecclesial body concerned beyond the limits of the confessional fellowship, if not of the *una sancta* (one, holy, catholic and apostolic church). The WARC suspended two white South African churches from its membership on this account, declaring that the theological defence of apartheid (which had been affirmed by interpreting Calvinism as justifying the South African whites' self-image as a divinely chosen people) is a heresy and that exclusion of non-whites from eucharist is a sin.

In such an atmosphere, many at Vancouver could see that a "conciliar process" meant not only a cooperative enterprise (which, of course, it was) but also one in which covenantal[54] commitment to global justice, peace and the integrity of creation could come to be seen as constitutive of the gospel itself. The conciliarity of such a process and its implications soon came to be tested in the preparations and execution of the world convocation at Seoul in 1990.

The new notion added to the theme-cluster, that of the "integrity" of creation, was adopted at the behest of the Orthodox. It aroused much interest while calling forth strenuous criticism. From the "sustainability" of a just, peaceful way of life on earth, basically an anthropological, societal concern, the focus now moved to an integrity attributed to creation itself, making "creation" virtually a partner in the dialogue. The question now

---

[54] The term "covenant", so familiar to the Reformed and other Protestant traditions, did not prove illuminating for all. Different churches use it in different ways, and some not at all. Disagreement likewise surfaced over the biblical roots of the term. Was the "covenant" not established by God once-for-all in Jesus Christ? How could it now refer to a mutual commitment made by the churches with one another? How was it related to the 17th-century and contemporary uses of the notion of "social contract". See *Commitment to God's World*, p.68.

was not only what standard of living, expressing distributive justice for all human beings, could be sustained into the foreseeable future. It asked instead what ways of life truly respect the created order for what it is? And then, of course, one has to *say* what it is: how it is to be regarded in its own existence.

Such questions naturally touched off new debates between moralists for whom concern focused on the human realm as such, and those who saw the creation itself as somehow living, possessing rights of its own, a world in which human beings are participants but not necessarily the centre of all value. A process of study followed involving local, national, regional and confessional groups across the globe. Conferences and assemblies on JPIC took place in Europe, Latin America and the Pacific. The 1989 European Ecumenical Assembly at Basel, sponsored by the Conference of European Churches and the Council of European Bishops Conferences, was the most substantial of these pre-Seoul meetings.[55] It proved to be important, quite apart from the Seoul convocation itself, in stimulating ecumenical thought and action within Europe, not least in the dimension of Protestant-Roman Catholic relationships. Other contributions, representing specific theological perspectives, came from the Reformed, the Orthodox, and the Roman Catholic Pontifical Council on Justice and Peace.

The Seoul convocation (1990)

What happened when the attempt was made to give the idea of ecclesial communion a specific ethical content? The WCC's 1990 Seoul convocation on "Justice, Peace and the Integrity of Creation" was intended by its organizers to help build a stronger conciliar fellowship in the ecumenical community around shared moral principles. Indeed, for some, the intention of the phrase "conciliar process" was to give such principles a status as marks of the mutual commitment implied in WCC membership, or as implied by the Nairobi assembly's adoption in 1975 of the notion of "conciliar fellowship", as earlier formulated by Faith and Order at Louvain (1971).[56] But in the preparatory process some saw a "conciliar process" as implying an ecclesiological commitment they were unprepared to make. It was largely, if not entirely, for this reason that the Roman Catholic Church withdrew its agreement to co-sponsor the event and scaled back its participation in the

---

[55] The 1989 Basel assembly was praised for the way it combined the features of a formal church assembly with those of a popular Kirchentag. An excerpt from its report, *Peace with Justice: The Official Documentation of the European Ecumenical Assembly, Basel, Switzerland, 15-21 May, 1989*, Geneva, Conference of European Churches, 1989, is provided in *The Ecumenical Movement: An Anthology*, pp.251-53.

[56] Indeed, it appears that the intent of some did indeed go beyond the formulas of Toronto, Louvain or Nairobi, namely to give affirmations growing out of the programme on Justice, Peace and the Integrity of Creation (the lineal descendant of the Life and Work movement within the WCC structure) a formal ecclesiological significance, i.e. to make moral commitments part of the *esse* of the church as theologically and juridically defined. It seems to have been, among other things, a retreat from this sort of commitment, seen as an unwarranted theological escalation of the meeting's original agenda, that led the Roman Catholic Church to withdraw from sponsorship of the Seoul meeting, although many Roman Catholics were present. The notion of "a genuinely universal council", of course, already had a long ecumenical history with many nuances of meaning. The term goes back at least to the Bristol (1967) Faith and Order Commission meeting, and found mention at Uppsala (1968) in the section report on "The Holy Spirit and the Catholicity of the Church." See *The Uppsala Report*, WCC, 1968, p.17. See also "The Importance of the Conciliar Process in the Ancient Church for the Ecumenical Movement", WCC Studies no. 5, WCC, 1968.

Seoul meeting. The nature of "conciliarity" with reference to global social issues was never sufficiently clarified.[57]

Other deep and divisive differences appeared at Seoul. Some of these were familiar from earlier ecumenical gatherings. There surfaced again two older models of Christian social and political responsibility: those of the "responsible society" and the model of a "just, participatory and sustainable society" (JPSS). The first was seen as Western Christian "realism", the other as a reaffirmation of third-world revolutionary political action for social justice.[58] Tension also arose between local, regional and global analyses of threats to life and appropriate responses by the churches. Differences appeared both in the degree of preparation by delegates and in their expectations. Differences in understanding regarding the meaning of "covenant" remained unresolved.

The Seoul meeting was presented at the outset with an analytical document dealing with the challenges facing the people of the planet. This work was generally well received, yet thought by many delegates to propose overly ambitious global reality-definitions couched in Western academic language too abstract to make contact with local experience in all its variety and profusion. The conference finally produced a set of four covenants and ten affirmations reflecting the contextual and ecumenical experience of the people present, drafted in the course of the meeting and considerably modifying the preliminary documents.

The "four covenants" dealt with (1) a just economic order, including liberation from debt; (2) true security for all in nonviolent cultures; (3) cultures that can live in harmony with creation's integrity; and (4) an end to racism and discrimination, dismantling patterns of racist behaviour.[59]

The affirmations came with elaborate explanatory texts: topic sentences or phrases give the flavour for purposes of this chapter. The document affirmed that all exercise of power is accountable to God, God's option for the poor, the equal value of all races and peoples, that male and female are created in the image of God, that truth is at the foundation of a community of free people, the peace of Jesus Christ, the creation as beloved of God, that the earth is the Lord's, the dignity and commitment of the younger generation, that human rights are given by God. Each clause is elaborated in three stages: the affirmation itself, and then two statements: one of resistance and the other of commitment. This structure implies that in each area of concern one is either on principle deeply opposed to something or strongly identified with it, with little in between.

The effort made after Seoul to persuade the churches to enter a covenant based on the ten affirmations did not wholly succeed. A feeling arose that the language adopted, grounded in actual experience as it was, could not be given clear (that is, unequivocal)

---

[57] It may also be that a classic linguistic confusion added to the difficulties, in that the single English word "council" can have different sets of meanings distinguishable in Latin, French and German. Clearly the WCC itself is a "council" in the sense of the Latin *consilium*, the French *conseil* and the German *Rat*: i.e. a consultative body making no claims to conciliarity in the Nicene or Constantinopolitan sense. But a "conciliar commitment" could also imply the larger, more portentous meaning, as in the Latin *concilium*, French *concile*, or German *Konzil*. Did the Seoul planners mean "conciliar commitment" as a step on the way to an "ecumenical council" of the whole church. If so, the claim went much too far, especially for Roman Catholics and Orthodox, but not for them alone.

[58] See *Commitment to God's World*, p.69.

[59] See the report of Seoul: D. Preman Niles ed., *Between the Flood and the Rainbow: Interpreting the Conciliar Process of Mutual Commitment (Covenant) to Justice, Peace and the Integrity of Creation*, WCC, 1992.

meanings across a variety of contexts. In different cultural and confessional situations their implications could not be foreseen.

Furthermore, the content of the affirmations also drew sharp criticism. Considering the conditions under which they were drafted, lacunae and weaknesses were inevitable. Slavery and torture, still existing in the world, were not specifically mentioned. Perhaps these issues fell under the heading of human rights, and possibly of other affirmations as well. But perhaps the most important questions were theological. As Charles West wrote in the wake of the meeting: Where are the elements of grace and forgiveness? Where is the evangelical witness to the saving work of God in human society?[60] And where, some asked, was there continuity with the ecumenical tradition in social ethics that runs from Oxford (1937) to Geneva (1966) to MIT (1979)?

Seoul undoubtedly failed to fulfill the expectations with which its planners had begun their task.[61] But, simply by eliciting comments such as those just mentioned, it contributed to the debate on ecumenical ethics, giving ecumenical social thought a new awareness of the diversity of approaches to the themes of JPIC owing above all to differences of conceptual frameworks. Some expected JPIC to come up with answers to questions first raised, in a Western idiom, at Oxford 1937, and were disappointed. But for many, Seoul 1990 turned out to be more a "liturgical event" than either a theological or a social-scientific consultation. Indeed, it was intended to be different in structure, programme and content from MIT (1979), not to speak of Oxford (1937). Others said that Seoul merely used biblical quotations as sticks with which to lambaste the secular order, offering running comment on every point in the world's agenda, encouraging simple-minded activism without adequate input from "experts" in the fields of sociology, politics or economics. Again others argued that the concept of "expertise" is now different. The expert is now someone actually in a situation of oppression. The Seoul process brought together people with first-hand experience of threats to their survival. It marked a rediscovery of social movements as part of the search for relevant ecclesiology.

The ten affirmations, moreover, did live up to their affirmative name. They were hopeful because they presupposed that by God's grace something can be done about the state of creation and of the human condition. They were valuable indications of the content that ought to be found in a moral communion of ethical engagement with the world. But, above all, they themselves helped create the kind of space needed for an effort to think out and live out what such a communion could require. As entry-points for the wide range of local case studies in the subsequent Theology of Life programme, they "serve[d] as a preliminary definition of the framework and space in which people can build up confidence and trust".[62]

The surfacing of a "loyal opposition"

The period of planning for Seoul, and the reaction afterwards, witnessed a resurfacing of general criticism about WCC social thought: criticism that had been smouldering at least since the adoption of the JPIC programme after Vancouver (1983). What might be called a "loyal opposition" – by persons with impeccable ecumenical credentials, in contrast to opposition from outside the movement altogether or from rival visions – began

---

[60] Charles West, "Ecumenical Social Ethics Beyond Socialism and Capitalism", in *The Ecumenical Review*, 43, 3, July 1991, pp.329-40.
[61] *Commitment to God's World*, pp.70ff.
[62] Martin Robra, "Theology of Life: Justice, Peace, Creation", in *The Ecumenical Review*, 48, 1, Jan. 1996, p.35.

to make itself felt. It could perhaps be said that foundations for this critical perspective began as early as 1985 in a special issue of *The Ecumenical Review* honouring the career of Paul Abrecht, who retired in 1983 as director of the Department of Church and Society.[63] Here, as if in response to the change in perspective marked by Vancouver, the legacy of "responsible society" thinking passes in review. The keynote piece by W.A. Visser 't Hooft is "Oldham's Method in Abrecht's Hands". Ronald Preston, in "Critics From Without and From Within", alludes to growing criticism of social witness in programmes other than those of Church and Society. But criticism soon begins to come from Abrecht's own pen. In a subsequent issue of *The Ecumenical Review*,[64] Abrecht took on the "liberation ecumenism" which he perceived to have displaced "responsible society" thinking and its successor programmes, as having difficulty coping with the challenge of the modern scientific-technological world-view. To demand that industrially developing nations receive a just share of the world's resources is understandable where social justice is taken as the primary issue, but it avoids the question of the uses of science and technology as such. Furthermore, the "action-reflection" approach suggests that commitment should precede reflection: that "reflection (in the form of conceptual or theological understanding) can never determine the action but only strengthen or defend what is already decided".

According to Abrecht, the ecumenical model, spoken or unspoken, for the "new world economic order" since about 1970 had been some form of socialism.[65] The 1960s' theology of revolution soon became liberation theology, which by Nairobi (1975) inspired an ecumenical commitment to struggle against the world capitalist system. This movement was unprepared for the fall of socialism in Eastern Europe and for revelations of the social, economic and political injustices of that system. At Seoul "the populist revolutionary ideology was simply assumed as the starting point without supporting analysis or consideration of alternative points of view". Abrecht concluded,

> Cut off from its historic theological-ethical roots and obliged to recognize that the concept of a revolutionary transformation of the world economic and social order is an illusion, ecumenical social thought faces a predicament of historic proportions. How shall it be reconstructed? What, precisely, is the function of the church in modern society?

Writing for *The Dictionary of the Ecumenical Movement* in 1991, Charles West took a different but equally critical tack. He expressed profound suspicion of the ideological bias in recent ecumenical theology and social ethics, in the form of a demand that solidarity with the oppressed be the starting point for all theological and ethical action and reflection. Ultimately the issue is that between divine and human power in our expectations for history:

> Can the world be redeemed by replacing the principalities and powers that now dominate it with others representing the people and the poor? Is the justice achieved by human struggle itself subject to the judgment of God and the correction of further struggle for the corruption which is present in its relative goodness? Are there resources in the Christian community to empower believers in their struggle against injustice while at the same time believing in and praying for divine forgiveness and transformation of us all?[66]

---

[63] "Church and Society: Ecumenical Perspective. Essays in Honour of Paul Abrecht", in *The Ecumenical Review*, 37, 1, Jan. 1985.

[64] Paul Abrecht, "From Oxford to Vancouver", in "Fifty Years of Ecumenical Social Thought", *The Ecumenical Review*, 40, 2, April 1988, pp.147ff.

[65] Paul Abrecht, "Ecumenical Social Thought in the Post-Cold War Period", in *The Ecumenical Review*, 43, 3, July, 1991, pp.305ff.

[66] Charles West, "Power" in *Dictionary of the Ecumenical Movement*, p.923 (2nd ed.).

An informal group of church leaders, theologians, social ethicists and lay persons active in public life met three times in the period 1990-93 to voice further fundamental criticisms. In a document titled "The Future of Ecumenical Social Thought",[67] this largely European and North American group argued that the WCC "lacks competence and credibility in its social witness, and that it fails to do justice to the diversity of situations confronting Christians, the different opinions they hold, and the variety of methods they employ in their social thinking". According to this document, the WCC defines an "orthopraxis" which excludes honest dissent, fails to be properly modest and selective in electing issues for attention, claims a "prophetic" stance without grasping that the biblical prophets did not claim to be "prophetic" and were not salaried bureaucrats, distrusts technical competence as "elitist", and fails to develop adequate theological foundations for its work. WCC social thought in the early 1990s, this document claims, also failed adequately to respond to events in Eastern Europe, the situation of the churches there, the collapse of totalitarian communism and the situation in the former Soviet Union. Better informed, more nuanced, treatments of the growing global market economy and of new environmental issues were needed, and not forthcoming.

THE SEVENTH ASSEMBLY, CANBERRA (1991)

Canberra was the first assembly to meet after the fall of the Berlin wall, the end of the cold war and the annexation of Eastern European nations in varying degrees to the economic systems and values of the West. Not surprisingly, then, this assembly also marked a season in which the great debate in ecumenical social ethics (whatever the terminology) between thinking of the "responsible society" type and of the "revolutionary solidarity" sort began to unravel, the East-West orientation replaced by a North-South perspective. Sometime in the 1980s, the former dialectic had begun to evolve into something less ideological and more pragmatic. In a certain way, both "responsible society" thinking and revolutionary socialism of the liberation type had been following the long-term assumptions, or perhaps the *grands récits* (Fernand Braudel) of their respective first and second worlds, while competing for dominance in the third world, whose very name reflected the former East-West world paradigm. But two things had begun to happen. What now was called "the South" began, at least in the persons of its theologians, to stake out its own perspectives and positions in a manner determined to be "non-aligned" politically, economically and theologically.[68] And, secondly, the *grands récits* themselves began to lose *cachet* as narratives descriptive of human fulfilment. They lost the spiritual quality, the worthiness to be trusted, they had possessed for millions of adherents, among them Christian leaders.

And, with this loss of spiritual charisma, these ideological utopias began to appear much less coherent philosophically. Intellectual foundations on both sides began to be

[67] "A Statement to the World Council of Churches on the Future of Ecumenical Social Thought", privately printed, with an introduction by John Habgood, Archbishop of York, Dec. 1992. This document is signed by twenty persons in addition to Archbishop Habgood: a veritable roster of ecumenical leadership on social questions mostly active in the movement prior to the 1970s. The one non-European member was Vítor Westhelle, professor of theology and ethics at the Escola Superior de Teología, Sao Leopoldo, Brazil.
[68] The Ecumenical Association of Third World Theologians, or EATWOT, founded in 1977, took this non-aligned position, but also incorporated the "third-world" notion into its name, thereby adopting nomenclature which depended for its sense on the existence of rival "first" and "second" worlds.

questioned. Much of this was already happening before the "wall" came down, and may have had something to do with its fall. "Deconstruction" of the great political ideals was in the air. This does not mean that all the qualities and political practices of the liberal spirit and of the socialist conscience disappeared. They only ceased to be connected with large expectations about human fulfilment. They ceased to be *believed in* as ideological syntheses, but remained useful in practical ways. What was left after the deconstruction were human-science insights and techniques of all kinds, pragmatic perspectives, a host of well-remembered experiences ready to be put to work in getting along and improving the practical human condition. Theologians could no longer attach themselves to great syntheses of the human spirit, East or West, and be confident of being carried forward along a self-evident course of human development, making what contribution they could to such inevitabilities. Something new was needed. This turned out to be an emphasis on the work of the Spirit in faith communities to generate ethical perspectives based on the churches' own traditions.

The delegates at Canberra could not have been fully aware of all this. The assembly moved along lines flowing from the conclusions reached at Seoul. It was preoccupied by divisive moral questions triggered by the Gulf war raging as the assembly met,[69] and by debates on syncretism touched off by the keynote address of a young Korean theologian, Chung Hyun Kyung. The theme "Come, Holy Spirit – Renew the Whole Creation" marked a further step in the process described by Raiser: away from Christological concentration and towards a fully trinitarian understanding of God at work to gather a "household of life".[70] The Orthodox voiced deep concerns, particularly with the appearances of "syncretism" in the keynote address, and their representatives expressed difficulty in even participating in the forms of discourse current at Canberra.

This assembly stressed the inevitable linkages between justice issues and environmental concerns. A distinction emerged between mere "growth", the strategy of the cancer cell, and "development", the strategy of the embryo. The latter strategy puts things in the right places in the right amounts at the right time. Development of the earth by human beings needs to follow the embryonic strategy.[71]

An important lesson had been learned in the JPIC process. It is vital, even in the midst of efforts to achieve the unity of the church and the moral coherence of human community and in the face of criticism from European and North American theologians

---

[69] Intense debate over the Gulf war again disclosed the deep divisions among Christians about the moral defensibility of warfare. An amendment by a German delegate, Konrad Raiser, to the assembly's deliberation on this subject proposed the following added sentence: "We call upon [the churches] to give up any theological or moral justification of the use of military power, be it in war or through other forms of oppressive security systems, and to become public advocates of a just peace." After being approved, the amendment was rescinded as delegates began to see its far-reaching implications. Two years later Raiser would be elected the WCC's fifth general secretary.

[70] Konrad Raiser's book *Ecumenism in Transition: A Paradigm Shift in the Ecumenical Movement?*, WCC, 1991, articulated for many the frustrations and the possibilities of the movement at this juncture. First published in German in 1989, the English language edition contains case studies and a postscript which update the text to include references to the Seoul convocation and the Canberra assembly that followed it in 1991. Raiser discusses the relation between the ecclesiological significance of the WCC, a subject of continuing debate, and the Council's aim to make the mutual search for justice, peace and creation's integrity a "conciliar process". Such a process, he wrote, needs guiding markers or touchstones arrived at not by superior central authority, but as the results of insights gained in striving together for the truth. These need to be provisional and revisable, their authority depending on reception by the fellowship of believers and their truth being constantly tested.

[71] Michael Kinnamon, *Signs of the Spirit*, WCC, 1991, p.63f.

and ethicists, to avoid approaches largely from above and largely from the North. Older visions of the oikoumene had been formulated theologically from centres of cultural, political and economic domination and unknowingly betrayed those origins even where strenuous efforts were made to include contributions from many cultures. The Theology of Life programme, which grew out of the deliberations at and after Canberra, sought to appropriate this lesson organically.

A Theology of Life programme

The Canberra assembly had clearly seen the destructive consequences of rapidly burgeoning global economic activities for creation and therefore called for better links between ecological and economic concerns. This, combined with the need to appropriate the learnings of Seoul, led in 1992 to a reorganization of the WCC's Unit III under the name "Justice, Peace and Creation". Units formerly working on these concerns independently were brought under one umbrella. A year of efforts to integrate these concerns organically led first to studies in the field of civil society,[72] but subsequently to a realization that all of the Unit III themes had to do with resistance to "threats to life". All of them had to do with fostering life in abundance.

Here Raiser's paradigm of a "household of life" was having its influence. But the guiding mind and hand were now those of Larry Rasmussen, co-moderator of the Unit committee.[73] It was affirmed that the vision of an "ecumenical earth", advocating a life-centred understanding of the oikoumene which embraces all God's creation and requires an openness to the insights of many cultures and faith communities, can contribute to a life-centred spirituality and ethic.[74]

Was the "theology of life" effort a response to the alleged "failure" of Seoul, or was it just the next step?[75] If the ten affirmations could not be adopted at the level of a "conciliar" commitment (implying at least some degree of centralized authority), then they could be carried forward in the form of a global-local hermeneutics of specific contexts, each of them unique in its own way. At this stage hope was expressed that hermeneutical criteria could be developed for grasping "areas of convergence" among the different communities of faith.[76] On the one hand was the danger of imposing foreign categories on the experience of peoples and cultures. On the other hand lay the danger of too easy

---

[72] The civil society studies, under the leadership of Israel Batista, had some success in northern hemisphere countries. See, for example, the report of a consultation on theology and civil society at Loccum, Germany, in June 1995, edited by Fritz Erich Anhelm (Loccumer Protokolle 23/95, Evangelische Akademie Loccum, 1996). The civil society initiative, however, encountered resistance elsewhere, particularly in India and Africa, owing to the impression that many of the non-governmental organizations thought to constitute "civil society" had already been coopted by "the system" and did not make good on their promises to the people.

[73] See Larry Rasmussen, "Theology of Life and Ecumenical Ethics," in David G. Hallman ed., Ecotheology: Voices from South and North, WCC, 1994. Also Earth Community, Earth Ethics.

[74] A concern for creation's wholeness and for both thinking and action carried on in that perspective was first introduced to the ecumenical movement in an address by Joseph Sittler at the New Delhi assembly of 1961. Excerpts from that address may be found in The Ecumenical Movement: An Anthology, p.288f. More recently, see Earth Community, Earth Ethics.

[75] This account of the Theology of Life programme is largely derived from a descriptive essay by Martin Robra, "Ecumenical Social Thought and Action in the 1990s: Theology of Life – Justice, Peace, Creation", an (apparently) unpublished manuscript underlying lectures given at the University of Birmingham and Westminster College, Cambridge, 1998.

[76] These methodological expectations for the Theology of Life programme are recorded from a 1994 memorandum from Julio de Santa Ana to Martin Robra and Sam Kobia.

an acceptance of differences. Consistent with maintaining the identity and integrity of all involved, might participants come to agree on some shared aspects of reality? It was important that the stories be told first without imposition of supposed "agreements" representing the views of the powerful. But then might some form of hermeneutical method be found to lift up what was being communicated in common? With such hopes, the Theology of Life programme embarked on its effort to hear and share a multitude of voices across the globe.

From 1994 onward, the ten affirmations of Seoul came to be used as entry-points for more than twenty case studies in different parts of world. Each study confronted one Seoul affirmation with the experience of people in a particular context. The values expected of participants were a willingness to listen, an openness to being surprised, a readiness to receive and remember. The underlying assumption was that theological commonalities and differences, raised up in local, regional and worldwide struggles, all of them interconnected, could deepen understanding in each place and for all involved. The "theology of life" effort thus sought in each place to create and maintain an open space, a theatre for the presentation of the gifts and contributions of others. Acceptance, understanding and affirmation were necessary *preconditions* to dialogue. The effort was to see connections and build bridges between different symbols of life.

The culmination of this programme prior to the 1998 Harare assembly was the sponsorship of an event modelled on the *sokoni* (the Swahili word for the traditional African market-place): a space for exchanges of all kinds – goods, information, ideas, plans, stories, music, gossip, deliberation[77] – in Nairobi, Kenya (1997), at which concerns related to resisting the forces of death and promoting the cause of life were shared among persons of widely differing ideologies and cultural backgrounds.

Margot Kässmann, in a report to the 1997 central committee titled "Glimpses of the New Ecumenical Movement",[78] described this event as one linking local experience with global action and reflection. In ways similar to those employed in the Decade of Solidarity with Women, it expressed what it means to be the one church of Christ across all boundaries. The *sokoni* saw a global agenda being discussed with local people, and local experience becoming a mirror in which to see the worldwide agenda anew. The *sokoni* specifically did not try to bring local experience to a level of concept in order to relate it to other realities. Rather, the findings of other case studies were re-contextualized within the immediate reality at hand. Differences become a medium for seeing one's own reality in a new way. The *sokoni* became a safe space, above all, for women. People did not present papers. They talked about their lives. Living theology was the result: a theology of life. Here was a move from domination to new forms of conviviality of different communities and cultures. No one, Kässmann asserted, could leave such an experience unchanged.

The hope of Theology of Life leadership, indeed, was not to leave the ecumenical movement unchanged. Here was a perspective on ecumenical interchange designed to create and maintain open space for the sort of discourse rapidly becoming needed in a world of pluralism and advancing intellectual decolonialization, a process of "globalization from below". For some participants this called for the de-emphasis of patterns of

---

[77] Larry Rasmussen "The Right Direction, But a Longer Journey", in Thomas F. Best and Martin Robra eds, *Ecclesiology and Ethics: Ecumenical Ethical Engagement, Moral Formation, and the Nature of the Church*, WCC, 1997, p.107f.

[78] Quoted at length by Martin Robra in a document of 28 Jan. 1998, containing elements of addresses by Robra at the University of Birmingham and at Westminster College, Cambridge.

doctrinal theology historically linked with imperialism and colonialism in order to listen to marginalized peoples and give shape to the vision of an "ecumenical earth". Yet it was also noted that this very programme had its own context: that of churches and ecumenical organizations distorted by assymetrical distributions of power. It followed that, if Theology of Life were to have a future, it might not be as a distinct programme under this title but rather as a new vision for ecumenism itself.

Ecclesiology and ethics

In 1993 a series of consultations began involving Faith and Order persons and resources (located structurally in another unit of the WCC) with those of Unit III concerning the relations between ecclesiology and ethics. This effort made explicit many of the questions lying behind the hesitations felt at Seoul, and at the same time took up the historic tensions separating the movements for Faith and Order and Life and Work, between concern for what the church *is* and what the church *does*.[79] This study process in many ways paralleled the "theology of life" inquiry, but in such a way as to draw Faith and Order concerns into the mix. The first consultation, at Rønde, Denmark, in 1993, took up some "unfinished business" from the JPIC process, asking how the Faith and Order watchword *koinonia* was related to it, affirming (after the American ethicist Stanley Hauerwas) that "the church not only has, but is, a social ethic, a *koinonia* ethic". This consultation also reopened the question of the ecclesial significance of groups working for justice, peace and the integrity of creation outside the church, and explored the significance of calling the church, in its own right, a "moral community".

Acceptance of the latter formula among the churches was far from unanimous. The nature of the resistance depended on what the claim was thought to mean.[80] But, in general, disquiet was found in quarters whose concern was that the church must *be* the church, and would do more for humankind by being so than by risking *defining itself* in terms of the particular present-day moral issues. Some also feared that seeing the church as moral community could open the door to a new Pelagianism, undercutting confidence in salvation by grace alone. Others said that connecting moral interests too closely to ecclesiology could supplant the centrality of the eucharist, diluting the church's essential sacramental being. Still other voices insisted that for the church to become involved in seeking the well-being of the society (what is implied by "ethics" in this discussion) is to be taken in by the surrounding culture, to accede to whatever role that culture gives to "religion". There was also fear of a loss of momentum in the agendas of both units. The unity thrust of Faith and Order, it was thought by some, could be diluted by questions of social ethics; the moral proposals of JPIC could be stalled in the seemingly endless unity debate.

A second consultation at Tantur, outside Jerusalem, in 1994, sought to take these and other criticisms into account. It focused again on the ecclesial significance of ethi-

---

[79] *Ecclesiology and Ethics*, p.vii.

[80] "Costly Commitment," §55 (in *Ecclesiology and Ethics*, pp.24-49) comments on misunderstandings of the intent of this term. "We recognize that the term 'moral community' has engendered considerable debate, not least at Tantur. Difficulties have arisen through the term being *misheard* as a full description of the ethical character of the ecclesia. Certainly Rønde did not intend any reductionism of the church, leading to moralism or a self-righteous triumphalism. For Rønde the identity of the church as a 'moral community' is a gift of God, a part, though not the whole, of the fullness of the church. The term 'moral' has also been *misheard* as 'moralistic', thus confusing our understanding of the ecclesia with such movements as Moral Rearmament or with the 'Moral Majority', or as representing the ethical character of the ecclesia as an individual or 'ghetto' morality."

cal action-reflection, allowing that ecumenical action-reflection is intrinsic to the church's nature, producing a classic and well-received series of questions:

> Is it enough to say... that ethical engagement is intrinsic to the church *as* church? Is it enough to say that, if a church is not engaging responsibly with the ethical issues of its day, it is not being fully church? Must we not also say: if the churches are not engaging these ethical issues *together*, then *none of them individually is being fully church?*[81]

Tantur also dealt with the mixed reactions to the Rønde document from the fifth world conference on Faith and Order at Santiago de Compostela, Spain, in 1993 and found greater precision in assessing the significance of communities of moral witness outside the church as such. "Though not ecclesial", these communities might "have implications for the way in which we understand church in so far as such communities embody prophetic signs of the reign of God..."[82] Finally, Tantur began to explore one way the church claims its moral identity, namely through the practice of moral formation. This breakthrough insight was largely the work of Rasmussen. It is not only the explicit "teaching" of the church but also the whole life of the church – its liturgy, its organizational style, its personnel practices – in short, its "body language" as an organization that "teaches" its faith and values.

The third "ecclesiology and ethics" consultation took place in Johannesburg in 1996 to deal further with the conditions of moral formation in both church and world. This meeting stressed the manner in which the world, encircling us and working within us, exercises formative power, sometimes producing notable "malformation". Churches themselves, of course, are able to "malform" their members without such outside help. The consultation also traced ways in which an authentic formation can take place, not least through worship and the celebration of the sacraments. The close relationship as well as distinctions between "moral communion" and "sacramental communion" were explored, not always to everyone's satisfaction. Equally controversial were suggestions concerning the WCC as "marker and space-maker for an ecumenical moral communion".[83] A final section of the report, experimental and controversial in nature, probed the idea of "resonance" across divisions of space, time, culture and ideology as different interpretations of the meaning of Jesus Christ recognize in one another the authentic "voice" of the Master.[84] "Each context of discipleship shapes us in a certain perspective on the world and thereby generates a community having a certain recognizable character. The Holy Spirit instigates an energy-field of resonance *among* these perspectives."[85]

The *sokoni*, a culminating event in the Theology of Life programme, became, in Rasmussen's hands, a touchstone by which the conclusion of the Johannesburg meeting could be judged.

> The most promising way forward is not that of finding the language of normative common ground as that might be offered by theologians and agreed to by heads of communions. This understanding of ecumenical formation is essentially doctrinal and jurisdictional. The most promising way is by arranging a common table, open to participation by the

---

[81] "Costly Commitment", §17, in, *Ecclesiology and Ethics*, p.29.
[82] *Ibid.*, p.xi.
[83] "Costly Obedience", §§98ff, in *ibid.*, p.81.
[84] For more detail, see accounts of the "theology and ethics" study in Duncan Forrester, *The True Church and Morality*, WCC, 1986, and Lewis S. Mudge, *The Church as Moral Community: Ecclesiology and Ethics in Ecumenical Debate*, WCC, 1998.
[85] "Costly Obedience," §88, in *Ecclesiology and Ethics*, p.98. See also Mudge, *The Church as Moral Community*, pp.13,128.

whole people of God, to see what emerges as living church when faith is freely shared on the burning issues we face.[86]

On the Faith and Order side, and for many others, this view seemed to involve potential costs to the integrity and ascertainability of the tradition of faith itself. In the enactment of the *sokoni* the church quite literally became a space in which economic, political and other questions – issues of human well-being as such – were brought into the transforming context of the gospel. Ecclesiology and social thought were close to becoming one. But what criteria of authenticity in the faith could be derived from this sort of enterprise? The actual Johannesburg report did not go as far as Rasmussen's critique would have demanded. It spoke of the need for a new kind of Faith and Order "language" and perhaps the adoption of hermeneutical methods in which the many traditions of faith could serve as guiding threads.

Economic globalization and sustainable societies

The theme of societal sustainability in the context of economic globalization also resurfaced in the 1990s. Brought to focus originally in the long debates on "development" in which the WCC resisted a focus on gross domestic product (GDP) numbers, the "globalization" threat took on new urgency with the so-called "new economic order" proclaimed after the collapse of Eastern European state socialist regimes. Unit III began once again to look at issues first raised in the 1970s under the rubric of JPSS and also did important work on climate change. It joined the debate surrounding the work of the UN Commissions on Social Development and Sustainable Development, linking these studies to the "theology of life" effort. Rasmussen's *Earth Community, Earth Ethics*, although a personal statement, offers highly useful insight into this thinking. The Harare assembly's background document on globalization provided indications concerning the relationships between these themes in an attempt to develop criteria for just and sustainable communities, and for the institutional arrangements that make space for them.

Missing from the pre-Harare period was any truly thorough analysis from Unit III of the phenomenon of economic globalization itself, which might have given opportunity, and a frame of reference, for the development of criteria for economic sustainability out of the Theology of Life case-study material. The latter was diverse, and no substitute for economic analysis as such, yet of value in illustrating the local consequences of large-scale economic decisions. During this same period, the Ecumenical Institute at Bossey was the setting for different efforts to address issues of democracy, economics and the sustainability of societies. Four consultations in memory of Willem Visser 't Hooft dealt with these issues. The first, in 1993, "discussed the tension between economic growth and sustainability, asking whether it is possible to affirm 'sustainable growth' or whether this very concept is a contradiction in terms". The second, in 1995, "focused on the relation between labour and sustainability, considering the question of employment from the perspective of a sustainable society". The third, in 1997, "considered the possibility of sustainable society and sustainable development in the context of the ongoing process of accelerated globalization".[87] The fourth consultation, in 1999, followed the line of the preceding three, focusing attention on "matters

---

[86] Rasmussen, "The Right Direction, But a Longer Journey", p.107.
[87] Julio de Santa Ana, "Introduction", in Julio de Santa Ana ed., *Sustainability and Globalization*, WCC, 1998, p.vii.

related to the construction of a sustainable society". Questions concerned "what should be done to put into action the agreements and conventions elaborated by the international community..." in the form of "contracts that oblige nations and other international agencies to participate in actions favourable to environmental sustainability. What can churches and Christian communities contribute to the formulation and enforcement of democratic contracts?"[88]

The force of this cumulative work on society, sustainability, democracy and economic globalization was not adequately brought to bear upon the eighth assembly, partly because the work was scattered and no comprehensive analysis reached the pre-assembly materials, and partly for reasons having to do with the organization of the assembly itself, as will be indicated below.

THE EIGHTH ASSEMBLY, HARARE 1998

The Harare assembly is still too recent an event for adequate historical judgments to be made. But it would be fair to say that Harare provided few new ideas or programmatic initiatives in the realms of ecumenical social thought and action: certainly nothing compared with the creativity of Uppsala or Vancouver. Part of the explanation may lie in the assembly's high degree of preoccupation with the WCC's institutional future. Pressure from Orthodox member churches regarding difficulties of their participation in WCC studies and official events was by no means irrelevant to the handling of social thought at Harare. Delegates were reminded that a largely different way of approaching social questions had for years been present among Orthodox representatives, yet not adequately incorporated into the common work. A pre-assembly meeting of Orthodox at the invitation of the WCC had detailed these difficulties, many touching on the question of social thought.[89]

Harare was notable as well for the highly local and situational character of the representations of social witness brought to the assembly. Receiving this material was a programme called *padare*, in the majority Shona language a market-place similar to *sokoni* in Swahili, to which persons from every corner of the earth brought reports of what was going on in their own settings: analyses, programmes, observations of every sort. Yet the *padare* was isolated from decision-making sessions of the assembly, and participants had little opportunity to enter findings into the official record. For the first time, an assembly had no "sections" in which the delegates, aided by preliminary staff work, could draft carefully worded statements on topics related to the main theme, in

---

[88] Julio de Santa Ana, "Preface: Democracy for a Sustainable Society in the Context of Economic Globalization", in Lewis S. Mudge and Thomas Wieser eds, *Democratic Contracts for Sustainable and Caring Societies: What Can Churches and Christian Communities Do?*, WCC, 2000, p.vii.

[89] See Thomas FitzGerald and Peter Bouteneff eds, *Turn to God, Rejoice in Hope: Orthodox Reflections on the Way to Harare*, WCC, 1998. This document notes that with respect to many issues in the moral sphere "Christians have not been able to come to a common mind" (p.11). And, further, "The treatment of such issues under the banner of 'human rights' has both positive and negative potential: on the one hand, it would affirm our common calling to treat all human persons with love and respect in view of their being created in the image of God. On the other hand, we would not want to be prevented, on the basis of 'human rights', from stating that certain life-styles and practices are not God-ordained" (p.11).

this case, "Turn to God – Rejoice in Hope". Section reports in the past had provided important benchmarks indicating the "state of the question" in ecumenical social thought at any given time.

Much conversation in the *padare* concerned the human impact of "globalization", both in the economic sphere and in the realm of communications. And hence, much talk had to do, directly or indirectly, with tactics and strategies of resistance. In the *padare*, several discrete theological strategies of resistance to economic and communications "globalization" were beginning to be linked together into a coherent whole. One could not avoid the sense of a world church composed of multiple cultural particularities. Awareness of the pluralism of Christian faith-expressions was of course not new to participants in the assembly. But at Harare it was clear that this localizing movement had taken hold and gone further even than had been evident at Canberra. Even among long-convinced ecumenists, there appeared to be less confidence than had been the case seven years before that academic theologizing – Eastern or Western – could build bridges between cultural particularities in faith.

As the sway of "liberation" formulas declined, the importance of "culture" grew. Social insights and initiatives at Harare came from no one central place. There was no single dominant theological style or concept at work either between the diverse cultural expressions of each of the themes. Moreover, no new overall expression of ecumenical social thought appeared to be growing out of these parallel problematics. No brief description can do justice to the complexity of what was going on. Out of this maelstrom, for example, came proposals for projects concerning ethnicity and violence in various locations, again without an overall strategy apart from close attention to particulars and the learnings one could gain from them.

The world church was, then, a "space" in which such mutual learning could go on. The general secretary's report at the opening of the assembly made extensive use of this ecumenical metaphor. Konrad Raiser spoke of the "free space" of the sabbath day that foreshadows the greater space of the Jubilee, the year of liberation and reconciliation. He went on to apply the "space" metaphor in several other ways: space where ecclesio-moral communion can come to fruition, space ample enough for diversity "and for open mutual confrontation of differing interests and convictions", space for the church to be a truly inclusive community, the earth as space provided by the Creator for all living things to live together in sustainable communities.

But, then, how do different localities within the "space" of the church communicate with one another? In such a vision of transformed social reality, what is the criterion of catholicity? Paraphrasing the Johannesburg "ecclesiology and ethics" report. Raiser proposed that the oikoumene be understood as

> ...an "energy field" of mutual resonance and recognition generated by the Holy Spirit. By choosing resonance and recognition as our metaphors we are able to turn to a biblical formula found in the Johannine literature... The sheep know the shepherd's voice (John 10:3, cf. Rev. 3:20). Discipleship means hearing, being drawn, being formed, by the voice: not just its sound but also the content, the authentic note of a way of speaking by which we are shaped, attesting to an identifiable way of being in the world, yet a way of being having many different forms.... The focus of ecumenical recognition is that the other community has an acted commitment analogous to one's own, and one's own commitment is analogous to the other's. The analogy exists because of a shared recognition-pattern of moral practice in the Spirit. People... recognize that others "have the same spirit"... Such recognition is something holistic, never merely doctrinal or jurisdictional but also including

both doctrinal and jurisdictional elements. It is recognition of a lived reality: a sense of moral communion. This is what *oikoumene* means.[90]

Many at Harare heard these words with appreciation. But many also wanted something more tangible and precise. In a day of burgeoning pluralism, *was* there one gospel for the whole world? And, if so, what criteria would help one identify it?

CONCLUSIONS

The period treated in this chapter thus ended with many questions unresolved. Abrecht was right in his 1968 prediction. Things have indeed become more, rather than less, difficult. Ecumenical social thinking remains "a precarious enterprise". Even the earlier "responsible society" rubric, with its emphasis on the moral responsibilities that go with leadership in Western democratic societies and loosely connected as it was to neo-orthodox perspectives, did not escape criticism in its later stages for being overly "directive" rather than properly "directional".[91] It did, nonetheless, offer at least some guidance in formulating "middle axioms" of value as guiding principles in reaching specific situational judgments. But the principled decision in significant sectors of the movement, beginning as early as 1966, to stand in solidarity with the strategic and moral judgments made by poor and oppressed people in their own right put in question many of the traditional North Atlantic ways of connecting theory with practice, opening the door to myriad situated theory-practice and practice-theory combinations, each relative to particular circumstances at particular times.

The convictions that Jesus Christ is the Lord of creation and history and that the scriptural witness to him demands a "preferential option for the poor" have in no way diminished over these years. But clarity, not to speak of agreement about what this means for moral and theological reflection, is still hard to come by. Did the "preferential option" involve also an "epistemological privilege"? And, if so, how exclusive was such a focus on the thinking of the poor themselves intended to be? For some, the change in perspective begun as early as 1966 involved a fundamental deconstruction of the whole former edifice of Christian social thought for the purpose of adequately hearing the world's "subjugated languages",[92] of sufficiently attending to peoples' "local knowledge".[93]

How far was it true, as critics outside the Council alleged, that the turn from "responsible society" thinking to the "preferential option" amounted to an adoption of "liberation theology" and hence was socialist or Marxist in inspiration? Were damaging accusations, especially between 1980 and 1985, of communist connections and Marxist tendencies in the WCC justified? Often overlooked by critics was the fact that the WCC

---

[90] "Report of the General Secretary", Harare document no. PL 4-1, p.7. In the interest of full disclosure, the writer needs to acknowledge having originally drafted the words in "Costly Obedience" (*Ecclesiology and Ethics*, p.78) quoted by Konrad Raiser at Harare. Similar language appears (by WCC permission) in my book *The Church as Moral Community*, p.128f.

[91] See Paul Ramsey, *Who Speaks for the Church?: A Critique of the 1966 Geneva Conference on Church and Society*, Nashville, Abingdon, 1967, pp.45ff.

[92] "Subjugated languages" is a term used by Michel Foucault. See *Power/Knowledge: Selected Interviews and Other Writings, 1972-1977*, New York, Pantheon, 1981, pp.81ff.

[93] "Local knowledge" is Clifford Geertz's favoured expression. See *Local Knowledge: Further Essays in Interpretative Anthropology*, New York, Basic, 1983.

is a council of *churches*. Many of the member churches in the southern hemisphere were in fact working in "liberation theology" terms during these years. Hence the WCC was necessarily involved. The principle of theological contextualization together with the principle of solidarity with those seeking liberation meant that the WCC encountered liberation theolog*ies* in many forms. But the Council never sponsored a consultation whose task was to explore and articulate such a theology as that of the organization itself. Much less did the WCC, even as it assisted liberation movements in several lands, ever adopt an explicitly Marxist analysis or agenda. Some, such as Ulrich Duchrow, have for years urged the Council to go much further, if not in a specifically Marxist direction, in condemning the developing global economic order.[94]

Did the WCC, then, without embracing liberation theology explicitly, simply take its relevance for granted?[95] This much can be said: Liberation theology taught a solidarity of resistance to oppressive and dehumanizing forces in which the WCC was deeply involved. The enemy was identifiable. Sober analysis disclosed a world in which both Western capitalism and Eastern totalitarianism were creating conditions that threatened to shut down human life. In some versions of this resistance solidarity, the energy came from a psychology of victimization and resentment. In other versions, notably Paulo Freire's *Pedagogy of the Oppressed*, erstwhile victims were urged to become the subjects of their own historical destiny. In few, if any, of these analyses were the poor understood as a "class" in the Marxist "proletarian" sense of that word.

What is to be said of the rationale of such "resistance solidarity" now? Liberation theology has taught the ecumenical movement an enormous amount about the life of human beings in situations other than those of the developed nations. It has given the world a new form of the church, the "base community". The liberation theologies of different continents and human communities – Latin American, African, Asian, feminist – have linked up sufficiently to provide a cross-cultural agenda for a human solidarity coming-to-be. One thinks of Robert MacAfee Brown's book *Kairos: Three Prophetic Challenges to the Church*,[96] which seeks to derive precisely such a sense of common humanity emerging in opposition to oppression by showing the close parallels of vision and expression linking liberation documents from South Africa, Latin America and Asia.[97]

But liberation thinking is now in at least its third, perhaps its fourth, stage of conceptual evolution. In some settings, it has had to adapt to the collapse of state socialist regimes in the former Soviet Union and Eastern Europe, and therefore to the discredit-

---

[94] The German theologian Ulrich Duchrow has constantly urged the WCC to take a more radical position with reference to the global economic order, insisting that threats to human life posed by the expansion of capitalism and consumerism be considered a status confessionis, or question of the basic integrity of faith. While publishing and drawing upon Duchrow's work, the WCC has resisted pressures to go this far. See Duchrow, *Conflict Over the Ecumenical Movement*, WCC, 1981; *Global Economy: A Confessional Issue for the Churches*, WCC, 1987; *Europe in the World System, 1492-1992: Is Justice Possible?*, WCC, 1992; *Alternatives to Global Capitalism*, Utrecht, International Books, 1995.

[95] See *Commitment to God's World*, p.50. Van der Bent records that at a 1971 SODEPAX consultation on "theology of revolution" Gustavo Gutiérrez did present a major paper on "A Theology of Liberation" which provoked intense discussion.

[96] Grand Rapids MI, Eerdmans, 1990.

[97] Of course something more than common theological formulas or conceptual parallels between theologies developed in different cultures is needed to generate relationships between human beings that deserve the name "solidarity". Perhaps only working side by side within a particular situation for a particular cause can produce genuine "solidarity", and even then, or especially then, possibilities for the emergence of serious differences are always also at hand.

ing of socialism, if not in theory, at least in what it has so far turned out to have been in practice. It seems that this adaptation has by now been largely accomplished. Admiration of state socialist regimes, or of Marxist analysis per se, was never a large element in liberation theory. Indeed, in many parts of the world the problem has been quite different, if not less difficult: namely, to articulate a liberation position appropriate to the "non-aligned", that is, a theology ideologically independent of economic views held in either East or West.

Over this period, liberation theology has been practised ecumenically, not as a form of Marxism, but simply as a biblical theology used directly to assist the poor in interpreting their experience and to gather them into base communities for worship, study and action. The poor have been understood as exploited human beings belonging to many cultures, including those of ethnic minorities and of women, who deserved to be preserved in their integrity and to have their voice.[98] A realization is now growing that recognition of the voices of many cultures is more than a capitulation to pluralism or social fragmentation. It is *also* a means of access to expressions of a more basic level of human experience than mere economic theory or class analysis can reach, an opening to "thick descriptions" of what it *is* – in many different situations – to be poor and powerless and afraid, and also to what it *is* – in equally diverse circumstances – to live in hope.

Of course a "simple" biblical theology is always more than that. Liberation hermeneutics have attracted criticism from within the theological community as well as from beyond. The habit of moving directly from certain passages in the Bible to judgments about contemporary life may be appropriate to a method which uncritically honours all progressive opinions arising from scripture study conducted within situations of oppression and injustice. But such a method lacks adequate attention to the coherence of the reasoning processes which derive operational principles from the Bible (i.e. "middle axioms") and apply them cautiously to particulars. As Ans J. van der Bent put it, "The World Council of Churches... needs to examine critically its fondness for moving from the Bible to judgments about the modern world without clarifying the intermediate steps."[99] The intermediate assumptions clearly exist even if they are unspoken. They need to be made more explicit and subject to criticism.

But ideological suspicion and vulnerable hermeneutical methods have not been the only issues. Much of the criticism of ecumenical social thought since Vancouver from northern-hemisphere sources has turned on a perceived lack of argumentative care and thoroughness – often defined in terms of North Atlantic academic standards. This has been the core of the criticism mounted over a number of years by Ronald Preston, and particularly in his *Confusions in Social Ethics*.[100] Preston, for example, attacks the 1990 Seoul convocation and the use of its results as a basis for the Theology of Life pro-

---

[98] The 1993 book by Gustavo Gutiérrez, on the 16th-century saint of Spanish America Bartolomé de las Casas (1484-1566) (*Las Casas: In Search of the Poor of Jesus Christ*, Maryknoll NY, Orbis, 1993), clearly shows this liberationist move towards cultural inquiry. But at the same time, Gutiérrez lifts up Bartolomé's recognition of the impact of Spain's greed for gold on the Indians of the New World, an estimated 20 to 25 million of whom died because of wars, disease and hard labour. Central to Las Casas' existence was his conviction "that in the Indian, as the poor and oppressed, Christ is present, buffeted and scourged" (p.18).

[99] *Commitment to God's World*, p.170. Cf. José Míguez Bonino, "Middle Axioms", in *Dictionary of the Ecumenical Movement*, p.761.

[100] Ronald Preston, *Confusions in Social Ethics*, Grand Rapids MI, Eerdmans, 1995, especially pp.167ff.

gramme. It is a "delusion", in his view, to see the ten affirmations as a kind of ecumenical catechism. He would prefer that discourse in the field of ecumenical social ethics be carried on using a Faith and Order model in some form, with careful, patient, mutual examination of opposing views and diverse perspectives, "a forum for examining disagreements, with the aim of clarifying them, and if possible modifying or resolving them". For all that, Preston states his conviction, "to put it bluntly... that Christians from the first world need to speak up more".

There are obvious reasons why Western expertise has been increasingly silent in WCC settings. Chief among these has been an internalization of the liberationists' criticisms, generating the fear that any form of ethical reasoning produced in the North Atlantic community may in fact be a form of ideological self-deception or false consciousness. As most thinkers have come to realize, talk of "responsible society" can serve to hold at bay the realization of Western complicity in the conditions making for global poverty. Over-consumption, the exploitation of global resources, the pollution of the earth, all lend credence to such a charge. Whether immanent social criticism, such as that practised by J.H. Oldham, Reinhold Niebuhr or others, must *always* be ideologically tainted remains an open question.

How, as many European and North American ecumenists may ask, can thinkers representing the traditional Christianity of the northern hemisphere get back with integrity into the conversation about ecumenical social thought? One way could be to stop making a fetish of guilt feelings and to realize that the West is a culturally specific space in its own right, with its own earthy issues and traditions of ecumenical social thinking, but nevertheless one situation among many. Combine with this the realization that, as the world becomes one through the technologies of communication, the global conversation becomes one as well. No part of the globe can now impose its arguments and conceptualizations on other places. Ecumenists everywhere are now conversing about the same things. The South certainly wants at least some of what the North has to give, if the gift can be given without exploitation or condescension.

Yet what gift has the North to give? It will not be a simple re-introduction of "responsible society" thinking. Expertise, careful analysis, skillful argument, even "moral realism", need not be wedded to status quo conceptualities. Nor are these qualities peculiar to thinkers of the North alone. The churches have access to political thinkers, economists and other experts in every land. Conversation with them could reconnect the WCC with the work of compatible NGOs and technical experts of all kinds, in an effort to examine the emerging world economic order in critical detail. Serious criticism of economic "globalization" is now emerging within, as well as outside, the nations contributing major energy and resources to the "system".

Much might be gained also by resuming active cooperation between the WCC and the Roman Catholic Church on issues such as these. It was perhaps unavoidable that SODEPAX had to be discontinued in 1980. That step marked a suspension of close collaboration in ecumenical social thought, even if relationships never entirely ceased. And collaboration has of course continued across communions among academic ethicists. But Roman Catholic involvement in the WCC's work in the area of church and society has never paralleled the highly active membership in Faith and Order.

But is the WCC ready for closer collaboration with Rome? Critics imply that the WCC has produced little of late with the authority, clarity and broad public recognition of, say, the US Roman Catholic bishops conference pastoral letters on nuclear deterrence and the economy.[101] In comparison with the WCC product, it is further argued, the great social encyclicals of this period, *Laborem Exercens* ("On Human Work" 1981) attacking the current Western capitalist system and asserting the priority of labour over capital, and *Sollicitudo Rei Socialis* ("On Social Concern" 1987) developing the "solidarity" and interdependence of humanity and opening up the concept of "structural sin", evince a remarkably informed thoroughness and tightness of argument. The encyclical *Veritatis Splendor* ("The Splendour of Truth" 1993), while not strictly speaking a social pronouncement, has led the development of natural law theory in a more scriptural and Christological direction which has attracted thinkers outside the Roman Catholic world towards a reappraisal of its possibilities. Such theory, in various forms, has also begun to have an influence upon secular social and legal thinking. It does, at least, offer ways of reasoning which connect Christian assumptions with specific moral issues in contemporary society which the WCC would be wise to consult. Another observation, less frequently uttered in public, also bears upon the links between ecumenical social thought and what is going on outside the WCC. Between 1968 and the Vancouver assembly in 1983, the WCC was at least in dialogue and tension with moral issues occupying the secular agenda. Typically, the Council came late to these debates, but it eventually came. Racism, development, human rights and the environment were prominent in the secular news media well before the WCC developed programmes to direct member churches' attention to such issues. But at, and after, Vancouver there begins to be a "disconnect" between WCC studies and events on the world scene. An example is the crucial decision of the Cancún summit (Mexico 1982) to implement deregulation and begin the construction of a new global financial market. It was a fateful turning point that seems to have passed undetected in the continued pursuit of the "development" theme at the assembly the next year. This in turn opened the decision to pursue "covenanting" around the issues of JPIC to the criticism of being "out of touch". Yet in recent years work by Unit III on questions of climate change and its participation in the debate surrounding the UN commissions on sustainable development and social development, together with the four Visser 't Hooft memorial consultations on globalization in Bossey at the close of the 20th century, appear to have done the most that could be done to keep the WCC seriously in the international dialogue.

Apart from these efforts, and without sufficient critical thought and adequate connections with the discourse of the international community, it is understandable that WCC social pronouncements have at times fallen into the genres of "prophetic" condemnation of present political and economic reality, or romantic, utopian, even messianically visionary speculation about possible human futures. For many readers, these traits, where present, have rendered WCC social pronouncements unpersuasive.

---

[101] If the comparison is not limited to the last fifteen or so years, the WCC can point to the brilliant and comprehensive preliminary materials for both the 1966 Geneva conference on Church and Society and the 1979 MIT conference on "Faith, Science and the Future", not to speak of the deeply impressive symposium on nuclear war published in 1983 as *Before It's Too Late*. Other examples could be adduced. Still, these are all analytical studies of issues, not moral pronouncements made on the basis of ecclesiastical authority.

Yet it is not clear that the critics of WCC social thought have sufficiently understood what the WCC is, and has been trying to do, over this period of time. One must consider the Council's basic nature and limitations. Comparison, for example, between Roman Catholic and WCC social pronouncements sets the Council, a fellowship of incredibly diverse churches worldwide, an impossible task. The role of the WCC may not be to produce deeply researched moral pronouncements – except perhaps in a few cases where there is broad and overwhelming agreement among the member churches – so much as to foster reflection and action among the member churches, usually in specific forms depending on the issues involved and the regions affected. The WCC has no authority to speak in the manner of the Holy See. But the Roman Catholic Church itself has felt for some time the impact of theological pluralism and multiculturalism within its own ranks.

Furthermore, the Council has carried on a principled enterprise of decentring ecumenical social thought and action so as to give voice to all localities of the global church. This has been no easy matter, but it has been indispensable. The decentring process has already had its impact on ecumenical efforts of every kind, and seems about to have an impact as well on the structuring of the Council itself and on its relation to other ecumenical institutions. The world of ecumenical discourse is rapidly becoming pluralized and fragmented, with a majority of Christians on earth now living in the southern hemisphere which is home to rapidly growing and varied forms of Pentecostalism, independent churches of all kinds, and myriad other contextual expressions of faith.

It is arguable indeed that shared social thought and action has for some time been proceeding more effectively in regional and local situations than in centres such as Geneva, Istanbul, Moscow and Rome. Collaboration between WCC member churches and both Roman Catholic and Orthodox dioceses and parishes has been significant in many localities, often in ways that at least imply greater mutuality of insight than has been achieved in global conversations. The same is true for other forms of collaboration, between both traditional and post-traditional (e.g. African Instituted [Independent) churches, and between Christian churches and non-Christian bodies, over the promotion and defence of human rights, programmes of solidarity with the poor, strategies for combating racism: all have thrived at the "periphery", bringing enrichment to the movement as a whole and instruction to its leaders, yet at the same time underscoring how diverse these many situations are, how hard it is to generalize in describing them.

Of necessity, then, the "social location" of ecumenical social thought, mentioned in the first paragraph, is itself in process of change. Pressure from the Orthodox churches for structures more hospitable to their participation is at present driving this change process, but their interests are obviously not the only ones involved. With a shift in its social location from WCC interests and programmes to many centres in many places, the character of ecumenical social thought itself is bound to evolve. A quarter-century from now, a chapter on "ecumenical social thought" will not be able to focus mainly on the WCC, its agencies, meetings and other activities. It will rather need to describe some new and more complex configuration of ecumenical initiatives.

This chapter has already posed the questions that follow: How do such myriad locally specific forms of social witness in the gathering of God's people talk to one another? How can they share standards of adequacy and faithfulness? Can there exist a common language of Christian social thought today? Is it time to try to construct some sort of "theory of communicative action"[102] for the world church, some sort of shared ecumenical "hermeneutic" for reading diverse expressions of the gospel's social meaning? Such a space of sharing could and should bring together not only the myriad localities in which the gospel is preached and heard, but also the many traditions of moral reasoning which the different Christian confessions – and different schools of thought within and among the confessions – have produced.

But then there is something more to be said. Running through this entire period is the affirmation that social witness is not merely a function of ecclesiality but rather of its essence. To believe that Jesus Christ founds a household of life is to believe that resistance to the powers of death in society is intrinsic to churchly being. Hence the question of catholicity, of wholeness, is being articulated in new forms for which long-standing northern-hemisphere answers alone are insufficient. While European (and, by derivation, North American) notions of catholicity pose questions for the new multitude of contextual ecclesial expressions, so also do these expressions pose questions for the traditional formulas. What role, one may ask, might a search for greater mutual understanding in social thought have in the effort to achieve unity in the sacramental or ecclesiastical sense?[103]

One cannot speak of the essence of the church today without inquiring how it comes to *be* contextually as an enacted vision of what human society is called by God to become. But likewise, one cannot speak of a moral unity of humankind without some grasp of what is involved in realizing the unity of the church. These insights were grasped as early as the 1971 Louvain Faith and Order meeting. But they are still more pressing today.

What paths lead towards the future? An attractive hypothesis suggests that the more culturally specific a theological-moral language is, the more it is likely to be energized by a shared sense of the action of the Holy Spirit and grounded in what we make of our common earth. Culturally specific treatments of the gospel's implications for life on this planet, however institutionally and theologically elaborated, may find ways to communicate by way of common earthy concerns and common apprehension of the Spirit's presence. The idea of "global theological flows" articulated by Robert Schreiter[104] seems to illumine much of what is now taking place. So too does the idea of "resonance", relating diverse apprehensions of the gospel across what appear to be impassable divides.

But here speculation must end. One has to say that no single, coherent body of ecumenical social thought has emerged from these years, but rather a highly instructive *history* of the interactions of many ideas and circumstances. To understand even the outlines of this experience is to grasp something of the complex combination of institutional and theologically visionary factors involved, as well as of the formidable challenges that lie ahead.

---

[102] "Communicative action" is, of course, an expression coined by the German social philosopher Jürgen Habermas. See Habermas, *The Theory of Communicative Action*, 2 vols, Boston, Beacon, 1984.
[103] *Who Speaks for the Church?*, p.13.
[104] Schreiter's book *The New Catholicity* (Maryknoll NY, Orbis, 1997) has caught the imagination of a number of students of the present ecumenical situation. By "global theological flows" Schreiter refers to the phenomenon of communication among myriad concrete situations, in which – without any specific conceptual sharing, common social analysis or particular institutional mediation – discourse flows globally on such issues as human rights, the environment, economic globalization, the rights of women and other similar issues.

BIBLIOGRAPHY

Abraham, Kuruvilla C. ed., *Christian Witness in Society : A Tribute to M. M. Thomas*, Bangalore, Board of Theological Education, Senate of Serampore College, 1998, 226p.

Abrecht, Paul and Koshy, Ninan eds, *Before It's Too Late: The Challenge of Nuclear Disarmament*, WCC, 1983, 391p.

Abrecht, Paul, "Ecumenical Social Thought in the Post-Cold War Period", in *The Ecumenical Review*, 43, 3, July 1991, pp.305-28.

Abrecht, Paul et al. eds, *Faith, Science and the Future: Preparatory Readings for a World Conference, Cambridge MA, July 12-114*, WCC, 1979.

Abrecht, Paul, "From Oxford to Vancouver: Lessons from Fifty Years of Ecumenical Work for Economic and Social Justice", in *The Ecumenical Review*, 40, 2, April 1988, pp.147-68.

Bent, Ans J. van der, *Commitment to God's World: A Concise Critical History of Ecumenical Social Thought*, WCC, 1995, 243p.

Berg, Aart van den, *Churches Speak Out on Economic Issues: A Survey of Several Statements*, WCC, 1990, 100p.

Best, Thomas F. and Robra, Martin eds, *Ecclesiology and Ethics: Ecumenical Ethical Engagement, Moral Formation, and the Nature of the Church*, WCC, 1997, 121p.

Brown, Robert McAfee and Brown, Sydney Thomson eds, *A Cry for Justice: The Churches and Synagogues Speak*, Mahwah NJ, Paulist, 1989.

Brown, Robert MacAfee, *Kairos: Three Prophetic Challenges to the Church*, Grand Rapids MI, Eerdmans, 1990, 158p.

"Church and Society: Ecumenical Perspective: Essays in Honour of Paul Abrecht", *The Ecumenical Review*, 37, 1, Jan. 1985.

Davis, Howard, *Will the Future Work?: Values for Emerging Patterns of Work and Employment*, WCC, 1985, 122p.

Derr, Thomas Sieger, *Barriers to Ecumenism: The Holy See and the World Council on Social Questions*, Maryknoll NY, Orbis, 1983, 102p.

Dickinson, Richard D.N., *Poor, Yet Making Many Rich: The Poor as Agents of Creative Justice*, WCC, 1983, 219p.

Drimmelen, Robert van, *Faith in a Global Economy : A Primer for Christians*, WCC, 1998, 156p.

Duchrow, Ulrich, *Conflict over the Ecumenical Movement*, WCC, 1981, 443p.

Duchrow, Ulrich, *Europe in the World System, 1492-1992: Is Justice Possible?*, WCC, 1992, 104p.

Duchrow, Ulrich, *Global Economy: A Confessional Issue for the Churches*, WCC, 1987, 231p.

Ellingsen, Mark, *The Cutting Edge: How Churches Speak on Social Issues*, WCC, 1993, 370p.

Francis, John, *Facing up to Nuclear Power: A Contribution to the Debate on the Risks and Potentialities of the Large-Scale Use of Nuclear Energy*, Edinburgh, St Andrew, 1976, 244p.

Gaay Fortman, Bas de and Klein Goldewijk, Berma, *God and the Goods: Global Economy in a Civilizational Perspective*, WCC, 1998, 100p.

Gill, David M., *From Here to Where: Technology, Faith and the Future of Man*, WCC, 1970, 111p.

Gros, Jeffrey and Rempel, John D. eds, *The Fragmentation of the Church and Its Unity in Peacemaking*, Grand Rapids MI, Eerdmans, 2001, 230p.

Hallman, David G. ed., *Ecotheology: Voices from South and North*, WCC, 1994, 316p.

Hallman, David G., *Spiritual Values for Earth Community*, WCC, 2000, 134p.

James, Leslie R., *Toward an Ecumenical Liberation Theology: A Critical Exploration of Common Dimensions in the Theologies of Juan L. Segundo and Rubem A. Alves*, New York, Peter Lang, 2001, 132p.

Kinnamon, Michael and Cope, Brian E. eds, *The Ecumenical Movement: An Anthology of Key Texts and Voices*, WCC, 1997, 562p.

Klein Goldewijk, Berma and Gaay Fortman, Bas de, *Where Needs Meet Rights: Economic, Social and Cultural Rights in a New Perspective*, WCC, 1999, 146p.

Küng, Hans, *A Global Ethic for Global Politics and Economics*, London, SCM Press, 1997, 315p.

Limouris, Gennadios ed., *Justice, Peace and the Integrity of Creation: Insights from Orthodoxy*, WCC, 1990, 126p.

Mudge, Lewis S., *The Church as Moral Community: Ecclesiology and Ethics in Ecumenical Debate*, WCC, 1998, 192p.

Mudge, Lewis S. Mudge and Wieser, Thomas eds, *Democratic Contracts for Sustainable and Caring Societies: What Can Churches and Christian Communities Do?*, WCC, 2000, 197p.

Musschenga, Bert and Gosling, David eds, *Science Education and Ethical Values: Introducing Ethics and Religion into the Science Classroom and Laboratory*, WCC, 1985, 115p.

Niles, D. Preman ed., *Justice, Peace and Integrity of Creation: Documents from an Ecumenical Process of Commitment [Final Report]*, London, Council for World Mission, 1994, 228p.

Niles, D. Preman, *Between the Flood and the Rainbow: Interpreting the Conciliar Process of Mutual Commitment (Covenant) to Justice, Peace and the Integrity of Creation*, WCC, 1992, 192p.

O'Brien, David J. and Shannon, Thomas A., *Catholic Social Thought: The Documentary Heritage*, Maryknoll NY, Orbis, 1992, 688p.

Pasztor, Janos ed., *Energy for My Neighbour: Perspectives from Asia: Towards More Just and More Sustainable Policies of Energy Development*, 1981, 158p.

Peace with Justice: The Official Documentation of the European Ecumenical Assembly, Basel, Switzerland, 15-21 May, 1989, Geneva, Conference of European Churches, 1989, 334p.

Preston, Ronald, *Confusions in Social Ethics*, Grand Rapids MI, Eerdmans, 1995, 202p.

Raiser, K., *Ecumenism in Transition: A Paradigm Shift in the Ecumenical Movement?*, WCC, 1991, 140p.

Raiser, K., *To Be the Church: Challenges and Hopes for a New Millennium*, WCC, 1997, 116p.

Rasmussen, Larry, *Earth Community, Earth Ethics*, WCC, 1996, 366p.

Reeves, Marjorie ed., *Christian Thinking and Social Order: Conviction Politics from the 1930s to the Present Day*, London, Cassell, 1999, 238p.

Santa Ana, Julio de, *Good News to the Poor: The Challenge of the Poor in the History of the Church*, WCC, 1977, 124p.

Santa Ana, Julio de ed., *Separation without Hope? Essays on the Relation between the Church and the Poor during the Industrial Revolution and the Western Colonial Expansion*, WCC, 1978, 192p.

Santa Ana, Julio de ed., *Sustainability and Globalization*, WCC, 1998, 143p.

Schlossberg, Herbert, Samuel, Vinay and Sider, Ronald J. eds, *Christianity and Economics in the Post-Cold War Era: The Oxford Declaration and Beyond*, Grand Rapids MI, Eerdmans, 1994, 186p.

Schmemann, Alexander, *For the Life of the World*, Crestwood NY, St Vladimir's, 1977, 151p.

Schmitthenner, Ulrich, *Contributions of Churches and Civil Society to Justice, Peace and the Integrity of Creation*, Frankfurt, Verlag für Interkulturelle Kommunikation, 1999, 332p.

Shaull, Millard Richard, "Revolutionary Challenge to Church and Theology", in *Princeton Seminary Bulletin*, 60, Oct. 1966, pp.25-32.

Shinn, Roger L. and Abrecht, Paul eds, *Faith and Science in an Unjust World: Report of the World Council of Churches' Conference on Faith, Science and the Future, Massachusetts Institute of Technology, Cambridge, USA, 12-24 July 1979*, WCC, 1980, 2 vols.

Stackhouse, Max L., *Christian Social Ethics in a Global Era*, Nashville, Abingdon, 1995, 135p.

Stückelberger, Christoph, *Global Trade Ethics: An Illustrated Overview*, WCC, 2002, 234p.

Taylor, Michael, *Christianity, Poverty and Wealth: The Findings of 'Project 21'*, WCC, 2003, 98p.

Webb, Pauline ed., *Faith and Faithfulness: A Tribute to Philip A. Potter*, WCC, 1984, 128p.

West, Charles, "Ecumenical Social Ethics beyond Socialism and Capitalism", in *The Ecumenical Review*, 43, 3, July 1991, pp.329-40.

13
Justice and Peace in a World of Chaos

Peter Lodberg

At the fourth assembly of the World Council of Churches, Uppsala 1968, the film *An Armed World* was shown. The purpose of the showing was to shock the assembly delegates into a new awareness of the disturbed state of the world. The film, however, offended a number of delegates and youth participants who saw it as an exercise in cold-war propaganda rather than as a presentation of the major concerns of peace and justice. According to these critics, the film's point "seemed not to be the dangers and destructiveness of war and injustice, but the supposed necessity of maintaining the balance of nuclear terror – a balance always loaded in favour of the West".[1]

This episode illustrates underlying conflicts and tensions, within the ecumenical movement in general and the WCC in particular, in relation to peace and justice during the period of the cold war. In subsequent years, the East-West conflict was enlarged to include the North-South dimension. Nuclear disarmament was seen in wider perspective, as a struggle that included a search for concrete criteria that could identify the marks of a new social order. In the vocabulary of the ecumenical movement, the language of "a responsible society" was replaced by the vision of "a just, participatory and sustainable society" and, in turn, at the sixth assembly of the WCC, Vancouver 1983, the key criteria became "justice, peace and the integrity of creation".

These new words and concepts reflected a profound change that was taking place in the WCC with regard to issues of peace and justice. The scale of the destructiveness of modern warfare and the inequalities of modern economic life had given rise to a new kind of theological reflection on traditional "Life and Work" issues.

In volume 2 of *A History of the Ecumenical Movement*, Paul Abrecht concluded his chapter on "Ecumenical Social Thought and Action" by referring to the importance of the world conference on Church and Society held in Geneva in July 1966.[2] That signal event identified Christian reflection and discussion concerning world development not just in terms of new and expanding forms of aid and assistance, but more in terms of a fundamental need for revolutionary change within the social order itself.

After the 1966 Geneva conference, ecumenical social ethics had to be evaluated against the backdrop of radical changes in science and technology, in politics and in

---

[1] Norman Goodall ed., *The Uppsala Report 1968: Official Report of the Fourth Assembly of the World Council of Churches, Uppsala, July 4-20, 1968*, WCC, 1968, p.57.
[2] Paul Abrecht, "The Development of Ecumenical Social Thought and Action", in Harold E. Fey ed., *A History of the Ecumenical Movement*, vol. 2, 1948-1968, 2nd ed., WCC, 1986, p.250ff.

family life. Conference participants were aware of potential dangers in such developments, but the overall picture was optimistic, marked by a confidence that growing economic prosperity could provide the solution to most social problems. The church, together with its social theology, was challenged to view positively these dynamic advances in social achievement and to leave behind the negative view of science and technology that had characterized earlier discussions.

In the life of the WCC, the Geneva conference marked a new beginning, a reorientation of the Life and Work tradition. As a consequence, the WCC and the Roman Catholic Church jointly established an exploratory committee on Society, Development and Peace (SODEPAX). Its task was to give advice on matters of social justice. Its reports did not have official WCC status, but, perhaps just because of that, they had considerable impact on ecumenical work concerning issues of development and peace.

The first SODEPAX conference was held in Beirut in 1968,[3] and later there followed conferences in Montreal[4] and Baden.[5] Initially, SODEPAX was marked by an optimistic view of global development. This was typical of the time, for development was then seen to offer unlimited growth in productivity and thus to guarantee improving incomes, in the West at least. However, later analyses of the structures supporting global technological and economic development made it clear that fundamental changes in the socio-economic structures in developing countries could not be made without far-reaching shifts in the terms of international trade that would necessarily prosper the poorer producer nations at the expense of industrialized countries. SODEPAX accompanied its analyses of both the practical and theoretical relationships between development, revolution and liberation with theological and ecclesiological arguments which established an intentional role for the churches in the economic, social and political affairs of societies.

SECULAR THEOLOGIES

For the first time in its history, the WCC at the Geneva conference of 1966 took the initiative in provoking discussion regarding the theological dimensions of "the secular". This was a move from strictly confessional theology, whether Protestant, Roman Catholic or Orthodox, to theology that was praxis-oriented and took its material from the actual socio-economic and political challenges of the global situation. At the Geneva conference a theology of revolution, formulated largely by Richard Shaull, a North American with considerable experience in Latin America, was extremely influential. Subsequently, SODEPAX was inspired both by the theology of liberation represented by Rubem Alves and the political theology espoused by Jürgen Moltmann.

With an expression borrowed from Yves Congar and Gustavo Gutiérrez, these theologies can be characterized as "theologies of temporal realities", even though their advocates did not necessarily agree among themselves on every issue.[6] Nevertheless, they all shared a similar hermeneutic that sees *humanum*, as it is revealed in the history of Je-

---

[3] Denys Munby ed., *World Development: The Challenge to the Churches, Conference on World Cooperation for Development, Beirut, Lebanon, 21-27 April 1968, Official Report*, Geneva, SODEPAX, 1968.

[4] *The Challenge of Development: A Sequel to the Beirut Conference of April 1968, Montreal, Canada, May 9-12, 1969*, Geneva, SODEPAX, 1968.

[5] *Peace – The Desperate Imperative. The Consultation on Christian Concern for Peace, Baden, Austria, 3-9 April 1970*, WCC, 1970.

[6] Gustavo Gutiérrez, *A Theology of Liberation*, Maryknoll NY, Orbis, 1981, p.45.

sus Christ, to be the cornerstone both for theology and ecclesial practice. Theologies of revolution and liberation and other political theologies, which after the Uppsala assembly provided the theological basis for WCC activity with respect to justice and peace, agree that human experiences of suffering and injustice are essential to a proper understanding of the biblical story of salvation. Shaull, Alves and Moltmann point to actual history as the place where all theology must begin and end.

The way was thus opened for seeing the sciences that deal with peoples' historical experiences – sociology, political science and the science of culture – as integral to theological work. They were not considered simply as helpful tools that could be used to make the church more effective or visible in the world. Rather, they were seen to offer methodologies that could help in an integrated way to effect a self-understanding of theology that demanded that critical questions be asked of old theological assumptions. After Uppsala, the theological focal point of the WCC changed from metaphysics to anthropology, from that which is inner and personal to that which is public and historical. A new historical-theological language was in the process of being created, a language capable of giving expression to the conflict, suffering and death experienced daily by many people all over the world.

This was particularly clear in Jürgen Moltmann's interpretation of the Uppsala theme, "Behold, I Make All Things New".[7] Moltmann argued that the eschatological tradition of hope concerned not only the future but was of great importance for the renewal of Christian faith in a revolutionary present. The political relevance of the tradition was expressed, according to Moltmann, by the language of "messianic hope", which interpreted the Exodus-event as a religious-political liberation. This eschatological realism was central to the Uppsala assertion that *everything* is made new.

Moltmann interpreted history as messianic. In that history, there runs a stream of renewal that flows from Christ who died in this world and was raised into God's new and just world. According to Moltmann, this changes the way in which time is perceived – the present is not to be understood essentially from the past, but rather from the future. Hope and prophecy become the key theological notions which interpret the world and give guidance to life in both church and society. Christian hope, which takes its content from the events of Christ's history of salvation, must take account of this future, the future hoped for in the midst of present sufferings, in order to establish practical initiatives to overcome instances of injustice and violence. Moltmann argued that critique, protest, creativity and action were all tools to be used to create more freedom for the future. Thus, in an illustrative way, he agreed with Shaull and Alves that new criteria for theology and faith had to be found in praxis. As a theological criterion, orthopraxis becomes more important than orthodoxy. "Political theology unites the old cosmological theology and the new theology of existence in the eschatological understanding of history with the messianic tasks of men in history."[8]

In Moltmann's political theology, *Messiah*, as the incarnate Son of God, is understood as the humanization of God for the sake of the humanization of men and women. Shaull and Alves, further, provided important theological insights to supplement and interpret

---

[7] Jürgen Moltmann, *Religion, Revolution and the Future*, New York, Scribner's, 1969, pp.129-47. See also Ernst Feil and Rudolf Weth, *Diskussion zur Theologie der Revolution*, Munich, Kaiser, 1979, pp.65-81.

[8] *Religion, Revolution and the Future*, pp.219f.

Moltmann. Their impact was seen in several theological consultations after Uppsala as, for example, the SODEPAX theological conference in Cartigny, Switzerland, in 1969. "To make and to keep human life human" (Paul L. Lehmann) became a major ecumenical theological project and, in this light, the WCC and its member churches were challenged to develop instruments to promote the humanizing of the world.[9] All of this implied a major shift in the understanding of soteriology – from "redemption", meaning a ransom paid by Christ, to "liberation", the securing of freedom from both present and future evil.

A JUST, PARTICIPATORY AND SUSTAINABLE SOCIETY

As a consequence of the developments in ecumenical theology, delegates to the fifth assembly of the WCC, Nairobi 1975, tried to formulate a new ideal for society to succeed the older idea of "the responsible society", first articulated at Amsterdam in 1948. The result was the quest for "a just, participatory and sustainable society" which was to be sought "taking into account both the need for a new international economic order and the concern for self-reliant and participatory forms for development which respond to the pressing needs of the people, and particularly programmes that help and encourage self-reliance and self-identity of the member churches".[10]

Nairobi's choice of "just" as a "middle axiom" suggested the need for an ethical basis to all political and social relationships. The use of "participatory" instead of "democratic" indicated dissatisfaction with the ways in which both capitalism and socialism, in all known forms, had treated democracy. "Participatory" implied an interpretation of democracy in the light of African democratic experiments, especially that of Julius Nyerere's *Ujamaa* socialism, known throughout the world as emphasizing a "self-reliance" model of social development.

Additionally, the importance of environmental issues for ecumenical social ethics was stressed by the notion of "sustainability", a notion identified by the WCC more than ten years before its introduction by the Brundtland report, *Our Common Future*, in international discussions of environment and development. An advisory committee for the search for a Just, Participatory and Sustainable Society (JPSS) was appointed by the WCC central committee in 1977; it made reports to the central committee in 1979 and 1982.[11] Further, the theology of liberation more directly found its way into the WCC in the late 1970s and early 1980s. This meant that the growing theological independence of many churches in Asia, Africa, Latin America and the Pacific, regardless of confessional heritage, found free space in the WCC.

---

[9] See also "Salvation and Social Justice in a Divided Humanity", report of section 2 at the 1973 Bangkok assembly on "Salvation Today". In this report the dynamic of salvation history is changed from ecclesiology to missiology and it is stressed that God and the kingdom of God have a concrete history in the world; salvation is not an eternal static reality, but is experienced in concrete historical situations. Bangkok formulated its provocative insight as follows: "In this sense it can be said, for example, that salvation is the peace of the people in Vietnam, independence in Angola, justice and reconciliation in Northern Ireland and release from the captivity of power in the North Atlantic community or personal conversion in the release of a submerged society in hope, or a new life-style amidst corporate self-interest and lovelessness". *Bangkok Assembly 1973: Minutes and Report of the Assembly of the Commission on World Mission and Evangelism of the World Council of Churches, December 31, 1972 and January 9-12, 1973*, WCC, 1973, p.90.
[10] David M. Paton ed., *Breaking Barriers, Nairobi 1975: The Official Report of the Fifth Assembly of the World Council of Churches, Nairobi, 23 November - 10 December, 1975*, WCC, 1995, p.299.
[11] See Koson Srisang ed., *Perspectives on Political Ethics: An Ecumenical Inquiry*, WCC, 1983.

At the same time as these developments were taking place, ecumenical ecclesiology was challenged by the conviction that the perspective of the poor is critical to the identification of the *locus theologicus*. When the poor – as individuals, class or nation – are seen as the hermeneutical key to the gospel's message of liberation, there are serious consequences for the church. José Míguez Bonino, an Argentinian scholar, president of the WCC from 1975 to 1983 and chairperson of the advisory committee for JPSS, argued that the poor point the way to a proper understanding of the message of salvation in the Bible. In consequence, Bonino argued, the issue at stake was the very nature of the church, its *esse*. He formulated this insight in relation to Benoit Dumas's book *The Two Alienated Faces of the One Church*:[12]

> Dumas's basic thesis is that the poor belong to the understanding of the mystery of the church or, if you wish to use other language, that the poor belong to the understanding of the very nature of the church. He says... in our present situation as churches the church does not recognize itself in the poor. It may recognize the poor as a very important part of the world, but the church does not recognize itself in the poor and the poor do not recognize Christ in the church. But this situation is one of lost identity, of self-alienation for the church, a situation in which the church is not altogether the church. The church which is not the church of the poor puts in serious jeopardy its churchly character. Therefore this becomes an ecclesiological criterion.

The poor, Bonino affirmed, are an ecclesiological criterion, no longer *objects* for the work of the church (preaching, diakonia, mission, education) but the church's *subjects*. The poor test the church as to whether or not it is or is not a true church. The tradition of a particular church can be rich, even possessing a lengthy history because of right theology, but it counts for nothing if it is not also the church of the poor, because it is in and among the poor that the suffering Christ is present.

According to Bonino and the JPSS study, God in Christ has chosen the poor as his people to save the world. And the fact that the poor, as God's people, are an ecclesiological criterion is the beginning of a new world order that will be just, participatory and sustainable. Thus, it is not the *faith* of the poor in some sort of confessional form that is the ecclesiological criterion, but rather the *fact* of poverty, something that can be measured with economic and sociological tools.

The JPSS study did not deal directly with the ecumenical discussion of church unity. However, JPSS implied indirectly that the present-day ecumenical movement has to occupy a position close to the classical Life and Work maxim: practice unites while dogma divides. Unity is not advanced solely by negotiation or organizational adjustment; it also requires common theological and socio-political reflection on those experiences which mirror the deepest intentions of the faith *(intentio fidei)*.

The JPSS study favoured the "covenant community" and "the people of God" as key ecclesiological symbols which maintain the interdependence of orthopraxis and orthodoxy, ethics and ecclesiology. It tried to find ecclesiological expressions that have both a biblical foundation and are open to important interpretations of political realities. To speak of the church as a "covenant community" is to say that the church is chosen by God. At the same time it opens up the idea of equality as an ideal in society at large. The term "people of God" offers an alternative and parallel structure. On the one hand, it is a fellowship of equal human beings; on the other hand, it tests a society to ascertain

---

[12]José Míguez Bonino in Julio de Santa Ana ed., *Towards a Church of the Poor: The Work of an Ecumenical Group on the Church and the Poor*, WCC, 1979, p.98.

whether it gives its citizens a participatory role in those socio-political decision-making processes that have an impact upon their everyday lives. The JPSS study thus ended up by translating different exemplary ecclesiological symbols and models so as to express the interdependence between the church and the world, between ecclesiology and ethics, between the history of salvation and secular history. It avoided dualistic error and also idealistic fallacy.

The JPSS study never really reached a conclusion, but it did help in the development of a coherent theological agenda that began to guide the work of the WCC and the ecumenical movement in areas of social ethics. The sixth assembly of the WCC, Vancouver 1983, changed the language and added a new dimension in its concern "to engage member churches in a conciliar process of mutual *commitment (covenant) for justice, peace and the integrity of all creation*".[13]

JUSTICE, PEACE AND THE INTEGRITY OF CREATION

The theme of the Vancouver assembly, "Jesus Christ – the Life of the World", was interpreted as a confession of the One who won victory over death in order that people might have abundant life. The assembly possessed a vision which resulted in a call for a global Christian response to the realities of an endangered planet. "Justice, Peace and the Integrity of Creation" (JPIC) were each understood as a dimension of an indivisible whole which was itself a response to a threefold threat to life: injustice, war and violence, and environmental disaster.

At the same time, social and ethical commitment was seen as vital to ecumenical ecclesiology and integral to the search by a "conciliar process" for church unity. In the Protestant tradition, this meant that human-rights issues, racism and nuclear deterrence were not to be regarded as merely *adiaphora* (theologically non-essential) but as issues which the church *by its nature* is required to face.

This new focus for ecumenical social ethics was introduced by the then WCC deputy general secretary, Konrad Raiser, in preparatory material for the assembly. He argued that the churches of the late 20th century had to put even more stress than the churches of the Reformation on the cross of Christ as the sign of God's struggle and victory over the powers of evil and destruction in the world.[14] This meant that Christian commitment and the confession of faith had to include a prophetic dimension which confirms the power of life in a world threatened by death and destruction. Because all life had its basis in Christ, according to Raiser, to confess Christ is not an action programme designed to solve the world's problems. Rather, such confession expresses an eschatological realism that anticipates God's final action. Thus, the Vancouver assembly, from a starting point of theology as confession, sought to combine ethics and ecclesiology on the basis of an eschatological frame of reference, centred around the cross as the criterion for Christian ethics and as a mark of the church *(nota ecclesiae)*.

When the JPIC process, initiated at Vancouver, culminated at the world convocation on "Justice, Peace and the Integrity of Creation" held in Seoul, Korea, 5-12 March 1990, perhaps the greatest frustration, according to Douglas John Hall, was "the failure to

[13] David Gill ed., *Gathered for Life: Official Report of the Sixth Assembly of the World Council of Churches*, WCC, 1983, p.255.
[14] Konrad Raiser, "Choosing Life rather than Death", in William H. Lazareth ed., *The Lord of Life: Theological Explorations of the Theme "Jesus Christ – the Life of the World"*, WCC, 1983, pp.57ff.

combine the quest for a globally appropriate profession of faith with commitments to theological and ethical positions that had been hammered out on the anvils of specific historical contexts".[15] Nevertheless, the representatives of member churches, movements and Christian World Communions formulated a "Final Document: Entering into Covenant Solidarity for Justice, Peace and the Integrity of Creation" that contained many valuable "points of no return" for ecumenical social ethics. God's covenant, which is open to all and holds the promise of life in wholeness and right relationships, was spelled out in ten affirmations:

- We affirm that all exercise of power is accountable to God.
- We affirm God's option for the poor.
- We affirm the equal value of all races and peoples.
- We affirm that male and female are created in the image of God.
- We affirm that the truth is at the foundation of a community of free people.
- We affirm the peace of Jesus Christ.
- We affirm the creation as beloved of God.
- We affirm that the earth is the Lord's.
- We affirm the dignity and commitment of the younger generation.
- We affirm that human rights are given by God.

Additionally, the Seoul participants affirmed a fourfold covenant, a commitment which the delegates accepted in solidarity with one another. The four areas of covenant committed them to a determined search:

- for a just economic order, on local, national, regional and international levels, for all people;
- for the true security of all nations and people; for the demilitarization of international relations; against militarism and national security doctrines and systems; for a culture of nonviolence as a force for change and liberation;
- for building a culture that can live in harmony with creation's integrity; for preserving the gift of the earth's atmosphere to nurture and sustain the world's life; for combating the causes of destructive changes to the atmosphere which threaten to disrupt the earth's climate and create widespread suffering;
- for the eradication of racism and discrimination on national and international levels for all people; for the breaking down of walls which divide people because of their ethnic origin; for the dismantling of the economic, political and social patterns of behaviour that perpetrate, and allow individuals, consciously and unconsciously, to perpetrate, the sin of racism.[16]

Between Vancouver and Seoul, many local and regional ecumenical events took place, helping to give the issues of JPIC high profile on the agenda of the churches. In 1988, the Pacific Conference of Churches had a JPIC assembly in Malua, Western Samoa, under the theme, "Renewing Our Partnership in God's Creation". In May 1989 in Basel, Switzerland, the Conference of European Churches and the (Roman Catholic) Council of European Bishops Conferences jointly convened a European assembly on "Peace with Justice for the Whole Creation". This was the first major meeting of Catholic, Orthodox and Protestant churches since the great schism of the 11th century.

---

[15] Douglas John Hall, "The State of the Ark: Lessons from Seoul", in D. Preman Niles ed., *Between the Flood and the Rainbow: Interpreting the Conciliar Process of Mutual Commitment (Covenant) to Justice, Peace and the Integrity of Creation*, WCC, 1992, p.35.
[16] *Ibid.*, pp.164ff.

In September 1989, the Christian Conference of Asia held a mission conference in Cipenas, Indonesia, under the theme "Peoples of God, People of God" and the Latin American Council of Churches (CLAI) convened a meeting in December 1989 in Quito, Ecuador, on JPIC using "land" and the "international debt crisis" as foci for discussing the importance of JPIC for Latin America.

Confessional families also took a keen interest in the JPIC process. The assembly of the World Alliance of Reformed Churches meeting in August 1989 in Seoul, Korea, had justice, peace and the integrity of creation as the theme of one of its sections. This was also the case at the eighth assembly of the Lutheran World Federation, meeting in Curitiba, Brazil, in January-February 1990.

The Roman Catholic Church in February 1989 published *A Catholic Contribution to the Process of Justice, Peace and the Integrity of Creation*. Arguing from the tradition of "the common good", this study declared that "the goods of this world are in fact, by their origin, destined for all".[17] The order of creation is described on the basis of respect for justice, peace and the integrity of creation. Five "middle axioms" were formulated on peace, human rights, exercising an option for the poor, development and ecological sustainability.

Thomas Derr has analyzed the difference between the Seoul final document and the Roman Catholic contribution to the JPIC process to illustrate the relationships between theological methods, organizational structures and various traditions of social-ethical teaching in respect to cooperation between the WCC and the Vatican.[18] While the WCC had come to favour an action-reflection model in which political contexts were of primary importance for the interpretation of the biblical message of justice and peace, the Vatican maintained a method of formulating general ethical principles in the tradition of middle axioms, a method followed by the WCC in its early years.

Orthodox churches also took a keen interest in the JPIC process, offering insights into the theological preparation of the Seoul convocation. Of particular importance was the third preconciliar pan-Orthodox conference (Chambésy, Switzerland, 1986) on "the contribution of the Orthodox church to the realization of peace, justice, liberty, brotherhood and love among peoples and to the suppression of racial and other discrimination".[19] An inter-Orthodox consultation was held in Sofia, Bulgaria, in 1987, when the document, "Orthodox Perspectives on Creation" was issued. Later, in May 1989, an inter-Orthodox consultation in Minsk, USSR, adopted the document "Orthodox Perspectives on Justice and Peace". The Orthodox church reacted against what it regarded as an irrelevant theology based only on the horizontal secularized ethic of classical humanism. According to Gennadios Limouris, the "Orthodox contribution to, and their task in, the JPIC process was to draw a social ecclesiology from the biblical tradition and the church fathers, and to try to theologize on these areas through its lived and experienced ecclesial life".[20] As an alternative, only "Christian personalism", according to Orthodox insights, offers a "chance of giving an adequate answer and resolving the present problems, for, unlike capitalism, individualism and Marxist collectivism, it has insisted for

---

[17] See WCC-JPIC Resource Materials 6.3, p.6.
[18] Thomas Sieger Derr, *Barriers to Ecumenism: The Holy See and the World Council of Churches on Social Questions*, Maryknoll NY, Orbis, 1983.
[19] See *Episkepsis*, 369, Dec. 1986.
[20] Gennadios Limouris, "New Challenges: Visions and Signs of Hope. Orthodox Insights on JPIC", in *Between the Flood and the Rainbow*, p.111.

many decades on the basic worth of the human person as subject (not object) and sought his fulfilment only in communion with all other individuals".[21]

The JPIC process provided important space for an ecumenical discussion concerning social ethics, but the process also showed that the debate was just beginning. It was extremely difficult to find common theological ground, and the whole idea of "conciliarity" had to be surrendered in light of pressure from many, including the Roman Catholic and Orthodox churches. There are still, however, elements of the original theological framework of the JPIC process in the final message from Seoul:

> Now is the time to recognize that there is a long process still before us. We will take to our churches and our movements the affirmations and commitments we have made in Seoul, inviting others to join in. Together with them we struggle for the realization of our vision. We are accountable to one another and to God. We pray that we do not miss the kairos to which we have been led by God.[22]

ECUMENICAL INVOLVEMENT IN INTERNATIONAL AFFAIRS

In the period after 1968 the WCC, especially through its Commission of the Churches on International Affairs (CCIA), continued to be a centre of inspiration and coordination for ecumenical involvement in international affairs. The struggle for justice, peace and human rights and the struggle against war, violence and racism have been issues on the agenda of the WCC since its inception.

A WCC-sponsored world consultation on inter-church aid, refugee and world service at Larnaca, Cyprus, in 1986 formulated the beginning of a consensus: "An ecumenical political ethic has to do with the evaluation of the understanding and exercise of power in faithfulness to the gospel for the sake of social justice, human dignity and authentic community."[23] A declaration from this consultation encouraged churches to assist victims of conscience and, where possible, to intervene with government authorities on behalf of such victims. In situations where the human rights of people were systematically and continuously violated, the churches were challenged to go beyond assistance and make efforts to rescue the victims. Churches are duty bound to address the root causes, the structural origins of such violations of human rights.

The main purpose of ecumenical involvement in international affairs was seen to be based on the integrity and dignity of politics. Good order in society should be maintained and, where undermined, restored. The churches are not required to establish themselves as a political force outside existing political structures or to identify themselves exclusively with one party or ideology. Ecumenical involvement is to be based on critical solidarity with the political system as the means necessary for the promotion of the welfare of all human beings.

Nevertheless, ecumenical confidence in international political structures decreased in the late 1970s. In public statements and publications the CCIA took a critical stance towards international politics and political institutions. This became especially clear in

---

[21] *Ibid.*, p.125.
[22] *Now is the Time. Final Document and Other Texts: World Convocation on Justice, Peace and the Integrity of Creation, Seoul 1990*, WCC, 1990,
[23] WCC, Commission of the Churches on International Affairs, *The Churches in International Affairs: Reports 1983-1986*, WCC, 1986, p.16.

the 1983 Vancouver assembly statement on peace and justice.[24] This statement described the growing threat to peace and justice from nuclear weapons, weapons that claim victims even in the absence of war. Additionally, local and national conflicts and economic threats to peace and stability were singled out as immediate dangers to the well-being of societies. According to the statement, concern for the common security of nations must be reinforced by a concept of "common security": "True security for the people demands respect for human rights, including the right to self-determination, as well as social and economic justice for all within every nation, and a political framework that would ensure it."[25]

This statement, further, affirmed the nation-state as the most significant pragmatic structure in society and still the best instrument for securing stability and social justice. But the nation-state was not to be sacralized; rather, it was to be seen in a wider global perspective that also included the United Nations as a necessary political institution. The growing refusal of many governments to use the UN to preserve international peace and security and to provide for the peaceful resolution of conflicts was criticized and the failure of the United Nations Conference on Trade and Development VI to establish a meaningful North-South dialogue was especially regretted.

Many churches, national and regional ecumenical councils, and local church groups agreed with Vancouver, when the delegates said:

> The churches today are called to confess anew their faith, and to repent for the times when Christians have remained silent in the face of injustice or threats to peace. The biblical vision of peace with justice for all, of wholeness, of unity for all God's people is not one of several options for the followers of Christ. It is an imperative in our time.[26]

But the Vancouver statement also provoked criticism and debate. In the assembly plenary, Bishop John Habgood of the Church of England argued for a more pragmatic, less "utopian" emphasis. His intervention signalled a fundamental disagreement within the ecumenical movement concerning the theological framework for the WCC's work on justice and peace. This resulted, in 1990, in an informal group of "friends of the WCC" addressing an open letter to Emilio Castro, then general secretary. Among these persons, along with Habgood, were such veteran ecumenists as Ronald H. Preston and Paul Abrecht. The letter criticized the WCC on the grounds that it no longer served as a facilitator in society because its social theology and ethics had lost the quality of genuine dialogue, analysis and study.

In 1992, this same group circulated a pamphlet on "The Future of Ecumenical Social Thought", explaining the raison d'être of the earlier open letter. Preston, professor emeritus of social and pastoral theology at the University of Manchester, England, advocated "Christian realism" in opposition to what he called the WCC's "theology of eschatological realism".[27] According to Preston, "Christian realism" represented a social theology committed, to be sure, to the gospel's radical challenge to social, economic and political injustice while taking realistically those parametres within which persons in

---

[24] *Gathered for Life*, pp.130-38.
[25] *Ibid.*, p. 134. At Vancouver, delegates were reminded of the real human consequences of national and international policies. A memorable instance was a presentation by Darlene Keju-Johnson of Micronesia, who as a child had been irradiated by radio-active fall-out from US nuclear testing in the Pacific.
[26] *Ibid.*, p. 132.
[27] Ronald H. Preston, *Confusions in Christian Social Ethics: Problems for Geneva and Rome*, London, SCM Press, 1994, pp.70ff.

public positions in pluralistic societies must move, especially if they are required to satisfy a majority of the electorate. According to Preston, the adoption of the theology of eschatological realism had turned the WCC into an institution that favoured the social commentary of non-professional pastors at the expense of informed lay experts, the participation of pressure groups at the expense of serious professional discussion among experts and political decision-makers, and utopian thinking instead of realistic awareness of the ambiguities of life. Christian unity had thus become identified with either ideological conformity or political solidarity.[28]

ACTIVE EFFORTS TOWARDS HUMAN RIGHTS

Beginning in the 1970s, there was indeed a shift of emphasis in the work of the CCIA. This became clear in respect to human rights when the WCC central committee, meeting in Addis Ababa in 1971, called the CCIA and member churches to become actively involved in efforts to actualize human rights.[29] This call resulted in serious attempts to formulate an ecumenical consensus regarding a common and enlarged understanding of human rights and the churches' responsibility in respect to them. An international consultation on "Human Rights and Christian Responsibility" held in St Pölten, Austria, in October 1974 marked an important turning point. According to Eric Weingärtner, delegates to that meeting were asked to deal with the question of "how to relate standards of human rights to the cultural, socio-economic and political settings of different parts of the world... [the] emphasis being laid on finding more effective means of international cooperation for the implementation of human rights".[30]

St Pölten helped to formulate at least two distinct positions in the area of human rights. One school of thought stressed individual rights and especially the absolute precedence of religious liberty. The theological focus for this way of thinking was the individual person as created in the image of God. In contrast, a second school of thought stressed the relational nature of the human person as created in the image of the triune God. Human dignity was not to be separated from the well-being of the entire human family – all rights were equally important, with religious liberty but one among many.

This latter position was also taken by the Nairobi assembly in 1975, when it recognized the indivisibility of the whole complex of human rights and therefore endorsed an integral approach to them.[31] For the first time in ecumenical history a consensus was reached concerning the content of human rights,[32] identified as:

– the right to basic guarantees for life;
– the right to self-determination and cultural identity;
– the rights of minorities;
– the right to participate in decision-making;

---

[28] See also Ans J. van der Bent, *Commitment to God's World. A Concise Critical Survey of Ecumenical Social Thought*, WCC, 1995, pp.178f.
[29] "Memorandum and Recommendation on Human Rights" (appendix XI), in WCC Central Committee: *Minutes and Reports of the Twenty-Fourth Meeting, Addis Ababa 1971*, p.269-272.
[30] "A Decade of Human Rights in the WCC: An Evaluation" (appendix I), in José Zalaquett, "The Human Rights Issue and the Human Rights Movement: Characterization, Evaluation, Propositions", in *CCIA Background Information*, 3, 1981, pp.45.
[31] *Breaking Barriers*, pp.102-107.
[32] See Gerald D. Gort, "The Christian Ecumenical Reception of Human Rights in IAMS", in *Mission Studies*, 11/1, 21, 1994, pp.76-107.

- the right to dissent;
- the right to personal dignity;
- the right to religious freedom.[33]

This consensus was put to the test by disagreement about how to respond to the signing in August 1975 of the Final Act of the Helsinki Conference on Security and Cooperation in Europe. It was argued that the so-called "third basket" of humanitarian issues in the Helsinki accord made it imperative for the WCC to protest publicly against human-rights violations in Eastern Europe. At the same time, spokespersons from the third world challenged the CCIA not to devote its resources to human-rights issues in Europe to the extent that necessary work in the southern hemisphere would be neglected.[34] As a double response, an international Human Rights Advisory Group (HRAG) was established within the CCIA in 1978 and a Churches' Human Rights Programme for the Implementation of the Helsinki Final Act was set up in 1980 under the joint sponsorship of the Conference of European Churches, the National Council of the Churches of Christ in the USA and the Canadian Council of the Churches.

In its report to the Vancouver assembly, the working committee of the Churches' Human Rights Programme for the Implementation of the Helsinki Final Act stressed, on the basis of a series of regional consultations held in 1981-82, the following priorities for the churches:
- the position of women;
- the situation of racial minorities;
- labour conditions and unemployment;
- the negative effects of the modern information revolution;
- threats to religious liberty for all.[35]

Further, the HRAG identified, at its 1986 meeting in Glion, Switzerland, three problem areas for renewed attention:
- the increasing use of genocide "as a systematic policy" by certain governments;
- threats to religious liberty in the form of state control;
- the undermining of the process of democratization and the pursuit of social and economic justice by militarization, the exploitation of the arms trade and the impact of crippling foreign debt.[36]

The HRAG also recommended ecumenical involvement in the establishment of continuous interfaith dialogue to promote full religious freedom for all. In 1991 at Canberra, the seventh assembly of the WCC confirmed the direction of the human-rights work taken by the CCIA. It both highlighted the God-given vocation of the churches to resist all forms of injustice and enlarged the human-rights discussion to include the special responsibility of churches and Christians for stewardship of the natural environment.

---

[33] *Breaking Barriers*, pp.103-106.
[34] Erich Weingärtner, "Human Rights on the Ecumenical Agenda: A Report and Assessment", in *CCIA Background Information*, 3, 1983, pp.22-29.
[35] Report to the 1983 Vancouver assembly by the Churches' Human Rights Programme for the Implementation of the Helsinki Final Act, in Eric Weingärtner, "Human Rights on the Ecumenical Agenda: A Report and Assessment" (appendix I), in *CCIA Background Information*, 3, 1983, pp.68-71; cf. *Gathered for Life*, p.143.
[36] "Priorities in the Human Rights Work of the Commission of the Churches on International Affairs, Human Rights Advisory Group, Glion, Switzerland 1986", in *The Churches in International Affairs, Reports 1983-1986*, WCC, 1987, pp.33-37.

Rights do not belong only to human beings but also to nature, an emphasis sharpened by the severity of the emerging global ecological crisis.[37]

Thus, the content of human rights in ecumenical reflection and action since 1968 has broadened. The first generation's concern for individual rights and the second generation's for social rights have been enlarged to include a third generation's concern for peoples' rights to self-determination. Furthermore, a fourth generation of environmental rights and a fifth category, called by Gerald D. Gort "future-generation rights" need now to be added to the agenda. At the same time the high priority given to "solidarity with the poor" aids in the uncovering of economic root causes of violations of human rights. An emphasis on global, structural impediments to the realization of human rights is thus a crucial part of present ecumenical thinking.

PEACE AND DISARMAMENT

In his study of how churches speak on social issues, US Lutheran ethicist Mark Ellingsen observes pronounced unanimity in recent church social statements concerning peace.[38] This consensus cuts across geographical and confessional lines and is the result of a long process in which every major ecumenical gathering dealing with social issues has given high priority to the establishment of peace.[39]

The world conference on Church and Society in 1966 argued in favour of nuclear pacifism, and even though this was not a position taken by the Uppsala assembly in 1968, that assembly, which strikingly and for the first time issued a call allowing for selective conscientious objection, in its statement "Towards Justice and Peace in International Affairs" asserted that "the concentration of nuclear weapons in the hands of a few nations presents the world with serious problems: (a) how to guarantee the security of the non-nuclear nations; (b) how to prevent the nuclear powers from freezing the existing order at the expense of changes needed for social and political justice".[40] Nevertheless, as the late North American Mennonite theologian, John Howard Yoder, pointed out, it was not until Vancouver in 1983 that an all-out rejection of nuclear weapons was embraced by the WCC.[41]

During this period, questions were also raised concerning "just-war" theory in a nuclear age, not least in the WCC study on "Violence, Nonviolence, and the Struggle for Justice" (1971-73) which analyzed the issue of war in a broad context. Deterrence was seen not only as a consequence of technical scientific and international developments, but also understood as a function of social, cultural and psychological interests. In view of the increasing worldwide trend to militarism, itself contrary to the Christian view of a world of justice and peace, the Nairobi assembly recommended that the WCC convene a special consultation on the nature of militarism preparatory to the creation of a programme to combat militarism.[42]

The proposed programme, which was to have paralleled the Programme to Combat Racism, was turned into a study project, and never materialized. This points to an interest-

---

[37] Michael Kinnamon ed., *Signs of the Spirit: Official Report Seventh Assembly, Canberra, Australia, 7-20 February 1991*, WCC, 1991, pp.54-95 (sections I and II) *passim*.
[38] Mark Ellingsen, *The Cutting Edge: How Churches Speak on Social Issues*, WCC, 1993, p.56ff.
[39] *Commitment to God's World*, p.107ff.
[40] *The Uppsala Report 1968*, p.62f.
[41] John H. Yoder, "Peace", in Nicholas Lossky et al. eds, *Dictionary of the Ecumenical Movement*, 2nd ed., WCC, 2002, pp.893ff.
[42] *Breaking Barriers*, p.140.

ing dilemma or paradox in the WCC. On the one hand, through its special fund of the PCR, the WCC supported liberation movements even when they used force in their struggle for liberation; but on the other hand, it organized studies to prevent the use of military power in and between nation-states. According to the analysis of Wolfgang Huber and Hans-Richard Reuter, this shows that

> An ethics of peace, by definition, must draw upon a consistent ethics of the use of force lest it merely serve to justify, without explicit criteria, force "from below" in response to the widely repudiated "force from above".[43]

The steady deterioration of prospects for world peace and the escalation of the arms race in the period 1976-82 drew the attention of many churches to their responsibility to act before it was too late. An international public hearing on nuclear weapons and disarmament was held in Amsterdam in 1981,[44] agreeing with the Palme commission of the UN that proposed common security as an alternative to deterrence. It was clear to the participants at Amsterdam that nuclear war could under no circumstances be just or justifiable, and that a "limited" nuclear war was unlikely to remain limited. The concept of nuclear deterrence was rejected as morally unacceptable and as incapable of safeguarding peace and security in the long run. The Vancouver assembly in 1983 affirmed the results of the Amsterdam hearing and cited the challenge to the churches:

> We believe that the time has come when the churches must unequivocally declare that the production and deployment as well as the use of nuclear weapons are a crime against humanity and that such activities must be condemned on ethical and theological grounds.[45]

Discussions after Vancouver demonstrated that the conviction that a just war could be ethically defended remained in respect to conventional warfare; the system of deterrence as a temporary expedient leading to progressive disarmament was still widely accepted in many churches. This was clear also in the intensive debate during the Canberra assembly in 1991. An amendment to the public statement on the Gulf war was proposed by Konrad Raiser, then a delegate of the German Evangelical Church. Raiser would have added the following sentence: "We call upon [the churches] to give up any theological or moral justification of the use of military power, be it in war or through other forms of oppressive security systems, and to become public advocates of a just peace."[46] The language of the amendment was taken from the world convocation on JPIC in Seoul. In spite of Raiser's advocacy, the amendment was defeated, after a long and heated debate because of objections to what was called the statement's "pacifist nature".

After Canberra, discussion was perpetuated by the many ethnic conflicts and civil wars that had spread, becoming ever more violent, since the destruction of the Berlin wall in 1989. The WCC and, indeed, the whole ecumenical movement thus continued to be engaged in the process of rethinking issues related to war and peace in the post-cold-war period. A background document, "Resurgent Racism, Ethnicity and Nationality Conflicts", received by the WCC central committee in Johannesburg in 1994, raised questions following the disintegration of the former socialist states of Eastern and Cen-

---

[43] Wolfgang Huber and Hans-Richard Reuter, *Friedensethik*, Stuttgart, Kohlhammer, 1990, p.165; translated from the German.
[44] Paul Abrecht and Ninan Koshy eds, *Before It's Too Late. The Challenge of Nuclear Disarmament: The Complete Record of the Public Hearing on Nuclear Weapons and Disarmament Organized by the World Council of Churches, Amsterdam 1981*, WCC, 1983.
[45] *Gathered for Life*, p.137.
[46] *Signs of the Spirit*, p.203.

tral Europe. It was decided to establish a Programme to Overcome Violence with the purpose of challenging and transforming the global culture of violence in the direction of a culture of just peace. The aim was to confront and overcome "the spirit, logic and practice of war".[47] A Decade to Overcome Violence was approved by the WCC's eighth assembly in Harare (1998).

COMMUNICATION FOR PEACE AND JUSTICE

The 20th century has experienced an explosion in the use and distribution of mass media. Pope Pius XII (1939-58) was one of the first church leaders to speak affirmatively concerning the potential value of the mass media, encouraging church bodies to use the media positively, especially for the propagation of Christian teaching. Some of his concerns were subsequently reflected in *Inter Mirifica*, the 1963 decree on the means of social communication of the Second Vatican Council, and in the 1971 pastoral instruction on the means of social communication, *Communio et Progressio*. However, a number of Roman Catholics and others criticized these documents for being too triumphalistic in tone and limited in scope.

In 1965, at the behest of the WCC, a group of professional journalists and broadcasters met with an ecumenical group of theologians at Bossey, Switzerland. According to Pauline Webb, the British broadcaster who served as a vice-moderator of the central committee between the Uppsala and Nairobi assemblies, this was the first international conference organized by the churches to discuss the relationship of theology to mass communication.[48] There was "apparent agreement that, with the advent of radio and television, the role of the printed page is not the same as it once was and will probably continue to change... [T]here was recognition of the inadequacy of any one means of communication – pulpit-press-broadcasting, the institutional church or the spoken and unspoken witness of the individual Christian – to carry the whole burden of God's revelation of himself."[49] The outcome of the consultation was the preparation of a statement subsequently adopted at the Uppsala assembly, *"The Church and the Media of Mass Communication"*.[50] Optimistic in tone, this statement defended the different media as enriching human life and culture. The media were seen as possible tools through which to promote some of the basic structures of a responsible world society. Further, the media were seen to provide a forum for discussing the crucial issues of the time and to give minority views a public hearing.

Uppsala thus placed the media on the agenda of the ecumenical movement, and throughout the 1970s the issue of communication was dealt with in a still wider context. SODEPAX, for example, emphasized the role of the media in relation to the developing world, and at St Pölten in 1974 the CCIA was critical of Western media in their selective presentations of world affairs.

When debate over the Programme to Combat Racism arose, the ecumenical movement was to go through a learning experience concerning the operations of the mass media. The WCC was challenged in a qualitatively new way to communicate effectively

---

[47] World Council of Churches Programme Unit III Justice, Peace and Creation, and CCIA, *Programme to Overcome Violence: An Introduction*, WCC, Geneva 1995.

[48] Pauline Webb, "Communication", in *Dictionary of the Ecumenical Movement*, p.223ff. See also Larry Jorgenson ed., *The WCC and Communication: A Survey of the Discussion So Far*, WCC, 1982.

[49] Jorgenson, quoting S.F. Mack and E.C. Parker, in *The WCC and Communication*, p.10.

[50] *The Uppsala Report 1968*, pp.389-401.

through the use of what had previously been regarded as "secular" media. This new alertness to the media shaped the Council's awareness of communication itself as an issue. There was a need for reflection on the power of the media and how the lives of people and institutions were influenced by the growing global network of communication.

In 1981, a consultation took place in Versailles, France, between representatives of the WCC, the World Association for Christian Communication, the Lutheran World Federation and three Roman Catholic agencies. A discussion document on "The Search for Credible Christian Communication" was prepared at this consultation and subsequently circulated among some four hundred churches, media institutes and individuals involved in the media. This paper attempted to stimulate greater awareness of the influence of the media on the whole of life, recognizing the injustice of an international communication order in which the tools of mass communication are owned by Western commercial interests responsible to no one but themselves.

The Versailles paper served as a briefing document for the 1983 debate at the Vancouver assembly where the issue of communication was dealt with as one of eight assembly sections. The report from that section, "Communicating Credibly", in contrast to the earlier Uppsala statement, was sharply critical of the various mass media and their impact on modern society. The section report formulated criteria for credible communication: "Does the communication make peace, build justice and promote wholeness? Does it present a complete picture, or is it based on national or sectarian prejudice?"[51]

Many of the issues discussed in the Vancouver report were taken up at the first world congress of the World Association for Christian Communication (WACC), Manila 1989. That organization's foundation dated back to 1950 and at the time of the Manila event it had some 600 individual corporate members (e.g. church agencies and communication institutions). In a "Manila Declaration" more than 450 people from over 80 countries formulated a list of concerns about the state of communication in relation to peoples' rights and dignity; communication was acknowledged to be part of every aspect of life. The declaration supported the call of UNESCO, through its celebrated MacBride report, for a new, more just and more efficient new world information and communication order (NWICO).[52] Such an order would change the structures of power in the mass media and information industries. Ordinary people especially, according to the Manila declaration, were victims of media power and were treated more and more as objects rather than subjects. "This is particularly true for women, manual labourers, indigenous minorities, senior citizens and children."[53] As an alternative, congress participants committed themselves to a vision of democratic communication that included democratization of the churches' own media, media awareness training within the family, and support for communication professionals who under certain conditions are persecuted or even killed for telling the truth. Advocacy journalism was favoured as serving the struggle for human rights, environmental protection and the exercise of people's power. "Ultimately, Christian communicators have no other option but to throw in their lot with the poor, oppressed and marginalized who bear the hallmark of God's communication."[54]

---

[51] *Gathered for Life*, pp.103-110.
[52] "Communication and Community: The Manila Declaration", in *Statements on Communication by the World Association for Christian Communication*, London, WACC, 1995, pp.12-16.
[53] *Ibid.*, p.14.
[54] *Ibid.*, p.15.

AFTER 1989: A NEW INTERNATIONAL DISORDER

Ninan Koshy, who served as the director of the WCC's Commission of the Churches on International Affairs from 1981 to 1991, has pointed to the fact that for the first four decades of its life the history of the WCC coincided with the history of the cold war, and that conflict inevitably made an impact on the ecumenical movement.[55] Yet it is important to note that the reverse was also true: the many initiatives of the ecumenical movement – on local, national and global levels – made an impact on the cold war itself. In many places, congregations and church bodies worked as bridge-builders between nations and churches that were separated or even seen as enemies because of the tensions between East and West. Albeit with difficulty, churches on both sides of the iron curtain were often able to create spaces of cooperation and community in which there was relative stability that benefited people in local situations. To a certain although limited degree, most churches in Eastern Europe were able to meet for worship although the living of committed Christian lives was costly, marked as it often was by harassment and frequent persecution.

For the churches, to build bridges it was necessary that cooperative relations be forged between church leaders and political authorities. This created a de facto acceptance by church leaders of the legitimacy of governmental structures; however, it also forced political authorities to recognize the existence of both the churches and the ecumenical movement as significant expressions of religious life in their own right and not simply as beneficiaries of state tolerance. Throughout the cold war, a mutual dependency was in fact created between the churches and the ecumenical movement on one side, and communist regimes on the other side.

In the German Democratic Republic (East Germany) especially, this mutuality of interests opened the way for the churches and the ecumenical movement to make a significant impact on the course of the cold war. As early as the Vancouver assembly, delegates from East German churches called for an "ecumenical council" to address issues of peace and justice. The inspiration for this initiative came not least from Dietrich Bonhoeffer's call, issued at the 1934 conference of the universal Christian council for Life and Work in Fanø, Denmark, for an ecumenical council of peace that would bring preparations for war in Europe to a halt. As already discussed, the Vancouver assembly did initiate a "conciliar process" for justice, peace and the integrity of creation, and in East Germany this process inspired churches to become meeting places for many persons who gathered to pray and work for the implementation of JPIC by democratic means. Most analysts agree that the peaceful revolution of 1989 in East Germany was closely related to the work for peace and justice which took place in the churches.

Even though the cold war, at least in Europe and North America, was experienced by many as a relatively stable, politically bi-polar situation, it was surely not a static phenomenon without consequence for global politics. The WCC's effort to witness in the realm of international relations had to take account of the fact that the cold war was marked in East and West by differing and often conflicting perceptions, suspicions, and ideological struggles concerning peace, justice and freedom.[56]

The fall of the Berlin wall in November 1989 became the symbol of peaceful revolution in Germany, and it had dramatic consequences for the entire world. Immediate re-

---

[55] Ninan Koshy, *Churches in the World of Nations: International Politics and the Mission and Ministry of the Church*, WCC, 1994, pp.104-105.
[56] *Ibid.*, p.105

action to the collapse of the communist systems of Eastern Europe was a mixture of both joy and anxiety. Yet subsequent developments in deadlocked situations soon gave way to hope for a new and more peaceful international order. In two areas where the WCC had been actively involved for peace and justice, there were immediate signs of hope. In South Africa, the release from prison of Nelson Mandela in 1990 was a signal event in the struggle for liberation and reconciliation within that nation. Additionally, in another area of consistent WCC engagement, the Oslo agreement between the government of Israel and the Palestine Liberation Organization likewise gave hope – subsequently placed in great jeopardy – for new momentum towards peace and justice in the Middle East.

In this situation, the WCC was also able to bring together the general secretaries of the National Council of Churches of Korea (Republic of Korea, South Korea) and the Korean Christian Federation (Democratic People's Republic of Korea, North Korea) at its 1991 assembly in Canberra. This was the first time that the small Christian community of North Korea was represented at an international ecumenical event. Additionally, at the same assembly the China Christian Council, absent from the WCC since 1956, re-established the presence of mainland Chinese Christians within the ecumenical movement. Both these events demonstrated the new possibilities for cooperation between the churches after the tumultuous events of 1989.

The Canberra assembly, however, also showed dramatically that to view the post-1989 world only with optimism would be an illusion. The assembly was held in the shadow of the first Gulf war, and delegates were uneasy about their own safety. At the assembly, the atmosphere was tense and at times even hostile when consideration was given to how the WCC should react to escalations of violence and to the war itself. Could – and should – the ecumenical tradition of dealing with issues of peace and justice, developed during the cold war, be maintained in the new situation? As has been pointed out, that tradition rested on a bi-polar, East-West, view of the world that saw things as relatively stable. The new situation was increasingly seen as uni-polar with the United States as the only military superpower. As indicated above, while most persons at Canberra rejected a pacifist attitude towards war, they did call both for an immediate cease-fire between Iraq and the coalition led by the US and for a negotiated settlement of the conflict within the context of the United Nations.[57]

This action raised for the delegates the question of how major international decisions were to be made in the post-cold war era. The UN was criticized for its dependency upon one powerful nation, the US, or upon one group of nations, the coalition led by the US. A critical examination of the emerging new world order was called for. The delegates stressed as a basic principle that no one government or group of governments should either take or be allowed to take primary responsibility for the resolution of major conflicts beyond their own borders.[58] In this critique of the UN there is, however, support of that institution as the only legitimate political instrument for handling the global conflicts that had escalated in number and violence in the new uni-polar world.

GLOBALIZATION AND HUMAN RIGHTS

New developments in international politics and in the global economic system have made it necessary for the World Council of Churches to formulate new insights and

---

[57] *Signs of the Spirit*, pp.205ff.
[58] *Ibid.*, p.211.

visions so that the churches may be helped better to understand and act in areas related to peace and justice. In the mid-1990s, the concept of *globalization* became a catchword to describe the dynamics of a new international *disorder*. At the eighth WCC assembly, Harare 1998, it was agreed that globalization is not simply an economic issue; it was also seen as a cultural, political, ethical and ecological issue, and as such it must be approached from the perspectives of the poor.[59]

The Harare assembly pointed to the fact that the vision behind globalization is a vision competing with Christian commitment to the oikoumene, the unity of humankind and the whole inhabited earth. Harare called the churches to reflect on the challenge of globalization from the perspective of faith and thus to resist the unilateral domination of economic and cultural globalization. Delegates expressed their appreciation for the call issued by the 23rd general council of the World Alliance of Reformed Churches in 1997 for a committed process of recognition, education and confession *(processus confessionis)* regarding economic injustice and ecological destruction, and encouraged all WCC member churches to join in such a process.[60]

With the use of the term *processus confessionis,* the challenge of globalization was placed in a theological context, lending it a dimension that has accompanied the ecumenical movement's socio-ethical reflection on a host of issues: justice for the Jewish people in the 1930s, apartheid in South Africa, disarmament in the post-second world war era, the unending struggle for justice for the poor. Theologically, both *processus confessionis* and *status confessionis* identify concrete issues of peace and justice not as secondary matters for the Christian faith but as matters that belong to the *esse* of both faith and church. In continuation of the conciliar process for justice, peace and the integrity of creation, churches, ecumenical groups and social movements are encouraged to form alliances with others in civil society in order to formulate alternative responses to the activities of transnational corporations, globalized communication media and financial institutions such as the International Monetary Fund and the World Bank.

By its use of the term "civil society", the Harare assembly pointed to another key concept that since 1989 acquired considerable weight not only in ecumenical discussion but in political science as well. This is a concept, rooted in Plato and Aristotle, that has been used in a variety of contexts throughout human history. It was used prior to 1989 by human-rights groups in Eastern Europe to describe the creation of free space where an oppressive state could not interfere in the activities of its citizens. In the WCC, civil society has been interpreted in accord with the ecumenical socio-ethical tradition used in formulating a vision of a society both justly peaceful and ecologically sustainable. Thus, the new international disorder does not require new analytical tools; rather, old traditions are to employ new concepts.

This is also clear from the Harare statements on human rights.[61] On the occasion of the 50th anniversary of the Universal Declaration of Human Rights, 10 December 1998, the assembly issued a statement of gratitude both for that declaration and for the United Nations as such. The statement described human-rights work within the Council and expressed appreciation for a growing awareness on the part of the churches of the importance of human rights. What is distinctive about the Harare statement, however, is the

---

[59] Diane Kessler ed., *Together on the Way: Official Report of the Eighth Assembly of the World Council of Churches,* WCC, 1999, p.183.
[60] *Ibid.*
[61] *Ibid.*, pp.191-206.

crucial place given to globalization as an element for understanding the conditions required for the realization of human rights. In the view of the assembly, globalization involves both the erosion of the power of the state to defend individual and group rights, and the weakening of the authority of the United Nations as a guarantor and promoter of collective approaches to human rights. This reality led the Harare assembly to reaffirm the position taken by the Nairobi assembly in 1975 that human rights are indivisible. The assembly also deplored the re-politicization of international human-rights discourse, a trend which, illustrative of the thesis of Samuel Huntington concerning "the clash of civilizations" especially between North and South but increasingly also between East and West, is a sign of a global conflict in which churches are well advised not to become involved.[62] Rather, the churches are to work for the safeguarding of freedom of belief for all, the most fundamental human right.

The Harare assembly of the WCC set old discussions of peace and justice into a new framework brought about by the new international context of growing disorder and a globalized, uni-polar world. This has, in turn, brought many old questions – thought by some to have been solved – back to the ecumenical agenda. Among presently burning issues is that of the future of the secular state when challenged by ethnic and religious expressions of nationalism: new states are being created along old ethnic lines, often reinforced by confessional or religious identities, and this has serious consequences for ecumenical and inter-religious relations. Much that the ecumenical movement endeavoured to keep together, paradoxically, was held in dynamic tension within the context of the bi-polar system of the cold war; the social equilibrium today threatens to fall apart in a uni-polar world.

BIBLIOGRAPHY

Abrecht, Paul and Koshy, Ninan eds, *Before It's Too Late. The Challenge of Nuclear Disarmament: The Complete Record of the Public Hearing on Nuclear Weapons and Disarmament Organized by the World Council of Churches, Amsterdam 1981*, WCC, 1983, 391p.

Anderson, Digby C. ed., *The Kindness That Kills: The Churches' Simplistic Response to Complex Social Issues*, London, SPCK, 1984, 170p.

Baum, Gregory and Wells, Harold, *The Reconciliation of Peoples, Challenge to the Churches*, WCC, 1997, 195p.

Bent, Ans J. van der, *Christian Response in a World of Crisis: A Brief History of the WCC's Commission of the Churches on International Affairs*, WCC, 1986, 80p.

Bent, Ans J. van der, *Commitment to God's World. A Concise Critical Survey of Ecumenical Social Thought*, WCC, 1995, 243p.

The Churches in International Affairs: Reports, WCC, 1970-.

Derr, Thomas Sieger, *Barriers to Ecumenism: The Holy See and the World Council of Churches on Social Questions*, Maryknoll NY, Orbis, 1983, 102p.

Derr, Thomas Sieger, *Ecology and Human Liberation: A Theological Critique of the Use and Abuse of Our Birthright*, WCC, 1973, 11p.

Duchrow, Ulrich, *Shalom: Biblical Perspectives on Creation, Justice and Peace*, WCC, 1989, 198p.

Ellingsen, Marc, *The Cutting Edge: How Churches Speak on Social Issues*, WCC, 1993, 370p.

Eskidjian, Salpy and Estabrooks, Sarah eds, *Overcoming Violence: WCC Statements and Actions 1994–2000*, WCC, 2000, 130p.

---

[62] Samuel P. Huntington, *The Clash of Civilizations and the Remaking of World Order*, New York, Simon & Schuster, 1996.

Gopin, Marc, *Between Eden and Armageddon, the Future of World Religions, Violence and Peacemaking*, Oxford, Oxford Univ. Press, 2000, 312p.

Gros, Jeffrey and Rempel, John D. eds, *The Fragmentation of the Church and Its Unity in Peacemaking*, Grand Rapids MI, Eerdmans, 2001, 230p.

Gutiérrez, Gustavo, *A Theology of Liberation*, Maryknoll NY, Orbis, 1981, 323p.

Huber, Wolfgang and Reuter, Hans-Richard, *Friedensethik*, Stuttgart, W. Kohlhammer, 1990, 365p.

Huntington, Samuel P., *The Clash of Civilizations and the Remaking of World Order*, New York, Simon & Schuster, 1996, 367p.

Jacques, Geneviève, *Beyond Impunity: An Ecumenical Approach to Truth, Justice and Reconciliation*, WCC, 2000, 71p.

Kässmann, Margot, *Overcoming Violence: The Challenge to the Churches in all Places*, WCC, 2000, 96p.

Koshy, Ninan, *Churches in the World of Nations: International Politics and the Mission and Ministry of the Church*, WCC, 1994, 120p.

Limouris, Gennadios, *Justice, Peace and the Integrity of Creation: Insights from Orthodoxy*, WCC, 1990, 126p.

Mudge, Lewis S. and Wieser, Thomas, *Democratic Contracts for Sustainable and Caring Societies. What Can Churches and Christian Communities Do?* WCC, 2000, 197p.

Munby, Denys, *World Development: The Challenge to the Churches. Official report and papers, conference on Society, Development and Peace, Beirut, 1968*, Washington, Corpus, 1969, 208p.

Now Is the Time. Final Document and Other Texts: World Convocation on Justice, Peace and the Integrity of Creation, Seoul 1990, WCC, 1990, 60p.

Preston, Ronald H., *Confusions in Christian Social Ethics: Problems for Geneva and Rome*, London, SCM Press, 1994, 202p.

Reuver, Marc, *Christians as Peace Makers: Peace Movements in Europe and the USA*, WCC, 1988, 84p.

Santa Ana, Julio de ed., *Towards a Church of the Poor: The Work of an Ecumenical Group on the Church and the Poor*, WCC, 1979, 210p.

Schmitthenner, Ulrich, *Contributions of Churches and Civil Society to Justice, Peace and the Integrity of Creation*, Frankfurt, Verlag für Interkulturelle Kommunikation, 1999, 332p.

Solms, Friedhelm, *Welchen Frieden wollen die Kirchen?: Beiträge zur ökumenischen Diskussion II*, Heidelberg, Forschungsstätte der Evangelischen Studiengemeinschaft, 1988, 174p.

Violence, Nonviolence and the Struggle for Social Justice: Exploring Strategies for Radical Social Change, WCC, 1971, 8p.

Williamson, Roger ed., *The End in Sight?: Images of the End and Threat to Human Survival*, Uppsala, Life and Peace Institute, 1993, 181p.

14
Racism and Ethnicity

Hugh McCullum

The ecumenical movement has generally accepted the notion that human beings are made in, by and for community, a human characteristic that finds expression in many forms and under many names. How then do race, ethnicity and nation – so often the basis for relationship and community – also become misused, distorted, manipulated and turned against each other? Indeed, in the last thirty or more years of the 20th century, the world was fractured by racial, ethnic and nationalist conflict. Are they the same thing in different forms? Are they overlapping forms of identity? Ethnicity and nation and (to a certain extent) race imply a degree of common culture. Some believe such commonalities to be natural – possessing shared language, origin, historical experience and religion. But they have all been the result of the interplay of historical and cultural factors. Such identities are therefore fluid, constantly being reconstructed. So they are never pure. More pertinent are the dividing lines between different groups, and the racist attitudes held by a group which sees itself as superior to others. Race is constructed on the basis of perceived external features; for example, skin colour.

This has monumental consequences. The justification of the European colonial conquest in the 18th and 19th centuries went hand in hand with racism. Claiming superiority, the colonizers took for themselves the right to oppress and exploit others. Alleged white superiority continues to be at the root of the most pertinent forms of racism today. But race, ethnicity and nation can be related in different contexts. Sometimes race coincides with ethnicity or nation, so that all members of the given ethnic group share the same racial features. In other instances a nation or state may be divided along racial lines with ethnicity as a sub-category. In the US, for example, with its pervasive white-black divisions, both racial categories subsume significant ethnic diversity.

As theologians, social scientists and historians began to reflect on, and address, the horrific increase in civil war and violence in the latter part of the 20th century based on ethnic, racial and national wars and unrest, they became especially concerned to address how *conflict* based on these identities – even when the groups have lived in peace alongside each other for a long time – can lead to such devastating destruction. Sometimes this has resulted from a threat, perceived or real: competition for a scarce resource; a sense that one group is prospering at the expense of another; perhaps from a new aware-

• This chapter has been drawn up based on material supplied by Thomas F. Best, Burgess Carr, Barney Pityana, Elisabeth Salter, Marilia Schüller, Bob Scott and Baldwin Sjollema.

ness that behind the issues of racial, ethnic or national identity may lie fundamental socio-economic injustices.

In other cases, it seems clear to those analyzing these various identities that the threat arises not so much from the interactions between the groups concerned as from external manipulation. Many current conflicts in the last four decades may be traced back to divisions which surfaced in the colonial past – often, in some extreme cases, created by the colonial powers. The outstanding example of this may be Rwanda, where European and African social scientists [and theologians] and colonial regimes defined Hutu and Tutsi as separate peoples, whereas previously there had been no such consciousness.

Problems arising from colonial history continued to impact the violent 20th century, especially after the second world war. The concept of the nation-state was often imposed in the colonial era on social and political situations which had not gone through the same historical and political processes as in Europe, thus forcing colonial territories to conform to the Western model of nation. This imposition of an irrelevant pattern of social organization often ignored ethnic and racial realities which had developed in the pre-colonial period. Before colonization these territories had their own indigenous systems, some of which were at least as highly developed and stable as those of the colonizers' own countries: for example, African and Asian kingdoms and the Aztec, Mayan and Incan empires of Latin America. The colonial enterprise was based on transferring indigenous wealth, both material and human, and therefore played off one ethnic community against another (the policy of divide-and-rule). This resulted in the creation of states that are quite artificial and do not follow pre-colonial – but still important – ethnic, racial, political and cultural contours. Unfortunately, there have been very few successful attempts to find alternatives to the colonial models of nation-building.

The churches could and should have been forces for human liberation throughout the colonial period, but instead they were too often a force of oppression. Churches and religious groups, and the ecumenical movement, needed to emphasize the liberating elements of their faith and ensure that its spiritual resources were brought to the search for just and liberated communities. Too often the church could not play that role because it had been too closely identified with one state or one ethnic group or one race striving for a dominant position in society. In other places, religion became the state religion, resulting in an intimate identification of the two to the disregard of the racial and ethnic realities, which were thus unable to play their proper role in society and be a prophetic and courageous sign of the transformation of racism and ethnic conflict. Thus, the churches' response to ethnic or racial violence ought not be to eliminate or suppress the causes of violence but to seek healing and redemption and to restore, or create, positive relationships among those concerned.

Peace-making in situations of racial, ethnic or national violence means re-establishing, if not establishing for the first time, relationships between groups who must coexist in shared space, even though terrible deeds may have been done by one or by all. In these circumstances *reconciliation* becomes a vital theme – one which, however, is so often abused that we must name and reject some of the main ways in which it has been cheapened. These include situations where the reconciliation process has been rushed, thereby ignoring justice; and others in which those in power use a simple, shallow or hasty understanding of reconciliation in order to avoid some of the hard issues that arise in the course or aftermath of the conflict.

THE STRUGGLE AGAINST APARTHEID

As Konrad Raiser, then the general secretary of the WCC, said in the 1994, few issues have more profoundly marked the life of the ecumenical movement and the World Council of Churches, and how people perceive them, than the struggle against racism and in particular the involvement in South Africa.

> It was as a consequence of this struggle and its programmatic expression in the Programme to Combat Racism that a decisive shift in ecumenical perspective began to manifest itself. Instead of continuing to interpret world reality from the perspective of those responsible for maintaining "order", the ecumenical movement declared its solidarity with the victims of the structures of injustice and with their struggle for liberation. The condemnation of racism as sin and the rejection of its theological justification as heresy were decisive in shaping ecumenical reflection about the unity of the church in its constitutive relationship to the quest for justice in human community.[1]

From the time of its formation in 1969 until its twenty-fifth anniversary in 1994, through intense struggle and controversy the Programme to Combat Racism helped to teach the ecumenical movement about new relationships and different perspectives between the worldwide Christian community and the people and churches of South Africa and, indeed, all of southern Africa. Later in this period of history, the WCC was forced to enter into the murky waters of ethnicity and national identity, noting repeatedly, as did the poet T.S. Eliot in 1937 (at the Oxford conference on church, community and state), that forms of worship and theology have been fractured by race, class and social group.

In his foreword to Pauline Webb's *A Long Struggle*, Raiser further said that the ecumenical movement and the WCC must keep this memory alive, "not to foster ecumenical triumphalism" but to retain the lessons learned. The victories for South Africa that culminated in 1994 must never be lost. Racism has in no way been eradicated and the ecumenical commitment to the promotion of justice and human rights wherever people are excluded because of race, gender, sexual orientation, class, ethnicity, nation or belief, and denied their dignity as persons created in the image of God, cannot waver.

South Africa is a relevant beginning to the story of the ecumenical movement's involvement in the issues of racism, ethnicity and other forms of extreme nationalism in the last decades of the 20th century, for the churches throughout the world were preoccupied with the removal of apartheid and the establishment of a democratic society in that country. The stories of that campaign are a powerful introduction to some of the contemporary debates about racism – especially in America and Europe – and ethnicity in the work of the WCC and its member churches.

In a sad and little-recognized irony, in the very month and year, April 1994, that the worldwide churches and society were jubilantly celebrating the first free, multi-racial and democratic elections in South Africa, a few thousand kilometres to the north one of the worst instances of post-second world war genocide was being perpetrated in Rwanda. And the world and the worldwide churches, including the WCC, ignored it, save for a handful of staff from the All Africa Conference of Churches who were acutely frustrated by the bureaucratic inaction of Geneva (the WCC) and New York (the UN security council and the office for peace-keeping.)

---

[1] "Foreword", in Pauline Webb ed., *A Long Struggle: The Involvement of the World Council of Churches in South Africa*, WCC, 1994, p.vii.

Many thought the WCC had learned to combat racism, and the PCR had played a huge role especially in liberating southern Africa, but ethnic violence was beyond churches' capacities in Rwanda, perhaps the most "Christian country" in Africa, and the ecumenical movement, like the world, turned its back on the horrific slaughter of 800,000 Tutsis and moderate Hutus in just ten weeks.[2] When it was over, convulsed by liberal guilt churches poured into Rwanda with aid and pastoral care, overwhelming the peoples' critical need for justice and reconciliation. Justice, it was feared by those who had stood on the sidelines in the years building up to the genocide, would cause more violence and less reconciliation so the best offer was a kind of cheap psychological pastoral care offered by young, inexperienced Europeans to a people traumatized beyond comprehension since every family had lost dozens of members in the most violent way. Churches, often themselves complicit in the genocide, had no skills in dealing with ethnic hatred promoted by extremists.

The struggle of black South Africans against the repressive apartheid regime was recognized, in most parts of the world, as the classic struggle against racism, but it was not by any means the first in which churches had been involved, as may be seen when slavery and the Armenian and Jewish Holocausts are recalled.

The cruel dynamics of institutionalized racism were widely known and understood outside the country even as they were being denied within South Africa. The end of constitutional apartheid, the release from prison of Nelson Mandela in 1990, and the eventual elections which saw him become president of the country in 1994, were cause for great celebration around the world. Racism had been defeated; black South Africans had won their liberation from oppression and regained their dignity.

Yet within a few years the (then) newly appointed chairman of the South African human-rights commission, Barney Pityana, who had been head of the black South African Students Organization under the apartheid regime, was lamenting the situation. Despite the constitutional advances, he maintained that black people, the majority of the electorate, continued to suffer exclusion in critical areas of national life, such as the media, universities, research institutes and business. Neither were they fully represented in shaping national policies and the economy.

By the end of 1997 President Mandela joined the fray. In his farewell address as president of the African National Congress (ANC), to the fiftieth national conference of the movement at Mafeking, he said that whites remained dominant in key spheres of national life, evidenced by media hostility towards the government's policies. Mandela charged that the media "uses the democratic order as an instrument to protect the legacy of racism". He went on to assert that "despite its professions of support for democracy, [the mass media] limits the possibility to expand the frontiers of democracy, which would derive from the empowerment of the citizen to participate meaningfully in the process of governance through timely access to information".

Also in 1997, Shaun Johnson, a journalist with the Independent Newspapers in South Africa, wrote a newspaper article headed "Race: a question the Rainbow Nation and the ANC can no longer duck":

> White South Africa needs to understand what its black compatriots mean when they bemoan the lack of fundamental transformation of the society. It is about deep-seated attitude change and the taking of personal responsibility for reconciliation and reconstruction.

---

[2] Hugh McCullum, *The Angels Have Left Us: The Rwanda Tragedy and the Churches*, WCC, 1995, repr. with afterword 2004.

The new democracy was wrestling with the tools, the approach and the language to use in creatively discussing the issues of race. An inextricable link was made between race relations, development and reconstruction. Johnson recognized that as long as whites continued to hold the keys to economic development, race relations would not improve and reconciliation would remain a distant dream.

The work of the Truth and Reconciliation Commission, under the leadership of Archbishop Desmond Tutu, went some way to tell the stories of pain and suffering from the past and unmask the methods of the apartheid regime, but it was able to do little to challenge the fundamental divisions which continued to exist in the society. This was the dilemma which faced Mandela's successor as president, Thabo Mbeki. It is a challenge that remains. And along with Rwanda, the Balkans, Sri Lanka and a host of other ethnic and class conflicts, it also serves as an indication that the story of the WCC's involvement in the struggle against racism and ethnicity is unfinished.

RACISM AND ETHNICITY WITHIN ECUMENISM 1921-69

Ecumenical theology denouncing racism was not invented by the World Council of Churches. Long before the founding assembly in 1948, the Student Christian Movement (SCM) in 1921 had made theological affirmations against racism, as had the International Missionary Council in Jerusalem 1928, declaring, "Any discrimination against human beings on the ground of race or colour, any selfish exploitation and any oppression of man by man is a denial of the teaching of Jesus."[3] These and many other statements were strong for their time, but there was little or no active follow-up during or after the Holocaust of the Hitler years in Germany.

Apartheid was enacted in South Africa two years after the WCC was formed. Some churches expressed concern. In 1952 W.A. Visser't Hooft, the first WCC general secretary, visited South Africa, and the WCC Evanston assembly in 1954 reaffirmed that "any form of segregation based on race, colour or ethnic origin is contrary to the gospel and incompatible with the Christian doctrine of man and the nature of the church of Christ".[4]

Six years later the shots rang out at Sharpeville, the ANC was banned and their leaders were exiled. The armed struggle began and internationally a new era dawned in the anti-apartheid movement. The English and Afrikaans branches of the Dutch Reformed Church came into conflict. Anglican Archbishop Joost de Blank of South Africa asked the WCC to expel the Nederduitse Gereformeerde Kerk or NGK (Dutch Reformed Church) from its membership.

The forerunners for a more radical, action-oriented opposition to white racism included the Cottesloe consultation in 1960, with representatives of eight WCC member churches in South Africa. Compared with the enormity of the Sharpeville outrage, the Cottesloe statement was timid. The organizers said the purpose of the consultation was "to seek under the guidance of the Holy Spirit to understand the complex problems of human relationships in this country, and to consult with one another on our common task and responsibility in the light of the word of God". The statement said that the pres-

---

[3] *The Christian Mission in the Light of Race Conflict: Report of the Jerusalem Meeting of the International Missionary Council, March 24-April 8, 1928,* vol. IV, London, Oxford Univ. Press, 1928, p.238.
[4] W.A. Visser 't Hooft ed., *The Evanston Report: The Second Assembly of the World Council of Churches,* London, SCM Press, 1955, p.158.

ent tension in South Africa was the result of a long historical development and all groups bore responsibility for it. At a time when national independence and decolonization were blossoming all over Africa, the consultation offered cautious support for African nationalism:

> In so far as nationalism grows out of a desire for self-realization Christians should understand and respect it. The danger of nationalism is, however, that it may seek to fulfil its aim at the expense of the interest of others and that it can make the nation an absolute value which takes the place of God. The role of the church must therefore be to help direct national movements towards just and worthy ends.[5]

Though Cottesloe achieved no common pronouncement regarding apartheid, it did declare that "no one who believes in Jesus Christ may be excluded from any church on the grounds of his colour or race". The NGK responded to Cottesloe by withdrawing from membership in the WCC.

DEFINITIONS OF RACISM

It was in this context that the WCC and others began to try and define racism, although from the beginning there were some who were, and still are, wary of precise definitions that may invite legalistic arguments and wrangling over semantics. They prefer the definition of racism to be the description of the actual experience of those who feel discriminated against. Situations vary so much that it is unwise to be dogmatic, and prudent to be sensitive to the accounts of victims. One definition, by British social scientist Charles Husband of the university of Bradford, is distilled from many other sources:

> Racism refers to a system of beliefs held by members of another group who are assigned a "race" category on the basis of some biological or other invariable, "natural seeming" characteristic which they are believed to possess; membership of this category then being sufficient to attribute other fixed characteristics to all assigned to it. Racism is the application of "race" categories in social contexts with an accompanying attribution of invariable characteristics to category members.[6]

The WCC's Notting Hill consultation on racism at London, England, in 1969 included a number of "principles useful in formulating contextually based definitions and theories" about racism.

1) Racism is first and foremost a *system* of domination and oppression.
2) Initially racism's basic motivations were economic, but at different stages of development racial domination has been maintained for political, social, cultural, religious, military and psychological reasons.
3) Manifestations of racism are socially determined and dependent on such factors as the racial character of the societal context; the nature of the competitive economic environment; the degree of the perceived threat posed by the oppressed racial group(s); the nature of the economic, political and cultural resources that the oppressed group commands; and the level of demand for these resources in the local, national and international political economy.

---

[5] "The Cottesloe Declaration", in F.C. Fry, W.A. Visser 't Hooft, R.S. Bilheimer, *Mission in South Africa, April-December 1960, Prepared by the WCC Delegation to the Consultation in December, 1960*, WCC, 1961, p.30.
[6] Charles Husband, Introduction, in *Race in Britain: Continuity and Change*, London, Hutchinson, 1982.

4) Racism is both overt and covert. It is enforced and maintained both consciously and unconsciously by the legal, cultural, religious, educational, economic, political and military institutions of society.
5) Undergirding systems of racial domination are myths of racial superiority and inferiority. The systems are built on notions of superior and inferior groups. Individual racist actions are expressions of a process of *group interaction.*
6) Racism confers certain privileges on the dominant group. It is the creation and defence of these *group* privileges that sustains and perpetuates racism.
7) Racism can be a matter of result rather than intent. Dominant group actions – intended or unintended – can produce patterns of racial domination.
8) Racism is one of the three major sub-systems of domination in the modern world. It interacts with classism and sexism to produce the broad pattern of oppression and exploitation that plagues the world.[7]

A far simpler description for racism and ethnicism is "discrimination plus power".

DEMANDS FOR ACTION

This tension between prophecy and reconciliation came to the fore at the world conference on Church and Society in 1966 – whose theme was "Christians in the Technical and Social Revolutions of Our Time". It challenged the churches to adopt a new and radical approach in the struggle to combat racism. The tension became the core issue in defining theological practices for the churches in the matter of race as they approached the fourth assembly in Uppsala in 1968.

In the period between the Church and Society conference and the Uppsala assembly, the world went through a global racial revolution. Unsurprisingly, the epicentres of the revolution were located in South Africa and the US.

In southern Africa independence for Botswana (1966), Lesotho (1966) and Swaziland (1968) precipitated the acceleration of South Africa's Bantustan policy with its violent displacement of the African population from urban townships and their resettlement in the so-called "homelands".

In the US, the assassination of Malcolm X, followed by that of Martin Luther King and Robert Kennedy, ignited a tidal wave of violence on university campuses and in inner cities across the country. Riots in Chicago had prevented King from coming to Geneva to deliver a sermon during the Church and Society conference in 1966. He had accepted to preach at the opening worship service at the Uppsala assembly in 1968. His tragic death created the conditions that compelled the WCC to deal with its own "crisis of imagination" with regard to race. Instead of just one high-profile event at the forthcoming assembly featuring an international figure of King's stature, a strategy needed to be developed to ensure that the issue of racism got the attention it deserved at Uppsala.

Six of the seven black executive staff of the WCC, supported by a few friends and with powerful encouragement from then general secretary Eugene Carson Blake, took this responsibility upon themselves. The group had less than two months to prepare. But in that brief period, a dozen experts from around the world were invited to produce a document on the global scope of racism and come to Uppsala to participate in the work of the

---

[7] "Working Descriptions of Racism", in Appendix II of Barbara Rogers, *Race: No Peace without Justice,* WCC, 1980, page 123.

programme units and sections, so as to ensure adequate discussion of the race issue in the work of the WCC after the assembly.

At the assembly itself, James Baldwin, son of a Pentecostal preacher and a widely celebrated black American novelist, and Lord Caradon (Sir Hugh Foot), the permanent representative of the United Kingdom to the UN and member of a famous Methodist family, spoke. Baldwin introduced himself as someone who had always been outside the church, even when he had tried to work in it. "I address you as one of God's creatures whom the Christian church has most betrayed," he began. Recapitulating the long tale of racial injustice, Baldwin charged that "long ago for a complex of reasons, but among them power, the Christian personality split itself into two – into dark and light – and is now bewildered and at war with itself... I wonder if there is left in the Christian civilizations the moral energy, the spiritual daring, to atone, to repent, to be born again?"

Lord Caradon, speaking as a diplomat and a politician, offered an assessment of the effect on racial relations of the end of colonialism, and of the prospects for reducing tensions and achieving racial understanding. He lamented the apathy of many Western nations, which he said "could turn to antipathy, instead of a greater readiness to help the new nations..." As though to put Baldwin's dualism into a global development perspective, Lord Caradon went on to speak passionately about the "widening gulf between the two worlds – that of the affluent, comfortable, complacent white people of the old nations, and the hungry, overcrowded, discontented coloured people of the new". He said that this worsening of relationships between the races was all the more dangerous "because it is now inextricably tied to the problems of poverty, population and youth. These last three problems, dangerous in themselves, become explosive when allied to the race issue." He said he believed the remedies to racial tension required international collaboration and a sober estimate of the limitations they faced. "Vain gestures and sweeping declarations will solve nothing." A campaign would have every "right to look for courageous leadership to the World Council of Churches".[8]

The impact of the fourth assembly on the struggle against racism cannot be overstated. In response to the call for action that went beyond words, the assembly decided that the WCC should "undertake a crash programme to guide the Council and the member churches in the urgent matter of racism".[9] The assembly left it to the central committee to determine the mandate, scope and focus of such a programme to combat white racism. For the first time in the history of the WCC, the fourth assembly used and defined the terms "racism" and "white racism":

> By *racism* we mean ethnocentric *pride* in one's own racial group and preference for the distinguishing characteristics of that group; belief that these characteristics are fundamentally biological in nature and are thus transmitted to succeeding generations; strong negative feelings towards other groups who do not share these characteristics coupled with the thrust to discriminate against and exclude the out-group from full participation in the life of the community.
>
> By *white racism* we mean the conscious or unconscious belief in the inherent superiority of persons of European ancestry (particularly those of northern European origin) which entitles all white peoples to a position of dominance and privilege, coupled with the belief in the innate inferiority of all darker peoples, especially those of African ancestry, which justifies their subordination and exploitation. By focusing on white racism, we are

---

[8] Norman Goodall ed., *The Uppsala Report 1968: Official Report of the Fourth Assembly of the World Council of Churches, Uppsala, July 4-20, 1968*, WCC, 1968, p.130.
[9] *Ibid.*, p.242.

not unaware of other forms of ethnocentrism which produce inter-ethnic and inter-tribal tensions and conflicts throughout the world today.

We believe, however, that white racism has special historical significance because its roots lie in powerful, highly developed countries, the stability of which is crucial to any hope for international peace and development. The racial crises in these countries are to be taken as seriously as the threat of nuclear war. The revolt against racism is one of the most inflammatory elements of the social revolution now sweeping the earth. It is fought at the level of mankind's deepest and most vulnerable emotions – the universal passion for human dignity. The threatened internal chaos in those countries in which racial conflict is most intense has immediate worldwide impact, for racism under attack tends to generate and spread counter-racism. We submit that this crisis will grow worse unless we understand the historical phenomenon of white racism, what has distinguished it from other forms of inter-group conflict, and what must be done to resolve the conflict on the basis of racial justice.[10]

The Uppsala assembly declared that racism is "a blatant denial of the Christian faith". It identified the linkages between racism and economic exploitation.

a) Racism is linked with economic and political exploitation. The churches must be actively concerned for the economic and political well-being of exploited groups so that their statements and actions may be relevant. In order that victims of racism may regain a sense of their own worth, and be enabled to determine their own future, the churches must make available economic and educational resources to under-privileged groups for their development and full participation in the social and economic life of their communities. They should also withdraw investments from institutions that perpetuate racism. They must also urge that similar assistance be given from both the public and private sectors. Such economic help is an essential compensatory measure to counteract and overcome the present systematic exclusion of victims of racism from the mainstream of economic life. The churches must also work for changes in those political processes which prevent the victims of racism from participating fully in the civic and governmental structures of their countries.

b)... The churches must eradicate all forms of racism from their own life. That many have not done so, particularly where institutional racism assumes subtle forms, is a scandal.[11]

NOTTING HILL 1969

The turning point in the WCC's opposition to racism came when the eloquent words of Uppsala were translated into challenging action.

The urgency with which Eugene Carson Blake convened a staff group on racism was a clear indication of the high priority he attached to this issue. His instructions were direct: the staff team was required to report in a matter of weeks on proposals to implement the Uppsala recommendations in accordance with the central committee guidelines formulated at the meeting immediately following the assembly. They were to focus attention on "the problems of white racism", in southern Africa, the US and Europe.

Work began immediately on planning a consultation to be held in Notting Hill, London, in 1969. Some eighty participants, with first-hand experience of dealing with racism issues, land issues and Indigenous culture, came from Australia, Canada, Korea, New Zealand, Peru, the United Kingdom, the US and, of course, from southern Africa (Angola, Mozambique, Southern Rhodesia and South Africa).

---

[10] *Ibid.*, pp.241-42.
[11] *Ibid.*, p.66.

Planning for Notting Hill involved the identification of high-profile individuals in churches, state, liberation movements and academia, and activists. George McGovern, a US senator from South Dakota and presidential candidate in the 1968 Democratic primaries, was selected to chair the consultation. McGovern had been a delegate from the United Methodist Church at Uppsala.[12] Blake himself served as secretary. The Archbishop of Canterbury, Michael Ramsey, and the president of FRELIMO (Front for the Liberation of Mozambique), Eduardo Mondlane, agreed to speak at a public meeting at Church House, Westminster, London.

Within days of accepting the invitation, Mondlane was assassinated in Dar es Salaam, Tanzania, by a parcel bomb. Oliver Tambo, chairman of the ANC, a devout Anglican, was invited to replace him. Shortly thereafter, the archbishop of Canterbury sent his chaplain to Geneva to inform the WCC of his withdrawal from the panel because he could not appear on the platform with a "terrorist". Bishop Trevor Huddleston spoke in his place but was pelted with eggs and screamed at abusively by right-wing British white supremacists.[13] However, Archbishop Ramsey did agree to chair a panel on the role of the churches and the WCC in the elimination of racism. In the preface to the report of the consultation, Blake drew attention to the fact that over the last forty years one ecumenical meeting after another had produced some "thirty statements, documents and resolutions castigating racial prejudice and discrimination".

Notting Hill was different. It was a defining moment described by some as a *kairos* time, that moment when every person is confronted with a "traumatic experience in the matter of race before she or he can look and see the world as it really is". Blake himself called it "an event... a happening", and Pauline Webb, who was at the time a vice-moderator of the central committee, chose the Hebrew word *dabar,* which signals both divine action and prophetic exhortation. "The word of God *happened* to us," she said.[14]

THE PROGRAMME TO COMBAT RACISM

The results of the Notting Hill consultation played a crucial role at the central committee meeting in Canterbury in 1969, which recommended that the WCC set up "an ecumenical programme for the elimination of racism". However, more important than any programme, Notting Hill had appealed to the churches for a profound and renewed commitment, specifically from the WCC, to offer a convincing moral lead in the face of this great and growing crisis of our times.

Racism is not confined to any one country or continent. It is a world problem. Neither is white racism its only form. Words like "Holocaust" in Europe, "genocide" in Rwanda, "ethnic cleansing" in the Balkans conjure up a host of crimes against humanity that cover the 20th century with shame.

The central committee paired the Uppsala call for a programme on racism with the Notting Hill assessment of the relationship between racism and power. Introducing the debate on the report of Notting Hill, Blake noted that, despite the statements of the churches since 1924, "the fact is that Christians have not deracialized their own struc-

---

[12] McGovern became the presidential nominee of the Democratic Party in 1972, unsuccessfully opposing the re-election of Richard Nixon.

[13] Piers McGrandle, *Trevor Huddleston: Turbulent Priest*, New York, Continuum, 2004.

[14] WCC, Central Committee, *Minutes of the Twenty-Third Meeting, Canterbury, 1969,* p.36.

tures and life... We must ask why we have failed... We must decide whether a new programme of study and action, with the emphasis on action, should not be undertaken."[15]
A prospectus was developed to ensure that such a commitment would be a concrete part
of the life of the WCC. It encompassed the scope of a new ecumenical programme for
the elimination of racism; an outline of a five-year programme; structure, staff and
finances.

The 1969 central committee expanded on that:

- Racism is not an unalterable feature of human life. Like slavery, it can and must be
  eliminated. In the light of the gospel and in accordance with its methods, Christians
  must be involved in this struggle and, wherever possible, in association with all people
  of goodwill.
- Racism today is not confined to certain countries or continents. It is a world problem.
  White racism is not its only form. It is recognized that, at this moment in some parts
  of the world like Africa and Asia, other forms of racism and ethnocentrism present the
  most crucial problems. There is a strong element of racism in current forms of antisemitism as well as in discrimination against the lower castes in India.
- It is the coincidence, however, of an accumulation of wealth and power in the hands of
  the white peoples, following upon their historical and economic progress during the
  past four hundred years which is the reason for the focus on the various forms of white
  racism in the different parts of the world. People of different colour suffer from this
  racism in all continents...
- In our ecumenical fellowship there are churches from every part of the world, some of
  whom have benefited and some of whom have suffered from racially exploitative economic and political systems. What is needed is an ecumenical act of solidarity which
  would help to stem the deterioration in race relations. To do this our action must cost
  something; it must be affirmative, visible and worthy of emulation...
- The churches must move beyond charity, grants and traditional programming to relevant and sacrificial actions that lead to relationships of dignity and justice among all
  men [and women] and become agents for the radical transformation of society. There
  can be no justice in our world without a transfer of economic resources to under-gird
  the redistribution of political power and to make cultural self-determination meaningful. In this transfer of resources a corporate act by the ecumenical fellowship of
  churches can provide a significant moral lead.[16]

The challenge to the WCC to launch the Programme to Combat Racism with special
emphasis on humanitarian aid to, among others, liberation movements in southern
Africa marked a defining moment in the history of the ecumenical movement. Without
doubt its prime mover was Eugene Carson Blake.

"If our churches were right in Uppsala to call racism a denial of the gospel, then we
should not be amazed to find that combating racism raises deep questions of faith." He
knew this to be true because the road he had travelled to become the general secretary
of the WCC had exposed him to the host of psychological and sociological difficulties encountered in combating racism. His convictions came from earlier experiences in which
he had met the problem of racism face to face: as a missionary in Lahore, Pakistan; as a
pastor in California, and when he had been arrested and taken into police custody for
participating in the work and witness of the National Council of Churches (USA) against
white racism at home. The Notting Hill consultation was one small step towards fulfill-

---

[15] *Ibid.*, p.143.
[16] Plan for the Ecumenical Programme to Combat Racism, in *Minutes of the Central Committee Meeting,
Canterbury, 1969*, pp. 271-73.

ing the mandate of the Uppsala assembly calling Christians "to seek to overcome racism wherever it appears".

There were those in certain churches who denied the existence of racism in Europe and alleged that Blake was transporting an "American virus" to the continent. In much of the earlier debate in the central committee this undertone was implied, in some cases explicitly so. But Blake was unrelenting in challenging the churches, in the words of Anglican Bishop Ernest Reed of Canada, "to put the World Council of Churches behind a definite programme for the eradication of racism".

Some felt that the ecumenical programme was too radical, others that it did not go far enough. One European member of the central committee spoke of the risk that "racism would be confused with other kinds of injustice, or rationalized as a conflict between rich and poor or between social classes. It [racism] is not only a matter of flesh and blood, it is a matter of demonic powers." A member from Switzerland, referring to his own country, said that many would deny racism existed. But "the question must then be asked whether racism was, in fact, demonstrated through foreign policy, investment practices and so on".[17]

> The draft document for the programme on racism was considered item by item. Several amendments and verbal changes were proposed and adopted. An anxious moment came when E.A. Payne, a president of the WCC, expressed his strong opposition to transfer US$200,000 of WCC reserve funds of the WCC to a special fund of the Programme to Combat Racism, describing the proposal as "financially questionable and morally wrong". This and several other motions were defeated, allowing the central committee to use some of the WCC reserves to start the Special Fund to Combat Racism.

Thus it was that on 22 August 1969 the proposal for the Programme to Combat Racism (PCR), as revised by the central committee, was adopted without opposition but with six abstentions.

There were two other actions at Canterbury that put the PCR in broader perspective. Firstly, the Church of Jesus Christ on Earth by the Prophet Simon Kimbangu, Congo-Kinshasa (now the Democratic Republic of the Congo) became the first African Independent Church admitted into membership in the WCC. The AICs (later known as African Instituted Churches) represent Africans' quest for that liberation for which Christ has set us free. It is more than coincidental that the WCC launched the PCR at the same meeting that one of Africa's Independent Churches, that had survived some of the worst forms of colonial and racist oppression, became a member of the WCC.

Secondly, the central committee adopted a statement on the Middle East in which the rights of the Palestinians were acknowledged, as was their need to be protected. The long-term implications of this for the political dialogue between the WCC and the Palestine Liberation Organization (PLO) cannot be over-stated.

The first phase of the PCR's work included support for decolonization and the struggles for liberation in southern Africa. A significant aspect of this was the campaign against apartheid in South Africa. Through these efforts the WCC spearheaded the worldwide campaign for sanctions and boycotts of South African products, trade and investment, and gave humanitarian grants to the liberation movements. This commitment continued to grow and the strategies became more sophisticated as the apartheid regime

---

[17] From the statement made by Jacques Rossel, *Minutes of the Central Committee Meeting, Canterbury, 1969*, p.37. Cf. R. Douglas Brackenridge, *Eugene Carson Blake: Prophet with Portfolio*, New York, Seabury, 1978, pp.147ff.

continued. One measure of the success of the programme would come in June 2004, when PCR's first director, Baldwin Sjollema, would receive the Oliver Tambo Order, the highest civil honour of post-apartheid South Africa.

The main priority for the PCR was solidarity with the liberation movements in southern Africa, analysis of the apartheid situation in South Africa and how international investment in the country acted to support apartheid. The PCR commission meeting in New York in 1972 proposed that the WCC central committee call for the withdrawal of investments from South Africa, as part of the economic isolation of the country. The subsequent central committee debate was heated, but it was finally agreed that the WCC should withdraw its funds from corporations directly involved in investment or trade with South Africa and that member churches should be called on to begin stockholder actions and disinvestment themselves.[18] In 1973 the PCR published a list of 650 corporations involved in South Africa. It gradually expanded its programmatic work to include economic, legal, educational and other aspects of the unmasking of racism. Church and community groups throughout the world could thus seek support for their own projects and programmes under these headings.

The PCR was called on to produce documentation and undertake research on the situation of minority groups throughout the world and, to a lesser extent, the plight of Indigenous Peoples, especially the Aboriginal peoples in Australia, the Maori of New Zealand, the First Nations of Canada and the US, and the Indigenous of Latin America. On behalf of the WCC, the PCR became associated with a number of significant international conferences on Indigenous issues. The genocidal effect of colonization on Indigenous nations throughout South America and the Caribbean and the failure of governments and churches to acknowledge this helped fuel the worldwide debates on racism.

In 1975 the Commission on Faith and Order and the PCR jointly sponsored a consultation at Louvain, Belgium, on the theme "Racism in Theology and Theology in Racism", which attempted to respond to a 1974 central committee request for further theological reflection on problems connected with the struggle against racism. It was the first of several consultations on the relationship between theology and spirituality and racism. Faith and Order called for a theological clarification of all the issues which had been highlighted in the WCC process, rather than merely trying to provide justification for what had been done. Faith and Order's studies included recognition of structural violence in church and state and reflection on Christ's bias for the oppressed. The report from the Louvain consultation stressed "the necessity of collective repentance in corporate action and reflection".

The Commission on World Mission and Evangelism also played a role. It allocated some of its funds to the basic PCR budget, made a contribution to the special fund and began to review missionary literature and the training of missionaries, looking for indications of material and attitudes that would reinforce racism. The commission also asked mission boards to disinvest from South Africa.

Seven years after Uppsala, the Nairobi assembly of 1975 unconditionally condemned racism as a sin, affirmed that the church is too often infected with racism, and that racism is structurally enforced by international trade patterns and military interests. Fur-

---

[18] WCC, Central Committee, *Minutes of the Twenty-Sixth Meeting, Geneva, 1973*, p.55.

thermore, the Council deepened its understanding of institutionalized racism with the following analysis:

> Institutionalized racism, in its many structural forms, resists most challenges with careful concessions calculated to preserve its power... Racist structures reinforce each other internationally. Self-serving policies of transnational corporations operate across boundaries with impunity; weapons or mercenaries are supplied internationally to the local elite; the worldwide communications networks are manipulated to reinforce racist attitudes and actions. It is precisely because of this worldwide web of racist penetration that the churches must seek out policies and programmes at the ecumenical and international levels. Such programmes can expose the international systems which support racism and provide an effective counter-response to them.[19]

THE SPECIAL FUND TO COMBAT RACISM

Along with establishing PCR itself, the 1969 central committee in Canterbury set up a special fund to combat racism. The meeting had agreed that in the struggle against racism "there can be no justice in our world without a transfer of economic resources to undergird the redistribution of political power and to make cultural self-determination meaningful". The Special Fund became the touchstone for most of the work of the PCR for the years ahead.

The first grants from the Special Fund were approved by the WCC executive committee in 1970. Within four years there was a pattern of distribution for the annual grants. Between 1970 and 1975, during which more than US$1 million was distributed, 65 percent went to liberation movements in southern Africa – Angola, Mozambique, Namibia, South Africa and Zimbabwe; black, aboriginal and Chicano groups in Canada and the US received 12 percent; and the rest was divided between Latin America, the Caribbean, Australia, New Zealand and Europe. The executive committee had agreed that southern Africa should be given priority and that wherever possible grants should be substantial and not merely token. Throughout the history of the special fund, until the end of constitutional apartheid in South Africa in 1994, this division of funds remained almost the same, half of each year's funds being shared among the liberation movements, with the African National Congress and the Pan-Africanist Congress receiving the most.

The grants to the liberation movements were the cause of noisy and often acrimonious debates and protests among some member churches. While the level of funding did not decline – in fact, it rose steadily – an increasing amount of time and energy had to be spent by WCC staff in defence of the grants, especially on the principle of the ecumenical movement giving funding to those engaged in armed struggle. The increasing controversy caused the central committee meeting in Utrecht in 1972 to confirm its commitment to the PCR unanimously, and to extend the special fund to US$ 1 million annually, calling on member churches for increased support. The committee members said "the Fund made the WCC 'move beyond charity' and involve itself, even if only symbolically, in the redistribution of power". However, the 1974 central committee in West Berlin revised that figure to "a minimum of $300,000 which should be raised and distributed each year".

---

[19] David M. Paton ed., *Breaking Barriers: Nairobi 1975: The Official Report of the Fifth Assembly of the World Council of Churches, Nairobi, 23 November-10 December 1975*, London, SPCK, 1976, p.112.

In the early 1970s over half the contributions from member churches to the special fund came from Germany, the Netherlands and Sweden, another pattern that was to continue for many years.

The WCC itself became a focus of many of the adverse reactions to the anti-apartheid campaign. The moderator of the central committee from 1975 to 1983, Archbishop Edward Scott of the Anglican Church of Canada,[20] was excoriated several times on national television in his own country, the US and international and other media, and accused of approving money to provide missile systems to Zimbabwe's Popular Front used to shoot down civilian aircraft in which some passengers were missionaries – a charge easily disproved, but nonetheless damaging in the hands of the propagandists of Ian Smith's Rhodesian media assisted by the highly sophisticated and well-funded propaganda of South Africa's ministry of information. The WCC was accused of supporting terrorism and communism against which both Rhodesia and South Africa were defending "civilization and Christianity". Publications such as *Readers Digest* were virulent in their attacks on Scott and the WCC in this period.

The WCC and the member churches were, thus, caught up in a strong commitment to the struggle against apartheid, including having to answer accusations of providing funding for armed guerrillas in southern Africa. The WCC stand against apartheid and the work of the PCR rapidly became the most recognized part of the Council's outreach. It was also a time when, because of their mutual focus on apartheid in South Africa, churches in some countries for the first time began to work closely with community groups and protest movements.

The decade ended with the then general secretary, Philip Potter, proposing to the 1979 central committee meeting in Kingston, Jamaica, that a process of consultation be set up "on how the churches might be involved in combating racism in the 1980s". The meeting urged the PCR to continue its concentration on opposing investments, trade and bank loans to South Africa; authorized the PCR to make the issue of land rights and racially oppressed Indigenous Peoples a priority; commended the PCR to study children's and school textbooks as well as Christian educational material for their racist content; and finally requested the PCR to give major attention to racism in Asia.

LEARNING FROM THE RACIALLY OPPRESSED: 1980–2000

Potter's challenge was taken up in a series of regional or national consultations which culminated in a world consultation on racism in Noordwijkerhout, the Netherlands, in 1980 on the theme "The Churches Responding to Racism in the 1980s", to which the regional consultations sent written reports. The 115 participants divided into workshops on land rights and genocidal practices, racism in church structures, the economic basis of racism, national security doctrines, migration, and racism and theology, and case studies were presented on institutional racism (using Namibia and South Africa). The final statement referred to the contribution of the PCR and the special fund in the previous ten years but contrasted this prophetic role with the "organized racism in some church structures".[21] One of the catch-phrases that emerged from the consultation was

---

[20] Hugh McCullum, *Radical Compassion: The Life and Times of Archbishop Ted Scott* (foreword by Desmond Tutu), Geneva, WCC / Toronto, Anglican Book Centre, 2004.

[21] *Churches Responding to Racism in the 1980s: The Report of the World Consultation on Racism Called by the World Council of Churches, held in Noordwijkerhout, Netherlands, 16-21 June 1980* (spec. ed. taken from *PCR Information* nos 6,8,9), WCC, 1983, p.79.

that churches should review the racism "in their own backyard", a challenge that was taken up only by a few churches. Not surprisingly, the consultation called for a strengthening of the PCR's programme work. Its report to the August 1980 central committee emphasized:

- the all-pervasive and diverse nature of racism;
- the infection of the churches themselves with racism; and
- the interlocking of racism and political and economic domination.

The PCR's mandate was widened to deal with issues of casteism and minority rights, including Indigenous Peoples, and later to include an emphasis on women as principal victims of racism.

Throughout this period also, the WCC continued to lead in international pressure on the South African government to abolish apartheid and cease its destabilizing activities in southern Africa. In 1986 Archbishop Scott was appointed a member of the seven-person Commonwealth Eminent Persons Group (EPG), along with Dame Nita Barrow of Barbados, a president of the WCC, to try to bring an end to apartheid. They were among the first to meet Nelson Mandela while he was still in prison. Within South Africa, anti-apartheid forces found a staunch ally in Denis Hurley, the progressive and ecumenically minded Catholic archbishop of Durban.

As a mark of the changes then under way in the country, the general secretary of the WCC, Emilio Castro, made a historic visit to South Africa in 1991 which culminated in a consultation in Cape Town. In the Cape Town statement the churches committed themselves to

> expose and eradicate all forms of apartheid which persist in the economic, social, cultural and political structures of South African society... also to uncover and fight against all forms of exploitation which threaten to carry apartheid into a new society in disguised forms. Racism, sexism, economic exploitation and cultural prejudices often act in cohesion to undermine the sense of humanness *(ubunti/botho)* which God is offering us.[22]

That statement set an agenda for the church in a democratic South Africa and affirmed the principles that were consistently at the heart of the ecumenical movement's engagement in the struggle against apartheid.

The Ecumenical Monitoring Programme in South Africa (Empsa) was inaugurated in 1992. Its objective was to continue to support the church and peoples of South Africa in establishing democratic institutions in an environment of peace and fairness. By sending teams of ecumenical monitors to South Africa during the transition period when violence was rife and the negotiations for a democratic settlement were poised on a knife-edge, the ecumenical community continued its historic programme for democratic transformation of the country.

After the release of Nelson Mandela from prison in 1990 and the election of the ANC as the government of South Africa in 1994 with Mandela as president, the general secretary of the South African Council of Churches, Frank Chikane, told the central committee,

> By its actions the WCC was not merely a pioneer in the struggle against racism – it provided spiritual, moral and political leadership; it acted as a catalyst for international action

---

[22] The Capetown Consultation Statement, published in "From Cottesloe to Capetown", *PCR Information*, 30, 1991, p.98.

against the South African regime at a time when no one was prepared to touch such a controversial issue.[23]

As the political climate in Europe changed, leading up to the collapse of the Berlin wall in 1989, it became clear that the agenda of the churches had to change to reflect these developments. The WCC's seventh assembly in Canberra, Australia (1991), affirmed the work of the ecumenical movement on racism and urged that it continue to be a priority. The assembly also recommended that the PCR take responsibility for issues of ethnicity as well as racism. It highlighted particular aspects of racism of profound concern to the churches: the suffering of the black diaspora, increased racial tensions occurring as a result of mass migration, and the disturbing currents of racism and ethnicity in regional conflicts. The programmes of the PCR following Canberra took account of these new thrusts: ethnicity, racism in the US, and racism in Europe.

An important contribution to the ecumenical debates on racism was made at the 1990 world convocation on "Justice, Peace and the Integrity of Creation" in Seoul, Korea. It was significant because it articulated the sentiments of grassroots Christians from around the world. Although racism had been an issue in the planning stages, it was not chosen as one of the themes around which Seoul participants would enter into a covenant of solidarity and mutual commitment. However, during the convocation itself, some participants successfully argued that racism should be added to the covenantal liturgy. As a result, the participants formed a covenant with one another in which they pledged to eradicate racism and discrimination on national and international levels for all people. They called for the "dismantling of the economic, political and social patterns of behaviour that perpetuate, and allow individuals to consciously and unconsciously perpetuate, the sin of racism".[24]

The central committee meeting in 1992 held a deliberative session on "racism in the church". One of the keynote speakers, Methodist Bishop Ayres Mattos from Brazil, posed the question,

> How can we show the unity of the church as *koinonia* when we know that our churches are divided by racism and ethnic conflict? What does the confession of the apostolic faith mean if it does not help to overcome injustice in our day-to-day relations?

Indigenous Peoples

The 1980 central committee recognized that the issue of land rights was at the heart of the struggle for survival of Indigenous Peoples. In 1981, the WCC sent a delegation to Australia to express solidarity with the Aborigines and to consult with the Australian churches about their responses to racism. The delegation travelled through each state of the country and its report covered housing, land rights, legal rights, employment, education, spirituality and culture. Recommendations were sent to the state and federal governments as well as to the Australian churches and the WCC. When published in Australia the report caused considerable controversy, not least among political leaders.[25] Partly in response to that report, the 1982 central committee approved a statement on land rights which included a recognition of "racist beliefs which identify Indigenous People as being sub-human, and which refuse to acknowledge the very existence of their

---

[23] WCC Central Committee, *Minutes of the Forty-Sixth Meeting, Geneva, 1995*, p.70.
[24] Preman D. Niles ed., *Between the Flood and the Rainbow: Covenanting for JPIC*, WCC, 1989, p.189.
[25] Elisabeth Adler et al., *Justice for Aboriginal Australians, Report of the WCC Team Visit to the Aborigines, June 15 to July 3, 1981*, Sydney, Australian Council of Churches, 1981.

spiritual, cultural, social, political and legal systems". The central committee recommended to member churches to "become politically involved on the side of Indigenous Peoples and join the struggle against those powers and principalities which seek to deny the land rights and human rights of Indigenous Peoples".

In 1989 the PCR sponsored a major global consultation on "Land Is Our Life" in Darwin, Australia. Its declaration, "Indigenous Nations in Global Crisis", called on the international community to "consider the connection between racism and the consequent historical denial of Indigenous rights, including land rights and the inherent right to self-determination". The accompanying petition invited the WCC to recognize that "Indigenous lands have been taken by the churches without the consent of the Indigenous People of that land".[26]

A significant aspect of the WCC seventh assembly in Canberra, Australia, was the participation of representatives of the Aborigines of Australia. Their representatives had been involved in the planning for the assembly and the Aboriginal tribe whose traditional lands covered Canberra were the first to welcome delegates to the assembly. The assembly had been preceded by a WCC delegation to a number of Aboriginal communities – a follow-up to the WCC delegation in 1981 which had called for drastic changes in government policies on Aboriginal affairs. The 1991 delegation caused a similar national stir, drawing a sharp response from then Prime Minister Bob Hawke when he addressed the seventh assembly. The plenary presentation by Aboriginal participants also had a strong impact, effectively placing Indigenous rights in the forefront of the assembly. A statement from the assembly entitled "Move beyond Words" called the member churches to "conversion, active and ongoing repentance and reparation for past sins as a prelude to reconciliation. Only by so doing can we hope to gain or retain and be worthy of the trust and respect of Indigenous Peoples."[27]

In 1995 a full-time Indigenous consultant joined the WCC staff, a position which a few years later became part of the core staff. The Indigenous Peoples programme facilitated the participation of Indigenous representatives in UN forums, especially the annual sessions of the working group on Indigenous Peoples, the protracted negotiations on a UN draft declaration on the rights of Indigenous Peoples, and the establishment of a permanent forum for Indigenous Peoples within the United Nations itself.

The programme also supported capacity-building within Indigenous nations and communities in Latin America, Asia, Europe and the Pacific, and brought African Indigenous communities together for the first time. Its particular emphasis was on Indigenous spirituality and the land. This took practical form, for example, in an international consultation of representatives of fifty Indigenous nations and communities, "Indigenous Land Claims and Mining Transnationals", held in London in 1995.

The dalits of India

A new aspect of the PCR's work after the Canberra assembly was on casteism. The assembly statement had "affirmed the growing consciousness of Indigenous Peoples' struggle for freedom, including those of the dalits of India". This had come about as a result of the PCR Commission meeting in Madras, India, in 1989 which had studied the situation of the dalits. Formerly known as the untouchables, they are now recognized as

---

[26] "Land is Our Life", in *PCR Information*, 25, 1989.
[27] Michael Kinnamon ed., *Signs of the Spirit – Official Report: Seventh Assembly, Canberra, Australia, 7-20 February 1991*, WCC, 1991, p.217.

being among the Indigenous Peoples of India. The Commission resolved to give greater visibility to the phenomenon of caste-based discrimination. The PCR strengthened its ties with the dalit communities and, in 1992, supported the establishment of the Dalit Solidarity Programme (which later became the Dalit Solidarity Peoples). The DSP brought together, for the first time in the history of India, dalits of Muslim, Hindu, Sikh, Buddhist and Christian faith communities. By 2000 the movement had spread to over twenty states, and the global community had begun to understand that discrimination against dalits in India was as serious a violation of human rights as was apartheid in South Africa.

The Ogoni people of Nigeria

In response to a request from the Movement for the Survival of the Ogoni People (Mosop) in Nigeria, a joint WCC-All Africa Conference of Churches team was sent in 1996 and its report was distributed to all member churches.[28] Thereafter the PCR facilitated the participation of Ogoni representatives in international forums while at the same time conducting discussions with the churches in Nigeria about the Indigenous ethnic groups in the country, particularly in the delta area. This process culminated in a memorandum and recommendations to Nigeria at the central committee meeting at Geneva in 1997 which, after hearing reports on a dialogue between the WCC and Shell International, called on the major oil company to have open and direct discussions with the churches in Nigeria, urged them to negotiate in good faith with the freely chosen representatives of the Ogoni people, and encouraged the churches in Nigeria in their witness for human rights, justice and peace in Nigeria through interfaith dialogue with followers of Islam.

Women under Racism

In addition to advocacy for the rights of Indigenous Peoples, the PCR also recognized the interconnections of race, gender and class, with a focus on women. The Women Under Racism (WUR) Programme of the PCR encouraged and facilitated the participation of black, Indigenous, dalit and ethnic minority women in ecumenical discussions, providing a collective voice on justice issues around the exclusion or marginalization of women. A WUR global gathering was held in Trinidad and Tobago in October 1992, attended by eighty women of colour from all regions who established a network called Sisters (Sisters In the Struggle To Eliminate Racism and Sexism). It became a means of international cooperation between women of colour, holding regional meetings in Asia, Europe and Latin America as in the case, for example, of a September 2000 workshop in Taiwan on women under racism in Asia. A direct outcome of that workshop was the campaign "Asia-Pacific Women Overcoming Racism and Intolerance", launched in 2001 and jointly sponsored by the National Council of Churches in the Philippines, the Christian Conference of Asia and the WCC.

Women from the Sisters network were also enabled to attend the UN World Conference on Population and Development in Cairo in 1994 and the UN World Conference on Women held in Beijing, China, in 1995.

---

[28] Deborah Robinson, *Ogoni: The Struggle Continues*, WCC, 1996.

Racism in the US

In 1989 the National Council of the Churches of Christ in the USA (NCCCUSA) sent a letter to the WCC noting an increase in attacks against racial and ethnic groups across the US and indicating that police brutality had reached alarming proportions. In addition, minority communities were being devastated by drugs, crises in both the education and health fields, unemployment and growing poverty. After Canberra, American members of the central committee and other governing bodies approached the PCR for help in exposing the international community to the deep levels of anger, frustration and powerlessness experienced by African Americans, Native Americans, Asian Americans and Latinos. The eruption of racial violence in Los Angeles in April 1992 sent shock waves across the country. Within weeks the WCC and the NCCCUSA had assembled an ecumenical team, led by WCC general secretary Emilio Castro, to visit Los Angeles to demonstrate ecumenical concern for the underlying issues of economic and racial injustice in the city.

Various communions within the United States came to recognize that race was a leading "contemporary church-dividing issue" hindering their progress towards visible unity in Christ. An exploration of this topic was undertaken in the 1980s by the Consultation on Church Union, a broad-based unity movement that included three historically African American churches as well as a number of other denominations. Similarly, at a national convention in 1994 the Pentecostal movement in the United States vowed to overcome racial distinctions in a formal action of repentance and rededication that came to be known as "the Memphis Miracle".[29]

In 1993 the WCC and the NCCC co-sponsored a campaign to investigate violations of human rights in the US, raise the level of awareness of racism as a violation of human rights, and:
- to provide the opportunity for local and regional organizations of racially oppressed to form partnerships; and
- to challenge local congregations to confront those human-rights issues and to inform the international ecumenical community and the UN.

A series of hearings were held in seven cities in October 1994. More than 175 people testified before a WCC eminent persons team led by a WCC president, Aaron Tolen from Cameroon.

Racism in Europe

The case of the small enclave of Nagorno-Karabagh, claimed by Armenia as part of its historical territory, yet geographically within Azerbaijan and made part of Azeri territory under Soviet rule, serves as an example of racism in Europe. The Armenian (Orthodox) Apostolic Church, to which the majority of Armenians belong, is one of the most ancient churches in Christendom. The Azeris are almost all moderate Sunni Muslims under a sheikh who is spiritual head of all Muslims in the Caucasus region. At the break-up of the Soviet Union, the two countries became engaged in bitter conflict over Nagorno-

---

[29] *The COCU Consensus: In Quest of a Church of Christ Uniting*, Princeton, Consultation on Church Union, 1985, pp.8-10; and the chapter on North America in this volume. See also Bishop B.E. Underwood, "The Memphis Miracle", http://www.pctii.org/arc/underwoo.html. In 1979, the US Catholic bishops had issued a powerful pastoral letter on racism in society and the church, *Brothers and Sisters to Us: www.osjspm.org/cst/racism.htm.*

Karabagh, and in the early 1990s hundreds of thousands of refugees fled from one territory to the other, to escape the fierce fighting and destruction of their homes and livelihood.

The leaders of the Armenian church – one of the WCC's founding members – and of the Azeri Muslims were respected and listened to in their own countries. What were those voices saying, in the name of their respective faiths, to help bring peace and reconciliation to their countries, torn apart by new enmities? Were their leaders to take the easy path, conscious only of their ethnic and national identities? Or could they speak out prophetically together as religious leaders, finding ways of engaging in dialogue, overcoming violence and asserting their common humanity? After delicate negotiations, the WCC and the Conference of European Churches were successful in arranging a meeting in February 1993 between the two major spiritual leaders and their advisers. The statement they issued, and their personal commitment to calling for an end to the armed conflict, a negotiated settlement, the freeing of all political prisoners and the setting up of a fund to help victims on both sides of the conflict, was a modest but important step forward along the road to peace. It also showed that, even when religious identity and ethnic or national origin are inextricably linked, this need not be a barrier to solutions that pay attention to the needs of all. The armed conflict between the two countries led eventually to an uneasy but sustained peace, in which the efforts of the religious leaders to go beyond their difference and to speak out together played a modest role.

Not all conflicts rooted in ethnic or national loyalties were dealt with in this high-profile way. The protection of minorities within states often calls for urgent action, and for speaking out on behalf of the suffering, as well as for humanitarian aid and support. It calls, too, for patient confidence-building, education, and the establishment of trust and understanding by promoting dialogue between groups and individuals with deep antagonisms born of oppression and suffering. An ecumenical conference on the rights of minorities, held in Budapest, Hungary, in 1993, pointed out that

> one of the major challenges in Europe today is the need to adjust to the reality of living in multi-ethnic countries... While recognizing that each minority situation is different, it is necessary to examine the common underlying factors, in order to find strategies to maintain stability in Europe, and to protect the rights of national, ethnic, linguistic and religious minorities.

After extensive discussions throughout Europe, in cooperation with the Conference of European Churches, a churches' declaration on racism in Europe and a plan of action were presented to the central committee in 1992 and commended to the member churches in Europe for their study and action.

The central committee affirmed the need for policies of affirmative action (in Europe) and also noted that "promoting racism should be considered a heresy". In 1994, after discussion between the PCR and the Churches Commission on Racial Justice (UK), the archbishop of Canterbury invited European church leaders to issue a joint statement. Over sixty Protestant and Catholic leaders responded. They spoke of their alarm at the rising tide of racism, xenophobia and antisemitism in Europe and called on all Christians, and peoples of other faiths, to eradicate racism "from ourselves, churches, countries and continent".

The PCR launched a research project on the churches in Europe and their initiatives to combat racism, xenophobia and racial violence. It produced reviews of initiatives taken by churches in Germany and Austria, published in December 2000, and in France and Great Britain, published in August 2001.

Racism, genocide and ethnicity

According to statistics compiled by US political scientist R.J. Rummel, more than 170 million people were murdered by their own governments in the 20th century. These far outnumber the estimated 15-50 million persons who were killed during the same period by wars between states. Many of these deaths have been the result of ethnic conflicts which take on a wider meaning than race.[30] In modern times, following the genocide of the Armenians and the Jewish Holocaust of the Nazi era, the world has been horrified and largely ineffectual in the face of ethnic cleansing in the former Yugoslavia, genocide in Rwanda and Cambodia, ethnic strife in Sri Lanka, religious warfare in Northern Ireland, the violent break-up of parts of the former Soviet Union, north-south racial and religious war in Sudan, and the slaughter of Indigenous Peoples of Central and South America.

Some of the reasons for these factors, which turned the 20th century into one of the most violent and bloody in the history of the world, are the following:
- the break-up of multinational states such as the Soviet Union and Yugoslavia after 1989;
- dissatisfaction with the failure of decolonization and development to bring the expected economic prosperity;
- population pressures leading to increased competition over land and for diminishing resources;
- weakening of the nation-state due to globalization of the economies, massive increases in communications technology and the growth of regional and international organizations;
- waning influence of traditional religions, cultures and ideologies, coupled with new aggressive forms of fundamentalism; and
- improved legal standards for the protection of minorities, providing legitimacy for the disfavoured and those demanding self-determination.

The violence that often characterizes ethnic or national conflicts has always been a particular concern of the WCC which, as far back as the first assembly in 1948, stated,

> War as a method of settling disputes is incompatible with the teaching and example of our Lord Jesus Christ. The part which war plays in our present international life is a sin against God and a degradation of man.

The call from the Canberra assembly for issues of ethnicity to be taken seriously had its first response in a Churches Commission on International Affairs (CCIA) and PCR joint consultation in Lusaka, Zambia, in 1994 to analyze and review ethnic conflicts on the African continent, just after the 100-day Rwanda genocide. This was followed by a joint CCIA, PCR, Lutheran World Federation and World Alliance of Reformed Churches consultation on ethnic conflicts throughout the world, held in Sri Lanka in 1994. Under the title "Ethnicity and Nationalism: A Challenge to the Churches", it heard reports of case studies in Fiji, Hungary, Malaysia, Nagorno-Karabagh, Nigeria, Rwanda, Sri Lanka, Sudan, Taiwan and the former Yugoslavia. Some cases were described as "inter-religious", some as "intra-religious". All conflicts were recognized as complex and fraught with unresolved historical issues, overt action from outside forces and tensions based on negative images the parties in conflict had of each other. Once again, as in the case of racism, the church was challenged "to reassess critically its own history and evaluate its

---

[30] Theo Tschuy, *Ethnic Conflict and Religion: Challenge to the Churches*, WCC, 1997.

own involvement in ethnic conflicts and nationalistic desires for power". It was also challenged "to examine and explore its relations with peoples of other faiths, moving beyond passive tolerance to constant, critical and creative dialogue with them".

The moderator of the central committee, Aram I, Catholicos of Cilicia, in his report to the 1996 meeting highlighted the major issues of ethnicity, stating that the whole question of security is at the heart of ethnic conflicts and tensions. He spoke of the desire for security as the "natural drive" of all ethnic groups and cited two specific manifestations of that: affirmation of identity and the right to self-determination. He called on the churches to recognize and repent of their own complicity in many cases of ethnic conflict and tension, and asked them to transcend their ethnic boundaries and unite around the vision of a holistic and just society.

These reflections on ethnicity repeatedly highlighted the potential role of the churches. Christians, on either side of an ethnic divide, were challenged to identify their primary loyalty, and their priorities in situations of oppression and conflict. An international ecumenical consultation, meeting in Morges, Switzerland, in 1998, pointed out,

> The right to self-determination should be understood as ensuring every individual, regardless of ethnicity, religion, gender or political status, [the right] to participate fully in every aspect of the social, economic, cultural and political processes that affect their lives.[31]

The common underlying factors are many and complex, and unless they are addressed, not only by the churches but also by political authorities, no amount of military might or peace-keeping initiatives will have long-lasting effect. In Europe, new nation-states that inherited the national minorities of the past – for example, Hungarians and Germans in Romania, and Slovak and German-speakers in Hungary – face the challenge of being living examples of how society should treat its minorities. As a report of the Leuenberg Church Fellowship pointed out:

> The ethnic minorities in the new nation-states are an enrichment, on the one hand, but on the other they also constitute a potential for conflict. In this sense, it is a challenge for the churches not to become involved in the activities of such political and nationalist groups, as either make hegemonic claims that transcend the state or try to assimilate or discriminate against the minorities. On the contrary, it is the task of the churches to point emphatically to the universality of human rights, the fundamental strength of a democratic society in which the citizens participate and the idea of social pluralism.[32]

The more that different ethnic and national groups interact and share language and memory, culture and tradition, the more likely communities are to hold together in times of stress and conflict, rather like building a wall with bricks that overlap with each other rather than building it with one brick directly over another. Where the line of separation excludes all others, the sense of marginalization and oppression grows and renders reconciliation increasingly hard to achieve.

However, nation-states with much at stake are often quite unscrupulous in trying to manipulate religious sensitivities and loyalties for their own aims. A case in point is the church-state relationship in many Orthodox churches. More particularly in south-east Europe, the Orthodox churches are national churches, and for Orthodox adherents the

---

[31] "Statement by the International Ecumenical Consultation, Morges, Switzerland, 1998", in Clement John ed., *Human Rights and the Churches: New Challenges. A Compilation of Reports*, WCC, 1998.
[32] *Church-People-State-Nation: A Protestant Contribution to a Difficult Relationship*, South and South-East Europe Regional Group of the Leuenberg Fellowship, 1995-2000.

nation is the repository of the faith. When the state is clearly antagonistic to the Christian faith, the church is faced with an impossible dilemma.

When war broke out in the Balkans between Serbia, Croatia and Bosnia, the ecumenical bodies were fully aware that state authorities in all three parts of the former Yugoslavia would be quick to see the potential in support for their actions from religious leaders – Orthodox, Roman Catholic and Muslim. Ethnic identity in a situation of conflict becomes vital, even when different ethnicities have been living side-by-side and intermarrying for centuries, as in Bosnia in particular. Apart from members of the small Protestant and Jewish communities, most Serbs, Croats and Bosnians, whether religious or not, felt loyalty to one or the other of the major faiths. It was only when one community began to attack another that the old intercommunal relations broke down, and faith and ethnic or national loyalty became inextricably linked.

In the early 1990s, when conflict in the Balkans was at its height, the task the WCC and the Conference of European Churches set themselves was to encourage the leaders of the Serbian Orthodox church to disassociate from the violence and aggression of the Serbian government, to assure the church of the support of the ecumenical community, and to encourage the Orthodox church leaders to denounce aggression and speak out for justice. That action was complicated by the reluctance of some member churches to support the Serbian Orthodox church, choosing rather to denounce what they saw as its complicity or silence in the aggression of the Serbian state.

A WCC effort to develop a systematic theological approach to ethnicity was a consultation, "Racism and Ethnic Conflicts in the Countries around the Baltic Sea", held in Lund, Sweden, in 1992 by the PCR. The consultation produced a report, "A Call for a New Community", and affirmed the inter-relatedness of ethnicity and racism. A summary of the consultation concluded that,

> Lund was successful in answering a need for mutual sharing and reflection on the "new" version of an old problem with which the churches and Christians are presently confronted and how they may deal with it. In the course of the consultation, various key issues emerged and were clarified. A theological framework for the search for new community was offered. And the consultation did provide some clues and practical suggestions on what could be done to overcome racism and ethnic conflict in the countries around the Baltic.[33]

An example of how the ecumenical community sought to show critical solidarity with its members during the crisis in the Balkans was the central committee's message to the countries of former Yugoslavia, in January 1994. It expressed deep concern for the tragic conflict, stressing that "every effort must be deployed, with imagination, determination and patience, for peace to be attained and kept". It also urged an end to the fighting, through peaceful negotiation, drawing attention to the fact that the conflict brought immense suffering to all sides. It added,

> We also condemn the manipulation of religious symbols and religious feelings for war aims, and call for the protection of the human rights of all, especially of religious, national and other minorities, and for the ending of all "ethnic cleansing"... We exhort our member churches... especially to resist every attempt to use religious sentiment and loyalty in the service of aggressive nationalism... [and promised] continuing efforts, through humanitarian relief, moral and spiritual support and dialogue with the political negotiators,

---

[33] *A Call for a New Community: A Consultation on Racism and Ethnic Conflicts in the Countries around the Baltic States, Lund, Sweden, 9-12 Ocober 1992*, WCC, 1993.

to bring succour to the suffering, strength to those under intolerable pressure, and an end to the war.

The central committee was restating the first principle, the over-riding need to remain faithful to the call of Christ to be peace-makers, while pointing to the dangers of ethnic cleansing and unbridled nationalism.

In the Jubilee year of 2000, Pope John Paul II laid special emphasis on the need for the Catholic church to repent historic instances of racial hostility and ethnic discrimination. In his travels he asked forgiveness from representatives of many cultural groupings, and in public prayers he asked for God's healing and reconciliation. Pratical steps were recommended in the international theological commission's "Memory and Reconciliation: The Church and the Faults of the Past".

For ecumenical bodies to arrive at a common understanding of what constitutes justifiable action to promote or defend ethnic or national identity, and what is unacceptable ethnocentricity or nationalism, is to say the least often problematical. Facing the issue in its guidelines for the churches, the *Charta Oecumenica*, negotiated at the end of the 20th century and signed in April 2001 by the presidents of the Conference of European Churches and the Council of European Bishops Conferences, states clearly, "We commit ourselves to counteract any form of nationalism which leads to the oppression of other peoples and national minorities and to engage ourselves for non-violent resolutions." There are, however, situations where the blatant abuse of human rights is so manifest that it calls out for strong words and sustained action. A message from the WCC general secretary, Konrad Raiser, to the Conference on Peace and Tolerance in Kosovo in 1998, illustrates such a circumstance. The conflict in Kosovo between Serbian government forces and ethnic Albanians caused the displacement of tens of thousands of civilians – a humanitarian disaster. The message affirmed that "the use of force and intimidation cannot secure a lasting and just solution to this complex and painful conflict" and called for a negotiated settlement "based on the establishment of full democracy and respect for the human rights of all communities, majority and minority, and the due recognition of the need for tolerance and peaceful co-existence". The WCC in addition pledged to continue to provide assistance to the victims of the humanitarian crisis, "regardless of their origin".[34]

PCR ROLE IN WCC REDUCED

The WCC spent more than a decade widening the scope of its concern about the varying expressions of racism and ethnicity. The PCR's method of operation was radical, in that it always sought to get to the roots of institutional and structural inequalities. Seeking partnerships for effective action was a fundamental part of the PCR methodology, inviting representatives of oppressed peoples and communities to develop common strategies and speak in international forums. Once again, the churches were drawn into alliances with civil society. This process has been essential in identifying and documenting the experiences of racially oppressed peoples throughout the world.

But it was the very expansion of the programmatic work on racism which began to affect the visibility of the PCR. During the period of international focus on apartheid, the

---

[34] Message to the Conference on Peace and Tolerance in Kosovo; a meeting of religious leaders of the Serbian Orthodox, Roman Catholic and Islamic communities in Kosovo, organized by the Appeal of Conscience Foundation, London, UK, Oct. 1998.

PCR had become one of the best-known WCC programmes. Post-apartheid, with the PCR's resources and energy allocated to a variety of areas, the focus was less clear because of the diversity of struggles. Some long-term PCR supporters became frustrated by what they saw as a loss of visibility and downgrading of the PCR's place within the overall WCC structure. Financial contributions to the PCR's work dropped dramatically after the release from prison of ANC leader Nelson Mandela, causing cutbacks in staff and project work. Other WCC programmes, such as Women, Youth, and Faith and Order began to develop anti-racism perspectives for their own work, thus broadening even further the WCC's focus on racism.

The challenge for the 21st century is to move the churches at every level from idealistic statements of purpose to mission strategies. The recognition that racism can no longer be justified is due in part to the policies of the ecumenical movement which have contributed handsomely towards the universal rejection of all forms of racism and racial discrimination. What is now needed is a clear answer to the question first posed by Eugene Carson Blake at Canterbury in 1969. Why is it that, despite the churches' teaching over so many years, racism continues to prevail in society, including within the church? Strategies should now be directed at engaging the church in its own transformation so that every Christian can become an agent of change in the world.

The activities of the WCC have had an impact on international developments. The WCC reflects, to the extent that it is consistent with the ecumenical vision and its own objectives, the experiences of the victims and the oppressed. Also, by its actions of solidarity and prophetic statements, the Council has put its reputation as a moral arbiter in world affairs to the test. Finally, the WCC's consistent action and statements against racism have managed to isolate the ever-dwindling influence of the purveyors of racism and give courage and support to all Christians committed to the struggle against racism. Racism has no place in the mainstream of human existence.

BIBLIOGRAPHY

Adler, Elisabeth, et al., *Justice for Aboriginal Australians: Report of the World Council of Churches Team Visit to the Aborigines, June 15-July 3, 1981*, Sydney, Australian Council of Churches, 1981, 91p.

Adler, Elisabeth, *A Small Beginning: An Assessment of the First Five Years of the Programme to Combat Racism*, WCC, 1974, 102p.

Beckmann, Klaus-Martin, *Anti-Rassismus Programm der Ökumene: Dokumentation einer Auseinandersetzung*, Witten, Eckhart, 1971, 261p.

Bent, Ans J. van der ed., *World Council of Churches Statements and Actions on Racism 1948-1985*, WCC, 1986, 107p.

Brackenridge, R. Douglas, *Eugene Carson Blake: Prophet with Portfolio*, New York, Seabury, 1978, 239p.

A Call for a New Community: A Consultation on Racism and Ethnic Conflicts in the Countries around the Baltic States, Lund, Sweden, 9-12 Ocober 1992, WCC, 1993, 74p.

Churches Responding to Racism in the 1980s: The Report of the World Council of Churches Consultation on Racism Called by the World Council of Churches, Held in Noordwijkerhout, Netherlands, 16-21 June 1980, WCC, 1983, 132p.

Dostal, W. ed., *The Situation of the Indian in South America: Contributions to the Study of Inter-Ethnic Conflict in the Non-Andean Regions of South America: Symposium, Bridgetown, Barbados, 25-30 January 1971*, WCC, 1972, 453p.

Final Report of the Seminar on the Role of Religion and Religious Institutions in the Dismantling of Apartheid, November 22-25, 1991, WCC, 1991, 88p.

For the Record: 1989: Papers and Addresses, WCC, 1990, 143p.

From Cottesloe to Cape Town: Challenges for the Church in a Post-Apartheid South Africa: The WCC Visit to South Africa, October 1991, WCC, 1991, 132p.

John, Clement ed., *Human Rights and the Churches: New Challenges, A Compilation of Reports*, WCC, 1998, 121p.

McCullum, Hugh, *The Angels Have Left Us: The Rwanda Tragedy and the Churches*, WCC, 1995, 115p., repr. with afterword 2004, 158p.

Mbali, Zolile, *The Churches and Racism: A Black South African Perspective*, London, SCM Press, 1987, 228p.

Meyers-Herwartz, Christel, *Die Rezeption des Antirassismus-Programms in der EKD*, Stuttgart, Kohlhammer, 1979, 378p.

Minutes of the Working Group on Racism, Ethnicity and Indigenous Peoples, Geneva, 24-28 June 1993, WCC, 1993, 78p.

Mutambirwa, James, *South Africa: The Sanctions Mission: Report of the Eminent Church Persons Group*, London, Zed, 1989, 135p.

Robinson, Deborah, *Ogoni: The Struggle Continues*, WCC, 1996, 106p.

Rogers, Barbara, *Race: No Peace without Justice*, WCC, 1980, 132p.

Sjollema, Baldwin C., *Isolating Apartheid: Western Collaboration with South Africa; Policy Decisions by the World Council of Churches and Church Responses*, WCC, 1982, 136p.

Tschuy, Theo, *Ethnic Conflict and Religion: Challenge to the Churches*, WCC, 1997, 160p.

Vincent, John J., *The Race Race*, London, SCM Press, 1970, 116p.

Webb, Pauline ed., *A Long Struggle: The Involvement of the World Council of Churches in South Africa*, WCC, 1994 133p.

Women under Racism: A Decade of Visible Action, WCC, 1990, 90p.

15

Science, Technology, Ecology

Stanley Samuel Harakas

A wide range of views exist regarding the relationship between faith and science. There are those who hold that science has destroyed Christian theology and faith. Others point to a deep divide between science and theology, with Christianity as an anti-cultural alternative to the scientific approach to knowledge and life. A somewhat less negative perspective is expressed in a Christian approach that divides science and the concerns of science sharply from the Christian faith into two unrelated and mutually exclusive realms.

Others, however, have assumed a more positive and dialogical relationship.[1] Ecumenical approaches to science and technology seek contact points and affirm openness to science from a Christian faith perspective. The alternatives listed above, consequently, are not usually found in ecumenical discourse regarding science and technology since ecumenism seeks to investigate the relationship between science and Christian thought. Through the catholic and outreach dimensions of Christianity, science is inevitably connected to Christian theology. The lynchpin for the connection is the doctrine of creation.

How this relationship is approached and how it functions, however, is a matter of some debate. For some, science is incomplete without a theological perspective; for others, what is known scientifically redefines belief, not only in dealing with externals, but also with the core of the Christian faith. Others seek a melding of scientific and theological knowledge or the road of complementarity towards scientific and theological experience and thought. Still others declare that the necessary approach combines several inter-related perspectives. On the one hand, there is the necessity of a theological perspective for science and technology to be able to function properly in social and moral dimensions (not science's primary methodology). This view assumes some necessary re-

---

• Some material for this chapter has been supplied by Steve de Gruchy.

[1] A short but thorough tracing of the development of the debate within Christianity regarding the relationship of Christian thought and the philosophical traditions leading to the dominance of scientific method can be found under various headings in Linwood Urban, *A Short History of Christian Thought*, revised and expanded edition, New York, Oxford Univ. Press, 1995. Richard H. Bube has placed these logically potential relationships between science and religion into seven categories. The range he describes is as follows: Pattern 1: Science has destroyed Christian theology; Pattern 2: Christian theology in spite of science; Pattern 3: Science and Christian theology are unrelated; Pattern 4: Science demands Christian theology; Pattern 5: Science redefines Christian theology; Pattern 6: A new synthesis of science and Christian theology; Pattern 7: Christian theology and science: complementary insights. Richard H. Bube, *Putting It All Together: Seven Patterns for Relating Science and the Christian Faith*, New York, Univ. Press of America, 1995.

formulation and additions to theological understanding as a result of scientific and technological developments. In addition, this perspective claims that some areas require a synthesis of scientific and theological understandings. Concurrently, this may require that in other areas there is a need to maintain a sense of complementarity in which scientific, technological and religious perspectives and values interact to form a more holistic approach which does not allow for the reduction of one or another approach.

The result is less a comprehensive theory and more a mosaic of many components mutually illuminating the human condition. This approach respects the integrity of the scientist and the value of the theologian; of science and faith; of objective knowledge of the physical world as it is and of the significance of the theological vision for the world's well-being. In broad terms this view characterizes most of the ecumenical encounter with science and technology. Historically it has avoided both the wholesale antitheses between science and religion on the one hand and the submersion of faith to science or science to faith on the other.

The ecumenical approach to science, technology and the environment, especially in its World Council of Churches expression, assumes a mutually informative relationship between Christian faith and science. This chapter seeks to sketch out the history of that relationship in the church's ecumenical life during the period 1968-2000, not as a description of a solution to the ongoing tensions, but as a serious effort to grapple with broadly conceived scientifically related issues. These concerns are not foundational theoretical issues. Rather, they arise from the empirical need for faith to address trajectories in science that require warning, response and, in some cases, proscription as well as prescription from the Christian theological, pastoral and ethical perspective of the churches.

EARLY ECUMENICAL EFFORTS

Prior to the period under review, themes in the World Council of Churches which dealt with issues related to science and technology included the first assembly's (Amsterdam 1948) "The Responsible Society";[2] the second assembly's (Evanston 1954) concern with "Rapid Social Change";[3] and the third assembly's (New Delhi 1961) third-world perspective on nuclear weapons, and the proper and responsible use of technology. During the same period, the Roman Catholic Church also addressed issues related to science and technology, especially at Vatican II and particularly in *Gaudium et Spes* (The Church in the Modern World).[4]

---

[2] Paul Abrecht, "The Development of Ecumenical Social Thought and Action", in Harold E. Fey ed., *A History of the Ecumenical Movement: Vol. 2: 1948-1968: The Ecumenical Advance*, 3rd ed. WCC, 1993, pp.241-42.

[3] The report of the conference called for by Evanston was published as *Dilemmas and Opportunities: Christian Action in Rapid Social Change. Report of an International Ecumenical Study Conference, Thessalonica, Greece, July 25-August 2, 1959*, WCC, 1959.

[4] The Council was a watershed in the life of the Roman Catholic Church, as a concentrated effort to bring it into the 20th century. Nevertheless, the Roman Catholic Church had a long history of involvement with the world through its theological and philosophical view of the social nature of persons, augmented by the high place of mutuality, love and justice in its teaching. The issue of the relationship of the church with the world in modern times was dealt with in the papal social encyclicals, such as *Rerum Novarum* (1891), *Quadragesimo Anno* (1931), *Summi Pontificatus* (1939), *Mater et Magistra* (1961) and *Pacem in Terris* (1962). One of the most important teachings of Vatican II regarding the contemporary world, in which in many ways the modern technical, economic and social structures of the world set the agenda for the church, was the Pastoral Constitution on the Church in the Modern World, published in 1965 as *Gaudium et Spes*. The intent of *Gaudium et Spes* was to delineate a

One year after the end of Vatican II, in 1966 the World Council of Churches held a conference in Geneva on the theme "Christians in the Technical and Social Revolutions of Our Time". There was wide-ranging participation of third-world lay representatives among the 420 delegates. Roman Catholics had prominent roles as speakers and observers. This was the first major WCC conference devoted solely to issues of social ethics and it had a wide impact. Its four preparatory volumes of essays were studied around the world. Among its speakers were scientists who spoke on scientific and technological issues, but these issues were not destined to become the central concern of the conference. As might have been expected, the social issues (political, economic and cultural) dominated the concerns of the participants. Science and technology were considered primarily as instruments for the exercise of power in reference to political, economic and cultural issues. Some of the scientists and representatives of technology objected that their concerns had been neglected and insisted that the report include acceptance of scientific and technological development in a theological context, coupled with a warning that science and technology could also have negative effects.[5] These concerns were, indeed, included in the official recommendations, though it was to be over a decade before serious ecumenical action would take place.

A voice expressing concern about the impact of science and technology also came from the joint WCC-Roman Catholic effort on Society, Development and Peace (SODE-PAX). Its focus was on social issues, specifically with economic development and issues of international relations. But the impact of science and technology could not be avoided and it pursued vigorously some of the concerns shared by Vatican II and the Geneva conference. The process took an unexpected direction when the issues of the environment leapt into prominence in several parts of the world. The question of the impact of science and technology on the environment became clearer in the context of the cold war. The fears arising from nuclear proliferation alerted the southern hemisphere to the consequences of post-colonial exploitation in the guise of industrial pollution and the continuance of economic, technological and political subservience of the South to the technologically advanced North. The older social concerns now seriously began to be integrated with the issues of the development of science and technology and the economic and social development of peoples.

The precursor to a focused approach to science and technology in the ecumenical movement was the activist fourth assembly of the WCC in Uppsala, Sweden (1968),

---

way of relating to the world by the church, "through the world". Its trajectory was not to present the church as opposed to the world, but in the world, with the goal of its transformation in the image of Christ, fostering the development of humanity to its fully human dimensions, rooted in the culture of the people. See Charles Moeller, "The Church in the Modern World: The Pastoral Constitution "Gaudium et Spes", *Lumen Vitae*, 21, 3, 1966, pp.291-306. While its reception in the Roman Catholic Church was tempered by conservative and liberal perspectives (the first concerned about an over-involvement in social concerns and the latter concerned by not enough involvement), the centrality of the consequences of modern developments on persons was acknowledged as a key value. See Kenneth R. Himes, "Mixed Reactions: The Reception of *Gaudium et Spes*", in *New Theology Review*, 3, 1, 1990, pp.5-17. It was not long before the impact of this view on science and technology was noted and the problems that it raised for the church were lifted up for attention, including issues of bio-ethics. See, for example, Hartmut Kress, "Autonomie in der Ethik. Zur Problematik und zum Gehalt eines ethischen Leitbegriffs (Autonomy in Ethics. On the Difficulty and on the Value of an Ethical Leading Idea)", in *Theologische Literaturzeitung*, 118, 6, 1993, pp.475-86. Kress bases his comments on the impact of *Gaudium et Spes*.

5 Paul Abrecht and M.M. Thomas eds, *World Conference on Church and Society, Geneva, July 12-26, 1966. Christians in the Technical and Social Revolutions of Our Time*, WCC, 1967.

whose theme was "Behold, I Make All Things New". In addition to mandating social programmes, it established the Commission on the Churches' Participation in Development and the Christian Medical Commission. The concern of the WCC unit on Church and Society turned to issues of science and technology.

SCIENCE AND TECHNOLOGY IN ECUMENICAL FOCUS

The first half of the 1970s[6] was marked by two WCC projects related to development issues but which impacted directly on the theme of science and technology: the Humanum and Futurum study projects, both of which concluded in 1974. They were preceded by concern regarding development in the secular world, especially by the UN First and Second Development Decades in the 1960s and 1970s. Clearly, they also provoked discussion within the member churches and within the WCC. These ecumenical study programmes raised the issue of "the human" and "the quality of life" as definitive concepts.

Several conferences explored the meaning of these terms. In general the trend was away from the traditional theological approach, opting for a more empirical approach to the discovery of criteria for a humane life. Initially the quality of life issue focused on the emerging technology of the biological manipulation of human nature. The Humanum Studies, however, linked themselves more closely to the secular debate, with a focus on science, technology and their economic impact on human life. Criticism was levelled against manipulation as a threat to human living and the quantitative approach to development, exemplified by the reliance on the gross national product (GNP) as an indicator of development. "Quality of life" thus was used as a counterpoint to traditional development theory. In any case, it served to bring the church into direct dialogue with social planners and decision-makers.

Two major and divergent views were developed in the five-year Futurum project, formally known as the WCC study programme on the "Future of Man and Society in a World of Science-Based Technology". This effort culminated in a conference on "Science and Technology for Human Development", sub-titled "The Ambiguous Future and the Christian Hope", held in Bucharest, Romania, in 1974.[7] The first of the two major views at the conference focused on the unique values and distinctive identity of the Christian and the church in the world. It emphasized the discontinuity between church and world. The discussion tended to present the role of the church as a prophetic community, challenging the status quo and calling for new ways of life. Remarkably, this approach, which reflected the Western social protest movements, found strong Orthodox support, especially when illumined by the values of the monastic tradition which ascribes a modicum of value to the commonly held requirements for human life, such as shelter, basic needs and just treatment, but not to conspicuous consumption. Quality of life was understood rather as the gifts of the Holy Spirit arising out of communion with God, regardless of external circumstances. For many, this was a critique of the quanti-

---

[6] The following few paragraphs are revised from material presented in Stanley Harakas, "An Orthodox Theology of Development: Justice and Participation from the Theological and Humanitarian Points of View: Christology, Pneumatology and Ecclesiology", a paper presented at the Orthodox consultation on "Just Development for Fullness of Life: An Orthodox Approach", Kiev, USSR 22-30 June 1982. *Just Development for Fullness of Life: A Responsible Christian Participation*, WCC, 1982, pp.49-81.

[7] The full report of the conference was published in *Anticipation*, 19, Nov. 1974. See pp.5,12,14-16,18,20,24,35-37.

tative approach to development and a reaffirmation of the vertical and transcendent dimension of the quality of life.

The second model, arising from the "Future of Man and Society" project, contradicted the previous one, focusing instead on continuity with the world and the fundamental place of the material in the understanding of quality of life. It sought measurable indicators in the individual and communal dimensions. Among these were such things as a stable population, fixed material wealth per person, low level of pollution, adequate food and a restricted use of non-renewable resources. Less successful was the effort to identify non-measurable indicators of quality of life. This perspective tended to have a clear secular expression, though not unrelated with theological and religious values. On the individual level these values included personal freedom, creativity, human relationships and ethics. On the social or communal level they included the principle of participation, the strengthening of the sense of community and new approaches to technology, which sought to oppose the "technologizing" of the totality of the human experience and political structures.

These two dynamics coalesced throughout the conference and found their way into the final report. The primary concern was development, but the relationship of this issue, with the increasingly strong presence of science and the technology which it produced, was evident in many of the report's sections.

The first part dealt with "the significance for the future of pressures of technology and population on environment and of natural limits to growth". The exaggerated hopes in the potential of science and technology for providing economic and social well-being for all the people of the world were cut down to size:

> We begin to perceive that the future will require a husbanding of resources and a reduction of expectations of global economic growth. We do not expect that all humanity can live as the most extravagant have been living, and we no longer believe that the spillover of wealth from the top will mean prosperity for all.

The "new ecumenical vision of the future" called for "an appropriate 'asceticism' for our time" that would serve to allocate the world's resources "with concern for the common good". Highlighting the themes of justice, interdependence and freedom, the report examined the short- and long-term dimensions of the impact of science and technology on human life and well-being. The need for fair distribution of food and availability of energy resources occupied the attention of the conference. A discussion of the pros and cons of nuclear energy took place. Much of the argumentation was "science informed", which also directed significant suggestions towards alternative energy sources.

Also highlighted at Bucharest was environmental deterioration, including the human impact on the climate, the beginning of a series of climate-change studies by various agencies of the WCC, scientific information and projections regarding potential harm arising in the future regarding food production, and energy resources.

The first part of the report presented the concept of a sustainable and just society as a response to the issue of environmental deterioration. Concerned about the effects of current trends upon the poor, the report said that "today the worldwide quality of life will be increased by material growth among the poor and by stabilization and possibly contraction among the rich . . . the goal must be a robust, sustainable society".

The second part, on "self-reliance and the technological options of developing countries", recognized that in developing countries research and development systems were not addressing the issues of their nations and regions. Ways must be defined to assist developing peoples to find "the right use of modern scientific knowledge".

"Quality of life and the human implications of further technological change", the third part of the report, spoke both of measurable social indicators of the quality of life and essential, but immeasurable, indicators of the quality of life. This effort to balance the conflicting approaches also characterized the report's assessment of technology: "But technology's capacity to enhance the quality of life is also a fact, which is why poorer people everywhere look to it with hope. The course indicated is the adaptation of technological processes to suit the values of individual cultures."

The fourth part of the report addressed "human settlements as a challenge to the churches", and it was a laundry list of the consequences of technological development as the world has come to experience its transmuting power: poverty, economic disparities, unemployment and under-employment, inadequate housing and public services, segregation, squatter settlements, urban ghettos, and the corrosive effects of pollution in the urban environment.

Though the major portion of part five of the Bucharest document dealt with issues of social justice on a global scale, the first section, titled "justice and technology in Christian perspective" spoke directly to science and technology. Once again, there was an effort to obtain a balance between the accomplishments and potential, and the misuse of science due to the human factor, both positively and negatively understood. The bulk of this section, true to its development purpose, focused on the impact of science-based technological development on various locations in the world and the various approaches needed to address their problems. In discussing the responsibilities of affluent societies for world social justice, two alternative approaches were presented, one a radical and the other an ameliorative approach.

The sixth part of the report on the "theological understanding of humanity and nature in a technological era" spoke first of Christian hope rooted in the faith understood both experientially and eschatologically. The document then applied the same theological perspective to the issue of ecology under the rubric "the ecological crisis and a theology of creation". It affirmed a "partnership rather than an opposition between science and faith," claiming concurrently that "many scientists and theologians still feel a contradiction between them". Ecological problems are seen as useful issues for fostering cooperation between science and faith. The report affirmed both continuity and discontinuity between the human and the non-human in creation, but claimed human responsibility for the balance of creation. It concluded with a call for an ecumenical dialogue between theology and science.[8]

---

[8] The full text of this recommendation is as follows:

2. Ecumenical Dialogue between Theology and Science

Because of the ecological crisis and its destructive effects on social justice throughout the world, science and technology as well as theology are challenged to proceed with self-examination, to find new approaches. Science-based technology has been the instrument of this crisis, endangering life without knowing whether it has the means for countering future threats. **Science** has developed into an instrument of domination for the exploitation of nature and the mobilization of human resources. **Theology**, in pursuing the doctrine of *dominium terrae*, has opened the door to thoughtless exploitation and destruction.

We therefore recommend that the various units of the WCC, including the Sub-unit on Church and Society, the Theological Education Fund, Faith and Order and the Programme Unit on Education and Renewal, continue the work begun after Uppsala and undertake a further study-programme on "rethinking theology" in view of the crisis of science and theology. This will involve a creative dialogue between theologians, scientists and philosophers of science, focusing in particular on:

An ecumenical hearing on the risks and potentialities of the further expansion of nuclear power programmes was held in Sigtuna, Sweden, in 1975, attended primarily by scientists, with strong representation from third-world nations. The report of the hearing[9] addressed issues regarding planning the energy supply system, nuclear risk assessment and the criteria for public acceptability, radiological hazards and operational experience with nuclear power programmes, the relationship between nuclear energy and nuclear weapons, as well as the challenge of nuclear energy to the churches. The hearing tended to offer a hesitant approval for at least interim use of nuclear power, anticipating the development of energy sources which did not carry as much negative risk.

The fifth assembly of the WCC (Nairobi 1975) reflected the concerns of the third world and liberation themes and expressed the repentance of the first world for the sins committed against the third world. The assembly endorsed the programme emphasis of the 1966 Geneva conference on technical and social revolutions and its continuing work. The central committee adopted a programme emphasis on the struggle for a "just, participatory and sustainable society" (JPSS). The latter theme had also been proposed by the Bucharest conference.

THE BEGINNINGS OF JPSS

Within the WCC there was some resistance to the new theme. To nations suffering from poverty, a warning against economic growth seemed to be a message of despair. Others feared that well-intentioned people, weary of strenuous conflicts for justice, welcomed a turn to a gentler environmental interest. Ecologists answered that if the dream of overcoming the gap between rich and poor by making everybody rich was illusory, the concern for distributive justice was all the more urgent.

Nairobi continued to encourage ecumenical attention to questions related to faith, science and technology, and ecology and human survival. The development section, "Human Development: Ambiguities of Power, Technology and Quality of Life", reflected conflicting approaches to the development question. The assembly delegates focused on the unjust structures of society, which were seen as exclusively arising out of the white, Northern, developed industrial societies. Essentially inspired by secular views on exploitation, class conflict and revolutionary solutions, the cry for justice for the oppressed was strongly and powerfully stated. The assembly lifted up the paradox that economic and technological development carry with them economic commitments and problems as illustrated by the energy crisis and environmental pollution. Even development aid and assistance were seen as perpetuating the subservient status of the third-

---

a) the world-view projected by modern science and technology, the assumptions and attitudes underlying and fundamental to it, and the extent to which theological and ideological factors have influenced it;

b) the attempts to overcome the rupture between nature and history as conceptualized in philosophical and theological thought;

c) the extent to which the alienation of the self from others and from the rest of creation arises from the objectifying and manipulatory tendencies in modern science and technology;

d) a re-examination of the scientific quest for truth in the light of the social, cultural, political conditions which provide the framework for the orientation of scientific work;

e) the theological search for a comprehensive concept which overcomes the fragmenting theologizing in relation to God, creation, humanity and the church.

9 *Anticipation: Christian Social Thought in Future Perspective*, 21, Oct. 1975.

world nations. This contributed to a long-standing theme, that of self-reliance in developing societies, i.e. placing more responsibility in the hands of the undeveloped and underdeveloped peoples themselves. The most significant new direction from Nairobi was uniting the emphases of justice and sustainability. Charles Birch from Australia defined the issue clearly:

> A prior requirement of any global society is that it be so organized that the life of man and other living creatures on which his life depends can be sustained indefinitely within the limits of the earth. A second requirement is that it be sustained at a quality that makes possible fulfilment of human life for all people. A society so organized to achieve both these ends we can call a sustainable global society in contrast to the present unsustainable global society. If the life of the world is to be sustained and renewed... it will have to be with a new sort of science and technology governed by a new sort of economics and politics. That is what the sustainable global society is all about. It will not come without radical and revolutionary transformations in science and technology and in economics and politics. The decisions we have to make are not just economic and political ones, they are also scientific and technical.[10]

When the central committee following Nairobi announced JPSS as one of the WCC's four major programme emphases, it concurrently authorized the working committee on Church and Society to plan for a conference to explore the theme. In part, the working committee said:

> The twin issues around which the world's future revolves are justice and ecology. "Justice" points to the necessity of correcting real distribution of the products of the earth and of bridging the gap between rich and poor countries. "Ecology" points to humanity's dependence upon the earth. Society must be so organized as to sustain the earth so that a sufficient quality of material and cultural life for humanity may itself be sustained indefinitely. A sustainable society which is unjust can hardly be worth sustaining. A just society that is unsustainable is self-defeating. Humanity now has the responsibility to make a deliberate transition to a just and sustainable global society.[11]

The working committee produced a widely distributed volume of preparatory readings for a conference to be held in 1979 on "Faith, Science and the Future". Recognizing that the churches' language is often metaphorical in character providing a vision of understanding, the section pointed to the difficulty of relating Christian understandings to science and technology. "Faith cannot turn this vision into a pseudo-science. Yet Christians believe that such language expresses a faith that contributes to the understanding of humanity, nature and God – and the human activity called science."[12]

In discussing "energy for the future", in the context of developed, developing and under-developed and as yet undeveloped societies, the potential and threat of nuclear energy joined the "participatory" and the "just" aspects of the theme. The negative aspects of nuclear energy development had already impacted on developed nations, provoking concerns about limitations and controls. To the developing nations, especially those with limited fossil or other sources of energy, this concern appeared to be another form of oppression, limiting their own growth potentials.

[10] David N. Paton ed., *Breaking Barriers, Nairobi 1975: The Official Report of the Fifth Assembly of the World Council of Churches, Nairobi, 23 November-10 December 1975*, London, SPCK, 1976.
[11] Charles Birch et al. eds, *Faith, Science and the Future: Preparatory Readings for a World Conference Organized by the World Council of Churches at the Massachusetts Institute of Technology, Cambridge, Mass., USA, July 12-24, 1979*, WCC, 1978, p.5.
[12] *Ibid.*, p.21.

Christian reactions to the development of nuclear power were traced from a welcoming acceptance through an increasingly less optimistic view, to a radical disavowal of nuclear energy. It had become clear that there were insurmountable problems with the manufacture, distribution and reliability of nuclear energy, many of which were technically beyond the purview of the churches. Without technical knowledge, no ethical evaluations could be made, while on the other hand technical development without ethical guidance was seen as a recipe for uncontrolled and irreversible injustice, if not disaster. The readings were not clear about solutions, but were firm about the need of the WCC to be involved in the debate about nuclear energy.

> It would appear from the nature of the problem – its centrality in future plans of many industrialized countries; the difficulty of finding alternative energy sources; the absence of simple, absolute solutions; the polarization of the debate; the existence of moral and ethical dimensions so far largely unperceived (or if so, selectively unattended) – that the churches can and must contribute.[13]

FAITH, SCIENCE AND THE FUTURE: THE MIT CONFERENCE

The conference, held at the Massachusetts Institute of Technology in 1979, was remarkable in its size and composition. More than four hundred delegates were present, about half of whom were physical scientists and technical experts, while the other half were church leaders, theologians, social scientists, and people from government, business and industry. The meeting also included speakers from Buddhism and Islam, in addition to Christian theologians. Other speakers, chosen for their technical competence, included Christians, Jews and agnostics. There were also speakers on technical topics who came from varied religious traditions, including non-believers. A significant contingent of young people was also present and participating.

The conference was organized into ten sections: (1) the nature of science and the nature of faith, (2) humanity, nature and God, (3) science and education, (4) ethical issues in the biological manipulation of life, (5) technology, resources, environment and population, (6) energy for the future, (7) restructuring the industrial and urban environment, (8) economics of a just, participatory and sustainable society, (9) science/technology, political power and a more just world order, and (10) towards a new Christian social ethic and new social policies for the churches.

The realistic and comprehensive tone of the conference was highlighted by the title of the two-volume report: *Faith and Science in an Unjust World*,[14] indicating a strong awareness of the context in which both faith and science functioned, which did not allow for facile ideologies nor for social irrelevancy. The MIT conference was immersed in the struggles of the times and fully aware of the difficult ambiguities being faced by the world as the decade of the 1970s was drawing to a close.

In his introductory presentation, Philip Potter, then general secretary of the WCC, traced the outlines of the history of the ecumenical concern with science and technology, including the problems associated with their impact on issues of economic and social justice. Potter took into account the concern of scientists who demanded attention to nuclear energy issues and to the confrontation of the problem of nuclear weaponry and the

---

[13] *Ibid.*, p.120.
[14] Roger L. Shinn and Paul Abrecht eds, *Faith and Science in an Unjust World: Report of the World Council of Churches' Conference on Faith, Science and the Future: Massachusetts Institute of Technology, Cambridge, USA, 12-24 July 1979*, 2 vols, WCC, 1980.

threat of nuclear war. Three and a half months earlier, on 28 March 1979, the most serious nuclear accident to take place in the US occurred at Three Mile Island, near Harrisburg, Pennsylvania. The theoretical dangers of nuclear energy for which scientists were particularly alert had materialized less than a thousand kilometres away. The potential for the evil consequences of technological advance was strikingly and patently evident and could not be ignored. While recognizing the tremendous value and contribution of science and technology, Potter did not hesitate to lift up its social and ethical dangers:

> Science and technology are not neutral or value free, but are instruments of power, and that means political power. How, then, can science and technology become the vehicles, not for legitimizing and perpetuating the structures of injustice, but for opening up the possibilities for structures of social control, which include all the people?[15]

He added this significant judgment: "To my mind, this is the central issue before this conference. It is the issue because we are concerned about faith and the future." It is about faith, he continued, because there is a profound need for repentance "towards God in Christ and towards our fellow human beings".

The presentations at the conference were wide-ranging and sometimes contrasting. However, in the judgment of Roger Shinn, professor of social ethics at Union Theological Seminary, New York, and editor of the plenary presentations, the variety and divergence was far from absolute. In his evaluation, if not at the beginning, at least by the end of the conference,

> there were no "scientific utopians" evident. That is, in contrast to a considerable literature of the past century, nobody was confident of a "technical fix" for the basic problems of societies and individuals . . .. There appeared to be universal recognition that the world's major problems require changes in social structures and in the values and commitments embodied in those structures.

Similarly, "nobody was confident of a 'religious fix' for the basic social problems of this century". The demise of scientific utopianism was matched by the demise of a facile appeal to religious conversion or even to greater commitment, as a panacea to the human problems of poverty, hunger or disease. Both parties to the dialogue understood that intense effort and reflection were demanded to work out the "difficult scientific, technological, economic and political issues. There was no claim that the churches were able to tell scientists the ethical formulas that would make their work benign." Shinn also made the interesting and telling observation that in no major arguments were scientists and technical experts united *en masse* against theologians and representatives of churches. "In the big debates – and there were some – scientists and theologians stood together on *both* sides of the issue."[16]

The first set of plenary presentations[17] responded to the question "What is science?" Astronomer Hanbury Brown went beyond the traditional understanding of science as a search for objective and verifiable truth to a recognition that its alliance with industry and government has impacted on the field significantly. He further indicated that

---

[15] *Ibid.*, vol. 1 , p.28.

[16] *Ibid.*, p.11.

[17] In this necessarily brief description, the summaries of Roger Shinn will be a guide. Readers are directed to the talks and presentations themselves for a fuller understanding of the content of the talks.

science's concepts are abstractions which exist in a mutually complementary fashion. He admitted the reality of other – religious – ways of approaching the mystery of existence. One response from South America was less accommodating, and challenged confrontationally the impact of modern science on the lives of many of the less privileged people of the world. Another, from Africa, was more affirmative to the potential contribution of science, but asked for its redirection to meet basic human needs.

This was followed by "What is faith?" Metropolitan Paulos Mar Gregorios of the Orthodox Syrian Church of the East responded that faith is "not so much an emotional-intellectual commitment of the will to someone who stands over against you, as allowing oneself to be trustingly carried, nourished, supported, by God, and the consequent strengthening and transformation of human personality and society".[18] A feminist response by Rosemary Radford Ruether cast the relationships of science and faith in terms of the creation of a new "scientific priesthood" in the service of political power used by white, Western males to dominate all others, including the "rape of the earth".

"Rethinking theology" dealt with nature, humanity and God from an ecological perspective, "Science and Technology as Promise and Threat" with themes of scale, complexity and risk management. A section was devoted to perspectives on the issue of faith and science in Islam and Buddhism. Presentations from Asia, Africa and South America, in large part informed by liberation theological perspectives, emphasized the negative consequences of science-based technology as an instrument of exploitation, while affirming the potential value of science and technology when used in the light of genuine human need.

Developed nations also made their case, accepting the challenges directed to them, calling for a transition to a just, participatory and sustainable society, while recognizing the problems and difficulties involved, including the significant impact of governmental policies and agencies. Industrialized socialist countries were present and dealt with Marxist views on the limits to growth, with approaches of Christians living in the socialist societies of the German Democratic Republic and Hungary. Further problem areas included "economics of the just and sustainable society", "energy for the future", "the biological revolution: the ethical and social issues", "the gathering and processing of information" and "disarmament".

Each section had a student vice-moderator, "thus assuring a student voice in the organizing of the work of the sections as well as in their continuing discussion".[19] While the students presented strongly worded statements and impacted significantly on the conference, they also gained a deeper understanding of the contemporary social impact of science upon society, especially in its negative dimensions.

The summary statement of all of the reports was cast in the form of an inquiry regarding the relationship of science and ethics: "The values inherent in science are incomplete without the incorporation of humanistic values." It continued,

> Competence in science may or may not be associated with love and passion for justice. The direction and application of scientific research depend largely upon the values in the culture (including its political and economic institutions) surrounding the scientist. The scientists in our midst have made this point forcefully and they are showing how scientists can contribute to the criticism and the shaping of cultural values.[20]

[18] *Faith and Science in an Unjust World*, p.49.
[19] *Ibid.*, p.10.
[20] *Faith and Science in an Unjust World*, vol. 2, p.151. Following references to pp.152 and 165.

The report concluded its discussion on science and ethics with a quotation from the "Genetics and the Quality of Life" consultation held in 1975: "There is no sound ethical judgment in these matters independent of scientific knowledge, but science does not itself prescribe the good."

On the issue of the relationship between technology and ethics, the conference delegates held that technology alone is not adequate to resolving the wide range of problems faced today and that it is necessary to examine all technical developments for their ethical aspects "before technical and social processes move to decisions without adequate attention to their ethical implications".

Practical recommendations were made regarding the sharing of scientific knowledge and technological capabilities widely throughout the world, expanding educational opportunities and participation, and continued "discussions and interactions among scientists, social scientists, theologians and lay people on the ethical aspects of the increasing influence of science and technology on our societies".

The goal of a "just, participatory and sustainable society" highlighted the need for science and technology to take seriously the ethical implications of their activities. The thrust of the MIT conference was to maintain a balanced stance between faith and ethics on the one hand and science and technology on the other. If there was sharpness in the reports and the general message of the conference, it came from those whose lives and societies had suffered a negative impact economically and socially from the advances of science and technology. But even the representatives of the advanced capitalist and socialist societies recognized that threats to human existence were too evident in the scientific and technological developments which had a negative impact on the ecosystem and the dangers of the widespread commercialization of scientifically based technology – in particular nuclear energy and the potential for nuclear war.

Arguably, the conference on "Faith, Science and the Future" was one of the most sustained, inclusive, reflective and honest ecumenical efforts at addressing the issues raised in the 20th century regarding faith, science and technology. Subsequent efforts were focused more narrowly on specific areas of concern. For those aware of its treatment of the broad theoretical issues as well as concrete problems such as the environment, biological manipulation of life, problems of energy use and misuse, and economic and political use of science-based technology, it became a springboard for continuing ecumenical concern.

JESUS CHRIST – THE LIFE OF THE WORLD

The sixth assembly of the WCC was held in Vancouver in 1983 under the theme "Jesus Christ – the Life of the World". Some of the themes of the MIT conference entered into the programme in issue groups dealing with topics which had become associated with the relationship of faith, science and technology. They included participation, healing and sharing life in community, confronting threats to peace and survival, and struggling for justice and human dignity.

Of significance for the relationship of faith with science and technology was the proposal that the WCC involve itself in a new theme of study and action. As Ans J. van der Bent put it,

> A recommended WCC priority was the engagement of member churches "in a conciliar process of mutual commitment (covenant) to justice, peace and the integrity of all cre-

ation", whose foundations were "confessing Christ as the life of the world and Christian resistance to the demonic powers of death in racism, sexism, caste oppression, economic exploitation, militarism, violations of human rights, and the misuse of science and technology".[21]

Though originally intended to be a programme priority for the WCC, "Justice, Peace and the Integrity of Creation" (JPIC) expanded quickly to churches which were not members of the WCC, other ecumenical organizations of a regional and national character and various movements for whom these social issues were central. This initiative was, of course, broader than the concern with science and technology and broader than a concern for Christian ethics. The ethical imperative was set within the faith perspective of the church, particularly as it expressed itself in Vancouver. JPIC developed out of the need to lead the churches and others to a mutual commitment in a conciliar process towards the implementation of those goals.

It was decided to convene a consultation in recognition of the truth that there were many differing perspectives on the vital issues related to justice, peace and the integrity of creation. Conceived as closely inter-related, and rooted in the Christian belief in the trinitarian God as Creator, Redeemer and Sustainer of the world whose liberating grace was at the heart of its gospel, the themes of justice, peace and the integrity of creation were studied at regional conferences during the decade of the 1980s.

Following the Vancouver assembly, two world-shaking events occurred which heightened the concerns lifted up by ecumenical encounter with science and technology, and especially their environmental impact. In December 1984, perhaps the worst industrial accident in history occurred in India. At a Union Carbide Company pesticide plant outside the city of Bhopal (pop. 672,000), a tank holding 45 tons of a poisonous chemical *(methyl isocyanate)*, used in the manufacturing of pesticides, was released into the air. More than 2500 people died.

Then on 25-26 April 1986 at Chernobyl, Ukraine, a meltdown in a nuclear reactor occurred, with radiation levels reaching as much as 2500 times normal levels. Within days 135,000 people were evacuated from a wide area around the plant. Nuclear fallout was observed the day after in Scandinavia and subsequently several nations have reported medical consequences attributed to the disaster.[22]

The seriousness of these events, including the disaster at Three Mile Island, having taken place in first-, second- and third-world countries, impacted strongly on worldwide public consciousness. Ecological awareness had gained an imperative which made the concerns highly relevant in the midst of planning for a world convocation on JPIC following the Vancouver assembly.

Regional JPIC meetings were held in September 1988 in the Pacific; in 1989 in Europe and Latin America. Orthodox conferences were held in Sofia in 1987 and Minsk in 1989; a Roman Catholic meeting at the Vatican took place in 1989, and the Reformed churches met in Seoul in 1989. In the planning for the world convocation, non-Christian faiths and others were also included, since the issues of JPIC were not exclusively Christian concerns.

---

[21] "WCC Assemblies", in Nicholas Lossky et al. eds, *Dictionary of the Ecumenical Movement*, 2nd ed. WCC, 2002, p.1236.

[22] *Time Magazine*, 1 Sept. 1986. *Time: Almanac of the 20th Century*. CD-Rom, Cambridge MA, Softkey International, 1994.

The methodology for forming a conciliar process which linked together theological, ecclesiological and ethical concerns was addressed by a JPIC conference in 1986 and by the central committee in Geneva in early 1987.[23] Contributions at the meetings affirmed the need to maintain a dynamic interplay among biblical, patristic, theological, ecclesiological, ethical, scientific, sociological (e.g., race relations, women and Indigenous Peoples), economic, environmental and other aspects.[24]

Many have raised the issue of the meaning of the term "integrity of creation" since it was coined at Vancouver. A sharp critic of the social ethics of the WCC, Ronald H. Preston, expressed wonder at how the term came to have significant importance:

> In the Vancouver assembly report, there is only a passing reference to the new phrase, and it is a puzzle how it came to be taken up so vigorously shortly afterwards. It looks as if the enthusiasm of a few, probably including influential staff members, carried the day, when there was no similar *ad hoc* group for any other theme. But this is surmise.[25]

Whatever the case, Preston adds,

> However, the theme has clearly had a growing resonance in public discussion, at least in the "West". It has now appeared in papal and in United Nations documents. For some time the third world was suspicious of it, as a device by the wealthy to keep their material privileges by rousing alarm at the global consequences if they spread to the third world. Now the third world has come to see that there are global problems from which it cannot be insulated.

He adds that "the integrity of creation" "has become a lynchpin of its work; indeed there are attempts to make it *the* lynchpin".

Geraldine S. Smyth, a much more sympathetic analyst of the ecological focus of ecumenical endeavour, also notes its obscure place in the work of the Vancouver assembly:

> Many have wondered how and whence came the term "integrity of creation" in the aftermath of the Vancouver assembly. The index to the assembly report offers only four entries under creation, and no mention of integrity. In no way was this term conceived as a theological cornerstone to the JPIC process. Often indeed, one gets the impression that despite the insistence on JPIC as one process and struggle for life, the third element is an appendage, and the emphasis is anthropocentric.

Under the leadership of Preman Niles, the JPIC initiative replaced the slogan "Just, Participatory and Sustainable Society" (JPSS). Smyth notes that "according to Niles,

---

[23] See WCC Central Committee, *Minutes of the Thirty Eighth-Meeting, Geneva, 1987*, pp.51-57 and appendix VII. For a full treatment of these two meetings and, indeed, the theme of the development of the concept of the "Integrity of Creation", see Geraldine S. Smyth, *A Way of Transformation: A Theological Evaluation of the Conciliar Process of Mutual Commitment to Justice, Peace and the Integrity of Creation, World Council of Churches, 1983-1991*, New York, Peter Lang, 1995.

[24] *A Way of Transformation*, pp.40-56, with the conclusion that "the Glion and the Geneva meetings emerge less as bringing the first phase of the JPIC process to consolidation, than as broadening the methodology and opening up the central questions. This theme of life was constant in these three years, though with the beginnings of a clearer trinitarian framework from Kinshasa on, and with the growing awareness that JPIC concerns are not the preserve of the ecumenical movement... The integrative potential of the 'life' motif was increasingly seen to relate to the universal threats to life, to our common humanity and our responsibility to recognize our continuity with nature and to relate to the earth in a life-giving way", p.57.

[25] Ronald H. Preston, *Confusions in Christian Social Ethics: Problems for Geneva and Rome*, Grand Rapids MI, Eerdmans, 1995, pp.119, 120.

JPSS had come to be resented by churches and ecumenical movements in the South as favouring the interests and hierarchical approaches of the North, which some thought would be corrected by the covenanting and commitment aspects of JPIC. Whatever [they thought] about justice and peace elements of the new conciliar process, not many, North or South, knew what to make of the third element, 'integrity of creation'."[26]

OUR COMMON FUTURE – A CHALLENGE TO THE CHURCHES

In 1986 a joint planning consultation of the Faith and Order Commission and the Church and Society Commission met on the theme "Creation and Kingdom" in York, UK. It raised numerous questions and planned several consultations to explore the implications of creation, new creation, nature, integrity, and science for the ecumenical development of the theme "integrity of creation".

In 1988, the first international consultation on the theme of the integrity of creation was held in Granvollen, Norway, under the sponsorship of JPIC and other ecumenical agencies. The meeting began with a keynote address by Norway's prime minister, Gro Harlem Brundtland on the theme "Our Common Future – A Challenge to the Churches". The theme of the deteriorating environment in relation to economic development gave a tone of urgency to the meeting. The consultation set itself the task of engaging the churches with the ecological problem over the long term through a programme of study and action.[27] Its report was not a position paper, but was designed to provoke reflection and discussion and action in the ecological sphere among the churches. A realistic description of the suffering of peoples as a result of the unjust destruction of the environment at the hands of the modern industrialization-based economic system was apparent from the beginning of the document. It witnessed to the brokenness of creation and its impact on justice and peace: alienated land, water pollution, the destruction of war, radio-active destruction of ecological systems, sickness and death, deforestation, the impact on women, the poor and, in particular, Indigenous Peoples.

The Granvollen report seeks to engage the issue theologically in a broad-based fashion, including "creation", "redemption" and "new creation" themes. The trinitarian foundation is evident. Other dimensions of the theme highlighted in the report are the inter-relatedness of all elements of the creation, commitment to the value of life as a gift of God, the importance of a mind-set of stewardship for creation, and the *koinonia*, or the communion of all things with God. The church is thus seen as fostering the sense that all Christians have a special priesthood on behalf of the creation, glorifying God for it, offering it up for his service, and seeking its healing and sanctification.

While much more would be done to develop the meaning of the "integrity of creation", Granvollen served to open many opportunities for further reflection and to bring together many varied views and insights, broadening the search for understanding and application in future concerns. In the context of science and technology, Granvollen provided a theological and ethical standing place for the ecumenical movement to address critically the dark side of scientific and technological development. Explicating a theo-

---

[26] *A Way of Transformation*, pp.59, 60.
[27] Granvollen Final Document, "Integrity of Creation: An Ecumenical Discussion", in *JPIC Resource Materials* 3.2, 1988.

logical foundation for the "integrity of creation" was not, however, an antagonistic confrontation, for it was admitted that the churches were implicated in the negative dimensions of science and technology. JPIC's focus on the "integrity of creation" was more of an invitation to repentance and reconciliation and restoration. These efforts led to a world convocation to move beyond reflection to action.

The following year the specific concern of nuclear energy and its ethical and human dimensions became a focus of reflection and study at a meeting sponsored by the Church and Society sub-unit at Kinshasa, Zaire (later Democratic Republic of the Congo), in 1989, building on the work of the MIT conference a decade earlier. Wesley Granberg-Michaelson summarized the focus of the Kinshasa consultation on nuclear energy, highlighting:

- questions related to the storage and handling of nuclear waste;
- nuclear proliferation;
- questions of safety related both to present reactors and a possible new generation of reactors; and
- the ethics of nuclear energy.

In addition, the working committee directed that discussion should take place within the broader framework of present and projected world energy needs in both industrialized and developing countries. It also requested that nuclear energy be evaluated as one possibility among varied energy options, each with its own environmental, social and economic costs and hazards. Finally, the committee asked that the consultation consider the possibility of, and limits to, improving energy generating and consumption efficiency.[28]

The working committee report indeed addressed these issues. Among its points were an emphasis on participation in decision-making on questions of nuclear energy by groups other than narrow governmental and technical agencies. Under the heading "Nuclear Energy and Technical Issues", the committee pointed to existing fast-breeder nuclear reactors, which posed "especially serious potential problems associated with controlling fission in their cores and with their sodium coolant systems". The report consequently held that "on safety grounds alone, their future development should not be supported". By far the longest section of the report dealt with "questions of safety in nuclear energy", which addressed technical questions and the issue of adequate safety training for nuclear reactor personnel. Other issues addressed were nuclear waste, the future design of nuclear reactors, the evaluation of the full costs of nuclear energy, access to information regarding nuclear energy to facilitate participation in the light of ethical and theological considerations. The report concluded with biblical and theological analyses on the themes of human responsibility for creation and the need to cultivate wholesome attitudes to creation and technology.[29]

SEOUL 1990 AND RIO 1992

The world convocation on "Justice, Peace and the Integrity of Creation" took place in Seoul, Korea, in 1990.[30] Prominent in its methodology was the use of the "covenant"

[28] Preface to Kristin Shrader-Frechette ed., *Nuclear Energy and Ethics*, WCC, 1991, p.9. Following references to pp.220-22.

[29] *Ibid.* The report is found in pp.219-27, and is preceded by thirteen conference papers. Following the introduction by the editor, Kristin Shrader-Frechette, entitled "Moral Consensus and Nuclear Power", three sections of papers concern historical, policy and ethical issues.

[30] *World Convocation on Justice, Peace and Integrity of Creation: 1990; Seoul, Report*, WCC, 1990.

motif. The convocation, which was popular in character and practical in intent, produced ten "affirmations" and an "act of covenanting". Of the ten affirmations, those dealing with the peace of Jesus Christ, creation as beloved of God, the earth as the Lord's, and human rights as given by God, had direct relationship with some of the faith, science and technology discussions. Among the "affirmations", calls for action based on faith presuppositions advancing justice in the economic order, demilitarization, the protection of the environment and the reduction of global warming were prominent.

The following year the seventh assembly of the WCC took place in Canberra, Australia under the theme "Come, Holy Spirit – Renew the Whole Creation". The sections and sub-themes were led by the ecological concerns evident in the recent activities of the WCC. The sub-themes were: (1) Giver of life – sustain your creation!, (2) Spirit of truth – set us free!, (3) Spirit of unity – reconcile your people!, and (4) Holy Spirit – transform and sanctify us! Canberra encouraged the continuation of the work of JPIC, a focus that remained in the WCC even after fundamental restructuring because of economic limitations.[31]

In 1992, the UN sponsored the "Earth Summit" held in Rio de Janeiro. Officially designated the United Nations Conference on Environment and Development (UNCED), the large gathering included official representation from 178 nations, with 117 heads of state in attendance. Associated with it was a Global Forum with 7892 NGOs from 167 countries participating. The division between the underdeveloped and developing countries of the southern hemisphere and the industrially developed nations of the North was even more pronounced in Rio de Janeiro than at the ecumenical conferences and meetings which preceded it. One of the great disappointments of the conference was the reluctance of the industrialized nations, especially the US, to support fully the ecological aims of this UN initiative. Nevertheless, significant documents were signed which could contribute, at the least, to moulding opinions and influencing actions among and within the nations.

Among these documents were "The Convention on Biological Diversity" which encouraged nations to take an inventory of their plant and animal life and to take action to protect endangered species. Another was the "Global Warming Convention", a binding treaty imposing the reduction of emissions of carbon dioxide, methane and other gases conducive to the increase of the "greenhouse" effect. In addition, the Declaration on Environment and Development

> laid down 27 broad, non-binding principles for environmentally sound development. Agenda 21 outlined global strategies for cleaning up the environment and encouraging environmentally sound development. The Statement of Principles on Forests, aimed at preserving the world's rapidly vanishing tropical rain forests, is a non-binding statement recommending that nations monitor and assess the impact of development on their forest resources and take steps to limit the damage done to them.[32]

---

[31] Michael Kinnamon ed., *Signs of the Spirit. Official Report, Seventh Assembly, Canberra, Australia, 7-20 February 1991*, WCC, 1991.
[32] "United Nations Conference on Environment and Development", in *Britannica CD, 2.0.* Encyclopaedia Britannica, 1995.

The ecumenical discussion preceding the Earth Summit had mirrored many of these concerns even prior to the JPIC and JPC programmes.[33] However, the ecological concerns of the WCC came to a focus in Rio. In conjunction with Unced the Council, functioning as an NGO, met to address the same themes as the UN gathering. Its theme was "Searching for the New Heavens and the New Earth". Wesley Granberg-Michaelson described its magnitude in significant detail:

> The World Council of Churches convened a major ecumenical meeting which was one of the myriad events at the Earth Summit. For the first seven days of June, a group of 176 people from 54 countries and over 70 different churches met in an area on the north side of Rio called Baixada Fluminense. There they reflected, worshipped, discussed and responded to the issues of the Earth Summit from the perspectives of churches worldwide. And they were embraced in lively fellowship by the Catholic and Protestant churches in this area – a place known as one of the most violent in Brazil, typifying the realities of suffering, social strife and economic despair which mark much of Brazilian life.[34]

The gathering's "Letter to the Churches" was not optimistic about the ecological state of the planet, or about the potential for improvement. "We have come inevitably to the conclusion that the prevailing system is exploiting nature and peoples on a worldwide scale and promises to continue at an intensified rate," it said.[35] It expressed repentance for the church's insensitivity to the environmental danger. And, more positively, it urged that attention be paid to the worldwide consequences of the ongoing degrading of the environment, in the form of support for the Unced declarations and conventions. In its theological dimensions, it rooted its appeal in the theology of the Holy Spirit.

In addition to the letter, the connection between Christian faith and the technological issues related to ecology were addressed by the WCC meeting in "An Evaluation of the Unced Conventions". This document encouraged the churches to take the Rio declaration seriously and to act on it "to press for changes in their own societies and internationally".[36] The evaluation chose, among many potential issues, to highlight the concern for bio-diversity, climate change, and forests in industrialized as well as developing areas of the world.

These interests and concerns continued to attract the attention of the WCC in the years following. An example of active involvement of the WCC was its representation at the second world climate conference in 1990. Subsequently, ecumenical participation took place in the UN Intergovernmental Negotiating Committee's five sessions. This body drafted "The UN Framework Convention on Climate Change", which was signed by 155 nations at the Rio Earth Summit. In subsequent implementation meetings, the

---

[33] Creation in one way or another had been addressed at the Evanston assembly (1954), the New Delhi assembly (1961), and meetings in Salonika (1959), Montreal (1963), Mexico City (1963), Bangkok (1964) and Geneva (1966). For references see Pierre Beffa et al. eds, *Index to the World Council of Churches' Official Statements and Reports: 1948-1994*, WCC, 1995, p.160. In the period from 1968 to 1977 treatments of ecological topics, creation, pollution, environment and the quality of life were to be found in the report and preparations for the Nairobi assembly (1975), the Humanum Studies (1969-75), and meetings in Montreal (1969), Geneva (1970), Baden (1970), Montreux (1970), Ibadan (1973), Zurich (1973), Bucharest (1974), Accra (1974), Colombo (1974), and Chiang Mai (1977). *Ibid.* See entries on "ecology", p.104, "environment", p.105, "human survival", p.111, "pollution", p.126 and "quality of life", p.122.

[34] Wesley Granberg-Michaelson, *Redeeming the Creation. The Rio Earth Summit: Challenges for the Churches*, WCC, 1992, pp.xi-xii.

[35] *Searching for the New Heavens and the New Earth: An Ecumenical Response to UNCED*, 2nd ed., WCC, Unced Group, n.d., p.9.

[36] *Ibid.*, pp.12-15.

WCC also participated and was involved in the Berlin climate summit, held in early 1995.

Part of the WCC effort in this area has been to inform the member churches about the problems of climate change. A consultation was held in the Netherlands in 1993, where the Council disseminated its study document "Accelerated Climate Change – Sign of Peril, Test of Faith". A policy statement on climate change was adopted by the 1994 central committee meeting in Johannesburg. Translated into many languages, it is a foundation for educating member churches on the issue of climate change. The churches' primary concern was "the impact that climate change will have on vulnerable peoples and ecosystems, especially those of island states and other low-lying areas",[37] in particular the Pacific Islands. WCC activities regarding climate change included cooperation on a petition campaign in industrialized societies, a regional support programme and the development of an "ethical response team" for the representation of the Council's views on climate change to "governments, scientists, United Nations officials, business and non-governmental organizations".[38]

It is important to note that much of the debate about science and technology throughout the latter half of the 20th century took place within the context of the cold war, and this gave obvious urgency to the question of nuclear technology. The collapse of communism in the Eastern bloc countries after 1989 substantially reduced concerns about a nuclear holocaust. To a large extent this issue is no longer significant in ecumenical discussions about technology, although it is clear from tensions in the Asian sub-continent that the use of nuclear weapons is still a real possibility. On the other hand, the end of the cold war saw the unrivalled ascendancy of the neo-liberal economic project known as the Washington Consensus. Discussions in the last decade of the century shifted to the role science and technology play in the context of globalization, in which "Western" science and technology, often represented by the products and pollution of giant multinational corporations, play such a powerful role in the lives of the people of the globe. This socio-economic context brings the ethics of the bio-technology industry into sharp relief.

THE CHURCHES' REFLECTION ON TECHNOLOGY AND SCIENCE

The ecumenical movement has provoked religious and theological reflection on the issue of science and technology in a way that has transcended the earlier confrontational approaches associated with evolution. While conservative and fundamentalist Protestant groups hold to "creation science" views, many churches have conformed to a more ecumenical and inclusive approach to the scientific endeavour and to its technological applications in modern life.

Reflection and grappling with the faith and ethical dimensions of science and technology have not only been addressed by the World Council of Churches, but by individual ecclesial bodies as well. Because of the perception by most Christians that their faith is integrally connected with ethics and the proper use of the material world, international confessional bodies, national ecclesial jurisdictions, regional and local church bodies have also spoken about the impact of science and technology. In Western Christianity many church groups have addressed issues that either directly or indirectly relate to

---

[37] *Overview of the World Council of Churches' Programme on Climate Change*, WCC, 1995, p.6.
[38] *Ibid.*, p.17.

science and technology. In a useful critical summary of the statements and other documents produced by ecclesial groups, Lutheran ethicist Mark Ellingsen analyses these areas: apartheid and racism, economic development and unemployment, ecology, nuclear armaments (peace and war), divorce, remarriage, polygamy, abortion, genetic engineering, social justice, and socio-political ideologies. The majority of these areas have either a direct or indirect relationship with the scientific and technological spheres.[39] Ellingsen's book *The Cutting Edge: How Churches Speak on Social Issues* makes reference to statements on social issues by over 270 churches, ecclesial bodies and agencies.

One of the most valuable aspects of Ellingsen's study is his analysis of the theological arguments used by various ecclesial bodies in reflection on social issues. Of particular interest for this chapter is his analysis of the theological arguments developed by various churches and ecclesial groups on issues related to science and technology. In the area of ecology, among the bodies whose statements are mentioned are the American Lutheran Church, the Baptist Union of New Zealand, the Evangelical Church in the Rhineland, the US National Council of Churches, the Canadian Council of Catholic Bishops, the papal encyclical *Redemptor Hominis* (1979), the Methodist Church of Malaysia, *The Resolutions of the Lambeth Conference (1988)*, the World Alliance of Reformed Churches and the Mennonite Church (USA), among many other churches and church-related bodies. At least 19 different theological warrants are given for various positions promulgated on ecological issues.[40]

Possibly the most significant contribution of one single church body to this field in the last thirty years of the century was the work of the Science, Religion and Technology (SRT) Project of the Church of Scotland.[41] The Project was established in 1970 to examine the impact of technology on society. It focused on issues of importance to technical experts, policy-makers, researchers and the public, and through the years contributed a Christian perspective to public debate in Britain and wider society in the area of science and technology. The SRT Project's most characteristic method of work was to draw to-

---

[39] Mark Ellingsen, *The Cutting Edge: How Churches Speak on Social Issues*, WCC, 1993.

[40] On this issue, Ellingsen writes: "All church statements explicitly addressing this issue call on the churches to work for better ecological balance. The only possible exception is a 1977 statement of the Evangelische Landeskirche in Baden, 'Wort zur Kernenergie', which insists that the concern with ecology must not be permitted to conflict with economic development. Differences emerge over the warrant they use to authorize their positions and how they relate ecology to the use of energy, particularly nuclear energy."

He lists the following theological warrants for these statements: "(1) Appeal to creation/view of human persons, (2) appeal to creation and Christology/the gospel, (3) appeal to creation, subordinated to the gospel/Christology, (4) appeal to creation and Christology, with creation subordinated to Christology, (5) appeal to creation, supplemented by warrants drawn from the second or third article of the creed, (6) appeal to creation, supplemented by and perhaps subordinated to warrants drawn from the second or third article, (7) appeal to creation and eschatology, (8) appeal to Christology/the gospel, (9) appeal to Christology/the gospel, supplemented by first-article warrants, (10) appeal to Christology/the gospel, supplemented by first- and third-article warrants, (11) appeal to the gospel and eschatology, (12) appeal to loci drawn from all three articles of the creed, (13) appeal to all three articles of the creed, with creation subordinated to redemption/Christology, (14) appeal to all three articles of the creed, with anthropology perhaps the prevailing warrant, (15) appeal to the Bible, (16) appeal to the commandment to love, (17) appeal to Christian ethical considerations and social responsibilities, (18) appeal to the concept of stewardship, (19) appeal to the nature of the Christian life-style/sanctification, (20) no clear theological warrant given for position." *Ibid.*, p.203. For the complete entry on "ecology" see pp.203-25.

[41] The information for this section is taken from the SRT Project web site which offers much information on contemporary discussions on the areas covered in this essay. See <www.srtp.org.uk

gether a multidisciplinary team, so that scientists, technical experts, theologians, representatives of civil society and other policy-makers could explore a specific issue in a collaborative manner. Such working groups and other SRTP research focused on nuclear power and its risks, polluting and military technologies, the internet, computer networks and information security, global warming and energy policy, patenting and bio-technology, genetically modified food and animals, cloning and stem cells, as well as the more general area of the interface of science and religious belief and the ethical limits of technology.

Conscious of the way in which the ethical issues of science and technology are framed by economic and political interests, Donald Bruce, the director of the SRT Project for the last decade of the century, wrote that the project was begun

> to address wider issues being raised by modern technology. Its concern was not only that the church would be well informed, but to stimulate balanced debate in the public at large and amongst those working within technology itself. On all the many issues it has examined, the SRT Project has sought to examine fairly and honestly, with no vested interests. Its reports and publications seek to present such a balance. Over the years our experience leads us to believe that there is no substitute for listening to all sides of the question, preferably round the same table. There are usually no easy answers, but with the insights of Christian ethics, SRT has often thrown new and relevant light on difficult and complex issues.[42]

The SRT Project always had a strong ecumenical emphasis. It worked with Action for Churches Together in Scotland, and the environmental issues network of the Churches Together in Britain and Ireland. It was involved with the church and society commission of the Conference of European Churches, was a founder member of the European Christian Environmental Network, and worked closely with the World Council of Churches from the 1970s. The Project also made many submissions to British parliamentary and government committees, as well as the European Parliament and Commission. It played a particularly significant role in European discussions about genetic engineering, owing to its early decision (1993) to set up a working group study on the ethics of genetic engineering in non-human life forms, which involved a range of specialists and leading figures in animal and plant genetics in Scotland and led to the publication of *Engineering Genesis*[43] in 1998.

THE ORTHODOX CHURCHES AND SCIENCE AND TECHNOLOGY

The Orthodox churches, in particular, because of their embodiment of the ancient patristic Eastern Christian tradition, have had an important impact on ecumenical reflections on science and technology, especially in the area of ecology. Orthodox theologian and long-time staff member of the WCC Gennadios Limouris has compiled Orthodox ecumenically related statements and texts in his volume *Orthodox Visions of Ecumenism*.[44] It is not generally recognized that the Orthodox in modern times have a his-

---

[42] See <www.srtp.org.uk/whatisrt.shtml>
[43] Donald and Ann Bruce, *Engineering Genesis: The Ethics of Genetic Engineering in Non-Human Species*, London, Earthscan, 1999.
[44] Gennadios Limouris ed., *Orthodox Visions of Ecumenism: Statements, Messages and Reports on the Ecumenical Movement – 1902-1992*, WCC, 1994. An earlier collection of Orthodox contributions to ecumenical reflection was Constantin G. Patelos ed., *The Orthodox Church in the Ecumenical Movement: Documents and Statements 1902-1975*, WCC, 1978.

tory of dealing with social issues of a wide variety, though this is indeed the case.[45] More recently, Paulos Mar Gregorios, a president of the WCC (1983-91) and the moderator of the world conference on "Faith, Science and the Future", contributed significantly to the Orthodox input on science and technology as related to the Christian faith. The year prior to the MIT conference Metropolitan Gregorios published a significant contribution presenting a cosmic, holistic, spiritual, ethical and theological perspective on the issue, titled *The Human Presence: An Orthodox View of Nature.*[46] In subsequent years he published volumes expanding and deepening the Orthodox approach to science and technology in his works *Science for Sane Societies*[47] and *Cosmic Man.*[48] At the MIT conference Gregorios made a plenary presentation on "Science and Faith: Complementary or Contradictory", in which he critically assessed the current methods of science and called for a "non-conceptual apprehension" of the created world in a liturgical, worshipful orientation. Nevertheless, the view was a corrective stance, coming down on the "complementary" aspect of his title:

> Such a non-conceptual apprehension cannot short-circuit or bypass the conceptual problems of science and its paradoxes, but must pass through them into the "cloud of unknowing", through the "taught ignorance" that goes beyond conceptual knowledge into silent adoration. Faith needs science, must come to terms with it, and work for new perceptions in both faith and science, through respectful collaboration and healthy self-criticism.[49]

Among the several other Orthodox contributions was a presentation by Fr Vitaly Borovoy, focusing on an area which was to receive significant Orthodox attention in the years to come – ecology: "Christian Perspectives on Creation in a Time of Ecological Unsustainability".[50] In it, he reaffirmed the crisis of the environment as a result of modern scientific attitudes and technological abuse. He issued a call to Christian faith and human action to overcome the ecological crisis, with special reference to the Russian philosopher-theologian Nicolay Fedorov (1828-1903), who called for a common struggle of all people against the corrupting forces of the ecological crisis.

The concern for the environment was included in two important Orthodox consultations held under the auspices of the JPIC sub-unit. These were a 1987 consultation on the theme "Orthodox Perspectives on Creation", in Sofia, Bulgaria,[51] and a consultation on "Orthodox Perspectives on Justice and Peace", held in Minsk, then in the Soviet Union, two years later, where some connection was made between ecology and peace and justice.[52] Geraldine Smyth provides a summary of the message of those two consultations:

---

[45] See chapter one, "The Tradition of Social Concern in the Orthodox Church", in Stanley Samuel Harakas, *Let Mercy Abound: Social Concern in the Greek Orthodox Church*, Brookline MA, Holy Cross, 1983. An extensive bibliography is found in the footnotes beginning with works published in the 1920s by Orthodox authors.

[46] WCC, 1978.

[47] Madras, Christian Literature Society, 1980.

[48] New York, Paragon, 1988.

[49] Roger L. Shinn and Paul Abrecht eds, *Faith and Science in an Unjust World: Report of the Churches' Conference on Faith, Science and the Future – Massachusetts Institute of Technology, Cambridge, USA, 12-24, 1979. Vol. 1, Plenary Presentations*, WCC, 1980, p.55.

[50] Ibid., pp.80-86.

[51] "Orthodox Perspectives on Creation", Inter-Orthodox Consultation, Sofia, Bulgaria, Oct. 24-Nov. 2, 1987, in *JPIC Resource Materials*, 74.1, 1988. Also in *Orthodox Visions of Ecumenism*, pp.116-26.

[52] "Orthodox Perspectives on Justice and Peace", Minsk, 1989, in *JPIC Resource Materials*, 6.4, 1989. Also in *Orthodox Visions of Ecumenism*, pp.150-57.

It was to be expected that one particular theological perspective which the Orthodox churches would bring to JPIC would be a trinitarian view of creation. This in fact emerged in the two conferences which were held in Sofia (1987) and in Minsk (1989). At Sofia, the human being was seen in the Orthodox understanding as "microcosm" of the whole creation, in order to stress the inextricable nexus between God, humanity and the rest of creation. There is an emphasis on human freedom, on the call to be co-worker with God and on the exercise of a priestly function for a reintegrated and transfigured creation. The doctrine is presented along traditional lines of creation ex nihilo, and there is an insistence that the cosmos has an integrity of its own and reflects the beauty of the Creator. The word "wholeness" recurs...

At Minsk, the creation perspective on justice and peace shows in a fresh way the interconnecting spirals linking justice, peace and creation. There is a particular dwelling on koinonia – the disruption of communion with God as the root of idolatry, injustice and exploitation. Jesus, by his death and resurrection, has made eternal peace between God, humanity and the created world. But Christians are called to "work synergetically"... with the spirit of God in the oikonomia for the eschatological transfiguration of creation through acting against injustice and active peace-making.[53]

These documents were an important starting place. They received from both Orthodox[54] and non-Orthodox[55] criticisms and correctives, but the "wholeness" of the vision that Orthodox brought to the issue of the integrity of creation was significant both for the Orthodox themselves and for their partners in dialogue.

In preparation for the WCC's Canberra assembly the Orthodox met in Crete at the end of 1989 to reflect on the theme of the assembly, "Come, Holy Spirit – Renew the Whole Creation". Limouris, who edited the proceedings, highlighted in his introduction the trinitarian, pneumatological, ecclesiological and sacramental dimensions of the theme as addressed by the consultation.[56] The author of this chapter, in his contribution "Giver of Life – Sustain Your Creation", addressed the role of the Holy Spirit and the material creation from theological, scientific and ecological perspectives. While connections among them are real, he cautioned that formulating theological doctrine on the basis of empirical science was extremely dangerous for theological truth. "[U]nlike the perspectives of science, which sees the physical world as primary, theology's perspective is different. It recognizes the Spirit as the die and the form and the mould in which the creation rests and has its being . . . Thus, from a patristic perspective it is not so proper to say that the Holy Spirit participates in the material world, but rather, it is more accurate to say that the material world participates in the Holy Spirit!"[57]

The report of the consultation thus bound the ecological concerns to the themes of the Holy Trinity, and "transcendence, communion, church, sacramental and particularly eucharistic life, transformation and glorification through holiness, foretaste of the kingdom within history through a constant *metanoia* and struggle against the powers of sin and evil".[58] In the face of a whole range of consequences bringing "disintegration and death", the report said,

---

[53] *A Way of Transformation*, pp.65-66.

[54] Of particular importance was Gennadios Limouris, "From Sofia to Minsk: Towards Seoul Seeking Justice, Peace and the Integrity of Creation: Orthodox Insights", *JPIC Resource Materials*, 7.5 .

[55] See *A Way of Transformation*, pp.66-68, from what appears to be a liberation theology perspective, and Konrad Raiser on ecumenical ecclesiological reasons (*Ecumenism in Transition*, WCC, 1991, pp.118-20.)

[56] Gennadios Limouris ed., *Come, Holy Spirit – Renew the Whole Creation: An Orthodox Approach to the Seventh Assembly of the World Council of Churches, Canberra, Australia, 6-21 February, 1991*, 4-6.

[57] *Ibid.*, p.91. The difference in these priorities would explode at Canberra to create sharp divisions between the theological methods implied in them.

[58] *Orthodox Visions of Ecumenism*, p.162, 163.

we call upon the Holy Spirit to intervene and sustain God's creation. We acknowledge and confess that salvation can only come from God, and that the Holy Spirit as the "giver of life" can help us find a way out of this vicious circle of life and death, of light and darkness, in which creation is caught up.

The ecological concern in the Orthodox church received an intensified focus on 1 September 1989, when Ecumenical Patriarch Dimitrios proclaimed an annual observance to be known as the Day for the Protection of the Environment.[59] Under the present Ecumenical Patriarch, Bartholomew, an active programme of "ecumenical seminars" was developed throughout the 1990s. Two, held on vessels on the Black Sea and the River Danube, issued a call to clean up these polluted bodies of water. In a presentation given during a pastoral visit to the US Patriarch Bartholomew addressed the human practices that lead to ecological destruction. He drew widespread reaction, including this report from James M. Wall in *The Christian Century* (US): "Bartholomew has been called the 'green patriarch' because of his strong support for earth issues... He declared, 'To commit a crime against the natural world is a sin. When we lose species, land and creatures, we lose a part of God's creative process, not through natural selection but by deliberate destruction on the part of an economic system driven by the god of profit.'"

THE BIOLOGICAL MANIPULATION OF LIFE

Several other specific areas regarding developing scientific discoveries and technological expansion came into the focus of ecumenical concerns. The revolutionary developments regarding genetic engineering and bio-technology were one case in point. Genetic engineering and bio-technology hold great promise for human good, but also provoke significant concern and anxiety.

The field of bio-ethics as a modern discipline can be dated from the publication of the *Encyclopedia of Bioethics* in 1979.[60] Christian thinkers and church leaders from the earliest period had addressed issues which are considered today to be part of the discipline of bio-ethics, such as physical life, health, illness, sexuality, abortion, medicine and death.[61] Nevertheless, in the modern sense of the term bio-ethics can be understood as having its origins in 1953 with the discovery of the DNA molecule. Twenty years later scientists announced the theoretical scientific ability to alter the gene structure of living organisms. While some hailed the therapeutic potentials of the new methodology, others feared the consequences which could arise from such power.

The potentialities of human intervention in biological processes previously beyond manipulation created numerous ethical and social questions. Some of the issues arising from the new developments dealt with various means of assisted reproduction, genetic screening for inherited illnesses, somatic and reproductive gene therapy, and the elimination and the creation of whole lines of plant and animal life through gene manipulation. Issues of control also came quickly to the fore. For example, questions regarding the public assumption of the costs of the development of gene manipulation and the private commercial exploitation of the research results were provoked. The impacts of this revolutionary new technology on women, minorities and third-world peoples are other

---

[59] *Ibid.*, pp.171-72.
[60] Warren T. Reich ed., *Encyclopedia of Bioethics*, 5 vols, New York, Free Press/Macmillan, 1978. See also 2nd ed. 1995.
[61] Donald L. Numbers and Darrel W. Amundsen, *Caring and Curing: Health and Medicine in Western Religious Traditions*, New York, Macmillan, 1986.

vital and important issues. Associated with all these concerns were numerous related bio-ethical questions.

The earliest WCC attention to the issue of human experimentation took place at a consultation in 1968 at the Ecumenical Institute in Bossey, Switzerland.[62] In the following decade, the Church and Society sub-unit of the WCC brought together in a series of meetings scientists, policy-makers and theologians to address some of these issues. Their work culminated in a consultation co-sponsored by the sub-unit and the Christian Medical Commission in Zurich in 1973. Its report was published with the title *Genetics and the Quality of Life*,[63] and served as the basis for the MIT conference discussion on bio-ethical questions. The two main plenary presentations by microbiology professor Jonathan King and Christian ethics professor Karen Lebacqz raised the moral and social hazards of the new biological developments. King suggested,

> In the area of human experimentation and genetic manipulation, the WCC should take an active role in ensuring that the development of very sophisticated technologies for helping a small number of individuals does not obscure the pressing need for eliminating the causes of disease and genetic damage.[64]

The fourth section of the MIT conference was devoted to "Ethical Issues in the Biological Manipulation of Life".[65] The report is divided into six parts, the last of which consists of a comprehensive set of recommendations. Themes discussed included eugenics, genetic counselling, prenatal diagnosis and abortion, artificial insemination, genetic engineering, behaviour control, self-medication, tranquillizers, accountability, self-induced drug experience, personality and experience, genetic determinants of human personality and the debate about socio-biology, the impaired personality and other ways of manipulating the human mind. The final two substantive sections dealt with distributive justice in the use of scarce medical resources, and experimentation on human and other vertebrates. These topics are listed here, neither because they exhaust the potential themes of bio-ethics, nor because the responses made are irrefutable or exhaustive. They simply show a wide-ranging concern.

The general impression derived from the report, however, serves to illustrate the broad ecumenical faith perspectives regarding contemporary science and technology. The old defensiveness of religion before science is no longer present. While there is an acceptance of the place of science and technology in the modern world, the unquestioning awe before science that characterized the pre-atomic period has also dissipated. Present throughout the report, and illustrative of the ecumenical stance before science and technology, is a balanced appreciation for its promise, but also a realistic assessment of its potential unintended and intended negative consequences.

While the Christian Medical Commission meeting in Zurich in 1973 and the WCC conference on "Faith, Science and the Future" at MIT in 1979 both anticipated the ethical implications of the emerging field of genetic engineering, it was only by the last decade of the century that society was confronted by the actual reality of genetic manipulation. Perhaps the most celebrated event was the "cloning" of Dolly the sheep at the

---

[62] J. Robert Nelson, "Bio-ethics", in *Dictionary of the Ecumenical Movement*, p.116.
[63] *Genetics and the Quality of Life: Report of a Consultation – Church and Society/Christian Medical Commission – Zurich, June, 1973*, WCC, 1973. Also published as Charles Birch and Paul Abrecht eds, *Genetics and the Quality of Life*, Potts Point NSW, Oxford Publ., 1975.
[64] *Faith and Science in an Unjust World*, vol. 1, p.271.
[65] *Ibid.*, vol. 2, pp.49-68.

Roslin institute in 1997; but there was an almost daily discovery of new genetic information, a race to decode the human genome, and an explosion of hope that diseases such as cancer, Parkinson's, diabetes and Alzheimer's would find a cure via genetic engineering. This drew a range of Christian scholars into discussion with this new technology, but there was very little time for formal ecclesial or ecumenical responses. The SRT Project of the Church of Scotland was perhaps the first institutional forum to seek a coherent response.

Alongside the bio-medical ethical issues involved in human genetic engineering, the 1990s saw the emergence of a new range of ethical issues to do with the manipulation of non-human forms of life, and particularly plants. The so-called "green revolution" of the 1970s led to the widespread use of fertilizer and agrochemicals in the developed and developing worlds, and to the emergence of giant multinational companies with a financial interest in supplying the food market. Genetic engineering introduced the possibility of changing the genetic make-up of seeds, and thus of making them able to withstand certain environmental pressures, or certain herbicides. Ethical concerns were raised about the manipulation of life involved in creating these genetically modified organisms (GMOs), as well as the impact that this might have upon bio-diversity. However, this issue took science and technology beyond the ethics of the laboratory because of the way in which food supply, hunger and poverty are linked to economic justice, and the way these issues are further exacerbated by the very global economy which is driven by the bio-technology companies. Many of the central themes raised by the MIT conference, and particularly the location of science and technology in an "unjust world", began to return as fundamental loci for theological reflection.[66] However, in thus making the connection between science, technology, globalization and economic injustice, these emerging debates about bio-technology and genetic engineering signalled many of the concerns which would characterize the church's response to science, technology and the environment in the last years of the century and on into the new millennium.

THE SPREAD OF CONCERN 1995-2000

Recent WCC-sponsored or approved projects in the area of religion, science and technology tend towards the practical implementation of initiatives in specific areas of concern, rather than theoretical questions on the human relationship with science and technology. The WCC's eighth assembly at Harare in 1998 did not directly address science, technology and faith in any of its reports. The only report that consciously embodied to some extent the approaches developed earlier was the statement on globalization.[67] The unit on Justice, Peace and Creation concerns (JPC) has based its work on "a life-centred ethic" with a quotation from the Harare globalization statement:

> It is our deep conviction that the challenge of globalization should become a central emphasis of the work of the WCC, building upon many significant efforts . . . The vision behind globalization includes a competing vision to the Christian commitment to the oikoumene, the unity of humankind and the whole inhabited earth. . . We should not subject ourselves to the vision behind [globalization], but strengthen our alternative ways towards visible unity in diversity, towards an oikoumene of faith and solidarity.

---

[66] Note that the WCC established a working group on the theme in 2001, just after the period covered by this volume.
[67] The reader is referred to the WCC website wcc-coe.org for further documentation.

Globalization is understood as subjugating all values to "corporate globalization, which is guided by the neo-liberal economic model and supported by modern technology and media". The concern is the pervasive impact of corporate globalization not only in the economic and political spheres, but also in that it "has cultural, ecological, ethical, religious and even ecclesiological implications as well".[68]

The JPC web-site also devotes significant space to the issue of climate change, continuing a programme in place since 1988 in the WCC. This programme called for technological changes in energy, transportation and economic policies that would significantly challenge the climate-changing impact of industrial emissions, carefully monitoring and participating as an NGO in the Rio Earth Summit in 1992 and the Kyoto Protocol deliberations in Japan in 1997. The WCC took a position in opposition to a condition of the protocol allowing for "emission trading" between developed and undeveloped nations. A consultation on "Equity and Emission Trading" in May 2000 in Saskatoon, Canada, based its conclusions on different and more just approaches to the issue.[69]

Climate change was also a concern of the WCC at the sixth Conference of the Parties (COP6) in the Framework Convention on Climate Change (UNFCCC) in The Hague, in 2000:

> The delegation challenged the world's richer polluting countries to actually reduce carbon dioxide emissions that raise world temperatures rather than "buy their way out of the problem through paying for projects in other countries". David Hallman, coordinator of the WCC's climate change programme, said, "emissions trading is unethical and risks exacerbating inequities between rich and poor countries". The WCC proposed the adoption of a "global atmospheric commons model" at COP6 and discussed this at an ecumenical workshop co-sponsored by Dutch churches.[70]

Another JPC concern is with the impact of "new technologies such as micro-electronics and bio-technology". In reference to the latter, the World Trade Organization agreement on Trade-Related Aspects of Intellectual Property Rights (TRIPS) "debate on patenting of life, and proliferation of genetically modified organisms (GMOs) especially through agribusiness, are probably the most important areas of concern at this moment". It has indicated opposition to the patenting of life forms, cloning of human beings, and express concerns about the risks involved in the "manipulation of the human genome line, misuse of knowledge of human genes, and dangerous consequences of the proliferation of genetically modified organisms".

---

[68] In the Justice, Peace and Creation concerns web page section "Ecumenical Earth" one of the paragraphs in the entry titled "A Life-Centred Ethics" reinstates the concept of "sustainable communities", from much earlier WCC reflection: "In this context of growing inequality, concentration of power, social exclusion and ecological destruction, people are longing for *life with dignity in just and sustainable communities*" (emphasis in original).

[69] "An alternate approach, which would be more sustainable and equitable, could be a Global Atmospheric Commons Model, which would be based on an equitable allocation of emission rights such as per capita convergence (i.e. long-term sustainable) level. Countries which use the global atmospheric commons in excess of the convergence level would have to pay a user penalty into a Global Atmospheric Commons Fund. The fund would assist impoverished countries and those with economies in transition to move towards a non-carbon economy focusing on renewable energy sources such as solar, biomass, wind and small scale hydroelectric." Included on the JPC site are a summary, as well as the text of the full statement.

[70] "Destroying the Atmosphere is a Sin", in *WCC News*, Dec. 2000, no. 4, p.4. See also WCC press release PR-00-34, 14 Nov. 2000, "'You can work for life or for death. We in the WCC have opted for life' – Ecumenical Team at the UN Climate Conference in the Hague" by Mirjam Schubert.

The JPC periodical *Echoes* focused one of its issues on the theme "Earth as Mother", in a particularized approach to ecological issues, indicating the impact and importance of ecological concerns to Indigenous Peoples, various regions in Africa, and women.[71] In 2000 *Echoes* also published an article on genetic engineering titled "Silent Death: The Possible Abuse of Genetic Engineering for Biological Warfare". The author, Jan van Aken, is co-founder of the Sunshine Project, which "gathers information on the potential harmful military use of bio-technology. The Project is concerned that abuse of some scientific advances may undermine international agreements on peace, disarmament and environment."[72]

As part of the WCC's Mission and Evangelism programme, a small but consistent and ongoing effort was the work on "health, healing and wholeness". An example of its concerns was its involvement in the fight against AIDS during the 13th international AIDS conference in Durban, South Africa, in 2000. It worked to enable the International Christian AIDS Network to participate in the conference, running a workshop on innovative approaches by Christian groups.[73] Also involved in AIDS work, especially in Africa, were Church World Service and the National Council of the Churches of Christ in the US through "A Resolution on AIDS in Africa" in 2000. Church World Service has emphasized innovative ways, including low-cost nutritional supplements, to seek to overcome the ravages of this disease in Africa that takes 6000 lives a day.

Concern with AIDS worldwide was adopted as one of two focuses for a new ecumenical effort, the Ecumenical Advocacy Alliance that was launched in Geneva on 9 December 2000 when "WCC general secretary Konrad Raiser said the time has come to take a courageous new step together to promote justice, peace and the integrity of creation". Out of 170 suggested topics for the Alliance's efforts for the next four years, two issues were selected: global economic justice, with a focus on global trade, and the ethics of life, with a focus on HIV/AIDS.[74]

AFTERWORD

The last half decade has seen widespread sensitivity and concern with issues that can be understood as being related to faith, science and technology, beyond the direct influence of the WCC and other organized ecumenical efforts.

Any science-based technology is capable of helping improve life. However, often unintended negative consequences can arise for some or all, especially for those on the periphery. Christians concerned for the well-being of others must speak and act on behalf of those who cannot speak and act in the halls of power and authority. Where possible, faith must enable the disadvantaged to demand and achieve justice, peace and the integrity of the created reality of which all are an integral part.

Concern for issues of faith, science and technology has moved in the final half-decade of the 20th century to practical questions, and it is clear that there will be continued ecumenical involvement with these issues as a consequence of the churches' commitment to Christian ethics and action in obedience to the triune God of all creation.

---

[71]"The Earth as Mother", in *Echoes*, 16, 1999.
[72] Issue 18, 2000, pp.30-34.
[73]*WCC News*, Aug. 2000, p.4
[74] "Global trade and HIV/AIDS first priority for new Ecumenical Advocacy Alliance", WCC press update, 11 Dec. 2000, The full text of the Alliance document, "A Covenant for Action", as well as of this communiqué are available by request or on this website: Communiqué A Covenant for Action.

BIBLIOGRAPHY

Abrecht, Paul et al. eds, *Faith, Science and the Future: Preparatory Readings for a World Conference, Cambridge, Mass., July 12-14, 1979*, WCC, 1978, 236p.

Birch, Charles and Abrecht, Paul eds, *Genetics and the Quality of Life*, Oxford, Pergamon, 1975, 232p.

Burning Issues: Papers from the Consultation in Cambridge, June 20-26, 1977, and Papers from the Consultation in Zürich, July 11-16, 1977 (Anticipation, 25, 1979) WCC, 1979, 79p.

Bube, Richard H., *Putting It All Together: Seven Patterns for Relating Science and the Christian Faith*, New York, Univ. Press of America, 1995, 213p.

"Church and Society: Ecumenical Perspective: Essays in Honour of Paul Abrecht", *The Ecumenical Review*, 37, 1, Jan. 1985.

Coste, René, *Sauvegarde et gérance de la création*, Paris, Desclée, 1991, 290p.

Derr, Thomas Sieger, *Ecology and Human Liberation: A Theological Critique of the Use and Abuse of Our Birthright*, WCC, 1973, 111p.

Ellingsen, Mark, *The Cutting Edge: How Churches Speak on Social Issues*, WCC, 1993, 370p.

Facing up to Nuclear Power, WCC, 1975, 43p.

Francis, John and Abrecht, Paul eds, *Facing up to Nuclear Power: A Contribution to the Debate on the Risks and Potentialities of the Large-Scale Use of Nuclear Energy*, Edinburgh, Saint Andrew Press, 1976, 244p.

Gill, David Muir, *From Here to Where?: Technology, Faith and the Future of Man: Report on an Exploratory Conference, Geneva, June 28-July 4, 1970*, WCC, 1970, 111p.

Gosling, David, *A New Earth: Covenanting for Justice, Peace and the Integrity of Creation*, London, CCBI, 1992, 108p.

Granberg-Michaelson, Wesley, *Redeeming the Creation: The Rio Earth Summit: Challenges for the Churches*, WCC, 1992, 90p.

Hallman, David G. ed., *Ecotheology: Voices from South and North*, WCC, 1994, 316p.

Hallman, David G., *Spiritual Values for Earth Community*, WCC, 2000, 134p.

Harakas, Stanley Samuel, *Let Mercy Abound: Social Concern in the Greek Orthodox Church*, Brookline MA, Holy Cross, 1983, 188p.

Just Development for Fullness of Life: A Responsible Christian Participation, WCC, 1982, 138p.

Limouris, Gennadios ed., *Justice, Peace and the Integrity of Creation: Insights from Orthodoxy*, WCC, 1990, 126p.

Limouris, Gennadios ed., *Orthodox Visions of Ecumenism: Statements, Messages and Reports on the Ecumenical Movement 1902-1992*, WCC, 1994, 283p.

Moltmann, Jürgen, *Creating a Just Future: The Politics of Peace and the Ethics of Creation in a Threatened World*, London, SCM Press, 1989, 103p.

Mudge, Lewis S. and Wieser, Thomas eds, *Democratic Contracts for Sustainable and Caring Societies: What Can Churches and Christian Communities Do?*, WCC, 2000, 197p.

Murray, Robert, *The Cosmic Covenant: Biblical Themes of Justice, Peace and the Integrity of Creation*, London, Sheed and Ward, 1992, 233p.

Niles, D. Preman ed., *Between the Flood and the Rainbow: Interpreting the Conciliar Process of Mutual Commitment (Covenant) to Justice, Peace and the Integrity of Creation*, WCC, 1992, 192p.

Niles, Preman ed., *Justice, Peace and the Integrity of Creation: Documents from an Ecumenical Process of Commitment: Final Report*, London, Council of World Mission, 1994, 228p.

Niles, D. Preman, *Resisting the Threats to Life: Covenanting for Justice, Peace and the Integrity of Creation*, WCC, 1989, 85p.

Now Is the Time: Final Document and Other Texts: World Convocation on Justice, Peace and the Integrity of Creation, Seoul, 1990, Report, WCC, 1990, 60p.

O'Brien, David J. and Shannon, Thomas A. eds, *Catholic Social Thought: The Documentary Heritage*, Maryknoll NY, Orbis, 1992, 688p.

The Official Documentation of the European Ecumenical Assembly, Basel, Switzerland, 15-21 May 1989, Geneva, CEC, 1989, 334p.

Pasztor, Janos ed., *Energy for My Neighbour: Perspectives from Asia: Towards More Just and More Sustainable Policies of Energy Development*, WCC, 1981, 158p.

Paulos Mar Gregorios, *Cosmic Man*, New York, Paragon, 1988, 274p.

Paulos Gregorios, *The Human Presence: An Orthodox View of Nature*, WCC, 1978, 104p.

Paulos Gregorios, *Science for Sane Societies: Reflections on Faith, Science and the Future in the Indian Context*, Madras, CLS, 1980, 176p.

Preston, Ronald H., *Confusions in Christian Social Ethics: Problems for Geneva and Rome*, Grand Rapids MI, Eerdmans, 1995, 202p.

Rasmussen, Larry L., *Earth Community, Earth Ethics*, WCC, 1996, 366p.

Santa Ana, Julio de, *Sustainability and Globalization*, WCC, 1998, 143p.

Schmitthenner, Ulrich, *Contributions of Churches and Civil Society to Justice, Peace and the Integrity of Creation*, Frankfurt, Verlag für Interkulturelle Kommunikation, 1999, 332p.

Science and Technology for Human Development: The Ambiguous Future and the Christian Hope, Report [of the] World Conference Held in Bucharest, Romania, 24 June-2 July 1974, WCC, 1974, 43p. (*Anticipation*, 19, Nov. 1974).

Shinn, Roger L. and Abrecht, Paul eds, *Faith and Science in an Unjust World: Report of the World Council of Churches' Conference on Faith, Science and the Future, Massachusetts Institute of Technology, Cambridge, USA, 12-14 July 1979*, 2 vols, WCC, 1980.

Shrader-Frechette, Kristin ed., *Nuclear Energy and Ethics*, WCC, 1991, 233p.

Smyth, Geraldine S., *A Way of Transformation: A Theological Evaluation of the Conciliar Process of Mutual Commitment (Covenant) to Justice, Peace and the Integrity of Creation, World Council of Churches, 1983-1991*, Dublin, no publ., 1992, 2 vols.

Solms, Friedhelm ed., *European Churches and the Energy Issue: Official Statements, Reports, Comments, 1975-1979*, Heidelberg, Forschungsstätte der Evangelischen Studiengemeinschaft, 1980, 193p.

Sustainable Growth: A Contradiction in Terms?, Geneva, Visser 't Hooft Endowment Fund for Leadership Development, 1993, 112p.

Thomas, M.M. and Abrecht, Paul, *Christians in the Technical and Social Revoutions of Our Time: The Official Report [of the World Conference on Church and Society] with a Description of the Conference*, WCC, 1967, 232p.

Urban, Linwood, *A Short History of Christian Thought*, rev. & expanded ed., New York, Oxford Univ. Press, 1995, 461p.

Wellman, David J., *Sustainable Communities*, WCC, 2001, 206p.

16
Diakonia in the Ecumenical Movement

Richard D.N. Dickinson

Critics of the ecumenical movement and the World Council of Churches in particular are fond of saying that the movement and Council have become obsessed with social issues at the expense of church unity and spirituality. Such criticism comes from outsiders as well as many who remain loyal to the Council. That is an easy, though misguided, assertion prompted by the churches' major commitments of energies and resources over the past forty years to diaconal, or "service", ministries. Clearly, a review of the WCC's activities – in meetings, conferences, publications, and deployment of financial resources – during the post-1965 period reveals diakonia as a major preoccupation. What critics miss, however, is the integral connection between issues of church unity, spiritual growth, theological reflection and diaconal witness.

This emphasis on diakonia, Christian witness through service, has deep ecumenical roots. From its inception the ecumenical movement, merging Life and Work, Faith and Order, and the International Missionary Council, has understood diakonia to be a central feature of its identity. That identity has been shaped not only through theological and biblical reflection, but also through the social traumas of the past century: the great depression, two world wars and many more limited conflicts, the Holocaust, struggles against political, economic and cultural colonialism, the enormous inequities between the rich and poor, and – more positively – the worldwide, UN-generated emphasis on "development".

Thus, more recent ecumenical emphasis on the nature and shape of diakonia has grown out of the seed-beds of major conferences at Stockholm, Lausanne, Tambaram, Oxford, Amsterdam and Evanston. More specifically, that emphasis is rooted in the suggestive and still-important ecumenical discussions about "responsible society" and "middle axioms" as foci for Christian views of society. It is deeply indebted to the discussions in the mid-1950s on the role of churches in the midst of "rapid social change", leading to the too-often overlooked Salonika conference in 1959.[1]

While this chapter focuses on those churches actively associated with the WCC, it is important to recognize that the Roman Catholic Church also played a significant role in lifting up issues of diakonia before the world. The germinal document on joy and hope *Gaudium et Spes* ("The Church in the Modern World") of Vatican II appeared in 1966 and sounded an alarm:

---

[1] *Dilemmas and Opportunities: Christian Action in Rapid Social Change: Report of an International Ecumenical Study Conference, Thessalonica, July 25-August 2, 1959*, WCC, 1959.

> In no other age has mankind enjoyed such an abundance of wealth, resources and economic well-being, and yet a huge proportion of the people of the world is plagued by hunger and extreme need... At no time have men had such a keen sense of freedom, only to be faced by new forms of slavery in living and thinking.[2]

Just a year later, Paul VI argued strenuously for the poor in his encyclical *Populorum Progressio* ("Development of Peoples"), giving an eloquent description of the inequities between nations and the reasons – unjust trade, for example – for them. Clearly, the pope was not only calling for more compassion, but also for a sacrificial promotion of justice. Even though the early prospect of closer collaboration between the WCC and the Roman Catholic Church through Society, Development and Peace (SODEPAX) did not fully materialize, on many issues there is a continuing partnership of witness between the two bodies.

Further, to concentrate on the diaconal witness of the WCC – while necessary for this volume – underplays two other main church-related actors: the growing involvement of evangelical and Pentecostal bodies, and the vast number of local and regional efforts by church groups in struggles for justice and dignity.

For the WCC, undoubtedly the watershed event was the 1966 Geneva world conference on Church and Society, conceived and organized by the Council's Study department,[3] the seminal event that catalyzed and set the tone for four decades. Why did Geneva 1966 have such an impact?

Following an extremely significant consultation, called by the WCC Division of Inter-Church Aid, Refugee and World Service (DICARWS) at Swanwick, England, in July 1966, on the role of diakonia in contemporary society, the Geneva world conference seemed to be a *kairos* moment when forces converged with inescapable urgency and power. There emerged a new force in the ethical reflection of the churches. The organizers of the conference made a concerted effort to hear voices from the third world, from persons on the "underside of history", to use the apt and provocative phrase of Gustavo Gutiérrez. They took seriously the diversity of cultural environments in which Christians and churches seek to live faithfully. The debate became more truly ecumenical, more world encompassing, than ever before.

This chapter on diakonia reviews the major moral, conceptual and operational changes and emphases that have emerged over the past decades. Finally, it suggests a typology of theological grounding for these changing emphases. Because the topic is so broad, reflections will be drawn largely, although not exclusively, from the experiences of DICARWS (later known as CICARWS, the Commission on Inter-Church Aid, Refugee and World Service) and the WCC Commission on the Churches' Participation in Development (CCPD, established in 1970).

It is important to acknowledge that by paying primary attention to CICARWS and CCPD the erroneous view that the ecumenical movement starts with and radiates from Geneva may be reinforced. The reality is different. Much of the vitality, creativity and social relevance of the movement as a whole have been incubated in the corporate life and struggles of Christians in local and regional settings. The WCC is a crucial part, but only

---

[2] "Gaudium et Spes: Pastoral Constitution on the Church in the Modern World", in Austin Flannery ed., *Vatican Council II: The Conciliar and Post Conciliar Documents*, vol. 1, Collegeville MN, Liturgical Press, 1992, p.906.

[3] Paul Abrecht and M.M. Thomas, *Christians in the Technical and Social Revolutions of Our Time*, WCC, 1967.

a part, of that larger ecumenical network. The many specific contributions stemming from Asia, Africa, Latin America, the Pacific, the Middle East – to say nothing of regional and denominational meetings and experiences – have shaped the ecumenical vision of diakonia.

However, to concentrate on the work of CICARWS and CCPD may not be as limiting as it first appears. As a living organism, the ecumenical family as a whole is influenced by all its other parts. Concerns, experiments, new insights are not the monopoly of any one part. Mutuality, reinforcement and challenge move quite naturally across the spectrum. Indeed, there has been so much cross-fertilization that it has often seemed that there was too much duplication of effort. At times, there may have been an inclination to think bureaucratically and competitively, to protect turf. The larger picture, happily, is one of mutual edification and challenge, of differing angles of vision on the same realities, of emerging common perspectives.

CONCEPTUAL CHANGES

What is the most effective way to describe conceptual changes over this period? A chronological approach is in keeping with the WCC's emphasis on a dialectical interaction between theory and practice, each informing the other in a pattern of "action/reflection". Changes in concepts are often a response to new situations, and changes in practice are often responses to new theories. Of course, this chronological review does not do full justice to the complexity of the debate. Further, these church debates have been greatly influenced by enormously rich and probing secular debates about development, e.g., in the United Nations. Social scientists have become major partners of the churches in these conversations. What follows is an effort to identify crucial changes in how the ecumenical family has thought about diakonia.

Moratorium

Precipitated in part by the moratorium on grants challenge, the ecumenical churches were forced into a sustained process of reflection on the nature of diakonia. A moratorium on aid through grants had been called for by a number of Christians in Africa and Asia as a challenge to force "donors" and "recipients" to explore and rectify the problems on both sides created by such grants. What was diaconal responsibility in the midst of new challenges and emerging insights from third-world churches? Did a preoccupation with sharing material resources tacitly impede the deeper meanings of the gospel? In what sense do all parties in an exchange have "empty hands"[4] – a capacity to receive as well as to give?

At a deeper level there was a growing awareness that societies vary dramatically in basic values. What is "development"? Consider, for example, how "liberation theology" has been variously underscored in Africa, Asia and Latin America. No one understanding of development, or of diakonia, fits all situations; no single tactic is appropriate to all.

Moral urgency

In 1965 most people were naïve enough to imagine that the biggest challenge facing the churches was that they were not sufficiently aware of the scandalous disparities between

---

[4] *Empty Hands: An Agenda for the Churches. Study Guide on the Ecumenical Sharing of Resources for Use by Churches, Local Congregations and Other Groups*, WCC, 1980.

the world's one-third relatively affluent people and its two-thirds poor. The primary problem was lack of moral urgency. The challenge to churches, governments and intergovernmental organizations was to make more financial resources and technical assistance available to the poor, and to arouse public consciousness to the plight of the poor.

Not only did the poor need greater financial assistance; in many cases they needed technical advice, even though the technical level of projects was frequently rudimentary or intermediary. Relying on a "stages to growth"[5] paradigm for development, some argued that large numbers of projects could be based on "appropriate technology", which, for many in the poorer countries, came to symbolize that the rich thought that second-best technology was good enough for the poor. Predictably, this debate was so psychologically volatile that it became confused with the "small is beautiful" approach to development. In any case, the WCC started Specialized Assistance for Social Projects (SASP) to assist projects with technical advice. For several years a network of advisers made themselves available to assist in technical aspects of development projects. Increasing emphasis was put on sharing of information and advice from one project to others, often South to South. By 1975 the SASP function had been reduced significantly, though remnants remained within CCPD.

By the time of the joint 1968 Roman Catholic-WCC Beirut conference on development and the Uppsala assembly of the WCC the same year, a more complex perspective on development was emerging. Under the influence of the charter of Algiers and the Group of 77,[6] some argued vehemently and cogently that the poor needed more equitable trading relationships far more than outright aid. There was considerable deliberation about the terms of aid and the explicit or implicit "strings attached" to most aid. Recognizing that a great deal of aid benefited the donor as well as the poor, a widespread debate emerged about the "myth of aid". Already by the mid-late 1960s, there was a growing conviction that simple moral urgency – even as difficult as it was to arouse – was only a small step in the right direction. The Swanwick consultation of 1966, under the leadership of Leslie Cooke, pointed in new directions, from relief towards justice and root causes.[7]

Justice, self-reliance, economic growth

By the early 1970s, conversations about development became much more complex. Following the Uppsala assembly, the Commission on the Churches' Participation in Development was formed in 1970. Two major Montreux conferences, in 1970 and 1974, began to flesh out components of the meaning of development. Largely under the influence of the Indian agricultural economist, Sam Parmar, three elements were deemed essential: justice, self-reliance and economic growth. This appears to be the first time in ecumenical discussion that "self-reliance" occupied a prominent place, and subtly it began to shift attention from aggregate economic indices – though growth still played a key role since, as Parmar argued at Montreux in 1970, "we are not in the business of redis-

---

[5] W.W. Rostow, *The Stages of Economic Growth*, Cambridge, Harvard Univ. Press, 1960.

[6] The Group of 77 was established in June 1964 by 77 developing countries at the end of the first session of the UN Conference on Trade and Development (UNCTAD) to provide the developing world with a means to articulate and promote collective economic interests. UNCTAD adopted the Algiers Charter in 1967 as a call to third-world solidarity to work together to end the deteriorating economies of the developing world through its own actions.

[7] Commission on Inter-Church Aid, Refugee and World Service, *Consultation Digest, Swanwick, 1966*, WCC, 1966.

tributing poverty"[8] – to what happens, or should happen, to individuals and groups in the development process. How were the identity and living conditions of the poor changed for the better? This focus on people, as individuals and communities, became a core criterion in promoting and assessing what the churches should be about.

It was no accident, therefore, that greater justice in trading relationships was perceived to be a central feature of authentic development. Trading under the right terms would not only generate far more money for poor countries than even greatly increased aid, but would also reflect more fully a genuine reciprocity in which the poor are contributors rather than beggars, self-reliant rather than totally dependent. A further benefit of more attention to equitable trade rather than direct aid was that already considerable disenchantment had set in with the willingness or capacity of governments to help those in their countries most in need. Big infrastructure projects could be only a part of the picture. Thus the importance of better trading relationships – e.g. modestly higher prices for raw materials such as sugar, copper and coffee, fairer tariff provisions – came to be a major preoccupation of some ecumenical conversations, even though these improved trading relationships were seen as complementary to, and not a substitute for, generous direct aid. Since the churches were not themselves in significant trading relationships with poorer nations, their role vis-a-vis trade was primarily to advocate greater justice.

Comprehensive development

A main feature of development thinking in the early 1970s was a commitment to working comprehensively and strategically, with clear priorities and a plan of action. Development was to be systematic, planned and cumulative. Many ecumenical efforts had seemed too random, too laissez-faire, unconnected with any overall plan. CCPD's first major initiative was to select six "counterpart groups", later called "partners", in as many different countries. These counterpart groups were supported through the Ecumenical Development Fund. They clustered "comprehensive" development schemes under one umbrella, combining several different but complementary initiatives – e.g., improved and diversified farming, development of cooperatives and marketing. By 1974, the initial counterparts were in Cameroon, the Caribbean, Ethiopia, India, Indonesia and Uruguay. Despite the obvious dangers of creating long-term dependencies, such counterparts were to plan, supervise and evaluate their own programmes, with the tacit understanding that support from outside would be sustained for at least several years. While minuscule in relation to the enormous global needs, these counterpart groups would be experiments pointing towards a new style of church-sponsored programmes.

Towards the late 1970s the partner group strategy had declined dramatically. Some had experienced internal management difficulties; some were becoming cumbersome and costly bureaucracies; self-reliance was threatened and funds coming through Geneva were being claimed for other purposes. But most significant in the decline of partner groups were changing perceptions of development and the emergence of new initiatives thought to be more congruent with these new ideas. Nevertheless, these partner groups had been an important stage in the evolution of the churches' diaconal service.

---

[8] Pamela Gruber ed., *Fetters of Injustice: Report of an Ecumenical Consultation on Ecumenical Assistance to Development Projects, 26-31 January, 1970, Montreux, Switzerland*, WCC, 1970, pp.48-49.

Root causes and structural realities

As reflection on the nature of development deepened, increased attention was focused on root causes rather than superficial symptoms. What good were Band-Aids while the world's poor were being overwhelmed with insuperable structural obstacles? Did even massive aid, more justice in trading relationships, greater technical assistance, or inter-governmental cooperation really serve the needs of the poor if the system itself simply reinforced and perpetuated the privileged position of the already powerful? Criticisms of the predominant models of development became more telling. Aggregate measure-ments of development progress, like gross national product, caloric consumption and per capita income were seen not to reveal much about the fate of real people, especially the poor.

The view that there are evolutionary, perhaps necessary, "stages of growth" was dis-credited because it obscured the fact that often the conditions of development are not evolutionary and predictable but rather revolutionary and unpredictable. The assump-tion that affluence and prosperity at the top of the economic ladder gradually will trickle down to benefit lower economic echelons was attacked. A growing body of empirical evidence suggested that wealth more likely trickled up. In short, the reigning growth paradigm for development, based largely on free-market capitalist assumptions, was for many no longer convincing.

Structural analysis was pursued on many fronts. For example, the drought in the Sahel region of North Africa in the 1970s prompted an in-depth analysis which revealed that, while lack of rain for seven years was an immediate exacerbating cause of massive hunger, the issues were deeper and more systemic. Studies of transnational corpora-tions led to increasing pessimism that, left on their own, they could be engines of change to improve the lot of the poorest of the poor. An eight-year study of national indebted-ness revealed stunning facts about the nature, extent and injustice of such indebtedness, with little prospect that the poor could escape that burden without revolutionary new thinking about external debt itself. One of the most successful attempts to assess root causes of underdevelopment was CCPD's establishment of an Advisory Group on Eco-nomic Matters (AGEM), a group of eight to twelve economists working with a smaller number of ethicists, mandated to assess economic aspects of the development process. The churches of the ecumenical movement, therefore, played important roles in de-mythologizing the dominant paradigms of development and articulating alternative cri-teria by which to measure true development.

Liberation

Halfway through the UN Second Decade for Development, in the mid-1970s, there was growing frustration and disillusionment that so little progress had been made. The ac-tual number of people living below the poverty line had increased. A New International Economic Order was widely called for among many third-world development theorists and the UN Conference on Trade and Development (UNCTAD) strongly urged new trad-ing relationships, such as indexing the price of exports of poor countries to match the escalation of prices of exports from the richer nations. When that failed, a "basic needs" approach, less threatening to the rich, was advocated in 1976, whereby a safety net for all people would be assured. Even that modest effort failed.

In ecumenical circles, too, a new vision was emerging. Latin Americans, especially vulnerable to the economic and political power of North America and Europe, offered a different analysis. Theologians from Latin America, joined later by others from throughout the world, concluded that it was deceptive to talk about "development". What was really needed, they asserted, was "liberation" from the structures of dominant power exercised by more industrialized countries. Some found a "domination-dependence" analysis compelling – a view that instead of potential partnership between the rich and the poor, in reality the case was that the affluence of the powerful was made possible by a progressive impoverishment of the poor.[9] The more tightly poorer nations were linked to materially prosperous nations, the more dependent and impoverished they would become.

A number of ecumenical theologians found this description appealing. They found biblical support in the Exodus account of the liberation of the Hebrew people from an obstinate Pharaoh who, although repeatedly promising freedom, would never free his slaves. Realistically, a liberation emphasis seemed to be truer to history: the recalcitrance of the rich; unpredictable turns of history rather than evolutionary development; the central importance of people for genuine development; and the necessity for concerted people's power. These factors had been important in winning political emancipation. Now, they might be required also to gain economic freedom and prosperity.

Some cautioned that the liberation theme, albeit an important contribution, should not completely replace other understandings of development. Would a liberation model cost the poor even more? Did the liberation model take economic realities too lightly just at a time when the churches, at long last, were struggling with hard economic questions? Did the zero-sum game implicit in the enrichment-impoverishment thesis make sense? Was there never any potential partnership between the rich and the poor? Was the notion of liberation too romantic in regard to the elimination of structures of order and too naïve about people's power? Despite such reservations, the liberation motif became a powerful idea in ecumenical reflections.

People's participation

Montreux II, in 1974, highlighted further the central importance of people as the direct object and means of development. Ecumenical reflections on diakonia and development put a premium on people's participation. There were practical reasons: unless people themselves were involved in the process, any changes would likely prove superficial and short-term.

But a deeper, theological and biblical reason also lay behind this growing commitment to participation. People are made in the image of God; they are co-creators in their own right. Further, they are the objects of Christ's redemptive acts. As such, they are called to be not only objects of other people's purposes, but subjects involved in defining and shaping their own future.

The struggle to participate is more profound than simply sharing material goods produced by society. The struggle for racial justice, as exemplified in the WCC Programme to Combat Racism, is about "having", "belonging" and "being", to use the apt terms of Kyle Haselden[10] when referring to the "race problem" in the United States. Participation means equitably to receive a fair share of things. It also means to share in the shaping of the goals and processes of one's society. Justice is not only distributive; it is also com-

---

[9] Commission on the Churches' Participation in Development, *To Break the Chains of Oppression: Results of an Ecumenical Study Process on Domination and Dependence*, WCC, 1975.

[10] Kyle Haselden, *The Race Problem in Christian Perspective*, New York, Harper, 1959.

mutative. Finally, justice requires that people be treated with respect and dignity even when their values and way of life differ from the majority's. In stressing the notion of participation, the WCC was making fundamental affirmations about human nature and also about the nature of God in Christ.

Role of "the poor"

Emphasis on people's participation led naturally to a new appreciation for the poor as agents, rather than the mere objects, of development. This emphasis on the poor was based upon three basic reasons that became ever clearer. First, it was because the poor were in special need of justice. Second, the poor were strategically placed to fight for justice because moral suasion of the rich and powerful seemed relatively unproductive. Some even argued that unless the poor themselves fought for and earned their rightful place in society, they would never develop their own sense of freedom and authentic power. Third, it was gradually seen that the poor and oppressed – at the margins because of gender, race, economic situation, etc. – have particular experiences and angles of vision that are crucial to the development process. It was thought not accidental that God covenanted with a slave community, that Jesus the Messiah was born into that community, that Jesus himself called social outcasts to be his disciples.

By the time of the WCC's 1975 Nairobi assembly, CCPD had adopted the view that development is "a liberating process aimed at social justice, self-reliance and economic growth. It is essentially a people's struggle in which the poor and oppressed are and should be the active agents and immediate beneficiaries... The role of the churches... is to support the struggle of the poor and the oppressed towards justice and self-reliance."[11] Within ecumenical circles there was considerable talk of "God's preferential option for the poor", a phrase made especially important by the Latin American Roman Catholic bishops. Some within CCPD circles asked whether churches themselves should become peoples' movements struggling for justice and human dignity, should become churches *of* the poor. The 1980 Melbourne conference on world mission and evangelism eloquently called on churches to "surrender their attitudes of benevolence and charity; [because] the voluntary joining in the community of the poor of the earth could be the most telling witness to the good news".[12] However, this radical identification of the church with the poor has never become definitive for the ecumenical family as a whole. While unwilling to identify the church exclusively with the poor, ecumenical development strategy was profoundly influenced by this stress upon the poor as the objects and agents of change. Perhaps the most dramatic and revolutionary efforts to implement this vision of development were pursued by the Urban Industrial Mission (later the Urban Rural Mission) in the WCC Division of World Mission and Evangelism. Too little attention has been accorded those bold experiments.

Sustainability

It was only natural that growing disenchantment with Western growth models of development was heightened by growing awareness of ecological limits. The earth simply could not sustain a development predicated on the earth's people, then four billion, putting demands on the environment equal to those imposed by North Americans. The

---

[11] Julio de Santa Ana, *Good News to the Poor*, WCC, 1977, p.114.
[12] *Your Kingdom Come: Mission Perspectives. Report on the World Conference on Mission and Evangelism, Melbourne, Australia, 12-25 May 1980*, WCC, 1980, p.177.

churches of the ecumenical movement recognized this huge challenge early. A new consciousness of limits, both in natural resources and in the capacity of the earth to absorb pollution, subsequently moved to deeper theological questions about the very nature of creation itself and humanity's relationship to it.

As early as the Bucharest conference of 1974, sponsored by the WCC's Department of Church and Society,[13] the churches were struggling towards a more adequate and profound theological understanding of sustainability, limits and creation. A purely anthropocentric understanding of nature became indefensible. Further, there are not only physical limits to growth, but social, psychological and spiritual ones as well. During subsequent years the links between ecological vulnerability and issues of justice and the well-being of the poor have become ever clearer.

The 1988 Church and Society consultation at Glion, Switzerland, "Creation and the Kingdom of God", provides an excellent example of the churches' struggle with ecological questions. God's presence in all creation reveals to us that in addition to human beings other creatures are also subjects that have a claim upon us. Non-human creatures are not merely objects to be used for our pleasure and instruments for human purposes. We are in fact part of a community of life which forms a single inter-related whole, and in which subjects other than ourselves have their own intrinsic value.[14]

It was inevitable that increasing disenchantment with a growth model for development should also lead to a fundamental questioning of life-styles, especially among the affluent. A "new asceticism" was advocated as early as the 1974 Bucharest conference. Was it not hypocritical to argue for population control, which would affect mostly the poorer countries, or for reducing pressures on the natural environment, while the main culprits were the consumerist life-styles of the rich? Perhaps worse than hypocritical, the rich seemed obtuse not only to the social justice issues, but also to the deep spiritual questions of consumptive life-styles. Simpler life-styles, then, were a corollary of sustainability questions, and such life-style changes became a more prominent theme in the period following the WCC assembly in Vancouver (1983). Life-style, however, should not be construed simply as individualistic asceticism. Rather, it involves larger issues of how life is engaged, individually and corporately, in the promotion of values, policies and conditions within the basic structures of society.

"Just, Participatory, Sustainable" and "Justice, Peace and Integrity of Creation"

As debates about development, liberation, "the poor" and sustainability swirled around, many Christians yearned for positive direction, for more than negative denouncements and inconclusive analyses; they longed not for clarity about what was wrong, but for goals for which they could strive. In the late 1970s the goal of a Just, Participatory and Sustainable Society (JPSS) was affirmed. This was not intended as a static model or blueprint, but as a framework for common reflection and action. To experienced ecumenists, JPSS echoed earlier ecumenical conversations about a "responsible society" and "middle axioms", themes so central to ecumenical social thought in the 1940s and 1950s. Originally intended as a programme priority for the WCC by its Vancouver assembly, JPSS

---

[13] Department of Church and Society, "Science and Technology for Human Development: The Ambiguous Future and the Christian Hope. Selected Preparatory Papers for the 1974 World Conference in Bucharest, Romania" (mimeogr. draft), WCC, 1974.

[14] Sub-units on Church and Society and Faith and Order, *Creation and the Kingdom of God: Consultation with Faith and Order*, WCC, 1988, p.73.

was expanded and transformed into "Justice, Peace and the Integrity of Creation" (JPIC), which became the centrepiece of ecumenical social thought for the subsequent decade. Both JPSS and JPIC provided positive themes around which to articulate an ecumenical vision and to mobilize action.

The role of women

Empirical data from studies of development highlight the crucial role that women play in economic life, especially in poorer and less industrialized societies. Anecdotal evidence is often more compelling than statistics, but the UN Development Programme estimated that in 1993 women contributed $11 trillion to the $16 trillion "invisible economy" of the world. In most countries women do more work than men.

> [M]en receive the lion's share of income and their economic contribution is recognized, while most of the work of women is not compensated or acknowledged. In the South, women's share of the workload averages about 13 percent higher than men's share, and in rural areas 20 percent higher.[15]

Thus, the crucial role of women in development has come to be recognized as involving not only scandalous injustice, which it surely does, but as a major economic factor.

Churches have deepened the issue by showing that the worldwide marginalization and oppression of women pertains to what economists term "opportunity costs", or the ways in which the human community, and women themselves, are deprived of their potential, frequently actual, intellectual, artistic and spiritual gifts. While women are considerable contributors to economic wealth, their overall contributions to their societies cannot be measured by economic functions alone.

A 1974 conference in Berlin on "Sexism in the Seventies"[16] was a wake-up call to the churches to play a prophetic and leading role in challenging, within both church and society, traditional views of women. The WCC's Nairobi assembly in 1975 amplified this call, and the adoption in 1981 by the executive committee of a "quota" system for women's representation in various ecumenical meetings, commissions, etc. was a more than symbolic step forward. In part, through an active women's desk within the WCC, the position and role of women in church and society has been a very important part of ecumenical discussions during the last decade and they continue to have profound influence upon the churches' understanding of diakonia.

Micro/macro interplay

A corollary of the emphasis on the poor as agents of development has been a growing recognition of the need to balance macro-level analysis of the work of the churches in diakonia with the micro-level of work. While it was important to consider macro questions such as trading patterns, debt, concentration of economic power, policies of the UN, the International Bank for Reconstruction and Development, the International Monetary Fund, ecological limits to growth, and the growing monopoly of information through new technologies, diakonia also required struggles at the grassroots with real communities of people in their everyday lives. At a consultation on church and service convoked by CICARWS in 1978 at the Orthodox academy of Crete, macro- and micro-dimensional aspects of diakonia were spoken about explicitly:

---

[15] Rob van Drimmelen, *Faith in a Global Economy: A Primer for Christians*, WCC, 1998, pp.77-78.
[16] *Sexism in the 1970s: Discrimination against Women. A Report of a World Council of Churches Consultation, West Berlin, 1974*, WCC, 1975.

by macro-dimensional diakonia was meant "the development of a fellowship of solidarity; the mission with a diaconal dimension and the commitment to social justice and liberation", and by micro-dimensional diakonia was meant the "concrete measures taken by the church to remedy the concrete distress of individuals and groups by concrete means".[17]

This stress on the importance of micro-level efforts was particularly fortunate at a time when ecumenical leaders from the more technologically developed nations were increasingly agitated about "limits to growth" and "sustainability". Had the concerns of Western churches dominated the agenda in the late 1970s, including the 1979 WCC conference on "Faith, Science and the Future", they might have overwhelmed the needs and perspectives of the poorer countries once again. While the concerns of this conference,[18] which was held at the Massachusetts Institute of Technology (MIT) at Cambridge, Massachusetts, in the US, about sustainability and the power of technology were well founded, the everyday pressing needs and contributions of the poor could not be overlooked. Thus, while there are certain tensions between micro- and macro-level analyses, they are complementary.

Diakonia and koinonia

In the mid-1980s and the 1990s five forces converged to reshape the understanding of diakonia (service to the poor, political action on behalf of justice, renewal through action) as consciously and intimately linked with koinonia (community, fundamental unity, the call of the church to be the church):

1) growing disillusionment with the meagre results of development efforts;
2) an impatience with generalized global analyses which seem to ignore or dismiss local realities;
3) a deepening sense that constantly to emphasize global and systemic change, important as it is, heightens a sense of powerlessness and impotence to change anything – the dynamics of the JPIC conference at Seoul in 1990 dramatically highlighted this insistence upon local experiences and direct participation in change;
4) a growing concern that genuine development must include more than material considerations; it must provide for the wholeness of human beings in communities; and
5) a maturing appreciation of the Orthodox emphasis on the intimate relationship between liturgy and service.

This conscious linking of diakonia and koinonia signals a significant evolution in ecumenical thinking.

Civil society

In the 1990s there was a growing conviction that the most promising aspect of development is the role played by "civil society". Variously defined, a civil society is one in which non-obligatory and non-governmental communities of people come together to achieve limited objectives deemed worthwhile for the health of people at the local level. Daniel Bell argued that a "demand for a return to civil society is a demand for the return to a manageable scale of social life, one which emphasizes voluntary associations, churches and communities, arguing that decisions should be made locally and should not be con-

---

[17] *An Orthodox Approach to Diakonia: Consultation on Church and Service*, Orthodox Academy of Crete, November 20-25, 1978, WCC, 1980, p.24.
[18] Roger Shinn, ed., *Faith and Science in an Unjust World*, 2 vols, WCC, 1980.

trolled by the state and its bureaucracy".[19] Julio de Santa Ana has defined civil society as "that sector of social reality in which human interests that are not rooted in the family or in economic power or in state administration seek to affirm themselves and defend their rights and prerogatives".[20]

A common feature of reflection on civil society is that official governmental and intergovernmental agencies alone cannot be relied on to promote the welfare of the poorest and most vulnerable sectors of the populace. At the same time, there is no illusion that the institutions of civil society are in themselves sufficient to achieve justice and well-being for all. Working together on a local level on concrete issues can empower marginalized peoples. The Canberra assembly of 1991 noted that "around the world we see that small groups of people of all races and classes, filled with courage and hope, can make a difference".[21] Section II of the assembly endorsed the importance of civil societies:

> Churches must recognize the increasing importance of the "civil societies", those non-governmental public organizations which express the interests and concerns of the people. It is in the "civil societies" that the energy of people aimed at greater emancipation and justice emerges. Churches belong to this "civil society" in the large majority of nations. They must put part of their resources towards the growth, the development, the empowerment and consolidation of these societies.[22]

Globalization

The 1980s and 1990s saw an enormously intensified concentration of economic power – globalization in various guises. This concentration was given great impetus by several factors:

- the demise of the USSR which freed laissez-faire market forces from significant restraints;
- euphoria in many countries about the prospects of market capitalism for producing prosperity;
- new technologies of communication and decision-making which, among other things, exploded the amount and speed for moving money across national boundaries; and
- the rise of powerful cross-national organizations such as the World Trade Organization.

The ecumenical family has seen globalization as a great threat to its own understanding of the goals of social change: equity and social justice, environmental health and sustainability, people's participation, self-reliance, social cohesion and community. Indeed, the Harare assembly in 1998 called the vision behind globalization "a competing vision of the oikoumene". Further, the driving forces of this new form of domination are economic powers which may be as insidious as political colonizers, and a subtle but powerful ideology which assumes that the most promising way to improve the quality of life for all people is to give free rein to market forces.

---

[19] As quoted in Julio de Santa Ana, "The Concept of Civil Society", in *The Ecumenical Review*, 46, 1, Jan. 1994, p.2.

[20] *Ibid.*, p.3.

[21] Michael Kinnamon ed., *Signs of the Spirit: Canberra 1991. Official Report, Seventh Assembly, World Council of Churches*, WCC, 1991, p.62.

[22] *Ibid.*, p.78.

In addition to being an economic issue, globalization is "a cultural, political, ethical and ecological issue". In short, "the increasing concentration of power – economic, political, cultural, military – is dramatically shaping the world of the present and future in ways that are not benign".[23]

This critique of globalization was echoed in the 1999 meeting of the WCC's central committee, at which many spoke urgently for the Council to confront the challenge of globalization. This was to be achieved in several ways, not least in a concerted attack on the huge indebtedness of poorer countries.[24] The Jubilee movement, finding its roots in the biblical notion of sabbatical and jubilee years, mobilized churches across the world to attack indebtedness. This movement made a notable – yet not complete – impact.

Next phases

It is impossible to know how emerging forces within the churches and society at large will affect the WCC's changing understanding of diakonia. At its October 1993 meeting, Samuel Kobia, then the new director of the Council's Justice and Service unit, openly wondered what steps were ahead in WCC diaconal work. He suggested that "networks" and "solidarity", while useful pointers in the right direction, were not wholly adequate for the new day. He stated that "the new focus may not be entirely clear, but we need to move on. The shift suggests that we move out of a period when the struggle was defined in terms of confrontation as a way of understanding our activity. The shift has now taken us into rebuilding, reconstruction, reconstitution, reconciliation."[25] Did this signal a return to the earlier emphasis on collaboration, rather than struggle, between the rich and poor, an emphasis which had been at the heart of the development debate in the 1960s and early 1970s?

Two things are certain. One is that the churches will be driven forward in their reflection as much by emergent and unpredictable social forces as by the workings of an inner theological logic. It was ever so. The other certainty is that a diaconal impulse remains a central conviction and commitment of many in the ecumenical family. In 1999 one such long-term Orthodox leader, Protopresbyter Georges Tsetsis, openly expressed his fear that the diaconal function and commitment of the Council could be too weak. He appealed to the programme committee to "ensure that diakonia will continue to be a *sine qua non* component of the Council's work".[26]

IMPLEMENTING A CHANGING VISION

While changing emphases in diaconal reflections have occurred during the past four decades, strenuous efforts have been made to reflect these changes in day-to-day decision-making within the churches. Admittedly, while considerable progress has been made at the conceptual level, there has been only modest success in devising organizations and procedures that respond adequately to a growing commitment to share power with the poor. Yet important changes have been made.

Churches have developed different means of organizing their diaconal efforts. In many northern countries, churches and ecumenical bodies developed specialized min-

---

[23] Diane Kessler ed., *Together on the Way: Official Report of the Eighth Assembly of the World Council of Churches*, WCC, 1999, pp.254,255,259.
[24] WCC Central Committee, *Minutes of the Fiftieth Meeting, Geneva, 1999*, pp. 32ff.
[25] "Report of Unit III Commission to Central Committee", WCC, Oct. 1993, p.46.
[26] *Ibid.*

istries to be responsible for development and emergency relief (e.g., Presbyterian World Service within the Presbyterian Church [USA], Christian World Service within the National Council of Churches in Australia). In other countries, specialized ecumenical diaconal ministries were created outside of formal church structures and today enjoy varying degrees of autonomy from the churches although they all have church representation on their governing bodies (e.g., International Organization for Development Cooperation [ICCO] in the Netherlands, Christian Aid in the UK, DanChurch Aid, Norwegian Church Aid). Most of these church agencies or specialized departments were created in the aftermath of the second world war to mobilize greater resources for reconstruction and for responding to the needs of millions of displaced Europeans. Over the years, however, these specialized agencies have developed into professional operations concerned with long-term development, environmental sustainability, emergency relief, refugee assistance, gender issues and human rights.

Today, they are powerful actors on the international scene both because of the resources they mobilize and because of their church-based constituencies and networks. Like their secular counterparts, these agencies emphasize partnerships with ecumenical organizations in the South, rely to varying degrees on government funding, and are increasingly engaged in advocacy. In a highly competitive world, they are under growing pressure to become more effective in raising funds and more efficient and accountable in operations. This creates tension with long-standing ecumenical partners in the South.

In the late 1980s, CICARWS initiated a process of annual consultations with the heads of these agencies known as the Heads of Agencies Network (HOAN) which has become an important forum for discussing collective agency approaches to particular issues of mutual concern. Responding to suggestions from HOAN, the WCC in 2000 initiated a round-table meeting to explore ways in which the agencies and the WCC could work together more effectively. Another suggestion from HOAN, to devise more open and effective ways of carrying out advocacy, led the WCC to launch a broadly consultative process which resulted in the formation of the Ecumenical Advocacy Alliance in late 2000. While created under WCC leadership, the Alliance draws on a broader constituency and includes participation by Roman Catholic organizations, regional ecumenical bodies, ecumenical networks, international ecumenical organizations, churches and agencies. These specialized ministries of the churches, whether church or independent agencies, are shaped by the same forces discussed above, particularly globalization and the growth of civil society.

Ecumenical diaconal activity is of several main types – outright grants, loans, technical assistance, exchanges of personnel, formal networks, development education and studies.

Outright grants

Historically, ecumenical diaconal work has been thought of primarily as outright relief – for example, the 2001 response to the catastrophic earthquake in Gujarat, India, which killed 30,000 people – and as project assistance. As indicated earlier, projects themselves have evolved from interchurch relief efforts towards longer-term programmes aimed at root causes of poverty, sustained self-reliance and development. While considerable progress has been made at the conceptual level, there has been only modest success in devising organizations and procedures that respond adequately to the growing commitment to sharing power with the poor. This commitment itself has grown steadily over the years, but actual implementation has lagged, not necessarily because of the recalcitrance of donors, but because of a failure of imagination on how best to share power. Yet several positive changes can be discerned.

A frequently minimized change was the emergence, in the late 1950s and early 1960s, of regional ecumenical groups, first in East Asia and later in other regions. The formation of such regional groupings, while often spontaneous, did not occur without some hesitation or outright opposition. Some feared that regional groups might compete with the more inclusive WCC. Yet prominent Asian Christians insisted, foretelling later developments, that mission and diaconal assistance were always two-way; that they had riches, material and other, to share with the traditional Western donor churches and agencies. Today it seems difficult to understand that some ecumenically minded church leaders in Europe and the US once looked upon regional groupings as a possible diversion of the larger ecumenical movement. In retrospect, the emergence of such regional groups has enormously enhanced rather than hindered genuine ecumenism, giving scope and voice for the great diversity of the church. Today the church is surely more truly ecumenical than at any previous stage in history. This emergence of regional ecumenical groups was a first stage in the decentralization of power and decision-making. Yet, it must be admitted that as recently as the Canberra assembly in 1991, relationships between Geneva and the regional ecumenical organizations "was not fully defined or resolved; some tensions persisted".[27]

Another early development in practical diakonia was the effort to coordinate project initiatives, to avoid unnecessary duplication or even competition. Among the early steps was development of the Herrenalb categories[28] in the mid-1950s to minimize overlapping between DICARWS and the Commission on World Mission and Evangelism (CWME). With the abolition of these categories in 1966 and an agreement on a single project list, the WCC made steady progress towards a system of projects for the entire Council, thus cutting across divisions which reflected only the WCC organizational structure. By the mid-1970s fuller collaboration on a Council-wide common project list was achieved. Yet, even then major efforts such as the CCPD's Ecumenical Development Fund (EDF) and the special fund of the Programme to Combat Racism remained outside that joint list. Nevertheless, collaboration on a single list was a major step forward in streamlining the process of decision-making. Task forces for certain regions were also developed to share expertise and knowledge.

In a parallel development, from the mid-1960s on there was increasing experimentation with round-tables where potential recipients participated along with donors, to make decisions about projects.

Similarly, consortia were developed for projects or regions, ensuring that recipients would not be beholden to, or at the mercy of, a single donor. Such consortia not only reduced recipients' dependency, they also enhanced the sense that the recipients were on a more equal footing with the donor partner. Consortia had the additional advantage of enabling churches to suggest and respond to more comprehensive and longer-lasting development programmes, as distinguished from projects. Increasingly, when recipients were given responsibility for evaluating their own programmes, including the criteria for evaluation, there was a further, albeit modest, sharing of power by recipient churches and groups. Little by little, accountability was being shared. Unfortunately,

---

[27] *Signs of the Spirit*, p.175.
[28] These categories were drawn up following two conferences, the second of which was held in Herrenalb, Germany.

however, a sense of dependency often persisted because recipient groups were usually unable to sustain their programmes without financial assistance from abroad. This persisting dependency was a major source of concern, as discussions during the 1979 CCPD Commission meeting in Cameroon illustrate.[29]

CCPD's "counterpart" (after 1979, "partner") groups were supported by the EDF, which was established by the executive committee in 1970 with the intent both to give greater power to recipients of aid and to promote new styles of development cooperation. While a major reason for the establishment of this fund was markedly to increase monies for development work, the EDF had two more subtle but explicit and important purposes: first, "to ensure that national, regional and sub-regional groups have both the initiative and the final say about the utilization of funds for development work in their respective areas", and secondly, "to ensure that programmes of development supported and carried out by the churches are those in which the main emphasis is given to the promoting of social justice and self-reliance".[30]

The early 1970s were a time of earnest discussions, especially within CICARWS, about the limitations of the entire project system. Some despaired that it could be sufficiently modified, but the Nairobi and Vancouver assemblies expressed their confidence that if significantly modified the project system would remain important. Yet questions persisted. For example, how could recipient churches and groups really establish priorities? The more the ecumenical community emphasized self-reliance and development, as distinguished from relief, the more important it became to think and act strategically. Who is in the best situation to define priorities when needs in differing contexts differ so markedly?

Gradually the official project list, covering all WCC desks, was modified to include priority proposals emanating from the churches and church bodies within each region. These were accorded top preference by funding bodies with guarantees, within certain established limits, that all such priority projects and programmes would be financed. Beyond these priority areas, other projects and programmes could be listed and receive assistance even if not endorsed fully by regional screening groups. To give more flexibility, and to reduce the time necessary for processing project applications, after the 1986 world consultation "Called to be Neighbours – Diakonia 2000", held at Larnaca, Cyprus, CICARWS adopted a "special action fund" and moved more intentionally to set up task forces addressing certain regions or countries. This was cumbersome and politically controversial, but the once scatter-shot project listings had moved substantially in the direction of priorities determined not by donors but by recipients.

In the mid-1990s a new instrument was set up, Action by Churches Together (ACT International), co-sponsored by the Lutheran World Federation (LWF). This new humanitarian agency drew on the resources of about 75 churches and aid agencies, which in 1999 contributed almost US$100 million dollars for humanitarian assistance. Basically a coordinating rather than an operational office for the churches, ACT is a global network governed by protocols which reflect a sophisticated understanding of how best to channel resources in emergency and relief situations. Because ACT has partners in regions where disasters occur, their joint perspectives on local realities play a significant role in fashioning responses to specific emergencies.

---

[29] *Minutes of the Meeting Held in Yaounde, Cameroon, June 17-22, 1979*, WCC, 1979, pp.6-8.
[30] *Fetters of Injustice*, p.135.

Perhaps the two most radical diaconal efforts to enhance recipient power were carried out under the auspices of the Programme to Combat Racism (PCR) and the Urban Industrial Mission, later Urban Rural Mission (URM).

Soon after the Uppsala assembly in 1968 the PCR became responsible for administering a WCC special fund to combat racism, from which annual grants were made to racially oppressed groups and organizations supporting the victims of racism based on explicitly designated gifts. Grants were clearly designed to help transfer power, as the 1970 committee insisted.[31] Recipient groups were approved by the executive committee based on several criteria adopted by the central committee at its 1971 meeting in Addis Ababa, which stressed that racism was a worldwide concern even though much of PCR's attention and energy in its first years was focused on southern Africa. Among the criteria were:

– goals and policies of recipient groups were not to be in conflict with those of the WCC itself;
– grants were not to be regarded as welfare but were to support ongoing programmes to combat racism;
– programmes were to aim at "conscientization", awareness-building, and thus required organizational stability and strength; and
– priority was to be given to programmes combating racism in the region of southern Africa.

When URM was formed out of Urban Industrial Mission and Rural Agricultural Mission in 1978, it was in a period of escalating militarization and violence in many parts of the world, increasing exploitation of people by governments and transnational corporations. People's struggles proliferated. And most were ruthlessly crushed. The primary method used by URM during this period was organizing the victims of oppression and marginalization for empowerment, enabling them to participate in the decision-making processes which affected their lives. Community organizing activities within national and global liberation perspectives, undergirded by leadership development, training, documentation and information exchange were complemented by theological reflection.

While controversial, the objectives of both URM and PCR were to respond to mission and service imperatives emanating from local action groups. Many of these action groups – predominantly in Asia, Africa and Latin America – were committed to working with people's movements whose aims were to organize for fundamental social and political change. Many such movements were only marginally related to churches and on occasion were, while actively promoting self-reliance and development as they envisaged it, actually at odds with the churches. It was the philosophy of PCR and URM to let local action groups define their own programmes; the role of the churches should be to support their struggles and not to interfere with their internal decisions. It is hardly surprising that groups willing to give financial support to PCR and URM have been relatively rare.

Leslie Cooke's wry warning in 1966 could not have been more apt. He observed that the more involved in real development – as distinguished from relief – the churches were, the more controversial and sometimes unpopular their diaconal witness would become.[32] These often controversial programmes – PCR and URM – have been among the

---

[31] Adler, Elisabeth, *A Small Beginning: An Assessment of the First Five Years of the Programme to Combat Racism*, WCC, 1974, p.5.
[32] Swanwick World Consultation, p.127.

most stimulating, provocative and imaginative of church efforts to exercise diaconal ministry.

With the restructuring of the WCC in the 1990s, the Council moved in the direction of a more unified and coordinated diaconal effort. After the Canberra assembly, the concentration of diaconal programmes in Sharing and Service provided an institutional basis for the sustained reflection and experimentation still necessary for the years ahead.

Loans

Two ecumenical organizations illustrate a second type of diakonia. Although established in 1946, the Ecumenical Church Loan Fund (ECLOF) only became closely linked to the WCC in 1964. Originally designed to provide low-cost loans to European churches recovering from the second world war, ECLOF's mandate grew "to foster human development in general and, in particular, to promote socio-economic justice and self-reliance for the alleviation of poverty". By 1996, two-thirds of ECLOF's grants were devoted to such purposes.[33] Most of the loans went to poor sectors of the population where it is difficult to obtain commercial loans, or where repayment is on frequently extortionate conditions. In 2000, for example, ECLOF made available 5393 loans, averaging about US$ 1800; the total loan volume was about $9.8 million. Loans are not expected to exceed US$50,000 and some can be as small as US$100. Intentionally, about half the total loaned in 1996 was for projects initiated by women or focused on women as primary beneficiaries.[34] Many loans can be repaid in local currency. When loans are repaid, the funds become available for other projects in the region, thus reinforcing the South-South character of the overall programme.

ECLOF development loans are used for a great many purposes: to develop family or village-size fish farms, to catalyze cooperatives, to start or promote cottage industries, to buy seeds and fertilizers, to run training programmes, etc. ECLOF concentrates 80 percent of its loans in the South. Despite the supposedly high-risk character of many loans, the repayment rate has been remarkably high. Decentralization of decision-making has also become a basic feature of the programme, now largely administered through national ECLOF committees that exercise considerable freedom to select and assist the management of loans, within general guidelines agreed to in advance in Geneva.

A second example of a loan-making diaconal programme is the Ecumenical Development Cooperative Society (EDCS), established by the central committee at Berlin in 1974. "[EDCS's] mission is to mobilize investment capital in order to provide loans to poor people for viable and productive business enterprises which operate on principles of justice" or, more mundanely, "to support poor people in their efforts for self-reliance".[35] In 1989 the EDCS director admitted that the requirement of commercial viability did not relate directly to the poorest of the poor, but argued, nevertheless, that such projects indirectly benefited the poorest sectors.

Share capital rose dramatically from about US$26 million in 1989 to US$85 million in 1996, with a lending capacity of US$94 million. The dividend to shareholders rose from zero to 2 percent in 1996.[36] The WCC made a commitment to have 10 percent of

[33] Ecumenical Church Loan Fund, *Annual Report*, WCC, 1993.
[34] Ecumenical Church Loan Fund, *Report 1996: Fifty Years of Fair Credit to Promote Human Development*, WCC, 1997, pp.42-43.
[35] EDCS, *Annual Report 1996*, Amersfoort, Netherlands, EDCS, 1997, p.1.
[36] *Ibid.*, p.3. This report also provides factual detail about how funds are received and expended by EDCS.

its capital in EDCS by 2000. Unfortunately, support from member churches has been disappointingly modest (5 percent of share capital in 1989). EDCS's 16-member board of directors is marked by significant gender and geographic diversity. In addition to the headquarters staff in the Netherlands, EDCS has 15 regional managers.

When compared with commercial loan rates, EDCS rates are comparatively low at 9 percent. Projects range broadly: salt-water aquaculture, fishing cooperatives, pig-meat production, women's marketing cooperatives, irrigation schemes, furniture factories, etc. The rate of loan failure has been a modest 10 percent, even though loans are extended to comparatively vulnerable groups. One aim of EDCS has been to demonstrate that economic projects can be managed in such a way that they are financially viable even as their premium is on "social return" or social benefit as distinguished from profit.

Perhaps EDCS's most interesting organizational innovation is the sharing of power – all shareholders have but one vote, whether they have invested hundreds of shares or only one. Only churches and church-related groups, rather than individuals, may be shareholders. "EDCS has developed into an organization which is mainly supported by grassroots groups investing in initiatives for just, participatory and self-reliant development."[37] Never intended to replace outright grants, EDCS was conceived both as a way to complement grants through invested capital and reasonable credit, and as a vehicle for dramatically increasing the churches' participation in development.

Networks

One of the most striking ecumenical developments since 1968 has been the growth of networks of people for mutual information, stimulation, encouragement and common action. Such networks are often based on geography, common interests and similar struggles, and on a sense of solidarity. Most of these networks are primarily designed not for material sharing, but for the sharing of non-material gifts. They are often informal, maintaining low profiles and serving as alternatives to more structured organizations. Three illustrations of such networks are instructive.

In the 1970s and 1980s, CCPD responded to the dream of persons in India committed to social justice and dignity for the underclass, Dalits or outcastes. Many different groups were discovered to be struggling with extraordinary courage and almost no material resources. A network of such groups was formed, designed to give technical assistance and advice where appropriate, and to provide contacts and solidarity with others who were facing similar questions so that they could be sustained in their often lonely struggle. CCPD came to realize the importance of these networks, not only for the practical information they conveyed, but also for the psychological and moral support they engendered. In CCPD circles this became known as "spirituality for combat", a term originating with M.M. Thomas, moderator of the central committee from Uppsala to Nairobi. Interestingly, some have argued that the term should be "spirituality *with* or *through* combat".

The ecumenical family has been committed to protecting these often vulnerable groups by giving space and encouragement as signs of solidarity even as their internal life and decision-making processes are respected. In some cases, these networks have been so fragile or controversial that they have also been given modest financial support,

---

[37] *Minutes of the CCPD Commission Meeting, Manchester, UK, June 25–July 3, 1989*, WCC, 1989, p.97.

with specific information about the groups being made available only to limited numbers of persons. From EDF funds, CCPD with no public announcement in 1988 made modest grants of US$1500 to $3000, called "programme assistance", to 24 such efforts.[38]

A second example of networks is the impressive work of the WCC Human Rights Resource Office for Latin America (Hrrola), as distinguished from the Human Rights Advisory Group (HRAG) of the WCC Commission of the Churches on International Affairs (CCIA). Focusing originally on Latin America, this office fostered human-rights networks that emerged as crucial expressions of diakonia. One of their significant contributions has been to protect numerous individuals and groups from arbitrary treatment. Also of considerable significance, and perhaps as important as the mobilization of efforts for particular individuals and groups, has been the work of Hrrola in conscientization concerning the abuse of human rights across the world. Sadly, the need for such networks on human rights has become even greater in recent years, although the work of Hrrola was phased out during the restructuring of the 1990s.

The Global Ecumenical Network on Uprooted People (GEN) is an expression of one of the ecumenical movement's historic and pressing areas of service. Since its inception, the WCC made refugee work one of its main diaconal activities. Over the years this work expanded to include not only refugees pushed out of their national homeland, but uprooted peoples of many differing kinds. Despite impressive efforts, the number of uprooted peoples in the world grew to 150 million people, of whom 100 million were migrant workers, 15 million refugees and approximately 35 million internally displaced persons. In the 1990s the problem of uprooted peoples was compounded not only by political turmoil, often precipitating internally displaced persons, but also by a growing reluctance of formerly "host" nations to welcome newly uprooted persons. Repatriation to one's home country was often fraught with great danger.

In the midst of this enormous tragedy, networks became important instruments of advocacy, resettlement and emergency assistance. In addition to GEN, numerous other networks of collaboration emerged, either to deal with problems of the uprooted in general, or to focus on specific situations. An example of the former would be Action by Churches Together (ACT), which responds more immediately and effectively to major emergencies. An example of the latter would be Gricar, a programme of accompaniment for returning Guatemalan refugees.

Not all networks were centralized; they often spread throughout many regions. Melaku Kifle, coordinator of the WCC's Refugee and Migration Service, warned in 1997,

> There is a tendency to judge the success of an emergency or rehabilitation response by the number of funds channelled and how many projects have been supported. As significant as this is, the measuring stick should be the extent to which such assistance has enabled beneficiaries to assume full control of their situation and move from relief to development.[39]

Networks reinforce an understanding that Geneva itself is not the centre of the witness of the churches; rather, Geneva is to be seen as but a part of a broadening network of diaconal action.

---

[38] Ibid., pp.131-32.
[39] Global Ecumenical Network Meeting on Uprooted People, Launch of the 1997 Ecumenical Year of Churches with Uprooted People, March 1-4, 1997: Report, WCC, 1997, p.6.

Development education

Originally, development education played only a marginal role in diaconal strategies. It was conceived primarily to counteract abysmal ignorance in the richer countries about the steadily worsening situation of poorer peoples. This basic orientation is reflected in the recommendations of the 1969 WCC-sponsored consultation on development education. Most of these were couched in terms of more effective educational techniques and strategies.

But as understandings of diakonia and development became more complex, stemming largely from greater awareness of how the rich are structurally implicated in the plight of the poor, the importance of "consciousness raising" in both richer and poorer countries became more apparent. In the Nordic countries, the Netherlands and Great Britain, development education became a prominent part of diakonia, but in many other parts of the world, including the US, development education remained a poor cousin in budget building. Five principal concerns have characterized development education:

1) How can the structures and programmes of churches (e.g. church-school materials, theological education) more effectively promote commitment to the Just, Participatory and Sustainable Society effort (JPSS, later Justice, Peace and Integrity of Creation-JPIC)?
2) How can development education be changed from a purely informational concept to one that aims at changed awareness, alterations in life-style, and political action? Development education is to be not only about new knowledge but about *metanoia*, changed beings. Such new life-styles are not merely private; they apply both to individual attitudes and behaviour, and to influencing public policies and actions.
3) How can churches learn from the experiences of the poor without imposing their own assumptions on the promotion of development?
4) How can Christians and churches actually be involved in the struggles of the poor because, as Paulo Freire taught,[40] only through such engagement does one truly learn?
5) How can global issues be linked to local ones?

Advocacy and alliances

One of the less visible but highly important diaconal ministries of churches is to advocate for the poor and excluded. Advocacy differs from education in that, by definition, it takes sides on controversial matters. It may be exercised in many ways, two being illustrative. One is for official church bodies to make statements on pressing social issues, such as apartheid in South Africa, land rights for Indigenous Peoples, the rights of uprooted peoples in Guatemala, nuclear testing, world food disorder, and specific conflicts such as the Gulf war.

A less direct advocacy role is to join others, especially non-governmental organizations, in expressing the conscience of the churches in a wide variety of arenas such as the debt crisis, land mines, global warming, fresh-water depletion, deforestation, the structural adjustment conditions of the International Monetary Fund, concentration of economic and political power, etc. Such collaboration, often related to UN activities, has since 1965 been a prominent feature of much church life.[41] As mentioned above, the Ecumenical Advocacy Alliance now offers a new model for advocacy by churches on a

---

[40] Freire, Paulo, *Pedagogy of the Oppressed*, transl. by Myra Bergman Ramos, New York, Herder and Herder, 1972, p.56 *et passim*.
[41] Cf. Mark Ellingsen, *The Cutting Edge: How Churches Speak on Social Issues*, WCC, 1993.

limited number of issues. The WCC is also a prominent collaborator with other non-governmental organizations.

The decades under review saw a tremendous amount of reflection and experimentation in regard to diakonia. Konrad Raiser, former general secretary of the WCC, has asserted that the era of exploration is not over:

> Our ecumenical reflection, which has focused far too long on the imperatives of the global situation, has to start from the everyday lives of people, their struggles and their hopes, their powerlessness and their inherent energies for life in community. The prophetic voice of challenge to those in power has to be supplemented by the voice of encouragement and support for those who sustain the web of life. We have to recognize that we have too easily identified the call to unity with the obligation to maintain a particular system of doctrine and church order. The new challenge is to develop new ways of recognizing diversity while affirming relatedness (catholicity), to learn mutual accountability and to develop a hermeneutics of unity.[42]

THEOLOGICAL GROUNDING

As might be expected in so diverse an ecumenical movement, theological and biblical bases for diaconal efforts have been understood in various ways. Indeed, recognizing the diversity of theological traditions within the ecumenical family, the Vancouver assembly in 1983 called for the development of a "vital and coherent theology", but the Canberra assembly in 1991 lamented that "at the end of the road from Vancouver to Canberra it must be said that, despite all the efforts so far made, the task we were set still remains ahead of us".[43] Some thought this diversity a sign of strength; others considered it a weakness. Risking simplification, one can detect six main theological and biblical bases for diakonia running through the literature. These differing bases, however, are not contradictory or exclusive; they intersect, complement and reinforce each other. They are emphases or strands rather than conflicting positions.

Imago Dei

Created in the image of God, humankind is held by Christians to have an inherent right to be treated justly and with dignity. Denial of justice and dignity, either by individuals or institutional structures, violates God's intentions or purposes in creation itself. While not a natural law in a philosophical sense, the inalienable rights of human beings are not contingent upon the civil laws of societies, but are rooted in creation itself. This view is shared by many who do not accept biblical Christian perspectives. It was exemplified in the statement from the 1987 consultation on the ecumenical sharing of resources – "Sharing Life in a World Community" – at El Escorial, Spain:

> Recognizing that all God's children are made in God's own image, which we see in Genesis 1:26 as a plural image, we acknowledge that "there is neither Jew nor Greek, slave nor free, male nor female"... A call to koinonia calls us to re-examine such theological understandings that eliminate women or other groups in the community from sharing the life of Christ in all its fullness.[44]

[42] Konrad Raiser, "Toward Koinonia in the Household of Life", keynote address to the meeting of the US Conference for the WCC, Louisville, Kentucky, April 1, 1993, p.3.
[43] *Signs of the Spirit*, p.137.
[44] Huibert van Beek ed., *Sharing Life: Official Report of the WCC World Consultation on Koinonia, "Sharing Life in a World Community"*, WCC, 1989, p.42.

Teleological orientation

This perspective emphasizes the unfinished character of creation and humankind's participation in an ongoing movement towards the eschatological reign of God – whether this is "realized" or seen as a dramatic breaking into history through direct divine intervention. Individuals and groups have God-given roles to play in God's unfinished creation. Humanity's rights and dignity are grounded not only, or even primarily, in their created character, but in what women and men are called to become in the larger, God-inspired human enterprise. To deprive individuals of their God-given rights is not only to violate them as individuals; it is to challenge – but not defeat – God's ultimate purposes. The JPIC convocation at Seoul in 1990 claimed an inseparable relationship between justice and human rights. Human rights have their source in God's justice which relates to the enslaved, marginalized, suffering people in concrete acts of deliverance from oppression (Ex. 3:7b). The term "human rights" must be clearly understood to refer not only to individual rights but also to the collective social, economic and cultural rights of peoples: the right to sovereignty and self-determination for peoples to work out their own models of development and to live free of fear and free of manipulation is a fundamental human right.[45]

Spiritual dangers of wealth

Many ecumenical gatherings have warned the churches not to become utopian about human prospects. Sin pervades every situation. It is especially important that Christians not confuse current hopes for material progress with the reign of God. This perspective focuses more on the affluent than the poor. The affluent, through their indifference towards the poor and their self-satisfaction and pride, tend to lose all sense of dependence upon non-human creation, other persons, and God. That denies wholeness as well as justice; the suggestion has been made that churches should advocate not only a minimum wage, but also a maximum one. One measure of justice is the discrepancy between the earnings of the highest 20 percent and lowest 20 percent of the population.

The Salonika conference of 1959, "Christian Action in Rapid Social Change", offered a powerful warning. Given humankind's sinful nature, economic and social life will never be free from abuse and arrogance. While material progress is desirable, it is not an answer to humanity's deepest problems of alienation and sin. The then director of the Commission on World Mission and Evangelism, Emilio Castro, addressing the 1973 Bangkok world mission conference, asserted that "the rich nations are spiritually and morally underdeveloped, functioning on the philosophy of aggressive individualism and corporate egoism".[46]

Jesus' teaching

Often diaconal ministries are justified primarily by an appeal to the life and teachings of Jesus, especially as presented in the synoptic gospels. Jesus represents a new ethic in the world – a self-emptying, other affirming, *kenotic*, ethic. Jesus' compassion for the poor, his disdain for those who arrogantly abuse their power, his championing the cause of the outsider and marginalized, his preference for the humble and poor in spirit, his fre-

---

[45] Preman Niles ed., *Between the Flood and the Rainbow: Interpreting the Conciliar Process of Mutual Commitment (Covenant) to Justice, Peace and the Integrity of Creation*, WCC, 1992, pp.175-76.
[46] *Bangkok Assembly 1973: Minutes and Report of the Assembly of the Commission on World Mission and Evangelism of the World Council of Churches*, WCC, 1973, p.53.

quent references to the Hebrew scriptures which focus on justice, are keys to understanding diaconal witness.

Cross and resurrection

For many in the ecumenical movement, a diaconal commitment is rooted not so much in original creation but in God's incarnation in history, the cross and resurrection of Christ the Son. While intimately connected, God's redemptive acts are distinguished from God's initial but now fallen creation – creation cannot by itself overcome this alienation. Jesus' death and resurrection demonstrate and actualize God's radical, forgiving love for all creation.

> We all have experienced, in one way or another, the transforming power of Christian service... As Christians, we believe that God is manifest through all creation and God's servants become instruments of calling to repentance, obedience and love, proclaiming the force of the kingdom of God.[47]

The centrality of the cross in diakonia is expressed clearly in the report of section IV at the 1980 Melbourne world mission conference:

> The eye of faith discerns in that cross the embodiment of a God who out-suffers, out-loves and out-lives the worst that powers do. In the decisive events which followed the crucifixion, something radically new happened which seems best described as a new creation. An altogether new quality of power appeared to be let loose among humankind.[48]

Eucharist and koinonia

For many in the ecumenical community, especially those nurtured by the Orthodox tradition, diakonia is a logical and necessary extension of the eucharist, the sharing of *koinonia* at the Lord's table. The consultation at Chania, Crete, in 1978 on "An Orthodox Approach to Diakonia" was particularly rich and suggestive:

> Christian diakonia also flows from the divine liturgy in which our offerings are sanctified by Christ's offering and requires our active cooperation *(synergeia)* with God in the exercise of our free will which is rooted in our common agreement *(symphonia)* (Matt. 18:19). Diakonia is therefore an expression of the unity of the church as the body of Christ. Each local celebration of the eucharist is complete and universal, involving the whole of creation, and is offered for the material and spiritual needs of the whole world...Christian diakonia is not an optional action, duty or moral stance in relation to the needy, additional to our community in Christ, but an indispensable expression of that community, which has its source in the eucharistic and liturgical life of the church.[49]

The 1986 consultation at Larnaca, Cyprus, "Called to Be Neighbours", reiterated this view:

> Diakonia demands of individuals and churches "a giving... not out of what they have, but what they are". This means recognizing that our whole life and action as persons and communities is an act of adoration and service of God, of sharing with God in the work of saving and redeeming the world.[50]

---

[47] Klaus Poser ed., *Diakonia 2000: Called To Be Neighbours: Official Report, WCC World Consultation, Inter-Church Aid, Refugee and World Service*, Larnaca, 1986, WCC, 1987, p.124.
[48] *Your Kingdom Come*, p.209.
[49] Gennadios Limouris ed., *Orthodox Visions of Ecumenism: Statements, Messages and Reports on the Ecumenical Movement, 1902-1992*, WCC, 1994, p.70.
[50] *Diakonia 2000*, p.18.

This understanding was echoed at El Escorial the following year:

> Perhaps the strongest biblical paradigm of sharing is the eucharist. In the sharing of the bread and the wine we celebrate the communion with him who died for us and was raised, so that we share in his life, through the Holy Spirit, and receive life abundantly... Only when the eucharist is really celebrated as the body broken for the world will it create and sustain a fellowship in which life is shared with all people... This sharing goes beyond the... churches to the oikoumene, the whole inhabited earth.[51]

Beyond this simple typology, it should be stressed that theological method has been severely tested since 1965. It is not the province of this chapter to discuss those rumblings, but four main challenges to traditional theological method illustrate the point:

- The "action/reflection" method of reciprocity between social engagement and theological reflection, so prominent in the early work of CCPD in particular, roots theology in everyday experiences. In particular, the stories of the people, rather than linear theological reflection alone, need to be explicitly present in theological method.
- There has been a growing insistence that all theological reflection is contextual – so radically contextual that common ground is sometimes difficult to discern. At the least, the hegemony of Western theology is no longer widely tolerated.
- God's presumed "preferential option for the poor" must have profound consequences for theological method.
- The view that "to know God requires that one be involved in the work that God is doing" sets a new epistemological requirement for the study of theology. The Melbourne conference in 1980 insisted that the churches must "evangelize themselves" since they often have been in collusion with oppressive powers, and have acted in ways which, within their own life, deny the gospel. The impact of these social and diaconal themes on theological method is not yet fully apparent but promises to be profound.[52]

A RETROSPECTIVE VIEW

In retrospect, what have been the most significant achievements of the past 35 years in relation to diakonia? One could conclude that, in view of minuscule progress in alleviating poverty, little has been accomplished. One could also conclude that, in some respects, recent emphasis on "civil society" returns ecumenical reflection and action to an earlier diaconal style. And, given relatively modest success in really enhancing participatory decision-making, one could argue that little progress has been made in the ecumenical sharing of resources. Notwithstanding such dour assessments however, these past decades have made important achievements. Six of these should be celebrated, though not exaggerated:

1. Simply on the informational level, there is far greater global awareness of the huge and growing gap between the rich and the poor. Concepts such as "third world", "below the official poverty line", "limits to growth", were not part of the general vocabulary at the beginning of this period. This heightened consciousness of the realities of poverty

---

[51] *Sharing Life*, pp.41-42.
[52] The Australian scholar John N. Collins has called into question in a most stimulating fashion much theological reflection concerning diakonia, including that found in a number of statements from the WCC and its units. Cf. John N. Collins, *Diakonia: Re-Interpreting the Ancient Sources*, New York, Oxford Univ. Press, 1990.

and the daily struggles of millions of people simply to survive is a small but important step forward.

Important as is this heightened awareness, it is more important that today there is far more analytical sophistication about what factors are at the root of poverty and exclusion. Poverty is no longer understood as mere happenstance, the result of indolence, lack of education, differing cultural assumptions and values – or even of unlucky weather or unfortunate environmental deficits. In a systemically inter-related world economy, poverty clearly involves the reality of oppression, intended or otherwise. Further, there is now an attendant awareness that material well-being is only a part of what is at stake in holistic development. There is far less optimism than in a previous era that more direct aid, in and of itself, can substantially improve the condition of the poor. Development is now more adequately understood as a complex of political, economic, psychological and cultural factors.

In the mid-1960s, it would not have been likely that a WCC document would make the following statement about economic growth:

> Growth for growth's sake is the strategy of the cancer cell. Growth for growth's sake is increase in size without control, without limit, in disregard for the system that sustains it. It ultimately results in degradation and death.[53]

2. During these 35 years there have been an unprecedented number of efforts by the churches not only to relieve suffering and destitution, but also to promote long- term improvement in people's living conditions. Literally tens of thousands of projects and programmes have been supported, and millions of individuals directly affected: fish farms, community organizations, production and marketing cooperatives, credit facilities, literacy programmes, new health schemes, integrated village development, training, afforestation. Programmes supported through CICARWS and other departments of the WCC represent only a small part of the total effort of the churches. Traditional support for building or repairing churches or building and running hospitals and educational institutions has been widely supplanted by less institutional and more people-centred development efforts. Ever greater attention has been paid to assisting communities rather than individuals per se and self-reliance and long-lasting benefits are consciously more central. New areas have opened up, such as greater concentration on women's roles in church and society. In short, the range, volume and complexity of church-generated development assistance programmes – all expressions of diakonia – have been impressive.

An important aspect of this multiplication of projects and programmes has been the forging of significant networks of people across national, ethnic, racial, class, gender and even religious boundaries – networks of people who share aspirations for the improvement of the lot of the poor. Today these networks are vital nerve centres for the whole church. They often generate a sense of power and self-reliance among the poor, promote contact between the privileged and the poor, and relate churches to communities of the poor. Such networks have also enhanced South to South relationships. Sometimes sharing is as concrete as learning how to use a bicycle to lift water for irrigation; at other times sharing through networks reaches deeper levels, reinforcing the sense of identity and dignity.

[53] *Signs of the Spirit*, pp.63-64.

3. The outstanding achievement of these past years in respect to diakonia is the degree to which people "on the underside of history" have developed a new awareness of themselves as subjects of history rather than merely as the objects of the history of others. Within nations and among individuals, this is undoubtedly the most significant, lasting and profound change of recent years. Many people in poverty had accepted that it was their fate to be poor, enslaved or oppressed. They had accepted a particular location in society, often content to seek reprieve or meaning in other-worldly religious expectations. Today, there is among many a new sense of self-worth and identity.

Although this new consciousness often has secular political and cultural roots, the role of the churches in its formation cannot be ignored. Movements for freedom and equality in the third world have profoundly influenced the churches' shift from distributive to commutative justice, from a diakonia based upon humanitarian assistance and relief to one based on the right and responsibility of people, created in the image of God, to participate in shaping the world and their own identity. Through biblical and theological reflection, churches have deepened the sense that to be truly human means to be co-creators in a process towards a yet unfinished creation.

4. If a new consciousness has emerged among the poor, a somewhat parallel and healthy change is also taking shape among the more affluent who often assumed that their world-views and values are normative for all peoples. Penetrating discussions concerning the goals and processes of development have deepened sensitivity to the pluriform nature of values. Development for what? Material goals only? Laissez-faire capitalism? Socialism? Mark Juergensmayer[54] has suggested that "a new cold war" is already taking shape between those who assume that Western, technological, scientific, secular orientations are the wave of the future, and those who believe that traditional values that emphasize community, human relationships and religion are the desired goals of social change.

In ecumenical circles there has evolved a growing consciousness of the limits and partiality of every religious and cultural perspective, including a deepened perception of the diversity of theological emphases among those who call themselves Christian. This diversity, within unity, has been one of the most vexing but enriching aspects of ecumenical reflection. The particularities of Christian faith and practice in each and every place confront the assumption that there is now one church, one faith, and one basic way to live out that faith. Western perspectives on Christian faith, so long considered normative, have been partially relativized. The class character of much theological reflection – formulated by those regarded as "the winners" of history – has been more fully unmasked. The debate about diakonia has induced, among many, greater humility about one's own faith and a complementary openness to listening to and learning from others of differing faiths and ideologies. What are the limits to diversity? That debate is sharpened by the recognition that even within the Christian community there are many – especially among the poor – who are now challenging the assumptions and practices of dominant churches. Charismatics, Pentecostals and Indigenous Christian communities are as much a challenge to mainline ecumenical Christianity as are believers from non-Christian religious traditions.

5. Not only are there new ways of thinking about diakonia; there are also new ways of living out these new understandings of service. Well-intended assistance and service

---

[54] Mark Juergensmayer, *The New Cold War? Religious Nationalism Confronts the Secular State*, Berkeley, Univ. of California Press, 1993.

are often fraught with dangers. Too often they are counter-productive – as when aid perpetuates and reinforces dependency. The ecumenical movement has experimented with different ways to enable the poor to exercise power in decision-making and much has been learned in that process so that today there is considerably more mutuality and sharing of power than was true in 1965. And it has been discovered that direct sharing of material resources is surely not the only, perhaps not always the best, shape for contemporary diakonia. Surely efforts such as those aimed at changing the structural adjustment requirements of the International Monetary Fund and the World Bank could be even more beneficial to the poor.

6. Finally, in the 1960s there was considerable discussion about the relation of service to mission; they are now seen as complementary. And diakonia, moreover, is increasingly understood as congruent with the search for the visible unity of the church. Promoting Christian unity is part of the struggle to realize and express the unity of all creation. Christian unity transcends ecclesiastical or church unity. Christian unity encompasses that unity of all creation towards which churches aspire. A statement from the CICARWS commission meeting in 1987 captured this diaconal obligation especially well:

> Diakonia is service to the whole human being, to all humanity, and to the whole creation. Just as Jesus shared himself with us through the eucharist, we are invited by him to share our lives with others. Our commitment to justice must be manifest through active solidarity with those who suffer, with all God's creation. Diaconal action will therefore demand suffering and self-emptying *(kenosis)* but always celebrating the hope of the resurrection.[55]

BIBLIOGRAPHY

Abrecht, Paul and Thomas, M.M., *Christians in the Technical and Social Revolutions of Our Time*, WCC, 1967, 232p.

Beek, Huibert van ed., *Sharing Life: Official Report of the WCC World Consultation on Koinonia, "Sharing Life in a World Community"*, WCC, 1989, 148p.

Boseto, Leslie et al., "Ecumenical Diakonia", in *The Ecumenical Review*, 46, 3, July 1994, pp.301-10.

Collins, John N., *Diakonia: Re-Interpreting the Ancient Sources*, New York, Oxford Univ. Press, 1990, 368p.

Commission on Inter-Church Aid, Refugee and World Service, *Consultation Digest, Swanwick, 1966*, WCC, 1966, 23p.

Diakonia: Towards Christian Service for Our Time: Useful Information for Church Workers in Africa, WCC, 1990, 72p.

Dickinson, R.D.N., *Poor, Yet Making Many Rich: The Poor as Agents of Creative Justice*, WCC, 1983, 219p.

Dilemmas and Opportunities: Christian Action in Rapid Social Change: Report of an International Ecumenical Study Conference, Thessalonica July 25–August 2, 1959, WCC, 1959, 104p.

Drimmelen, Rob van, *Faith in a Global Economy: A Primer for Christians*, WCC, 1998, 156p.

Early, Tracey, *Simply Sharing: A Personal Survey of How Well the Ecumenical Movement Shares Its Resources*, WCC, 1980, 84p.

Empty Hands: An Agenda for the Churches. Study Guide on the Ecumenical Sharing of Resources for Use by Churches, Local Congregations and Other Groups, WCC, 1980, 60p.

Ferris, Elizabeth G., *Beyond Borders: Refugees, Migrants and Human Rights in the Post-Cold War*, WCC, 1993, 310p.

---

[55] *Minutes of the CICARWS Commission Meeting at Chavannes-de-Bogis, Switzerland, June 23-27, 1987*, WCC, 1987, p.32

Gruber, Pamela ed., *Fetters of Injustice: Report of an Ecumenical Consultation on Ecumenical Assistance to Development Projects, 26-31 January, 1970, Montreux, Switzerland*, WCC, 1970, 164p.

Jacques, André, *The Stranger within Your Gates: Uprooted People in the World Today*, WCC, 1986, 87p.

Klinken, Jaap van, *Diakonia: Mutual Helping with Justice and Compassion*, Kampen, Kok, 1989, 134p.

Kudadjie, J.A., *Towards Abundant Life: Official Report of the Africa Consultation on Diakonia, Nairobi, 31 March-7 April, 1989*, WCC, 1989, 103p.

Mshana, Rogate ed., *Wealth Creation and Justice*, WCC, 2003, 94p.

An Orthodox Approach to Diakonia: Consultation on Church and Service, Orthodox Academy of Crete, November 20-25, 1978, WCC, 1980, 64p.

Padilha, Anivaldo, "Diakonia in Latin America: Our Answers Should Change the Questions", in *The Ecumenical Review*, 46, 3, July 1994, pp.287-91.

Poser, Klaus ed., *Diakonia 2000: Called To Be Neighbours: Official Report, WCC World Consultation, Inter-Church Aid, Refugee and World Service, Larnaca, 1986*, WCC, 1987, 133p.

Raiser, Konrad ed., *Ökumenische Diakonie, eine Option für das Leben : Beiträge aus der Arbeit des ÖRK zur theologischen Begründung ökumenischer Diakonie*, Frankfurt, Lembeck, 1988, 156p.

Resource Sharing Book: Programmes, Projects and Services, WCC, 1983-1997, 15 vols

Robra, Martin, "Theological and Biblical Reflection on Diakonia: A Survey of Discussion within the World Council of Churches", in *The Ecumenical Review*, 46, 3, July 1994, pp.276-86.

Santa Ana, Julio de, *Good News to the Poor*, WCC, 1977, 124p.

Shinn, Roger and Abrecht, Paul eds, *Faith and Science in an Unjust World*, WCC and Philadelphia, Fortress, 1980, 2 vols

Slack, Kenneth, *Hope in the Desert: The Churches' United Response to Human Need, 1944-1984: Essays to Mark the Fortieth Anniversary of the Work of the World Council of Churches*, WCC, 1986, 143p.

Strohm, Theodor ed., *Erneuerung des Diakonats als ökumenische Aufgabe*, Heidelberg, Diakoniewissenschaftliches Institut, 1996, 262p.

To Break the Chains of Oppression: Results of an Ecumenical Study Process on Domination and Dependence, WCC, 1975, 63p.

Together in God's Service: Toward a Theology of Ecclesial Lay Ministry: Papers from a Colloquium, National Conference of Catholic Bishops Subcommittee on Lay Ministry, Washington, United States Catholic Conference, 1998, 199p.

17
Under Public Scrutiny

Martin Conway

The present ecumenical situation can best be described by the paradoxical statement that the ecumenical movement has entered into a period of reaping an astonishingly rich harvest but that, precisely at the beginning of the 21st century, it is more seriously called into question than ever before.[1]

As the wider context of this comment by Visser 't Hooft in 1968 makes clear, he was referring principally, in his "astonishingly rich harvest", to the comprehensiveness of the ecumenical movement now that all the Orthodox churches were members of the WCC and that the Roman Catholic Church had established "a great network of close fraternal relationships". But he was also referring to the "many inside and outside our churches, particularly among the younger generation, who have their deep doubts about the relevance of the ecumenical movement and turn away from it with a sense of disappointment". He could not know of the storms that were soon to engulf the movement that he had done so much to shape, let alone of the public and indeed political ferocity of these storms. Yet the remark admirably sums up the dual character of one of the most significant dimensions of the ensuing period of ecumenical history, when the movement came under near-constant fire from several different quarters, and thus had to learn to live and move in a very much more public and confrontational field of forces than seems previously to have been the case.

Not that the earlier periods were free from critiques or controversies, as earlier volumes in this series have made clear. But these controversies were almost all contained within the world of the Christian family. The new feature since the 1960s has been the overtly public nature of so much of the controversy. In earlier times the more "public" view of the rise and growth of the ecumenical movement, in the comments of politicians and social leaders, was on the whole encouraging and supportive. Now, no doubt in reaction to the increased public effectiveness of the movement, some such voices were to become – and remain – strongly, indeed angrily, hostile and condemnatory.[2]

---

[1] From "The Mandate of the Ecumenical Movement", the address by Dr W.A.Visser 't Hooft, first general secretary of the World Council of Churches, to the Uppsala assembly in 1968. Norman Goodall ed., *The Uppsala Report 1968: Official Report of the Fourth Assembly of the World Council of Churches, Uppsala July 4-20, 1968*, WCC, 1968, p.316.

[2] Two preliminary remarks about what follows: comments are needed to place this critique in context. (a) While this volume aims to cover the ecumenical movement as a whole, in its many manifestations, and at its various levels – local, national and international – almost all of this chapter will be devoted

The episode in the history of the ecumenical movement which most clearly marks the transition into the period under review was the Church and Society conference held in 1966 in Geneva, under the title "Christians in the Technical and Social Revolutions of Our Time". Three new features were deliberately planned:

- The majority of the participants were drawn from the laity rather than clergy or church officials, so that people could speak of that which they were handling in their working lives.
- Of the 420 participants, roughly equal numbers came from the third world, and from North America and Western Europe, thus following the example already set in Tambaram 1938 by the International Missionary Council.
- The central committee had agreed that the conference should be empowered to speak to, rather than for, the churches and the WCC, thus giving it freedom to explore issues and suggest new approaches.[3]

It is important to recall how startling – to the participants, to the journalists present, almost half of them from the secular press, and through these to the churches at large – was the characteristic "feel" of the voices from the third world. For instance, the *New York Times* reported,

> The sharpness with which the conference on Church and Society... criticized American policies in Vietnam reflects not only a concern for peace but also a fundamental shift of the balance of power within the World Council of Churches...

More generally a French journalist wrote:

> The confrontation of persons coming specially from insurrection battlefields or engaged in a political revolution, sometimes violent, with defenders of the Western order could have led them to turn their backs on each other. Instead, it led to a dialogue as genuine as it was harsh. To a certain extent that extraordinary conference may start a new orientation of the World Council.

The conference message said:

> [The church] can hope to contribute to the transformation of the world only as it is itself transformed in contact with the world. The God who sent his Son to the cross and manifests his power in weakness has brought us to this point and offers his people new opportunities of service and witness in it. In this conference, we have been led to perceive some of these new opportunities, and have been challenged to prepare ourselves for this task of service.

---

to the criticisms and controversies that have surrounded the World Council of Churches. Similar critiques have on occasion arisen concerning more local and national efforts of the movement, though often in some relation with the concurrent debates around the WCC. If these are largely overlooked, it is partly because it would have been near impossible to assemble an adequately representative spread of evidence from around the world, and partly because it is an undeniable aspect of the vocation of the WCC precisely to embody and make visible a movement that is going on in all sorts of ways in all sorts of situations, and thus to draw the fire of those who criticize or object. (b) This chapter was originally planned as the place where the "outside" critiques of the movement would be chronicled and assessed. As the work towards it developed it became plain, at least to this author, that it is impossible and undesirable to draw any clear line of separation between inside debates and outside critiques; especially with the international and cross-cultural development of the mass media, in print and electronically, as one of the outstanding features of the second half of the 20th century, these distinct levels of debate are found to be constantly feeding into and out of one another.

[3] The material here draws on Paul Abrecht's account in chapter 9 of Harold E. Fey ed., *A History of the Ecumenical Movement*, vol. 2, 1948-68, 2nd ed., WCC, 1986, p.251.

A perceptive if anxious Swiss journalist opined,

> Who has God's wisdom to interpret the evolution and the revolutions of nations? The enterprise is more than hard; it is impossible and can only lead to a major heresy, that of using God as one's own instrument. It is not difficult to discern the spiritual motives of the protagonists of a "theology of revolution"; they refer to the revelation of Christ not only as Lord of the church but of the world.[4]

FIVE STRANDS IN THE RUNNING CONVERSATIONS

"Guns for guerrillas" – reactions to the Programme to Combat Racism

The atmosphere of the ecumenical movement changed decisively in a couple of days in early September 1970. The WCC executive committee, meeting in Arnoldshain, West Germany, awarded a first set of financial grants from the special fund of the newly created Programme to Combat Racism,[5] and issued a straightforward press release reporting the decision and giving a few lines of information on each of the 19 organizations which received grants.[6]

There were screaming headlines the next day in British newspapers, which had virtually nothing to do with the press release issued in Germany. The South African secret service, known as BOSS (Bureau of State Security), with whose ways the WCC staff were to become all too well informed as the controversy continued, had seized an opening to grab the initiative. The news had been telegraphed immediately to Prime Minister John Vorster, brother to one of the principal leaders of the Dutch Reformed Church, whose white section was a vital religious and ideological pillar of the apartheid regime. The headlines came from a rapidly convened press conference where Vorster spoke of the shock and horror at this news of people calling themselves church leaders giving money to organizations that were actively killing and terrorizing people in his part of the world.

Similar headlines appeared in most countries of the rich white West, especially in West Germany. Their effect in the US was to be no less long-lasting, though somewhat less "shocking" because of the lively events and debates to do with race relations there in the years of Martin Luther King, Jr and Malcolm X. Throughout the West the press enjoyed the controversy for months, as political and other leaders, including not a few church people, took up the heady mixture of themes which these grants involved: religion and politics, race relations, the morality of violence, attitudes to the third world – with particular focus on attitudes in the West to its former "colonial subjects".

Within the churches, much attention focused on the apparently inadequate action of the WCC communication department because the press release from Arnoldshain did not reach national church offices until a day or two after Vorster's outburst. The church leaders who would have wanted to present the decision in quite a different way often complained bitterly that they had been left uninformed – although they had full knowledge of the discussions at the Uppsala assembly in 1968 and at the central committee in

---

[4] These quotations from the "Ecumenical Chronicle" containing the message and press comments on the conference in *The Ecumenical Review*, 19, 1, Jan. 1967, pp.59-77.

[5] Elisabeth Adler, *A Small Beginning – An Assessment of the First Five Years of the Programme to Combat Racism*, WCC, 1974, remains one of the fullest and most authoritative accounts, if of course written from the point of view of a WCC "insider", of the crucial early years of the Programme.

[6] *Ibid.*, p.40.

Canterbury a year earlier where the objectives of the PCR and the special fund had been debated.

The ensuing public discussion was, especially in the West, heated to a degree that, 25 increasingly affluent years after the end of the second world war, Western Europe had largely forgotten. As Church of England Bishop Kenneth Sansbury generously acknowledged,[7]

> But there are not only the ignorant and suspicious who fight shy of the PCR, there are also some who have studied the WCC material carefully and at the end come up both hostile and angry. Typical of such people was D.W. Yates, diocesan secretary of the diocese of St Albans, who writing in his personal capacity expresses total opposition, not only to the programme [PCR] but to the WCC and all its works. "I suggest", he writes "the whole debate is being carried on in a vacuum, as though the whole matter was quite separate from what else is going on in the world today around us. In fact, however, I am convinced that the greatest threat to society today is the existence of a well-organized international subversive movement, totally ruthless and dedicated to the violent overthrow of the standards which are accepted as civilized. The bodies involved in this movement seem largely to be extreme Marxist and atheist in their outlook and there is no doubt that once in power Christianity would receive short shrift from most of them." Yates believes that these bodies use "any local grievance that happens to be at hand" – racial and cultural tensions in Africa, the sad history of religious strife in Ireland, and so on... He says that, while many bishops and clergy support the WCC, he knows of "hardly any laity who do except for the few people intimately involved". "This is a burning issue in many parishes and our diocesan stewardship department tells me that the PCR is the biggest hindrance to increased giving to the church at the present time." He sums up his views by saying, "I want to see the Church of England totally dissociate itself from the WCC."

That long quotation can stand for thousands of letters and other protest actions that significantly altered the agenda and the priorities of church leaders in the West.

Another dimension often forgotten is the less heated but no less passionate development in other parts of the world of support for the "positive discrimination" in favour of the oppressed and the underdogs that the grants represented. Baldwin Sjollema, first director of the PCR, recalls,[8]

> The WCC was receiving a good deal of support as well, notably in messages from the All Africa Conference of Churches and from President [Kenneth] Kaunda of Zambia, but as importantly from informal signs of support from black people in South Africa itself, both inside and outside the churches. Invariably, however, they did not want to be quoted for fear of reprisals.

Eight years later, in 1978, the PCR granted $85,000 to the Patriotic Front in Rhodesia, then engaged in the civil war settled a year later by an agreement in which Zimbabwe was born. Reactions to the grant in the British press were almost an exact re-run of the earlier episode. The front-page headline of the *Daily Express* of 11 August 1978 ran, "Rhodesian mission-killers get cash-aid – courtesy of world's churches. BLOOD MONEY." And its editorial included the following,

---

[7] In his full study of the events and the underlying issues, as they came to be seen and discussed in Britain: *Combating Racism – The British Churches and the WCC Programme to Combat Racism*, London, British Council of Churches, 1975, pp.78, written expressly for the BCC, of which he had been general secretary until 1973, to help the British churches' delegates to the Nairobi assembly of the WCC in 1975 prepare for their decisions about the PCR.
[8] In his chapter "Eloquent Action" in Pauline Webb ed., *A Long Struggle – the Involvement of the World Council of Churches in South Africa*, WCC, 1994, p.16.

What the founder of the Christian faith would think of the World Council of Churches we are not able to say. But we recall that He was very specific in His predictions about the fate of those who harm little children. Those who hand over the cash, under whatever pretext, are just as guilty as those who do the dirty work – even if they say nice prayers in the morning. "By their fruits ye shall know them." Well, we know the Patriotic Front. Now we know the World Council of Churches.

Two months later a feature writer in *The Times* of 21 October provided a remarkably different perspective:

The acceptance of violence by African Christians today simply reflects the refusal of the churches of Europe to take the nonviolent demand of the gospel seriously. Western outrage expressed at the giving of symbolic financial gifts to guerrillas is surely ludicrous, coming as it does from Christians who uncomplainingly pay taxes to finance nuclear missiles which are intended to defend our way of life by "taking out" whole cities at a time.

The *Daily Mail* of 23 August, referring to the announcement that the Salvation Army was to withdraw from the WCC (a slight, if understandable, overstatement of the actual decision), headed an editorial "Sense and Salvation" which included the sentences,

Its resignation from the World Council of Churches for that body's financial support for the murderous Patriotic Front in Rhodesia is an act of massive common sense. We must hope that it will start a fashion.[9]

To sum up these episodes there was no better comment than that made for Bishop Sansbury's study by Canon David Paton:

The central issue in the debate about the PCR is the threat to the rich and powerful represented by a deliberate siding with the poor and the weak who happen also to be coloured. At bottom I do not think that the thrust of the programme has been misunderstood. I think it has been understood quite well, and people no more like it than the Sadducees liked that preacher from Nazareth. I have always thought that at bottom it was an issue about the gospel, and I still so think.[10]

"A movement with questionable politics" – constant undertow in the US

Especially in the US the controversy about the PCR was nourished by a long-standing current of anxiety about developments in the mainline and liberal churches attributed to their involvement in the WCC. This current can be found in many quarters but two sources of this undoubtedly powerful anxiety that has accompanied the ecumenical movement for more than thirty years must be outlined here:

1. The *Reader's Digest* is a familiar example of North American publishing, sold and read all over the world, with an attractively folksy blend of short, instantly readable articles, assorted jokes and invitations to buy merchandise. In terms of magazine publishing it is a striking – if lightweight – example of what is now known as globalization, the drive to extend the supposed "good things" of the "Western way of life" throughout the world.

Over the last thirty years it has published a number of articles condemning the WCC and the National Council of the Churches of Christ in the USA. In successive issues of October and November 1971 there were articles by Clarence Hall entitled "Must Our

---

[9] I gratefully acknowledge the source of these quotations from 1978 in Pradip Ninan Thomas's MA dissertation "Media Reportage of the WCC Programme to Combat Racism – A Study of How the British Press Reported on the Grant Given in 1978 by the WCC PCR to the Patriotic Front in Zimbabwe", Leicester, unpubl. diss., Centre for Mass Communication Research, 1983.
[10] The quotation comes from K. Sansbury, in *Combating Racism*, p.25.

Churches Finance Revolution?" and "Which Way the World Council of Churches?" In August 1982 there appeared "Karl Marx or Jesus Christ? Which Master Is the World Council of Churches Serving ..." by Joseph A. Harriss, followed ten years later in February 1993 by "The Gospel According to Marx – Why Have the Interests of the WCC Strayed So Far Afield from Christianity? Top Secret KGB Files Suggest One Reason" by Harriss, described now as "currently a senior editor with *The Digest*'s European Bureau in Paris, who has covered international affairs, including religion, for thirty years".

Both writers had visited the WCC offices in Geneva. Their articles are an accomplished mixture of vivid pictures and selected "facts" or quotations that enable them briefly, but damningly, to portray the WCC as veering from misguided anti-Americanism to deliberate obedience to the dictates of Marxist infiltrators from the Soviet KGB. The third paragraph of the 1993 article, following a judgmental picture of the opening of the Canberra assembly of the WCC in 1991, reads,

> Today the WCC, which includes 322 churches in over 100 countries, is a caricature of the ecumenical movement founded in 1948 by mostly American and European religious leaders. In its desire to accommodate radical anti-Western and third-world pressure groups, the Council has drifted from its original goal of Christian unity into the choppy waters of "secular ecumenism" – ministering to society through political activism. Now *Reader's Digest* reveals a major reason why: for decades this vast organization has been a target for manipulation by decidedly un-Christian forces.

That one paragraph encapsulates several of the emphases that appear time and time again: that the ecumenical movement has betrayed its original, purely religious, goals; that "third-world pressure groups" have taken charge over against what Americans would have wished; that it has abandoned the goal of Christian unity; and that it has let itself be steered by Soviet-Marxist influences and ideas. Almost any paragraph from these articles reveals a comparable barrage of misleading and deliberately tendentious material. Here are two paragraphs which appear towards the end of the 1982 article:

> *Soul-searching time.* The WCC today faces a growing backlash. It began with Protestant laity, who have been voting with their feet and their pocket-books. The United Presbyterian Church, which gives more per capita than any other American WCC affiliate, has lost nearly one million members in the last decade. As one Presbyterian lay representative has observed, "We hear deep resentment about the World Council from many church members. They simply feel that the WCC is dominated by people with a leftist ideology." Financial support by US congregations for activities like the WCC has dropped drastically, to less than half of what these activities received in the past.
>
> The grassroots backlash is now gaining the support of theologians and professional churchmen. Lutheran theologian Richard John Neuhaus, for instance, says, "The WCC has almost become an anti-ecumenical organization by using social and political criteria to distinguish good guys from bad guys. This creates much sharper divisions in the church than any of the old denominational and doctrinal problems did." Says West Germany's Peter Beyerhaus, head of the International Christian Network, "If we don't succeed in bringing the WCC back onto a course that represents its true calling, it would be far better to simply dissolve it."

2. That evident purpose of encouraging US Christians to withdraw moral and financial support to the ecumenical movement, nationally and internationally, is mirrored in the more sophisticated but basically similar intent of Ernest W. Lefever, founder in 1976 and subsequently president of the Ethics and Public Policy Center in Washington DC. Having been present at the first assembly of the WCC at Amsterdam in 1948, presum-

ably in his student days, he has written and published two successive volumes[11] devoted to the WCC which focus on its "questionable politics",[12] as seen from a Republican and Reaganite angle of perception.

The same themes as in the *Reader's Digest* articles reappear here, with a fuller and apparently more representative spread of quotations from WCC documents. The view is centrally political rather than theological; little account is taken of the Council's work in Faith and Order, congregational renewal, Bible study, etc., yet there is a constant thread of accusation that the WCC is abandoning a proper Christian concern for church unity in favour of worldly and political preoccupations. Moreover, while there is a steady accusation of "lack of balance" in the WCC's statements on current political events, the view of the author is no less unbalanced, geared as it is to a US-centred outlook which gives little understanding, let alone respect, to views from any other quarter. Here are some paragraphs from the penultimate, overview chapter, "A Persistent Double Standard", on the period between Nairobi to Vancouver:

> From a rational Western perspective, the WCC was using a rubber yardstick or invoking a double standard, but the matter is more complex. The Council denounced alleged curbs on religious freedom in the Philippines and refused to condemn documented and massive repression of religion in the Soviet Union. According to Western reason and the rule of law such behaviour is a perfect example of the double standard. But from the vantage point of revolutionary logic, including "liberation theology", any action that promotes liberation (read: revolution) is right and that which impedes it is wrong. During the past twelve or more years the WCC generally invoked the single standard of revolutionary logic, having abandoned the canons of social and political responsibility proclaimed at the 1948 Amsterdam assembly. If we assess WCC behaviour by the Amsterdam understanding of the Christian moral tradition, Council leaders strayed far from the founders' intention. Egregious examples of how far include the WCC's unwillingness to condemn the Soviet invasion of Afghanistan or to criticize openly religious persecution in the USSR and its praise of the repressive Marxist regime in Nicaragua and condemnation of the democratically elected government in El Salvador.[13]

> Does this mean that the WCC staff in Geneva and other key Council leaders were taking orders from Moscow? Hardly. There has been, of course, increasing Soviet influence, even pressure, on Council deliberations at every level since the Russian Orthodox Church was admitted to membership in 1961. The 100-plus Soviet bloc delegates at Nairobi and Vancouver, along with third-world and Western sympathizers, were very active both in the open and behind closed doors. Evidence suggests that the leading Soviet delegates were under strict orders to push the Soviet world-view and prescription on all key issues. WCC leaders were aware of this. They were also aware that each Russian Orthodox delegation included at least one KGB agent. "Of course we know that," said the late Cynthia Wedel, a former North American president of the Council, to this writer, adding that it was far better to have Soviet delegates in the WCC than outside.

> The USSR was also successful in increasing the number of Soviet and Soviet bloc staffers at the WCC Geneva headquarters, where key policy decisions on the international agenda are made. In a real sense, the development of the WCC parallels that of the UN general assembly and secretariat. In both institutions the influence of the Soviet bloc states

---

[11] Ernest W. Lefever, *Amsterdam to Nairobi: The World Council of Churches and the Third World* and *Nairobi to Vancouver: The World Council of Churches and the World, 1975-1987* (both: Washington DC, Ethics and Public Policy Center, respectively 1979 and 1987).

[12] A phrase which I owe to a chapter heading in the useful doctoral thesis of Jimmie Dean Ward, "A Critical Evaluation of the Ecumenical Movement in Light of Southern Baptist Perceptions", University Microfilms International, pp.236 submitted for the degree of Th.D, New Orleans Baptist Theological Seminary, 1987, available in the library of the Ecumenical Centre, Geneva.

[13] *Nairobi to Vancouver*, pp.78ff.

and their third-world friends has dramatically increased since the 1950s, when Western members could command a majority vote on any important issue. Now, through coalition politics based on the number of member states, a Soviet-third world alliance can ensure a majority vote. At Vancouver ... there were 336 delegates from the West, compared to 511 from the Soviet bloc and the third world. At Nairobi, there were approximately 300 Western delegates and 350 from the Soviet bloc and the third world. Generally, most delegates from Asia, Africa and Latin America supported the Soviet view along with many from Western countries.[14]

On a different tack, here is Lefever in his closing chapter, "Future of the WCC", reflecting on the long-term implications of his diagnosis:

In a larger sense, the ecumenical movement as manifest in the WCC and the US National Council of Churches – especially in the past two decades – has failed in its culture-forming mission in the Western world. It should be noted here that the main thrust for creating the modern ecumenical movement came from the dynamic interaction of Protestant pluralism in the United States, symbolized by the establishment of the Federal Council of Churches in 1908 and the International Missionary Council in 1921. The character of ecumenical activities since then has reflected in a large measure the changing theological and ecclesiastical trends in mainline Protestant America. From colonial times until recent years in America, the Protestant tradition has performed well the culture-forming task, including the development of a widely shared political ethic. But since the mid-1960s, as Richard John Neuhaus and others have pointed out, the Protestant mainline has forfeited this crucial culture-forming role out of fatigue, lack of creativity, and self-alienation from the classic Christian tradition. Hence the ecumenical movement's social witness has become obsolescent, marginal, irrelevant, or worse.[15]

Other chapters in this volume will provide the material by which to test and evaluate these views. There can be no doubt that the steady criticism of this sort has been a considerable burden to leaders of the WCC member churches in the US and beyond.

"The battle for world evangelism" – the prime evangelical critique

Often with many of the same ideas and expectations as those in "secular" quarters, the period between the WCC's Uppsala (1968) and Nairobi (1975) assemblies saw an upsurge of much more sharply focused critique – indeed, of pointed antagonism and threatened "competition" – in the area of "world mission", and especially of the understanding and practice of evangelism. Again, this largely stemmed from the US, but it had important allies in West Germany, the Netherlands and the UK, and had great influence also in the third-world churches closely linked to the more evangelical mission agencies in the West.

In distinction from the general readerships targeted by the *Reader's Digest* and Lefever, the writers to be mentioned here had in mind a Christian audience. Yet their critique, both by its content and by the precision of its aims, will have considerably augmented the effect of the more general attacks and the comparable TV programmes.[16]

Here the thesis, baldly stated, is that the International Missionary Council, in the years running up to its integration into the WCC in 1961 and still more thereafter, progressively watered down, even abandoned, the prime commitment to evangelism un-

---

[14] *Ibid.*, pp.80f.

[15] *Ibid.*, p.89.

[16] Mention is frequently made, for instance in Lefever's *Nairobi to Vancouver*, p.87, of the "segment" broadcast in CBS-TV's "Sixty Minutes" programme of 23 January 1983. From 1981, critiques of the WCC often included negative information provided by the media-conscious Institute on Religion and Democracy, or IRD.

derstood as the proclamation of the gospel of Christ in favour of a social, at worst revolutionary, approach to "salvation" seen as worldly "progress".

In terms of institutional development, the changes in the IMC were answered by the Billy Graham congresses on evangelism in several areas of the world, starting in Berlin (1966) and climaxing in Lausanne (1974), where many had been expecting the creation of a new IMC. In practice, and thanks not least to strong voices from Latin America (René Padilla and Samuel Escobar among the invited speakers at Lausanne, Emilio Castro on behalf of the wider ecumenical movement, and Orlando Costas as one of the most influential writers), that did not happen. With John Stott, chief drafter of the Lausanne Covenant, bringing a sharp but positive and effective challenge to the Nairobi assembly (1975), considerable efforts were devoted towards reconciliation between the supposedly differing commitments, to such good effect that talk about all-out confrontation soon dwindled. There are still important differences in emphasis and approach; no one should take it for granted that a comparable hostility will never grow again. But through the efforts of such very different people as David Bosch, Emilio Castro, Raymond Fung and Walter Arnold, the climate has improved to an extent few could have foreseen in the early 1970s.

At that time there was a massive critique addressed by American Evangelicals to the Commission on World Mission and Evangelism (CWME) which within the WCC had succeeded to the mandate of the IMC. Two large books may be taken as witnesses, both growing out of doctoral theses: *The Battle for World Evangelism* by Arthur P. Johnston,[17] and *The World Council of Churches and the Demise of Evangelism* by Harvey T. Hoekstra.[18]

Johnston was the more combative. His opening survey and his discussion of the history of mission and evangelism within the ecumenical agencies are dominated alike by awareness of the "three billion who have never heard the gospel" and by a concern for the purity of the evangelical truth of the scriptures. As he traces the story from the beginnings of the IMC at the Edinburgh conference of 1910 up to the Mexico City world mission conference of 1963 and the Uppsala and Nairobi assemblies, he sees it all unmistakably as an outsider, suspicious at first and increasingly hostile to developments that he summarizes as "the crystallization of another gospel" at the Uppsala assembly, so that finally the Bangkok world mission conference of 1973 "codified another mission for the ecumenical and conciliar movement". In the conclusion of his full chapter on the Edinburgh conference, he is already clear where things will go:

> The scriptures have not promised to make a man or a society perfect in this present age, yet nothing contributes more to the ultimate needs of the world than evangelism. Nevertheless, the goal of biblical evangelism is not a Christianized world or a Christlike world but a world evangelization that will bring back the King. New York 1900 was evangelical in the historic sense of the word. Edinburgh 1910 was no longer evangelical but ecumenical, upholding a pluralistic, progressive theology. After Edinburgh 1910, evangelism hesitated, then faltered and almost died in the IMC.[19]

No wonder then that nothing in the later history persuades Johnston of any significant movement in the right direction. After reviewing the story up to the mid-1960s, in particular Philip Potter's speech "Evangelism and the World Council of Churches" to the 1967 central committee as director of CWME, he concludes,

---

[17] Wheaton IL, Tyndale House, 1978, pp.416.
[18] Wheaton IL, Tyndale House, 1979, pp.300.
[19] *Ibid.*, p.52.

> Evangelicals have been right in rejecting ecumenical evangelism. Evangelicals within the movement and without have been slow to discern the basic theological deviations. The debilitating effects paralyze a personal verbal witness, church growth, church extension and mission. The complexity of the philosophical-theological nuances of its Barthian theology, however, is not likely to have an appeal beyond an intellectual elite. Ecumenical theology of evangelism lacks the spirituality and the dynamic of the word and the Spirit.[20]

So also at the end of the book, after a full and by no means uncritical discussion of the distinctive emphases of the Lausanne Covenant and its consequences for the evangelical constituency, he is still warning,

> Evangelicalism by its very nature is ecumenical. It loves and seeks fellowship with "born-again" believers wherever they are found. Para-church evangelical evangelism, however, may be most vulnerable to the post-Vatican II theological relativism expressed in multiple forms of conciliarity – from councils, assemblies and synods to the new congeniality on the local levels. This raises the legitimate question as to the point when evangelical cooperation becomes compromise and complicity in error and "another gospel". There are biblical guidelines beyond which evangelicalism cannot go without falling into evangelistic impotency and, eventually, self-destruction. The complete truthfulness and final authority of scripture provides the essential parameters for Evangelicals.[21]

Hoekstra, earlier a missionary of the Reformed Church of America in Ethiopia, is much more of an insider. His church was a founder member of the WCC; he surveys the history with a closer awareness of the main motives; he spent six weeks in Geneva to check his evidence and test out his approach with the WCC staff there, and above all he participated in the Nairobi assembly and is evidently excited by the depth and truth of the change there. In earlier chapters he traces how "mission (was) in transition" at the New Delhi assembly and the Mexico City conference, how Uppsala "reconceptualized mission" into what he baldly calls "new mission", and how this was "implemented" by the Bangkok conference. So he fully expected the WCC staff to have it "ratified" at Nairobi. But the Holy Spirit had other ideas; "many delegates", especially those from Norway, came determined to ensure that a true evangelism was restored into the WCC programme:

> The fifth assembly laid a base for the WCC staff and central committee to respond with a new commitment, new programmes and people to back up that commitment. ... It has once again become fashionable to speak of evangelism in the churches.[22]

At the same time:

> There is, sadly, one real disappointment. The fifth assembly failed to recognize adequately the tragic fact of the nearly three billion people who remain unreached with the gospel. Even if every recommendation were carried out faithfully, the great missionary task of the church would remain unfinished.[23]

The book concludes with a fair degree of scepticism over whether the WCC overall will really back up in practice the undoubted commitment of some of its member churches and staff to launch genuine programmes of evangelism in true continuity with the "classical" missionary tradition. He closes with eloquent pleas to the churches to

---

[20] *Ibid.* p.119.
[21] *Ibid.*, p.359.
[22] *The World Council of Churches and the Demise of Evangelism*, p.153.
[23] *Ibid.*, p.156.

keep pressing this concern on an organization all too likely to say some of the right things on occasion but then to lose sight of them again as other tasks come along.

Both writers are unashamedly North Americans; they are no less unashamedly "evangelicals", in the sense of having a commanding loyalty to one particular "party" within what they know to have been for centuries a worldwide church with many other such traditions; moreover, they are both heart and soul committed to evangelism as they know it, and apparently take little interest in anything else the ecumenical movement, let alone the WCC, may be about. Neither book conveys much sense of a "dialogue", let alone a dialogue of equals. The central question is: Does the WCC measure up to what it ought to be? In neither case can a straight "yes" be given.

The same is true for the parallel critique developed at the same period in West Germany by Peter Beyerhaus of Tübingen[24] and Rolf Scheffbuch of the church of Württemberg,[25] among others. In that country too, despite the testing period of Hitler and the ensuing world war, the post-war period had seen a growing split between "Evangelikale" (in German the normal spelling of the word has been used since the Reformation for what in English is called "Protestant") and "Ökumeniker" (a misleading term if it appears to designate a narrow "party" over against other such). This split reached a point of particular sharpness at the time of the Bangkok world mission conference, but has moderated since, without by any means disappearing. A critique of comparable ferocity was published in the last months of the century by Gerhard Besier, Gerhard Lindemann and Armin Boyens, the latter a staff member of the WCC in the 1960s, focusing on their view of the WCC's failure adequately to support dissident Christians in the countries under Soviet domination during the cold war.[26] Their detailed research, supported by a large grant from the interior ministry of the government of German chancellor Helmut Kohl, betrays in every chapter an unquestioning "Western free-market" ideology, so that the scandals that blew away Kohl's credibility at the precise time the huge book was published have also left Besier and Boyens with little credibility.

Two useful summaries present the main lines of the argument.

1. In a survey[27] drawn up in 1970, i.e. before the Bangkok conference but in the light of the Uppsala assembly, Helmut Aichelin, Reinhard Frieling and Marianne Koch identified seven areas of question where *evangelikal* critics were becoming increasingly anxious about developments in the international ecumenical movement:

– The "super-church": Are we moving towards a time of colossal organizations that will abolish all sense of human-scale community?

---

[24] A prolific author, and progenitor of the Frankfurt Declaration on the Fundamental Crisis in Christian Missions of March 1970 by a group of concerned theologians and mission supporters. See his *Humanisierung: Einzige Hoffnung der Welt?*, 1970, transl. as *Missions: Which Way?*, Grand Rapids MI, Zondervan, 1971, pp.120, with a foreword by Donald McGavran and a preface by Harold Lindsell; and his *Bangkok '73 – Anfang oder Ende der Weltmission? Ein gruppendynamisches Experiment*, Bad Liebenzell, Liebenzeller Mission, 1973, pp.255.

[25] A delegate to the Nairobi assembly and editor of the book *FRAG-würdige Ökumene*, Neuhausen-Stuttgart, Hänssler, 1974, pp.96, which documents the preparations, discussions and follow-through of a particularly important visit to Geneva by an impressive group from the Ev. Landeskirche of Württemberg, including a long letter from Philip Potter, by then general secretary of the WCC, though writing also out of his experience as director of the CWME from 1965 to 1972.

[26] Gerhard Besier, Armin Boyens and Gerhard Lindemann, *Nationaler Protestantismus und Ökumenische Bewegung: kirchliches Handeln im Kalten Krieg (1945-1990)*, Berlin, Duncker und Humblot, 1999.

[27] In Arbeitstexte nr. 7, "Gegen-Ökumene: Kritische Stimmen zur Ökumene aus Protestantismus und Katholizismus", mimeographed, published by the *Evangelische Zentralstelle für Weltanschauungsfragen*, Stuttgart, Sept. 1970.

- Are we seeing the early stages of a "theology of unity" that will prove domineering and dominating to any local and particular way of believing and acting as Christians?
- In regard to ecclesiology, must we not look for a more adequate doctrinal basis than the basis of the WCC? There are objections to the Council's proscription of proselytism, and fears about its universalist outlook.
- There are fears of a "hidden confessionalism" among the partners in the ecumenical dialogue, not least among the Orthodox, discussion with whom reveals a much sharper division between East and West than between Catholic and Protestant.
- But there are still many fears about the centralizing and institutionally self-concerned power of Rome, not least now that such friendly noises are being heard about Catholic commitment to the "one ecumenical movement".
- Other fears are aroused by the term "secular ecumenism": Is the WCC proposing to abandon the central evangelistic purpose of the church in favour of some secular political crusade?
- Already some of the political declarations and attitudes to be met in the WCC arouse fears of a misleadingly over-simplified dogmatism, and an undemocratic glorification of "revolution" that are false and dangerous.

2. Writing in the *Lutheran World* in 1975, the Latvian theologian Gunnars Ansons surveys "Ecumenism under Tension: Evangelical versus Social-Political Forces" at some length, and concludes,

> I believe this chapter of differences on social issues can be closed. In future, the debate between Evangelicals and the rest of Christendom will be on understanding the Bible as the word of God, and on its authority, with the whole host of subsidiary questions of historicity, exegetical principles, and the philosophical backgrounds of different parts of the scriptures as well as of their present exegetes. ... No doubt the social issues will continue to cause tensions and misunderstandings, but the ground has been cut from under them. "Liberals and Evangelicals are closer to each other today than either camp realizes," Richard Quebedeaux writes in his book *The Young Evangelicals: Revolution in Orthodoxy*.[28]... The really important ecumenical questions in relations with Evangelicals will have to do with the understanding of the scriptures rather than with social ethics or ecclesiology.[29]

One-sidedness comes all too easily: complementary examples from interfaith dialogues concerned with the Middle East

The concentration in the previous two sections on voices in North America and Western Europe may be usefully complemented by briefer accounts of quite directly comparable "unbalances" in the attitudes, expectations and suspicions voiced by very different spokespersons within both the majority Muslim communities in Arab lands, and the widely based but energetic international Jewish communities.[30]

The Arab world

The far-flung Muslim communities are not short of people eager to point out the weaknesses and failings of the Christian world, and not least of its World Council of Churches. There is, however, no overall unanimity among its Arab critics. The over-

---

[28] New York, Harper & Row, 1974.
[29] *Lutheran World*, 3, 1975, pp.210-11.
[30] The writer gratefully acknowledges the considerable help provided for this section by colleagues much more directly informed about both milieux, though as always the responsibility for any mistakes must be his.

whelming majority of these see any such international Christian organization as essentially an American-controlled instrument devoted to Protestant missionary "conquest" of Islam. Others, fewer in number but more sophisticated and better informed, being subtly aware of the inner, cultural and religious power of West European forces, see the Council in terms of a liberal movement engaged in some sort of Christian self-secularization, no less intent, in the long run, on the undermining of Islam.[31]

The former equate the WCC directly with the evangelical wing of Protestant Christianity, especially in its Reaganite, North American forms. The WCC is seen as closely linked with the US government, particularly with the Central Intelligence Agency (CIA). This identification has become all the more familiar and pervasive since 1983, when Muhammad Hasanayn Haykal included it in a chapter in one of his books dealing with the Coptic church in Egypt.[32] One of the most elaborate Islamic studies on contemporary missionary strategies among Christians simply does not differentiate between the WCC and the powerful US-based evangelical mission agencies.[33] Here the call made by Christians for dialogue with Islam is seen as serving the purpose of preparing for new efforts of mission, as a more subtle approach which aims no less directly at de-Islamizing Muslims. From another angle it is seen as a religious-cultural weapon in the campaign for Western political and economic domination of the Muslim lands.

In the latter case, the WCC is recognized as a Christian organization taking a markedly different line to that familiar in the Roman Catholic and Orthodox churches. These often agree with Islam in seeking to preserve a sense of the "sacred" in public life, and therefore in reaffirming the role of moral values and of religion as a positive force in the life of a people. The kind of dialogue for which the WCC is heard to call is interpreted rather as some sort of syncretism, involving a relativistic attitude to all religious truths, and therefore as a form of anthropocentrism superseding obedience to God. Saoud al Mawla, an intellectual who is both committed to Muslim-Christian dialogue and active in the field, criticizes the WCC for an implicit – indeed, often more than implicit – theology that speaks of Islam as either a culture or an ideology, in both cases no more than a human world-view, expressing a search for truth, but not as obedience to a revelation from God.[34] He sees it as a natural consequence of this orientation that the WCC is acting as an agent of cultural uniformization serving the same powers as economic globalization. Indeed, he also sees it as significant of precisely this subservience to a wider power that the WCC should have a specific committee responsible for dialogue with Judaism (i.e. the Committee on the Church and the Jewish People), while its concern for Islam is handled through the more general Sub-unit on Dialogue with People of Living Faiths and Ideologies.

---

[31] See, for instance, Rafiq Habib, *Who Sells Egypt? The State, The Elite, The Church?* (in Arabic), Cairo, Misr al Arabiyya lil nashr, 1994, where the author highlights especially a supposedly German inspiration.

[32] M.H.Haykal, *The Autumn of Anger* (in Arabic), Cairo, 1983. The author is a widely read and highly respected public figure in Egypt. This book, like others by him, was a best-seller and has been translated into a number of European languages. He explicitly states here that his sources are primarily Christian. He quotes, in extenso, an anonymous document published in Egypt in the late 1950s, *The Coptic Church Confronts Colonialism and Zionism*, no date or publisher.

[33] See Muhammad 'Am'ra, *The Strategies of Christianization in the Islamic World, or The Protocols of the Christianization's Priests* (in Arabic), Malta, Islamic World Studies Centre, 1992.

[34] Saoud al Mawla, *Muslim-Christian Dialogue and the Need for Taking a Risk* (in Arabic), Beirut, 1996, p.34.

Whatever the differences in these two basic approaches, they converge in a critique of the Council's claim of universality, often expressed in the form of a "truly ecumenical outlook". Both views see this as a cloaked form of pursuit of a single world government, which in turn is supposed to be the ultimate aim of the Jewish-Masonic conspiracy that has for so long attacked the house of Islam.

These same Muslim voices will therefore readily join in stigmatizing the philozionism of the WCC. They see this as arising out of a combination of Protestant biblical theology, guilt feelings towards the Jewish people, and Jewish influence in the international arena, strongly aligned to the political interests of the West.[35]

So also these same voices speak as one about the impact on the lives of Christian communities in the Arab-Islamic world of their partnership with international bodies in the ecumenical movement. Any such partnership is seen as exacerbating their feelings of cultural alienation, their concentration on their own interests as minorities, and as diminishing their loyalty to their own nations. It is seen as a corrupting influence on the clergy and on Christian lay elites alike.[36]

These ideas are to be found in many different, but seldom original publications. They come equally from more conservative Muslim circles and from radical Islamist opposition groups. Most of the writers are journalists who reflect, in other ways also, the suspicion of certain Arab governments towards the degree of Western influence in international organizations seeking contacts in their countries.

The resulting image of the WCC in the Arab-Muslim world has proved to be one that can be changed at best very slowly. It has to be understood that the voices of "friends" of the ecumenical movement, whether Christian or Muslim, are almost inevitably less audible than those of its detractors. Most of the movement's friends use a language which, since it le properly sober, is unlikely to communicate to a wider public. Arab media are no less sensationalist and interested in controversy, in their own way, than the media of the West.

Other friends choose to be reserved. Their own public credibility may suffer from being associated with the WCC. They may prefer to avoid risks, especially on matters they regard as less than urgent or of lower priority. They may not feel a strong enough commitment to the ecumenical movement to stand out publicly in its defence. Many of them may well also lack sufficient knowledge or information about what is really going on in the movement, let alone of the deeper reasons for it.

While the influence of the publications here referred to should not be over-estimated, it should not be minimized either. For it rests on a deeply-rooted suspicion of Western Christianity and what have long been considered to be its hidden, or semi-hidden, motives. That suspicion, in turn, feeds off a no less long-standing view of complex social and cultural phenomena in strange and unfamiliar societies as best interpreted in terms

---

[35] Saoud al Mawla goes so far as to suggest a direct link between the foundation of the WCC in 1948 and the creation of the state of Israel that same year: *Muslim-Christian Dialogue and the Need for Taking a Risk*, Beirut, 1996, p.49.

[36] See, for example, M.H. Haykal, *The Autumn of Anger*. It is because of the long-standing respect and credibility accorded to this author that he has been widely quoted as drawing from reliable Christian sources, even though he deliberately chose not to quote any names in view of the nature of the information given orally to him. Since they were never convincingly denied, these same accusations have found their way, quoted now as established facts, into an otherwise entirely serious and reputable academic study "Le renouveau copte: La communauté comme acteur politique", by Dina al Khawaga, thèse de doctorat en sciences politiques, Institut d'études politiques de Paris, mai 1993.

of conspiracies against Islam. Nor should it be overlooked that although most of these writers are Muslims, they draw eagerly on Christian critics of the WCC and of the ecumenical movement – the Protestant academic, for instance, Rafiq Samuel Habib, who is a prolific author, or William Sulayman Qaladah, a Coptic jurist and historian. The former has been writing recently on modern Islamic and Christian political-religious movements. The latter was much preoccupied by attempts to Westernize the Coptic church. Nor must it be forgotten that the reproaches and accusations put forward by persons like these will surely be shared to some extent by Christian leaders in the various churches.

Jewish-Christian dialogue

The situation in the dialogue between Christians and Jews is of course different in detail, but there are also several similarities. Any commentator in this field must begin by taking into account a notable assymetry in this dialogue, which often disconcerts Christians. Assymetry between two dialogue partners must be accepted as a likely element in any dialogue, not least when this is between two religious communities. But there is a quite specific assymetry, rooted in their different histories and theologies, between Jews and Christians.

"While an understanding of Judaism in New Testament times is an integral and indispensable part of any Christian theology, for Jews a 'theological' understanding of Christianity is of a less than essential or integral significance."[37] From the beginning it has had to be understood in all contacts between such bodies as the WCC and the Vatican with Jewish organizations that their conversation could not be limited to theological issues. It has been important – indeed obvious – for Jews to make sure that Christians, through dialogue, should become and remain allies in confronting antisemitism. Jews have all along also felt it necessary to try and make their Christian partners aware of the feelings of the Jewish community about any attempts by Christians to evangelize Jews. And there has from the outset been a clear priority to make Christians sensitive to the importance of the state of Israel for the entire Jewish people.

Real-life issues have thus predominated over theological concerns in the agenda of the International Jewish Committee for Interreligious Consultations (IJCIC), the body established in the 1970s to take responsibility for dialogues with the Vatican and the WCC. The IJCIC is an umbrella organization of the major Jewish world bodies: the World Jewish Congress, the American Jewish Committee, the Anti-Defamation League, the Israel Committee for Interreligious Consultations, and the Synagogue Council of America. The issues mentioned above have predominated in the official meetings, though not wholly to the exclusion of theological questions raised by one side or the other.

The records show that the IJCIC has all along monitored closely what the WCC was doing in any field of interest to them. Statements and documents of the Council have been studied by the IJCIC and commented on in the common forum known as the liaison planning committee. This has frequently served as a place where contentious issues could be discussed and controversial positions clarified. Since its last meeting in 1994 the role and activity of the IJCIC has apparently declined, because its central organizational component, the Synagogue Council of America (itself comprising the three major

---

[37] From "Ecumenical Considerations on Jewish-Christian Dialogue", WCC executive committee, 1.4.1982.

streams of modern American Judaism, the Orthodox, the Conservative and the Reform), has collapsed on account of the withdrawal of the Orthodox Jews.

From the beginning the major issue on the agenda between the IJCIC and the WCC has been the question of the Israeli-Palestinian conflict. The Amsterdam assembly expressed a certain bafflement: "We do not undertake to express an opinion", but since the six-day war in 1967 the WCC has found it necessary to articulate a position. It has all along concurred with the comparable resolutions of the UN, emphasizing repeatedly two major points: (1) "the right of every state in the area, including Israel, to live in peace within secure and recognized boundaries, free from threats or acts of force";[38] and (2) "the mutual recognition of the Israeli and Palestinian people on the basis of equality is the only guarantee for peace in the region".[39]

During the 1970s the IJCIC repeatedly reproached the WCC for being biased towards the Palestinian understanding of the conflict, and saw it as under pressure from its members and others to espouse the Arab view. Rabbi Marc Tannenbaum of the American Jewish Committee took this as an additional reason for Jewish organizations to keep the dialogue with the WCC going, lest the churches fall into the arms of the enemies of the Jewish state. "The absence of ongoing communication between leaders and representatives of the WCC and its member denominations, and world Jewish bodies, has resulted in a vacuum which has been quickly filled by Arab and pro-Arab forces who have brought great pressure on the WCC to adopt a one-sided position on the Middle East crisis." A request to the WCC for two million dollars for refugee work among Palestinians is seen as "an indication of the nature and size of pressures that are being pressed increasingly upon Western Christians by the Arab world".[40]

Moreover the programme on Christian-Muslim dialogue carried on by the WCC is seen as having negative repercussions on the Council's thinking about the Middle East conflict. It has been said that Muslims took up this dialogue "in order to influence their Christian partners to condemn Israel's policies, even its existence". The World Muslim Congress, with which the WCC is in dialogue, is said "to have adopted the most extreme antisemitism".[41]

Several other reasons are seen to be involved in the WCC's hostility to the state of Israel. By virtue of the theological positions of some of its member churches, the WCC is said to harbour "Christian anti-Zionism". Further, the perceived pro-Palestinian stance is seen to result from the close relationship the WCC has with the third world. "The WCC is deeply involved with the third world, and this connection dictates its politics, including its identification with the Palestinian-Arab cause."

The Jewish author Paul Giniewski suggests that the WCC, by its very denunciation of antisemitism, is providing arguments for antisemites and to the enemies of Israel:

> The World Council of Churches... could be providing arguments to antisemites and to the enemies of Israel. It is in its support for the Palestinians that the WCC document openly

---

[38] "Statement on the Gulf War, the Middle East and the Threat to World Peace", in M. Kinnamon ed., *Signs of the Spirit: Official Report: 7th Assembly, Canberra, Australia, 7-20 February 1991*, WCC, 1991, p.214.

[39] E.g. in the statement by Emilio Castro, WCC general secretary, on the Palestinian declaration of independence, 12.12.1988.

[40] From *News from the American Jewish Committee*, 18.12.1970, p.4.

[41] Geoffrey Wigoder, *Jewish-Christian Relations since the Second World War*, New York, Manchester Univ. Press, 1988, pp.20, 110-112.

reveals its fundamental position. It denounces "the oppression of Palestinians by Israelis", "this unjust and oppressive occupation", and affirms its "solidarity with the Palestinian claim for a national identity and an independent state".[42]

The February 1991 statement concerning the Gulf war, made after long discussion by the WCC Canberra assembly, was "carefully read" by the IJCIC and harshly criticized – so much so that the IJCIC "questioned the future of the relationship between the two (bodies)".[43] Seymour Reich, chairman of the IJCIC, publicly expressed disappointment that the WCC had not given voice to the concerns of the Jewish organizations, i.e. a statement against antisemitism. When Emilio Castro, then WCC general secretary, made a public statement on antisemitism to the European churches, this was not considered enough. Reich voiced his "dismay" about the Council's "insensitivity and indifference towards the fate of the state and the people of Israel as well as their behaviour during the agonizing events" [the Scud missiles over Israel]. Reich's letter maintains that there is a "hidden bias, unbalance of judgment and a lack of concern for the Jewish people".[44]

Another sensitive point has been the unwillingness of the IJCIC to accept that the WCC might engage in relations with Jewish individuals, groups or organizations other than itself, or those it had recommended. The executive secretary of the Dialogue sub-unit at the time, Allan Brockway, phrased this as "the IJCIC's desire to be the 'gate-keeper' of the WCC's contact with the Jewish community".[45] Controversy arose again, in the early 1990s, around Brockway's successor, Hans Ucko. The IJCIC reproached the Council for employing in this post a person of Jewish origin.[46] Particular criticism was expressed by the Orthodox Jewish constituency, which objected to any relationship with the WCC while the present secretary was employed.[47]

Nonetheless, Rabbi David Rosen, a long-standing partner in the dialogue, has suggested[48] that the chief goals of the IJCIC for dialogue with Christians have been to a certain extent achieved: the church has committed itself to fight antisemitism, and the Vatican has recognized the state of Israel. The question of mission to Jews may still be on the agenda of some churches, but it is not left unquestioned within internal Christian discussions. Could the Jewish-Christian relationship being explored in dialogues between the Jewish and Christian world organizations now have reached a juncture beyond which quite new avenues of concern may be explored?

---

[42] P. Giniewski, *La croix des Juifs*, Genève, Editions MJR, 1994, pp.227-28 (author's translation).

[43] Interview with Gerhard Riegner in *Jerusalem Post*, 9 May 1991.

[44] Letter from Seymour D. Reich, chairman of IJCIC, to general secretary Emilio Castro, 26 April, 1991.

[45] Jean Halpérin, representing IJCIC in a letter dated 4 June 1985, voiced the concern that "the invitation to a Jewish consultant... took place without prior consultation with IJCIC".

[46] For instance, in the World Jewish International Congress Report, November 1992: "Another obstacle to a solid relationship past and present, say Jewish observers, is the Protestants' selection of a Jew who converted to Christianity to be the official representative working with the Jewish community."

[47] "'It communicates that their (sc. the WCC's) attitude is 'we'll sock it to the Jews', said F. Schonfeld, the Orthodox co-chair of the interfaith committee of the Synagogue Council of America... 'We will not have any dealings with the WCC... if he remains in charge of Jewish-Christian matters.'... 'They're fully aware that Ucko is an impediment. The ball is in their court.'" From "Jews and Protestants renew dialogue after years of frosty relations", by Debra Nussbaum Cohen, 2 November 1992.

[48] In "How has the Fundamental Agreement between the Holy See and Israel affected the Dialogue ?", his address at the International Jewish-Catholic Symposium, 10 February 1997.

"Succumbing to secular values and considering them universal"[49] – the never-finished discussion with the Orthodox

The church which, earlier than any single other communion, acted in a way that led to the founding of the World Council of Churches, was the Ecumenical Patriarchate of Constantinople, with the encyclical from its holy synod addressed "Unto the Churches of Christ Everywhere" in January 1920.[50] At the Amsterdam assembly in 1948 all the churches in communion with the ecumenical patriarch, except those in countries ruled by communist governments, became founder members of the WCC. Yet as early as 1963 the noted Orthodox theologian Alexander Schmemann was warning,

> Officially the Orthodox participation in the WCC looks like a well-established tradition, raising no questions or doubts. ... But does this official optimism correspond to the real situation? To this question I must quite honestly give a negative answer... first, that there exists a discrepancy between the official Orthodox position in the WCC and the real Orthodoxy, and, second, that this discrepancy constitutes an urgent issue for the WCC which, if it is not understood on time, may sooner or later lead to a major ecumenical crisis.[51]

Prophetic words. At the time, Geneva-watchers would have found them incomprehensible. The Orthodox participation in the WCC had been greatly strengthened by the entry of the Russian Orthodox Church and its sisters of Romania, Bulgaria and Poland at the 1961 New Delhi assembly. To be sure, the Orthodox were still – as they had been since 1948 – in a minority among the participants, numerically speaking. The major crisis appeared publicly in August 1973 in two texts sent to the central committee. One was a "Declaration of the Ecumenical Patriarchate on the Occasion of the 25th Anniversary of the WCC";[52] the other a "Message of Patriarch Pimen of Moscow and All Russia and the Holy Synod of the Russian Orthodox Church".[53]

The former was a well-rounded summary of ecumenical advance, but included judicially phrased warnings about a dangerous lack of balance. After a lengthy catalogue of "contemporary social evils" it continued,

> These all make up the untold sufferings of striving humanity in our time. The World Council of Churches knows itself called from within the family of mankind to make some effort to tackle the challenges of these many and ever-increasing demands. That throws up, however, the question whether it is these issues and only these which properly constitute the objectives and orientation of the World Council.

Later, it devoted several paragraphs to essential tasks of the Council, including this:

---

[49] From § 24b of *Common Understanding and Vision of the WCC: Preliminary Observations on the Reflection Process*, the final document of the inter-Orthodox consultation held in the Orthodox Centre of the Ecumenical Patriarchate, Chambésy, Geneva, 19-24 June 1995, published in G. Lemopoulos ed., *The Ecumenical Movement, the Churches and the World Council of Churches*, WCC, 1996, pp.63. The full sentence runs: "We have the impression that the WCC is succumbing to the pressure of adopting secular values, considering them universal and, therefore, acceptable by all churches or the cultural ethos in which these churches live and witness." (p.15)

[50] Fuller details in the opening chapter of W. A. Visser 't Hooft's *The Genesis and Formation of the World Council of Churches*, WCC, 1982, pp.1-8.

[51] From his "Moment of Truth for Orthodoxy" in Keith Bridston and Walter D. Wagoner eds, *Unity in Mid-Career: An Ecumenical Critique*, New York, Macmillan, 1963, re-published in Daniel B. Clendenin ed., *Eastern Orthodox Theology – A Contemporary Reader*, Grand Rapids MI, Baker, 1995. Schmemann taught at St Vladimir's Seminary in the USA.

[52] Most readily available in G. Limouris ed., *Orthodox Visions of Ecumenism – Statements, Messages and Reports on the Ecumenical Movement 1902-1992*, WCC, 1994, pp.50-54.

[53] Published in *International Review of Mission*, 63, 249, January 1974, pp.125-29.

The WCC must equally take seriously the reactions of our contemporaries to what the churches are offering, however justified or unjustified these reactions may be.... Any pursuit of aims foreign to its nature or which could move it away from its original and specifically churchly, spiritual goals, is on this account to be strictly avoided.[54]

The Russian message concentrated on the findings of the Bangkok world mission conference, and in many ways echoed the evangelical critique summarized in the previous section. For instance, it spoke of "perplexity and regret that are increased by examination of the conference documents":

> ... the deviation from positively indicating these personal and eternal dimensions of salvation as integral to the true understanding of salvation in the part of the report that is specially devoted to theological reflections can easily be assumed as a deliberate trend towards one-sided and detrimental understanding of salvation in the spirit of boundless "horizontalism". ... There is no room left for the main "vertical" dimensions that would have indicated that salvation requires personal perfection as a part of a social organism called upon to fight against the sin that is both in and out in order to achieve the fullness of life in the vital communion with God in both the temporal and eternal worlds.

Two paragraphs later:

> In the documents there are statements that have no clear and direct confirmation by the scriptures. The following passage from document 39 concerning the dialogue with peoples of living faiths can serve as an example: "Our dialogue will be open and free... As to apparently irreconcilable differences we shall remember Our Lord's promise that the Spirit will lead us into all truth." But are the words from the gospel said about the dialogues between different religions? And doesn't this rather free application of them come into contradiction with the exegetical tradition of the ancient undivided church?[55]

These challenges gave rise to a series of efforts: visits, articles in journals, invitations to Orthodox to share in meetings they might otherwise have missed, and above all a series of consultations called specifically to enable Orthodox leaders to consult together about key questions arising. The texts produced by no less than 21 such meetings between 1975 and 1991 are published in the book compiled by Gennadios Limouris (see note 51). Of these, Sofia 1981, Chambésy 1986, Canberra 1991 and its follow-up in Chambésy the same year all quite deliberately and carefully address the "crisis" of understanding and confidence between the Orthodox churches and the ecumenical movement as symbolized and led by the WCC. These efforts have achieved much, not least in helping the WCC itself to fulfil the hope its leading Orthodox staff member in 1973, Nikos Nissiotis, formulated at a meeting to take stock of the two major letters:

> The WCC has to recapture this wholeness of the Christian presence and accept the exchange of charismata as one of its most primary tasks and to act in humility without triumphalisms or self-sufficiencies in a mutual correction of traditions.[56]

Yet the unease is by no means overcome. Despite the many meetings and the hundreds of pages produced, and despite outstanding addresses by three leading Orthodox theologians of different backgrounds, the consultation called by Syndesmos on behalf of the Orthodox youth movements in 1995 raises anew a long list of "difficulties we face"

---

[54] These two quotations from §§11-12 and 22g-22h, in *Orthodox Visions of Ecumenism*, pp.52,53,54.

[55] *International Review of Mission*, 63, 249, Jan. 1974, p.128.

[56] From an unpublished working paper for the WCC week of meetings, November 1973, "Orthodox Criticism of the WCC", p.11.

– theological, cultural and procedural – and lays most of the obligation to discover "solutions" to these squarely on the WCC and its "majority" Protestant churches.

In fact, Schmemann already had discerned in his 1963 article the roots of the problem in a way that neither the Protestants nor the Orthodox themselves have known how to overcome. He stated baldly,

> To explain this failure, two facts are of paramount importance. One is the isolation of the Orthodox church from the Christian West, the other the specifically Western character and ethos of the ecumenical movement.

Spelling these out at length, he discussed the "basic terms of reference of the ecumenical encounter and conversation":

> From the Orthodox point of view the only really common language, the only workable set of references in such a conversation, would be supplied by that tradition which at one time was accepted by all Christians as the common and universal teaching of the church; that tradition was precisely the tradition represented by Orthodoxy.... Hence, the only adequate ecumenical method from the Orthodox point of view was that of a total and direct doctrinal confrontation, with, as its inescapable and logical conclusion, the acceptance of truth and the rejection of error. Throughout all its history Orthodoxy knew only those two categories: the right belief (orthodoxy) and the heresy, without any possibility of compromise between them. Heresy was looked at not so much as intellectual distortion, but as a deficient faith, endangering salvation itself. It was, therefore, truth, and not unity, which in the Orthodox opinion and experience had to be the real goal of the ecumenical movement, unity in this experience being nothing else but the natural consequence of truth, its fruit and blessing.

Still more, he insisted on the "falsehood of the Orthodox position within the WCC":

> Because of the Western religious situation, the structure of the Council is based on the denominational principle. Since no common definition of the "church" is to be found, any group with some degree of organizational autonomy must be accepted as "church" even if this term does not belong to its self-determination. This principle adequately reflects the Protestant view of the ecumenical movement, but is radically incompatible with the views of the Roman and Orthodox churches. What is involved here is not a question of prestige... but a question of ecumenical truth and reality.... By accepting the denominational principle and applying it to themselves, the Orthodox betrayed once more their own ecumenical mission and function, namely, representing the wholly different pole of the experience of the church, or, in other terms, the church herself in all her reality and unity. This, however, is to be achieved not by the routine repetition of her claim to be the true church, but by the firm affirmation of the simple fact that in any ecumenical encounter the Orthodox church is always and by her very nature the other half standing together with, and yet always against, the totality of the Protestants. As long as this real opposition is not expressed in the very structure of the WCC, the position of Orthodoxy in it will be misleading and confusing for both the Orthodox themselves and their Protestant brothers.[57]

By the time of the Harare assembly in 1998 the WCC was determined to confront many fundamental issues through a Special Commission on Orthodox Participation in the WCC, to report in 2002.

CRITICISMS AND CONTROVERSIES: WHAT HAS BEEN LEARNED?

There can never be a final resolution, let alone summary, adequate to the range of debates upon which this chapter has touched. This is not the place to try to "answer" the

---

[57] In the Baker Books reprint (note 50 above), pp.205, 206-207 and 209-10.

critics or "resolve" the controversies. But it is a place to reflect on what has been learned within the ecumenical movement as a result of so much demanding criticism. At least seven long-range and, on the whole, positive lessons for ecumenical awareness and obedience have been widely learned as a result.

Where there is no criticism, there will be no movement

A former colleague on the WCC staff has remarked, "In the five years I have been home since my time in Geneva, I can't recall any occasion when people were seriously critical of the ecumenical movement." That is surely neither healthy nor encouraging. The things of God will never advance if people simply shrug their shoulders about it all.

It is the ecumenical movement in which Christians and the churches are engaged

The phrase "ecumenical movement" is familiar as a technical term, but many have forgotten the precise meaning it carries. (The same is true for the less accurate term popularized by the Second Vatican Council, "ecumenism".) The word "ecumenical" points to all Christians or the whole church, in their service of all humankind or the whole world. The word "movement" is used to indicate that it is God the Holy Spirit who is leading along paths that cannot be known in advance, towards the wholeness of God's kingdom. The central concern of the ecumenical movement is not for the good repute of any party or institution, but quite simply for what God is calling his servant people to be and do in each new situation.

Precisely because it is the obedience of "the whole church" that is in question, the movement must involve a constant flow of debate, question, criticism and, where necessary, controversy about any and every point on which there is as yet no clear agreement. God gives us to each other as partners and servants, as human beings with our diverse outlooks, hopes and priorities. Especially when we are trying to handle and heal the great divisions between Christians, let alone outbreaks of new divisions between Christians or between different ethnic or religious communities, we cannot suppose that agreement will easily be found.

Yet God gives us one another also as people who can at best discover possibilities of friendship and understanding even in situations of hostility and rejection. That is what "ecumenical movement" is about. The Holy Spirit can open paths of reconciliation even in the depths of hatred. Even sharply polemical voices may on occasion be needed to disturb complacency or error, and to prompt self-criticism and repentance. For these last are the essential building blocks of all ecumenical movement.

The movement is far from reaching its goal: neither in a fully reconciled and effectively united church, still less in a harmonious, mutually enriching world community. Constant debate is necessary to clarify where the movement should be trying to go next. People who disagree with the current dominant view should be welcome, provided only that contributions are made in good faith and not in the service of alien gods. The point of ecumenical bodies like the WCC is not to insist they are right but to seek for what can prove to be closer to the purposes of God for God's church and world.

Ecumenical leaders do well to spend time on those "outside" the movement

The value of any one criticism always need to be discerned with care; just because they are critical does not mean that they are necessarily speaking the truth. Nonetheless, these years of controversy teach that any ecumenical grouping would do well to take note of any Christian neighbours who do not see fit to take part in the ecumenical striving. Why not? Are there ways in which our group, despite being devoted to the good of the whole, may actually seem hostile or unattractive to these others? What could any of us be doing to heal the rift, and to discover what God requires of us together?

In this chapter there has been brief mention of the role played by Emilio Castro in moving between the WCC and those responsible for the meetings of Evangelicals at Lausanne, Pattaya and Manila that could easily have proved overtly competitive with the WCC and thus destructive to the overall participation of Christians in world mission. That was one notable example of a type of ecumenical obedience and leadership needed at every level of church life.

One often difficult dimension concerns relationships between churches and groups where one is larger than another, or has a historical position felt to be "superior". Most of us are quick to sense we are being patronized by a larger partner, and may be the more aggressively passionate in refusing some well-meant advance. Relationships between groups are at least as sensitive as between individuals. We must expect just as many unexpected twists in handling larger historical, cultural or political divisions as in handling immediate personal relationships within a family or neighbourhood. But the problems are never an adequate excuse for not trying. Each advance, however small, is an encouragement for the total movement.

It is easy to speak of one world but hard to handle the tensions

As the 20th century drew to a close, there were few people anywhere who were not jolted out of total isolation into some awareness of the wider world. The ecumenical movement has been for many Christians a welcome eye- and heart-opener to partnership with people of very different backgrounds to our own. Those privileged to travel and make friends in different cultures can easily take for granted that God has created a whole world and set us in a total human family.

In fact, tensions and divisions abound despite all the traffic of crossing frontiers, and the structures for inter-group and inter-national contact. Within an institution such as the WCC, both conferences and the day-to-day staff contacts will throw up disagreements no one was expecting. Many of these are newly created; but many also can be traced back to some long-present difference between cultures or nations or churches that has never been fully resolved and which still continues to influence us.

Churches are apt to think of themselves as special, as shaped by the Holy Spirit and so free from some of the surrounding evils of the world. We do well to strive for such freedom. Yet the ecumenical movement has had to learn, painfully, that our churches are almost always shaped more deeply than they know by the dominant ideas and expectations in the surrounding culture. One proven way towards liberating one another is to give time to careful debate of the current topic of public concern: the Vietnam war at the Bangkok world mission conference, or the Gulf war at the Canberra assembly of 1991. From such debates, often at times heated and difficult, the outcome of which will not make everyone happy, the sensitive listener learns more about the total complex of facts, expectations and yearnings than they knew beforehand from their own background, and will be the better equipped to approach whatever situation of tension and division lies ahead on the path God is setting. The purpose of such debates is not for the WCC to "go political", but rather for all present to be engaged in an attempt to learn more of what the Holy Spirit may be wanting of the whole people of God today.

Much has been learned about the ways of the mass media

The atmosphere of criticism and controversy is one in which journalists flourish. With the ever-increasing power of broadcasting, electronic and print media, leaders of the ecumenical movement do well to school themselves in ways of handling journalists, and their own tongues. Christians depend, no less than others, on mass media both to learn what is going on around them, and to let other people know what we are doing; but by the same token we are at least as likely as others to be misused by these organs of contemporary life.

First, the principal motive of almost any journalist will be that of "selling the product", i.e. of making what is said or written attractive to the editor and the public. But not any public – the specific public which reads that particular newspaper or listens to that radio station. The news is those parts of what has happened that are judged by the media to be likely to win readers, to interest their listeners and viewers; this may both skew the angle of perception and cause lasting harm to the people whose lives are portrayed.

Second, there are always ideological and economic interests at work: a "free press" is at best an ambiguous claim. Even where an individual journalist is trying to record objectively, what appears on the screen has been through producers and editors, and is subject to the dictates of owners who have their own agendas of power and control. At least one can take steps to be aware of what those are likely to be, and so to guard against the most probable distortions.

Third, in the international sphere, the press is a striking example of the globalization that is widely felt to be culturally and economically damaging to the interests of smaller nations. Events become known because of the interests at work in the newspapers, radio and TV stations and, most pervasive of all, the worldwide web. The example mentioned above, of Prime Minister Vorster in South Africa, by swift work with the international press, broadcasting his view of the PCR special fund grants around the world before church leaders had heard about them, is in fact typical of many other stories. It is difficult to know how to handle these forces so as to make them serve the purposes of God, but from now on this must be high on the agenda of any serious ecumenical endeavour, especially at the international level.

Fourth, in the generally secular culture that reigns in most journalistic milieux, matters of religion will often be subject to several distorting pressures. On the whole, the church is not news, unless it offers high entertainment value. It is seen as a source of stories that are either "good for a laugh" or stern warnings against radical fundamentalism or moral decline. Sharp controversy is next best, while an act of reconciliation will usually be overlooked unless it is startlingly unexpected or effective. Debate on questions of faith or ethics is mostly held to be of no news value unless it can serve as a peg for the controversial views of a particular person or group. More generally, religion is not expected to offer solutions, only material for entertaining argument or discord. So the ecumenical movement has a lasting problem to win a fair hearing.

And yet, fifth, there is no way of getting information made available quickly to those who need – and will want – to know it except by the public channels of press and broadcasting.

The WCC has learned to set standards of open access for the press

Already at the 1968 Uppsala assembly the WCC had published a text on "The Church and the Media of Mass Communication"[58] which served as a basis for policy decisions to make the Council's life as fully open as possible to the public media. In a carefully

---

[58] From Norman Goodall ed., *The Uppsala Report 1968: Official Report of the Fourth Assembly of the World Council of Churches, Uppsala July 4-20, 1968*, WCC, 1968, pp.390.

balanced approach, the text does not hesitate to call the media to the best use of its powers:

> The Christian conviction is that the God of Jesus Christ is already at work everywhere in his creation. Hence the world of communication is his theatre of operations. The Christian claims that God wants the media to be useful to man and his communities and invites people to mould and use them according to that purpose.
>
> The media can enrich human life considerably.... As never before they make it possible for men to share experience with the hope that men may grow in awareness, understanding and compassion. The media provide some of the bone structure for a responsible world society.
>
> Modern life gives freedom at a price: willingness to take responsible, self-disciplined action in defence of man's new liberty.
>
> By and large the contribution of the media to interconfessional understanding has been as important for the ecumenical movement as the invention of the printing press was for the Reformation. Different denominations had to learn to cooperate as they shared in work of broadcasting departments and religious production. Members of other groups became "acceptable", and as the impressive quality of their life became visible the hitherto unquestioned singularity of one's own confession had to be re-examined.
>
> Increasingly the churches will have to learn to live in an open situation where their message will carry weight by its own authenticity, by the inherent quality of the truth of what they say and do rather than from any accepted authority.

That last sentence rings with the echo of Archbishop William Temple's dictum, built into the Council's rules,[59] that any authority the Council's statements may claim shall "consist only in the weight which they carry by their own truth and wisdom".

On that basis the WCC has put much effort, especially at its major conferences and meetings, into offering access as openly as possible to journalists and broadcasters. This is expensive both in staff time and financial cost. It has on occasion given rise to not a little annoyance, yet overall the conviction remains that, provided the Council's staff are prepared to put time and care into working with the media, and to trust in the Holy Spirit's possibilities of overcoming suspicion with friendship, most of the publicity gained will turn out to be serviceable to the long-term goals of the movement.

The 1983 Vancouver assembly provided striking confirmation of both sides of that balance. Its opening ceremonies were harassed (many would have said hijacked) by disciples of Northern Ireland's Ian Paisley, protesting in garish tartan outfits about the "heresies" and other sins of the World Council, and attracting the attention of all the TV crews with a model skeleton that was thrust into prominence. This and other side-shows provided by various opponents were given abundant space in the media, to such an extent that many Vancouver citizens were asking "whatever sort of show is this so-called World Council of Churches?" At the same time, however, the WCC had given permission for the Canadian Broadcasting Corporation to be the official broadcaster with rights to film the sessions of the assembly in their entirety, and to broadcast them live on the national and regional network and to feed to broadcasters worldwide. In face of the sceptical question aroused by the protesters, it was possible to invite people to turn on their television sets and watch what was actually going on and being said. This proved so genuine and attractive that the work of the protesters faded from memory almost as soon as their raucous colours and cries had moved on.

---

[59] *Uppsala Report*, Rule X, "Public Statements", clause 2, pp.480f.

A disciple who had learned the master's skills

A lunchtime press conference at that same Vancouver assembly proved a striking demonstration of both the dangers of the mass media and the value of learning to handle them creatively.

Bishop Desmond Tutu was at the time general secretary of the South African Council of Churches. In connection with the hearings of the Eloff Commission into financial mismanagement of the SACC, Tutu had his passport withdrawn, which made it unlikely that he could attend the assembly. However, with his fellow-countryman Allan Boesak giving a stirring keynote address, South Africa was not escaping attention. There was all the more excitement when news arrived that Tutu had suddenly been given his passport back and would be arriving after all. His first appearance came shortly before midnight on 6 August 1983 during a prayer vigil at the end of a celebration of the Transfiguration, which was also in memory of the nuclear bombing of Hiroshima. He spoke briefly, memorably, and in an atmosphere of intense expectation. So there was a huge crowd at next day's press conference, almost all from the rich, Western countries, especially Canada and the US.

It was soon obvious that the journalists were engaged in some sort of contest to see who could produce the most "tricky" question designed to get him saying something controversial that could be trumpeted by the journalist as the latest of Tutu's wild sayings. Virtually every question was a "trap".

But he was ready for anything. Time after time, he listened to the "question" with a cocked head, grinned as he realized the nuance involved, and began: "We...ell, that's an interesting one. What would you say if I were to suggest that in those circumstances a Christian would have to wonder ..." and his voice would rise to the height of the question and leave them there, with his counter-question hanging in the air, posing a challenge to the assumptions of their opening gambit.

That hour is the nearest I have ever heard to the kind of cat-and-mouse game that was played with Jesus in the temple in the week that led up to Good Friday: question met by counter-question which nevertheless made the questioner face up to a quite new answer to his original trick question. The humour and inventiveness involved was remarkable, but still more the courage, freedom and mastery, witnessing to a depth of spirituality and a grasp of truth that could outface all the "powers and principalities of this world", with an authority that "carried weight by its own authenticity", that stemmed from a wisdom higher than all other.

BIBLIOGRAPHY

Aagard, Anna Marie and Bouteneff, Peter, *Beyond the East-West Divide: The World Council of Churches and "The Orthodox Problem"*, WCC, 2001, 118p.
Adler, Elisabeth, *A Small Beginning – An Assessment of the First Five Years of the Programme to Combat Racism*, WCC, 1974, 102p.
Aichelin, Helmut, Frieling, Reinhard and Koch, Marianne, "Gegen-Ökumene: Kritische Stimmen zur Ökumene aus Protestantismus und Katholizismus", mimeogr., in *Arbeitstexte*, 7, September 1970, Stuttgart, Evangelische Zentralstelle für Weltanschauungsfragen.
Ansons, Gunnars, "Ecumenism under Tension: Evangelical versus Social-Political Forces", in *Lutheran World*, 3, 1975, pp.199-212.
Beek, Huibert van and Lemopoulos, Georges eds, *Turn to God, Rejoice in Hope: Orthodox-Evangelical Consultation, Hamburg, 30 March-4 April, 1998*, WCC, 1998, 109p.

Berneburg, Erhard, *Das Verhältnis von Verkündigung und sozialer Aktion in der evangelikalen Missionstheorie, unter besonderer Berücksichtigung der Lausanner Bewegung für Weltevangelisation (1974-1989)*, Wuppertal, Brockhaus, 1997, 413p.

Besier, Gerhard, Boyens, Armin and Lindemann, Gerhard, *Nationaler Protestantismus und Ökumenische Bewegung: Kirchliches Handeln im Kalten Krieg (1945-1990)*, Berlin, Duncker und Humblot, 1999, 1074p.

Beyerhaus, Peter, *Bangkok '73 – Anfang oder Ende der Weltmission? Ein gruppen-dynamisches Experiment*, Bad Liebenzell, Liebenzeller Mission, 1973, pp.255. In English: *Bangkok 73: The Beginning or End of World Mission?*, Grand Rapids MI, Zondervan, 1974, 192p.

Beyerhaus, Peter, *Hoffnung der Welt?*, MBK Verlag, 1970. Engl. transl.: *Missions: Which Way?*, Grand Rapids MI, Zondervan, 1971, 120p.

Bria, Ion, *The Liturgy after the Liturgy: Mission and Witness from an Orthodox Perspective*, WCC, 1996.

Clapsis, Emmanuel, *Orthodoxy in Conversation: Orthodox Ecumenical Engagements*, WCC, 2000, 236p.

Conway, Martin, "Lessons from Nairobi", in *The Churchman*, 90, 2, April-June 1976, pp.86-109.

Conway, Martin, *Look, Listen, Care – One Man's Experience and Interpretation of the Sixth Assembly of the World Council of Churches, Vancouver 1983*, London, British Council of Churches, 1983, 62p.

Fackre, Gabriel, *Ecumenical Faith in Evangelical Perspective*, Grand Rapids MI, Eerdmans, 1993, 230p.

Gill, Theodore A. Jr, "American Presbyterians in the Global Ecumenical Movement", in Milton J. Coalter et al. eds, *The Diversity of Discipleship*, Louisville, Westminster John Knox, 1991, 416p.

Hall, Clarence, "Must Our Churches Finance Revolution?", and "Which Way the World Council of Churches?", in *Reader's Digest*, October and November, 1971.

Harriss, Joseph A., "Karl Marx or Jesus Christ? – Which Master is the World Council of Churches Serving?" in *Reader's Digest*, August 1982, pp.130-134.

Harriss, Joseph A., "The Gospel According to Marx – Why have the Interests of the WCC Strayed So Far?" in *Reader's Digest*, February 1993, pp.68-73.

Hoekstra, Harvey T., *The World Council of Churches and the Demise of Evangelism*, Wheaton IL, Tyndale, 1978, 416p.

Johnston, Arthur P., *The Battle for World Evangelism*, Wheaton IL, Tyndale, 1979, 300p.

Lefever, Ernest W., *Amsterdam to Nairobi: The World Council of Churches and the Third World*, Washington DC, Ethics and Public Policy Center, 1979, 114p.

Lefever, Ernest W., *Nairobi to Vancouver: The World Council of Churches and the World, 1975-1987*, Washington DC, Ethics and Public Policy Center, 1987, 149p.

Nicholls, Bruce J. and Ro, Bong Rin eds, *Beyond Canberra: Evangelical Responses to Contemporary Ecumenical Issues*, Oxford, Regnum, 1993, 144p.

Ramsey, Paul, *Who Speaks for the Church?*, New York, Abingdon, 1967, 189p.

Sabev, Todor, *The Orthodox Churches in the World Council of Churches: Towards the Future*, WCC, 1996, 100p.

Sansbury, Kenneth, *Combating Racism – The British Churches and the WCC Programme to Combat Racism*, London, British Council of Churches, 1975, 78p.

Scheffbuch, Rolf, *FRAG-würdige Ökumene*, Neuhausen-Stuttgart, Hänssler, 1974, 96p.

Thomas, Pradip N., "Media Reportage of the WCC Programme to Combat Racism – A Study of How the British Press Reported on the Grant Given in 1978 by the WCC PCR to the Patriotic Front in Zimbabwe", Leicester, Centre for Mass Communication Research, 1983, unpubl. diss.

Ward, J.D., "A Critical Evaluation of the Ecumenical Movement in Light of Southern Baptist Perceptions", University Microfilms International, 236p., submitted for the degree of Th.D, New Orleans Baptist Theological Seminary, 1987.

Webb, Pauline ed., *A Long Struggle: The Involvement of the World Council of Churches in South Africa*, WCC, 1994, 133p.

Wheeler, Barbara G. and P. Mark Achtemeier, *The Church and Its Unity*, Louisville KY, Presbyterian Church USA, 1999, 34p.

Part III

18
The Significance of Regional Ecumenism

Georges Tsetsis

For the last four decades regional ecumenism has undoubtedly been one of the more significant developments within the one ecumenical movement. Growing out of the need to enhance fellowship and cooperation between churches in particular geographical areas, regional ecumenical activity demonstrates that the goals of the global ecumenical movement cannot be attained unless churches are able to apply them in the milieu where they live and witness. Moreover, it should immediately be acknowledged that the creation of regional ecumenical organizations (REOs) in the early 1960s, particularly in the southern hemisphere, was partly a response to the political needs of the time. Churches living in what was then called the third world were greatly affected by the geopolitical contexts in which regional coalitions had been formed in order to affirm identities – economic and military as well as cultural and social – over against the Northern powers dominating the world scene. REOs were formed, therefore, not only to promote Christian unity and enable joint action, but also to make the voices of the churches heard at regional as well as world levels.

Regional councils exist and operate today in all the major geopolitical areas of the globe except North America, although the two national – as distinct from regional – councils of churches in that part of the world (the National Council of the Churches of Christ in the USA – NCCCUSA, and the Canadian Council of Churches – CCC) fulfill functions similar to REOs. The principal aims of these regional councils are to help member churches promote Christian unity, shape a common response to socio-political and ethical issues of regional concern, and serve as a bridge between churches of the region and global organizations.[1]

It is worth noting that while the origins of both the Christian Conference of Asia (CCA) and the Middle East Council of Churches (MECC) go back to 1921 and 1929,[2] the genesis and formation of other regional councils coincide with the development of the WCC following its 1961 assembly at New Delhi. Indeed, with the exception of the Conference of European Churches (CEC) which was formed in 1959, all REOs came into being in their present forms between 1963 and 1982, a period when the WCC acquired its

---

[1] Thomas F. Best, "Councils of Churches: Local, National, Regional", in Nicholas Lossky et al. eds, *Dictionary of the Ecumenical Movement*, 2nd ed., WCC, 2002, p.257-58.
[2] Weber, Hans-Ruedi, "Out of All Continents and Nations: A Review of Regional Developments in the Ecumenical Movement", in Harold E. Fey ed., *A History of the Ecumenical Movement*, vol. 2, 1948-1968, WCC, 1986, pp.67,79.

global dimension by receiving into its membership an impressive number of churches from Africa, Asia and Latin America as well as those Orthodox churches of Central and Eastern Europe which for a variety of reasons, mainly political, had been unable to participate in the WCC's first assembly at Amsterdam in 1948.

Thus the All Africa Conference of Churches (AACC) was formed in 1963, the Pacific Conference of Churches (PCC) in 1966, the Caribbean Conference of Churches (CCC) in 1973, and the Latin American Council of Churches (CLAI: Consejo Latinamericano de Iglesias) in 1982. At the same time and because of new ecclesial realities in their region, Asian Christians, cooperating since 1921, formed the East Asia Christian Conference (EACC) in 1959 which in 1973 became the Christian Conference of Asia (CCA). A similar development occurred during the same period in the Middle East where the Near East Council of Churches, made up since 1929 of several Anglican and Protestant churches and mission agencies and operating mainly as a mission-oriented body, was transformed in 1974 into the MECC. The MECC, fully representative of the churches of the region, became the only ecumenical body of predominantly Orthodox character.

Regional councils have their own characteristics and differ considerably in terms of history, context, membership, structure and decision-making processes. The Roman Catholic Church enjoys full membership in three REOs – the Caribbean, the Pacific and the Middle East. In spite of their particularities all REOs share with the WCC the affirmation that they are a "fellowship of churches which confess the Lord Jesus Christ as God and Saviour according to the scriptures and therefore seek to fulfil together their common calling to the glory of the One God, Father, Son and Holy Spirit".

It goes without saying that emerging ecumenical and socio-political realities in the regions have not left the World Council of Churches indifferent. At its third assembly in New Delhi in 1961, speaking about Christian unity, the WCC highlighted local ecumenism by emphasizing unambiguously that "[t]he place where the development of the common life in Christ is most clearly tested is in the local situation, where believers live and work", and by stressing the need for an increase in opportunities of growing together as local churches, through common worship, Bible study groups, prayer cells, joint visitation and common witness in our communities.[3]

Along the same lines, the assembly at Uppsala in 1968, while calling Christians to manifest their "unity in Christ by entering into full fellowship with those of other races, classes, ages, religious and political convictions, in the place where we live",[4] also sought practical ways of cooperation between the WCC and regional councils in the fields of development, diaconal work, ministry towards refugees and migrants, and world mission and evangelism.[5] Recognizing that since New Delhi the formation of regional councils or conferences with an increasing ecumenical role constituted a new challenge, the assembly encouraged the Division of World Mission and Evangelism "to help regional organizations to relate to each other in the framework of the policy of mission in six

[3] Report of the section on unity, third assembly of the WCC, New Delhi, 1961, in W.A. Visser 't Hooft ed., *The New Delhi Report: The Third Assembly of the World Council of Churches*, 1961, London, SCM Press, 1962, p.116-35.
[4] A message from the fourth assembly of the World Council of Churches, in Norman Goodall ed., *The Uppsala Report 1968: Official Report of the Fourth Assembly of the World Council of Churches, Uppsala, July 4-20, 1968*, WCC, 1968, p.5.
[5] *Ibid.*, pp.254-66.

continents". It was a strong conviction of the Uppsala assembly that regional conferences ought to be "stimulated and supported to become new vehicles of mission in their own regions and in all the world".[6]

The WCC's willingness to foster relationships with regional and national councils was underscored by the creation at Uppsala of a secretariat on relationships with national and regional councils headed by an associate general secretary. Acting upon the recommendation of its structure committee, the assembly wished thus "to give continuous attention to the development of relationships of mutual helpfulness between the WCC and national councils of churches (NCCs) and other Christian councils". The function of such a secretariat, assisted by an *ad hoc* advisory committee, would be to:

1) develop patterns of relationships and cooperation whereby the WCC, NCCs and other Christian councils can strengthen each other and best serve the needs of their constituencies;
2) assist such councils in utilizing the resources of the WCC and to assist divisions of the WCC to relate their programmes to the needs of such [regional and local] councils;
3) keep before all the divisions and departments of the WCC and its member churches the significance of such councils in the fulfilment of the purposes of the ecumenical movement.[7]

A further step towards improving and consolidating relationships between the WCC and regional conferences was the recognition by the central committee in 1971 of REOs as "essential partners in the ecumenical enterprise", having the right to attend assemblies and central committee meetings through fraternal delegates and/or advisers, to receive copies of all general communications sent to WCC member churches of their regions, to be kept informed of important ecumenical developments and to be consulted with regard to WCC programmes in their regions.[8] Regional councils were thus considered dynamic forms of regional ecumenism, partners with the WCC in one common enterprise and not merely instrumentalities for Geneva's concerns.

A year later, the central committee, meeting at Utrecht, The Netherlands, in a deliberate effort to place REOs at the centre of the ecumenical debate and also to engage member churches in meaningful regional activities, called on the WCC member churches "to review and evaluate the authenticity and sincerity of their commitment to one another through the instrumentality of existing national and local councils of churches".[9] This unequivocal call was motivated by the fact that in many cases councils appeared to be "an ecumenical façade behind which churches remain as un-ecumenical as ever".[10]

In the mid-1970s the WCC acknowledged the absence from the interchurch scene of any coherent and coordinated approach to issues affecting the worldwide ecumenical agenda. This concern was clearly expressed by its fifth assembly in Nairobi in 1975. Believing that many ecumenical structures at regional, national and local levels pursue the same or similar objectives as the WCC itself – the promotion of visible unity, renewal, common witness and service in the world – the assembly held that as the ecumenical

[6] *Ibid.*, pp.231-32.
[7] *Ibid.*, p.365-66.
[8] WCC Central Committee, *Minutes of the Twenty-Fourth Meeting, Addis Ababa, Ethiopia*, 1971, p.217.
[9] WCC Central Committee, *Minutes of the Twenty-Fifth Meeting, Utrecht, The Netherlands*, 1972, p.38.
[10] *Ibid.*, p.221.

movement advanced, relationships ought to be reviewed in order to ensure a maximum of concerted and complementary action:

> In the past years, many new developments have taken place. Many councils have now an expanded membership, e.g., one regional and nineteen national councils have Roman Catholic membership. Regional councils have acquired new significance in the life of the churches. Many councils at all levels have developed new programmes. These and other developments make it imperative to reflect afresh on the relations between the WCC and other ecumenical bodies.

Because of these developments the Nairobi assembly instructed the central committee "to encourage further reflection on this matter and recommend steps to increase cooperation with such councils and define anew the WCC's relationship with them".[11]

Regrettably, in the years following the Nairobi assembly, no significant progress was made regarding relationships between the WCC and regional councils. On the contrary, a kind of competitiveness, an increasing tension, even a real crisis emerged. This was often due to the fact that regional councils, having been assured of direct independent funding by overseas agencies and having developed a multitude of programme activities, were tempted not only to challenge the World Council's regional activities, but even to question the WCC's constitutional right to deal directly with its member churches.

This "love-hate" relationship continued for a number of years with certain key questions emerging, largely during periodic meetings between REO and WCC leaders. These questions concerned: (1) the growing complexity of relationships caused by the Roman Catholic presence in *some* REOs; (2) the necessity of finding a *modus operandi* for the implementation of WCC programmes and projects; and (3) the effect of the WCC resource sharing programme on the regions.

Inspired by its theme, "Jesus Christ – the Life of the World", the WCC's sixth assembly at Vancouver in 1983 pointed out that life in Christ "is to be expressed through maturing ecumenical relationships among the churches... locally and regionally" if churches wished to grow towards unity of faith, eucharistic fellowship and service. The assembly delegates stipulated that "fostering ecumenical relationships with and between churches, communities, groups and ecumenical organizations on all levels should become a priority for the WCC".[12] As a consequence, after Vancouver greater efforts were undertaken to find ways for clearer dialogue and cooperation between REOs and the WCC.

Unfortunately, in the years between assemblies, the WCC was able to promote its relations only with NCCs. A consultation in October 1986 involving some 70 national councils of churches around the world attempted to clarify their mission in a given national situation, as well as their role in the context of the overall ecumenical movement.[13]

It was not until the seventh assembly in Canberra in 1991 that a turning point occurred in relationships between the WCC and REOs. After having acknowledged the fact

---

[11] Policy Reference Committee II, Report on Relationships in David M. Paton ed., *Breaking Barriers: The Official Report of the Fifth Assembly of the World Council of Churches, Nairobi, 23 November – 10 December, 1975*, London, SPCK, p.195.

[12] Report of the Assembly's Programme Guidelines Committee in David Gill ed., *Gathered for Life: Official Report, VI Assembly of the World Council of Churches, Vancouver, Canada, 24 July – 10 August 1983*, WCC, 1983, pp.251,253.

[13] Cf. Thomas F. Best ed., *Instruments of Unity: National Councils of Churches within the One Ecumenical Movement*, WCC, 1988.

that regions set their own priorities which often cannot easily be fitted into a global network, and admitted that there were increasing examples of inter-regional cooperation without the involvement of the WCC, Canberra urged churches to find new ways of formulating, initiating and funding regional ecumenical activities. According to the assembly such activities ought to reflect present-day ecumenical realities and be implemented on the basis of the following affirmations taken from a prior joint document, "Guiding Principles for Relationships and Cooperation between the Regional Ecumenical Organizations and the World Council of Churches":

1. The oneness of the ecumenical movement implies the recognition of the principle of complementarity in their relationships and functions, globally, regionally, nationally and locally.
2. The ecclesial nature of the councils or conferences of churches confers a preferential character on their relationships with each other, with churches and church organizations.
3. Their primary function within the one ecumenical movement is to serve, enable and challenge the local churches in the one common mission which includes the manifestation of visible unity among the churches.
4. Their relationship is one of partnership based on sharing of information, mutual trust, help and reciprocity.[14]

A meeting of the WCC and REO general secretaries, directly after the seventh assembly, helped clarify matters, and it was agreed that both the WCC and REOs are necessary instruments of the same ecumenical movement. It was affirmed that there must be: (1) a complementarity of ministries and avoidance of overlapping, (2) regular exchange of information, (3) mutual consultation on matters dealing with a given region, (4) a clearer mutual sharing of respective agendas, and (5) a closer relationship between REOs and WCC central committee members within a region.[15]

In an effort to translate these principles into a common policy, the central committee at its 1992 Geneva meeting dedicated a full session to this issue. Churches which are constituent members of both REOs and the WCC were to take an active part in a process of establishing a viable working pattern of relationship and cooperation between these entities. This move was prompted by the fact that both REOs and the WCC had in common: (1) the conviction that the ecumenical movement is one and it is wider than the ecumenical bodies they represented, (2) a commitment to foster the one ecumenical movement, (3) an openness to dialogue and cooperation with people of other faiths, and (4) a commitment to work with all people for the establishment of justice, the affirmation of peace and the renewal of creation. Thus, the central committee approved four "guiding principles" almost identical to those stipulated in Canberra, which constitute a framework of cooperation between REOs and the WCC, based on mutual trust, reciprocity, information sharing, mutual consultation and programmatic collaboration. According to these principles, the REOs and the WCC affirm that:

1. The ecclesial basis of the councils or conferences of churches qualifies their relationships with each other, with churches and organizations.

---

[14] Report of the Reference Committee, in Michael Kinnamon ed., *Signs of the Spirit: Official Report Seventh Assembly, Canberra, Australia, 7-20 February 1991*, WCC, 1991, p.175.
[15] WCC Central Committee, *Minutes of the Forty-Fourth Meeting, Geneva, Switzerland*, 1992, p.51.

2. The oneness of the ecumenical movement implies the recognition of the principle of complementarity in their relationships and functions, globally, regionally, nationally and locally.
3. Their primary function within the one ecumenical family is to serve, to enable and to inspire the member churches, NCCs [national councils of churches] and other Christian councils and each other in the common calling aimed at fostering the visible unity of the church and its witness in the world.
4. Their relationship is one of partnership based on their common faith and commitment.[16]

A consultation on "The Significance and Contribution of the Councils of Churches in the Ecumenical Movement", sponsored by the Joint Working Group of the WCC and the Roman Catholic Church, held in Venice in 1982, rightly remarked that councils of churches are instruments designed to help the churches move from "co-existence" through "cooperation" to deeper "commitment". It went further, by characterizing these councils as provisional "structures of *koinonia*" which can enable the churches to make "irreversible steps" in their common ecumenical pilgrimage.[17]

The WCC – in fundamental agreement with the wider ecumenical family – did not think differently at the eve of the third millennium when its central committee adopted a policy statement, "Towards a Common Understanding and Vision of the World Council of Churches" (CUV). After a thorough assessment both of the achievements and the shortcomings of the WCC over the past five decades, and after having again emphasized the oneness of the ecumenical movement and the servant role of the WCC within that movement, the statement called all those who are engaged in the ecumenical enterprise to work for

> the establishment of more structured relationships and better coordination of activities among the councils on all levels. All councils, in so far as they serve the ecumenical vision of wholeness and healing, are gifts of the same Spirit and expressions of the same fellowship in Christ. The oneness of the ecumenical movement worldwide should be evident in each local, national or regional council of churches, just as the WCC must remain firmly in touch with the reality of local communities where Christians are gathered to worship and serve.[18]

One of the two policy reference committees of the eighth assembly (Harare 1998), dealt extensively with the relationship of the WCC to regional ecumenical organizations as highlighted in the CUV document. Further, it considered a number of related issues, giving special emphasis to the possibility of decentralizing the work of the WCC. It also pointed out that the inter-relatedness of the agendas of the WCC and the REOs and the need for coordination were no longer questioned: "The challenge is to move to a common ecumenical agenda which will not only require coordination but steps towards an integration of ecumenical structures."[19]

In the light of these considerations, the Harare assembly encouraged the WCC and the REOs to engage in reflection on a common ecumenical agenda, to design ways of

[16] *Ibid.*, pp.155-57.
[17] "Councils of Churches Called Way to Unity," in *The Ecumenical Review*, 34, 3, July 1982, p.300.
[18] *Towards a Common Understanding and Vision of the World Council of Churches: A Policy Statement*, WCC, 1997, pp.21,22.
[19] Diane Kessler ed., *Together on the Way: Official Report of the Eighth Assembly of the World Council of Churches*, WCC, 1999, p.162.

consultation and decision-making regarding responsibilities for ecumenical programmes, and to develop a common approach to relationships with the Roman Catholic Church and with evangelical and Pentecostal churches and organizations.

Having in mind the above considerations, is it utopian to expect regional councils and conferences one day to become organic parts of the WCC? Such a hope is legitimate in light of the reality that all those who foster interchurch relations and cooperation clearly affirm that, in fact, they serve the one ecumenical movement on local, regional and world levels.

BIBLIOGRAPHY

All Africa Conference of Churches, *Abundant Life in Jesus Christ: 6th General Assembly, All Africa Conference of Churches, Harare, Zimbabwe, 25-29 October 1992: Programme and Information Book*, Nairobi, All Africa Conference of Churches, 1992, no pag.

Amanze, James N., *A History of the Ecumenical Movement in Africa*, Gaborone, Pula Press, 1999, 320p.

Best, Thomas F. ed., *Instruments of Unity: National Councils of Churches within the One Ecumenical Movement*, WCC, 1988, 179p.

Civil Society, the State, and African Development in the 1990s: Report of Study and Workshop: Receding Role of the State in African Development and Emerging Role of NGOs, Arusha, Tanzania, 2-6 August 1993, Nairobi, All Africa Conference of Churches, 1993, 143p.

Conference of European Churches, *The Report of the Conference of European Churches 10th Assembly "God Unites, in Christ a New Creation", 1-11 September 1992, Prague, CSFR*, Geneva, CEC, 1993, 332p.

Conference of European Churches, *Thy Kingdom Come: Report of the Fourth European Ecumenical Encounter, 28 September to 2 October 1988, Erfurt, GDR*, Geneva, CEC, 1989, 97p.

Cuthbert, Marlene, *Caribbean Ecumenical Consultation for Development 6: The Role of Women in Caribbean Development: Report on Ecumenical Consultation July 19-23, 1971*, Barbados, Caribbean Ecumenical Consultation for Development, 1971, 56p.

Directory of Christian Councils, WCC, 1985, 244p.

Forman, Charles W., *The Voice of Many Waters: The Story of the Life and Ministry of the Pacific Conference of Churches in the Last 25 Years*, Suva, Lotu Pasifika Productions, 1986, 211p.

Gavi, Chiramwiwa ed., *Jubilee 2000: Economic Justice for Churches in Eastern and Southern Africa: A Report on a Workshop on Economic Justice Organized by the FOCCESA*, Harare, EDICESA, 1999, 120p.

Hao, Yap Kim, *From Prapat to Colombo: History of the Christian Conference of Asia (1957-1995)*, Hong Kong, Christian Conference of Asia, 1995, 205p.

Hope in God in a Changing Asia: 10th General Assembly, Christian Conference of Asia, Colombo, Sri Lanka, 10-14 June, 1995, Hong Kong, Christian Conference of Asia, 1995, 40 p. (also in CCA News, 30, 3-5, March-May 1995).

Kürschner-Pelkmann, Frank, *Von Babel nach Jerusalem: Der Beitrag der Christenräte zur Einheit*, Hamburg, Evangelisches Missionswerk, 1991, 215p.

Mugambi, Jesse N. K. ed., *The Church and the Future of Africa: Problems and Promises*, Nairobi, All Africa Conference of Churches, 1997, 216p.

Noll, Rüdiger and Vesper, Stefan eds, *Reconciliation: Gift of God and Source of New Life: Documents from the Second European Ecumenical Assembly, 23-29 June 1997, Graz, Austria*, Graz, Styria, 1998, 331p.

Peace with Justice: The Official Documentation of the European Ecumenical Assembly, Basel, Switzerland, 15-21 May, 1989, Geneva, CEC, 1989, 334p.

Pobee, John Samuel ed., *Africa Moving towards the Eighth Assembly, Harare*, WCC, 1998, 113p.

Quintero, Manuel ed., *Renaciendo Para una Esperanza Viva: Cronica de la Tercera Asamblea General del CLAI, Concepcion, Chile, 25 Enero al 1 Febrero de 1995*, Quito, Consejo Latinoamericano de Iglesias, 1995, 184p.

Report of the 9th General Assembly, Christian Conference of Asia, Manila, Philippines, June 4-12, 1990, Hong Kong, Christian Conference of Asia, 1990, 153p.

Schmidt, William John, *Architect of Unity: A Biography of Samuel McCrea Cavert*, New York, Friendship Press, 1978, 330p.

Steindl, Helmut ed., *Les Eglises d'Europe: L'Engagement oecuménique: documents des rencontres oecuméniques européennes (1978-1991)*, Paris, Cerf, 1993, 739p.

Utuk, Efiong Sam, *Visions of Authenticity: The Assemblies of the All Africa Conference of Churches, 1963-1992*, Nairobi, All Africa Conference of Churches, 1997, 271p.

Waruta, Douglas W. ed, *African Church in the 21st Century: Challenges and Promises*, Nairobi, All Africa Conference of Churches, 1995, 155p.

19
Africa

Mercy Amba Oduyoye

> The ordinary African had rarely regarded the multiple and variety of churches as a scandal. The diversity was accepted with that typically African sense of fatalism which looked at the inevitable things as *shaura la Mungu*, a matter to be left to God.[1]

It is with the above assertion by John Baur as background that we look at more than three decades of ecumenism in Africa, from 1968 to 2000. Is this illustrative of "typically African fatalism" or are there other forces at work? Is the African scene in the sense of "ecclesial ecumenism" very different from that of other parts of the world?[2]

The 1960s for much of Africa was the decade of euphoria: political independence, European colonies becoming sovereign nations and Christian missions transformed into African churches. By the end of the 20th century, the euphoria had faded into near despair. None of these projects have been in any way concluded. New and utterly unpredictable wars, violence, the collapse of nation-states, renewed economic neo-colonialism and unparalleled disease struck the continent, leaving it reeling in pain un-imagined in colonial times. For many, "freedom was just another word for nothing left to lose". New Christian missions and new forms of colonialism are contemporary Africa's bleak experience.

Individuals appointed on behalf of the platform of Euro-American mission churches had participated in the International Missionary Conference as far back as 1910 and a few had provided Africa with a presence at the inaugural assembly of the World Council of Churches in 1948. The mid-1950s saw more intentional involvement in the ecumenical movement and African Christians in the World Student Christian Federation (WSCF), the YMCA and the YWCA. The Christian unions and scripture unions had also planted persons at strategic points in the academic world. At the beginning of the period under review, Africa's formally structured ecclesial ecumenical presence (All Africa Conference of Churches – AACC) was less than a decade old. For Africa the period of this history should begin in the mid-1950s, the reason being, according to Clement Janda, that "Africa began emerging from its colonial past in the 1950s: Ghana (1952), Sudan (1956), and then a great many others until 1990 when Namibia finally was liberated from South Africa, thus ending the struggle for independence on the continent". In

---

[1] John Baur, *2000 Years of Christianity in Africa: An African History 1962-1992*, Nairobi, Pauline Publ. 1994, p.361.
[2] Ecclesial ecumenism is used to cover the efforts to unite churches and to attempt visible unity in terms of conciliar movements and cooperation of churches.

1994 the last hold-out of white colonial and racist power fell with the formal end of apartheid in South Africa and the election of a multi-racial, unitary democratic state led by Nelson Mandela.

Janda, a former general secretary of the AACC from Uganda, continued,

> The period of colonization witnessed strong control of churches by foreign missionary boards and agencies, hence there was very little chance, if any, for the ecumenical enterprise in Africa. It was therefore not accidental that the idea to form a pan-African grouping of churches started in 1958 in Ibadan, Nigeria, resulting in the founding of the AACC in 1963.

An additional factor is that in most cases "running parallel with the decolonization process was the formation of national councils of churches [NCCs] in many parts of Africa". For Africa "the greatest thing" that happened in ecumenism, again according to Janda, was the impact of Vatican II. It enabled the Anglican and Roman Catholic churches to pioneer the formation of the Sudan Council of Churches, followed by similar councils in Swaziland, Lesotho, Liberia, Namibia and Uganda that also included the Orthodox churches in Africa. Recognitions of each other's baptism and joint religious education courses were the most visible achievements.

However, direct participation by African churches in the ecumenical movement belongs to the years covered by this history. Africans have served the WCC, the AACC, the national councils of churches and other ecumenical structures in increasing numbers and in a variety of positions, making it possible for African perspectives to be aired in the global, continental and national arenas of decision-making. True, Africa's financial participation in the ecumenical movement has been far below that of Europe and North America, but in other ways African hospitality has never failed to facilitate ecumenical gatherings and encounters. Voices, votes and cheque books make it possible for ecumenism to be a movement but the spirit of ecumenism does not depend entirely on these. When the central committee of the WCC was held in Enugu in 1960, Francis Akanu Ibiam, the first indigenous governor of colonial Eastern Nigeria, was a president of the Council. The meeting brought the global ecumenical image closer to Christians in Africa and Africans saw themselves as a significant component.[3]

Later, when Ibiam sided with his people during the Biafran war and was forced into exile, he renounced his English knighthood and Christian name in protest against Britain's unquestioning support for Nigeria's inhuman treatment of the Ibo people. The WCC provided leadership in the Biafran humanitarian aid programme that placed the Council squarely in the mode of ecumenical humanitarian aid regardless of the political tensions it raised. When the WCC's fifth assembly was forced to re-locate at short notice from Indonesia to Nairobi in 1975, churches in Africa rose to the occasion. They feel integral to the ecumenical movement. They are neither guests nor alms-seekers.

The Nigerians who were present at the WCC's Uppsala assembly in 1968 came from a country in the midst of a bitter and vicious civil war. Biafra had seceded from Nigeria and declared its independence in 1967. The militarily superior Nigerians were using food and other sanctions as a weapon to starve the dissidents into surrender. Using newly developed mass media techniques and technologies, churches mobilized around

---

[3] For an overview of the previous period, see J.S. Pobee, "Africa", in Nicholas Lossky et al. eds, *Dictionary of the Ecumenical Movement*, WCC, 2002, pp.5-12. Cf. Mercy Amba Oduyoye "The Development of the Ecumenical Movement in Africa with Special Reference to the AACC 1958-1974", in *Africa Theological Journal*, 9, 3 Nov. 1980.

the world. Those allied with both the WCC and the Vatican worked to feed millions of hungry Biafrans. Jointchurchaid (JCA), the Scandinavians, Canadians and Americans, set up aid to starving civilians by flying food into Biafra in the face of the Nigerian air force – JCA rapidly became known the world over as the Jesus Christ Airline. Ecumenically, support for the Biafrans came in the form of joint action by the WCC and official Roman Catholic agencies like Caritas.

Ibiam led the Biafran delegation to Uppsala to garner ecumenical Christian support for a cause which the world had been erroneously told was a Muslim (north-Nigeria) versus Christian (east-Biafra) struggle but which was really a result of failed colonialism and Western covetousness of Biafra's oil. Bola Ige came as leader of the WCC delegation from the federal Nigerian side, determined to counter this impression of Nigeria's corruption and instability. Both came from the Student Christian Movement of Nigeria where they had been friends and colleagues. Whatever the merits of each side, the fact is that Christians from a war-torn African countries felt themselves accountable to the ecumenical family represented at Uppsala.

Many will point to the Uppsala assembly as a watershed and the preceding conference on Church and Society, held in Geneva in 1966, as the root of the divergences that Uppsala introduced. "Behold, I Make All Things New" – the assembly's theme – signalled a significant change in the speed and intensity of the ecumenical current, but for Africa it was not tantamount to a change in course – the ecumenical ship was not entering new seas. Such a change, if there ever was one, had to wait for the 1980s and the 1990s when response to political developments became inescapable.

The centre of critique was the roots of poverty in the third world and the need for developments that would uproot poverty. Focus was specifically on the WCC's promotion of the Programme to Combat Racism and other justice issues including women and other people on the margins of power structures, the young and the differently abled. But it was also in 1966 that the World Council of Christian Education (WCCE) and the Sunday School Association merged in Nairobi in preparation for joining the WCC to become its office on education. For African Christians, Sunday schools were institutions in the mission structures which they held dear and which they had struggled to maintain, with varying degrees of success. This became a point of commitment that the AACC was to inherit and promote through curriculum development programmes.

From the African point of view there was never a paradigm shift. Challenges continued to pile up and the churches coped as best they could. If there was a shift at all, it was in terms of more direct participation in determining what the challenges were. At the 25th anniversary evaluation of the Mindolo Ecumenical Foundation, located at Kitwe in the Copper Belt of northern Zambia, in 1983, it was noted that a marked shift had occurred from training leaders for churches to training leaders for wider service. This change was to enable Christianity in Africa to be associated with the struggle for integral development, said to be a part of the church's mission. As Clement Janda, also a former director of Mindolo, put it,

> Mindolo was ecumenical but broader than "church". It therefore remains for Africans an acceptable face of ecumenism and the church's mission.

However, this ecumenical understanding of the church's mission has been consistently challenged by other forms and expressions of Christianity and of the mission of the church in Africa – an ecumenism that is beyond the institutional churches and beyond denominations.

The "evangelical" became more visible in Africa with the establishing of the offices of the Association of Evangelicals of Africa and Madagascar (AEAM) in 1966 in Nairobi. From their work among students to their pan-African conferences the impression was given that they were promoting the denial of "structural sin" and locating all of Africa's ills in the sins of the individual. This meant that individual conversion marked by a world-denying spirituality was pitted against the struggle for justice which was then depicted as one of the primary aims of the ecumenical movement. Often the "evangelical" approach was labelled "anti-ecumenical". But in all of Africa's churches, there were both "evangelical" and "ecumenical" elements.

ORGANIZED EXPRESSIONS OF CHRISTIANITY

The founding assembly of the AACC, at Kampala, Uganda, in 1963, was an announcement that a broad base had been born, determined to hold Africa together. It was to be an expression of ecclesial ecumenism. Pan-African unity was spreading like a *veld* fire across Africa. The Organization of African Unity (OAU) was also founded in the same year. Continental unity was in the air and the ecumenical movement was to be one of the ways of promoting it. Yet it is also a fact that in all these movements and especially in those with a Christian basis, Africans were never entirely free to take their own decisions. Like the Western mission churches, the ecumenical movement in Africa would remain in contact with its Western partners and the nature of their relationships would remain a challenge to their Christian charity. Similarly, the OAU faltered and failed for fifty years, only to be reborn in 2000 as the African Union. The OAU fell victim to fixed, inflexible colonial borders drawn a hundred years earlier by monarchs and politicians in Berlin. Pan-Africanism, born with such great hopes, was unable to overcome the heritage of its colonial masters.

The announcement of the birth of the AACC under the theme "Freedom and Unity in Christ" was communicated across the continent with drums, once symbols of African "paganism". Member churches were mainly those emerging from Western missions in Africa, and the two Oriental Orthodox churches of Africa, the Egyptian Coptic and the Ethiopian Orthodox. The most important factor of the "new" was that decisions were being taken in Africa by Africans.

A further development of ecclesial ecumenism in Africa was represented by the African Instituted (Independent) Churches (AICs) which set up headquarters in 1978 in Nairobi and constituted more than 15 percent of the total Christian population of sub-Saharan Africa. These *independent* expressions of Christianity came into being or were *instituted* by the initiatives of Africans, and carried a radically biblicist message. They are a place "to feel at home" in response to the generally negative reaction of Western missionaries to African culture, and of Africans who were alienated from the gospel yet dressed in European garb. To that extent AICs represent an indigenizing movement in Christianity. In a sense they are a renewal movement, a celebrative religion, a religion of the Holy Spirit. Yet the historic churches have long been suspicious of AICs, some going so far as to call them a heathenization of Christianity, and they rarely found a place in the ecumenical movement. Only three, the African Israel Church Nineveh with more than 100,000 members, in Kenya, the Church of the Lord (Aladura) from Nigeria, which claimed a membership of one million in 2000, and the Church of Jesus Christ on Earth by the Prophet Simon Kimbangu, or Kimbanguist Church, from the Democratic Republic of Congo, which claimed some five million members, had become WCC members by the year 2000.

The YMCAs and YWCAs remain expressions of extra-ecclesial ecumenism in Africa but with no particular relationship to the AACC. The WSCF carried its close association with the WCC into its regional expressions and therefore collaborated intentionally with the AACC, while the Student Christian Movements (SCMs) at the national level sought affiliation with national councils of churches (NCCs). For a long time the SCMs were the only expressions of Christian unity in secondary and tertiary institutions apart from formal worship services which were often in the mode of one denomination or the other.

Before the "Decree on Ecumenism" *(Unitatis Redintegratio)* was published during the third session of Vatican II (1965), it was not possible for the Roman Catholic Church in Africa to participate officially in Protestant-Orthodox ecclesial ecumenism. But, as elsewhere, Roman Catholic observers could attend ecumenical events. At the 1969 AACC assembly at Abidjan, Ivory Coast, Roman Catholic Archbishop Kodwo Amissah of Ghana, one of four observers from that church, made what was hailed as a significant statement on "eucharistic hospitality". To date African Christians are no closer to this vision than believers elsewhere. This is for many the signal failure of ecumenism in Africa. Ecclesial ecumenism by the beginning of the period under review had seen some expansion but that growth was mainly from the arrival of three AICs.

Several radical Protestant evangelical churches of European and American origin continued to shun ecclesial ecumenism.

Several persons who had observed, studied or participated in the ecumenical movement since the 1950s entered a period of mourning at what by the 1980s seemed to them a paradigm shift in the being of the movement. Ogbu Kalu, professor of church history at the University of Nigeria, Nsukka, captured this in a note sent to the writer:

> Between 1968 and 1980 the tendency to emphasize church unity as a key goal in [African] ecumenism suffered defeat. Most union talks collapsed; the re-emphasis on the unique identity of each denomination loomed large in the early 1980s.

The Christian World Communions (CWCs), especially the Anglican, Lutheran, Reformed, Baptist and Methodist, were active in Africa. Together with the Roman Catholic Symposium of the Episcopal Conferences of Africa and Madagascar and its regional manifestations, they demonstrated an ability to unite their members. When they operated on a principle of "each on behalf of all", they were able to demonstrate an ecclesial ecumenism beyond their own communions.

Other indicators of ecumenism in Africa are the theological associations: the Ecumenical Association of Third World Theologians (EATWOT); the Association of African Theologians; the associations of theological institutions, with their continental voice in the Conference of African Theological Institutions; and the Circle of Concerned African Women Theologians, all are efforts at theologizing in different ecumenical contexts. The latter, for instance, is unique in having Muslim women as members and being open to women theologians from other faith communities in Africa. Religion and culture is their theological locus.

The profile of ecumenism in Africa from 1968 to 2000 can be outlined under five headings:
- the struggle for justice and development;
- the scope and dynamism of churches together in response to the African context;
- ecclesiology and ecumenism in which the NCCs and other ecumenical structures are discussed;

- multiple postures/one mission, a review of the responses of movements of Christians along non-denominational lines and those of the AICs; and
- ecumenical concerns that continue to engage the attention of African Christians, churches and ecumenical bodies.

JUSTICE, DEVELOPMENT AND DE-DEVELOPMENT

The first major consultation of African theologians took place in Ibadan, Nigeria, in 1966, on the theme of biblical revelation and African beliefs. The participants predicted that "the continent of Africa will see unparalleled events and changes during the rest of the century". They could not have foreseen that these events would take the form of civil wars and carnage among Africans such as we have witnessed. They may have thought of the dismantling of apartheid in South Africa; the independence of the then Southern Rhodesia, now Zimbabwe; and that of South-West Africa, now Namibia, forcing European descendants in Africa to recognize the humanity of the African and to begin to deal more equitably in the trade of Africa's resources. The Decade of Development declared by the United Nations ended, ushering in an uncertain atmosphere in the 1970s. The ecumenical scene was preoccupied with the struggle against decolonization, neo-colonialism and apartheid. Little justice had been done and development was threatening to become de-development.

Africa was still in the throes of the struggle to rid itself of the spiritual and economic legacies of slavery, colonialism, and the lively and tenacious presence of racism. Hence the watchword of the 1974 AACC assembly in Lusaka, Zambia, "the struggle continues" (*a luta continua*, as it was better known in Portuguese) was entirely appropriate. Lusaka saw the ecumenical task as one of enabling the churches to enter a mode of disengagement from dependence to a commitment to liberation. The assembly called for "disengaging ourselves from those things that may hinder our active participation in the mission of God in Africa". Kenyan Presbyterian John Gatu's interpretation of disengagement as "moratorium" became a bone of contention. He pleaded for a complete halt in the sending of missionaries and funds from European and North American churches to the churches of Africa in order to enable the Africans to develop their own identity and to define their mission for their time and place. Moratorium was a challenge to the assumption that without the large-scale presence of Western missionaries, Christianity could not survive in Africa. Some members of foreign mission boards and Northern "sending" churches distorted the moratorium call in reports to their constituents. Instead of embracing moratorium as a new relationship of mutuality enabling African churches to attain full maturity, certain boards forced "daughter" churches into submission by simply withholding all funds. Even after the AACC's 1974 assembly endorsed moratorium as "the most viable means of giving the African church the power to perform its mission in the African context",[4] leaders of resource-starved receiving churches were led to denounce the call for a moratorium as "satanic" or "emotionally political".

For those who saw the liberation praxis as necessary for the church in society, moratorium was a positive contribution of the AACC to the ecumenical movement. It forced the churches and mission partners to rethink mission. It became clear that in Africa the mission paradigm was one of putting the horse before the cart. Instead of establishing churches that would be *in* mission, Africa's missionaries had planted missions which

---

[4] Quoted in Gerald H. Anderson, "Moratorium", in *Dictionary of the Ecumenical Movement*, pp.797-98.

they hoped would become churches and hopefully in some future date *undertake* mission.

Missiologists looking at Africa now reflect in terms of "transforming mission".[5] Churches in Africa are often churches in name and outward structures only. There is no spring of living water in them so they cannot be in mission without continual injection of the mission spirit of churches from outside Africa, often solicited by the African leaders of Western churches in Africa. The ecumenical leaders of Africa in the 1970s called the attention of the churches to this situation, hoping that a fresh approach would be developed. For Africa, to be engaged in development was to be engaged in justice, and the 1967-70 civil war between Nigeria and Biafra, with overtones of its colonial and resource extraction, simply heightened this.

What has been written about the Biafra situation documents the intricacies of diplomacy, control of petroleum resources and promotion of militarism for the sake of the arms industry. In the same way, the endless conflict in Sudan is a religious one complicated by a history of Arab racism and the slave trade. In 1983 large amounts of oil were found in south Sudan, the benefits of which would accrue to Khartoum, leaving the black African south without the benefit of their resources. For the WCC, the AACC and the Christian councils of Nigeria and breakaway Biafra, to be engaged in justice and development meant not only to undertake relief during the conflict, but also to be engaged in reconciliation, reconstruction and development. RRD has become a mark of ecumenism in Africa, following the winding up of the ecumenical programme for emergency action in Africa.

To do justice in Africa meant to see to the education and development of people; to become involved with their socio-political and economic development; and to respond in a humanitarian way to the emergencies, natural and man-made, that continued to plague the continent. For the ecumenical family this meant calling the churches to respond together with compassion and justice. Diakonia became a cardinal mark of ecumenism in Africa and it took the form of providing relief in emergency situations, scholarships for leadership development and training personnel for the churches. For many, these became the raison d'etre of the ecumenical movement.

Nation-building and economic development of the 1960s began to recede as a process of "de-development" set in in the 1980s. Simultaneous with this were the continuous flash-points in Sudan, Ethiopia, Mozambique and Angola, the Horn of Africa, and parts of the continent still under colonial domination. Military coups as a preferred method of changing governments occurred all too often in parts of west Africa.

Churches and councils from outside Africa worked with and through African churches to mitigate the human cost of civil wars, coups and massive movements of refugees and displaced people and other disasters such as starvation, famine and drought. They brought relief, medical care and shelter while keeping the world's attention focused on those imprisoned for resisting apartheid, and providing for the education and legal assistance of those on trial for opposing racism, injustice and human-rights abuses. It is for these reasons that the ecumenical movement has come to stand for involvement in Africa's struggle on the side of that which is life-sustaining rather than the promotion of ecclesial unity. This was seen by some as a deviation from the central concern of ecumenism.

---

[5] See David J. Bosch, *Transforming Mission: Paradigm Shifts in Theology of Mission*, Maryknoll NY, Orbis, 1991, for his discussion on the paradigm shift in mission theory and practice.

The period 1985-95 were years that no one could ignore and Ogbu Kalu rightly observes that there were a variety of responses to Christian activism. Those who were not in favour of this intensive involvement of the church in social action fought back. People from various denominations came together "for common fellowship without abandoning denominational roots". There was rapid growth of the Full Gospel Business Men's Fellowship and Women Aglow in west Africa. These were significant ecumenical bodies that challenged the secular ecumenism of service clubs. The response of the Western churches was to "radicalize their liturgy and spirituality". Institutional ecumenism of the church-union model was abandoned for strategies designed to protect the flock against newer and different forms of ecumenism.

Right up to the fall of the Berlin wall in 1989, the extra-ecclesial ecumenical structures in Africa and the youth departments of the WCC and the AACC were intensely involved with people's development, especially in leadership and skills training. NCCs were calling attention to church-state relations, often to the state take-over of church schools and even hospitals and clinics. Inter-religious relations were becoming critical as Christians and Muslims vied for media attention and for state recognition of religious festivals. All of this receded as attention turned to human-rights abuses and democratization ushered in by Gorbachev-era *perestroika*. The irony is that, whereas the fall of the Berlin wall inaugurated a move towards a united Europe, the walls created in Africa by Europeans sitting in Berlin in 1883-84 became even more obstructive for Africans one hundred years later.

With the globalization of the world's economy, the indebtedness of African countries to the world financial institutions, and the concomitant economic structural adjustment programmes, the process of de-development was inevitable. De-development has become a factor that defies resolution. Whether the language is nation-building or human resource development, nothing much is achieved as long as the initiative is seen as outsiders' efforts to develop Africa. The dispossessed of Africa are the basic challenge of extra-ecclesial ecumenism and one which the churches have barely faced individually, let alone become able to talk of jointly.

Ecumenism in Africa has attempted to evolve in this highly unstable context of disorganized political, military, economic and social changes. In many countries, the decades under review have seen very little peace. Civil war and military coups have suffocated the future of Nigeria, the most densely populated country in the continent. Added to this are Ethiopia, Eritrea, Somalia, Sudan, Uganda, Angola, Mozambique, Namibia, Liberia, Sierra Leone, Rwanda, Burundi, the Democratic Republic of Congo (formerly Zaire), not forgetting the struggles against white supremacy in Rhodesia and apartheid in South Africa. The continued stranglehold of the West on the economies of Africa through colonial trade pacts and ownership of land and means of production was aggravated by the global slump of the late 1970s and 1980s, resulting in the debt crises that still distort the lives of Africans socially, politically and economically. The themes studied by ecumenical bodies underline this context, which is a deep challenge to the ecumenical movement in Africa.

THE SCOPE AND DYNAMISM OF CHURCHES TOGETHER

The ecumenical movement responded initially to these crises with studies of "rapid social change", and then the churches moved into goodwill missions in conflict areas to promote reconciliation, participate in reconstruction of devastated communities, and help redevelop broken human spirits – the traditional three RRRs, reconciliation, reconstruction and redevelopment used so effectively in countries like Namibia. More recently, churches and ecumenical institutions have emerged as a significant part of civil society with influence sufficient to affect the state as it struggles to formulate or implement policies and take concrete action to effect change in the living conditions of people. On the ecumenical scene a noteworthy example is the beginning of interchurch aid among African churches. Ecumenical cooperation among the AICs in Kenya took the form of mutual help in building village churches. With the nationalization of schools in Kenya in 1970, churches got together to develop a joint syllabus and common textbooks for religious and moral education in schools and thereby saved religion from being thrown out of school entirely.

Under the directorship of E.A. Adeolu Adegbola, the Institute of Church and Society at Ibadan, Nigeria, developed cooperation between member churches of the Christian council and the post-Vatican II Pastoral Institute of Ibadan, a study centre of the Catholic church. A series of six textbooks on Christian religious studies for primary schools in Nigeria with the title *Together in God's Family* were published jointly. Limited as these efforts were, they demonstrated that ecumenical religious education is feasible and indeed desirable.

Cooperation has become the norm for Bible translation, under the auspices of the United Bible Society and the Roman Catholic bishops conferences. A meeting of Catholic and Protestant biblical scholars in 1967 laid the ground rules for the translation of local-language Bibles. By 1977 there were 78 Bibles being translated by an ecumenical team. Using the same Bibles in schools made a great impact on young Christians in the 1970s. There is joint work in this area in many African countries.

Ecumenism in Africa also took the form of joint efforts to provide higher education in theology. The departments of religious studies in Legon, Ghana; Ibadan, Nigeria; and Makerere, Uganda; began in the 1950s and the 1960s with the approbation of the churches, and staff and students came from all churches. This enabled several churches to encourage their seminaries and joint theological institutions to affiliate with these departments and for students to take their diplomas in theology examinations. The current moves in Kenya, Uganda, Zimbabwe and Ghana to establish Christian universities and the increasing numbers of denominational seminaries may prove to be a setback to this tradition of ecumenical theological education, a practice which at least ensured that there was some common ground for dialogue among persons who would later meet around ecumenical tables.

Roman Catholics have participated fully in some departments of religion. In Yaoundé, Cameroon, they shared the united school of theology which catered to French-speaking students north of the Democratic Republic of Congo but in addition maintained its seminaries and other theological institutions nationally. Then there are the international schools like the Pastoral Institute, Gaba (1967), later moved to El Doret, Kenya (1976); the Pastoral Institute, Ibadan; the Catholic Institute of West Africa, Port Harcourt, Nigeria; and the Catholic University of Eastern Africa which was inaugurated during the papal visit to Kenya on the occasion of the eucharistic congress in 1985.

These provided locations for people to meet ecumenically. Meanwhile, several ecumenical theological institutions and informal groups, and joint research promoted by the AACC and the Association of Members of Episcopal Conferences of Eastern Africa during the period 1976-81, continued to struggle to provide ecumenical education and resources, and to prepare theologians who could contribute an ecumenical perspective to the theological developments in Africa.

The establishment of national councils of churches (NCCs) was the first visible expression of the churches' "given unity" and the intention to make this unity operational. There are now more than twenty NCCs in Africa. Where they exist, they consist mainly of Protestant churches although Roman Catholic membership is becoming increasingly common. At the beginning of our period of history they were few: Congo, Gambia, Lesotho, Swaziland, Sudan, Uganda, Malawi and Madagascar. The formation of the New Sudan Council of Churches (NSCC) as a council in exile was a major ecumenical development in Africa. As the Sudanese church leaders have insisted, the coming into being of the NSCC is purely circumstantial. The ongoing (since 1983) civil war in Sudan made it impossible for the Sudan Council of Churches in Khartoum to cater ecumenically for the many Sudanese Christians in southern Sudan and the neighbouring countries, notably Kenya and Uganda. The NSCC is also a commentary on the prevailing situation in southern Sudan. The word "new" signifies the emergence of a new Sudan in the "liberated areas" in the south and west of the country. The NSCC was established in 1990 and took over the relief and other activities borne by the Sudan desk and ecumenical support programme until then under the auspices of the National Council of Churches of Kenya.

The Christian Association of Nigeria was formed in 1976. In 1986 it was revitalized by the threat of the Islamization of Nigeria, and as a result all the ecclesial communities in Nigeria are members. Christian leaders meet more often to review their mission in their various national contexts and take common action in terms of joint statements.

There are also less formal and sometimes ad hoc gatherings for cooperation among Christians that are manifestations of the spiritual unity of the church. An ecumenical study group, the Cercle d'études oecuméniques (Circle for Ecumenical Study) brought together Roman Catholics and Protestants in Yaoundé. Supported by the Catholic bishops conference and the Federation of Protestant Churches, it took off in 1964 and showed signs of being an expatriate, mainly European study group.[6] Nevertheless, it is of immense significance since in the eyes of Africans it was these same Europeans who brought a divided church into Africa. Ghana has a committee of cooperation between the Christian Council of Ghana, mainly Protestant, and the Catholic Secretariat. At the end of his section on ecumenism in Africa, Baur concludes:

> The picture of the church in Africa after thirty years of ecumenical history is disappointing. What has been achieved is a relatively general peaceful co-existence, but little cooperation and much less congruence. Almost nobody feels the urgency to go further, and it would be difficult to distribute the blame for this lethargy.[7]

Baur goes on to propose his theses of "African fatalism, conservatism, care for identity and feeling at home in a small community", adding that the situation of ecumenism demonstrates that these traits are "seen to be stronger than the African gift for dialogue, reconciliation, hospitality and universal human love". But there are other ways of viewing ecumenism beyond the ecclesial concerns for visible church unity.

The Student Christian Movements, constituent members of the WSCF, operate in 27 African countries with a contextualized policy that empowers them to respond to local needs while remaining an integral part of a global ecumenical vision. The SCMs in Africa consider themselves as a reservoir of leadership, a catalyst for change and a labo-

---

[6] *2000 Years of Christianity in Africa*, p.476.
[7] *Ibid.*, p.364.

ratory for new ideas.[8] The federation has also provided ecumenical leadership for NCCs and other ecumenical bodies. Holding its centenary in Yamoussoukro, Côte d'Ivoire, in 1995 brought the global nature of the federation forcefully home to African youth, while its theme, "A Community of Memory and Hope Celebrating Faithfulness", was just the affirmation of ecumenism Africa needed to make, for in Africa the ecumenical ideal is to see the continent "as a house where God lives" (Eph. 2:22).

Christian youth associated with the AACC have kept alive the dynamism of the ecumenical movement in Africa by holding several national, sub-regional and pan-African meetings to voice their concerns. There has been much lamentation over the dearth of leadership for the ecumenical movement since the beginning of the 1980s. Some have attributed this to the lack of intentional cultivation of the spirit of ecumenism among the young people of the churches. Others, like Janda, have said that this loss of strong ecumenical leadership may in itself have given rise to many church groups, most of them right-wing in orientation.

The most intractable challenge for pan-Africanism is weak communication across the continent. Before the establishment of the AACC, the Africa Literature Centre opened in Kitwe, Zambia, to foster Christian communication in Africa. The facility was located at the training centre which later became the Mindolo Ecumenical Foundation. To date some 1200 journalism and art and design diplomas have been issued to people from all over the continent.[9] Mindolo is only one of the several ecumenical and lay centres that have come together in the Association of Christian Lay Centres in Africa (ACLCA). For more effective networking this body took a decision in 1994 to sub-regionalize. Decentralization is becoming an ecumenical way of working because of the size and difficulties of communication and the necessity for staying grounded in the immediate context while remaining connected in the wider one.

The AACC communication centre was added to these ecumenical efforts in 1963 and together they facilitated communication as well as adding other services. The most recent addition to the AACC's effort is a library project and archival space along with Africa Press Service which has existed for many years and serves to keep the ecumenical bodies in the region connected through the sharing of information.[10] African Christian publishing houses, most of them belonging to NCCs, have participated actively in the World Association for Christian Communication and enabled the churches to provide publishing services, an area that until recently was the monopoly of European houses.

The dynamism of ecumenism is promoted even more effectively when persons meet around common concerns. It is, therefore, not without some justification that Mampila Mambu, a theologian from the Democratic Republic of Congo, laments that, while all

---

[8] Kangwa Mabuluki, "An Old Federation of Young People", in *Tam Tam* (a publication of the All Africa Council of Churches), June-July 1995 pp.9,14-15. In Africa persons who have served both the AACC and the WCC in the period under review include Jose Chipenda WSCF Africa secretary, later AACC general secretary; Aaron Tolen, WSCF Africa secretary and later a WCC president (1991-1998) and Mercy Amba Oduyoye, president of WSCF 1973-77 and a deputy general secretary of WCC 1987-94; co-initiator of the Circle of Concerned African Women theologians.

[9] From correspondence with Clement Janda, former general secretary of AACC who had served as director of Mindolo Ecumenical Foundation, former staff of the WCC and also a member of SCM.

[10] For a list of ecumenical centres and other ecumenical agencies in Africa see D.B. Barrett, *World Christian Encyclopedia*, Nairobi, Oxford Univ. Press, 1982, for statistics under country profiles and p.929.

large churches participate in ecumenical conversations at the international level, few of them have promoted a similar practice of ecumenism at the local level.[11]

The East Africa Revival Movement (EARM) is another form of reshaping spirituality. An indigenous initiative founded in Rwanda in 1947, its membership is drawn from the missionary-founded denominational churches and AICs in the whole of East Africa. EARM fellowships hold weekly, monthly and annual ecumenical events. Its objective has been stubbornly consistent – the spiritual nurture of individual Christians. Deliberately apolitical, the movement refrains from commenting on political issues. Its members are openly pietistic. They feel duty-bound to give a testimony of their Christian life privately and publicly. The movement insists that its members must live and be seen to live their message. Its moralistic style of life has made it a moral oasis in an otherwise corrupt and corrupting society. Interestingly, the EARM is financially independent. It is one of the few indigenously founded movements that are sustained by locally derived resources. It has energized ecumenical leadership in East Africa: virtually all the prominent church leadership in the national churches are, or have been, members. Its influence on students and academics has sent many to international, regional and national ecumenical organizations. Its faithful members, who number more than one million, tithe regularly and this remains EARM's main source of funding. The EARM has successfully resisted the temptation to institutionalize and has remained very much a movement.

ECCLESIOLOGY AND ECUMENISM

Whereas Africa has seen some fresh developments in conciliar ecumenism such as the two Christian councils of Sudan,[12] the waters of ecclesial ecumenism remain stagnant in terms of uniting churches. We have already referred to the failures in Ghana and Nigeria.[13] Added to these are the 1961-72 abortive attempt at an east African church union consultation to bring together some churches in Tanzania and Kenya. There have, however, been two dramatic efforts, the formation of the Church of Christ in Zaire in 1972 and the following year's visit to Rome of Pope Shenouda III of the Coptic church following the return to Cairo by Rome of the relics of St Mark in 1968 and a move towards a common statement on Christology in 1971. The Zaire effort, however, produced what was in effect a loose federation of Protestant churches as each constituent part remained autonomous in all but name. Much more significant was the agreement of the Oriental Orthodox churches of the Middle East in 1987 which enabled them to transcend the rift created by the council of Chalcedon. This has been hailed as one of the greatest ecumenical events of our time and involved two churches in Africa, the Patriarchate of Alexandria and the Coptic Orthodox Church.

---

[11] *2000 Years of Christianity in Africa* (p.363) suggests that this contributed to the establishing of AACC-AMECEA joint research.

[12] As Sam Kobia explains: The Sudan Ecumenical Forum (SEF) was set up in 1994 by the World Council of Churches to provide the space and opportunity for the SCC and NSCC to coordinate their work. SEF is also an important ecumenical platform for dialogue between the Sudanese churches and their ecumenical partners. It further provides a model of coordinated ecumenical accompaniment and solidarity with the Sudanese churches and people, especially in the area of peace and advocacy.

[13] See Ogbu Uke Kalu, *Divided People of God: Church Union Movement in Nigeria, 1875-1966*, New York, NOK Publ., 1978.

In many African countries conversation about uniting churches began to seem inappropriate as major CWCs held on to their members. As an example, Tanzania at independence in 1964 had a population distributed equally among three religions: African, Christian and Islamic. Of the Christians the majority were Roman Catholic, Anglican or Lutheran. The most effective Christian union that has been demonstrated in the country was the coming together in 1963 of the seven Lutheran synods to become the Evangelical Lutheran Church of Tanzania. The World Alliance of Reformed Churches' attempts to bring Reformed churches into closer cooperation at the national level, as in Nigeria and South Africa, is only slowly showing signs of coming to fruition.

For the rest, each denomination keeps to itself and together they stay distinct from the African Instituted Churches (AICs). Here it is interesting to note that Tanzania is unique in having escaped break-aways from the Western churches that have given Africa more AICs like the Church of Christ in Africa (People of Love) created by a rivalry within the Anglican diocese of Maseno in Kenya and the *Legio Maria* (Legion of Mary), an attempt to establish a Roman Catholic "African" church. While more AICs come into being, such direct splits from Western churches are rare. Further, the AICs are themselves grouping together on national levels and now have a continental conciliar expression in the Organization of African Instituted Churches.

An innovation in conciliar fellowship in Africa is the sub-regional manifestation of NCCs in the form of fellowships which came together in the 1980s and 1990s. A fellowship of NCCs in west Africa, a counterpart to the political structure of the Economic Community of West African States (Ecowas), became necessary and possible and can accompany the NCCs as they seek to serve a zone torn by civil wars, *coups d'état* and economic traumas. The challenge to minister more effectively is what brought them together in 1994. The Fellowship of Councils of Churches in Eastern and Southern Africa (Foccesa), formed in 1986 with a membership of 12 NCCs (South Africa, Namibia, Botswana, Angola, Malawi, Mozambique, Kenya, Tanzania, Lesotho, Swaziland, Zambia, Zimbabwe), seeks to find regional answers to regional problems. It keeps the churches and councils attending to refugees, matters of peace and security in the region, gender and partnership relations, economic justice and the coordination of national and other ecumenical institutions.[14] The impact of Foccesa on coordinated ecumenical response to regional challenges was a motivation for the formation of the Fellowship of Christian Councils in Western Africa (Fecciwa) in 1994 and the Fellowship of Churches and Councils in the Great Lakes and Horn of Africa (Fecclaha) in 1998. The latter decided to focus sharply on peace and reconciliation in that volatile region. Headquartered in Nairobi, Fecclaha promotes an ecumenical space for churches in collaboration with the civil society to work together for peace, healing of memories and conciliation in specific countries and in the region generally.

The AACC has taken a decision to launch a new structure to bring it closer to the regions. Having moved from a decentralized operation in 1974, the AACC has gradually reverted to decentralization in acknowledgment of the size and complexity of Africa.

---

[14] The formation of Foccesa was done in full consultation with the AACC and the WCC, with the latter having played a major role in facilitating the setting up of Ecumenical Documentation and Information Centre (Edicesa) to document and channel information from South Africa during the apartheid era. Today Edicesa, which is based in Harare, Zimbabwe, provides the secretariat for Foccesa. With the formation of Fecclaha in 1998, Foccesa became Foccisa – Fellowship of Councils of Churches in Southern Africa.

Africa is vast and it is expensive in personnel and funds for any pan-African organization to stay visible and effective at the "grassroots". Uniting churches have been replaced by inclusiveness and participation, mutual respect and the quest for wholeness of humanity in Africa. Whereas competition among missionary societies meant that African Christians related more to their CWCs than to the local expressions of ecclesial ecumenism, they continued to strive together for the so-called social ecumenism that keeps them alive to their mission in society. The ecumenical movement in Africa poses the question, "Is uniting churches a *sine qua non* for a visible demonstration of the church's unity?" Churches of Western origin whose partners stay away from ecclesial ecumenism in Europe and North America follow that policy in Africa. Those which remain in the ecumenical stream and the ecumenical vocation continue to hold to the vision of visible unity and attempt to live out the prayer of Jesus that those given to a Christ-centred vision of life should also be seen to be one; that is, live out the given unity in overt ways.

The African Instituted Churches[15] began to merge into larger groups, first in South Africa, then in Nigeria. The process culminated in the formation of the Organization of African Instituted Churches (OAIC). While the phenomenal growth of the AICs was constantly recognized, not much was done to court them towards the existing ecclesial ecumenism in Africa. It was not until after 1975 that Prophet Zakayo Kivuli's African Israel Church Nineveh, which had begun in Kenya in 1942, was accepted into membership of the WCC, followed by the Kimbanguists of the DRC and later the Church of the Lord, Aladura, from western Nigeria. Among themselves they try to live out the visible unity of the church in overt ways.

The 1980s saw the emergence of religious entrepreneurship, which Paul Gifford describes as Africa's new Christianity.[16] The establishment and spread of these prosperity-preaching gospel churches has been greatly influenced by Pentecostalism, especially from North America, but also to a lesser extent Brazil, Europe and New Zealand. On the face of it they appear to be fundamentalist. However, Gifford prefers to identify them more with "experientialism" than with "fundamentalism". Harvey Cox made such a distinction in describing the essence of similar churches in Latin America.

Televangelism in Zambia has grown in leaps and bounds, particularly in the 1990s, partly because of the encouragement and support from the constitutionally Christian state. The same applies to Kenya where on Sundays continuous Christian television programmes run from morning to evening. Both in Kenya and Zambia these programmes are foreign products and they include well-known shows like "The 700 Club" and "The Road to Happiness". A few locally made shows are also screened including the South African "Rhema Church Hour".

One main characteristic of the prosperity gospel churches is that they are non-denominational. Their members are drawn basically from mainstream Protestant churches and to a lesser extent the Roman Catholics. It is extremely rare that the prosperity churches seek to evangelize and convert non-Christians. That would be a daunting task and entail going out into deep rural areas hitherto rarely visited by these

---

[15] The "I" in AIC is variously interpreted as Independent, Initiated or Instituted. The latter is used here as in the name of the Organization of African Instituted Churches. The naming of these churches is in itself a missiological issue.

[16] Paul Gifford, *African Christianity: Its Public Role*, London, Hurst, 1997, p.333. Harvey Cox, *Fire from Heaven: The Rise of Pentecostal Spirituality and the Reshaping of Religon in the Twenty-First Century*, London, Cassell, 1996.

churches. In their regular urban services, as well as the huge conventions they hold from time to time, they use Westernized forms of mechanized media including music – electric guitars, electronic keyboards and percussion.

After the end of the long civil war in Uganda in 1986, there was enormous Pentecostal religious growth. These include parent churches from Canada and New Zealand in the Pentecostal assemblies. Most notable of all is one of the newest, the Kampala Pentecostal Church (KPC), founded in 1984, which has grown so enormously that by the mid-1990s each of its three Sunday morning services in the capital city of Uganda was attended by 5000 worshippers. Its congregation is ecumenical in that most of its members were originally Roman Catholics or Anglicans and Protestants. The KPC impact among youth is so great that thousands of parents encourage their children to join.

The Nairobi Chapel (NC) in Kenya is the KPC's equivalent, if on an even more grandiose scale. The astronomical growth of the NC between 1994 and 2000 is such that its weekend services start on Saturday evenings. It conducts six services, each attended by more than 6000 worshippers, the majority of whom are drawn from young professional elites. The leadership comes from more than twenty denominations, the principal pastor is Presbyterian-trained and one of the assistant pastors is an Anglican priest. They understand themselves to be a part of the local ecumenical community, albeit not linked to institutional ecumenism. They do not accept the label "pentecostal" and are politically progressive, advocating for social democratic change. Their ministry to adolescents includes elaborate rites of passage. Worship, including African cultural and religious values such as community responsibility, respect for the elderly, mutual age-group responsibility, integrity and honesty, greatly influences the spirit and orientation, making the services highly appealing to youth and young adults.

With the weakening of local SCMs and the WSCF, churches like the NC are critical sites for ecumenical formation. While theirs is not the mainstream ecumenical theology, they nevertheless respond to the spiritual needs of the younger African generation in a way that conventional ecumenical formation processes do not.

ECUMENICAL CONCERNS

In 1976 the general committee of the AACC meeting at Cairo adopted the "Confession of Alexandria", following an ancient Christian practice and conscious of their heritage in the ancient north African church of Alexandria. They listed the churches' current concerns as "economic justice, the total liberation of men and women from every form of oppression and exploitation, and [a concern for] peace in Africa". They further stated the churches' search for "authentic responses to Christ as Lord over the whole of our lives". The committee affirmed "that the struggle for human liberation is one of the ways we confess our faith in an incarnate God". Ecclesial ecumenism had to restate publicly that it remained, and intended to remain, a movement to enable the churches in the development of a Christianity that was orthodox and catholic both in its outreach and in its cultural authenticity.

Authenticity and relevance have always been concerns of Africa but much more so since the Western missions became churches. The AACC assembly at Lusaka in 1974 signalled the movement from theological conservatism to a fresh and empowering gospel, and criticized rigid and timid church structures inadequate to the challenges of the continent. For the AACC, this was not new: its inaugural assembly in 1963 reported in drumbeats, and the second assembly at Abidjan in 1969 had sent out these same signals. But these emphases have been seen by some Christians, both African and non-African, as extra-ecclesial and therefore not the proper business of the AACC. Nevertheless, the themes of AACC assemblies continue to reflect the concerns of ecumenism in Africa and those of many churches as well as the majority of humanity in Africa.[17]

These themes, assembly messages to the churches, other ecumenical events and deliberative sessions are reflected in the efforts of other ecumenical bodies. Best known is the anti-apartheid struggle of the South African Council of Churches (SACC), ecumenical institutes, and individual Christians and some of their denominations. Of particular note is the Kairos document of 1985 which was reflected upon, and emulated, worldwide but not often enough among churches and ecumenical families in Africa. This powerful theological document called Christians to reflection from a biblical and theological perspective, to discover how to respond as Christians to what it called a situation of death. In South Africa "the moment of truth" (kairos) was defined as "the moment of grace and opportunity, the favourable time in which God issues a challenge to decisive action". The document critiques "state theology", which justifies theologically the status quo. It also criticizes "church theology", which in only "a limited, guarded and cautious way... is critical of apartheid". Instead the document promotes "prophetic theology" as an alternative, in which biblical teaching on suffering and oppression is considered in relation to a social analysis of the structures of oppression in South Africa.

In South Africa, the Kairos document is regarded as a theological watershed. It called for Christian action against a state which it described as having "no moral legitimacy" and which had become "an enemy of the common good". For the church to be the church, it must stand "unequivocally and consistently with the poor and the oppressed". But not all churches in South Africa were prepared to receive this "Challenge to the Church" (the subtitle of the Kairos document).[18]

Kairos documents were developed across the continent and around the world, using similar analysis. Shortly before the WCC's eighth assembly in Harare in 1998, a group of Zimbabwean Christians published a Zimbabwean Kairos document, denouncing "poverty, ill-health, bad governance, corruption, fear and hopelessness" in their country. The document was produced by the Ecumenical Support Services using the same methodology as the South African document, arguing that the Zimbabwe nation "had been plunged into a political, economic and, above all, moral crisis shaking its very foundation". It particularly criticized the ruling ZANU PF party of President Robert Mugabe, claiming that "despite our hopes and expectations [at independence and the end of white minority rule] in 1980, today we find new black political and economic elites within the same structures". The Zimbabwe churches were also criticized, since "while some have constantly challenged injustice, both before and after independence, many have failed to educate their members about abuses of power by authorities".

---

[17] Assembly themes of the AACC 1981-1997: Nairobi 1981, "Follow Me... Feed My Lambs", expressing faith and hope and a prayer that God would hasten the liberation of Africa (John 21; 15-19) see *Official Report of the 4th AACC Assembly, Nairobi 1981*, Nairobi, AACC, 1982; Lomé 1987, "You Shall Be My Witnesses" (Acts 1:8;), see Richard Sakala ed., *Official Report of the 5th AACC Assembly, Lomé 1987*, Nairobi, AACC, 1988; Harare 1992, "Abundant Life in Jesus Christ", held in the context of "deep crisis on the African Continent", as the then general secretary Jose Belo Chipenda said. See *Official Report of the 6th AACC Assembly, Harare 1992*, Nairobi, AACC, 1994. The assembly at Addis Ababa in 1997 took the theme "Troubled but not Destroyed" (2 Cor. 4:8-9). See *Tam Tam*, 2, 1996.

[18] Willis H. Logan ed., *The Kairos Covenant: Standing with South African Christians*, New York, Friendship, 1988, pp.16-18.

During the assembly itself, a plenary session dealt with "*ubuntu* and the African kairos". *Ubuntu* refers to an African sense of belonging and sharing and finding identity. The plenary session ended with a liturgical act of "commitment to a journey of hope" by all Africans "from the continent and the diaspora" to work for a better Africa, saying "never again" to the many forms of suffering and humiliation that the continent's people have known, and joining in an act of "covenant with God". The assembly was called to accompany them on their journey of hope and the delegates sang *Nkosi Sikilel'i Afrika* (God Bless Africa) as a symbol of mutual ecumenical solidarity.

The WCC's Nairobi assembly in 1975 had shed fresh light on the many ramifications of the concept of, and the search for, unity aided by the theme "Jesus Christ Frees and Unites", reinforcing what the AACC and the SACC were calling for.

The deep crises on the continent are of immediate and urgent concern to all. Ecumenism has to do with the visible unity of the church and with demonstrating the spiritual unity of Christians, unity not only for its own sake but also because it is the mission of God entrusted to the church. Ecumenism has to do with the integrity of the whole human race, its unity and well-being as much as with the integrity of the whole creation. With a fresh understanding of ecumenism and unity, it seems clear that the churches have entered a phase of mutual respect and a higher level of cooperation. It was therefore not surprising that where churches did act together, it was to deal with the unity of humankind and justice in human relations.

MULTIPLE POSTURES, ONE MISSION?

In the 1960s it seemed as if Africa would be torn apart by "evangelicals" and "ecumenicals". It was not enough to tear Africa apart with Christian denominationalism, one more division had to be played out, namely, who were the true Christians seeking the soul of Africa for Christ, and who were the Marxists in cassocks, only interested in wrenching wealth from the rich for the benefit of lazy Africans. Even at the WCC assembly in Nairobi 1975 there was a group denouncing ecumenism.

Once again Africans were being thrown into confusion. The Association of Evangelicals in Africa and Madagascar (AEAM – born in 1966, shortly after the AACC was founded) and the AACC were made to look like antagonists.

Further, there came into being the African Evangelistic Enterprise. Clement Janda observed the growth of other ecumenical structures in the post-Lusaka period (1974) set up primarily to counter the impact of the AACC third assembly. Prominent among these, he pointed out, was the Pan African Christian Leadership Assembly (PACLA).[19]

Two global Christian organizations meeting at the same time in Nairobi in 1975 – the WCC and the International Congress of Christian Churches (ICCC) – was no accident and succeeded in demonstrating one of the uglier sides of Christianity, its divisiveness and lack of real unity. The ICCC, run by fundamentalist conservative American Carl McIntyre, was deliberately planted in Nairobi at this time with the main objective of countering the WCC assembly. This was not an isolated incident, however. Several WCC assemblies and central committees were forced to deal with McIntyre's diatribes although his following gradually petered out in the 1980s.

---

[19] PACLA's first assembly was held in Nairobi (1976) barely a year after the fifth assembly of the WCC, also held in Nairobi. PACLA gathered churches under the guise of evangelical appeals, an expression which was aimed at countering the "liberal" WCC and AACC theology.

African Christians torn by traditional denominationalism were now to be further introduced to the divisiveness generated by varieties of theological stance. Other more overtly anti-ecumenical groups began to flood the African scene, often in the guise of fighting communism during the period that Africa was a field of struggle for the two principal proponents of the cold war, the US and the USSR. This continued division of Africa was another extension of colonialism as the superpowers saw the continent as a place to play out their struggles for victory. Several conservative evangelical movements with their funding and ideological bases in the US and apartheid South Africa and often with ties to the US Central Intelligence Agency infiltrated nations and churches in the name of fighting communism. Most had the effect of dividing and confusing African Christians. The lack of an active search for ecclesial unity therefore had roots other than the "fatalism of Africans". At the same time the Ecumenical Association of Third World Theologians began encouraging African theologians to craft Christian theology relevant to this context and adequate to respond to the challenges to the faith of African Christians.

Another variety of ecumenism observed by Ogbu Kalu was the non-structural ecumenism that thrived from 1985 and beyond. Kalu describes this as the "re-shaping of spirituality". The average African had rarely regarded the multitude and variety of churches as a scandal. This diversity was accepted with that sense which looked at inevitable things as *shaura la Mungu* (a matter to be left to God). People from various denominations came together for "common fellowship without abandoning denominational roots". Kalu cites the rapid growth of the Full Gospel Business Men's Fellowship and Women Aglow in West Africa. These were to challenge the secular ecumenism created by the various service clubs like Rotary and Lions.

The rift and rivalry between ecumenism and evangelicalism began to mend as African Christians found themselves face to face with the enormous extent of poverty, oppression, war and human-rights abuses. As Kalu observes, between 1975 and 1995, there was a rapid deterioration of the African environmental, socio-political, economic and infrastructural systems. Civil wars and disease devastated communities and nations. Africa has known violent religious strife, mainly generated by Christian and Muslim fundamentalism. In Nigeria this stimulated the formation of a wider conciliar fellowship named the Christian Association of Nigeria (CAN). CAN's watchword, "Jesus is Lord", has enabled Christians of various hues to join together to comment on political authority. As Kalu puts it, "Sensitive minds have awakened to what used to be called social ecumenism – re-discovering the diaconic, stewardly responsibilities of all people." According to Kalu it is the degeneration of the ecosystem that has brought people together to face a common enemy. "To the extent that such social activism and dialogue have taken place within the Christian perspective, ecumenism has been practised."[20]

It is interesting that PACLA II, held in December 1994 almost twenty years after the first assembly, was organized by the AEAM and the African Evangelistic Enterprise (AEE) in cooperation with the AACC and with a fund-raising policy that actively courted funding from the WCC while the list of participants included Roman Catholics. At the

---

[20] Kalu argues that the issue is not simply that the worsening economic backdrop forced people into a heightened religious response. In his mind, the data on the vertical growth rate of Pentecostalism in the midst of the oil boom in Nigeria does not fit this sociological interpretation offered by Paul Gifford.

inauguration of AEAM it appeared as if this would be the beginning of competition between the ecumenical and evangelical wings of Christianity. The AEAM, while it may be known for lack of openness to non-evangelicals, may be seen as a seminal embodiment of ecumenism in that its membership includes people from various denominations who cooperate and share fellowship. In local areas, however, its churches often function as para-churches. Influenced heavily by its moneyed supporters from the North, the AEAM needs to find an African identity.

The AACC assembly of 1987 affirmed a "spirituality that is not merely other-worldly, but expresses itself in an authentic and genuine liberation process in our villages as in the world". At the open air service the preacher, Rose Zoe-Obianga, then secretary of the women's programme of the Federation of Protestant Churches in the Cameroon, spoke on the assembly theme, choosing the text "You shall be my watchman". She observed that there was a landmark change in the AACC, a revival enabling it to accompany churches as they responded to natural, socio-economic, socio-cultural and political challenges. In 1992 at Harare there was further optimism reflected by the theme "Abundant Life in Jesus Christ", but five years later in Addis Ababa (1997) the last assembly of the century had a more sobering theme, "Troubled but not Destroyed", which may well have summed up the ethos of ecumenism in Africa. By the time of Addis Ababa, the woes of Africa were gathered up in the theme: Sudan, Rwanda, Burundi, Liberia, Sierra Leone, Zaire, Nigeria, all were flashpoints of internecine strife, abject poverty and the horror of the HIV/AIDS pandemic.

Ecumenism in Africa has continued its involvement in conflict resolution and crisis alleviation undertaken through member churches and with the mediatory services of "international affairs" programmes of ecumenical bodies. All the churches will continue to accompany a new phase of African struggle for stable governance.

The AACC, the Symposium of the Episcopal Conferences of Africa and Madagascar, the LWF and the WCC together with NCCs of the countries concerned have all been part of these ecumenical efforts. Together with promoting dialogue and providing humanitarian aid, much has been done in the area of partnership towards the old themes of reconciliation, reconstruction and development. In much of Africa that has predominantly Muslim populations, coupled with being French-speaking, the Christian presence is largely Roman Catholic and ecumenical cooperation has not become a way of life. But even in these areas ecumenical aid was effective, for example in the Sahel region of West Africa during the severe droughts of the 1970s and 1980s with a programme based in Burkina Faso.

THE HEALING MINISTRIES: FACE OF DEATH AND HOPE

The acquired immune deficiency syndrome (AIDS) caused by infection with the human immunodeficiency virus (HIV) was first diagnosed in 1981 although it had been spreading silently for at least two decades before that. By the year 2000, more than 36 million people worldwide were living with HIV and some 22 million had already died. Hardest hit was sub-Saharan Africa and especially southern Africa where between 20 and 30 percent of all people were infected and more than 13 million children had been orphaned. Countries especially hard hit include Botswana, Kenya, South Africa, Swaziland, Uganda, Zambia and Zimbabwe.

Churches all over the world began, very belatedly, providing care for people affected by HIV/AIDS but faced the problems of particular sexuality, gender relations, discrimination and the unconditional acceptance of people living with AIDS. The WCC's executive committee said in 1987,

> The AIDS crisis challenges us greatly to be the church in deed and in truth: to be the church as a healing community. AIDS is heart-breaking and challenges the churches to break their own hearts, to repent of inactivity and of rigid moralisms.

No other calamity since the slave trade has depopulated Africa at the rate AIDS has done. It is a plague of genocidal proportions. The African churches were faced with the need to change language, policy, behaviour and mobilize their own resources to reverse the epidemiological trend and give to those infected. Churches in particular have the capacity to influence the behaviour of people so as to render them less vulnerable to HIV, and to promote an attitude of care and love. Uganda is a prime example where close cooperation between government, churches and NGOs has led to a reduction of the infection rate of nearly 50 percent. The joint efforts resulted in delayed sexual intercourse among young people (abstinence), reduced numbers of casual sex partners (fidelity) and an increase in condom use.

The churches' healing ministries were first introduced to Africa during the era of colonialism and foreign missions and they have been continued ever since with hospitals, clinics and care-giving by churches in ecumenical cooperation. From the 1970s, ecumenical endeavours shifted to community health and to the participation of people in their own health-care provisions. The application of community-based health care to the effort to contain the HIV/AIDS pandemic has been a most significant arena of ecumenical cooperation. The WCC programme "Health, Healing and Wholeness" signalled the need for churches to pay attention to primary as well as preventive health care.

In HIV/AIDS, the tragedy is that the very means by which human life comes into being has become the source of death and raises the threat of non-being.

> We are called to transform this tragedy by linking life to a moral cosmology as the means to reclaim the intrinsic value of being in the world. That is why a new expression of the theology of life in the context of the HIV/AIDS pandemic would be liberating indeed.[21]

The receding role of governments in Africa in providing basic health care, much of which was inherited from colonial churches and taken over by the states, and the growing involvement of the private and NGO sectors demand an urgent response from the ecumenical movement in Africa. An alternative institutional framework needs to be established to meet pressing needs and consolidate the links between the socio-economic realities and health-care demand, especially for women. With the feminization of poverty in Africa there is an urgent need for affirmative action in health-delivery systems. Contemporary medical training in most African countries does not equip care-givers with skills for dealing with the consequences of domestic and other forms of violence, especially rape and sexual assault on children. Domestic violence and its consequences have become a continental public-health issue, greatly linked to HIV/AIDS.

> The need for global partnership in facing the crisis of HIV/AIDS is critical indeed. But we must always return to the values and norms of experiences with living communities in Africa. The people of Africa have always cherished an integrated vision of social reality. It is this connection between human experience and the structure or systems that yields an integrated understanding of the value of life.

---

[21] Samuel Kobia, *The Courage to Hope: The Roots for a New Vision and the Calling of the Church in Africa* (Risk Book Series, 102), WCC, 2003, p.178.

Thus the various belief systems... in Africa remind us that we live in a moral universe nurtured by the web of life-giving and sustaining relationships among all beings that inhabit the earth, including ancestral spirits.

The human condition is at the heart of our experience, and it is held together not by dualistic systems or inanimate objects but by institutions of affection that guarantee human happiness. New methodologies and preventive measures against the spread of HIV/AIDS, especially among young people, are necessary. Building institutions with ethical responsibilities for moral life, especially in the midst of communities, is essential.[22]

TOGETHER AS A FAMILY

As in 1963 the AACC and the whole ecumenical movement in Africa continue to "help member churches by accompanying and encouraging them in their attempt to remain faithful and relevant".[23] In 1996 the organization was described as

an ecclesial association comprising 142 churches and Christian denominations present in 39 African countries... and concerned with the spiritual, social, economic and political needs of Africa and its people.

The ecumenical concern for evangelism and frontier ministries, the building of a home for Christ in Africa and the evolution of a new society together with the debate on liberation and moratorium of the 1970s and 1980s remain. But these no longer divide the ecumenical movement nor create leadership crises. It has become clear to Africans that to be authentically Christian, they have to be authentically African, that is, approach life in an integrated fashion and live with integrity.

One of the facets of rooting ecumenism in Africa is the attempt to heal the major rifts in the Western church resulting from the Protestant Reformation. Vatican II followed by papal visits to Africa have been a source of inspiration as well as openness towards African culture, other religions and ecumenism. Papal visits to Yamoussoukro, official capital of Cote d'Ivoire, in 1980, the World Eucharistic Congress in 1985, and the 1989-90 centenary of the Roman Catholic Church's "second coming" into Africa, put an emphasis on the church as the "whole people of God" and thus opened the way for lay persons to take seriously their social and political obligations. International churches and institutions gave the Roman Catholics a sense of Africanness and, together with their episcopal conferences, generated an ecumenism in Africa. The pope's 1995 encyclical *Ut Unum Sint* ("That They May Be One") has demonstrated to African Roman Catholics his commitment to ecumenism, making it possible for Christians from that tradition to be open to sharing gifts in the ecumenical context, thus building upon Vatican II.

The most significant expression of rooting ecclesial ecumenism in Africa has been the establishment of councils of churches. Christian councils, usually pre-dating the WCC, are associated with the International Missionary Council, and national councils of churches, most of them also older than the AACC, continue as the public face and voice of ecclesial ecumenism. Some, like the National Council of Churches in Kenya, 57 years old in 2000, and the South African Council of Churches, have seen years of intensive socio-political and economic involvement of member churches. The costs have been high. In the 1980s, the NCCK undertook intense educational work in political conscientization of churches towards democratic change in Kenya. This prophetic critique led

---

[22] *Ibid.*, p.180.
[23] *Tam Tam*, 2, 1996.

to the banning in 1988 of *Beyond*, the council's news magazine. Following the banning, the council revived *Target* which had been discontinued.

Many were the martyrs of this period of liberation from the end of colonialism to the present. The role of the SACC in the anti-apartheid struggle made the ecumenical celebration of the release of Nelson Mandela a landmark in inter-religious relations in South Africa and a prelude to the most inclusive democratic national constitution that Africa has known. But needless to say, other landmarks have been the refugees and mortalities of this struggle. The road "accident" that killed Anglican Bishop Alexander Muge of Kenya in 1992 recalled for many the martyrdom of Anglican Archbishop Janani Luwum of Uganda in 1977. The slaughter of hundreds of thousands of Tutsis and moderate Hutus in Rwanda's church compounds of all denominations in 1994, the maiming and massacres in Liberia and Sierra Leone in the same decade that saw South Africa free, the world war-size conflicts between Eritrea and Ethiopia and the millions killed in the Democratic Republic of Congo as the century ended crossed all boundaries between denominations and faiths and even Christian councils, as failed states divided along ethnic and tribal lines.

For NCCs in Africa, national unity has taken priority over church unity. The councils stand for a dynamic approach to ecclesial unity with the growing participation of Roman Catholics. Joint projects and specialized committees have become a way of expressing unity and these are found in several countries.[24] Councils that have the full and vigorous participation of AICs are not common, but the establishment of groups like the Christian Association of Nigeria may signal future development in ecclesial ecumenism in Africa.

The Ecumenical Association of Third World Theologians and the Ecumenical Association of African Theologians have both undertaken to develop theologies addressing Africa's ecumenical concerns. The WCC promoted the Ecumenical Decade: Churches in Solidarity with Women (1988-98) and the AACC pan-African women's conference in 1987 drew many African women into the ecumenical movement. Women theologians have come together to establish an ecumenical forum for research and writing on women, religion and culture and have named themselves the Circle of Concerned African Women Theologians. Initiated by an all-Africa women theologians conference in 1980, it was formally convened in 1989 in Accra, Ghana. The Circle held three pan-African conferences and several national and area workshops which produced a number of theological publications.

For the churches in Africa and the NCCs, globalization has become a signal challenge to the meaning and practice of diakonia. In response to African problems exacerbated by events following the collapse of Soviet-influenced communism, non-governmental organizations of all shapes and forms began to take over social services from governments. Alongside these emerged in the early 1990s non-structured social action-oriented Christian groups. They are unrelated to any specific churches and have many of the same characteristics and features as the secular NGOs – they often revolve around a "charismatic" individual and are not accountable to any definite constituency; they are primarily urban-based, venturing only occasionally into rural areas to deliver

---

[24] Cameroon, Ghana, Kenya, Liberia, Madagascar, Malawi, Mozambique, Namibia, Rwanda, South Africa, Tanzania, Tunisia, Zaire and Zimbabwe are examples of councils with Roman Catholic participation at one level or another.

services; the leadership tends to be elitist in life-style with external sponsorship in terms of funding and ideas. Samuel Kobia of the WCC calls them churches' NGOs.

The negative impact of the work of these NGOs and churches on local ecumenical organizations is quite strong. Slowly they have occupied the spaces that were long occupied by the national councils of churches and local denominations. That is the case with regard to emergency relief as well as diaconal work, especially development. The NGOs have less bureaucracy and are therefore quicker to respond to emergency situations. They have, therefore, been able to attract funding even from donors who were traditional sources of financial support for NCCs and churches. This has led to the weakening of NCCs whose activities and life depended on external financial support. This fact should prompt soul-searching by the NCCs concerning their mission and calling to be the church in Africa in the third millennium.

An aspect of ecumenism in Africa that does need urgent support is the Project on Christian-Muslim Relations (PROCMURA). This dialogue is evidence of the theology of pluralism that ecumenism in Africa needs to recognize and promote. Questions were first raised as far back as 1960 in Nigeria as independence first began: What is the responsibility of Christianity in the areas of the north which are predominantly Muslim? Should the church attempt to evangelize in these areas? Should the church expect to have the right under the constitutional guarantee of religious freedom to propagate its faith in these areas? If so, how does one proceed? PROCMURA is an effort to get churches in Africa to cooperate on this issue of common concern raised by earlier questions.

REVIEW

Acy Peters, general secretary of the Christian Council of Gambia, wrote that the ecumenical movement in Africa came into being as a "watch dog" and "advocate" for the poor because better results for Christianity were envisaged if the approach was a collective one. She observed that in the process Africans found themselves engaged in all kinds of areas, as spiritual needs could be addressed only if physical needs first were taken care of. The development of ecumenism in Africa is clearly a response to the demands related to the churches' mission in Africa. Since the re-emergence of globalized capitalism as the world's sole power, there is serious concern that the ecumenical movement is being affected in a fundamental way. With the shift to profit and market ideologies, it is feared that the movement may have to abandon slogans like "preferential option for the poor" and the language of liberation for mottos more recently popular in Western circles. For Clement Janda, "the challenge to the ecumenical movement in Africa in the latter years of the 1990s was to stay on course with its programmes of being the voice of the voiceless". That uniting churches have not been a favoured form of ecumenism in Africa has nothing to do with the speculations of Baur on the African character, if ever there was justification for such a generalization of a continent's whole people. One can also suggest that the form of ecumenism favoured by Africans may arise out of the theology of pluralism that those who deal in terms of hierarchies and structuralism may not appreciate. The struggle for cooperation rather than union is itself an effort at ecumenical living.

One aspect of ecumenical living to which Africa has made a laudable contribution is worship. When the Kimbanguist Church of Zaire (later Democratic Republic of Congo) became a member church of the WCC, it brought a manner of praying that was unique.

Other AICs like the Church of the Lord Aladura offered songs that moved worshippers. *Worshipping Ecumenically: Orders of Service from Global Meetings*[25] reflects the amazing development in ecumenical worship since the WCC's Vancouver assembly in 1983. African music has been part of the contextualization of ecumenical worship so that it reflects the "image of God in all humankind".

When the Centre for Applied Religion and Education at Ibadan graduated its first students in ecumenical learning in 1995, the graduate who spoke on behalf of the class described how ecumenical learning had transformed his biblical interpretation and his concepts of salvation. He said there were similar ecumenical efforts going on in Africa and transforming theological perspectives, and the effects could not be minimized. Even the attempts at cooperation to meet the immense needs of refugees and other traumatized people of God in Africa were commendable given the power of the forces that insisted on sowing dissent and division in Africa.

Ogbu Kalu should have the final word:

> To the extent that social dialogue has taken place within a Christian perspective, ecumenism has been practised. The roaring lion outside has quietened the bickering within.

BIBLIOGRAPHY

Abundant Life in Jesus Christ: 6th General Assembly, All Africa Conference of Churches, Harare, Zimbabwe, 25-29 October 1992, Nairobi, All Africa Conference of Churches, 1992, no pag.

Alberts, Louw and Chikane, Frank eds, *The Road to Rustenburg: The Church Looking Forward to a New South Africa*, Cape Town, Struik Christian Books, 1991, 286p.

Amanze, James N., *A History of the Ecumenical Movement in Africa*, Gaborone, Pula Press, 1999, 320p.

Ankrah, Kodwo E., *Development and the Church of Uganda: Mission, Myths and Metaphors*, Nairobi, Acton, 1998, 197p.

Appiah, Evelyn V. and Pobee, John Samuel, *Africa Pre-Assembly of the World Council of Churches, Winneba, August, 1990: A Report*, WCC, 1990, 144p.

Appiah-Kubi, Kofi and Torres, Sergio, *African Theology en Route: Papers from the Pan-African Conference on Third World Theologians, December 17-32, 1977, Accra, Ghana*, Maryknoll NY, Orbis, 1979, 214p.

Baur, John, *2000 Years of Christianity in Africa: An African History 1962-1992*, Nairobi, Pauline Publications 1994, 560p.

Bosch, David J., *Transforming Mission: Paradigm Shifts in Theology of Mission*, Maryknoll NY, Orbis, 1996, 587p.

Ela, Jean-Marc, *African Cry*, Maryknoll NY, Orbis, 1986, 154p.

Equipping the Laity for Social Transformation: A Resource Manual for Courses on Leadership in Lay Training, Accra, Asempa, 2000, 216p.

Follow Me – Feed My Lambs: Official Report, 4th General Assembly, All Africa Conference of Churches, Nairobi, Kenya, 2-12 August 1981, Nairobi, All Africa Conference of Churches, 1982, 124p.

Gavi, Chiramwiwa ed., *Jubilee 2000: Economic Justice for Churches in Eastern and Southern Africa*, Harare, EDICESA, 1999, 120p.

Gifford, Paul, *African Christianity: Its Public Role*, London, Hurst, 1997, 368p.

Kobia, Samuel, *The Courage to Hope: The Roots for a New Vision and the Calling of the Church in Africa* (Risk Book Series, 102), WCC, 2003, 218p.

Logan, Willis H. ed., *The Kairos Covenant: Standing with South African Christians*, New York, Friendship Press, 1988, 184p.

---

[25] Per Harling ed., WCC, 1995. Also *Thuma Mina: Singing with Our Partner Churches*, Basel, Basileia, 1995.

M'Biti, John S., *Bible and Theology in African Christianity*, Oxford, Oxford Univ. Press, 1986, 248p.

M'Passou, Denis, *Mindolo, a Story of the Ecumenical Movement in Africa: To Mark the 25th Anniversary of Mindolo Ecumenical Foundation*, Kabulong Lusaka, Multimedia Publ., 1983, 118p.

Mugambi, Jesse N.K. and Magesa, Laurenti eds, *The Church in African Christianity: Innovative Essays in Ecclesiology*, Nairobi, Initiatives Publ., 1990, 205p.

Mugambi, Jesse N. K. ed., *Democracy and Development in Africa: The Role of the Churches*, Nairobi, All Africa Conference of Churches, 1997, 196p.

Mulunda-Nyanga, Ngoy Daniel, *The Reconstruction of Africa: Faith and Freedom for a Conflicted Continent*, Nairobi, All Africa Conference of Churches, 1997, 145p.

Njoroge, Nyambura J. and Réamonn, Paraic eds, *Partnership in God's Mission in Africa Today: The Papers and Reports of the Consultation on African Women and Men of Reformed Tradition, 9-15 March 1994*, Geneva, World Alliance of Reformed Churches, 1994, 94p.

Nyomi, Setri ed., *Ecumenical Youth Ministry in Africa: A Handbook*, Nairobi, All Africa Conference of Churches, 1993, 160p.

Oduyoye, Mercy Amba, *Hearing and Knowing: Theological Reflections on Christianity in Africa*, Maryknoll NY, Orbis, 1986, 168p.

Okullu, Henry, *Church and State in Nation Building and Human Development*, Cincinnati OH, Forward Movement, 1987, 141p.

Pityana, N. Barney and Villa-Vicencio, Charles eds, *Being the Church in South Africa Today*, Johannesburg, South African Council of Churches, 1995, 173p.

Pobee, John Samuel ed., *Africa Moving Towards the Eighth Assembly*, Harare, 1998, WCC, 1998, 113p.

Rasmussen, Lissi, *Christian-Muslim Relations in Africa: The Cases of Northern Nigeria and Tanzania Compared*, London, British Academic Press, 1993, 132p.

Réamonn, Paraic ed., *Farewell to Apartheid? Church Relations in South Africa*, Geneva, WARC, 1994, 96p.

Shank, David A. ed., *Ministry in Partnership with African Independent Churches: Papers Presented at the Conference on Ministry in Partnership with African Independent Churches, July 1989, Kinshasa, Zaire*, Elkhart, Mennonite Board of Missions, 1991, 436p.

Shorter, Aylward, *The Church in the African City*, London, Chapman, 1991, 152p.

Shorter, Aylward, *Evangelization and Culture*, London, Chapman, 1994, 164p.

Spong, Bernard and Mayson, Cedric, *Come Celebrate! Twenty-Five Years of the South African Council of Churches, 1968-1993*, Johannesburg, South African Council of Churches, 1993, 148p.

Uka, Emele Mba, *Missionaries Go Home? A Sociological Interpretation of an African Response to Christian Missions: A Study in Sociology of Knowledge*, Bern, Peter Lang, 1989, 313p.

Utuk, Efiong Sam, *Visions of Authenticity: The Assemblies of the All Africa Conference of Churches, 1963-1992*, Nairobi, All Africa Conference of Churches, 1997, 271p.

Waruta, Douglas W. ed., *African Church in the 21st Century: Challenges and Promises*, Nairobi, All Africa Conference of Churches, 1995, 155p.

You Shall Be My Witnesses: Official Report, General Assembly, All Africa Conference of Churches, Lomé, 18-25 August 1987, Nairobi, All Africa Conference of Churches, 1988, 250p.

Young, Josiah U., *African Theology: A Critical Analysis and Annotated Bibliography*, Westport CT, Greenwood, 1993, 257p.

Youth Peace Training Manual: All Africa Conference of Churches Youth Training Manual, Nairobi, All Africa Council of Churches, 1999, 189 p.

20
Asia

K.C. Abraham and T.K. Thomas

During recent decades there has been a general decline in the churches' commitment to ecumenism. Church union negotiations seem to have lost their momentum. In spite of post-Vatican II developments and better, even innovative, cooperation among churches in general, a mood of ecumenical exhaustion seems to have set in. At the same time, however, ecumenism has itself acquired a wider meaning. The unity of the human family, in fact of the whole of creation, is increasingly being recognized as the goal of the ecumenical movement, and the overcoming of divisions in the Christian church is by many no longer seen to comprise the full ecumenical mission.

The 1960s and 1970s were a period of growing disillusionment and political uncertainty in Asia. Quite a few countries had to deal with situations of ethnic conflict, large-scale corruption, human-rights violations and the rise of religious fundamentalism. Even in societies with a measure of political stability, governments found it difficult to provide the necessary infrastructure for people to maintain a reasonable standard of life.

The countries that gained independence from colonial rule embarked on massive efforts to develop national resources and eliminate poverty. Development through economic growth based on rapid industrialization was the over-riding concern. The three ingredients in this enterprise were the local elite consisting mainly of rulers and those who wielded power, external resources largely in terms of aid from the developed world and multinationals, and trade. The goal was not only to eliminate poverty but also to catch up with the first world in modernization which was often confused with Westernization. So was development confused with growth. But as the Indian economist C.T. Kurien points out, growth by itself is not a sufficient condition for the removal of poverty. "At least two other conditions are required: the increase in output must be of the things that the poor need and, when such goods become available, the poor must have access to them".[1]

A few Asian countries, pre-eminently Japan but also South Korea, Taiwan and Singapore, have become economically powerful. China and India have demonstrated their potential for technological development. But among Asian countries are also a few of the world's poorest. All of them, however, rich and poor alike, have given in to the compulsions of the world market which has emerged as the dominant economic force. Thus the economies of most, including Vietnam, Laos and Cambodia, have undergone a process

---

[1] C.T. Kurien, *Economic Reforms and the People*, Delhi, Madhyam Books, 1996, p.62.

of liberalization and globalization. Even the economies of the People's Republic of China and the "Socialist Secular Democratic Republic of India" are now linked to the global economy which is largely under capitalist control.

So the global market, largely shaped by the logic of capitalism, seems to have conquered. After the disintegration of the Soviet Union and the collapse of socialism in Eastern Europe, the economies of Asian countries have by and large succumbed to the demands and dictates of the market.

Asia is the home of the major religions of the world, and all of these religions have come under the influence of modernism. Their responses to the challenges of modernism provide a new context for the ecumenical movement. The traditional cultures of Asia have always had a strong religious foundation which has provided much of the cultures' integrating principles as well as a certain legitimacy for social structures and political authority. The rise of technological rationality and the consequent secularization of society during the last few decades pose serious threats to this overall religious orientation. To be sure, except in the Philippines, Australia and New Zealand, Christians are still minority communities in all Asian countries and even the extraordinary church-growth phenomenon in South Korea has had no real impact in other countries.

The renascent nationalism of the 1950s and 1960s gave rise in several Asian nations to movements of religious revival which, in countries such as India, Sri Lanka and Pakistan, resulted in large-scale violence and "communal" conflicts. In the wake of gathering disillusionment with nation-building and the apparent failure of official development policies, the reaction to modernization and secularization led to an upsurge of religious fundamentalism and in some countries to alliances between politics and religion. A word that was first used to describe militant Evangelicals in the United States, "fundamentalist", is now widely used in Asia when referring to followers of traditional religions who possess political ambitions. The Bharatiya Janata Party (BJP) or the Indian People's Party, with its ideology of *hindutva* – a term that is widely used to convey the essence of cultural nationalism – is one of the largest political parties in India and its membership is drawn almost entirely from the Hindu majority. The Rashtriya Swayam Sevak Sangh (literally "the national society for voluntary service"), a fundamentalist movement within Hinduism, was responsible for the demolition of the mosque in Ayodhya in 1992, the worst manifestation of Hindu fanaticism in independent India. In parallel fashion, the demand for a separate Sikh state in India was made by fundamentalist groups within Sikhism.

Fundamentalist intolerance is most common in monotheistic religions, especially when their followers form the majority of the population. Pakistan is an Islamic republic, and Hindu and Christian minorities often complain that they are treated as second-class citizens. The separate electoral system introduced in 1979 by the military government of General Zia-ul-Haq for local elections and extended in 1985 to national and provincial elections confined Pakistani religious minorities – Hindus, Christians, Parsis and Buddhists – to separate electorates. In effect this system is a form of religious apartheid.

The Malaysian society is more multi-ethnic and multi-religious, but here too fundamentalist groups have been active, committed to the preservation of Islamic identity and resisting the secularization of the Malay culture. The first prime minister of the country, Tunku Abdul Rahman, once declared that "a Malay who abandons his religion ceases to be a Malay".

Indonesia has the largest Muslim population of any country in the world. Unlike Pakistan, it is not an "Islamic" republic, and its state philosophy of *Pancasila* ("the five pillars") stressing belief in one supreme God, humanity, nationalism, democracy and social justice was expected to provide a secular framework for the peaceful coexistence of people with different religious affiliations and from different ethnic groups. Its failure to serve effectively as the constitutional guarantee of interfaith amity in Indonesia and to protect the unity of the country is a striking example of the limitations of rule by decree.

The emergence of East Timor as an independent nation is one of the important recent developments in the region. This island was under Indonesian military rule and the peoples' demand for freedom culminated in a referendum under the supervision of UN and other observers. Over 78 percent of the 800,000 people of East Timor voted for independence on 30 August 1999. The unexpected repression that followed left the newly independent country devastated. It received massive humanitarian aid, but only after a UN peace-keeping force had brought the Indonesian militia under some measure of control. The Christian Conference of Asia and the WCC have supported the freedom struggle of the people of East Timor and are involved in the massive rehabilitation programme in the country.

Frequently behind the facade of communal harmony fundamentalist groups remain active throughout Asia. Even in the Philippines, with around 48 million Christians and eight million Muslims, Islamic fundamentalism has been a force to reckon with. The Christian contribution to reconciliation, both from the Roman Catholic and Protestant churches, has been minimal, confined to small ecumenical groups.

No wonder the fundamentalist resurgence within Asian religions is often seen as a threat to the "Christian presence" in Asia – in the literal sense of that expression. Islamic fundamentalism is perhaps the most insidious and intolerant today – as Christian fundamentalism from time to time has been in the past – and Charles Amjad-Ali has a case when he reminds fellow Christians in Pakistan that "Islam and the Muslims force us much more towards ecumenicity than either the plurality of philosophies and ideologies which are the dialogical partners in the West or Hinduism and Buddhism and other such religions in other parts of Asia". Islam directly challenges Christian theological and doctrinal positions, and the refusal of Christians to convert to Islam questions the "validity and veracity of Islam as being the ultimate revelation within the monotheistic tradition". The differences among Christians in matters of faith and order are of no importance to Muslims, and therefore Christians in Pakistan have "an automatic opportunity for ecumenism" which does not obtain anywhere else.[2] This approach is pragmatic; it commends ecumenism for survival in a minority context and expresses much the same fear as in Benjamin Franklin's blunt statement: "If we do not hang together, we shall all be hanged separately." But hanging together can also mean the negation of ecumenism as understood today. It can mean living in a ghetto, a perennial temptation for religious communities in minority situations.

The missionary goal of winning Asia for Christ is still cherished in certain quarters, but Asian theologians have been urging Christians to discern the work of Christ in peoples' struggles for justice, stressing the need for religious communities to be a part of, and to work for, truly human communities. In response to the developments described above, several peoples' movements outside the formal political processes have emerged in recent years – social-action and human-rights groups and organizations of marginal-

---

[2] Charles Amjad-Ali ed., *A Look Towards the Mountains*, Rawalpindi, Christian Study Centre, 1993, pp.4ff.

ized peoples, women, dalits, the minjung and Indigenous Peoples. These movements are committed to social change, though their analyses of the situation and their strategies for change differ widely. Action groups and peoples' movements present important challenges to the church and its mission. They remind Christian people that they should work for a renewed community which allows space for different identities to flourish, and that they should mobilize the liberating vision of religions to build just and participatory communities.

The Christian response to all this has varied from country to country and even within countries. In the main it involved, on the one hand, a return to institutional securities and other-worldly piety and a decline in whatever ecumenical commitment the churches once had and, on the other hand, resistance to the sponsoring of radical causes, increasing scepticism about church-related ecumenism, and a search for broader ecumenism.

THEOLOGICAL RESPONSES

Context continues to be a decisive factor in the development of Asian theology. Contextualization was in its early phase apologetic and polemical. The relation between Christian faith and the major Asian religions was the theme that received serious attention at that time.

A new stage was set when Asian theologians such as Raimundo Panikkar and D.T. Niles acknowledged the incognito presence of Christ in Asia's history and religions long before the missionaries came to Asia.

During the period under review, theology emerged out of an active interaction between the gospel and the religious philosophies of Asia. Concepts, doctrines and symbols of other religions were used freely, though critically, by Asian churches both to deepen their experience of Christ and to interpret the Christian faith. Alongside this there was – in an attempt to remove the general perception of Christianity as an alien faith – also a vigorous search for an Asian face of Christ. Theologians were convinced that the Christ reality was greater than formal Christianity and that the Christ was present, though unacknowledged, in the religions and cultures of Asia. Dialogue thus became the chief mode of theological discourse. In such dialogue, as Stanley Samartha says, "It is not *ideas*, but *people*, not religious systems, but living faiths, that are involved."[3] Aloysius Pieris of Sri Lanka deepened the dialogue when he related Marxist insights on liberation to the religious experience of liberation in an effort to forge a new theology of Asia. He declared in his book *Towards an Asian Theology of Liberation* that "theology in Asia is the Christian apocalypse of the non-Christian experiences of liberation".[4]

A second stream in recent Asian Christian theology had its origin in the churches' encounter with the socio-political realities of their contexts. In a number of his writings M.M. Thomas dealt with the Asian revolution from the perspective of the gospel. According to him, colonization, though often ruthless and exploitative, was the bearer of a process of humanization in Asian societies, however ambiguous, especially through the introduction of technology and industry and of liberal ideas of freedom and justice.

---

[3] Stanley J. Samartha, *One Christ – Many Religions: Towards a Revised Christology*, Maryknoll NY, Orbis, 1991, p.33.
[4] Aloysius Pieris, *Towards an Asian Theology of Liberation*, Edinburgh, T. & T. Clark, 1988, p.86.

Christ, the promise of a new humanity, he argued, should be confessed as the trans-forming and judging presence of God. For him the struggle for human dignity is a preparation for the gospel.⁵

The Christian Conference of Asia (CCA) has provided a forum for Asian thinkers to reflect deeply on the events of the gospel story from within the social and cultural con-texts of the region. Such reflection leads to the affirmation that confessing faith in Christ involves constructive participation in the social and political revolutions of the day and in the building of nations based on justice and freedom. The methodology governing such theology is that of contextualization. Shoki Coe of Taiwan, who contributed signifi-cantly to the growth of Asian theology, indicated that this process involves a dynamic in-teraction between the text and the context. Contextual theologians also proposed a criti-cal Asian principle as a method for doing theology in their situation.

Thirdly, the theme of "people" has assumed a special significance in Asian theologi-cal discussions. CCA programmes such as the Urban Rural Mission (URM) and the themes of CCA meetings and conferences have for years focused on "people", seeing them as the subjects of history and of the church's mission. Appropriating insights from recent biblical scholarship, Asian theologians interpret the term "people of God" not to mean a single tribe but a heterogeneous group of powerless, marginalized and dispos-sessed men and women, victims of injustice and social and political oppression, who are longing for justice and liberation. They claim that for the most part it was with people in this understanding of the term that Jesus associated. In programmes organized by the CCA and the Asian section of the Ecumenical Association of Third World Theologians (Eatwot), Asian Christian thinkers have explored the implications of people-centred the-ology, focusing on the areas of Christology and ecclesiology, and particularly on soteri-ology, interpreting salvation in terms of liberation and humanization.

"Living in Christ with People" was the theme of the 1981 CCA assembly. There, on the one hand, people were identified as the poor and powerless, "the politically op-pressed, economically exploited, socially marginalized and culturally deprived".⁶ On the other hand, there were repeated reminders about the danger of deifying people, as when Masao Takenaka of Japan warned against the temptations to romanticism and to "equate people with the Messiah". But in spite of the recognition that people are both sinned against and sinning, that "the people and their struggles are *simul iustus et peccator*, both just and sinful", the more idealized notions about people and their struggles have per-sisted, especially in CCA-URM circles.

In Korea the focus has been on the theology of the "minjung". David Kwang-Sun Suh, an exponent of minjung theology, explains the origin and meaning of the word:

> "Minjung" is a Korean word, but it is a combination of two Chinese characters "min" and "jung". "Min" may be translated as "people" and "jung" as "the mass". Thus "minjung" means "the mass of the people, or mass, or just the people".

Minjung theology developed during a period of oppressive military dictatorship in Ko-rea, when the "development" ideology imposed by the government led to the systematic

⁵ See Douglas J. Elwood ed., *What Asian Christians Are Thinking: A Theological Source Book*, Quezon City, New Day Publ., 1976, p.267. See esp. M.M. Thomas, *The Acknowledged Christ of the Indian Ren-aissance*, London, SCM Press, 1970.
⁶ See Yap Kim Hao, *From Prapat to Colombo*, Hong Kong, Christian Conference of Asia, 1995, pp.106ff.

suppression of human rights and a widening gap between the rich and the poor. A variety of Christian groups have been actively involved in the struggle.

> Theology of minjung is a creation of those Christians who were forced to reflect upon their Christian discipleship in basement interrogation rooms, in trials, facing court-martial tribunals, hearing the allegations of prosecutors, and in making their own final defence. Theology of minjung is the socio-political biography of Korean Christians in the 1970s.[7]

Another minjung theologian, Suh Nam Dong, identifies the most important element in the political consciousness of the suppressed people in Korea as *han*, a deep "feeling that arises out of their unjust experiences, a feeling of unresolved resentment against unjustified suffering".[8] Theology is rooted in the *han* of the suffering people; its task is to retell and reflect on the stories and social biography of the minjung and their hopes and aspirations in the world and its history. Minjung theology is a political theology arising out of concrete experiences of suffering and often expressed through cultural symbols. It sees culture as a source of power for people's liberation, and interprets people's life in music, drama and masked dances, representing, often satirically, their sense of frustration as much as their will to resist. It is committed to women's liberation and to the reunification of Korea. It articulates, in brief, a theology of liberation in the Korean context.

The emergence of dalit theology in India has resemblances in certain respects to the rise of minjung theology in Korea. Dalits are the untouchables, subjected for centuries to caste discrimination and social oppression. Gandhi called them *Harijans*, God's people, but they rejected the belated recognition and chose to be called dalits, meaning the "broken and oppressed people". According to A.P. Nirmal, a prominent dalit theologian, pathos and suffering are the essence of dalit existence, and it is the experience of suffering that mediates to dalits the knowledge of God. "We proclaim and affirm", Nirmal writes, "that Jesus Christ himself was a dalit – despite his being a Jew."[9] Dalit Christians have been in the forefront of the struggle, and their theological reflections are a valuable contribution to contextual theology in India.

In recent years women in Asia, mainly through their work with the Asian Women's Resources Centre for Culture and Theology, EATWOT, CCA and similar organizations, have been reflecting on the patterns of domination that keep them powerless and dependent on patriarchal structures. Through their involvement in several movements that focus on specific areas of discrimination – such as gender discrimination in the workplace and unjust wages, denial of the right to own property, dowry-related atrocities and sexual exploitation – women have gained the courage to dream of a brave new world, positively affirming their environment, futures, and the destiny of all people. Theological reflection on this experience is both critical and constructive. There is a

> growing consciousness of the indispensability of a partnership between women and men in the process of change and liberation. This partnership is an important point in Asian culture which we need to rediscover and recover.[10]

---

[7] Yong-Bock Kim ed., *Minjung Theology – People as the Subjects of History*, Singapore, Christian Conference of Asia, 1981, pp.17ff.

[8] *Ibid.*, p.27.

[9] A.P. Nirmal in Raju Sail ed., *Transcending Boundaries: Perspectives on Faith, Social Action and Solidarity: A Festschrift in Honour of Bishop A. George Ninan*, Bombay, Vikas Adhyan Kendra, 1995, p.80.

[10] Marianne Katoppo in Virginia Fabella ed., *Asia's Struggle for Full Humanity: Towards a Relevant Theology. Papers from the Asian Theological Conference, January 7-20, 1979, Wennappuwa, Sri Lanka*, Maryknoll NY, Orbis, 1980, p.147.

Women realize that the scriptures, written and interpreted by men, can distort the truth and be a source of oppression, and there have been several attempts by Asian women to reinterpret the scriptures, reading them from the perspective of the suffering of women and their struggle to come to a new ordering of human relations and a more caring relationship with creation. Women's movements all over Asia are predominantly multi-religious. In their struggle they respect the liberation strands in all faiths. They try to tap the unexpected protest potential in religious traditions, forge links with the past, and find cultural roots for protests today.

This method of doing theology with people's symbols and images holds great promise. Indications are that there will emerge a distinct voice in theology that comes out of the deepest yearnings of the people of Asia. Choan-Seng Song's *Theology from the Womb of Asia*, Kosuke Koyama's *Mount Fuji and Mount Sinai*, and Masao Takenaka's *God Is Rice* make, in different ways, important contributions in this area. The Programme for Theology and Culture in Asia under the leadership of C.S. Song is providing a forum, through its workshops and publications, for deepening this concern. According to Song,

> there is something deep in folklore and fairy tales – culturally and spiritually deep. In them we find popular theology at its most unsophisticated and yet at its most profound, at its simplest and yet at its deepest, at its most unadorned and yet at its most moving.[11]

Harvey Perkins's important book *Roots for Vision* is "an extended reflection on how the gospel not only impinges on but also inspires – breathes the spirit into – the church's mission to be with the poor and in the struggle for justice, peace and freedom for all the human family". The book has a more descriptive subtitle: *Reflections on the Gospel and the Church's Task in Re-peopling the De-peopled*. Early in the book he explains what he means by re-peopling and de-peopling:

> It helps me to underline that the "de-peopling" process is the result of the political, economic, social and cultural structures of community; that the "re-peopling" process is not merely ameliorating conditions of poor people, but restoring them to a place in society from which they can claim their rights, and not become marginalized or oppressed by the structures of society again.[12]

In theological reflection on people, whether in books or consultations, de-peopling seems to receive greater attention than re-peopling. We know our context, but we do not seem to know how best to respond to it, with the result that we have not quite succeeded in really seeing people as the subjects of theology. The question can be, and has been, asked: "Is this yet another instance of using people?" God's preferential option for the poor and the crucial place of the poor in the church's mission have found wide acceptance among theologians, but their implications for the programatic thrusts of Asian churches have not been clearly worked out.

"Development" was still a good word when Harvey Perkins was in charge of the CCA's development and service desk. For him it meant the process of re-peopling. The Indian economist Samuel Parmar's emphasis on economic growth, self-reliance and social justice was formative for the ecumenical understanding of development, the first of these being the means of promoting the other two. But during the post-Soviet period,

---

[11] C.S. Song, *Tell Us Our Names: Story Theology from an Asian Perspective*, Maryknoll NY, Orbis, 1984, p.ix.

[12] Harvey L. Perkins, *Roots for Vision: Reflections on the Gospel and the Churches' Task in Re-Peopling the De-Peopled*, WCC, 1985, p.4.

development has been increasingly identified with globalization and the triumph of capitalism. The response to globalization varies from country to country. Nations which once were called the "tiger-economies" of East Asia – a term describing the astounding economic miracle which started in Japan decades ago and later spread to so-called "little tiger" countries such as South Korea, Taiwan, the Philippines, Thailand and Malaysia – owed their prosperity to full participation in the process of globalization. Recent economic crises and the devaluation of currencies have made the tigers of Asia look more like kittens, creatures of Western capitalism, pampered and then ignored. Theologians in these countries are only beginning to grapple with the problems of globalization and the ambiguities of market economy. In southern Asia, especially in India, there are strong reservations among economists regarding the growing control of the global market over the economies of developing nations. And theologians such as Sebastian Kappan and Samuel Rayan see globalization as a new stage of capitalism and warn against the dangers it poses. But the fact remains, as Feliciano V. Carino of the Philippines points out, that "there is a dry spell in present Christian social and political thought which makes the prospects of a creative Christian witness and response relatively gloomy". He continues,

> The irony of our condition is that precisely at a time in which Christians and Christian institutions have gained some respect for their involvement and moral courage in the social and political arena, no body of Christian social and political thinking has emerged that could be given equal respect or real attention.[13]

This is also largely true of the response of Asian theologians to the ecological crisis. The crisis raises serious questions, but an Asian perspective on it has not yet emerged. The romantic view of nature that is evident in some of the green movements has been questioned. Theologians in Asia would like to emphasize the need to see the ecological crisis as a justice issue. Kim Yong Bock writes,

> The issue of the relationship between human life and nature is not merely the question of how to deal with the natural environment, but that of total creation, which involves justice, participation and peace as an integral unit.[14]

Other writings on environmental and ecological issues place emphasis on spirituality – a creative form of spirituality which is life-giving and dynamic. The Asian section of EATWOT has developed this theme in relation to the experiences of women and Indigenous Peoples and their struggles for justice. It has given rise to a renewed interest in the spirituality of other religions – Buddhism, Taoism and Hinduism – which cherish a cosmic vision in their hope for the future and celebrate an earth-centred spirituality.

UNITED AND UNITING CHURCHES

Asia has its share of united churches – and also of church union negotiations that have not come to fruition, as the one in Sri Lanka which floundered, first in litigation and then because of the long drawn-out ethnic conflict in the country. The Church of South India (CSI) was one of the first and most promising among United churches. Its for-

---

[13] From a presentation on "Our [CCA] Ecumenical Agenda: A Perspective on Present Tasks and Future Work."

[14] Yong-Bock Kim, "Justice, Peace and the Integrity of Creation", in *Voices From The Third World*, 16, Bangalore, EATWOT, 1973.

mation in 1947, through the coming together of the South India United Church (itself formed through the union of Presbyterian and Congregationalist denominations) and Anglican and Methodist (British) churches was an event of immense historical importance. This union of episcopal and non-episcopal churches marked a momentous ecumenical breakthrough, and it happened a few weeks after India became an independent nation and almost a year before ecumenism found institutionalized expression through the formation of the WCC.

On 27 September 1997 the CSI celebrated the fiftieth anniversary of its formation. The CSI has served as a catalyst for other church union movements, especially in North India and Pakistan. Further, the CSI has grown through the years, both numerically and institutionally. It started with 14 dioceses in four south Indian states. With 21 dioceses and a membership of nearly 2.5 million people, it is the largest Protestant church in India today. Its involvement in educational and medical work is impressive. There was considerable opposition when the CSI decided to ordain women, but this is now well accepted.

In spite of all this, there is a general feeling that the CSI has failed to live up to expectations. The main criticism is that today it is a denomination like other denominations. Unity has become "visible" and real, but it has not extended to other churches. Dialogues with the Methodist church of India (American) and the Lutheran churches have not led anywhere. Nor has unity gone beyond denominational cohesion. The CSI today is one United church, and that is no small accomplishment; but tensions persist because of caste, regional and linguistic differences within the body.

Episcopacy, as it has developed in the CSI through the years, was a target of criticism in papers presented at seminars held in connection with the jubilee celebration. The CSI's basis of union describes the bishop as "the chief pastor and father in God", but he – there are as yet no women bishops in the CSI – has apparently become the executive head and a symbol of power. Yet another point of criticism is that the laity is largely marginalized, and women have not found their legitimate place in the decision-making bodies. "Unity for mission" and "unity for renewal" were familiar slogans in the 1940s and 1950s, but theological discussions on mission in context and on the church's role in the life of the nation were more or less confined in later years to presentations at synod meetings.

In varying degrees such criticisms apply to most churches in India. It is no mean achievement that in the CSI unity has endured, but what is disappointing is that its immense ecumenical potential has not been exploited through relevant witness in the pluralistic context of the country and through theological contributions and programmes of action which address issues of the "renewal of human community" in India.

After over four decades of negotiations the Church of North India (CNI) was formed in 1970. The uniting bodies were the Anglican dioceses in North India, the British and Australian Methodist churches, the Council of the Baptist Churches in Northern India, the Church of the Brethren and the Disciples of Christ. The Methodist Church of Southern Asia, which had been actively involved in the negotiations, at the last moment decided not to join the union. The motto of the United church is "unity, witness, service".

Following the example of the CSI, the church adopted an episcopal structure, but it does not subscribe to any specific interpretation of episcopacy. It began its life as a United church with a service of unification of the ministries, with mutual laying-on of hands. Both infant baptism and believer's baptism have been accepted as alternative practices.

In an evaluation of the church's record, one of the bishops of the CNI mentions among its achievements the overall conviction that it is a "visible expression of our oneness in Christ", the reality of eucharistic fellowship, of common ministry, and of one administrative structure which accepts "the episcopal, presbyterian and congregational elements in church order, as the means through which the lordship of Christ in his church may be realized". The negative points he makes, however, are deeply disturbing. "The engagement in the field of mission and evangelism by the United church seems to be less than the sum total of what was being done by the various denominations before the union." In liturgy and worship the new church has not been able to preserve denominational traditions, nor could it compensate for that loss by making its own contributions to corporate worship, which has led to a certain impoverishment in "liturgical koinonia". Further, the CNI has become "an island church", a denomination that has no world communion to relate to. The gains, concludes the bishop, "have been superficial, while the new burdens of litigations, dissensions and lack of accountability have become unbearable".[15]

That is a negative assessment of the church's record, made from a conservative understanding of ecclesial identity. The CNI with 23 dioceses covers a vast area. Its membership of over a million people, most of them from poor backgrounds, forms a small minority within a very large and predominantly Hindu population which is becoming increasingly conscious of its Hindu identity and political power. How does the church in such a situation become a sign of God's kingdom of justice?

The CNI and the CSI have much in common. The Mar Thoma Church is a reformed Oriental Orthodox church, with a liturgical tradition that is largely Orthodox and a mainly Protestant theology. Also known as the Malankara (Indian) Orthodox Church which has always cherished the tradition of St Thomas, it has had friendly relations with the churches that came together to form the CNI and the CSI, and has developed a relationship of full communion with the United churches. The three churches had a joint theological commission which recommended in 1975 the establishment of a

> joint council of the three churches to express our joint concerns for the mission of Christ in our country today, to give concrete expression to our relationship of full communion already existing and also to continue to initiate negotiations for a wider manifestation of the unity of the church so that the world may believe.

The joint council was duly formed and its work during those early years was ecumenically encouraging. As decided by the council, eucharistic liturgies of the three churches were published in one volume, to encourage the celebration of one another's order in local congregations. The second Sunday in November was to be celebrated as a festival of unity. Among other recommendations of the council were the formation of regional councils, holding joint meetings of women, youth and clergy, and participation in one another's decision-making bodies. But the decisions were hardly communicated and rarely interpreted to local congregations. The proposal that the three churches have a common name, Bharat (Indian) Christian Church, made by the joint theological commission, was accepted by the two United churches but rejected by the Mar Thoma Church whose members, with their tradition of celibate episcopacy and old liturgy, and

---

[15] S.B. Joshua, "The Future of the Ecumenical Movement: From the Perspective of a Member of a United Church", in Thomas F. Best and Günther Gassmann eds, *On The Way to Fuller Koinonia: Official Report of the Fifth World Conference on Faith and Order*, WCC, 1994, pp.147,148.

their fond attachment to the heritage of St Thomas, were totally unprepared for the radical erosion of ecclesial and social identity such a change of name would involve. During the celebration of the eucharist, prayers are offered in all three churches for the moderators of the CSI and the CNI and the metropolitan of the Mar Thoma Church, but a common name is obviously much more problematic.

The joint council continued to meet from time to time but there was no significant advance in dialogue or relationship and the congregations remained largely unaware of its existence. In 1999 it was, however, given a new lease of life. At a meeting of the leaders of the three churches the joint council was renamed Communion of Churches in India and its objectives were further elaborated and clarified.[16]

Church union in Japan did not happen through decades of ecumenical dialogue as in most other places. It was imposed by government pressure in the early 1940s, through the religious bodies law. Thirty-four denominations were forced to come together to become one church, the Nippon Kirisuto Kyodan, the United Church of Christ in Japan (UCCJ). Among them were Reformed, Methodist, Presbyterian, Lutheran, Congregationalist, Holiness, Baptist, Disciples, and other groups including one-third of the Episcopalian congregations.

There was no agreement on matters of doctrine, liturgy or church structure and it was inevitable that when the religious bodies law was no longer in force and the postwar constitution guaranteed religious liberty, several groups would withdraw from the United body in order to resume their old denominational identities. Among them were the Episcopalians, the Lutherans, and parts of the Holiness, Baptist and Presbyterian groups. The Kyodan thus became one among several denominations. It had achieved only uniformity, not unity. What was perhaps more important was the fact that through its formation Christianity was recognized, along with Buddhism and Shintoism, as one of the religions of Japan. After the war "state Shinto", which was thought of as the national religion, was dissolved. Emperor Hirohito publicly renounced his divinity, and the separation of religion and state was enforced. Shinto became one of the religions, though there were later attempts to restore its primacy, invariably provoking Christian protests.

The Kyodan was now free to address real ecclesial and ecumenical issues. A new confession of faith was drawn up, giving the church a basis for doctrinal agreement. Years later, on Easter day 1967, the moderator of the church issued a statement confessing "the responsibility of the Kyodan during the second world war". Deeply self-critical, the confession admitted that the Kyodan, established under government pressure, had compromised itself by cooperating with the imperial regime. It asked for God's forgiveness and for the forgiveness of Asian people who were the victims of Japanese aggression. It expressed the church's determination to play a critical and prophetic role in the future. The confession had far-reaching repercussions, including the long and acrimonious controversy over the Kyodan's participation in the proposal to have a Christian pavilion at the Osaka world exposition in 1970. Those who were opposed to the proposal argued that Expo 1970, through advertising Japanese technology and material success, would lead to the economic exploitation of Asian nations and that the churches should not be

---

[16] For an account of this meeting, and the recommendations made, see *The Ecumenical Review*, 52, 1, Jan. 2000, pp.11-19.

a party to it. The controversy in turn raised radical questions regarding the administration of the Kyodan, its confession of faith, and its pattern of ministerial training.

In spite of continuing discontent among sections of people, both conservative and progressive, the UCCJ has been able to take stands on important social and political issues in Japan. It has fought discrimination in Japanese society, especially the treatment of the Buraku people, through the Buraku liberation centre, and it has provided consistent support for the large number of Koreans in Japan who were for years exploited and marginalized by the Japanese. It has denounced trends towards the revival of emperor worship, and taken a firm stand whenever democratic values and the freedom of religion came under threat. The church has established covenant relations with the Korean church in Japan and with churches in Taiwan and Korea.

Church union negotiations in Australia have a long history. They started in earnest in 1901, the year Australia became a nation with its own constitution and a federal parliament. Involved in the dialogue were the Methodist, Congregational and Presbyterian churches. Attempts to form a United church failed in the 1950s and 1960s because of Presbyterian dissent. Negotiations continued, however, until a revised basis of union was accepted by the churches, and the Uniting Church in Australia (UCA) was formed on 22 June 1977, though some Congregationalists and quite a number of Presbyterian congregations chose to remain apart.

The churches that came together were of European origin, but the present membership of the Uniting church reflects the multicultural character of Australian society. From its early years it has witnessed to the conviction that union is not an end in itself, only a means to renewal in faith and mission and engagement with the world. Its concern for social justice and the bold stand it has taken on issues such as apartheid, nuclear tests, and mining near Aboriginal sacred sites has often proved controversial. It has consistently supported the claims and rights of the Aboriginal people. One of the significant developments in the Uniting Church's life is the Uniting Aboriginal and Islander Christian Congress. In 1996, joining the Anglican and Roman Catholic churches, the Uniting Church apologized to the Aboriginal people for cooperating with the government policy of assimilation which separated children from their families in order to assimilate them into white society.

The UCA is a young church, but it has already made an ecumenical impact even though the unity it has achieved is by no means complete, and there are unresolved problems. It is still *Uniting in Worship* – the title of a worship resource book it published a few years ago – and in witness. Perhaps it is a little premature to describe it as "the most exciting Christian venture in Australia's history", but it has indeed been "an independent Christian voice" in its setting.[17]

The United Church of Christ in the Philippines (UCCP) was founded in 1948 by the union of similar but far from identical heritages – the United Evangelical Church of the Philippines, itself a union of Congregational, Presbyterian and United Brethren traditions, the Philippine Methodist Church, and an earlier union of a number of evangelical churches called the Evangelical Church in the Philippines. The church is run on presbyterian lines, though the area overseers are called bishops. Responsible for its government are congregational councils at the local level, district annual conferences at the regional level, and the general assembly that meets every four years at the na-

[17] Muriel Porter, *Land of the Spirit? The Australian Religious Experience*, WCC, 1990, p.74.

tional level. The church is often described as a "United and Uniting Church". The Church of Christ (Disciples), which had voted against the union in 1948, joined the UCCP in 1962.

The UCCP is the largest Protestant church in a predominantly Roman Catholic country. The church's cooperation with Roman Catholics depends, as in other Asian countries, on the attitudes and orientation of local priests and pastors. Issues of justice and common social problems sometimes lead to joint action. Catholic priests and nuns and Protestant pastors and church workers have from time to time rallied round issues of militarization and martial rule. The most impressive instance of such joint protest was during the 1985 uprising of the people which resulted in the overthrow of the Marcos regime, a unique display of people's power.

The Church of Pakistan was formed in 1970 through the union of Anglican, Lutheran, Methodist and Scottish Presbyterian traditions. Its diocese of Dhaka was reorganized as an autonomous church, the Church of Bangladesh, after East Pakistan, one of the five provinces of Pakistan, became an independent state in 1972. Christians form only a small part of the population in both countries, and most of them belong to the poor sections of society. The churches have been active in educational and medical work, but many of their institutions have now been nationalized. Though minority religious communities in these countries are supposed to have full rights, much of the kind of Christian mission enterprise that is generally taken for granted is likely to provoke opposition. In Pakistan, violation of "the blasphemy law" can attract the death penalty and, from a fundamentalist Islamic perspective, some of the ecumenical goals may well come within that law's purview.

This account of United churches in the Asian region is by no means complete. Another example would be the Church of Christ in Thailand, which celebrated its fiftieth anniversary as an autonomous church in 1984.

There has been a marked loss of momentum in church union negotiations. There have been few instances of what M.M. Thomas described as "risking Christ for Christ's sake", and of "putting the Christian faith alongside other faiths, and alongside rationality and other human values which we share with others, allowing the examination of each, including our faith, in the categories of the others",[18] or of the churches undergoing what Aloysius Pieris calls the double baptism, "in the Jordan of Asian religions" and "on the cross of Asian poverty".[19]

Does it now mean, then, that the goals of organic unity, structural integration, and "the fullness of lived koinonia" are only ecumenical illusions? Not necessarily. But it certainly does mean that education for church union at the congregational level should have received far more attention than it did. In a sense church unions in Asia have been imposed from above, through negotiations that went on for decades, sometimes long after the pioneers with their informed passion for unity had left the scene. People acquiesced rather than participated in many of these unions. Perhaps a case can be made for the kind of movement from below which has led to the formation of "ecumenical congregations" and "local ecumenical partnerships" in some Western countries and "cooperative ventures" in Aotearoa-New Zealand.

---

[18] M.M. Thomas, *Risking Christ for Christ's Sake*, WCC, 1987, p.7.
[19] *Towards an Asian Theology of Liberation*, p.86.

THE CHRISTIAN CONFERENCE OF ASIA

The East Asia Christian Conference (EACC), later renamed Christian Conference of Asia, was the first regional ecumenical organization to be formed; in May 1997 it celebrated its fortieth anniversary. The modest anniversary function held at the Hong Kong YMCA was attended by members of the CCA general committee, the executive committee of the Hong Kong Christian Council, and representatives of churches and Christian organizations in Hong Kong. It was a time gratefully to remember the CCA's ecumenical witness in the past, to renew its ecumenical vocation, and to rethink the implications of that vocation in the fast-changing Asian context. It was also a time to express the CCA's solidarity with the churches and the people of Hong Kong, on the eve of Hong Kong's reversion to Chinese rule.

CCA assembly themes, taken together, have a story to tell, a story of the changing self-understanding of the CCA, of changing perceptions of the churches' role in Asian societies, and of changing theological emphases. Earlier themes were stubbornly Christian in their formulation and content. Even though the way these early themes were dealt with often broke through the exclusiveness of their formulation, they nevertheless reflected the inward-looking ethos of the small Christian communities in Asia – and the nervousness of their missionary mentors. Then there was a change. The theme of the third assembly, which met in Bangkok in 1964, was "The Christian Community within the Human Community". Christian identity is affirmed, but it is no longer seen as separate from or unrelated to the identities of others. Christians share a common history with those who are not Christians; their destiny is bound up with that of the whole human community of Asia. In the documents that came out of the assembly are statements like these:

> When we offer ourselves in worship as the gathered people, and when we offer ourselves in service, scattered in the world, we engage in the one liturgy. In the temple we are confirmed as God's children, in the world we are set as God's sign. Our discussion as Christians of economics, politics and society are therefore conversations about Jesus Christ, that is to say, an attempt of faith to discern him in the social changes of our nations, and to discover what it means to respond to his call in relation to these changes.

In 1968, at the fourth CCA assembly, the theme was the Pauline affirmation, "In Christ All Things Hold Together", which sounds like a relapse into Christian triumphalism. It was, however, more a kind of undergirding, a return to the source which is now seen as Christ and not the church. And that is what makes "Christian Action in the Asian Struggle" possible, the theme of the 1973 assembly in Singapore. Then, almost as a corrective to the monopolistic undertones in "Christian Action", the theme of the Penang assembly in 1977 was "Jesus Christ in Asian Suffering and Hope". Implicit in that formulation is the call to discern the presence and activity of Christ in the struggles of Asian peoples; the theme unfolds the logic of earlier ones. The Christian community within the human community of Asia must witness to the Christ who is himself involved in Asian suffering and hope, and whose involvement in the life of Asian people precedes the brief history of the churches in Asia. That witness must take the form of "Living in Christ with People", the theme of the seventh assembly, held in Bangalore in 1981. And then, providing the theological rationale for such living in Christ, came the affirmation that "Jesus Christ Sets Free to Serve", the theme of the eighth assembly in Seoul in 1985.

CCA assembly themes thus seem to reflect a changing understanding of mission. The early themes focus on evangelism, and what is new about them is their call to unity.

They urge the churches to go beyond comity and cooperation to unity and togetherness. Then we see a change in the thematic orientation, from a largely introverted understanding of mission to a more contextual one, situating the Christian community within the human community and, with it, a more comprehensive and universalistic understanding of the mission of the Christ in whom all things hold together. And that seems to lead, with almost inexorable logic, to an action-oriented stance. The context is the Asian struggle and what it calls for is Christian action. Such action must proceed from, and be informed by, the "previousness" of Christ, and Christ's presence within the pain and suffering of the struggle.

That leads, in turn, to the affirmation of our calling to live in Christ and to live with people, not in that order, not the one after the other but rather simultaneously and inseparably. And that because "Jesus Christ sets free to serve", not a phrase this time but a complete sentence with a subject and a predicate – and no object. It does not say who is set free and whom to serve – an omission that seems to point to the measure of the freedom that Christ offers. By now we have come a long way from the "Christian Prospect in East Asia".

The theme of the ninth assembly, which met in Manila in 1990, was "Christ Our Peace: Building a Just Society"; the theme of the tenth assembly, in Colombo in 1995, was "Hope in God in Changing Asia". In both, the goal of mission is understood as social transformation and not church growth. The theme of the most recent assembly, which met in North Sulawesi, Indonesia, in June 2000, was "Time for Fullness of Life for All".

We cannot claim, however, that all these themes reflect the theological and ideological orientation of the CCA's member churches. Asian churches are not committed to building just societies and they do not live in Christ with people or see Jesus Christ in people's sufferings and hopes more than churches elsewhere. Yet these themes have had a cumulative impact. There is a growing appreciation among groups of people that the churches' task is not to speculate about the Christian prospect in Asia but to become a Christian presence in Asia, and that the Christian community must live within and for the human community.

What was unfortunate, however, was the fact that the CCA had to pay a price for all this. A few of the statements that came out of CCA meetings and some of its programmes, along with the themes of its more recent assemblies, created the impression that the CCA was becoming ideologically radicalized. The 1970s and 1980s had seen the emergence of a number of action groups and peoples' movements, some genuinely committed to and involved in the struggles of the poor and the oppressed and others apparently using the rhetoric of liberation mainly to impress aid agencies. In a few countries their relationship with the churches was marked by tension if not by open hostility and they often found a ready home in ecumenical organizations such as the WCC and the CCA which the churches sometimes resented. At the 1983 general committee meeting of the CCA, during a lively discussion of the issue of churches and action groups, Bishop Emerito Nacpil of the Philippines remarked that the CCA's close relationship with action groups had given rise to the perception that the CCA too was an action group.[20]

Not that the CCA was unaware of such criticism. The general committee meeting in 1979 wanted the CCA to undertake a study of "multinational style para-church organi-

---

[20] *From Prapat to Colombo*, p.123.

zations" which, through their programmes of charity, methods of preaching and structures of operation, caused confusion among Christian people in Asian countries. That was to be expected. But the meeting was also self-critical; it sounded a warning against the insidious temptation among activist groups that pursue human liberation to exploit the suffering of people. The end, that of making human life truly human, is a noble one, but as an editorial comment in the issue of CCA's monthly news magazine that reported on the general committee meeting said,

> Before we know where we are, there is a whole network of vested interests, spawned by a concern for human suffering, sustained by the systematic advertisement of human suffering and supported by resources that come from elsewhere, borne on rumours of development. Suffering, which is the result of exploitation, now begins to look like an area of exploitation.[21]

The 1973 CCA assembly marked a new phase in the life of the regional body. The EACC was renamed the Christian Conference of Asia; its constitution was revised; the rules and procedures were amended. It was given a new structure and a new team to head the general secretariat. A presidium of four took over from the chairman and vice-chairman. All the activities were grouped under three programme clusters: message and communication, justice and service, and life and action. So far the CCA had managed with a small office in Bangkok, with most members of its staff, many of them part-time, working from their home countries. Now it had a centralized structure and small staff, most of whom moved to Singapore where the CCA was based till 1987.

In December 1987 the CCA was "dissolved" by the Singapore government and its expatriate staff "expelled" from the country.[22] An official news release said that the CCA had breached the undertaking it articulated when it moved its headquarters to Singapore: "not to indulge in any political activity or allow its funds to be used for political purposes". It had been using Singapore, the news release said, as a base to support "liberation movements" in other Asian countries and it had been providing covert help to subversive elements in Singapore. The CCA received messages of support from churches and Christian organizations around the world, but the member churches in Singapore and their national council withdrew their membership. The closing of the Singapore office led to another period of dispersion, this time out of necessity and not of choice. The work of the CCA was carried out from offices in Osaka, Manila, Chiang Mai and Hong Kong until June 1993 when the centre which had been acquired in Shatin, New Territories, Hong Kong, was declared open, and soon after the staff came together once again and the process of centralization was completed.

When D.T. Niles became chairman of the EACC in 1964, U Kyaw Than took over as general secretary. Yap Kim Hao, from Malaysia, succeeded Kyaw Than, and served in that position for three full terms. After him, Park Sang Jung of South Korea, John Victor Samuel of Pakistan, and Feliciano V. Carino of the Philippines served as general secretaries. At the end of the century, the general secretary was Ahn Jae Woong of Korea.

The relationship between the Federation of Asian Bishops Conferences (FABC) and the CCA has entered a new stage with the setting up of an Asian Ecumenical Committee

---

[21] *CCA News*, 15 March 1979, p.2.
[22] Ron O'Grady's book *Banished: The Expulsion of the Christian Conference of Asia from Singapore and Its Implications*, Hong Kong, CCIA International Affairs Committee, 1990, gives an account of the expulsion of the CCA and its ramifications.

(AEC). The Asian mission conference which met in 1989 had resolved to strive towards a more representative expression of Asian ecumenism and to explore the possibility of working towards Catholic membership in the CCA or in "a successor Asian ecumenical structure". The 14-member AEC, with equal representation from the two bodies, met in Colombo in January 1997. Among the projects recommended by the committee were a joint pastoral visit to the churches in East Timor, in collaboration with the Indonesian bishops conference and the Communion of Churches in Indonesia; and the publication of a worship book for ecumenical gatherings in Asia, reflecting the rich and varied cultural heritage of Asian churches. An earlier example of FABC-CCA collaboration is the Ecumenical Coalition on Third World Tourism (ECTWT), organized with the two bodies as charter members. The ECTWT had its origin in a pioneering study on tourism initiated by the CCA in 1975. Following an international workshop on tourism held in Manila in 1980 and attracting the participation of other third-world regional ecumenical bodies, the ECTWT was set up in 1982. Based in Bangkok, the coalition addresses the ethical and cultural implications of third-world tourism and promotes positive programmes for change.

By the end of the 20th century, the Christian Conference of Asia had contributed significantly towards the development and promotion of an Asian theological agenda. In cooperation with the networks of theological education in Asia, primarily the Association of Theological Education in South East Asia, the Board of Theological Education of the Senate of Serampore College in India and the Programme for Theology and Culture in Asia, together with other ecumenical organizations, CCA organized a Congress of Asian Theologians, whose first meeting was held in Suwon, Korea, in 1997. CATS aims at providing "ecumenical space" and a continuing structure for the sharing of theological work and for promoting cooperation in theological studies and reflection.

Since 1974 the CCA has been celebrating the Sunday before Pentecost as "Asia Sunday". It commemorates the inauguration of the regional body on the eve of Pentecost in 1959 and gives an opportunity for Asian churches to pray for one another and to thank God for their growing sense of togetherness. In 1996, Asia Sunday focused on the theme, "Indochina: Let There Be Shalom". The CCA has a long history of involvement in the countries of Indochina and what started as a relief programme later developed a service and development thrust; during the post-war period the emphasis has been on reconstruction and rehabilitation.

The Asian ecumenical course, started in 1975, has become an annual event making a major contribution to ecumenical formation. The month-long programme involves a period of exposure to Asian realities and discussions in depth on the region's ecumenical future. Publications on Asian art, Asian theology, the Asian context of material poverty, religious pluralism, the ubiquitous URM presence in Asian struggles, reports of and statements from consultations and conferences – these form only a part of *There Is No End*, the title of a bibliography of Asian ecumenical documents from 1948 to 1981.

The CCA has had its share of setbacks, as when it was summarily sent out of Singapore by a government known equally for its efficiency and its paranoia, or when the Indonesian churches, reacting to the insensitive way the politically controversial East Timor issue was discussed at the Seoul assembly in 1985, decided to stay out of all CCA's decision-making bodies for a period. The CCA has also had its share of internal conflicts and financial crises. The level of ecumenical support it receives from member churches and councils has not always been encouraging. But in spite of all these, the CCA constituency has registered a steady growth; by the end of the 20th century, it was made up of 109 churches representing all the major confessional and ecclesiastical traditions, together with 16 national councils.

NATIONAL COUNCILS OF CHURCHES

The *Directory of Christian Councils* published by the World Council of Churches in 1985 is an impressive testimony to ecumenism in our time. Listed in it are 90 councils in 78 countries. Their names vary, due to national or historical reasons: a few are called missionary councils, but the most common name is Christian council, as in the Hong Kong Christian Council, or council of churches, as in the National Council of Churches in Pakistan. The difference between the two is mainly one of membership; only churches can have full membership in councils of churches, though interdenominational or para-church organizations such as the YMCA, the YWCA and Bible societies can become associate members, while along with churches they can have full membership in Christian councils.

Listed in the directory are all the national councils in the Asian region, except the National Council of Churches in Taiwan. All of them, including the Maori Council of Churches in New Zealand which was formed in 1982, have membership in the CCA; the only exception is the NCC of Singapore. Most of them are associate councils of the WCC and affiliated to the Commission on World Mission and Evangelism. Roman Catholics are full members of the NCCs in New Zealand, Australia, Malaysia and Taiwan.

The Australian Council of Churches, the predecessor of the National Council of Churches in Australia (NCCA), was formed in 1946. Among its main concerns and activities were faith and order issues, overseas aid and development, resettlement of refugees, defence of human rights, extending consistent support for Aboriginal land rights, and church and society issues.

The formation of the NCCA on 3 July 1994 at St Christopher's cathedral, Canberra, marked a significant ecumenical development in the region. As Keith Rayner, the primate of the Anglican Church of Australia, said in the inaugural sermon, the fact that the Roman Catholic Church, numerically the largest in the country, has joined the fellowship of the Council means that the NCCA, with its blend of Catholic, Orthodox, Anglican and Protestant traditions, has in it "an almost unequalled representation of world Christianity". In a contribution entitled "Towards the National Council of Churches in Australia", NCCA general secretary David Gill pointed out a year earlier that, in addition to the Anglican and Protestant churches, the NCCA would have, unusual among national councils of churches, "a significant number of Eastern and Oriental Orthodox jurisdictions: Armenian Apostolic, Antiochian, Assyrian, Coptic, Greek, Romanian and Syrian. The decision of the Catholic bishops brings in not only their 28 Latin rite dioceses but the Maronite, Melchite and Ukrainian dioceses of the Eastern rite as well." Gill concluded his article,

> How the people of St Agatha's congregation on one side of the street deal with the folks of Wesley Uniting Church on the other, and what difference this makes to their efforts to be more truly the church in that place, is what, at the end of the day, the National Council of Churches in Australia is all about.[23]

---

[23] David Gill, "Towards the National Council of Churches in Australia", in *A Yearbook for Australian Churches*, Hawthorn, Christian Research Association, 1994.

The constitution of the enlarged Council has a section dealing with issues of ecclesiology – "The Church, the Churches and the NCCA". This makes clear that the NCCA is not a church; the member churches bring to it their own understanding of the nature of the church. They are not to give up or compromise such understandings, but it is hoped that there will be an ongoing dialogue of ecclesiologies within the fellowship of the Council.

The Council of Churches in Indonesia (DGI) was established in 1950 as "a place for consultation and for common efforts of the churches" in the country. Its goal was to work towards a united Christian church in Indonesia. The churches had come into being in various parts of the country to serve particular ethnic groups, and they represented most ecclesial traditions except the Orthodox and the Episcopalian. During the first three decades of the work of the DGI, although the member churches got to know one another, there was no tangible move towards unity or common witness. In 1984, on the basis of five documents on unity that the member churches had endorsed, it was decided to change the name of the DGI from the Council of Churches to the Communion of Churches in Indonesia (PGI or CCI). The word "council", explains CCI general secretary Joseph M. Pattiasina, emphasizes the organizational aspects of unity while "communion" highlights the ecumenical and spiritual gains achieved through the experience of fellowship.

The five documents dealt with the basic task and common calling of the churches, the common understanding of the Christian faith, the issue of mutual recognition and acceptance, the constitution of the CCI, and the question of self-reliance in theology, human resources and funds. Behind the documents lay the conviction that unity is a process and not a product, and that it cannot be divorced from ongoing signs of renewal and growth in cooperation and mutual understanding. The documents also provided for variety and diversity within the unity, and the affirmation of the identity of member churches within the overall framework of their common identity in Christ, a point that received special emphasis in the third document which dealt with mutual recognition and covered almost all aspects of church life. As Fridolin Ukur, a former general secretary of the CCI, has said, "After 34 years in the fellowship of the council of churches in Indonesia, the 54 member churches proclaimed that the churches in Indonesia are a communion of churches and are part of the one holy, catholic and apostolic church."[24] Not that their unity is complete and final. At the twelfth assembly of the CCI held in 1994 in Jayapura, participants discussed at length how the unity that had been discovered and affirmed could become real at congregational and denominational levels so that it could lead to the formation of a united Indonesian Christian church. The unity CCI seeks must be meaningful within the history and for the future of the Indonesian nation, and the ecumenical movement it represents includes this dimension of national commitment.

In Japan, Christians form less than one percent of the population but the Christian voice does not go unheard. Often it is a voice of dissent and protest within a culture of conformity and, in the main, it is articulated by the National Christian Council in Japan (NCCJ) which has among its members a number of Christian agencies and associations, apart from churches and organizations, such as the Bible Society, the YMCA and the YWCA. The Council registers its protest whenever there is violation of the post-war peace constitution of the nation. It is totally opposed to any move that appears to en-

---

[24] Thomas F. Best ed., *Living Today Towards Visible Unity*, WCC, 1988, p.109.

courage the re-militarization of the country and it has consistently denounced the lingering rituals of emperor worship, sponsoring protests every time government officials visited the Yasukuni shrine, a Shinto war memorial and a symbol of Japan's imperial past. The NCCJ regularly takes up the causes of minorities in Japan – the Koreans, the Ainus, the Burakumins, the Okinawans and migrant workers from other Asian countries, all of them victims of discrimination. Thus the Council condemned the practice of fingerprinting foreign residents and has been fighting the Japanese alien registration law.

With its phenomenal church growth, Korea has also gone through an unprecedented denominational proliferation. Membership has gone steeply up in the Roman Catholic Church and even more so in several Protestant denominations. The Christian message was brought to Korea by Presbyterian missionaries and both the Presbyterian democratic structure and the room it had for respect for elders appealed to the Korean people. Presbyterians outnumber all other Christian groups and they are represented by a large number of church bodies. In recent years there were attempts to bring them together into some kind of coalition, and the Council of Presbyterian Churches formed in 1995 has now several groups in its membership. All the churches are deeply committed to evangelism. According to a 1994 survey carried out by the Korean Research Institute for Missions, there were nearly 3000 Korean missionaries working in various countries throughout the world, over 1500 of them in Asian countries. But shared expressions of the enthusiasm for evangelization are rare, an exception rather than the rule. These churches have different approaches to most political, economic and ecumenical issues.

In contrast to the situation in quite a few Asian countries, the church in South Korea does not have an image problem. It is fast-growing, and well accepted by people. Christians were in the forefront of resistance during the period of Japanese occupation and in more recent decades Christian groups have been actively involved in the struggle for democracy and in the defence of human rights. One of the concerns of quite a few churches today is the reunification of the divided peninsula. The council of churches in Korea is deeply involved in the movement for reunification, as it was in the struggle against dictatorship and the violation of human rights under authoritarian regimes.

Founded in 1924 as the National Christian Council, the National Council of Churches (NCCK) was formed in 1946. For many years it had only six churches in its membership: the Presbyterian Church of Korea, the Anglican Church of Korea, the Presbyterian Church in the ROK, the Evangelical Church in Korea, the Salvation Army and the Korean Methodist Church. The Korea Assemblies of God joined in 1996, which may well open the way for other conservative denominations to take up membership in the Council. The NCCK's unification committee was formed in 1982 and its first statement, the "Declaration of the Churches for Peaceful Reunification", was adopted in 1984. The fiftieth year of the division of the country into North and South Korea, 1995, was commemorated as a Jubilee Year for Peaceful Reunification. The main goals of the committee were to increase exchanges between Christians in South and North Korea and to make reunification acceptable to the Korean churches.

The NCCK took the initiative in forming a committee consisting of representatives of 43 Korean denominations which declared that the Unification Church of Sun Myung Moon is "not Christian". The work of the committee led to seminars and theological studies and a concerted attempt to boycott the products of companies related to the Unification Church.

Through years of costly struggle against dictatorial regimes, the NCCK has won the respect of people and the right to coordinate all ecumenical efforts in the country. A word that was not popular in Korean Christian vocabulary, "ecumenical", has lately attained wide acceptance because of the work of the NCCK.

The National Council of Churches in the Philippines (NCCP) was founded in 1963. The immediate predecessors were the National Christian Council formed in 1929, the Philippine Federation of Evangelical Churches (1939) and the Philippine Federation of Christian Churches (1949). Among the main functions and concerns of the NCCP are the promotion of ecumenical cooperation and of united witness and common actions on matters affecting the religious, moral, social and civic life of the nation. The NCCP is committed to defend fundamental human rights and uphold the principle of the separation of church and state.

The umbrella organization of the ten mainline Protestant churches in the country, the NCCP consistently opposed martial law after its imposition in 1971. Its long-term programme emphasis, "Transformation of Church and Society", was meant to create political awareness among the people and to help them understand problems facing the country such as militarization, corruption, violation of human rights, and the oppression and exploitation of people. Preceding the historic February 1985 uprising and its unique manifestation of people power, there was a period of political conscientization in which the Council had played an important role. Nor did the pilgrimage of hundreds of thousands of people to Epifanio de los Santos Ave and the four days of "people-power revolution" – sometimes described as a koinonia of Catholics and Protestants and a good many Muslims as well – and the end of the Marcos regime automatically and immediately lead to the establishment of a democratic government. The NCCP statement on the February uprising said,

> Beyond the power already achieved by the people must be their continuing empowerment to fully actualize their potentials in sharing the collective task to rebuild the nation. The wounds of the nation are deep and grievous. The healing of these wounds does not come from patching-up treatment, but from radical transformation of our lives and values as a government and as a people.

The NCCP has continued to contribute to this "participative and collaborative work" of achieving "reconciliation with justice".

The NCCP and the Catholic bishops conference have two working committees, one on peace and the other for the preparation of a basic module on ecumenism, jointly conceptualized by the NCCP and the bishops conference through an ecumenical affairs commission, for use in the local dioceses and parishes in the country.

The China Christian Council (CCC) is neither a national council of churches nor a church in a normal understanding of the word; it is somewhere between the two and operates as both. For all practical purposes it is the Protestant church in China, officially recognized, representing the majority of Christians in the country and, since 1991, a member of the World Council of Churches. The CCC marks the re-emergence of the Chinese church on the ecumenical scene.

The first volume of A History of the Ecumenical Movement contains a number of references to the Chinese churches and the work of foreign missions in China. The chapter on "Ecumenical Bearings of the Missionary Movement and the International Missionary Council"[25] devotes several pages to a survey of the growing cooperation among

---

[25] Ruth Rouse and Stephen Charles Neill eds, A History of the Ecumenical Movement 1517-1948, 3rd ed., WCC, 1986, chapter 8, pp.351ff.

Chinese churches, and refers to the significant contributions of ecumenical leaders such as T.T. Lew, T.Z. Koo, T.C. Chao and Ms Wu I-Fang. It draws attention to a massive volume, *The Christian Occupation of China*, containing the findings of "the most comprehensive and detailed survey of the missionary enterprise in any country", published at Shanghai in Chinese and English in 1922, and to the national Christian conference held in the same year under the chairmanship of Cheng Ching-yi. The history affirms that "the church in China was coming of age", but a footnote at the end of the section reminds readers that "th[e] account of progress towards union in China refers only to the period before the communist victory in 1949, which has created many new difficulties for the Chinese churches and for the moment rendered impossible their participation in the worldwide ecumenical movement."[26]

In the second volume of *A History of the Ecumenical Movement* there is only one brief reference to the Chinese church. It is in the chapter on "Mission to Six Continents", and deals with "The End of Missions in China":

> The most massive effort of Protestant missions during the century preceding the period of this survey had been directed to China. The Chinese church, though small, seemed full of immense promise. Yet, within a few years of the establishment of communist rule in China, missions had been completely eliminated from the country and much of the fruit of their century of work had apparently been destroyed.[27]

The church in China has gone through traumatic experiences, especially during the late 1950s when religious and cultural life began to be systematically suppressed as the Chinese Communist Party (CCP) consolidated its power, and even more so during the decade of the cultural revolution (1966-76) when all religious institutions were closed. It seemed then that all religions, including Christianity, had disappeared from China. After Deng Xiaoping assumed control in 1978, the CCP repudiated its past policies and promised greater freedom to people. This marked the beginning of what later came to be known as "Christianity fever", an expression that by 1990 began to be used even in official publications. By then there were nearly 6000 open churches in the country, some 15,000 registered meeting points, and about five million believers.

Organized by the WCC, a 13-member team visited China in 1996, and reported that according to official estimates there were at the time ten million baptized Christians in China and the number was growing steadily. Members of the WCC team were impressed by the overall level of religious tolerance, though they also came across instances of repression. Generally, Christians are allowed to practise their faith, provided they belong to churches registered with and operating under the local religious affairs bureau. Quite often, however, the cadres entrusted with the responsibility of supervising religious affairs, as Bishop K.H. Ting pointed out in a speech he gave at the national people's congress in 1993, "do not believe in religion, nor do they understand religion or the religious feelings of believers".[28] The government, however, has consistently denied that there is religious persecution in China. An official white paper on "The Situation of Religious Freedoms in China" released in October 1997 perhaps in response to the widespread criticism that several religious groups – underground Christian congregations, Tibetan Buddhists and certain Islamic organizations – are regularly subjected to perse-

---

[26] *Ibid.*, pp.380,387.
[27] Harold E. Fey ed., *A History of the Ecumenical Movement, vol. 2, 1948-1968*, 2nd ed., WCC, 1986, chapter 7, p.173.
[28] *Bridge*, 59, June 1993.

cution, asserts that only criminals are punished, alleging that some of the heads of "pseudo-religions" are in fact criminals. According to official statistics provided in the paper, around one hundred million Chinese citizens practise Buddhism, Islam and Christianity. Among them are ten million Protestants, including 18,000 preachers ministering at 12,000 churches and 25,000 meeting points. The paper promises to protect the religious freedom of all citizens, provided that those who practise religion register with the government and "hold aloft the banner of patriotism".

The China Christian Council and the Three-Self Patriotic Movement of the Protestant churches in China (TSPM) are the two national Christian bodies in the country. For years Bishop Ting was president of both organizations. The TSPM had its beginnings in the early 1950s; it assumed the name Three-Self Patriotic Movement in 1954, thus making it clear that its purpose was to make the church self-governing, self-supporting and self-propagating within the overall climate and necessary discipline of patriotism. It had its critics in China and outside, and perhaps they had a case. But the TSPM did ensure the church's survival. Had it not existed "the church could hardly have survived in China in any form at all. It is a reasonable argument that in the circumstances, compromise was the only possible course of action."[29] The Catholic Patriotic Association which held its first national congress in 1957 is a parallel Roman Catholic body. Through its formation the government effectively split the Catholic church into two, an open Chinese Catholic church and an underground "Roman" church, faithful to the Vatican.

The formation of the China Christian Council was announced in 1980, when China opened its door to the world after years of isolation, at the first meeting of the TSPM in twenty years. The National Christian Council had been dissolved years before, as were denominational structures. The CCC was to operate both as a council of churches and as the post-denominational national church. Its functions were to be more pastoral and ecclesiastical and less politically oriented than those of the TSPM. But one cannot make a clear distinction between the two organizations and TSPM/CCC must often be seen as a single entity. In its early years the main task of the TSPM was to eliminate foreign ecclesiastical influences, bring together the various Protestant bodies, and secure Christian support for communist party policies. In spite of its limitations, TSPM/CCC made an enormous contribution to the church and Christian life in China. It has reclaimed and restored thousands of church buildings and erected new ones; it has established several Bible schools and support ministries. Thanks to its initiatives, the churches now have a common catechism, more than a million copies of which have been printed, and a common hymnal. In 1994 the circulation of *Tian Feng* ("Heavenly Wind"), the church monthly, exceeded 100,000. A good many simple biblical commentaries have been published, as have also guides for preachers in rural areas and devotional books for ordinary members of congregations. By 1994 almost ten million copies of the Bible had been printed and distributed. "The Bible now ranks second only to the *Selected Works of Mao Zedong* among books published in China!"[30] There have been a large number of lay training programmes, mainly focusing on the Bible but also dealing with issues such as preaching, church administration and government policy.

---

[29] Alan Hunter and King-Kwang Chan, *Protestantism in Contemporary China*, Cambridge, Cambridge Univ. Press, 1992, p.62.
[30] Philip L. Wickeri, "Issues Facing the China Christian Council" (unpublished paper), 1994, p.7. See also Wickeri's *Seeking the Common Ground: Protestant Christianity, the Three-Self Movement and China's United Front*, Maryknoll NY, Orbis, 1989.

The CCC faces a number of problems. Its ecclesiological status remains unclear. At some point it will have to answer questions like these:

> How can the CCC become a stronger institutional expression of the body of Christ? How should national, provincial and local Christian communities be related ecclesiologically? What is the role of the laity and different orders of ministry in the life and witness of the Chinese church? To what extent should sacraments and liturgical practice assume a greater role in the worship of the church? Can space be created for ecumenical discussion with Chinese Catholics?[31]

Another problem the CCC faces is the generation gap within its own leadership. For three decades, from 1949 to 1979, very few church leaders received theological education, with the result that church personnel at present are either very old or very young and there are often severe generational disagreements. The clergy-laity ratio in China is among the lowest in the world. Except for administering the sacraments, lay people do all the work. The incredible growth of the Protestant church in China during the last few decades was largely the result of the work of lay people, and China has much to teach the rest of the world concerning the ministry of the laity. But the situation is ecclesially precarious.

The CCC meets with considerable resistance from groups and house churches that do not want to be identified with it, and even less with the TSPM. Several denominations, with or without overseas support, are succumbing to the temptation to reassert their autonomy, notably the True Jesus Church, the Seventh-day Adventists, and the "Little Flock" or Christian Assemblies. The Chinese church has always had an otherworldly orientation; for many Christians personal piety and individual salvation have become more important often in reaction to the communist ideology with its rejection of the world to come. Given the political climate, it is not possible for the CCC to offer a theological critique of China's current modernization programme or shift to market economy. The CCC will have a difficult time ahead if it endeavours to develop social awareness among members of the church.

One of the Chinese church's important links with the outside world is the Amity Foundation which was set up in 1984 and is largely run by Christians. This foundation manages a number of projects in areas such as health care, rural development and education. The printing press it established with the help of the United Bible Societies has been of immense importance for the church's publishing programme, especially the printing of Bibles. Amity enables the Chinese church to receive outside assistance for social welfare projects without compromising its principle of self-support. The *Amity News Service*, based at an overseas coordination office in Hong Kong, communicates "the news and views of the China Christian Council as a service to the international Christian community".

There is a great deal of speculation concerning house churches in China, but not much authentic information. Many of the reports that appear outside China romanticize their role and exaggerate their overall impact. In a book entitled *Households of God on China's Soil*,[32] Raymond Fung brought together 14 stories of house churches told by Chinese Christians actually involved in them. In the foreword to the book Emilio Castro wrote that the stories "describe how small Christian communities, through one of the most radical upheavals in human history, kept their faith in Jesus Christ – and how their

---

[31] *Ibid.*, p.10.
[32] Raymond Fung ed., *Households of God on China's Soil*, WCC, 1982.

faith kept them". The stories are of small groups of people who have persevered in their faith in a climate of persistent pressure and under the constant threat of persecution. The house churches were "classic examples of spiritual dissent from a prevailing orthodoxy". These autonomous communities are surely a part of the church in China, but their relationship to the CCC, the official, united or uniting Protestant body, ranges from indifference and suspicion to antagonism. Quite a number of house congregations are convinced that the TSPM has compromised the faith and that its agenda is dictated more by political opportunism than Christian conviction. The CCC, however, has repeatedly sought to establish contacts with groups and communities which are not part of its fellowship. Bishop Ting said in a speech in January 1994, when he was still president of the CCC, that from the point of view of faith, a great many Christians with whom the CCC has no contacts "are our brothers and sisters in Christ with whom we must seek to be reconciled. We must strive to serve them, to protect them and to unite with them."[33]

CONCLUDING NOTES

In general, churches in Asia continue to project a conservative image. Evangelical campaigns and traditional programmes have a greater visible impact than ecumenical ways of working and witnessing. This is particularly true of churches in Bangladesh, India, Indonesia, Malaysia, Pakistan, Sri Lanka and Singapore. Many churches observe the annual Week of Prayer for Christian Unity and hold common services during the seasons of Christmas and holy week, but there are very few sustained ecumenical programmes. The re-emergence of the church in China is indeed a major development, but its postdenominational character owes more to political compulsions than to ecumenical convictions. National councils of churches have a growing membership today in many Asian countries, but relatively little impact on the life of the churches. By and large councils have become necessary and increasingly bureaucratic organs for negotiating with local and national governments and with churches and ecumenical bodies outside the country. In nations where such negotiations are not vital for the survival of the churches, councils of churches have remained weak and generally ineffective. They are institutions that often serve the churches more as an ecumenical facade than as vital agents and instruments of the ecumenical movement. Of course there are notable exceptions and this essay has dealt with some of them.

The emergence of voluntary organizations, action groups, academies and study centres within Asian churches is indeed a significant development. In many cases, they are ecumenical in their composition and operation. They address the two basic realities of Asian existence: endemic material poverty and pervasive religious and, until recent years, ideological pluralism. As a result of the work of such academies and study centres, Asian church history is slowly being rewritten. This history is increasingly recognized as far more than the history of foreign missions. Basically it is the story of the gospel's impact on communities and cultures; it is the story of the acceptance of Christian faith by a minority and the appropriation of Christian values by far more people within the majority communities. As a result, theology is receiving a new orientation. By adopting the format of story-telling, it now emphasizes not so much the role of the theologian as that of the people. In fact the marginalized and the minjung have emerged as both the testing ground of theology and its spokespeople. Theology arises from praxis; it is no longer

---

[33] *ANS (Amity News Service)*, special issue, 3 March 1994.

deductive but inductive. Theology is not so much addressed to non-believers as to non-persons; it is dialogic rather than apologetic. Whether the approach is sacramental, as with many Roman Catholics, or activist, as with many peoples' movements, there is a growing emphasis on inclusiveness and an avoidance of apodictic stances.

Among hopeful signs in Asian churches are new forms of ecumenical cooperation:
- around service to human need, providing relief and aid for refugees and victims of "communal conflicts";
- around the development debate and developmental projects, and in vocational training, community health and similar services;
- through coming together to struggle for justice and defend human rights and democratic values, under the Urban Rural Mission umbrella and in local action groups;
- through ecumenical theological dialogue which creates contextual theologies, like the dalit and the minjung, and which sees "people" as a central theological category.

Many questions remain largely unanswered for the Asian churches. Where are we, after years of debate on "confessing the faith in Asia", and formulating the memorable phrase "the Christian community within the human community", and after all the consultations and publications on interfaith dialogue? Has dialogue received the theological attention it deserves from an Asian perspective? Is dialogue still understood as a strategy for survival – or as preparation for evangelism in modern disguise? Can ecumenism, understood either along traditional lines or as a common quest for justice, peace and the integrity of creation, survive in the climate of homogenization brought about by technological innovation, market values and a culture of consumerism? Are we ready to affirm ecumenism as basic to our call for pro-existence and community-building?

BIBLIOGRAPHY

Achutegui, Pedro S. de ed., *Towards a Dialogue of Life: Ecumenism in the Asian Context: First Asian Congress of Jesuit Ecumenists, Manila, June 18-23, 1975*, Manila, Loyola School of Theology, 1976, 337p.
Amaladoss, Michaël, *Life in Freedom: Liberation Theologies from Asia*, Maryknoll NY, Orbis, 1997, 180p.
Amirtham, Samuel and Bautista, Liberato eds, *Those Who Would Give Light Must Endure Burning: Report of the Consultation on Spirituality for Justice and Peace, November 26-30, 1986, La Sallette Shrine, Silang, Cavite, Philippines*, Quezon City, National Council of Churches in the Philippines, 1987, 151p.
Asia Youth Assembly, *Out Of Control: Official Report of the Asia Youth Assembly, Delhi, September 25-October 10, 1984*, Singapore, Christian Conference of Asia Youth, 1985, 208p.
Bautista, Liberato and Rifareal, Elizabeth eds, *And She Said No! Human Rights, Women's Identities and Struggles*, Quezon City, National Council of Churches in the Philippines, 1990, 188p.
Carr, Dhyanchand ed., *Christ and God's People in Asia: As Seen by the Participants of the Consultation on the Theme "Through a New Vision of God towards the New Humanity in Christ", Kyoto, 1994*, Hong Kong, Christian Conference of Asia, 1995, 143p.
Christ Our Peace: Building a Just Society: Bible Studies on the Theme of the 9th Assembly of the Christian Conference of Asia, Osaka, Christian Conference of Asia, 1990, 94p.
Chunakara, Mathews George ed., *Indochina: From Socialism to Market Economy*, Hong Kong, Christian Conference of Asia, 1996, 125p.
Elwood, Douglas J. ed., *What Asian Christians Are Thinking: A Theological Source Book*, Quezon City, New Day Publishers, 1976, 497p.
England, John C. ed., *Living Theology in Asia*, London, SCM Press, 1981, 242p.

Fabella, Virginia ed., *Asia's Struggle for Full Humanity: Towards a Relevant Theology. Papers from the Asian Theological Conference, January 7-20, 1979, Wennappuwa, Sri Lanka,* Maryknoll NY, Orbis, 1980, 202p.

Fabella, Virginia and Lee Park, Sun Ai eds, *We Dare to Dream: Doing Theology as Asian Women,* Hong Kong, Asian Women's Resource Centre for Culture and Theology, 1989, 156p.

Fullness of Life for All: CCA Joint Program Area Committees Meeting, Bangkok, 21-24 February 2001, Hong Kong, Christian Conference of Asia, 2001, 143p.

Fung, Raymond ed., *Households of God on China's Soil,* WCC, 1982, 78p.

Furtado, C.L., *The Contribution of D.T. Niles to the Church Universal and Local,* Madras, CLS, 1978, 264p.

Gandhi, P. Jegadish and Cheriyan, George eds, *Globalization: A Challenge to the Church: Papers and Documents from the South Asian Consultation on "Recolonization, Globalization and the Role of the Church", 16-19 March, 1998, Bangalore, India,* Nagpur, National Council of Churches in India, Urban-Rural Mission, 1998, 153p.

George, K. M., *Church of South India: Life in Union (1947-1997),* Delhi, ISPCK, 1999, 290p.

Gowing, Peter ed., *Understanding Islam and Muslims in the Philippines,* Quezon City, New Day, 1988, 176p.

Hao, Yap Kim, *From Prapat to Colombo,* Hong Kong, Christian Conference of Asia, 1995, 205p.

Holden, Peter, *Tourism: An Ecumenical Concern: The Story of the Ecumenical Coalition on Third World Tourism,* Bangkok, Viscom, 1988, 170p.

Hunter, Alan and Chan, King-Kwang, *Protestantism in Contemporary China,* Cambridge, Cambridge Univ. Press, 1992, 291p.

Image and Reality in the Ecumenical Movement, Quezon City, National Council of Churches in the Philippines, 1987, 85p.

John, Clement, *Seoul to Manila: The Christian Conference of Asia from 1985 to 1990,* Hong Kong, Christian Conference of Asia, 1990, 145p.

Kim, Yong-Bock, *Messiah and Minjung: Christ's Solidarity with the People for New Life,* Hong Kong, Christian Conference of Asia, 1992, 380p.

Kim, Yong-Bock ed., *Minjung Theology – People as the Subjects of History,* Singapore, Christian Conference of Asia, Commission on Theological Concerns, 1981, 196p.

Kitagawa, Joseph M., *The Christian Tradition beyond Its European Captivity,* Philadelphia, Trinity, 1992, 307p.

Mei-Jung, Yvonne Lin ed., *Asian Consultation on Tourism and Aboriginal Peoples: Community Control, Cultural Dignity and Economic Value,* Taidong, Huadong Community Development Centre, 1989, 134p.

Moving Heaven and Earth: An Account of Filipinos Struggling to Change Their Lives and Society, WCC, 1982, 191p.

Nacpil, Emerito P. and Elwood, Douglas J. eds, *The Human and the Holy: Asian Perspectives in Christian Theology: First All-Asia-Consultation on Theological Education for Christian Ministry, Manila, 1977,* Maryknoll NY, Orbis, 1980, 367p.

O'Grady, Ron, *Banished: The Expulsion of the Christian Conference of Asia from Singapore and Its Implications,* Hong Kong, CCIA International Affairs Committee, 1990, Hong Kong, Christian Conference of Asia, 103p.

Panikkar, Raimundo, *The Unknown Christ of Hinduism: Towards an Ecumenical Christophany,* Maryknoll NY, rev. 1981, 195p.

Park, Kyung Seo, *Reconciliation, Reunification: The Ecumenical Approach to Korean Peninsula, Based on Historical Documents,* Hong Kong, Christian Conference of Asia, 1998, 237p.

Peoples of Asia, People of God: A Report of the Asia Mission Conference 1989, Osaka, Christian Conference of Asia, 1990, 161p.

Perkins, Harvey L., *Roots for Vision: Reflections on the Gospel and the Churches' Task in Re-Peopling the De-Peopled,* WCC, 1985, 284p.

Pieris, Aloysius, *An Asian Theology of Liberation,* Edinburgh, T. & T. Clark, 1988, 144p.

Porter, Muriel, *Land of the Spirit? The Australian Religious Experience,* WCC, 1990, 102p.

Religions and Ideologies in the Asian Struggle: Asia Regional Fellowship, 4th Assembly, Chiang Mai, Thailand, May 19-24, 1987, Quezon City, Asia Regional Fellowship, 1987, 154p.

Sahu, Dhirendra Kumar, *The Church of North India: A Historical and Systematic Theological Inquiry into an Ecumenical Ecclesiology,* Frankfurt am Main, Peter Lang, 1994, 354p.

Samartha, Stanley J., *One Christ – Many Religions: Towards a Revised Christology*, Maryknoll NY, Orbis, 2000, 222p.

Song, C.S., *Tell Us Our Names: Story Theology from an Asian Perspective*, Maryknoll NY, Orbis, 1984, 407p.

Takenaka, Masao, *Cross and Circle*, Hong Kong, Christian Conference of Asia, 1990, 417p.

Thomas, M.A., *Towards Wider Ecumenism*, Bangalore, Ecumenical Christian Centre, 1993, 323p.

Thomas, M.M., *Risking Christ for Christ's Sake*, WCC, 1987, 122p.

Ting, Kuang Hsun, *The Church in China*, London, British Council of Churches, 1982, 20p.

Weingärtner, Erich, *Human Rights: Solidarities, Networks and the Ecumenical Movement*, Quezon City, National Council of Churches in the Philippines, 1988, 29p.

Wickeri, Janice and Wickeri, Philip eds, *A Chinese Contribution to Ecumenical Theology: Selected Writings of Bishop K.H. Ting*, WCC, 2002, 115p.

21
Caribbean

Carlos F. Cardoza-Orlandi

In the conceptual topography of the ecumenical movement, the Caribbean is that region which includes the islands of the Caribbean Sea and some countries in Central and South America which border on the Caribbean. It is a region of considerable diversity, but there is a common history of colonialism, neo-colonialism, imperialism, exploitation and conquest, as well as of resistance, dignity and struggle for survival. Religious, political and social unity were at first imposed from without but were ultimately modified and shaped by each island community to its own needs, and this includes the current manifestations of the ecumenical movement.

The original Indigenous people of the Caribbean have been almost wiped out except for a few in Dominica and Trinidad. There were Indians with their own culture, languages and religious practices but the harsh treatment meted out to them by colonial churches and settlers, which amounted to a genocide, left them almost exterminated on their own land, with their religious practices stamped out.

The slaves who came later from Africa to work the plantations also had their own cultures and religions but these too were erased by the early missionaries; both Catholic and Protestant considered them demonic. Christianity, largely Anglican and Roman Catholic, quickly became the "language" of the settlers. French and Spanish colonizers brought Catholicism to the French Antilles, Cuba, Trinidad, St Lucia and Dominica, while the Church of England became prominent on the British Antilles. Later came Methodists, Presbyterians, Baptists and Moravians. These influences still prevail.

Following the period of slavery came indentured labour, workers from India, Indonesia and China (the latter settled in Cuba) bringing their own religions and customs especially to such countries as Trinidad and Tobago, Surinam and Guyana.

Since the 1960s, the Caribbean religious and social history has been marked by energetic forces that are altering the landscape. Comparatively recent developments related to cheaper and more available travel are leading to increased sharing between the islands. The Caribbean is still in process of transformation from enclosed and self-sustained island societies, tied to whichever European nation first settled and colonized them, to interdependent societies participating in common social, economic, political and ecclesiastical institutions. Indeed, it was in the 1950s and 1960s that regional institutions first developed with the avowed aim of encouraging the fledgling alliances which were then beginning to make themselves manifest.

The four decades from the 1960s to the 21st century have been a convulsive period in the history of the region, characterized by dramatic cultural, political and economic transformations. Pregnant with hopes and expectations, this period has also witnessed political interventions, threats of intervention, *coups d'état* and invasions. The Caribbean has been transformed in these years from an area of tourist exploitation to a region seeking political independence, economic stability and cultural identity.

In the midst of this exciting turbulence, the Caribbean churches – African Methodist, Anglican, Baptist, Congregationalist, Lutheran, Moravian, Pentecostal, Presbyterian, Roman Catholic and United, among others – have struggled to discern the will of God. North Americans and Europeans have also participated in this journey of the people of God seeking God's redemptive and liberating power in and for the region.

To facilitate this reflection we shall use the image of rhythms. Music is a gift which God has given to the Caribbean people. Rhythms, particularly the style known as *polyrhythm*, is an outstanding aspect of Caribbean music. Polyrhythm is two or more basic rhythmic patterns going on at the same time. For the Westerner, polyrhythm may create both the sensation of absolute mastery of rhythm and the sense of being "offbeat". It is confusing and yet fascinating.

The ecumenical endeavours in the Caribbean are a combination of many rhythms. Some rhythms came from outside the region; others were created by Caribbean people and churches. Many are a blend of both.

THE CARIBBEAN: MANY RHYTHMS, MANY CULTURES

The Caribbean is much more than a region on the map. It is full of diversity. Spanish, French, English, Dutch, Creole, Patois and Amerindian languages are all spoken. Indeed, one fascinating linguistic phenomenon in the Caribbean has been the emergence of new forms of communication created out of the linguistic interaction of colonial languages with African and Amerindian languages. All Christian traditions, including that of the Eastern Orthodox, as well as Islam, Hinduism, Sikhism, Buddhism, and a variety of Afro-Caribbean religions such as Rastafarianism, have their followings. Political systems operative in the area include liberal democracies, authoritarian dictatorships, communist states, commonwealths, colonies and dependencies.

The Caribbean nations share many similarities, for example a history of colonialism and neo-colonialism. They share a history of "the annihilation of the original inhabitants in most of the territories",[1] followed by a history of slavery, exploitation and oppression. The *mestizaje* and *mulataje* – mixed breeds – witness to the cultural and biological interpenetrations of the different ethnic groups that constitute the Caribbean people. A history of political interventions, military threats and economic dependency leaves little space for national autonomy. Despite the "polyrhythm", the phrase "out of many one people"[2] still portrays who the Caribbean people are.

In 1951, the International Missionary Council (IMC) appointed E.J. Bingle to conduct a survey of the situation of the churches in the Caribbean, published in 1954 as *From Cuba to Surinam*. In 1957, the IMC held a Caribbean consultation in Puerto Rico, which produced the report entitled *The Listening Isles*. It "recommended a system of correspondents in the English-, French- and Dutch-speaking areas in the fields of Christian

---

[1] Lewin L. Williams, *The Caribbean: Enculturation, Acculturation, and the Role of the Churches*, WCC, 1996, p.2.
[2] This is the national motto of Jamaica.

education, theological education, home and family life, and special south Caribbean problems".[3]

The 1960s, argues David Chaplin, brought the West Indies at long last out of the colonial era into the modern world of independent nations and raised the inevitable problem of the search for identity.[4]

The question was whether the churches could respond appropriately to the demands of the time. Dale Bisnauth describes the historical and ecclesial issues in this important period:

> Up to quite recently, religious affiliation on the part of the Caribbean people was linked to their places on the social scale. Those places were not unrelated to the distribution of power in the society, or at any rate to the perception as to how power was distributed. Thus, in a British colony, Anglicans would be high in the social gradation, with Methodists and "Scots" Presbyterians sharing a middling position, and Congregationalists and Baptists being fairly low. The most deprived classes would hold to some form of cultic beliefs which represented, in turn, some form of syncretism. Because the social consensus subscribed to recognizes membership in the Christian church as one of the symbols of social worth, where there were Hindus and Muslims these were relegated to the fringes of society. So, also, were those practitioners of "African" rites who did not belong to Christian congregations.[5]

The history of colonialism, the hierarchical nature of Caribbean society, and the old establishment of the church were difficult stumbling blocks to overcome.

In 1970, in Port-of-Spain, Trinidad and Tobago, the black power movement painted the statues of the saints in the Roman Catholic cathedral black. The Roman Catholic archbishop interpreted the event as a challenge to the church to become Caribbean.[6] The people had symbolically spoken.

RHYTHMS BECOME POLYRHYTHMIC: THE CARIBBEAN CONFERENCE OF CHURCHES

The CCC celebrated its inaugural assembly in Kingston, Jamaica, in November 1973, under the theme "The Right Hand of God". The meeting took place in a large hotel, although the year before the pre-assembly consultation had boycotted the governor-general's cocktail party in Trinidad on the grounds that it was "incongruent" with Caribbean aspirations of decolonization. At the same time, a concerted effort was made to have delegates not only from each country but also from every area of the churches' life. Special care was taken to ensure a strong representation of youth and women.

A special theme song was written for the occasion. It was the culmination of a vision which, like a symphony, had one theme but several variations, many instruments but a single orchestra and leader, writes Horace Russell, a Jamaican theologian and long-time member of the WCC's Faith and Order Commission. "Yet it was more than that," wrote Russell. "The CCC is like the polyrhythm in Caribbean music: fascinating and confusing at the same time. It combines not only many beats but also 'off-beats'. The event was

[3] David I. Mitchell, *With Eyes Wide Open*, Kingston, CADEC, 1973, p.198.
[4] David Chaplin, in Robert W.H. Cuthbert, *Ecumenism and Development: A Socio-Historical Analysis of the Caribbean Conference of Churches*, Bridgetown, Barbados, Caribbean Conference of Churches, 1986, p.59.
[5] Dale Bisnauth, "Religious Pluralism and Development in the Caribbean: Questions", in *Caribbean Journal of Religious Studies*, 4, Sept. 1982, p.22.
[6] Allen Kirton, personal interview, Atlanta GA, 30 Dec. 1996.

the writing of new Caribbean music in an ecumenical, linguistic and cultural interaction of European, Asian, African and Amerindian languages." In continuity with the previous ecumenical programmes, the assembly stated that at the heart of the CCC "lies the conviction that the renewal of the Christian community is an instrument for the total human development of Caribbean people".[7] Thirty-seven churches signed the inaugural document and it became one of three regional councils with Roman Catholic membership (the others were in the Middle East and the Pacific).

The preamble of the CCC's constitution defined the purpose and goals of the institution as follows:

> We, as Christian people of the Caribbean, separated from each other by barriers of history, language, culture, class and distance, desire because of our common calling in Christ to join together in a regional fellowship of churches for inspiration, consultation and cooperative action. We are deeply concerned to promote the human liberation of our people, and are committed to the achievement of social justice and the dignity of man in our society. We desire to build up together our life in Christ and to share our experience for the mutual strengthening of the kingdom of God in the world.[8]

The CCC continued to develop two basic programmes: Christian Action for Development in the Eastern Caribbean (CADEC) and Action for the Renewal of the Churches (ARC), both of which had been started in 1968, some time before the CCC was formed. In addition, the Conference took up the important task of developing a Caribbean theology, a theology of decolonization. In fact, this theological endeavour characterizes the CCC's ecumenical and ecclesial framework. Such a theology needed to emerge in order to provide depth to the faith and activity of the CCC:

> We have seen that the vision of the "new Caribbean man" can also become a theological perspective if Caribbean man is seen as being made in the image of God, and that to pursue this vision in social and historical terms can become the main agenda of Caribbean Christian praxis.[9]

A crucial sub-programme of CADEC was *Caribbean Contact*, the CCC's newspaper which became an important source of information for churches in the region. In the midst of political turmoil, military interventions and invasions, particularly in Grenada, and misleading information from the official media services, *Caribbean Contact* kept the churches well informed and in touch with the difficult transitions of the region. It also provided information regarding grassroots activities and development projects. Its editorials included a variety of perspectives on Caribbean politics, economics and ecumenical issues. Its impact was such that it progressively became an important newspaper all over the region. The CCC's other media channel was "Caribbeat", a radio broadcast which reached more than 14 regional stations. These have now both been replaced by *Christian Action,* a quarterly newspaper.

The CCC's general assembly which meets every five years is the chief governing body; in the interim, the Conference is run by a continuation committee. The general secretariat is located in Trinidad, the easternmost Caribbean island. At the 1997 assembly it was decided to downsize and it was envisaged that the CCC would operate through councils of churches or other ecumenical bodies in the islands and territories through-

---

[7] Assembly I:87, quoted in *Ecumenism and Development*, p.76.
[8] Caribbean Conference of Churches' Constitution, in Kortright Davis, *Mission for Caribbean Change*, Bern, Peter Lang, 1982, p.198.
[9] *Mission for Caribbean Change*, p.175.

out the region. Also at that assembly, the councils of churches were accepted as "fraternal members".

The ARC sponsored programmes on Caribbean church women, Caribbean ecumenical youth action, the local/national councils, the educational renewal agency, and family life education. They have been evaluated consistently since 1975. To maintain a polyrhythm is a difficult task. However, the CCC, despite its economic limitations, was able to keep the programmes running and to hold most of them in place.

Three important achievements need to be mentioned in this history of the ecumenical movement in the Caribbean. The CCC was the first ecumenical institution to include the official participation of the Roman Catholic Church. The interpretation of the Second Vatican Council documents, particularly those on liturgy, divine revelation, the church, the church in the modern world and ecumenism, contributed to the active participation of the Antilles episcopal conference of the Roman Catholic Church from the CCC's beginning.

Secondly, the CCC adopted a resolution which embraced all the official languages of the Caribbean. Recognizing the multilingual and multicultural reality of the region, the CCC has never wanted to establish a single official language for its assemblies.

Thirdly, perhaps the most controversial decision of the CCC was the invitation it extended to the Cuban churches to become members. The political turmoil of the period, particularly Jamaica's democratic socialism, Guyana's socialist project and Grenada's revolutionary government, raised suspicions as to the ideological and political inclinations of the CCC, which was often accused, particularly by some elements in the US and their missionary enterprises in the region, of being Marxist.[10]

The CCC faced difficult and important issues. By promoting and developing a Caribbean theology and a theology of decolonization, the Conference clearly identified the legacy of colonialism in the churches and in the region in general. In its programmes, it opted for the poor, who constitute the majority of the Caribbean people. These theological and ecumenical positions crystallized the CCC's option for development and liberation.

Pentecostalism is one of the fastest-growing churches, drawing adherents from every sector and country. Once referred to as a poor person's religion, it has grown increasingly sophisticated, reflecting its American influences, which is causing some concern to the more established churches. The new Pentecostal churches do not join the ecumenical movement, instead forming their own alliances, but they are widely recognized as having social, political and economic influence in the life of the region.

THE ASSEMBLIES: LOUDER AND CLEARER POLYRHYTHMS

The second general assembly of the CCC, held in Georgetown, Guyana, in 1977, focused "on working together with Christ for human rights, for full human development, and for Caribbean unity". Once more, the emphasis was on the topics of development and unity.

The focus of the third general assembly, held in Willemstad, Curacao, in 1981, was on the Lord's prayer. Under the theme, "Thine is the Kingdom, the Power and the Glory", the member churches called for "a greater urgency" in "ecumenical action at the national level within Christian councils, where the action to promote truth, goodness, justice, love and peace can be most concrete".

---

[10]Ashley Smith, personal interview, United College of the West Indies, Kingston, Jamaica, 15 Jan. 1997.

Willemstad discussed the relationship between the CCC and the national councils. The CCC was seeking to promote unity within a theological commitment to development and to justice, while most of the national councils tended to support the existing order. Indeed, one of the most significant tensions in the history of the ecumenical movement in the Caribbean has been the engagement in the struggle for decolonization and liberation while at the same time benefiting from the status quo. Frequently, the national councils found themselves pulled by the opposing forces of denominations and the energy and commitment of the CCC.

At the fourth general assembly which met in Barbados in 1986, the struggle against the colonial legacy was again evident. While recognizing that some churches were happy with the status quo, the Conference reaffirmed its commitment to liberation from all unjust structures including those of militarization, especially in its nuclear form.

The fifth general assembly, in Port-of-Spain, Trinidad and Tobago, in 1991, addressed ecological issues which were at the heart of the discussions:

> We appeal to you to be more alert to wanton destruction, pollution, litter, unsanitary conditions, and the disposal of toxic wastes. We urge you both to stretch your hands and raise your voices for the healing of the land and the health of the people. Be a part of every good cause which is dedicated to peace and justice, community-building and the awakening of political consciousness. Do not be afraid! Encourage your pastors also to speak loudly and to act boldly when the safety of the people, the welfare of the community or the integrity of the nation is imperilled. Act in concert if you can, act alone if you must, but act! The time has come for the church to make the difference between what is and what ought to be![11]

THE CONTINENTAL ENCOUNTER

In 1991, the Canadian Council of Churches, the National Council of the Churches of Christ in the USA, the Caribbean Conference of Churches, the Latin American Council of Churches and the Ecumenical Council of Cuba celebrated a continental encounter and wrote a declaration entitled "Continental Encounter for the Pastoral Accompaniment of the Churches and the People of Cuba". This declaration, which summarized the struggles of the Cuban people during the revolution, established "short-, medium- and long-term" tasks according to the following priorities:

1) to achieve the total lifting of the blockade of the United States against Cuba;
2) to provide humanitarian help, especially medicine and food for children, women and elderly who are suffering the impact of the blockade;
3) to promote an exchange at the people-to-people level between Cuba, Latin America, Canada and the US, in different sectors, i.e., grassroots groups, women, youth, etc.;
4) to establish alternative networks of information to educate our people in relation to the Cuban reality;
5) to commit ourselves, both the Christians in Cuba and in the continent, to deepen the dialogue ecumenically with other Christians (Evangelicals, Pentecostals and Roman Catholics), so that our witness in favour of life will be an expression of the unity of the church;

---

[11]Quotations from Adolfo Ham's chapter "Caribbean Ecumenism and Emancipatory Theology", in Oscar Bolioli, *The Caribbean: Culture of Resistance, Spirit of Hope*, New York, Friendship, 1993, pp.116, 107, 109.

6) to stimulate the churches in Cuba and abroad to recognize the unity of the Cuban people, in the spirit of reconciliation, as a necessary element to conquer the difficulties that have come up in these times of crisis: that unity shall include the Cuban community abroad.[12]

The most controversial issue since the beginning of the CCC, Cuba, continues to be a relevant and important ecumenical priority in both the northern and southern hemispheres.

To celebrate the 500th anniversary of Christopher Columbus's Atlantic journey in 1992, the Caribbean African American Dialogue and the Caribbean Conference of Churches met together and produced the "Verdun Proclamation". The consultation

> paused to reflect on these five hundred years... in order to sharpen our consciousness of our historical condition, thereby to understand better our present realities and to be able to chart a course for our total liberation and self-realization.[13]

The "Verdun Proclamation" presented four "concerns" for the future of African-American and Caribbean people: racism, Caribbean cultural identity, economic democracy and the search for a Caribbean theology. Though the theme of Caribbean identity has always been part of the CCC's ecumenical discussions, it seems to be more integrated in this declaration than in other documents. Previous declarations and assembly statements emphasized development. Here, the search for cultural identity, which is set within the economic situation, is given theological significance.

In 1993, the CCC held a consultation on religions and inter-religious dialogue in the Caribbean, whose report was published in *At the Crossroads: African Caribbean Religion and Christianity*, edited by Burton Sankeralli. This volume has a series of excellent articles on themes such as syncretism, the retention of Africanisms in Caribbean Christianity, popular Caribbean religiosity, and Islam and Hinduism in the Caribbean.

In 1997, the sixth assembly of the CCC in Havana, Cuba, took the theme "Celebrating a New Vision, New Hope, New Life", and affirmed the search for a Caribbean theology. When bankers and accountants called for neo-liberal structural adjustments and for the sovereignty of market forces, it was left to the churches to make a prophetic defence of justice for the poor. International debt threatening all poor nations was soundly condemned. Neo-colonialism and external political interventions were denounced, while greater respect for the order of creation was called for. National councils were encouraged both to promote unity and participate in the struggles of the poor. Finally the whole hemisphere was challenged to give fresh attention to curtailing drug trafficking and drug abuse.

This assembly crystallized the CCC's commitment to build stronger and healthier relationships with churches in the Caribbean. The assembly recognized the importance of such a task in a time of regional fragmentation and division. The CCC plans to extend, develop and strengthen programmes with national councils of churches, in order to be a witness to solidarity and unity in the region.

---

[12] *Ibid.*
[13] Caribbean African American Dialogue and Caribbean Council of Churches, "The Verdun Proclamation" in James A. Scherer and Stephen B. Bevans eds, *New Directions in Mission and Evangelization, vol. 2: Theological Foundations*, Maryknoll NY, Orbis, 1994, pp.199-207.

THE CONTEMPORARY CARIBBEAN SCENARIO

In the lead-up to the 21st century following the Havana assembly, the CCC described its present context as one in which the region is grappling with endemic poverty, the second highest incidence of HIV/AIDS infection in the world, drug trafficking and addiction, and the phenomenon of uprootedness as people are – for various reasons – internally displaced. Data for the region indicate that approximately 400,000 adults and children were living with the disease in 2000; of new cases of AIDS, a growing number were women and the disease was the leading cause of death among 15-45 year-olds. Increasingly the social, economic and development impact of HIV/AIDS was being recognized.

Food security continued to be a major issue for the region, especially because of globalization and the expected (by 2005) Free Trade Area of the Americas (FTAA). Some countries remained a hotbed of volatile and violent political instability. Domestic violence and drug-related crime were also on the increase and posed a threat to developmental processes.

Given this scenario, the CCC devised and adopted a new approach for the dawning century, one that is described as holistic, multidisciplinary, multisectoral and which – given the pan-Caribbean spread of its membership – takes into account the comparative advantages of the CCC in responding to social issues. In its regional development programme, the CCC states that there are few other organizations that have the base, reach and ability effectively and efficiently to deliver human and societal programmes and projects. "By their very nature, the churches, as civil society actors, are well-poised to have a real, sustainable and positive impact on some of these seemingly intractable social problems."[14]

The CCC policy at the start of the new millennium is one of intensifying ecclesial engagement with its 34 member churches in all four linguistic constituencies (Dutch, English, French and Spanish), and commitment in responding to the complex social ills affecting the region. Every programme undertaken is designed to bolster and strengthen member-church initiatives through education, sensitization and advocacy, with provision of funding and technical expertise where needed. The five major programmatic initiatives are:

1) A *cluster of human development programmes called Priority Regional Initiatives (PRIs)*:
    To strengthen the member churches' response to, and impact on, social issues affecting the region, especially the HIV/AIDS epidemic, the resultant breakdown in family life, violence, illicit drugs, food security and uprootedness.
2) A *cluster of sustainable socio-economic development programmes*: To deal with the increasing levels of poverty and inequitable distribution of wealth by poverty eradication programmes; a self-development of peoples fund; disaster management and mitigation, preparedness and response; sustainable development; and safeguards for the poor and marginalized.
3) A *regional advocacy and communications programme*: To give a voice to the poor and oppressed, always an integral part of the CCC. All programming has a major component of advocacy, communication and public relations to inform and engage the Conference constituency and the wider public regionally and internationally. Media

---

[14] In *Caribbean Regional Development Programme*, Caribbean Conference of Churches, Port of Spain, 2000.

agencies across the region are linked in partnership with the Caribbean Community (CARICOM – the official governmental grouping of 14 countries in the region).

4) *A new programme implementation framework*: To develop a cadre of highly skilled clergy and church activists equipped to address constructively the region's social issues by forming ecumenical social action groups and acting in partnership with the UN, CARICOM and NGOs.

5) *The Caribbean Regional Ecumenical Institute*: The hub of the Conference's various thrusts. The work of the institute provides the theological and developmental thinking that informs all other activity. At this critical period in the story of ecumenism in the Caribbean, the church needs to develop a Caribbean hermeneutic, with a view to discovering the oneness that is appropriate for reality in the region. The institute provides courses for clergy and church workers in mission, spirituality, evangelism, development theology, social action, community mobilization and programme project management.

WILL THE POLYRHYTHMS OF THE CARIBBEAN PREVAIL?

There are lessons and challenges that the ecumenical movement in the Caribbean as a whole needs to learn and face. The first is for Caribbean denominations and national councils to recognize the crucial contribution of the CCC during this politically turbulent period. As an ecumenical organization, the CCC has battled on different fronts with a wide range of very complex issues. Nevertheless, it has continued to focus on its goals, particularly those of human rights and the integrity of the political sovereignty of the Caribbean's several nations. The Conference has sought to provide adequate vehicles of information when the imperial powers have tried to isolate country from country. At the same time, it has responded as a relief agency in various crisis situations. To struggle in such difficult circumstances and yet still be alive is a testimony to God's support and accompaniment.

As the CCC faces transition once more, much of the ecumenical responsibility will devolve on the national councils. Will they sustain and give continuity to the vision of the CCC? Will they seek to do Caribbean theology and continue to abrogate the colonial heritage that prevents Christian churches from becoming Caribbean? Will they begin to support their own projects economically? Will they be able to overcome a long tradition of dependency?

Another lesson for the ecumenical movement in the Caribbean is that the CCC has the ability to work beyond the region, in Latin America and North America, in partnership with African-American and Amerindian groups. As the over-arching ecumenical bodies experience contraction because of decreasing economic resources, partnership between regions will be necessary in order to promote and sustain the ecumenical imperative. On the other hand, partnerships with marginalized ethnic groups in North America, including groups with roots in the Caribbean, will also be critical as common problems and challenges are encountered.

Three challenges confront the churches in the Caribbean. First, the CCC and other ecumenical organizations face the problem of economics. Regrettably, dependency continues to perpetuate the colonial heritage both of the Caribbean and of those who offer paternalistic support. The economic system that provides the funding for a significant number of projects is the same system that exploits the people.

Secondly, national councils, denominations and local churches need to commit themselves to grassroots ecumenical projects. The ecumenical imperative needs to resonate with and arise from the base. Out of all this comes the need to integrate development and liberation projects with the religious needs and aspirations of the people in the pews.

Thirdly, the CCC and other ecumenical organizations of the region need to address interfaith issues. The presence and development of other religious expressions, particularly those born outside the Caribbean context, represents an ecumenical challenge to the mission of the churches in the Caribbean. In the past the emphasis on issues of development and justice marginalized the spiritual life and fervour of the region. Can the CCC and other ecumenical bodies articulate the theological relationship between material and spiritual need? How will a Caribbean theology of religions respond to the voices of those lacking the basic necessities of life? How will a Caribbean theology of decolonization include a theology of religions perspective?

Moreover, will the CCC be able to establish relationships with the many Pentecostal and neo-Pentecostal movements in the region? These churches represent an increasing majority among Christians and the poor. This is by far the most critical challenge for the CCC.

There is one aspect of polyrhythm that is an advantage for those who live in the Caribbean: the ability to become compatible with other rhythms without losing the beat. The CCC and other ecumenical institutions need to play their own rhythms so that they can adapt to others. The struggle for life in the Caribbean is compatible with the struggle for life in Africa, Asia, Latin America, the Pacific and certainly in the urban areas of the Western hemisphere. With an ability to be compatible, the gift of polyrhythms can allow us to cross-fertilize and share life and God together.

Caribbean people love music! They have rhythm! Can they express ecumenical rhythms in the Caribbean with integrity? Can they learn other rhythms without compromising their commitments? Can they continue to play their music with rhythms of hope and joy? With the help of God, and for the glory of God, they will!

BIBLIOGRAPHY

Bisnauth, Dale, "Religious Pluralism and Development in the Caribbean: Questions", in *Caribbean Journal of Religious Studies*, 4, Sept. 1982.

Bolioli, Oscar, *The Caribbean: Culture of Resistance, Spirit of Hope*, New York, Friendship, 1993.

Cuthbert, Robert W.M., *Ecumenism and Development: A Socio-Historical Analysis of the Caribbean Conference of Churches*, Bridgetown, Barbados, Caribbean Conference of Churches, 1986.

Davis, Kortright, *Mission for Caribbean Change*, Bern, Peter Lang, 1982.

Kurlansky, Mark, *A Continent of Islands: Searching for the Caribbean Destiny*, New York, Perseus, 1991, 324p.

Mitchell, David I., *With Eyes Wide Open*, Kingston, CADEC, 1973.

Sankeralli, Burton, *At the Crossroads: African Caribbean Religion and Christianity*, Trinidad and Tobago, Caribbean Conference of Churches, 1995.

Schalkwijk, J.M.W., "Mission in the Micro-World of the Southern Caribbean", in *International Review of Mission*, 60, April 1971.

Scherer, James A. and Bevans, Stephen B. eds, *New Directions in Mission and Evangelization, vol. 2: Theological Foundations*, Maryknoll NY, Orbis, 1994.

Williams, Lewin L., *The Caribbean: Enculturation, Acculturation, and the Role of the Churches*, WCC, 1996.

22
Europe
Keith Clements and Todor Sabev

From the early 1960s to the late 1990s, significant long-term developments and dramatic changes occurred in Europe affecting the political, economic, cultural and religious scene on the continent. These events precipitated major changes in European perceptions, both about Europe itself and the world beyond. In turn the churches' understanding of themselves, their relations to one another and their role in society was challenged.

The construction of the Berlin wall in 1961 symbolized, literally concretely, the cold-war division of Europe into communist East and capitalist West. Consequently, a major focus of ecumenism for much of the period was the attempt to ensure that the churches of East and West remained in fellowship despite all the political and ideological differences under which they lived. This became more urgent in view of the perpetual state of nuclear-armed confrontation between NATO and the Warsaw Pact countries. Europe, conscious of having given birth to two world wars in the century, remained fearful of being the locus for a third conflict which could engulf the planet in total and irrevocable destruction.

The period saw the finale of European imperial and colonial rule in Africa, Asia and elsewhere in the South. In some cases independence emerged relatively smoothly and peaceably, in others (southern Africa, for example) only after long and bitter armed struggle. Europeans were confronted with a view of themselves no longer as beneficent patrons of "under-developed" countries but as racist practitioners of injustice – injustice which continued in the entrenched neo-colonial economic dominance they wielded over the South even after political independence had been granted. European Christians and churches were particularly affected by this new consciousness, since they had deep and long-standing links with many countries of the South through their missionary history and continuing relationships with churches there. At the fourth assembly of the WCC at Uppsala in 1968 the churches of the South sounded this call for justice as never before. A natural consequence of this new and unavoidable challenge was that European issues, with the exception of the intractable East-West divide, now had to compete strenuously for space on the European Christian and ecumenical agenda with "the wider world". A new "heresy" was identified: "Eurocentrism".

Nevertheless, the churches could not ignore the important social and political developments taking place within Europe. Chief among these in Western Europe was the

---

• This chapter also includes material from Günther Schulz and Robin Gurney.

process of economic and, later, political integration. On the basis of the treaty of Rome (1957), six countries – Belgium, France, the Federal Republic of Germany, Italy, Luxembourg and the Netherlands – formed the European Economic Community (EEC). By 1986 this group had grown, with six more signatories of the Single European Act: Austria, Denmark, Greece, Ireland, Sweden and the United Kingdom. This act set out plans for a single European market, which came into being at the end of 1992. The European Union (EU), as it was now called, expanded in membership, numbering some 15 member states in 2001 – adding Spain, Portugal and Finland. The EU operates through its council of ministers, the European Commission based in Brussels and the European Parliament which meets in both Brussels and Strasbourg. Other important political structures include the European Court of Justice in Strasbourg and, for security issues, the Western European Union.

All these developments, which in part reflected an attempt to overcome the national antagonisms that had resulted in two world wars, also led to concern that Western Europe was adopting a "fortress" attitude, against both Eastern Europe and the economically oppressed countries of the South.

However, pan-European impulses were also at work. The Helsinki Final Act of 1975 codified a commitment by Eastern and Western European countries, including the Soviet Union, together with the US and Canada, to seek to implement a common understanding of security, economic development and human rights which would be in the interests of all the signatory states. Concern for human rights was of particular interest to the churches, in view of the extensive repression of religion in the communist East. It was significant that this issue surfaced conspicuously that same year at the fifth assembly of the WCC at Nairobi.

With certain exceptions, most European societies in this period experienced an advancing secularization, seen not only in a steady numerical decline in committed allegiance to the churches but in an increasing marginalization of institutional Christianity from public affairs. In communist countries this was occasioned by ideologically led governmental policies. In Western Europe, it was a result of the erosion of the social significance of traditional religion in societies increasingly dominated by the ethos of technology and an individualistic, consumerist culture. At the same time, prophecies in the 1960s of an entirely "secular" society were to prove illusory, for two main reasons. First, the increasing presence of immigrants, especially from Asia, raised the profile of other world faiths – especially Islam – in Europe. Second, New Religious Movements appeared, some of which were highly sectarian, others syncretistic and sometimes closely allied with ecological concerns and a new appreciation of nature. The overall result has been a Europe more secularized and much more religiously pluralistic than previous generations could have imagined.

For this reason the "secularization thesis" has been challenged in recent years,[1] not least from within some of the historic churches which still claim a significant role in the social and cultural life of their respective countries. For example, in the Lutheran "folk churches" of Scandinavia the picture is at least ambiguous. While relatively few Scandinavians seem to dissociate themselves from their churches (into which the great majority have been baptized), only a small minority regularly attend worship, and

---

[1] A classic exposition of this thesis is found in A.T. van Leeuwen, *Christianity in World History*, London, Edinburgh House, 1964; cf. Charles C. West, "Secularization", in *Dictionary of the Ecumenical Movement*, 2nd ed., WCC, 2002, pp.1031-34.

the degree to which Christian faith existentially affects daily life and public affairs is open to debate. It is perhaps safest to say that post-modern European society is increasingly fragmented into compartments, even within the life of individuals, and that religious faith, while certainly still alive, neither dominates life nor is an integrating factor.[2] Similarly, the extent to which, in the post-communist societies of the East, a unifying "Orthodox culture" can survive the inroads of secular pluralism remains to be seen.

What proved to be the long-term effective challenge to the Soviet socialist hold on Eastern Europe began in the early 1980s in Poland, where national loyalty to the Roman Catholic Church had remained unshaken. From Poland, too, had come Pope John Paul II, elected in 1978. He quickly made the situation of religion in Europe as a whole one of his chief concerns.[3] Meanwhile, in 1985, Mikhail Gorbachev emerged as the new president of the Soviet Union. His policies of *glasnost* and *perestroika* revealed a desire for a new openness within the Soviet Union and between that state and the rest of Europe. Change swept through Eastern Europe from late 1989. The breaching of the Berlin wall came to symbolize the rapid transition to democracy of almost the entire former Soviet bloc countries and even, eventually, Albania, the most rigorously closed and repressively anti-religious communist country of all. The Soviet Union itself was dissolved in 1991.

THE EASTERN EXPERIENCE: A CLOSER VIEW

The events that took place between 1989 and 1991 in the Eastern region undoubtedly marked a turning point in the continent. Apparently immovable political, social, economic and cultural conditions were fundamentally changed and these upheavals naturally affected the church and the ecumenical situation. Relationships of churches and Christians to society and in society as well as to the ecumenical movement and its councils were fundamentally shaken in a number of ways.

1. Churches and other faith communities were afforded new and guaranteed status under revised national church laws. They were recognized as associations under public law, with new obligations. Their role in and for society was redefined. The churches saw themselves as integral parts of the emerging reformed societies but often held exaggerated expectations. All the churches with a dominant presence in particular countries, e.g. Roman Catholic in Poland, Lithuania, Croatia and Slovenia; Orthodox in Bulgaria, Romania, Serbia and Russia; Protestant in the former German Democratic Republic (GDR), Latvia and Estonia, had the opportunity (by no means always positive) to regain former privileges or demand new ones. Where they took this opportunity they were incorporated into new social systems, and were expected to provide these with models of behaviour and instruments of interpretation. In difficult ethical and social matters, society looked to the churches for guidance. At the same time, the new societies distanced themselves from traditional Christian norms; in other words secularization, which had long been advancing under communism, entered a new and more extreme phase in, for example, the former GDR, Poland, the Czech Republic and Hungary. Amidst incredible new challenges, they had to find a Christian life-style for themselves, seeking to articulate new and convincing answers for their own peoples or communities.

---

[2] See S. Barrow and G. Smith eds, *Christian Mission in Western Society*, London, CTBI, 2001.
[3] G. Weigel, *Witness to Hope: The Biography of Pope John Paul II*, London, Harper&Collins, 2001.

2. Concurrently, relations with the ecumenical movement and worldwide Christianity declined in importance. The ecumenical movement found that it could offer only hesitant answers for the problems raised by the unexpected and unparalleled transition from socialist-style societies to new "reforming" societies, and the role of the churches in them. Ecumenical relations also lost some of their external importance. These had served to help believers to maintain the position of the church in their respective societies. Churches and monasteries near capital cities or in historically or culturally important places, which were often visited by ecumenical delegations or church dignitaries from abroad, could not readily be closed down.

After the 1989-91 changes, ecumenical activities fell away. For experienced ecumenists, however, ecumenical relations acquired a new importance as it was realized that the vast range of new tasks that awaited them could be properly reflected on theologically, and practical solutions found, only if the experience of worldwide Christianity were taken into account. Furthermore, in all the churches in the East it had been recognized that the WCC was independent of social and political systems, serving religious goals and symbolizing a third way in the struggle between antagonistic forces. Its independent position and voice were important in reassessing the past and setting directions for the future.

3. Among themselves, the churches' relations also changed after 1989-91. Prior to the events of these years, against the tide of both official and actual atheism, churches and communities in Eastern and South-eastern Europe, finding themselves in similar circumstances, recognized one another. Under persecution, ecumenical relations had grown with shared joys and sorrows but once the unifying hostile pressure was lifted, churches went their own way. This divide was often encouraged by influential entities from Western countries and affected the everyday lives of the faithful.

COMMUNIST RULE AND THE COLD WAR

For many churches and groups the period of communist rule, and certainly the last third of it, was not a time of constant brutal persecution. Of course, they all faced an unrelenting current of opposition, sometimes stronger, sometimes weaker. Phases of confrontation (e.g. 1958-62 in all the socialist countries) alternated with phases of a good modus vivendi (e.g. the GDR 1978-86) or a bad one (e.g. Soviet Union 1952-58). Conditions for the churches and ecumenical relations were different in each socialist country and there were considerable differences within individual countries.

The East-West division of Europe was complete by the time of Stalin's death (1953). Indeed, the building of the Berlin wall (1961) may be seen not so much as a symbol of the division as an early sign of the deep crisis in the socialist world system. Above all, it was a sign of the inability of that system to manage the crisis by its own means in ways appropriate to the times. Seen like this, it seemed inevitable that the wall would eventually fall and take the whole system with it. Through their witness to the freedom of God's love, which breaks all ideological bonds – Western and Eastern alike – and especially through the conciliar process in the GDR in 1988-89, the churches, notably in the GDR, Poland and the Czech Republic, contributed appreciably to liberation.

Protestant and Catholic Christians in the GDR were in a special situation. Only here and in Latvia and Estonia was the majority church Protestant. This challenged both the Protestant tradition, the socialist state and socialist society seeking to be established. Until 1968-69 the Protestant churches in the GDR remained members of the Evangelical

Church in Germany (EKD). Christians were allowed to form a political party, the Christian Democratic Union (CDU), to do diaconal work, and to receive aid, especially from the churches in the Federal Republic of Germany. All churches and faith communities in the GDR benefited from the unique position of the Protestant churches there. The few Orthodox congregations in that country, headed by the exarch of the Moscow patriarchate, enjoyed special rights, including an exemption from censorship for their publications.

The Russian Orthodox Church (ROC) and all the churches in the Soviet Union had different experiences. The ROC had been brutally persecuted in the attempt to eliminate it from the life of society and liquidate it "legally", and the church in the Soviet Union almost disappeared from public life.

The end of communist rule and the cold war were greeted with relief and euphoria not only in Western Europe but also among those who had most keenly felt the oppression in their own countries, not least the churches there. A new day of democracy and human rights, peace and shared economic prosperity throughout "our common European house" (to use Gorbachev's phrase) seemed to have dawned. However, the 1990s proved to be a decade of deferred hopes and disillusionment. For some Eastern European countries, and for the former Soviet Union itself, the attempts at a rapid transition to a market economy resulted in economic impoverishment and social chaos. Tragically, national and ethnic antagonisms re-emerged and flared into conflict, most catastrophically in the countries of the former Yugoslavia and the smaller states of the Caucasus region. The fact that religion has been a factor in the identities of the warring parties has been deeply sobering to the European Christian conscience, and has provided one of the most searching challenges to ecumenism.

At the end of the 20th century, therefore, ecumenism in Europe was challenged to face anew how to enable the churches to witness together for a Europe at peace with itself and contributing to a just world order.

The Eastern European churches' response to the cold war was to strengthen bonds with churches elsewhere: bonds within their respective worldwide communions, but also with the WCC and the Conference of European Churches (CEC). This permitted them to ease their isolation, and opened up new hope of survival and protection. The contacts made in this way were barely tolerated by the communist authorities but in exchange for this "freedom" they demanded loyalty to their domestic and foreign policy. From the 1960s until the late 1980s the churches faced the dilemma of either going underground, as some did, or finding a modus vivendi through conformity and collaboration with the civil authorities. While many church leaders opted for the second alternative, most believers sought a way between the two, a decision which inevitably led to confrontation.

Until the end of the 1980s the limited space for the churches' mission was determined by materialistic ideology and atheistic propaganda. "The separation of church from state and of school from church" was a general rule, but the degree of separation differed from place to place. Some Protestant churches, for example, refused any financial allowances from the socialist state. The juridical status of the Orthodox churches in Romania and Bulgaria was explicitly recognized. In Poland, Czechoslovakia and Hungary, Orthodox churches benefited from legislation which favoured minority confessions over against the powerful Catholic church, and allowed them to organize religious instruction. Similar opportunities were available to the majority Orthodox church in Yugoslavia and to some extent in Romania, with a right to official holidays. Protestants and

Roman Catholics in the German Democratic Republic never ceased their diaconal activity. Apart from Albania, governments allowed churches to retain certain land and buildings and to have their own publishing houses and factories for producing candles and other items used in worship. Some churches were granted subsidies and other help in order to maintain buildings and monasteries recognized as cultural monuments. A significant number of communities benefited from state pension funds. But with such favours often came dependency on the state.

While all communist countries restricted religion and tried to suppress and eliminate the role of churches in society, political realities created inconsistencies. In East Germany and Poland especially, concessions were granted. There was also variety and evolution in the mandate and operation of governmental offices for church-state relations. Those affected most by laws and practices overseeing Christian communions were the Catholics (both Western- and Eastern-rite) and the "neo-Protestants", though all suffered to some degree.[4]

THE RUSSIAN ORTHODOX CHURCH

A large majority of Orthodox Christians live in Eastern Europe, and there are four Orthodox sister churches in adjacent countries: the Ecumenical Patriarchate in Turkey, and the Orthodox churches in Cyprus, Greece and Finland. An Orthodox diaspora, small in numbers but significant in witness, is found in several Western European countries. By far the largest Orthodox church, that of Russia, requires special attention.

In the 1960s and 1970s, the ROC's basic policy was to maintain its position internally in Soviet society and externally among the Orthodox churches and within world and regional Christianity, i.e. the WCC (from 1961), the CEC and the Roman Catholic Church. The participation of Russian Orthodox observers at Vatican II in the autumn of 1962, in the midst of the Krushchev persecution (1958-62), was a significant event. The ROC profited from the rise of Russian nationalism, the revaluing of Russia's past, the preservation of its monuments (including churches and icons). In the WCC and the Christian Peace Conference (CPC), it did not hesitate to adopt, with only slight deviations, Soviet foreign policy positions. These strategies were promoted by the head of the church's office of external relations, Metropolitan Nikodim (Rotov) of Leningrad, a president of the WCC from 1975 until his death in the arms of Pope John Paul I on a visit to the Vatican in 1978.

World Christianity – the WCC the CEC, the Vatican and the Christian World Communions – helped to sustain this shaky, constantly endangered and questionable modus vivendi. After the end of the Krushchev persecution, the ROC pursued its liturgical life as an assertion against Soviet atheism. In spite of censorship, information about church life, including a periodical review, books and occasionally Bibles, were printed.

For the ecumenical movement, the modus vivendi meant that, within certain limits, contacts with the ROC and other churches in the socialist countries were possible. Thus these churches could participate in the life of world Christianity and were not excluded – as they had been in the Stalinist era – from the theological and ecumenical process at international levels. On the eve of the WCC's third assembly at New Delhi (1961), and more intensively later, the ROC began various theological conversations (EKD 1959, the

---

[4] Cf. Erich Weingärtner ed., "Church within Socialism: Church and State in East European Socialist Republics", in *IDOC Europe Dossiers*, 2-3, Rome, IDOC International, 1976.

Roman Catholic Church 1967, Lutheran Church of Finland 1970, the Federation of Evangelical Churches in the GDR 1974, the Lutheran World Federation 1981, the World Alliance of Reformed Churches 1988). The St Sergei-Holy Trinity Monastery in Zagorsk (now Sergiev Posad) became a centre of ecumenical contacts. Material and information on the ecumenical movement and the dialogues were published. The training academies received theological literature, and the publishing house of the Moscow Patriarchate was donated up-to-date equipment by the EKD.

However, both the ROC and the ecumenical movement paid a price for this – too high a price, according to Soviet Union dissidents.[5] The charge has been that – because they wanted to maintain stability and recognized the downside of the capitalist economic system – both the ROC and the ecumenical movement failed to express any fundamental criticism of Soviet conditions and of the socialist state.

Following the Helsinki Accords (1975), the priest Gleb Yakunin and the lay man Lev Regelson took up the issue of human rights and religious freedom in their country, and addressed a letter to the WCC assembly in Nairobi which sparked a heated debate. To avoid upsetting their relationship with the government, ROC delegates prevented the assembly from endorsing concerns expressed in the letter. Nevertheless, human rights and religious freedom in the Soviet Union were always on the ecumenical agenda.

The ROC's ecumenical witness was also endangered by its efforts to strengthen its influence over the ecumenical community in order to guarantee its existence within its own country. Indeed, Orthodox churches as a whole steadily increased their presence on WCC governing bodies. Through the CPC, controlled by the ROC, issues of social ethics or peace-keeping were introduced into the ecumenical debate and influenced churches in the third world.

Like all Orthodox churches, the ROC was also involved in elaborating *Baptism, Eucharist and Ministry* (BEM 1982). The ROC accepted in principle the text on baptism, but raised considerable objections to that on eucharist. The strongest criticism, however, was of the section on ministry. In spite of this the BEM texts are regarded in the ROC, even today, as important theological work in the ecumenical movement.[6]

After 1989-91 the ROC had to come to terms with bitter disappointment. As no other church in Europe, it had resisted organized atheism with its own life-blood, with tens, perhaps hundreds of thousands of martyrs. After its "liberation" many Western churches and mission agencies, instead of coming joyfully to its aid, seized the opportunity of its weakness and lack of experience in the new conditions to engage in mission or, as the Orthodox see it, proselytism, in Russia – and, indeed, in the whole of Eastern Europe.

---

[5] Files on WCC Relationships with Member Churches in the USSR during the 1960-80s (Archives of the WCC): Documentation on E. European Churches: Relations with Eastern Europe – Files of Lukas Vischer (hereafter "Relations with E. Europe"), nos 2-4,6-8 (Archives of the WCC); Dimitry Pospielovsky, *The Russian Church under the Soviet Regime, 1917-1982*, vol. II, Crestwood NY, St Vladimir's, 1984, pp.327-363,424,434ff.,455ff.; Jane Ellis, *The Russian Orthodox Church: A Contemporary History*, London & Sydney, Croom Helm, 1986, pp.290-355,369-454; H. Bell and J. Ellis, "The Millennium Celebrations of 1988 in the USSR", in *Religion in Communist Lands*, 16,4, 1988, pp.292-328; Claire Seda Mouradian, "The Armenian Apostolic Church", in Pedro Ramet ed., *Eastern Christianity and Politics in the 20th Century* (Christianity under Stress, vol. I), Durham NC, Duke Univ. Press, 1988, pp.353-74; C.J. Peters, "The Georgian Orthodox Church", in P. Ramet ed., *Eastern Christianity and Politics in the 20th Century*, pp.299ff.
[6] Cf. V. Borovoy and A. Buevski, "The Russian Orthodox Church and the Ecumenical Movement", in *Orthodoxy and Oikumene: Documents and Materials 1902-1997*, Moscow, 1998 (in Russian).

The collapse of the state system motivated many lay people to turn to the church. They considered and experienced Orthodoxy as the new "ideology" underpinning the state. This, however, did not help ecumenism, as opposition in the Russian synod of bishops in 1994, 1998 and 2000 illustrated. Relationships with the WCC were deeply affected, and a much reduced representation from that church participated in the 1998 Harare assembly.

The re-emergence of the uniate churches, especially in the Ukraine, and their turning to their traditional home, the Vatican, for support, further complicated relations with the ROC. A four-party commission (1989-90) of representatives from the Vatican, the ROC, the uniate churches and local Orthodox churches issued repeated calls for Christian fellowship and respect for traditions. Despite many such appeals the issue of the uniate churches remains an open wound, especially in the area of the ownership of church buildings and properties.

The withdrawal of the Georgian and Bulgarian Orthodox churches from membership in the WCC and the CEC in 1997 and 1998 created further ecumenical tensions, even though both churches have stated that they will not retreat from their basic ecumenical responsibility.

OTHER ORTHODOX CHURCHES IN EASTERN EUROPE

In the Balkans, an extreme Stalinist regime brought great suffering to the Orthodox Church of Albania. Repressed and isolated by an ideology which declared itself the "first atheist state in the world" (1967), the church barely survived except in private religious practice. However, after 1990 Albania too embarked on a democratization process that allowed the reconstitution of the Orthodox church in that country by the Ecumenical Patriarchate. Under the inspired leadership of Archbishop Anastasios, the Orthodox Church of Albania experienced a remarkable resurrection in its liturgical, pastoral and diaconal life.

The Bulgarian and Romanian patriarchates also maintained a strong self-consciousness of national Orthodox fellowship. This made them vulnerable to adapting religious life to political reality and a "forced church-state coexistence". Representatives of the Orthodox and other Romanian churches had seats in the grand national assembly and in the United Socialist Front. The spirituality and commitment of the faithful (15-17 million in the 1980s) sustained the mission of the Orthodox Church of Romania. In Bulgaria, the public function of the church was less visible. The six million baptized members of the Bulgarian Orthodox Church were affected by the decline of the religious vocations. Lay brotherhoods and sisterhoods contributed to the church's mission and modest social work, but during the 1970s their activities virtually came to a halt. A significant expression of ecumenical commitment and "new openness" was the range of international meetings in the Bulgarian capital, contacts with local churches and communities, state authorities and pioneers of the ecumenical movement. In 1969 a mood of dissent appeared in both Romania and Bulgaria. In Bulgaria this showed itself in resistance to the introduction of the "new-style" church calendar labelled by some as Western and ecumenical. In the 1980s Bulgarian religious dissidents joined the movement for human rights.

A Christian ecumenical committee for the defence of religious rights was formed in Romania, and in the late 1980s protests erupted against the demolition of churches within the grandiose plan of the Nicolae Ceausescu government to destroy many villages and move their inhabitants to new "urban agro-industrial centres".[7]

The Romanian "systematization" plan was one of a few occasions when East and West tensions surfaced openly on the agenda of the WCC's governing bodies, leading to heated debates in the central committee in 1988, 1989 and 1990. Romanian church representatives spoke out strongly against the attempt in 1989 by the committee to make a public statement. Their course of action, which was eventually sustained, was to continue the monitoring process begun under the auspices of the general secretaries of the WCC and the CEC in 1988. Under dramatically changed circumstances – the Ceausescu regime had fallen and its leaders were executed at Christmas 1989 – another heated debate erupted during the 1990 meeting of the central committee. While resisting calls by some members to express repentance for "our failure to speak out forthrightly" in 1989, the committee adopted a statement regretting "its mistaken judgment in failing to speak adequately" about the situation.

During the cold-war period, the difficulties facing the Serbian Orthodox church were less severe and more sporadic. The multinational character of Yugoslavia, the existence of three major religious communities (Orthodox, Roman Catholic, Muslim) and several smaller ones, and the detachment of Yugoslavia from the Eastern bloc allowed for a certain liberalization of state policy, encouraging church resistance and aspiration to freedom. The church had a strong understanding of itself as guardian over the Serbian people and their culture, and its concern focused on the Christian family, youth and education. In the hostile atmosphere created by anti-religious propaganda in the 1970s, both the Orthodox church in Serbia and Catholic church in Croatia were accused of nationalism and political clericalism. For a short time, these domestic conditions and the strength of ecumenical spirit in Europe as a whole led to a rapprochement between Orthodox and Roman Catholics in Yugoslavia.

In another complicating move, political forces interested in nation-building persuaded Orthodox bishops in the Yugoslav republic of Macedonia to request ecclesiastical autocephaly in 1967 from the Serbian Orthodox patriarchate. When the request was refused, they unilaterally proclaimed the independence of the "Macedonian Orthodox Church" the following year. The resulting schism is still not healed.

WCC staff reports from the first half of the 1980s speak of improvements in church-state relationships. The Orthodox church was allowed to initiate and carry out some building projects, including the unique St Sava memorial church and (with the aid of international ecumenical organizations) the construction of a theological faculty in Belgrade. The number of theological students and clergy had increased, and there was a slowly growing interest in religion.[8]

---

[7] Trevor Beeson, *Discretion and Valour: Religious Condition in Russia and Eastern Europe*, rev. ed., Philadelphia, Fortress, 1982, pp.333-40,345ff.,354ff.,377ff.; Alan Scarfe, "The Romanian Orthodox Church", in *Eastern Christianity and Politics in the 20th Century*, pp.222ff.; Report of Piet Bouman on Bulgaria, 31 May 1974, Relations in E. Europe, no.7-8 (Archives of the WCC); Alf Johansen, "The Bulgarian Orthodox Church", in *Occasional Papers, Religion in Eastern Europe*, 1, 7, Dec. 1981, pp.3-12; Marin Pundeff, "Churches and Religious Communities", in Klaus-Detlev Grothusen ed., *Handbook on South Eastern Europe, vol. VI: Bulgaria*, Göttingen, Vandenhoek & Ruprecht, 1990, pp.559-62.

[8] Pedro Ramet, "The Serbian Orthodox Church", in *Eastern Christianity and Politics in the 20th Century*, pp.240-48; Peter J. Babris, *Silent Churches: Persecution of Religion in the Soviet-Dominated Areas*, Illinois, Research Publishers, Arlington Heights, 1978, pp.378 ff.; *Discretion and Valour*, pp.303ff.,334ff.,345ff.; Uffe Gjerding, "Report on Visit to Yugoslavia, 11-18 December 1984", in Files on the Europe Task Force and WCC Relationships with the Serbian Orthodox Church (Archives of the WCC).

Despite better legal provisions, the Orthodox churches of Poland and Czechoslovakia also faced problems. In Poland there was concern over concessions granted by the state to the majority Catholic church at the expense of other churches. To a large extent, the Orthodox were apolitical, though they took part in the Christian Peace Conference, developing a theology of peace, justice and service and seeking to organize religious instruction, diaconal activities, youth work and theological education – mainly ecumenically. Financial support from the state to the churches in both Poland and Czechoslovakia was an incentive to religious revival and ecumenical work.[9] These two local Orthodox churches succeeded in publishing Bibles, periodicals and books, and they enjoyed religious broadcasting.

During the decades of communist power in Eastern Europe, valuable support for Orthodoxy, particularly in the Balkans, came from the Church of Greece, in coordination with the Ecumenical Patriarchate. The Church of Greece offered spiritual and moral help, sometimes with the mediation of the Greek government, as well as providing scholarships, Bibles and literature. The Orthodox Church of Finland, although small in size, maintained good ecumenical relations by supporting considerable Orthodox witness in neighbouring countries.

THE ECUMENICAL PATRIARCHATE

During the period under review, the Ecumenical Patriarchate was severely affected by the tense relationships between Greece and Turkey over the issue of the division of Cyprus. The Greek Orthodox flock of the Ecumenical Patriarchate living in Istanbul (Constantinople) and the neighbouring dioceses became direct victims of the intercommunal hostilities on Cyprus only a few years after its independence (1960). Between 1963 and 1975, tens of thousands of Orthodox believers emigrated to Greece, other European countries and beyond, leaving the see of Constantinople with only a small number of faithful. In addition, the 150 year-old theological school of Halki was closed down in 1971 on the basis of a Turkish governmental decree terminating the functioning of private schools of higher education, even though Halki was never considered as such by the authorities. Notwithstanding these difficulties the Patriarchate was able to develop inter-Orthodox and ecumenical activity during this period.

The historical meeting of Patriarch Athenagoras with Pope Paul VI, in Jerusalem in January 1964, as well as the lifting of the anathemas between Rome and Constantinople on 7 December 1965 the same year were outstanding events that contributed to the reduction of the 1000-year-old tensions between the two churches.

The visits of Ecumenical Patriarchs Athenagoras (1967), Dimitrios (1987) and Bartholomew (1995) to Rome, Canterbury and Geneva were signs of Constantinople's deep commitment to the ecumenical movement. This commitment was reiterated during the working sessions Bartholomew had with the WCC and CEC leadership during his visit to Geneva.

In addition to inter-Orthodox and international dialogues, the Patriarchate maintains regular bilateral relations with the Church of England and the EKD, churches of coun-

---

9 Files on the Europe Task Force and WCC Relationships with the Orthodox Churches of Poland and Czechoslovakia (Archives of the WCC); Relations with E. Europe, no.7; *Silent Churches*, pp.267-328; S.G. Hruby, L. Laszlo and St. Pavlowith, "Minor Orthodox Churches in Eastern Europe", in *Eastern Christianity and Politics in the 20th Century*, pp.320-30.

tries which host significant numbers of people of Greek Orthodox origin. These contacts are not only for discussions on theological issues, but also pastoral questions related to the presence of Orthodox in a non-Orthodox environment.

THE CHURCH OF GREECE

The Church of Greece, a participant in the ecumenical movement since the 1920s and among the founding members of both the WCC and the CEC, has always manifested some reserve, if not hostility, towards the movement and its institutional expressions, particularly the WCC. A major crisis arose following the military coup d'état of April 1967, when the WCC's executive committee in 1968 expressed concern about the treatment of political prisoners and Greek migrant workers critical of the military government and whose families at home were threatened. What upset Archbishop Hieronymus of Athens was the executive committee's decision to seek the help of experts in order to appraise the new proposed Greek constitution. The archbishop, in a letter to Eugene Carson Blake, the WCC general secretary at the time, considered the executive committee's decision a "flagrant interference" in the internal affairs of Greece. In the ensuing months a concerted press campaign against the WCC culminated in a boycott of the fourth WCC assembly at Uppsala.

Relations with the WCC and the ecumenical movement returned to normal following the collapse of the military regime and restoration of democracy. In spite of the official, but cautious, commitment of church authorities in Greece, there remains a latent anti-ecumenical climate fermented by conservative circles within the official church and by dissident groups such as the Old Calendarists whose raison d'etre is combating the "pan-heresy of ecumenism". It is unfortunate that this slogan, formulated in the last three decades in Greece and Serbia, became popular among fundamentalist dissident Orthodox groups in the Balkans and the Caucasus, causing considerable damage to the life and witness of local Orthodox churches. The withdrawal of the Orthodox churches of Bulgaria and Georgia from the WCC and the CEC in 1998 is a direct outcome of this aggressively anti-ecumenical campaign.

PROTESTANT CHURCHES IN EASTERN EUROPE

In the socialist countries of Europe, Protestant churches and communities included those regarded as "traditional" and "national"; those with a long history in the country; those of national minorities; and the so-called neo-Protestant churches, which arose from more recent missionary activity. These churches varied greatly in their practice of ecumenism and understanding of church-state relationships.

The now scarcely imaginable differing experiences of the Protestant churches in the two German states, within hostile social systems, forced the Evangelical churches in the GDR to withdraw from the EKD (as they were required to do by the GDR's 1968 constitution). Against the will of the state these churches formed the Federation of Evangelical Churches in the GDR in 1969, defining itself as a "fellowship of witness and service" and the "church in a socialist society". This formula was constantly misinterpreted during and after the cold-war period. It was simply meant to claim a firm place for the church and for Christian witness in the socialist society of the time.

The confrontation surrounding the stationing of Soviet missiles in the GDR and the corresponding arms build-up in the NATO countries led to the emergence of a Christian peace movement, Swords to Ploughshares. Initially strongly opposed by the authorities, it was eventually tolerated in a toned-down form (1980-83). In a complicated process, Protestant churches tried to accept the socialist form of society as their living space and to join in shaping it as responsible Christians in a spirit of "critical solidarity", a phrase which arose out of Bishop Albrecht Schönherr's 1978 conversations with GDR President Erich Honecker.

Meanwhile, ecumenical activities were tolerated by the authorities within certain limits, partly out of concern for their own image and partly because of the move away from the EKD. In 1971, the WCC executive committee met in Bulgaria, the first ecumenical governing body to meet in a socialist country since the central committee in Hungary in 1956, shortly before the Hungarian uprising.

From 1974 to 1990 theological talks were held with the Russian Orthodox Church in Zagorsk, and with the Bulgarian Orthodox Church in Herrnhut. Orthodox theologians and churches took a great interest in these conversations as they wanted to see how Christians lived and witnessed to their faith in a socialist society.

Preparations for the five hundredth anniversary celebrations of the birth of Martin Luther (1983) led to a reassessment of the Reformation in the GDR. The publication of writings from the Reformation and the festivities themselves, some organized with the aid of the state, were impressive.The greatest ecumenical mission event in the GDR was the "Conciliar Process for Justice, Peace and the Integrity of Creation" (1988-89) in which all the churches, including the Roman Catholic Church and many local congregations, took part. Here, the questions of Christian witness and life in a socialist society were openly discussed, a fact which led to great tensions with the official ideology and its representatives.

The life and witness of the Protestant churches in Czechoslovakia, Hungary and Poland were shaped on the foundations of a theology of service, a biblical understanding of peace and justice, and a search for convergence between Christian social ethics and socialist humanism. Until his death in 1970 Josef Hromádka of the Evangelical Church of Czech Brethren was a visionary leader in this "new thinking". A Christian-Marxist dialogue gained momentum and flourished. The churches of socialist central Europe were deeply involved in the ecumenical movement through national councils of churches, the CEC, the Christian World Communions and the WCC. The Polish theological seminary functioned ecumenically, with Protestant, Orthodox and Old Catholic sections.

The Warsaw pact military intervention in Czechoslovakia in August 1968 crushed the hopes for a credible "socialism with a human face". In the following years most of the churches in Eastern Europe experienced renewed repression and were compelled to identify themselves more closely with state policy. During the 1970s attempts to normalize interchurch cooperation in Czechoslovakia and other communist countries were repressed and controlled by the political authorities. This provoked resistance and renewed struggles for religious liberty and saw the emergence of movements such as the New Orientation group in the Evangelical Church of Czech Brethren, Protestant and Catholic support for Charter 77, and involvement in the Polish Solidarity trade-union movement. There was also an underground movement within the Reformed Church in Hungary and renewal groups in that country's Lutheran church.

From the late 1970s certain improvements in religious life and relationships with the state became evident, and the public role of the churches became more visible. Greater internal independence led to closer ecumenical collaboration, a growth in the national

Bible societies, religious education, theological schools and publishing facilities, and financial help from foreign churches.

Although Protestantism in Romania, Yugoslavia and Bulgaria differed from country to country, there were common features, particularly with regard to state policy, church-state relations and attitudes towards "foreign" religious communities in Orthodox lands. The traditional Protestant family in Romania consisted of a large Reformed church and a small Lutheran church of Hungarian descent, German Lutherans, Baptists and Unitarians. They worshipped in their own languages, published periodicals and organized catechetical classes. The Protestant churches in Yugoslavia avoided political compromise and nationalistic rivalries, slightly expanded their religious activity and enjoyed some growth.

Protestant churches in Bulgaria lived in isolation and harsh conditions for almost three decades, but in spite of this the Pentecostal churches and the Church of God (unregistered) increased their membership. Adventists, Congregationalists and Methodists also faced difficulties but continued to witness. A certain ecumenical openness on the part of the Orthodox church meant that a few Protestant pastors could be trained at the theological academy in Sofia. The leader of the Congregational church took part in the commission for a new edition of the Bible and joined the Bulgarian Orthodox delegation at the WCC assemblies in Uppsala and Nairobi. Bulgarian Protestant church representatives attended meetings of the Christian Peace Conference as well as ecumenical conferences hosted by the Bulgarian Orthodox Church.

The trend of the 1980s in these three Balkan countries was a slow positive change and religious revival, though Protestants in Bulgaria still endured a certain persecution, as did neo-Protestants in Yugoslavia. The most severe tensions were in Romania: German-speaking Lutherans were leaving the country, and an economic crisis, nationalistic political pressures and cultural discrimination against Hungarians in Transylvania produced a growing stream of emigrants towards the western borders. In 1986 there was an ecumenical "Call for Reconciliation" from Hungary, but tensions escalated. The refugee problem, exacerbated by the Ceausescu government's "systematization" plan, prompted a series of appeals and protests, challenging the Romanian authorities and deploring the inconsistency of church representatives. Several religious leaders whose credibility had been eroded by their response to this situation later issued open letters of confession and regret. Dissent continued to increase, with the Baptists, following traditional emphasis on religious rights for all communities, playing a major role. All this climaxed in 1989 in the revolutionary events in Timisoara, where the Hungarian Reformed pastor (later bishop) Laslo Tökes played a catalytic role. The uprising in Bucharest followed shortly afterwards.

In the USSR, the largest and most dynamic Protestant bodies were the Baptist, Lutheran and Pentecostal churches. Until the mid-1960s the All-Union Council of Evangelical Christian Baptists (AUCECB) was the registered "common" structure for most. But within ten years all were recognized as independent communities. In 1965 the Baptist *Initsiativniki* – reformers who refused state registration in order to avoid any restriction on witness – founded their own union, the Council of Churches of Evangelical Christians-Baptists (CCECB). Its leadership was forced to work clandestinely, while the Soviet authorities granted the "official" Protestant bodies space for religious activity. A growing social commitment, begun in the 1970s and continued in the 1980s, made it possible to expand the work of the AUCECB. The non-conformist Baptists were exposed to severe repression, as were the dissident wings of the Pentecostal and Adventist movements, and the Jehovah's Witnesses experienced terrible suffering during the period 1979-84.

The Lutheran churches in the Baltic republics, though restricted, found peaceful and practical ways of serving their people. Participation in the Christian Peace Conference, sharing with the Baptists in educational correspondence courses, and moral protection and support from the Lutheran World Federation and sister churches in neighbouring countries, sustained their reduced form of mission. In the late 1980s *perestroika*, coupled with Baltic nationalism, brought further renewal and freedom.

German Lutherans in the Soviet Union lived for many years in isolation, deprived of pastoral care. In the first half of the 1980s they were provided with Bibles and hymnals, a consistent source of encouragement for all Protestant communities in Eastern Europe throughout the cold war. Although the situation for these churches improved, it did not prevent the exodus of many members from the USSR.[10]

ECUMENICAL PARTNERSHIPS IN EASTERN EUROPE

The period from the 1960s to the mid-1990s saw only limited cooperation in ecumenical partnership between the Eastern European Orthodox and Protestant churches on the one side and the Roman Catholic Church on the other. However, there was a growing spirit of collaboration and rapprochement. The churches gave preference to bilateral and multilateral dialogues, rather than the wider ecumenical activities in which the Roman Catholic Church was involved. The most visible expressions of Protestant-Catholic-Orthodox relations were the European ecumenical encounters of CEC and the Council of European Bishops Conferences (CCEE), the CEC assemblies, and the consultations and publications which encompassed the major aspects of church life in Europe.[11]

During the 1980s, an important WCC-CEC joint enterprise (in cooperation with the US and Canadian churches) was the Churches' Human Rights Programme for the Implementation of the Helsinki Final Act, and a number of meetings of the human-rights working committee took place in Eastern Europe. In the latter period, ecumenical cooperation focused on mission, reconciliation, human rights, solidarity with women and diakonia.[12]

The United Bible Societies, with their independent structures, wise strategy, suitable methodology and appropriate assistance from the world Christian family, developed a wide network and enhanced church life all over Eastern Europe.

THE ROMAN CATHOLIC RESPONSE

The Second Vatican Council inspired new vision and an accommodation of the Catholic church within the specific cultural and political environment in Eastern Europe. Influenced by the *Ostpolitik* of the West German government, hostility between East and

---

[10] See the rich documentation on the Protestant churches in E. Europe, in Files on WCC Relations with Member Churches, Specialised Task Force on E. Europe, and various meetings held in E. European countries (Archives of the WCC); Relations with E. Europe, no. 5-7; cf. *Church within Socialism*, passim; a series of scholarly, well documented articles in Sabrina P. Ramet ed., *Protestantism and Politics in Eastern Europe and Russia: The Communist and Post-Communist Eras* (Christianity under Stress, vol. III), Durham, Duke Univ. Press, 1992, passim.

[11] Files of the CEC (archives of the CEC); Helmut Steindl ed., *Documents des rencontres oecuméniques européennes (1978-1991)* Paris, Cerf, 1991, passim.; *Informationes Theologiae Europae*; *Internationales ökumenisches Jahrbuch für Theologie* 1992-95.

[12] *Ibid.*; Robin Gurney, *The Face of Pain and Hope: Stories of Diakonia in Europe*, WCC, 1995, passim; unpublished report to the CEC assemblies in Graz, 1997, pp.52ff.,86ff.,96ff.,108ff.,112,116ff.

West shifted into the diplomacy of detente, resulting in a more effective protection of Catholic church life. The changing realities of religious life and ecumenical engagement depended on historical legacy, local context and relations between majority and minority churches, as well as on the slow penetration of the renewing energy of Vatican II.

The normalization of diplomatic relations between the Holy See and the socialist governments began with a partial agreement with Hungary in 1964, developed with Yugoslavia and Poland in the 1970s, but was finalized with other countries only on the eve or at the beginning of the post-communist era. Meanwhile, state authorities sought to keep Catholics in their countries independent from the juridical authority of the Vatican, a move resisted by both the local churches and the Vatican. The governments also sought to make both clergy and lay people sympathetic to state policy on national and international issues, and to coopt priests associations. *Pacem in Terris* ("Establishing Universal Peace") in Czechoslovakia, the Berlin conference of Catholics, the association of Catholic priests in Yugoslavia and "peace priests" in other countries were instrumental in raising ecumenical awareness and taking steps towards interchurch dialogue and confidence-building in a divided Europe.

Under the circumstances and with conservative leadership, some clergy remained silent on social and political issues, for example in the GDR and Bulgaria during the 1960s. Subsequently, theological articulation of the church's role in new societies and grassroots dissent resounded within Catholic communities in most parts of Eastern Europe, giving a distinctive Roman Catholic impulse to ecumenical thinking and common witness.

Clearly, the most active Catholic family in Eastern Europe was in Poland, whose mission influenced the whole life of the nation. The most difficult fate was experienced by a significant number of Eastern-rite Catholics (uniates), whose churches had been forcibly merged with the Orthodox churches in the USSR, Romania and Czechoslovakia.

THE WCC AND ECUMENICAL PARTNERS IN EASTERN EUROPE

From the 1960s, many Eastern European church delegates attended ecumenical meetings, for example one in 1981 devoted to clarifying the vision of unity and strengthening relationships between the WCC and Orthodox constituencies. At the Bossey Ecumenical Institute, the presence of an Orthodox faculty member and an annual seminar on Orthodox spirituality provided opportunities for mutual learning and enrichment. Greater Orthodox membership on WCC governing bodies, commissions and staff led to more sharing of responsibility in the Council's leadership. Relations were strengthened by the presence of permanent representatives of the Ecumenical Patriarchate and the Russian Orthodox Church at the ecumenical centre.

Through its Orthodox member churches and staff, the WCC contributed to ecumenical themes, publications and meetings with people of living faiths, organized by the Orthodox centre in Chambésy (Switzerland) in preparation for the great and holy pan-Orthodox council.

During the mid-1970s, the World Council encouraged specific bilateral dialogues between Orthodox and Protestant churches, and after the WCC Canberra assembly in 1991 it supported joint initiatives and meetings between Orthodox and Evangelicals. The multilateral dialogues, assisted by the Faith and Order Commission, enhanced the Orthodox bilateral dialogues carried out by international theological commissions of churches and CWCs.[13]

From the 1980s, Orthodox student and youth work in Eastern Europe was facilitated through Syndesmos, the international organization of Orthodox youth, which also helped develop ecumenical relations with non-Orthodox youth organizations. In the 1970s and early 1980s, the World Student Christian Federation staff visited some Eastern European countries and secured participation of students in regional and international events.[14]

For the whole period under review, the East European Protestant churches, like the Orthodox, shared in the WCC programme concerns of unity, mission, renewal and service. All participated in the WCC, CEC and CPC ministry of peace, mutual confidence-building, disarmament and environmental concerns. Priority was given to studies and actions important to Christian witness in socialist society, for example, "Giving Account of the Hope That Is in Us", confessing the faith together, witness of the gospel in the Eastern countries, science and technology for human development, international public hearing on nuclear weapons and disarmament, the churches in Eastern Europe and ecumenical sharing of resources. Most of these were subjects of WCC consultations with churches in socialist Europe.

Thanks to the ecumenical movement, numerous leaders and staff of the WCC, the CEC and other organizations as well as representatives of West European and North American churches visited the churches in Eastern Europe in the period 1960-80 and return visits were made to the ecumenical centre, Geneva. Similarly, the many meetings of the WCC, the CEC, the CWCs and other ecumenical partners held in Eastern Europe provided occasions for mutual information-sharing, strengthening relationships and designing new projects.

The solidarity, exchanges and help rendered to both Orthodox and Protestant churches through the WCC's Commission on Inter-Church Aid, Refugee and World Service and other ecumenical agencies in the 1960s-80s took the following forms: (1) scholarships for young theologians and students from Eastern countries to study abroad, as well as possibilities for Western Europeans to become acquainted with theology, traditions and contemporary life in Orthodox institutions (e.g. in Romania); (2) invitations to eminent non-Orthodox professors to lecture in Moscow, Leningrad, Belgrade, Bucharest and Sofia; (3) support of semi-official visits of pastors, church groups and tourists to Eastern Europe; (4) equipment of theological schools in Yugoslavia and other countries; (5) carrying out of social and diaconal programmes of the Church of Greece and church-related projects in Eastern Europe; (6) assurance of economic stability for Orthodox diaspora communities, with implications for the ministry of their respective mother churches; (7) medical treatment in Western Europe, purchase of medicines and equipment; (8) supply of theological literature; (9) disaster relief; (10) holidays for pastors and their families at the ecumenical Casa Locarno, Switzerland.

The Protestant churches in the GDR and neighbouring countries and the Russian and Balkan Orthodox churches, including the Church of Greece, were involved in the Pro-

---
[13] Constantin Scouteris, "Christian Europe: An Orthodox Perspective", in *The Ecumenical Review*, 45, 2, April 1993, pp.151-68; Todor Sabev, *The Orthodox Churches in the World Council of Churches: Towards the Future*, WCC, 1996, pp.10ff.,44ff., Gennadios Limouris ed., *Orthodox Vision of Ecumenism: Statements, Messages and Reports on the Ecumenical Movement 1902-1992*, WCC, 1994, pp.55-188.
[14] Manuel Quintero, "Notes on WSCF Ostpolitic", in *WSCF Journal*, August 1990, p.24.

gramme to Combat Racism and participated in the Palestinian refugee humanitarian programmes. They also shared in the WCC material aid to some countries in Asia and Africa.[15]

In the 1970s-80s, leaders of state offices for religious affairs in the communist states (except Albania and Bulgaria) visited the ecumenical centre in Geneva, together with church representatives from those countries. These occasions served to discuss publicly church-state relations, share information on ecumenical activities and the contribution churches in Eastern Europe could make, and grapple with the tenacious difficulties inherent in the issues of human rights and religious liberty.

The WCC, sister ecumenical bodies and churches in Eastern Europe joined in paving the way for Billy Graham's historic evangelism campaigns in Yugoslavia (1967); Hungary (1977 and 1989); Poland (1978); the GDR, Czechoslovakia and the USSR (1982); and Romania (1985). These spectacular events gathered millions of people, had tremendous impact on ecumenical relations and confidence-building, and created new perceptions of religion.[16]

The WCC also expressed concern over the future of Russian monasteries and communities, as well as the fate of religious dissidents and their reinstatement to the priesthood. Difficulties faced by Russian Baptists, the Reformed in Armenia, Lutherans of German origin in the USSR and Protestants in the Balkans were all raised with the Orthodox churches. Help with particular cases was sought through diplomatic channels, international institutions, and influential church and public figures.[17]

As a follow up to the 1979 WCC-CWCs project to face together challenges to religious freedom, a WCC-CEC consultation on human rights, with specific reference to Eastern Europe, was held in Geneva in 1983. After 1988, numerous letters and official statements of the WCC, the CEC, the CWCs, churches and ecumenical officers expressed deep concerns and disappointments over human-rights issues in Romania.

During the transition period from communism to democracy, the WCC, the CEC and other partners accompanied the churches in fellowship, providing both moral and material support. A series of consultations with church delegates was initiated and sponsored in Geneva, Bossey, Moscow and Rome (1990-91) to evaluate the new situation brought about by the fall of communism and to discern the calling of the churches within the new socio-political context. In 1990, the central committee of the WCC adopted a "Statement on Issues Arising out of the Developments in Central and Eastern Europe". Other consultations also effected change: the Bossey seminar with students on "Christian witness in a situation of radical change" (1991), an Orthodox symposium on curriculum development (1994), "Church-state relations in a Christian perspective" (1991), "Eastern European women today" (1994), mission and proselytism (1995), workshop on missionary and ecumenical formation of Orthodox youth (1995), Orthodox-evangelical consultation (1995), and a preparatory meeting for the conference on world mission and evangelism (1996).

An important consultation on "Uniatism: an ccumenical response towards the healing of memories", sponsored by the WCC and the CEC in 1992, considered the basic aspects of uniatism – historical, ecclesiological, ecumenical, pastoral and legal – and made

---

[15] Cf. *ibid.*; files on CICARWS, 1960s-80s (Archives of the WCC).

[16] *Ibid.*; Documentation compiled by T. Sabev on Rev. Billy Graham's visit to churches in E. Europe (Archives of the WCC).

[17] *Ibid.*; Relations in E. Europe, no. 5-7; *EPS*, no. 2, 15 Jan. 1976; Albert H. van der Heuvel, "The Churches and Human Rights", in *Mid-Stream*, 16, 2, April 1977, pp.189ff.; *Discretion and Valour*, p.290.

recommendations to the churches.[18] It was preceded by visits to the churches concerned in Ukraine, Belarus, the Czechoslovak Socialist Republic and Romania.

The WCC and its partners responded to emergency needs for food, medicine and relief supplies. Humanitarian aid of some form was channelled to most churches in the former socialist countries. A special appeal provided for the spiritual, social and diaconal ministry of the Albanian Orthodox Church, and of others facing difficulties.

Churches from all over Europe maintained dialogue in conflict situations in most former communist states. They contributed to stabilizing the peace process, the healing of wounds, the rejection of prejudice, and the protection of religious and ethnic minorities, all helping to pave the way for democracy.[19]

The ecumenical movement and the Christian World Communions played an important role for Protestant Christians and churches and the smaller Orthodox churches in Eastern and Southern Europe. The administrative structure of the Federation of Evangelical Churches in the GDR, for instance, was originally based on the structure of the WCC. Many congregations appreciated keenly the Pentecost messages from the presidents of the WCC, and the Week of Prayer for Christian Unity was carefully prepared and observed. Contacts with the ecumenical community, and the knowledge of its commitment to them, reassured the Christian community in Eastern Europe that it was part of the life of world Christianity, with a share in shaping the ecumenical process as committed, equal and respected members.

The impetus for the conciliar process on Justice, Peace and the Integrity of Creation which led to one of the high points for the ecumenical movement, the European Ecumenical Assembly in Basel in 1989, came largely from the Protestant churches in the GDR at the WCC assembly in Vancouver in 1983.

Although ecumenism had an impact in all areas of Protestant church life, it barely permeated to the larger church membership, and its influence at parish level remained insignificant. In the Orthodox churches it was even less known and practised. The structural expressions of ecumenism in some countries were symbolic institutions, e.g. the national council of churches in the former Yugoslavia. In some parts of Europe ecumenism was more festive, representative, ostentatious and formal than real. Eastern European ecumenism was fragile, immature, limited in width and depth. It was also closely observed and politically repressed, a "koinonia under the cross" (Heinz J. Held). Nevertheless, it was authentic and fruitful, beneficial to church mission and interchurch relations; thus Marxist ideological workers were nervous, continually criticizing the WCC and "modernistic theological approaches" which were said to support religion "against progress".

THE CHRISTIAN PEACE CONFERENCE

During the strained 1960s-1970s, the Christian Peace Conference (CPC) was a promoter of ecumenical commitment and social ministry of the East European churches. Founded in 1958-60 under the leadership of Josef Hromádka and Bohuslav Pospisil of the Comenius theological faculty in Prague, and supported by German theologians such as Helmut Gollwitzer and Heinrich Joachim Iwand, it offered a forum for theological

---

[18] See documents on all these meetings in the files on the Churches in E. Europe in the Post-Communist Era (Archives of the WCC).

[19] Files on the WCC General Secretariat, Programme Units, Orthodox task force and Europe task force, 1990-1996.

discussions and practical work on the topical peace and justice agenda embraced by churches, groups and individuals from many regions, not least from the "non-aligned" countries of the third world. Despite conformity with communist policy, the CPC equipped constituencies in Europe to engage in dialogue and tackle challenges to Marxist ideology and atheism, to acquire space in public life, a sense of Christian mission in the socialist society and common witness in a divided oikoumene. It created suspicion among some circles in the West – and among some dissidents in the East – on account of its apparent acceptance of much of the official Eastern governmental ethos.

The tragic events of 1968 in Prague prompted a crisis in the CPC leadership and for many of its members, and the movement consequently lost strength and specific purpose. After 1990 the Conference underwent a self-examination and faced a deepening financial crisis. Its office in Prague would close in 2001. This called for a reshaping of vision and determining a new course of struggle for peace and reconciliation at world level.[20]

CHURCHES IN POST-COMMUNIST SOCIETIES

The dramatic changes of 1989-90 in Eastern Europe demanded radical responses from both churches and ecumenical bodies. Meetings at various levels assessed the situation and provided means for a new beginning. Changes in legislation on religious denominations and church-state relations were required in order to provide for the restitution of church property, allow the formation of associations and institutions for social activities, permit religious education in public schools and on church premises, and restore the celebration of Christmas and Easter as official holidays. Some of these demands were met immediately, others were implemented partially, still others deferred. Church governing bodies assembled for a self-assessment of their witness, suffering, guilt or innocence during the communist period, and to undertake a process of rehabilitation. Some church leaders who had compromised with the communist regime were asked to resign.

The state offices for religious affairs were reorganized with new mandates to ensure the liberty and autonomy of religious life and to facilitate church-state and interchurch relations. Ecumenical witness was strengthened in the work of national Bible societies, charitable organizations, chaplaincy services and other initiatives. Structures for sharing foreign humanitarian aid (in Romania, for example) were an impulse towards wider ecumenical contacts.

Evangelization – or re-evangelization – emerged as a source of confusion and competition, raising accusations of proselytism and anxiety about the influence of parachurch groups, new sects and New Religious Movements. In Russia more than three hundred mission, education and charitable societies initiated complex operations ranging from preaching, to education, to business.

The churches' commitment to overcome the legacy of totalitarianism and to nurture democracy as a Christian social value was expressed in the preparation of elections, membership in parliaments and other elected bodies, participation in public organizations and critical support for state policy. But the churches did not escape the tensions and ambiguities inherent in the transition to pluralistic societies, sometimes succumb-

---

[20] See Milan Opočenský, "Christian Peace Conference", in *Dictionary of the Ecumenical Movement*, pp.172-74.

ing to triumphalism, nationalism, xenophobia and antisemitism. The deeper involvement of the church in politics and an emphasis on intrinsic church-nation-state relations sometimes compromised the churches' witness and diminished the ability to offer Christian ethical guidance to their nations, a situation which had implications for both the internal renewal of the churches and their capacity to be agents of healing in society.

Political, ethnic and religious conflicts in several countries, most acutely around the break-up of Yugoslavia, inhibited Christian unity and mission. During the war in Croatia and Bosnia, Orthodox, Catholic, Protestant and Muslim leaders, with the assistance of ecumenical bodies, maintained dialogue and appealed for respect for human rights and reconciliation. Although the primary concern of the Serbian Patriarchate was with fractures of its dioceses and the suffering of its people, it deplored atrocities and violence committed by all parties to the conflicts. In this context, the destruction of each other's places of worship became an all-too-frequent tactic in the overall strategies of ethnic cleansing.

The Orthodox Church of Albania, which had been resurrected to new life, dedicated itself to a ministry of reconstruction, renewal and reconciliation. During the Kosovo conflict in 1999, it played an important role in delivering relief and providing refugee services. The Ecumenical Patriarchate and the Church of Greece made numerous appeals for peace and justice in Europe, particularly in the Balkans. In addition, Greece offered considerable assistance to the churches in this region, especially in the provision of humanitarian aid, educational support and scholarships, as well as Bibles.

Similarly, churches in the Commonwealth of Independent States and the Baltic states gave priority to unity, peace and the prevention of religious and ethnic hatred. In 1994 they organized an interconfessional conference on Christian faith and human enmity. A Romanian-Hungarian conference on reconciliation held under the auspices of the CEC in 1990 initiated a rapprochement on various levels. In the early 1990s, the Moscow Patriarchate performed a delicate mediation between opposing elements in the government and society, then undertook a peace mission to Chechnya.

The legalization of Eastern-rite Catholic churches (uniates) led to a sharp deterioration in relationships between the Orthodox and the Roman Catholic Church over matters of dioceses and church property in Ukraine, Romania and Slovakia. The reestablishment of Roman Catholic ecclesial structures and communities, as well as of some historic Protestant churches, within traditional Orthodox jurisdictions, further impeded the ecumenical spirit, especially in Russia. Finally, intra-Orthodox disputes over jurisdiction in Ukraine, Moldova and Estonia, as well as schismatic movements within the Russian Orthodox Church and the Bulgarian Patriarchate, also had a negative effect on the unity and witness of the church. Opposition to ecumenism became a central issue in the internal tensions within several local Orthodox churches in Eastern Europe; and in the late 1990s both the Bulgarian and the Georgian Orthodox churches withdrew from the WCC and the CEC. Despite these obstacles and reverses, the spiritual bonds of *koinonia* were not extinguished, even if they became less intimate than many had hoped during the initial months of euphoria following the changes of 1989-90.[21]

---

[21] Files on WCC Relations with E. European churches, Europe Task force, specialised Task force on E. Europe, and Orthodox Task force (Archives of the WCC); *Catholicism and Politics in Communist Societies*, pp.86ff.,98ff.,139-40,173-77,204-205; *Protestantism and Politics in Eastern Europe*, pp.9-10,104-5,173-208,213,217-19,221ff.,232-33,252-53; Timothy Ware, *The Orthodox Church*, London, Penguin, 1993, pp.162ff.

WESTERN EUROPEAN CHALLENGES

The ecumenical movement in Western Europe during this period was also complex. Structural unions between churches, formation of local, national and regional councils of churches or other bodies promoting interchurch cooperation, formal agreements between churches at national or international levels, movements among lay people, women and youth across confessional lines – all these and more were examples of ecumenism. Underlying them all was a sense of the scandal of disunity which, precisely because the crucial divisions within Christianity arose within Europe, imposed on the European churches a particular obligation to overcome them. This sense of obligation was compounded by the awareness that it was among the "younger" churches of the former mission fields outside Europe that much of the most obvious ecumenical progress had been and was being made. But it was Western Europe that provided the stage-setting for an event of immense ecumenical significance: the Second Vatican Council which met from 1962 to 1965. In Europe the impact of the Council on Roman Catholics was much less marked in the communist-dominated East than in the West (not until the late 1990s, long after the dramatic changes of 1989-91, were the documents of Vatican II translated into certain of the Central and Eastern European languages, such as Czech).

The chief expressions of Western European ecumenism may be briefly surveyed.

Structural unions of churches

Only three cases of united churches being formed by organic, structural union have occurred in Europe during this period: the United Reformed Church in the UK in 1972 (Presbyterian, Congregational and from 1981 the Churches of Christ, joined in 2000 by the Scottish Congregational Union); the United Protestant Church of Belgium in 1979; and the union of the Waldensian Church and the Evangelical Methodist Church of Italy, also in 1979. By the year 2000 decisive steps had been taken towards the formation of the Protestant Church in the Netherlands, bringing together the Reformed Churches in the Netherlands, the Netherlands Reformed Church and the Evangelical Lutheran Church in the Kingdom of the Netherlands. None of these involved unions between churches maintaining the historic episcopate and those not so doing, and most involved only churches of the Reformed family. It was on the crucial issue of the mutual recognition of ministries that the scheme for union between the Church of England and the Methodist Church failed in 1969 and 1972.

Formal agreements between churches

A number of groupings of churches were formed in Europe during this period, on the basis of a measure of doctrinal agreement and commitment to common witness. In 1969 the process began which, based on a reading of article 7 of the Augsburg confession and a number of more recent Lutheran-Reformed consultations, led to the 1973 Leuenberg agreement: church fellowship was declared among the Lutheran, Reformed and United churches in Europe. By 1988, some 80 churches (including a number in South America) were signatories. In 1983, the fifth centenary of the birth of Martin Luther, the archbishop of Canterbury, Robert Runcie, on a visit to Germany proposed that closer relations be formed between the Church of England and the Protestant (Lutheran, Reformed and United) churches of Germany, then still divided between East and West. Conversations were entered into, producing a report in 1988 on the basis of which the Meissen agreement was formally declared in 1992, by which time the Evangelical Church of Germany (EKD) had itself been reunited following the fall of the Berlin wall in 1989. The Meissen agreement is a mutual acknowledgment by the Church of England and the EKD of belonging to the one apostolic faith and mission, of being churches where the word of God is truly preached and the sacraments rightly administered, and of each other's ministries as given by God and instruments of God's grace. It does not, however, imply a complete interchangeability of ministry: the difference of view represented by the Anglican episcopal succession on the one hand and the German churches of the Reformation on the other is openly acknowledged. Further discussions are taking place on the nature of *episcope* and on practical steps towards active cooperation and fellowship.

In many ways parallel to the Meissen agreement and very similar in content, the Porvoo agreement, formalized in 1996, arose out of a long history (dating from before the first world war) of conversations and ad hoc agreements between the Church of England and some of the Nordic (Norway and Sweden) and Baltic (Estonia and Latvia) Lutheran churches. Again it was Archbishop Runcie who suggested, in 1988, that the time might be ripe for more considered and purposeful steps towards Anglican-Lutheran unity, in the light both of these earlier agreements and of more recent multilateral statements of the WCC (in both Meissen and Porvoo, statements such as *Baptism, Eucharist and Ministry* were highly significant in providing a common basis for understanding). But whereas in Meissen the Anglicans were dealing with non-episcopal churches, the Lutheran churches of Scandinavia and the Baltic had maintained the historic episcopate (with the exception of the Church of Denmark, which finally was not a party to the agreement). Porvoo includes the establishment of a common ministry in the historic succession and therefore has implications going well beyond its immediate European context, since it links the Nordic churches into the worldwide Anglican communion.

The Church of England also engaged in conversations with the Moravian Church in Britain, leading to the Fetter Lane common declaration of 1996, setting out a series of mutual recognitions and commitments. In this way, by establishing a local ecumenical partnership wherever there is a Moravian congregation in England relations will take on a distinctively intensive quality, while the British and Irish Anglican churches as a whole entered into dialogue with the French Lutheran and Reformed churches.

National ecumenical bodies

Most countries in Western Europe had national ecumenical bodies, aiming at cooperative work among the churches, dating from well before the period under review. However, several new councils of churches were formed around or during this period: the Federation of the Protestant Churches in Italy (1967), the Council of Churches in the Netherlands (1968), and the Portuguese Council of Christian Churches (1971). In addition, certain restructuring of existing ecumenical bodies occurred, as with the British Council of Churches (founded 1942) which in 1990 dissolved and was replaced by the Council of Churches for Britain and Ireland (now called Churches Together in Britain and Ireland), with the Roman Catholic Church in England, Wales and Scotland coming into full membership. The Roman Catholic Church is also a full member in a number of other councils: the Netherlands, Finland, Denmark and Germany. Ecumenical councils existed during the cold-war period in Poland, Czechoslovakia and Yugoslavia, and following the division of Czechoslovakia into the Czech Republic and Slovakia separate councils were formed in these two countries. But the formation of new councils in post-Soviet Eastern Europe has proved slow and difficult.

Ecumenical responses to Western European political institutions

Beginning in the 1960s, one of the most significant features of ecumenical life in Western Europe was the series of attempts to relate Christian concern to the political institutions of European unity, centred in Brussels (the European Commission) and Strasbourg (the European Parliament, the European Court of Human Rights, etc).[22] In the early days of the European Commission in Brussels, a small number of commissioners felt the need to examine more closely the bearing of their Christian faith on their work. With the support of local ministers they created the Ecumenical Association for Church and Society (EACS), which organized Bible studies, prayer groups and discussions of the ethical aspects of the construction of Europe. Contacts between EACS and the Protestant, Anglican and Orthodox churches of the member states of the European Economic Community (as it was then called, later the European Union) led to the foundation in 1978 of the European Ecumenical Commission for Church and Society (EECCS) with a small full-time staff in Brussels and, subsequently, Strasbourg. The EECCS from the beginning worked closely with the parallel Roman Catholic organization in Brussels, the Catholic Office for Information on European Issues (OCIPE), and there has been increasingly close cooperation with the Commission of the Bishops Conferences of the European Union (COMECE). The EECCS developed considerable expertise during the later 1970s and 1980s, in both mediating to the member churches the issues arising out of the work of the EC, and in enabling dialogue with the decision-makers on European policy from the perspective of Christian social concern. Since the Single European Act and the formation of the single market at the end of 1992, the increasingly integrated economic and social policies of the EU, with all their implications for justice and equality, have underlined the need for a united Christian voice especially in view of the eastward expansion of the EU.

Of equal ecumenical concern were the implications of unifying Western European policies for the wider world. In 1974 an ecumenical conference on Christians and the future of Europe was held at Roehampton, England, including Roman Catholic participation. This was followed in 1975 with the foundation by EACS and OCIPE of the European Ecumenical Organization for Development (EECOD). This aimed at increasing the European churches' awareness of the issues involved in third-world development, the role played by the European Community, and to inform national and Brussels-based decision-makers of the churches' views. The EECOD worked closely with the EECCS and shared the same building in Brussels.

Founded in 1964 in Geneva, the Churches' Committee for Migrants in Europe (CCME) joined the other ecumenical organizations in Brussels in 1978. It was set up as an independent church agency on the recommendation of the WCC, to keep churches and public opinion in Europe informed about the problems of migrant peoples in Europe and to promote their individual and collective rights. Again, the significance of its task has been borne out by the increasing signs of racism and xenophobia in Europe, not least since the changes of 1989-91.

---

[22] On the earlier historical background to engagement with issues of European unity see J.A. Zeilstra, *European Unity in Ecumenical Thinking 1937-1948*, Zoetermeer, Boekcentrum, 1995. On more recent responses of the churches, see D. Edwards, *Christians in a New Europe*, London, Collins, 1990; and K. Blei, *On Being the Church across Frontiers: A Vision of Europe Today*, WCC, 1992.

Despite frequent tributes to the importance of their work, by the mid-1990s all such organizations were working under increasingly stringent financial constraints. The EECOD was dissolved in 1995. A vitally important move, however, was the integration of the EECCS with the Conference of European Churches, a process completed in 1999.

Lay movements and "unofficial" ecumenism

The 1960s saw a rapid growth in laity education movements: well-resourced centres such as the evangelical church academies in Germany, or less formal bodies such as the Audenshaw Foundation in Britain. The Ecumenical Association of Academies and Laity Centres in Europe, which grew out of the European Association of Academy Directors (1956) played a vital part in creating a Europe-wide network of such bodies. Membership by the 1990s numbered some ninety centres (mainly Protestant) in 16 European countries. Its emphasis upon the import of faith for secular responsibilities in society, government and industry often generated a healthy tension with the ecumenism primarily concerned with ecclesiastical issues of doctrine and order. Closely allied to this lay-centred ecumenism was the specialist work of industrial mission. On a European level this operated through the European Contact Group (formed in 1966). Of increasing ecumenical significance has been the biennial German Protestant Kirchentag (church day), founded after the second world war. By the late 1980s, not only was this huge event attracting over 100,000 Germans, mainly young and lay, for worship, Bible study, and theological and political debate, but it was also attracting some 2000 visitors from elsewhere in Europe and beyond, making it the largest ecumenical meeting of such frequency anywhere in the world.

For many European Christians, their primary ecumenical awareness has been engendered by a search for a new spirituality and experience of community. The most widely influential centre for such encounter, especially for young people, has been the Taizé community in France. Taizé's contribution extends far beyond those who actually live or visit there, not least through its music and liturgy. Taizé chants have fostered a kind of common liturgical culture now familiar to worshippers in all Christian traditions. Other communities are also important in drawing together people from diverse confessions – and sometimes nationalities – in prayer, celebration and reconciliation. Among these the Iona community in Scotland, the Agape community in Italy, the Imshausen community in Germany, and the Corrymeela community in Northern Ireland are notable.

Finally, for many Christians "ecumenism" happened as they engaged in campaigning on burning social issues. These campaigns often took their participants beyond the official positions of their respective churches (or of the ecumenical bodies) and they found a new solidarity with others in prophetic faith and witness. In the 1960s, and again during the 1980s, nuclear disarmament was one such issue. Solidarity with the anti-apartheid struggle in South Africa was a crucial focus for many throughout the 1970s and especially in the 1980s. Environmental and ecological issues came to the fore from the late 1980s onwards. There was a danger of fragmentation of such activity into a plethora of single-issue movements, but the network Kairos Europa for example, which arose around the 1992 commemorations of Europe's encounter with America by Christopher Columbus five centuries earlier, sought to discern the common factors linking the marginalized in European society and in the wider world, and to provide a critical challenge "from below" to the dominant economic and spiritual ethos of contemporary Europe.

PAN-EUROPEAN ECUMENICAL ACTIVITIES/ORGANIZATIONS
Conference of European Churches

The period saw the consolidation of the main regional ecumenical body, the Conference of European Churches (CEC).[23] This originated in the 1950s from conversations among European church leaders from both halves of the continent, on the need to discover, maintain and strengthen the bonds of unity between the churches separated by the lines of differing political ideology and military confrontation. The stated purpose of CEC was "to discuss questions concerning the churches in Europe and to assist each other in the service which is laid upon the churches in the contemporary . . . situation". Anglican, Lutheran, Reformed, Orthodox, Old Catholic and Free Church Protestant churches all were involved, from throughout Europe.

The notable absence from this membership was the Roman Catholic Church. However, from 1964 CEC developed a close working relationship with the Consilium Conferentiarum Episcoporum Europae (CCEE – Council of European Bishops Conferences) and a joint CEC-CCEE committee was set up.

Up to this point CEC had relied upon part-time staffing, but at the assembly at Pörtsach, Austria (1967), steps were taken to introduce a full-time secretariat the following year. A further change took place around this time. Hitherto, the main profile of CEC had been provided through its assemblies. These continued to be significant, but were held less frequently: 1971 (Nyborg), 1974 (Engelberg, Switzerland), 1979 (Crete) – and then not until 1986 (Stirling, Scotland). Several factors were significant in this change. One was the increasing size of the assemblies themselves (membership increased to around 120 churches by the late 1980s) and the logistical problems this presented. More important was the conscious shift towards concentrating more of the work not in top-level representative gatherings (which led to some criticisms of the overly "clerical" ethos of CEC), but rather in study programmes and consultations on specific topics. This in turn led to the establishment of special desks alongside the general secretariat. The first was a study secretariat, and this was followed by a secretariat for finance and interchurch service (later separated into two separate desks). Interchurch service then took on the task of coordinating the European churches' working group on asylum and refugees.

Until the later 1980s, the CEC could virtually justify its existence simply by being the body which bridged the East-West divide. It was a powerful symbol of ecumenical solidarity, and one of the few means by which representatives of the churches in the communist East could meet with brothers and sisters in the West. Its pan-European nature however was more than symbolic, and certain crucial issues affecting Christianity in a divided and often oppressed Europe required active attention, notably that of human rights. The Helsinki Final Act of 1975 was followed closely by the CEC, especially its provisions on religious freedom and other basic human rights. In conjunction with the National Council of the Churches of Christ in the USA, and the Canadian Council of Churches (both the US and Canada also being signatories to Helsinki) the CEC established the churches' human rights programme to monitor the implementation of Helsinki, and in particular the "human dimension" section of the Conference on Security and Cooperation in Europe (later the Organization for Security and Cooperation in Europe). Peace, justice and human rights also became an autonomous programme

---

[23] R. Gurney ed., *CEC at 40: Celebrating the 40th Anniversary of the Conference of European Churches, 1959-1999*, Geneva, CEC, 1990.

within the CEC, with its own secretariat. Finally, desks for women's issues and communications were established.

The Stirling (1986) assembly signalled the retirement of Glen Garfield Williams, the first general secretary, and the arrival of Jean Fischer, a Swiss Protestant lay man with much previous experience of ecumenical aid and development work. Stirling was also significant for other reasons. Two motions from churches in the East and West German republics proposed a European assembly as part of the worldwide conciliar process for justice, peace and the integrity of creation, set in motion by the WCC sixth assembly in Vancouver (1983). A truly ecumenical peace assembly was envisaged, and the cooperation of the CCEE invited and accepted. Thus was born the (first) European Ecumenical Assembly on "Peace with Justice" (Basel, May 1989).[24]

On many counts Basel could claim to be one of the most significant European ecumenical events in the entire period under review, and it certainly awakened the ecumenical conscience in a new way. CEC-CCEE cooperation had already generated a number of important "ecumenical encounters", at Chantilly (France, 1978), Logumkloster (Denmark, 1981), a much larger gathering at Riva del Garda (Italy, 1984), and at Erfurt (Germany, 1988). The Basel assembly however was unprecedented both in size and in scope. Official delegates – in equal numbers from CCEE and CEC churches – totalling seven hundred came from every country in Europe together with thousands of unofficial participants. It was aptly described as combining the features of a church assembly and a Kirchentag. Peace, human rights, economic justice within Europe and between Europe and the third world, the place of women in church and society and – perhaps more conspicuously than ever before in ecumenical history – human environmental and ecological responsibility formed the agenda of this week of worship, celebration, Bible study and rigorous ethical debate. The vision of what peace with justice could mean for a Europe still divided was spelled out both in the brief message and the final document of the assembly.

In many ways, the Basel assembly represented the high-point of the ecumenical movement for Justice, Peace and the Integrity of Creation not just within Europe but in the whole world. Furthermore, in addition to the sense of achievement at the Basel event itself, the dramatic changes which within months overtook Eastern Europe lent in retrospect a prophetic aura to the assembly.

The ending of Soviet-led socialism in Eastern Europe and the break-up of the USSR proved complex in their consequences for the pan-European ecumenical movement. At one level, there was deep thankfulness that the days of officially imposed state atheism were over, and with the new freedoms, international fellowship could be strengthened without political hindrance. At another level, new problems arose. One was sheer economics. Many post-communist societies endured extreme economic hardship, the churches no less than other sectors of society, and it is ironic that just as travel to the West became politically more possible, it became financially far more difficult. Furthermore, because such official ecumenical activity as was allowed during the communist period could take place only with the sanction of the state, in some quarters in the East "ecumenism" as such came to be regarded as tainted with the old order. In some cases, not least in Russia, such an anti-ecumenical attitude has accompanied a strongly resur-

---

[24] *Peace with Justice: Official Documentation of the European Ecumenical Assembly, Basel, Switzerland, 15-21 May 1989*, Geneva, CEC, 1989.

gent nationalist feeling. The benefits of belonging to a wider ecumenical family could no longer be taken for granted in some quarters in the East.

Church responses to the "new Europe"

The events of 1989-91 threw all the European churches and ecumenical bodies into a new and uncertain situation. The "old" grounds for ecumenical cooperation seemed no longer adequate, as signs of a new confessionalism emerged. If, in the East, the old common enemy of the atheistic state had disappeared, against what and for what was a common Christian front now required? In this situation it was not surprising that a desire emerged to find new confessional identities and roles in relation to the changed context. This impulse was not necessarily counter to ecumenism, since it could be argued that without such a new-found identity the various traditions would be in no position to approach each other with integrity. But it did mean a certain readjustment of priorities.

A series of major meetings took place in Europe during 1991-92 indicative of this change of mood and of attempts to deal with it. In 1991 the CEC called a church leaders meeting in Geneva which was attended by many of the heads of member churches, affording the opportunity for first time face-to-face contact. Later that same year a special European bishops synod was convened in Rome by Pope John Paul II. The overall mood was that of celebrating the survival of the church throughout the repression of the communist period, and of a resurgence of hope that Christianity could again unite Europe. The final document emphasized the need and opportunity for a "new evangelization" of Europe. In March 1992, at the invitation of the newly elected Ecumenical Patriarch Bartholomew, a summit meeting of Orthodox primates took place in Istanbul. Their statement clearly reflected the experience of suffering of Orthodox churches under communism. Again, the search for European unity was welcomed, and the Orthodox contribution to this was affirmed. But, significantly, the ideal of a "Christian Europe" was spoken of, not triumphalistically as some detected in the Roman Catholic statement, but as a commodity under threat: from secularization, from proselytism by non-Orthodox Christians, and from Islam.

That same month, a special ad hoc assembly of Protestant leaders met in Budapest to consider the significance of the legacy of the Reformation for the new European scene. Here, a "Christian Europe" was rejected, being suspected as covering a desire by some churches for the restoration of their power and privilege in alliance with the state. This gathering was more open to the secularizing process than were its Catholic and Orthodox counterparts. A Protestant power-bloc to rival the other two main confessional families was not envisaged. Rather, a more modest role was proposed for contemporary Protestantism: for example the doctrine of justification by faith alone was suggested as answering the need for honesty in dealing with the guilt of complicity in the wrongs of the recent past. Finally, in the summer of 1992, the CEC's tenth assembly took place in Prague on the theme "God Unites – In Christ a New Creation". That assembly revealed a greater awareness of the plethora of items the churches might undertake in the new Europe, rather than a capacity to set clear goals within a coherent understanding of the churches' mission.[25] During the Prague assembly severe criticisms were voiced, particularly from former Czech dissidents, of the role that CEC and other ecumenical bod-

---

[25] *God Unites – in Christ a New Creation: Report of the 10th Assembly of the Conference of European Churches,* Geneva, CEC, 1993.

ies had allegedly played in relating to the official leadership of churches, rather than to dissidents, during the communist period.

The Balkans conflict

If such gatherings revealed newly differing perceptions and emphases within the main Christian groupings in Europe, an even more severe testing of ecumenical commitment came with the outbreak of armed conflict on the continent. In 1989, the final document of the Basel assembly, while recognizing the re-emergence of regional and national conflicts, had declared: "There are no situations in our countries or on our continent in which violence is required or justified." Yet within two years, the break-up of Yugoslavia was prompting the outbreak of open military conflict between Serbia and Croatia, followed in 1992 by the appalling destruction, bloodshed and so-called "ethnic cleansing" in Bosnia-Herzegovina which resulted in the greatest refugee crisis in Europe since the second world war. Conflicts in the former Soviet Union, especially between Armenia and Azerbaijan, and in Chechnya, further darkened the scene.

It was the conflicts in the former Yugoslavia which presented the ecumenical bodies with the most acute challenges, since the warring sides differed by religious affiliation: Roman Catholic (Croats), Orthodox (Serbs) and Muslim (mostly Bosnians and Kosovars). The CEC, in conjunction with the CCEE and the WCC, sought to create and maintain dialogue between the religious representatives within the communities at war through round-tables and consultations. Such attempts drew criticisms from some quarters in the West that in placing the emphasis on dialogue, the CEC and the WCC were evading a judgment on where the main responsibility for the war lay and how aggression should be countered.[26]

Diakonia, reconciliation

At the same time the ecumenical bodies were deeply involved in coordinating diaconal work among the victims of all conflict regions, and other centres of need in Europe. The European regional group was a joint CEC-WCC body set up to agree on priority projects in Europe and to advise on diaconal issues and resource sharing. Increasingly by the mid-1990s, after decades of concentration on the third world, the European churches' aid and development agencies, many created to meet the needs of a devastated continent strewn with refugees immediately after the second world war, were once again being called upon to help bind the wounded on their own doorstep. Fortunately, a number of these agencies had long experience of working together through the WCC, and also at times of forming a common network of advocacy in relation to the European Union structures. More recently a number of agencies have moved towards a more "bilateral" policy of relating directly to partners in the recipient countries, throwing into question the role of the ecumenical networks as a means of channelling aid.

By the later 1990s, the most significant fact about the ecumenical movement in Europe was its determination neither to depend upon the euphoria such as that which briefly swept Europe in 1989-90, nor to be lost in the uncertainties and disillusionment that followed. A further meeting in the series of ecumenical encounters sponsored by

---

[26] For background to WCC actions, see E. Weingärtner and E. Salter eds, *The Tragedy of Bosnia: Confronting the New World Disorder*, WCC, 1993. The controversy on the ecumenical stance is exemplified in A. Hastings, "SOS Bosnia", in *Theology*, July-August 1994; and K. Clements and A. Chandler, "A Live Bishop Bell in 1994: A Response to Adrian Hastings", in *Theology*, Jan.-Feb. 1995.

the CEC and the CCEE took place at Santiago de Compostela, Spain, in 1991 on the theme of common mission and witness in Europe. In addition, following the tenth CEC assembly, the joint committee on Islam in Europe, which had in fact been in operation since 1987, was reconstituted. Then, at a joint meeting of the CEC central committee and the CCEE plenary assembly in Assisi in 1995, it was decided to convene a second European Ecumenical Assembly in succession to Basel 1989. This took place in Graz, Austria, in June 1997 under the theme "Reconciliation – Gift of God and Source of New Life". It was followed immediately by the CEC's eleventh assembly. The Graz assembly, constituted in a similar fashion to the Basel event, attracted even more participants than Basel: some 10,000 overall. Special trains brought large numbers of Christians from Eastern Europe and, for the first time in ecumenical history, this enabled people from this part of the continent to make an impact in their own right rather than being simply the objects of Western concern.[27] Among the fruits of Graz was the establishment of a European Christian environmental network, but the most highly-publicized (and in some quarters controversial) was the process set up for the production of the Charta Oecumenica. This is a set of principles, guidelines and commitments for the European churches to be adopted in their relationships to each other, and to their mission of evangelization, peace and justice.[28]

Women and European ecumenism

European women have figured among the outstanding names in ecumenical leadership since the second world war: Kathleen Bliss, Suzanne de Diétrich, Pauline Webb, Madeleine Barot, to name but a few. Yet in the early stages of the life of the CEC women often tended to be excluded. It was after the Stirling assembly in 1986 that women began to play a fuller role. In 1993 a woman executive secretary was appointed to work half-time for the Ecumenical Decade of the Churches in Solidarity with Women (1988-98), as well as half-time for interchurch service. In 1994 the WCC and the CEC jointly hosted a conference at Ballycastle in Northern Ireland on issues of violence against women, resulting in the Ballycastle declaration challenging the churches on this issue. How the issue of reconciliation between women and men in the church would be handled at the second European Ecumenical Assembly was a matter of some controversy in the planning process.

On a less formal but vital level, the Ecumenical Forum of European Christian Women has been a meeting-point for Anglican, Protestant and Orthodox women in Europe. It grew out of discussions in Brussels in 1978, stimulated partly by the feeling of women that they were excluded by the CEC, and partly by their desire to work with Roman Catholic women. This latter motive ensured the continuance of the Forum after the point when women did begin to play a fuller part within the CEC, together with the possibility of raising radical issues and pursuing feminist theology. The Forum has held five assemblies. Also, in 1996, a European women's synod was held at Gmunden, Austria. This gathering, open to any women who wished to attend, attracted more than 1000,

---

[27] *Reconciliation – Gift of God and Source of New Life: Documents from the Second European Ecumenical Assembly in Graz*, Geneva, CEC, 1998.

[28] *Charta Oecumenica: Guidelines for the Growing Cooperation among the Churches in Europe*, Geneva, CEC, 1991 (original text in German). See also Viorel Ionita and Sarah Numico eds, *Charta Oecumenica: A Text, a Process, and a Dream of the Churches in Europe*, WCC, 2003.

mostly Roman Catholics. Among its statements was the declaration that "there can be no reconciliation in Europe without justice for women".

Violence against women in the home, in society and within the churches themselves was one of the issues most prominently highlighted in Europe during the Ecumenical Decade of the Churches in Solidarity with Women. The presidents of the CEC and the CCEE in 1999 addressed a joint letter to the churches calling them to face the matter more honestly and effectively, and the CEC produced a booklet on the subject in several languages. Further, one of the most shameful features of the so-called "new" Europe of the post cold-war era has emerged in the trafficking of women and children, mainly from East to West, for sexual exploitation. The CEC held a major consultation on the issue at Driebergen in the Netherlands in 1999, and measures to help the churches oppose the evil are being followed up through an ecumenical working group with Roman Catholic involvement.

CONCLUSION

The foregoing survey illustrates that one cannot speak of "the ecumenical movement in Europe" during this period without recognizing its many different components, not all of them easily harmonized with one another. Moreover, an in-depth evaluation of some aspects is still awaited, not least concerning the stances of the official church leadership in the East during the cold war, and the strategies of the ecumenical bodies towards the East. A readiness to face an honest appraisal of that period will be a component of a truly ecumenical integrity in the coming years. At the same time, but for the striving for solidarity on the part of ecumenical organizations, manifested in many concrete forms of aid and support, not only would the fundamental principle of the *una sancta* transcending national and ideological divisions have been without witness, but the situation of the churches in the East would have been unimaginably more difficult than in fact it was.

Equally, there has arisen a continual dissatisfaction within the churches, not least in the West, with the endemic tendency towards confessional and national self-sufficiency, and indeed a continental "fortress attitude" towards the rest of the world. The achievements of organic union between the churches may be sparse. But the growth in closer fellowship and deepening dialogue is undeniable. It is even the case that many of the "anti-ecumenical" stances now being expressed, for example, from within the Orthodox churches carry an implicit desire to clarify what "ecumenism" should mean, and by no means constitute a rejection of ecumenism as such. The real challenge for the European churches is whether, together, in face of the many political, social and cultural forces now reshaping the life of their continent, they can lay out a vision for their region which is truly unifying on the basis of values inherent in the gospel, and can exemplify that vision in their own life together.

BIBLIOGRAPHY

Ackermann, Bruno, *Discernment and Commitment*, Kampen, Kok, 1993, 222p.

Althausen, Johannes, *Was kommt nach der Volkskirche? Oder: Wie lassen sich Strukturen überlisten?: Die "Strukturstudie" des ÖRK in der DDR 1962-1973, erlebt, neu erforscht, dokumentiert und ins Gespräch gebracht*, Rothenburg, Ernst Lange Institut für Ökumenische Studien, 1997, 166p.

At Thy Word: Mission and Evangelism in Europe Today: Report of the Fifth European Ecumenical Encounter, 13-17 November 1991, Santiago de Compostela, Spain, Geneva, CEC, 1992, 192p.

Beeson, Trevor, *Discretion and Valour, Religious Conditions in Russia and Eastern Europe*, Philadelphia, Fortress, 1982, 416p.

Blei, Karel, *On Being the Church across Frontiers: A Vision of Europe Today*, WCC, 1992, 81p.

Boerma, Conrad, *The Poor Side of Europe: The Church and the (New) Poor of Western Europe*, WCC, 1989, 131p.

Clements, Keith, *The Churches in Europe as Witnesses to Healing*, WCC, 2003, 128p.

Craig, Maxwell ed., *For God's Sake, Unity: An Ecumenical Voyage with the Iona Community*, Glasgow, Wild Goose, 1998, 185p.

Ecumenical Dialogue on Reconciliation: Belgrade, 19-22 February 1996, Conference of European Churches, Theological Faculty, Serbian Orthodox Church, Geneva, CEC, 1996, 88p.

Edwards, David L., *Christians in a New Europe*, London, Fount Paperbacks, 1990, 257p.

Europe on the Move: Documentation from a Special meeting of European Church Leaders, Geneva, Switzerland, 23-25 April 1990, Geneva, CEC, 1990, 108p.

Gill, Sean, D'Costa, Gavin and King, Ursula eds, *Religion in Europe: Contemporary Perspectives*, Kampen, Kok Pharos, 1994, 213p.

Greinacher, Norbert and Mette, Norbert eds, *The New Europe: A Challenge for Christians*, London, SCM Press, 1992, 123p.

Gurney, Robin ed., *CEC at 40: Celebrating the 40th Anniversary of the Conference of European Churches (CEC) 1959-1999*, Geneva, CEC, 1999, 98p.

Gurney, Robin, *The Face of Pain and Hope: Stories of Diakonia in Europe*, WCC, 1995, 70p.

Hume, Basil, *Remaking Europe: The Gospel in a Divided Continent*, London, SPCK, 1994, 107p.

Hurley, Michael, *Christian Unity: An Ecumenical Second Spring?*, Dublin, Veritas, 1998, 420p.

Ionita, Viorel and Numico, Sarah eds, *Charta Oecumenica, a Text, a Process, and a Dream of the Churches in Europe*, WCC, 2003, 113p.

Link-Wieczorek, Ulrike ed., *Polnische Impressionen: Ökumenisch-theologische Fragen im Europa nach der Wende*, Frankfurt am Main, Otto Lembeck, 2000, 222p.

Linn, Gerhard ed., *Hear What the Spirit Says to the Churches: Towards Missionary Congregations in Europe*, WCC, 1994, 139p.

Lodwick, Robert C. ed., *Remembering the Future: The Challenge of the Churches in Europe*, New York, Friendship, 1995, 126p.

Luxmoore, Jonathan and Babiuch, Jolanta, *The Vatican and the Red Flag: The Struggle for the Soul of Eastern Europe*, London, Chapman, 1999, 351p.

MacSpadden, Lucia Ann ed., *Reaching Reconciliation: Churches in the Transitions to Democracy in Eastern Europe and Central Europe*, Uppsala, Life & Peace Institute, 2000, 243p.

Noll, Rüdiger and Vesper, Stefan eds, *Reconciliation: Gift of God and Source of New Life: Documents from the Second European Ecumenical Assembly, 23-29 June 1997, Graz, Austria*, Graz, Styria, 1998, 331p.

Peace with Justice: The Official Documentation of the European Ecumenical Assembly, Basel, Switzerland, 15-21 May, 1989, Geneva, CEC, 1989, 334p.

Ramet, Pedro ed., *Catholicism and Politics in Communist Societies*, Durham NC, Duke Univ. Press, 1990, 454p.

Ramet, Pedro ed., *Eastern Christianity and Politics in the Twentieth Century*, Durham NC, Duke Univ. Press, 1988, 471p.

Ramet, Sabrina Petram ed., *Protestantism and Politics in Eastern Europe and Russia, the Communist and Postcommunist Eras*, Durham NC, Duke Univ. Press, 1992, 441p.

The Reception of BEM in the European Context: Report of the Four Study Consultations on BEM of the Conference of European Churches 1984-1985, Geneva, CEC, 1986, 199p.

The Report of the Conference of European Churches 10th Assembly "God Unites, in Christ a New Creation", 1-11 September 1992, Prague CSFR, Geneva, CEC, 1993, 332p.

Sabev, Todor, *The Orthodox Churches in the World Council of Churches: Towards the Future*, WCC, 1996, 100p.

Steindl, Helmut ed., *Die Kirchen Europas: Ihr ökumenisches Engagement: Die Dokumente der europäischen ökumenischen Begegnungen (1978-1991)*, Köln, J. P. Bachem, 1994, 573p.

Strohm, Theodor ed., *Diakonie in Europa: Ein internationaler und ökumenischer Forschungsaustausch*, Heidelberg, Universitätsverlag C. Winter, 1997, 518p.

Toth, Karoly ed., *Steps Towards Reconciliation: Ecumenical Conference on Christian Faith and Human Enmity, Kecskemét, August 21-27, 1995*, Budapest, Ecumenical Council of Churches in Hungary, 1996, 196p.

Vorster, Hans ed., *Ökumene lohnt sich: Dankesgabe an den Ökumenischen Rat der Kirchen zum 50jährigen Bestehen*, Frankfurt am Main, Otto Lembeck, 1998, 432p.

Witte, John and Bourdeaux, Michael, *Proselytism and Orthodoxy in Russia: The New War for Souls*, Maryknoll NY, Orbis, 1999, 353p.

Weingärtner, Erich ed., "Church Within Socialism: Church and State in East European Socialist Republics", in *IDOC Europe Dossiers*, 2-3, Rome, IDOC International, 1976, 262p.

Zeilstra, Jurjen Albert, *European Unity in Ecumenical Thinking, 1937-1948*, Zoetermeer, Boekencentrum, 1995, 454p.

23
Latin America

Dafne Sabanes Plou

At the Edinburgh world missionary conference in 1910, cooperation between Protestant missions in Latin America was not included on the agenda. The decision not to discuss this issue was taken in light of the fact that German mission societies and the Church of England both viewed Latin America as a territory historically linked to the Roman Catholic Church and held that it would be "anti-Catholic" to speak of Protestant missions on the continent.[1] To avoid a debate that could create obstacles to broad ecumenical cooperation in mission development, the organizers of the Edinburgh conference limited its agenda to the "non-Christian world".[2] However, in 1913 the Committee on Cooperation in Latin America (CCLA) was formed, which would play an important role in Protestant church work for most of the 20th century.

In 1916 the CCLA organized the Panama congress on mission in Latin America, a milestone for Christianity in the region. The leaders of missionary societies working there, however, who were not in agreement with the organizers of Edinburgh, studied Protestant work in each country and saw the need for joint church action and cooperation. The congress emphasized education and the setting up of schools as an important step in strengthening the Protestant presence in South America.

In 1949, the first Latin American evangelical conference (CELA I) took place in Buenos Aires.[3] It was the first initiative of this kind taken by the 18 churches which alone decided on the agenda and the message produced by the conference. Evangelization, the presence of Protestantism in Latin America, and cooperation between different church bodies were among the major themes. It was the first time also that delegates from churches so diverse had come together – Episcopalians, Lutherans, Methodists, Congregationalists and Baptists, Reformed and Presbyterians, Nazarenes and Pentecostals.

• The author is grateful to José Míguez Bonino for his contribution to this chapter.
[1] John A. Mackay, *The Latin American Churches and the Ecumenical Movement*, New York, NCCCUSA, Committee on Cooperation in Latin America, Division of Foreign Missions, 1963 – *Las iglesias latinoamericanas y el movimiento ecuménico*, Comité de Cooperación, New York, 1963, p.11.
[2] Juan Sepúlveda, "Misión y unidad: una historia de encuentros y desencuentros", in *Unidad y misión en América Latina*, Comisión de Teología del CLAI, Quito, Ecuador, 2000.
[3] The majority of Protestant churches in Latin America prefer to be known as evangelical churches, although the use of that word is most often not the same as in, for instance, North American conservative churches. The connotation is similar to the German usage, *evangelisch*, i.e., a church that belongs to and preaches the gospel.

In the early 1960s Latin America was deep in economic, political and social change. The urbanization and industrialization process, which had been growing during the 1950s, increased in the 1960s, bringing with it a rise in urban marginalization; agriculture was not modernized, and there was a growing dependence on foreign capital, not only in industry but increasingly also in the financial and service sectors. In the political arena, social, labour and student movements grew stronger as the socialist revolution took place in Cuba. A conviction that one could defeat the imperialism imposed by foreign powers and governments in Latin America – particularly by the US – awakened an important social movement.

Politically, the blockade of Cuba and a bloody military coup in Brazil, followed by systematic repression of social movements and their leaders, led to a doctrine of "national security" which buttressed the state terrorism that was to characterize Latin American politics throughout the 1970s and part of the 1980s. Meanwhile, economic and political thinking in Latin America was changing substantially. A new theory appeared, that of "dependence", which held that the logic of existing capitalist structures did not allow for development to be accompanied by economic and social integration.[4]

The second Latin American evangelical conference (CELA II), in Lima in 1961, was an important stage in developing dialogue and cooperation in Latin America. It called for a deeper involvement of the churches in the social reality of the continent. It emphasized a common vocation for unity, but ideological differences between and within the churches thwarted the creation of an entity that could embody the desire to foster cooperation. Some voices denounced CELA II as a communist event, which provoked the brief detention of three ecumenical leaders, John A. Mackay, José Míguez Bonino and Tomas Ligget, accused of exerting Marxist influence. Such tensions, arising from differing views of Christian social responsibility, were to continue for a long time, hindering ecumenical cooperation between churches.

Among the church-related movements arising at this time were church and society in Latin America (ISAL – Iglesia y Sociedad en América Latina), which stimulated an innovative dialogue between theology and the social sciences, and the Latin American Protestant commission for Christian education (CELADEC – Comisión Evangélica Latinoamericana de Educación Cristiana), which professed an "evangelical option on behalf of the poor" and a decision to contribute "to the construction of a Latin American church" as "a coherent response to the historical interests of the poor and their liberation in every Latin American situation".[5]

The churches in Latin America were close to the people and thus shared in their fears and hopes. They were already engaged in social action, but the creation of a series of structured ecumenical entities provided the instruments necessary for intellectual theological analysis. All these movements stimulated the internal life of the churches and strengthened their witness in society.

In 1963, representatives of church organizations from Argentina, Brazil, Chile, Mexico, Peru and Uruguay met in Rio de Janeiro and issued the "Corcovado Declaration", calling for the establishment of the provisional evangelical committee on Christian unity in Latin America (UNELAM – Comisión Provisional Pro Unidad Evangélica Latinoameri-

---

4 Emilio Castro, *Amidst Revolution*, Belfast, Christian Journals, 1975, pp.12-25.
5 "Educación es vida, XX aniversario de CELADEC", report of the seventh CELADEC general assembly, where the 20th anniversary of the birth of this movement was celebrated, Lima, Peru, 1982.

cana). UNELAM was founded in Montevideo, Uruguay, in 1964, and held its constitutive assembly in Campinas, Brazil, in 1965. Benjamin Moraes from Brazil was elected president and Emilio Castro from Uruguay was designated part-time general secretary. Its main objective was to stimulate cooperation in the life, mission and witness of the churches throughout Latin America. UNELAM was to fulfill the CELA II mandate of convening a third Latin American evangelical conference.

An important landmark in the development of ecumenical thought with relation to the social commitment of Christians in Latin America was the world conference on Church and Society held in 1966 in Geneva. Forty-two Latin American delegates participated, and UNELAM organized a follow-up consultation on church and society in Sao Paulo, Brazil, in 1967.

A NEW CALL TO ECUMENISM

The third Latin American evangelical conference (CELA III) was held in 1969 in Buenos Aires, with 206 delegates from 23 Latin American countries and 40 denominations. For the first time, observers from the Roman Catholic Church were invited, an indication of the new ecumenical openness introduced by Vatican II and the second general conference of Latin American bishops (CELAM II) in Medellín, Colombia, in 1968. Pentecostal church leaders were also involved for the first time.

The theme of CELA III, "Debtors to the World", was based on Romans 1:14, "I am a debtor both to Greeks and to barbarians, both to the wise and to the foolish." For CELA III analysts, among them the theologian Orlando Costas, this conference made evident the need to define the prophetic mission of the Protestant churches in Latin America, in light both of the social, political and economic changes then taking place, and the new challenge of dialogue with the Roman Catholic Church. In this sense, CELA III represented the emergence of a new theology and a new model of mission in which "the church can find itself only in its service to Jesus Christ in the world", a service which requires "the incarnation of the church in the life and conflicts of society".[6]

However, there were definite divergences between the delegations from the different churches and countries at CELA III. Many churches did not agree with the proposed dialogue with Roman Catholics, as they did not believe in their sincerity. Para-church movements shook the meeting with a fiery document that was extremely critical of the position of the churches regarding the social changes taking place, and that accused them of adopting a conservative socio-political stance that legitimated US imperialism.[7]

However, the Vatican II "Decree on Ecumenism" (*Unitatis Redintegratio*) and subsequent ecumenical directives orienting the Roman Catholic Church towards ecumenism opened the door for dialogue between Catholics and Protestants. First contacts took place between clergy and teaching theologians during Vatican II, but it was not until CELAM II in 1968 that the foundation was laid for ongoing dialogue. The organizers of the bishops conference invited a group of Protestant observers and, according to José Míguez Bonino, a president of the WCC from 1975 to 1983 and an official observer both at Vatican II and Medellín, these observers participated more freely and openly than had been possible at Rome. The bishops often quoted explicitly from Protestant documents,

---

[6] Orlando Costas, *Oaxtepec 1978 – Unidad y misión en América Latina*, San José, CLAI, 1980, p.87.
[7] Dafne Sabanes Plou, *Caminos de unidad*, Quito,CLAI, 1994, p.80.

and certain observers helped to prepare the final statements of the conference, an indication of the depth of spiritual encounter.

The final documents expressly mentioned ecumenism at only three points related to cooperation, social issues and education. Nevertheless, the significance of these points for non-Roman Catholic churches was considerable, given the emphasis on the incarnation of the gospel in the struggles and needs of the people of Latin America.

LIBERATION THEOLOGY AND ANTI-ECUMENICAL REACTION

The philosophical breakthrough that took place in the social sciences in Latin America during the 1960s was of great importance since it was on the basis of the "theory of dependence" that a "theology of liberation" began to appear. The dialogue between the social sciences and theology was manifest in grassroots or base communities *(communidades de base)*, in Catholic and Protestant youth organizations, and in ecumenical para-church movements.

Liberation theology, however, was not the fruit of academic reflection; its origins were rather in the pastoral activity of the churches. Priests and ministers working at grassroots level made a valuable contribution to the formulation of this theology. Initial mimeographed documents were circulated and studied throughout the continent after Vatican II and Medellín. They were used by para-church movements and groups of priests and religious who began to organize themselves in the various countries. The Peruvian Roman Catholic Gustavo Gutiérrez, an adviser to the student movements in his country, as well as Protestants such as Rubem Alves from Brazil and Míguez Bonino from Argentina, studied the possible theological basis for a praxis of social change on the continent. The term "liberation theology" was used for the first time in print in 1971 by Alves and Gutiérrez. The latter took it as the title of his work, *Teología de la Liberación: Perspectivas (A Theology of Liberation: History, Politics and Salvation)*, which was to prove fundamental in the development of this new approach to Christian theology.

Despite all these positive encounters, the Latin American ecumenical movement was forcefully opposed during this period. In the 1950s hundreds of former US missionaries to China were expelled from that country. Many came to Latin America, and their presence strengthened evangelical fundamentalism and its criticisms of progressive trends.

In 1969, Protestant Evangelicals held a first Latin American evangelism congress (CLADE I) in Bogota, Colombia, under the theme "Action in Christ for a Continent in Crisis". According to reports from the 920 participants, the congress was a valuable experience but "many were disillusioned by its social myopia and lack of theological depth". For these participants, CLADE I failed because it "did not give priority to the problems of poverty, oppression and social, economic and political corruption". They also criticized the fact that the congress did not recognize the opportunities offered by the changes taking place in Roman Catholicism.[8] In contrast, the missionary Peter Wagner published *Teología Latinoamericana, ¿radical o evangélica?* (Latin American Theology: Radical or Evangelical?) in which he criticized ecumenical Protestantism. Several younger Evangelicals protested this publication, pointing out that it created divisions among Protestants at a time when there were good opportunities for dialogue and joint work.

---

[8] Dayton Roberts, "El movimiento de cooperación evangélica", in Consejo Latinoamericano de Iglesias (en formación), *Oaxtepec 1978: Unidad y misión en América Latina*, San José, CLAI, 1980, p.60.

THE POLITICAL SCENE OF THE 1970s

The victory of Popular Unity in Chile in 1970 revived the hope of grassroots and social movements that it would still be possible to bring about essential changes in Latin America by democratic means. With the triumph of Salvador Allende in Chile and the emergence of other governments with popular support – in Argentina, Peru, Bolivia and Honduras – hope for social and political change seemed to rest on the democratic participation of the people themselves.

Reaction came swiftly, however. In 1969, Nelson Rockefeller, the governor of New York state and an adviser to President Richard Nixon, issued the celebrated "Rockefeller report" which expressed concern over the nationalist positions adopted by several Latin American governments and the strong determination of the Latin American people to work for social change. The report paid particular attention to the demands of "internal security" in order to safeguard the huge North American interests in the continent. A number of political analysts hold that US secretary of state Henry Kissinger was instrumental in reinforcing the role played by Latin American armed forces during the 1970s. He encouraged a series of military agreements that made them the "police over their own peoples, militarizing their civil and political life and structuring a system of norms outside of the political constitutions, known as national security norms, that were to become the spinal column of the reactionary and monopolistic forces that pushed for the establishment of a new fascism".[9]

In just a few years, those countries where social and grassroots movements had begun to effect significant change suffered repressive military coups – in Uruguay and Chile (1973), El Salvador (1974), Peru and Honduras (1975), and Ecuador and Argentina (1976) – that stifled all hope for change by initiating policies that involved the systematic violation of human rights and the death, disappearance and exile of opponents.

The dominant and powerful groups, whose supremacy was threatened by the social activism of workers and *campesinos*, backed the military regimes and completely ignored violations of human rights. The doctrine of national security encouraged joint actions of repression, such as the "Condor Operation" in the Southern Cone, in which military forces from several countries came together to persecute, imprison and even assassinate political opponents who were refugees or exiled from their own countries.

In 1977, with the arrival of the Carter administration in Washington, the international situation in relation to the military governments in Latin America changed. President Jimmy Carter began with a policy of "planetary humanism", which reflected a foreign policy with a discernable moral dimension, in part to compensate for defeat in Vietnam and the Watergate scandal. American policy on Latin America underwent important changes: a softening in its relations with Cuba, an acceptance of demands made by Panama concerning the canal, and a campaign against the violation of human rights in many Latin American countries ruled by military dictatorships. Actions by the Carter administration reinforced public denunciations of violations in international fora and encouraged the formation of North American and European solidarity groups and organizations dedicated to support Latin American democracy, aid exiles, and save the lives of those who had been kidnapped and detained.

---

[9] Moisés Cherñavsky, *Doctrina de seguridad nacional*, Asamblea Permanente de Derechos Humanos, Buenos Aires, 1983. Cf. also Thomas L. Schubeck, *Liberation Ethics: Sources, Models, and Norms*, Minneapolis MN, Fortress, 1993, pp.106-16.

ECUMENISM BETWEEN THE CHURCHES

CELA III endorsed the first four years of UNELAM's work, and encouraged UNELAM to disseminate the resolutions of CELA II and to hold regional meetings leading towards a fourth CELA event. UNELAM thus moved from being a provisional commission to becoming a stable structure. In 1970, it held its second general assembly and became a regional organization for coordinating ecumenical activities. Studies were promoted on themes relating to ecumenism, the political role of the churches, nonviolent action for social change, theological reflection on mission, the role of women in church and society and relations to the Pentecostal movement. Most ambitiously, UNELAM worked on a distinctively Latin American Christology. It also promoted programmes related to Indigenous matters and the organization of Bible study workshops. It issued two publications: *Servicio Evangélico de Información* (Evangelical Information Service), and *Testimonio Cristiano* (Christian Witness), a magazine on the training of lay people.

In 1972, at a consultation in Asunción, Paraguay, UNELAM together with the WCC's Programme to Combat Racism (PCR) denounced the racial discrimination of the Indigenous Peoples and supported the creation of organizations for defending their rights. In a joint project, PCR and UNELAM formed ecumenical work groups, which included Roman Catholics, to concentrate on specific areas where Indigenous communities were oppressed. UNELAM was also concerned about the situation of Latin American women; in 1975, the International Year of Women, encounters and seminars were organized in different countries for women who were leaders in their churches and regions.

The main strength of UNELAM was that it related closely, in all aspects of its work, to the churches which participated fully in the organization. However, the juridical basis of UNELAM was councils of churches and church federations, which at the time were going through a difficult period of internal readjustment, especially as they were having to face military dictatorships. Many people in the ecumenical movement were persecuted because of their political stands and were forced to go into exile. In addition, reconciling "progressives" and "conservatives" was increasingly difficult. The ideological conflict present throughout South and Central America only aggravated these difficulties.

In 1975, largely at the initiative of UNELAM, a broad consultation involving 144 national church bodies from Latin America and the Caribbean sought to discover the will of the churches in relation to Christian unity. Many felt that UNELAM's work had reached an end and that something new was needed, perhaps the creation of a body representing all the churches in the whole continent. Thus it was that in 1977, at a meeting in Panama with delegates from 85 national church bodies from the entire continent, Central America and the Hispanic Caribbean, the decision was taken to convene a major assembly of churches to consider the creation of a more representative regional ecumenical organization.

UNELAM's call for a continental assembly of churches resulted in the September 1978 Oaxtepec, Mexico, assembly: 194 delegates took part, representing 110 church bodies and ten ecumenical organizations from 19 Latin American and Spanish-speaking Caribbean countries. Twenty-five percent of these delegates represented Pentecostal churches, itself an important ecumenical milestone. This assembly met under the theme "Unity and Mission in Latin America".

The assembly was based on what were called "four foundations": the eucharist, led each day by a different denominational family, which encouraged deeper ecumenical understanding; Bible study based on the epistle to the Ephesians; study and analysis of the

Latin American situation in the church socially, politically, economically and culturally; and personal encounter between delegates.

Assembly delegates agreed to create the Latin American Council of Churches (In Formation), with four main objectives:
– to work for unity within the Protestant family;
– to base this search for unity on a number of basic doctrinal principles;
– to express this unity in concrete witness at all levels of church life;
– to manifest the solidarity of the churches with the people and their hopes.
Bishop Federico Pagura of the Methodist Church in Argentina was elected president and a four-year period for full constitutional formation was set, thus providing an opportunity for other churches and ecumenical groups to affiliate.

Practical ecumenical action was particularly visible at the time of the Nicaragua and Guatemala earthquakes in 1974 and 1976. Relief efforts by the churches and other expressions of international solidarity were pivotal in the rebuilding of devastated areas and in attending to thousands of victims.

PROBLEMS FOR THE ECUMENICAL ORGANIZATIONS

The para-church ecumenical movements, which had often been founded by laity, also underwent significant changes from the mid-1960s, changes which distanced them from the churches and also from their populist roots. The groups became intellectual and exclusive and a virtually automatic connection began to appear between revolutionary political activism and participation in these organizations. Criticism of the "institutional church" intensified and mutually enriching contacts between churches and these movements became minimal.

The notion that evangelism and social action were antagonistic sharpened this separation and isolated the para-church movements. Further, political persecution wreaked havoc among the movements' leadership, since many were imprisoned, some died for their cause, and others chose exile. The result was the creation of a new organization, Latin American ecumenical social action (ASEL – Acción Social Ecuménica Latinoamericana) with headquarters in Mexico.

The understanding that these progressive movements had of the churches changed in light of the churches' actions against dictatorships in the struggle for human rights and in defence of life. So the church was rediscovered and understood as both object and subject of mission, and the strained relations that had existed for a decade began to improve.

In the dynamics of the interdenominational dialogue that took place during this period, the birth of the Latin American theological fellowship (FTL – Fraternidad Teológica Latinoamericana) should also be noted as an important instance of cooperation among young leaders from the more conservative Protestant churches. This organization was founded by pastors and theologians dissatisfied with CLADE I, who felt it was time for an Indigenous leadership to arise among Latin American Evangelicals. It was seen as necessary to curb the strong influence of fundamentalist missionaries who dominated both Protestantism and CLADE I. This leadership asserted that the task of evangelism should not be divorced from social concern or from the massive political changes taking place in the region. The FTL was to concentrate on evangelical theological reflection within the Latin American context, during which it became acutely aware of the changes taking place on the continent.

The FTL was constituted in Cochabamba, Bolivia, in 1970, precisely to promote theological reflection and encourage the publication of Christian literature, including the significant journal *Boletín Teológico*. No official ties were established with any church body; members were individuals and did not officially represent churches. During the 1970s, the FTL sponsored consultations on a variety of themes including social issues. Although its leaders participated in the World Congress on Evangelism in Lausanne in 1974, they distanced themselves from the most conservative and fundamentalist currents present in that congress.

From its very beginning the FTL maintained institutional independence, and its leaders were Protestants representing different trends of thought. Thus, while some of its members participated actively in the Latin American Council of Churches, others were found in other organizations. FTL leaders were critical of the lay para-church movements in light of their avant-garde political positions and their distance from the churches. They felt that the reflection taking place within these organizations had been determined by an ideology based solely on the political, social and economic situation of Latin America. In spite of these objections, however, the FTL recognized their efforts to influence the real situation of the Latin American people. In this sense, the FTL also emphasized the need to do theology in dialogue with concrete reality, in the service of praxis. It saw theology as an instrument of transformation.[10]

In 1972, endorsed by a number of Roman Catholic priests, Protestant pastors and laity committed to liberation theology, the movement Christians for socialism (Cristianos por el Socialismo) was born in Chile, holding its first international event that year with delegates from several Latin American countries. Although independent of the churches, this movement has had an important influence on ecumenical thinking linked to the new theological trend. Subsequently, however, the Roman Catholic Church in Chile condemned this movement and after the coup of 1973 it was ruthlessly repressed by the state.

THE STRUGGLE FOR HUMAN RIGHTS

The military coup in Chile on 11 September 1973 which resulted in political imprisonments, assassinations, torture, disappearances, and the forced exile of resisters prompted the churches to react in defence of human rights. The Roman Catholic Church, alongside Lutheran, Methodist, Pentecostal and Orthodox churches and the Hebrew community of Chile, formed the cooperation committee for peace in Chile. At the same time, the ecumenical national refugee commission was formed.

The cooperation committee's work benefited thousands of victims of political persecution, but due to pressure from the military government it went out of existence on 31 December 1975. The following day, in full accordance with the other churches, the Roman Catholic Church created a vicariate of solidarity. The Protestant churches continued to work through the Christian churches' foundation for social aid (FASIC), formed on 1 April 1975 and representing both the refugee service of the World Council of Churches and the United Nations' High Commissioner for Refugees. The vicariate and FASIC worked closely together with the support of the WCC.

---

[10] René Padilla, "Iglesia y Sociedad en América Latina", in *Fe cristiana y América Latina hoy*, Buenos Aires, Certeza, 1971, pp.119-47.

This collaboration of the WCC in the Latin American struggle for human rights was reinforced by the creation of its Human Rights Resource Office for Latin America, sanctioned by the WCC's fifth assembly at Nairobi in 1975. At the end of that same year, the permanent assembly for human rights was created in Argentina with the participation of political, social and religious leaders. In February 1976, the ecumenical human rights movement was also created in Argentina by six Protestant churches and two Roman Catholic dioceses. The first of these groups worked mainly on denouncing human-rights violations and the second assisted victims of repression, both with WCC support. Protestants and Catholics also worked together in defence of human rights in the church committee of Paraguay, the peace and justice service of Uruguay, and in the Sao Paulo archdiocese in Brazil. In Central America, a WCC human-rights office carried out important work in protesting human-rights violations in Nicaragua, Guatemala, Honduras and El Salvador, as well as in aiding refugees who were fleeing from political persecution and the massacres of resistance leaders and Indigenous communities that were convulsing those countries.

INCREASED ECUMENICAL DIALOGUE

In 1954, the International Missionary Council created a Fund for Theological Education to encourage and develop theological education in missionary areas. A WCC committee visited Latin America to survey existing conditions and needs, and this was followed up by the publication of theological texts, the holding of joint theological seminars, and the creation of resources for training. In 1971 in Buenos Aires the evangelical theological faculty and the evangelical Lutheran faculty joined to become the higher evangelical institute of theological studies (ISEDET – Instituto Superior Evangélico de Estudios Teológicos), involving nine Protestant churches. In Costa Rica, also in 1971, the Latin American biblical seminary (SEBILA) became independent and made significant academic changes to adapt to a Latin American perspective; 19 Protestant churches were to back this entity.

The dialogue between Catholic and Protestant liberation theologians was intense during these years as an international movement of progressive theologians began to take shape. In 1975, the first Latin American theological encounter took place in Mexico, followed by another meeting on "Theology in the Americas", held in Detroit, US. It was at this conference that Latin American theologians first encountered North American black, Chicano and feminist theologians. In 1976 the Ecumenical Association of Third World Theologians (EATWOT) was created, bringing together scholars from Latin America, Africa and Asia in annual meetings.

Several ecumenical and social science-based centres for theological dialogue and reflection were set up in different countries: the department of ecumenical research and the Victor Sanabria centre in Costa Rica; the Bartolomé de las Casas centre in Lima, Peru; the Antonio Valdivieso centre in Managua, Nicaragua; the Gumilla centre in Caracas, Venezuela; and the Montesinos centre and the theological research centre in Mexico. To this list should be added the ecumenical documentation and information centre set up in Brazil the previous decade.

Christian-Marxist dialogue also held an interesting place within the ecumenical debates of this period, in particular that developed by the group *Exodo* in Costa Rica, and that between Christians and Sandinistas in Nicaragua. The latter resulted in a seminar on "Christian Faith and the Sandinista Revolution", organized by the Central American university and the Central American historical institute in Managua in 1979, where Father Amando López, SJ, coordinated sessions that involved the participation of both Sandinista commanders and Christian theologians.[11]

But the main and richest theological debate of the 1970s arose from the preparatory document for the third Latin American bishops conference, in Puebla, Mexico, in 1979. According to historian Enrique Dussel, "this is, perhaps, the most important theological debate that has taken place in the history of Latin American theology" since the one started by Las Casas and Sepúlveda in Spain during the period of colonial domination.[12] Puebla, with newly elected Pope John Paul II in attendance, was the second bishops conference to develop and approve the church's preferential option for the poor and place itself squarely and openly in solidarity with workers and *campesinos* and all Latin Americans who were living under repression. The theology of liberation was fully affirmed by most bishops, as well as ecumenical solidarity. The debates were lively and open and watched closely by the new pope and the Vatican as a section of conservative bishops close to military regimes and those thought to be part of Opus Dei, the growing reactionary movement in the Roman Catholic Church which had originated in Spain, attempted to return to old roles where church and state were close and interdependent. That part of the church played the part of chaplaincy to the established order, following unquestioningly the oppressive regimes.

Of particular concern to the Puebla meeting was the place of Indigenous Peoples throughout the region and especially in Guatemala, Bolivia, Nicaragua and other countries where Indians existed in large numbers and were among the poorest and most exploited of all Latin Americans.

Puebla came at a critical time for Protestant and Catholic churches to work together for justice and peace as a priority of the churches' mission. Once again, Protestant observers were invited and one working group on dialogue for communion and participation dealt specifically with the issue of ecumenism. In the Puebla document concrete references to the practice of ecumenism appear, in several forms: "practical social", "spiritual", "doctrinal", "biblical", "dialogue" and "witness" ecumenism.

Puebla, however, established clear limits for ecumenical dialogue. According to the document, ecumenism should take place at the institutional level and for many bishops this was the only form of ecumenical manifestation allowed. In that perspective, ecumenism emanating from the grassroots was marginalized, ignored and often rejected because it "overstepped" those boundaries.[13]

ECUMENISM FOR JUSTICE AND PEACE IN THE 1980s

The triumph of the Sandinista revolution in Nicaragua in 1979 bolstered hope throughout Latin America for significant social change. The fact that several well-known active Christians had taken part in the struggle against the dictatorship of Anastasio Somoza and subsequently became part of the revolutionary government seemed to open up interesting perspectives for many ecumenical Christians who believed in the need to work for revolutionary transformation in the region.

[11] "Apuntes para el estudio de la realidad nacional", no. 3, extraordinario, 1979, Managua, Año de la Liberación.
[12] Enrique Dussel, *Historia de la teología en América Latina*, San José, DEI, ed. rev., 1985, p.426.
[13] *Caminos de unidad*, p.149.

The dialogue between religious communities and the Sandinistas was backed by the declaration "On Religion" made public by the Sandinista National Liberation Front on 7 October 1980. It indicated that "our experience proves one can be a Christian and at the same time a consistent revolutionary; there is no insurmountable contradiction between these two things".[14] Ominously, however, reaction against this view had already been organized. A group of experts who were to be close to President Ronald Reagan, the "Santa Fe committee" of the Council for Inter-American Security, prepared a document advocating a new policy for inter-American relations. It set the foundation for crucial policies of the Reagan administration.

The document began by affirming that war and not peace is the norm ruling international affairs. It asserted that a third world war was imminent and that Latin America and Southeast Asia were to be the scenes of the confrontation. To meet what the document described as the "Soviet-Cuban aggression" which was affecting Latin America, it was again necessary to impose the doctrine of national security. This would allow the US to protect "the independent nations of Latin America from communist conquest", thus helping "to preserve the Hispanic American culture from being sterilized by international Marxist materialism".[15] The document also held that internal subversion in Latin America was a fact and that the US needed to combat such subversion through its foreign policy, which would involve both suspending the defence of human rights and active opposition to liberation theology.

The 1980s also saw the start of the external debt crisis, which had tremendously negative consequences for the continent. According to reports by the UN Economic Commission for Latin America, the lack of economic growth and investment in public measures that could activate the economy stemmed from the fact that large sums of money were required to cover interest on foreign debt. This forced an additional 71 million people to live below even the minimal poverty level. There was a regression from the economic level of the 1960s, and the 1980s became known as the "lost decade". New Latin American democracies that followed the military dictatorships found themselves tied to the decisions of both international financial powers and the major banks that were external creditors. Some analysts have described these democracies as "controlled" because, even though they were backed by popular vote, they could do little or nothing on behalf of the well-being and development of their people. The pressure of corporations and transnational interests required payment on the debt rather than the satisfaction of social needs. Towards the end of the decade, there were social uprisings in several countries, but there were no substantial changes in the economic policies monitored closely by the International Monetary Fund and the World Bank.

THE BIRTH OF THE LATIN AMERICAN COUNCIL OF CHURCHES

Toward the end of 1979, the second Latin American evangelism congress (CLADE II) was held in Huampani, Peru, under the theme "May Latin America Hear His Voice". The organizers decided that not more than ten percent of the participants should come from outside the continent, a decision not well accepted by some of the Northern missionary

---

[14] Quoted by Enrique Dussel in *Hipótesis para una historia de la teología en América Latina*, "Iglesia Nueva" series, Bogota, Indo-American Press Service, 1986.
[15] In "Final Synthesis" of the Santa Fe Document, cited by Cherñavsky, *Doctrina de seguridad nacional*, p.11.

organizations which found it hard to tolerate such independence. This congress, however, marked an important stage in Protestant reflection since a better understanding of the Latin American context, hermeneutical renewal, and a deeper reflection on Protestant social ethics clearly emerged in the presentations and deliberations.

During the four years between the Oaxtepec meeting of UNELAM and the constituting assembly of the Latin American Council of Churches (CLAI – Consejo Latinoamericano de Iglesias), 1978-82, the board and secretariat of this organization in formation established its presence throughout the continent. CLAI strengthened its ties with those churches that favoured its formation and worked to establish new relations with denominations and churches that had still not decided to join the new ecumenical body. It also maintained dialogue with already existing ecumenical entities and with international ecumenical organizations such as the World Council of Churches. Part of this latter collaboration consisted in organizing the highly significant Faith and Order meeting in 1982 in Lima, with the participation of 150 theologians from around the world.

Most of the different meetings and consultations held during this period issued clear statements expressing CLAI's commitment to the Latin American reality and its firm intention of continuing to promote the search for a united ecumenical witness on the continent. Among CLAI's tasks was the creation of the pastoral ministry of consolation and solidarity, which called churches once more to assume responsibility in the socio-political field, a field of considerable importance. This ministry accompanied and encouraged different groups in the active defence of human rights, contributed to a ministry to affected persons and channelled emergency resources to situations of natural disaster and war. CLAI also promoted prophetic ministry on the part of its member churches and organizations and encouraged a process of theological reflection on the issues involved.

Nevertheless, not everything was easy for this new organization. As pointed out in the board of directors' report to the constituting assembly, it had to avoid the tensions between "those who wanted to reduce us to immobility and those who wanted to push us towards unbridled activism". It also had to forget old disputes that were "sterile and wearisome" and avoid "all false dichotomies between the personal and social dimensions of the gospel, which have caused so much damage in the past".[16]

The constituting assembly of CLAI was held in Huampani, Peru, in November 1982, under the theme "Jesus Christ, a Vocation Committed to the Kingdom". One hundred and forty-one delegates participated, representing 79 churches and six partner organizations. The Pentecostal churches were once more in the majority, with more than 20 percent of the participants. The assembly ratified Bishop Pagura in the presidency and 85 churches and six ecumenical organizations affirmed their membership.

CLAI structured its work around five regional secretariats: Andean, River Plate, Brazil, Middle America and Hispanic Caribbean, and Greater Colombia; and several programmatic secretariats: women, children and family; Indigenous People and blacks; pastoral care, spirituality and human rights; evangelism and worship; and promotion and communication. From its inception the Council followed the principle of not replacing the churches or duplicating their work, but rather encouraging interdenominational actions that faced priority problems. Although there was a programme concern for evangelism in the areas both of pastoral care and spirituality and ministry to Indigenous People and blacks, there was also evangelizing work. In the first case, this happened through

---

[16] "Informe de la Junta Directiva", in CLAI (en formación), *De Oaxtepec a Huampaní*, Lima, CLAI, 1982, pp.11-20.

the sharing of resources and education so that "suffering is assumed in a Christian way, with a political, social and theological understanding of its roots and with formation towards changing what can be changed". In the second, an attempt was made to evangelize by seeking unity based on the community and cultural values of the Indigenous Peoples and their struggle for land.[17] Other CLAI initiatives that took on importance during the organization's early years were the Central American pro-peace programme and a new dialogue with Roman Catholicism.

At CLAI's second general assembly, in Indaiatuba, Brazil, in 1988, the initial activities were viewed positively and the image of the organization continued to gain strength. The theme, "The Church: Towards Hope in Solidarity", called member churches to renewed participation based on their struggles, concerns, needs and daily experiences. Bishop Pagura was re-elected president. On this occasion, the highest percentage of delegates came from Lutheran churches.

Just before the Indaiatuba assembly, a Latin American and Caribbean encounter of ecumenical organizations had taken place in Quito, Ecuador. This marked an important moment of regional ecumenical dialogue since it strengthened the commitment of the ecumenical organizations to a church in solidarity with the poor and the grassroots movements. Representatives from 94 ecumenical groups attended, broadening CLAI's scope of action through their work and support. The encounter became known by the name *Mauricio López*, in memory of the ecumenical leader who "disappeared" in 1977 under the military dictatorship in Argentina.

CONTINUED ACTION FOR HUMAN RIGHTS

The 1980s were characterized by the violence of dictatorships and internal wars, particularly in Central America. The decade began with the assassination on 24 March 1980 of Archbishop Oscar Arnulfo Romero in San Salvador, and the rape and murder of four American religious sisters, and ended with the killing of six Jesuit priests and their two assistants in November 1989, also in San Salvador. Among them was theologian Ignacio Ellacuría, rector of the Central American university, who had participated actively in ecumenical dialogue in the region. There was, during this period, considerable ecumenical assistance to victims of repression and to thousands of refugees who fled from war to a precarious existence in Honduras and Mexico, even as there was an international ecumenical effort to denounce widespread violations of human rights. More than 70,000 lives were lost to right-wing death squads in ten years of internal conflict.

Guatemala, with more than forty years of US-backed military dictatorships as the core of state power, found itself with at least 150,000 dead, 40,000 disappeared, 50,000 widows, 80,000 orphans and more than 60,000 refugees in neighbouring countries, and a million internally displaced persons, the vast majority being Mayan Indians. Resulting from the army's scorched-earth policy, the Guatemalan churches lost many priests, pastors, religious sisters, catechists, health promoters and faithful, the majority of whom were Indigenous.

In view of the growing impunity of Latin American military dictatorships, ecumenical action in defence of human rights grew stronger. Even as violations became more acute in Central America, nations in the southern part of the continent which had lived

---

[17] "Informe de la Junta Directiva del CLAI," in CLAI, *De Huampaní a Indaiatuba, 1982-1988*, Quito, CLAI, 1988, p.20.

under dictatorships – dictatorships worn down by their own peoples and by international opinion – began to take steps towards democracy. The government of Raúl Alfonsín in Argentina was the first to set the foundations for the prosecution of the military for crimes against the civil population when it created a national commission to investigate the "disappearance" of people during dictatorship. Bishops Carlos Gattinoni, Methodist, and Jaime de Nevares, Roman Catholic, both presidents of the permanent assembly for human rights, and Rabbi Marshall Meyer, were all members. Their report, entitled *Never Again (¡Nunca Más!)*, stands in a series of investigations that produced similar documents in Uruguay, Paraguay, Brazil and Chile. They all uncovered the existence of concentration camps, torture, forced abductions of people and thousands of political assassinations. The WCC human-rights office played a significant role by cooperating with churches and ecumenical entities so that the truth about these serious violations would come out.

In Argentina, the investigation provided evidence needed for the 1985 trials against the military juntas. The ecumenical human-rights movement and the permanent assembly for human rights also helped in the investigations. The WCC human-rights office increased its support for the Mothers and Grandmothers of the Plaza de Mayo in their search for the nearly five hundred children who had disappeared with their parents during the period of dictatorship. In Uruguay, it was with the peace and justice service, under the coordination of the Jesuit Luis Pérez Aguirre, that such ecumenical collaboration took place. In Brazil, the archdiocese of Sao Paulo, under Cardinal Paulo Evaristo Arns, carried out a detailed investigation with ecumenical assistance coordinated by Presbyterian minister Jaime Wright. This investigation consisted in secretly microfilming military files that proved that the systematic torture of political prisoners had been an essential part of the Brazilian military justice system. In Paraguay, a church committee made a detailed investigation of human-rights violations during the thirty years of the dictatorship of Alfredo Stroessner, and in Chile, once democracy had been achieved in 1990, a truth and reconciliation commission carried out its own investigation, with support from human-rights organizations and the Christian Churches' Foundation for Social Aid.

In 1988, the WCC human-rights office and the CLAI pastoral ministry for consolation and solidarity organized an inter-regional encounter on "Human Rights in Asia and Latin America", with delegates from Chile, Argentina, El Salvador, Taiwan, South Korea and the Philippines. This experience reaffirmed the importance of establishing closer South-South ecumenical ties in order to develop common strategies for work in the area of human rights.

Actions of solidarity on the part of the churches and ecumenical organizations were important during the Mexico City and El Salvador earthquakes of 1985 and 1986. Thousands of victims received emergency assistance and also benefited from resettlement programmes.

STRIVING FOR PEACE IN CENTRAL AMERICA

By reading the public documents, declarations and official letters sent by CLAI leaders throughout the decade of the 1980s,[18] one can follow in detail the ecumenical work for

---

[18] Found in *Comprometidos con el Reino (2)*, Quito, CLAI, 1988.

peace in Central America. CLAI created a pro-peace programme and cooperated with other ecumenical bodies: the Caribbean Conference of Churches, the WCC through its Human Rights Resources Office for Latin America, and the National Council of the Churches of Christ in the USA. These ecumenical bodies supported the Contadora group and the efforts of the Esquipulas summit in 1987, where an historic peace accord was signed between the presidents of five Central American countries (Costa Rica, Nicaragua, Guatemala, Honduras and El Salvador).

This programme in Central America effectively mobilized many human, spiritual, economic and diplomatic resources, showing the importance of ecumenism in international relations, both between nations and between churches and other Christian organizations. In 1987, after the signing of the Esquipulas II agreement, a delegation from the ecumenical organizations visited the five Central American countries, meeting with the presidents and visiting national reconciliation commissions and church authorities.

On Easter Sunday 1988 in Nicaragua, a representative group of Christians from Central America addressed a document to the churches and to the world at large, "Kairos Centroamericano". The document pointed out that the region had been experiencing "an opportunity of grace, a decisive hour, a particularly active time within the area of the history of salvation". This declaration was inspired by the 1985 Kairos document of South African church leaders and had as its immediate context the peace process initiated by the Esquipulas II agreement. Sixty delegates from ecumenical churches, groups and organizations in the region signed the document which uses analysis based on liberation theology and the base communities. It was aimed at Christians in Central America and the US in the conviction that these were the people most directly involved in the conflicts in the region. According to many scholars, these Kairos documents were a new theological genre characterized by a contextual theology; they were drawn up collectively, and were confessional and prophetic in nature, the result of extensive ecumenical interchange.

Earlier, ecumenical work for peace had also played a role during the 1982 Malvinas-Falkland Islands war between Argentina and Great Britain. As soon as the war started, the British Council of Churches invited representatives from Argentine Protestant churches to a meeting in the United Kingdom. Because of the hostilities and the cancellation of flights between both countries, only José Míguez Bonino, who happened to be teaching in Brazil at the time, was able to attend. It was nevertheless an important occasion for dialogue and mutual understanding. When the war ended, the British Council of Churches organized a visit of Argentine church leaders to Great Britain. The delegation was sent by a consultative council formed of churches affiliated with ISEDET, the ecumenical theological seminary in Buenos Aires. During this visit, Argentine delegates had the opportunity to talk with leaders of British churches and to visit local parishes and other church organizations in order to communicate their churches' position on the war and their commitment to peace and friendship between the Argentine and British people.

ROMAN CATHOLIC CRITICISM OF LIBERATION THEOLOGY

In 1980, CELAM, the Latin American bishops conference, organized a seminar for Central American bishops. This marked the beginning of sharp criticism of liberation theology by the Roman Catholic hierarchy. A first indication of rejection of this theology by some bishops had already occurred in 1974 at a seminar in Bogota, where the secretariat of CELAM was located. This seminar, meeting under the theme "Liberation: Dialogue in CELAM", did not initially seem to have major repercussions. However, it was in 1980 that the Santa Fe document was published, in which the conservative think-tank known as the Council for Inter-American Security pointed to the danger of Marxist ideology which it saw in liberation theology. Rejection of a dialogue between Christians and Marxists was also made clear in the highly critical visit made by John Paul II to Nicaragua in 1983 where he publicly chastised several activist proponents of liberation theology, both clergy and lay.

In 1984 the Vatican issued two instructions. The first, "Instruction on Liberation Theology", seriously criticized the movement. The document generated an important theological debate both in Latin America and the US and Europe. By then, the Ecumenical Association of Third World Theologians (EATWOT) had encouraged the development of forms of liberation theology throughout the Christian world. The Vatican's questioning specifically touched Brazilian theologian Leonardo Boff. Boff's book *The Church: Charisma or Power* questioned the Roman church's exercise of "earthly power" in contrast to its calling to be a prophetic church committed to the poor and to building the kingdom through service and in the midst of poverty.[19]

Later in the year, the Vatican Congregation for the Doctrine of the Faith published another document, "Instructions on Some Aspects of Liberation Theology". This created an even larger theological controversy than that caused by the preparatory papers for the Puebla conference in the 1970s. Leonardo Boff was silenced by the Vatican for a full year. The work of liberation theologians, however, continued with force, particularly in Central America where the centre of much Latin American ecumenical thinking had moved. The dimensions of this work were expanded by reflection on the meaning of martyrdom, since there were many priests, pastors, catechists and faithful Christians – Catholics and Protestants – in Central America who were being persecuted and murdered for their loyalty to the gospel.

DIALOGUE AND THE "PEOPLE'S CHURCH"

Although the controversy over liberation theology placed the conference of Latin American bishops at a distance from the organized ecumenical movement, dialogue and joint work continued at the level of several dioceses and of CLAI, as well as at the parish level, particularly in the ecumenical base communities and within the movement of the so-called "people's church" *(iglesia popular)*, grassroot groups that took a radical prophetic line in relation both to society and to the church.

In 1986, the first consultation of Latin American and Caribbean bishops and pastors was held in Cuenca, Ecuador, sponsored by the conference of Ecuadorian bishops, CLAI and the Caribbean Conference of Churches. The theme was "Contemporary Religious Movements: A Challenge to the Churches". This event was an important landmark in ecumenical dialogue within the region since, as stated in the final document, it called Roman Catholics and Protestants to decide on "an attitude of ecumenical dialogue not only among ourselves, but also with the leaders and other members of religious movements", and also to "face the challenge posed by contemporary religious movements, maintaining our own faith in a better way in order to help our people to recover the truth

---

[19] *Historia de la Teología en América Latina*, p.67.

of the gospel". In addition, it agreed to promote ecumenism beyond mere dialogue, living in liberating solidarity with the poor so that ecumenical initiatives might arise from authentic encounters at the grassroots.[20]

Christian participation in grassroots movements developed into what some theologians considered to be a new ecclesiology based on the so-called "people's church". The popular church was seen as the one convened by the poor as they received the word of God and evangelized.[21] This movement was evident mainly in Central America and Brazil, where the largest growth both of base communities and of other Christian communities committed to the worker and *campesino* movements took place. The hierarchy of the Roman Catholic Church split over these developments. Some bishops saw them as responses to the Puebla document in which the base communities had been pointed to as "hubs of evangelism", "motors of liberation" and "a source of ministries". More conservative bishops considered them to be an alternate location of power that had to be opposed.

In the 1980s, several ecumenical enterprises became more active, including the movement of biblical scholars and theologians and the programmes of several centres for theological study and reflection. The ecumenical research centre also continued to carry out important work through its offices in Sao Paulo and Rio de Janeiro. This centre had been founded in the 1960s and had been instrumental in bringing together important Portuguese- and Spanish-speaking scholars and leaders, both Roman Catholic and Protestant. In 1982, the ecumenical centre for evangelization and education of the people was founded in Sao Paulo and became an important regional training centre for ecumenical and grassroots leaders. Also during this decade, the movement arose in both Protestant and Roman Catholic circles of women theologians and biblical scholars who carried out their study and reflection from clearly feminist perspectives. Many of these persons became members of the Ecumenical Association of Third World Theologians.

THE SOCIO-POLITICAL SITUATION AT THE END OF THE 1980s

Towards the end of 1988 the committee that in 1980 had published the Santa Fe document released another statement known as Santa Fe II. In it they underscored the emphases made previously and also pointed out new problems facing US relations with Latin America. Additionally, the statement indicated possible ways for strengthening US interests south of the Rio Grande.

The authors of Santa Fe II were mainly concerned about the displacement of millions of persons due to "Marxist violence, poverty, bad governmental administration and the increase in general of anarchy and corruption in Latin America". Clearly the US at that moment was concerned about a possible "export" of the Nicaraguan revolution to other countries, and about the drug trade, particularly from Colombia to North America. The document also pointed to the trend of the new Latin American democracies towards statism, emphasizing the need for the US to participate actively in developing national private capital markets and a free enterprise system in order to speed the dismantling of public enterprises and thus the privatization of all public property.

Santa Fe II showed concern about the "subversive-terrorist threat" perceived in Nicaragua. It supported "a sophisticated development of the doctrine of low intensity

---

[20] *Cuenca Declaration*, §41.
[21] Pablo Richard, *La Iglesia Latinoamericana entre el temor y la esperanza*, San José, DEI, 1980.

conflict" which had been supported by military aid to counter-revolutionary forces – the Contras – based in Honduras. Although, according to the analysis, the Contras had lost power and prestige, President Daniel Ortega's Sandinista government had to participate in so many peace negotiations that it lost political power. In addition, the constant threat of an escalation of the war and the increasing poverty of the Nicaraguan people made it difficult in the democratic elections of 1990 for the Sandinistas to win against the conservative coalition parties.

Just days before Christmas 1989, US troops invaded Panama as part of its "fight against drugs" and apprehended General Manuel Noriega, the head of state. In this invasion, B-52 planes indiscriminately bombed poor areas, killing an unknown number of civilians. It was clear that the recommendations of Santa Fe II were being implemented; they were to influence the political, social and economic life of Latin America during the next several years.

In the economic sphere, the external debt crisis remained critical; there were no possibilities for an early solution to the problem. The fall of authoritarian socialist governments in Eastern Europe strengthened capitalism and the view that the "free market" was the only option for third-world countries. In Latin America at the beginning of the 1990s, there were already 183 million people living in poverty, and a third of them, 88 million, had reached "extreme poverty". Meanwhile, the structural adjustments required by international financial institutions prevented governments from investing in a better quality of life for the people. The deterioration of health, education and security systems, the lack of investment in infrastructure and consequent widespread unemployment was evident throughout the continent. In accordance with free-market principles, economies were unregulated, causing the destruction of many local industries and trade. Latin American countries entered the 1990s with the obligation of paying billions of dollars in interest on a foreign debt which itself amounted to one and a half billion dollars.[22]

FIVE HUNDRED YEARS OF EUROPEAN PRESENCE

A significant task for Latin American ecumenism at the beginning of the 1990s was the commemoration of five hundred years of European presence in the Americas. It was important to take fully into account the integrity of the first inhabitants, avoid triumphant talk about an "encounter of cultures", and admit openly and confessionally the oppression and genocide caused by Christopher Columbus's "discovery" of 1492.

CLAI began with a consciousness-raising process following its 1988 assembly in Indaiatuba. The assembly's final message pointed out that "we are more and more aware of the immeasurable crimes committed in our continent by white (and Christian) people against other races. Countless millions of Indigenous have been killed throughout history, since the arrival of Columbus in these lands... Like the blood of Abel, the voice of the blood spilled by these throngs clamours from earth to God."[23]

Following the assembly, CLAI initiated a "five-hundred year programme" which led to a continental encounter on "Martyrdom and Hope" in Cochabamba, Bolivia, in 1992, just before the UN International Year of the World's Indigenous People in 1993. This encounter was a rich experience for Latin American ecumenism, because it not only expressed solidarity with the Indigenous Peoples, but also acknowledged five hundred

[22] José Maria Vigil ed., *Sobre la opción por los pobres*, Managua, Ed. Nicarao, 1991.
[23] *Mensaje a los Pueblos*, 2.b, II asamblea general del CLAI, Indaiatuba, 1988.

years of martryrdom and resistance by Indigenous Peoples in their own lands against the various processes of colonization and evangelization carried out by Europe. Cochabamba encouraged heightened awareness and education in the churches and in society. The churches rejected the marginalization and discrimination that affected – and still affects – the life of Indigenous communities. The Indigenous Peoples initiated the process, opening up a dialogue between the descendants of the conquerors, the native communities, and the black communities that came to Latin America through the slave traffic from Africa. The meeting formally expressed its support of Rigoberta Menchu, a Mayan woman from Guatemala, for the Nobel Peace Prize and made clear its solidarity with the demands of her people, the Kachiquel Quiche Indigenous People of Guatemala.

As well as affirming the rights of the Indigenous Peoples and the ecumenical commitment to support their struggle, CLAI made specific references to the major role played by native and black women in the life of their peoples. The meeting also set up a series of programmes addressing different situations and needs in aboriginal and black peoples communities and worked to combat racism and discrimination in society. Both the WCC and international ecumenical solidarity movements were present and witnessed the commitments and challenges raised for the ecumenical movement in Latin America.

An "Assembly of the People of God", held in Quito in 1992, brought together hundreds of delegates, Protestant clergy and Roman Catholic priests, laity from progressive hierarchies, base communities and the Indigenous and black movements. The assembly proposed new ways to overcome racism on the basis of broad and intercultural ecumenical dialogue.

CATHOLIC-PROTESTANT RELATIONSHIPS

In 1990 and 1993, the ecumenical organizations responsible for the Cuenca meeting in 1986 arranged two encounters between Protestant and Roman Catholic leaders. The 1990 event took place in Kingston, Jamaica, under the theme "Foreign Debt and the Drug Trade"; the second was in Nova Iguaçu, Rio de Janeiro, Brazil, on "Democracy in Crisis and the New World Order". On both occasions it was the Santa Fe II document which identified the issues: the growth of the drug trade, social violence and exploitation rooted in the external debt crisis, and the imposition of neo-liberal economic systems that limited the consolidation of democracy in the region.

In 1992, the fourth conference of Latin American bishops was held in Santo Domingo, Dominican Republic, again with John Paul II in attendance. Although it had been intended that the conference would celebrate five hundred years of evangelization in the Americas, this was rendered impossible by a strong movement against any form of celebration of the European presence in the Americas. Rather, the bishops requested, on behalf of the Roman Catholic Church, forgiveness from both the Indigenous People and people of African origin for the abuses committed during the conquest and subsequent years.

There was no active ecumenical participation at Santo Domingo, as there had been at Medellín and Puebla in 1968 and 1979. The Vatican was primarily interested in consolidating its hegemony over the Latin American bishops, and the conference was largely marked by internal struggle between the papal representatives and the Latin American bishops.

The attitude expressed at Santo Domingo led CLAI not to invite Catholic observers to its own third general assembly in 1995, in the belief that it was time for the Protestant churches to set their own priorities for dialogue with Roman Catholicism. In an analysis of this situation presented to the CLAI assembly, Argentinian Methodist theologian José Míguez Bonino stated that "the Roman Catholic Church sees itself, at the end of the century, as the spiritual and ethical force that defines a new civilization. It accepts the dominant economic model, complementing it with a social doctrine that tries to humanize it and moralize it." Even though he was clear that not all Catholics accepted this fundamentally conservative position, Míguez Bonino had no hesitation in affirming that "this will be the dominant framework for Roman Catholicism in the near future". He was of the opinion that the changes experienced within Latin American Catholicism between Medellín and Santo Domingo showed that the concern for the political and economic situation had been supplanted by a concern for culture, which presupposed an identification of Latin American with Roman Catholic culture. For Míguez Bonino, this created serious difficulties for issues such as religious freedom – hegemonic Roman Catholicism impeding significant advances in religious equality. Moreover, ecumenical dialogue would appear to be limited since the Roman Catholic Church referred to new evangelical independent churches throughout the continent as "sects".

In spite of these insights, Latin American Protestant leaders were perhaps not prepared for the declaration of the Vatican's Congregation for the Doctrine of the Faith in the year 2000, "*Dominus Iesus:* On the Unicity and Salvific Universality of Jesus Christ and the Church". Walter Altmann, the Brazilian Lutheran theologian then president of CLAI, regretted that 35 years of ecumenical history was being ignored, and emphasized that "ecumenism is still vitally important because it responds not to a passing state of affairs but to fundamental biblical convictions". Altmann reaffirmed CLAI's "commitment to the search for unity, to persevere in an open and sincere dialogue among the Protestant churches and between them and the Catholic church, with the assurance that faith in Jesus Christ as our Lord and Saviour unites us more than the divisions we still suffer".[24]

EVANGELICAL, PENTECOSTAL AND NEO-PENTECOSTAL GROWTH

Ever since their creation at the beginning of the 20th century, the Pentecostal churches in Latin America have been linked and committed to union in mission; thus, their involvement with the ecumenical movement has been seen from that perspective. Many are involved with CLAI and form an important sector of its membership. Some Pentecostal churches are also members of the WCC, and their theology and spirituality have contributed in a very special way to the life of the ecumenical movement. At the same time, the Pentecostal movement in Latin America has different manifestations and its churches have different origins. Consequently there are a considerable number which are not involved in ecumenical activities and others that are quite opposed to them. However, in all cases these churches have experienced continual growth. This has entailed consistently "new faces" of the church and new forms of relationships in society, in political, social and cultural areas.

---

[24] *Declaración del Consejo Latinoamericano de Iglesias "Dominus Iesus"*, Sept. 2000.

In 1998 the Latin American meeting at Buenos Aires prior to the eighth assembly of the WCC observed that

> the main churches in terms of initiative, commitment, missionary expansion and public presence are no longer those that gave rise to the WCC but rather the so-called churches of the poor in their multiplicity of manifestations. This form of church is oriented towards a "spiritual" and sometimes charismatic church which, although professing to reject the world, is a profoundly 'corporal' church that generates health, life and joy amidst death.

It would be fair and more precise not to associate the term "neo-Pentecostals" with the Pentecostal movement; perhaps "New Religious Movements" would be more correct. Secondly, there are marked theological differences, even though in matters of ritual there might be common points of emphasis. These New Religious Movements construct their message from a theological perspective that assures converts their lives will improve radically on the material level. This approach has been called the "theology of prosperity".

The final document of the Latin American pre-assembly meeting stated,

> The excluding and mercantilist system that predominates demands the prophetic voice and courageous witness of our churches. This requires new reflection that will lead the churches to act ethically in the public sphere. We are committed to witness against the current idolatrous system... In the midst of violence, fragmentation and despair on the one hand, and generosity, hope and the search for what is new on the other, we are called jointly to build a culture of peace and solidarity.

The growth of Pentecostal and other charismatic churches in the 1990s caused the Roman Catholic Church to become even less involved in ecumenical activities since it perceived that its numerical majority and overall influence were being challenged. Mainline churches did not experience a growth in membership, but they witnessed the establishment of many new independent evangelical churches, the result of the work of local charismatic leaders or of American missionaries. Initially, there was little contact between them, but dialogue began in a number of local councils where ministers from different denominations met regularly to pray and study together, to share concerns, and to engage in joint actions like the "March for Jesus" that takes place annually in different countries. These councils also initiated a desire for legislation granting equality for all religions. In countries like Argentina and Chile, mainline, Pentecostal and evangelical churches formed associations to work on this issue.

The World Council of Churches in collaboration with CLAI sponsored a consultation with evangelical free churches in Quito, Ecuador, in 1993 and another with Pentecostal churches in Lima in 1994, thus opening up a new form of dialogue with churches that are not members of the WCC but have a strong presence in Latin America. Two Pentecostal churches joined the WCC in 1961, and they now represent 20 percent of the membership of CLAI. Ecumenical dialogue with these churches is an element in the process of relating to Pentecostalism both as an important expression of popular Protestant religious life and as a movement that is posing new ecclesiological, theological and pastoral challenges for ecumenism.

The theological level and depth achieved in the dialogue between Latin American Protestants was reflected at the third Latin American evangelism congress (CLADE III), held in Quito in 1992 and organized by the Latin American theological fellowship (FTL). A total of 1080 persons from the entire region reflected on the theme "The Whole Gospel for All the Peoples from Latin America". They emphasized that evangelization can be separated neither from social responsibility nor from the historical processes taking place. It was also recognized that the theological work carried out by the FTL is a service to the churches instead of simply a dialogue with the academic world. As in the two previous CLADE events, the task of evangelization continued to be centred on witness, celebration and reflection.

DEVELOPMENTS IN THE 1990s

When CLAI held its third general assembly in 1995 at Concepción, Chile, its theme was "Reborn to Living Hope", a theme which recognized important elements in the changes taking place in Latin American Protestantism – the growth of Pentecostal churches and the charismatic movement, and a deep commitment to the marginalized sectors of society. "Unity has necessarily to be celebrated as a concomitant expression of diversity, offering Jesus Christ as its witness, who summons the church, sustains it and sends it out to the world," the assembly's final declaration stated. This meeting reaffirmed the work carried out in the areas of ecumenism, evangelization and the struggle for peace.

In 2000, the fourth Latin American evangelism conference (CLADE IV) took place at Quito, 1300 people coming together under the theme "Evangelical Witness towards the Third Millennium: Word, Spirit and Mission". It was organized jointly by the FTL and CLAI.

A significant contribution to ecumenical work during the 1990s was the creation of a "liturgy network" by CLAI to enliven worship life in churches in the region. Launched in 1991 and coordinated by Ernesto Barros Cardoso, a Brazilian Methodist, the network brought about a wide renewal of worship through new musical and liturgical resources, and an important exchange between the churches that both strengthened the identity of Latin American worship and opened new spaces for appreciating the diversity of its cultural and musical expressions.

A comparable recent development in several countries – albeit in another area – has been the establishment of Christian political movements and even evangelical political parties marked by direct participation of clergy and lay people. Confronted with this situation, the WCC has – with the main leaders of the evangelical churches in Latin America – encouraged a process of study, reflection and publication on the level of participation of churches and official Christian groups in political life. The growth of the Protestant movements in Latin America made this reflection process an absolute priority for the present missionary situation of those churches.

In the second half of the 1990s, two strong social movements – linked to the issues of social exclusion and the external debt crisis – were born. The first, "Cry of the Excluded", arose in Brazil in 1995 as an answer to the growing exclusion of countless people due to the neo-liberal structural adjustments imposed by international financial institutions. Millions of people took part in annual demonstrations for "bread, work and life" sponsored by this movement. Four Latin American personalities associated with the movement spoke to the general assembly of the United Nations in 2000: Bishop Federico Pagura, a Methodist from Argentina and a WCC co-president; Rigoberta Menchu and Adolfo Perez Esquivel, Nobel Peace Prize laureates; and Frei Betto, a well-known Brazilian Catholic theologian. They denounced the suffering of thousands, presenting alternative solutions to overcoming the situation of exclusion that abuses many people and deprives them of dignity and well-being.

In 1999 leaders from social movements and Protestant and Roman Catholic churches signed the Declaration of Tegucigalpa (Honduras) in which the external debt oppressing third-world countries was denounced as immoral and its abolition was demanded. This declaration initiated the Latin American Jubilee 2000 movement, linked to the global movement of the same name. In 1998 and 2000, a "tribunal on the external debt", condemning the payment of the debt as unethical, illegal and politically unjust and indefensible, was convened. In Brazil, the tribunal's organizers included the national conference of bishops, Caritas, the National Council of Christian Churches (CONIC), the ecumenical coordination of services and the landless movement; in Argentina, representatives of social movements participated together with Catholic and Protestant bishops, presidents of evangelical churches, many priests and religious, ecumenical organizations and the CLAI regional secretariat.

CONTINUATION OF WORK FOR PEACE

The ecumenical commitment to peace in Latin America concentrated during the 1990s on Guatemala where war had dragged on for over thirty years, and Peru where the extremist Marxist guerrilla group Shining Path wreaked havoc among the civilian population. Peace endeavours also continued in El Salvador where churches actively defended human rights, helping to bring about the signing of peace treaties in 1992.

In Guatemala several ecumenical organizations – CLAI, the WCC, the National Council of the Churches of Christ in the United States, the Lutheran World Federation – joined forces to bring representatives from the military, the national revolutionary unity movement and civil society together at the same table to prepare peace accords. Roman Catholic and Protestant churches were also involved. In November 1993 the first peace encounter took place in Washington DC, followed by a second meeting in Guatemala in April 1994 and a third in Oslo in September of that same year. The statements released at the end of these meetings confirmed the advances achieved and the commitment of the churches to build peace in that country.

Early in the 1990s, the WCC, through its Human Rights Resources Office for Latin America, sponsored two visits to Peru where the rebellion of Shining Path and the war against it was costing thousands of lives and where human rights were regularly violated. On both occasions, human-rights abuses committed by the Peruvian state as well as by the rebel forces were considered. Local peace and human-rights organizations together with the evangelical council of Peru collaborated in both efforts.

Mandated by its 1995 general assembly in Concepción, CLAI launched a peace programme. This "peace plan", started in three countries divided by long-standing internal conflicts – Guatemala, Colombia and Peru – was actively to involve churches in each country's peace processes. The plan also encouraged evangelical leadership to develop training programmes on issues such as education for peace and human rights, administration of justice, peace mediation and pastoral actions for peace. It also advocated church involvement in social movements for peace. In Colombia, a fellowship of Christians for reconciliation and peace was formed, an organization representing evangelical and Protestant churches which became a qualified actor in the peace process.[25]

NEW THEOLOGICAL EMPHASES

The Vatican attack on liberation theology, embodied in the silencing of Leonardo Boff, eventually led to the suspension of his priesthood. Nevertheless, the Brazilian theologian

---

[25] CLAI, *Forjadores de Paz*, Informe del Plan de Paz 1997-1999, Quito, 1999.

continued to produce new reflections – using the methodology of liberation theology – on themes such as social democracy and Christian responsibility towards creation.

The work of a considerable number of ecumenical seminaries and theological institutes was strengthened in the 1990s. In 1988, the third CLAI general assembly approved the creation – with the support of the WCC, the National Council of Churches (USA) and the Evangelisches Missionswerk of Germany – of the Latin American Community for Theological Education (CETELA) which brought together several entities. The first president, the American Eugene Stockwell, promoted its first Latin American consultation in 1991, with the support of the WCC programme for theological education. CETELA thus became a key referent for the development of Latin American theological reflection. It based its work on the Latin American identity and heritage, holding that theology is not an end in itself but rather a service to God's mission to the world through the church. In regular theological encounters, CETELA supported education open to cultural pluralism and interdisciplinary work involving anthropology, sociology, economics, gender theory and other sciences. Emphasis was also on the relation between theology and pedagogy as a means of renewing theological education in the region.

The five hundredth anniversary of the European conquest of the Americas prompted significant theological reflection, particularly with regard to the issues of repentance and forgiveness as seen from an Indigenous perspective. The 1990s also saw increasing work by women theologians and biblical scholars, as well as efforts in Indigenous ministries and those based on the African American culture. In all these areas denominationalism has been overcome, and ecumenical work has strengthened in such groups and initiatives as the association of theological schools, the theological reflection encouraged by CLAI and the FTL, the Ecumenical Association of Third World Theologians and many others.

With regard to new areas of reflection, the ecumenical research department in Costa Rica together with CETELA have made important contributions to the study of such issues as spirituality, Pentecostalism, anthropology and culture, gender issues, neo-liberalism and exclusion. The meeting held by CETELA in 1995 in Colombia on "Abya-Yala Theology at the Turn of the 21st Century" (Abya-Yala is a Panamanian Indian expression used – instead of European expressions such as "in Latin America" or "Ibero-America" – to refer to the continent and emphasize the theological reflection of the traditional inhabitants of Latin America) included persons who have traditionally been excluded from theological work.[26] In 1997, at the fifth theological encounter, CETELA and EATWOT reached important agreement on coordinating their work.

Participants in the Panama congress of 1916 may well have thought that their ecumenical cooperation would initiate a process for Latin American unity in Christian witness capable of influencing churches and society. They could never have dreamed of the tremendous process of renewal that would take place within the Roman Catholic Church and the ecumenical openness of that church as well as of many evangelical churches. Neither could they have dreamed of the astounding numerical growth in non-Catholic Latin American churches. The process which began in Panama remains ongoing, enriched by the contribution of people, movements and churches that hold an ecumenical vision integral to the Latin American identity with its cultural and racial diversity. All who hold that vision are led by faith and ready to commit themselves daily in situations

---

[26] A selection of papers from this meeting were published in the book *Por una sociedad donde quepan todos* (For a society where everyone fits in).

of adversity that mark the life of their people. They struggle for new social relations based on justice, equity and solidarity. They give witness to the gift of God's liberating love, the love that calls churches to give way to the Holy Spirit so that the Spirit's unifying power may bring a new time for the reign of God in Latin America.

BIBLIOGRAPHY

Alvarez, Carmelo E., *Celebremos la fiesta: una liturgia desde América latina*, San José, DEI, 1986, 100p.

Araya, Victorio, *El Dios de los pobres: el misterio de Dios en la teología de la liberación*, San José, DEI, 1983, 244p.

Bastian, Jean-Pierre, *La historia del protestantismo en América Latina*, Mexico, CUPSA, 1990, 307p.

Brysson, Maryse, *America Latina: Resistir por la Vida*, Santiago, Rede de Centros y Organismos ecuménicos de Latinoamérica y el Caribe, 1993, 173p.

Buss, Théodore, *El movimiento ecuménico en la perspectiva de la liberación*, Quito, CLAI, 1996, 327p.

Castro, Emilio, *Amidst Revolution*, Belfast, Christian Journals, 1975, 111p.

Celebrando la esperanza: Documentos de la segunda asamblea general del Consejo Latinoamericano de Iglesias, Indaiatuba, Sao Paulo, Brasil, 28 de octubre al 2 de noviembre de 1988, Quito, CLAI, 1989, 274p.

Cook, Guillermo ed., *Crosscurrents in Indigenous Spirituality: Interface of Maya, Catholic and Protestant Worldviews*, Leiden, E. J. Brill, 1997, 329p.

Costas, Orlando E., *Theology of the Crossroads in Contemporary Latin America*, Amsterdam, Rodopi, 1976, 32p.

Dussel, Enrique D. ed., *The Church in Latin America 1492-1992*, London, Burns & Oates, 1992, 501p.

Eagleson, John and Scharper, Philip eds, *Puebla and Beyond, Documentation and Commentary*, Maryknoll NY, Orbis, 1979, 370p.

Hennelly, Alfred T. ed., *Santo Domingo and Beyond: Documents and Commentaries from the 4th General Conference of Latin American Bishops*, Maryknoll NY, Orbis, 1993, 242p.

Irarrazaval, Diego, *Inculturation, New Dawn of the Church in Latin America*, Maryknoll NY, Orbis, 1999, 134p.

Una lectura de Puebla, Lima, CELADEC, 1980, 102p.

Medellín, Reflexiones en el CELAM, Madrid, Biblioteca de Autores Cristianos, 1977, 525 p.

Memoria Clai 1990, Quito, CLAI, 1991, 54p.

Meyer, Gérson ed., *Cosecha de esperanza: iglesia, hacia una esperanza solidaria*, Quito, CLAI, 1988, 2 vols.

Míguez Bonino, José, Dias, Zwinglio M. et al., *Puebla y Oaxtepec: una critica protestante y catolica*, Mexico, CUPSA, 1980, 133p.

Oaxtepec 1978: unidad y misión en América Latina, San José, CLAI, 1980, 228p.

Oshige, Fernando ed., *Por eso es que tenemos esperanza: homenaje al Obispo Federico J. Pagura*, Quito, CLAI, 1995, 150p.

Quintero, Manuel ed., *Renaciendo para una esperanza viva: cronica de la tercera asamblea general del CLAI, Concepción, Chile, 25 Enero al 1 Febrero de 1995*, Quito, CLAI, 1995, 184p.

Richard, Pablo, *La Iglesia latinoamericana entre el temor y la esperanza*, San José, DEI, 1980, 103p.

Sabanes Plou, Dafne, *Caminos de unidad : Itinerario del dialogo ecuménico en América Latina 1916-1991*, Quito, CLAI, 1994, 170p.

Santa Ana, Julio de, *Ecumenismo y liberación: reflexiones sobre la relación entre la unidad cristiana y el reino de Dios*, Madrid, Paulinas, 1987, 323p.

Torres, Sergio and Eagleson, John eds, *The Challenge of Basic Christian Communities: Papers from the International Ecumenical Congress of Theology, February 20 – March 2, 1980, Sao Paulo, Brazil*, Maryknoll NY, Orbis, 1981, 283p.

Valle, Carlos A. ed., *Semilla de comunión*, Buenos Aires, La Aurora, 1983, 164p.

24
Middle East

Jean Corbon

This chapter deals with the history of the ecumenical movement in the last three and a half decades of the 20th century, looking at it chronologically, under four headings: the first structures (1966-74), the role of the Middle East Council of Churches (1974-2000), convergence in church renewal (1980-2000) and, lastly, the unresolved problems (1991-2000).

To help readers find their way through the first stage without too much difficulty, it is useful to begin by giving a few important reference points, first on the ecumenical geography of the region, then on the principal elements of its socio-political, economic and cultural context and, finally, on the immediate prehistory which made it possible for the first structures to be set up at the end of the 1960s.

THE ECUMENICAL GEOGRAPHY OF THE MIDDLE EAST

In current usage, the Middle East comprises the countries lying between the Asian shores of the Mediterranean Sea in the West and the eastern border of Iran in the east, and from Armenia in the north to the tip of the Arabian peninsula in the south. Culturally distinctive local churches developed in this region during the first four centuries of the common era around the great centres of evangelization, the cities of Antioch, Alexandria, Etchmiadzin (Armenia, c. 300) and Seleucia-Ctesiphon (Mesopotamia, 5th century). From the second part of the first millennium onwards, the human geography of these churches was disrupted, with displacements taking place both for internal doctrinal, cultural and ethnic reasons and as a consequence of the Byzantine-Sassanide wars and, later, Arab and Turkish invasions. During the second millennium, the displacement of populations was more terrible still, while at the same time internal schisms came from the West, with the creation of Eastern churches united with Rome and proselytism by the Latin and Protestant churches.[1]

The history of Christianity in the Middle East has been, since the first century, a history of diversity manifested in the course of evangelization originating from Jerusalem, the spiritual pole of three continents: Asia, Africa and Europe. As regards the ecumenical geography, three issues are important for an understanding of the present problems.

---

[1] The Ecumenical Patriarchate and the Armenian Patriarchate of Constantinople, situated in the western part of Asia Minor, are not covered by this chapter.

First, there is the *internal fragmentation* of the churches which sprang up around the four great metropolises mentioned above. Instead of four groups of churches homogeneous in faith and canonical structures, the Middle East today has four Orthodox churches of Chalcedonian tradition (Alexandria, Antioch, Jerusalem and Cyprus), four Oriental Orthodox churches of pre-Chalcedonian tradition (Armenian Apostolic Church, Assyrian Church of the East, Coptic Church of Alexandria, Syrian Church of Antioch), seven Catholic churches (Armenian, Chaldean, Coptic, Greek-Melchite, Latin, Maronite and Syrian) and lastly, the Evangelical Episcopalian, Lutheran and Presbyterian churches and various "evangelical" communities such as the Adventists and the Baptists. Only a few among the ten to twelve million Christians who continue to live in the region call themselves Christians of the Arab world. They prefer their historical names, whether reflecting a salient ethnic and cultural particularity (Armenian, Assyrian etc.) or meant to specify primarily a linguistic, liturgical and ecclesial tradition (Greek-Orthodox, Maronites, Copts, Syrians etc.)

Secondly, the – still continuing – dispersion of the faithful has created a patchwork of *ecumenical mosaics.* In most countries in the region it is not unusual to find the twenty churches mentioned above present in the same territory. This phenomenon is most noticeable in the countries on the shores of the Mediterranean, which have become staging posts for emigration. Christians in the Arab world often present themselves as "Arab Christians". Notwithstanding its ambiguity, this inclusive name has fewer disadvantages than "Christian Arabs" or "Christians of the East". Depicting oneself as an Arab Christian highlights an identity shared with Muslims but antecedent to Islam.

Thirdly, the *emigration* of Christians from the Middle East is the most tragic result of the successive divisions of the churches and their displacement. In the absence of reliable statistics, and taking only the Arab countries in the region, there are thought to be some 12 million Christians (of whom 8 million are Copts and 200,000 Protestants), that is, 10 percent of the total population. Whatever the emigrants' cultural, canonical or economic ties with their mother church, the history of the past two centuries leaves no doubt that there is no hope of the flow of migrants returning. Nor are the same causes likely to stop producing the same effects if they go untreated. This is the radical challenge facing the ecumenical movement in the Middle East today. To understand all the dimensions involved, it is essential to set this in the overall socio-political, economic and cultural context of the region.

THE POLITICAL, SOCIAL, ECONOMIC AND CULTURAL CONTEXT

In the 1960s, the newly created states in the region, and the various political regimes which ruled them, did not enjoy enough legitimacy to achieve genuine independence, foster social progress and secure national integration. Most political systems were authoritarian, even if some of them had, in a formal sense, democratic political institutions. The Ottoman heritage, with its "hierarchical pluralism" consecrated by the millet system (broadly speaking, a socio-cultural and communal framework based on religion and ethnicity which reflected linguistic differences of the millets consisting essentially of people who belonged to the same faith), continued to influence political culture and social relations. The abolishing of the Islamic Caliphate did not extinguish the longing for Islamic unity. Also, the adoption by the ruling elites of modern secular models of polity and society did not succeed in creating new loyalties at the expense of the traditional ones.

The silence of the Yalta agreements (between Churchill, Stalin and Roosevelt in 1945) on the region allowed the US and the USSR to press their rival ambitions of controlling the strategic crossroads, energy resources and sea routes that made the Middle East central to any design for world domination. Much of the geopolitical confrontation was by proxy. The state of Israel, created in 1948, came to function as a bridgehead for American influence, strategic and otherwise, which forced some Arab countries, especially those that were threatened by Israel's military superiority, to seek Soviet support.

Since the dispossession of the Palestinians, Israel was perceived by Islamic states as a powerful, Western, settler, colonial entity. The imperative of facing its challenge overshadowed other national priorities in many cases.

The defeat of the Arab uprising in 1967 and the occupation by Israel of additional Arab territories had a tremendously negative impact on the whole of the Middle East, not just the countries that were involved directly in the war. One manifestation of special concern to churches was the passionate and far-reaching controversy concerning the role of religion. Many political movements espoused secular and revolutionary ideologies that held traditional values, attributed to religion, responsible for the traumatic defeat of the Arab states. Simultaneously, revival of Islamic movements gained a wider audience as they vilified the secular and modernist regimes whose failure and discrediting were proclaimed a consequence of their moving away from Islam.

At the social level, authoritarian regimes did little to encourage the population, far less the minorities, to take responsibility for the development of their country. In the 1950s, certain non-confessional groups and agencies tried to promote the freedom to do so, but they had the disadvantage of having been set up by Christians; moreover, because they were secular in character and open to all religions they were suspected of being breeding grounds for communism. Some of these organizations would be taken over by governments; others maintained their autonomy but were clearly operated at the direction of sponsors in the West. Except in Lebanon, what was called at the time Christian political commitment amounted in fact to little more than activities in the area of social assistance.

It is important to draw attention here to an inherent feature common to the societies in the region: a person's identity is inseparable from the group to which he or she belongs – family, clan, district, village, confessional community. These multiple and overlapping identities limit individual freedom and responsibility. To be sure, they do not constitute a protection against the ills of individualism, in the sense of manifesting little concern for the common good. In the same way, loyalties to various groups favour clientelism in which the leader is the sole authority. Obviously, relations between the churches are also marked by this paradox, which is a stumbling block for the ecumenical movement.

Once one is aware of this context, with its lack of social cohesion, it is perhaps easier to grasp the deeper underlying reasons for the conflicts which have broken out since 1947. The main trigger, of course, was Israel. Through provision of aid to Israel the West discharged its guilt over its own antisemitism, yet this often had the effect of detonating explosions by remote control. But the explosive itself is a local product. Basically, the peoples of the region, whatever their ethnic group, culture or religion, aspire to live a life in human dignity, security and peace. Every so often this aspiration, repressed by the great powers and their local agents, explodes, producing the wars that have marked the period: 1947-48 (creation of the modern state of Israel), 1956 (Suez), 1967 (six-day war), 1973 (October, or Yom Kippur war), 1975-90 (a dozen wars, of which Lebanon bore the brunt), 1980-88 (Iraq-Iran), 1988 (Intifada), 1991 (the Gulf), January 2001 (beginning of the second Intifada). In these wars, the lives and welfare of the people of the Middle East are not taken with the same seriousness as economic and political advantage. The failure to do so, which is criminal in terms of the law, and above all of the Christian faith, generates state terrorism directed against the peoples of the region who resist by using the feeble means at their disposal, sometimes including desperate acts of violence. The deep underlying cause of these conflicts is essentially the injustice inflicted on these peoples, from which they are condemned never to break free. We shall see how the churches' conscience was roused in the course of these decades, causing them to proclaim the gospel with ever-increasing clarity in the face of these conflicts.

The economic dimensions of the regional context reveal what is really at stake in the conflicts. Industrial activity remains low, while only the regions along the Nile, Euphrates and Tigris rivers have rich soil resources. The economic stakes are concentrated in the underground resources (water and oil) and in the tertiary sector (commerce, banking and tourism). In this semi-arid zone, water is and always has been a source of conflict at every level. Today it has become an issue of survival between states: Egypt/Sudan argue over the Nile; Israel/Syria-Lebanon over the sources of the Jordan; Turkey/Syria/Iraq over the dams on the Euphrates. Oil – quite apart from the rivalries among the producer countries – is the primary strategic target of the US on account of the Saudi Arabian reserves, thought to be the world's largest. Further reinforcing this neo-colonialist subjection is the fact that oil revenues have done little to promote human development for the peoples of the oil-producing countries. Indeed, the region is locked in under-development thanks to the banking system put in place following the oil embargo in 1973 (October war), designed to prevent oil and petrodollars from being concentrated in the same hands. As for Christians, they endure this carefully organized anomaly together with their fellow citizens.

Lastly, it is at the cultural level that the most fundamental challenge of the Middle East is experienced in everyday life, namely, how to live together. The problems involved in this challenge call into question the very being of Christians and of the church. They may be expressed in the form of four inherent paradoxes:
- Plurality/unity, placing demands that often conflict upon the churches and other religious traditions.
- Tradition/modernity and their implications for public education and the formation of character.
- Religion/society as forces in the building of regional community.
- God/humanity in the mystery of the incarnation, and consequences of the divine-human relationship for Christian social action.

THE FIRST-FRUITS OF ECUMENISM IN THE MIDDLE EAST

While it is true that it was in the Middle East that divisions first appeared among the churches, it is no less true – even if not widely known – that efforts to restore communion among the churches have gone on there constantly for the past fifteen centuries.[2] The diversity of churches has not always been the result of their divisions. A gen-

---

[2] The most outstanding example concerns relations between the Byzantines and the Armenians. Cf. P. Dzoulikian, "Deux évêques arméniens du XIIe s. apologistes de l'union", in *Proche-Orient chrétien*, 61, 1961, pp.36-43.

uine ecclesial sense, especially among the Orthodox, has never ceased to perceive the church's unity in plurality not as an antinomy of principles, but as the essential mystery of the divine Three-in-One. Accordingly (long before the "ecumenism" of the 20th century), the unity they sought could not be conceived merely as uniformity and, moreover, could only be recovered by resolving the original causes of division, without avoiding the issues and rushing into what amounts simply to collaboration among Christians. In other words, in this region, the prime perspective in the quest for unity is that of the church and its being and raison d'etre in the world.

In this spirit, in 1902 Joachim III, the Ecumenical Patriarch of Constantinople, addressed an encyclical letter to all the Orthodox churches, calling on them to seek points of encounter with other churches. In the patriarchates of the region, Alexandria, Antioch and Jerusalem, the call was heard, but how could they seek "points of encounter" with churches that had come to the East to whittle away at Orthodox believers and "convert" them to Catholicism or the Reformation? In 1920, the Ecumenical Patriarchate addressed an encyclical letter to the other churches inviting them to join together to form a "communion [koinonia] of churches".[3]

In 1932, under the aegis of the International Missionary Council, the Protestant communities which sprang from the proselytism of Western missionary societies set up the Near East Christian Council in Beirut, later to become the Near East Council of Churches after the New Delhi assembly (1961), with the admission to that council of the Syrian Orthodox Church of Antioch. But the breath of ecumenism really touched most circles within the churches in the region in the wake of the second world war, remaining for many long years an underground movement (1942-59), but finally emerging into the light of day (1959-66).

After having been viewed suspiciously or ignored by the church authorities, the ecumenical movement now came out of its clandestine existence, helped by four events: the convocation of the Second Vatican Council, first announced in January 1959, at which one of the major concerns would be ecumenism; also in 1959, the first pan-Orthodox conference in Rhodes, which studied the matter of relations with other churches; in 1960, the establishment of the Secretariat for Promoting Christian Unity in Rome; and, in 1961, the third WCC assembly at New Delhi, which brought all the Orthodox churches of the Middle East into membership.

This, then, was a first ecumenical springtime. All the churches in the region, except the Catholics, could now meet, if not locally, then at least in Geneva and in all the departments of the WCC. Epiphany 1964 in Jerusalem, the occasion of the historic meeting between Pope Paul VI and Ecumenical Patriarch Athenagoras I, marked a new beginning in relations among the Catholic, Orthodox and Armenian Apostolic churches.[4] On 7 December 1965, Paul VI and Athenagoras I lifted the mutual excommunications of 1054: the long process of cleansing the churches' memory could begin. Meanwhile, on a modest scale, the charismatic breath of unity inspired the setting up of minimum basic structures for dialogue and cooperation in the Middle East. The architects were young people, who opened the ecumenical office for youth and students in the Middle East, and a few adults, who formed an ecumenical group for pastoral ministry, intended

[3] "Encyclical of the Ecumenical Patriarchate", 1920, in C. Patelos ed., *The Orthodox Church in the Ecumenical Movement*, WCC, 1978, pp.40-43.
[4] Cf. J. Corbon, "Nouvelles perspectives oecuméniques au Proche-Orient", in *Proche-Orient chrétien*, 64, 1964, pp.129-47.

to draw the Catholic churches into the ecumenical movement. This brings us to the start of the first attempts at the creation of appropriate structures.

THE FIRST STRUCTURES (1966-74)

By the mid-1960s, it became necessary for the churches in the Middle East to establish commissions for their ecumenical relations. This was done either in each country or on a broader basis in 1966 and the following year. These commissions were to serve as official reference and decision-making points for major issues. For the day-to-day routine of ecumenical service – information, education, prayer, cooperation – the church leaders relied on the practical support of the structures set up spontaneously in the preceding years.

Noteworthy here is the decisive part played by Gabriel Habib, general secretary of the ecumenical office for youth and students in the Middle East. For more than thirty years he was the mainspring of the ecumenical movement in the region,[5] concerned from 1961 onwards to involve it in the dynamic of world ecumenism. From Beirut, where the ecumenical office was based, branch offices were set up in the main capitals in the region, in Europe and in the US. Gradually, the churches were thus able to take a stance on the urgent problems arising out of the tensions in the region.

The first problem was the Israeli-Arab war of June 1967, the tragic consequences of which continued to bar the way to a "just and lasting peace". The first ecumenical response was made in terms of the faith, in view of the ecstatic support given to Israel by certain Christians in the West, who saw the "six-day war" as the fulfilment of the promises made to the people of the Old Testament and of eschatological expectations arising from a particular reading of the New Testament book of Revelation. The stakes were high: no less than the Christian meaning of the Promise, the Land, the People of God and, ultimately, of messianism – hence the memorandum published in 1968 by the theologians of the Middle East on "Christian Faith and Religious Zionism".

But the Christian faith was not the only thing at stake. A human tragedy of injustice towards the Palestinian people, endorsed by the great powers in defiance of international law, challenged the conscience of Christians around the world to show solidarity. A world conference of Christians for Palestine was organized. The first and most important session was held in Beirut in 1970. All aspects of the tragedy were examined – religious Zionism again, but also the information conveyed by the media, international law, the status of the "refugees", humanitarian aid, relations with governments, the UN, the non-governmental organizations, Palestinian cultural continuity, and resolutions pressing for a plural, democratic, secular state in the holy land, where all ethnic, religious and cultural communities would enjoy the freedom and equality worthy of a constitutional state. Other regional meetings (Europe and the Americas) extended this first series of discussions up to 1975.

The second problem facing the ecumenical office was the under-development of the region. There could be no question here of the churches compensating, even distantly, for the failure of governments to fulfil their responsibilities. It was simply a matter of coordinating their forces to promote the human development of their members and, by extension, their fellow-citizens. In 1968, the inaugural assembly of the committee on So-

---

[5] Habib was the founder of the ecumenical office for youth and students in 1961, and general secretary of the MECC from 1977 to 1994.

ciety, Development and Peace (SODEPAX), a new joint body for social development, justice and peace formed by the WCC and the Vatican, was held in Lebanon. This occasion saw the launching of two SODEPAX groups, one in Egypt, succeeded in 1975 by a pastoral agreement between the Coptic Orthodox Church and the Roman Catholic Church, the other in Lebanon, sponsored by the Catholic and Greek Orthodox ecumenical commissions. Serious preliminary investigations were carried out in view of the latter project, but it was brought to an abrupt end in 1975 by events in Lebanon.

Another decisive event for the regional scene was the fourth assembly of the WCC in Uppsala (1968). New Delhi had already distanced the WCC from proselytism by Western missionaries, commending to the churches a position paper on "Christian Witness, Proselytism and Religious Liberty".[6] At Uppsala the ecumenical position was clearer still. The WCC opted resolutely for regionalization of ecumenical endeavour and gave priority to aid for local churches. At the same time, this was also the direction chosen by the Secretariat for Promoting Christian Unity (Rome). From Uppsala to Nairobi (fifth assembly), the decolonization of ecumenism was virtually completed. The Orthodox, Catholic and Reformation churches of the Middle East were thus sent back to their regional base to resolve their common problems. At Uppsala the masterly opening address on the main theme given by the Greek Orthodox Metropolitan of Latakia, Ignatios Hazim,[7] contributed in no small way to this ecumenical progress.

It was at this point that new structures for dialogue and cooperation began to take shape. In the field of ecumenical information, *Al-Montada*, a bi-monthly newsletter in Arabic, French and English published in Beirut, was distributed to a growing number of countries in the region and beyond. The period saw a growth of awareness at various levels. During the summer of 1969, a catechetical congress in Lebanon with emphasis on ecumenism was attended by more than six hundred participants from all the churches. Thereafter a project began to take shape for a harmonized catechism based as much as possible on the Antiochene tradition common to most of the local churches. The general principles had been approved prior to the congress by the ecumenical commissions. Between 1970 and 1975, mixed teams of catechists submitted several common texts for the approval of the competent authorities, but here again the violent events in Lebanon in 1975 which impacted the entire region meant that the project had to be shelved *sine die*.[8] During the same period, a joint Orthodox-Catholic team had also prepared audiovisual materials for this harmonized catechism.

At another level, less broadly based but more crucial for the ecumenical movement, the theological students of the churches present in Lebanon began to meet periodically, from 1966 onwards. Then there were also the many meetings and consultations for youth and students organized by the ecumenical office, in Egypt, Jordan, Lebanon and Cyprus, on major topical themes – Christian political engagement, the challenges of Zionism, Arab Christian culture, Muslim-Christian relations, Christian reading of the Bible, common witness, the contemporary significance of the fathers of the church.

---

[6] See Paul Löffler, "Proselytism", in *Dictionary of the Ecumenical Movement*, Nicholas Lossky et al. eds, 2nd ed., WCC, 2002, pp. 940-41.
[7] Text (in French) in *Proche-Orient chrétien*, 68, 1968, pp.236-47. In English, in Norman E. Goodall ed., *The Uppsala Report 1968: The Official Report of the Fourth Assembly of the World Council of Churches, Uppsala, July 4-20, 1968*, WCC, 1968, pp.293-303.
[8] For the history of this project, cf. J. Corbon, "Une catéchèse orthodoxe-catholique est-elle possible dans les Eglises d'Antioche", in *Proche-Orient chrétien*, 90, 1990, pp. 56-78.

In this context, where young people in general and future pastors in particular had the opportunity to educate themselves for their ecumenical responsibilities, an appropriate structure was set up in 1968. This was the Association for Theological Education in the Near East (ATENE[9]). Originally the objective was more academic than ecumenical, the intention being to provide institutes of higher education in the region with instruments for cooperation in teaching and research. The association therefore published annotated catalogues of library resources, especially manuscripts, and organized an ambitious programme to translate essential books from Arabic into French and English and vice-versa. Finding the teams of translators proved difficult, but eventually it was lack of funds which obliged the association to review its objectives after 1975.

These efforts in the fields of information and education promised progress in regard to communion in the faith among the churches in the region. A project for an ecumenical institute for the Middle East, similar to Bossey, was the subject of various conversations and "working papers", but the differences in level among the theological institutes made it necessary to wait for internal renewal to take place in each church. Moreover, the rising tension in the region from 1967 to 1973 was hardly conducive to the development of gatherings for prayer for Christian unity, except in Egypt.

There, in 1973, the installation of His Holiness Patriarch Amba Shenouda III as pope of the Coptic Orthodox Church opened the way for a new ecumenical breakthrough. His visit to the Maronite patriarch and other Christian hierarchs in Lebanon was particularly cordial. Then came his meeting with Pope Paul VI and their common Christological declaration putting an end to the dissensions of the 5th century over the unity of the person of Christ, true God and true Man. This marked the official creation of the joint commission for theological dialogue between the Coptic Orthodox Church and the Roman Catholic Church, followed by a joint group responsible for pastoral relations in the local situation.

Again in 1973, on the initiative of the ecumenical office for youth and students, an unofficial meeting between Orthodox and Oriental Orthodox theologians was held in the Greek Orthodox Institute of Theology in Balamand (north Lebanon), which produced a common Christological statement similar to that of Popes Paul VI and Shenouda III. This text from Balamand was taken up again and improved 15 years later, this time at the international level, when the Orthodox and Oriental Orthodox churches officially declared their doctrinal agreement on the mystery of Christ.

ROLE OF THE MIDDLE EAST COUNCIL OF CHURCHES (1974-2000)

After the WCC's New Delhi assembly the new Near East Council of Churches (NECC), originally the Association of Protestant Missionary Societies, was joined by an Orthodox member, the Syrian Church of Antioch. Talks began with the other Orthodox churches, but came to nothing because the fifty-fifty basis proposed by the NECC was unacceptable to the Orthodox churches, which numbered ten million faithful as against two hundred thousand Protestants. The negotiations resumed after Uppsala and arrived at a formula by which the three church families – Chalcedonian Orthodox, Oriental Orthodox

---

[9] ATENE became ATIME (Association of the Theological Institutes in the Middle East) in 1980, after its affiliation with the MECC, and defined its objectives: membership of theological institutes in Lebanon, Egypt, the Holy Land and Iraq, consultations among teaching staff, regular meetings for students, publication in Arabic of the most ancient Christian texts, for the use of students.

and Protestant – would be equally represented in the organs of the future Middle East Council of Churches (MECC).

The constitutional basis of the new body did not count the numbers of member churches but grouped them in the three "families". The term is no more theological than the word "denomination" adopted by the WCC in Amsterdam, but it is closer to what in current ecumenical ecclesiology is understood by "communion". Indeed, in the Oriental Orthodox family, the Armenian, Coptic and Syrian churches are in full communion in the faith and the sacraments; likewise, in the Orthodox family, the Patriarchates of Alexandria, Antioch and Jerusalem and the autocephalous Church of Cyprus are in full communion, including canonical communion. As to the Reformation family, despite the divergences between the Evangelical Episcopalian Church (which belongs to the Anglican communion and is now known as the Episcopal Church of Jerusalem and the Middle East), and the Lutheran and Presbyterian churches, the common basis accepted by the WCC at New Delhi was sufficient to bind them together as a single family.

And so at the end of May 1974 this new fellowship came into being at the first assembly of the Middle East Council of Churches (MECC) in Nicosia, Cyprus. The observers and guests from Geneva were surprised by the absence of the Roman Catholic churches since they had been involved in ecumenical cooperation for two decades. The truth of the matter was that they had never been invited to the negotiations, for various reasons, the most obvious of which were the requirement of an initial financial payment and, above all, the more or less conscious distrust of a Catholicism that was considered, rightly or wrongly, as better organized and therefore more dangerous.

But the years passed, and with them the prejudices. Unofficial talks were blocked by questions of procedure, including the prospect of having to alter the Council's constitution and the distribution of responsibilities with the transition from three to four families. In 1985, on the eve of the fourth assembly of the MECC, for the first time in the history of the region a "summit" meeting was held in Nicosia attended by the heads of all the churches in the Middle East, including the seven Catholic churches and the Assyrian Church of the East. In the end the Catholic churches[10] were admitted as the fourth "family" at the MECC's fifth assembly in 1990.

The MECC is not a superchurch nor a branch office of the WCC, but a body which exists to serve the churches of the region, and it is an essential structure for dialogue and cooperation among the churches. Its purpose is:
- to promote communion and ecumenical awareness among the churches so that each one may, through prayer, study and action, share in the rich tradition and experience of the others;
- to furnish the means of common research to help understand the respective traditions;
- to broaden the field of cooperation among the churches in fulfilling the church's essential mission, which is to proclaim the gospel of salvation; to carry out and coordinate appropriate forms of service to express the churches' common concern for all human beings; and
- to be a regional reference point in the world fellowship of Christian churches (relations with the WCC, national and regional councils and other ecumenical bodies).

---

[10] Armenian Catholic Church of Cilicia; Chaldean Catholic Church of Babylon; Coptic Catholic Church of Alexandria; Greek Melkite Catholic Patriarchate of Antioch, Alexandria and Jerusalem; Latin Patriarchate of Jerusalem; Maronite Church of Antioch; Syrian Catholic Church of Antioch.

600 | chapter 24

The priority objectives of the MECC relate very concretely to the present problems of the churches in the Middle East: (1) continuity of the Christian presence, especially by remedying the causes of emigration; (2) renewal of the spiritual quality of church life, over and beyond the churches' socio-cultural identities (cf. overcoming the "confessional" mentality); (3) Christian unity; and (4) common witness by the churches.

The assembly, meeting in principle every four years, comprises 96 members (24 per family). It elects four presidents, one from each family, the general secretary and three deputies who, together with 24 elected members, form the executive committee, which is the Council's real decision-making body. The three main service units are: education and renewal, with programmes for youth, women, family, church-related schools, Christian education and scholarships; faith and unity, with programmes on inter-Christian dialogue, Christian witness, inter-religious dialogue, theological education; and life and service, the unit which, understandably given the situation in the region, takes up most staff and resources in order to serve needy populations, especially in Palestine, Lebanon, Iraq and Sudan. Other programmes which depend directly on the general secretariat, besides the administrative services, are information, documentation, publications, human rights, justice and peace, Islamic-Christian relations and the Council's regional desks.

The MECC is only a service organism; in other words, the decisions taken and the application of such decisions are the churches' responsibility. If they are to be effective, they have to be translated at the level of each church, which is autonomous in its decisions, and at the same time they can be translated only in fellowship with the other churches. These two requirements are inseparable. Progress in communion among the churches and the renewal of each one of them are interdependent. The problems of the Middle East are such that none of the churches can now exist without co-existing, nor operate without cooperating. This has become obvious over the past quarter of a century.

CONVERGENCE IN CHURCH RENEWAL (1980–2000)

Starting in 1973, the Middle East was struck by a succession of traumatic "cyclones", to which no end is yet in sight. Having disposed of the Vietnam tragedy, US strategists turned their attention to the Middle East as a principal arena in the geopolitical contest between East and West. It was fortunate that the MECC had been set up just at that time, as it enabled Christians to face the challenges of survival together, and in solidarity with their fellow-citizens. It is also wonderful, even though it has gone unnoticed by the media, that this journey through hell was, and continues to be, a time of grace and renewal for the churches.

The "October" 1973 or Yom Kippur war was brought to a close through the promise of an honourable peace between Egypt and Israel in which no one would lose face. The result, of course, was the Camp David agreements in 1978, thanks to which Egypt recovered the Sinai, while the Palestinians were forgotten. But at the end of 1973, the Arab League declared an oil embargo; the West caught cold, and went into economic recession. The oil producing nations' "crime" was considered unpardonable by Western corporate interests. From a Middle Eastern perspective, ensuing events were deliberately orchestrated in the West to punish regional leaders.

The partition of Cyprus had prevented the Soviets from using it as a base (1974), and there was a temporary reconciliation between Iran and Iraq, ensuring their neutrality (Algiers, 1975) when Israel launched its intervention into Lebanon in 1975. To many observers in the Middle East, the aim of the operation seemed clear: millions of unwanted

Palestinians on Israeli territory were to be resettled in Lebanon. As the strongest opposition to this resettlement came from the Maronite Christians, these same observers were not surprised to see them forced to leave their country due to tensions among the 18 Lebanese communities and the dozen or so Palestinian organizations through which each Arab country sought to turn the "sacred cause of Palestine" to its own advantage. In the process, the whole infrastructure of Lebanon was systematically destroyed and Beirut, the petrodollar centre of the region, saw its banks scientifically pillaged, with the exception of those that were owned by Americans or Soviets.

By 1978, Egypt was out of the game, absorbed once more in its own population and economic problems. Some 90 percent of Lebanon was occupied by Syria, while 10 percent of the south of its territory had been amputated by the Israeli army, and the water courses had been diverted towards Galilee in defiance of UN resolution 425. As a result of Israeli military action and US diplomacy, Lebanon and the Palestinians had been effectively neutralized in their opposition to Israel. Lebanon had been proclaimed democratic, pluralist and anti-war; meanwhile, the Palestinians were anathematized as terrorists.

This left in play the eastern side of the region, the more important in terms of the "new world order". There, it seemed, Iran was developing imperial aspirations. But in 1979 the extremist Islamic republic was born. Once again, Iraq and Iran were pitted against one another. In 1981, Israeli air strikes destroyed the nuclear power station at Tamuz (Iraq). Then Iraq, having been encouraged through US support to counter Iranian Islamic extremism, outraged the US administration by its invasion of Kuwait (1990). There was a "first" Gulf war, the flames of which were still smouldering at the onset of the second Gulf war of the next decade.

This particular view of the conflicts of the past three decades is not irrelevant to our subject. For it took a long time for the peoples of the Middle East, overwhelmed by so much suffering,[11] to realize the significance of these absurd and calamitous events. At first the churches reacted by responding to emergencies. Practising the gospel meant aid, forgiveness, patience, hope. Their condemnations of violence and injustice were not heard beyond the frontiers. The real scale of the tragedy became apparent, in the region as a whole, at the end of the 1980s, and one may ask whether it was fully appreciated by international opinion even at the end of the century.

More even than the scale of the tragedy, the heads of churches in the Middle East clearly grasped the real issues at stake, first of all individually in their own territory and then, gradually, together in solidarity. The stakes for all inhabitants of the region were socio-economic, cultural and religious, acutely so for the Christians there, a steadily shrinking minority. Pope Shenouda III was among the first to speak out against the situation and his boldness earned him five years of exile in the Wadi Natrun desert. The presence of the general secretary of the MECC in Cyprus after 1984 was a standing protest by the churches against Turkey's occupation of part of the island, while the Greek part served as an ecumenical meeting place for the whole region. The MECC issued countless reports and statements on all the sensitive topics in the region during those terrible years. Locally, in Lebanon, Syria and the holy land, the voices of the church hierarchs and the Christian press, where it was free to do so, never ceased to cry in the wilderness, recalling the demands of justice and peace. In Iraq, where more than a million Christians enjoyed a measure of religious and cultural freedom, the Chaldean

---

[11] Concerning Lebanon, cf. "Deux bilans statistiques de 16 années de guerre", in *Courrier*, 24, III, 1994, p.25.

(Catholic) patriarch began in the summer of 1990 to speak out in defence of his Muslim and Christian fellow-citizens well before international and church bodies in the West.

After operation "Desert Storm" (February 1991), the Catholic patriarchs of the East (Maronite, Greek-Melchite, Chaldean, Armenian, Syrian and Latin) visited Pope John Paul II to review the disastrous situation in the region and consider what was to be done. This led to the establishment of the Council of Catholic Patriarchs of the East, to allow for closer coordination of their pastoral ministry and involvement in MECC. But another profound outcome of this meeting was the decision to "start with Lebanon", with a special assembly of the synod of bishops on Lebanon, convened on 12 June 1991 by John Paul II, as a matter of solidarity among all the Catholic churches around the world.

It is noteworthy that the significance of synodality as a motor of church renewal had frequently been stressed and practised in the Greek Orthodox Church of Antioch, the Coptic Orthodox Church of Egypt and the Armenian Apostolic Church of Cilicia (Antelias, Lebanon) during the 1980s. Now, the Catholic churches in the holy land have likewise been engaged in a synodal process. This convergence inevitably draws attention to three aspects of the ecumenical movement in the Middle East:

• During these years of trial and tribulation the time had come for "judgment to begin with the household of God" (1 Pet. 4:17). The Lord always comes in poverty and in being humbled his church is purified. Communion among the churches is not possible without humility.

• The synodal renewal taking shape in all the churches in the region is also the fruit of slow and almost imperceptible processes of renewal started in previous decades, with the spread of reflection on God's word, more or less timid reforms in liturgical ministry, the rediscovery, above all by young people, of the spiritual fathers and the authenticity of their ecclesial tradition, the renewal of prayer from the heart, the spirituality of marriage and the family, new cultural demands in the training of future pastors and lay leaders. Looking at the breadth and depth of renewal in all churches in the region, it is clear that through this convergence the Holy Spirit is writing and guiding the ecumenical movement, amidst all the troubles and manoeuvrings of secular politics, as the leaven of unity at work in the dough of this world.

• During these dark years, signs of hope have been given to the churches on the path towards full communion. In 1980, theological dialogue started between the Roman Catholic Church and the Orthodox churches, one of the most important results being the Balamand document (1993) which "rejected uniatism as a method of achieving unity between Orthodox and Catholics and affirmed the right of the Eastern Catholic churches to exist and to respond to the pastoral needs of their faithful".[12] In 1983, Armenian Orthodox Catholicos Karekin II met Pope John Paul II, as did the Greek Orthodox Patriarch of Antioch, Ignatios IV, in 1983. The same year saw the common Christological statement by John Paul II and Ignatius Zakka I, the Syrian Orthodox Patriarch of Antioch. A line was finally drawn under the Christological divisions of the 5th century in 1988, with the Christological accord between the Chalcedonian Orthodox churches and the Oriental Orthodox churches. As for the Assyrian Church of the East, once the great missionary church of Asia from India to China, but the one which has suffered most from the vicissitudes of history, it too was restored to communion with its sister churches in 1994, as mentioned above.

---

[12] *Dictionary of the Ecumenical Movement*, p. 867.

EVOLVING PROBLEMS (1991-2000)

The ecumenical movement of the 20th century has taught us to be more careful in distinguishing the "non-theological factors" influencing or determining the divisions among the churches. At the end of the second millennium, how are we to distinguish the two sets of problems prevailing in the present situation in the Middle East, one non-theological and the other essentially ecclesial? These two sets of problems are "evolving" in the sense that the given elements are now better known, but a solution has yet to be found. There is also a certain analogy between the basic elements of the overall context and those of the ecumenical movement, namely, the fundamental quest for identity and the undeniable fact of difference, in short, the dialectic of the "one" and the "many".

To use an expression that has become symbolic, we may say that the whole problem of the Middle East turns on the "peace process". Here, four major problems interact and challenge the churches. They are Judaism, Islam, Jerusalem and religious extremism.

The churches' relations with Judaism

There is confusion over the question of relations with Judaism, because it is approached either in terms of the conflictual and, ultimately, tragic situation of the Jewish communities which lived in a supposedly "Christian" Europe for almost two millennia, or else in terms of the political situation prevailing de facto in the Middle East since 1948. If the question is to be clarified, it has to be posed in terms of relations between the Christian churches and the Jewish communities in the Middle East, but these relations have a quite specific history and problematic of their own.

Jews and Christians lived in peaceful coexistence as religious communities in the region from the beginnings of Christianity until 1948. They had in common not only a scriptural and liturgical heritage, but also a scientific, philosophical and literary Semitic culture which, with its Muslim partner, had contributed greatly to human civilization. Furthermore, and this needs to be stressed, these two communities of believers never attained independent political status in the form of national territory, state or army. They had always been ethnic-religious communities incorporated in empires governed by others – Roman, Byzantine, Parthian, Sassanide, Arab, Persian, Ottoman, British. Under Muslim rule they were minorities, tolerated and protected by the dhimma as "the people of the Book". With the collapse of the Ottoman empire and the independence of the countries in the region, these two communities had hopes of attaining the status of full citizenship, without religious discrimination. In the event, the only country not to have a "state religion" turned out to be Lebanon, but then, in 1948, came the creation of the state of Israel, with Judaism as its state religion. From then on, two questions entered the relations between the churches of the region and Judaism as a religion, both as yet unresolved:

1. The creation of the Hebrew state despoiled the Palestinian people of their rights to exist as a people, nation and state. In the face of this injustice, the position of the churches in the region has been simply to demand that justice be done for the Palestinians in the name of human rights and the international law of nations. Their position is not antisemitic; on the contrary, they reject racial and religious discrimination. Nor is it confessional; it is based on reason and justice. Nor does it take sides; the United Nations charter and the Declaration of Human Rights are accepted by the vast majority of states.
2. The state religion is Judaism in Israel and Islam in the other countries of the region, except Lebanon. Its religious pluralism guarantees equality for all citizens, whatever

their religious convictions, and freedom of conscience and expression for all confessions. But elements within the Israeli state sought to safeguard the security of its future borders (a unique case in the age of the UN) by destabilizing the region in order to encourage the formation of confessional states in its own image, based on ethnic-religious identity: Druze, Alaouite, Sunni, Shiite.... and Christian mini-states. Lebanon was the very opposite of a religious nation-state, the contradiction of the theocratic model whether Jewish or Muslim, and it was the first country to be destabilized.

For the churches of the Middle East, the question is vital and the answer seems simple: no to theocracy of every kind, be it imposed in the name of Christianity, Islam or Judaism. The reasons for this are also clear. At the close of the 20th century the churches have no wish to see the Middle East slipping back into the Middle Ages of political discrimination under the banner of religion. Both the logic of human rights and their faith in Christ forbid the churches from being accomplices of such institutionalized injustice. Christian-Jewish dialogue in the region will remain blocked so long as the strictly religious level of such dialogue continues to be overshadowed by the political dynamic and its injustices.

The churches' relations with Islam

The churches' efforts, certainly in the past twenty years, have been concerned with everyday life – getting to know and respect one another, demonstrating loyal and committed citizenship, free and responsible involvement in all possible areas of national development, and the concern not to play the game of party politics. With the meaning of humanity in the light of Christ as their sole criterion, the different churches can thus bear common witness in the societies in the region. Pastoral guidelines, from whichever "family" of churches, all go in the same direction. The latest bears the title "Together before God for the good of the individual and society. Coexistence between Muslims and Christians in the Arab world".[13] The MECC also organizes periodic consultations at which Muslims and Christians from several countries in the region exchange points of view on social problems without seeking to publish a final document. There too, as in everyday encounters, the important thing is to move from co-existence to community.[14]

The holy city, Jerusalem

Jerusalem is the "holy city" for Jews, Christians and Muslims, not just in the holy land but worldwide. What is to become of it at the outcome of the final "peace process", whatever that is and if it ever succeeds? As early as 1948, and again after 1967, but especially since the Israeli government declared Jerusalem to be the "one eternal capital" of Israel, all kinds of proposals have been made concerning the ultimate status of the holy city. It is not the role of the churches to present plans, nor even to negotiate about them at the political level. Their contribution to truth, justice and peace is to recall certain facts that are liable to be disregarded, for instance that the "living stones" (the faithful) are more

---

[13] Pastoral Letter from Council of Catholic Patriarchs of the East, Christmas 1994
[14] Reports in almost all the issues of *Courrier*, cf. 1 (1-1987), pp.19-23; 3 (3-1987), p.34; 10 (1-1990), p.34, on religious pluralism; 11 (2-1990), p.18 among Lebanese intellectuals; 13 (1-1991), p.25 on children; 14-15 (2/3-1991), p.78 on emigrants and refugees; 18 (3-1992), p.39 on moral education in schools; 21 (3-1993), p.53 on the summit meeting of religious leaders in Lebanon; 24 (3-1994), p.50 on Islamic-Christian dialogue and its difficulties. Note that Lebanon today has five institutes of Islamic-Christian studies.

important than the "holy places". For in Jerusalem, the mother church of all the churches, Christians of all communions are present today, but above all those whose roots are in the holy land. Moreover, both Israeli Jews and Palestinian Muslims and Christians have the right to live in Jerusalem and have access to their holy places.

However, the never-ending problem of Jerusalem, the constant symbol of human folly and inability to realize unity in diversity, also has to do with the eschatological drama,[15] and reminds the churches that they are called to unity, so that the world may believe in the One whom God has sent. The King of Peace does not conquer his city by ruse or violence; it is by the cross that he gathers in God's scattered children. And so the problem of Jerusalem, in its historical, political, human and religious dimensions, is the subject of consultations among moderate Israelis and Palestinians, Muslim and Christian chiefs in the region and, obviously in the framework of the MECC or locally, leaders of the Christian churches.[16]

Religious extremism

What may be designated by the generic term of religious extremism has appeared as an epiphenomenon of the regional conflicts. It is not the preserve of certain Muslim group-ings, whatever the Western media may think, but is also rampant on the fringes of Jew-ish groups in Israel and even, though without the same arsenal at their disposal, among certain Christian minorities. These outbreaks of extremism have more than one trait in common: a deep-rooted fear of threat to their identity, revolt against injustice and hu-miliation, anger against leaders of their community accused of siding with the oppres-sors and, lastly, the refusal to coexist with those who are "other", and hence their exclu-sion. This phenomenon of social pathology is then theorized according to the cultural tradition of each group and may develop beyond the stage of ideological paranoia to the extreme stage where the believer is convinced that he or she is acting under divine or-ders and power.

In the face of the extremism of Islamic fundamentalist groups, especially in Egypt and Palestine, the churches share the governments' diagnosis that the causes of the phe-nomenon are economic and political, with the proviso that steps be taken to remedy these. This gives occasion for dialogue and collaboration between Muslims and Chris-tians with a view to human development and national independence. As for the sepa-ratist tendencies of small Christian groups (Syrians, Copts and the "Lebanese Forces" of the 1980s) encouraged, let it be said, by Israel, the heads of churches concerned now in-sist on real Christian conversion as understood by the church and on the need to cleanse confessional mentalities (Ta'ifiyya).[17]

ECCLESIAL PROBLEMS

It will help to situate the ecclesial problems during the developments of the past two decades in the Middle East in their wider context by recalling the elements of the re-

---

[15] Cf. the lecture given by the Latin Patriarch of Jerusalem, Mgr Michel Sabbah, on "Les chrétiens de Terre Sainte aujourd'hui et le dialogue des religions", in Courrier, 28 (1-1996), pp. 50-57.

[16] Cf. the international consultation on the significance of Jerusalem for Christians and of Christians for Jerusalem, January 1996, in *Courrier*, 28 (1-1996), pp. 26-28. In June 1996 a conference of Christian and Muslim religious heads on the future of Jerusalem was held in Lebanon. Report in *Courrier*, 29-30 (3-1996).

[17] Besides the regular exhortations by the hierarchs on this subject, it is the theme of a pastoral letter from the seven Catholic patriarchs.

gion's ecumenical geography outlined at the beginning of this chapter. From the Iranian plateau to the valley of the Nile and from Armenia to the Yemen, this region is one, complex and strife-torn though it is. Its interdependence is given in its human, cultural and religious geography. The church of God, diverse and even divided because it is first of all one, serves and cares for this body of humanity. For this humanity loved by God – from which the church springs to bear witness to that love – the words of St Paul are true: "If one member suffers, all suffer together with it" (1 Cor. 12:26). Today more than ever before, the suffering inflicted on one people of the region also causes the others to suffer, including Israel, which will never know security unless it consents to live in interdependence and justice. One of the ecclesial problems for the future is thus the revival of the churches' diakonia, which is directly in line with the movement of renewal for unity. From this point of view, the churches face three challenges – two which have to be prevented and one which has to be opened up to hope.

1. The challenge of displacement leading in the end to emigration has grown steadily worse during the 1990s and into the second millennium. In Iraq, towns and villages in the north have been deserted by Christians ; the same is true of the Syrian and Assyro-Chaldean Christians in south-east Turkey so that the largest parts of the Syrian and Assyrian churches are to be found in northern Europe, the US and Australia. The Christians in the Lebanese mountains, "displaced by the events" (as official language puts it), are in fact confined in one confessional area, which was precisely one of the objectives of destabilizing the country in the first place. Luxury blocks are being built and the centre of Beirut restored, but poverty is on the increase and any young people who can do so are leaving, for good. In Israel and the "territories", the impossible struggle for survival, for Muslims and Christians alike, is adding month by month to the brain drain and the exodus of workers to free countries. The challenge here, we should have no delusions, is the diminishing size of the flock that remains.

2. The second challenge is that of the aggressive proselytism practised by those known as "evangelicals", coming mainly from the US. In the 1980s, the MECC counted several hundred of these "commandos" based in Cyprus. They are resolutely anti-ecumenical, for they see ecumenism as an invention of the devil. With the Bible in one hand and dollars in the other, they are often taken for Jehovah's Witnesses by the people – which they are not. They are Christians concerned to proclaim their version of the gospel, but in their zeal they are misguided. Not only does each one of them interpret the Bible according to his or her own judgment, but they know nothing at all about the churches of the East. Naively convinced, like the Protestant missionary societies of the century before them, that the Christians of the region worship pieces of wood (the holy icons) and know nothing of God's word, they engage in proselytism on all sides. The avowed aim, according to their radio station in Israeli-dominated South Lebanon, is to destabilize the churches so that all that remains are undefined groups of baptized believers. Understandably, the Israeli government makes use of them to realize its dream of a Hebrew state surrounded by confessional vassal mini-states. A (so-called) "international Christian embassy"[18] was set up in Jerusalem, for instance. Likewise, it was in the wake of Israeli tanks, in 1992, that the evangelical shock troops infiltrated Lebanon under cover of humanitarian aid to repair the damage done by their Zionist sponsors. In some of the Gulf states, the churches have

---

[18] Cf. *Courrier*, 19 (1-1993), p. 27.

even had to intervene with the authorities to prevent the witness of Eastern Christians from being equated with the provocative proselytism of the evangelicals. Against this background, the MECC began in 1987 to publish a number of documents on the Western evangelicals and, above all, started a dialogue with some of their leaders to explain to them the real situation of the churches in the region.[19] The fact remains that the challenge of this neo-colonialism can be met only by a further spiritual and pastoral renewal brought about by the local churches, in solidarity.

3. The renewal of the churches has been highlighted several times as the path towards full communion among them. We have also seen that the dialectic between plurality and unity lies at the heart of the problems of the region and of its churches. In the 1980s, the question was, "what kind of unity?" and the answer was: not uniformity, nor federalism, nor uniatism, but communion in catholicity, in which the churches recognize one another as churches and serve that communion in conformity with the same apostolic tradition.[20] That is all very well, but what does this communion in catholicity presuppose? How are the churches to prepare themselves to receive this gift? Today, in this decade beginning the third millennium, it has become clear that the ecumenical challenge is that of the churches' common roots. Having grown into different branches, the church of the Middle East has been in danger of forgetting its common roots.

This call, to find their way back to the profound mystery of the church as it took root in this region, concerns first and foremost the Latin and the Reformation churches. The contribution of these two Western traditions has of course had some positive aspects but, whether Latin or Reformed, these Christians are also Eastern by cultural heritage, as well as being ecclesially uprooted... Among all of them, the search for their unbroken Eastern identity is palpable today.

The same challenge is addressed to the Eastern churches united with Rome, though in a different perspective, in that they have also become spiritually, theologically and canonically latinized. In fact, for the past thirty years, they have been seeking to get back to the authentic sources of their tradition. Lastly, the Orthodox churches are also aware that orthopraxy, or "right practice", has sometimes distorted and obscured their original orthodoxy, or "right doctrine", and a return to the sources is precisely one of the objectives of the renewal going on at present.

The challenge of this ecumenism based on common roots is not archeological nostalgia nor ethnic-religious nationalism. It is quite simply – and the fundamentals are always simple – that the churches are together seeking their common roots: the word of God and its living Tradition, through the fathers and the liturgy. Basically, it means taking seriously all that makes the churches local, that through which, in the Middle East, they sacramentally represent the mystery of the one, holy, catholic and apostolic church. This challenge is progressively being taken up and in this the "little flock" that remains is the bearer of hope.

---

[19] Cf. the open letter from the general secretary of the MECC to Western fundamentalist evangelicals, in *Courrier*, 4 (1-1988), pp.51-54; Towards a clarification of "missionary activities" in the Middle East, in *Courrier*, 6 (3-1988), pp.29-30; an open letter from the general secretary of the MECC to the Congress of Evangelicals in Manila, in *Courrier*, 8-9 (2/3-1989), pp.52-53; 2nd consultation between MECC and Western evangelicals, in *Courrier*, 18 (3-1992), pp.55-56.

[20] Cf. "Quelle unité?", last chapter in the book by J. Corbon on *L'Eglise des Arabes*, Paris, Cerf, 1977, 2nd edition in Arabic published by MECC in 1996.

BIBLIOGRAPHY

Assaad, Marie and Padolina, Priscilla eds, *Local Ecumenism – How It Is Manifested: Joint WCC/MECC Regional Workshop, Cairo, Egypt, 9-12 November 1985*, WCC, 1986, no pag.

Ateek, Naim, Duaybis, Cedar and Schrader, Marla eds, *Jerusalem: What Makes for Peace! A Palestinian Contribution to Peacemaking*, London, Melisende, 1997, 241p.

Cragg, Kenneth, *The Arab Christian: A History of the Middle East*, Louisville, Westminster John Knox, 1991, 334p.

Durst, Stefan, *Jerusalem als ökumenisches Problem im 20. Jahrhundert*, Pfaffenweiler, Centaurus, 1993, 403p.

Fry, Ian and Leahy, Peter eds, *Trouble in the Triangle, Book 1: Christians, Jews and Muslims in Conflict: A Critical Reassessment of the Relationship between Christianity, Judaism and Islam*, Fitzroy, Vict., Compton Arch, 2000, 902p.

Jaeger, David-Maria A. ed., *Papers Read at the 1979 Tantur Conference on Christianity in the Holy Land*, Tantur, Ecumenical Institute for Theological Research, 1981, 432p.

Kimball, Charles Anthony, *Angle of Vision : Christians and the Middle East*, New York, Friendship, 1992, 120p.

Nicholl, Donald, *The Testing of Hearts: A Pilgrim's Journal*, London, Marshall Morgan & Scott, 1989, 307p.

Raheb, Mitri, *I Am a Palestinian Christian*, Minneapolis, Fortress, 1995, 164p.

Ucko, Hans ed., *The Spiritual Significance of Jerusalem for Jews, Christians and Muslims : Report on a Colloquium, Glion, Switzerland, 2-6 May 1993*, WCC, 1994, 81p.

Virtue, David W., *A Vision of Hope: The Story of Samuel Habib*, Oxford, Regnum, 1996, 136p.

Wessels, Antonie, *Arab and Christian? Christians in the Middle East*, Kampen, Kok Pharos, 1995, 255p.

Who Is My Neighbour? Report on an Ecumenical Visit to the Middle East, 10-24 March 2001, London, Churches Together in Britain and Ireland, 2001, 135p.

Williamson, Roger ed., *The Holy Land in the Monotheistic Faiths*, Uppsala, Life and Peace Institute, 1992, 190p.

25
North America
Paul A. Crow, Jr

The late Yale historian Sydney E. Ahlstrom noted that the 1960s – searching, turbulent, revolutionary – ended a 400-year period of consensus and commonality in North American religious history. The 1960s (the end of "a Great Puritan Epoch" in Anglo-American culture) was a time "when the old foundations of national confidence, patriotic idealism, moral traditionalism, and even of Judaeo-Christian theism, were awash. Presuppositions that held firm for centuries – even millennia – were widely questioned.... The nation was confronting revolutionary circumstances whose effects were... irreversible." Christians began to experience "deep social and institutional dislocations".[1]

By the end of the 20th century, long heralded as the ecumenical century, cultures and the churches in the United States and, to some extent, Canada, reflected "altered landscapes", to use the imagery of a book by leading American church historians.[2] By this they meant that the culture in which churches in America and Canada made their witness had changed dramatically.

1. The most visible change in this period has been the "crisis" or changing role of the "mainline" churches, those Protestant churches which from the colonial period until the second world war exercised a dominant influence in culture.[3] In defining consensus, moral values, and the Christian political and economic role of the church, they enjoyed the privileges of an unofficial "establishment".

In the 1970s and 1980s an ecumenical shift occurred as these churches began to experience severe decline in membership, major losses in offerings especially to their national agencies, and in public influence, the distrust of institutions, internal conflicts and theological uncertainty. Because of these developments the privileged Protestant mainline churches no longer enjoyed the influence and power they once had exercised.

- There is no regional ecumenical conference for North America. Both the Canadian Council of Churches and the National Council of the Churches of Christ in the US are independent.
[1] Sydney E. Ahlstrom, *A Religious History of the American People*, vol. 2, New Haven, Yale Univ. Press and Image Books, 1975, pp.614-20.
[2] David W. Lotz ed., *Altered Landscapes: Christianity in America 1935-1985*, Grand Rapids MI, Eerdmans, 1989.
[3] They included the American Baptist Churches, the Disciples of Christ, the Episcopal Church, the Evangelical Lutheran Church in America, the Presbyterian Church (USA), the United Church of Christ (earlier the Congregational Church) and the United Methodist Church. In Canada a similar list would include the United Church of Canada, Anglicans, Presbyterians, Disciples of Christ and Lutherans.

More significantly, a common civil faith that once united Americans around the same national values and identity lost its power to hold people together. All this provoked an identity crisis in each of these churches.

Because these churches were the creators and primarily leaders of modern ecumenical institutions – councils of churches, unity negotiations, mission agencies and projects – their crisis has inevitably brought traumatic change, instability and inevitable reordering to the long-serving ecumenical bodies and institutions.

2. Ecumenism in the US has experienced a dramatic pluralism that has many expressions – race, gender, ethnic identity. Diversity or pluralism has long been a positive characteristic of American religious life. Yet the definition of what it means to be American is no longer determined by a melting-pot sociology, politics or theology. Immigration, birth rates and demographics have brought North America to the point where African Americans, Hispanics, Asians and others form significant and distinct communities. Multiculturalism is an emerging reality and a challenge for those who cherish unity as a gift and goal for the church.

The increased role of women in church and society represents another sign of diversity in North American Christianity. In most Protestant and ecumenical theological seminaries women constitute approximately fifty percent of the students and future ministers. From 1968 to 2000, Protestant congregations increasingly accepted women as both lay leaders and ordained ministers.

Expanding pluralism has produced in North America a new phenomenon of ethnic denominations such as Latino Pentecostals, Korean Presbyterians, Solomon Islands Congregationalists, Vietnamese Catholics and Cambodian Methodists. By the mid-1980s Presbyterian (USA) statistics revealed that Koreans were the fastest growing segment – in members and new congregations – of that church. Among the Disciples of Christ, Hispanics are increasing at a much higher rate than any other constituency. Methodists in southern California report that their congregations worship in 24 languages. The implications for liturgy, music, theology and ecumenical consciousness promise dramatic change and renewal.

Will such pluralism expand the sense of catholicity among the churches of North America, or become the source of new forms of competition and division? Two issues will determine the outcome: whether these new identities can be affirmed as part of the one church of Christ in time and space, and whether the American churches embrace pluralism without denying their Christian identity.

3. Another trend over the past thirty years that affects the ecumenical movement in North America is variously called the "new voluntarism", radical individualism, or "privatized" religion. Sociologists of religion have charted this powerful development. Largely characteristic of Americans born since the second world war (baby boomers), this religious instinct is marked by inward concern, individual choice and a self-serving Christianity.[4] Canadian sociologist Reginald Bibbey calls it "religion à la carte".

This voluntarism breeds a suspicion of institutional Christianity. The norms of faith and practice are determined by the individual, not by churches or traditions. This un-

---

[4] Robert Wuthnow, *After Heaven: Spirituality in America since the 1950s*, Berkeley, Univ. of California Press, 2000; *The Restructuring of American Religion*, Princeton, Princeton Univ. Press, 1990; Wade Clark Roof and William McKinney, *American Mainline Religion: Its Changing Shape and Future*, New Brunswick NJ, Rutgers Univ. Press, 1987; see also Robert D. Putnam, *Bowling Alone: The Collapse and Revival of American Community*, 2nd ed., New York, Touchstone, 2001; Robert D. Putnam and Lewis Feldstein, *Better Together: Restoring the American Community*, New York, Simon & Schuster, 2003.

derstanding of Christianity or religion claims little relationship with others. Which church one joins is determined largely through a congregation's marketing strategy.

Such a privatized, voluntaristic Christianity is, to quote Wade Clark Roof, "the most insidious, most challenging of all the trends in eroding religious commitment". Rather than lifting up the church as a communion *(koinonia)*, privatized Christianity defines faith in terms of the separate, spiritual journeys of atomistic individuals. In this sense a privatized Christian is vulnerable to the sectarian spirit and a "tribalism" that defines others as outsiders because they are not "our kind of people".

Such an attitude inevitably causes the decline of commitment to North American denominations which in the past were teachers of the Christian tradition and sources of religious identity. The full Christian tradition is not being handed on, say many observers. Instead the focus now is primarily local and with little appreciation for the wider global church. Even the denominational influence is muted by the cafeteria-style influence of television preachers, para-church organizations, new religious cults, wandering gurus. The new popular idea of the church is based in the church-growth movement with its strategy of non-denominational congregations of 2000 to 10,000 members, for whom marketing strategies are more central than confessional or theological perspectives. In this sort of atmosphere, voices calling for the unity of the church will have to make their witness more articulately and address it to a far more pluralistic culture.

4. The American and Canadian religious landscape has been transformed by the engagement of new ecumenical partners – the Roman Catholic Church, conservative Evangelicals, Pentecostals and Holiness churches. After Vatican II, the Catholic church moved effectively into the mainstream of religious life in both countries. The seismic effect of that council of bishops, cardinals and theologians was to place the Roman Catholic tradition in the midst of the modern world and to commit Catholics to ecumenism and the search for visible unity in partnership with other Christian traditions.

Following this spirit, the US conference of Catholic bishops called upon every bishop and diocese to appoint a diocesan ecumenical officer to nurture the understanding of ecumenism among the parishes and priests. National dialogues between Roman Catholics and Orthodox and Protestant churches have brought these divided Christians closer to each other and to a common faith. Another sign of this ecumenical leadership came in the 1980s when the American Catholic bishops issued pastoral letters – to all Americans, not only Roman Catholics – on peace and nuclear armament and the economy. In these teaching documents, observe Wade Clark Roof and William McKinney, "a once-suspect Catholic leadership had become a major, if not the major, religious voice articulating a public vision for America". Hence, Roman Catholics have greatly influenced the American ecumenical situation by being open to the spirit of Christian unity through theological dialogue, contemporary liturgy, democracy, lay leadership in partnership with priests and bishops and more vital parishes.

In 1975 the mainline Canadian churches formed a unique group of ecumenical justice coalitions with full membership in all of them from the Canadian conference of Catholic bishops.

The American ecumenical situation has also been affected by numerical growth, upward mobility, and movement towards the centre of conservative Protestant, Pentecostal and Holiness churches. Once sectarian and socially marginal, these members of the body of Christ now exercise an increasing influence in North American Christianity and are reaching for common ground with other evangelical Christians. They too are moving from the margins towards the political and theological centre. Unfortunately ecumenical bodies such as councils of churches, as well as many conservative Evangelicals, remain ambivalent about the next steps towards cooperation. These churches increasingly reflect a nascent ecumenism and are a part of the future of the ecumenical movement.

United States of America

THE CONCILIAR MOVEMENT IN THE USA

Unlike the "ecumenical councils" of the early Christian centuries, the "conciliar movement" of the late 20th century was the product of divided churches searching for their given unity in Christ. The criteria for judging their validity lies in the degree to which they have enabled the churches to find their full unity in the one faith and eucharistic fellowship. No council can fulfill its purpose, declared the Montreal world conference on Faith and Order (1963), "without being concerned deliberately with unity. As a council of churches, or as *churches in council*, it manifests a growing mutual understanding of the churches and their will to find ultimate unity."

The National Council of the Churches of Christ in the USA

The centrepiece of 20th-century conciliar ecumenism in the US was the National Council of the Churches of Christ (NCCCUSA), constituted in December 1950, and its predecessor, the Federal Council of Churches of Christ in America (1908-50). The history of both is largely liberal in theology and activist in facing the Christian implications of social and political issues. Both played strong, visible roles among the churches and in the American society.

The original constituency of the NCCC included 29 churches – 25 Protestant and four Eastern Orthodox with a combined membership of nearly 40 million – and 12 interdenominational agencies. From the beginning its members reflected a wide spectrum of churches, ranging from Presbyterian and Reformed; Disciples of Christ; Congregational (later United Church of Christ); Methodist, including African-American; Baptist, Lutheran, Episcopal, Moravian, Church of Brethren, Friends and Orthodox (Russian, Syrian, Antiochian, Romanian, Ukrainian and Greek). Among the agencies that entered the NCCC were those committed to religious education; relief, refugee and development work; Bible translation; home mission, overseas mission, broadcasting and film; missionary education, curriculum and publications; stewardship; youth and university student movements; church women; and the interseminary movement.

Early in its life the NCCC made strong commitments to those dimensions of Christian witness that were to distinguish its history. In its first triennium the churches participated in historic work done on a new translation of the Bible, producing the Revised Standard Version (RSV) in the early 1950s. The RSV gained the distinction of being officially authorized by all major Christian churches: Protestant, Roman Catholic and Eastern Orthodox. In 1974 Protestant and Roman Catholic scholars produced the RSV *Common Bible*, with the apocryphal or deuterocanonical books included. In 1989 ecumenical scholars working through the NCCC produced the New Revised Standard Version (NRSV).

Central to the NCCC's work from the beginning was Church World Service, a worldwide network that expresses the churches' commitment to relief and refugee work, development, caring for the poor and the marginalized through spiritual and material aid. In the 1970s and 1980s these ministries began to encompass the whole global human family in Asia, Africa, Latin America, the Pacific and the Middle East. Throughout its history CWS has represented 70-80 percent of the budget of the NCCC. Beyond the large amount of funds involved, these compassionate ministries are carried out ecumenically, bringing CWS into direct partnership with the World Council of Churches' programme on interchurch aid, refugee service and development, and other ecumenical partners. The broadening of the concepts of CWS and the churches came in 1981 when the WCC's central committee adopted a public statement on "The Churches and the World Refugee Crisis", in which refugees came to include victims of social, economic and political injustice and armed conflicts.

The National Council has been courageous – if not always successful – in its participation in the struggle for racial justice, the war on poverty, and international peace: the work of the commission on religion and racism (1963); the Freedom Summer in Mississippi (1964); the march on Selma, Alabama (1965), coordinated with Martin Luther King, Jr; the Delta ministry (1966-74), a self-help programme for poor share-croppers in Mississippi; and the Crisis of the Nation programme (1967), focused on the poverty that damaged the lives of poor and African Americans in the ghettos of US cities.

In its prophetic social advocacy the NCCC has represented the minority liberal conscience among primarily American Protestants, although their occasional partnership with Roman Catholics and Jews on certain issues has been significant and courageous. Some church leaders would call this witness radical. The Council was thought by many to be out of touch with its constituency, many of whom could not accept its radical commitments. On the other side, black leaders became impatient with the pace of reform on the part of white power structures and began to create their own structures for empowerment. A dilemma of the ecumenical movement is therefore illustrated in the history of the NCCC. At times it courageously named parts of the Christian agenda – human rights, peace, racial dignity – but often it has been ineffective in teaching this responsibility to the churches.

At the height of the cold war the NCCC took another courageous initiative in establishing dialogue between church leaders in the US and the USSR. By the mid-1980s, several waves of American pastors and key church leaders – totalling over 2000 – travelled for seminars to the USSR. There is no doubt that the friendships and discoveries of these groups were a sign of Christian unity and contributed to the fall of the walls separating the West and the East.

The participation of the Orthodox churches in the NCCC has been important but problematic. The reasons are important to address – the Orthodox immigrant mentality, Protestant insensitivity to authentic openness in Orthodox participation, different ecclesiologies. For the Orthodox the NCCC has been and remains dominated by a Protestant leadership and agenda. Some Orthodox parishes have been active in local councils of churches, especially in their humanitarian projects. In an important development the Standing Commission of Orthodox Bishops in America (SCOBA) issued guidelines for Orthodox Christians in ecumenical relations which encouraged limited and cautious involvement. The over-arching hesitancy of the Orthodox bishops, theologians and laity lies in the conviction that the NCCC advocates "positions that run contrary to historic Christian teachings and the concern that Orthodox positions are not taken seriously within the various departments of the Council".[5]

---

[5] Thomas F. FitzGerald, *The Orthodox Church*, Westport CN, Greenwood, 1995, p.126.

The most severe crisis in Orthodox-NCCC relations came in October 1991 when Scoba suspended Orthodox participation in the Council. The action came in the wake of the general board's consideration of the application for membership of the Universal Fellowship of Metropolitan Community Church, a denomination of mostly gay and lesbian members and ministers. In 1986 the general board – after intense debate and by a 70 percent majority – voted not to receive this church in membership but to continue the dialogue. This debate signalled what was at that time undoubtedly the most divisive issue in the ecumenical movement, an issue that has traumatically polarized most mainline churches and ecumenical bodies in the US. Other divisive issues which the Orthodox identified and which required some intentional dialogue were such activities by the NCCC and its member churches as the new inclusive language lectionary that altered texts from the RSV, approaches to the ordination of women and feminist theology. After a joint NCCC-Orthodox commission reviewed these issues and clarified some of the misunderstandings, Scoba decided "temporarily" to reinstate its membership in the NCCC. The full participation of the Orthodox remains a critical need for the NCCC and all other ecumenical bodies, but by the year 2000 there had been little constructive work in this area.

The Roman Catholic Church's links with the NCCC and the American ecumenical movement officially began as a result of Vatican II (1962-65). The bishops encouraged Catholic participation in local celebrations of the Week of Prayer for Christian Unity. In 1966 the National Conference of Catholic Bishops created a committee on ecumenical and inter-religious affairs that established relationships with the NCCC as well as national bilateral dialogues with various Protestant and Orthodox churches. By 1968 over 5000 study groups using the *Living Room Dialogues*, a guide for Protestant-Catholic-Orthodox laity, had been organized. In the mid-1970s the bishops permitted Roman Catholic membership in the Faith and Order commission of the NCCC.

By the late 1960s the changing landscape of the American culture, the emerging crisis of denominational and ecumenical students, and the conflict between differing agendas among Christians posed the need for rethinking the nature of the NCCC and a new structure for its witness. Thus began a long process of attempts to address these issues.

In 1963 a major study produced a new constitution and bylaws and a mild reorganization of the Council. In 1972 the Council integrated its several units and increased the participation of various minority groups. In 1979-80 a panel on ecumenical commitment and NCCC purposes probed the meaning of what would be involved in "authentic ecumenical commitment" by the churches, and identified eight disparities between what the churches affirm about Christian unity and what they do or do not do as members of the NCCC or in other ecumenical relations. The panel's theological report, *Foundations for Ecumenical Commitment*, approved in 1981, was highly fruitful in its proposals. The new vision was articulated in a constitutional revision that redefined the nature and purpose of the NCCC.

No document of the NCCC has ever been as biblical and theological or addressed as clearly the nature of a conciliar body and its implications for the churches. The concept of a cooperative agency that serves the practical needs of the churches was jettisoned. The purpose of the Council was to call the churches "to visible unity as a sign of the unity of humankind and to enable the churches to act responsibly together in living out that wholeness in witness and service to the world". The hope was that the churches would move beyond "interdenominational collaboration to covenantal bonds". This vision was voted by the NCCC's general board, but it was never claimed or enacted by the member churches. The same hopeful possibilities were revisited by a presidential panel on future mission and resources, which in 1984 basically restated the 1980 vision with a slight change in image. The NCCC is called "a community of Christian communion" and specific "marks of our commitment" were set forth for the member communions. In 1995 this interminable process of organizational adjustment proposed the downsizing of NCCC units.

World Council of Churches

Within American conciliar life the US Office of the WCC has played a valuable role. Sometimes called the "New York office", its identity and functions can be traced to the very beginnings of the WCC.

Opposition to and criticism of agencies of the ecumenical movement within the US has not been lacking. Some of these "apostles of discord" have been highly active and visible in the American media, often funded by major support of right-wing groups. From early days the Federal, the National and the World Council Churches have been targets of open opposition from fundamentalists and extremists like Carl McIntyre, who popularized the fear of the ecumenical movement creating a "super church" or leading its churches into Marxist ideology.[6]

The severest attacks on both councils came in three articles in *The Reader's Digest* in 1973, 1983 and 1993. Also in 1983 the CBS television show "60 Minutes" did a television version of these attacks – claiming the councils misused funds and lost the trust of the churches by supporting liberation armies in Africa and elsewhere and by involvement in similar political activities around the world. The churches in the NCCC and the WCC were able to disprove the charges. Research at the time brought forth evidence that assistance to those who made these erroneous attacks was given in the form of funds by the Institute on Religion and Democracy, a neo-conservative research institute in Washington that received a large percentage of its funds from right-wing foundations. After considerable time, the churches have proved that these critiques were gross distortions, but unfortunately the correct interpretation did not always reach the pews and pulpits.

In the final days of the 20th century both the WCC and the NCCC, like most ecumenical institutions, were riding in troubled waters. The changing leadership in the American churches and cultures; the distrust of all institutions, including religious ones; the post-modern critique of the possibility of consensus; the challenge of pluralism and the increased presence of churches outside the ecumenical circle; the sharp decline of contributions and resources – all posed dramatic challenges to conciliar bodies.

Local and regional ecumenism

A principal barometer of ecumenism in the US is the witness of hundreds of local, metropolitan, county and state councils of churches. Indeed, one could say that the chief locus of the joys and trials in the search for unity and mission is evident in the histories,

---

[6] Other sharp critics are James de Forest Murch, C. Marcella Kirk, K.L. Billingsley and Ernest W. Lefever. See *Amsterdam to Nairobi: The World Council of Churches and the Third World*, 1979; and *Council of Churches and the World, 1975-1987; From Mainline to Sideline; The Social Witness of the National Council of Churches*. Each critiqued the NCCC and the WCC for their support of "liberation" movements and political involvements in third-world countries. Less polemical scholars include Paul Ramsey (*Who Speaks for the Churches?*) and Dean M. Kelly (*Why Conservative Churches Are Growing*).

the untold stories of struggle for caring and justice, the networking around Christian councils in cities and towns in all parts of the nation.[7]

In its original structures the NCCC created the office for councils of churches (since renamed twice) with the aim of working intimately with local and state councils, providing assistance in programme planning and evaluation in leadership training and financial matters. Apart from interfacing with other units of the NCCC these offices worked closely with the Association of Council Secretaries and its successor the National Association of Ecumenical Staff, and with professional organizations of council staff which met annually for collegial support and to reflect upon concerns and developments in the conciliar movement. In 1970 the NCCC created the Commission on Regional and Local Ecumenism which became a pivotal network of local, state and regional ecumenical bodies.

Vatican II changed the character of local and regional councils of churches. The updated code of canon law (1983) placed the primary responsibility for teaching and witnessing to ecumenism upon the local bishop. By 1993, 110 dioceses out of 180 in the US had ecumenical officers, who worked within the National Association of Diocesan Ecumenical Officers. At the national level the US Catholic bishops created the Secretariat for Ecumenical and Interreligious Affairs, located in Washington, DC.

In many places Catholic dioceses began to live out the spirit of Vatican II by seeking membership in different councils. Both the invitation and the acceptance for membership were motivated, said a 1988 consultation on Roman Catholic participation in state ecumenical agencies, "by the need to demonstrate the basic oneness of Christ's church and the vision to see that social issues in the state need to be addressed together out of a common understanding of Christ's mandate for justice and compassion". The coming of Roman Catholic participation broadened these councils ecclesiologically and brought new priorities to the ecumenical table – the centrality of worship, a eucharistic understanding of the goal of unity, commitment to ecumenical formation of priests and laity. It also brought a new generation of conflictive issues – abortion, the ordination of women and aid to parochial schools. In all cases, when they became members Roman Catholics took that membership seriously.

In the late 1960s the major changes in Western culture and the "altered landscape" in the US created a crisis in local and regional ecumenism. The sources of the cultural side of this crisis, as a study by Arleon L. Kelley and Kathleen Hurty reveals, were the urban, racial and social upheavals – recognized in the late 1960s but continuing even at the end of the century – and the trauma in America over the Vietnam war. The myths of innocence and progress were gone for ever. In the same way the crisis of the mainline churches dealt a body-blow to ecumenical organizations – in terms of decreased funding, ownership and the sense of a common agenda. This crisis challenged the viability of many councils and many did not survive. In 1976 only half as many ecumenical organizations existed as in 1967. Across the country, individually and collectively in the 1980s and 1990s, councils tried to analyze the evident changes and their implications. The responses were mixed; some appeared constructive and hopeful, others unprofitable:

---

[7] See the book of essays *A Tapestry of Justice, Service and Unity: Local Ecumenism in the United States 1950-2000*, Arleon L. Kelly ed., Tacoma WA, National Association of Ecumenical and Interreligious Staff, 2004.

- Some councils pressed for deeper theological and ecclesiological reflections. In his 1983-84 survey Grover Hartman, dean of local and regional executives, observed that the most vital conciliar organizations place Faith and Order at the heart of their life. If this is true, the new dimension of the theological task before the churches lies in the relationship between theology or ecclesiology and ethics, between what the church *is* and what the church *does*. Those pursuing this insight say that any ethical decision-making is integrally related to the church's worship, its confession of faith, its witness and service to the world.

- Some councils have boldly embraced a model of inclusiveness in their vision of unity and in their daily witness. Past models of ecumenical bodies involved primarily white men, people of power from powerful churches, liked-minded and like-cultured churches. This created a marginalization of others – women, people of colour, the poor – that caused these groups to look at the ecumenical movement with a hermeneutic of suspicion. The presence and participation of lay baptized Christians, especially "the new voices", required a recasting of the ways councils worked.

- In response to the new pluralism in the cities and villages of America, some Christian councils reconstituted themselves as interfaith organizations. The National Association of Ecumenical Staff changed its name to the National Association of Ecumenical and Interreligious Staff. This move has been one of the most controversial ecumenical developments in recent decades. While interfaith dialogue and work for the common good in society was more essential in the last decade of the 20th century than ever before, many have argued that any interfaith dialogue requires a common Christian perspective. Otherwise divided churches will have little to contribute.[8]

- Councils have placed enormous time and resources in restructuring their organizations. In his extraordinarily helpful study, funded by the Lilly Endowment and evaluating the present state of local and regional ecumenism in the US, Gary Peluso points out that "changing agendas require changing structures". Yet the bane of most of the North American churches and ecumenical agencies in recent decades has been what he calls "structural tinkering" – incessantly restructuring a denomination's or local council's structure and blithely assuming that the new structures will resolve the dysfunctions of the church today. The experience of ecumenical restructuring is clear. Renewal will come from engaging the ecumenical vision within the new realities that face the ecumenical movement.

Thus at the end of the 20th century these local and regional ecumenical bodies, so fundamental to the fabric of ecumenism in the US, are at the crossroads.

Church Women United

A gem in American ecumenism, unheralded by historians, has been Church Women United, the movement of ecumenical cooperation among church women. The historical roots of this movement can be found in the missionary societies of 19th-century Amer-

---

[8] Diane C. Kessler, executive director of the Massachusetts Council of Churches, identifies the fundamental issue at stake: "How inclusive can Christianity be of various cultural assumptions and practices before it violates its fundamental theological basis? What are the proper grounds for and what is the appropriate purpose of evangelization? Who is within the saving realm of God, and on what grounds do Christians base these claims? What is the purpose of the unity we seek for the churches and why are we seeking it? How does that unity relate to the unity of all humankind, indeed of the cosmos?" "New Angles in a Lively Debate: Should Ecumenical Organizations Be Christian or Interfaith?", in *Mid-Stream*, 32, 4, Oct. 1993, p.34.

ica, most of which were founded by women. These societies were part of a wider women's movement of the time which witnessed on behalf of temperance, anti-slavery, voting rights for women, prison reform and the visible leadership of women in higher education, business and industry.[9]

In 1950, the United Council of Church Women (founded in 1941 and bringing together three national women's groups and representatives of seventy Protestant denominations) was one of the interdenominational agencies to form the National Council of Churches, becoming the general department of United Church Women in the new structure. The decision to join the NCCC was taken with no little anxiety over the possible marginalization of women in leadership positions as well as concern that their prophetic witness on social and political issues might be controlled. Later years proved that the integration did not work.

In 1971 United Church Women exited from the NCCC and again became an autonomous body, changing its name slightly to Church Women United (CWU). The primary factors for this withdrawal were a commitment "to trust church women united to church women" and a discontent with its financial obligations within the NCCC structures (e.g., its payments for administrative central services were far more within the NCCC than the costs would have been were it on its own). With its self-governance and priority-setting regained, CWU became more dynamic and reached for new challenges. As women became more integrated into the leadership of the churches, they began to address more aggressively the issues confronting Christians in the larger society. A consultative office was established at the Church Center for the UN in New York City. A national programme was set in motion that addressed the ills of racism, illiteracy among children and adults, discriminatory housing for minorities, hunger among school children, economic development in Africa, Asia and Latin America.

CWU became more inclusive, seeking to attract church women who had not been significant participants in any ecumenical organizations – younger women, professional women, and women of racial and ethnic minorities. Bridges began to be built with Roman Catholic and Orthodox women locally, nationally and internationally. Its ecumenical purpose was defined in new by-laws:

> to encourage church women to come together in a visible fellowship to witness to their faith in Jesus Christ as divine Lord and Saviour and, enabled by his Spirit, to go out together into every neighbourhood as instruments of his reconciling love.

In triennial assemblies and local gatherings during the past three decades Church Women United's strategy has been effective. In 1984 a Washington office was established to advocate and seek to shape policy in the US government. In 1985 a project known as "The Imperative" pledged the resources of CWU to break the cycle of poverty among children and women by eliminating the root causes of poverty and prejudice against the poor. In the early 1990s programmes were set up to overcome violence against women and the impoverishing economic conditions that confront all women.

Among ecumenical organizations in the US, none lives with more vitality and viability than Church Women United. Its vision and witness live in local communities, express its strong Christian faith, and focus upon caring for God's little ones.

---

[9] See Robert Grimm and Kathleen S. Hurty, "Prayer, Power, and Prophetic Action: Church Women United", in *A Tapestry of Justice, Service and Unity*, pp.71-102.

VISIBLE CHURCH UNITY IN AMERICA

In the 20th century, many church leaders and local Christians concluded that cooperation among permanently separated churches is not enough. The fellowship that results
from cooperation does not necessarily bind together the life and faith of the churches.
However, there is widespread scepticism about plans of unity that call for the merger of
church structures or polities. Models affirmed most positively by US churches in the late
20th century tended to be those characterized by unity in diversity. The form of unity
sought was one that could overcome division, but a unity where theological, ethnic,
racial, national and cultural differences are held together in dynamic tension as a sign
and the first-fruits of God's purpose to reconcile all things in Christ. This sort of unity
has been called "organic union", "visible unity", "full communion", "conciliar fellowship", "fully committed fellowship", "reconciled diversity", *"koinonia* in faith, life and
witness" and "covenant communion".

Each of these models of visible unity had a particular nuance that enriched the understanding and goal of ecumenism. Yet it was commonly understood that each model
called the churches to the same fundamental expressions:
- confessing together the one apostolic faith;
- recognizing a common baptism and celebrating the eucharist together;
- mutually accepting and reconciling the ordained ministries;
- engaging in common mission, justice and caring for the world.

United Methodist Church

This church was formed in 1968 by the uniting of the Methodist Church and the Evangelical United Brethren (EUB) Church, both themselves products of earlier mergers. In
1946 the Evangelical Association and the Church of the United Brethren united – both
reflecting the faith of immigrants from Germany and German-American revivalists. In
1938 the estranged Methodist Episcopal Church and the Methodist Episcopal Church,
South – separated in 1844 over the slavery issue and tensions related to the coming
American civil war – reunited. The EUB and Methodist Episcopals were joined in 1968
by a small Methodist Protestant Church to constitute the United Methodist Church, the
second largest Protestant church in the country. In this act, all American Methodism became one church except for the three African American Methodist churches which had
been forced out of the Methodist and Episcopal churches because of racism in 19th-
century America.

Presbyterian Church (USA)

On 10 June 1983 the Presbyterian Church (USA) was brought into being, uniting the former Presbyterian Church in the US – with congregations and presbyteries primarily in
the American South – and the former United Presbyterian Church in the United States
of America. These two communions were once one church until divided in 1861 by the
animosities of the American civil war.

Church union negotiations began again in 1969 at the initiative of the Southern
Presbyterian Church. In 1977 the general assemblies of both churches looked favourably
upon the possibility of reconciliation yet urged a gradual process. The proposed future
was focused on cooperation and joint mission at every level of church life, the creation
of union presbyteries, holding joint general assemblies every other year, the sharing of
programme funds, the cross-deployment of presbytery and national staff, and the joint

commissioning of overseas fraternal workers. These interim steps drew these two churches together so that within a decade 250,000 Presbyterians belonged to union congregations and presbyteries. Also the emphasis upon missional and functional unity began to soften the distrust and alienation between these two churches with the same name, doctrine and polity. Ministers and lay people in both traditions became aware of each other and the need to be visibly one. By 1978 the two general assemblies referred a plan of union to the presbyteries for study and response. In 1983 the plan was approved and union was inaugurated with a great celebration.

The Presbyterian Church (USA), like other mainline churches, has reverberated between the crisis of identity, creative attempts to relate the gospel to a radically changing culture, periodic but short-lived attempts to restructure the church, and internal conflict between conservatives and moderates. In the 1980s and 1990s Presbyterians were typical of mainline US churches: the deepest differences were now *within* traditions rather than between them. So, too, Presbyterians and certain other mainline churches reflected the ills of a merger mentality that thwarts the desire for a united church which can comprehend differences. In spite of such struggles, however, Presbyterian ecclesiology and mission kept alive a strong commitment to the search for a wider unity.

Evangelical Lutheran Church in America

On 1 January 1988, the Evangelical Lutheran Church in America was created by the merger of the Lutheran Church in America (LCA), the American Lutheran Church (ALC) and the small (150 congregations) Association of Evangelical Lutheran Churches. In this act two-thirds of all Lutherans in the USA (5.3 million members and over 11,000 congregations) found life in one ecclesial fellowship. Two of these churches were earlier mergers of ethnic Lutherans from Scandinavia and continental Europe. The ALC, mostly mid-Western in locale and outlook, was constituted in 1960; the LCA, largely reflecting north-eastern roots, was formed in 1963. The AELC was a 1978 ecumenical breakaway from the arch-conservative and anti-ecumenical Lutheran Church-Missouri Synod.

In 1978 the LCA and the ALC approved "A Statement on Communion Practices" that called for intercommunion and provided guidelines for eucharistic sharing in inter-Lutheran and ecumenical gatherings. In 1981 an opinion poll taken in all three churches revealed overwhelming approval of a move towards Lutheran unity. In 1982 the three churches established a commission for a new Lutheran church to facilitate the union and to draft a plan of union. Negotiations lasting from 1979 to 1987 revealed hopes, hesitancy and even conflict over serious issues: the nature of the church (ALC focused on the congregations, LCA on synods or districts); relations between congregations and larger expressions of the church; the nature of the office of bishop or district president (elected in the LCA for life, in the ALC for a term); the importance of quotas – women, minority racial and ethnic groups, clergy and laity – elected to conventions and committees; the church's role in society; and future ecumenical relations.

A policy statement entitled "Ecumenism: The Vision of the ELCA" (1991) made ecumenism and Christian unity a fundamental part of the new ELCA's life and witness. Guided by this vision, Lutherans in the US have been energetic partners in bilateral dialogues with Roman Catholics, Eastern Orthodox, Episcopalians, Reformed, Methodists and others. In 1989 the ELCA's church-wide assembly voted to delay action on the report of the Lutheran-Episcopal dialogue. Then in a dramatic action at the 1997 church-wide assembly, Lutherans failed to approve by the constitutional two-thirds vote the concordat of agreement with the Episcopal Church, which earlier in the same summer had overwhelmingly approved the concordat calling for full communion. Ironically, the same Lutheran assembly voted by over 90 percent to enter into pulpit and altar fellowship with three Reformed churches – the Presbyterian Church (USA), the United Church of Christ and the Reformed Church in America. After the traumatic negative vote, ELCA and Episcopal leaders initiated a process to revise the concordat and successfully brought the agreement "Called to Common Mission" to the church assemblies in 1999 and 2000.

Consultation on Church Union and Churches Uniting in Christ

The boldest and most comprehensive attempt at visible church unity in the US has been the nine-church Consultation on Church Union (COCU). The definitive moment for this multilateral movement towards reconciliation was an electrifying sermon preached on 4 December 1960 at San Francisco by Eugene Carson Blake – then stated clerk of the United Presbyterian Church and later general secretary of the WCC. Entitled "A Proposal Towards the Reunion of Christ's Church", his sermon called for a united church "catholic and reformed", but COCU quickly added "evangelical", a third mark of the church. Blake's fundamental motive was the conviction that "God requires us to break through the barriers of nearly five hundred years of history of our churches, and to find a way together to unite them so that by manifesting the unity given us by our Lord Jesus Christ, his church may be renewed for its mission to our nation and to the world so that the world may believe".[10]

The public responses in the churches and the media were hopeful. The four original churches envisaged by Blake were the United Presbyterian Church, the Episcopal Church, the Methodist Church and the United Church of Christ. Eventually these churches were joined by the African Methodist Episcopal Church, the African Methodist Episcopal Zion Church, the Christian Methodist Episcopal Church, the Christian Church (Disciples of Christ), and the International Council of Community Churches. Churches Uniting in Christ was officially constituted by the churches at its first plenary in 1962.

In 1970 a commission brought before the churches "A Plan of Union for the Church of Christ Uniting", an enhanced version of the theological consensus drawn up in the "Principles of Church Union" in 1966, with structural proposals for the organization and governance of the united church. Also included were theologically crafted liturgies for the different occasions. Common regional and national judicatory structures were envisioned. Unique in the plan was the proposal to bring local congregations of different races, cultures and economic strata together in a "parish", a cluster of congregations from diverse traditions including at least one African American congregation. However, the parish concept failed to understand how fundamental the congregation – where Christian identity and worship are located – is to Americans' understanding of the church.

Statistics reveal that the plan of union was one of the most widely distributed (500,000 copies) and studied (responses from 3000 study groups and individuals) ecumenical documents. The thousands of responses from member churches and local

---

[10] Eugene Carson Blake, "A Proposal towards the Reunion of Christ's Church", in *Mid-Stream* 37,3-4, July/Oct. 1998, pp.285-97.

study groups affirmed the theological vision of the church, reflected in "Principles of Church Union" and "A Plan of Union", but the proposals for structural union were rejected. These nine churches were not yet ready to enter into full organic union, but neither did they want to disband the Consultation. The churches called for a model of visible unity that would encourage diversity.

A part of the catholic creativity of COCU's witness was the development of liturgical texts and services for use in the proposed united church and even in other ecumenical contexts. In 1968 the commission on worship — one of the most gifted and productive working groups — published the first COCU liturgy: *An Order of Worship for the Proclamation of the Word of God and the Celebration of the Lord's Supper*. A second eucharistic liturgy, *Word Bread Cup*, appeared in 1978, reflecting a less formal style, a more flexible order and a wider cultural context. Other worship texts published were: *An Order for the Celebration of Holy Baptism with Commentary* (1973); *Guidelines for Interim Eucharistic Fellowship* (1973); *An Affirmation on Mutual Recognition of Members in One Baptism* (1974); *A Lectionary* (1974); and *An Order for Thanksgiving for the Birth or Adoption of a Child* (1980). These liturgical texts were used rather widely throughout the US and were carriers of the vision of a united church.

At the 1971 plenary, there were early signs of a changing cultural situation in the US. In 1972 the general assembly of the United Presbyterian Church – the founding church – in a surprise action voted to withdraw from COCU. The following year the Presbyterians voted to return to full participation. What seemed like a blip on the ecumenical screen proved to be a sign of key factors that in the coming decades would haunt every ecumenical venture – increasing apathy towards ecumenism, uncertainty about denominational identity, distrust of leadership beyond the congregation, differing visions of justice and unity.

COCU developed a new strategy to express unity among local congregations. Two models creatively gave signs of unity in local communities: "Generating Communities" which encouraged engagement together in mission, and "Interim Eucharistic Fellowships" which brought congregations together for a common celebration of the Lord's supper, prayer for and study of Christian unity. In the meantime COCU sought to discover a model of visible unity with diversity which addressed the deepest divisions that separate the human community – racism, sexism and disability.

Eventually two decisions were made: to issue and claim "The COCU Consensus" (1985), a revision of the theological chapters in "A Plan of Union"; and to commit COCU to the model of "covenant communion".

In 1988 a new phase of COCU's history began with the issuance of a new concept and document, "Churches in Covenant Communion: The Church of Christ Uniting". The essence of "covenant communion" was clearly described: it implied not the consolidation of forms and structures, but what the early church referred to as "communion in sacred things". Such unity meant becoming one in faith, sacraments, ministry and mission. This kind of unity was visible and organic, whether or not organizational structures were to be consolidated.[11]

Covenant communion or "covenanting" represented both an act by which the churches committed themselves to each other and a process that drew the churches into

---

[11] Consultation on Church Union, "Churches in Covenant Communion" and "The COCU Consensus", combined and revised edition, Princeton, Consultation on Church Union, 1995.

more mature relationships and common life. In covenanting, diversities remain within the one body while the covenanting churches gradually become one. Each church was to maintain as long as they wished their own structures and traditions, yet the churches would intentionally express their unity in faith, sacraments, ministry and mission.

These proposals were before the member churches for more than a decade. Recurring points of controversy included the nature of ordained ministry and especially the office of bishop, varying understandings of apostolic succession, the role of the covenanting council in relation to existing denominational structures, and COCU's commitment to overcoming racism.

By the time of the 18th COCU plenary in 1999, it was understood that the process required new direction and energy. This was sought in a combination of official responses to the 1988 plan from the nine member churches, and a "spiritual discernment process" in plenary aimed at achieving a consensus on the prospect of continuing towards visible unity of the church.[12]

In the end, the plenary produced and adopted a proposal for a new covenant relationship to be known as Churches Uniting in Christ (CUIC).[13] It also adopted and commended to the churches a companion statement, "A Call to Christian Commitment and Action to Combat Racism".

The document addressed by the plenary to the churches described nine "visible marks" characterizing Churches Uniting in Christ: (1) mutual recognition of one another as authentic expressions of the one church of Jesus Christ; (2) mutual recognition of members through one baptism; (3) mutual recognition of ordained ministry; (4) mutual recognition that each affirms the apostolic faith of scripture and Tradition as preserved in the Apostles' and Nicene Creeds; (5) provision for the regular celebration of the eucharist together, acknowledged as the heart of the church's life; (6) "engagement together in Christ's mission on a regular and intentional basis, especially a shared mission to combat racism"; (7) opposition to exclusion from church or society based on "such things as race, age, gender, forms of disability, sexual orientation and class"; (8) commitment to an ongoing process of theological dialogue; (9) appropriate structures of accountability and means for consultation and decision-making, flexible and adaptable to local circumstances.

The nine COCU church delegations approved the proposal unanimously – with a word of warning that "unreconciled issues of ordained ministry" would have to be worked out within the fellowship of CUIC, sooner rather than later. Authority and oversight would clearly be key issues in the "ongoing process of theological dialogue" to which CUIC was pledged.

The plenary extended again an open invitation to other churches to become involved in covenanting. The US conference of Catholic bishops continued as an observer of the process, and the Evangelical Lutheran Church in America and the Northern Province of the Moravian Church officially accepted the status of partnership in dialogue and mission.

As the 20th century drew to a close, it was clear that all nine of the member churches would approve a "public declaration and liturgical celebration" of CUIC to be held in Memphis, Tennessee, in 2002.

---

[12] See *Mid-Stream*, 34, nos 3-4, July-Oct. 1995, "The Promise of the Consultation on Church Union"; 37, nos 3-4, July-Oct. 1998, pp.275-456, "Preparatory Papers on the Consultation on Church Union's Plenary, St Louis, Missouri, Jan. 20-24, 1999".

[13] Thomas F. Best and correspondents, "Survey of Church Union Negotiations 1999-2000", in *The Ecumenical Review*, 54, 3, July 2002, pp.402-06.

The potential of Churches Uniting in Christ represents a new depth and vitality in American churches' search for faithfulness, reconciliation and renewal. Its potential gifts are enormous for a society torn by debilitating denominational and cultural divisions. The presence of the three African American churches requires the other communions to address the question of racism – the most divisive reality in America – and to search for visible unity with justice and inclusiveness. In CUIC the unity of the church and the renewal of human community are seen as the same mandate of the gospel.

Yet Churches Uniting in Christ have yet to address the "altered landscape" of Christianity in America. The internal and cultural crisis of the mainline communions calls for the restatement of the biblical vision and the conversion of a new generation to the unity of the church.

Ecumenical partnership between the Christian Church (Disciples of Christ) and the United Church of Christ

Following decades of bilateral conversations on means towards unity, these two churches explicitly did not perceive their goal as an organizational merger of existing structures and institutions. Theirs would be a visible unity with diversity; a unity that would encourage the fuller participation of all members, especially the laity, racial and ethnic minorities, youth and women in the life and leadership of the church; a unity that would resolve the historic divisions that prevented common mission and sharing the Lord's supper; such a unity would emerge step by step along a common faith journey. This sort of unity was given the name of "ecumenical partnership".

After a decade of significant work, the 1985 Disciples general assembly and the UCC general synod declared that ecumenical partnership exists between the churches, basing the new relationship on ten "Theological Affirmations for Our Life as Ecumenical Partners" and focusing their continuing life together on common mission, common theological work and common worship. In 1989 another step came with the declaration of full communion, to be expressed through the common confession of Jesus Christ; the recognition that members of each partner church are members of the one universal church of Jesus Christ and linked to one another as members of one body; the celebration of the Lord's supper together in all levels of church life; the recognition of the ordained ministers of each partner church as "truly ministers of word and sacrament"; common mission and witness in the world, especially by embodying God's justice, peace and love to the poor and oppressed. These marks of ecumenical partnership were reminiscent of COCU's elements of covenant communion in the same period, thus illustrating the continuing commitment to make this unity expressive of the goal of Churches Uniting in Christ.

In the last decade of the century these marks of covenant communion began to find fuller expression. In 1994 the Division of Overseas Ministries (Disciples) and the United Church Board for World Ministries (UCC) took a courageous decision by forming a common global ministries board which knits together all overseas mission. The crowning expression of full communion came in 1997 when services for the reconciliation of ministries were celebrated in the national assemblies of both churches.

Faith and Order

An irony of the modern ecumenical movement lies in the fact that the origins of the Faith and Order movement took form first in the United States. History reveals that Christian witness in America has been overwhelmingly pragmatic, volunteeristic, focused on action rather than theology – all in contrast to a vision of church unity that is confessional, sacramental and ecclesiological. Yet the initiative towards a world conference on Faith and Order came in 1910 from the general convention of the Protestant Episcopal Church (Anglican) and was on the same day seconded by the general assembly of the Disciples of Christ.[14]

Faith and Order became a permanent presence of ecumenism in the US and Canada in September 1957, with the convening of the North American conference on faith and order at Oberlin, Ohio. Under the theme "The Nature of the Unity We Seek", the churches addressed an assorted but propitious agenda: the gospel and the imperative to unity; doctrinal consensus and conflict; baptism, the Lord's supper, unity and the organizational life of the churches; unity and the life of congregations; the role of cultural factors in the disunity and unity of the church; racial and economic stratification; ecumenism on university and college campuses; the impact of the mobility of the population. One of the results of the Oberlin conference was the creation in 1958 of the Faith and Order department in the NCCCUSA.

Within the last three decades Faith and Order in the US has shown imagination in its work.[15] A courageous study addressed "The Ecclesiological Significance of Councils of Churches", asking the key question, "Is the reality of the church expressed in councils of churches?" The reply was cautiously positive. While councils do not and cannot administer the sacraments, ordain people to the ministry, constitute proper church order, define the faith, "there are convincing signs of the presence and activity of God the Holy Spirit in the council of churches movement". Signs of the Spirit, claimed the report, are in their witness to the lordship of Jesus Christ over the world, compassion and service to the needs of people in God's name and calling the churches to reconciliation.

In the late 1960s and early 1970s a new imaginative model of "living-room dialogues" was developed with the intention of taking Faith and Order and other ecumenical issues to lay people in local communities across the US. The plan brought together 12-15 lay people – Roman Catholic, Orthodox and Protestant – in informal settings in homes.

Gradually, the Faith and Order circle was expanded to include official members of churches beyond the membership of the NCCC, the Roman Catholic Church, the Southern Baptist Convention and the Lutheran Church-Missouri Synod. This circle later widened to include representatives of the Pentecostal, Holiness, Church of Christ and Seventh-day Adventist communions.

Faith and Order was also the catalytic centre for the symbolic though unofficial participation of Roman Catholics in the NCCC. Onto the Faith and Order staff came the first Roman Catholic members. From this staff also came the probe as to whether or not the Roman Catholic Church might become a full member of the Council, along with Orthodox and Protestant churches. However, hesitancies in both camps has left this ecumenical option unfulfilled.

In the 1970s Faith and Order broadened its agenda to include the full participation and concerns of women, African Americans and Hispanics. Studies were pursued on

---

[14] See Paul A. Crow, Jr, "The Formative Role of the American Churches in the Origin and Development of the Faith and Order Movement", in *Story Lines: Chapters on Thought, Word, and Deed for Gabriel Fackre*, Skye Fackre Gibson ed., Grand Rapids MI, Eerdmans, 2002, pp.157-72.

[15] See Jeffrey Gros, FSC, "The Vision of Christian Unity: Some Aspects of Faith and Order in the Context of United States Culture", in *Mid-Stream*, 30, 1, Jan. 1991, pp.1-19; and Melanie May, "Faith and Order in the USA: A Future Glance", in *Mid-Stream*, 31, 4, Oct. 1992, pp.289-300.

"The Community of Women in Church and Society", pressing the reception of the WCC's Nairobi statement on unity (1975), and the spirituality of the struggle for human rights.

Studies in the 1980s centred on traditional Faith and Order issues present in the bilateral dialogues, church union processes, and the witness of the patristics churches. Other issues of particular relevance to the changing American culture were also addressed: the unity of the church and the struggle for justice, and the reality of AIDS. In this period of energizing developments, major attention was given to the WCC's convergence text *Baptism, Eucharist and Ministry* (1982) and a study on the apostolic faith.

Twelve American member churches of the WCC made official responses to BEM. To assist the reception process for BEM in the US, the Faith and Order commission of the NCCC sponsored three conferences across the country. The substantial issues in US churches' responses to BEM included: authority, scripture and Tradition; the role of women in ministry; the ministry of all the baptized; the distinction between *episcopos* (bishop) and *episcope* (oversight); the place of non-sacramental and Pentecostal churches in relation to the BEM ecclesiology; gender-inclusive language; the tension between the Life and Work and the Faith and Order agendas.

At Lima, Peru, in 1982 the WCC Faith and Order Commission also officially initiated a new theological programme, "Towards a Common Expression of the Apostolic Faith Today". The US Faith and Order commission soon launched a study to explore this theme within the American context. Extraordinary reflections came as this study was nuanced by the experiences of the African American churches and by the ecclesiological perspectives of non-credal communities such as Pentecostal, Holiness, Southern Baptist and Peace (Mennonite) churches. Faith and Order concerns speak dramatically to the American context, but it takes interpretation to raise its place on the churches' agenda.

BILATERAL DIALOGUES IN THE US

In the early 1960s, prompted largely by the ecumenical vision of Vatican II, another approach to church unity was initiated and began to assume prominence in the one ecumenical movement. Two churches or families of churches committed themselves to "bilateral dialogues", official theological explorations addressing specific issues that separate these traditions. Some sought only mutual understanding between these traditions. Others had the deeper intention of full communion and the reconciliation of their historical memories and relationships. Some bilaterals were international, usually with more visibility and public attention, while others drew the same churches into bilaterals within a national context.

The flourishing of bilateral dialogue since Vatican II is due primarily to two factors. The earlier multilateral theological encounters in the settings of the Faith and Order movement and united churches such as the Church of South India had prepared the ground for a more intimate relationship between two churches. The simpler bilateral allows the churches to know more comprehensively the ecclesiology, worship and ethics of the partner communion. Second, as the Roman Catholic Church took initiatives in "the restoration of unity among all Christians" and "making the first approach" towards other churches – as mandated by the "Decree on Ecumenism" – it preferred the model of bilateral dialogues.

The bilaterals in the US constitute an interesting mosaic. All have contributed to the ecumenical vision in a nation particularly defined by church divisions. The literature related to these bilateral dialogues is so prolific that we cannot in this chapter cover it all. Yet it is important to identify the partners and the measure of progress towards visible unity which each represents. Without any gradations of status or priority, all represent God's rich gifts to the church and the ecumenical movement.

The following bilaterals stand among the significant dialogues in the US between 1962 and 2000: Lutheran-Reformed (1962); Lutheran-Episcopal (1969); Lutheran-Baptist (1979); Lutheran-Orthodox (1983); Lutheran-United Methodist (1977-79); Disciples of Christ-Roman Catholic (1967-74); Roman Catholic-Southern Baptist (1974); Roman Catholic-Lutheran (1965); Roman Catholic-Orthodox (1965); Roman Catholic-Oriental Orthodox (1980); Roman Catholic-Polish National Catholic; Roman Catholic-Presbyterian and Reformed (1965); United Methodist-Roman Catholic (1966); Pentecostal-Roman Catholic; and United Methodist-AME, AMEZ, CME; Anglican-Orthodox (1983).

Among the common themes there is considerable convergence.[16] At the same time certain dialogues have made particular theological breakthroughs that could eventually serve the whole ecumenical movement beyond the two particular partners.

Significant agreed statements on the centrality and meaning of the eucharist have been made by the Lutheran-Roman Catholic (1968), the Lutheran-Episcopal (1981) and the Anglican-Orthodox (1988) dialogues. Each dialogue reflects the influence of the World Council of Churches convergence text *Baptism, Eucharist and Ministry* (1982). The United Methodist-Roman Catholic dialogue did solid work on the untypical topics of "Holiness and Spirituality of the Ordained Ministry" (1976) and "Holy Living, Holy Dying" (1988) which expressed common ground on the ethical issues involved in the care of the dying. This latter statement reveals that even ethical and pastoral principles must be based on scripture, Tradition, experience and reason. Issues related to the ordained ministry, especially the ordination of women and the episcopacy, have been creatively dealt with in the Lutheran-Episcopal context. Unique to the Roman Catholic-Orthodox dialogue are six texts on pastoral care for wives, husbands and children in Orthodox-Catholic marriage.

In the Lutheran-Roman Catholic US dialogue two ecumenical issues which have long evoked controversy – the papacy and the role of Mary – have found considerable consensus that will be a resource for the cause of unity beyond these two churches. In the rather lengthy common statement on "Differing Attitudes towards Papal Primacy" (1973), American Lutheran theologians admitted the possibility of "a specific office of ministry to serve the church's unity and universal mission". This model of attaining the universal unity of the church is spoken of as a "Petrine function", that is, represented in the bishop of Rome.

Another historically divisive issue since the 16th-century Reformation which has received constructive treatment in US bilateral dialogues is the role of Mary in the church. Some hopeful beginnings have been made in the Lutheran-Roman Catholic dialogue, as seen in its report on "The One Mediator, the Saints, and Mary" (1990).

There is a unique dialogue between the large and powerful United Methodist Church and three African American Methodist traditions: the African Methodist Episcopal,

---

[16] One finds many common themes – the gospel; mission and the world; baptism; the eucharist; the ministry, especially the historic episcopate; ecumenical methodology; and ecclesiology. The fruits of the theological convergences are recorded in the many reports issued individually by the different dialogues, but also are published in volumes like *Building Unity: Ecumenical Dialogues with Roman Catholic Participation in the United States* (1989) and *Growing Consensus: Church Dialogues in the United States, 1962-1991* (1995).

African Methodist Episcopal Zion and Christian Methodist Episcopal. This dialogue has been sporadic, but in the mid-1990s was rejuvenated. Its significance lies in the fact that slavery and racism created division. While the polities, worship, concepts of ministry and episcopacy reflect the same Methodist tradition, any visible church unity is haunted and forestalled by the unreconciled memories of a history of racism and white Methodist domination.

In the triennium of 1984-87 the NCCC's Faith and Order commission reviewed all the American bilaterals and identified 34 findings or constructive ecumenical insights that will move the churches from separation to reconciliation. Then this report pressed the churches to translate their theological agreements into a new official relationship of unity, saying,

> Cumulatively considered, these agreements indicate that the ecumenical movement has reached the stage for moving beyond finding commonalities and formulating consensus; the ecumenical movement has now reached the stage of proposing to the churches a new agenda for proceeding to the reception of the results and for proposing common action based upon this new level of ecumenical agreement.

NEW FRONTIERS OF CHRISTIAN UNITY

Black ecumenism

A phenomenon of ecumenical Christianity in the US in recent times is African American ecumenism, a development of the black consciousness movement of the 1960s and its theological component, black theology. In her important study, *Black Ecumenism: Implementing the Demands of Justice*, Mary R. Sawyer, posits this description of the contemporary black ecumenical movement:

> Their agenda is empowerment and liberation. Their goal is participation as equals among equals in an ethnically pluralistic American society and in a universal Christian church comprised of culturally defined particularities. Their strategy is cooperative, interdenominational action involving the historic black denominations and black enclaves within predominant white denominations, both Protestant and Catholic.[17]

The black or African American churches – primarily Methodist, Baptist and Pentecostal – were born to care for those excluded from the traditional churches and who suffered the sins of slavery, segregation, and personal and economic oppression. These Christians understood themselves to be part of the church universal, yet they were marginalized from full fellowship and participation in the American church and culture. The long-awaited reversal began in the 1960s, as their ethnic pride, confidence and solidarity became strong enough to bring new self-identity and empowerment.

Black ecumenism has had two expressions which coexist in American ecumenism. The first involves the participation of African American churches in the traditional 20th-century ecumenical movement in the US. The second is expressed among those organizations committed to the unity of the African American churches. The contrast in goals and agenda between the two is clear. These latter institutions pursue cooperation in social, economic and racial empowerment that comes from identification with poor and marginalized people. Their priority, empowerment and liberation, is achieved through the struggle for justice, rather than theological consensus.

---

[17] Philadelphia, Trinity, 1994.

The tension and scepticism between these two visions of ecumenism was boldly stated in the report of a 1984 NCCC Faith and Order consultation on "Towards a Common Expression of Faith: A Black North American Perspective". For black ecumenism, Christian unity is possible only when justice is achieved and there is "acceptance of suffering under Christ's work of liberation and when there is commitment to his mission". Moving towards the church universal means defining faith and ecclesiology with the experience of black Christians being at the centre, not on the periphery.

The NCCC was an arena where the new black theology was listened to and creatively engaged. Yet in 1969 the NCCC and its member churches were taken aback by the angry demands of James Forman and the Black Manifesto, demanding $500 million in "reparations" from the white churches and synagogues because their institutions and members had profited from the exploitation of black people. This traumatic demand was a cry of oppressed people and a moment of alienation among Christians in America. At least a dimension of the ecumenical agenda in America was clarified, even if it was not claimed by the majority.

Black ecumenism took on other institutional expressions. The Congress of National Black Churches (CNBC) was formed in 1978 to bind the black churches into a federation for common action on behalf of the black agenda. A former CNBC chairperson defines the focus in these words: "We act out of a common understanding of the church in the black community as a liberating instrument, in the sense that it frees us to be ourselves, to conform to the significance that we consider important, rather than necessarily conforming to the demands of the Europeanized cultures." By the 1990s the CNBC had become the most trusted and developed of all black ecumenical efforts. It is revealing that when the Lilly Endowment decided in 1997 to contribute $6 million for the restoration of burned black churches in the South, their gift was made to the CNBC, not to the NCCC or any other predominantly white conciliar body.

Born in the 1960s, another expression of ecumenism among black Christians is the National Black Evangelical Association (NBEA). The NBEA draws together African Americans who identify themselves within the conservative evangelical and missionary traditions, yet who are committed to the cultural goals of the black power movement. Many of these black pastors attended white evangelical colleges and seminaries, and previously ministered to white evangelical congregations. Their official objectives are "to promote and undergird a dynamic Christian witness among Afro-Americans and to help all evangelicals to find involvement with vital social issues". By "social issues" they refer to hunger, poverty and racism.

Two other manifestations of ecumenism in the US among African Americans are the Black Theology Project – a Christian group of black scholars committed to the promotion of historic and contemporary black religious thought and action – and Partners in Ecumenism, a project of the NCCC which tried to intensify the response of white Christians and institutions to black concerns and to identify a place for the black church as an equal partner within the church universal. PIE lasted as a viable organization only about a decade (1978-88), but it contributed towards raising the level of participation of blacks in the American ecumenical movement.

Anyone who has been part of the ecumenical movement must confess that the church in the US and throughout the world is and remains shamefully divided by racism. What many have experienced as revolutionary events are surely expressions of God's judgment on a church divided by ethical, racial, cultural and tribal loyalties. When the expectations of what Christian unity means can become common for the whole people of God, then ecumenism will become a different, more inclusive movement. When this transformation takes place, each part of the body of Christ will come to understand God's grace more deeply.

Orthodoxy and ecumenism in a new land

The Orthodox faith came to North America in 1794 when monks from Russia, travelling with fur traders, established a mission on Kodiak Island in Alaska. After the sale of Alaska to the US (1867), this mission spread to other parts of North America, and eventually the episcopal see was transferred from Sitka, Alaska, to San Francisco, California, then to New York City (1905). In the same period other Orthodox Christians came to the continental United States, largely due to the influx of immigrants from Greece, Asia Minor, Carpathia, Russia, Eastern Europe and the Middle East.

When the National Council of Churches was constituted in 1950, four charter members were the Russian Orthodox Church in North America, the Syrian Antiochian Orthodox, the Romanian Orthodox and the Ukrainian Orthodox churches. Two years later the Greek Orthodox Archdiocese of North and South America, the largest Orthodox community in the US, elected to join. Yet the involvement of these churches has been marginal. In 1970 the Russian and Serbian Orthodox united into the Orthodox Church in America. The same year the OCA was unilaterally granted an independent status by the Moscow Patriarchate – but without the approval of the patriarch of Constantinople. The complexity of this decision gave them the status of a permanent autonomy but without autocephaly.

Two Orthodox schools of theology have become centres of Orthodox participation in ecumenism: St Vladimir's Orthodox School of Theology (Orthodox Church in America) at Crestwood, New York, and the Holy Cross School of Theology (Greek Orthodox) in Brookline, near Boston, Massachusetts. The Orthodox presence, however, requires a new intentionality on the part of the other churches to take their witness seriously and to allow the Orthodox ethos to be present in ways that make them full partners. In such a full ecumenism, prophetic witness and common faith will both be priorities.

Evangelical, Pentecostal and Holiness churches and the future of ecumenism

Those who live outside North America find it difficult to understand and assess the presence and power of conservative and fundamentalist Protestants in the US. They are significant players in the American religious scene, and their aloofness from the ecumenical movement has to be addressed. Whether or not, or in what sense, they will participate and, by God's grace, draw close to those churches officially involved in ecumenism remains a providential possibility but not a foregone conclusion.

Evangelicals generally stress two essentials: the acceptance of the Bible as the sole, inerrant authority in faith and practice, and agreement that the only means of salvation is a life-transforming experience given by the Holy Spirit through personal faith in Jesus Christ.

Evangelical churches and their para-church mission organizations have their own disagreements and conflicts. These centre around dispensationalism, the inerrancy of the scriptures, millenialism, the calling to social witness in the world. Paradoxically, alienation frequently occurs within churches that are Spirit-filled which allow the more progressive leaders to acknowledge their need for reconciliation – the theme of the ecumenical movement.

These churches have several organizations that seek to play a cohesive role among Evangelicals. For example, the National Association of Evangelicals (1942) is a loose affiliation of diverse churches and individuals organized for common evangelical witness.

While the early motivations of the NAE were sharply critical of the National Council of Churches of Christ, especially for its liberal witness in society, a changed spirit has moved among Evangelicals since the 1950s. The latest positive development was an encouraging symbolic act in 1996 when the executive director of the NAE gave a speech to the general assembly of the NCCC in Chicago.

At the international level, Evangelicals participate in the World Evangelical Fellowship (WEF 1951) which in the 1980s began to attend as an observer certain meetings of the WCC and the annual gatherings of the secretaries of Christian World Communions. The Lausanne Congress on World Evangelism, a large international gathering of Evangelicals convened in 1974 by the Billy Graham organization, produced the Lausanne Covenant, which articulates among other things the conviction that the evangelistic task calls the churches to visible unity. This covenant offered a creative opportunity for dialogue between the WCC and the WEF, but the moment was missed. When this dialogue begins, many ordinary members in the mainline churches in the US will have more confidence in the WCC.

Among Pentecostals one can sense a cautious openness for ecumenical dialogue. Cecil M. Roebeck, Jr, professor of church history at Fuller Theological Seminary at Pasadena, California, and the major Pentecostal participant in WCC and NCCC Faith and Order commissions as well as the Pentecostal-Roman Catholic international dialogue, often addresses what he calls "the irony" between Pentecostals and ecumenical bodies like the NCCC and the WCC:

> Two of the 20th century's most significant developments, the formal ecumenical movement and the vigorous Pentecostal movement, have developed in almost total isolation from one another. Yet each has been reticent to acknowledge the activity of God in the other.

Other hopeful developments should be recorded. Since 1983 a partnership has been operative between the NCCC and the Society for Pentecostal Studies. Two SPS members are on the Commission of Faith and Order. In 1986 a consultation took place on Pentecostalism, sponsored jointly by the Commission on Faith and Order and the David Du Plessis Center for Christian Spirituality at Fuller Theological Seminary. The report of that consultation urged more contact and participation between classical Pentecostals and the historic churches represented in Faith and Order.

Canada

THE DISTINCTIVE CHRISTIAN EXPERIENCE IN CANADA

While Canadians and Americans share a continent and some cultural and religious commonalities, they are distinct countries. Those who glibly assume Canada is a northern extension of the US rightly receive the ire of Canadians who cherish their own religious, cultural and political history. Triumphalism by Americans and defensiveness and a degree of nationalism by Canadians have resulted in few church-to-church links across the border and discouraged partnerships in ecumenical arenas such as the World Council of Churches.

The similarities are noticeable. Canadians and their neighbours to the south are by nature religious people. Christians, Jews and more recently people of other faiths have had formative influences on both societies. Both are voluntary religious societies, in that neither allows an established church with state-affirmed status and privileges regarding law, education and taxation. Both countries are pluralistic in religion and culture.

On the other side of the ecclesial ledger, there are distinctive differences in the impact the churches have had upon Canadian cultural formation. While Canadian churches reflect a pluralism, they are not as diverse as their neighbours in the US. Hundreds of denominations proliferate across the US, many with memberships ranging from 500,000 to 12 million. Canada has a population of 36 million in which nearly 10 million are nominally identified as Protestants compared with 12 million equally nominal Roman Catholics. It used to be that most of the Catholics were French in language and culture, but since the independence movement began in the 1970s the Catholic church in Quebec has been in serious decline. The majority of practising Catholics in the 1960s tended to reflect such ethnic groups as the Irish, Scottish, Italian, German, Polish and Ukrainians of the Eastern rite. Protestants were largely Anglo-Saxon. By 2000 that ethnic reflection was mirrored by Canada's official multiculturalism and the most liberal immigration policies in the world in which most new Catholic and Protestant growth came from immigration, especially from the South. Five mainstream Protestant churches – United, Anglican, Presbyterian, Lutheran, Baptist – constituted 80 percent of the Protestant population in 1968 but their numbers are dwindling fast as the country becomes increasingly secular. The remaining non-Catholics include the Orthodox, Disciples of Christ, Mennonites, the Salvation Army and fast-growing Pentecostal, evangelical and Holiness churches. In the period covered in this volume, the weight of pluralism in Canadian religion has shifted. Traditional Protestants have faded in their influence. Reflecting on the depreciated role of the Protestant churches, John Webster Grant, a prominent church and ecumenical historian, observes,

> What is certain is that the major Protestant churches no longer serve as Canada's moral arbiters as they were once accustomed to do. Ironically, this role largely dropped away during the prosperous 1950s rather than the tumultuous years (late 1960s and 1970s) that followed.[18]

The second difference in the way Christianity developed in Canada is the strategic role played by the churches in the immigration of peoples. The hospitality of Protestants and the Canadian Council of Churches as well as Roman Catholics – often with government assistance – helped newcomers to find land, jobs and acceptance in rural and urban communities across Canada. Both Canada and the US are societies of immigrants, in different waves and in different decades, but Canadians seem to remember that reality more positively. This hospitality and the demands of a harsh environment encouraged a sense of community among old and new Canadians. For this and other reasons Canadian Christianity does not reflect as dominant a radical individualism as that which marks, sometimes scars, US Christianity. Community and shared social responsibilities come easier for Canadians, a fact that conditions their sense of church.

---

[18] John Webster Grant, *The Church in the Canadian Era*, Burlington, Ont., Welch Publ., 1988, pp.227-46; Grant ed., *The Church and the Canadian Experience*, Toronto, Ryerson, 1963.

A third contrast is seen in the absence in Canada of any doctrine of "manifest destiny", the belief of founders and religious leaders in early US history that God uniquely blessed and gave a particular destiny to their nation to bring God's kingdom to all the world. This sort of "spiritual patriotism" or "messianic mythology" is absent in Canadian consciousness or in their churches.

CHURCH UNION

On 10 June 1925 all Methodists, Congregationalists and the majority (71 percent) of Presbyterians united to constitute the United Church of Canada. At the time this was celebrated by churches all over the world as the most dramatic act of Christian reconciliation in modern church history. Such a multilateral union was unprecedented. The motives for such a bold union in Canada were basically twofold: to bring strength and a sense of mission to Christians and congregations throughout a sparsely populated country marked by a frontier situation, and to have a church with a Canadian identity. During the years of negotiation (1904-25) the constant justification given for a united church was that division and competition among Christians have "no practical relevance" on the frontier. The missionary situation required more resources of leadership and money than any one tradition could provide. Furthermore, the existence of many local union congregations in western Canada made a national union essential. Equally important was the belief that the development of one political confederation required a comprehensive national church that would draw together all regions and Christians, thereby bringing a Christian character to the nation.

Distinct to this Canadian union was the absence of Anglicans and only the partial participation of Presbyterians. In the 1920s the Church of England in Canada was basically English in character as well as name. A large proportion of its funds and bishops came from England. There were still illusions of a future Anglican establishment in Canada, an illusion which exists to this day among the Anglo business, cultural and academic elites.

When the time came for decision, the Congregationalists and Methodists approved the basis for union almost immediately. A severe blow came to the union process, however, when after very hostile debates almost one-third of the Presbyterians decided not to enter the united church. The underlying reasons had to do with the fear of the "extinction" of Presbyterian identity, the loss of church property and differing conceptions of evangelism and social action. The Presbyterian Church in Canada remains today as a separate church.

More realistic possibilities came in 1964 through an initiative from western Ontario. After some serious theological work the Anglican diocese of Huron and the United Church London conference published the so-called London-Huron plan, setting forth elements for a constitution of a united church and a service for the reconciliation of ministries which followed the pattern of the North India proposals for union. This regional initiative stimulated the formation of a national commission of Anglicans and United Church leaders and theologians.

The penultimate stage after several years of denominational work came in 1967 when the two churches formed a general commission on church union with five special commissions – constitution, legal, doctrinal, liturgical and the church in the world. Between 1967 and 1972 intensive work and interpretation was done by more than two hundred lay and clergy representatives.

In a providential act two small churches, both with roots in the US, came closer. In 1968 the Evangelical United Brethren Church in Canada – whose parent body in the US was uniting that same year with the Methodists to become the United Methodist Church – became a part of the United Church. In 1969 the Christian Church (Disciples of Christ) in Canada entered full membership, becoming the third church in the ongoing negotiations. The participation of the EUB and the Disciples influenced the chemistry of the conversations in a way that diminished the power plays of the two large churches.

The Canadian union process reached its high-water mark in 1972, when the general commission on church union unanimously approved a plan of union and sent it to the three churches for study, prayer and action. The plan founded the proposed new church upon the faith witnessed to by Christians down throughout the centuries. At the heart of the vision of the Church of Christ in Canada – the proposed name – was also a commitment to mission as "the community of Christ the servant, to be itself a servant community", to speak God's liberating word, to accept and care for all of God's people and "to search for justice and to struggle against the forces that subvert the human and the humane". Both practices of adult baptism by immersion and infant baptism and later confirmation were encouraged as different modes that witness to the one baptism into Christ. The Lord's supper or eucharist, "where we agree on essential elements, we expect variety in administration", would be "at the heart of our worship". The ordained ministry of the United Church would include deacons, presbyters and bishops. The three traditions composing the United Church would however have the freedom "to interpret its provisions for ministry in the light of their awareness of the work of God within the histories of the communions to which they have belonged".

During the decision-making period, the United Church of Canada and the Disciples of Christ indicated that the plan of union gave a credible expression to a "new embodiment of the one church of God". However, Anglo-Catholics, conservative Evangelicals and Anglican social action proponents unwittingly made a negative phalanx against any form of union. A survey of the rank and file of both large churches also revealed insufficient congregational support for visible organic union. In 1975 the Anglican house of bishops ceremonially affirmed their "primary and deep commitment to the unity of the body of Christ", but rejected the plan as "unacceptable". This action concluded with a pledge to apply to the Canadian churches the principle proposed by the Lund world conference on Faith and Order (1952): to "act together in all matters except those in which deep differences of conviction compel them to act separately". Unfortunately, the Anglican bishops ignored another important principle set forth by the Lund conference: "The measure of unity which it has been given to the churches to experience must *now* find clearer manifestation."

This action brought confusion and deep disappointment among the other negotiating churches. The Anglicans had played a major role in shaping the principles and plan of union. It was the Anglicans who earlier in the century had proposed, even required, full, organic union as the primary ecumenical model. On 31 January 1976 the commission on union and joint mission was dissolved.

The United Church of Canada's people remained distraught over the Anglican rejection. The Disciples themselves looked away from the United Church, whose often radical theological and social conceptions and occasional attitudes of arrogance made them uncomfortable. For the first time in its history, the United Church of Canada was not in negotiations for reconciliation and visible unity with any church.

CONCILIAR ECUMENISM

In 1938 when the international conference of the World Council of Churches-in-process-of-formation drafted the WCC's constitution, several cooperative interchurch ventures came together in the World Council of Churches Canadian committee. Between 1942 and 1944 a series of planning meetings led to the formal constitution of the Canadian Council of Churches (CCC), four years before the WCC and six years before the NCCCUSA.

The early years of the CCC were rather heady. The new ecumenism brought the churches out of their isolation into a common witness and the more effective use of their resources. This ecumenical framework gradually led the staff of the larger churches – Anglicans, Presbyterians and United Church of Canada – to identify common concerns and to develop common programmes under the aegis of the CCC.

From its beginning the Council developed certain characteristics that defined its nature and methodology, particularly in contrast to the NCCC in the US. First the CCC intentionally worked in partnership with the World Council of Churches. It is not accidental that the CCC's basis is identical with that of the WCC.

Second, the CCC has often worked with the Canadian government, especially in national development. In the late 1980s an average of CAN$1.5 million of government funds were processed annually through the CCC to various countries in the third world and into refugee programmes. In both instances these humanitarian witnesses were made with government partnership.

Thirdly, the budgets, staffs and organizational plans have been modest, never equalling the large, bureaucratic proportions of the NCCC. The largest staff in the CCC's history was ten full-time persons; the largest budget was slightly over CAN$500,000.

In Canada as in the rest of the world the 1960s brought enormous interest and energy to the ecumenical task. After many more Orthodox churches came into membership of the WCC at New Delhi in 1961, the Orthodox churches in Canada began to look towards formally joining the CCC. In the same period there developed a restlessness in Canada with the structures and focus of ecumenical bodies, particularly the Canadian Council of Churches. A certain segment of the leadership of both the United and Anglican churches of Canada began to press for a more radical form of ecumenism, and for a restructured CCC occupied less with the churches and more with the crisis of humanity. It was more than the structures of the Council that was at issue in these overtures: under evaluation was the nature of ecumenism itself. A report from the 1969 CCC assembly states the changing vision:

> Different understandings exist as to the basic roles of the Council – whether it should be to develop ecumenical programmes independent of the church structures or to work primarily within the church structures; whether it should seek to build up interchurch programmes under Council administration, or whether its role should be primarily catalytic – i.e., to facilitate common action by the churches on the growing edges of the contemporary Christian mission, carrying out in its own name only such pilot projects as would promote this objective.

As ecumenism bifurcated between the common action of the churches and the action of individuals and consortia on particular issues, the search for Christian unity was marginalized by those committed only to a radical witness. As this happened, the Council was put into crisis and severely weakened.

In 1971 the Council was restructured into three commissions: world concerns, Canadian affairs, and faith and order. In the aftermath of Vatican II discussions began to take place about the possible relationship between the CCC and the Canadian conference of

Catholic bishops. New issues confronting Canadian society and the whole world brought forward another and globally unique form of ecumenical witness for social justice known as the interchurch coalitions for justice: economic justice, poverty, immigration, racism, human rights in Africa and Latin America, solidarity with women, ecology, the liberation of Indigenous Canadians, bio-ethics and the ministry to youth. Throughout its history the CCC has developed special relationships with churches and councils in different regions of the world – the Caribbean, Middle East, South Africa and the long-time Canada-China programme. These coalitions were fully ecumenical, independent of the CCC and nearly destroyed the structural base of the Council.

In 1998 the membership of the CCC included 16 communions: Roman Catholic, Orthodox, Anglican and Protestant.

As the impulse towards an ecumenism that focuses on justice, peace, and the integrity of creation became more dominant, the "coalitions for justice" became a special feature of the Canadian ecumenical scene. Each coalition addressed a particular concern of the Christian community in Canada and was led by particular advocates either within or outside denominational offices. Coalitions allowed committed individuals and groups with expertise to move together without the approval of church bodies.

The difference between a conciliar witness and a coalition witness can be seen in their focus, structures and methodology. As one advocate of coalitions describes, they are

> marked by a shift from service and educational priorities to justice and advocacy; from the gathering of Protestants to the inclusion of Roman Catholics and the Orthodox communions; from a formal organizations of churches into a broad-based network of action groups; from a focus upon social problems to a global awareness of one humanity inhabiting a common ecology.[19]

In the 1980s the CCC changed its structure in order to allow social coalitions to work in relationship with the Council through its commission on justice, peace and the integrity of creation. By the late 1990s, eleven coalitions were engaged in this relationship.

Canadian ecumenism has developed nothing like the network of local and regional councils of churches in the United States, but there are regional councils in the Maritime Provinces, Saskatchewan and British Columbia. Fifteen cities have councils of churches witnessing under various names. Since Vatican II, Roman Catholic participation in local ecumenism has spread.

In 1971 the Catholic bishops appointed a six-member delegation to the CCC's commission on Faith and Order. In the last three decades of the 20th century Faith and Order in Canada centred much of its work on baptism. In 1972 a major study began with the goal of various churches declaring the mutual recognition of each other's baptism. The potential of a common theology and practice of Christian initiation was significant for the unity of the church. By 1975 consensus was achieved and five churches – United Anglican, Presbyterian, Lutheran and Roman Catholic – announced that any one of these churches would recognize the validity of a baptism of the other churches.

In 1985 a national consultation on baptism, eucharist and ministry was convened in Quebec. The focus was on the pastoral and administrative implications, if and when the churches were able to recognize their tradition in the BEM text. One of the conclusions was the acceptance of the validity of all baptisms "administered according to the estab-

---

[19] Christopher Lind and Joe Mihevic eds, *Coalitions for Justice*, Ottawa, Novalis, 1994.

lished norms of the Christian churches, when conferred with flowing water, by pouring, sprinkling or immersion, accompanied by the trinitarian formula". A year or so later this historic agreement and the unity it represented was shaken when the general council of the United Church of Canada proposed that the historic trinitarian language – "Father, Son and Holy Spirit" – be expanded to include "Creator, Redeemer and Sustainer" or other contemporary formulas. However, following the BEM consultation, the process turned to identifying those common elements that should be included in an ecumenical catechesis on baptism. The result was the publication in 1992 of a consensus text entitled *Initiation into Christ: Ecumenical Reflections and Common Teaching on Preparation for Baptism.*[20]

In the mid-1970s difficulties developed within the CCC about the direction and method pursued by the Faith and Order commission. There was also concern that the commission did not represent a broad enough spectrum of churches and views. The fact that Faith and Order work was primarily in English and not bilingual as the nation was officially, was harshly judged. These concerns were taken up at a conference in 1977 that identified the fundamental methodological tension in the Faith and Order movement around the world. Two different approaches or methods were being pursued. The first concentrated on the historic church-dividing issues – baptism, eucharist, ministry, scripture and Tradition, etc. The second reflected theologically on those issues that divide the human community and also the churches – racism, poverty, oppression. While not excluding the traditional approach, the CCC decided to focus its Faith and Order work on the contextual, world-centred agenda. Furthermore, in 1989 the commission's name was changed from Faith and Order to Faith and Witness. This change represented a broadening of the mandate to include matters of mission and social ecumenism as well as interfaith relations.

This recast mandate was captured in 1991 in a new working theme "Living and Proclaiming Jesus Christ in a Religiously Plural Society". Under this focus work has been done on interfaith dialogue, inclusive language, interfaith marriages, AIDS, advocacy for Indigenous Canadians, and bio-ethical issues. This theological shift leaves some church leaders in a quandary, especially those committed to the visible unity of the church understood as a sign of the unity and renewal of the human community. One result of this choice by the CCC was that the energy for church unity shifted to the bilateral dialogues.

BILATERAL DIALOGUES

Interchurch bilateral dialogues play a key role in Canadian ecumenism. Their significance became greater after Vatican II when the Canadian conference of Catholic bishops became a collegial part of ecumenism in Canada, symbolized by their associate membership (1986) and full membership (1997) in the Canadian Council of Churches.

Anglican-Roman Catholic dialogue

Begun in 1971, this Canadian bilateral dialogue has done promising theological work. Participants include ordained and lay people, women and men, systematic and pastoral theologians. Its work has been focused largely on the Anglican-Roman Catholic Inter-

---

[20] Canadian Council of Churches, Commission on Faith and Witness, Winfield, Wood Lake Books, 1992, 50pp.

national Commission (ARCIC I and ARCIC II). In an innovative act towards reception, nine Anglican and nine Roman Catholic bishops came together to discuss the theological and practical implications of the unity this dialogue offers. These bishops jointly issued two important pastoral documents: "Pastoral Guidelines for Interchurch Marriages between Anglicans and Roman Catholics in Canada" (1987) and "Pastoral Guidelines in the Case of Clergy Moving from One Communion to Another" (1991). In 1994 a pastoral letter encouraged their priests and lay people to participate in the ecumenical movement. One of the characteristics of the Canadian dialogue has been the fact that theological reflection is grounded in experience. The central issue now being pursued is the possibility of the recognition of ministries – an age-old source of alienation since the Roman Catholic Church in the action of Pope Leo XIII in 1896 declared Anglican orders to be "null and void". The prospects of any recognition of ministries became more problematic in the 1970s when Canadian Anglicans accepted the ordination of women and in the 1990s ordained women bishops.

In Canada as in the US some Anglicans have expressed the preference to seek reconciliation with the Roman Catholic Church, while marginalizing relationships with Protestant churches. This approach has been rejected in Canada.

Roman Catholic-United Church dialogue

Since 1925, when the United Church of Canada was constituted, there has been a decided distance between these two communions. This distance was widened by the ultramontane character of Catholicism in French-speaking Quebec, noted for its strict loyalty to the absolute authority of the pope and to an authoritarian adherence to Catholic piety. It was ameliorated only with the rise of mid-century secularism and the ecumenical impact of Vatican II, causing the walls between these two churches – both with ambitions to be the moral conscience of the country – to fall. The two largest churches in Canada began official dialogue in 1975.

The style of the Roman Catholic-United Church dialogue has been not to produce theological consensus texts, as have other national and international bilaterals. Their intent has been to seek greater understanding of the doctrinal issues that have historically divided Catholics and Protestants and to examine critically those popular attitudes that shape the perceptions and misconceptions of one another. In this spirit the dialogue group has discussed personal understandings of fundamental Christian beliefs such as prayer, the role of the church, ministry, the meaning of the Lord's supper or eucharist.

From 1990 to 1995 this dialogue turned its attention to evangelism/evangelization in Canada. The result was a working paper bearing the title "Sharing the Good News Today" (1995). The text speaks of evangelism (preferred Protestant term) and evangelization (preferred Roman Catholic term) as the process by which Christians "make all people aware of the good news of Jesus Christ, that God's unconditional and reconciling love sustains the universe and is available to all". Every aspect of the church's life – conversion, teaching, witness, promoting justice and peace, interfaith dialogue – is an expression of evangelism/evangelization. Because of the differing ethos of these two churches, this dialogue has important possibilities for Christian witness in Canada.

Lutheran-Roman Catholic dialogue

In the early 1970s the Lutherans overtook the Presbyterians, becoming the third largest Protestant church in Canada. Following the lead of their sisters and brothers in the US, the various groups of Lutherans, except for the Lutheran Church-Missouri Synod, united in 1986 under the name of the Evangelical Lutheran Church in Canada. The first steps towards dialogue between Lutherans and Catholics took place in regional groups in Montreal, Saskatoon and Toronto in 1968. In 1973 the possibility of national dialogue was considered, but was delayed because the process of Lutheran merger was underway. A national dialogue between the newly formed ELC in Canada and the Canadian conference of Catholic bishops – a product of a similar dialogue in the US – was initiated in 1986. Later meetings explored the questions of ministry and ordination, and discovered helpful general agreements, especially on the divine institution of ministry, the sacramental dimension of ordination and the permanent gift of ordination. While some differences were acknowledged about ministerial orders and apostolic succession in ordained ministry, Lutheran and Catholic theologians expressed a common commitment to "the historic succession of ordained ministers as an expression of the church's apostolicity". For Lutherans the three forms of the ordained ministry – deacon, presbyter and bishop – are defined differently than for Roman Catholics. Areas of special disagreements between Lutherans and Roman Catholic are – as with Anglicans – over women in the ordained ministry and the papal office. Regarding the papacy, Canadian Lutherans take the same position as Lutherans elsewhere: "Lutherans have acknowledged that there may be a place for a ministry and visible sign of the unity of the church insofar as [this office] is subordinated to the primacy of the gospel by theological reinterpretation and practical restructuring." While new language was being used, most realized that the papacy remained an obstacle to unity for the immediate future. Yet this dialogue encourages the practice of interchurch marriages, common baptisms and funerals, and cooperation in mission.

Anglican-Lutheran dialogue

Anglican and Lutheran relations are nurtured by the fact that both churches have roots in the 16th-century Reformation. In 1975 regional meetings took place in Kitchener (Ontario), Saskatoon (Saskatchewan) and Edmonton (Alberta). From these conversations cooperative ministries in isolated areas, theological dialogue in seminaries, and meetings of Anglican bishops and Lutheran district presidents began to take place.

In 1983 a joint commission was set up. In the meantime the Evangelical Lutheran Church in Canada came into being. The commission produced agreed statements on justification, eucharist, apostolicity and the ordained ministry. Recommendations for interim eucharistic fellowship were approved. Different interpretations of the episcopate were acknowledged. While Lutherans had begun to use the name of "bishop", their statement acknowledged "they do not possess the apostolic succession as Anglicans understand it... [Lutherans] have been willing to agree to the efficacy of the historic episcopate in preserving the gospel, but not to its necessity".

Orthodox churches and ecumenism

The Orthodox presence in Canada increased in the closing decades of the century. Six Orthodox churches – Eastern and Oriental – were members of the Canadian Council of Churches. No official dialogue involved the Orthodox churches, except a diaconal partnership between Anglicans and the Armenian Apostolic Orthodox Church. There were informal relations, mainly in Toronto, among Anglicans and Armenians, Copts, Ethiopians, Syrians and Malankara Syrian Orthodox.

CONCLUSION

After innovative leadership in the church union movement, the Canadian churches have accepted friendly cooperation – in councils and social justice coalitions – as the middle option in ecumenism. Bilateral dialogues represent a measure of visible unity between two traditions, yet they do not address the difficult issue of visible unity in a pluralistic church and in an increasingly fragmented society. As a new century begins, neo-denominationalism reigns over the ecclesiological scene, while a resurgent evangelicalism and Pentecostalism – within the larger denominations and among a host of small fundamentalist bodies – is a reality to be taken seriously in any honest assessment of the ecumenical future. All this is taking place in a time when secularism more and more defines values and goals and when the interfaith character of Canada is expanding. Yet the defining reality for the Canadian experience at the end of the 20th century, says historian Mark A. Noll,[21] is that Canada is not so much *a* Christian nation as *two* Christian nations, Roman Catholic and Protestant. The future depends upon whether this division is addressed as a matter of cultural and political power plays, or is reconciled by humble churches finding visible unity through offering their spiritual gifts to manifest a community of love.

BIBLIOGRAPHY

Andrews, James E. and Burgess, Joseph A. eds, *An Invitation to Action: A Study of Ministry, Sacraments, and Recognition: Final Report of the Lutheran-Reformed Dialogue III (1981-1983)*, Philadelphia, Fortress, 1984, 126pp.

Baer, Hans A. and Singer, Merrill, *African-American Religion in the Twentieth Century: Varieties of Protest and Accommodation*, Knoxville, Univ. of Tennessee Press, 1993, 267pp.

Ball, William B. ed., *In Search of a National Morality: A Manifesto for Evangelicals and Catholics*, Grand Rapids MI, Baker, 1992, 298pp.

Best, Marion, *Will Our Church Disappear? Strategies for the Renewal of the United Church of Canada*, Winfield, Wood Lake Books, 1994, 137pp.

Best, Thomas, F, "Survey of Church Union Negotiations 1999-2000", in *The Ecumenical Review*, 54, 3, July 2002, pp.402-406.

Black, Donald, *Merging Mission and Unity: A History of the Commission on Ecumenical Mission and Relations*, Philadelphia, Westminster, 1986, 180pp.

Booth, Rodney M., *The Winds of God: The Canadian Church Faces the 1980s*, WCC, 1982, 128pp.

Burgess, Joseph A. and Gros, Jeffrey eds, *Building Unity: Ecumenical Dialogues with Roman Catholic Participation in the United States*, New York, Paulist, 1989, 499pp.

Burgess, Joseph A. and Gros, Jeffrey eds, *Church Dialogues in the United States, 1962-1991*, New York, Ramsey, Paulist, 1995, 688pp.

Churches in Covenant Communion: The Church of Christ Uniting, Princeton, Consultation on Church Union, 1989, 102pp.

Findlay, James F., *Church People in the Struggle: The National Council of Churches and the Black Freedom Movement, 1950-1970*, Oxford, Oxford Univ. Press, 1993, 255pp.

Fournier, Keith A. and Watkins, William D., *A House United? Evangelicals and Catholics Together: A Winning Alliance for the 21st Century*, Colorado Springs, Navpress, 1994, 367pp.

Geyer, Alan, *Ideology in America: Challenges to Faith*, Louisville KY, Westminster/John Knox, 1997, 139pp.

Gunnemann, Louis H., *United and Uniting: The Meaning of an Ecclesial Journey: United Church of Christ 1957-1987*, New York, United Church Press, 1987, 215pp.

---

[21] *A History of Christianity in the United States and Canada*, Grand Rapids MI, Eerdmans, 1992, 576pp.

Hjelm, Norman A. ed., *Out of the Ashes: Burned Churches and the Community of Faith*, Nashville, Thomas Nelson, 1997, 113pp.

Hogson, Janet, *Vision Quest: Native Spirituality and the Church in Canada*, Toronto, Anglican Book Centre, 1990, 213pp.

Kelly, Arleon L. ed., *A Tapestry of Justice, Service and Unity: Local Ecumenism in the United States 1950-2000*, Tacoma WA, National Association of Ecumenical and Interreligious Staff, 2004, 527p.

Lind, Christopher and Mihevic, Joe eds, *Coalitions for Justice: The Story of Canada's Interchurch Coalitions*, Ottawa, Novalis, 1994, 397pp.

Lotz, David W. ed., *Altered Landscapes: Christianity in America 1935-1985*, Grand Rapids MI, Eerdmans, 1989, 387pp.

MacKinney, William, *The Responsibility People: Eighteen Senior Leaders of Protestant Churches and National Ecumenical Agencies Reflect on Church Leadership*, Grand Rapids MI, Eerdmans, 1994, 377pp.

Moede, Gerald Frank ed., *The COCU Consensus: In Quest of a Church of Christ Uniting, Approved and Commended to the Churches by the 16th Plenary of the Consultation on Church Union, November 30, 1984*, Princeton, Consultation on Church Union (COCU), 1985, 55pp.

Nickle, Keith F. and Lull, Timothy F. eds, *A Common Calling: The Witness of our Reformation Churches in North America Today: The Report of the Lutheran-Reformed Committee for Theological Conversations, 1988-1992*, Minneapolis MN, Augsburg, 1993, 88pp.

Niebuhr, Gustav, "American Religion at the Millennium's End", in *Yearbook of American and Canadian Churches 1999*, Eileen W. Lindner ed., Nashville, Abingdon, 1999, 408p.

Noll, Mark A., *A History of Christianity in the United States and Canada*, Grand Rapids MI, Eerdmans, 1992, 576pp.

Norgren, William A. and Rush, William G. eds, *Toward Full Communion and Concordat of Agreement: Lutheran-Episcopal Dialogue, series III*, Minneapolis MN, Augsburg, 1991, 119pp.

Petersen, Rodney L., *Christianity and Civil Society: Theological Education for Public Life*, Cambridge MS, Boston Theological Institute, 1995, 165pp.

Radner, Ephraim and Reno, R.R. eds, *Inhabiting Unity: Theological Perspectives on the Proposed Lutheran-Episcopal Concordat*, Grand Rapids MI, Eerdmans, 1995, 247pp.

Rasmussen, Larry L., *Moral Fragments and Moral Community: A Proposal for Church in Society*, Minneapolis MN, Fortress, 1993, 176pp.

Reid, Daniel G. ed., *Dictionary of Christianity in America*, Downers Grove IL, Intervarsity, 1990.

Sawyer, Mary, R., *Black Ecumenism: Implementing the Demands of Justice*, Philadelphia, Trinity, 1994, 251pp.

Vanderwerf, Nathan H., *The Times Were Very Full: A Perspective on the First 25 Years of the National Council of Churches of Christ in the USA, 1950-1975*, New York, National Council of the Churches of Christ in the USA, 1975, 128pp.

Watley, William D., *Singing the Lord's Song in a Strange Land: The African American Churches and Ecumenism*, WCC, 1993, 69pp.

Wuthnow, R., *After Heaven: Spirituality in America since the 1950s*, Berkeley, Univ. of California Press, 2000, 277pp.

26
Pacific

The area known as the Pacific comprises the immense ocean of the same name, and the small volcanic and coral islands scattered across it. It covers one half of the maritime surface of the earth: about 176 million square kilometres, of which only about 10 million are land. Of this land surface, Australia and New Zealand make up 9.2 million square kilometres. This chapter deals with the inhabitants of the little land surface that is left, and the micro-states and churches.

The Pacific islands fall into three major cultural, ethnic sub-regions – Polynesian, Melanesian and Micronesian. Taken together, they have become a Christian majority area as a result of early activities by Protestant and Roman Catholic missionaries. As in other parts of the world, the international missionary movement became the cradle of the modern ecumenical movement.

The arrival of Christianity in these small island states in the late 19th and early 20th centuries was looked upon by many Islanders as "the dawn of a new day". The impact of the gospel was like a strong wind of change, or the rising sun appearing over the horizon giving light. Christ, the light of the world, was heralded across the Pacific. The arrival of the Europeans as missionaries, traders and travellers was also described as "the fatal impact": the missionary activities they brought with them included "denominational cargoes of controversy and division which were dumped on the Pacific shores".[1] Each group believed their good news was better than the others. Converts to one denomination were encouraged to bring other people to their group. As evangelization progressed, both Protestants and Catholics found that their "cargoes of controversy and division" were beginning to affect communities negatively: villages and families were divided because of their denominational affiliations and loyalties.

The work of evangelization was carried out mainly through the activities of Pacific Island missionaries. Although missionary societies and religious orders founded churches and eventually ceded them autonomy, most of the Pacific region was converted through the activity of Pacific Islander missionaries proceeding broadly from east to west in a process of church growth, culminating in the New Guinea Highlands region. The records of indigenous missionaries kept at the Pacific Theological College chapel in Suva, Fiji, tell of thousands of men and their families who left their own islands to

• This chapter is based on material supplied by Kafoa Solomone, John Garrett and Faitala Talapusi.
[1] S.A. Tuilavoni, "The Pacific Church within the Universal Christian Family", in *Background Reading to the Fourth Pacific Conference of Churches Assembly 1981*, Suva, PCC, 1981, p.72.

preach the good news in others. From Tahiti in the east Pacific to Papua New Guinea in the west, they were like waves carrying coconuts to other places. These Islanders through their faith carried the coconut of the gospel to other islands. Despite the early story of mission as that of denominational divisions, the dawn of the new day in the light of God was upon the Pacific people.

After the second world war, the mission stations achieved partial independence from missionary oversight. Island church leaders helped negotiate political independence of their island states. This important phase of transition from mission to church led to the 1961 conference of churches and missions held in Malua, Western Samoa (Samoa since 1997), organized by the International Missionary Council and the WCC for all the churches and missions in the region. The chairman, Amanaki Havea[2] from the Methodist Church in Tonga, spoke of the characteristics of the worm wood-borer, commonly called in the Pacific *afato*. It lives by eating dead wood. Any number of borers can live and bore holes in the same wood, but no one *afato* dares cut its hole to get in the way of the other borers inside. A Polynesian proverb from this *afato* experience translates as "the fellowship of the *afato* or *afatoism*: they live together but do not know each other".

The churches in the region had existed for more than one hundred years but none dared to make its way into the presence of others. The Malua conference revealed that the Pacific churches had many good things to share. The convictions of the conference reflected those of the founding assembly of the WCC in 1948 that "we intend to stay together", and of the WCC's 1954 assembly, "we intend to grow together". This was the beginning of ecumenism in practice in the Pacific. The previous divisions and separations were deplored, and the days of flying denominational flags whereby Catholic and Protestant passengers in their respective canoes never greeted one another came to an end.

After Malua many denominational flags were lowered and the ecumenical flag was raised. After several days of worship, study, fellowship, consultation and sharing at Malua, participants found that each was enriched by the others. The spirit of ecumenical awareness grew as the Spirit of God blew afresh.

THE PACIFIC CONFERENCE OF CHURCHES

The Malua conference was like a mountaintop experience to those who were present – they did not want it to be lost. A continuation committee was set up to carry further the resolutions approved at the conference, and the members visited different island churches to share the spirit of Malua. Vavae Toma of the Congregational Christian Church of Samoa, secretary of the continuation committee, was known as the "living link" for ecumenism in the Pacific. His purpose throughout these visits was to help the local churches appreciate the spirit of Malua. A pattern of fellowship and cooperation began to take shape during the five years of the committee's life. Apart from the informal ecumenism that emerged at the local level, two ecumenical institutions were set up.

The Pacific Conference of Churches (PCC) and the transconfessional and regionally inclusive Pacific Theological College (PTC) were landmarks in translating the spirit of the Malua conference. The PCC under its first general secretary, Setareki Tuilovoni of the Methodist Church in Fiji, helped in the formation of national Christian councils of churches in the newly independent states of the Pacific. The agreed aims of the PCC

---

[2] Amanaki Havea, "Church Unity in Diversity in the Pacific", in *Background Reading to the Fourth Pacific Conference of Churches Assembly 1981*, p.67.

closely followed the aims and basis of the WCC, as adapted to the special needs and concerns of member churches in the islands: the furtherance of a spirit of ecumenism; work for justice, peace and development; consultation on church relationships; promotion of participation in the wider ecumenical movement; mutual help between island churches and with organizations in other parts of the world (interchurch aid). According to its constitution the PCC's goal is:
- to promote a spirit of ecumenism among the churches in the Pacific;
- to help member churches to evaluate their work in mission, and to plan together so that wherever possible their resources in people and money can be used in joint action for mission;
- to help create a greater awareness of issues of justice, peace and human development facing the people and nations of the region and the world;
- to facilitate mutual consultation on issues affecting church relationships and other subjects of common concern among the churches;
- to promote the participation of the Pacific churches in the wider ecumenical movement;
- to be a means whereby the churches of the Pacific may help each other and help churches and other organizations in other parts of the world in times of natural disaster and special need, or are helped by the churches in other parts of the world in times of similar natural disaster or need; and
- to undertake such cooperative activities, on behalf of member churches, as the assembly may from time to time approve.

From 16 founding members the PCC has grown to more than thirty members, and it has developed programmes that help the churches to complement their own efforts in fostering a common journey for the people. The PCC's programmes followed mainly the lines of those developed earlier by the WCC. In 1981 the PCC assembly agreed to create three programme clusters:
1. Mission, unity, renewal, witness and dialogue: theological education; dialogue between the churches; dialogue between people of other living faiths; development of Pacific theology; unity in mission; church unity; ecumenical sharing of resources, personnel, material and information; development and planning (e.g. Pacific advisory group, Pacific mission board).
2. Justice and development: social and international issues (e.g. nuclear, trade, migration); land tenure and education (family, culture, role of traditional leaders, etc.); communication.
3. Ecumenical relationships: development and cooperation between national councils of churches; cooperation between churches; strengthening global partnership.

Added to these clusters were the youth and women's desks.

The justice, peace and development (JPD) desk was active in monitoring and taking appropriate action in the name of the PCC on issues of human-rights abuse, ecological and environmental threats, political independence of island states, preservation of cultural inheritance, tourism, development, racism, unemployment, the threat of AIDS, and other social ills such as prostitution, child abuse, domestic violence and alcoholism. The nuclear issue (tests and their impact on the environment and people as well as radio-active-waste dumping in the Pacific) was a particular concern for all Pacific Islanders. The JPD was one of their main sources of information.

In 1982 the steady growth of the PCC was temporarily reversed following a decision to reduce staff and programmes drastically in the hope of decreasing the dependence on foreign funds. However, the dependence remained and from 1986 on there was re-newed and steady re-growth.

While the goals are clearly laid out in the constitution, the churches are often more preoccupied with their own problems and priorities and they tend to forget that the PCC is also theirs.

THE PACIFIC THEOLOGICAL COLLEGE

The second institution set up in the wake of the 1961 Malua conference, the PTC, founded at Suva, Fiji, in 1966 with help from the Theological Education Fund of the World Council of Churches,[3] is an interdenominational regional college designed to train Pacific Islander clergy at accredited graduate level. At the outset, the college drew most of its students from among alumni of existing local denominational colleges and seminaries in other parts of the Pacific. Later it developed courses and relationships with the Melanesian Association of Theological Schools and the South Pacific Association of Theological Schools. PTC graduates eventually became leaders in their home churches, committed to the furtherance of the ecumenical movement and to conversations about prospects for visible unity and union in their own island countries. As concern for the service and status of women in the Pacific Island churches developed, the PTC offered a women's programme for individual women students as well as wives of students, stressing the role of women in the church through theological education by extension. The extension programme involved visitation of island churches especially, at first, in Micronesia. In 1972 the Roman Catholic Pacific regional seminary was built within walking distance of the PTC in Suva and worked cooperatively with the PTC from its in-auguration. As a result, faculty and students could expect understanding and coopera-tion when they worked in the Pacific in their own island states.

The second PCC assembly, meeting at Davuilevu, Fiji, in 1971,[4] heard reports of many activities launched in parallel with programmes of the WCC: a Pacific Islands Christian education council, which devised agreed curricula; a communication pro-gramme to promote book production and other media; a marriage and family life semi-nar; and a women's programme. Following this assembly, the staff expanded to include linkage with the Church and Society activities of the WCC, and eventually to participate in joint action for development and peace within SODEPAX, and joint action for mission. The Roman Catholic Church at this stage began to be involved, having been represented until then only through observers. During the mid-1960s, when reforms of the Second Vatican Council were being implemented, the prospect of full Roman Catholic mem-bership in the PCC matured, and at the third PCC assembly in Port Moresby, Papua New Guinea, in 1976, the episcopal conference of the Pacific entered full membership. It set up administrative headquarters in Suva, Fiji, and worked in close consultation with the PCC.

By creating the PCC and the PTC and producing the Sunday school curriculum, the Pacific churches affirmed the ecumenical commitment forged at Malua.

---

[3] C.W. Forman, "Theological Education in the South Pacific", in *Journal de la Société des océanistes*, 24, 15, 1968, pp.152-67.

[4] *The Fourth World Meets: Report of the Pacific Conference of Churches Assembly, Davuilevu, Fiji*, Suva, PCC, 1972.

LOCAL INITIATIVES

The wind of friendship and cooperation which was felt at the Malua conference was a significant experience for the Pacific churches, and encouraged them to analyze their local situation and reality. The saying "denomination divides and culture unites" interpreted well the inherent state of affairs in most places. People affiliated to different churches did not worship together, yet their culture brought them together as one people. As churches became aware of this contrast with the new spirit of cooperation, local initiatives were put in place to address the situation. There are many stories of local ecumenical journeys that attempted to reconcile the divisions. Stories, not reports were related – it is important for Pacific people to *tell* their stories, not *write* reports. There are stories of villages with more than one church where they all came together to grieve the loss of someone, to rejoice in the marriage of another and to work in joint fellowship and worship. There are stories of the late 1960s and early 1970s when most of the island states became independent; Samoa (1962), Nauru (1968), Fiji (1970), Papua New Guinea (1975), Solomon Islands (1978), Kiribati (1979) and Vanuatu (1980). All these transitions went smoothly except in Vanuatu. There the churches were divided on independence, and the national council of churches was instrumental in resolving the crisis, networking with the PCC, the WCC and the UN.

Translations of the Bible in some islands were achieved through ecumenical cooperation. In Vanuatu, after twenty years of work the NCC printed its Bible in Bislama and launched it in 1999. The Protestant and Catholic church leaders in Ponpei, Micronesia, initiated translations which were completed within five years. Women's groups started interdenominational fellowships and the Papua New Guinea church council had two chairwomen and a woman general secretary. Women's involvement and participation, still limited in other Pacific churches, is nevertheless growing as more women take on leadership roles in the ecumenical environment.

The 1970s and 1980s saw the formation of many national councils of churches, started originally by the mainline churches present in Malua and joined later by other denominations. Some Islanders migrated to New Zealand, and in 1971 formed a body called the Pacific Islanders synod within the Presbyterian Church of Aotearoa New Zealand. This synod is now a member of the PCC. These stories and many more reflect the ecumenical journey of the local people.

However, despite these bright spots, ecumenism is still a long way from realizing the vision of Malua. In some places it is but a name; in others it is enthusiastically embraced by church leaders although distrusted by some as interference. There seem to be two types of misunderstanding of ecumenism. Some (mis)understand the ecumenical movement as an umbrella-church under which everything or every church is the same. They sometimes say, "It's good nowadays because Catholics and Protestants are one happy family, so we can worship and pray in either church, it does not matter which." The other understanding is that ecumenism is doing more than its mandate. It is seen by certain people as an anti-government body. It often speaks out in matters of justice, peace, environmental concerns, human rights and so on. But these people consider ecumenism should only be "churchy", and deal only with "spiritual" things and not with others, even if there are injustices, lack of peace, poverty, etc. An ecumenical body may do charity work, but it should not speak out against government or the cultural chiefly system of control. This brings to mind the words of Archbishop Oscar Romero of El Salvador who was murdered for this "option for the poor", when he said, "When I give bread to the poor, they call me a saint; but when I speak of injustice, they say I am a communist!" This is also the attitude of some government leaders when challenged by the Pacific churches.

Ecumenism in the Pacific is about the process of achieving Christian unity and, eventually, the unity of all humankind in a common search for the ultimate meaning of life or salvation. It involves what we do together to achieve that goal. It is taken for granted that there are certain types of unity but they may be subsumed under two broad headings: spiritual unity and visible unity. Both are of vital importance to ecumenical unity.

CHALLENGES AND CONCERNS

The local and regional awareness of the Pacific as the arena of life for the people has intensified the concern for its well-being. In the last three decades of the 20th century, the churches attempted to alert governments and people to challenges and issues of concern.

From the very beginning of the PCC, the well-being of the islands' churches and their people was at the top of the ecumenical agenda. Unity in what we do and in what we believe are vital components of those concerns. In the first church and mission consultation that gave rise to the PCC and throughout the pages of the reports of each assembly, these concerns have been voiced repeatedly. The Pacific churches claimed the right to self-determination for the islands, in politics, economics, and expressions of church life and faith – the right to be free from foreign interference that threatens or destroys their means of livelihood.

High among the concerns of the churches were injustice and poverty; corruption among government and community leaders; environmental degradation – nuclear pollution and toxic-waste dumping in rivers and sea, deforestation and over-logging, mining and destruction of the natural habitats of flora and fauna; the adverse effects of Western culture on local cultures; rising crime rates; race relations; political issues such as independence, democracy and human rights.

As in other parts of the developing world, the young churches of the Pacific voiced aspirations for full self-propagation, self-government and self-support. Self-propagation was not novel in the Pacific; church growth had, in many places, been regionally furthered by Islander missionaries since the 1820s. Self-government, largely within structures introduced by white missionaries of varying confessional backgrounds, evolved easily as Islanders assumed presiding and directing roles. Self-support came more slowly as patterns of missionary financial assistance continued, often in close consultation with the WCC's Commission on Inter-church Aid, Refugee and World Service. The Roman Catholic Church operated along parallel but different lines through its Congregation for the Evangelization of the Peoples. Inclusive strategies were coordinated in the region through meetings of the Pacific advisory group, attended annually by the WCC and Roman Catholic representatives.[5] The financing and staffing of the Pacific Conference of Churches and the Pacific Theological College largely depended on such ongoing advice and support. Simultaneously, evangelical churches in French-speaking areas were helped through the Evangelical Community for Apostolic Action (CEVAA – Com-

---

[5] "Major External Sources of Finance and Aid for the Churches", in Kerry James and Akuila Yabaki eds, *Religious Cooperation in the Pacific Islands*, Suva, Univ. of the South Pacific, 1989.

munauté évangélique d'action apostolique), a Reformed worldwide agency that took over previous contacts and responsibilities largely through the French Evangelical Department of Apostolic Action (DEFAP – Département évangélique français d'action apostolique), the successor body of the Paris Evangelical Mission.

ECOLOGICAL ISSUES

One of the constant worries of the churches was the effect of various commercial ventures on the islands' environment and peoples. From its inception the PCC has been in the forefront of the struggle for a cleaner and more stable environment, and this issue has always been a priority in discussions of PCC general assemblies. National councils of churches were the agents directly involved where the issue was most pressing.

Environmental concerns were a major emphasis at the PCC's sixth assembly in Vanuatu in 1991, meeting under the theme "Proclaiming a Living Hope". Its sub-theme stated,

> Stewardship of the Pacific inheritance is to look at the inter-relatedness, inter-relationship and interdependence of the rights and dignity of human beings and of the whole humanity respectively in relation to sustainability of all living creatures. We are created to be both scientists (to know more about the creation) and pastors (to care for the whole creation), or to be both kings and priests of our Pacific inheritance including our families, villages, tribes as well as our environment.
>
> The Pacific Ocean and all that is therein are our God-given gifts, to be looked after. We are the sovereign stewards and managers of our area. We believe that many respectable and recognized leaders of the world have not yet known us very much. We do not think that they know we exist.
>
> We must be recognized, heard, respected, honoured, and our struggles and cries for our stand for a nuclear-free Pacific and for justice, peace and integrity of creation must be responsibly responded to by those who caused the testing of nuclear weapons and dumping of nuclear wastes, etc.[6]

On some large islands of the Pacific deforestation is a reality. Logging companies have succeeded in persuading tribes and clans in the interior and highlands to sell them logging rights. Consequently, there is destruction of the habitats of rare native flora and fauna as well as the source of livelihood for some of the people who live in these rain forests. Papua New Guinea, the Solomon Islands, Fiji, New Caledonia and Vanuatu are the islands most affected by logging and its side effects.

In early 1996 Britain, France and the US signed the South Pacific Nuclear Free Zone Treaty (Rarotonga Treaty) in Suva, Fiji. France had called an end to its series of nuclear undersea testing at Moruroa Atoll (Tahiti). The Pacific churches led the opposition to these tests, and the PCC had actively cooperated with the Evangelical Church of French Polynesia in protesting against the tests and the arrogant behaviour of the French government. Since 1961 the churches were concerned and called for a halt to nuclear testing.[7] France finally declared an end to its tests, but the churches still continue to conscientize the people about the presence and dangerous effects of radio-active matter in

---

[6] *Proclaiming A Living Hope: Pacific Conference of Churches Sixth Assembly, Port-Vila, Vanuatu, 1991*, Suva, PCC, 1992, p.115.

[7] C. Forman, *The Voice of Many Waters: The Story of the Life and Ministry of the Pacific Conference of Churches in the Last 25 Years*, Suva, Lotu Pacifica, 1986, pp.112-14. Peter Salamonsen, *Report for the 7th Pacific Conference of Churches Assembly in Arue, Tahiti, 1997*, pp.2-4.

the ocean, whether by emission or by dumping.[8] Every PCC assembly has dealt with one or other related aspect of this issue.

The people of the islands of Micronesia, in particular the Federated States of Micronesia and the Marshall Islands, still suffer from the effects of nuclear testing by the US on these islands (1946-68). Deformities, countless tumours and all kinds of cancer have developed after eating or drinking radio-active, contaminated food and water. In addition, some of the people no longer live in their traditional islands/atolls because they were "relocated" for the tests and have remained in exile ever since.

The local churches and the PCC with the collaboration of the WCC and many concerned NGOs voiced strong opposition to the continued dumping of nuclear and toxic-waste materials in the Pacific ocean. As far back as 1976, the PCC assembly stated,

> We, the Pacific Conference of Churches, condemn the continued use of the Pacific by foreign powers still occupying areas of the region, for nuclear-weapons testing, storage, waste dumping; the mining of uranium for destructive purposes; and the disregard of the stated wishes of the peoples of the region for self-determination in this matter. The assembly also endorses the resolution of the executive committee [February 1974] for the creation of a Pacific nuclear-free zone.[9]

It is an ongoing struggle to raise this in the world arena. One of the most effective voices on nuclear testing, the rights of Island people and the responsibility of powers like the US belonged to the late Darlene Keju-Johnson of the Marshall Islands. At the WCC's assembly in Vancouver (1983) and subsequent negotiations involving governments, the WCC, the PCC and the Christian Medical Commission, she brought these issues into the international spotlight.[10]

The people and the ecumenical movement of the Pacific repeatedly called for the world to take seriously the threat of climate change. The atolls spoke from experience of the threat of high tides. Many are low-lying coral islands where the people live close to the sea – for example, in such countries as Kiribati, Tuvalu and the Marshalls. Thus the depletion of the ozone layer and a subsequent warming of the earth would spell disaster for these islands and their people. The islands will either submerge completely or lose much of the land mass where the people now live. Conscientizing people about this problem was one of the key projects of the PCC. Seminars on this subject were organized across the Pacific with the help of the WCC.

POLITICAL ISSUES

The churches and the ecumenical movement in the Pacific were deeply involved in the peoples' search for political independence. In the late 1960s and 1970s, this was an issue for which the ecumenical movement helped to seek peaceful solutions. Movements for full political independence for both Tahiti (as Maohi Nui) and New Caledonia (as Kanaky) were supported by major churches in both territories.

Political unrest in the late 1990s in some island states challenged the ecumenical movement and its resolve to seek both liberation and peace. This tension has been recognized in studies of the sometimes conflicting demands of overcoming violence and es-

---

[8] See Suilana Suwatibau, "Nuclear Issues in the Pacific", in *Report of the Pacific Conference of Churches Fifth Assembly September 14-24, 1986, Apia, Western Samoa*, Suva, PCC, 1986, pp.232-37.
[9] *Report: Third Pacific Conference of Churches Assembly, Port Moresby*, Suva, PCC, 1976.
[10] Thomas F. Best ed., *Vancouver to Canberra 1983-1990*, WCC, 1990, p.126.

tablishing justice. The churches, acting together, have called for compensation and rehabilitation of land laid waste by mining on Nauru and Ocean Island, where the world's richest deposits of calcium phosphate were extracted for many years, mainly under colonial powers and with insignificant compensation to local landowners. The people of Ocean Island were completely "relocated" to Rabi, an island in the Fiji group.[11]

On the large island of Bougainville violent disputes over land rights, which led to the closure of a large mine at Panguna, culminated in Bougainvillean movements for secession from Papua New Guinea. Attempts to end the violence and reach an agreed solution were approved and promoted by the PCC when Bishop Patelesio Finau and Rev. Leslie Boseto together tried unsuccessfully to visit Bougainville and mediate agreement, with endorsement by Bougainville's churches – a Catholic majority and a United church minority of Protestants.

In West Papua, formerly Irian Jaya, a province of Indonesia, a movement for political independence has emerged, with active participation of local Christians and supportive sympathy from other parts of the Pacific Islands.

There were other interesting ecumenical developments outside of the PCC. In 1987 a military coup in Fiji – following elections that put in power the labour party, which was predominantly Indo-Fijian but headed by a Fijian – was staged to ensure that political power would always be held by Fijians. As a result, a great deal of distrust and bitter feeling came to the surface especially along racial lines. A group of people from different religious persuasions came together to pray for harmony and reconciliation, and sought to inform the ordinary people about spiritual values as a means of reducing and calming racial tension. The group called itself Interfaith; it was composed of Christians (both Catholics and Protestants), Muslims and Hindus. They came together in a time of national crisis because they thought what they had to offer together was worthwhile. And although things quietened down on the political front in Fiji, what these people started could be a way forward in the relationships between world religions in the Pacific.

THE CHURCH UNITING

One of the expressed wishes of the churches at the Malua conference was for some organic unions between the scattered churches in the Pacific. Very few appeared – an exception being the United Church in Papua New Guinea and the Solomon Islands, which integrated former Methodists and Congregationalists. This church has since divided into two separate but related churches, partly on account of the Bougainville crisis.[12] Conversations about possible union between Anglicans and Roman Catholics in Papua New Guinea finally met with a negative response from Rome, which maintained its previous pronouncement that Anglican orders are invalid.[13]

---

[11] J. Garrett, *A Way in the Sea: Aspects of Pacific Christian History with Reference to Australia*, Melbourne, Spectrum, 1982, pp.43-47; Barrie Macdonald, *Cinderellas of the Empire*, Canberra, 1982, pp.247-49; Maslyn Williams and Barrie Macdonald, *The Phosphateers*, Melbourne, 1985. See also *Report for the 7th Pacific Conference*, pp.2-4.

[12] Finau's interventions on behalf of reconciliation in Bougainville are in David Mullins ed., *He Spoke the Truth in Love: A Selection of Tongan Bishop Patelisio Finau's Writings and Speeches*, Auckland, Catholic Publ. Centre, 1994, pp.179-184.

[13] Theo Aerts and Peter Ramsden eds, *Studies and Statements on Romans and Anglicans in Papua New Guinea*, Port Moresby, Catholic Bishops Conference of Papua New Guinea, 1995.

Though there are not many Uniting churches, the national councils of churches are engaged in the discussion. However, at the local level more churches are working and worshipping together than ever before.

Underlying doctrinal questions familiar within the Faith and Order movement had rarely been faced together in the Pacific except when, with the help of the United Bible Societies, cooperative Bible translation in many local languages was initiated jointly by Roman Catholics and other churches. In every part of the region, reduction of languages to writing and the spread of literacy came originally through church and mission influence. Foreign missionaries were among pioneer linguists and ethnographers, since they stayed longer in Oceania and learned more at village level than traders, transient social anthropologists or colonial administrators. The use of varying words and expressions in Bible translation has become a source of dialogue between Catholics and Protestants. Working together on biblical translation has been a fertile seedbed for consideration of the deeper meanings of words used for God, church and churches in the Bible and in worship.[14] Biblical theological reflection led to deeper study in the local context of the issues of church, ministry, sacraments, and Tradition and traditions. Faith and Order work was facilitated locally by the Ecumenical Association of Third World Theologians at two consultations in Suva in 1994 and 1996. Women's theology was consequently taken more seriously within previously male-dominated churches. Publication of the report of the Lima meeting of the Faith and Order Commission in 1982 led to presentation of a paper by Thomas Best of the WCC's Faith and Order Commission, on *Baptism, Eucharist and Ministry* (BEM) at the PCC's assembly in 1986. This paper sought a (belated) response to the Lima document on BEM and consideration of related issues broached in a related book.[15]

By the year 2000 awareness of ecumenical developments in the world as a whole diminished. The appearance of many newer self-styled fundamentalist and Pentecostal groups fomented reaction against the World Council of Churches, which was thought to be either "liberal" or politically leftist – or both. At the same time, within Protestant, Anglican and Roman Catholic churches in the region, the charismatic movement adopted forms of ecstatic worship, including speaking and praying in tongues. The practices also spread among some "mainline" church leaders and laity.[16] There seemed to be a void left by the mainline churches that the new groups filled. This new phenomenon caused some soul-searching for the Pacific churches. While they were busy with finding ways to work together and to seek eventual unity, these new groups were introducing new divisions on top of the existing ones. Furthermore, the new religious groups were by nature not ecumenical. The ecumenical task for the future is to find ways to initiate dialogue and work with these groups.

Many Pacific Islanders felt at home in this setting, possibly because ecstasy was closer to pre-Christian religious behaviour than the formal liturgies and services intro-

---

[14] For an example see Jacques Nicole, *Au pied de l'écriture: histoire de la traduction de la Bible en tahitien*, Papeete, Ed. Haere po no Tahiti, 1988, pp.273-79. The laity of all churches speak and think together increasingly as a result of Bible study and forms of worship in the vernaculars of the islands since implementation of the norms of the Second Vatican Council's Constitution on the Liturgy.

[15] *Report of the Pacific Conference of Churches Fifth Assembly*, pp.169-75. M. Thurian and G. Wainwright eds, *Baptism and Eucharist: Ecumenical Convergence in Celebration*, WCC, 1983.

[16] A survey of new groups was commissioned and published by the Pacific Theological College: Manfred Ernst, *Winds of Change: Rapidly Growing Religious Groups in the Pacific Islands*, Suva, PCC, 1994.

duced by the older missions. Many syncretic local cults in the Pacific were led by prophets and promised a coming kingdom of earthly prosperity and material rewards.[17]

"Renewal fatigue" set in after earlier implementation of programmes of the WCC and the reforms of the Second Vatican Council. Many younger church leaders seemed relatively unaware of ecumenical origins and motivation. They were once described by Sione 'Amanaki Havea as "a generation that knew not Joseph" (Ex. 1:8). He appealed to them not to lose the earlier momentum.

THEOLOGICAL SCHOOLS AND LOCAL THEOLOGY

Until 1966 each church trained its ministers in its own local theological school. The Catholics sent their seminarians overseas (New Zealand, Australia, US, France). The setting up of regional theological schools like the Pacific Theological College (the only ecumenical college for the Pacific), the Pacific Regional Seminary of the Pacific Catholic bishops conference (1972) and the Bomana Holy Spirit seminary for the Papua New Guinea and the Solomon Islands bishops conference (1963),[18] brought about a new era in the life of the churches in Pacific. Students were encouraged to contextualize their theological thinking. Ecumenical gatherings such as the PCC assemblies urged the development of a "Pacific theology". By 2000, results were beginning to show not only in the way local church leaders spoke about the gospel but also in the way the people understood it, as well as in worship. Theological topics such as the theology of the coconut, theology of the kava, the Pacific Christ, have emerged. The use of various local rituals during worship is quite common – the Catholics seem to be more at ease here than their Protestant counterparts. These ideas and practices became accepted due in part to training in the theological colleges where inculturated or contextualized thinking and practice are encouraged. Furthermore, many more local theologians took up the teaching posts in these institutions, and they were more comfortable with the thought patterns and cultural items brought into theological parlance by the students.

The Pacific Theological College and the Pacific Regional Seminary are situated quite close together in Suva. Both institutions grant a bachelor of divinity degree and the PTC grants a master in theology degree. They also have a close working relationship which in the beginning was forced upon them by necessity, e.g., lecturer shortage in one or the other institution necessitated the exchange of lecturers or students from one to the other. This exchange has since developed into one based in ecumenical conviction. Thus the future leaders of the Pacific churches, both Catholic and Protestant, get to know each other. This in turn facilitates ecumenical dialogue and cooperation.

Local theological schools have come a long way since the days of training local ministers. Today, most islands have their own theological schools that train both men and women up to the level of bachelor in divinity. The graduates do not necessarily go into

---

[17] Wendy Flannery ed., *Religious Movements in Melanesia Today*, Goroka, Melanesian Institute for Pastoral and Socio-Economic Service, 1983, 3 vols; Garry Trompf ed., *Prophets of Melanesia*, Suva, Univ. of the South Pacific, 1977.

[18] The Roman Catholics had a seminary in Lano, Wallis Island, that trained local priests for the Vicariate of Western Oceania, and for the French-speaking seminarians in Paita, New Caledonia, but it had been stopped in the 1930s. See John Broadbent, "Early Catholic Attempts at Forming a Priesthood in the Pacific", in Doug Munro and Andrew Thornley eds, *The Covenant Makers: Islander Missionaries in the Pacific*, Suva, Pacific Theological College, 1996, pp.115-23.

the ministry. The Pacific Theological College and the Pacific Regional Seminary are in a special way the power houses of the church in the Pacific. The friendships that develop there among all the future leaders of the churches is a foretaste of what is to come in ecumenism in the Pacific.

In connection with Pacific theology, the Ecumenical Association of Third World Theologians held two consultations in the Pacific in 1994 and 1996 and in the latter meeting a Pacific chapter was set up with fifty theologians as members. Within the EATWOT membership, more and more women have made their presence felt in the theological arena. But given the cultural confines, the struggle of women for recognition of their role in church and society is still in its early stages.

On the doctrinal front, there is a somewhat disinterested approach by many of the Pacific Islands' churches. This aspect does not seem to rank high in the PCC's priorities. Although the *Baptism, Eucharist and Ministry* document came out of the Faith and Order Commission meeting at Lima in 1982, it was not until the sixth assembly of the PCC in 1991 that the general secretary, Sione Motu'ahala, asked in his report how many churches in the Pacific "have taken the BEM document seriously".[19] Work on this important document was listed as an educational agenda item for some of the churches in the Pacific, but nothing seems to have come of it.

In a PCC meeting with ecumenical partners at the WCC in 1992, a programme was presented for the discussion of this document: 1992, baptism; 1993, eucharist; 1994, ministry. The PCC, through its mission and unity desk, ran three workshops on baptism for Polynesia, Micronesia and Melanesia, and an agreed statement on baptism went to the PCC assembly at Tahiti in 1997 for approval.

With regard to the eucharist, the late Roman Catholic bishop Patelisio Finau of Tonga expressed a dream when he became the chair of the PCC in 1991 that he wanted to see the unity of the churches in receiving communion together from the same eucharistic table by the year 2000. Part of the disappointment with that PCC assembly was that not much had been done to explain the BEM document's text on eucharistic sharing. The unrealized vision awaits its hour as other basic preoccupations of the ecumenical movement increasingly occupy centre stage. Encouragement for the dialogue on this important issue is needed for all the churches in Oceania.

There seems to be a yearning for a common sharing of the eucharist among the churches, but at the same time there is a certain reluctance to talk out differences. Yet these differences have to be understood in order to reach some sort of agreement on common sharing. On the other hand, we could start from the opposite pole by sharing together, then engage in dialogue to understand one another and our various denominational traditions. However, we are slow to do either.

The BEM consultations mark a new stage in the history of ecumenism in the Pacific. We have moved from what we have in common to discuss what divides us. And the most unitive of all Christian rites, the eucharist, is the most divisive – we still cannot receive the eucharist together. We have moved further along the road to unity both by continuing with issues that concern our physical livelihood, and by entering the more profound spiritual aspect of our life as Christians.

---

[19] *Proclaiming a Living Hope*, p.124.

ECUMENISM IN THE PACIFIC TODAY

In conclusion, it is important to note some of the people who have been at the forefront of the Pacific ecumenical journey. The movement owes its existence to the hard work by some Islanders with a vision of the different denominations uniting in Christ: to name only some, Vavae Toma and Fetaui Mataafa of the Congregational Christian Church in Samoa, Setareki Tuilovoni, Lorine Tevi and Sevati Tuwere of the Methodist Church in Fiji, Amanaki Havea of the Tonga Methodist Church, Patelesio Finau of the Roman Catholic Church in Tonga, Leslie Boseto of the United Church in Papua New Guinea and the Solomon Islands, Jabez Bryce of the Polynesian Diocese of the Church of England and Baiteke Nabetari of the Kiribati Protestant Church.

Ecumenism has come a long way in the Pacific. It has done much good in bringing together opposing poles in the spectrum of Christianity. Better understanding among the churches is a common canoe. However, a proper and true understanding of ecumenical bodies has to be clarified for the people at the grassroots. Encouragement for ecumenism at all levels has to be maintained. Theological contextualization and inculturation of the gospel still have a long way to go, but they are already on the way. The regional theological schools are bringing this aspect to their education, and the ecumenical movement has committed itself to this inculturation.

There has also been a shift of basic concerns. While programmes and projects are still run on social, environmental and political issues and concerns, there is a longing for more doctrinal and theological discussions which have in fact started. The Pacific churches are looking afresh at the concept of ecumenism, and they take seriously the social, political, economical and cultural impact of the modern world on the lives of their people.

BIBLIOGRAPHY

Adler, Richard, *Religious Cooperation in the Pacific Island*, Suva, Univ. of the South Pacific, 1983, 231p.

Aubert, Marie-Hélène and Rivasi, Michèle eds, *The French Nuclear Tests in Polynesia, Demanding the Truth and Proposals for the Future*, Lyon, Centre of Documentation and Research on Peace and Conflicts, 1999, 143p.

Breward, Ian, *A History of the Churches in Australasia*, New York, Oxford Univ. Press, 2001, 474p.

Chandran, Joshua Russell ed., *The Cross and the Tanoa: Gospel and Culture in the Pacific*, Suva, South Pacific Association of Theological Schools, 1988, 111p.

Coop, William L. ed., *Pacific People Sing Out Strong*, New York, Friendship, 1982, 96p.

Ernst, Manfred, *Winds of Change: Rapidly Growing Religious Groups in the Pacific Islands*, Suva, PCC, 1994, 357p.

Flannery, Wendy ed., *Religious Movements in Melanesia Today*, Goroka, Melanesian Institute for Pastoral and Socio-Economic Service, 1983, 3 vols.

Forman, Charles W., *The Island Churches of the South Pacific: Emergence in the 20th Century*, Maryknoll NY, Orbis, 1982, 285p.

Forman, Charles W., *The Voice of Many Waters: The Story of the Life and Ministry of the Pacific Conference of Churches in the Last 25 Years*, Suva, Lotu Pasifika Prod., 1986, 211p.

Garrett, John, *Footsteps in the Sea: Christianity in Oceania to World War II*, Suva, Institute of Pacific Studies, 1992, 514p.

Garrett, John, *To Live among the Stars: Christian Origins in Oceania*, WCC, 1982, 412p.

Garrett, John, *Where Nets Were Cast: Christianity in Oceania since World War II*, Suva, Institute of Pacific Studies, 1998, 499p.

May, John D'Arcy, *Christus Initiator: Theologie im Pazifik*, Düsseldorf, Patmos, 1990, 151p.
Nicole, Jacques, *Au pied de l'écriture: histoire de la traduction de la Bible en tahitien*, Papeete, Tahiti, Ed. Haere po no Tahiti, 1988, 343p.
Pacific Conference of Churches, *Report of the 4th Assembly, May 3-15, 1981, Nuku'alofa, Tonga*, Suva, PCC, 1981, 298p.
Pacific Conference of Churches, *Report of the Fifth Assembly, September 14-24, 1986, Apia, Western Samoa*, Suva, PCC, 1986, 385p.
Proclaiming a Living Hope, Suva, PCC, 1992, 238p.
Siwatibau, Suliana, *A Call to a New Exodus: An Anti-Nuclear Primer for Pacific People*, Suva, Lotu Pasifika Prod., 1982, 96p.
Towards a Relevant Pacific Theology: The Role of the Churches and Theological Education, Suva, Lotu Pasifika Prod., 1986, 189p.
Trompf, G.W. ed., *The Gospel is not Western: Black Theologies from the Southwest Pacific*, Maryknoll NY, Orbis, 1987, 213p.
Vernier, Henri, *Au vent des cyclones, missions protestantes et Eglise Evangélique à Tahiti et en Polynésie Française: 1797-1963-1985*, Paris, Les Bergers et les Mages, 1986, 465p.
Weingärtner, Erich, *New Caledonia: Half-Way to Independence? Ecumenical Seminar on Matignon Accords and the Kanak People's Future*, WCC, 1994, 54p.
Wright, Cliff and Fugui, Leslie eds, *Christ in South Pacific Cultures: Articles by South Pacific Islanders about the Relationship of Traditional Culture to Christian Faith: Group Work Suggestions, Poems*, Suva, Lotu Pasifika Prod., 1985, 117p.

Part IV

27
The Changing Shape of the Ecumenical Movement

John Briggs

The last third of the 20th century witnessed a period of history full of momentous change. The full measure of human achievements was everywhere apparent – efficient worldwide travel, the exploration of space, information technology that could reduce to a single key-stroke both complex calculations and intricate analytical processes, the conquest of many killer diseases, and processes of bio-technology that brought as much fear as hope. The contribution of science clearly enriched human experience. Because, however, the enquiring mind is a fallible human intelligence, which lacks moral omniscience, every advance possesses ambiguity and must be submitted to critical evaluation.

Advances in technology – transport, communication, development of international trade – have all played a critical part in globalization which creates a particular kind, perhaps a false type, of global unity. It is a unity which brings with it fragmentation and dislocation for many people, as more and more parts of the human family become excluded from full participation in determining their own futures. This pattern cannot, therefore, form any kind of model for the unity the ecumenical movement seeks to foster.

Moreover, since the eclipse of communism – and in large measure, socialism – politics has lost touch with the world of ideology and become increasingly discredited as politicians, tainted by corruption or the fear of corruption, have lost the confidence of those who elected them. A vacuum of ideals has been created, while the pragmatism that all too easily fills the gap is made to sanctify an uncritical consumerism devoid of any values apart from the delivery either of greater profits, or the material wealth which, it is imagined, will make for greater personal gratification. Winning in life's lottery becomes the ultimate goal.

The moral foundations which once served as a basis for acceptable human behaviour have been corroded; everything becomes privatized into a matter of personal choice. Hopes of a "new world order", representative of order rather than disorder, seem so distant from reality that expectations give way to pessimism and despair, for the world remains in chaos. Wars still inflict death upon combatants and, even more, on noncombatants. Millions have been driven from their homelands and depend upon the compassion of men and women of faith for the restoration of some measure of human dignity. People remain divided from each other on the basis of race, gender, class, religious confession and ethnic difference so that xenophobia reinforces other fears. Militarism enjoys a new lease of life.

The end of the bipolar confrontation of the cold war has hardly given way to the peaceful and purposeful world which had been eagerly anticipated. Rather, a single superpower uneasily manoeuvres its massive power against the forces of an international terrorism, all too easily identified with confessional division. So appealing is the cause that young people are readily recruited to the role of suicide killers.

In consequence, the expectations of the Enlightenment, and its Marxist and positivist offspring, have failed to materialize, as an easy confidence in the benefactions of science has given way to a cynical post-modernism. Hope in human scholarship and technological dexterity is seen to be misplaced. Old secular certainties are shattered: "Computers", as one Russian scientist remarked, "know no morality". The inhabitants of the concrete city, which is the context of life for so many of the world's population, find themselves rootless if not uprooted and, therefore, uncertain of their future.

Colonialism has all but disappeared, but in its wake has come a form of economic dominance that witnesses the growth of transnational corporations, whose budgets dwarf the total gross national product of many a sovereign state in the developing world: every year it takes more days' work to secure basic technological necessities such as tractors, irrigation pumps or engines for manufacturing. A national debt which overpowers social welfare becomes a formidable opponent of the survival of human life itself within the poorest nations. At the same time richer nations combine together in powerful economic and political unions that all too often stack up diplomatic and trading power at the expense of the weakest.

Glasnost and *perestroika* have not yielded the security and improvement in living standards which were initially imputed to them. They have, however, successfully created a form of pluralism that a people, disciplined by both church and state to a life of limited choice, find hard to comprehend. Free trade in ideas, especially religious ideas, is a reality to which it takes time to acclimatize, and the transition can easily bring with it much fear and apprehension. Under the guise of the democracy of such pluralism, East European and third-world countries have been bombarded by North American sectarian agents, who have at their command technologies that are beyond the hopes of access for many traditional church groups. Such action easily provokes the charge of proselytism, with all this entails for the unity of the church, for as has been well said, "Mission without ecumenical awareness becomes proselytism; ecumenism without mission becomes selfish and sterile."

In fact, a persecuting communism helped majority Orthodox churches discover both smaller Protestant minorities within their own nations, and the value of international ecumenical fellowship, for solidarity with the suffering church was a significant aspect of ecumenical concern throughout the latter years of the 20th century. The ending of the cold war, however, brought with it not only new freedoms but new suspicions. The fragility of ecumenical relationships within such a context was demonstrated by the withdrawal of the Georgian Orthodox Church from the World Council of Churches and the Conference of European Churches in May 1997 and of the Bulgarian Orthodox Church from these bodies in July 1998. Even within the Orthodox family of churches the jurisdictions of the Ecumenical Patriarchate and the Moscow Patriarchate found themselves in conflict over the allegiance of the Estonian-speaking faithful, following the independence of the Baltic republics. Similar conflicts appeared between the Russian and Romanian Orthodox churches following the independence of Moldova.

While apartheid may have come to an end in South Africa, racism still finds a comfortable existence in most societies, including in that country, and "ethnic cleansing" and genocide appear as actions that the world is powerless to prevent. The power of ethnicity and tribalism unsettles the peace of human society in many parts of the world, and it is all the stronger when buttressed by confessional differences. Elsewhere Indigenous people cry out against the seizure of their lands, and an unjust economic order fashions "economic migrants" who are denied the status of true refugees. Ecumenical vigilance is ever necessary both to control old enemies and to recognize their new disguises.

One thing is certain: a self-evident surge of secularism has not killed religion, or indeed superstition, as appeals to luck, fate and astrology still attract popular fancy. At the same time there is a resurgence of other world faiths: Western historians confident of their secularist presuppositions still have to learn how to spell "Ayatollah", while their colleagues in anthropology undertake comparative studies in varieties of fundamentalism. Exploring the ways in which different religions can live together in the modern world makes dialogue a vital aspect of mission, especially when it is seen that dialogue is not a substitute for evangelism, and that it does not imply a species of religious syncretism that attributes only a relative value to the saving truth which is revealed in Jesus Christ.

THE ROMAN CATHOLIC CHURCH

The 1960s can be seen as a watershed in the ecumenical movement, given the hopes born out of the Second Vatican Council (1962-65) which began a vital process of bringing the Roman Catholic Church up to date. The fruits of this ecumenical pilgrimage can be seen in more occasions of shared worship, genuine and open bilateral dialogues, and the ability to gather with other Christians around a common Bible. Modernization of the church and its liturgy has made it easier for other churches to relate to the Roman Catholic Church, while old landmarks of division and suspicion seem to have dwindled. The Pontifical Council for Promoting Christian Unity, in responding to the WCC's "Common Understanding and Vision" document,[1] clearly states that "there is a true and real, even if imperfect, koinonia existing between the Roman Catholic Church and other churches and ecclesial communities" and it is on that "real but imperfect" koinonia that future work must build.

Charismatic influences have also played their part in breaking down barriers between the Roman Catholic and sister churches, for such influences operate without respect for confessions across denominational divides. Institutionally both Orthodox and Protestant churches have found a more welcoming tone in documents emanating from the Pontifical Council for Promoting Christian Unity under the successive presidencies of Cardinals Bea, Willebrands and Cassidy, over against the more conservative and dogmatic judgments articulated by the Congregation for the Doctrine of the Faith, as identified with the authorizing signature of Cardinal Ratzinger.

---

[1] In 1989 the WCC's central committee launched a process of study and consultation on "Towards a Common Understanding and Vision of the World Council of Churches". This process was deemed necessary, as "the context in which the WCC works today – the world situation, the situation in the churches and the situation in the ecumenical movement – differs radically from that of 1948, when the Council was founded. In the light of these changes, it is critically important to renew the churches' commitment to the movement and to the Council, based on a new articulation of their shared understanding of what the WCC is and vision of what it ought to be" (*From Canberra to Harare 1991-1998*, WCC, 1998, pp.1-2). Following a process of consultation with the churches, the CUV document – as it has come to be known – was presented to the Council's eighth assembly in Harare in 1998. See also the last section of this chapter.

The eirenic purposes of the papal encyclical *Ut Unum Sint* ("On Commitment to Ecumenism"), 1995, with its evident spirit of humility, and its clear recognition that ecumenism is an organic part of the church's life and work, are clear, even if serious divisions between the Roman Catholic Church and the Eastern and Protestant churches remain and are recognized as such by both sides. But in the encyclical there is a ready acknowledgment that every church needs the help of all others in seeking the unity Christ desires for his church. In that context it will be wise to explore which ecclesial practices and structures might be inimical to the gospel, and what, for the mutual understanding of one another, legitimate diversity may mean. Legitimate diversity is a problematical concept for, clearly, diversity of basic belief cannot be intended when the search is for "the unity of churches in one faith and eucharistic fellowship". Therefore, there are core beliefs, as outlined in the constitution of bodies like the World Council of Churches, which require the assent of all members; however, beyond such fundamentals, Christian tolerance must teach us to learn to live happily with elements of diversity in emphasis and practice.

Ecumenical leaders, who experience the full participation of the Roman Catholic Church at national and regional levels, find it hard to understand why such constitutional participation is not possible at a global level. It is here that the special catholicity claims of the Roman Catholic Church most urgently impinge upon the church status of all other Christian confessions, and where further conversations must take place.

NEW PATTERNS OF CHURCH LIFE

One of the most conspicuous markers of this period has been the shift in the centre of gravity for membership of the Christian church from the North to the South; Europe and North America, with their post-Christian populations, are now properly on the receiving end of missionary endeavours from the South. With a loss of influence, both in the worldwide church and in their own societies, a number of mainline churches, both in Europe and in North America, have faced considerable uncertainty as to where they are going. This very often has contrasted sharply not only with the growth of the churches of the southern hemisphere but with a buoyant Pentecostalism and evangelicalism nearer home, which has been highly successful in exploiting the techniques of the church-growth movement. Success has sometimes been the parent of stridency, particularly as focused within the US, there represented by the activities of the many tele-evangelists, and a wide variety of fundamentalist groups. During the Reagan, George H.W. Bush and even Clinton years, this was seen to effect a critical alliance between conservative religion and conservative politics, an alliance which retains potency in the US, particularly in the years leading up to and following the second Gulf war. Such fundamentalist groups often also have perceived a correlation between material wealth and spiritual health. This can be seen in the espousing of a self-confirming form of prosperity theology which has been widely exported by both American and Korean missionaries.

There is, however, another tradition of evangelicalism, in the US as elsewhere, which is shared, for example, by Indigenous Latin American Pentecostals. Working out a commitment to a holistic understanding of Christian mission, this offers a radical critique of the political scene: Jovito Salonga, voicing a common concern among third-world delegates, told those assembled for the second International Congress on World Evangelization sponsored by the Lausanne Committee and held in Manila in 1989,

We achieve spirituality when we are out there in the busy streets or in the crowded market place, among the oppressed and the poor, identifying ourselves with the lowliest of them and struggling for a free, open society where the weak shall be strong and the strong shall be just.

Such commitments lead to both the correction of old stereotypes and the development of new and unanticipated alliances. This means that commentators have to be more discerning in their analyses, and commentaries certainly need to distinguish evangelicalism, in its several forms, conservative or radical, from fundamentalism and from sectarianism.

Within the structures of the WCC it has not always been easy to persuade the churches that the Council has been faithful in keeping central on its agenda the concerns of the former International Missionary Council, whose work was integrated into the WCC in 1961. Faithfulness in this area has, for almost forty years, been a test of WCC credibility within a fairly broadly defined evangelical constituency. The document "Mission and Evangelism: An Ecumenical Affirmation" (1982) was well-crafted to reassure Evangelicals of the WCC's commitment to evangelism but, though approved by the central committee, it has not had as wide an impact on the life of the Council as that of *Baptism, Eucharist and Ministry*, which appeared at exactly the same time.

It could be argued that different advocates come to the WCC with different agendas. Some wish to champion an other-worldly concern for salvation, even when spelled out in the context of holistic mission: others seek a more down-to-earth engagement with hurting humanity's experience of violence and injustice; for still others the essential commitment is to the search for the unity of the church in life and faith. That is perhaps to say that the predecessors of the Council – Faith and Order, Life and Work, the International Missionary Council – still have advocates who wish to give clear voice to these particular emphases, especially when the reshaping of the work of the Council is being considered. On the other hand, strong voices would claim that that era of competition is passed, and the search for unity, as in John 17, is not for its own sake but essentially for missionary purposes. This is to affirm that the mission of the church is fundamental to its being and certainly to its unity. Equally clearly, that same commitment to mission must necessarily involve both gospel proclamation and a radical engagement with issues of justice, peace, and a holy respect for the created order. Any attempt to separate vertical responsibility to the triune God from horizontal solidarity with God's children in desperate need must be seen as false.

CHURCH AND PARA-CHURCH

In Europe state churches until the mid-1900s seemed to exhibit considerable strength, at least as seen from the membership claimed on the basis of baptism and confirmation.

They have been able to command impressive budgets supported by the church-tax system. Historic churches are beautifully maintained, while ecclesiastical headquarters have been able to sustain a wide range of services and mission agencies, all generously supported. These churches have also carried the lion's share of funding ecumenical enterprise all round the world, including the work of the World Council of Churches and the Lutheran World Federation. Indeed, they have been glad to carry a quite disproportionate burden in this respect, and other churches have been content for them to do so. With the reuniting of Germany, with the movement of the tax burden from direct to indirect taxes, and with more people opting out of this partnership, that ability to fund global ecumenism has understandably come under increasing pressure. The churches themselves have had to engage in reducing their payrolls and to give notice to their ecu-menical partners of a new lower level of support, a reduction in income which is prov-ing almost impossible to replace from other sources. At the same time such mainline churches, which have traditionally been conceived of as folk churches, are also having to come to terms with a newly divergent pluralism which questions whether they can, in any meaningful sense, be seen as the conscience of the nation or its moral intelligence.

While the routine and discipline of parish life leave many unmoved, there remains a religious consciousness, in Germany at least, which can still command huge attendances and stir people's religious aspirations through the biennial Kirchentag. Elsewhere, as in Great Britain, para-church experiences, in a more evangelical key, such as Spring Harvest and Greenbelt, capture the enthusiasm of the young. Communities like Taizé in France or Iona in Scotland, each with a commitment to an updated community life, support for liturgical reform, an ongoing search for Christian unity, and an engagement with an ur-ban-industrial agenda, continue to offer renewal of faith through pilgrimage experiences, which in their turn make for the renewal of the life of the local church.

Sociologists of religion, such as the British scholar Grace Davie, have suggested that a residual level of belief still exists in apparently secular societies which exhibit declin-ing church commitment, thus her phrase about the many who engage in "believing without belonging". Elsewhere in Europe there exist "movements" of people who still es-pouse a Christian commitment but who have become disillusioned with the life of the local "church", leading commentators to speak of "a church beyond the church". Ecu-menical relations with, or support of, such groups sometimes confuse or distress the leaders of mainline churches who, by contrast, retreat into confessionalism.

At the very least the question needs to be posed as to where the "church" is in these confusing patterns? What criticisms does the organized church need to hear? What dis-ciplines are required of those committed to Christ to stand firm with other Christians in their own locality? To what extent are the "movements" not merely agencies of the church, but themselves aspects of "being church"? An ecumenical movement which lim-ited its function to fostering interchurch fellowship would be just as untrue to its calling as a conscientious activism that had lost touch with its ecclesial roots. At the heart of the ecumenical movement there must exist a church that exists for others, not just for itself.

A resurgence of confessionalism has, thus, put all ecumenical work at a disadvan-tage. More particularly, an abuse of the venerable tradition of congregationalism – but more truly a form of neo-parochialism – has led to a situation in which rich congrega-tions coexist with poor denominations, and therefore with an under-funded ecumenism. Local ventures can be funded in abundance, whereas the same resources are not avail-able for work elsewhere. It is not, however, a matter of finance alone: there is also a pathological sense of self-sufficiency of the local, apparently successful, congregation, unconcerned for the welfare of the other, or the whole. Such an abuse is a function of the privatization of religion which has an ill-defined understanding of the catholic and the corporate. Indeed, there have emerged de facto denominations which, in fact, con-sist of but a single mega-congregation, innocent and ignorant of all sense of the catholic.

TRADITION AND CHANGE

Tradition has often found it difficult to accommodate itself to pluralism and change, as the debate within the Anglican communion over the ordination of women, and subse-quently their consecration to the episcopate, has demonstrated. The articulation of the churches' attitude to those of gay and lesbian orientation has similarly been, and promises to be, fraught with difficulty in some places. Like the ordination of women, it has occasioned new grounds of division between those who, in the name of justice, passionately desire change, and those who, equally passionately, believe that they, in the interests of truth, are called to defend a sacred inheritance. Because of these tensions the leaders of the Orthodox churches have found themselves increasingly embarrassed by the discussion of such issues in a way that they find it difficult to interpret in terms other than as a form of advocacy.

The churches, while realizing that their own record is far from perfect, have played a major part in championing the rights of women, who all too often have been the victims of prejudice and bias, not to mention violence and abuse. Moreover, in so far as it is poor women who are the worst exploited and who suffer most, reference should be made to "the feminization of poverty". Although many churches are committed to working for a better deal for women in both church and society, others continue to reinforce the prejudices of secular society by their own exclusivity; the church has not always been the inclusive community it was intended to be, where barriers of class and race, gender and colour are overcome in the unity of all God's people in Christ. Patriarchal structures, long accepted as the order of things, are now challenged in many Protestant churches by feminist theology which already has found some support among Catholic women. Aware of the hurts caused by male dominance, ecumenical leaders have encouraged the use, wherever possible, of inclusive language and the avoidance of gender-biased thought forms, recognizing, however, that the Bible speaks of both the Fatherhood of God and the Sonship of Christ.

All such issues are potentially divisive, separating those who favour change from those who believe fundamental truth is enshrined within existing formularies. Concern is not confined to such issues in themselves, divisive as they have proved, but relates to the issue of authority in the handling of scripture, the significance of universal Tradition, and the competing claims of synod and bishop within the government of the church. Thus a new threat to the unity of the church is posed, when ethical judgments as much as theological beliefs may form the grounds for division, both within and between churches. Tragic in itself, it becomes the more tragic as such conflicts consume energies which divide, at the expense of building up the church's common witness.

The question is therefore raised whether, for the sake of the unity of the church, there are in fact limits to the diversity that the worldwide church, and its ecumenical instruments, are able legitimately to accept. Certainly the most foot-loose radicalism which seems overtly to abandon all commitment to Christian truth can become a burden even to those struggling to discover the path of relevant contextualized discipleship in the modern world, not to mention an offence alike to Orthodox and conservative evangelical members of ecumenical bodies.

SHARED RESPONSIBILITIES

A post-colonial world was soon discovered to be a post-missions world in so far as national churches in newly independent states quickly became independent players. Other large and growing fellowships were proud to see themselves in contra-distinction to mission-founded churches, as for example African Instituted Churches (AICs). Such churches may now be seen to constitute a separate Christian world communion for, though based in Africa, AICs also possess a powerful diaspora whose members find common ground with other independent Afro-Caribbean groups both in Europe and the Americas.

With the expulsion of missionaries from China following the communist take-over in 1949, Christians in the West prayed for the survival of the church in China. At that time the Christian community was significantly less than one million strong. Today, there is great debate as to the size of the church in China. Whether within churches affiliated to the China Christian Council, whose representatives were present at the Canberra and Harare assemblies (their membership of the WCC was re-established at Canberra), or within the house-church movement, a not altogether separate entity, it is clear that the Chinese-promoted church of today is many times larger than the church inherited from missionary endeavours before the revolution. Moreover, it is a much more genuinely Chinese church than formerly. When in 1997 Hong Kong became a special administrative region of the People's Republic, the hope was that its Christian community might experience a similar pattern of growth.

Many churches, both in the South and in the former Eastern bloc, need the support of those churches in the North and West. In such a situation care has to be taken to avoid any form of "donor dictatorship", determining which programmes will be funded and which not. By contrast, the ecumenical sharing of resources has emerged as a conceptual framework that frees the churches from being either sending or giving agents, or accepting or receiving bodies, replacing such a pattern with more genuine forms of partnership. Guidelines for such a way of working, drawn up at the WCC's consultation on "Sharing Life in a World Community" in El Escorial, Spain, in 1987, were adopted by the central committee the following year. But that is not the end of the story, for policy can become practice only by the intentional actions of the member churches and their mission agencies. The ecumenical sharing of resources is not restricted to church partnerships but provides a model for the wider sharing of life with all peoples in response to the biblical imperatives of compassion and justice, seeking to give voice to the voiceless and power to those currently without opportunity to improve their lot.

Christian compassion is, properly, no longer satisfied with simply providing aid. Western consumers have to be educated into more responsible patterns of purchasing. Governments have to be persuaded to act in support of a new economic order. Mission agencies, formerly supporting large aid programmes, now prefer to invest resources in long-term development, even though they may entertain increasing doubts as to the ability of development programmes to deliver economic and, therefore, political independence.

A WORLD OF MANY FAITHS

In a world where religion is all too easily made the cause of racial conflict, it is incumbent on the historic communities of faith to be in dialogue with one another, so that the religious elements of any potential conflict may be identified and, where possible, defused. At the very lowest level, the human rights of those of other faiths must be defended as vigorously as one's own, a position clearly adopted by the Anabaptists of the 16th century in their search for freedom from persecution, and now guaranteed in most national legal codes. However, abuses remain and the law is slow to intervene to defend the persecuted minority. But beyond this minimum, one would expect much more common ground between the historic faith communities, where the great goals of peace, justice, freedom, human dignity, and all that makes for human happiness derive from fundamental faith commitments.

Christianity shares, in a special way, with the Jewish community an Old Testament inheritance, while the New Testament contains clear guidelines for interfaith relationships between Christians and Jews. In a similar way Christians and Muslims share a common Abrahamic tradition and have lived together in many communities for a millennium and a half. There is a history, for which both sides need to repent, but there have also been times of sharing together and of common suffering, calling for mutual support.

Issues of dialogue have focused on different understandings of mission, the possibilities of diaconic cooperation, youth and faith, religion and the state, ethics and development, with the hope that mutual respect might follow from such exchanges. It is important to understand that dialogue does not require the surrendering of either party's religious convictions or identity. Indeed, genuine dialogue puts a premium on each side being faithful to the fullness of revelation as perceived by it, and only on that basis emphasizing a common humanity or commitment to search for community of interest within a divided world. What is involved is a turning away from historical prejudices, the need to judge one's neighbour's faith by its best manifestation and not by a suspicious delight in its past failures and weaknesses, for it is incumbent on both parties to proceed in growing knowledge rather than ignorance, so that even where there is no agreement there can be mutual respect and trust.

A PROPHETIC MINISTRY

The World Council, in both voice and action, is called to a prophetic ministry: on many occasions it has spoken to an urgent international situation in the name of the churches within its membership. In espousing such a prophetic style of leadership the WCC has often, of necessity, been ahead of some of its member churches. It may have been that its policies were formulated not by the consensus of all the churches, but by those church leaders most committed to making the Council an instrument of radical change.

This can be illustrated by the contrasting enthusiasm and suspicion provoked by the Programme to Combat Racism in different parts of the constituency. Some churches were quite clearly opposed to the way in which grants were made from the Special Fund to political organizations who were combatants in a conflict, even though grants were made available for humanitarian purposes only. Very clearly, and as a matter of conscience, they accordingly withheld support for this. Others, by contrast, welcomed this act of solidarity with an oppressed majority. A third group only slowly came to see the justification of this programme after apartheid had been abandoned by the South African government, when the testimony of the gratitude of the black population for the stance adopted by the WCC became very clear. The PCR represented a major programme of the Council which gave clear definition to its uncompromising determination to attack racism wherever it appeared, an alertness that is still needed at the beginning of a new millennium.

By contrast, the programme concerned with the search for a Just, Participatory and Sustainable Society encountered difficulties, just because the ideas involved were new, complex and not well understood without patient explanation. Again, in due time the Council was seen to be undertaking important pioneering work in alerting the Christian churches to the urgency of developing an ecological ethic to address the increasing crises of the environment threatening the world's very existence. New resistance structures have to be developed in the face of the most powerful nations in the world selfishly denying that, in any meaningful sense, there is a crisis which requires them to change their behaviour.

Hence the development of the Justice, Peace and Integrity of Creation (JPIC) priorities which have been perceived to be intrinsically inter-related, as they urgently press their claims upon Christian discipleship as part of a spiritual quest. These were not seen as three separate issues but three aspects of the one dislocation of human existence from the created order as God intended it. Though coined at the Vancouver assembly of the WCC (1983), it was not long before other organizations were picking up the "JPIC" language. The hope at Vancouver had been for "a conciliar process of mutual commitment" which would see all member churches committing themselves to a common stand on these three issues. But for some churches the language of "conciliar process" could be used only within the canons of their church order, and thus it had to be abandoned for the purposes of JPIC. The language of mutual covenant, which had different nuances of meaning in different church traditions, hardly fared better, but the inter-relatedness of issues of justice, peace and respect for creation continues to be at the heart of the ecumenical vision for the life and work of the churches, both separately and together.

The Decade to Overcome Violence, proposed and adopted at the WCC Harare assembly in 1998, picked up a perennial concern of the ecumenical movement. It sought to alleviate the abuse done to the poor and destitute in the great urban areas of the world. Clearly the poor, the marginalized and the excluded must be at the heart of the churches' concern, if the churches are to be instruments of Christ's kingdom and not simply institutions concerned about their own survival.

Such a ministry has to be partly educational – to educate the Council's own constituency; partly programmatic, engaging directly with the issues; and partly representative, articulating a Christian voice within bodies like the UN, and from time to time speaking directly to specific governments on issues such as conflict resolution, human rights, development economics, social and economic justice, and the threats to the environment.

THE WCC AND THE FUTURE

At the founding assembly of the WCC in Amsterdam in 1948, the churches made a declaration that they "intended to stay together". With others joining them along the way in their search for the unity of all God's people, they have managed to do this despite evolving differences in social circumstance and religious outlook. Even in the darkest moments of the cold war, the Council was able to foster links between churches in the East and the West, though this was sometimes at the cost of secular suspicions in the West that it was far too friendly to international communism.

Today, however, questions are raised as to whether the ecumenical movement, in its ongoing pilgrimage, has run out of steam, lost its vitality, forgotten where it is going. Is there still a need for a worldwide fellowship of churches? Are the activities of the WCC still relevant to the life of its member churches? Doubtless the movement has not always been faithful to its mission and has missed particular opportunities for more courageous witness. Equally, ecumenism is in danger of under-estimating its own significance: because it has so often been the leader in new thinking, at the moment of the inception of new ideas it tends to suffer from isolation. When, however, time is allowed for the percolation of those ideas down into the life of the churches, and not only WCC member churches, the Council can be seen to have been remarkably influential, especially when judged by the interests of the church worldwide, and not simply the churches of Europe and North America.

While WCC membership has increased very considerably in its fifty years of existence, with its more than three hundred member churches now more representative of Christendom, both in terms of ecclesiastical and cultural traditions and geographical spread, questions have been raised as to whether the increased membership remains as committed to the goals of the ecumenical movement as were the founding partners. It would be foolish to pretend that the present time is the only moment in history when the churches have proved slow to follow where the Council led, or when local church leaders became weary of the task and engaged in only minimal effort to involve people. The fellowship of the World Council of Churches is not, itself, beyond the need for repentance for the mishandling of mutual relationships, or the need to claim from other Christians that forgiveness that makes for new beginnings. The Council will not offer hope for a renewal of community in the world unless its members first find a way to handle past mistakes and become reconciled to one another.

The quality of member churches' commitment is questioned not simply because of the small number of churches either able or willing to contribute financially towards the support of the work of the Council, but because of a more general reluctance to take on the responsibilities of belonging to the ecumenical family, not least in the local situation which must always be the fundamental point at which any ecumenical commitment has to be tested. In other words, some have perceived an increase in membership to accompany a reduction in participation and a lack of willingness to own the work of the Council by some churches, large and small. Developing patterns of meaningful participation in a worldwide body with limited financial means is not easy. Because of these concerns, the Council's central committee deemed it right both to reassess its own sense of priorities and to spell out the obligations of membership in terms of the mutual accountability that commitment to one another implies. This has been construed as showing solidarity with those who suffer – moving from the local to the global – praying for and providing material assistance to those in need, refraining from any action which might give hurt, worshipping together as often as is possible, seeking to be enriched by learning of each others' traditions, and (as the 1950 Toronto statement of the central committee affirms) trying "to learn of the Lord Jesus Christ what witness he would have them to bear to the world in his name".

Membership of this fellowship entails handling disagreements soberly, maintaining mutual respect, engaging in dialogue, eschewing any sense of scoring points. Because there is an obligation to help one another to be faithful to the gospel, it means challenging any member perceived to have moved away from the fundamentals of the faith or to be in a state of disobedience to the gospel. As the "Vision" document affirms, "The integrity of the fellowship is preserved through the exercise of responsibility for one another in the spirit of common faithfulness to the gospel, rather than by judgment and exclusion." Beyond this, each member body has a conscientious responsibility to give careful consideration to implementing within its own fellowship agreements arising out of enterprises involving joint theological study and reflection.

Member churches are selective; when the Council articulates a position they already hold, then it may be seen to be offering wise leadership; but when it advocates a position which is uncomfortable to the member church, then it is quietly ignored, so that little genuinely collegial fellowship emerges, and it becomes questionable whether the Council possesses a mechanism for common decision-making. One may in fact question whether the Council has made any significant progress in seeking to work out the principles of "conciliar fellowship".

Within the last decade or so, few new schemes for church union have been forthcoming. Such schemes as were proceeding seemed more aware of difficulties than achievement. In many countries the capacity for Protestant churches to split further has also been apparent, and poses problems when these dividing churches separately seek membership of the WCC. At the same time, in all too many denominations the ecumenically committed find themselves a campaigning minority who find it increasingly difficult to enlist the support of others. Such advances as are being achieved – such as the Meissen and Porvoo accords – seem to arise more from bilateral conversations than from the work of the World Council.

Considerable creative theological debate within Faith and Order has witnessed a more general and heartening "de-confessionalization" of theology; now the same process of "de-confessionalization" needs to be applied to mission so that it becomes the mission of the whole church and not of any party or sect, thereby ensuring that it transcends all confessional boundaries, replacing credal competition with mutual cooperation. In this respect the time is ripe, in the context of the start of a new millennium, for a fresh attempt to articulate a common understanding of the essentials of the Christian faith.

Notwithstanding the convergence witnessed in the BEM document, little formal progress seemed to have been made on the issue of intercommunion between Protestants and either Roman Catholics or Orthodox, though intercommunion between different traditions of Protestants had become the widely accepted practice. Indeed, just because many churches have come so far on their journey together in enjoying fellowship at Christ's table, there is a weariness with the fact that the ancient churches seem incapable of taking the issue forward. This places a considerable burden, within the ecumenical fellowship, on the representatives of those churches. Even intercommunion between Eastern and Oriental Orthodox Christians is still not possible, even though it is agreed that, after prolonged investigation and discussion, the old Christological debates no longer divide them.

Clearly for the Orthodox, as for Roman Catholics, this is a difficult issue. But there is also a burning passion that impels the concern of others. The Church of Sweden writes,

> To understand the eucharist as an eschatological sign removed from... contemporary life in the ecumenical movement is... unacceptable. It is incomprehensible that this the most visible and tangible means of God's grace should be unavailable to us as a fellowship of churches. The eucharist is a means of unity, a meal for pilgrims, as well as an expression of the deepest possible togetherness, a foretaste of the goal. We can no longer afford to be divided when celebrating the eucharist.

Over against such a passionate plea, the ancient churches affirm that the precondition for intercommunion must be prior recognition that there already exists a unity in faith between the several parties: communion follows unity, rather than being an instrument of securing that unity. It is the manifestation of our unity in faith.

In other areas, too, there are few signs of advance: over against the vibrancy of the youth movement of former years which provided life-changing experiences for many young people, today it is a struggle to keep any significant youth or student movement, representative of all the churches, in place. While women's participation has been advanced, the place of the lay man in the ecumenical movement is more yesterday's story than today's achievement. This is all the more important if it is judged that the student and lay movements, rather than the clerical and ecclesiastical mind, provided the batteries for much that was achieved in earlier years.

"TOWARDS A COMMON UNDERSTANDING AND VISION"

It is not surprising, therefore, to discover that the ecumenical movement, as it faces a new chapter in its existence, has set itself the task of trying to articulate a Common Understanding and Vision (CUV) for its work. As it seeks to build on, and consolidate, the first fifty years of ecumenical work, the WCC also must prepare for the ecumenical task facing it in a new millennium. The vision put before the churches has to be large enough and compelling enough to secure the commitment of both individuals and institutions for the next half century. It must have the power to command that sort of commitment which responds to the ecumenical movement, not only as something to be respected, but something deserving of deep affection and sacrificial service. It needs to raise the profile of the Council above that of being just another institution, with all its rules and regulations, programmes and procedures, to being a living vehicle for the incarnation of the missionary purposes of Almighty God.

It needs to celebrate what God has already given his people, and will then seek to inter-relate the search for unity, the common witness of the people of God in mission and evangelism, the demonstration of Christ-like love in diakonia, and the relentless promotion of justice and peace. In this, the church has always to be partisan, especially as it is the world that so often sets the agenda on these issues. The enigma here is that ecumenical commitment itself is in danger of being the parent of division. As the CUV document itself bears witness,

> New sources of division have appeared both within and among churches. In some churches, things which have been said or done ecumenically have proved so contentious that ecumenical commitment is itself rejected as heretical or even anti-Christian.

The unity of the church must reflect that New Testament understanding of koinonia which already exists among the churches because essentially they share together in the One in whom the faith and being of the church is founded. Without that sharing in Christ there can be no church. Thus the unity of the church has often been seen as both gift and calling. The recognition of our unity in Christ is an occasion to give thanks for what God has given to the people of God; at the same moment, this gift of unity breeds a holy discontent and spiritual longing for the so-much-more to which Christ continues to call his church. This has been recognized by Patriarch Bartholomew as perhaps the most compelling "ecclesiological challenge" of our times. It involves the recognition that, although the church has throughout history been marred by division and schism, there already exists a God-given unity that needs to be more fully realized. For the WCC, this means both accepting the churches as they are, as authentic witnesses to the gospel, yet constantly challenging them to be on the move, searching for that more complete koinonia God wishes for them. Thus, if in no other way, then by its very existence the Council prompts each of its members to consider what they can do to advance the unity of Christ's church: as the Pontifical Council for Promoting Christian Unity affirms in its response to the CUV document, "The shared gift implies a common calling." This means not just occasional collaboration but a calling to solidarity in life and witness, as common convictions are received by the churches and worked into their day-to-day programmes.

To achieve unity, the churches need to surrender their hold on the partial, the transient and the provisional, in an aspiration for the greater fullness offered by the Lord of the church. Thus each part of the church needs to submit its life to being formed anew so as to become the means of being God's renewing agency in the world, both by calling its people to belief in God, and in seeking to bring healing to the whole human community. Discussions of the life of the church must never be separated from concern for the advancement of the kingdom of God in the world.

In all this the churches together need to learn again how to be risk-takers, knowing that God's truth is larger and more robust than all their many attempts to conserve it. The living out of faith is more important than all the talk about it promoted by ecclesiastical bodies. As the WCC Canberra assembly affirmed in 1991, the movement desperately needs,

> a mobilizing portrait of reconciled life that will hold together an absolute commitment to the unity and renewal of the church and an absolute commitment to the reconciliation of God's world... We need to affirm the vision of an inhabited world [oikoumene] based on values that promote life for all.

It must continue to be a major problem for the World Council of Churches that it represents a selection of churches rather than the whole of Christianity. The absence of the Roman Catholic Church from formal membership, however much patterns of common work are developed, must remain a defect within the ecumenical fellowship which justifies the description of its koinonia as "real but imperfect". Another flaw is the absence of large and growing evangelical and Pentecostal churches from the WCC's central councils, even if there is a developing fruitful process of dialogue. This certainly raises the question whether the WCC with its formal membership is the only way for Christian churches to relate to one another. Already the Council has ceased to describe itself as "the privileged instrument of the ecumenical movement", now seeing itself, alongside other organizations within a polycentric ecumenical movement, as "uniquely privileged" in its ability to serve the common good.

The World Council of Churches is by constitutional description "a fellowship of churches which confess the Lord Jesus Christ as God and Saviour according to the scriptures and therefore seek to fulfill together their common calling to the glory of the one God, Father, Son and Holy Spirit". Time and again member churches have reiterated their confidence in the WCC, just because it is a council of member churches who thereby have the responsibility for determining its activities and actions. This basis accordingly offers the Council considerable strength and makes it something different from just another, or indeed a specially ecclesiastical, NGO, a role which had considerable attractions in the 1980s but which has rightly been laid to one side. The WCC should not see itself, or allow itself to be seen, as primarily a programme agency, acting on behalf of the churches in a number of good causes. Rather, the essence of its business is "the relationship of the churches to one another. The Council is the churches together in fellowship on the way towards visible unity..."

For some, this means that the World Council of Churches necessarily has some kind of ecclesial significance, although it is not itself a church, much less some kind of superchurch. Others, however, would find any such language not only unacceptable but threatening. The Council by its very nature lacks juridical power to impose its mind upon disaffected or reluctant churches. It cannot bind them or command their adherence to a particular action. Its opinions and judgments need to commend themselves to the membership by their intrinsic nature as being for the good of the kingdom, that is to say, the only power they have is that which they possess in their substance, and which the churches recognize that they possess. Thus the churches must be free to reject the counsel of the WCC, though respect for the fellowship suggests that the communication of an honest expression of dissent is more respectful of the common fellowship than simply ignoring the world body: the obligation is not to give consent, but to enter into conversation with those recognized as fellow member churches to be partners in one common mission.

Within its own life, the Council has to develop methods of respecting both majorities and minorities as it develops its work. As one church makes clear in its response to CUV,

> It is vital that space is given to minorities in the church to speak up and challenge what is being taken for granted in the dominating church structures, so that the "prophetic word will not be despised".

Because constitutionally the Council exists as a fellowship of churches, ecumenical partners can relate to it only indirectly, that is to say by being present but without voting rights, even though it is the resources provided by such partners that very often keep the Council going. These partners, therefore, justifiably ask for a place in the making of decisions concerning the application of the funds they make available. Some would go further and pose the question whether the concept of "member church" does not define the meaning of church too narrowly. Is not the providing of compassionate aid in the name of Christ to the most needy also a way of "being church", and therefore should not the agencies have a full seat at the WCC table?

This has raised the question whether there is a need to create an ecumenical forum to which member and non-member churches (some of whom, independently of the WCC, already have institutional links with either Faith and Order or the Conference for World Mission and Evangelism) can exercise equal rights. Such a forum could also welcome regional ecumenical organizations and national councils of churches as well as the main Christian World Communions, which are themselves dedicated to advancing church relations on a global confessional basis. A forum could also, surely, find a place for such pioneering ecumenical bodies as the Bible Society, the YMCA and the YWCA, the WSCF and the several mission agencies that make possible much of the work the Council undertakes. All this becomes the more important as limitation of financial resources requires that the Council's style of work be "cooperational" rather than "operational", that is to say, increasingly its role must be to facilitate or animate rather than to implement or operate. In embracing a wide membership, the forum would follow through the principle that effective decision and action should be taken as near as possible to the people affected.

The Council needs to face up to the need for radical change, the full dimensions of which cannot yet be spelt out. As an early draft of the CUV document expressed it,

> Structures and operations are not ends in themselves. Thus, its [the Council's] work should be done in the awareness that, for institutions as for persons, the act of self-emptying opens up space for God to show us new ideas, provoke new initiatives and help to build relationships of trust apart from institutional structures.

In this respect the opening years of a new century will be of great importance as new ways are crafted for fulfilling the one ecumenical vision. There are dangers to be avoided; "the challenge to avoid being drawn into an institutional preoccupation that obscures the wider ecumenical movement's evangelical commitment to the mission of God" and therefore the need for all churches "to engage in a self-critical review of their commitment to membership and participation", "to find new ways for discernment and decision-making... that will enhance the quality of the fellowship while at the same time empowering it for clear and decisive action".

In his helpful "Visions for the Future", delivered at Harare in celebration of the Jubilee of the World Council of Churches, veteran servant of the ecumenical movement Philip Potter concluded by affirming,

> What is abundantly clear is that the WCC, as a fellowship of churches and as an instrument of the ecumenical movement, has as its continuing raison d'etre to declare by word and deed the unity of all God's people; to witness to the saving and renewing grace and power of the gospel of God through Jesus Christ in the fellowship of the Holy Spirit; and to serve and advance the well-being of all people.

Part V

General Bibliography

The great tradition of providing useful bibliographies, inaugurated with the first two volumes of the history of the ecumenical movement, is maintained in the present work, albeit with some changes.

The bibliographies now appear at the end of each chapter to provide broader documentation and to offer suggestions for additional reading. Each bibliography includes a modest number of items, gathered according to certain principles. The vast majority of entries are in English, recent, and do not duplicate the same record existing in other chapters. Considered in their totality, the bibliographies of all chapters list about one thousand titles, recent and focused to provide informative and interesting tools for further study.

But this traditional approach has its limitations. We live today in a changing age of information technology. The contemporary reader will not hesitate to use bibliographical resources available on the Internet. The library of the World Council of Churches has made its catalogue available on line at this address:

http://www.wcc-coe.org/wcc/news/library/index-e.html

The ecumenical collection *stricto sensu* offers more than 50,000 references available on request. This applies to most books cited in the bibliographies which are in the WCC library's holdings, apart from a few exceptions.

A general bibliography also has been prepared and appears below. It contains books and periodicals that are quoted in most chapters plus some other indispensable references. And finally, the reader will not forget the many ecumenical resources available locally, and also very often presented on the Internet.

Arzier, August 2004

Pierre Beffa
Librarian, Ecumenical Centre
1987-2002

Books

And So Set Up Signs...: The World Council of Churches' First 40 Years, WCC, 1988, 74p.

Barrett, David B., Kurian, George T. and Johnson, Todd M. eds, *World Christian Encyclopedia: A Comparative Study of Churches and Religions in the Modern World*, Oxford, New York, Toronto, Oxford Univ. Press, 2001, 2 vols.

Beffa, Pierre ed., *Index to the World Council of Churches' Official Statements and Reports 1948-1994*, WCC, 1995, 184p.

Bent, Ans Joachim van der, *Historical Dictionary of Ecumenical Christianity*, Metuchen NJ, Scarecrow, 1994, 599p.

Bent, Ans Joachim van der, *Six Hundred Ecumenical Consultations 1948-1982*, WCC, 1983, 246p.

Bent, Ans Joachim van der, *Vital Ecumenical Concerns: Sixteen Documentary Surveys*, WCC, 1986, 333p.

Best, Thomas F., *Vancouver to Canberra, 1983-1990: Report of the Central Committee of the World Council of Churches to the Seventh Assembly*, WCC, 1990, 275p.

Bilheimer, Robert S., *Breakthrough: The Emergence of the Ecumenical Tradition*, WCC, 1989, 235p.

Bria, Ion ed., *Dictionnaire oecuménique de missiologie: cent mots pour la mission*, Paris, Cerf, 2001, 393p.

Bria, Ion, *The Sense of Ecumenical Tradition: The Ecumenical Witness and Vision of the Orthodox*, WCC, 1991, 120p.

Brosseder, Johannes, *Internationale ökumenische Bibliographie – International Ecumenical Bibliography – Bibliographie oecuménique internationale*, Mainz, Matthias Grünewald, 1967-to date

Fahey, Michael A. ed., *Ecumenism: A Bibliographical Overview*, Westport CT, Greenwood, 1992, 384p.

Fey, Harold E., *A History of the Ecumenical Movement: The Ecumenical Advance 1948-1968*, WCC, 2nd ed. 1986, 590p.

Gassmann, Günther, *Documentary History of Faith and Order, 1963-1993*, WCC, 1993, 325p.

Gill, David Muir ed., *Gathered for Life: Official Report, Sixth Assembly World Council of Churches, Vancouver, Canada, 24 July – 10 August 1983*, WCC, 1983, 355p.

Goodall, Norman ed., *The Uppsala Report 1968: Official Report of the Fourth Assembly of the World Council of Churches, Uppsala July 4-20, 1968*, WCC, 1968, 513p.

Goosen, Gideon, *Bringing Churches Together: A Popular Introduction to Ecumenism*, WCC, 2001, 173p.

Gros, Jeffrey, Meyer, Harding and Rusch, William G. eds, *Growth in Agreement II: Reports and Agreed Statements of Ecumenical Conversations on a World Level, 1982-1998*, WCC, 2000, 941p.

Hastings, Adrian ed., *A World History of Christianity*, London, Cassell, 1999, 594p.

Johnson, David Enderton ed., *Uppsala to Nairobi 1968-1975: Report of the Central Committee to the Fifth Assembly of the World Council of Churches*, London, SPCK, 1975, 256p.

Kessler, Diane C. ed., *Together on the Way: Official Report of the Eighth Assembly of the World Council of Churches, Harare, Zimbabwe, December 3-14, 1989*, WCC, 1999, 406p.

Kinnamon, Michael and Cope, Brian E. eds, *The Ecumenical Movement: An Anthology of Key Texts and Voices*, WCC, 1997, 548p.

Kinnamon, Michael ed., *Signs of the Spirit: Official Report: Seventh Assembly, Canberra, Australia, 7-20 February 1991*, WCC, 1991, 396p.

Krüger, Hanfried, Löser, Werner and Müller-Römheld, Walter eds, *Ökumene-Lexikon: Kirchen, Religionen, Bewegungen*, Frankfurt am Main, Otto Lembeck, 1987, vols

Limouris, Gennadios ed., *Orthodox Visions of Ecumenism: Statements, Messages and Reports on the Ecumenical Movement, 1902-1992*, WCC, 1994, 283p.

Lossky, Nicolas et al. eds, *Dictionary of the Ecumenical Movement*, 2nd ed., WCC, 2002, 1324p.

Meyer, Harding and Vischer, Lukas eds, *Growth in Agreement: Reports and Agreed Statements of Ecumenical Conversation on a World Level*, WCC, 1984, 514p.

Nairobi to Vancouver: 1975-1983, Report of the Central Committee to the Sixth Assembly of the World Council of Churches, WCC, 1983, 238p.

Paton, David M. ed., *Breaking Barriers: Nairobi 1975: The Official Report of the Fifth Assembly of the World Council of Churches, Nairobi, 23 November – 10 December, 1975*, London, SPCK, 1976, 411p.

Raiser, Konrad, *Ecumenism in Transition: A Paradigm Shift in the Ecumenical Movement?*, WCC, 1991, 132p.

Rouse, Ruth and Neill, Stephen C. eds, *A History of the Ecumenical Movement 1517-1968*, WCC, 3rd ed. 1986, 866p.

Uhl, Harald ed., *Taschenlexikon Ökumene*, Frankfurt am Main, Otto Lembeck, 2003, 300p.
Van Elderen, Marlin ed., *From Canberra to Harare: An Illustrated Account of the Life of the World Council of Churches 1991-1998*, WCC, 1998, 52p.
Van Elderen, Marlin and Conway, Martin, *Introducing the World Council of Churches*, WCC, 2001, 198p.
Wainwright, Geoffrey, *The Ecumenical Movement: Crisis and Opportunity for the Church*, Grand Rapids MI, Eerdmans, 1983, 263p.
Yearbook: World Council of Churches, WCC, 1995-2003, annual vols.
Minutes of the... Meeting of the Central Committee of the World Council of Churches, WCC, 1948-to date
Canterbury 1969, Addis Ababa 1971, Utrecht 1972, Geneva 1973, Berlin 1974, Nairobi 1975, Geneva 1976, Geneva 1977, Kingston 1979, Geneva 1980, Dresden 1981, Geneva 1982, Vancouver 1983, Geneva 1984, Buenos Aires 1985, Geneva 1987, Hanover 1988, Moscow 1989, Geneva 1990, Canberra 1991, Geneva 1991, Geneva 1992, Johannesburg 1994, Geneva 1995, Geneva 1996, Geneva 1997, Harare 1998, Geneva 1999, Geneva 2000, Potsdam 2001, Geneva 2002, Geneva 2003.

Periodicals

Bulletin ENI: Ecumenical News International, Geneva, 1994-to date
Dialogo ecuménico, Salamanca, 1966-to date
The Ecumenical Review, Geneva, 1948-to date
Ecumenical Trends, Garrison NY, 1972-to date
Ecumenism, Montreal, 1965-to date
Ecumenist: A Journal for Promoting Christian Unity, Ramsey NJ, 1962-to date
Information Service, Pontifical Council for Promoting Christian Unity, Rome, 1967-to date
International Review of Mission, Geneva, 1912-to date
Irenikon, Chevetogne, 1926-to date
Journal of Ecumenical Studies, Philadelphia PA, 1964-to date
Mid-Stream, An Ecumenical Journal, Indianapolis IN, 1961-2002
Ökumenische Rundschau, Frankfurt, 1952-to date
One in Christ, A Catholic Ecumenical Review, Turvey, Bedford, UK, 1965-to date
Una Sancta, Freising, 1947-to date
Unité des chrétiens, Paris, 1975-to date

Abbreviations

AACC	All Africa Conference of Churches
ACT	Action by Churches Together
AGEM	Advisory Group on Economic Matters
AICs	African Instituted (Independent) Churches
AIDS	Acquired Immune Deficiency Syndrome
APRODEV	Association of WCC-Related Development Organizations in Europe
ARCIC	Anglican-Roman Catholic International Commission
ATESEA	Association of Theological Education in South East Asia
BWA	Baptist World Alliance
CBCs	church base communities
CBF	Catholic Biblical Federation
CCA	Christian Conference of Asia
CCC	Caribbean Conference of Churches
CCIA	Commission of the Churches on International Affairs
CCJP	Committee on the Church and the Jewish People
CCLA	Committee on Cooperation in Latin America
CCPD	Commission on the Churches' Participation in Development
CEC	Conference of European Churches
CELA	Latin American evangelical conference
CELADEC	Comisión Evangélica Latinoamericana de Educación Cristiana (Latin American Protestant commission for Christian education)
CELAM	Latin American bishops conference
CETELA	Latin American Community for Theological Education
CEVAA	Communauté d'Eglises en mission (Community of Churches in Mission)
CICARWS	Commission on Interchurch Aid, Refugee and World Service
CIMADE	Comité inter-mouvements auprès des évacués (Intermovement Committee for Evacuees)
CLADE	Latin American evangelism congress
CLAI	Consejo Latinoamericano de Iglesias (Latin American Council of Churches)
CLLT	course for leaders in lay training
CMC	Christian Medical Commission
CPC	Christian Peace Conference
CUV	Common Understanding and Vision
CWCs	Christian World Communions
CWM	Council for World Mission
CWMC	Community of Women and Men in the Church
CWME	Commission on World Mission and Evangelism
DEFAP	Service protestant de mission (French Protestant Missionary Service)
DOV	Decade to Overcome Violence

EAA	Ecumenical Advocacy Alliance
EACC	East Asia Conference of Churches
EATWOT	Ecumenical Association of Third World Theologians
ECLOF	Ecumenical Church Loan Fund
ECOWAS	Economic Community of West African States
ECTWT	Ecumenical Coalition on Third World Tourism
EDCS	Ecumenical Development Cooperative Society
EDF	Ecumenical Development Fund
EECCS	European Ecumenical Commission for Church and Society
EKD	Evangelische Kirche in Deutschland (Evangelical Church in Germany)
ESM	Ecumenical Shared Ministry (USA)
ESR	Ecumenical Sharing of Resources
FECCIWA	Fellowship of Christian Councils in Western Africa
FECCLAHA	Fellowship of Churches and Councils in the Great Lakes and Horn of Africa
FOCCESA	Fellowship of Councils of Churches in Eastern and Southern Africa
FTL	Fraternidad Teológica Latinoamericana (Latin American theological fellowship)
GATT	General Agreement on Tariffs and Trade
HOAN	Heads of Agencies Network
HRAG	Human Rights Advisory Group
HRROLA	Human Rights Resource Office for Latin America
IBRD	International Bank for Reconstruction and Development
ICCJ	International Council of Christians and Jews
ICRC	International Committee of the Red Cross
ICVA	International Council of Voluntary Agencies
ICYE	International Cultural Youth Exchange
IEF	International Ecumenical Fellowship
IEOs	international ecumenical organizations
IFACAT	International Federation of Action by Christians for the Abolition of Torture
IFIs	international financial institutions
IFOR	International Fellowship of Reconciliation
IJCIC	International Jewish Committee for Inter-religious Consultations
ILO	International Labour Organization
IMC	International Missionary Council
IMCS	International Movement of Catholic Students
IMF	International Monetary Fund
IOM	International Organization for Migration
IRD	Institute on Religion and Democracy
ISAL	Iglesia y Sociedad en América Latina (Church and Society in Latin America)
ISEDET	Instituto Superior Evangélico de Estudios Teológicos (Higher Evangelical Institute of Theological Studies)
JPC	Justice, Peace and Creation
JPIC	Justice, Peace and the Integrity of Creation
JPSS	Just, Participatory and Sustainable Society
JWG	Joint Working Group between the Roman Catholic Church and the WCC
LCWE	Lausanne Committee for World Evangelization
LEP	Local Ecumenical Project
LWF	Lutheran World Federation
MECC	Middle East Council of Churches
MIT	Massachusetts Institute of Technology
NAFTA	North American Free Trade Agreement
NCCCUSA	National Council of the Churches of Christ in the USA
NCCs	national councils of churches
NECC	Near East Christian Council/Near East Council of Churches
NEPAD	New Partnership for Africa's Development

NGO	non-governmental organization
NRMs	New Religious Movements
NWICO	New World Information and Communication Order
OIRR	Office on Inter-religious Relations
PCC	Pacific Conference of Churches
PCID	Pontifical Council for Inter-Religious Dialogue
PCPCU	Pontifical Council for Promoting Christian Unity
PCR	Programme to Combat Racism
PTE	Programme on Theological Education
RCC	Roman Catholic Church
REOs	regional ecumenical organizations
SCM	Student Christian Movement
SODEPAX	Joint Committee on Society, Development and Peace
TSPM	Three-Self Patriotic Movement
UBS	United Bible Societies
UNCTAD	United Nations Conference on Trade and Development
UNELAM	Comisión Provisional Pro Unidad Evangélica Latinoamericana (provisional evangelical committee on Christian unity in Latin America)
UNESCO	United Nations Educational, Scientific and Cultural Organization
UNHCR	United Nations High Commissioner for Refugees
UNICEF	United Nations International Children's Emergency Fund
UNIDO	United Nations Industrial Development Organization
UNRRA	United Nations Relief and Rehabilitation Administration
URM	Urban Rural Mission
USSR	Union of Soviet Socialist Republics
WACC	World Association for Christian Communication
WARC	World Alliance of Reformed Churches
WCC	World Council of Churches
WCCE	World Council of Christian Education
WCFs	World Confessional Families
WCOLC	World Collaboration Committee of Christian Lay Centres, Academies and Movements for Social Concern
WCRP	World Conference on Religion and Peace
WEF	World Evangelical Fellowship
WELG	Women's Ecumenical Liaison Group
WHO	World Health Organization
WMC	World Methodist Council
WSCF	World Student Christian Federation
WVI	World Vision International
YMCA	Young Men's Christian Associations
YWCA	Young Women's Christian Association

Index

Authors and Contributors

K.C. Abraham, a presbyter of the Church of South India, was director of South Asia Theological Research Institute of Serampore University, India, and previously director of the Ecumenical Christian Centre, Whitefield. A former president of the Ecumenical Association of Third World Theologians and a member of many committees of the Christian Conference of Asia and the WCC, he has written extensively on issues such as church and society, Christian ethics and pluralism.

Paul Abrecht, American Baptist Churches in the USA, was director of the WCC's Sub-unit on Church and Society 1948-83.

Ulrich Becker, a pastor of the Evangelical Lutheran Church of Bavaria, Germany, is professor emeritus of the University of Hanover. After eight years as director of the WCC's Sub-unit on Education 1977-85, he was professor of theology and religious education at the University of Hanover until 1995. Since 1992 he has been president of the Institute for Development and Adult Education (IDEA), Geneva. He has published several books and articles on the New Testament, biblical didactics, ecumenical and inter-religious learning and ecumenical theology.

Pierre Beffa was director of the World Council of Churches library and archives 1987-2002.

Thomas F. Best, an ordained minister of the Christian Church (Disciples of Christ (USA)), is acting director of the WCC's Faith and Order secretariat.

Carlos F. Cardoza-Orlandi, an ordained minister of the Christian Church (Disciples of Christ) in Puerto Rico, the USA and Canada, is associate professor of world Christianity at Columbia Theological Seminary, Decatur, Georgia, USA. He participates in intercultural and inter-religious activities in the Atlanta area, the Caribbean and Latin America. His areas of research and writing include the history of the Christian movement and mission theologies in the third world, and intercultural and inter-religious studies.

Burgess Carr, Protestant Episcopal Church, Liberia, was on the staff of the World Council of Churches' Commission of the Churches on International Affairs in the 1970s and a general secretary of the All Africa Conference of Churches.

Gwen Cashmore, Church of England, was director of the WCC's Sub-unit on Renewal and Congregational Life 1983-86.

Emilio Castro, an ordained minister of the Evangelical Methodist Church in Uruguay, was director of the WCC's department on world mission and evangelism 1973-83, and WCC general secretary 1984-92. Under a WCC scholarship, he pursued post-graduate work in Basel in 1953-54 under the guidance of Karl Barth. His main responsibilities before joining the WCC were coordinator of the Committee on Christian Unity in Latin America (UNELAM) 1965-72, president of the Evangelical Methodist Church of Uruguay 1970-72, and vice-president of the Christian Peace Conference 1964-68.

Keith Clements, a minister of the Baptist Union of Great Britain, has been general secretary of the Conference of European Churches since 1997. A graduate of the universities of Cambridge and Oxford, he was tutor at Bristol Baptist College and part-time lecturer in theology at Bristol University before taking up the post of secretary for international affairs in the Council of Churches for Britain and Ireland, which he held from 1990 to 1997. He was a member of the WCC's Plenary Commission on Faith and Order 1985-98. With a specialist interest in Dietrich Bonhoeffer, he has written extensively on 20th-century church history, theology and ecumenism.

Martin Conway, Church of England, was president of the Selly Oak Colleges in Birmingham, UK, with oversight of their international, interdenominational and interfaith training programmes. He has been study secretary of the WSCF in Geneva, full-time secretary for chaplaincies in higher education in the Church of England in London, WCC publications secretary and editor in Geneva, and assistant general secretary of the British Council of Churches, responsible for unity, mission and renewal. In 1994 he was awarded a doctorate of letters by the archbishop of Canterbury for his theological contribution to the ecumenical movement.

Jean Corbon, priest of the Greek Melchite Catholic Church, was executive secretary of the Association of Theological Institutes of the Middle East 1980-92. He taught liturgy, ecumenism, ecclesiology and Orthodox theology at the Universities of the Holy Spirit in Kaslik and of St Joseph in Beyrouth. Theologian-interpreter at Vatican II, he was member of the WCC's Faith and Order Commission (1972-79), the Joint Working Group between the Roman Catholic Church and the WCC (1991-98), the Mixed International Commission for Theological Dialogue between the Roman Catholic Church and the Orthodox Church (1980-2001), and the International Theological Commission of the Vatican (1986-96).

Paul A. Crow, Jr, was president of the Council on Christian Unity of the Christian Church (Disciples of Christ) in the United States and Canada. He has also been a pastor, professor of church history and ecumenical theology, and the first general secretary of the Consultation on Church Union, 1968-1974. He was a member of the WCC's Faith and Order Commission 1968-98, and a vice moderator, 1991-98, a member of its central committee 1976-98, and moderator of the board of the Ecumenical Institute Bossey 1975-83. He served as the first co-moderator of the international bilateral dialogue commission of the Disciples of Christ and the Roman Catholic Church 1975-98 and general secretary of the Disciples Ecumenical Consultative Council 1975-98.

Richard D.N. Dickinson, Christian Church (Disciples of Christ (USA)), was president of Christian Theological Seminary, Indianapolis, Indiana, US. Ordained in the United Church of Christ, he has served on several WCC committees and commissions over the past 35 years, including several years as moderator of the Commission on the Churches' Participation in Development. As a member of staff of the Council, he was responsible for development issues during preparations for the Uppsala assembly. His area of special interest is justice and dignity for the third world.

Alan Falconer, an ordained minister of the Church of Scotland and director of the WCC's secretariat on Faith and Order 1995-2004, is minister of the Cathedral Church of St Machar in Aberdeen, Scotland.

John Garrett, a minister of the Uniting Church in Australia, is a research associate of the Pacific Theological College and honorary fellow of the Institute of Pacific Studies at the University of the South Pacific in Fiji, where he is a citizen. He lives in retirement in Sydney, Australia.

K.M. George, a priest of the Malankara Orthodox Syrian Church, is principal of the Orthodox Theological Seminary, Kottayam, Kerala, India. He is also chairperson of the Federated Faculty for Research in Religion and Culture, Kerala, and vice-president of the Joint Ecological Commission, Kerala. His responsibilities within the WCC include the moderatorship of the programme committee, and membership of the central and executive committees. He has also been associate director of the Ecumenical Institute, Bossey, 1989-94, and senior secretary for national affairs of the National Council of Churches of India 1986-89. He is a member of the Oriental Orthodox-Eastern Orthodox theological dialogue commission.

Steve de Gruchy, United Congregational Church of Southern Africa, is the director of the theology and development programme in the University of KwaZulu-Natal, South Africa, and a member of the WCC working group on genetic engineering.

Robin Gurney, Methodist Church, UK, was communication secretary for the Conference of European Churches 1990-2002.

Stanley S. Harakas, a priest of the Greek Orthodox Archdiocese of America, is Archbishop Iakovos professor of Orthodox theology emeritus at Holy Cross Greek Orthodox School of Theology, Brookline, Massachusetts, where he taught from 1966 until his retirement in 1995. He served as acting dean and dean of Hellenic College 1969-75 and dean of Holy Cross School of Theology 1970-80. He has been active in the ecumenical movement on local, state and international levels, and in 1986 was the inaugural appointee to the first endowed chair at Holy Cross. He is the author of numerous books and articles, and has written religious columns and editorials in Greek-American newspapers since 1980.

Norman Hjelm, Evangelical Lutheran Church in America, was director of the commission on Faith and Order of the National Council of the Churches of Christ in the USA, 1991-96. After 22 years as director and senior editor of Fortress Press, Philadelphia, in the US, he became director of communication for the Lutheran World Federation in Geneva in 1985, also serving as acting deputy general secretary for planning. Between the Canberra and Harare assemblies of the WCC he was a member of its advisory committee on communication.

John George Huber, a pastor of the Lutheran Church Missouri Synod, USA, served for 31 years in ministry at University Lutheran Church in La Jolla, California, acting also as pastor to the University of California at San Diego campus.

Michael Kinnamon, an ordained minister of the Christian Church (Disciples of Christ (USA)), is the Allen and Dottie Miller professor of mission, peace and ecumenical studies at Eden Theological Seminary in St Louis, Missouri, USA. He formerly served as an executive secretary of the WCC's Faith and Order secretariat and general secretary of the US Consultation on Church Union. He is currently moderator of the commission on justice and advocacy of the National Council of the Churches of Christ in the USA. He is author of several books on the ecumenical movement and co-edited *The Ecumenical Movement: An Anthology of Key Texts and Voices*.

Birgitta Larsson, Church of Sweden, was executive director of the Church of Sweden Mission 1991-96 and professor at the Lutheran Theological Seminary in Hong Kong 1999-2004. As a missionary of her church working with the Evangelical Lutheran Church in Tanzania 1969-75 and 1980-84, she developed an interest in African church history and devoted her thesis to that subject. She served as a member of the WCC's central committee 1983-98 and of the Commission on Unit II: Churches in Mission, 1991-98.

Peter Lodberg, Evangelical Lutheran Church in Denmark, was associate professor of ecumenics at the faculty of theology, University of Aarhus, Denmark, 1994-2001, and is currently general secretary of Danchurchaid. He was a member of the WCC's central committee 1983-98.

Martin E. Marty, Evangelical Lutheran Church of America, is the Fairfax M. Cone distinguished service professor emeritus of the history of modern Christianity at the University of Chicago, US. The author of more than fifty books, he has produced titles dealing with ecumenism since the 1960s. Since 1956 he has been associated with the ecumenical magazine *The Christian Century*. His two fields of research are American religious history and comparative movements across national boundaries, for example the Fundamentalism Project of the American Academy of Arts and Sciences.

Melanie A. May is vice-president for academic life, dean of faculty, and John Price Crozer professor of theology at Colgate Rochester Crozer Divinity School in Rochester, New York, USA. She has been a member of the WCC Commission on Faith and Order since 1984, serving as vice-moderator since 1998, and was a member and moderator of the National Council of the Churches of Christ in the USA Commission on Faith and Order 1988-95. A lifelong member of the Church of the Brethren, she is also a member and ordained minister in the American Baptist Churches USA.

Harding Meyer, Evangelical Lutheran Church of Hanover, Germany, was professor and director of the Institute for Ecumenical Research in Strasbourg, France, 1971-93. Previous assignments include a professorship in systematic theology at the theological faculty of the Lutheran Church in Brazil, Sao Leopoldo, 1958-67, and the post of research secretary for ecumenical affairs at the Lutheran World Federation, Geneva, Switzerland, 1967-71. He holds several honorary doctorates, and has been a guest professor in New York, Rome, Toulouse and Philadelphia.

José Míguez Bonino, Argentine Evangelical Methodist Church, is professor emeritus of systematic theology at the Higher Evangelical Institute of Theological Studies (ISEDET) in Buenos Aires. He was a president of the WCC 1975-83.

Tarek Mitri, Greek Orthodox Patriarchate of Antioch and All the East, is executive secretary for Muslim-Christian relations with the WCC.

Lewis S. Mudge, Presbyterian Church (USA), is the Robert Leighton Stuart professor of theology emeritus at San Francisco Theological Seminary and the Graduate Theological Union, Berkeley, California, US. He chaired the theological commission of the US Consultation on Church Union 1978-85, and was co-moderator of the second international Reformed-Roman Catholic dialogue commission 1984-90. He has served since 2002 as a member of the Bossey research group on ecumenical social ethics, and continues to teach courses on ethics in an age of globalization and related subjects at the Graduate Theological Union.

Simon Oxley, an ordained minister of the Baptist Union of Great Britain, is responsible for work on education and ecumenical formation in the WCC.

Barney Pityana, an ordained minister of the Church of the Province of Southern Africa, director of the WCC's Programme to Combat Racism 1988-92, is vice chancellor of the University of South Africa, Pretoria.

Dafne Sabanes Plou, Evangelical Methodist Church in Argentina, is a free-lance journalist and communicator who writes mainly on social movements, human rights, communications and church and society issues. She was a member of the WCC committee on communication 1985-98. She participates actively in the World Association for Christian Communication, and the women's networking support programme of the Association for Progressive Communications. She is author of *Caminos de Unidad*, a publication on the ecumenical movement in Latin America and the Caribbean 1916-91, published in Spanish and Portuguese.

Joan Puls, Roman Catholic Church, is president of the School Sisters of St Francis in Milwaukee, Wisconsin, USA.

Elisabeth Raiser, Evangelical Church in Germany, was a lecturer at the Atelier oecuménique de théologie in Geneva 1993-2001, and president of the ecumenical Kirchentag in Berlin 2003. She was president of the Ecumenical Forum of European Christian Women 1990-94, and has participated in numerous ecumenical conferences and assemblies as delegate of her church or representative of the Forum. She holds a doctorate in history, and has authored many articles on women in the ecumenical movement.

Larry Rasmussen, Evangelical Lutheran Church in America, is Reinhold Niebuhr professor of social ethics at Union Theological Seminary, New York, USA.

Martin Robra, an ordained minister of the Evangelical Church of Westphalia, Germany, is programme executive for ethics and ecology with the WCC.

Horace Russell, an ordained minister of the Jamaica Baptist Union, is dean of chapel and professor of historical theology at the Eastern Baptist Theological Seminary in Philadelphia, Pennsylvania, USA.

Todor Sabev, Bulgarian Orthodox Church, was deputy general secretary of the WCC, moderator of the programme unit on faith and witness, and co-secretary of the Joint Working Group between the Roman Catholic Church and the WCC 1979-93. A specialist in Orthodox theology and church history, he contributed to preparatory work for the great and holy Orthodox council, and the opening of Eastern European churches' membership in the WCC and the Conference of European Churches.

Elizabeth Salter, Religious Society of Friends (Quakers), Britain Yearly Meeting, was on the staff of the WCC's Commission of the Churches on International Affairs 1990-94, with special responsibility for Europe and for peace issues, setting up the Programme to Overcome Violence.

Julio de Santa Ana, Evangelical Methodist Church in Uruguay, was director of the WCC's Commission on the Churches' Participation in Development 1979-82.

Marilia Schüller, a lay theologian from the Methodist Church in Brazil, is programme executive for combating racism in the WCC.

Günther Schulz, Protestant Church in Germany, was director of the Ostkirchen-Institut [institute for the history and present situation of churches in Eastern Europe] of the Evangelical Theological Faculty of the Westphalian Wilhelms University in Münster, Germany, 1992-2001. The Institute publishes a yearbook, *Kirche im Osten*.

Bob Scott, Anglican Church of Aotearoa, New Zealand and Polynesia, was on the WCC staff with the Programme to Combat Racism 1988-98, and with Communication 1998-2002.

Israel Selvanayagam, a presbyter in the Church of South India, is currently principal of the United College of the Ascension, one of the Selly Oak Colleges in Birmingham, UK. He was formerly on the staff of the Tamilnadu Theological Seminary, Madurai, India, as a lecturer in religions and dialogue, and coordinator of the programme on interfaith dialogue. He has written extensively on dialogue, both in Tamil and English.

Baldwin Sjollema, Uniting Protestant Churches in the Netherlands, worked at the WCC 1958-81, as secretary for migration, then as first director of the Programme to Combat Racism. From 1982 to 1987 he was in charge of the ILO programme against apartheid. South African President Thabo Mbeki presented him with the Oliver Tambo Order in 2004.

Kafoa Anthony Solomone is a faculty member of the Pacific Theological College, Suva, Fiji.

Faitala Talapusi, an ordained pastor of the Congregational Christian Church, Samoa, is lecturer at the Ecumenical Institute, Bossey.

T.K. Thomas, Mar Thoma Church, India, was publications editor for the WCC 1981-91. Early in his career he edited the liturgy of the Church of South India and other church-related material, before earning a Fullbright scholarship in 1957. After a period at the Madras Christian College, he joined the national council of YMCAs in 1964 as their literature secretary, then became editorial secretary of the Christian Literature Society 1969-76. He acted as communication secretary of the Christian Conference of Asia 1976-81.

Lukas Vischer, a pastor of the Federation of Swiss Protestant Churches, was on the staff of the WCC's Faith and Order secretariat 1961-79, first as executive secretary, then as director. From

1980 to 1992 he was professor of ecumenical theology at the Evangelical Reformed theological faculty of the University of Bern, Switzerland. He has authored several publications on ecumenical and ecological issues.

Hans-Ruedi Weber, Federation of Swiss Protestant Churches, worked at the WCC 1955-88, first in the Laity department, then at the Ecumenical Institute at Bossey, and finally as director of biblical studies. After graduating in theology at Bern university he continued post-graduate studies at Leiden, Geneva and Lausanne universities. Before and after his WCC assignments he worked as theological teacher in Indonesia and the Fiji islands.

Charles West, Presbyterian Church (USA), is professor emeritus of Christian ethics of Princeton Theological Seminary, NJ, USA.

Philip Wickeri, Presbyterian Church (USA), is professor of mission and evangelism at San Francisco Theological Seminary, San Anselmo, California, USA, and was associate director of the Ecumenical Institute, Bossey, 1956-61.